D0166228

RESOURCES FOR EDUCATING CHILDREN WITH DIVERSE ABILITIES

●

BIRTH THROUGH EIGHT

Penny Low Deiner

UNIVERSITY OF DELAWARE

HARCOURT BRACE COLLEGE PUBLISHERS

Fort Worth   Philadelphia   San Diego   New York   Orlando   Austin   San Antonio
Toronto   Montreal   London   Sydney   Tokyo

Publisher	Earl McPeek
Executive Editor	Christopher Klein
Acquisitions Editor	Carol Wada
Production Manager	Andrea A. Johnson
Production Management	Publications Development Company of Texas

Photo credits:

Charlotte Branblett, p. 344
Beverly Childs, p. 53
James J. Childs, p. 269
Pat Childs, pp. 8, 14, 20, 31, 42, 49, 74, 78, 81, 92, 114 (right girls), 175, 208, 215, 233, 252, 287, 298, 311, 321 (left), 336, 358, 402, 443, 488, 517, 522, 524, 547, 556, 559, 579, 589, 595.
Robert Cohen, p. 505
Jane I. Davidson, pp. 259, 493, 605
John T. Deiner, pp. 27, 87, 284, 354 (right), 383, 412, 599
Paige L. Deiner, pp. 160, 472, 605
Penny L. Deiner, pp. 3, 10, 17, 23, 45, 52, 59, 63, 67, 99, 106, 109, 114, (left, boy) 118, 130, 134, 149, 153, 157, 162, 168, 170, 194, 186, 191, 205, 219, 223, 240, 244 (all), 249, 267, 274, 279, 290, 292, 295, 302, 316, 321 (right), 323, 331, 343, 354 (left), 364, 367, 372, 375, 389, 395, 410, 437, 455, 468, 485, 502, 515, 552, 563.
Charlie Miller, pp. 37, 231

Cover photograph: David de Lossy/The Image Bank

ISBN: 0-15-505471-6
Library of Congress Catalog Card Number: 98-075254

Address for Domestic Orders
Harcourt Brace College Publishers, 6277 Sea Harbor Drive, Orlando, FL 32887-6777
800-782-4479

Address for International Orders
International Customer Service
Harcourt Brace & Company, 6277 Sea Harbor Drive, Orlando, FL 32887-6777
407-345-3800
(fax) 407-345-4060
(e-mail) hbintl@harcourtbrace.com

Address for Editorial Correspondence
Harcourt Brace College Publishers, 301 Commerce Street, Suite 3700, Fort Worth, TX 76102

Web Site Address
http://www.hbcollege.com

Printed in the United States of America

3 4 5 6 7 8 9 0 1 066 9 8 7 6 5 4 3 2

Harcourt Brace College Publishers

To my husband, John,
who is still my most critical editor, and
the marriage that continues to survive this writing process.
And to our daughter Paige
who is embarking on her own journalistic career.

PREFACE

The landscape of early childhood is changing and with it the field of early childhood education. These changes reflect the increases in the number of young children from diverse ethnic and cultural backgrounds and the inclusion of young children with diverse abilities. With increasing numbers of women in the workforce most young children, including those with diverse abilities are in some early care and education setting.

The importance of the early childhood years has been recognized as a time of rapid growth, but also as a critical period that will influence later development. Neurological studies have confirmed that for children to develop optimally they need secure attachments to caring adults and caregiving that is respective, responsive, and stimulating. At the same time that we have recognized the importance of these early years, families with young children have become our poorest population with approximately a fourth living below the poverty line. For children of color, the figure approaches a half. Poverty brings many significant disadvantages for young children making this population more developmentally vulnerable increasing the number of children born with disabilities and those acquiring them in early childhood. These children plus those who might have died in the past, but are now living with diverse abilities, are impacting early care and education settings and the educators and caregivers who work in these settings.

Today, children with diverse abilities are being included in early care and education settings, in regular classrooms as well as in community activities. There are fewer special events and more inclusive events. These changes have come about because of new insights into how children develop and learn. This text is designed to make these changes a challenge you can meet.

Organization

This book is divided into three parts and 24 chapters. Part One, "Early Childhood Intervention" introduces the field the changes in the field and the current issues we are struggling with. It provides an historical overview of early childhood and special education, the impetus and barriers to inclusion and the move to thinking of early childhood education and early childhood special education as one field. Information is also provided on the early identification and assessment of children. Two chapters focus on families and their roles and how to work with families that empower them while being respectful of their values and decisions. The first part closes with information on individualizing programming and methods to incorporate individualized programs into inclusive early care and education settings.

Part Two, "Educating Children with Diverse Abilities" focuses on the adaptations and accommodations needed to include children with diverse abilities in regular settings. The goal of these chapters is to take a functional approach to modifying the child's behavior and the learning environment. This part provides disability specific information but weaves this back into the fabric of general development while acknowledging that children often have more than one area of need. Accommodations that are necessary to allow *some* children to participate are also designed to expand the learning and creative opportunities of *all* children in the class. These nine chapters have a similar format: Each begins with a vignette followed by a descriptive overview and discussion of the diverse abilities that most frequently need accommodations. It includes information on the definitions and prevalence, causes of particular disabilities, and early signs. This is followed by information on assessment and intervention and guidelines for adapting programing area and curriculum. Each chapter concludes with a summary, educational resources for obtaining further information, and references.

Part Three, "Curriculum and Activities for Inclusion" focuses on program planning and national standards for curriculum that apply to the early childhood years. Five general curriculum areas are addressed and goals are generated for each curriculum area. The curriculum areas are then divided by chapter and subareas and activities are given that are designed to be part of the early childhood general education curriculum and also part of a child's individualized educational program. The final chapter in this book addresses planning and activities for infants and toddlers with diverse abilities.

The book concludes with a Children's Bibliography that topically annotates books for young children designated by age. These books all specifically relate to the understanding of diverse abilities or related areas such as fears, death and dying, or family disruption. The book concludes with the indexes: the activities in the book, a subject index, and an author index.

Summary of Overall General Changes

This book is the third edition of *Resources for Educating Children with Diverse Abilities: Birth through 8.* The first edition was published in 1983. The major changes in the text are reflections of changes in our knowledge, in the legislation that underlies early childhood education, and what professionals deem to be best practice in early childhood education.

The text has been updated throughout. These changes include:

- An assumption that all early childhood educators and caregivers will teach all children (with appropriate supports). Therefore, the text has been written to be responsive to the needs of all educators who teach children with diverse abilities. It is written for what we thought of in the past as regular educators, special educators, and caregivers.

- A further assumption that all educators are decision makers. These decisions have consequences for educators and for the children they teach. They also lead to further decisions. Throughout the book an effort is made to view educators as decision makers and to provide them with enough facts to make informed decisions.

- The text emphasizes people first language and increased awareness of the implications of the language used in reference to individuals with disabilities. When appropriate, the term *diverse abilities* is used where others might use disabilities as a positive frame for looking at what a child can do. The emphasis is on abilities, not disabilities.

- There is a greater emphasis on culture and ethnic diversity throughout the book and also practices that increase awareness of and are respectful of cultural and ethnic differences.

- All chapters have an updated annotated list of educational resources that are designed to provide additional information to educators or are sources of information that can be shared with families. These resources include organizations, print material, and electronic material. Both parents and educators most frequent request is for more information. This change responds to that request and the increasing importance of electronic materials as a potential source of information.

- Information about the major issues the field is struggling with are included such as the issue of full inclusion, family partnerships, and developmentally appropriate practices as they apply to children with diverse abilities.

- The children's bibliography has been focused more clearly on disability related issues and expanded and updated.

- This text is supported by a Web site that provides updated information, application activities, suggestions for presenting the materials, overheads, and examination questions that can be downloaded.

Summary of Specific Changes

Part One: Early Childhood Intervention

- The four family chapters have been collapsed into two and more clearly focused on children with diverse abilities.

- The newly articulated developmentally appropriate practices (DAP) have been incorporated into the chapters on program planning.

- The text is responsive to the changes that the 1997 Amendments brought to the Individuals with Disabilities Education Act (IDEA).

- Personal stories and vignettes from parents, educators, and children appear throughout the book to illustrate particular points. The stories are real although the names and circumstances have been modified to protect the privacy of those who so willingly shared their stories.

Part Two: Educating Children with Diverse Abilities

- Although each chapter stands alone, the interrelatedness of specific conditions is emphasized.

- The chapter on early growth and development has been eliminated but relevant concepts have been incorporated into each chapter to show how a particular disability impacts development at ages 0-3, 3-6, and 6-9 and to aid in early identification.

- The glossary has been eliminated, however, the words have been defined in the text as they are used. They are also listed in the subject index.

- The chapter on learning differences has been separated and expanded to focus on information about learning disabilities and attention deficit/hyperactivity disorder while at the same time looking at areas of overlap and co-occurrence information has been added on dyslexia or reading disorder.

- The chapter on health impairments has been modified to reflect changing incidence figures. For example, the sections on allergies, asthma, and AIDS have been expanded.

- A chapter on advanced cognitive development has been added.

Part Three: Curriculum and Activities for Inclusion

- A chapter on curriculum for inclusion was added as now all children must participate in the general education curriculum. This chapter highlights the national standards that apply to early childhood developed by the various professional organizations

- The activities were revised to reflect the national standards as the basis for developing goals for activities. This will allow the activities to be easily incorporated into both the early childhood curriculum and a child's individualize educational plan.

- The activity chapters contain only activities. Informational text has been incorporated into other areas or eliminated because of duplication. The activities have been numbered to make finding them easier.

Using the Text

The text is designed to be used flexibly to fit educator and student needs. Although complementary, each of the three parts of the book are independent, as are the chapters. Course sequences, the availability of practicum settings, different service delivery systems, or instructor preference may influence the order in which the chapters are read.

The activities and resource material provided in the book are just that, resources for current and future use. As such, they will be useful in both preservice and inservice education and with all educators and specialists in early childhood. They can be shared with families. They can be referred to, used, and modified throughout one's career. Above all, this text is meant to be used. Five years from now we hope this book has handwritten comments in the margins noting where you have updated information that has changed, noting activities that succeeded as well as revisions for those that flopped, noting update and additions to the addresses, telephone numbers, electronic resources, and highlighting useful information and guidelines.

Acknowledgments

No author writes a text without the academic and emotional support of colleagues, students, friends, and family. Although their contribution is different,

each in his or her own way influenced the final outcome. Let me begin with students: those who took my courses, those I supervised in field placements, my advisees, and even those who just stopped by to chat. For me, students who asked questions that challenged my thinking and forced me to clarify my ideas were an inspiration. They made it clear that what I thought was common sense needed to be taught until one had an experiential base to draw on. They helped me see the need to qualify, quantify, and package materials for preservice teachers who have not been in the field. Just as important were graduate students and cooperating teachers who were including children with diverse abilities in their classrooms. They were clear about ideas that sounded wonderful and idealistic but were not practical. Robin Gross and Kristine Moser helped with the children's bibliography and the educational resources.

I want to particularly acknowledge the schools and teachers who allowed me or a colleague to take pictures. Although I am grateful for the pictures, I also wish to express appreciation for the information gained and the support and willingness that went beyond the pictures themselves. The University of Delaware's Laboratory School, directed by Alice P. Eyman, was an invaluable resource, particularly its master teachers, Jane Davidson, Nancy Edwards, and Nadine Heim, and its support staff, Connie Kelly and Connie Sims. Especially helpful support was provided by the Meadowood Program Preschool and its principal, Lynne Meyer-Berlin. The Leach School at Castle Hills and its head teacher Melanie Chadwick were also invaluable as was my reception at the Delaware Curative Workshop and teachers Maryann Koziol, Valerie Martin, and Celeste Ryan. Additionally, Joanne P. Gichner's willingness to invite me into her family daycare home provided another perspective, and Diana Mertens hosted a group of diverse children so pictures could be taken. Two schools in Arizona also willingly participated in pictures for this latest edition. I was particularly impressed with the inclusion of children with severe disabilities at Meyers-Ganoung and the thoughtfulness of Principal Nancy Harden.

I want to thank my colleagues in the Department of Individual and Family Studies at the University of Delaware particularly Kate Conway-Turner who invited me into her home to take pictures, and Rob Palkovitz whose office is down the same small corridor and who empathized with this seemingly endless process. Daniel Shade helped me find additional electronic resources. And Rebecca Knight, my favorite reference librarian, taught me more about tracking down references than I ever wanted to know. I am also grateful for friends and colleagues who reviewed parts of the manuscript and provided valuable suggestions: Charlotte Bramblett reviewed the chapter on Chronic Health, Marc Wojtkiewiez provided suggestions relative to physical disabilities. I am also grateful to the professionals and families who shared their stories with me.

I am indebted to individuals in the Delaware Department of Education, in particular Martha Brooks,

George Smith, Thomas Pledgie, and Martha Toomey who invited me to meetings about the implementation of the 1997 Amendments to the IDEA and who shared ideas with me about the development of the IEP and the implications of instructional objectives, standards, and benchmarks.

Friends play an exceedingly important role in the process. I wish to acknowledge Harriet Ferguson and Lorna Wells, neighbors who never failed to support me throughout the long publication process. And, Grace Lowe, who in the second edition at the eleventh hour provided not only psychological support but invaluable help with the Children's Bibliography. In the third edition, David Beers helped me track down some of the more elusive legal references and his wife Peggy offered perspective and encouragement. And, it will take a year to repay the dinners we owe Ginger and Jack Henriksen because I was too busy to cook.

It is difficult to express how Pat Childs has influenced all three editions of this book. She had progressive ideas in the 1980s and continues to have them today. She continues to influence my awareness of the challenges individuals with disabilities face and the skills that children will need to meet these challenges. Her input has been more frequent with the addition of e-mail. Her insights shaped the manuscript and expanded the concept of inclusion. Her willingness to take pictures for the book and evaluate mine certainly increased the visual quality of the book.

One of the impetuses for revising this text was the need to print a Canadian edition of the text. I was impressed with the Canadian reviews and suggestions, one of which was to include a chapter on children who were cognitively advanced which had been dropped from the second edition. I wish to acknowledge the Canadian reviewers: Connie Winder, George Brown College; Dianne Laking, Institute for Early Childhood Education and Developmental Studies; Claudia Painter, Langara College; and Lana-Lee Hardacre, Conestoga College. I used these reviews extensively as I updated the book. I also owe a special thanks to the reviews of the manuscript that eventually became this text: Alice Sterling Honig, Syracuse University; R. J. Gallagher, University of Kansas; and Dennis Showers, State University of New York at Geneseo. They provided not only constructive criticism, but encouragement that the book was worth the investment of both their time and mine. The team I worked most closely with at Harcourt College Publishers included JoAnne Weaver, Carol Wada, and Christine Abshire. I also thank Nancy Marcus Land and her staff at Publications Development Company for their work in getting both the U.S. and Canadian editions published.

This book is simultaneous coming out in a Canadian edition. I wish to acknowledge the two Canadian authors Lou Dyck and Lana-Lee Hardacre, both of whom teach at Constoga College, and the Harcourt Brace Canadian editors, Joanna Cotton and Christine Langone. Talking with them helped increase my awareness of the field of early childhood education itself, the implications of legislation, and the shared yet separate pasts of the two countries.

I also wish to acknowledge my family. My husband, John, to whom I am still married and who is still my most critical editor and our youngest daughter Paige. She was a 3-year-old when the first edition of this book was published and is now a freshman at American University. Although she has asked me on numerous occasions not to write any more books, she started college with a major in communications and international studies. Her goal is to be a human rights advocate. Our older two children, Jamie and Michael, are both completing graduate degrees on the West Coast. Jamie's interest is in speech and language therapy, and Michael's is in neurobiology. Perhaps families influence their children in more ways than we know.

Finally, I owe a great deal to children, our own children, their peers, and the children of friends whom I have observed, as well as the children I taught who in reality taught me—not so much the easy ones, but the ones who challenged me.

PENNY LOW DEINER

CONTENTS

PART ONE

Early Childhood Intervention

Chapter 1

EDUCATING AND CARING FOR YOUNG CHILDREN IN A CHANGING SOCIETY

Change is everywhere: Education and care for young children is changing, the children we educate and care for are changing, the families of these children are changing, what we know about early childhood is changing, and the context in which education and care is provided is changing. These changes are causing us to ask questions about the role of educators and caregivers and the educational process.

For young children, the early care and education system is problematic: It is fragmented and disjointed. Families develop their own packages of care and education based on what is available, what they can afford, and how they can manage the many scheduling demands of child care, education, home, and work. This is further complicated if a child has diverse abilities. Concerns for young children revolve around the quality of care they receive and the long-term implications of lack of quality care. As children get older, the concerns focus more on academic issues such as too little reading, too little accountability, and too much violence. The solutions are diverse. Some see the current state of early care and education as an indictment of the educational system, others see it as a challenge, but *all* agree that this is a topic that needs discussion.

The mission of education is changing. Schools are having to respond to increasing problems of society such as poverty, substance abuse, violence, and discrimination (Putnam, 1993). There is concern about the level of academic standards in schools for all children including those with diverse abilities. Many of these children were excluded from the educational system in the 1970s or were educated in segregated classrooms and separate schools.

Education and care issues for children are changing. In the past, educators were viewed within the context of the classroom and were seen as well-trained, educated professionals whose exclusive job was to teach children beginning at age 5. Some educators even objected when parents "taught" their children at home and those children came to school already knowing skills that were to be taught there.

Today, the role of educator is less clear, especially in early childhood. The most widely recognized term for those who teach children from birth through age 8 is *early childhood educator.* However, this term does not acknowledge the role of caregiving which is an important aspect of working with young children. Bettye Caldwell tried unsuccessfully to introduce the term *educare* (Daniel, 1995). The president of the National Association for the Education of Young Children, Jerlean Daniel, proposed the term *developmentalist.* She feels this term serves three functions: It presents an accurate view of our way of working with and providing services for children and their families; it allows for a variety of program delivery modes; and it provides a rationale for involvement in child and family public policy issues (Daniel, 1995). The developmentalist perspective allows one to simultaneously look at the child himself, his experiences and maturational level, and the interaction of these within the larger societal context.

We will use the terms *developmentalist, educator, teacher, early childhood educator,* and *early childhood educator and caregiver* interchangeably to refer to individuals who care for and educate young children including children with diverse abilities.

There is also confusion with the term *early childhood special educator.* In the past, young children with disabilities were taught solely by early childhood special educators. Today, early childhood special educators are often part of a team of teachers who teach all the children. Or, these special educators may work as consultants in the early childhood classroom. We refer to all adults who teach young children as early childhood educators. When individuals in early childhood special education serve as consultants, they are referred to as *early childhood consultants* or just *consultants.* This designation reflects their role in the class.

Educators today are part of teams: teaching teams, teacher-therapist teams, and teacher-family teams, individualized program teams, and others. These teams extend into the community and view early care and education as part of a comprehensive strategy to improve the quality of life for the nation's youngest citizens (Riley, 1996).

Children are changing. There were more children in educational settings in 1998 than at any time since the baby boomers set records in 1971 (Riley, 1996). These children are different from those who swelled the schools in the 1970s. The present population is far more diverse. There are increasing numbers of children from a variety of cultural and ethnic backgrounds, including those for whom English is a second language. Many of these young children live in poverty (approximately 1 in 5), many lack health coverage (approximately 1 in 8), and increasingly, children have been exposed to violence on television, in their homes, and in their neighborhoods (Carnegie Task Force, 1994; Children's Defense Fund, 1996).

Families and their structure are changing. There are increasing numbers of single parent families. In 1970 there were 2.9 million single-parent families. By 1994 this number increased to 9.9 million (U.S. Bureau of the Census, 1995). Over 1 million children have their parents divorce each year (National Center for Health Statistics, 1993). Between 40 and 60 percent of children born in the 1990s can expect to live some time in a mother-only household (Furstenberg & Cherlin, 1991). The remarried family system is increasing as approximately two-thirds of all divorced people in the United States remarry. Although the number is declining in both the United States and Canada, the number of individuals choosing nonmarital cohabitation after divorce is increasing (Wu & Balakrishnan, 1994). About 7 times as many couples chose to live together but not marry in 1994 as in 1970. Almost 1 child in 4 is born to a woman who has never been married (U.S. Bureau of the Census, 1995). Approximately 10 percent of couples are gay or lesbian, many with children. The number of children under 6 has increased by 10 percent between 1971 and 1991, but the number of poor children has increased by 60 percent; and 1 in 4 children under the age of 3 lives in a family whose income is below the federal poverty level (Carnegie Task Force, 1994; Eshleman, 1997).

Family functions are also changing. The breadwinner-homemaker family of the 1950s and 1960s has been replaced with single-parent or dual-earner families. Over half of the nation's youngest children are in the care of other adults while their parents work. The pressure of work and family obligations means that many parents have less time to enjoy, supervise, and play with their children (Hochschild, 1997).

These changes bring challenges and possibilities to early childhood educators and to us as individuals. It presents each of us with the possibility of learning and growing as an individual, an educator, a member of a team, a citizen, and as part of a greater community and nation. This book is designed to provide you with the beginning knowledge to face these challenges and the resources to include children with diverse abilities in early childhood settings.

This text is designed to give you information about educating and caring for children in today's changing world. It is intended to provide guidance for those who plan to teach young children and to be a resource for those who are already working in the field. Whether or not you welcome change, it is a reality that cannot be avoided. Change is complex, additive, and stressful. Changes in society affect the children in your classroom and how you will educate them.

The children are our future, but a number of the changes (increasing poverty, hunger, homelessness, and decreasing funding for schools and social programs) make children more vulnerable to adverse developmental outcomes. For some children, changes are temporary stressful conditions (for example, the birth of a new sibling or a move) and, with strong support, the children will resume their individual developmental trajectory. Other children's environmental circumstances are not amenable to change. These children will need more support for greater periods of time. We have a great deal of information on how to support and educate children in some of these changing circumstances. For other children, situations are so new that little guidance is available, and you will be the one breaking the path for others to follow.

Early Childhood Educators as Decision Makers

By the nature of their profession, early childhood educators have made a commitment to serve young children and their families. Basic principles they subscribe to include:

- A belief that *all* children are worthy of respect;

- An empathetic understanding of how children develop and learn;

- A knowledge base and the practical skills to create appropriate environments for young children;

- An inquiring mind and a problem-solving approach to challenging situations;

- A willingness to take risks in the service of children and their families and persist in the face of challenges;

- An eagerness to collaborate and learn from colleagues as well as professional literature;

- A respect for diversity and an openness to new experiences;

- An approach that includes adaptability, flexibility, and responsivity to both continuity and change in the field; and

- The ability to reflect on ideas and experience as a method of personal growth (Bredekamp & Copple, 1997; Green, 1995; Hyson, 1996).

Central to all of these principles is viewing change as a challenge for which you must prepare.

Changes in educational philosophy now call for the inclusion of children with diverse abilities in regular care and education settings including family day care, child care centers, preschools, and all private and public schools. Consequently, educators need to expand and adapt their knowledge base of child development, family studies, and educational theory to include information about adapting the learning environment to meet the needs of an increasingly diverse population. Educators must plan developmentally appropriate programs that meet the individualized needs of children as they are included in the on-going experience of education.

This requires a sense of adventure and creativity in using developmental principles and knowledge of diverse abilities to modify the learning environment. Some new or adapted methods and activities may need to be designed not only to meet the needs of children with diverse abilities, but for the good for all children. This text provides a guide on how to educate, enjoy, and include, *all* children in your classroom.

As an early childhood educator, you not only teach and care for young children, you are a role model. Your feelings and attitudes toward children are indicated by both verbal and nonverbal behavior. By modeling acceptance of children's differences, the child's peers will develop a positive attitude toward others with diverse abilities. Having an enthusiastic, positive, imaginative, and flexible decision maker who believes that all children are more similar than different and that modifying the environment so all children can learn together is more important than having the latest information about disabilities, demographic change, or even the latest educational theory.

Children are part of a family-centered unit and you and the family members should be partners in the decision-making process. Frequent and varied interactions with all families is essential. We need to develop techniques for communicating with parents on a regular basis and viewing children within the context of the family system. Families need to be empowered to generate solutions that work for them. Families must be supported as advocates for their children. Invite parents into your class and encourage their suggestions; they have lived with their child much longer than you have. Respect their knowledge as well as their child's knowledge.

As decision makers, educators make choices based on their knowledge of child development, how children learn, their perceptions of individual children; and their understanding of the social and cultural context in which children live and grow (Bredekamp & Copple, 1997). A primary purpose of this book is to assist in making thoughtful educational decisions.

Including All Children

All children are unique, yet they have much in common. Like adults, they all have strengths as well as limitations. All children have specialized needs some of the time. One child may have a cast on his broken leg for several months, while another may forget her toilet training when her baby sister is born, and another may show her anger during her parents' divorcing process. Needs change during crucial periods in children's lives just as with adults.

When children have diverse needs, whether temporary or permanent, there is a danger of considering only how different those needs make them; educators may lose sight of how much they resemble other children. When that happens, the educator may forget these children have the same basic educational needs as their classmates. They need friends, they need to develop a positive self-concept, and they need to see themselves as making a positive contribution to their class and society. The *whole* child must be planned for, not just the parts that are different. A child with a hearing loss needs to learn to speech read and use residual hearing. However, he or she also needs to make friends and be included in the everyday activities of the classroom.

Early care and education may be a new and possibly frightening experience for some children. A child who is seen as different has an added fear—fear of rejection by adults or peers. The child may have had few previous experiences away from the family, and may associate school with painful experiences in a hospital or doctor's office. More than others, children with diverse abilities may need reassurance and may take time to develop a trusting relationship with teachers and peers. It is the teacher's responsibility to make the child feel safe in her classroom.

Educators can help children understand individual differences by developing an awareness of the diversity among all children as well as their commonalities. As an understanding of themselves and others grows, children can learn strategies for interacting with all of their peers—a valuable lifelong skill.

What's in a Name?

Sometimes we focus only on what makes children unique. Nicknames are often based on these characteristics: "Lefty," "Red," and "Freckles." Sometimes nicknames are not as positive. A poster in my office reminds me of the negative aspects of some names:

> STICKS AND STONES CAN BREAK MY BONES,
> BUT NAMES WILL SURELY HURT ME.

The practice of naming, categorizing, or labeling children based on a disability or trait evolved gradually; no one planned it. It mirrors the traditional medical model where a professional diagnoses an illness and labels it.

The words people use, the order in which they use them, their tone of voice, and other nonverbal aspects of language affect the images we form about people. Language is powerful. If I describe Sarah as a "lazy, overweight girl," you get a very different picture than if I describe Sarah as "a lively girl who is intrigued with words." Language can value or devalue people.

Language is a reflection of how individuals in a society see each other (Blaska, 1993). For individuals living with disabilities, there is often sympathy, pity, or even horror. The association of disability with acts of violence and hate has been strong (Bogdan & Biklen, 1993). Such individuals are often portrayed negatively in the media, for example, Captain Hook in *Peter Pan*. The wicked witch in *Snow White* changed from a beautiful woman to a hunched-back ugly old woman who gave out the poisoned apple.

One of the ways society both maintains and changes attitudes and prejudice is through language. Think of the history of the terms "nigger," "Negro," "colored," "black," "African American." Changing terminology both reflects and stimulates changing attitudes. However, it seems easier to agree on what words *should not be used* than on what words *should be used*. There are a variety of problems that relate to labels and labeling. Of particular concern are the social consequences of a label and the overgeneralizations that accompany the labeling process (Zola, 1993).

Prejudice is "any oversimplification and overgeneralized belief about the characteristics of a group or category of people" (Bogdan & Biklen, 1993, p. 69). Prejudice toward individuals may be displayed by assumptions of inferiority. *Stereotypes* are more specific oversimplifications, such as the assumption that children with Down syndrome are always happy. To the extent that individuals and society act on prejudice and stereotypes about children who live with disabilities, discrimination and "handicappism" results.

Handicappism is "a set of assumptions and practices that promote the differential and unequal treatment of people because of apparent or assumed physical, mental, or behavioral differences" (Bogdan & Biklen, 1993, p. 69). One component of the "isms" is discrimination: handicappism, racism, sexism.

People First Language

Terminology in the field of disabilities is changing. Some of the changes are dramatic, others more subtle. However, the intent of all of the changes is to focus on people first and disabilities second. The terms handicap and disability are not synonymous. A *handicap* "is the cumulative result of the barriers imposed by society which come between an individual and the environment of an activity which the person wants to do" (Blaska, 1993, p. 28). An inaccessible building is a handicap for a child using a wheelchair just as a high bookshelf that is out of reach is a handicap for a short individual. A *disability* is a general term referring to a condition or functional limitation that interferes with major life activities such as walking, hearing, or learning (PACER, 1991). The term handicapped has been replaced by the term disability when the references is to an individual. This change is reflected in the names of the laws passed. The Education of the Handicapped Acts (EHA) were renamed the Individuals with Disabilities Education Acts (IDEA) in 1990. The word handicapped is still used in citing laws or environmental barriers, but not in reference to people.

Another important change focuses on *people first* language. Think about how you might introduce yourself. Who are you? How would you describe yourself? The description you give might vary with the situation, making some aspects of you more relevant

than others. An individual's disability is an aspect of the person. If not relevant, reference to the disability should be omitted. When used, the term disability should not be placed in a preceding adjective phrase, nor should people and conditions be confused. Also avoid grouping individuals into categories such as "the deaf" (Blaska, 1993).

Say:	Do Not Say:
a child with a hearing impairment	a deaf child
babies addicted to crack	crack babies
a child with a disability	disabled child
a child who has cerebral palsy	child who is cerebral palsied
a child who is gifted	a gifted child
individuals with disabilities	the disabled

When comparing children with disabilities and children without disabilities, do just that. If one refers to children without disabilities as normal children, the obvious implication is that children with disabilities are abnormal. Use terms such as normal development, typically developing, or children without disabilities. Be aware of the terms you use and be sure that they convey an accurate description of the child. Be wary of professionals and individuals whose language does not reflect a *people first* philosophy. If their language is out of date, their knowledge may be as well.

Some words used in the past to describe individuals with disabilities have negative connotations. They have created images of people who are to be pitied and who are not able. These words have been replaced with less value-laden terms, for example:

Say:	Do Not Say:
has epilepsy	is *afflicted* by epilepsy
has cerebral palsy	*suffers* from cerebral palsy
has AIDS	is a *victim* of AIDS
uses a wheelchair	is *confined to* a wheelchair
has Down syndrome	is *mongoloid*
is nonverbal	is *dumb* or *mute*
has a physical disability	is *crippled* or an *invalid*

Remember, it is not only what you say, but *how* you say it. Even appropriate language can be used in a misdemeaning way.

The term *special* has also come under scrutiny. We all like to feel special sometimes such as on our birthday, we enjoy special events such as concerts, and we may even have particular clothing that makes us feel special. However, we don't want to be special all of the time. Sometimes we want to be just like everyone else, part of the group. The question then becomes should there be special education? Why not just education that meets the needs of all children?

Using people first language requires us to utilize more words to describe an individual. Some people find this cumbersome, some unnecessary. Words shape attitudes. They are a reflection of the timeliness and accuracy of your knowledge.

Labels and Labeling

Given the concerns about the power of language, leaders in the field are questioning the use of labels and the need for labeling. They argue that the challenge for both research and implementation is for delivering effective, comprehensive services for all children based on their individual educational needs rather than their labeled disability.

Classification or labeling provides a basis for communicating about a child and helps organize information, it has potential hazards: the harmful effects on the child of being labeled, or mislabeled (Division for Early Childhood, 1996). Labels pick out a single characteristic of a child (usually not a strength) and call attention to this characteristic. A child with a physical impairment may be viewed as "a pair of legs": the picture of the child as a whole is lost.

Furthermore, diagnostic tools are not completely accurate, children may be mislabeled or the assessment may not accurately reflect the child's abilities. Labels given at a very young age may be on a child's record for his entire educational career, whether or not the labeled condition still exists. Future teachers may be biased by the label before they even meet the child. The expectations of both the teacher and the child may be lower because the child is labeled. Children may miss opportunities because it is assumed (because of the label) that they cannot do something.

In addition to having a potentially stereotyping, stigmatizing effect, the need for labeling has kept some children from obtaining needed services. Under the labeling system, educators had to wait until a disability was verifiable before intervention could officially begin. Early preventive actions were made difficult, and helping children who are *at risk* (but not diagnostically verified) was not supported through legislation.

Although the federal government specifies the categories of children who are eligible to receive funds for specialized educational services, it does not specify standards for classifying children. This has led to disparity by location and ethnic background.

For example, of students identified for special education in Georgia, 32 percent are categorized as having learning disabilities, in Rhode Island 63 percent have learning disabilities (Shapiro, Loeb, & Bowermaster, 1995). These states employ different criteria.

Looking at the United States as a whole, approximately 12 percent of elementary age children receive special educational services. In the 1994–95 school year, 439,626 children between 3 and 21 received special education or intervention services—an increase of 3.2 percent over the previous year. The number of eligible preschools receiving services rose 6.7 percent with a total of 524,458, and 165,253 infants and toddlers received early intervention services in 1993–94—an increase of 7 percent. About half of these children are served in regular education classes (Council for Exceptional Children [CEC], 1997).

Because the term *developmentally delayed* is used with most younger children, we have less information on the specific types of disabilities these children have. For children ages 6 to 21, specific learning disabilities account for 51 percent, speech and language impairments for 21 percent, mental retardation for 12 percent, and serious emotional disturbance for 9 percent of children with disabilities. The most rapidly growing categories are children with traumatic brain injuries, other health impairments, and autism (CEC, 1997).

The statistical profile of children in special education reveals another disturbing aspect of the labeling system. African American children are twice as likely to be labeled as mentally retarded as other ethnic groups.

In addition to concerns about the cultural bias of tests used to classify children, there is concern that, given the same profile, white children would be placed in the less stigmatizing category of learning disabled whereas African American children would be labeled mentally retarded. To the extent that the label of mental retardation will lower teacher expectations of performance, children labeled as mentally retarded will have fewer learning opportunities and may in fact learn less because of a label (Shapiro, Loeb, & Bowermaster, 1995).

To help the problem of mislabeling children, the 1997 amendments to the Individuals with Disabilities Education Act allows the use of the category *developmental delay* for children from birth through age 9. This is a category that had been available for young children (birth to 3) and became available for children

TABLE 1.1 PERCENTAGE OF STUDENTS WITH DISABILITIES IN THE PUBLIC SCHOOLS

	Native American	Asian	Hispanic	African American	Minority	White
In school	1%	3%	12%	16%	32%	68%
Mentally Ret	1%	1%	11%	34%	47%	53%
Speech Impair	1%	2%	9%	16%	27%	73%
Emotion Dis	1%	1%	6%	22%	29%	71%
Learning Dis	1%	1%	11%	17%	30%	70%

Statistical Profile of Special Education in the United States, 1994.

It is challenging to accurately assess young children. It requires contact with the child and his family to know whether behavior is typical of a child or a response to a new situation.

3 through 5 in 1991. The goal of this change is to alleviate the mislabeling of children during the early years (Division for Early Childhood, 1996). The developmentally delayed label is replaced by a more specific one (for example, learning disabilities) as the child gets older, or is dropped altogether if the delay is outgrown. This new legislation also allows states to serve young children who are "at risk" for developmental delays.

The term developmentally delayed solves some of the problems related to mislabeling. However, it is not a useful guide in designing educational programs for children. One modifies the environment very differently if the child has a delay in the development of communication skills or in motor skills. The emphasis of this text is on understanding the implications of developmental differences and on adapting the learning environment to enhance the development of children with diverse abilities. The focus is on broad developmental areas and how the learning environment can be modified to accommodate children whose development is different from the norm in these areas.

The most useful and positive approach for all children is to identify the child's strengths and then to build programming to develop these strengths. This

will, in turn, meet the child's needs. Saying "Juan has atypical visual development and can distinguish only light and dark" does not help design an appropriate program; it only describes the area of development that is of concern. It would be more useful to note that Juan has age-appropriate fine motor skills and plays frequently with small objects. He especially likes small cars and trucks. He follows two-step directions well. Then describe his needs—Juan will need alternative methods for handling activities that require fine visual discrimination. Several possible actions are now implied. The materials can be adapted (for example, larger objects with highly contrasting colors) or the activity can be expanded (a cooperative learning project with a variety of tasks) so that all children can enjoy and learn from the activity.

With statements about children's strengths and limitations, accommodations can be made and effective teaching can begin. The process of translating strengths and needs into individualized educational goals and developmentally appropriate programs and then designing and modifying activities to support this planning process is demonstrated throughout this book. The process of programming through strengths and interest is a dynamic one. A child who has atypical visual development may have a visual impairment for life, but that child's strengths and needs will change—not merely each year, but perhaps each week or day. Effective teaching is responsive to children and change, not categories and labels.

Prevention

In early childhood education, the concept of prevention is used in its broadest sense. It involves identifying factors that cause a particular disability or at-risk condition and then reducing or changing those conditions to optimize outcomes for children and families. Prevention is an underlying theme for all of early childhood.

Primary prevention is designed to reduce the incidence of disability and targets everyone. The goal is to change the environment to promote healthy individuals and to build skills in citizens as a whole to help them stay healthy. Laws that require individuals to wear seatbelts and young children to use car seats fall in this category (Pransky, 1991). Inoculations such as smallpox and the diphtheria, tetanus, and pertussis (DPT) vaccine are designed to prevent these diseases from occurring.

Secondary prevention, or intervention, focuses on groups that are *at risk* and is designed to change responses to particular situations or to change the situations. The government warning: "According to the surgeon general women should not drink alcoholic beverages during pregnancy because of the risk of birth defects," is targeted specifically to pregnant women, an at-risk group. Many conditions that place the fetus at risk are identified with warnings about the need for good prenatal care. Injury prevention is a focus during the early years. Child-proofing homes as infants become mobile is another example of secondary prevention. Intervention for at-risk children falls in this category. This is considered secondary intervention because the expectation is that intervention can reduce the risk. The focus is short-term and designed to change the situation or to provide skills to respond to the situation (Pransky, 1991).

Tertiary prevention targets those who have been identified as having a particular disease or disability and its purpose is habilitation. Early childhood education is a relatively new tertiary prevention tools. It is designed to teach children who have disabilities and to prevent secondary problems such as low self-esteem and behavior problems. Many see tertiary prevention as treatment.

Best Practice

All fields grow and change. The concept of *best practice* focuses on what scholars think is the best way to handle a situation at a particular time. What was best practice in 1950 is not best practice in 1999. Likewise, what is best practice as we move into the 21st century may no longer be best practice in 2020. This text reflects what is considered best practice in the late 1990s. Best practice is determined by input from a variety of sources: researchers and scholars in the field, professional and parent organizations, child advocates and others. A consensus about best practice frequently translates into legislation as a way of making best practice available to all. Current ideas relating to best practice in early childhood special education include the following:

- *Inclusion*—Children with diverse abilities should be included in neighborhood early care and education settings. Inclusive settings support sustained connections with well-selected materials and educational methods, typically developing peers, and knowledgeable, enthusiastic adults. This does not include settings that practice pull-out sessions or limit the child's involvement because of a disability.

- *Normalization*—When possible, children with disabilities should be placed in the same settings they would have been in if they did not have disabilities. The makeup of a setting should reflect "naturally occurring proportions"; this means all child care programs should include children with disabilities in numbers approximating their occurrence in the population (Irwin, 1993, p. 13). They should live in homes with caring parents, play in recreational facilities with their siblings and typically developing peers, and participate in the same activities as their age-mates.

- *Zero reject*—All children are included in early care and education settings irrespective of their level or type of disability.

- *Same range of program options*—The range of early care and education options (family day care, center care, nursery school, play groups, private schools, and public schools) should be available to all children. These options, or a combination of options, need to be available for the number of hours parents request for children with or without disabilities.

- *Comprehensive service delivery*—Services should take into account the child's needs across a broad range of areas and disciplines. Parents and professionals must become part of a team that focuses on the strengths and needs of the child. Teams include professionals whose areas of expertise complement each other yet who are individually and collectively committed to the development of the child. Procedures used need to be flexible to meet the needs of children from a variety of family structures.

- *Outcome-based*—The focus of intervention must be on the present and future skills that children need to have the best possible quality of life now and in the future. The curriculum needs to be broad, intellectually challenging, developmentally based, and individually appropriate. Proposed outcomes need to be grounded in an empathetic understanding of child growth and development within a culturally diverse context.

- *Family-centered*—Families need to be acknowledged as the experts regarding their children, and planning must be inclusive of and responsive to the family's needs and desires. Family-centeredness includes the recognition that the family is the constant in children's lives, though service systems and personnel change. Families are partners in the educational process; they deserve to be respected and empowered.

- *Culture- and gender-sensitive*—Children need to be viewed in the context of their family, community, and cultural/ethnic background. Early childhood education practices need to be sensitive to and responsive to children's cultural/ethnic background. Best practice includes multicultural and nonsexist experiences, materials, and equipment.

- *Early intervention*—Identifying children as early as possible supports planning designed to maximize children's potential for growth, minimizes the effects of the disability, and prevents secondary disabilities. New information stresses the importance of the early years for learning for all children (Carnegie Task Force, 1994). Early intervention is an investment for both the child and the nation.

- *Transition planning*—Preparing children to move from one service system to another (home to school, preschool to public school), as well as being sure the new (receiving) system is ready to meet the children's needs prevents gaps in services. It also reduces stress in parents, children, and early childhood professionals.

- *Resilience*—Traditionally, we have focused on the weaknesses or problems related to specific disabilities and viewed early childhood as a time to remediate these conditions for a child's long-term good. We are now focusing on the strengths and resilience that children have as a way of working toward positive outcomes. Although we know there are no "invulnerable" children, we are concentrating on what works and how it can work better.

- *Prevention*—Identifying factors that cause a particular disability or at-risk condition and then reducing or changing those conditions to optimize outcomes for children and families is an underlying theme for all of early childhood.

A number of sources provide more information on best practices in inclusive child care. See Bredekamp & Copple, 1997; DEC, 1996; DEC, NAEYC, & ATE, 1995; Derman-Sparks and the ABC Task Force, 1989; Hyson, 1996; Irwin, 1993; McDonnell & Hardman, 1988; & Pransky, 1991.

About the Text

This book is divided into three parts. Part One, Early Childhood Intervention, includes information about the profession of early childhood education and general information necessary to work with children who have diverse abilities. Chapters 1 and 2 introduce the text and the base for early intervention. Chapter 3 focuses on inclusion. Chapters 4 and 5 view children in the context of their families and the skills that are needed to work with families. Chapter 6 discusses the early identification and assessment of young children with diverse abilities. Chapter 7 discusses developing individualized programs, and Chapter 8 looks at how to use individualized program planning in inclusive settings.

Part Two, Educating Children with Diverse Abilities focuses on the adaptations and accommodations needed to include children with diverse abilities in regular classrooms. The chapters are grouped by developmental domains and ordered by the probability of your having a child with these needs in your classroom. (You are more likely to have a child with a behavioral disorder than a visual impairment.) Chapter 9 focuses the changes necessary to include children with emotional or behavioral differences. The next four chapters focus on differences primarily in the cognition and learning area. Chapter 10 looks at children with learning differences, including children who have learning disabilities and attention deficit hyperactivity disorder. Chapter 11 includes information on communications differences. Chapters 12 and 13 focus on including children with delayed or advanced development.

Chapters 14 to 17 include information on including children with physical, health, and sensory differences. Chapter 14 focuses on adaptations to include children with chronic health problems and Chapter 15 provides information for making accommodations for

Families vary in how important their culture is to them and how they embrace it.

and including children with orthopedic impairments. Chapters 16 and 17 focus on children with auditory and visual differences.

Many children with diverse abilities need modifications in more than one developmental area. For example, children with delayed development may also have language delays. Children with learning disabilities may also have a behavioral disorder. These modifications can be accomplished by integrating the information and guidelines from several chapters.

The format of Chapters 9 through 17 is similar. Each chapter begins with a vignette followed by a descriptive overview and discussion of the diverse abilities that most frequently need accommodations. It includes information on the causes of particular disabilities and the early signs. This is followed by information on assessment and intervention and information on adapting programming and curriculum. Each chapter concludes with a summary, references, and resources for obtaining further information about these developmental areas.

Part Three, Activities for Inclusion provides a variety of activities to help achieve goals that are both part of the child's individualized program and part of the regular educational curriculum. Chapter 18 provides an overview of the curriculum areas and the suggested standards for the regular curriculum in early childhood. It also gives information on the format of activities and how to use them. Chapters 19 through 23 contain activities designed to help children gain needed skills. They are grouped both by curriculum area and the goals the activities are designed to meet. Chapter 24 focuses on planning and implementing activities with infants and toddlers with diverse abilities.

The activities presented in the book—although good for all children—are designed to demonstrate effective accommodations for meeting the needs of children with diverse abilities. All activities include information about the specific programming area they are designed for, group size, goals and objectives for the activity, materials necessary, procedures for carrying out the activity as well as adapting it, and information about how to integrate this activity into the general curriculum. The expectation is that these activities will be integrated into an ongoing curriculum. The activities are numbered consecutively. The activities are also indexed by the goals they support.

Using the Text

The text may be used flexibly to fit teacher and student needs. Although complementary, each of the three parts of the book are independent, as are the chapters. Course sequences, the availability of practicum settings, different service delivery systems, or instructor preference may influence the order in which the chapters are read. Likewise, encountering a child in a practicum about whom you need more knowledge may make you seek out information before it is covered in the text.

The activities and resource materials provided in the book are just that, resources for current and future use. As such, they will be useful in student teaching experiences and also as part of regular program planning. They may profitably be shared with families. They can be referred to, used, and modified throughout one's teaching career. This text is meant to be used. Five years from now, we would expect your copy of this book to have comments in the margins noting where you have modified activities, addresses and telephone numbers updated and added to, and pages dog-eared and highlighted.

Summary

Education is crossing a new frontier and changing to meet the new demands. Educators are at the forefront of this change as they modify the learning environment to meet new educational standards and to include children with diverse abilities. Change brings challenges and new and different ways of being in the world.

Today's teachers must know what is considered best practice. They must focus on children first in their language usage, their attitudes, and their teaching practices. They need to view children with diverse abilities in the context of their families and culture with the expectation that these children will live,

grow, and learn in environments as similar as possible to those of their siblings and peers. Education will focus on prevention and the development of strength and resilience in these children as they develop and move among early care and education settings.

This text is designed to support best practice and to provide a knowledge base in early childhood education as it relates to including children with diverse abilities. It provides information about children and their families, developmental delays and disabilities, and information on individualizing programming. It is based on best practice and focuses on including children with developmental delays and disabilities in regular classes and providing activities that will meet their developmental and individual needs.

Educational Resources

Annie E. Casey Foundation. (1998). *Kids count data book: State profiles on child well-being.* Author.

Provides a summary for the nation and each state on a variety of indicators that place children at risk for developmental disabilities. Updated annually.

Carnegie Task Force on Meeting the Needs of Young Children. (1994). *Starting Points: Meeting the needs of our youngest children.* New York: Carnegie Corporation of New York.

Provides an overview of the first three years and their importance in development with suggestions for changing risk factors and strategies for action.

Children's Defense Fund. (1996). *The state of America's children.* Washington, DC: Author.

A review of how America's children are faring relative to a variety of indices both nationally and internationally. Updated annually.

The Council for Exceptional Children
1920 Association Drive
Reston, VA 22091-1589
(703) 620-3660 (Voice), FAX (703) 264-9446
http://www.social.com/health/nhic/data/hr0500
/hr0523.html

CEC has divisions for all major disability areas and is committed to advancing the quality of education for all children. Their web page is about the organization and contains links to other resources.

Division for Early Childhood (DEC) (at CEC, same address as above).

A division of CEC that focus on young children with disabilities. Has state divisions and holds national conferences as well as publishing a newsletter and journal.

ERIC Clearinghouse on Handicapped and Gifted Children (at CEC, same address as above)
http://ws1.kidsource.com/kidsource/content2
/Educating_Exceptional_kids.html

Send or call for a product flyer.

Healthtouch

http://www.healthtouch.com/level1/menu.htm

Provides information about health news, health products, drug information, a pharmacy search, and a health resource directory, which has links to other health-related pages.

HEATH Resource Center

One Dupont Circle, NW Suite 800

Washington, DC 20036-1193

(202) 939-9320, (800) 544-3284, FAX (202) 833-4760

http://www.und.nodak.edu/dept/dss/heath.htm

Has a variety of literature about many different disabilities.

National Association for the Education of Young
    Children

1509 16th Street, NW

Washington, DC 20036-1426

(202) 232-8777, (800) 424-2460, FAX (202) 328-1846

http://www.naeyc.org/naeyc

e-mail: pubaff@naeyc.org

Offers professional development opportunities to early childhood educators designed to improve the quality of services to children birth through 8. Publishes the journal Young Children. Has publications that focus on including children with disabilities in early care and education settings.

National Information Center for Children and Youth
    with Disabilities (NICHCY)

PO Box 1492

Washington, DC 20013-1495

(202) 884-8200, (800) 695-0285, FAX (202) 884-8441

e-mail: nichcy@aed.org, gopher aed.org (select "6"
    Disability Services)

Provides information and referral and technical to individuals working with children with disabilities. They publish a free newsletter and their many publications are available from their gopher address.

Resources for Rehabilitation

33 Bedford Street, Suite 19A

Lexington, MA 02173

(781) 862-6455, FAX (781) 861-7517

http://www.rfr.org

Provides information about national organizations that provide services to people with disabilities and chronic conditions as well as videotapes and computer technology such as bulletin boards, e-mail, and the Internet. Produced Resources for people with disabilities and chronic conditions, a valuable resource.

References

Blaska, J. (1993). The power of language: Speak and write using "person first." In M. Nagler (Ed.), *Perspectives on disability* (2nd ed., pp. 25–32). Palo Alto, CA: Health Market Research.

Bogdan, R., & Biklen, D. (1993). Handicapism. In M. Nagler (Ed.), *Perspectives on disability* (2nd ed., pp. 69–76). Palo Alto, CA: Health Market Research.

Bredekamp, S., & Copple, C. (Eds.). (1997). *Developmentally appropriate practice in early childhood programs serving children from birth through age 8* (Rev. ed.). Washington, DC: National Association for the Education of Young Children.

Carnegie Task Force on Meeting the Needs of Young Children. (1994). *Starting points: Meeting the needs of our youngest children.* New York: Carnegie Corporation of New York.

CEC. (1997). Eighteenth annual report affirms CEC's policy on inclusive settings: Full continuum of services a must. *CEC Today, 3*(7), 1, 4–5.

Children's Defense Fund. (1996). *The state of America's children.* Washington, DC: Author.

Daniel, J. E. (1995). Advancing the care and education paradigm: A case for developmentalists. *Young Children, 50*(2), 2.

Derman-Sparks, L., & the A.B.C. Task Force. (1989). *Anti-bias curriculum: Tools for empowering young children.* Washington, DC: National Association for the Education of Young Children.

Division for Early Childhood. (1996). *Developmental delay as an eligibility category (1–8).* Author.

Division for Early Childhood, Council for Exceptional Children, National Association for the Education of Young Children, & Association of Teacher Educators. (1995). Personnel standards for early education and early intervention: Guidelines for licensure in early childhood special education. *Communicator, 21*(3), 1–16.

Eshleman, J. R. (1997). *The family* (8th ed.). Boston: Allyn & Bacon.

Furstenberg, F. F., Jr., & Cherlin, A. J. (1991). *Divided families.* Cambridge, MA: Harvard University Press.

Green, J. W. (1995). *Cultural awareness in the human services: A multi-ethnic approach* (2nd ed.). Boston: Allyn & Bacon.

Hochschild, A. (1997). *The time bind: When work becomes home and home becomes work.* New York: Metropolitan Books.

Hyson, M. (1996). *NAEYC folio: Early childhood education.* Unpublished manuscript. Newark: University of Delaware.

Irwin, S. (1993). SpeciaLink: The road to mainstream child care. *Focus, 1*, 11–16.

McDonnell, A., & Hardman, M. (1988). A synthesis of "best practice" guidelines for early childhood services. *Journal of the Division of Early Childhood, 12*(4), 328–341.

National Association for the Education of Young Children. (1995). *Guidelines for preparation of early childhood professionals: Associate, baccalaureate, and advanced levels: Position statement of the National Association for the Education of Young Children.* Washington, DC: Author.

National Center for Health Statistics. (1993). *Marriage and divorce data.* Hyattsville, MD: U.S. Department of Health and Human Services, Centers for Disease Control, National Center for Health Statistics.

PACER Center, Inc. (1991). *It's the "person first"—Then the disability.* Author.

Pransky, J. (1991). *Prevention: The critical need.* Springfield, MO: Burrell Foundation.

Putnam, J. W. (1993). The movement toward teaching and learning in inclusive classrooms. In J. W. Putnam (Ed.), *Cooperative learning and strategies for inclusion: Celebrating diversity in the classroom* (pp. 1–14). Baltimore: Brookes.

Riley, R. W. (1996, February 28). *State of American education address.* Washington, DC: U.S. Department of Education.

Shapiro, J. P., Loeb, P., & Bowermaster, D. (1995). *Separate and unequal. Annual editions: Educating exceptional children* (8th ed., pp. 18–23). Guilford, CN: Dushkin.

Statistical profile of special education in the United States (1994, January). *Teaching Exceptional Children, 26*(3) (Suppl.).

U.S. Bureau of the Census. (1995). *Statistical abstracts of the United States* (115th ed.). Washington, DC: U. S. Government Printing Office.

Wu, A., & Balakrishnan, T. R. (1994). Cohabitation after marital disruption in Canada. *Journal of Marriage and the Family, 56,* 723–734.

Zola, I. K. (1993). Self, identity, and the naming question: Reflections on the language of disability. In M. Nagler (Ed.), *Perspectives on disability* (2nd ed., pp. 15–24). Palo Alto, CA: Health Market Research.

Chapter 2

HISTORICAL BASES FOR INCLUSIVE CARE AND EDUCATION

I have never faced a harder time in Greg's life than I am facing today. Going from infant to young adult is far easier than the challenges we face as adults away from the public school system. Greg will graduate in May and would like to obtain a full-time job. I'm not sure he will be successful. Our education system failed to teach him any real skills. Because of his physical disability, he can't take a physically intensive job. Because of his spastic speech, his present employer (part-time) will not give him a job working with the public. Greg is not extremely bright, so he can't go for one of those brainy jobs either.

I had hoped that the school would have been more involved in the community by adopting a co-op program, one where the school and employer would have worked hand-in-hand. The school would have supplied the training and additional aid that the employer did not have the time to provide or did not have the resources to provide. Instead, the school system pushed Greg out the door so they would have one less student to fret over. It's scary. We weren't prepared for this.

How would Greg's life be different if he were born in 1997 instead of 1977? Greg was born as we began to implement the Education for All Handicapped Children's Act in 1978. We were just beginning to realize then the potential of early intervention, the importance of early childhood, and the importance of including children with diverse abilities in regular classrooms.

What if Greg were part of your class today? How would you feel about his being there? Does he belong? How would you talk to Greg? How would you talk to his parents? Would you expect to interact with his brother? Would you be intimidated by his braces and his speech? What do you need to know to include the Gregs of today in your classroom? How will you program so that the Gregs of tomorrow have the skills to live as independent productive adults in the 21st century—to have equality and justice for all?

The inclusion of all children in early care and education is a relatively new paradigm. In 1970, the field of early childhood special education was mini-

mal and, much like regular education, was dealt with by early childhood special educators. If a child were born severely disabled, institutionalization was often recommended, or the child was kept at home and "made comfortable." Efforts to teach these children were considered to be a waste of time. Children with severe disabilities were often considered a bother, requiring too much time. The only concentrated effort was made in the area of self-help skills, these skills could ease the family burden and perhaps make the child eligible for school.

Children whose disabilities were not apparent at birth but who did not meet developmental milestones were typically dealt with by a physician. Advice was usually to "wait and see," or "keep the child under observation." Worried parents were treated as "overanxious," or, especially in the case of a first child, "inexperienced." Parents of later-born children were told that all children develop differently—each at his or her own pace. Given such an approach, it was frequently not until children reached school age that specific problems were diagnosed and an intervention program developed. The opportunity for intervention during the critical early years was wasted.

Historical Overview

Although the history of inclusive early care and education is relatively short, there is a long and interesting history of beliefs and decisions about how children with disabilities should be educated.

In the mid-1800s, little was known about disabilities or possible causes. Disabilities were frequently blamed on "sinful living" (Berkson, 1993). This particular legacy has influenced the field. People thought you could inherit lifestyle characteristics from your parents as well as what we now know to be genetic information (height, sex, and so on). It was commonly assumed that all disabilities were passed down through generations and that the only way to stop society from being overwhelmed with these individuals was to sterilize adults to stop reproduction (Berkson, 1993).

It was at the turn of the century that the work of Alfred Binet (1857–1911) allowed for the identification of milder disabilities that impacted school performance (Berkson, 1993). He showed that the scores of children classified as mentally retarded were similar to those of younger "normal" children.

Despite some advances, our knowledge of the contribution of heredity and environment to the developing child was far from complete as we moved into the 20th century. The eugenics movement began to gain popularity as it targeted specific racial/ethnic groups and individuals with disabilities. In Europe, particularly in Germany, the movement led to the genocide of ethnic minorities and individuals with disabilities. The United States began to pass compulsory sterilization laws so that individuals with disabilities could not reproduce. Although these laws were rarely enforced, they did lead to the practice of separating individuals with disabilities and maintaining them in institutions.

Although it became clear that those institutionalized had very different needs, institutions only provided for basic needs. The term "warehousing" was used to indicate there was no intent to include any rehabilitation, training, or education. Children with mild to moderate impairments were placed in segregated schools or separate classrooms in the public schools.

Beliefs About the Education of Young Children

The field of early childhood education is the result of several overlapping movements: "the kindergarten movement, the nursery school movement, the daycare movement, and more recently, the early intervention or compensatory education movement" (Spodek, Saracho, & Peters, 1988, p. 3).

The Kindergarten Movement

The first kindergarten was started by Friedrich Froebel (1782–1852) in Germany in 1837. Froebel, known as the "father of the kindergarten" developed the first educational toys which he called *gifts*. He held the then radical notions that children should be cared for and play in school, that they could learn through using toys, and that teachers needed training. The German word *kindergarten* means children's garden. Teachers plant ideas for children to use as they grow. Until the late 1800s, Froebel's ideas of teacher-directed learning had a major influence on the kindergarten movement.

John Dewey's (1858–1952) educational philosophy, known as the progressive movement, clashed with Froebel's approach. Dewey valued children and childhood. He felt that learning and living were inseparable and that social skills developed along with the three Rs. For Dewey, the teacher's role was one of support and encouragement. He felt that children should play with real objects, not "gifts," and that the setting should be child-oriented and child-directed.

The debate over what was developmentally appropriate in kindergarten continued until the 1930s.

The kindergartens of today, although retaining some of Froebel's basic concepts, reflect more strongly the progressive ideas of John Dewey.

Kindergarten remained on the fringe of the public school system until the 1960s. The 1960s brought in a new era of awareness regarding the importance of early care and education. As the public evaluated the problems in society, they began to view the early childhood years as a time to begin potential solutions.

The Nursery School Movement

The nursery school movement began with concern for young children and their health care. Women such as Margaret and Rachel McMillan in England developed nursery school programs for poor children as young as 2 years of age. They emphasized children who were active, happy, and busy. Their concern went beyond education to include medical and dental care, fresh air, sleeping, and hygiene. This was far more than custodial care, and some even felt that the nursery school environment poor children experienced was better than what well-to-do families could obtain (Gordon & Browne, 1993).

The Child Care Movement

Child care has a long history, dating from the mid-1800s. It was initially a philanthropic endeavor by upper-class women to care for children of the working poor and recent immigrants. Such group care later became part of the social welfare movement, and social workers trained paraprofessionals to care for young children (Klein, 1992).

The federal government became involved in child care during the depression of the 1930s. Child care was one aspect of the Works Progress Administration (WPA) program. Its purpose was three-fold: it provided work for unemployed teachers, care for children whose mothers were working because their husbands were out of work, and it used up surplus food the government was buying from farmers. The federal government's interest in child care continued through the end of World War II. Then, although some child care centers remained, the majority of them closed in the late 1940s (Barclay, 1985).

The early history of child care has had a direct impact on early childhood education. The historical connection of child care to the welfare system has caused much stigmatization. Child care was viewed as part of a service system that provided custodial care for children of families who needed help. Child care allowed mothers to work and hence kept them off "welfare" while at the same time preserving the family unit (Klein, 1992).

Over time, the nursery/kindergarten movement began to overlap with the child care movement. An important distinction between the two is that the nursery/kindergarten movement was based on education, not social welfare or a response to the needs of working parents. The nursery/kindergarten movement significantly influenced child care in two ways: Educators were interested in impacting the curriculum for children so that it moved beyond custodial care, and such education was recognized as a service to the general public, not as a welfare issue (Klein, 1992).

As more women of all social classes began to participate in the workforce, more care was required than a half-day preschool program. Working mothers, including those who had young children with disabilities, began to look toward full-day child care programs. This need for increased care inspired changes not only in the types of care and types of programs, but also in the diversity of children cared for.

As increasing numbers of children with diverse abilities were included in child care, the distinction between nursery/kindergarten and child care blurred. Some professionals see child care and early education as different, but overlapping, services for young children. Spodek and Saracho (1992), see no distinction, "Indeed, children's development is considered at risk if they are denied an educational program while they are attending a child care center" (p. 189). Agreeing with Spodek and Saracho, we use the term early care and education to include both preschool and child care settings.

The Special Education Movement

There have always been children with disabilities, but there have not always been educational services to address these children's needs. Although a few attempts were made to educate young "idiots," these were isolated and nonsystematic until the beginning of the 1900s. Before that time, it was assumed that society should protect these individuals by placing them in asylums. The originators of special education were young, ambitious European physicians.

Jean Marc Gaspard Itard (1775–1838), a French physician, is credited by many as the founder of special education based on the principles that he used to educate Victor. Victor, a boy of about 12, had been found wondering alone in the forest of Aveyron and was considered a "wild boy" or hopeless idiot. Itard did not cure Victor, but he made significant changes in Victor's behavior using a set of principles including individualized instruction, stimulation, sequenced learning tasks, a structured environment, immediate reward for correct performance, and focus on functional skills. He believed that all children can learn to some extent and they should be educated to that level (Hallahan & Kauffman, 1994).

Although all students could learn, some needed different educational experiences. Elizabeth Farrell, a teacher in New York City, attempted to modify educational practices to address the needs of children and youth with disabilities. In 1922, Farrell and special educators from the United States and Canada founded the Council for Exceptional Children (CEC) which exists today (Hallahan & Kauffman, 1994). They wanted to share their ideas about what worked and what did not in this emerging field.

After World War II, several factors, both ideological and legal, led to a movement toward *normalization* in the lives of individuals with disabilities. These factors came together in the social activism of the 1960s.

Moving Toward Normalization

In the late 1800s and early 1900s, all education was viewed as a *privilege* rather than a right, and children who were disruptive or mentally retarded were frequently excluded from school to preserve order, to protect teachers from excessive demands, and to spare the other children the "pain" of having to look at children with disabilities (Hallahan & Kauffman, 1994).

Schools impart not only academic information but also social values. To the extent that children are segregated from regular schools and classrooms, whether because of physical impairment or skin color, they are seen as deficient. Beginning in the 1950s, the courts have defended education as the *right* of every child regardless of race or disability.

Societal attitudes slowly began to change in the 1960s. There was a growing interest by early childhood educators in the concept of early developmental programming. The mandate for Head Start, first made in 1965, publicly acknowledged the nation's concern about the needs of young children from low-income homes, the value of early childhood education, and the concept that education begins before public school age. Head Start was viewed as compensatory education, that is, it acknowledged the possibility that educational programs could make up for inadequate early life experiences. Head Start was community-based and was concerned not only with education but also with nutrition and health. Parents were involved as planners, teachers, and decision makers. Education was being offered to children who were "disadvantaged." Parents of children with diverse abilities began to ask if their children, too, could not profit from early education.

The request of the parents of children with diverse abilities reflected their belief in normalization for their children. *Normalization* is an approach that ensures that children who require special services are not separated from experiences of normal life, that is, educational, social, and recreational environments are as close to normal as possible.

Some of the stigma of having a child with a disability was removed when public figures such as President John F. Kennedy acknowledged enjoying spending time with his sister who was born with Down syndrome. Authoress Pearl Buck and movie stars Roy Rogers and Dale Evans made having a child with a disability a fact of life by not only loving these children but even writing about them. Encouraged and acting within the context of the social activism of the 1960s, parents and professionals began to form organizations and take legal action. Parent organizations, such as the National Association for Retarded Citizens (ARC), and professional organizations, were founded and actively promoted the cause of children with disabilities. They succeeded in making the general public (and eventually the legislators) aware that "it can happen to anyone."

The first definition of developmental disabilities was written during the 1960s. Society learned that those with disabilities needed specially trained professionals and teachers. And, people began to believe that individuals with disabilities were being deprived of their constitutional and human rights.

A very different influence was also at work changing social attitudes and creating a demand for a solution. In the 1960s and 1970s, the cost of education was outstripping the funds available to pay for it. Constructing and maintaining separate buildings to provide programs for those with disabilities multiplied costs to parents and taxpayers. Salaries for a separate set of teachers, administrators, custodians, and other personnel was an additional factor. Elimination of the special schools would bring tremendous savings. Even after spending more money on support services, such as temporary foster care, family counseling, and traditional therapies, society still benefits financially from integrating children with disabilities into regular schools. Further savings are possible if, through early identification and appropriate programming, children with disabilities can become contributing members of society.

By the 1980s, many professionals embraced this approach to providing services to children and followed these guidelines:

i. Provide developmentally delayed children with the most extensive opportunities for social, emotional, and skill development, as early as possible;

ii. Compensate for dissimilarities for appearance and/or physical disabilities through appropriate dress, surgery, dental work, physical therapy, prosthetic equipment, and so on;

iii. Present and interpret the children to others in ways that clearly reflect how highly they are valued and how much they have in common with all children; and

iv. Shape the attitudes of other children and adults to be more accepting of "differences" (Health & Welfare Canada, 1980, p. 2).

The interest in normalization emerged concurrently with the increasingly high costs of institutional care, the growing awareness of abuse and neglect in large institutions, as exposed in public scandals. Increasingly, individuals with disabilities and their human rights became an issue.

Special Education

Within the public school system, the first special education schools and classes were established beginning in the early 1900s for children who were

Young children with disabilities were (and sometimes still are) grouped together and taught in separate schools in self-contained classrooms with an early childhood special education teacher and several paraprofessionals.

identified as "educable mentally retarded." Most of these programs were in separate schools, some private, some public. Children with sensory impairments were typically taught by specialists in residential schools. They came home only for holidays or the summer unless the family lived near such a school (Gearheart, Mullen, & Gearheart, 1993).

During the late 1920s, classes for students with physical impairments were added to the public school system in special schools or classes. As other disabilities were recognized in the 1950s, it became clearer that these children needed different educational approaches. Special education as a field has focused on "difference," and the view of difference has been to give attention to what is exceptional rather than what is the same.

Special education also traditionally focused on a particular age range, usually 6 to 18 or 21 years. It was further broken down into separate subfields such as mental retardation, learning disabilities, behavioral disorders, sensory impairments, and so on. These focused on specially devised instruction that is designed to meet the unique and unusual needs of an exceptional student (Hallahan & Kauffman, 1994). The traditional special education curriculum centered around teaching children with disabilities specific adaptive skills with teachers providing instruction one-on-one or in small groups.

Although special education was viewed more positively than institutionalization, many still felt that there were problems with the system. Parents felt powerless in the face of school administrators who did not want to include *all* children with disabilities and were not providing what parents considered to be an appropriate education and related services.

Legal Basis for Integration

Integrating children with disabilities has followed two paths, one in the area of civil rights, the other in education. It also has three distinct eras. Before going into these let's be sure we understand the basic system.

A law passed by congress is referred to as a Public Law (P.L.), followed by two numbers separated by a hyphen. The first number is that of the congress that passed the law; the 94th Congress passed P.L. 94-142. The second number refers to the sequential position in the laws that particular congress passed, in this case the 142nd law. Federal laws are often changed or amended. P.L. 94-142 was amended in 1997. These amendments change the law. Most professionals in the field know the names or numbers of significant laws. When a law is passed, regulations are detailed in the Code of Federal Regulations (CFR) to further explain the law. Individual states may go beyond what is required in the regulations. For example, some states include gifted and talented children in their special educational programming; however, all states have to meet the minimum requirements of the federal law.

The Early Years

The early years are those that led up to the passage of P.L. 94-142 in 1975. The 1954 case of *Brown v. the Board of Education of Topeka, Kansas,* focusing on the civil rights of Black Americans, had little to do with disabilities, but much to do with segregation in education. Separate education was declared not equal. Whether the separation is based on race or disability, the principle is the same:

> Separate educational facilities are inherently unequal. This inherent inequality stems from the stigma created by purposeful segregation which generates a feeling of inferiority that may affect their hearts and minds in a way unlikely ever to be undone. (Earl Warren, Chief Justice, United States Supreme Court, May 17, 1954)

Another case *Tinker v. Des Moines Independent Community School District* (1969) furthered civil rights for students. This case focused on whether or not students had the right to wear black arm bands to protest the involvement of the United States in the Vietnam War. The students wearing arm bands were quiet, passive, nondisruptive, and did not impinge upon the rights of others. The court ruling was interesting. It declared that children are *persons* under the Constitution of the United States and that they have civil rights independent of their parents, and further that they do not lose these civil rights when they attend school. This case set the stage for cases that used the violation of the First (right to free speech) and Fourteenth Amendments (right to due process) as their grounds for bringing suit.

As parents of children with disabilities became increasingly dissatisfied with the education of their children, they, too, sought legal remedies to make the educational system more responsive to their needs. Encouraged by an increasingly receptive public and strengthened by better organization and cooperation among parent and professional groups, parents began to press their cause in court and in congress.

Although progress was being made in educating children with disabilities in the public schools, advocacy groups such as the Children's Defense Fund made their position clear about the almost 2 million children who were not being served by the public school system in the Washington Research Report:

> [I]f a child is not white, or is white but not middle class, does not speak English, is poor, needs special help with seeing, hearing, walking, reading, learning, adjusting, growing up, is pregnant or married at age 15, is not smart enough or is too smart, then, in many places, school officials decide school is not the place for that child. In sum, out of school children share a common characteristic of *differentness* by virtue of race, income, physical, mental, or emotional "handicap," or age. They are, for the most part, out of school not by choice, but

because they have been *excluded.* (Children's Defense Fund, 1975, p. 4)

The move to educate *all* children without discrimination was supported by the Rehabilitation Act of 1973. Section 504 of that act focused on nondiscrimination in programs or activities receiving federal financial assistance and provides qualified individuals civil rights protection against discrimination in institutions that receive *federal* funds, including Project Head Start. The definitions used in Section 504 are far broader than those used in educational laws. The definition is "Any person who (i) has a physical or mental impairment which substantially limits one or more of such person's major life activities, (ii) has a record or such an impairment, or (iii) is regarded as having such an impairment." (Major life activities include self-care, performing manual tasks, seeing, hearing, speaking, breathing, learning, and walking.) Section 504 applies to all educational institutions that receive federal funds:

> The regulations governing Section 504 stipulate that No otherwise qualified handicapped individual . . . shall, solely by reason of his (or her) handicap, be excluded from the participation in, be denied the benefits of, or be subject to discrimination under any program or activity receiving *federal* financial assistance. (C.F.R. 104; P.L. 93-112)

A related piece of legislation, P.L. 93-380, The Family Education Rights and Privacy Act of 1974, often called the Buckley Amendment, gives parents of students under 18 and students 18 and over the right to examine records kept in the student's personal file, to have these explained. If found to be misleading or inaccurate, they may request the records be amended. Written permission from parents is required for these records to be released unless it is to other school officials (such as when students transfer) (NICHC, 1988). These laws, and the work of advocacy groups and parents, set the stage for the middle years.

The Middle Years

The passage of P.L. 94-142, the Education for All Handicapped Children Act of 1975 (EHA), marked the beginning of the middle years. The EHA is a series of laws focusing on the rights of children with disabilities to have a free appropriate public education. The intent of this legislation has been to require teachers to meet the needs of individual students with disabilities. Legislation in this area has moved increasingly to *mandate* or require states to provide educational services for younger children. Failure to comply with such a mandate can result in the loss of federal funding in other programs. In the past, the federal government authorized programs that states could choose to participate in. If states chose to participate, rewards were provided. Legislation also sup-

ported the concept that children should be educated in the least restrictive environment, that is, one that is closest to the one in which the child would have been educated if he did not have a disability.

As children move through public school, the relationship between Section 504 of the Rehabilitation Act of 1973 and P.L. 94-142 is important. All children who are eligible for services under P.L. 94-142 are also covered by Section 504. However, Section 504 includes disabilities that may not interfere with learning. For example, a child who has asthma may not have a learning problem, however, he may need accommodations in physical education. Likewise, a child who tests HIV positive may have no symptoms that interfere with learning, but may need some accommodations to stay in school. Section 504 includes these children and requires that accommodations be made for them. If at some point their disability does interfere with their ability to learn, they will also be covered under P.L. 94-142.

The passage of P.L. 94-142 in 1975 had a tremendous effect on the education of the school-age children with disabilities. It had much less effect on the education of young children with disabilities. Although children 3 to 5 "could" be included, that was not part of the original mandate. Educators had their hands full, and little energy was left over for concerns about younger children.

The government did create a Preschool Incentive Grant Program as part of P.L. 94-142 that encouraged states to serve children ages 3 through 5. It even authorized money for this purpose ($63 per child per year). Few states chose to participate because the $63 did not cover the cost of serving these children (Hebbeler, Smith, & Black, 1991).

The Later Years

Education for children with disabilities birth through 5 began evolving into a situation where there was more knowledge but without a state-level system of services. The need for greater interagency coordination was apparent as was the push to serve all eligible young children (Hebbeler et al., 1991).

P.L. 99-457 (1986) lowered the age of eligibility for mandated services to age 3, increased funding for preschool children (Part B), and established the Infants and Toddlers Program for children from birth through age 2 (Part H). The Infants and Toddlers Program was a discretionary one in which states were allowed to develop their own definitions of "developmentally delayed" and each state could decide whether or not they would serve children "at risk."

Individuals with disabilities have found that technology will support them in doing tasks that had previously been impossible. The federal government acknowledged the importance of the role of technology when they passed the Technology-Related Assistance for Individuals with Disabilities in 1988 (P.L. 100-407), commonly known as the Tech Act. This act was designed to help explore the potential of technology for meeting the needs of individuals with disabilities including young children and the elderly. Increasingly, the field has become dependent on assistive devices to enable children with disabilities to function in regular settings.

In 1990, the Education for All Handicapped Children Act (EHA) was renamed the Individuals with Disabilities Education Act (IDEA). These laws are designed to provide more and better services for children with disabilities and their families and to guarantee the rights of these children to equal educational opportunities. Additionally, these educational opportunities are to be provided in the "least restrictive environment." The emphasis is on placing and educating young children with diverse abilities in their own homes, child care settings, preschools, and regular public school classrooms, not setting up separate segregated settings for them.

The Americans with Disabilities Act (ADA) of 1990 extends civil rights protection and nondiscrimination requirements of Section 504 to *all* settings not just those that receive public funds. The ADA expanded this and opened all child care settings and private schools to children with disabilities.

This child uses a communications board to communicate with his teacher and classmates. One of the teacher's roles is to help him become more fluent in using the keyboard and more specific in his communication by showing which key to push. Communications boards vary based on the child's receptive and expressive language skills.

The IDEA was again reauthorized in 1997, P.L. 105-17. These changes are referred to as the 1997 Amendments. The major modifications for children address areas of behavioral intervention, transition, assessment, the IEP, and classroom implementation strategies CEC, 1997). The 1997 Amendments also strengthen the role of the parents in the educational process and made the federal government's position on least restrictive environment clearer.

Table 2.1 gives a chronological summary of the laws that relate to the education of children with disabilities.

The IDEA has a wide-ranging impact and contains specific terminology. Detailed information about the IDEA and its requirements and implications are given in Chapter 7.

Legislation and Litigation

The relationship between legislation and litigation is an interesting one. In many ways, litigation provides the impetus for new laws or clarifies and determines the limits or interpretation of existing laws. One case, *Pennsylvania Association of Retarded Children v. Commonwealth of Pennsylvania* (1971), a class action suit on behalf of the parents of 13 children, argued that the denial of a free public education for children with mental retardation was a violation of the Fourteenth Amendment of the Constitution of the United States. Education for *some* had to be education for *all.* In a settlement approved by the court, Pennsylvania agreed to provide education to all school-age children with mental retardation living in the state (including those in state institutions) within one year. A parallel decision, *Peter Mills v. Board of Education of The District of Columbia* (1972), added the stipulation that lack of funds was not an acceptable reason for excluding children.

Other decisions concerned children who had been misplaced by the system. In *Diana v. State Board of Education of Monterey County, CA* (1970), the court ruled that children must be tested in their primary language. Previously, children whose primary language was not English had been tested in English and sometimes wrongfully declared mentally retarded. This type of litigation was part of the early years and did much to provide the impetus for the passage of P.L. 94-142.

Once P.L. 94-142 was passed, litigation determined the minimum level of services that must be provided under the law. For example, the case of the *Board of Education of the Hendrick Hudson Central School District v. Rowley* (1982) provided guidelines on what "free appropriate public education" means. Amy Rowley was a child with a hearing impairment whose parents thought she would do better if she had an interpreter. They were probably right. However, Amy Rowley was functioning at the same level as her peers. The Supreme Court ruled against Rowley. Their interpretation was that the EHA was not intended to require any particular level of, or intensity of, educational services. Maximizing a child's potential

TABLE 2.1   PUBLIC LAWS SPECIFICALLY AFFECTING EARLY CHILDHOOD SPECIAL EDUCATION

Year	Public Law	Title and Significance
1968	90-538	*The Handicapped Children's Early Education Assistance Act (HCEEP).* This act established the development of model demonstration projects to serve young children with disabilities.
1973	93-112	*The Rehabilitation Act of 1973.* Section 504 of this law mandates equal opportunities for children with disabilities in preschools and schools that receive *federal* funds.
1975	94-142	*Education for All Handicapped Children Act of 1975 (EHA).* Mandates a free appropriate public education in the least restrictive environment for children and youth (5–21) with disabilities.
1983	98-199	*Education of the Handicapped Act Amendments of 1983.* Supported the development of model demonstration programs for preschool special education, early intervention, and transition.
1986	99-457	*Education of the Handicapped Act Amendments of 1986.* Established (Part B) mandated services for children 3–5 years. Established (Part H) an entitlement program for infants and toddlers 0–2.
1988	100-407	*Technology-Related Assistance for Individuals with Disabilities Act of 1988.* Technology refers to "any item, piece of equipment, or product system whether acquired off the shelf, modified or customized that is used to increase, maintain, or improve the functional abilities of individuals with disabilities." This act provides adaptive devices, whether commercially available or customized to individuals with disabilities (including young children) and the elderly.
1990	101-336	*The Americans with Disabilities Act of 1990 (ADA).* Extended civil rights protection to people with disabilities in all settings. Required that schools, employers, and government agencies provide reasonable accommodations to allow individuals with disabilities to participate to the fullest extent possible.
1990	101-476	*Individuals with Disabilities Education Act (IDEA).* These amendments to the EHA renamed the law. The act made language changes by replacing the term "handicapped" with "disability" and used "people first" language. Includes services to children with autism, traumatic brain injury, serious emotional disturbances, and attention deficit disorder, as well as transition and assistive technology services.
1991	102-119	*Individuals with Disabilities Education Act Amendments of 1991.* The terms "language and speech" have been replaced by communication, "psychosocial" by social or emotional, and "self-help skills" by adaptive development. "Case management services" are referred to as service coordination. Another important change is that "to the maximum extent appropriate," children are to be in natural environments, including the home, and community settings in which children without disabilities participate.
1997	105-17	*Individuals with Disabilities Education Act Amendments of 1997.* Changes include the ability to use the Developmental Delay eligibility category, at the discretion of states, for children through age 9, funding formulas have changed to include population and poverty data, Part C (Formerly Part H), infant and toddlers, allows young children who are not eligible for services to be monitored over time. States are required to establish and implement a mediation process. Discipline procedures have been clarified; there are also changes in the IEP, assessment procedures, and a clear emphasis that children with disabilities should participate in the regular curriculum and assessment procedures.

was too high a standard but providing only those services available to children without disabilities was too low a standard. The EHA requires the provision of a "basic floor of opportunity" consisting of "access to specialized instruction and related services individually designed to provide educational benefit to the handicapped child." If the child is educated in the regular classroom, the program should be "reasonably calculated to enable the child to achieve passing marks and advance from grade to grade."

Additionally, they defined a free appropriate public education to be personalized instruction with sufficient support services to permit a child to benefit educationally from instruction, at public expense, that meets the state's educational standards and

approximate grade levels used in the state's regular education and conforms with the IEP.

In the area of related services, *Irving Independent School District v. Tatro* (1984) expanded services to a child with disabilities. The Supreme Court determined that catheterization for a 3.5-year-old student, which can be provided by a school nurse or trained lay person, is a proper related service, not an excluded "medical service." The court approaches adoption of the "but for" test. It goes something like this: "but for" catheterization the child could attend public school. "The Act makes specific provision for services, like transportation, for example, that do no more than enable a child to be physically present in class . . . Services like catheterization that permit a child to remain at school during the day are no less related to the effort to educate than are services that enable the child to reach, enter, or exit the school" (adapted from Hartman, 1989).

Inclusion of children with AIDS in schools has been controversial and is expected to become more so. In *School Board of Nassau County, Florida v. Arline* (1987), the Supreme Court ruled that individuals with infectious diseases including AIDS are covered under Section 504 of the Rehabilitation Act. When they need special educational services, they will also be covered by the IDEA.

Determination of the law's meaning is an ongoing process. States that provide the minimum required by law are referred to as "floor-of-opportunity" states. States that provide services beyond those required by law are "maximizing" states.

The laws have required that increasingly younger children with disabilities be educated, even starting at birth. The question becomes who would do this? Special education started at school age. Early childhood education focused on young children without disabilities. How could these two be combined?

Theoretical Bases for Inclusive Early Childhood Education

Deriving some of its characteristics from special education, and others from early childhood education and child development *inclusive early childhood education* goes beyond applying traditional special education techniques to an earlier age and acknowledging developmentally appropriate practices; rather, it is a unique blend that has emerged into a field of its own. It includes aspects of family relations and family therapy, the creative arts, branches of psychology and sociology, and knowledge gained from compensatory education approaches. The field continues to change and expand in response to emerging information and innovative techniques.

Early childhood education is a field of study that concentrates on the development and education of children from birth through age 8. It is concerned with practice, research, and theory in the field. It includes areas such as parenting and teaching young children, child care, curriculum, administration, discipline, and age-based topics focusing on infants, toddlers, preschool, and early elementary school children. The field has a strong child development base, although it adheres to no single philosophy of educating children. It is committed to the principle that birth through age 8 are critical years for development and that good programs and programming are imperative during those years. The focus of early care and education is typically on the whole child, with a balanced program taking into account the child's developmental characteristics in a setting that is appropriately designed for children. The emphasis has been on developmentally appropriate practice and responsive caregivers (Bredekamp, 1987; Bredekamp & Copple, 1997). There is a debate as to whether the generally accepted, high-quality characteristics of early childhood programs for children without disabilities are equally appropriate and effective for children with disabilities.

Inclusive Early Care and Education

Inclusive early care and education is a blend of early childhood and special education. The focus is on children who have diverse abilities. Those working in inclusive early childhood education mix the excitement of helping mold a new profession with the unsettling position of having fewer "knowns." This profession emerged because neither special education nor early childhood education practitioners, while working separately, were able to make a maximum impact on the lives of young children with diverse abilities. Professionals from both groups found they were more effective when they blended their expertise.

Change in the field of inclusive early care and education is a result of interwoven social and legal factors. Much of the change has come as a result of research and experimentation. For example, findings in psychology have affected our philosophy of what education is and how it takes place. We now recognize the importance of individualizing our teaching. This has facilitated the provision of attention to individual needs that is essential when working with children with diverse abilities.

Most educational research has focused on how (and what) to teach rather than how children learn. Swiss psychologist Jean Piaget (whose work was published in English in the early 1950s) focused his research on *how* children learn. Piaget (1970) argued that the teacher's role is to set up an environment that a child can actively explore. Classroom activities, which are part of the environment, should incorporate both familiar and new aspects. Lev Vygotsky, a Russian researcher whose works were translated into English in the 1980s, focused on social interactions and language as the foundation for cognitive development. When examining the adult-child relationship, he looked at the range of tasks that children could not accomplish alone but could accomplish with the help of competent adults or peers. He called this the *zone of proximal development* (ZPD) (Vygotsky, 1934/1987). Techniques or strategies that adults use to allow children to accomplish more difficult tasks are called *scaffolding*. With language, scaffolding may include using gestures, actions, facial expressions, objects, or pictures to reinforce meaning and extend learning. From the work of Piaget and Vygotsky, scholars concluded that to learn, a child must actively interact with the environment and that the activities in the environment must be individualized to match and then expand the child's experience.

The work of Albert Bandura (1992) and others focused on how children learn by modeling other children. Segregating children at an early age meant that

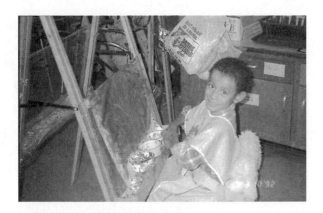

Including children with disabilities may require some accommodations. This boy needs to paint from a padded chair rather than standing up. The chair provides him with a more stable base, and the padding protects his skin.

children with disabilities had only peers with disabilities available as models. This segregation effectively resulted in teaching children to imitate such peers. With teacher support and exposure, children with disabilities can learn to model and play with nondisabled peers. All children can gain experience from an early age in interacting with a wide range of people.

Piaget and Vygotsky's work helped make integration possible by changing our philosophy and methodology of education. Bandura's work helped make inclusion imperative by demonstrating that segregation deprived children with disabilities (and those without) of a full education.

Differences in orientation of early childhood and special education have been topics of hot debates and challenges on both sides. For example, Graham and Bryant (1993) state:

> Environments for children with disabilities are typically less stimulating and developmentally appropriate than those for their nondisabled peers. Behavioral instruction methods such as reinforcement, modeling, shaping, and prompting are more prevalent in programs for children with disabilities and these methods have been shown to help them achieve developmental milestones. (p. 31)

Not only are the environments less stimulating, but there is some concern that an emphasis on behavioral methods doesn't adequately take into account the role emotions play as a motivator for learning. Emotions provide young children with a foundation to learn about feelings and to have wider and more complex emotional relationships. They influence developing a sense of self as well as being linked to culturally valued skills and standards (Hyson, 1994).

Much of the controversy focuses around the interpretation of developmentally appropriate practices. In response to this controversy, the National Association for the Education of Young Children has published guidelines specifying what is meant by developmentally appropriate practice (Bredekamp, 1987; Bredekamp & Copple, 1997) and operationalized this for curriculum and assessment for both children with and without disabilities (Bredekamp & Copple, 1997; Bredekamp & Rosegrant, 1992, 1995). Developmentally appropriate practice has three distinct features: age appropriateness, individual appropriateness, and social and cultural appropriateness. Age appropriateness focuses on the relationship between the materials and methods used based on the age group that is being served. This is particularly an issue when development is either much faster or slower than average. If a second grader reads at an eighth grade level, much of the available literature is inappropriate for him. Likewise if a second grader has the mental age of a 3-year-old, many of the materials used with second graders are inappropriate. The second aspect of developmentally appropriate practice requires that the environment, materials, and interactions with adults be consistent with the ability and needs of each individual child (Bredekamp, 1987; Bredekamp & Copple, 1997). It focuses on providing options for children rather than expecting all children to do the same thing at the same time. In early childhood education, this has frequently been interpreted as responding to a child's interests; in early childhood special education, it is viewed as responding to a child's needs. In reality, it is both. Individualized planning should take into account both children's *interests* and their *needs* (Bredekamp & Rosegrant, 1992). It is not an either or situation. The third factor, social and cultural appropriateness, relates to educating children in a way that is respective of and responsive to their family background.

Within a given classroom some children need more specialized services and planning than others. Some children may lack prerequisite skills and knowledge. Individualized planning, in addition to being based on the child's strengths and needs, must take into account the priorities of the family and the skills required for future school and nonschool environments (Carta, Schwartz, Atwater, & McConnell, 1992). Ongoing criterion-based assessment is necessary in order to monitor the child's progress toward these goals.

Educators working with young children with diverse abilities must have a wide range of teaching strategies to provide optimal care and education. These strategies need to be matched to individual children to facilitate learning. Some children with diverse abilities may need support to be actively involved and participatory. Services for young children with diverse abilities are family-centered, and families must play an active role in home-setting partnerships. Including children with diverse abilities in the early childhood program broadens expectations for educators' skills, and assumes that children will require more varied care and learning environments. Bredekamp and Rosegrant (1992) visualize these teaching techniques as being on a continuum that goes from nondirective to directive. The early childhood educator, as decision maker, decides about the appropriateness of the technique based on the individual child and the learning environment.

According to the National Association for the Education of Young Children (Bredekamp & Copple, 1997), the developmentally appropriate practice requirements really represent a matter of degree of interpretation rather than an underlying philosophical difference between early childhood education and early childhood special education. Others feel that developmentally appropriate practices are not specific enough to guide the learning of young children with diverse abilities. They caution that the intent of early childhood programs for children with diverse abilities is *intervention.* This intervention must be specifically designed for a particular child, given his individual situation and intervention should take precedence. "Programs serving young children with special needs must be outcome-based, with specific criteria, procedures, and timelines used to determine if individual children progress toward stated outcomes" (Carta et al., 1992, p. 7). This approach typically leads to teacher-directed programs leaving less room for child-centered activities.

The accountability principle that came to the forefront with the passage of P.L. 94-142 is one of the factors influencing programming for young children with diverse abilities. Parents not only wanted individualized programs designed for their children, but they wanted to ensure that their children were progressing toward the goals set for them. Hence, instructional objectives were determined to measure progress and to make teachers more accountable for learning. Carta et al. (1992) question the efficacy of applying developmentally appropriate practices to young children with disabilities. At this time, there is not, according to their review, an empirical research base to support this approach. However, working with developmentally appropriate practices as programming guidelines for working with children with disabilities has not been widely enough used to reach any conclusions.

The controversy about the effectiveness of the outcome-based intervention approach versus the developmentally appropriate practice approach to planning effective care and curricula emphasis is ongoing. We support the use of developmentally appropriate practices when planning for children with diverse abilities and emphasize the skills that developmentalists need to care for and educate a wide range of children. However, there is a need for more research to show whether or not these practices can be supported empirically. The issue of developmentally appropriate practices is one that students need to keep in mind as they enter the field.

If *all* children are part of regular settings and *all* children participate in the general curriculum, then *all* educators need to know sufficient techniques to care for and educate *all* children. One of the most powerful crossovers in inclusive early childhood education is that *all* educators are sharing the knowledge that each child is unique, that instruction needs to be individualized, that developmentally appropriate practices are important for all children, and that what

happens in classrooms is about *children,* not just about math, reading, and science.

New methods, support services, and technology now available make inclusion a more achievable goal. For example, team teaching, that is, a teacher trained in special education and a teacher whose focus has been regular education, together teach a group of children. This is now a common practice with young children and can help the developmentalist who has little experience with children with diverse abilities. The consultation model which involves a specialist coming into the classroom on a regular or as-needed bases to provide specific information, model behavior, technical assistance, and troubleshooting, allows developmentalists access to a professional support system.

The principles underlying inclusive early care and education hold the potential for meeting the needs of children from different socioeconomic groups, different cultural/ethnic backgrounds, and different abilities.

Summary

Education for children with diverse abilities has a long history that has involved exclusion and segregation. The move toward inclusion has resulted from changing social, legal, and educational philosophies that have led to individualized programming for children. Of particular importance are the legal requirements that all children have a free, appropriate, public education. In addition to including all children with diverse abilities, their families are included as well, not just as sources of transportation and the like, but as decision makers whose priorities, values, and needs must be reflected in the educational process.

Inclusive early childhood education is a dynamic new field. It requires professionals from early childhood and early childhood special education to rethink many of the ways they have operated in the past and come up with new solutions for a young diverse population. It is a field of growth and potential. You can help shape the direction of that growth and help fulfill the potential.

Educational Resources

Administration on Developmental Disabilities (ADD)
Administration for Children and Families
U.S. Department of Health and Human Services
370 L'Enfant Promenade, SW
Washington, DC 20447
(202) 690-6590, FAX (202)690-6904
A federal government agency that works with state and local governments to promote independence and productivity for those with developmental disabilities. Provides funding and information about the Developmental Disabilities Planning Councils, the Protection and Advocacy system and the University Affiliated Programs in each state.

Clearinghouse of Disability Information
Office of Special Education and Rehabilitative
    Services (OSERS)
Room 3132 Switzer Building
Washington, DC 20202-2524
(202) 205-8241, (202) 205-8723
    *Provides information about federal legislation
and programs for individuals with disabilities and
makes referrals.*

Commission on Mental and Physical Disability Law
American Bar Association
740 15th Street, NW, 9th Floor
Washington, DC 20005-1009
(202) 662-1570, TTY (202) 662-1012,
    FAX (202) 662-1032
http://www.abanet, org
e-mail: cmpdl@attmail.com
    *Provides technical consultation about issues re-
lated to the Americans with Disabilities Act and
provides searches of legal databases in the field of
disability.*

Office on the Americans with Disabilities Act
Department of Justice, Civil Rights Division
PO Box 66118
Washington, DC 20035-6118
(800) 514-0301, TDD (800) 514-0383
http://www.usdoj.gov/crt/ada/adahom1.htm
    *Enforces Tiles II and III of the ADA. Provides
publications, technical assistance, and consultation
on the ADA.*

Office of Civil Rights, Department of Education
300 C Street, SW
Washington, DC 20202
(202) 205-5413, FAX (202) 205-9862
http://www.ed.gov/offices/ocr
    *Enforces laws and regulations for individuals
in educational institutions. Complaints may be filed
at any of 10 regional offices.*

Office of Civil Rights, Department of Health and
    Human Services
330 Independence Avenue, SW (Cohen Building)
Washington, DC 20201
(202) 619-0585, FAX (202) 619-3437
http://www.hhs.gov/
    *Office which is responsible for enforcing laws
and regulation designed to protect the rights of individuals seeking medical and social services in institutions that receive federal assistance. Complaints
may be filed at the regional offices.*

Social Security Administration
Office of Public Inquiries
6401 Security Boulevard
Room 4-C-5 Annex
Baltimore, MD 21235
(800) 772-1213, TTY (800) 325-0778
http://www.ssa.gov/SSA_Home.html/
    *Provides information and publications on social
security benefits for individuals with disabilities.*

Special Education Resources Internet
http://curry.school.Virginia.EDU/go/specialed/
    *A well organized set of resources about special
education events, history, and interventions, focus
on disabilities, Internet resources, professionals and
parents.*

References

Americans with Disabilities Act of 1990, Pub. L. No.
101-336, 104 Stat. 327-378, 42 U.S.C. 12101.

Bandura, A. (1992). Social cognitive theory. In
R. Vasta (Ed.), *Six theories of child development*
(pp. 1–60). United Kingdom: Jessica Kingsley.

Barclay, L. K. (1985). *Infant development.* Fort
Worth, TX: Holt, Rinehart and Winston.

Berkson, G. (1993). *Children with handicaps: A
review of behavioral research.* Hillsdale, NJ:
Erlbaum.

Board of Education of the Hendrick Hudson Central
School District v. Rowley, 453 U.S. 176 (1982).

Brant, D. M., & Graham, M. A. (Eds.). (1993).
*Implementing early intervention: From research to
effective practice.* New York: Guilford Press.

Bredekamp, S. (Ed.). (1987). *Developmentally
appropriate practice in early childhood programs
serving children from birth through age 8*
(Expanded ed.). Washington, DC: NAEYC.

Bredekamp, S., & Copple, C. (Eds.). (1997).
*Developmentally appropriate practice in early
childhood programs serving children from birth
through age 8* (Rev. ed.). Washington, DC: NAEYC.

Bredekamp, S., & Rosegrant, T. (Eds.). (1992).
*Reaching potentials: Appropriate curriculum and
assessment for young children* (Vol. 1). Washington,
DC: NAEYC.

Bredekamp, S., & Rosegrant, T. (Eds.). (1995).
*Reaching potentials: Transforming early childhood
curriculum and assessment* (Vol. 2). Washington,
DC: NAEYC.

Carta, J., Schwartz, I., Atwater, J., & McConnell, S.
(1992). Developmentally appropriate practice:
Appraising its usefulness for young children with
disabilities. *Topics in Early Childhood Special
Education, 11*(1), 1–19.

Children's Defense Fund. (1975). *Washington
research report.* Washington, DC: Author.

Council for Exceptional Children. (1997). IDEA sails
through congress. *CEC Today, 3*(10), 1, 9, 15.

Diana v. State Board of Education of Monterey
County, No. C-70-37 (N.D. Cal., Feb. 5, 1970)
(unreported).

Education for All Handicapped Children Act of 1975,
Pub. L. No. 94-142, 89 Stat. 773-796, 20 U.S.C. 1400.

Education for All Handicapped Children Act of 1983,
Pub. L. No. 98-199, 97 Stat. 1357-1377, 20 U.S.C.
1400.

Education for All Handicapped Children Act of 1986, Pub. L. No. 99-457, 100 Stat. 1145-1211, 20 U.S.C. 1400.

Family Educational Rights and Privacy Act of 1974. Pub. L. No. 93-380, 88 Stat. 484 Section 513.

Gearheart, B., Mullen, R. C., & Gearheart, C. (1993). *Exceptional individuals: An introduction.* Belmont, CA: Brooks/Cole.

Gordon, A., & Browne, K. W. (1993). *Beginnings and beyond: Foundations in early childhood education* (3rd ed.). Albany, NY: Delmar.

Hallahan, D., & Kauffman, J. (1994). *Exceptional children: Introduction to special education* (6th ed.). Englewood Cliffs, NJ: Prentice-Hall.

Handicapped Children's Early Education Assistance Act of 1968. Pub. L. No. 90-538, 82 Stat. 901.

Hartman, B. (1989, May). *Overview of special education case law affecting Delaware.* Presentation at Roles and Functions of Due Process Hearing Panel Members, Dover, DE.

Health and Welfare Canada. (1980). *Children with special needs in day care: A guide to integration.* Ottawa, ON.

Hebbeler, K., Smith, B., & Black, T. (1991). Federal early childhood special education policy: A model for the improvement of services for children with disabilities. *Exceptional Children, 58*(2), 104–112.

Hyson, M. C. (1994). *The emotional development of young children: Building an emotion-centered curriculum.* New York: Teachers College Press.

Individuals with Disabilities Education Act of 1990. Pub. L. No. 101-476, 104 Stat. 1103 Section 901, 20 U.S.C. 1400.

Individuals with Disabilities Education Act of 1991. Pub. L. No. 102-119, 105 Stat. 587, 20 U.S.C. 1400.

Individuals with Disabilities Education Act of 1997. Pub. L. No. 105-17, 111 Stat. 37-157, 20 U.S.C. 1400.

Irving Independent School District v. Tatro, 468 U.S. 883 (1984).

Klein, A. G. (1992). *The debate over child care 1969-1990: A sociohistorical analysis.* Albany: State University of New York Press.

National Information Center for Children and Youth with Handicaps. (1988). *Questions parents often ask about special education services and Public Law 94-142.* Washington, DC: Author.

Pennsylvania Association of Retarded Children v. Commonwealth of Pennsylvania, 334 F. Supp. 1257 (E.D. Pa. 1971).

Peter Mills v. Board of Education of the District of Columbia, 348 F. Supp. 866 (D.C.D.C. 1972).

Piaget, J. (1970). Piaget's theory. In P. H. Mussen (Ed.), *Carmichael's manual of child psychology* (Vol. 1, 3rd ed., pp. 703–732). New York: Wiley.

Rehabilitation Act of 1973, Pub. L. No. 93-112, 87 Stat. 355.

School Board of Nassau County, Florida et al. v. Arline, 480 U.S. 273 (1987).

Spodek, B., & Saracho, O. N. (1992). Child care: A look to the future. In B. Spodek & O. N. Saracho (Eds.), *Issues in child care* (pp. 187–198). New York: Teachers College Press.

Spodek, B., Saracho, O. N., & Peters, D. L. (1988). Professionalism, semiprofessionalism and craftsmanship. In B. Spodek, O. Saracho, & D. L. Peters (Eds.), *Professionalism and the early childhood practitioner* (pp. 3-9). New York: Teachers College Press.

Technology-Related Assistance for Individuals with Disabilities Act of 1988, Pub. L. No. 100-407, 29 U.S.C. 2201.

Tinker v. Des Moines Independent Community School District, 393 U.S. 503 (1969).

U.S. Department of Education. (1988). *AIDS and the education of our children.* Washington, DC: Author.

Vygotsky, L. S. (1987). Thinking and speech. In R. Rieber & A. S. Carton (Eds.), *The collected works of L. S. Vygotsky: Vol. 1. Problems of general psychology* (pp. 37–285). New York: Plenum Press. (Original work published 1934)

Chapter 3

MOVING TOWARD
INCLUSION

After a struggle, another round of being the "squeaky wheel," we persuaded the principal and staff to let our son attend a traditional first-grade class for part of the day—about 2 hours every afternoon. The rest of the day he remained in a segregated classroom shared by other students with orthopedic disabilities—primarily those who used wheelchairs and were for the most part nonverbal. We believed inclusion was important for Don, but also for the "typical" children—we believed acceptance of differences should start early in life and we wanted to act on our beliefs—but we were weary from the fight. . . . Don was reluctantly allowed to attend this class, but no other child with a disability was invited even though other children were more "able" than he.

Don loved the inclusive class. At 7 he was still learning to drive a power wheelchair, and the paraprofessional said that he tried to drive by the segregated classroom to get to the inclusive setting. We knew it was working for Don.

One day I came to pick Don up early for an appointment. As I walked up the hallway, a line of first graders waited to go to the cafeteria. A few of Don's classmates in the segregated classroom silently rolled by the line of chattering children. I met Don in the office and began to go with him down the hallway to the outside door. As we neared the line of kids, I prepared myself for the usual stares or pointing fingers. Instead, I heard "Look, there's Don!" "Hi Don." "See you tomorrow, Don." "Will you be back tomorrow, Don?" I couldn't believe it! Those warm greetings meant more to me than any straight A report card could have meant. Don smiled and so did I—through lots of happy tears on the way home. I still cry when I think about it. I felt there may be hope for inclusion after all.

Don attends a "typical school" now. He's just one of the gang—the kids in the school have accepted his presence as normal and he has many friends there. However, one of the staff tells me that Don still gets those stares from one group of kids. They have a program at Don's school where gifted kids come once a week for enrichment.

These kids have never had the opportunity of getting to know a fellow classmate who happens to use a wheelchair. So, they still stare. . . . Will they ever get to know Don from the inside out or only the outside in? It's their loss, our loss, and society's loss.

Inclusion really works.

Have you ever been excluded? Chosen last? Had to watch while others participated in something you could not do? How did it feel. If this were an isolated event it probably didn't impact your self-concept, however, depending on the extent that you were excluded or even made fun of and laughed at, you may have felt isolated, lonely, and uncared for. Think about the first female to enter an all-male military school. Was she included? Inclusion is more than physical proximity; it requires all participants to change their values—to include all participants.

The landscape in early care and education is changing. Developmentalists are providing care and education to younger children, to children who come from more diverse cultural, ethnic, and economic backgrounds, and to children with diverse abilities. And they are doing this in inclusive settings.

Inclusion represents an ideal: that all children with disabilities will have their differences acknowledged and, where possible, will be educated to be equal participants in society. This objective means that children with diverse abilities should be provided with care and education in neighborhood settings, that their lives should be as normal as possible, and that intervention should not interfere with individual freedom. It seeks to restructure early care and education settings from a dual system that segregates children and educators by a labeling process to a system in which all children—regardless of race, socioeconomic status, gender, age, ability, religion, linguistic ability, or sexual orientation—are educated together in a unified educational system that meets the needs of *all* children. Although the inclusion movement has focused primarily on the needs of children with disabilities, its goal is to change education for all children (Forest & Pearpoint, 1990).

The scope of inclusion is broader than just traditional elementary school settings and includes all 27

TABLE 3.1 LEAST RESTRICTIVE ENVIRONMENT

Least Restrictive . . . . ▸ . . . . ▸ . . . . ▸ . . . . ▸ . . . . ▸

Setting	Child care, preschool, regular kindergarten	Child care, preschool, kindergarten with consultation	Regular setting with itinerant teacher/therapist
Children typically served	Children who haven't been identified; children with mild speech and language delays, conductive hearing losses, mild behavioral and emotional disorders, and health impairments	Identified children with mild to moderate disabilities and some children with severe impairments	Children with visual, hearing, physical, or communication impairments
Teacher's role	Teach all the children in the classroom, make referrals	Teach all the children, receive some training in disabilities, be part of the intervention team, implement IFSP or IEP	Teach all children; accommodate and work with itinerant teacher/therapist on intervention team
Specialist	No specialist	Early childhood special educator (ECSE)	Itinerant teacher (for visually, or hearing impaired, and others)
Specialist's role	Child may receive therapy outside of setting	Model, demonstrate, and provide technical assistance; write part of IFSP or IEP	Visit classroom, provide specialized materials and program, teach child in regular classroom, may pull child out for specialized instruction, help write IFSP or IEP
Features	Teacher meets child's needs; may be unaware of problem; rarely part of team for services outside the setting	Teacher teaches all children; ECSE provides technical assistant and consultation	Child is with peers: teacher can consult with and observe itinerant teacher, who is in a disability area, rarely early childhood

early care and education settings such as preschools, child care centers, and family day care homes. It offers the expectation that children with disabilities will take swimming lessons at the local Y, that they will have friends in their neighborhood, they will attend religious services with their family, and that they will join the Boy Scouts or Girl Scouts if they choose to do so. Inclusion creates a challenge for many adult professionals and volunteers. It requires that they expand and modify their roles to make reasonable accommodations to include increasingly diverse children, including those with developmental delays and disabilities, and their families.

In the care and education of young children, the concept of inclusion requires a paradigm shift, "a fundamental change in the way we think about differences among people, in the way we choose to organize schools for education, and how we view the purpose of that education" (Developmental Disabilities Task Force, n.d., p. 7). The hope is for a unified system of education in which there is no longer *special education* and *regular education,* just *education.*

Inclusion is one of the most controversial and least understood educational policies. Most educational professionals believe that *some* children with disabilities should be included in regular classrooms.

Some education professionals believe that *all* children should be included (Stainback & Stainback, 1990). "This movement toward more integration has led to some of the bloodiest professional battles ever waged in the field of special education" (Hallahan & Kauffman, 1994, p. 46).

Least Restrictive Environment

The ideas that led to inclusion are based on the concept of least restrictive environment (LRE). This concept was part of P.L. 94-142 passed in 1972. It is a legal concept that is designed to assure that:

> [T]o the maximum extent appropriate children with disabilities, including children in public or private institutions or other care facilities, are educated with children who are not disabled and special classes, separate schooling, or other removal of children with disabilities from regular educational environment occurs only when the nature or severity of the disability of a child is such that education in regular classes with the use of supplementary aids and services cannot be achieved satisfactorily. (IDEA, 1997)

. . . . ▸ . . . . ▸ . . . . ▸ . . . . ▸ . . . . ▸ Most Restrictive

Resource room/pull-out therapy	Special class/segregated intervention program in regular school	Special school or day setting	Residential school/ institution
Children who need therapy (OT, PT, speech, etc.) or help in a subject area (reading, math, etc.)	Children with moderate, severe, or profound impairments	Children with severe or profound impairments	Children with severe/profound impairments and those living where other services are not available
Teach all children, accommodate pull-out schedule, consult with specialists, make accommodations for child	Help nondisabled children socialize (playground, lunch); support children mainstreamed for part of the day; support reverse mainstreaming for part of the day; increase awareness of disabilities	Increase other children's awareness of disabilities	Increase nondisabled children's awareness of disabilities
Therapist or special education teacher Teach child part of the day and provide some technical assistance to teacher, write and implement most of IFSP or IEP	Early childhood special educator Teach children; write and implement IFSP, EIP; support regular or reverse mainstreaming	Early childhood special educator Teach children; write and implement IFSP, IEP	Special education teachers, therapists, nurses Teach child; write and implement ISFP, IEP; care for child's needs and educational program
Child is with peers most of the day; a specialist/ teacher provides more individualized instruction in a segregated classroom	Child is integrated some of the day	Child is segregated for the school day	Child is segregated all day; has little contact with family

Initial attempts at defining the characteristics of the least restrictive environment resulted in the concept of a continuum of services. Deno (1970) conceptualized a "cascade" system of services with "exceptional" children placed in regular classes with or without supportive services, moving to supplemental instructional services, part- and then full-time special classes, special schools, homebound instruction, and hospital, residential, or total care settings. As Deno envisioned this model, one moved down the cascade only as far as necessary and then returned up "as rapidly as feasible." This model has been expanded and augmented, but the essence of the model remains: Children with disabilities will be placed in increasingly integrated environments until there is just one level of service.

The continuum of services shown in Table 3.1 is an example of how we viewed the educational system. It highlights the children you might find in each level and the role of the teacher and of related specialists or therapists. It moves from the least restrictive environment on the left to the most restrictive environment on the right. It also serves as an historical view of the field. The norm is moving toward more inclusive settings.

Some argue that the concept of a continuum of services has not been useful in including children with disabilities in regular education, that in effect it has served to justify placements in more restrictive settings. Some advocate doing away with the concept of least restrictive environment because if there is a *least* restrictive environment there is also a *most* restrictive environment. The continuum of services not only affects the children with diverse abilities, but the other children, teachers, and therapists as well.

Current thinking is that it might be wiser to think of an "array" of services and that services should be designed to fit the needs of the child rather than placing the child in an existing service system. Instead of asking "Where should Alex be placed in the service continuum?" the question would be "What services does Alex need in the regular setting to function there?" Inclusion is more than physically placing children in regular classroom environments that were originally designed for children without disabilities. Inclusion changes the care and education for *all* children (DEC & NAEYC, 1993). The potential for all children to learn is clear from the comments of children in a first-grade class in Maine:

We have been friends with Matthew for a whole school year. We call him Matt. He likes school because he loves people. . . . Matt has trouble understanding everything people say to him, so he uses lots of picture signs and some sign language. That's just the way he was born. We help him by taking turns being his buddy. When we are his buddy, Matt likes us to hold his hand firmly. He feels real sure we know what we are doing if we hang on that way. Many times he will thank us with a big hug. It's nice to be appreciated. (Zeph, Gilmeer, Brewer-Allen, & Moulton, 1992, p. 31)

Including children with diverse abilities can improve education for all—academically, as well as socially and emotionally.

Designing services around children is the ideal sought by inclusion. When children with diverse abilities are included in the classroom setting, a team (including the parents) chooses what services the young child needs. The early childhood educator plays the major role in caring for and educating the children, and collaborates with parents and specialists on an early intervention team available to help the educator adapt her care, teaching, and programming to meet the needs of the children in her class or at home. Likewise, therapists and early childhood consultants must take into account the needs of the early childhood educator and the children in the class as they program for a particular child. This need for teamwork on the part of developmentalists, parents, early childhood consultants, and therapists requires a level of planning and cooperation that may be new for all. It may also include a different array of services than in the past.

What Is Inclusion?

The words *mainstreaming, integration,* and *inclusion* are used interchangeably by some. However, they have different connotations. Consider the concept of *mainstreaming.* If children are to join the mainstream, then obviously they were not part of it to begin with; they are being added to an existing group. In mainstreaming programs, children with disabilities are added to existing programs for typically developing children with minimal support. Increasing mainstreaming would mean that children with disabilities spend greater amounts of time in a regular classroom (Proctor & Baker, 1995).

Integration goes a step further and implies interaction between two groups of children with adequate support so that all children can participate. Integration provides the opportunity for children with diverse abilities to participate in academic, physical, or social activities with their nondisabled peers. "While integration is considered to be philosophically and educationally superior to segregation, such 'push in' arrangements remain inherently hierarchical and unequal" (Salisbury, 1991, p. 147).

Early childhood programs began using the term integration in the 1970s to describe programs where children with diverse abilities were combined with other children in the same setting (Bricker, 1995). The goal of integration was to correct the social discrimination associated with segregation and exclusion. Beginning in the 1990s, integration was being replaced by the term and concepts embodied by inclusion.

Inclusion is a value term indicating that all children belong in the same setting. Inclusion requires developmentalists, parents, and administrators to examine their value systems and to develop creative, effective programming for all children. "Rather than 'forcing' students with disabilities into an existing mainstream that is structured to teach everyone the same thing in the same way for the same amount of time, inclusion presumes a restructuring to accommodate individual student differences" (Proctor & Baker, 1995, p. 224). Inclusion promotes a process that will reconceptualize school for all.

Inclusion in and of itself is neither good nor bad. Many people fear that inclusion will result in all children being "dumped together" in the same arbitrary way they were previously separated out. And, if including children with disabilities is done poorly, without allocating time and resources, it can, and has created, a dumping ground (Council for Exceptional Children [CEC], 1996a). Successful inclusion involves placing children in an early care and education setting that provides the support that meets children's emotional, social, and educational needs. The purpose of inclusion is to help all children gain interaction skills that will be valuable throughout life, as well as to provide appropriate care and education for all.

For inclusion to be done well, there must be support services for teachers, parents, and children. When children with disabilities were channeled off into special schools, the role of specialized services in the regular school was primarily diagnostic. As soon as a child was identified as having a disability, the child was moved; the task of the regular school support services was finished. Despite their original limited function, inclusion has expended the roles of these professionals. School psychologists no longer just give tests, but also may do group or family counseling. Speech and language therapists and occupational and physical therapists now work in early care and education settings and young children's homes. Social workers, adaptive physical education teachers, and home-school liaisons may all be part of a school setting. Although some of these specialists have been around for a long time, their previous practice of always pulling children out of class has changed. Now they perform some or all of their work within the classroom, and often consult with the teacher to develop a classroom program for a child that complements the individual or small group therapy that the specialist is carrying out.

Although the field of early childhood education as a whole supports the idea of inclusion, there is disagreement about *who* should be included. Most agree that children with mild to moderate disabilities should be included in regular classes. Some believe that *all* children, including children with profound disabilities, should be included.

Everyone agrees that the child who uses an arm prosthesis should be included. However, it is less clear if a child who is medically fragile or self-abusive should be part of the classroom.

Incluoion of young with disabilities is increasing with the number of children served primarily in resource rooms declining. However, the pattern of inclusion varies by disability. Almost all children with speech and language or communication impairments are included in regular classes. Children with learning disabilities, orthopedic impairments, emotional and behavioral problems, and traumatic brain injury are usually in regular schools but have a combination of general education classes, resource rooms, and separate classes. Children with autism, mental retardation, and multiple disabilities are most often in separate classrooms (CEC, 1997).

What Is Full Inclusion?

Full inclusion means that all children, regardless of their developmental lcvcl or disability, are always included in whatever setting is appropriate and available to other children their age (Brault, 1992). Although acknowledging the challenges, proponents of full inclusion believe that *all* children can and should be provided with care and education in regular settings. They believe "the movement toward inclusive education is a process—a journey to create an educational system where excellence and equity walk hand in hand and where the highest values of the nation are respected, honored, and achieved" (Forest & Pearpoint, 1990, p. 187). They believe that inclusive care and education is for all; they even include children ". . . who have or could potentially exhibit severe aggressive behaviors" (Forest & Pearpoint, 1990, p. 187). The Association for Persons with Severe Handicaps adopted a resolution calling for the education of *all* students in regular neighborhood schools.

In the U.S. Department of Education's *18th Annual Report to Congress on the Implementation of the Individuals with Disabilities Education Act* (December 1996), it concluded that no single setting benefits all children and there needs to be a range of options that can be designed to meet the individualized needs of each child (CEC, 1997).

However, the 1997 Amendments to the Individuals with Disabilities Act (IDEA) makes the position of the U.S. Department of Education and the Congress that passed the legislation clearer on the inclusion of children with diverse abilities into regular neighborhood schools and classrooms. They should be there. They should participate in the regular education curriculum and in the assessment procedures with necessary accommodations provided. When this cannot happen, there must be a rationale justifying why it cannot. This legislation supports inclusion, but does not require full inclusion.

Concerns About Full Inclusion

There are a variety of concerns about full inclusion that relate to the impact some children with disabilities might have on the social and learning environment of other children in the class as well as the education of children with disabilities themselves. The inclusion of children with profound disabilities, particularly children with severe behavior disorders, and those who are profoundly mentally retarded cause the most concern. Children with severe behavior disorders may hit or bite without warning or behave in extremely violent and aggressive ways that put other children in the class at risk. These children may also display self-stimulatory or self-injurious behaviors that both put them at risk and are highly disruptive in a group (Greer & Greer, 1995). The concern about children who are profoundly mentally retarded is that they will gain little from the academic aspect of the class and will miss time they could have spent on learning basic skills. They learn best when tasks are broken down into very small steps and repeated many times (Greer & Greer, 1995). This style of teaching is rarely used in regular classrooms.

Children who are medically fragile are another group that is of concern. Their medical problems can be restrictive and life threatening. Although few question the social desirability of including these children in a regular classroom, the risk of infection needs to be evaluated. The concern in this case is that the children's medical condition will worsen because of exposure to the other children in the class. This may be related to either disease or injury.

Some professionals and parents feel that children with some disabilities learn better in segregated classrooms. For example, children with hearing impairments may be in segregated classrooms or at home to concentrate on learning sign language and auditory discrimination skills at a young age. Likewise, children who were exposed to cocaine prenatally may find the regular classroom so distracting that they lose control and find it difficult to learn.

Some parents may not want their children in inclusive settings. If we believe that parents are partners in the decision-making process, how do we respond to parents who do not want their children in an inclusive setting? Parents may feel that a segregated classroom is safer and easier for them to cope with and for the parents this is the "least restrictive environment."

If parents are truly part of the decision-making process for their children, how do we evaluate the decisions of parents of children *without* disabilities who oppose the inclusion of children with diverse abilities in the class? Don't they have a legitimate right to oppose the inclusion of children they believe to be potentially harmful, disruptive, or overly demanding of the teacher's time? Or, should only the parents of children with disabilities be included in the decision making? Tough questions with no easy answers. All families want what is best for their children.

For families with children who have diverse abilities, Bricker believes "We should be examining first the child's needs, then the family's values, the desired outcomes, and the short-term versus the long-term effects of specific approaches and placements" (1995, p. 183). Others support Bricker's position that although inclusion may be a worthwhile opportunity for some, it may be cruel for others. Smelter, Rasch, and Yudewitz (1995) also support the concepts that decisions about inclusion need to be made case by case. Others in the field (Turnbulls and Stainbacks) see Bricker's position as a reflection of the 1970s and a roadblock to progress. To the extent that decisions are made on an individual basis, the educational system will not change. They believe "If we can't just do it, could we at least get on with it" (Turnbull & Turbiville, 1995, p. 201).

These dilemmas are real and difficult to resolve. Inclusion is a complex issue. For many years, we expected children with disabilities to be educated in segregated settings and then we focused on characteristics of children that would make them candidates for part- or full-time integration into regular settings. The IDEA expects all children to begin their education in a regular classroom with the necessary support services. When these supports have been exhausted, we might consider moving children into segregated settings.

The real crux of the issue about full inclusion is its implications for the system as a whole. If one believes in full inclusion then one supports a paradigm shift to one educational system for all. If one believes that decisions should be made on a case-by-case basis, there will be separate systems and resources will be divided between them. Underlying support of equality for all is crucial to the success of inclusion. Whether "full" inclusion happens remains to be seen. The cumulative effect of legislation and litigation clearly supports moving toward greater inclusion.

There is, however, general concern about the overrepresentation of minority students in special education:

- More minority children continue to be served in special education than would be expected from the percentage of minority students in the general school population.

- Poor African American children are 2.3 times more likely to be identified by their teacher as having mental retardation than their white counterpart.

- Although African Americans represent 16 percent of elementary and secondary enrollments, they constitute 21 percent of total enrollments in special education.

- The drop-out rate is 68 percent higher for minorities than for whites.

- More than 50 percent of minority students in large cities drop out of school.

- The limited English proficient population is the fastest growing in our nation. . . . The Department of Education has found that services provided to limited English proficient students often do not respond primarily to the pupil's academic needs. These trends pose special challenges for special education in the referral, assessment, and services for our Nation's students for non-English language backgrounds (IDEA, 1997).

The cited discrepancies have lead the Department of Education's Office of Civil Rights (OCR) to increase the number of complaint cases it will review by 150 percent (CEC, 1995). The concern is that there is too high a proportion of ethnically diverse students in special education in general and particularly in programs for the mentally retarded and behaviorally impaired (CEC, 1995).

Why Was Inclusion Proposed?

Early supporters of inclusion were disenchanted with the way the traditional educational system worked. Special education itself has had limited academic success and there has been little consensus about the effectiveness of pull-out programs (Wang, Reynolds, & Walberg, 1986). There is consensus however, that children who have been labeled and segregated from their peers are often stigmatized and have low self-esteem (Guralnick & Groom, 1988).

Pull-out programs, where children are taken out of the regular class and placed in a special smaller class to do concentrated work in subject matter areas in which the child was performing below grade level expectation were the mainstay of mainstreaming. However, the underlying assumptions behind pull-out programs are questionable and inherently unequal. They focus almost exclusively on the child's weakest academic area. The special educators who teach these classes rarely observe the children they teach in regular education settings so they don't have a complete picture of the child's academic day, which includes areas of strength as well as social interactions with peers. While the child is out of the regular class, the children in the class are learning information this child will miss and hence be behind in other areas as well. This particularistic approach rarely encourages the transfer and generalization of learning.

It also requires children with diverse abilities to adjust to more transitions than their peers. The transition process itself identifies children who must learn in a segregated environment. Some feel this is an infringement on their civil rights (Yatvin, 1995).

Children are often identified for special educational services because they have "failed" regular education. Children who struggle but do not actually fail badly enough to be labeled are not given individualized services. These at risk children are viewed by many as falling between the cracks (Greer & Greer, 1995).

On the more positive side, from the perspective of children without disabilities, including children with disabilities is a way of helping them learn about diversity and developing positive attitudes toward children with disabilities. It provides the opportunity for them to learn prosocial and altruistic behaviors and to serve as positive role models in some areas (Wolery et al., 1993).

The number of early childhood programs that include children with disabilities is rising. Wolery (1993) and others found that between 1985 and 1989 the number of early care and education programs enrolling children with disabilities increased by 37 percent, with 74.2 percent of the programs enrolling at least one child with a disability. However, they found differences in the disabilities of the children enrolled in these programs. Many programs enrolled children with speech and language impairments (57.5 percent), developmental delays (30.6 percent), behavior disorders (24.1 percent), and physical disabilities (20.8 percent). Early care and education settings were less likely to enroll children with mental retardation, sensory impairments, and autism (Wolery et al., 1993). These disabilities are lower in occurrence than the previously cited ones; and best practice favors classifying young children as developmentally delayed rather than using a specific label (so they may be there under the developmentally delayed label).

Does inclusion work? We don't really know. There are so many levels of inclusion that research leading to a definitive answer is difficult. Also, it is a new practice and so there is little research to either support or refute its long term effects. There are also concerns about what the objectives of inclusion are. How do we decide whether or not it has been successful? The impact of inclusion is difficult to assess with younger children and even for children in elementary schools.

Barriers to Inclusion

There are many barriers to inclusion. Some of the major ones are discussed next.

Awareness

Inclusion is a new concept and may be misunderstood. Awareness of inclusion issues must not just lie with the parents of children with disabilities but with all of the stakeholders in the educational system: parents of all children, early childhood educators, administrators, paraprofessionals, legislators, business and community leaders. Even support staff such as bus drivers, secretaries, and cafeteria workers need to be aware of aspects of inclusion. Many stakeholders are not aware of legal requirements of the IDEA and the ADA to include children with disabilities in typical settings and the research that served as the foundation for these laws.

Strategies for disseminating this information are numerous, varying from newspaper articles about inclusive settings to visiting model programs. Professional journals in education, early childhood, and early childhood special education all contain information about inclusion. Meetings of international, national, and state professional organizations often have presentations on this topic. Positive attitudes are at the core of successful inclusion, including the belief that all children have the right to be included in the same programs they would attend if they did not have a disability. This doesn't mean that a child with muscular dystrophy will necessarily play the same sports as a child who does not have this disability, but rather, the question is "How can we include a child with muscular dystrophy or cerebral palsy in an activity in a manner that the child is physically and mentally capable of?" Disabilities are real, the intent is not to ignore the disability, but to meet the child's need to be included as a child with accommodations for the disability.

Successful programs have a shared vision that all children belong and all children can learn and have the opportunity to reach their potential. There is a sense of community that helps each child develop in her own way, with a sense of self-worth, with pride in each child's accomplishments and mutual respect (CEC, 1994). It may be that previously negative attitudes are changing significantly as negative staff attitudes and philosophical differences were listed infrequently as barriers to inclusion and that initial negative attitudes became more positive with experience in inclusion (Wolery et al., 1993).

Professional Preparation in Early Care and Education

Untrained staff and lack of consultative support is ranked as one of the main barriers to inclusion (Wolery et al., 1993). Many teachers feel that they are not prepared to teach and care for children with diverse abilities. Educators feel that they do not have good knowledge about disabilities per se and particularly about children with severe disabilities or those children who are medically fragile (Rose & Smith, 1993). They are genuinely concerned that they might do something that will hurt the child. They also feel they lack educational strategies to effectively teach children with diverse abilities. Parents, too, may wonder if all developmentalists are prepared to care for and educate their child. Teachers with a background in special education feel that they may not have the management skills to teach larger groups of children and lack child development knowledge. They also lack skills in the consultation role.

Inclusion has forced educators to consider new and different ways of teaching and providing care for children. Educators who previously did not include children with diverse abilities have to develop techniques for including them; likewise, educators whose total focus was teaching children with diverse abilities in small segregated groups must learn new methods of individualizing programming for these children in the regular classroom while at the same time including the child's peers. An additional group who may profit from inclusion are children who are "at risk for developmental delays." These are frequently low-achieving children who may be at risk, but who don't have diagnosable disabilities (CEC, 1996a).

Teacher skills are an essential part of strategies for inclusion. Often models include extensive initial training before inclusion but research has shown that training needs to be ongoing, and needs to provide technical assistance in solving problems as they arise (Bruder, Deiner, & Sachs, 1992; Greyerbiehl, 1993). Strategies to change teacher attitudes are both long- and short-term. The preservice teaching of students in higher education needs to be evaluated against the skills necessary for inclusive education. The Division for Early Childhood, Council for Exceptional Children, National Association for the Education of Young Children, and the Association of Teacher Educators (1995) have agreed on a set of personnel standards for early childhood special education and early childhood education. These guidelines are for teachers of children from birth through age 8. The goal is to get institutions that train teachers to adopt these standards in their teacher preparation programs. Wolery and others (1993) noted that only about 44 percent of associate degree programs, 61 percent of bachelor's degree programs, and 25 percent of master's degree programs in early childhood education offered one or two courses in special education. Fewer still required courses in teaching young children in inclusive settings.

Providing professional development for educators already in the field provides even more of a challenge. Some early childhood educators have been prepared for the inclusion of children with disabilities by workshops or courses about the law and disabilities characteristics. Although useful and necessary, this is only a first step. Teachers also need long-term technical assistance and support in adapting strategies and teaching methods to include children with disabilities (CEC, 1996a). Some have used a consultation model by having early childhood special educators go into a center to model behavior and to provide technical assistance to developmentalists (Bruder et al., 1992). Professional development opportunities which include individuals whose background is from early childhood education and those from special education in the same training has been found to be a positive strategy (Rose & Smith, 1993). Setting up professional development opportunities

for early childhood educators in child care settings and family day care homes is challenging because of the hours they work and the limited organized in-service training. However, there are models available for training here as well (Kontos & File, 1993).

Educational Standards and Assessments

Traditionally children with disabilities have been exempted from state educational standards and assessments. If they did take the tests, their scores were omitted from the overall results (CEC, 1996b). (It was felt that the inclusion of their scores would drive the scores down and schools would look bad in the eyes of the community.)

As children with diverse abilities are included in regular classrooms, they are also being taught the regular education curriculum of their peers. Some states are now saying that if *all* children should be in regular classrooms then *all* children should have to meet the standards of the state. States will need to provide testing accommodations for students with disabilities because of the requirements of the Americans with Disabilities Act. This too is a double-edged sword. Some children may not graduate from high schools because they cannot meet the standards (or they make take longer to graduate). However, to the extent that all children are included, more effort will be made to ensure that they meet the standards. This might provide the incentive for creative and innovating teaching. Without including children with disabilities in the testing there is no way to monitor their progress (CEC, 1996b).

Adult-Child Ratios

Adult-child ratios and class size are significant barriers to inclusion. Many adults in early care and education want fewer children per adult so they have the opportunity to individualize programming and respond to each child's needs (Wolery et al., 1993). The assumption is that including children with diverse abilities will increase the adult time spend in collaboration, planning, and carrying out plans.

Adult-child ratios, like many other aspects of inclusion, can be affected in surprising ways, and may result in requiring different skills. This example illustrates the number of adults and the professional and volunteer resources that may be necessary to support children with diverse abilities in a full day program. Working from this model makes some very different assumptions about the skills that early childhood educators need. A certain amount of start-up time is necessary to learn these skills.

Early childhood educators may have a paraprofessional or volunteer to help each child, and occasionally some related services professionals (for example, speech therapist) as well as an early childhood special education consultant in her class some of the

Rena has spina bifida (her spinal cord was not enclosed at birth) and hydrocephalus (excess cerebral spinal fluid on her brain). Rena's parents want her to attend and participate in the same early care and education setting as her older brother. Her physician supports this decision. Two early childhood educators were trained by a public health nurse to catherize Rena. This allows her to attend the full-day program. Rena also has large and fine motor challenges. A physical therapist demonstrated lifting techniques and positioning to all the early childhood educators and caregivers at the setting as well as the support staff and volunteers. This permits Rena to move safely and comfortably from her wheelchair to chairs at activity tables that have special straps designed for her. She can also join in floor activities with appropriate supports (pillow rolls). Rena's interest in drawing, painting, and gluing are facilitated by the adapted crayons and brushes recommended by the occupational therapist. The itinerant early childhood consultant follows up on the recommendations from the nurse, physical therapist, and the occupational therapist in his twice weekly visit to the center. During the visit, the early childhood consultant assists the two early childhood educators who have Rena in their group to plan and implement an individualized program for Rena. He also provides suggestions and support to three volunteers who are assigned to work with Rena (adapted from Deiner, Hardacre, & Dyck, 1999).

---

time. This means that early childhood educators not only have to have the techniques to teach all the children including those with diverse abilities, but they also need the skills to manage the adults. This situation frequently creates a problem when school systems decide to "try" inclusion; it is a situation that advocates want to avoid. This is a typical "add-on" type of problem except that not only the children, but the adults too are being added on.

Inclusion requires a paradigm shift in the educational system. Inclusion starts with the simple assumption that all children are part of the class and that they will participate in the class routine at a level that is commensurate with their abilities. The goal is to establish what is needed to effectively educate these children. Trying to incorporate the philosophy behind inclusion as an "add-on" can create chaos. For example, suppose we start with a regular first-grade class with 25 students and 1 teacher plus a paraprofessional for half of the day. The plan is to include a class of 10 children that have been designated as having learning disabilities and suppose that class has 1 teacher and 2 paraprofessionals. What is frequently done is that 2 of the children with learning disabilities are taken to the regular first grade by 2 paraprofessionals for the morning on Monday, 2 for the afternoon, and so on. The regular classroom teacher may then have to teach 27 children (or 35 children in a week) and supervise 3 paraprofessionals.

On the other hand, if we say that we have 2 teachers and 35 children to teach with the support of 2 and a half paraprofessionals, the opportunity for different solutions is immediately apparent. Each teacher could have a class of 17 children and a full-time paraprofessional and a part-time floater, or, class size could be dropped to 12 by using the money from the paraprofessionals to hire a third teacher. (Combining two regular classrooms provides no gains.) Working from this model makes some very different assumptions about the skills that teachers have and need. It may be that a different teaching model is preferable to having so many paraprofessionals.

In a co-teaching model, there are two trained teachers, one an early childhood educator, the other an early childhood special educator. (Paraprofessionals, volunteers, and grandparents don't qualify.) The model is used when children have diverse learning abilities. The educators are there and qualified to teach; they are expected to teach all of the children in the same room at the same time. They may divide their work up differently during the course of the day (Cook & Friend, 1996). At one point one educator may take the lead, while the other adult floats and trouble shoots. At another point, they may divide the content to be taught and teach small groups different information while others work independently.

They may parallel teach by dividing the children in the classroom in half so the groups are smaller. Or, they may team teach as each teacher takes turns leading a discussion or modeling appropriate behavior in some area (Cook & Friend, 1996). Regardless of the model, time needs to be allocated for collaboration and for learning to use various teaching models.

Communication, Collaboration, and Respect

We all feel that we probably do our jobs better than others with different training and orientation. We may get territorial and think others with less expertise will lose the gains we have helped children make. Specialists often are afraid of what will happen to "their" children at the hands of early childhood educators and children without disabilities. They probably chose a specialty because they felt a special affinity for children with diverse abilities and fear that others may not share those feelings.

The role of the early childhood educator changes dramatically when children with diverse abilities are no longer pulled out of class for special instruction or related services. These changes require close collaboration between educators, consultants, therapists, and other professionals involved with the child (for example, physicians and other medical specialists). Those in early care and education will share information about development, content, and curriculum sequences. Other professionals on the team will draw on information about disabilities and different learning strategies (Greer & Greer, 1995). Common planning and shared decision making will benefit all the children.

Many early childhood educators are concerned that if they include children with disabilities they will not receive the support they need from other professionals, particularly related service professionals such as speech-language therapists, physical therapists, occupational therapists, and early childhood special education consultants. They believe that it takes a team to meet the needs of young children with disabilities and are afraid the team will not be in place for them (Wolery et al., 1993). Some of these fears are well-founded.

The development of mutual trust and respect is one of the core components to inclusion. Strategies for success involve ongoing discussions and the willingness to share expertise with each other as well as working as teams (Rose & Smith, 1993). Communication among professionals is often difficult. When young children have diverse abilities the need to communicate may be greater but even more difficult because there are so many different individuals and institutions involved. The situation for these children may be tremendously complex. They may attend an inclusive preschool program for part of the day and then go to child care settings until their parents finish work. Often they have related services such as physical or speech and language therapy on a regular basis; they may have medical needs that require both regular and specialized medical care; they need regular assessment and evaluation and so on. The various professionals involved need to talk with and respect each other and to communicate necessary information in a way that all can understand. Communication frequently depends on the attitudes of professionals toward inclusion. The children, too, play a very important role in making inclusive settings successful. Collaboration requires that the staff and the children support each other. Differences cannot be ignored but must be respected, acknowledged, and even seen as cause for creative solutions.

Quality of Early Care and Education

There is frequently an underlying assumption that the quality of education for all students will decrease if children with diverse abilities are included. Parents of typically developing children are concerned that those with disabilities will hold back the class and require an inordinate amount of the teacher's time and attention (Rose & Smith, 1993). Conversely, parents of children with diverse abilities often feel that their children will not receive the needed service or specialized instruction they might get in a segregated class. There is also a concern that children with diverse abilities may be picked on or made fun of by other children. Children with disabilities need to develop the skills to handle this behavior in other children. Children without disabilities need to change their behavior.

Programs that include children with diverse abilities reported including a wider range of activities than other programs. Early childhood educators reported finding it relatively easy to adapt these activities to include children with disabilities (Wolery et al., 1995). An initial concern with including young children with disabilities was related to the social inclusion (Sale & Carey, 1995). Recent studies have indicated that there are social and communication benefits from the inclusion of children with disabilities (including those with profound disabilities) (Cole, 1991; Hanline, 1993). There still appears to be some basis for concern about social inclusion especially as children get older. Even in schools practicing full inclusion, children who would have been eligible or likely eligible for special education were significantly less likely to be chosen as preferred children to play with (Sale & Carey, 1995). Concern about children's peer relationships arise because their ability to establish relationships is a good predictor of their ability to make adjustments later in life.

Lack of Supports

Strategies for achieving quality education include consideration of the supports that are necessary to make inclusion successful and communicating the value of these supports to both the administration and parents. The education of all the children should be expected to meet high general educational standards. However, the levels of achievement, the specific content, and the method of instruction reflect the individual differences of children in the setting (CEC, 1995).

Lack of supports can take many forms. At times supports are not available because there is no common vision of what inclusion means and requires. Funding and budget cuts that limit money to hire trained paraprofessionals or make facilities accessible make support difficult. Lack of teaching materials or training to support inclusion, limited or no preparation or collaboration time with team members, too many nonteaching assignments (lunch duty, hall duty and so on), large classes, and no co-planning time can all contribute to a lack of support. (Greyerbiehl, 1993). Community supports may be unavailable due to physical location or the limited number of available professionals.

Overcoming lack of support becomes an administrative responsibility. The administration needs to improve leadership and to motivate and monitor commitment to the vision of inclusion. Sharing responsibilities on a setting-wide basis is necessary for all those involved in the planning and carrying out of strategies that are designed to ensure inclusion. The administration needs to provide a vision that all the stakeholders can believe in (CEC, 1996a). However, the vision is only the beginning. There must be a commitment to follow through on the vision.

Inclusion is not the only item on the American education agenda. However, it must be included when concerns are voiced about other topics such as literacy, math, and science. Consensus must be developed to reach *all* the goals on the agenda.

Educating young children involves dealing with conflict. Early childhood educators must be prepared not only to help children solve conflicts but also to provide them with a framework for solving problems and the social skills to interact with their peers.

Inclusive Program Planning

Parents, children, community activists, and professional organizations have concerns about inclusion. One critical issue in early childhood is the application of developmentally appropriate practices to curricula that include children with diverse abilities.

Developmentally Appropriate Practices

The concept of developmentally appropriate practices underlies planning for all of early childhood education. There are three major components: *age appropriateness, individual appropriateness,* and *social and cultural appropriateness.* These components are inextricably intertwined in one knowledge base consisting of the following:

1. *What is known about child development and learning.* Knowledge of age-related human characteristics permits general predictions within an age range about what activities, materials, interactions, or experiences will be safe, healthy, interesting, achievable, and also challenging to children;

2. *What is known about the strengths, interests, and needs of each individual child in the group.* This is necessary to be able to plan for and be responsive to inevitable individual variation; and

3. *Knowledge of the social and cultural contexts in which children live.* This ensures that learning environments are meaningful, relevant, and respectful for the participating children and their families (Bredekamp & Copple, 1997, p. 9).

Developmentally appropriate practices enhance learning and encourage independence. The role of the adult is to match the particular activity to the developmental level of the child in a way that supports more complex concepts and behavior while honoring the uniqueness of that particular child and adapting activities to her diverse abilities.

The National Association for the Education of Young Children (NAEYC) position statement clearly puts the adult in the role of decision maker, yet provides guidance for those decisions. Early childhood educators and early childhood special educators have sometimes made very different decisions related to these practices (Bredekamp, 1993). The argument seemed to be that "age appropriateness" was most important for children without disabilities whereas "individual appropriateness" was the major principle for working with children with disabilities. The position statement argues for the necessity of including both age and individual appropriateness as well as a consideration of cultural context (Bredekamp & Copple, 1997).

Adults can learn more about individual children by spending more time with these children. Increased information about cultural context comes with more frequent contact with families and other professionals who are part of the team that works children who have disabilities.

Related Services

There is consensus that it takes a team to care for and educate a child with diverse abilities. It is important to know what each team member (specialist) does and there are often many team members as was illustrated in Rena's case study. In inclusive settings, these professionals will come into the classroom and work with a particular child or a small group of children. Specialists in the classroom give the early childhood educator an opportunity to observe what they do and gain additional skills. This can then help children generalize and transfer the skills that the specialists initiated.

Because we are identifying and serving children earlier, available resources must be shared among more children than ever before. To benefit from your interactions with specialists, early childhood educators need three sets of skills:

1. They must learn enough about specialists' expertise and jargon to decide what questions to ask which specialists, to talk with them about a child, and to interpret their technical reports so they can use materials and suggestions from these reports in their program planning.

2. They need to observe specialists in the classroom, model, and expand their techniques with the feedback of the consultant.

3. They need to establish ongoing communication to keep all team members, including families, informed of progress, changes that need to be made, and issues that need consultation.

When you don't understand the jargon or how it applies in the classroom, ask the specialist, then ask them to demonstrate it, then demonstrate it to confirm that you are doing it correctly. It is okay to ask, and prudent to ask again to be sure you do understand. This is how a good program develops. You are the expert in early childhood education, the specialists may not understand your jargon either.

When therapy takes place in your classroom, both the early childhood educator and the other children have the opportunity to learn about the therapy and to ask questions of the specialist. In cases where the therapy cannot be done in the classroom, the educator should try to observe the child in therapy and request a brief description and explanation of the activities that occur during therapy. The specialist can help educators understand how a child's therapeutic needs will affect behavior in the class. The educator will need to ask how to carry out the therapist's goals in the class, and should invite the therapist to visit the class whenever possible.

Conversely, the early childhood educator can help the therapist or specialist understand what is happening in the classroom with the child and why. (For example, the specialist may not have any idea why dramatic play is important.) The early childhood educator should remember that a specialist is also a consultant. A child does not have to be in therapy to benefit from a specialist's knowledge.

Knowing what specialists do is important, especially when you need advice about problems a child may be having. The next part of this chapter discusses the types of specialists. The jargon specialists use is often difficult to understand. Start by asking parents their understanding of the terms. They have probably heard them many times before. Their understanding is useful to you in two ways: they may explain the terms very practically or you may discover that they don't understand either. Then, look up terms in an appropriate dictionary. Ask a colleague about the terms and consult with the specialist who wrote the report. When consulting a specialist, an effective communication strategy is to confirm or clarify points, restate what you think the specialist said in your own words, and ask if that interpretation is accurate. This technique is effective with parents as well. Sometimes educators ask questions to which they already know the answers, particularly on behalf of parents. Again, demonstrations are often effective. Say "Let me show you and tell me if I am doing right."

You need to understand the therapy goals and terms. The role of the early childhood educator is to help children generalize concepts and behaviors by using them in a variety of situations. To do this, you must understand the underlying goals, not just the terms. You need to educate the child and confirm that the parents too understand the goals.

Once you understand a specialist's report, you must translate it into strengths and limitations for which you can program. The process might work like this: The occupational therapist reports that "Mike fell off the nystagmus board following rotation." After doing some checking in the medical dictionary, you decide that Mike was probably dizzy! Mike probably needs practice in changing directions and starting and stopping to better develop the sense of balance which is located in the inner ear—his vestibular sense. Now, check with the medical report and parents to figure out why Mike might be dizzy and if you need to avoid or limit these activities. You might need to plan some creative movement activities with slow turns, as well as working on body awareness, flexibility, and static and dynamic balance.

Major Specializations

We have included an alphabetical listing of specialists who provide services for young children with diverse abilities. More detail is provided for the less familiar specializations. These specialists are members of the teams that work with early childhood educators in meeting the holistic needs of the child:

- *Child development consultants* usually have a master's degree and are trained in developmental principles and in the use of assessment measures for very young children. This consultant often works in a home-based setting and provides consultation to families, and in early care and education settings. This specialist may serve a liaison between the parents and the physician, and the parents and the educational setting.

- *Developmental psychologists* know about various aspects of child development and usually have a doctorate degree. Assessments are conducted that use observational techniques, especially of the child and the family. This specialist can use educational and psychological tests to aid in the diagnostic process and is likely to be on the multidisciplinary assessment team of young children. Developmental psychologists are knowledgeable about behavior management, counseling, and intervention strategies. Many school districts have developmental psychologists as part of the elementary school team.

- *Early childhood educators* provide care and education for children birth through age 8. They often informally and formally assesses the child's development, plans developmentally appropriate programs and selects activities to support children in all developmental areas including social/emotional, cognitive, language, and physical/motor development. Behavior management issues also are often addressed by early childhood educators. They have training in working with parents and may teach alone or with an early childhood special educator. They may work with children in the home, in centers, or in schools.

- *Early childhood special educators* have training in child development, early childhood materials and methods, and special education. Increasingly there is state certification for this position. This specialist often is part of a team teaching situation or may work as a consultant in the early childhood setting. (Increasingly students are earning dual certification in early childhood education and early childhood special education.)

- *Educational diagnosticians* usually work under the supervision of a psychologist and spend a great deal of time testing and observing children referred to them because of a suspected disability. They write the formal reports that are required for special educational services. They can discuss the test results with both the parents and the educators and are usually knowledgeable in other areas such as behavior management, counseling, and intervention strategies.

- *Family support workers* offer home-based services to the families of children with developmental delays. They provide emotional support, assistance with obtaining appropriate services; and information on issues that relate to the child. They also act as advocates for the family and child and assist in coordinating services for the family and child with other agencies.

- *Medical specialists* are frequently consulted when children have diverse abilities. The exact nature of the problem and the complexity of it will determine the number and specializations required. Specialists frequently needed are those in the fields of allergy and clinical immunology; arthritis and rheumatology, cardiovascular diseases (heart); dermatology (skin); endocrinology and metabolism (glandular diseases); gastroenterology (stomach and intestines); hematology (blood); nephrology (kidneys); neurology (nervous system); oncology (tumors); ophthalmology (eyes); orthopedic (bones) otolaryngology (ear-nose-throat); physical medicine and rehabilitation (muscular treatment and so on); psychiatry, surgery, urology (urinary tract); and so on. Within each of these specialties are subspecialties. When specialists further focus their specialty on children, the word pediatric precedes the specialization, for example, a pediatric rheumatologist.

- *Nurses* are often part of an early intervention team especially for children birth to 3. They may make home visits to address medical needs, screen or assess development, and recommend specific developmental activities. They also may refer the family to community resources and may be responsible for coordinating services for the family with a young child who has medical needs. Nurses also provide parents with follow-up education in health care, growth, and development.

- *Pediatric nurses* are registered nurses who specialize in young children. They have training in using developmental screening tools as well as additional training in family counseling and evaluation and child care. With infants, the pediatric nurse is frequently selected as the service coordinator. Pediatric nurses can work out of a hospital or community-based setting or from a state department of public health. For young children with disabilities, the pediatric nurse often makes home visits to help parents learn to better care for and meet the medical needs of their child, in addition to monitoring the health status of the child. Nurses often work with child development specialists for developmental intervention or infant stimulation.

- *Nutritionists* have training in the area of foods, the essential nutrients for a balanced diet, and the amount of nutrients necessary for energy, maintenance, and growth. They are concerned about all the processes by which the body uses food for energy, and growth. Children with feeding problems, food allergies, and children who fail to thrive are likely to have a nutritionist on their team.

- *Occupational therapists* work from a developmental rather than a medical base. They hold a degree from an accredited school with course work in biological and psychosocial sciences, foundations of medicine, sensory integration, psychiatry, and prevocational skill development. Their therapy emphasizes vestibular (balance as determined by the inner ear), tactile, kinesthetic (sensory knowledge of one's body movements), and perceptual motor (mental interpretation of sensation and movement based on these sensations) development, fine motor coordination, and self-help/ adaptive skills. The therapist's role includes assessment, intervention, and consultation in the areas of self-help/adaptive skills, adaptive behavior and play, and sensorimotor development. The occupational therapist may adapt the environment (for example, limiting distractions, combining gross and fine motor activities, making a task achievable), providing devices to help develop functional skills such as eating, dressing, and playing, and minimizing the impact of the disability. Occupational therapists often see children who are also seen by physical therapists and speech and language therapists.

• *Parents* are important specialists. They determine the priorities for their child and family. They know what the children want and need and, how they want these needs to be addressed. Parents give other team members information on how their child functions at home and help team members see the whole child in the context of the family and the culture in which they live. They update the team on an ongoing basis.

• *Pediatricians* are physicians who specialize in the medical treatment of children from birth to about age 12. The pediatrician is probably the most familiar professional to families with young children. Pediatricians may be the first to express concern about a condition or may be the first person to whom parents turn to express their concern. Children are seen by pediatricians for well-baby checkups and when the child is sick.

• *Physical therapists* are state-licensed health professionals who have completed an accredited educational program, largely medically based, which includes the study of biological, physical, medical, and psychosocial sciences, as well as course work in neurology, orthopedics, therapeutic exercises, and treatment techniques. Physical therapy is directed toward preventing disability, that is, developing, improving, or restoring more efficient muscular functioning and maintaining maximum motor functioning for each person. A physical therapist works with any child requiring prosthetic management training, wheelchair mobility training, or measurement for or use of other medically prescribed mobility devices. The physical therapist evaluates the child's range of motion, posture, muscle tone, strength, balance, and gross motor skills. Treatment usually focuses on increasing strength, improving balance skills, and facilitating gross motor development. Physical therapists are responsible for monitoring a child's orthopedic

needs and assisting the family in obtaining adaptive equipment, if necessary. They provide parents and educators with information about optimal ways for positioning and carrying the child for different activities.

• *Physicians* may be pediatricians, in family practice, neurologists, or other specialist. The physician's role includes determining medical needs and referring the family to specialists and programs that can provide intervention services.

• *Psychologists'* roles vary with the setting and the level of training they have as well as their specialization. A school psychologist is state certified and has typically completed either a master's or doctoral degree in school psychology. Course work varies from state to state, but generally includes psychology, counseling, standardized testing and its interpretation, child development, children with disabilities, and education. Most psychologists must complete an internship or practicum under a practicing psychologist. The duties of a psychologist in a school setting vary with the number of psychologists in the district and their individual skills. Most school psychologists spend a great deal of time testing and observing children referred to them because of a suspected disability. They must write the formal reports that are usually required to place children into any special education program. The psychologist may act as a consultant to the teacher or parents, which includes discussing test results or observations. Some psychologists emphasize individual therapy: either a child or a parent. Others make family therapy their primary function; they work with the child as part of the family unit.

• *Social workers* usually concentrate on the adults in the family. They may well look at family needs in relation to child rearing or coordinating the social service network. They are knowledgeable about resources and referral to community services (for example, Medicaid, respite care). Social workers usually work in the home and are often the best source of information about the types of intervention families are most likely to use. They are trained in family relations, counseling and advocacy skills, and working with agencies. Increasingly, public schools have social workers as part of their staff.

• *Speech and language therapists* are state licensed and have completed a degree program with an accredited college. Course work includes psychology, education, and anatomy, with an emphasis on speech and language development. The role of the speech and language therapist in early intervention includes assessment and intervention with oral-motor disorders (difficulties in feeding and swallowing as well as speech production) and communication delays and disorders. Their work includes sociocommunicative competence during preverbal and verbal areas of development; receptive and expressive language (both speech and nonverbal means of communication), and speech production and perception. Many young children with disabilities have associated problems with muscle tone that may effect the finer movements of the tongue and lips needed for feeding and speech.

Service Delivery Systems

Service delivery systems, individually or together, provide for the care and education of children with diverse abilities. Service delivery systems can be distinguished by their location, level of inclusion, the focus (child or family), and whether the system is formal or informal. Children are increasingly being served by a combination of service delivery systems. Depending on the child's specific disability, medical condition, family needs, the location of the community (especially rural versus urban), the available services and funding, a range of delivery services is possible.

Like the field itself, service delivery systems are struggling to find answers to questions such as:

- Should all service delivery systems be inclusive?

- Should service delivery systems be designed to meet the needs of the child or the total family?

- What level of participation/cooperation can be expected between parents and service delivery systems?

- How much input should parents have in the decision making process?

- How important is parent education and how actively should service delivery systems be expected to pursue programs in this area?

- How is the role of advocacy divided between parents and service delivery systems?

- What will adequate service delivery cost and who should pay?

Changing demographics are forcing service delivery systems to evaluate their policies in relation to their target population. Interagency collaboration is required to ensure quality programming for children. If mothers work, whether single or married, home-based services may not be a feasible option unless specialists are willing to work in the evenings or on weekends.

To meet the needs of the whole family, parents may develop complicated "packages" based on child care, early intervention, education, therapy, and health concerns. Children with disabilities who attend school programs often need care before and after school as well as during the summer. This need extends past the time when other children can be left at home independently (Fewell, 1986).

As part of an interagency team, educators need to be aware of and part of the entire service delivery system in which children participate. Many children come to school from child care and return there when school ends. The communication system must include parents, specialists, and all early care and education providers. As early childhood education has grown and families have changed, so has the diversity of available service delivery systems.

Varying theoretical differences influence the goals and supports that the delivery systems provide for children and their families. Viewing families as dynamic parts of a larger social system has brought about a change in how service is delivered. Empowering parents to make choices in the best interests of both their child and their family has affected both delivery systems and the thoughts and actions of professionals in the field of early childhood. Like the continuum of services in the least restrictive environment, service delivery systems may be either segregated or inclusive.

Segregated Service Delivery Systems

When services are delivered in segregated settings they may be one of several services that children take part in.

Home-Based Services. Home-based service delivery systems involve an early interventionist (typically a nurse, child development specialist, and/or early childhood special educator) visiting the family in their home on a regularly scheduled basis. This type of service delivery is frequently used for infants and medically vulnerable young children. This may be the only viable system of service delivery (for example, for children who are medically vulnerable to exposure to other children and their germs or in settings where rural distance or lack of transportation is an issue).

The consultant's responsibilities to the family and child include sharing information with the family about available resources and services, answering parental questions about the child's disability, and modeling and demonstrating activities and techniques for working with the child. The consultant may serve as a liaison between the medical and educational communities.

Success for this type of system depends on parents understanding and following through on the intervention. It is based on the consultant's building a relationship with the family by visiting at a scheduled time that is convenient. An obvious assumption in this type of service delivery system is that there is a parent or adult at home who is willing and able to meet with the consultant and follow through in delivering early intervention services. Most specialists work a daytime schedule; what frequently happens is that the mother, if not working, is the one who is home and then has the responsibility of carrying out the prescribed early intervention as well as interpreting for her spouse (if there is one) what the consultant said. With increasing instances of both parents being in the workforce, this type of delivery system may only work for a short period, and probably only for children whose disabilities are identified at birth. Unless this program is flexible enough to schedule evening and weekend appointments, it would only be available for families who have a parent at home during the day.

Service delivery systems are becoming more responsive to work/family issues. The necessity of child care is a reality for most families with young children today. Neither home nor center-based services totally meet the needs of these families.

Center-Based Services. Center-based service delivery systems may be situated in hospitals, schools, child care centers, or public or private agencies. The parents are usually responsible for bringing the child to the program, although some programs provide transportation. A center-based program often has a team of early intervention specialists. Some programs are designed for children with a specific disability, such as hearing impairment, while others serve children with a variety of disabilities. These programs usually have specialized materials and equipment. Parents can meet other parents of children with disabilities at these centers. Many of these programs are half-day, so they may represent only

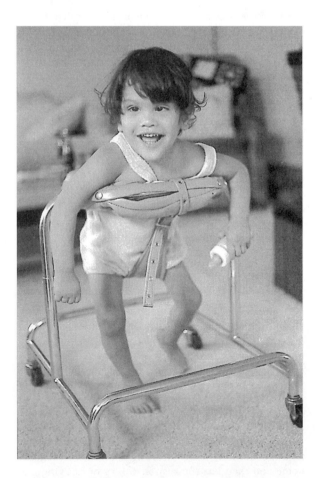

For some children, because of age, parental preference, or medical needs, a home-based early intervention is preferred until the child's needs can be safely met in an early childhood setting.

part of the service delivery system if the child needs full-time care. The New Mexico Developmental Disabilities Planning Council found that 40 percent of the children in segregated center-based programs were also in child-care settings before and/or after early intervention (Klein & Sheehan, 1987). These children spent an average of 26 hours per week in child care. Within this dual-service perspective, the child-care provider was responsible for adapting activities to allow young children with disabilities to participate and for supporting social integration. In this model, the child-care provider was not responsible for the educational component of early intervention services and was not considered part of the team, but rather a receiver of information from the team.

The staff of early intervention centers is usually well trained in early childhood special education, and therapists not only make active contributions to the child's program but may provide needed therapy in the setting as well. This staff would also do assessments as needed. Parents often feel more comfortable leaving young children in a setting with specialists. For a variety of reasons, including both philosophy and funding, these center-based services are likely to be segregated programs.

Home/Center-Based Services. Some programs are a combination of home- and center-based programs. In these programs children go to the center but are served by a home-based component as well. This service combines the advantages of both programs. Trained professionals are in charge of the programming, and parents can consult with them on a regular basis.

Public School Programs. Public schools play a major part in the service delivery system for children 4 and older and in some cases beginning in infancy. The intent of the Individuals with Disabilities Education Act (IDEA) is for children to be educated in the least restrictive environment (LRE). When public schools serve children below the kindergarten level, they are faced with a dilemma. They receive funds to educate children *with* disabilities beginning at age 3, but not for those *without* disabilities. They are also required to educate these children in the least restrictive environment. If they are to create inclusive environments, they must have the parents of children without disabilities pay for these public school services or they must integrate the children into programs outside of the traditional public school. Some public school programs have integrated young children with disabilities into Head Start settings that are in public schools. Others pay to include the children in regular preschools for all or some portion of the day. The 1997 reauthorization of the IDEA acknowledges that children without disabilities may profit from services designed for children with disabilities. However, it seems unlikely that public schools can afford 4-year-old programs just for the purpose of inclusion.

Hospital-Based Care. Most hospitals are designed for high-volume, short-term acute care. Their top priority is to preserve life. The focus is primarily on medical rather than social needs. When an infant is born very prematurely or critically ill, he is placed in a critical care unit. Not all hospitals have these units for neonates. They are staffed by neonatologists and neonatal nurses who "care for the critically ill and ventilator-dependent infants and . . . provide treatment for premature and sick full-term newborns during the most critical phase of their care" (Gilkerson, Gorski, & Panitz, 1991, p. 446). Infants may remain in the critical care unit for only a day or two for observation or up to a year or more for some of the most fragile infants.

When infants are medically stable, they are moved to an intermediate unit. It is at this point, as the child is exiting the critical care section and going to community-based programming, that early intervention is usually considered. Some infants who remain in the critical care unit for extended times receive early intervention services there.

Hospitals designed for the long-term care of children will have their own teachers who continue the school work that children would be doing if they were in school. There are many reasons why a child's medical condition may require hospitalization (uncontrolled seizures, technology-dependence, leukemia, and so on). The length of the child's stay and the seriousness of the illness will determine to a great extent how much contact a child will have with early interventionists. Larger hospitals have child life staff who provide stimulation and intervention to young children while they are in the hospital. They also work with children to prepare them for operations and other medical procedures.

Residential Care. A residential program is a treatment facility that is not a medical facility, where young children live in order to receive intervention/educational services. Residential programs are being phased out for all children, but particularly very young children. Their use is primarily for disabilities such as hearing and visual impairments. Children as young as 3 and 4 years who lived too far from the school to attend on a daily basis lived at the schools and came home to their families on weekends and during the summer. This practice is less common now than it was in the 1970s. Some children who are profoundly involved and whose parents cannot care for them live in nursing homes or state institutions and receive care and education there.

Inclusive Service Delivery Systems

There are a variety of settings in which children with and without disabilities come together. Once a child is old enough to attend kindergarten, this is the most likely setting. Before school age, children may be in a variety of inclusive settings.

Early Care and Education. Many children with disabilities are included in early care and education settings. The passage of the Americans with Disabilities Act (1990) required child care and preschool programs to use the same criteria for eligibility for all children. Children with disabilities must be accepted as any other child would be. Centers can deny admission on a case-by-case basis if the setting can show that accepting a child with a specific disability would "fundamentally alter" the services they provide or constitute an "undue burden" (Rose & Smith, 1994). Otherwise, the expectation is that these programs will make reasonable accommodations to prevent discrimination against children with disabilities. A reasonable accommodation might involve adding balls with bells or other sounds inside for children with visual impairments, a specialized swing for a child with physical impairments, or not permitting class pets if a child has a chronic allergy.

Placing children with disabilities in regular child-care settings is not a new idea (U.S. Department of Health, Education, and Welfare, 1972), but it has recently received a great deal of attention because of changing demographics and a changing philosophical environment.

Over 60 percent of mothers of children under 6 are in the workforce and the number is continuing to grow (U.S. Bureau of the Census, 1995). Between 5 and 10 percent of these children have disabilities (Salkever & Connolly, 1988). Parents of children with disabilities face increased financial demands: medical treatments, durable medical equipment, and supplies are expensive. However, a national survey of families with children who had physical disabilities (Harbaugh, in Seligman & Darling, 1989) found child care to be the largest single out-of-pocket expense. In 1990, families paid an average of $2,565 for family day care or $3,173 for center-based care for each child (Carnegie Task Force, 1994; Friedman, 1993; Galinsky, 1993). Care for children under 1 year is even more expensive in most settings. This expense hits low income families the hardest.

Families who make less than $15,000 annually spend 23 percent of their income on child care, whereas those who make $50,000 and over spend 6 percent of their income on child care (Carnegie Task Force, 1994). Families with low incomes are more likely to have children with disabilities and their children are likely to be in lower quality child care as are children from minority families (Galinsky, Howes, Kontos, & Shinn, 1994).

Family day care is the most common setting for children under 2 who are cared for outside the home (Clarke-Stewart, Gruber, & Fitzgerald, 1994) and constitutes at least 30 percent of child-care arrangements (National Center for Educational Statistics, 1992). Family day care probably serves more disabled children than any other arrangement (Fewell, 1986).

Child care for children with disabilities is used in one of two ways by service delivery systems: child care before and/or after early intervention or as a primary site for the delivery of early intervention services. In the latter case, related services may be provided in the child-care setting or elsewhere.

Programs that use child care as a primary intervention site typically use consultation models. The early childhood special education consultant and other professionals train the child-care provider to function as an early childhood interventionist with the support of consultants who visit the site on a regular basis, trouble shooting and modeling behavior. Consultants also provide a variety of technical assistance services ranging from specialized equipment and a selection of toys to phone consultation.

An overarching issue is whether the amount and quality of individual attention provided in child care is enough to meet the needs of children with disabilities. This is actually part of the much broader issue addressing adequacy of child care for all young children, particularly infants.

Head Start. Head Start began in the summer of 1965 as a comprehensive service system designed to deliver health, education, and social services to children and families who met low-income eligibility criteria. Since its inception, Head Start has had a strong commitment to parent involvement and inclusion with a mandate to include 10 percent of children with a diagnosed disability. Head Start uses the state definitions of disability for eligibility. In 1993, Head Start emphasized the regulations that require grantees to provide enrollment opportunities for children with disabilities as well as screening and referral services. The range of comprehensive services (medical, dental, and nutritional services) in addition to early childhood education is designed to serve children with identified disabilities as well as those at risk (Collins, 1993).

Increasingly, Head Start is beginning programs for children starting at birth (Pizzo, 1990). They are increasing their family focus. With growing numbers of young children living in poverty, Head Start is viewed as an effective way of "reducing childhood morbidity and mortality, supporting families, and providing a boost to the overall development of children" (Pizzo, 1990, p. 31). Head Start, however, has some of the same problems that child care has relative to low teacher salaries, and related concerns about program quality (Lombardi, 1990). In many cases, Head Start is using a consultation model to provide technical assistance when including children with disabilities.

Head Start programs are required to coordinate their efforts and responsibilities with the local school district (Rose & Smith, 1994). Collaboration with the public schools provides an inclusive setting for children with disabilities who do not meet Head Start income guidelines (10 percent of children do not have to be from low income families) and the school district often provides consultative services to the program. If the child's IEP is developed by Head Start, Head Start personnel have supervisory responsibility. If it is developed jointly with the public schools, there needs to be a written agreement between the two relating to this responsibility (Rose & Smith, 1994).

Many Head Start programs are moving from traditional half-day programs into all-day child care. Head Start is increasingly moving from a philosophy of parent involvement to a philosophy of *family* involvement and *family* (not just child) outcomes. They look at family outcomes related to family literacy, adult education, substance abuse, and health (Collins, 1993).

Respite Care

All parents need a break from caregiving. However, few babysitters are willing or able to care for children with disabilities. Respite care has become part of some service delivery systems. Respite care is one of the few services that is designed specifically for the *caregivers*. Respite care can be either inclusive or segregated.

A young child with a disability often needs time-consuming and perhaps complicated caregiving. The demands on time and finances leads to increased stress for the families. Often what families need is a break from care responsibilities to allow them time away from the child and time to focus, even if only briefly, on themselves.

Broadly defined, respite care is the temporary care of an individual with a disability for the purpose of providing relief to the primary caregiver. Respite care is part of a support system that helps keep children with developmental disabilities in the community by allowing families to go on vacation or even out to dinner and have time to rest and recuperate.

Respite care can be either primary (designed specifically to provide respite care only) or secondary (primarily designed to provide other services such as early intervention, but at the same time incidentally providing respite) (Salisbury, 1986). Child-care services for children with disabilities are secondary respite services. Child care is a potential setting for the provision of both respite care and early intervention services in one setting.

Service Coordination and Interagency Collaboration

Because young children with disabilities frequently require a variety of services, often from different agencies, the IDEA requires that a *service coordinator* be designated for infants and toddlers. Many agencies offer an array of services to families in a given community. Sometimes these services overlap; other times there are gaps in needed services. Some agencies are public and some private. Some agencies serve families in many different capacities, others in only one. Services and personnel within agencies change. The service coordinator is responsible for coordination with other agencies and persons and for assuring the implementation of the individualized planning process.

The impetus of the movement for a service coordinator was to help families obtain services for their child, and to coordinate those services within and between agencies. While service coordination has been identified as a need in the delivery of services to young children with disabilities and their families, some issues surrounding service coordination are not resolved.

The initial term relating to coordination used in the EHA, P.L. 99-457 (1986) was "case management," with the interpretation that parents could *not* be their own case managers. Many believed that the family, not a professional, was the most appropriate case manager, and that the family should play a more active role in securing resources to meet their needs (Dunst, Trivette, & Deal, 1988). Some felt that a dependency relationship was created when professionals played this role, and families would be unable to cope with the situation when the case manager left (when the child became 3 years old). Families themselves made it clear that they didn't consider themselves "cases" and they didn't want to be "managed." This issue was resolved to some extent in the reauthorization of P.L. 99-457 in 1991 when the term was changed to service coordinator and the role was defined as a coordinator of services (which families could do themselves if they chose) and affirmed families as the decision makers.

Any member of the team can be the service coordinator. But people have found it useful to have one contact person who is in charge of delegating responsibilities and being sure that appropriate follow-up has been completed. This individual coordinates professionals, paraprofessionals, and volunteers as well as others who participate. She also monitors what is happening to see that goals are being met.

Formal and Informal Social Support Networks

A social network is a group of people "who provide information leading the subject to believe he is cared for and loved, esteemed, and a member of a network of mutual obligations" (Cobb, 1976, p. 300). Research on social support for families of children with diverse abilities suggests that the presence of effective social supports can assist families in coping with stress and can enhance the well-being of these

Young children and their families need formal and informal support networks.

families (Stagg & Catron, 1986). However, while families with children with diverse abilities may benefit greatly from the existence of support networks, they are also less likely to have them available than are families with children without disabilities (Stagg & Catron, 1986).

Support networks can be formal or informal. Formal networks are generally made up of professionals involved with service agencies. Informal social networks are made up of friends, neighbors, and extended family members. Most families utilize informal social networks (Unger & Powell, 1980). There is concern that families with children with disabilities lack these informal networks and rather than having them rely on the support of professionals. Perhaps one role of professionals should be to help families in development rely on an informal support network rather than a formal one.

Support networks offer three major types of support: (1) providing material goods and services when needed; (2) providing emotional support by communicating the person's value and worth to them; (3) providing information about and referrals to other perhaps more formal, support systems. In general, social networks work best when they are reciprocal in nature (although in some extreme situations the process of having to "pay back" support can itself add to stress) (Unger & Powell, 1980).

Support empowers families to strengthen and add to their already existing networks. One relatively easy way for parents to increase the size of their support network is to meet parents of other children in their child's setting. These parents may have children with disabilities.

As part of normalization and inclusion, we are moving toward helping families develop informal social support networks. This is important, since professionals in an organization change or are assigned to different cases. Teaching families how to build their own social support network gives them a lifetime skill and one that is likely to continue to serve them.

Summary

Moving from an approach that separates children with disabilities to one that includes these children is a challenge to parents, educators, and children themselves. Although most professionals believe in inclusion, they differ on who they believe should be included and how. Advocates of full inclusion feel that all children regardless of the severity of the disability should be included and want to build a single educational system that meets the needs of all children without the need to label any child. Others feel that including children who are profoundly delayed or have severe behavior or medical problems is a disservice to both children with disabilities and those without.

There are many barriers to inclusion. Some people are unaware of what inclusion means, educators do not necessarily have the training to include children with disabilities, nor to work as part of teams, support services are not in place, and adult-child ratios make inclusion difficult. There is also concern about the overall quality of education in the United States and how much of a priority inclusion has within this overall education agenda.

Including children with disabilities changes the role of the educator and makes it more complex. As part of a team, the early childhood educator must learn the roles of other team members and methods of collaborating with them, and open up her classroom to them. Inclusion has a strong base in the law, however, whether or not full inclusion will come about is not clear.

Service delivery systems for young children with disabilities are changing in response to changing demographics and philosophies about how children with diverse abilities should be educated. Some service delivery systems, especially for very young infants or medically fragile ones, are home-based. Others are center-based, and some use a combination. Early intervention is increasingly only one of the services that young children with disabilities need. They may go from an early care and education setting to intervention and back. With the move toward inclusion of children with disabilities, intervention services are being incorporated into early care and education settings through the use of consultants. Increasingly, the needs of the total family are taken into account when planning and coordinating services needed by young children with diverse abilities. There are many excellent services available, however, coordinating the total range of services is a challenge.

Educational Resources

The Circle of Inclusion
http://circleofinclusion.org/
This website addresses the challenges and issues of inclusive program development with emphasis on collaborative programs between early childhood programs, local education agencies, and special education services. Geared toward educators.

Kids on the Block
9385-C Gerwig Lane
Columbia, MD 21046
(800) 368-KIDS (5437), (410) 290-9095,
   FAX (410) 290-9358
http://www.kotb.com/
Uses puppets, and publishes a series of children's books, and give programs to increase children's understanding of disabilities and siblings of a child with a disability.

Parent Education and Assistance for Kids (PEAK)
6055 Lehman Drive, Suite 101
Colorado Springs, CO 80918
(800) 284-0251, (719) 531-9400, (719) 531-9403,
   FAX (719) 531-9452
e-mail: PKPARENT@aol.com
Promotes the integration of children with disabilities into regular classes. Provides referrals and

technical assistance to school systems as well as a newsletter.

Pediatric Projects, Inc.
PO Box 571555
Tarzana, CA 91357
(800) 947-9094, (818) 705-3660, FAX (818) 705-3660
Produces toys and books to help children understand children with disabilities and chronic illnesses.

References

Americans with Disabilities Act of 1990, Pub. L. No. 101-336, 104 Stat. 327-378, 42 U.S.C. 12101.

Brault, L. M. J. (1992). Achieving integration for infants and toddlers with special needs: Recommendations for practice. *Infants and Young Children, 5*(2), 78-85.

Bredekamp, S. (1993). The relationship between early childhood education and early childhood special education: Healthy marriage or family feud? *Topics in Early Childhood Education, 13,* 258-273.

Bredekamp, S. (1997). Developmentally appropriate practice: The early childhood teacher as decision maker. In S. Bredekamp & C. Copple (Eds.), *Developmentally appropriate practice in early childhood programs* (Rev. ed.). Washington, DC: NAEYC.

Bredekamp, S., & Copple, C. (Eds.). (1997). *Developmentally appropriate practice in early childhood programs* (Rev. ed.). Washington, DC: NAEYC.

Bricker, D. (1995). The challenge of inclusion. *Journal of Early Intervention, 19*(3), 179-194.

Bruder, M. B., Deiner, P. L., & Sachs, S. (1992). Models of integration through early intervention—Child care collaborations. In S. Provence, J. Pawl, & E. Fenichel (Eds.), *The zero to three child care anthology 1984-1992* (pp. 46-51). Arlington, VA: National Center for Clinical Infant Studies.

Carnegie Task Force on Meeting the Needs of Young Children. (1994). *Starting points: Meeting the needs of our youngest children.* New York: Carnegie Corporation of New York.

Clarke-Stewart, K. A., Gruber, C. P., & Fitzgerald, L. M. (1994). *Children at home and in day care.* Hillsdale, NJ: Erlbaum.

Cobb, S. (1976). Social support as a moderator of life stress. *Psychosomatic Medicine, 38,* 300-314.

Cole, D. A. (1991). Social integration and severe disabilities: A longitudinal analysis of child outcomes. *Journal of Special Education, 25*(3), 340-351.

Collins, R. C. (1993). Head Start: Steps toward a two-generation program strategy, *Young Children, 48*(2), 25-33, 72-73.

Cook, L., & Friend, M. (1995). Co-teaching guidelines for creating effective practices. *Focus on Exceptional Children, 28*(3), 1-16.

Council for Exceptional Children. (1994).*Creating schools for all our students: What 12 schools have to say.* Reston, VA: Author.

Council for Exceptional Children. (1995). Department of education challenges schools on high number of minority students in special education. *CEC Today, 2*(3), 7.

Council for Exceptional Children. (1996a). Inclusion—Where are we today? *CEC Today, 3*(3), 1, 5, 15.

Council for Exceptional Children. (1996b). States act to include students with disabilities in standards. *CEC Today, 3*(3), 1, 9.

Deiner, P. L., Hardacre, L., & Dyck, L. (1999). *Educating children with diverse abilities.* Toronto, ON: Harcourt Brace Canada.

Deno, E. (1970). Special education as developmental capital. *Exceptional Children, 37,* 229-237.

Department of Education. (1997, October 22). Individuals with Disabilities Education Act: Proposed Rules, Federal Register, 55025-55135.

Developmental Disabilities Task Force. (n.d.). *Inclusive education: A background paper for state legislators* (1-11). National Conference of State Legislatures.

Division for Early Childhood, Council for Exceptional Children, National Association for the Education of Young Children, & Association of Teacher Educators. (1995). Personnel standards for early education and early intervention: Guidelines for licensure in early childhood special education. *Communicator, 21*(3), 1-16.

Division for Early Childhood and the National Association for the Education of Young Children. (1993). Position on inclusion. *Young Children, 49*(5), 78.

Dunst, C. J., Trivette, C. M., & Deal, A. G. (1988). *Enabling and empowering families: Principles and guidelines for practice.* Cambridge, MA: Brookline Books.

Education for All Handicapped Children Act of 1986, Pub. L. No. 99-457, 100 Stat. 1357-1377, 20 U.S.C. 1400.

Fewell, R. R. (1986). Child care and the handicapped child. In N. Gunzenhauser & B. M. Caldwell (Eds.), *Group care for young children* (pp. 35-46). Skillman, NJ: Johnson & Johnson.

Forest, M., & Pearpoint, J. (1990). Supports for addressing severe maladaptive behaviors. In W. Stainback & S. Stainback (Eds.), *Support networks for inclusive schooling* (pp. 187-197). Baltimore: Brookes.

Galinsky, E., & Friedman, D. F. (1993). *Education before school: Investing in quality child care.* New York: Scholastic.

Galinsky, E., Howes, C., Kontos, S., & Shinn, M. (1994). The study of children in family child care and relative care—Key findings and policy recommendations. *Young Children, 50*(1), 58-61.

Gilkerson, L., Gorski, P., & Panitz, P. (1991). Hospital-based intervention for preterm infants and their families. In S. Meisels & J. Shonkoff (Eds.), *Handbook of early childhood intervention* (pp. 445-468). Cambridge, MA: Cambridge University Press.

Greer, B. B., & Greer, J. G. (1995). Questions and answers about inclusion: What every teacher should know. *The Clearing House, 68*(6), 339-343.

Greyerbiehl, D. (1993). *Educational policies and practices that support inclusion of students with disabilities in the general education classroom.* Quality Life Concepts, West Virginia Developmental Disabilities Planning Council.

Guralnick, M. (1986). *Children's social behavior: Development assessment and modification.* Orlando, FL: Academic Press.

Hallahan, D., & Kauffman, J. (1994). *Exceptional children: Introduction to special education* (6th ed.). Englewood Cliffs, NJ: Prentice Hall.

Hanline, M. F. (1993). Inclusion of preschoolers with profound disabilities: An analysis of children's interactions. *Journal of the Association for Persons with Severe Handicaps, 18*(1), 28-35.

Individuals with Disabilities Education Act of 1997. Pub. L. No. 105-17, 111 Stat. 37-157. 20 U.S.C. 1400.

Klein, N., & Sheehan, R. (1987). Staff development: A key issue in meeting the needs of young handicapped children in day care settings. *Topics in Early Childhood Special Education, 7,* 13-27.

Kontos, S., & File, N. (1993). Staff development in support of integration. In C. A. Peck, S. L. Odom, & D. D. Bricker (Eds.), *Integrating young children with disabilities into community programs: Ecological perspectives on research and implementation.* Baltimore: Brookes.

Lombardi, J. (1990). Head Start: The nation's pride, a nation's challenge. *Young Children, 45*(6), 22-29.

National Center for Educational Statistics. (1992). *Home activities of 3- to 8-year-olds* (NCES 92-004). Washington, DC: U.S. Department of Education, Office of Educational Research and Improvement.

Pizzo, P. D. (1990). Family-centered Head Start for infants and toddlers: A renewed direction for Project Head Start. *Young Children, 45*(6), 30-35.

Proctor, T. J., & Baker, B. R. (1995). Inclusion: One way a professional development school can make a difference. *Childhood Education, 71*(4), 224-226.

Rose, D. F., & Smith, B. J. (1993). Preschool mainstreaming: Attitude barriers and strategies for addressing them. *Young Children, 48*(4), 59–66.

Rose, D. F., & Smith, B. J. (1994). Providing public education services to preschoolers with disabilities in community-based programs: Who's responsible for what? *Young Children, 49*(6), 64–68.

Sale, P., & Carey, D. M. (1995). The sociometric status of students with disabilities in a full-inclusion school. *Exceptional Children, 62*(1), 6–20.

Salisbury, C. L. (1986). Parenthood and the need for respite. In C. Salisbury & J. Intagliata (Eds.), *Respite care: Support for persons with developmental disabilities and their families* (pp. 3–28). Baltimore: Brookes.

Salisbury, C. L. (1991). Mainstreaming during the early childhood years. *Exceptional Children, 58*(2), 146–155.

Salkever, M., & Connolly, A. (1988). *Day care for disabled children.* Baltimore: Maryland Committee for Children.

Seligman, M., & Darling, R. (1989). *Ordinary families, special children: A systems approach to childhood disability.* New York: Guilford Press.

Smelter, R. W., Rasch, B. W., & Yudewitz, G. J. (1995). The times, they are a-changing. *Phi Delta Kappan, 76*(6), 484–486.

Stagg, V., & Catron, T. (1986). Networks of social supports for parents of handicapped children. In R. R. Fewell & P. F. Vadasy (Eds.), *Families of handicapped children: Needs and supports across the life span* (pp. 279–295). Austin, TX: PRO-ED.

Stainback, W., & Stainback, S. (1990). *Support networks for inclusive schools: Interdependent integrated education.* Baltimore: Brookes.

Turnbull, A. P., & Turbiville, V. P. (1995). Why must inclusion be such a challenge? *Journal of Early Intervention, 19*(3), 200–202.

Unger, D., & Powell, D. (1980). Supporting families under stress: The role of social networks. *Family Relations, 29,* 566–574.

U.S. Bureau of the Census. (1995). *Statistical abstracts of the United States* (115th ed.). Washington, DC: U.S. Government Printing Office.

U.S. Department of Health, Education, and Welfare. (1972). *Day care: Serving children with special needs* (DHEW Publication No. (OCD) 73-1063). Washington, DC: Office of Child Development.

Wang, M. C., Reynolds, M. C., & Walberg, H. J. (1986). Rethinking special education. *Educational Leadership, 55*(2), 128–137.

Wolery, M., Holcombe, A., Venn, M. L., Brookfield, J., Huffman, K., Schroeder, C., Martin, C. G., & Fleming, L. A. (1993). Mainstreaming in early childhood programs: Current status and relevant issues. *Young Children, 49*(1), 78–84.

Wolery, M., & Wilbers, J. S. (Eds.). (1994). *Including children with special needs in early childhood programs.* Washington, DC: NAEYC.

Yatvin, J. (1995). Flawed assumptions. *Phi Delta Kappan, 76*(6), 482–485.

Zeph, L., Gilmeer, D., Brewer-Allen, D., & Moulton, J. (Eds.). (1992). *Kids talk about inclusive classrooms: Creating inclusive educational communities: A monograph series* (No. 3). Orono: LEARNS, College of Education, University of Maine.

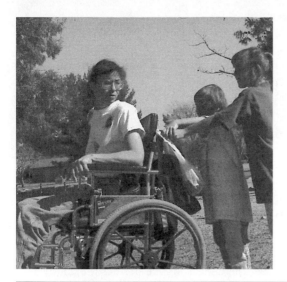

Chapter 4

UNDERSTANDING FAMILIES AS A SYSTEM

Although I tried to sound reasonable on the phone, this new demand appalled me. I rehearsed angry, self-justifying speeches in my head. Jody, I thought, is blind, has cerebral palsy, and his development is delayed. We do his physical therapy daily and work with him on sounds and communication. We feed him each meal on our laps, bottle him, change him, bathe him, dry him, put him in a brace to sleep, launder his dirty bed linens daily, and go through a variety of routines designed to minimize his disabilities and enhance his joys and his development. (All this in addition to trying to care for and enjoy our other young children and making time for each other and our careers.) Now you tell me that I should spend fifteen minutes every day on something that Jody will hate, an activity that will not help him walk or even defecate, but one that is aimed at the health of his gums. This activity is not for a finite time but forever. It is not guaranteed to help, but "it can't hurt." Well, it's too much. Where is that fifteen minutes going to come from? What am I supposed to give up? Taking the kids to the park? Reading a bedtime story to my eldest? Washing the breakfast dishes? Sorting the laundry? Grading students' papers? Sleeping? Because there is no time in my life that hasn't been spoken for, and for every fifteen-minute activity that is added, one has to be taken away (adapted from Featherstone, 1980, pp. 77, 78).

This passage vividly reminds us that children are part of a family system. To be effective we need to view children in the context of this system and evaluate our requests in this light.

The birth of an infant is a momentous occasion that affects all family members. At birth the infant begins an individual course of growth and development. However, she is born into a family. Her first relationships and first experiences of the world are with family members. She joins an existing family unit whose development is already in progress. The family unit may include one or two parents, biological or adoptive, step- or half-siblings, and extended family members. As the family incorporates the infant into its system, certain changes and adjustments are necessary in the ongoing process of family development.

Before the 1970s, our focus was on *children* with disabilities. Although we were aware they had parents, we rarely considered the fact that these children both impacted and were impacted by their families. Professionals saw parents as unknowledgeable to the point that they might interfere with the good we were doing for their children. Professionals, not parents, were the decision makers. Some parents may be wary because of stories they have heard or interactions they have had with unenlightened professionals. Today we attempt to collaborate and become partners with parents, but it helps to know how parents were viewed in the past.

Parents' Roles

One of the most destructive beliefs once held was that parents were the cause of their child's disability. Dr. Bruno Bettelheim contended that autism was caused by children's cold interactions with their "refrigerator parents" (Bettelheim, 1967). At one time we believed that mental retardation and other disorders were caused by parents' sinful living (Berkson, 1993). We now know these beliefs are generally erroneous.

However, in some cases, parents contribute to the "cause" of their child's disability. Approximately 25 to 39 percent of pregnant women smoke, and even more are exposed to passive smoke putting children at risk of *fetal tobacco syndrome*. Approximately 59 to 65 percent of women expose their embryo-fetus to alcohol during pregnancy which results in many children being born with *fetal alcohol syndrome* or *fetal alcohol effects* (Mason & Lee, 1995). Approximately 10 to 32 percent of women use illicit drugs and narcotics, primarily marijuana and cocaine, during pregnancy placing children at risk for *neonatal abstinence syndrome* and neurological problems (Curet, 1995). More than 90 percent of children newly diagnosed with HIV infection have acquired it from their mother (Rutstein, Conlon, & Batshaw, 1997). Are 49 these parents accountable for their children's disability? Does it matter that the disability was preventable? What about children who become disabled because of family violence or are injured because of inattentive parents?

Blaming is counterproductive. It makes parents defensive and does not help children grow and develop. Blaming builds barriers not partnerships.

Turnbull and Turnbull (1996) reviewed the roles parents had in the past. Some parents find organizations helpful, others distressful, others aren't aware of the organizations, and still others would not join even if they knew about them. Although there are many different organizations and support groups focusing on different disabilities, they all tend to have a similar membership: white middle-class parents. Families have the right to decide how they feel about support groups.

In the past, professionals *expected* parents to somehow find ways of obtaining needed services for their children. This was particularly true in recreation activities, religious activities, and organizations such as scouting or 4H. Parents were expected to be the path breakers: "They have created public awareness, raised money, operated services, and advocated for others to take over service operations" (Turnbull & Turnbull, 1996, p. 6).

As we learned more about the impact of the environment on young children, we wanted to teach parents to teach their children. The assumption was that parents lacked skills and so had to be taught. We offered them parenting classes or gave them information to read about discipline or disabilities. They sometimes had roles as adjuncts to professionals in that they were to carry out a home program to support what teachers and therapists were doing.

We frequently thought of parents as recipients of professionals' decisions. That is, we as professionals, made educational decisions in the best interest of their children and relayed those decisions to the parents. The parental role was not to question decisions, but to appreciate the time and effort that went into the decision making and to follow through. Although the law gave parents the right to make educational decisions for their child, professionals rarely expected parents to take on that role. And, in fact, parents frequently supported this position, saying "You're the expert," and abdicated their decision-making authority. Some professionals still believe they know what is best for children and expect parents to comply with their decisions.

We also used parents as political advocates. In the early 1970s, parents brought right-to-education suits against states and usually won. They joined with other parents and professional organizations to advocate for federal legislation and convinced congress to pass it. The role of parents as collaborators in political advocacy is an indication of the changing roles of parents and professionals. Educators, too, are empowered by this equity with families.

To collaborate with families, we need to know something about collaboration and a great deal about families:

Collaboration refers to the dynamic process of connecting families' resources (that is, motivation and knowledge/ skills) to an empowering context to make decisions collectively. (Turnbull & Turnbull, 1996, p. 11)

Expectations about the ways professionals will work with families have changed as have the families.

The Family

Defining families has become complicated. Families are easier to describe than define. For data-gathering purposes, the Census Bureau defines the family as "a group of two or more persons related by birth, marriage, or adoption and residing together in a household" (U.S. Bureau of the Census, 1991, p. 5).

Others emphasize different aspects of family. "Families comprise those that have a shared history and a shared future. They encompass the entire emotional system of at least three, and frequently now four generations, held together by blood, legal, and/or historical ties" (McGoldrick, Heiman, & Carter, 1993, p. 406). For children with disabilities, the idea of a functional household unit seems to be more relevant than concerns over blood lines and legal ties.

Viewing the multiple roles and responsibilities of people who are significant in children's lives requires us to make new assumptions about families, develop new service options, and view the family as an active, dynamic system. Theories about the tasks that families must accomplish, how families change over time, and how families interact provide a general framework for understanding families.

Theories of Family Development

Family developmental theories provide a way of looking at the interrelationships between developing individuals, the family unit, and socio-historical time.

Consider how different the life of a child with severe mental retardation would be if he were born in 1950, 1970, or 1990. In 1950, he probably would have been placed in an institution shortly after birth or at puberty. In 1970, the same child would have probably remained at home but had no early intervention and if admitted to school would have been in a special school. In 1990, this child would have had intensive early intervention, may have started his education at a local child-care center and now is in his neighborhood school and may be in a regular class.

Two particular patterns have influenced the family in the United States in the 1990s and hence the lives of children with disabilities who are born into these families. One is the relationship of women, mothers in particular, to the workforce. In 1960, only 18.6 percent of mothers with at least one child under 6 were in the workforce. In 1994, this number rose to 61.7 percent (U.S. Bureau of the Census, 1995b) and is expected to continue to rise.

A related trend has to do with the synchronization of family and individual goals. Historically, family goals took precedence over individual goals. The expectation was that individuals would subordinate their needs for the collective good of the family unit (Hareven, 1996). Some feel that today individualism has become so excessive and adults so focused on their own satisfaction they may fail to meet family obligations. They cite the high divorce rate, cohabitation, single-parent families, working mothers, and examples of this individualism. Some feel these situations are placing children at risk for developmental problems. The rise in individualism did not cause these problems, but some researchers see it as a contributing factor (Cherlin, 1996).

Few parents expect that their children will be disabled. Families having children with disabilities face not only the ordinary tasks of family life, but must also confront issues that are idiosyncratic to the specific disability and level of functioning of their child. The impact of the child on the family changes as the child grows. Learning about and adjusting to a child's diverse abilities impacts the entire family system.

Family Systems Theory

The family systems framework is a theoretical umbrella that makes assumptions about how families function. In the family systems framework, the focus is more on the relationships between family members than on the individual members themselves. Using family systems theory, one focuses on the family as a unit as opposed to focusing on one member of a family.

Family systems theory posits that families operate under the same rules that govern all systems. In family systems theory, families are viewed as powerful forces that can work for the good or detriment of individual family members (Gladding, 1995). Families are seen as continuously changing and reconstituting themselves. Families and their children are parts of open self-regulating systems. Families also interact with the larger social system.

To understand the impact a child with diverse abilities will have on a particular family, one needs to understand the characteristics of the family itself, as well as the individuals who make up the family and the particular challenges this family faces. This must be viewed within the current socio-historical time. Family characteristics and interactions provide *inputs* into the system.

Family Characteristics. Families are diverse. They live in geographically different areas and they differ in the economic and educational resources they have. The personal characteristics and styles of family members influence the family and how it operates. A family's cultural and ideological background influences how it perceives situations such as diverse abilities and how it react to them. Some families face special challenges in addition to having a child with diverse abilities such as living in poverty, drug or alcohol addiction, family violence, or divorce.

Characteristics of the Family. Families have different sizes and forms. The number of parents (including stepparents) and children (including step- and half-siblings) varies, the relationship with the extended family, and the presence of live-in family members who may or may not be related by blood or marriage influences the family (Turnbull & Turnbull, 1996). Larger families make the adaption to having a child with diverse abilities an easier one. There are many people to help with care and other chores and to absorb the parents' expectations. In two-parent families, there is another adult to help with the care or at least be supportive of the other adult. Single-parent families face the disadvantage of having no other adults in the household and there are usually fewer financial resources (National Center for Children in Poverty, 1995).

A family's economic resources, education, and occupation combine to form the family's socioeconomic status (SES). Families with a higher SES frequently can afford formal support systems, such as help with cleaning and child care to offset some of the demands of rearing a child with a disability. This does not necessarily mean that these families cope better than families with lower SES, but they do have more resources available to them.

The family's cultural/ethnic background, in combination with religious affiliations, influences the foods families eat, the rituals and celebrations they participate in, and values and perspectives they hold. Increasingly, the United States is becoming multiethnic and multiracial. Early childhood educators need to be aware of and value cultural differences, be cognizant of family values, and use culturally sensitive communication.

Families often perceive children and disabilities very differently. While some families view having a baby as a major crisis and the first months as a blur of adjustment, other families seem more able to accommodate these changes. Likewise when families discover their child has a disability, some may view it as a crisis, others as an adjustment, and still others as a relief. They may have feared worse.

The geographic location in which a family lives influences the services that are available. Metropolitan areas have a wider range of services than rural areas. Families with a child with a disability living in a rural area might have to travel long distances to obtain needed specialized or complex medical care. Problems in getting needed care also exist in large urban areas with primarily poor populations. Some families choose to relocate to obtain needed services.

Personal Characteristics. All individuals have personality characteristics that can be strengths or make families more vulnerable to the stresses of raising young children with diverse abilities. Adding a child to any family increases stress and when this child is diagnosed with a disability, an already stressful time is magnified.

Families are diverse. Family members have personality characteristics that make them more or less vulnerable to stress.

Individuals within families have different ways of reducing stress and coping. Some parents rely on professional support systems such as counseling to cope with stress, others use informal social support networks such as family and friends. Some families find religion or spiritual support helpful, others do not. Some families members find ways to positively reframe the circumstances as a way of coping. Others simply ignore the stress in hopes that it will go away or cure itself. It rarely does.

Children with disabilities make great demands on adult time. The health status of all family members is an important variable in coping. To the extent that adult family members have repeated or chronic physical or mental illnesses, or use drugs or alcohol excessively, their ability to cope in general and to care for a child with a disability are reduced.

Different conditions make different demands on the family system and the extent or degree of the condition impacts the family as well. Additionally, one must look at the match between the family's lifestyle and the child's abilities. To a family of musicians, a child with a profound hearing loss might require a far greater adjustment than that same child would if the parents themselves could not hear.

Some conditions, such as chronic illness, are episodic and require high levels of medical intervention at various times. Others, such as hearing impairment, require families to adapt their communication style permanently, whereas a physical impairment may necessitate physically altering the home. It is important to look at how the family perceives the impact of the disability.

The severity of the condition is an important variable. The more severe the disability, the more difficult it will be for the family to care for the child. Families may actually try to avoid becoming attached to a severely involved child for fear the child will die. Typically, young children with severe disabilities require more caregiving for a greater length of time. They also need a wide range of services involving many specialists; necessitating more appointments, more waiting, and more bills. However, the effect is not linear; one cannot necessarily assume that the more severe the disability the greater the impact on the family. Children with more severe disabilities are more easily planned for and controlled whereas children with milder disabilities are less predictable, especially over the long term.

Special Challenges. Some families face challenges others do not, such as poverty, homelessness, and living in violent neighborhoods. The condition of one family member such as having AIDS, being incarcerated or, addicted to drugs or alcohol may impact the whole family. Often these conditions are cumulative. Living in poverty means that families may not have adequate food, shelter, or have other basic needs met. This chronic stress may lead to violence, depression, and addiction. These conditions increase the probability of having a child with a disability; they also increase the possibility that an infant, born healthy, may become disabled through neglect or maltreatment.

Family Interactions

Family characteristics provide the *inputs* for the family system; family functions serve as the *outputs*. How these inputs are processed by the system we refer to as *family interactions*.

One assumption of family systems theory is that the sum is greater than the component parts. That is, you can't understand the family by working only with the child, nor can you appreciate the family's view if the mother is your only informant. Family members are both individuals as well as part of the family system. They must have the personal space to develop their uniqueness yet at the same time function together as a unit. The family unit tries to find a balance between separateness and connectedness. A child with a disability may change this balance. The interactions among the members are more significant than the characteristics of the family members themselves. To understand how families work, all the members need to be present. It is useful to look at the traditional subsystems within which families operate.

Like most systems, families are divided into subsystems. Boundaries define who is part of the subsystem and who isn't. Although families have many subsystems, the ones we are primarily concerned with are:

- *Marital subsystem* which focuses on the interactions of the marital or cohabitating couple.

- *Parental subsystem* which includes the interactions of the biological parents (in a nuclear family) and also the stepparents in a remarried family system with the children.

- *Sibling subsystem* which looks at the relationship among the siblings, half-siblings, and step-siblings.

- *Extended family subsystem* which includes the interactions of relatives and others who are regarded as relatives.

Not all families have these subsystems. A single mother does not have a formal marital subsystem nor does an only child have a sibling subsystem.

Marital Subsystem. The husband and wife, or couple, constitute the marital subsystem. The ability of the marital subsystem to establish a clear boundary allows them to grow and develop as a couple as well as fulfilling their other roles. The marital subsystem focuses on the interactions between marital partners or significant others who function as partners. The research on the impact of a child with a disability on the marital adjustment is inconsistent (Turnbull & Turnbull, 1996).

Parental Subsystem. In nuclear families, the same people who constitute the marital subsystem also are the parental subsystem. The parental subsystem focuses on the interactions between parents and their children. When the bond across generations (for example, the mother-child bond) becomes stronger than the marital bond the marriage is at risk. In remarried families, the parental subsystem may include step-parents as well as biological parents.

Mothers. For research purposes, mothers and families have been almost synonymous. Mothers are frequently the spokesperson for the family. Even today, if we give a family an assessment form to be filled out, it is usually the mother who does it. In these situations, valuable information is lost, and we don't truly have a picture of what the *family* wants and needs.

We know little about the different needs of mothers who work outside the home and those who do not. We do know that it is most frequently mothers who are required to adapt to sick children, early school dismissal, school vacations and the like. One of our concerns about mothers relates to *spillover.* That is, that stressful events (positive or negative) in one part of a person's life often spill over into other parts of an individual's life (Cherlin, 1996). To the extent that children with disabilities add stresses without additional resources, this can lead to a pile-up of stressors and spillover.

Mothers feel more supported (and less stressed) when their spouse is actively involved in parenting and, in turn, interact more positively with the child themselves. Mothers observe and imitate father's positive interactions with infants and vice versa. Because much past research focused on the child herself or the mother and child, we know less about fathers and their role in families with children with disabilities.

Fathers. Fatherhood is a hot topic of the 1990s. Professional and popular literature portrays a "new breed" of fathers who have high involvement, increased commitment, and spend greater amounts of time and energy in child-centered activities (Palkovitz, 1996). At the same time, we are being

Fathers interact with children differently than mothers. These differences are important for families and children. Fathers may need support in learning how to safely interact with their children to adjust to one another's strengths and limitations.

inundated with stories about the uninvolved "deadbeat" father who ignores his parenting obligation, resulting in a "good dad–bad dad" dichotomy (Furstenberg, 1988).

Fathers and mothers respond differently to being told their child has a disability. Usually fathers are less emotional and focus on long-term concerns, whereas mothers are more emotional and are involved with more immediate concerns about child care (Seligman & Darling, 1997). Males are also less likely to participate in formal or informal support groups. Often such groups are composed totally of women, they may be held during the day when the father can't attend, or involve sharing feelings which is uncomfortable. This leaves fathers out of one of the most common support systems available to mothers of young children with diverse abilities.

Some areas have developed fathers' groups in an effort to support fathers' need for information and support. Fathers play and interact with their children differently than mothers. Mothers tend to spend more time in routine caregiving behaviors (like diapering and feeding) while fathers tend to play more often in physical ways. Fathers are more likely to bounce and tickle younger infants and engage in more rough-and-tumble play as the child gets older. If the child has a disability, fathers need to know what types of play are safe, otherwise they might not play at all. Men are in no way inherently deficient in their ability to parent. A father's qualities as a parent are far more important than gender (Griswold, 1993). Some fathers see their role as discretionary, that is, the child requires the care of the mother but the play of the father is an extra. The father's attitude can set the tone of acceptance or withdrawal for the entire family. However, when fathers withdraw (either psychologically or physically), the system is affected and mothers must assume additional duties.

Two divergent forces influence the roles of working class mothers and fathers. When both parents need to work, child care becomes an important issue. It is both more expensive and more difficult to find child care for young children with disabilities. The growth of the service sector economy that requires non-day-shifts is also having an impact. The National Survey of Families and Households found that one-fourth of all dual-earner married couples had at least one spouse who worked an evening or rotating shift (Presser, 1994). One reason for this arrangement is to meet child-care needs.

Sibling Subsystem. Children with diverse abilities often require a greater amount of time, supervision, and attention than other children. Parents may need to spend time driving back and forth to doctor and therapy appointments, participate in early intervention programs, and work with the child at home. While all of this is good and very necessary, it is also important to consider the needs of other siblings in the family. As we have broadened our interest to include siblings, we have discovered that some siblings may be at psychological risk (DeLuca & Solerno, 1984).

Seligman and Darling have noted that "sibling relationships are usually the longest and most enduring of family relationships" (1989, p. 111). Siblings of children with disabilities have many of the same feelings that parents do. They may be very proud of each accomplishment their sibling makes. Or they may wonder why this has happened to them, and be sad or angry about it. There may be times when they are embarrassed by their sibling. They may feel jealous of the extra attention he receives and yet feel guilty for having those feelings. All of these feelings are normal and expected. While there will continue to be times when they are frustrated with their sibling (as with *any* brother or sister), most children will learn to accept and love their sibling.

Siblings of children with diverse abilities have additional needs. They need information. They want to know what's going on. Parents, in an effort to "protect" them, often don't tell them very much. Limited or poor information adds to their confusion. If the child wears a hearing aid, for example, siblings need to know what it is for, how it works, and what it does and does not do to aid hearing.

They need specific information about whether the disability is transmittable, how to talk to their friends about it, how to relate effectively to their sibling, and what family expectations are for their future role with their sibling.

Despite what siblings are told, many have a private version of why their sibling has a disability and may feel that in some way they are the cause of it (Seligman & Darling, 1989). Someone must learn about this private version and help siblings gain more accurate information about the cause of diverse abilities.

All children need time to develop friendships with other children close in age outside the family. Children also need private time with parents. If there are two parents in the family, each parent needs to spend some time alone with each child. Overburdening siblings with care responsibility can result in anger and resentment rather than acceptance. A child's sense of obligation for a sibling with diverse abilities can be a major concern and may require professional counseling. For the most part, siblings don't expect the situation to be "fixed"; they do, however, need a safe time and place to express their feelings and be accepted.

Siblings may need specific support in developing their own identity. They may need the opportunity to talk with other siblings of children with disabilities. If one is available, they may want to be a part of a support group. Parents often think that siblings are coping much better than the siblings see themselves coping (Wallinga, Paquio, & Skeen, 1987). Parents need to be aware of possible differences in perception about how well siblings are coping. Siblings need to be asked directly about their perceptions. Their parents cannot speak for them.

Extended Family Subsystem. The extended family plays an important role in many families. They frequently provide support for each other in a variety of ways, including babysitting. The birth of a child with diverse abilities may be an emotionally draining experience, particularly for the grandparents. "The same event that creates the need for emotional support in parents also wounds grandparents and renders them less able to supply it" (Gabel & Kotsch, 1981, p. 32). Even when extended family are willing to help, the care of the child may be very complex and grandparents may be less able to help without a lot of training. Families may need help in dealing with the feelings of the extended family as well as finding ways to include them.

In the next section, we discuss how those subsystems relate to each other. Some interactions are determined by the culture in which one is raised. Interactions can be looked at based on the dimensions of cohesion, flexibility, and communication.

Cohesion, Flexibility, and Communication

Families, as a system, need to find a balance between separateness and connectedness. Some families prefer to do many things together, whereas in other families, members prefer to do most things on their own. Families also need to find a balance between periods of stability and change. Olson, Portner, and Levee (1985) have developed the *circumplex model* to measure three elements: cohesion, flexibility, and communication.

Cohesion

Cohesion is defined "as a feeling of emotional closeness with another person" (Olson & DeFrain, 1997, p. 85). Cohesion emphasizes how much independence family members have, how decisions are made within the family, the amount of time families spend together, whether family members share interests or hobbies, and so on.

The circumplex model distinguishes four levels of cohesion: disengaged, connected, cohesive, and enmeshed (Olson & DeFrain, 1997). In disengaged relationships, the emphasis is on the individual whereas in enmeshed relationships the emphasis is on togetherness. Although there are times when these extremes are appropriate, individuals or families can become *stuck* at the extremes. Connected and cohesive relationships are more balanced.

Families that rate extremely high on cohesion are *enmeshed;* that is, the bonds are so close that there is little individual autonomy and family goals and needs are put before individual goals and needs. These families are characterized by overinvolvement and overprotection. At the other extreme of cohesion, families are described as *disengaged*. These families have high autonomy and individuality but experience very little closeness as a family and are not high on family solidarity. These families may be underinvolved; as a result, a child might be neglected. Most families fall somewhere between enmeshment and disengage-

ment; healthy families with young children are closer to enmeshment and move toward disengagement as the child approaches adolescence.

Understanding the level of cohesion in a family helps in choosing appropriate support services. For example, in an enmeshed family, it might be useful to train extended family members to provide intervention and respite care. Whereas in a disengaged family, this might not be useful.

Flexibility

Families differ in their ability to cope with periods of change and instability. All families experience these periods. Flexibility is "the amount of change that occurs in leadership, role relationship, and relationship rules" (Olson & DeFrain, 1997, p. 89). Like cohesion, there are four levels: rigid, structured, flexible, and chaotic. The extremes of rigid and chaotic may be appropriate for short periods of time, but too little change or too much change is problematic in the long haul. The more balanced positions of structured and flexible are seen as being healthier over the life cycle. The dimension of flexibility is important when families are under stress or need to adapt to a crisis (Olson, 1993).

Families with little control or structure are *chaotic*. These families have few rules, but even these change frequently and are rarely enforced. It may not be clear who is part of the family and who is not and there may be no one in charge of the family. Family members come and go apparently at will with little notice or planning. These families are unpredictable and sometimes stressful; they have little opportunity to develop relationships and common meaning. Family members cannot count on each other nor do they plan together for the future of family members. The family is like a sieve; change is the only constant. These families frequently have trouble complying with complicated care routines for children with disabilities.

Rigid families are the other extreme. They have a high degree of control and structure. They tend to repress change and growth. Roles are rigidly, and often traditionally, defined. The power hierarchy is clear and there is little room for negotiation. Rules are handed down and enforced. However, rules that are appropriate for young children may not change to meet needs of older children and there may be an unwillingness to modify rules to meet a child's individualized needs. When change is difficult for families, they may need time to plan for change and help in seeking and evaluating alternatives.

Communication

Communication is the facilitating dimension in the circumplex model and it both characterizes families as well as helps them change degrees of cohesion and flexibility. Olson and DeFrain (1997) see six dimensions of communication that relate specifically to families: listening and speaking skills, self-disclosure, clarity, staying on the topic, and respect and regard. Listening involves not only understanding content but empathizing with the feelings of the speaker and providing feedback. Speaking requires that one speaks for oneself with "I" statements, not for the entire family or others. Self-disclosure includes sharing personal feelings and ideas. Clarity involves the ability to send clear, discrete messages—not those with a double meaning. Staying on the topic is important in coming to closure and beginning to make plans about a particular area. Finally, respecting and regarding family members and their good intentions keeps communication open and positive. Communication allows well-functioning, balanced families to move from being close and cuddly with young children to gradually opening up to allow more space for older children. Communication allows families to modify and adapt roles and rules to include children with diverse abilities.

Family Functions

To survive, all families must perform certain functions. These functions meet the needs of family members and also have the long-range goal of helping family members become self-sufficient and independent. These functions are the same for all families, although families may fulfill these functions at different levels. Functions are interrelated, that is, if a family has economic problems, this may have a negative impact on family members' social, recreational, or educational activities (Turnbull & Turnbull, 1996; Zilbach, 1989). Children with diverse abilities impact these functions.

Affection. Successful families meet the needs of their members by exchanging verbal and physical intimacies and unconditional love (Summers, 1987). One's family, culture, and religion determine how affection is displayed. Some families are very affectionate both publicly and privately, others only express affection in private, and some have little outward displays of affection.

All children need to develop trust, become securely attached to their parents, accepted for themselves, and be loved and cared for. A child with diverse abilities may make unconditional love a challenge for families. As children grow older, the concept of sexuality often becomes confused and confounded with needs for affection.

Self-Esteem. A positive self-image is important for all members of the family. All family members need to see themselves as having competence and worth. Parents of children with diverse abilities need to support their accomplishments. This may be difficult when accomplishments seem insignificant or when the child is so gifted his accomplishments intimidate parents. Under these circumstances, parents may have difficulty seeing themselves as competent parents. Some families face multiple stressors.

Children need to have their strengths and accomplishments affirmed. Children's self-esteem is influenced by how they are viewed by their family, those who provide their care and education, their peers, and others in their lives. For individuals with disabilities to maintain a positive self-esteem requires persistence and a sense of humor. Siblings may be at risk regarding self-image if the family revolves around the child with diverse abilities.

Economic. Families vary greatly in the economic resources they have available to them. Few families have so much income available that they do not need to work. Most families must generate income and pay bills. Many families live in poverty. Research consistently shows that the addition of a child with diverse abilities increases expenses and may decrease income. Families often spend more money on these children than on their other children (Turnbull & Turnbull, 1996). Increased expenses result from: the cost of medical care and durable medical equipment, clothing that must be specially adapted, food for specialized diets, diapers, extra telephone costs, transportation to service providers, and child-care expenses. Although it is not clear which disabilities are the most costly, it appears that families with children who have autism spend more than families who have children with cerebral palsy, and these families in turn spend more on their children than those with mental retardation (Fujiura, Roccoforte, & Braddock, 1994). Many of these expenses are not covered by medical insurance, but are just as real.

Another way in which income is affected is through "lost opportunity." Income may be lost if a parent takes maternity or paternity leave, if a parent stops working, or if a parent must take time off to care for a sick child. Parents may not be willing to change jobs for fear of losing medical coverage, or they may turn down opportunities for advancement because it means a move or a change in hours that they cannot accommodate.

Daily Care. All families must perform tasks of daily life, such as cooking, cleaning, laundry, transportation, home repair, and so on. There has been a traditional, gender-based division of labor related to many of the daily care tasks. Female household tasks have traditionally been defined as cooking meals and cleanup, cleaning house, and care of clothing and laundry. Male or shared household tasks include out-of-door work, home repairs, garden and pet care, and paying bills. This is true whether or not women participate in the workforce. Although there have been trends that show a modest increase in the amount of male participation in female tasks, equity has not been obtained. In 1965, the split in household work was 90/10 with women doing the majority of the work; it rose to about 70/30 in 1985. If this rate continues for families with children under 5, the split would be 60/40 in 1995 (Cherlin, 1996).

Child care is considered "women's work." With young children, mothers do approximately four times as much caregiving as fathers (Palkovitz, 1992). Some children with diverse abilities require more care than other children for longer periods of time, and increase the number of daily household tasks that must be performed. The chronicity of care some families anticipate is 24 hours a day, 7 days a week, for many many years (Seligman & Darling, 1997). With the imbalance of household labor, child care in two-parent families, the number of single-parent families, and the increasing numbers of women also working outside the home, we are becoming concerned about *role overload* (that is, women having too many roles with conflicting demands) (Cherlin, 1996). This is a particular concern for single mothers with children with diverse abilities. A related problem in this area is *spillover*. Spillover, which can occur with or without role overload, occurs when the demands in one area of life spill over into another such as the work place causing individuals to be less effective and perhaps put their employment in jeopardy. The reverse, working at low-paying, dirty, or dangerous jobs, and being treated in a dehumanizing way may also spill over into the home and make parents less available to their children.

Socialization. All families and members of families need to experience the joy and even the disappointments of social relationships. Families need to be part of a larger social system. They need an informal support network of friends and neighbors to share the high and low points of life, to share ideas, and to commiserate. Social networks provide opportunities for children to practice social skills and develop friends.

Most families find their social life and outside leisure activities affected by having a child with diverse abilities. Some parents get so involved in the education of their child they forget the importance of their own and their child's social life. Sometimes families don't meet social needs because of finances or because including a child with diverse abilities makes the activity too difficult. Parents need a social life apart from their children. Overall, families with good support networks make it through crises better than those who lack such a system.

Recreation. Families need time to rest, relax, and recuperate. The enjoyment of leisure time is an essential component of individual and family life. For children who are particularly talented in an area of athletics, significant family time and resources may be devoted to this area. Other families may constrain recreational opportunities because of safety concerns or because of the effort it takes to plan and carry out these activities.

Families need enjoyable leisure time activities for themselves as a family unit and for the individuals in the family. Children with diverse abilities need to learn how to use leisure time and reap the benefits from using it wisely.

Education. Education and educational achievement are important in many families and cultures and less in others. For many children with diverse abilities, education is highly emphasized. We as educators should note that meeting educational needs is only one of many functions of families. Even though it is probably the one in which our interests overlap with families the most, it is not necessarily the most important function for families. For children with diverse abilities, families must make decisions about early intervention, the quality of early care and education settings, the type of setting in which to enroll their child, and the development and appropriateness of individualized programming. As children grow, the question arises as to whether or not the care and education setting for a younger child is still ideal as the child becomes older.

Caring for children and other dependent members, and meeting individual growth needs, are concerns of all family members.

The Changing Family Life Cycle

In theories relating to the family life cycle, families are conceptualized as a unit of interacting individuals moving through time. Some changes are predictable *(normative)*, such as when family members are born, grow up, and leave the home. Other changes cannot be predicted *(non-normative)*, such as discovering a child has a disability, or an untimely death. The family life cycle is one way of organizing information about the family.

In the United States, the structure, stages, and form of the family have changed radically since the 1950s. Also, the length, sequence, and composition of transitions tend to vary with social class as well as socio-historical time (Gladding, 1995). Some reasons for changes are related to later marriages, decreasing birth rates, increasing divorce and remarriage, and longer life expectancy.

Family structure has also changed, challenging the "normal" family life cycle even more. People are living together without marrying (about 3 percent), and women are having children without marrying (about 26 percent). More women are choosing never to marry (about 12 percent), and even more never to have children (15 to 25 percent). Approximately half of all U.S. marriages will end in divorce and last an average of 7 years. After 2 to 3 years, approximately 40 percent of individuals remarry and an additional 20 percent are in some type of nonmarital union. Remarriages are more likely than first marriages to end in divorces and they tend to do so in about 4 to 5 years. About 6 percent or more of the population is homosexual. (Carnegie Task Force, 1994; Cherlin, 1996; McGoldrick et al., 1993; Olson & DeFrain, 1997). Cultural variations, migration, and poverty reduce the number of "normal" family life cycles further. Among all the changes that have occurred, the changing role of women has probably most dramatically affected the shift in family life cycle patterns (Carter & McGoldrick, 1993; Piotrkowski & Hughes, 1993).

Regardless of variations, this model focuses on the negotiation of underlying processes of family expansion, contraction, and the realignment of the relationship systems to support the entry, exit, and development of family members in a functional way (Carter & McGoldrick, 1993). Another value of the family life cycle approach is that it shows the different tasks family units must accomplish at different points in time; how difficult it is to meet the needs of all the family members; and how patterns can change based on the developmental needs of the family and as family members interact with a changing society.

Some theorists think of the family life cycle as a kind of dance. There are times when families are very close (centripetal) and other times when families open up to give their members more freedom or personal space (centrifugal) (Combrinck-Graham, 1985). Childbirth is one of the centripetal or coming together times. Even adult children who had not previously been close with their parents frequently find ways of resolving relationship issues as the first child/grandchild is awaited. The stages, changes required by transitions, and challenges to the family life cycle are discussed next, as well as the concerns that arise when developmental tasks are not met.

Launching the Single Young Adult

The primary developmental task for this stage is for young adults to develop a sense of self in relation to the family in which they were reared. They need to consider the powerful influence their family has on their perception of reality, of who they are and if, who, when, how, and where they will marry. Families also influence their expectations for the remaining stages of the family life cycle including marital roles, choices about child bearing, and child rearing (McGoldrick et al., 1993). Young adults need to develop intimate peer relationships and establish themselves in relation to work or a career and financial and emotional independence.

Successful completion of this stage requires that the young adult separate from his family of origin without cutting them off or continually fleeing to them for emotional support. It is a time to formulate personal life goals, to establish a sense of self before joining with another, and to find new and different ways to relate to their family (Carter & McGoldrick, 1993).

The Joining of Families: Coupling

The beginning of a family unit can be viewed as the establishment of a common household by two people who may or may not be married, but have the expectation of becoming an interdependent couple. Coupling, whether a first or later marriage, or without marriage, involves renegotiating personal issues that previously were decided individually (Carter & McGoldrick, 1993).

Achieving a successful couplehood is challenging. Many of the challenges at this stage are related to separating from the family of origin and establishing boundaries that allow the couple the space to grow as

a twosome while at the same time maintaining connections to the extended family systems (McGoldrick et al., 1993). Major issues, such as deciding whether to have children or not, and minor issues, such as putting the cap on the toothpaste, are negotiated.

The more couples reward and complement each other in their roles, the better the relationship is likely to be. Successful and amicable negotiation of roles provides a positive base for the next stage in the family life cycle, should the couple have a child. If these issues have not been successfully negotiated, they will reappear as stressors in the next stage.

Becoming Parents: Families with Young Children

This stage of the family life cycle is characterized by adding a dependent member to the family. Becoming parents requires appending the role of parent to the role of partner. The young adult moves up a generation and performs the task of caregiving for the young child (Combrinck-Graham, 1985).

Transition to Parenthood. All family life cycle transitions, such as marriage or retirement, bring some accompanying stress, and the transition to parenthood is no exception. Becoming parents causes adults to clarify and reconsider their values and the decisions they made in young adulthood. The reality of the infant may be different from the expectation. A mother who initially planned to take a six-week leave from work and then place the infant in child care may decide that she doesn't want to do that. But, if she must go back to work, her situation becomes stressful. Likewise, a mother who quit her job to be with the infant full-time may decide that full-time child care is not as fulfilling as she thought, and so she wants to return to work. As with all joint decisions, the partner may not have changed his thinking or may have changed in different directions. Having a child with diverse abilities adds a dimension that most parents have not planned on.

The extent to which the newborn is divergent from the family's hopes and expectations can be particularly stressful. Children both affect and are affected by the systems in which they develop. The characteristics of the infant and the interaction of these characteristics with parenting styles are particularly important factors.

The Premature Infant. Children who are born prematurely are not what families expect. Parents may move from wondering if the infant will live to wondering what to tell people. They are concerned about the long-term implications for the infant's quality of life. Yet at this early stage, there are usually too many unknowns to make accurate predictions. For infants who are critically ill, long hospitalizations and separations from parents cause additional problems. Parents may have other children at home that need care.

Becoming a couple is an important family ritual. Although celebrated in different ways, children need to be included in rituals.

In addition to anxiety about the obvious problems for the infant, the couple may not have been physically or emotionally prepared for the early birth. Preterm infants often do not respond well. They offer unclear signals, and families have to work harder or modify their interaction to get a response. Barnard (1981) reported that with preterm infants having these characteristics, parents often showed signs of burn-out by the time the child was 1 year old.

Discovering the Disability at Birth. Reactions to having a child with diverse abilities both within and between families are highly individualistic and depend on the severity of the child's condition, supports available to the family, and the cultural context of the family as well as other factors. Parents have a variety of reactions when they are told that their child has a disability. Most professionals see some type of "grief cycle," in which parents move through stages on their way to acceptance of the child. The exact stages, sequences, and time spent in each are individual.

Most parents report feeling a sense of shock. They feel emotionally "numb." They may even show physical signs of shock. Shock often turns to denial; parents may deny the disability or the severity of it. For children who look "normal," this denial is easier. These reactions may be a way of buying time to adjust. Once reality is acknowledged, everything must change. This is also a time when families are suscep-

tible to quackery. There are many charlatans who offer cures for all manner of diseases and conditions.

Parents may feel angry at doctors, professionals, and even the child himself. Some feel a kind of mourning, feeling sad about the child they had expected but didn't get; in reality, mourning the death of the normal child. Featherstone (1980) compares the death of a child and the birth of a child with a disability:

> The most important difference between mourning a death and mourning a disability is that the child in question is not dead at all. . . . While death provides a moment's respite from ordinary demands, disability generates new tasks and necessities. (Featherstone, 1980, p. 234)

Chronic sorrow may continue off and on throughout the child's life. This episodic process becomes especially strong at normal transition times such as birthdays, school entry, and at times when families join for reunions or other traditional gatherings. Seeing how easy it is for other children to do certain things and how difficult it is for their child to do the same thing can bring back the sorrow or the anger. Even explaining the child's disability may activate the cycle for some parents. Rather than endure this, the family may reduce its social life and withdraw from all but medical associations with the community.

Parents often seek a "cause" for the disability. If a specific cause for the child's condition is identified, parents can use it to get their world back under control. By not doing whatever it was (drinking, smoking, and so on), they have nothing to fear. In social psychology this is called "just world belief" and in some cultures this is very powerful. People want to believe that the world is fair. Good things come to good people. If they do the right things, they will not meet bad ends. To admit that some things are just out of control means that they can be victimized at any time. For families with children with disabilities, the causes are often unknown. To the extent that they cannot find out why it happened, they cannot prevent it from happening again. If they want to have other children, they must do so with this risk in mind. It is stressful to not know the cause of a disability. Hope provides strength even when the hope is unrealistic. Having some degree of unrealistic hope may be helpful to the family if it is all they have to go on.

There is disagreement about whether the goal of families' accepting a disability is realistic. DeLuca and Solerno (1984) feel that it is not realistic to expect families to accept a child's disability, and that this should not be a goal; rather, that families adjust to the reality of the disability in their own diverse and unique ways. One parent told me that "you never reach acceptance. You love your child, but you never quite accept the disability."

The timing of the grief cycle is an important variable. Parents go through the stages in the cycle individually and in their own time. Often the person who spends the most time with the child reaches a level of acceptance before others. It adds to family stress when one parent wants to make adaptations to accommodate the child's disability and the other parent is still in a stage of denial and refuses to allow the adaptations. Most families eventually reach some degree of adaptation although families re-experience these reactions across the family life cycle as a continuing, evolving reaction to the chronic stresses of caring for a family member with a disability (Wikler, 1981).

Later Discovery of the Disability

For children whose disability is not identified at birth, a diagnosis is often made during early childhood. The process of identification is different for different family members. The family believes they have a normally developing healthy baby. One parent may think something is wrong, but is not sure. There is a sense of foreboding that is sometimes worse than knowing for sure that the child has a specific condition, particularly when that parent shares her concern with her spouse or friends and they deny her concerns. Mothers are typically the first to sense difficulties, if these weren't picked up by the physician at birth. Physicians may attribute mothers' concerns to lack of expe-

rience or anxiety. Getting confirmation is often a long process. Mothers often have concerns for months or even years before they are confirmed. Sometimes learning that the child really does have a disability is a relief. For example, parents may be relieved to find their child has a learning disability when their greatest fear was mental retardation.

Some, but not all, families with a child with diverse abilities experience marital strain (Gabel, McDowell, & Cerreto, 1983). The primary caregiver may form a very strong bond with the child, leaving considerably less time and attention for the marital relationship. At the very least, many families find their social life and outside leisure activities affected by the birth of a child with a disability. Families may require tremendous creativity to continue as before. Other families report that having a child with diverse abilities increased family closeness, pride in working together through difficult times, and increased sensitivity to the needs of others (Helsel Family, 1985).

Many couples try to manage child-care responsibilities and household chores while both parents work full time. The problem of finding and affording high-quality child care and negotiating issues of gender roles related to child care and the maintenance of the household are at the core of this phase (Piotrkowski & Hughes, 1993).

Transition to School. Most children enter school with some experience in early care and education settings. However, the transition to school may still be a major event. Parents and educators view children from different perspectives. It is important that you be aware of such possible differences, and consider how your personal perspective might bias your perceptions of parents' priorities. When parents and teachers evaluate behavior very differently, it is not necessarily because they disagree on the behavior per se, but rather because they approach the situation from different orientations. For example, parents may want a child toilet trained because of the expense of diapers, teachers may be more concerned about developmental appropriateness and the social implications of not being toilet trained at an age when most other children are. In this instance, the goals are the same. If the teacher were to decide that toilet training was not a school problem and that it was easier to have the child in diapers because then she didn't have to monitor the child's toileting and, besides, there were more important things for children to be learning in school, the goals would be incompatible as well as the perspective. To work together effectively, each needs to be aware of the other's values, goals, and perspective.

Some parental goals are universal. They are the same in all cultures and across diverse groups within the same culture. Parents are concerned about the physical health and survival of their child. They want their child, over time, to develop the skills and capacity for being increasingly more independent. They are concerned that necessary self-help skills, decision-making strategies, social, and cognitive skills are developing in a timely manner. Additionally, parents want children to learn about their culture and develop a system of values that will help guide them in decision making.

Teachers' goals vary considerably depending on the age of the child, the type of program the child is enrolled in, and the philosophy of both the teacher and the program. Initially, most teachers are concerned about children separating from their parents, joining the group, and observing some ground rules and routines set up for all children. Teachers tend to focus on a specific aspect of behavior or development.

Parents typically focus on broad, long-range goals that they have for their child, such as learning to talk or becoming more independent. Educators tend to concentrate more on short-range goals that can be accomplished and documented, such as learning color names. Parents view education at all ages from a very personalized perspective and focus on how it affects their child and how their child is progressing. Educators are concerned about all the children in the group. They may discuss relationships between children and how a child relates to the group.

Parents often have convictions about how their children should be reared or taught. They may be influenced by how they were raised, their culture and religion. These views may or may not be congruent with the educational philosophy of the setting. For example, some parents may believe that spanking children helps them behave. They encourage you to spank their son at the center so "he doesn't get too big for his britches." If you respond that you use logical consequences as a way of dealing with misbehavior, parents may volunteer to take care of incidents when the child comes home. This places educators in a dilemma.

Educators often have strong opinions about how children should be taught. These are sometimes based on requirements set up by licensing agencies and other regulations that govern education and early intervention. Additionally, educational programming is often based on a particular theory about how children learn. These developmental or educational theories are important for the educator who is guiding the program.

It is not unusual to discover that what parents and educators want for children is different. Educators need to think through these differences before approaching parents. It is imperative that families decide what is important to them and the areas in which they want to focus, and early childhood professionals frame their focus in a developmentally appropriate way.

The Family with Adolescents

As children move into adolescence, families must evaluate and establish qualitatively different boundaries than they used when children were younger. Adolescents need freedom with guidance. They want to be like their peers, thus parental authority is often challenged. Adolescents need flexible boundaries that allow them to be dependent and nurtured when they cannot handle things alone, yet they also need to experiment with increasing degrees of independence. Adolescence is even more complex when families have children with diverse abilities.

In families where children require physical care such as lifting in and out of bed or the bath, the size and weight gain in adolescence is an added problem. Likewise, children whose behavior is not under control become more of a threat to others.

There are also the added complexities of sexuality at this time. Biologically most people with disabilities mature sexually at about the same time as their peers. A variety of concerns surrounds the issue of sexuality. For some, it focuses around the genetic transmission of disabilities; for others, there are concerns about dependency-related victimization (Finkelhor, 1995).

Families at Midlife: Launching Young Adults and Moving On

This is the longest phase in the family life cycle. With low birth rates and longer life spans, parents now launch children almost 25 years before retirement. The process of launching young adults is a very gradual one that actually begins in infancy. The launching process begins when parents take an infant to a childcare setting or preschool (Zilbach, 1989).

When children have diverse abilities, they may never leave home as they may not be able to live independently. Parents realize that their caregiver role may be permanent. Some children may move into community living arrangements, but families may still be required to monitor the young adult's behavior and provide financial support. The responsibilities of caregiving may appear overwhelming at this stage, as, in addition to caring for an adult-child with a disability, parents may be responsible for their own parents as well.

The Family in Later Life

Adjusting to retirement is the major task of the later life stage in the life cycle. This may put strain on a marriage. Financial insecurity and dependence are also issues that elderly people face. It is also a time when couples must cope with the loss of friends, relatives, spouse, and perhaps a child. Grandparenthood, however, can offer opportunities for relationships with young children without the demands of parenthood. As parents face their own death, they may need to make financial and guardianship decisions related to their adult-child with a disability.

Viewing the family from the family life cycle perspective highlights some of the tasks that families must perform at various stages in the development of the family, how these tasks change over time, and how a child with diverse abilities impacts these tasks.

The tasks, obligations, and expectations vary with changing socio-historical circumstances. Feelings about divorce and cohabitation have changed just as feelings about how and where to educate children with diverse abilities have changed. It is not possible to understand any system without taking into account what else is happening in the world and what is considered to be "best practice." Best practice includes having some understanding of a child's ethnic/cultural background in addition to an understanding of families and how they work.

Cultural Diversity in Families

Families' views are influenced by their cultural background. What we think, how we act, the language we speak, and even what we eat are part of our wider cultural context. Looking at cultural diversity is a matter of "balance between validating the differences among us and appreciating the forces of our common humanity" (McGoldrick, 1993, p. 332).

The actual fabric of the nation is changing with increases in cultural diversity. The Children's Defense Fund predicts that by the year 2030, there will be 5.5 million more Hispanic children, 2.6 million more African American children, 1.5 million more children of other races, and 6.2 million fewer white non-Hispanic children than in 1985.

The following brief sketches provide some demographic information as well as concerns that will be relevant to your teaching. The resources and bibliographies at the end of the chapter can help you locate additional information. It is useful to start with a common understanding of terminology. A *racial* group is a socially defined group distinguished by selected, inherited physical characteristics. An *ethnic* group is distinguished by a sense of peoplehood or "consciousness of kind" based on a common national origin, religion, or language. If one's racial or ethnic group is subordinate to the majority in terms of power and prestige (not necessarily in terms of number of members), he or she occupies a *minority* status as well (Eshleman, 1997).

The key characteristics of any racial or ethnic group center around self and social definitions. In Hawaii and Jamaica, for example, the social meaning of black is very different than in Kansas and Georgia. To have a particular skin color, speech pattern, or manner of dress may lead others to perceive and label someone correctly or incorrectly, as a member of a specific racial or ethnic group (Eshleman, 1997). There are 5 main groups of racial/ethnic families in the United States. In many ways they are more similar than dissimilar to the dominant family forms that exist in the larger U.S. society. For European Americans, African Americans, Hispanic Americans, Asian Americans, or Native Americans, social status is positively related to marital stability. Children receive their basic identity and status within the family context. Parents ascribe to the basic achievement and mobility values that exist within the larger society. In other ways they are different.

African American Families

In the 1990s, African Americans formed the largest distinct racial/ethnic group in the United States; they numbered about 33 million or almost 13 percent of the population according to the 1990 census data (U.S. Bureau of the Census, 1995c). Of these, 27 percent are under the age of 15. African American children are more likely to live in poverty (46 percent) compared to 11 percent of white children, with slightly more than half living in homes with the father absent (U.S. Bureau of the Census, 1993). (We use the terms black Americans and African Americans interchangeably.) Because of their unique historical and social experiences, many African Americans have lifestyles and value patterns that differ considerably from the European American majority. The relations between whites and blacks in the United States has been a source of a number of major social issues in the past several decades: segregation, busing, and job discrimination to mention a few.

One of the most significant features of African Americans is the color of their skin. Black Americans who can "pass" as white are confronted with a different set of interactions than those with darker coloring. Darker skinned blacks are at a continuing disadvantage and experience more discrimination than fair-skinned blacks in the contemporary United States (Keith & Herring, 1991). The black community in contemporary America is a blending of individuals from three distinct ethnic groups: those born in America, those born in the Caribbean, and those born in Africa. They have diverse values, beliefs, lifestyles, and cultural preferences (Willis, 1998).

The migration of African Americans from rural to urban areas has followed the general population trend. With the exception of California, there are fewer African Americans in the West. By 1994, 86 percent of African American families lived in metropolitan areas, with 56 percent living in central cities (U.S. Bureau of the Census, 1995a).

African American families, like white families, fit no stereotypic view. Strengths such as strong family ties and flexibility in family roles, and caring parenting give some families and their children a strong support network. African American families have a strong work orientation and motivation as well as a strong religious orientation (Olson & DeFrain, 1997). The African American family is an absorbing, adaptive, and amazingly resilient mechanism for the socialization of its children and surviving in society (Eshleman, 1997).

African American families face challenges based on their history of discrimination and racism in the United States. Black males face a high risk of being killed as young men; there is a high rate of violence against each other. African Americans lack male role models and may feel powerless and have problems building positive self-esteem. They risk being judged as financial risks, because of inadequate education.

Major disparities still exist between blacks and whites. A persistent problem is that of black females finding mates. In 1993 there were almost 2 million

All families have an ethnic/cultural background. Educators need to respect this background and learn how it impacts the child's inclusion in the classroom.

more black women than black men. Because black males experience higher rates of unemployment and underemployment, it is difficult to attain a family income level that allows them to provide adequately for their families. When families (regardless of race) are constantly worrying about financial problems, marital difficulties often follow.

A disproportionate number of blacks live below the poverty line. Consequently, the incidence of poverty-related disability (poor nutrition resulting in iron deficiency that causes anemia, problems with attention, concentration and problem solving as well as lower IQ scores) is high. African American children are over represented in class for the mentally retarded (IDEA, 1997).

Although African American families are primarily nuclear families, they have a much stronger social support network than white families. The significance of such a support system is extremely important to families with children with diverse abilities. Relatives form a significant part of this support network. The importance of religion in family life at all social levels is another difference between African American and white populations. The religious community can provide a social life for the African American family as well as giving emotional support and help in caring for a child with diverse abilities.

Within African American nuclear families, the typical pattern appears to be egalitarian relationships where roles are flexible and tasks are often interchanged. Parents, males in particular, seem to be more authoritarian than in white families and encourage independence and responsibility earlier (Seligman & Darling, 1989). Children with diverse abilities who are unable to live up to this expectation provide added stress to family systems. African American women have been portrayed as having more power than in other cultures, but such female dominance is rarely true. Education is valued for upward mobility. Most women work either out of necessity or out of desire to enhance family income.

In the past, we did little to enhance children's understanding of their own culture. With growing cultural awareness and sensitivity, this should be changing. Some African Americans are now asking for their differences as well as their similarities to be acknowledged and encouraged. Because the tests that are used to determine learning ability and achievement are standardized on white populations, we don't know how black children learn best. Perhaps because of fear of discrimination we have not met their individual learning needs.

Learn more about the African American culture and incorporate this knowledge in your teaching. Examine your teaching materials. Do you have stories about African American children and representative dolls available? When you discuss families do you include a wide range of family configurations including multigenerational families, those who have others living with them, single-parent families, and those with working mothers? African Americans have a rich heritage with a strong sense of family, community, and culture.

Guidelines for Working with African American Families:

- Do not ignore race and pretend that African Americans are the same as whites but just happen to be black.

- Value the strengths of kinship bonds and included extended family members and friends who are involved with the family.

- Work with the family's informal support network (friends, neighbors, church) whenever possible.

- Begin by addressing people formally (Ms. Wapoles) until the individual asks you to change the form of address.

- Learn about the family's beliefs relative to health and medical care and make suggestions that are congruent with their beliefs. Adapt interventions to coincide with their values and lifestyle.

- Learn about the resources in the African American community.

- Separate the effects of poverty from the effects of culture and respond to each individually.

- Avoid stereotyping.

- Honor the home language of the family and child.

- Include African Americans on the child's IEP/IFSP team.

- Learn more about the African American culture by talking to and reading about this culture (adapted from Willis, 1998).

Hispanic American Families

Hispanic Americans constitute the second largest ethnic minority in the United States. They do not share a common racial background. The Hispanic population in the United States is increasing rapidly and may soon be the largest minority. There were almost 23 million individuals in the United States who claimed Hispanic origin in 1993 (about 9 percent). Most are American citizens; some are not, but are legal residents; some are here illegally. While the U.S. population as a whole increased at a rate of about 10 percent over the past decade, the Latino population increased by 48 percent. The population itself is diverse, with many subcategories, the most numerous being Mexican Americans (14.6 million, 64 percent), Puerto Ricans (2.4 million, 11 percent), Cuban (1.1 million, 5 percent), those from Central and South America (3.1 million, 13 percent), and those who are Hispanic but come from other areas (1.6 million, 7 percent) (U.S. Bureau of the Census, 1994).

Hispanic Americans are overrepresented in poverty groups. In 1993, the median income of Hispanic families was $23,912 whereas for non-Hispanic families it was $38,015 (U.S. Bureau of the Census, 1994). Among the Hispanic groups, Puerto Ricans (all of whom are U.S. citizens) have the lowest median family income and Cubans the highest.

Enchautegui (1995) points out the following barriers to our understanding and acting on the problems that Latinos face:

- *Misperceived identity.* Even though 64 percent of Hispanics living in the United States are native born, they are often perceived as immigrants. They are viewed as being here temporarily or seen as competing against whites for scarce resources.

- *No attention to the working poor.* Most reform efforts have been directed to the nonworking poor, and this overlooks the problems of Hispanic Americans who are poor, but most of whom are working.

- *Geographic concentration.* Three-fourths of all Hispanic Americans live in five states (California, Florida, Illinois, New York, and Texas). Consequently, programmatic attempts to deal with Hispanic American issues are often state or local rather than national efforts.

- *Political participation.* Only a third of all Hispanic Americans were registered to vote in 1992 compared to 64 percent of African Americans and 70 percent of white non-Hispanics.

- *Differences among subgroups.* By highlighting differences among the various Hispanic American subgroups, larger underlying themes common to the poverty experiences of Hispanic Americans have been overlooked.

Hispanic families have high family cohesion and flexibility. Families are important to them and they frequently have supportive kin networks. Many families have a strong ethnic identity and, despite the stereotypes, most have equalitarian decision making (Olson & DeFrain, 1997).

Like African American families, they face many challenges. A primary challenge is increasing their level of education and overcoming economic discrimination to gain financial resources. Families that do not speak or read English face additional challenges. They often have to cope with relocation issues at the same time as they try to maintain their family centeredness and ethnic traditions. After families are here for several generations, there seems to be a drift from the traditional ways and values (Olson & DeFrain, 1997).

The extended family plays an important role in Latino families. Siblings, cousins, and other relatives provide a support network that is helpful to families with children with diverse abilities. The overall attitude toward children is one of acceptance, putting less pressure on children to achieve milestones early. This attitude may make it easier to cope with a child who is developmentally delayed. However, concern with socialization and showing respectful well-mannered behavior may be difficult at later ages.

Depending upon their degree of identification with the traditional culture, some Hispanics may see disease and disability as punishment for wrongdoing. Medical settings may be intimidating to Hispanic parents. Hospitals may be thought of as places where people go to die. Visiting rules that are time-bound and exclude some family members may make families feel even more alienated. A diagnosis may not be acknowledged nor permission for testing may not be signed when it is initially proffered, as the mother may want to talk with the entire family about the advisability and implications of testing or treatment.

Because of family values, very young Hispanic children are less likely to be in early care and education settings. Mothers are generally expected to stay home and raise children. When this is not possible, the extended family frequently takes over the care of the young children. Some families may see sending children to school before kindergarten as a sign of deteriorating family values. Hispanic families who choose to send their children to child care or preschool need your support. Help them see this as an alternative to extended family care. They should not be made to feel that they are not fulfilling their roles as parents.

Communicating with Latino families who do not speak English may be challenging. Some families that speak Spanish may not read it. Children may come to school with good language skills in both Spanish and

English or with only rudimentary knowledge of English or Spanish. If the parents speak little or no English, it is important to have bilingual/bicultural support for parent-teacher conferences and to translate forms that are to be sent home. Use parents as a resource to learn about the culture and enrich the class curriculum.

The overall Hispanic American population is young and primarily urban. There are many distinctive differences among the Hispanic groups. Only a few of these will be highlighted but the differences are so great that it is important to know what specific group you are learning about and what aspects of the culture the individuals you are working with embrace.

Mexican American Families. Over one million Mexican Americans are descendants of the native Mexicans who lived in the southwest before it became part of the United States following the Mexican American War. They became Americans in 1848, when Texas, California, New Mexico, and most of Arizona became U.S. territory. There was also large-scale migration in the early 1900s caused by the chaos of the Mexican Revolution and the demand for labor on cotton farms and railroads in California. These four states, plus Colorado, contain the largest concentrations of Mexican Americans (Williams, 1990).

Strong family ties typify the Mexican American culture. They often live near nuclear and extended family members and share interests and concerns about welfare of the family unit. The needs of the family often supersede the needs of an individual. An individual may drop out of school to work to contribute to the family income.

The theme of family honor and unity is strong throughout Mexican American society and is irrespective of social class or geographic location. Godparents play an important role in families. Traditionally, expectant parents select a patron, a married couple, or an extended family member to be the child's sponsor. This is considered both a special honor and an obligation. The baptism ceremony establishes a social bond and godparents are thought of as being co-parents. The relationship is expected to last a lifetime, although this tradition is less strong in the 1990s than it has been in the past (Williams, 1990).

In the past, Mexican Americans adhered to the traditional ideal of manliness (*machismo*) which is equated with authority, strength, sexual virility, and prowess. The male was the patriarch who made important decisions. He was also the provider and protector for his family. He had the freedom of seeking other sexual partners, his wife could not.

In the 1990s, decision making is becoming more egalitarian. In general, however, Mexican American males still exert power over their wives and the women still fulfill the majority of child-care and household tasks. Mexican American families have a high fertility rate and interest in having children. Fathers show a definite interest in their children and their behavior. Given the size of the family, along with minimal skills and low level of income, it is difficult for many families to live above the poverty line (Williams, 1990).

Puerto Rican Families. Puerto Rican families are heavily concentrated in cities in the east, especially New York City. Many have low-paying full-time jobs, part-time jobs, or sometimes no job at all. Males previously came to the United States to work in manufacturing jobs that required little education and few skills. In the 1990s, there are few such jobs left.

More than other Hispanic groups, Puerto Ricans form families without benefit of marriage and have a high proportion of female-headed households. In 1993, 60 percent of Puerto Rican female-headed households lived below the poverty line (Enchautegui, 1995). This poses challenges to these families.

Guidelines for Working with Hispanic American Families:

- Look at yourself to determine your experience with culturally diverse people, especially those who speak English as a second language and those who have immigrated illegally.

- Assess your style of interacting with others, especially how you think about time. To the extent that you feel the pressure of time during your interactions and that documents must be signed *now,* families may interpret this as a lack of respect or concern.

- If families have immigrated recently, they may need time to adjust to the culture and how they will meet their basic needs while not having the energy to focus on the needs of a particular child. Particularly if the family is not legally documented, be clear about your role. Specifically how it relates to child welfare (you are not there to take their child away) and the Immigration and Naturalization Service *(La Migra)* (you will not inform them). In paperwork, use the term undocumented immigrants in reference to their status.

- Learn about the immigrants' country of origin and area of the country the family emigrated from. If the area is rural, they may need support childproofing their home and adjusting to other basic issues that are different.

- Do not assume that families who speak Spanish and/or English can also read it. They may have learned words in English, particularly in relation to their child they have never seen or heard in Spanish.

- Assess family's transportation needs. Is there public transportation and can they use it? If they have a car, are they comfortable driving on freeways and can they read maps?

- Talk with families about their feelings about physicians and hospitals and how comfortable they are with the concept and the actual physical place.

- Learn more about the Latino culture in general, as well as the specific country from which the families come. Attend Latin American community celebrations and watch films from and about Latin America. Find out what community resources are responsive to and supportive of Latin Americans in general and specific countries or areas in particular (adapted from Zuniga, 1998).

Asian American Families

As of 1997, over 4 percent of the U.S. population (10 million) were characterized as Asian Pacific Americans. The Asian American population has doubled each decade since 1970, representing the fastest growing minority population in the United States. This population is projected to reach 40 million (10 percent) by 2050 (Aponte & Crouch, 1995). Most of this growth was the result of immigration. They are not a homogeneous group. The major groups typically included in this category are: Chinese (1.6 million), Filipino (1.4 million), Japanese (848,000), Asian Indian (815,000), Korean (799,000), Vietnamese (615,000), Laotian (149,000), Cambodian (147,000), Thai (91,000), and Hmong (90,000). Although the term Pacific Islander appears as a subcategory in the U.S. census, this does not represent an ethnic group. Included in this subcategory are Hawaiians (211,000), Samoans (63,000), and Guamanians (49,000) (U.S. Bureau of the Census, 1992).

All these groups had different ancestors, languages, customs, and recency of immigration. Like the African Americans, they are concentrated (90 percent) in metropolitan areas. Like Hispanic Americans, they reside in specific states: New York, Texas, Illinois, and New Jersey. Asian and Pacific Islanders marry at the same rate as the European American population (82 percent) and there is a high level of family stability. Asian Americans are younger with a median age of about 30 compared to 34 for the U.S. population. They are better educated and have higher median incomes than all other groups. About 13 percent live below the poverty line (U.S. Bureau of the Census, 1995b). Their strengths lie in family loyalty and a strong family orientation. They respect their elders and have high levels of mutual support between generations. Their children are well disciplined and they place a high value on education.

They, too, face challenges in the United States. One challenge is the loss of ties with kin, particularly for those who have come to the United States more recently such as those from Vietnam, Cambodia, and Laos. They may distrust those outside of their group and have a stigma against seeking help. They have high expectations for themselves and their children. This is problematic when they have young children with diverse abilities that interfere with the ability to learn. Dealing with an excessive focus on work and emotional vulnerability are additional challenges (Olson & DeFrain, 1997).

Overall, Asian Americans value family very highly and tend to initially solve problems within private family settings. Family needs often have precedence over individual needs. Family ties are close and divorce rates are low with few female-headed households (13 percent). As a culture they avoid open confrontation, therefore they are unlikely to challenge professionals even when they may disagree. Communication is often indirect (Eshleman, 1997).

Some of the traditional cultural norms, such as speaking the native language, patriarchial authority, and traditional role expectations for wives and children, fade. By the second or third generation, children tend to accept English as their dominant language, they adopt the dress codes and musical preferences of their peers, and they pick up various dating and sexual patterns that are at odds with traditional and parental values. The family is seen as a harmonious group and anything, such as strong emotions, that might disrupt this harmony is expected to be suppressed. Children are expected to conform. In order to develop these values in children, parents may teach children that disobedience brings ridicule on the child and shame on the family. Traditional cultural values of patience and persistence are handed down. Family dependency is valued over independent achievement and cooperation over competition.

Asian American families place a high value on education. The parents generally show educators respect and expect their children to do the same. Children are expected to obey educators and not question what they say. They may need to learn the skill of asking questions of adults without questioning the authority that adults have. Children may need support in learning skills for getting along with peers. Stress the value of cooperation and helping others rather than one child's winning and others' losing. Talk about the differences between feelings and how these feelings can be expressed. Children may need your help in learning to express themselves in ways that do not conflict with family values. As you work this out, consult with the parents for their ideas and use parents as a resource for expanding your knowledge of the Asian cultures.

To facilitate learning and be more relevant, materials and programming need to take the child's culture into account. Be aware, however, of the differences among Asian cultures. Japanese and Chinese people have both similar and different values. Even among members of one group, there is great variation. Learn about the particular families you interact with and decide which generalizations apply and which do not.

Guidelines for Working with Asian American Families:

- When greeting (or saying good-bye), family members begin with the oldest family member and typically greet male members first. Use the appropriate title with either the last name (Chinese and Korean) or the individual's first name (Cambodian, Laotian, and Vietnamese), depending on the country of origin. Many women retain their own family name when they marry. It is appropriate to address her as Mrs. Onn (Miss Onn becomes Mrs. Onn when she marries, not Mrs. Kim).

- Initiate interactions slowly and cautiously. Ask general, not personal questions, but do not ask about U.S. foreign policy, the internal politics of their country of origin, or religion. Expect to be asked personal questions; this is a way of showing interest and concern.

- In general, avoid initiating physical contact particularly between men and women. This includes shaking hands or hugging another individual.

- Keep your language and voice reserved and polite. Control your emotions and avoid direct confrontation. Do not show anger or criticize the family.

- Focus your attention on the family as a system rather than only on the child.

- Consider the degree to which families embrace traditional values and beliefs particularly as they relate to spirituality and healing.

- Assess the English proficiency of the family and modify your language to accommodate their

Early childhood programs need to be responsive to cultural differences and acknowledge these differences in the way they plan for children.

level. Speak more slowly for families who are not as proficient. Do not correct their English. Do not assume that individuals who speak with an accent are not proficient.

- Become more aware of your nonverbal communication. Avoid sustained eye contact and winking or batting your eyes. Do not touch a child on the head, wave your arms, beckon, or point your index finger. These are considered to be signs of contempt.

- Learn the body language that is associated with negative and affirmative responses. Some families will not say no to you even if they disagree with your suggestions. Learn when yes means no.

- When sitting in a chair, keep both feet on the floor and your hands visible; if on the floor, point your soles away from others.

- If the family does not wear shoes in the house, remove your shoes before entering. Expect to be offered food or drinks and enjoy the hospitality. However, do not praise or compliment a particular household object or the family may feel compelled to give it to you.

- Families may offer you gifts. This frequently poses a dilemma as many agencies do not want you to accept these. If you do accept a gift, take it in both hands, express your gratitude, and do not open it in the presence of the giver.

- Include bilingual and bicultural professionals on the team (adapted from Chan, 1998a, 1998b; Mokuau & Tauili'ili, 1998).

Native American Families

For over 500 years Native Americans were referred to as Indians. There were, and still remain several hundred tribes or nations with 300 separate languages and dialects. Their population at the time Columbus landed (1492) was estimated to be about 10 million (Harjo, 1993). As of 1995, 2.2 million people, or slightly less than 1 percent of the population of the United States, claimed American Indian or Alaska Native origins (U.S. Bureau of the Census, 1995c). More than half of these Native Americans live on reservations, trust lands, or tribal designated areas. The others (46 percent) live in cities and communities part from designated areas. Growing numbers of Native Americans are leaving the reservations (Harjo, 1993).

The largest group, the Cherokees, comprise about 16 percent of the Native American population. The second largest group, the Navaho, comprise about 12 percent. Other groups, ranging from 6 to 2 percent, include the Chippewa, Sioux, Choctaw, Pueblo, Apache, Iroquois, Lumbee, and Creek tribes. They live mostly in the western region of the United States: California, Arizona, Oklahoma, New Mexico, Washington, and Alaska. It is important to know the characteristics of the particular tribe the family belongs to, as there is much intertribal variation and danger in overgeneralization.

About two-thirds of all Native American family households are comprised of married couples, with about 26 percent of households headed by females (U.S. Bureau of the Census, 1995c). Elders play a special role. Grandparents actively participate in passing on the cultural heritage. Of particular relevance is the teaching of living in harmony with nature and having respect for the land. Interracial marriage is common. Overall, Native Americans stress cooperation over competition and harmony with nature as opposed to trying to control nature. They are adult centered as opposed to child centered, and their time orientation is present instead of future.

The number of individuals choosing the designation Native American on census forms appears to be growing at a rate 4 times the national average. Primarily this is because many people who have previously called themselves European Americans are now identifying themselves as Native Americans (Eschbach, 1993). (Let me add a note of caution here. In collecting data one graduate student observed that 2 males marked that they were Native American. When questioned, they said that they chose Native American because they were born here. Individuals have the right to claim any origins they choose on forms. To the extent that individuals do not fill out forms accurately, for whatever reason, our information will be misleading.)

Like other groups, Native Americans are not a homogeneous people although they share many values in common. Like Hispanic Americans they are young, with a median age of 26.4 (for European Americans the median is 34.4). One of the most troubling statistics is life expectancy, which is estimated at less than 50 years (compared to 75 for the population as a whole). A high rate of infant mortality, alcoholism, tuberculosis, diabetes and other diseases, psychological distress, suicide, crime and accidental deaths all contribute to this low life expectancy.

While other minorities have struggled to gain a place in the United States, the experience of the Native Americans has been the opposite. They have struggled to avoid being subjugated and to preserve their land, water, traditions, and unique legal rights. Unlike any other minority group, Native Americans have negotiated over 600 treaties with the U.S. government and ceded billions of acres of land and untold natural resources (Harjo, 1993).

According to Harjo (1993) assimilation for Native Americans has meant cultural genocide. There has been a concerted effort to destroy Native American languages, traditions, customary laws, dress, religion, and occupation, This was done by encouraging Christian denominations to convert Indian nations, imposing an educational system that was designed to separate children from their families and instill non-Indian values, and by the federal government's breaking up tribal landholding in favor of individual landowners, and taxing the lands.

Education for Native American children has often been run by the Federal Bureau of Indian Af-

fairs. Traditionally, the schools have been boarding schools, located far from the children's homes, with European American educators. The focus of this education was to "de-Indianize" the Native Americans. It hasn't worked. Native Americans have in many instances not wanted to have their children included, but instead have wanted to foster close ties with the tribe. They want to improve the quality of education for their children by changing the standard curriculum to be more responsive to another view of American history. Until the 1970s, Native American children were taught in school that their traditions were savage or immoral (Harjo, 1993). Educators were actively trying to change and denigrate their way of life. Their school drop-out rates are high. In 1992 only about 5 percent of the Native American population was enrolled in college and a majority of these were attending two-year colleges (Harjo, 1993).

Some feel that one reason the drop-out rate for Native American children is higher than for the rest of the population is because of the biased view that educators and textbooks present. For example, many Native Americans view Thanksgiving as a day of mourning, not one of cooperation, celebration, and feasting. Remember that cultural diversity may impact the ways in which you celebrate holidays. Of all cultures, we tend to misrepresent this one to the detriment of the people the most.

Some children's ideas of Native Americans may be influenced by traditional "Cowboy-and-Indian" movies. Replace these ideas with more realistic ones and have children do more than make Indian headbands and give war whoops. Giving an in-depth view of Native Americans will help other children increase their knowledge and decrease their prejudices.

We come back to the question then what is the dominate culture in the United States. It depends. In general, the longer families have lived in the United States the more they move closer to the dominant value system.

Guidelines for Working with Native American Families:

- Ask parents who they want to include in meetings. Once this is established, include and show respect for the entire group.

- Listen to the family's ideas and concerns and acknowledge them, show interest. Provide emotional support and respect for the family.

- Build trust. Many Native American families have a history of negative experiences with public agencies and hence distrust them.

- Learn about communication styles. Some families find periods of silence and reflection an important part of their interactions, more at a pace that is comfortable for the family.

- Find out what families want, particularly if they need support in interpreting an assessment, and then explain these results to other family members.

- If the family speaks English as a second language, offer the skills of an interpreter, especially when an evaluation is explained or a new intervention introduced. (Most people like to learn new or technically dense information in their native language.) Choose an interpreter with the advice of the family, sometimes an individual from the community is a good choice; in other instances, this might violate confidentiality. If technical information needs to be interpreted, the individual chosen needs to understand the information in both languages.

- When you need a lot of information from families, set the stage by telling them you will be asking a lot of questions. Encourage them to ask for clarification if they don't understand and to feel free to consult with others before they answer.

- Some families who seek early intervention and specialized education also practice their tribal religion and consult with tribal healers. If a child is wearing amulets or has certain markings, do not remove these without the permission of the family. (If removed, give them to the family.) Do not ask a lot of questions about tribal ceremonies.

- If you know little about the family's culture, admit it, show your respect, ask them to tell you if you offend them in some way, and make a sincere effort to learn more about the culture.

- Even after arranging to meet with families at a particular time, always check before entering if it is a good time; if not, honor their decision and reschedule.

- Explain time lines and medical procedures fully to families. Be sure to explain the actual procedures in detail, the reason for them, and the available options.

- Encourage families to help in the selection of the service coordinator and when there are changes, allow time for the transition.

- As families change and grow in their understanding of their child's situation, they may want or need information that they had previously been offered but didn't seem useful then. Offer suggestions again, particularly opportunities to talk with other parents (adapted from Joe & Malach, 1998).

European American Families

As with other groups, we know descriptive information about this group. There are approximately 57.87 million European American family households in the United States with about 82 percent of these composed of married couples. We know their median family income in 1993 was $39,300 (U.S. Bureau of the Census, 1995c). Although we have many descriptive statistics, they shed little light on the culture and values of the "majority."

Traditional white Anglo-Saxon Protestant (WASP) values generally include such personal traits as control, personal responsibility, independence, individuality, stoicism, keeping up appearances, a "hard work" ethic, and moderation (McGoldrick, 1993). Complaining is viewed negatively. Increasingly this dominant culture is embracing the importance of individualism especially in gender-related issues. There are many subcultures of the dominant culture; we will provide three examples that illustrate this diversity. One caution is in order, when discussing ethic or cultural traits, we risk stereotyping people. Our intention is to provide evidence of diversity.

German Families. Germans are the most frequent immigrants to the United States and represent an estimated 60 million residents (about 23 percent of the population). The early waves of German immigrants came between 1880 and 1920 primarily for religious, economic, and political reasons (Lassiter, 1995). These early settlers migrated to rural areas with later waves seeking out major cities.

Irish Families. There are approximately 38.5 million individuals in the United States of Irish background, almost 16 percent of the population (Lassiter, 1995). Many came in large numbers in the 1840s because of the potato famine and the oppressive conditions in Ireland. They have often been here for 4 or more generations and think of themselves as American. Some traits this group shares are: They value language and poetry; they may believe that problems are a result of their sins and see problems as private matters and rarely seek help; they believe in suffering alone and in silence. Despite the "gift of gab," they rarely talk of feelings. They tend to have high rates of addiction, primarily alcoholism (McGoldrick, 1993).

Italian Families. The major Italian immigration to the United States was from the late 19th to the early 20th centuries. They continue to hold a strong cultural identity, making up about 6 percent of the Unites States population (about 14 million citizens) (Lassiter, 1995). Most are from southern Italy. Italians value family, both nuclear and extended, and the sense of security, affection, and relatedness that family brings. They have a strong ethnic attachment and may prefer to live in ethnic neighborhoods. The father is typically the undisputed head of the family and the mother its heart. Feelings are discussed, sometimes in colorful, expressive, and dramatic ways. There are often strong family boundaries and there is some information that is not talked about openly with individuals outside the family (McGoldrick, 1993).

Jewish Families. There are approximately 6 million Jewish people living in the Unites States (about 3 percent) (Lassiter, 1995). They tend to live in major cities. Most of the Jews in the United States came from Eastern Europe beginning about 1900 through the 1940s. This group tended to be family-oriented, value their culture, and take great pride in their children. Families are often democratic even across generational boundaries. They seek information, respect wisdom, and then make decisions. They value artistic and educational achievement. Raising successful children is important and is a major responsibility of parents, particularly the mother. Parents make sacrifices for children and experience personal pleasure in their children's accomplishments. Life-cycle rituals play an important role in family life. Sharing suffering is seen as an expression of loyalty for those who have suffered in the past (McGoldrick, 1993).

Although there may be a set of values that reflect the dominant culture, it too is heterogeneous and it is just as difficult not to generate stereotypes about European American groups as it is other. Learn your personal cultural background and where you fit in the culture. Value and respect the culture of others at the level at which they embrace it.

Guidelines for Working with European American Families:

- Speak about issues directly and honestly without using jargon. Be aware of regional differences in terms and vocabulary.

- Families have a tradition of being involved in their children's education and expect to take an active role; they want to be informed and have input into the process.

- Many families have active complex lifestyles, so meetings need to be scheduled to accommodate these commitments. They should start on time and have a stated end.

- Even among the dominant culture, there are many individual differences and preferences. These must be respected and honored.

Summary

As we are viewing children in a family-centered context, we are finding that we need to learn more about family systems. Our views of families are changing while the families themselves are changing. Parents have historically been viewed as having a variety of roles from being the cause of their child's disability to being a political activist. We are now viewing parents as having multiple family roles.

One way of viewing the family system is looking at the family life cycle and the developmental tasks families must perform. To understand a family, one must know about the particular characteristics of the family and its members, including the child himself and his abilities and the way a particular family perceives a disability. Families differ on their levels of cohesion and flexibility as well as their traditional patterns of interacting and communicating.

There are many subcultures in the United States including African Americans, Hispanic Americans, Asian Americans, Native Americans, and European Americans. Some generalizations can be made about each of these groups, but there are also many differ-

ences within each group. Professionals need to be supportive of the family's values and work to provide services in an acceptable way.

Educational Resources

Beach Center on Families and Disability
c/o Life Span Institute
University of Kansas
3111 Haworth Hall
Lawrence, KS 66045
(913) 864-7600, FAX (913) 864-7605
e-mail: beach@dole.1si.ukans.edu
A federally funded research and training institute that focuses on families and the successful functioning of families who have members with disabilities.

Chicana/o Latina/o Network
http://latino.sscnet.ucla.edu/
This site provides information about the Latin American community. It includes information on job opportunities, education, building community and family ties, and information on institutions providing services to Hispanic Americans.

The Circle of Brotherhood Association
http://www.acsu.buffalo.edu/~sww/circle.html
A group of African American men practicing, and dedicated to, the quality of life, successful manhood and parenting, economic growth and development, and the pursuit of excellence and spiritual development.

Department of Health and Human Services
Administration for Children and Families
Administration for Native Americans (ANA)
200 Independence Avenue, SW, Room 348F
Washington, DC 20201
(202) 690-5780
http://www.acf.dhhs.gov/programs/ana/
This agency provides grants, training, and technical assistance to eligible tribes and Native American organizations.

Facts for Families
http://www.aacap.org/web/aacap/factsFam/
This page can educate parents and families about some emotional problems that affect children such as child abuse, AIDS, divorce, and eating disorders.

Grandmothers' Wisdom Keepers
PO Box 20665
Knoxville, TN 37940
http://members.aol.com/ladinred/pages
/gwkhome.htm
This organization provides an opportunity for young children, particularly girls, to learn and preserve the old ways of Native Americans. This includes the skills, art, and traditions of the Native American people.

Lynch, E. W., & Hanson, M. J. (Eds.). (1998). Developing cross-cultural competence: A guide for working with children and their families (2nd ed.). Baltimore: Paul H. Brookes Publishing.

Provides information on cultural diversity and ways to assess oneself in this area as well as information about various cultures and ways of interacting with individuals from that culture.

National Association of Sibling Programs (NASP)
Sibling Support Project
Children's Hospital and Medical Center
PO Box 5371
Seattle, WA 98150
(206) 368-4911, FAX (206) 368-4816
e-mail: dmeyer@chmc.org

Keeps a database of programs for siblings of children with developmental disabilities and chronic illness.

National Black Child Development Institute
1023 15th Street, NW
Suite 600
Washington, DC 20005
(202) 387-1281, FAX (202) 234-1738
http://www.nbcdi.org/
e-mail: moreinfo@nbcdi.org

An institution founded to improve and protect the quality of life of African American children and families. Publishes a variety of pamphlets and magazines with information about parenting and child health, as well as a calendar with photos of African American children.

The National Council of Negro Women, Inc.
633 Pennsylvania Avenue, NW
Washington, DC 20004
(202) 737-0120
http://www.ncnw.com/
e-mail: info@ncnw.com

This organization's mission is to advance opportunities and the quality of life for African American women, their families and communities. Sponsors activities to promote community and family involvement, including a mentor program in the Washington, DC area.

Turnbull, A. P., & Turnbull, H. R., III (1996). *Families, professionals, and exceptionality: A special partnership* (3rd ed.). Upper Saddle River, NJ: Merrill.

Provides an overview of families and disabilities from a family life cycle framework particularly as it relates to the schools.

Urban Education Web
Urban/Minority Families
http://eric-web.tc.columbia.edu/families/index.html

This site provides on-line publications dealing with the education of minority families. Urban Education Web also provides links to other sites concerning minority families.

References

Aponte, J. F., & Crouch, R. T. (1995). The changing ethnic profile of the United States. In J. F. Aponte, R. Y. Rivers, & J. Wohl (Eds.), *Psychological*

interventions and cultural diversity (pp. 1–18). Needham Heights, MA: Allyn & Bacon.

Barnard, D. E. (1981). An ecological approach to parent-child relations. In C. C. Brown (Ed.), *Infants at risk: Assessment and intervention. An update for health-care professionals and parents* (pp. 89–96). Skillman, NJ: Johnson & Johnson.

Berkson, G. (1993). *Children with handicaps: A review of behavioral research.* Hillsdale, NJ: Erlbaum.

Bettleheim, B. (1967). *The empty fortress: Infantile autism and the birth of self.* London: Collier-Macmillian.

Carnegie Task Force on Meeting the Needs of Young Children. (1994). *Starting points: Meeting the needs of our youngest children.* New York: Carnegie Corporation of New York.

Carter, B., & McGoldrick, M. (1993). The changing family life cycle In F. Walsh (Ed.), *Normal family processes* (2nd ed.). New York: Guilford Press.

Chan, S. (1998a). Families with Asian roots. In E. W. Lynch & M. J. Hanson (Eds.), *Developing cross-cultural competence: A guide for working with children and their families* (2nd ed., pp. 251–354). Baltimore: Brookes.

Chan, S. (1998b). Families with Pilipino roots. In E. W. Lynch & M. J. Hanson (Eds.), *Developing cross-cultural competence: A guide for working with children and their families* (2nd ed., pp. 355–408). Baltimore: Brookes.

Cherlin, A. J. (1996). *Public and private families.* New York: McGraw-Hill.

Combrinck-Graham, L. (1985). A developmental model for family systems. *Family Process, 24,* 139–150.

Curet, L. B. (1995). Diagnosis and management of drug abuse during pregnancy. In D. R. Coustan (Ed.), *Human reproduction: Growth and development* (pp. 137–159). Boston: Little, Brown.

DeLuca, K., & Solerno, S. (1984). *Helping professionals connect with families with handicapped children.* Springfield, IL: Thomas.

Enchautegui, M. (1995). Policy implications of Latino poverty. *The Urban Institute/Policy and Research Report, 25,* 10–12.

Eschbach, K. (1993). Changing identification among American Indians and Alaska Natives. *Demography, 30,* 635–652.

Eshleman, J. R. (1997). *The family* (8th ed.). Needham Heights, MA: Allyn & Bacon.

Featherstone, H. (1980). *A difference in the family: Life with a disabled child.* New York: Basic Books.

Finkelhor, D. (1995). The victimization of children: A developmental perspective. *American Journal of Orthopsychiatry, 65*(2), 177–193.

Fujiura, G. T., Roccoforte, J. A., & Braddock, D. (1994). Costs of family care for adults with mental retardation and related developmental disabilities.

American Journal on Mental Retardation, 99(3), 250-261.

Furstenberg, F. F., Jr. (1988). Child care after divorce and remarriage. In E. M. Hetherington & J. D. Arasteh (Eds.), *Impact of divorce, single parenting and stepparenting on children* (pp. 245-261). Hillsdale, NJ: Erlbaum.

Gabel, H., & Kotsch, L. (1981). Extended families and young handicapped children. *Topics in Early Childhood Special Education, 1*(3), 29-38.

Gabel, H., McDowell, J., & Cerreto, M. C. (1983). Family adaptation to the handicapped infant. In S. G. Garwood & R. R. Fewell (Eds.), *Educating handicapped infants: Issues in development and intervention* (pp. 457-494). Rockville, MD: Aspen.

Gladding, S. T. (1995). *Family therapy: History, theory, and practice.* Englewood Cliffs, NJ: Prentice Hall.

Griswold, R. L. (1993). *Fatherhood in America: A history.* New York: Basic Books.

Hanson, M. J. (1998). Families with Anglo-European roots. In E. W. Lynch & M. J. Hanson (Eds.), *Developing cross-cultural competence: A guide for working with children and their families* (2nd ed., pp. 93-126). Baltimore: Brookes.

Hareven, T. K. (1996). Life course. In *Encyclopedia of Gerontology*, (Vol. 2, pp. 31-40). Academic Press.

Harjo, S. S. (1993). The American Indian experience. In H. P. McAdoo (Ed.), *Family ethnicity: Strengths in diversity* (pp. 199-207). Newbury Park, CA: Sage.

Helsel Family. (1985). The Helsels' story of Robin. In H. R. Turnbull & A. P. Turnbull (Eds.), *Parents speak out: Then and now* (2nd ed., pp. 81-100). Englewood Cliffs, NJ: Merrill/Prentice Hall.

Individuals with Disabilities Education Act of 1997. Pub. L. No. 105-117, 111 Stat. 37-157, 20 U.S.C. 1400.

Joe, J. R., & Malach, R. S. (1998). Families with Native American roots. In E. W. Lynch & M. J. Hanson (Eds.), *Developing cross-cultural competence: A guide for working with children and their families* (2nd ed., pp. 127-164). Baltimore: Brookes.

Keith, V. M., & Herring, C. (1991). Skin tone and stratification in the Black community. *American Journal of Sociology, 97*, 760-778.

Lassiter, S. (1995). *Multicultural clients: A professional handbook for health care providers and social workers.* Westport, CT: Greenwood Press.

Mason, E., & Lee, R. V. (1995). Drug abuse. In W. M. Barron & M. D. Lindheimer (Eds.), *Medical disorders during pregnancy* (2nd ed., pp. 465-486). St. Louis, MO: Mosby.

McGoldrick, M. (1993). Ethnicity, cultural diversity, and normality. In F. Walsh (Ed.), *Normal family processes* (2nd ed., pp. 331-360). New York: Guilford Press.

McGoldrick, M., Heiman, M., & Carter, B. (1993). The changing family life cycle: A perspective on normalcy. In F. Walsh (Ed.), *Normal family processes* (2nd ed., pp. 405-443). New York: Guilford Press.

Mokuau, N., & Tauili'ili, P. (1998). Families with Native Hawaiian and Samoan roots. In E. W. Lynch & M. J. Hanson (Eds.), *Developing cross-cultural competence: A guide for working with children and their families* (2nd ed., pp. 409-440). Baltimore: Brookes.

National Center for Children in Poverty. (1995, Winter/Spring). Number of poor children under six increased from 5 to 6 million 1987-1992. *News and Issues, 5*(1), 1-2.

Olson, D. H. (1993). Circumplex model of marital and family systems: Assessing family functioning. In F. Walsh (Ed.), *Normal family processes* (2nd ed., pp. 104-137). New York: Guilford Press.

Olson, D. H., & DeFrain, J. (1997). *Marriage and the family: Diversity and strengths* (2nd ed.). Mountain View, CA: Mayfield.

Olson, D. H., Portner, J., & Levee, Y. (1985). *FACES III.* St. Paul: Family Social Science, University of Minnesota.

Palkovitz, R. (1992). Changes in father-infant bonding beliefs across couples first transition to parenthood. *Maternal Child Nursing Journal, 4,* 141-154.

Palkovitz, R. (1996). The recovery of fatherhood? In A. Carr & M. S. Lan Leeuwen (Eds.), *Religion, feminism and the family.* New York: John Knox/Westminister Press.

Piotrkowski, C. S., & Hughes, D. (1993). Dual-earner families in context: Managing family and work systems. In F. Walsh (Ed.), *Normal family processes* (2nd ed., pp. 185 -207). New York: Guilford Press.

Presser, H. B. (1994). Employment schedules among dual-earner spouses and the division of household labor by gender. *American Sociological Review, 59,* 348-364.

Rutstein, R. M., Conlon, C. J., & Batshaw, M. L. (1997). HIV and AIDS: From mother to child. In M. L. Batshaw (Ed.) *Children with disabilities* (4th ed., pp. 163-181). Baltimore: Brookes.

Seligman, M., & Darling, R. (1989). *Ordinary families, special children: A systems approach to childhood disability* (2nd ed.). New York: Guilford Press.

Seligman, M., & Darling, R. (1997). *Ordinary families, special children: A systems approach to childhood disability.* New York: Guilford Press.

Summers, J. A. (1987). Family adjustment: Issues in research on families with developmental disabled children. In V. B. Van Hasselt, P. S. Strain, & M. Hersen (Eds.), *Handbook of developmental disabilities* (pp. 79-90). New York: Pergamon Press.

Turnbull, A. P., & Turnbull, H. R., III. (1996). *Families, professionals, and exceptionality: A special partnership* (3rd ed.). Upper Saddle River, NJ: Merrill.

U.S. Bureau of the Census. (1991). *Statistical abstracts of the United States.* Washington, DC: U.S. Government Printing Office.

U.S. Bureau of the Census. (1992). *The Asian and Pacific Islander population in United States: March 1991 and 1990* (Current Population Reports, Series P20-459). Washington, DC: U.S. Government Printing Office.

U.S. Bureau of the Census. (1994). *The Hispanic population in the United States: March 1993.* (Current Population Reports, Series P20-475). Washington, DC: U.S. Government Printing Office.

U.S. Bureau of the Census. (1995a). *The Black population in the United States: March 1994 and 1993* (Current Population Reports, Series P20-480). Washington, DC: U.S. Government Printing Office.

U.S. Bureau of the Census. (1995b). *Household and family characteristics: March 1994.* (Current Population Reports, Series P20-483) Washington, DC: U.S. Government Printing Office.

U.S. Bureau of the Census. (1995c). *Statistical abstract of the United States* (115th ed.). Washington, DC: U.S. Government Printing Office.

U.S. National Center for Health Statistics. (1994). *Advance report of final natality statistics* (Monthly Vital Statistics Report, 1992, 43, 5). Washington, DC: U.S. Government Printing Office.

Wallinga, C., Paquio, L., & Skeen, P. (1987). When a brother or sister is ill. *Psychology Today, 42,* 43.

Wikler, L. (1981). Chronic stresses of families of mentally retarded children. *Family Relations, 30,* 281–288.

Williams, N. (1990). *The Mexican American family: Tradition and change.* Dix Hills, NY: General Hall.

Willis, W. (1998). Families with African American roots. In E. W. Lynch & M. J. Hanson (Eds.), *Developing cross-cultural competence: A guide for working with children and their families* (2nd ed., pp. 165–208). Baltimore: Brookes.

Zilbach, J. J. (1989). The family life cycle: A framework for understanding children in family therapy. In L. Combrinck-Graham (Ed.), *Children in family contexts: Perspectives on treatment* (pp. 46–66). New York: Guilford Press.

Zuniga, M. E. (1998). Families with Latino roots. In F. W. Lynch & M. J. Hanson (Eds.), *Developing cross-cultural competence: A guide for working with children and their families* (2nd ed., pp. 209–250). Baltimore: Brookes.

Chapter 5

FAMILY-CENTERED COLLABORATION

I feel like a 25-year-old trapped in a 55-year-old body since gaining legal custody of the children—Jessica 3, Jeff 5, and John 8. It was bad when their mother left and our son had the children alone. We always knew he had a drinking problem, but we didn't want to admit he was really an alcoholic and that he was also addicted to drugs. He is now in treatment for his addictive behaviors that have affected us all. We hope someday he will be re-united with his children on a permanent basis and that his wife will change her self-destructive patterns and form a bond with her children. Until then, I guess the children are here to stay. After a year, we are learning more about the children ourselves and how to cope with each other better.

All of the children experienced anxiety when they first came. Although they knew us as their grandparents, we had seen little of them because they lived 3000 miles away. All of a sudden, we were thrust on each other. The two younger children adjusted more easily. John had difficulty adjusting to his new surroundings. He had fitful sleep, broken by nightmares, he couldn't focus on his schoolwork, but he seemed to get along well with his peers. He was very confused about why he and his brother and sister were separated from their parents. Probably because of the unstructured and chaotic life he was used to, he found the structure of our home both comforting and distressing. Because of the children's circumstances and the fact that our son had a learning disability, shortly after taking custody of the children we requested that they be evaluated. I lived with my son's frustration before we knew what to do about it.

John was evaluated first, as he was the only one in the public school system. Early in the school year, he had trouble staying focused on his work and attending to task. He seemed to be in his own little world. He was frustrated with school and completed few assignments. He struggled each night with his schoolwork. The evaluation results confirmed that he did not have a learning disability. However, they did indicate that he was abnormally impulsive and distractable. We then took him to our family physician who diagnosed him as having attention-deficit hyperactivity disorder. He recommended that we give him Ritalin. It seems to have helped a great deal. (I know others have had problems, but it worked for him.) He turned into a learning sponge. His difficult behaviors turned around. I'm really glad that he didn't have a learning disability like his father. I don't think I could bear the pain and humiliation again. Now that things are settling down a little, I'm beginning to worry about the medication. Will he have to be on it forever? He is starting to lose weight, I wonder about the long-term side effects.

Jeff was identified as at risk for a learning disability and was enrolled in a public preschool where he receives speech and language therapy. Jessica, the youngest and only girl, seems hesitant and very withdrawn. She is considered at risk because of her lack of speech. She has severe articulation problems and is extremely difficult to understand even when she does talk.

The children, even after a year, still have emotional problems. They frequently have nightmares, and they openly worry when I leave to go to the store. They need constant reassurance that we will not leave them. We need support as well.

Our lives have changed considerably. I had to quit my job to stay home with the children. I have tried to organize the household to provide a safe and structured environment, but it is hard at times. It takes a lot of energy to provide the children with good nutrition, love, and a stable environment. At times I wonder if we are doing the right thing. Although the children appear resilient, some of their behaviors worry me. Their life before was anything but normal, so it must be difficult for them to accept this new way of life.

S ome family systems and children are more at risk than others. There are many variations in family types that contain children with diverse abilities. Some occur because of divorce and remarriage, some because of single-parent situations, and some where grandparents become parents. These variations have implications for children, their families, and how we work with these families. They increase our need to know more about the families and to develop the skills to interact with all family members.

"We are family-centered." "We support family empowerment." "We believe in family support." "We look at parents as partners in the educational process." What does all this mean? What does it mean to the family described? These phrases are part of the new rhetoric. The question is whether this is just rhetoric, or really a new approach. In the past, professionals acknowledged parents as the primary caregivers, teachers, and socializers of their children, but then the tendency was for professionals to tell families how they should raise their children. True collaboration can offer advantages to teachers, families, and young children.

Parent-Teacher Collaboration

There is general consensus among all professionals that collaboration is important. The opportunity to set the stage for parent involvement arises during the first encounter with parents (Berger, 1995). With a focus on viewing children with disabilities in a family-centered way, it becomes important for developmentalists to be sensitive to the needs of families as a unit. Children with diverse abilities are likely to have two working parents, some of them will live in single-parent families with young mothers, and some with relatives.

Regardless of whom these children live with, it is likely that the adults will work and that the children will be in the care of others for some part of the day. This will influence your expectations about the level of involvement to which parents can commit.

Parents of children with diverse abilities, especially single parents, have many demands placed on them. Parents may not be free during the day to attend meetings. If parent meetings are scheduled in the evening, parents may have to hire a babysitter or, in a two-parent family, one adult will need to stay home and care for the child if child care is not provided at the meeting. If activities or meetings are held on the weekend, parents may feel that their only free days are being consumed. Expectations for parent involvement need to be couched in terms of the realities facing dual-earner families and single parents. Levels of collaboration that do not require attendance at the center itself need to be acknowledged and supported.

Stressors on the Early Childhood Educator

Educating young children, including those with diverse abilities, is physically demanding. In trying to be helpful to parents and responsive to their children, some teachers begin to feel burned out as they find themselves trying to be "all things to all people" (Galinsky, 1988, p. 6). Early care and education professionals may unconsciously make judgments about the parents of the children in their care. Generally, parents held in low esteem were those who limited their conversations with staff to talking only about their children, and those who were authoritarian in their control of their children. They were also more likely to be single minority parents with low incomes. Thus the parents who are likely to be the most stressed, have the fewest resources, and are most in need of social support are least likely to receive adequate support from developmentalists (Kontos & Wells, 1986).

Developmentalists often receive much less training in how to work with parents than they do in how to work with children. When everything is going well, there are few perceived communication problems. However, when early childhood educators and parents have a difference of opinion, the early childhood specialist may have few skills to resolve these differences. Adults (including teachers) typically rely on conflict resolution methods that result in patterns of verbal aggression and defending, withdrawal without resolution, or blaming. If a teacher has had a difficult day, she doesn't want to "take it out" on the child but may well blame the child's parents or any available parent (Galinsky, 1988).

Parental Stressors

Work/family stressors are a reality of the 1990s. College-educated women have moved to professional occupations in unprecedented numbers. Noncollege-educated women are most likely to be employed as clerical and service workers. They tend to marry non-college-educated men whose income has actually declined since the 1970s. The dual income is necessary to maintain the family's standard of living (Bianchi, 1997).

Some aspects of employment are more likely to increase parental stress. The more hours parents work, the more likely they are to feel conflict between their job and family responsibilities. Parents who have little control over scheduling their work hours experience more stress, as do parents with very demanding, hectic jobs. When supervisors are not supportive of work and family needs, there is likely to be lower job satisfaction and a higher degree of stress (Galinsky, Bond, & Friedman, 1993). Those women who want to work and have husbands who support their work and those women who don't want to work outside the home and do not are happier. Married women most vulnerable to role overload and depression are those who work outside the home, get little child care help from their husbands, and have trouble arranging adequate child care while they work (Ross & Mirowsky, 1988).

All single parents experience some role overload and parents of children with diverse abilities are particularly vulnerable. If children are difficult, parents feel unsure about their parenting skills as they try to decide how to respond to the demands of their child. This, too, adds stress. Parents may also feel very possessive of their child and are not sure they want to entrust anyone else with his care. They may not want their child to form a strong attachment to others because this makes them feel more insecure.

Communication is the key to successful collaboration (Shea & Bauer, 1991). Parents and educators each have history, personal style, and needs that should be acknowledged; each has different concerns, perspectives, and ideas about potential solutions. The communication skills of the teacher can increase or decrease mutual understanding.

Communicating with Parents

Communication is the process we use to give and receive information. It is an indicator of interpersonal functioning. To give and receive information, clear communications, both verbal and nonverbal, are essential. Communication includes speaking, listening, reflection of feeling, and interpretation of the meaning of the message (Berger, 1995). Communication is a complicated process because it takes into account not only the words spoken, but also nonverbal information such as tone of voice and body language that accompanies the words. Relying solely on the content of the spoken word is not effective. Researchers believe that in interpersonal communication only 7 percent of the meaning of a conversation is conveyed by the verbal message (spoken word). The way the words are spoken, the vocal and tonal quality of the message, accounts for 38 percent of the information gleaned, and 55 percent of the meaning is gathered from the visual message, or body language (Miller, Nunnally, & Wackman, 1975).

Important information should be conveyed face-to-face with parents and telephone conversations should be limited to nonemotional, factual information. People filter messages through their values and past experiences so that different people interpret the same information differently.

Berger (1991) identifies educators who are good communicators as those who:

- Give their attention to the person speaking, utilizing both eye contact and body language;

- Listen to parents to gather both the feelings and meaning behind statements; they clarify, reframe, and/or restate parental concerns and distinguish between factual information and feelings;

- Do not criticize, moralize, blame, or judge others; they discuss the child's good qualities before bringing up concerns;

- Match their style of giving information and the amount of information they share with the parents' ability to handle the information; they don't "dump" all the information on the parents at one time if they feel the parents will not be able to handle the information;

- Emphasize that problems are no one's fault; they work together to solve problems and plan for the future;

- Focus on one issue at a time and have enough specific information to document both concerns and progress, but keep the focus on strengths;

- Become allies with parents, view them as partners, and work to empower them to help their children; and

- Focus on the topic at hand, encourage parents to talk and share information, and talk only 50 percent of the time (adapted from Berger, 1991, pp. 156–157, 175–176).

Words are abstractions that stand for ideas. They make communication possible but also confound it. Clarity is especially difficult when people from diverse cultural backgrounds communicate. Context is important in determining the meaning of words. The word orange, for example, can be a fruit or a color; the context of usage allows us to distinguish between the two meanings. However, as ideas get more abstract, clarity is more difficult.

Communication Techniques to Avoid

There are some ways of communicating that are likely to be counterproductive with parents—or with anyone, for that matter.

Avoid Giving Advice. It is often tempting to give parents advice on how to solve problems that they are having with their child; it is rarely wise. It is appropriate to offer constructive suggestions, but even these should be given with care. Before giving suggestions, follow these steps:

1. Gather enough information about a situation to make the suggestions relevant.

2. Find out about the problem, when it occurs, how frequently it occurs, what parents have already tried to do to solve the problem, and whether or not these solutions were effective. Try to get as much specific information as possible before you offer any suggestions.

3. Offer your perception of the problem to see whether or not it is the same as theirs.

4. Support the parents in their efforts to solve the problem by commenting positively on what solutions they have tried (if this is appropriate).

If you do find the need to offer suggestions, do so in a casual, tentative, nonjudgmental way. Offer several suggestions (optimally four) rather than just one.

Avoid the Word Understand. Sometimes early childhood educators and caregivers respond to a parent's problem by saying, "I understand exactly what you mean." This response is likely to trigger in a parent thoughts such as, "How can she understand? She isn't me. She doesn't walk in my shoes. She isn't the one getting up in the middle of the night," and so on.

People who respond by "understanding" usually convey the impression to others that they really don't care. An empathetic response is far more appropriate: "It must be difficult to get up in the night when you know you have to go to work the next day."

Avoid Judging and Blaming. Although we consciously try not to judge parents, sometimes our language gives us away. When parents feel they are being judged or blamed, they frequently become defensive. Starting out a conversation with "As you know . . ." is almost always offensive. Using words such as "ought" or "should" also implies judgment. Saying "You should always make sure Chunga has her medicine" is different from saying "Chunga didn't get her medicine today and that makes it more difficult for us to work with her." The former statement is likely to evoke a defensive reaction from a parent. This can end up being a no-win situation that, with some thought, could easily be avoided.

Avoid Mind Reading. Mind reading is assuming to know what another person is thinking or feeling without asking. When a parent says, "Tell me what I need to know," she is assuming that you can read her mind. If you respond to that statement, you will tell her what you find interesting or what you would want to know if you were the parent. For example, you may tell her the particular activities that her son enjoys when what she really wants to know is whether or not he is a "behavior" problem. If he is not, you are unlikely to mention it. You may not figure out what the parent wants to know; ultimately, the parent will be dissatisfied with the exchange. It is more useful to help the parent clarify what it is she wants to know than to assume you can read someone's mind. Do this by asking the parent for more specific information: "I want to tell you about what concerns you have. Can you ask me questions about certain aspects of the day?" If the parent persists in wanting to know about what you think is important, you may have to offer her choices: "Would you like to know about his activities, his eating, or how he gets along with the other children? Help me decide where to start." This will usually get a parent to at least state a preference.

Being an active and explorative listener is a good way to avoid mind reading. A parent might ask, "Do you think Pat is happy here?" To simply say "Yes" doesn't answer the question. It may take some exploration on your part to find out what the parent is concerned about, such as "Can you tell me more specifically what you want to know?" The parent may say, "I worry because he always cries when I leave him and I wonder if he cries all day." Then you can appropriately respond, "Pat continues to cry for about five minutes after you leave. A teacher holds him and she walks around the classroom with him as she tries to figure out what may interest him. She typically finds something and he gets involved playing. He is involved until nap time, and then he frequently withdraws and gets a little weepy. We rub his back until he settles down. The other difficult time for him is when the other children's parents come to pick them up. He becomes anxious for you. I can see why you might think he was unhappy all the time when you only see his most difficult times. Do you have suggestions for ways of comforting him that work well for you that we might try?"

Suppose, on the other hand, you had said, "Pat really enjoys modeling clay; that keeps him happy for a long time." Although a truthful answer, the parent might come away from the conference feeling that you didn't answer her question (even though she never really asked it).

Much of the communication that takes place between parents and teachers takes place on an individual basis in brief, daily interactions. In addition to these daily exchanges of information, regularly scheduled conferences focus on each child's long-term development. There may be other times when the parents of all the children in the class meet. This is a time to talk about general philosophy and curriculum issues and inclusion. It also provides opportunities for parents to meet other parents who may become part of support networks. We will start with individual, regularly scheduled parent conferences.

Individual Parent-Teacher Conferences

Traditionally, there are at least three occasions throughout the year for parent-teacher conferences in early childhood education. The first occurs near the beginning of the year, the second about the middle of the year, and the final one near the end of the year. If there is an expectation that the child will change placements in a setting or move to a different setting, another conference may be used to plan for the transition. Routine conferences use the basic technique known as the "sandwich":

- Talk about the child's positive qualities and how she has adjusted and the developmental strides she is making.

- State your concerns about the child, if there are any, and give concrete examples.

- Conclude on a positive note.

Conferences don't just happen. They require much gathering and organizing of information and reflection about the meaning of the information gathered.

Preparing for the Conference

Gather and organize the notes you have about the child, including examples of activities, that you plan to share with parents. Give careful thought to the child as an individual, his likes and dislikes, personality traits, temperament, and the special qualities that you enjoy. Be prepared to talk about the child's group participation and how having a diverse ability impacts this. Have some of his or her favorite toys or activities available so parents can see them. (This also gives them information about developmentally appropriate materials they might use at home.) Make a short (5 minutes or less) videotape to show the parents how their child spends his time at the setting. They may be particularly interested in friendship patterns. Think about how to make parents physically and psychologically comfortable.

Conferencing with Parents

If the conference is held at the educational setting, the parents might view this as "teacher territory" and they may need help feeling relaxed and comfortable. Avoid jargon, accentuate the positive, talk in terms that are specific enough so that parents can take action on new information if they choose (Bjorklund & Burger, 1987).

Parents genuinely want to know what their child does while he is with you. Work older children bring home from school plus their verbal comments help parents understand how they spend their time. With younger children and those who have little communication, parental understanding is more difficult as the children don't convey the necessary information and they may have few "products" as examples of their activities. Parents want specific information about their child. Routinely share with parents the following types of information:

- *Videotape.* Show the parent how the child spends his day. If the child has some behaviors that are of concern to you and you want to point it out to the parents, videotape it so you can show them specifically what concerns you and when it occurs. This helps clarify the context.

- *Work samples.* Collect samples of the child's work and share these with parents. If there are differences you want parents to see show them the work of a child of a similar age and gender.

- *Anecdotal records and checklists.* Have available the records (originals and your summaries) that you have kept on the child to share with the parents and document your observations.

Sometimes, as you prepare for a conference, your concerns become heightened and you focus more closely on the developmental level of the child. This requires additional information.

Conferences About Developmental Concerns

No one wants to be the one to suggest that a child might have a developmental problem; however, at some point, you may have to do so. The role of the educator in this instance is to provide parents with the information they need to make a decision about whether follow-up is necessary, and if so, how to do

As you observe children, sometimes something catches your attention. Perhaps it is the child's gait or the way he holds his hands. Trust your instincts. Continue your observations and ask parents if this behavior occurs at home. If the behavior continues, explore with parents their concerns and develop with them possible intervention strategies.

it. This type of problem-solving conference requires careful preparation, records of observations, and factual information. Chapter 6 details the formal procedures necessary to make a prereferral decision. In this chapter, the focus is on packaging that information to be used with parents during a conference.

When you first suspect a developmental problem in a child, you may have only a vague feeling of uneasiness. You may feel that something about this child's behavior is outside your category of "normal." Trust yourself and think about the steps you need to take in the prereferral process. Watch the child closely, and write down your behavioral observations to determine what is bothering you. These notes are for you. They need not look beautiful and they might include the questions your observations generate as well as the observations themselves, for example:

Shawn seems to have trouble getting along with the other children. (More often than the others?)

I better start counting (frequency!) (Has this always been true? Better talk with his mother briefly when she picks him up and his teacher from last year (context). He cannot (will not?) stay at one center for over a minute or two. I need to time this (duration). He doesn't seem to be involved with the activities of other children (bored? over his head?) Is he enthused about other things (intensity)? Transitions are a problem too. Are there particular times when it occurs (time)?

Does Shawn have an emotional problem? Maybe he does and maybe he doesn't. Your role is that of gathering additional specific information, not providing a diagnosis. It is the parents' decision as to what to do with the information you gather.

Your first goal is to gather the information that you need to make a prereferral decision about your hunch, that is, either to talk with the parents, or to dismiss the hunch. After you have gathered enough information to determine Shawn's normal or baseline information, generate (and write down) your hypotheses and potential solutions. Modify your program in response to these solutions and continue your record keeping. If you are not seeing positive changes, have another set of eyes look at the child. The director or administrator of the program, principal, or other teachers might have suggestions as well as additional insights and observations about the child (Abbott & Gold, 1991; Salvia & Ysseldyke, 1995).

Gathering and Organizing Additional Information

If, after further observation and data gathering, you still believe there is a problem, the next step is to talk with the parents. Prepare yourself by keeping the following questions in mind: What do I need to know? How will I use this information? What is the most effective way to gather and convey this information? Be creative and thorough in gathering your information.

To the videotape, work samples, and records and checklists, add the following:

- *Programming modifications.* Be prepared to talk with parents about the ways you have modified your programming for the child and the results of these modifications. Be sure to date these.

- *Informal consultation.* Plan to share with parents your initial concern and how you worked though the process and the people with whom you shared your concerns and the feedback they gave you in the process. Be clear that this was informal, not part of the referral process.

- *Agencies, parents, and other professionals.* If parents share your concerns, they are likely to proceed further. They will probably ask you for suggestions about referral sources. Think about the types of services that parents may need and have the names of contact persons as well as phone numbers. They may want to know about Child Find or other agencies that serve young children. They may also want to know about private resources. They may even want to know if there are parents or parent groups that might provide some insights for them (adapted from Abbott & Gold, 1991).

Your role is one of expressing concern, providing information, and helping parents develop a plan of action that will support their decision making about their child. This process of confirmation will require referral services. States provide free evaluation for children 3 to 5; many states also provide these services free to children under 3. The Child Find Specialist is a contact person who knows the regulations for the state, the services provided, and the cost. Child Find is a good initial source of information.

Know going into the meeting that this may be the first of a series of meetings. Most parents need time to consider what you say and to look at their child in a new light. Give them time as well as information. Although you may have prepared all of the information for the conference, you may not use it all at the first conference. Conferencing is part of a process and the follow-up is as important as the conference itself (Bjorklund & Burger, 1987). Now, on to the conferencing itself.

Conferencing with Parents About Developmental Concerns

Welcome the parents, state your general concerns, then get input from the parents about their perception of the child's behavior both at home and at school. If they share your concerns and are appreciative that someone else has noticed, the conference will probably move quickly. If they don't share your concerns, you need to find out the basis for their perceptions. These are frequently based on experience with other siblings ("Jack didn't talk until he was 3 and he was always a loner") and/or lack of information about developmental norms or experience with other children. Sometimes learning about developmental norms can influence parents' understanding of the situation and help them differentiate between age-appropriate behavior and that which is not. They may attribute the behavior to particular circumstances ("Dottie's grandmother is in the hospital"). How you proceed depends on the parents' perception of the situation. They may provide you with information that causes you to rethink the issues.

The goal of the conference is to develop a plan of action. This plan may be additional observation or it may be that parents follow up on the referral process.

It should be clear who is responsible for doing what and when you will conference again. You will need to plan to meet again in the near future to evaluate what you each have learned.

The referral process, if parents make that decision, takes time. It may start with a developmental screening, depending on these results, it may move to more formal measures. Keep open lines of communication with the parents and support them in their efforts. This may be a stressful time and they may be reluctant to talk with others until they know the outcome of the assessment process. Parents themselves may disagree about whether or not to follow through on the assessment, and this may add to family stress. Remind yourself to avoid giving advice, mind reading, judging, blaming, or telling them you understand what they are going through. Support the process and the concerns that parents have. If the parents follow through on the assessment and find that their child is eligible for services under the IDEA, then the focus of concern moves more clearly into more formalized family-centered intervention.

Problem-Solving Conferences

On occasion, you will request a conference with the parents, or they with you, to discuss a specific concern. These conferences are different from the routine conferences or those about developmental concerns. They are problem-related and usually have one definite topic. A problem-solving conference should be scheduled when you notice a consistent change in a child's behavior, when his behavior in a specific area deviates significantly from the norms of development, or his particular behavior pattern consistently comes to your attention. This deviation is more than just having a bad day or behavior that is expected because of diverse abilities. A different, although overlapping, set of techniques is used for these conferences.

Scheduling the Conference

Arranging a problem-solving conference is a delicate matter. You don't want to alarm parents, but they do need to know the purpose of the conference. The time frame between scheduling the conference and holding the conference should be as short as possible. Parents are likely to be anxious when you request such a conference. Plan what you will say ahead of time. State your concerns generally; for example, you might begin by saying, "I have been observing Kate for several weeks. I am concerned about the amount of time she spends sitting alone. I have tried to adapt the program to better meet her needs, but she still has difficulty getting involved with activities. She wonders around the classroom. Could we set a time to meet and talk about this?" Parents may push for additional information. Give them general information, but don't have the conference itself. Explain that you have things to show them to help them better understand what is happening before you can jointly work

on solving the problem. Schedule the conference as soon as possible.

Preparing for the Problem-Solving Conference

As with all conferences, being well prepared is important. In these problem-solving conferences, however, much of the preparation has to do with preparing yourself. After you have made your observations and gathered all the information you have, proceed through the following steps. These steps should be thought through carefully before meeting with families; they provide guidance for the conferencing process:

- *Welcome the family and state your general concern.*

- *Define the problem.* An important aspect of this part of the conference is to separate facts from assumptions or generalizations. It is important to be specific and precise. To say that Brian "doesn't get along with the other children" is not precise enough. However, knowing that Brian bit Sally while they were both using playdough and that he hit Juan, knocking him off the tricycle, helps define the problem more clearly. It might be expressed like this: "I'm concerned about Brian's social interactions. In a typical day, he has at least three confrontations with his classmates, which usually involve hitting another child."

- *Express your concern.* At this point, it is useful to express concerns or how the behavior makes caregivers feel: "I am worried that one of the other children will get hurt and also concerned that the program is not meeting Brian's needs."

- *Determine the parents' perception of the situation.* It is useful to both describe the problem and express your concerns before you ask the parents how they feel about the situation. Parents may share your concerns or have very different ones. Some parents may respond that they don't view this behavior as a problem and may try to rationalize it ("He is all boy just like his Dad."). Another parent might be appalled that his son is being aggressive with others and want to "straighten him out at home." It is futile to try to problem solve without knowing how the parents perceive the problem. Although the "facts" might be agreed upon, how the facts are interpreted may be different.

- *Generate hypotheses.* Ask parents their hypotheses about the child's behavior. In general, behavior doesn't have either a single cause or a single solution. It is wiser to think through the problem fully the first time than to have a second conference over the same issue, having made no progress toward solution. Problem solving generally involves generating hypotheses about the cause of the problem and potential solutions. Generate some hypotheses of your own before the meeting. If your hypotheses are different from the parents, include them in the discussion.

- *Generate solutions.* Once you have at least four hypotheses about the cause of the problem, it is necessary to generate suggestions for solving the problem. It is important that all participants generate suggestions and that all suggestions are considered. Examine each suggestion, critique it, and then prioritize them. This may be a time when negotiation is necessary as the long- and short-term advantages of solutions are weighed (Brandt, 1995).

- *Develop a plan of action.* After defining the problem and looking at potential causes and solutions, a plan of action must be developed and then implemented. Troubleshooting approaches must also be developed and potential problems anticipated. (If the solutions were easy and obvious you would not have needed a conference.) The question you must now work through in your plan is why the obvious solutions have not worked and what will now be different. Verbally work through potential solutions and their consequences and decide on an initial plan of action.

- *Try out the plan.* Agree to try out the plan for a specified period of time and see how it works.

Don't modify the plan or evaluate the results until it has been tried for the specified time. Know that change is difficult; if it were easy your help wouldn't be needed.

- *Modify the plan.* Most plans need some modification to work effectively. It is important to think of problem solving as a process and not an event. Consider generating additional hypotheses about the cause of the problem and consider other solutions to see if they look any better in light of experience. Being prepared to try out a plan and then modify it based on new information is very different from expecting a plan to work the first time and to continue working. The modification may be done on an informal basis.

- *Evaluate the plan.* Schedule a time to evaluate the plan and to determine if it is working. If it is not working, modify the plan or generate a new one. Even if the plan seems to be working effectively, don't expect that the issue will stay solved forever. Circumstances and people change.

It is useful and empowering to share the process of problem solving with parents. All people face problems and having a plan is often useful. Framing problem solving as a process makes it less likely for people to decide that they failed to solve the problem if their initial efforts are not successful.

Whether children are included in parent-teacher conferences depends on the purpose of the meeting. When included, they should be active participants in the process.

Group Parent Meetings

Meeting with the parents in a large group requires another set of skills, particularly if this is the first time the parents have had children in an inclusive setting. Be prepared to make some initial statements about your personal philosophy, what you expect to have happen in your classroom, what inclusion is, and why it is happening.

Although what you say will be affected by your own circumstances, the tone and content might resemble the following:

> As we continue to study how children learn, we are discovering that it is beneficial to have a variety of children in the same classroom, rather than putting children in classrooms because of their similarities. This variety encourages children to learn about their own and others' strengths and needs.
>
> In our class, for example, there is a child who prefers to play alone most of the time, who rarely joins the group. The other children are learning skills for approaching her as well as an appreciation of the fact that there are times when each of us wants to be alone. When I require them to participate in group time yet don't require her to be part of the group, the children are learning to be flexible and to allow exceptions to rules when appropriate.
>
> These are difficult concepts for young children to learn, yet their efforts will be rewarded, for children's appreciation of individual differences in other children helps them learn more about themselves.

Avoid labeling children or citing children by name unless you are discussing many children. This approach becomes easier as you internalize viewing a diverse ability as one aspect of individual differences.

You need to be prepared for questions parents will ask. The following are some typical questions with possible answers.

Parent: *Why doesn't my child have an IEP/IFSP?*
Teacher: I take the individual needs of all the children into account when I plan my program. In some cases the exact form of programming that I use is dictated by law. In other cases I use a system of my own. I'd like to share this with you during an individual conference.

Parent: *Do you have enough time to teach all the children in your class when some of them have such diverse abilities?*
Teacher: I think all the children in the class have special needs some of the time, so on a particular day or week I may spend more time with one child than others. Overall, I think it evens out. I'm lucky to have Mrs. C. as a paraprofessional in the class. Her presence allows us far greater flexibility in programming. We can always use more help, so if any of you have time on a regular basis, I'd enjoy having you help in the room.

Parent: *Isn't it hard to teach children at so many different levels of ability?*
Teacher: I think the key to teaching children with varying abilities and interests is to plan activities that can be used at several different levels by children who are playing together. Many of the materials I use fall into this category. The playdough, for example, can be manipulated by all the children. Some children make specific shapes and then count them, others make impressions with cookie cutters, and some even make a "tea set." For some children, using playdough is primarily a creative activity; for others the main benefit lies in developing motor skills or having a sensory experience. There are many activities like this that I use for multilevel teaching and learning.

Parent: *My child says there is a child who cannot walk in his class. How does this affect the class?*
Teacher: Yes, we do have a child in our class who crawls or uses a creeper in the classroom. We have added ramps to make it easy for him to get outside. He needs some help getting out of the wheelchair and down on the floor, but in the same way that your child is working on tying his shoes, this child is working toward independence in movement.

Answers like these help parents see the process you use in teaching as well as the product. Group parent meetings are frequently followed by individual parent-teacher conferences. The principles of these are similar whether children have diverse abilities or not. The content itself, however, may be different, as parents of children with diverse abilities may have different questions and concerns.

Family-Centered Early Intervention

As services for children with diverse abilities have become more normalized, the role of the family has changed, as has the relationship between families and professionals. Services for young children are now expected to be family-centered. The role of working with families can be both new and exciting or frightening and overwhelming. Just as there are very different ideas about what inclusion means, there are also very different ideas about what family-centered *really* means. Researchers have suggested six major categories or principles of family-centered support:

1. *Enhancing a sense of community.* This involves bringing people together and building informal support networks between the family and the community. Interventions are then based on the needs and resources of those who live in the community.

2. *Mobilizing resources and supports.* The necessary resources and supports are responsive to the needs of the entire family, not just the child.

3. *Sharing responsibility and collaboration.* Parents and professionals work in partnership to support and strengthen the family. The relationship is based on mutual respect.

4. *Protecting family integrity.* Interventions are provided in ways that accept and respect a family's values and culture.

5. *Strengthening family functioning.* Interventions are built on strengths, not designed to remedy weaknesses. The goal is not to "fix" families.

6. *Practicing proactive human service.* Service delivery systems are consumer-driven, not designed to meet the needs of the professional (Dunst, Johanson, Trivette, & Hamby, 1991, p. 117).

In family-centered practice, family priorities mobilize the system. Families determine the role of the service coordinator. Families decide what will or will not be in the IFSP or IEP, and family concerns determine what areas of assessment are most important.

Just as many professionals have problems with including all children, many also have problems allowing parents to be "in charge" of their family and their children. Our profession is being stretched in new and different ways that require many and varied skills. As families express needs and desires, developmentalists are expected to respond. Although early childhood educators are not expected to be family therapists, they are expected to have a knowledge base in family assessment and skills in helping families determine their strengths and areas in which they want more information.

Family Assessment

The assessment of families is relatively new to early childhood educators. As programs strive to meet the mandates of the law, more information is needed on the identification of family strengths and needs and the role of family goals in the Individualized Family Service Plan (IFSP).

The role of the early childhood educator in family assessment is evolving and varies among programs. In some programs, the early childhood educator would have the lead role with the family and be expected to conduct interviews and family assessments. She would be the service coordinator. She would then be responsible for reporting information back to the team and, with the family, write the IFSP. In other programs, another professional would be the service coordinator and she would be a team member. Early childhood educators and caregivers need the skills for both roles. They need skills in interviewing families and using family assessments; they also need to be able to interpret the results of these interviews and assessments.

Family assessment plays an integral role in service delivery to young children with diverse abilities. If knowledge gained will not be used, there is no reason to gather the data. In assessing children and families, certain principles must be considered:

- *Family assessment appropriately follows child assessment.* Families of children who are not eligible for programming are not included in the assessment process.

- *Early childhood educators need to be trained and understand the purpose and usefulness of family measures.* While skilled, experienced professionals may find informal assessment to be the most effective mode of data collection, most of these same professionals gained this expertise by first having experience with the administration of formal family assessment measures.

- *The process of identifying family needs may be a goal in and of itself.* For many families, identifying what they want is a very new process offering great potential for them to learn about themselves. Initial family IFSP goals might be thought of as a "process IFSP" that focuses on *how* the family will go about selecting goals rather than the goals themselves. This may avoid determining goals that are later found to be inconsistent with what families want (Whitehead, Deiner, & Toccafondi, 1990). We are less skillful at measuring family strengths than needs.

- *The purposes family measures need to be made clear and the process must be respectful and useful to families and allow them to participate at the level they choose.* Families have varying reactions to the assessment process. While most are willing to participate, some do not see the relevance of family assessment to services for their child.

- *Families must be listened to and their input valued and acted on.* There is variability in the usefulness of assessment measures in generating family goals. Assessment tools can be viewed as a menu of choices: Only those items that are necessary and appropriate for a particular family should be chosen (Deal et al., 1989; McGonigel & Garland, 1988).

- *Families need to be informed of the results of any assessment used.* A structured, if informal, system of feedback to families, responsive to their needs and desires, is essential.

Identifying Family Strengths

Bailey and Simeonsson (1988) suggest five domains are important in the process of assessing family strengths, including: (a) child strength, needs, and characteristics; (b) parent-child interaction; (c) family needs, desires, and priorities; (d) critical events; and (e) family strengths. There may be times when additional information is useful, particularly when families are complex.

Selecting Family Assessment Measures.

The philosophy and scope of a program determines the appropriateness of various family assessment measures. The questions all programs need to ask are: "Why are we assessing families?" Is it solely to develop the IFSP? Are you thinking of starting a fathers' or siblings' group? Is the school's policy on inclusion being expanded? The answer to these questions will help determine the measures that are used. When selecting a family assessment measure consider the following issues:

- Is this what the family wants?
- Does the instrument provide useful information to the family as well as the program?
- Does the instrument identify strengths as well as desires? Can parents prioritize this information?
- Is the content sensitive to cultural differences?
- Is the content sensitive to changing family needs, priorities, and configurations?
- Is the reading level of the instrument appropriate for the family?
- How long will it take the family to complete the instrument?
- Who will interpret the results and bring that information back to the parents?
- Is the information necessary for program planning?
- Is the instrument itself technically sound? That is, does it have known reliability and validity?

Knowledge about measures can be gained by reading published review articles or by critiquing the measures themselves.

Most family assessments are a combination of formal and informal measures, including observations and interviews. An initial family visit might begin with a general interview to determine overall family strengths and priorities. That interview might be followed at a later visit with formal or informal measures addressing areas of expressed family strengths or needs that relate to the family's ability to optimize the development of their child or areas more broadly based. The goal is to tailor assessments to the family and planned intervention (Bailey, 1987; Johnson, McGonigel, & Kaufmann, 1989).

Informal Assessment.

As adults, we do not expect to be tested and we usually feel that we have the right to raise our children as we choose. We are not necessarily happy to have a sometimes younger, perhaps single, person assess us. This frequently is a parent's perception. For this reason, informal assessments often are useful, especially as you are building rapport with families. What is important is that you must focus on what you want to know.

The Family-Focused Interview. An interview may be the only way to obtain necessary information. To discover the family's perception of what they want, it is necessary to ask. Given the complexity of family life today, standard forms may not cover a particular family's situation; that is, the "fill in the blank" form may not have a blank to state that Dad's sister Rosy lives with the family. This is important information that can be generated from an interview.

An interview is more than just sitting down for a chat with a family. There are two essential elements: establishing rapport and gathering information. Winton (1988) describes five specific phases in the focused interview process. The *preliminary phase* involves planning before the interview. Any existing information needs to be organized and evaluated for discrepancies or areas that need further clarification. (This may have been obtained during the child's assessment.) A list of areas that need further exploration may be generated.

During the *introductory phase* of the interview, information about the purpose of the interview and its format and structure are clarified with the family and their permission to continue is requested. This is the time to establish rapport and a sense of trust. It is useful to clarify the time frame as well. Interviews should be scheduled at a time that is convenient for the family.

The *inventory phase* is the needs assessment itself. Here, listening skills are important. The interviewer needs to be sure that all relevant topics are covered. This is a time for families to talk about their strengths and their personal goals. Although the major role is one of listening, families may have had little experience in this area and may need some guidance. Few people ask families what they want for themselves and they may not have thought about it. It may be useful to make some suggestions to families based on what you know about the field in general and this family in particular. You might say, "Some families want all the information they can get about cerebral palsy. Others decide that they would rather learn just a little at a time." Depending on what they say, you might ask how they want to acquire that information: "Some families like to go to the library and take out books on cerebral palsy. Others would rather talk to the parents of a child who has cerebral palsy. Some find watching a videotape the most useful; others would rather have an Internet address, and some want to do all those things." Note that the interviewer doesn't show a preference or even follow up with a "What do you want to do?" The family may not be ready to decide yet. Listing options lets them learn what is available.

The *summary, priority, and goal-setting phase* is characterized by the interviewer's summarizing what has happened and framing the strengths into goals that are attainable. The beginning of this phase involves the interviewer's asking the family for clarification on what they really want, then prioritizing the information. These priorities may be translated into IFSP goals. The final phase is *closure.* The interviewer expresses appreciation to the family members for their time and effort. A schedule of future meetings is clarified, and so on. Be sure to allocate time for this phase.

Additional important information may be brought up as parents themselves pull information together. For example, a family who had decided not to discuss the terminal illness of a child with her brother may ask, "Do you think it is important that we talk to Mica about his sister?" They are not purposefully detaining you; it just took time for the implications of what had been said to be focused. Their question is important and needs to be answered. An appropriate response might be, "I want to support you in giving Mica information. Let's think about what he needs to know and the best ways for him to learn and develop a plan next time we meet."

If the interview was difficult, a follow-up phone call may help. Families may have shared very personal information with you and begin to wonder if this was a good decision (Winton, 1988). A brief phone call can offer them the reassurance they need.

In family assessments, it is important that all family members have some input; otherwise, we are simply assessing the parents or, more frequently, the mother. The particular and unique needs of fathers are missed if mothers are the ones filling out the forms or answering the questions. Sometimes the differences in perception of husbands and wives is the most interesting and enlightening aspect of the assessment process.

Siblings play an important role in the family and how it functions. There are few formal measures that assess siblings, yet their involvement is important both for their own well-being and for that of their sibling. If possible, schedule some time separately with the siblings. They might express different needs if their parents are not present.

Parent Education and Support Groups

Another form of educator-family collaboration is providing education and support groups. Educational groups offers exciting possibilities for working with parents to potentially enhance the development of their children as well as giving them the support of others who are sharing a similar experience. The goal of most parent education groups is to develop parenting and decision-making skills. The goal of support groups may be to provide information about a particular diverse ability or to offer social and emotional support or both.

Parent groups vary significantly in their structure and purpose. On a continuum from relatively unstructured groups in which a parent is the leader, to groups run by a professional instructor, meetings can also range from unstructured with no specific goals or curriculum to discussions led by professional experts who control the curriculum and the level of participation (Berger, 1995). These differences are inherently neither good nor bad, but the match between the parents and the structure may influence participation as well as what is learned.

Parents are adult learners and may reflect a wide variety of experiences, attitudes, and values. Successful groups support all levels of expertise in a risk-free environment (Berger, 1995). Evaluations of intensive family-oriented education programs have shown short-term positive effects in increased child competence and positive maternal behaviors and longer-term effects on increased levels of education, smaller family size, and an increased probability of the family's being self-supported (Powell, 1989).

One challenge for parent education is the different value systems that parents bring to the child-rearing situation. The academic field of child development has some clear guidelines regarding the types of parenting that are most likely to produce children who do well in school. This field supports reasoning over corporal punishment, authoritative rather than authoritarian parenting, responding to infants as quickly as possible in a gentle, responsive way rather than letting them cry it out, and so on. These views are not accepted by all parents, and it is often challenging to work with parents who have different values and do not want to be told how to rear their children (Theilheimer, 1991). Yet parent education programs are adapting. High-quality parent programs have the following characteristics:

- Equal relations exist between parents and staff, to empower parents in their child-rearing roles. Professionals do not take the role of expert and tell parents the "best" way to rear their children.

- Time is devoted to open-ended, parent-dominated discussions.

- There is a balanced focus between family and child concerns. Programs include information to support families in strengthening their social support networks and community ties.

- Programming is responsive to the needs and characteristics of the population served. Good programs are different, and they are designed to match the parents they serve. They are responsive to the cultural characteristics and values of the populations and to the income level and risks that families face (adapted from Powell, 1990).

Increasingly children with diverse abilities live in families who themselves are at risk either on a short- or long-term basis. To work effectively with these families, we need some understanding of their situation.

Working with Family Systems at Risk

The family has the potential for increasing or decreasing risk for children with diverse abilities. Some situations families face are temporary, others are more permanent.

Divorcing Families

The largest variation from the traditional family life cycle comes through divorce. In the 1990s, about half of all marriages in the United States ended in divorce. The divorce rate peaked about 1980, has declined slightly since then, and stabilized (Collins & Coltrane, 1995). Divorce is becoming more a norm than an exception to the norm. Of these divorces, approximately 60 percent involve children (Hetherington, Law, & O'Connor, 1993). In divorcing families, the children are likely to be young. High rates of divorce have been attributed to a variety of causes, such as the greater participation of women in the labor force with its concomitant economic independence, improved contraception, the welfare system, the increasing proportion of marriages involving premarital births, the women's movement, and the liberalization of divorce laws (Hetherington et al., 1993).

Families with young children are in what is often called the "pressure cooker" stage of the family life cycle. The most common time for divorce is during this stage, about six years after marriage, with rates peaking in the second and third years (U.S. Bureau of the Census, 1992). Differences in attitudes toward child rearing go to the very core of relationships and parents frequently find it difficult to compromise in this area. Few parents will tell you that they are contemplating divorce or that their marriage is unhappy. Children may begin to display signs of stress and some of the symptoms of underparenting.

Over 1 million children experience their parents' divorce each year (U.S. National Center for Health Statistics, 1994); however, the role that children play in divorce is not clear. The statistics indicate that parents who divorce typically have two young children. However, the patterns of unresolved conflict are likely to have operated within a family for a long time before the divorce. This means that children were exposed to unresolved disagreement, anger, and a model of ineffective problem solving. Troubled marital relations frequently make parents unavailable to their children and these children have high rates of behavioral problems before the divorce. This is a vicious circle in that the stress of dealing with a difficult, noncompliant, and antisocial child adds stress to a fragile marriage and may precipitate a divorce (Hetherington et al., 1993). Whatever the cause, it seems clear that families in the process of divorcing have disrupted family relationships, that both parents and children display disordered behavior, and that these behaviors will affect them as they move into the changes and challenges of establishing separate single-parent households.

You will probably be told about the divorcing process when the physical separation takes place. This is when parents must make practical decisions about who will be picking children up and what emergency numbers need to be added or changed. Finding out about the divorcing process may help explain a child's behavior.

For young children, divorce is a loss of a way of life. The predictable patterns of everyday life are replaced by different expectations and life experiences and a profound degree of uncertainty about what is happening. Household rules and routines change, and a single parent typically experiences task overload as he or she takes on the tasks that previously were shared by two.

Although we frequently have parent conferences at this point, in many cases parents are too involved in their own feelings to be available and sensitive to their children. If custody is an issue in the divorce, it is imperative that the early care and education center know who can pick up the child and who cannot. Very young children and children with diverse abilities, regardless of sex, are almost always in the custody of their mothers. Furstenberg and Cherlin (1991) identified three factors that impacted the child's adjustment to divorce: (a) the effectiveness of the custodial parent in parenting the child; (b) level of conflict between the mother and father; and (c) relationship of the child with the noncustodial parent. When the custodial parent is effective, levels of conflict are low and the relationship between the child and the noncustodial parent is maintained, the outcome is more positive for children.

In the first year following divorce, the average family income of women decreases by almost 40 percent. One cause of this is the partial, intermittent, or nonpayment of child support by 70 percent of fathers (Hetherington et al., 1993). This is particularly problematic when a child has a disability and the expected level of support makes the family ineligible for Medicaid. The average amount of child support received (regardless of disability) was under $3000 (Ahlbrug & DeVita, 1992). Lack of child support is a major reason why six times as many female-headed households live below the poverty line as compared to male-headed households.

The first years after divorce are also associated with diminished parenting by custodial mothers. Some mothers are frequently preoccupied, irritable, nonsupportive, and use erratically punitive discipline. Most children show some problems in the first two years following divorce. These problems are primarily in the social and psychological area. Young children demonstrate increased noncompliant, angry, and demanding behaviors. Sibling relationships are problematic, with conflict, aggression, rivalry, and disengagement (Hetherington, 1989).

Parental conflict does not end with divorce and indeed is often accelerated after a divorce. Conflicts often revolve around issues related to visitation rights and child support payments. Children can be caught in the middle of these conflicts. Older children seem to be able to adapt and negotiate, whereas young children don't have these skills.

For many young children, divorce is the first in a series of changes from a two-parent family to a one-parent family and frequently (with the remarriage rate for women 65 percent), again to a two-parent family (Carter & McGoldrick, 1993). These changes have many implications for children and their early care and education setting.

Young children frequently regress and lose skills they had previously attained such as toilet training. They may want to be held, they may bring an attachment object such as a blanket that had been given up. They may need support to try new activities and materials. Children who adjusted well to the educational environment may now cry when left and become anxious when it is time to leave and someone is not there to pick them up. This is an adjustment for children.

What children need in their early care and education setting is stability. They need familiar toys, familiar adults, and a familiar routine. They often have problems handling change. Their world seems out of their control and they seem adrift. They need a setting to help them become stabilized.

Cohabitation Families

Cohabitation is a living arrangement in which two adults who are not married to each other live in the same setting and have a sexual relationship (Cherlin, 1999). There has been a significant increase in couples who make this choice. The Census Bureau estimated that in 1995 there were 3.7 million cohabitating households (U.S. Bureau of the Census, 1996). There is more cohabitation among previously married people than never-married people. Estimates are that a fourth of births to unmarried women are born to cohabitating couples and even more have children from previous relationships (Cherlin, 1999). Although this trend is too new to know what it means for families and children with diverse abilities, it does mean that you are likely to have children in your setting living in cohabitating, but unmarried, families.

Early childhood settings need to portray many family situations and provide opportunities for input from parents and significant others. When cohabitating relationships change, children need the stability of a setting that has familiar activities and people. Centers make individual decisions about who they invite to conferences and group meetings. It is important to talk with a biological parent and determine the roles of the adults in a child's life to be sure to include these important figures.

Remarried Family Systems

Researchers predict that by the year 2000 there will be more stepfamilies than any other single type of family in the United States (Glick & Lin, 1986). Whether this predication becomes accurate depends on how one defines stepfamilies as at least 60 percent of divorced people live with another partner (usually the future spouse) before they remarry (Bumpass & Sweet, 1989). Additionally, women who have given birth outside marriage may later live with and marry a man who is not her child's biological father (Bumpass, Raley, & Sweet, 1995). Using a definition

of stepfamilies as having two adults who are married or cohabitating with at least one adult who has a child from a previous marriage or relationship acknowledges these living arrangements and reflects more accurately what is happening in society today (Cherlin, 1999). In 1987, 33 percent of the population was in some step situation and 20 percent of children under 19 were stepchildren or had half-siblings (Visher & Visher, 1993). Family systems, sometimes called blended families, are complex and highly variable. They include more than one household unit. All family members are affected emotionally, financially, and legally by the actions of the other household. The coparenting team is complex, as it includes both biological parents and their respective spouses and/or committed live-in partners. The new extended family includes multiple grandparents and stepgrandparents, and siblings consist of biological siblings, half, and stepsiblings from both households.

Approximately half of stepfamilies have a mutual child. If the child is born after the couple has formed a solid relationship, the birth of the child makes a positive contribution to the integration of the family; if before, there will likely be increased stress (Bernstein, 1989).

Remarried families are different from first-married families in a variety of ways. Stepfamilies form after a process of loss and change. Members of stepfamilies come together at different phases of their individual, marital, and family life cycles. Children and adults have experienced different traditions and ways of doing things. Parent-child relationships have preceded the couple relationship, rather than followed it. Children have a parent elsewhere, if not in reality, at least in memory. About half of children in stepfamilies have contact with their other parent, therefore there are shifts in household membership when the children move between households. There is little or no legal relationship between stepparents and stepchildren.

Children in step-families have greater diversity in the relationships they have with their siblings as well as with their biological parents and step-parents.

Children may move from living in a cohabitating situation to a remarried family or from a single-parent family to a remarried family. They may acquire not only another parent figure, but siblings as well. Children may be struggling with identity problems and trying to find their personal space. Educators need to be open to discussions with children who have siblings "some of the time" or who call their mother by her first name. Conscious efforts need to be made to include diverse families in stories and celebrations. We need to acknowledge many types of families.

Single-Parent Families

Single-parent families are those with one parent and dependent children. One of four children in the United States lives in a single-parent family. The number of single-parent families has more than doubled since 1970. The majority of single parents in the 1990s are single parents because of separation (19 percent) and divorce (42 percent), or because they have never been married (29 percent) (Karmerman & Kahn, 1989). The fastest growing group of single-parent families are headed by women who have never been married.

Single-parent families are as diverse as two-parent families. Approximately 80 percent of all single-parent families are headed by women. The number of single fathers living with their children has more than doubled since 1980, and they constitute about 18 percent of single-parent families with children (U.S. Bureau of the Census, 1997). This does not include custodial fathers who have remarried. Despite the increased number of single-parent families, there is still a tendency to look at these families as deviant, unstable, or dysfunctional. Society has not focused on the strengths of single-parent families or accepted them as viable family units with variability in style, structure, and values.

Never-Married Adolescent Single-Parent Families. The move away from the marital dyad is increasing for all families in the United States. In 1994, 80.8 percent of all teenage mothers were not married at the time of delivery. Grandmothers or other family members often take on parenting responsibilities. This provides a collective responsibility for the child, but often adds stress to the household (Annie E. Casey Foundation, 1994).

Adolescent motherhood is a complex and serious situation. The actual birthrate for teens has declined, but the proportion of all births that occur to unmarried teens has increased. This group accounted for 9 percent of all births in 1991 (Annie E. Casey Foundation, 1994). Estimates are that 80 percent of teenage pregnancies are unplanned (Alan Guttmacher Institute, 1993). Adolescent pregnancy occurs more frequently in the United States than any other developed country (twice as high as England and seven times as high as the Netherlands). Over one million adolescent girls become pregnant annually, and about half of these pregnancies go to term. Virtually all of these mothers keep their infants (Carnegie Task Force, 1994).

The stresses of single parenthood is complicated by being an adolescent. During adolescence, women experience multiple biological, social, cognitive, and psychological transitions and challenges. If an event such as an unwanted or unintended birth occurs during adolescence, school-aged adolescents are likely to be developmentally unprepared to adjust psychologically and socially to parenthood (Ketterlinus, Lamb, & Nitz, 1991). The concern is not just for the unexpected pregnancy, but also its implications for the child. Women with unintended pregnancies are less likely to provide good prenatal care, less likely to reduce or end the use of drugs, alcohol, and smoking, and, after the child is born, less likely to follow up on immunizations (Public Health Service Expert Panel, 1989). Correspondingly, the risks of child abuse and neglect, low birth weight, infant mortality, and disability are greater (Florida State University Center, 1997).

Those who were raised in single-parent households and who themselves were born to teenage mothers are also more likely to experience early childbearing. She is likely to have more children than the average and to spend more time as a single parent (Florida State University Center, 1997). Infants born to adolescents experience long-term consequences as well. They are 50 percent more likely to be born at low birth weight, 50 percent more likely to repeat a grade in school and less likely to graduate from high school. If female, she is 83 percent more likely to become a teenage mother. Males are 2.7 times more likely to be incarcerated. Regardless of sex, they are twice as likely to be abused or neglected and two to three times more likely to run away from home (Florida State University Center, 1997). Early intervention and high quality child care can change these statistics.

Risks do not end with the birth of a full-term viable infant. Only 1 to 2 percent of children are born with disabilities that are identifiable at birth, yet by school age we find that 10 to 12 percent of children are identified as needing special educational services. The interplay among risk factors in early childhood produces poor outcomes. The combination of low birth weight and low maternal education increases by 8 times the probability that the child will need special educational services (Florida State University, 1996). Adolescent mothers tend to be less verbal and less supportive of the infant's social/emotional development (Pope et al., 1993). Negative long-term child developmental outcomes have been found in the areas of intellectual development, social/emotional development, and school achievement (Harel & Anastasiow, 1985). We now believe that opportunities for learning and nurturing missed early in life cannot be fully regained; by 18 months, infants raised in impoverished environments have cognitive deficits that may not be totally reversible (Florida State University, 1996).

Among all the responsibilities parenting brings, the new mother is called upon to fulfill the functions of socialization and education for her child. This can be a difficult task for an adolescent who is still working on her own socialization. A teenage mother may not even understand that this duty exists. The mother's reactions to her child may focus more on discipline for individual acts and less on developing social skills as a whole. Many young mothers have difficulty understanding the reasons underlying the aggressive behavior of their children and have difficulty setting limits for the child's behavior. The teenage mother needs family support and guidance: "The complexity of assuming adult roles without cognitive, emotional, and social maturity can be catastrophic for both the young mother and her infant when there is not an extensive supportive environment" (Mercer, 1990, p. 72).

If an adolescent in poverty enters motherhood, it is unlikely that she will ever break free from the poverty. Even if teenage mothers do not start off in poverty, the outlook for their future is uncertain: 15 years after giving birth, teenage mothers were more often the head of single-parent households, and their children were more likely to be living in poverty (Mercer, 1990).

Regardless of the type of family in which children with disabilities live, some face more challenges than others. One of the most pervasive situations facing children with disabilities and their families today is poverty.

Families Living in Poverty

Poverty is a leading risk factor of negative outcomes for young children. Increasingly, families with young children are living in poverty in the United States. "Across all ethnic groups and family structures, more children under three live in poverty than do older children, adults, or the elderly" (Carnegie Task Force, 1994, p. 17). Between 1987 and 1992, the number of children 6 and under living in poverty grew from 5 to 6 million, putting the poverty rate at 26 percent. In 1996, the poverty line was $15,911 for a family of four (U.S. Bureau of the Census, 1997). Child poverty rates in the United States are two to nine times as high as those in other major industrialized countries (Children's Defense Fund, 1996).

Poverty is complex and multifaceted. It undermines families and the well-being of young children. Poverty affects parents who are overwhelmed by the work and cost of caring for young children. Substandard housing and crowded conditions increase the probability of infection, which may be compounded by poor nutrition and lack of medical treatment so that conditions that respond easily to medication at an early stage are left untreated and may become serious or chronic. Children (and adults) may not go to a physician for preventive check ups and immunizations.

Medicaid is one of two federal programs that were created by President Johnson in his War on Poverty (1965). Medicaid was designed to provide health insurance for families whose income falls below a certain standard. It is closely tied, in reality, and in people's minds to welfare. Although it is a federal program and the federal government creates minimum standards, the program is administered by the states and varies among states (Tilson, Ross, & Calkins, 1995). In 1995, approximately 36.3 million people were receiving Medicaid, with 51.1 percent of these children under 21 (Health Care Financing Administration, 1997). Not all physicians will accept Medicaid patients because of the fee structure set for their services and because of the time it takes to get their reimbursement (Tilson et al., 1995). Families who cannot get regular medical care may wait until things get "bad" then seek emergency room treatment. When children have disabilities, this lack of continuity in health care is a major concern.

Approximately 40 million Americans are uninsured. They don't qualify for Medicaid, their employers don't pay for coverage, and they don't earn enough to pay for it privately. Of these 40 million, approximately 10 million are children (Health Care Financing Administration, 1997). The combination of living in poverty, not having health insurance, being a member of a minority, and being a child increases health risks and the probability of a disability (Newachek, Hughes, & Stoddard, 1996).

Poverty adds to the stress that trying to cope with these problems produces. Families who are forced to spend their resources and energy on mere survival often do not have additional time or energy to encourage their children to develop language and other cognitive skills. Under circumstances such as these, children are more likely experience emotional trauma and to sustain accidents.

The human cost of poverty to young children is devastating. Low-income children are:

- Two times more likely than other children to die from birth defects;

- Three times more likely to die for all causes combined;

- Four times more likely to die from fires;

- Five times more likely to die from infectious diseases and parasites; and

- Six times more likely to die from other diseases (Children's Defense Fund, 1995, p. 19).

At-risk conditions are not mutually exclusive; in fact, they often appear in combination, and this interaction or additive quality increases the probability of creating a developmental disability. In addition, the interactive quality confounds early diagnosis and makes intervention more difficult. It is difficult to determine if a child with poor language skills has a conductive hearing loss due to middle ear disease, is distrustful of adults because of past experience with them, has received so little language stimulation that his vocabulary is inadequate, or lacks the expectation that language is a useful tool for getting what she needs.

In 1992, even full-time employment was not a guarantee against poverty. If an adult worked 35 hours a week at a minimum wage job ($4.25 in 1992), she would earn $7,438. This amounts to 66 percent of the poverty line for a family of three and 52 percent for a family of four (National Center for Children in Poverty, 1995). Although it would be possible for both parents to work in a two-parent household, the second salary, if minimum wage, would almost be negated by the cost of child care for one child and would be financially disadvantageous if there were more than one child.

Poverty is highest in urban areas, 35 percent, as compared to 19 percent in suburban areas. Statistically, children of color, living in inner cities, and having single mothers are overrepresented. Twenty-nine percent of children under 6 are Hispanic or African American, yet they represent 55 percent of all poor children. Children born to unmarried mothers are more likely to be poor (National Center for Children in Poverty, 1995). The Hispanic population with very young children is the poorest segment of the population; 73 percent of Hispanic single mothers and 30.8 percent of married couples live below the poverty line. African Americans with very young children fare little better, with 69.7 percent of single mothers and 21.4 percent of married couples living below the poverty line (Einbinder, 1992).

Poverty increases the probability that risk factors will be present simultaneously in the child, the parent, the parent's informal support system, and the neighborhood. The disadvantages of poverty permeate all of life, from health care and nutrition to quality of housing and neighborhoods to educational opportunities. The cycle of poverty is associated with poor maternal nutrition, low birth weight in babies, and increased substance abuse by pregnant women. These are all potential causes of developmental problems and additional potential stressors in an already stressed system. Women with low incomes have the highest rate of depression of any group (Halpern, 1990). Mothers who are depressed are less responsive and nurturing, less aware of their children's moods, and more restrictive. Children raised in extreme poverty are at risk for developmental problems. The causes are complicated, but include poor cognitive/language stimulation, poor nutrition, exposure to safety hazards, and poor health care. Adverse financial circumstances affect the entire family and include increased risk of marital dissolution, family disorganization, physical abuse, and neglect (Conger, Elder, & Lorenz, 1992).

Overall, 61.5 percent of single mothers with children under 3 live in poverty as compared to only 12.8 percent of married couples. The number of children receiving food stamps increased by over 40 percent from 1989 to 1992, reaching 13 million children (Children's Defense Fund, 1994). Poverty is rarely eliminated by public assistance: The combination of Aid to Families with Dependent Children (AFDC) and food stamps only raised the income levels of families to 65 percent of the poverty line in 1993 (Annie E. Casey Foundation, 1994).

As we look at areas like welfare reform, it appears that there will be more young children living in poverty in the foreseeable future. These children may not have their basic needs met nor may they have the support of families who are already stressed. Child care is frequently tied to work-related programs as both a service to the parents and to the child.

When children enter a child care setting, they need to feel safe and have their behavior framed as inexperience. Give them more time to manipulate and explore materials, especially those that may not be familiar. Support prosocial behavior and the situational aspects of behavior. Be clear about what behaviors are appropriate in the setting. Children need to increase the scope of their behavior and know what behavior to use in what situations; however, it is not safe to try to eliminate skills from a child's repertoire as there may be times when they mean his survival. Differences have to be accepted and discussed openly.

Homelessness

In the latter part of the 1980s, families with young children became the fastest growing segment of the homeless population. Reports indicate that about one-third of the homeless population are families, with the percentage being even larger in cities such as New York and Philadelphia (VanRy, 1993). Homeless families are diverse, but young, single-parent, female-headed households represent the largest portion of the homeless population nationwide (Kryden-Coe, Salamon, & Molnar, 1991). Accurate statistics of how many children are homeless are difficult to obtain because of the nature of the population and differences in definitions of homelessness. Estimates are that on any given night 100,000 children are homeless, with the majority of the children under 5 years of age (Carnegie Task Force, 1994).

Many of these homeless families have experienced high rates of violence and report that family violence was the primary cause of the homelessness. Often the mother took the children and left the abusive situation without time, emotional strength, or financial resources to find another secure place to live. Concern about additional violence may make having a permanent address an impossibility (Kryden-Coe et al., 1991). Homeless mothers typically had children before the age of 20, their children are under 10 years of age, and they had experienced unstable housing before they became homeless. They moved an average of 2.6 times in the 12 months before they became homeless (Winkleby & Boyce, 1994).

Living on the streets or in shelters has many effects on homeless children and their families. There are physical health problems related to homelessness; colds, tiredness, and generally not feeling well, are the most frequent and common health problems, as well as feelings of depression (VanRy, 1993). Homeless children may be hungry and have poor nutrition and increased health problems. When they are homeless their parents may not have places to put their children, therefore, there is little opportunity for the children to play and explore their environment. For a young child, becoming homeless may be devastating:

> ... the disruption of existing social networks, family routines, and emotional grounding in one's own home; the anxiety of an uncertain future and the fear and violence often associated with shelter living. For a child who is homeless, the play yard can mean a motel hallway; the bedroom, a back seat of the car. (Klein, Bittel, & Molar, 1993, p. 23)

Conditions related to homelessness frequently lead to developmental delays for young children; these are most apparent in motor, cognitive, and language development.

In the United States, an increasing number of early care and education settings are including homeless children. Their programs must be modified to help children feel safe and to help them develop age-appropriate skills and concepts. This is difficult, because although many of the children are in programs when their family is in a shelter, rules about how long a family can stay in a shelter vary, and programming is based on unstable funding sources and whether or not space is available. Some shelters have on-site child care settings, others use settings within the community. Regardless, child care is seen as an essential element in helping young children whose families are homeless (Klein et al., 1993). Many young homeless children are fearful. They frequently display emotional and behavior problems such as short attention span, withdrawal, aggression, speech delays, sleep disorganization, difficulty in organizing behavior, regressive behaviors, awkward motor behavior, and immature social skills (Klein et al., 1993; VanRy, 1993).

Parental roles may change as families move, and parents may not be emotionally available to their children when they are trying to cope with problems related to food, shelter, and finances. Poverty and homelessness are inextricably tied to the family and community. In many instances, these problems are compounded by violence.

Violent Environments

No one likes to think about violence and young children. When violence does occur, we want to believe that it is the exception and that it is reported to make headlines and sell newspapers. When we read these articles, we also want to believe that young children don't understand what is happening and therefore won't remember the experiences. Research findings negate such optimistic views. Children *do* remember and it influences their lives.

Researchers categorize violence in terms of (a) community violence, (b) domestic violence, and (c) physical and sexual abuse (Osofsky, 1993/1994). As stress to families increases, the probability for violence increases. Very young children are exposed to this violence and frequently are the victims of it. Young children *do* experience violence and it influ-

ences their lives. Because they don't have the language to express their feelings, it is the professional's role to comprehend what the meaning of this violence is for young children (Osofsky, 1993/1994). In addition to being the victims of violence, children are exposed to violence on television, in their homes and in the community.

Community Violence. The United States is one of the most violent nations in the world. This violence has reached down to our youngest and most vulnerable citizens. Almost four million children are growing up in "severely distressed neighborhoods." These neighborhoods are characterized by poverty, female-headed families, high levels of school dropouts and unemployment, and a reliance on welfare (Annie E. Casey Foundation, 1994). In these neighborhoods, fear of crime and violence undermines security and increases isolation. Many young children have witnessed a stabbing or shooting either in their home or in the neighborhood (Osofsky, 1993/1994). The average child has watched 8000 televised murders and 100,000 acts of violence before leaving elementary school (American Psychological Association, 1993). Watching violence on television is correlated with aggressive behavior.

Parents worry about their inability to protect their children from violence and to keep them safe even when they are home or in their own neighborhood. Low-income and minority parents report the most worries. Protecting their children is a basic family function. When they cannot do this, parents feel helpless and threatened. Although very young infants may not be aware of violence in the community, they are aware of their caregivers' fears and anxiety and will be influenced by the adults' coping strategies (Osofsky, 1993/1994).

Parents who raise children in violent environments may be depressed, sad, and anxious. Adults who are depressed tend to talk to children less and to be less responsive to their needs. They have difficulty controlling their emotions and their children experience more scoldings and shouts than hugs and kisses (Osofsky & Jackson, 1993/1994). Young children reflect this same depression and smile less and begin to withdraw into themselves. Adults may cope with violent environments in a variety of ways, becoming overprotective as a way of keeping their children safe. They might put young children to sleep in bath tubs to avoid random bullets and rarely take children outside or allow them to play on the playground.

Young children who are exposed to violence think about their world differently. Repeated exposure to violence is likely to have an even more significant effect and it is likely to be more pervasive as infants' and toddlers' understanding of events changes with increasing age. It will be difficult for such children to learn to trust others or to think about their environment as dependable and predictable. Traumatic events in infancy continue to negatively affect social, emotional, and cognitive growth into adulthood.

Children need safe places to play in the neighborhoods where they live.

Unlike older children, young children have a very small repertoire of behaviors with which to show their distress. The symptoms children display are related to the child's age, gender, and circumstances. Some very young children who have been maltreated or exposed to violence withdraw and may become depressed; others may become aggressive. Among young children who see parents fight, boys are more likely to become aggressive and girls to withdraw. Other symptoms may include disrupted patterns of eating and sleeping, fearfulness, and difficulties in attending (Cicchetti & Lynch, 1993).

Children living in violent environments need to know that their early care and education setting is safe. If children cannot feel safe, they cannot participate in activities fully. Part of their energy is spent being watchful and waiting, not engaging. Children learn over time that they are safe and only then become available for learning. Activities need to be repeated to gain control and mastery. Parents need to know that their children are safe before they can be concerned about their developmental level.

Domestic Violence. Domestic violence is viewed as a systematic pattern of gender-related abuse. Definitional problems and underreporting make it difficult to ascertain the actual extent of abuse. The National Coalition Against Domestic Violence estimated that three to four million women are beaten by their male partners every year (Alsdurf & Alsdurf, 1989). Domestic violence cases only get reported when victims seek assistance. It is estimated that for every call made to the police about domestic violence there are ten instances when the abuse goes unreported (Davis, 1988).

Domestic violence impacts children in three ways: it makes their primary caregiver less available to them, they may witness the abuse, and they may be injured by the abuse. Domestic violence is the leading cause of injury to women of childbearing age (15 to 44) (Ingrassia & Beck, 1994). It is estimated that 20 to 25 percent of adult women (15 million) have experienced physical abuse at least once from a male partner (Stark & Flitcraft, 1991). Twenty-one percent of all pregnant women are battered and 30 percent of all battered women are abused while pregnant (National Coalition Against Domestic Violence, 1994). We don't know the relationship of this abuse to children being born with disabilities. At least 3.3 million children witness parental abuse each year, including fatal assaults with guns and/or knives as well as hitting or slapping (Jaffee, Wilson, & Wolfe, 1988).

Domestic violence is a pattern of behavior rather than an isolated event. An abusive event typically starts with conflicts and arguments. Next, there is a tension-building stage. Hostility increases. At some point, the abuser's rage can no longer be controlled and he lashes out in physical aggression. After the aggression, the abuser is often kind and affectionate to try to make up for or minimize the seriousness of the abusive event (Alsdurf & Alsdurf, 1989). Abuse is not limited to physical force but can include the threat of force, coercion, intimidation, withholding financial resources, and isolation from friends and families (Fishbane, 1993). The effects of violence can make women emotionally paralyzed, submissive, and victims of learned helplessness, all of which have negative effects not only for the women themselves, but on the children they care for (Gondolf, 1988).

When there is violence in the home, there is also more likely to be maltreatment of children. Children with diverse abilities are frequently the ones targeted for this abuse. Children in families with a history of violence or abuse and neglect in the home are at risk medically, psychologically, and educationally. The topic of child abuse and neglect is dealt with in detail in Chapter 9.

Children in Foster Care

Sometimes, child rearing becomes so complicated by other stressful conditions, such as physical or mental illness, domestic violence and abuse connected with alcoholism or drug addiction, that the social service system decides that a child's safety is threatened (Lee

& Nisivoccia, 1989). At any given time in the United States, there are more than 250,000 children in out-of-home placements (Maluccio, Kreiger, & Pine, 1990). Abandonment and removal of children from their biological family is occurring more frequently. The increase in the number of children in out-of-home placements is related to increases in substance abuse and AIDS. Child removal is often an emergency response for their safety.

The attachment process is often affected when infants and toddlers are removed from their homes. Attachment is based to some extent on day-to-day interactions and having needs met for physical care, nourishment, and affection; therefore, families who cannot fulfill these functions place young children at risk (Solnit & Nordhaus, 1992). These young children are in double jeopardy. They live with caregivers who are unavailable to them and are at risk for the long-term implications detailed above, yet removing them from their homes may have negative consequences relative to attachment. "As a practical guide, for most children between the ages of two and five, a separation for more than two months is upsetting to the degree that it may lead to psychological harm" (Solnit & Nordhaus, 1992, p. 16).

More than others, children with diverse abilities are likely to be in out-of-home care. Families may be unable or unwilling to care for children with complex needs. Children may be distressed by their loss of family and familiar surroundings. They need support, consistency, and encouragement. The goal for these children is permanency planning. The first choice is to reunite them with their family of origin. Only after this possibility is exhausted will an adoptive family be considered.

In addition to being aware of the risks that families face and learning techniques of interacting with them, it is also important to learn about cultural sensitivity and working with families in a cultural context.

Working with Families in a Cultural Context

Individuals do not develop their language, rituals, rules, and beliefs in a vacuum. They are part of the cultural heritage handed down to them through their family. Cultural values are a way of life, a blueprint for living. Values are both learned and internalized by being part of a particular culture (Berger, 1991). A family's culture will have an impact on how they view having a child with diverse abilities and the solutions they seek.

Children come to educational settings with a cultural background, as do their families. Children and their families must be understood within the context of their cultural and ethnic background. The meaning of a diverse ability must also be understood in this context.

Learning about different cultural groups is necessary, but not *sufficient* because individuals and families are different and embrace different aspects of culture. Knowledge of culture has to be both generalized and individualized:

> Families from racial and ethnic minority groups are faced with the task of raising their children to live in their own culture as well as to function effectively as a minority member in a majority culture. (Rounds, Weil, & Bishop, 1994, p. 8)

When the person gathering information and those giving it are not from the same culture nor proficient in the same language, the communication process can be very difficult. Even when information is translated, there can be confusion. To be culturally sensitive, competent teachers must learn four tasks:

> First, they must clarify their own values and assumptions. Second, they must gather and analyze ethnographic information regarding the cultural community within which each family resides. Third, they must determine the degree to which the family operates transculturally; and finally, they must examine each family's orientation to specific child-rearing issues. (Hanson, Lynch, & Wayman, 1990, p. 126)

Cross, Bazron, Dennis, and Isaacs (1989) identify six elements that contribute to cultural competence:

1. *Acknowledging and valuing diversity.* This involves the recognition that there are cultural differences and that these differences play a role in what families believe about children and how they should be reared.

2. *Conducting a cultural self-assessment.* Before one can become aware of other cultures, one needs to take a close look at one's own culture and how this has shaped values and beliefs about children and diverse abilities. This is the lens through which you will view children and their families, and you need to be aware of the biases you hold. Becoming aware of one's own culture and its values increases the probability of becoming a culturally sensitive individual who can validate differences among people and appreciate their commonality.

3. *Recognizing and understanding the dynamics of difference.* Cultural differences contribute to both obvious and subtle differences in individuals. Obvious differences include such things as language, eye contact, and body language; more subtle aspects of culture may influence the amount of self-disclosure someone is comfortable with.

4. *Honoring diversity.* Child rearing practices are designed to socialize children into their own culture. With young children, daily caregiving routines reflect a culture's fundamental, deeply held values and beliefs (Nugent, 1994). Because children absorb their culture as part of the caregiving process, these practices are important to

many parents. Child rearing practices may provide the key to understanding socialization practices in different cultural contexts. If early care and education settings reflect only the values of the dominant culture, parents from other cultural backgrounds may be concerned about the practices used; likewise, children may be deprived of a part of their own culture.

5. *Acquiring cultural knowledge.* Cultures are dynamic. Learning about different cultures is an ongoing process. There are many different ways to learn. Lynch (1998) suggests starting with books and the arts, then talking and working with individuals from other cultures, participating in daily life activities, and learning the language. This is the foundation from which more individualized knowledge must build. Additional family information is necessary about variations within the cultural group, especially for families where migration was a factor. These include:

   • *Reason for immigration.* What was the family seeking and/or leaving behind? Were they fleeing from political persecution, poverty, or war, or were they brought against their will as slaves?

   • *Length of time since immigration.* How many generations has the family been in the United States?

   • *Place of residence.* Does the family live in an ethnic neighborhood?

   • *Order of migration.* Did the family come as a unit or did one member come first and others join later?

   • *Socioeconomic status.* What is the socioeconomic status (SES) of the family and their attitudes toward education and upward mobility?

   • *Religion and politics.* What are the family's religious ties to the ethnic group and are there strong political ties?

   • *Language.* What languages are spoken by family members and what are their levels of comfort and fluency in different languages?

   • *Intermarriage.* To what extent do family members have connections to other ethnic groups, and how frequently have intermarriages occurred?

   • *Attitudes.* What are the family members' attitudes toward the ethnic group and its values? (Adapted from McGoldrick, 1993)

6. *Adapting to diversity.* The final element in cultural sensitivity is using the information and insights acquired to adapt educational practices to meet the needs of the children and families that you serve. This may challenge you to expand your definition of family and their participation to include grandparents and various significant others in conferences. It will be useful to focus on the strength that a particular cultural background brings to children with diverse abilities and work with the strengths and priorities that families have set. At another level, adapting to diversity may cause you to look at the bulletin boards, books, and even dolls in the dramatic play area in a new light and to wonder about how comfortable families from various cultures feel in the educational setting.

Children with diverse abilities and their families come from a variety of ethnic and cultural backgrounds. Increasingly, the importance of culture for children and their families is being recognized. There is a constant need for developmentalists to be aware of their own cultural values, to be sensitive to the values of others, and to adapt their communication and programming to accommodate diversity. Intervention must be based on the family's definition of the situation, not the professional's.

Summary

Parent involvement is viewed as a positive factor in early childhood education. Programs and philosophies of parent involvement are changing in the direction of being more responsive to the characteristics of the population served. Collaborating and communicating with parents are essential parts of working with children with diverse abilities. Parents need information about their children, and early childhood educators need to know the parents' perspective regarding their children. The roles and expectations of parents and teachers are not always clearly defined. Differences in expectations about these roles as well as the ambiguity of the roles may be a source of tension between teachers and parents.

Early childhood educators often receive little training in o working with parents. Educators who are good communicators listen to parents and attend to them, focus on issues, and become allies with them. Communication can be improved by avoiding some common mistakes. Teachers and parents schedule routine conferences as well as conferences devoted to solving specific problems and developmental concerns. The latter conferences require more preparation and more detailed follow-up.

As families change, the changes pose challenges for professionals working with young children with diverse abilities. Research increasingly stresses the importance of the early years for a child's development and the possibilities these years hold for development. We also find that an increasing number of children with diverse abilities are being raised in conditions of poverty and are facing risks that no other group of children in our history has had to face: the prevalence of teenage mothers, divorce, single-parent families, remarriage, and lack of child care. Professionals must be cognizant of these challenges for children with diverse abilities.

Professionals in early childhood education have a great responsibility to both children and their families. To provide appropriate service, they need to find out what services families want and need. They need to coordinate these services in a useful fashion and help deliver the services in a way that is respectful of families from diverse cultures.

Educational Resources

Carter, B., & McGoldrick, M. (1988). *The changing family life cycle: A framework for family therapy* (2nd ed.). New York: Gardner Press.

Provides information about how the family life cycle stages are changing as they relate to women's roles, race/ethnicity, and poverty.

Child Trends, Inc.
http://www.childtrends.org

A nonprofit, nonpartisan research group that maintains a fact sheet on adolescent pregnancy and child bearing.

http://www.divorce-online.com

Reprints articles on divorce related topics including how divorce affects children.

The Family Network on Disabilities of Florida
http://www.gate.net/~fnd/

A page where parents can ask for help about a disorder and find services. It contains addresses for parent groups nationwide.

Father's Resource Center
http://www.parentsplace.com/readroom/frc
/index.html

An interesting site for fathers to browse information designed for them.

Kilbride, M. K. (Ed.). (1997). *Include me too! Human diversity in early childhood.* Toronto: Harcourt Brace, Canada.

Focuses on including children with diverse cultural backgrounds in early childhood settings.

Lynch, E. W., & Hanson, M. J. (Eds.). (1998). *Developing cross-cultural competence: A guide for working with children and their families* (2nd ed.). Baltimore, MD: Paul H. Brookes Publishing Co.

Discusses the development of cultural competence and provides information about a variety of cultures.

National Parent Network on Disabilities (NPDP)
1727 King Street, Suite 305
Alexandria, VA 22314
(703) 684-6763, FAX (703) 836-1232

Publishes a newsletter, "Networking" and is an advocacy group that publishes legislative alerts regarding federal policy that effects children with disabilities. It serves as an information and referral source for organizations and parents.

National Self-Help Clearinghouse
Graduate School and University Center/CUNY
25 West 43rd Street, Room 620
New York, NY 10036
(212) 642-2944

Makes referrals to self-help groups and clearing houses throughout the United States.

Our-Kids Homepage
http://rdz.stjohns.edu/library/support/our-kids/

This page is a support group for parents and caregivers of children with physical or mental disabilities. It also includes recommended readings, and links to other Internet resources.

PACER Center (Parent Advocacy Coalition for Educational Rights)
4826 Chicago Avenue South
Minneapolis, MN 55417-1098
(612) 827-2966, (800) 537-2237, TDD (612) 827-7770, FAX (612) 827-3065
http://www.pacer.org/

Offers information about laws, procedures, and parents's rights. Has a catalogue of publications.

Parent Information Centers (PIC)
Washington, DC

Funds PICs in almost all states to provide information and advocacy for parents of children with disabilities.

The Stepfamily Association of America
http://www.stepfam.org

Provides education and support to stepfamilies including a digest of facts and articles.

Walsh, F. (Ed.). *Normal family processes* (2nd ed.). New York: Guilford Press.

Woodbine House, Inc.
5617 Fishers Lane
Rockville, MD 20852
(301) 468-8800, (800) 843-7323

Publishes books for both children and adults about disabilities including Cory Moore's Reader's guide: For parents of children with mental, physical, or emotional disabilities.

References

Abbott, C. F., & Gold, S. (1991). Conferring with parents when you're concerned that their child needs special services. *Young Children, 46*(4), 10–14.

Ahlburg, D., & DeVita, C. (1992). New realities of the American family. *Population Bulletin, 47*(2). Washington, DC: Population Reference Bureau.

Alan Guttmacher Institute. (1993). *Facts in brief: Teenage sexual and reproductive behavior.* New York: Author.

Alsdurf, J., & Alsdurf, P. (1989). *Battered into submission.* IL: Intervarsity Press.

American Psychological Association. (1993). *Violence and youth: Psychology's response: Vol. 1. Summary report of the American Psychological Association's commission on violence and youth.* Washington, DC: Author.

Annie E. Casey Foundation. (1994). *Kids count data book: State profiles of child well-being.* Baltimore: Author.

Bailey, D. B. (1987). Collaborative goal-setting with families: Resolving differences in values and priorities for services. *Topics in Early Childhood Special Education, 7*(2), 59–71.

Bailey, D. B., & Simeonsson, R. J. (1988). *Family assessment in early intervention.* Columbus, OH: Merrill.

Berger, E. H. (1991). *Parents as partners in education: The school and home working together* (3rd ed.). New York: Merrill.

Berger, E. H. (1995). *Parents as partners in education: The school and home working together* (4th ed.). New York: Merrill.

Bernstein, A. C. (1989). *Yours, mine and ours: How families change when remarried parents have a child together.* New York: Scribners.

Bianchi, S. M. (1997). The changing economic roles of women and men. In R. Farley (Ed.), *Social diversity in the United States.* New York: Russell-Sage Foundation.

Bjorklund, G., & Burger, C. (1987). Making conferences work for parents, teachers, and children. *Young Children, 42*(2), 26–31.

Brandt, P. (1995). Negotiation and problem-solving strategies: Collaboration between families and professionals. In J. A. Blackman (Ed.), *Working with families in early intervention. Infants and young children series* (pp. 94–102). Gaithersburg, MD: Aspen.

Bumpass, L. L., Raley, R. K., & Sweet, J. A. (1995). The changing character of stepfamilies: Implications of cohabitation and nonmarital child bearing. *Demography, 32,* 425–436.

Bumpass, L. L., & Sweet, J. A. (1989). Estimates of cohabitation. *Demography, 26,* 615–625.

Carnegie Task Force on Meeting the Needs of Young Children. (1994). *Starting points: Meeting the needs of our youngest children.* New York: Carnegie Corporation of New York.

Carter, B., & McGoldrick, M. (1993). The changing family life cycle. In F. Walsh (Ed.), *Normal family processes* (2nd ed.). New York: Guilford Press.

Cherlin, A. J. (1999). *Public and private families* (2nd ed.). New York: McGraw-Hill.

Children's Defense Fund. (1994). *The state of America's children yearbook.* Washington, DC: Author.

Children's Defense Fund. (1995). *The state of America's children yearbook.* Washington, DC: Author.

Children's Defense Fund. (1996). *The state of America's children yearbook.* Washington, DC: Author.

Cicchetti, D., & Lynch, M. (1993). Toward an ecological/transaction model of community violence and child maltreatment: Consequences for child development. In D. Reiss, J. E. Richters, & M. Radke-Yarrow (Eds.), *Children and violence* (pp. 96–118). New York: Guilford Press.

Collins, R., & Coltrane, S. (1995). *Sociology of marriage and the family: Gender, love, and property* (4th ed.). Chicago: Nelson-Hall.

Conger, R. D., Elder, K. J., & Lorenz, F. O. (1992). A family process model of economic hardship and adjustment of early adolescent boys. *Child Development, 63,* 526–541.

Cross, T. L., Bazron, B. J., Dennis, K. W., & Isaacs, M. R. (1989). *Towards a culturally competent system of care: A monograph on effective services for minority children who are severely emotionally disturbed.* Washington, DC: Georgetown University Child Development Center.

Davis, N. J. (1988). Shelters for battered women: Social policy response to interpersonal violence. *Social Science Review, 25,* 401–419.

Deal, A. G., Dunst, C. J., & Trivette, C. M. (1989). A flexible and functional approach to developing individualized family support plans. *Infants and Young Children, 1*(4), 32–43.

Dunst, C., Johanson, C., Trivette, C., & Hamby, D. (1991). Family-oriented early intervention policies and practices: Family-centered or not? *Exceptional Children, 58*(2), 104–112.

Einbinder, S. D. (1992). *A statistical profile of children living in poverty: Children under three and children under six, 1990.* Unpublished document from the National Center for Children in Poverty. New York: Columbia University, School of Public Health, 1992. Cited in the report of the Carnegie Task Force on Meeting the Needs of Young Children. *Starting Points: Meeting the needs of our youngest children.* New York: Carnegie Corporation of New York.

Fishbane, R. H. (1993). *Annual report of the domestic violence coordinating council.* Delaware: Domestic Violence Coordinating Council.

Florida State University. (1996). *Teen pregnancy prevention final report.* Tallahassee, FL: Author.

Florida State University Center for Prevention and Early Intervention Policy. (1997). *Florida's children: Their future is in our hands.* Tallahassee, FL: The Task Force for Prevention of Developmental Handicaps, Florida Developmental Disabilities Council.

Furstenberg, F. F., Jr., & Cherlin, A. (1991). *Divided families.* Cambridge, MA: Harvard University Press.

Galinsky, E. (1988). Parents and teachers-caregivers: Sources of tension, sources of support. *Young Children, 43*(3), 4–12.

Galinsky, E., Bond, J. T., & Friedman, D. E.(1993). *The changing workforce: Highlights of the national study.* New York: Families and Work Institute.

Glick, P. C., & Lin, S. (1986). Recent changes in divorce and remarriage. *Journal of Marriage and the Family, 48,* 737–747.

Gondolf, E. (1988). *Battered women as survivors.* Lexington: Lexington Books.

Halpern, R. (1990). Poverty and early childhood parenting. *American Journal of Orthopsychiatry, 60*(1), 6–16.

Hanson, M. J., Lynch, E. E., & Wayman, K. L. (1990). Honoring the cultural diversity of families when gathering data. *Topics in Early Childhood Special Education, 10*(1), 112–131.

Harel, S., & Anastasiow, N. J. (Eds.). (1985). *The at-risk infant.* Baltimore: Brookes.

Health Care Financing Administration. (1997). *HFCA Statistics: Populations.* http://www.hcfa.gov/stat /hstats96/blustats.htm.

Hetherington, E. M. (1989). Coping with family transitions: Winners, losers, and survivors. *Child Development, 60,* 1–14.

Hetherington, E. M., Law, T. C., & O'Connor, T. G. (1993). Divorce: Challenges, changes, and new chances. In F. Walsh (Ed.), *Normal family processes* (2nd ed., pp. 208–234). New York: Guilford Press.

Ingrassia, M., & Beck, M. (1994, July). Patterns of abuse. *Newsweek,* 26–33.

Jaffee, P., Wilson, S., & Wolfe, D. (1988). Specific assessment and intervention strategies for children exposed to wife battering: Preliminary empirical investigations. *Canadian Journal of Community Mental Health, 7,* 157–163.

Johnson, B. H., McGonigel, M. J., & Kaufmann, R. K. (Eds.). (1989). *Guidelines and recommended practices for the individualized family service plan.* Washington, DC: National Early Childhood Technical Assistance System and the Association for the Care of Children's Health.

Karmerman, S. B., & Kahn, A. J. (1989). *The responsive workplace: Employers and a changing labor force.* New York: Columbia University Press.

Ketterlinus, R. D., Lamb, M. E., & Nitz, K. (1991). Developmental and ecological sources of stress among adolescent parents. *Family Relations, 40,* 435–441.

Klein, T., Bittel, C., & Molnar, J. (1993). No place to call home: Supporting the needs of homeless children in the early childhood classroom. *Young Children, 48*(6), 22–31.

Kontos, S., & Wells, W. (1986). Attitudes of caregivers and the day care experiences of families. *Early Childhood Research Quarterly, 1,* 47–67.

Kryden-Coe, J. H., Salamon, L. M., & Molnar, J. M. (Ed). (1991). *Homeless children and youth: A new*

American dilemma (pp. 19–24). New Brunswick, NJ: Transaction Press.

Lee, J., & Nisivoccia, D. (1989). *Walk a mile in my shoes.* Washington, DC: Child Welfare League of America.

Lynch, E. W. (1998). Developing cross-cultural competence. In E. W. Lynch & M. J. Hanson (Eds.), *Developing cross-cultural competence: A guide for working with children and their families* (2nd ed., pp. 24–47). Baltimore: Brookes.

Lynch, E. W., & Hanson, M. J. (1992). *Developing cross-cultural competence: A guide for working with young children and their families.* Baltimore: Brookes.

Maluccio, A. N., Kreiger, R., & Pine, B. A. (1990). *Preparing adolescents for life after foster care.* Washington, DC: Child Welfare League of America.

McGoldrick, M. (1993). Ethnicity, cultural diversity, and normality. In F. Walsh (Ed.), *Normal family processes* (2nd ed., pp. 331–360). New York: Guilford Press.

McGonigel, M. J., & Garland C. W. (1988). The individualized family service plan and the early intervention team: Team and family issues and recommended practices. *Infants and Young Children: An Interdisciplinary Journal of Special Care Pediatrics, 1*(1), 10–21.

Mercer, R. (1990). *Parents at risk.* New York: Springer.

Miller, S., Nunnally, E. W., & Wackman, D. B. (1975). *Alive and aware: How to improve your relationships through better communications.* Minneapolis, MN: Interpersonal Communications Programs.

National Center for Children in Poverty. (1995, Winter/Spring). Number of poor children under six increased from 5 to 6 million 1987–1992. *News and Issues, 5*(1), 1–2.

National Coalition against Domestic Violence. (1994). Pamphlet materials.

Newachek, P. W., Hughes, D. C., & Stoddard, J. J. (1996). Children's access to primary care: Differences by race, income, and insurance status (On-line serial). *Pediatrics, 97*(1), 11 pages. Expanded Academic ASAP: Item A17902931.

Nugent, J. K. (1994). Cross-cultural studies of child development: Implications for clinicians. *Zero to Three, 15*(2), 1–8.

Osofsky, J. D. (1993/1994). Introduction. In J. D. Osofsky & E. Fenichel (Eds.), Hurt, healing, hope: Caring for infants and toddlers in violent environments. *Zero to Three, 14*(3), 3–6.

Osofsky, J. D., & Jackson, B. R. (1993/1994) Parenting in violent environments. In J. D. Osofsky & E. Fenichel (Eds.), Hurt, healing, hope: Caring for infants and toddlers in violent environments. *Zero to Three, 14*(3), 8–12.

Pope, S. K., Whiteside, L., Brooks-Gunn, J., Kelleher, K. J., Rickert, V. I., Bradley, R. H., & Casey, P. H. (1993). Low-birth-weight infants born to adolescent mothers: Effects of coresidency with grandmother on child development. *Journal of the American Medical Association, 269,* 1396–1400.

Powell, D. R. (1989). *Families and early childhood programs.* Washington, DC: NAEYC.

Powell, D. R. (1990). *Parent education and support programs* (ERIC Digest). Urbana, IL: Clearinghouse on Elementary and Early Childhood Education.

Public Health Service Expert Panel on the Content of Prenatal Care. (1989). *Caring for our future: The content of prenatal care.* Washington, DC: Public Health Service.

Ross, C. E., & Mirowsky, J. (1988). Child care and emotional adjustment to wives' employment. *Journal of Health and Social Behavior, 29,* 127–138.

Rounds, K. A., Weil, M., & Bishop, K. K. (1994). Practice with culturally diverse families of young children with disabilities. *Families in Society: The Journal of Contemporary Human Services, 38,* 3–12.

Salvia, J., & Ysseldyke, J. E. (1995). *Assessment* (6th ed.). Boston: Houghton Mifflin.

Shea, T. M., & Bauer, A. M. (1991). *Parents and teachers of children with exceptionalities: A handbook for collaboration* (2nd ed.). Boston: Allyn & Bacon.

Solnit, A. J., & Nordhaus, B. F. (1992). *When home is no haven: Child placement issues.* New Haven, CT: Yale University Press.

Stark, E., & Flitcraft, A. H. (1991). Abuse and neglect of children. In M. L. Rosenberg & M. A. Fenley (Eds.), *Violence in America* (pp. 123–157). New York: Oxford University Press.

Task Force for Prevention of Developmental Handicaps—1991 update. (1991). *Florida's children: Their future is in our hands.* Tallahassee, FL: Developmental Disabilities Planning Council.

Theilheimer, R. (1994). Not telling young parents how to raise their children: Dilemmas of caregivers and parent group leaders at a program for out-of-school youth and their babies. *Zero to Three, 14*(4), 1–6.

Tilson, H. H., Jr., Ross, M., & Calkins, D. (1995). In D. Calkins, R. J. Fernandopulle, & B. S. Marino (Eds.), *Health care policy* (pp. 102–120). Cambridge, MA: Blackwell Science.

U.S. Bureau of the Census. (1992). *Marriage, divorce, and remarriage in the 1990s* (Current Population Reports P-23, No. 180). Washington, DC: U.S. Government Printing Office.

U.S. Bureau of the Census. (1996). *Marital status and living arrangements, March 1995* (Update). (Current Population Reports, Series P20-491). Washington, DC: U.S. Government Printing Office.

U.S. Bureau of the Census. (1997). *Poverty thresholds: 1996.* http://www.census.gov/hhes/poverty/threshld/thresh96.html.

U.S. National Center for Health Statistics. (1994). *Advance report of final natality statistics.* Monthly Vital Statistics Report, 1992, 43, 5. Washington, DC: U.S. Government Printing Office.

VanRy, M. (1993). *Homeless families.* New Brunswick, NJ: Garland.

Visher, E. B., & Visher, J. S. (1993). Remarriage families and stepparenting. In F. Walsh (Ed.), *Normal family processes* (2nd ed., pp. 235–253). New York: Guilford Press.

Whitehead, L. C., Deiner, P. L., & Toccafondi, S. (1990). Family assessment: Parent and professional evaluation. *Topics in Early Childhood Special Education, 10*(1), 63–77.

Whiteside, M. F. (1989). Remarried systems. In L. Combrinck-Graham (Ed.), *Children in family contexts: Perspectives on treatment* (pp. 135–160). New York: Guilford Press.

Winkleby, M. A., & Boyce, T. (1994). Health-related risk factors of homeless families and single adults. *Journal of Community Health, 19*(1), 7–18.

Winton, P. (1988). The family-focused interview: An assessment measure and goal-setting mechanism. In D. Bailey & R. J. Simeonsson (Eds.), *Family assessment in early intervention* (pp. 185–205). Columbus, OH: Merrill.

Chapter 6

ASSESSMENT

I probably wouldn't have kept the appointment except that I forgot to cancel it and felt guilty when they called to remind me that Diana was scheduled to have her hearing assessed. I had made the appointment several months ago when she was having a bout of ear infections and I was concerned about her hearing.

Because we weren't worried about this assessment, my husband went fishing, and Diana, then almost 3, and I went to the audiology clinic. We entered a soundproof room about the size of an elevator. I sat slightly behind her so she couldn't see me. The audiologist conditioned her to place a ring on a spindle each time she heard a noise. She learned easily. Then the testing actually began. I didn't pay much attention to what was going on until I realized that I could hear sounds but Diana wasn't doing anything. Then I began to pay close attention. She really couldn't hear the sounds. I was sitting there and I could hear them but she couldn't. I was dumbfounded. I didn't have to be told that she had a hearing loss. Next, they tried to get tympanic responses and said that her ear canals had fluid in them. They recommended that I take her to an ear doctor and he would probably suggest putting tubes in her ears to allow the fluid to drain. I sat there and heard what they said but didn't really absorb it. All I kept thinking was that I was her mother and I didn't know she couldn't hear. Somehow I should have known.

I was dazed as we left. I couldn't decide whether to take her to the child care center or not. She couldn't hear. Rationally, I knew that she went the day before and couldn't hear then, but now I knew. How could I have let this happen? Where was my husband when I needed him? I pulled myself together and decided, given my current state, that my daughter was probably safer at the child care center than she was with me and I really needed some personal space. I took her into the center, explained very briefly that I had her hearing tested and that she had a hearing loss of about 60 decibels. I turned as the tears began to come and ran to the car. I just sat

there and cried for a while. Then I decided there were a lot of things I needed to do. I went home and made an appointment for Diana with the otologist. I cried some more. Then I began to wonder why there was fluid in her ears. What caused it? I blamed my husband. He had allergies, it was his fault, she probably had allergies. And where was he now: fishing. I called the pediatric allergist and made another appointment. By now, it was time to go get Diana. I was early, but I needed to get her. The director met me at the door and invited me to come in and talk. The tears that were close to the surface welled up again. This was really ridiculous because I was almost certain the hearing loss was temporary and getting the fluid out of her ear canal would solve the problem, but this knowledge didn't seem to influence my behavior. By the time Diana and I got home, everyone else was there as well. I thought that now I would have the support system I needed.

I told my husband, Jim, and the two older children, Anne 15 and Seth 13, what had happened. No one believed me. Some support. I decided I might as well get dinner. As I was getting dinner, I could hear the older children hiding and calling Diana from another room to see if she could hear them. The hiding and calling seemed to go on forever. Jim wanted me to repeat in exact detail everything that happened. He too found the whole thing hard to believe. How could she talk if she couldn't hear? It made no sense to him. The assessment must be wrong. We'd find another audiologist. He'd go with me this time. Probably, the best thing that happened to me was I was too mad to cry.

We finally sat down to dinner with Diana still being asked questions amid the general uproar of a typical dinner. Midway through dinner, there was a storm with much lightning and thunder. The thunder was loud and startled everyone, everyone but Diana, that is. More questions: Did she hear the thunder? What thunder? It came again, no response. Dinner was very quiet after that, but now the family did believe she couldn't hear.

Young children are delightful, unpredictable, and difficult to make conclusive statements about. The child who "acts out" daily is angelic when you ask someone to come and observe; the child who is withdrawn cooperates beautifully during the observer's visit. Parents face similar problems when having their children assessed. A child who shuts his eyes during an eye examination makes it difficult to determine accurately what he sees. If another cries when earphones are put on, it is difficult to determine what she hears. The difficulty in getting representative behavior from children on a scheduled basis makes the role of early childhood professionals important. These specialists can provide baseline information about whether the behavior observed is typical of the child, is a reaction to the observation or the setting, or is perhaps caused by a physical condition such as coming down with a cold.

According to the National Association for the Education of Young Children:

> *Assessment* is the process of observing, recording, and otherwise documenting the work children do and how they do it, as a basis for a variety of educational decisions that affect the child, including planning for groups and individual children, and communicating with parents. (1991, p. 21)

Although similar, Salvia and Ysseldyke (1995) are a bit more succinct: "Assessment is the process of collecting data for the purposes of making decisions about students" (p. 5). Both emphasize the fact that assessments are used in decision making. *Assessment* is designed to determine a quality or condition, *evaluation* is using the assessment information to make decisions.

Until recently, we lacked means to identify and diagnose children with mild to moderate disabilities at very young ages. Now there are a variety of assessment tools designed for this purpose. In general, assessment instruments are shortcuts for observation. They have a variety of functions and formats. Some assessment tools you will need to use proficiently; others you will only have to know how to interpret and use the results.

Assessment procedures can be divided into two groups: formal and informal. Formal assessment procedures use measures that have been standardized and are usually given by psychologists, or educational diagnosticians. They are often given in a "battery" that usually includes intelligence tests, criterion-based tests, and/or other specialized instruments. Informal assessment is typically done by educators as they systematically find out whether children know expected academic information and when there is concern about physical development or behavior.

Assessment is a complex topic. There are many different ways to approach it. As early childhood educators have a major role in the early identification of young children with diverse abilities, the first part of the chapter is devoted to using assessment for identification purposes. Children who are receiving special educational services will already have been through the identification and assessment process. For children about whom there are concerns but no diagnosis, the assessment process provides four major decision-making points for educators. The initial one is a prereferral decision.

Prereferral Decisions

After the first week, you may reflect on the children in your class. Different children come to mind, incidents that make them stand out: your mind's-eye snapshot of what each is like. High points and those not so high. Triumphs and concerns. Sometimes, the concerns focus on a particular child. They start out small but then become a niggle in the back of your mind, stay there and grow. The scenario often goes something like this:

> Natasha is one of the youngest children when she enters your class. She is not as advanced as the other children, but that is expected. She doesn't seem to catch on as quickly as the other children, she seems small for her age. Informal conversation with her family reveals that she was a preemie weighing in at only two pounds. You casually inquire if her parents have any concerns. They don't. They did when she was younger, but when she started to walk they knew that she had finally "caught up." Her behavior is a puzzle to you, and your concern increases. You are convinced that there is something different that you should be doing with Natasha, but you aren't sure what.

All of us have some expectations about what normal, typical, or developmentally appropriate behavior is. Trust yourself. Watch the child more closely, noting what you observe to determine what is bothering you. The first decision you must make is whether or not the child's behavior is typical for a child her age. Is the behavior that you are observing so different from the norm that it will require different educational methods and materials? There are a variety of ways of making this decision, but most require observation and record keeping. You need to be sure that you aren't responding to a bad day but rather to a pattern of behavior that extends over time. You need to answer the following questions for yourself: What do I need to know? How will I use this information? What is the most effective way to gather this information? If you have a system of record keeping in place, use it; if not, some suggestions for informal assessments follow. Observation and record keeping are essential parts of the assessment process.

Record Keeping

There are many different systems of record keeping. Older children have test scores and report cards. Younger children provide more of a challenge.

Especially at the beginning of the year, a combination of record-keeping methods is most effective.

Anecdotal Notes. Probably the most common form of nonsystematic observation is keeping anecdotal notes on children's behavior. You might have a card for each child, a notebook with a page for each child, or a folder for each child. In a class of 25, some educators write notes about five children each day. There are some problems in this, in that significant events often happen to children on days when you aren't writing about them, and one tends to write about interesting events as opposed to developmentally important information. If your order of writing about children has been random, on Friday you may have to write notes on five children about whom you have nothing to write, and what you really want to do is go home. Frequently, going home wins. It is useful to note whom you have the fewest notes on and try to figure out why. These may be the children that you need the most information on.

Anecdotal notes are for you. They need not look beautiful and they might include questions your observations generate as well as the notes themselves. Your notes may resemble these:

(4/7) Suzy spilled her milk (more often than the other children?). She did not (cannot? will not?) put a simple puzzle together. She did not sit through group time (bored? over her head?). She played with Nathan in the dramatic play area but this ended when she couldn't be the baby. She ran to her cubby and stayed there until a teacher helped her reenter the group. (Was this a bad day?) (I better check and see if anything is going on at home.) (4/8) Talked to Mom and she said everything was fine at home.

To make anecdotal notes more useful, you might ask yourself *why* you observe the children. What is the purpose of observation? Typically, observations are used to make academic and social decisions (Salvia & Ysseldyke, 1995). When things are going well, they provide the information you need for parent conferencing. When you begin to develop concerns about a child, you need to refine your notes and combine them with behavior observations to help you target children and specific behaviors.

Behavioral Observations. Behavioral observations are useful ways of recording information on behaviors that draw your attention (such as hitting). They are less useful as an everyday assessment of how your program is going and as a way of assessing social patterns and what children are learning. The usual purpose of behavioral observation is to target behaviors that need some modification or those that indicate that a child's development is not following the usual track. Behavioral observations include information

about the situation as well as specific characteristics relative to behavior: duration, latency, frequency, intensity, context, and time (Salvia & Ysseldyke, 1995).

Duration. Behaviors have discrete beginnings and endings. It is relevant to know how long Suzy played in the dramatic play area before leaving and how long she remained in her cubby before a teacher helped her reenter the group. Think about how she spends her time. Picture her in your mind's eye; where do you see her? If you picture her sitting in her locker, find out how much time she spends there each day. Most digital watches have timers. Use yours for several days to find out how much time she spends in her locker. Duration is an important variable in other areas, including for children who wander, children who remain at activities for a short or long time, and so on.

Frequency. Frequency relates to how often a particular behavior happens. In this case, it is relevant to know how often Suzy goes to her locker during a day. If you record how many times during the day she seeks refuge there and the amount of time she spends each time, you can build a database. Compute a weekly and daily average using the frequency and duration data for the episodes.

Intensity. Intensity has to do with the magnitude or severity of the behavior. Some children whimper, others scream; sometimes a temper tantrum involves lying on the floor and sobbing, other times a child throws himself on the floor screaming, arms flailing and legs pounding. Find some consistent way to calibrate intensity. Perhaps a scale of 1 to 4, with 1 being low intensity, nondisruptive, 2 disrupts a small group of children nearby, 3 disrupts most of the class, and 4 disrupts the entire class and those in the hall or perhaps in adjoining rooms. Adding intensity to duration and frequency data provides additional insights.

Latency. Latency is the length of time between a request and the child's response to the request. It might be the time you ask children to start putting away their materials and when they actually start. This is a relevant variable when children are asked to do tasks that require higher order thinking, tasks that require change, and tasks children may not want to participate in.

Context. Context refers to what is happening in the classroom before, during, or after an event happened. We are looking for a probable cause for the behavior, what influences the duration of the behavior, and what role the response to the behavior has in maintaining the behavior. If the behavior occurred during group time, one might explore different possible solutions than if the behavior occurred during transitions (arrival and departure).

It is useful to find out whether behavior is consistent or inconsistent across settings and contexts (Salvia & Ysseldyke, 1995). It is particularly useful to know if you are seeing the same behavior as the parents. If the child is also in another setting, are they seeing the same behavior you are? If the behavior is consistent across contexts, you need to focus on the behavior itself. If it is inconsistent, there may be something in the environment that is triggering the behavior.

Time. Time refers to when during the day a particular behavior occurs. It is important to note if behavior happens at specific times of the day or if they seem to occur randomly throughout the day.

I once had a child who had a temper tantrum every day, starting on the first day of school. I checked with his mother and found that he "never" had temper tantrums at home. I observed his behavior and found that he only had one temper tantrum a day; it seemed unrelated to the children he was playing with or the activity itself, and it lasted about 10 minutes and disturbed most of the class. After trying a variety of different interventions, all of which failed miserably, I talked with his mother again and asked her to tell me about a typical day in his life when he was home all day. I found that his day began about 4:30 A.M. and he had breakfast at 5:00 A.M., then played until lunch which he had about 10:00 A.M., and then he played and had dinner at 4:00 P.M. and was in bed by about 6:00 P.M. Based on this information, I decided to note the time of the temper tantrums. They were consistently around 10:00 A.M. Having decided that the cause of the temper tantrums was hunger, I had a snack ready earlier or had an open snack set up as a center and children could eat when they were hungry. The temper tantrums stopped.

Behaviors that are typically targeted for observation and intervention are those that are harmful to the child or others (hitting, biting), behavior exhibited in an inappropriate context (using an outside voice inside, running inside), infrequently displayed desirable behavior (sharing, turn taking and other prosocial behavior), and stereotypic behavior that draws negative attention to the child (hand flapping and rocking) (Salvia & Ysseldyke, 1995). Anecdotal notes are typically done at the end of the day; behavioral observations are made during the day. That may make them more difficult for teachers unless they target specific behaviors. Behavioral observations are helpful in gathering information about particular children and specific behaviors, but checklists are more efficient in gathering general information on all of the children in a short time span.

Checklists. At the beginning of the school year, you might use a checklist to help you learn the children's names and to focus on general patterns of adjustment and behavior. Consider using a checklist that looks only at where children are in the room and that can be filled out in less than a minute (after a few days practice) during free play or center time. Use it several times during free play for about a week. If there are others in the classroom, encourage them to fill out the forms as well. The recorder initials the form and fills in the time and date.

To use a form such as that shown in Figure 6.1, first divide the room into areas. Then, write a brief description of what is in each area on a given day. (If the dramatic play area is a hospital, note that.) Then write the first names of the children in alphabetical order on the side. Play with your version of the form for a while, then duplicate what you use all the time so you only have to make additions for daily changes. Individualize this form to meet your purposes.

RECORDER _____								TIME _____		
UNIT/THEME _____								DATE _____		
				RECORDS						
CHILD'S NAME	AREA	ART	MANIPULATIVE	WATER/SAND TABLE	BOOKS	BLOCKS	DRAMATIC PLAY	LOCKERS	WANDERING	BATHROOM
	DAY'S ACTIVITIES									

Figure 6.1   Records Form

This form is most useful at the beginning of the year. First survey your room and name each different area. Then add to the form those areas beyond the double line, that is, other places children might be. For example, in addition to being in the bathroom, wandering around, or in the locker area, children might be at the nurses' office or in therapy. If these events happen frequently, add them to the chart; if they are unusual, they are not worth including. Indicate the theme and place a brief reminder of the day's activity below each designated area. Use the form by placing a check in the box beside the child's name to indicate where each child is in the room. Use the form as frequently as you are free to do so. It helps to have them on a clipboard at various places around the room.

Assume that in two weeks you have been able to fill out this form ten times. What can you do with the data you've generated? First, you need to put it all on one form. Some of the implications will become apparent. Some children play in many areas, some in only one or two. You might identify small groups of children who play together. If you haven't noticed them yet, children who appear in the last three columns (lockers, wandering, and bathroom) frequently are of concern. These are children who are walking around without purpose and not engaging in activities. They probably need your help. At this stage, you are asking more questions than generating answers. If you become interested in how long children are staying at activities, try to use the form at short intervals for a few days, and look at children who are in the same area of the room on at least two consecutive observations as well as those who are never in the same area twice. This allows you to generate some information about interest span. These data, coupled with anecdotal notes, begin to give you a foundation for looking at the children in your classroom in a more systematic way. You can do all this record keeping and teach at the same time. You may now decide that you need more specific data on children's skills.

Checklists can help focus attention on specific skills. Some you can more appropriately fill in after school is over. Useful examples and rationale for some of the checklists have been included. Especially with younger children, adding their age (in years and months) to a general skills checklist often is important, as children in a given class have a range of 12 to 18 months in age. For 4-year-olds, this is a fourth of their lifetime. It is a reminder that children are appropriately different. Try to add information to these charts a few times a week. Children that are inconsistent or need work in an area will become more evident. These are the children to observe more closely.

Transitions are a good time to collect information about children's skills. For example, as children move from a group situation to free play, it is easy to dismiss them in a way that helps keep track of their learning. With planning, you can be sure that all children are successful, and you have accurate records. If you are concerned with number and letter recognition, consider using the record-keeping forms in Figure 6.4. Include color and spatial concepts also. To do this effectively, you can use a calendar for number identification ("Put your finger on the 12 and then you may go to the block area") or recognition ("Tell me the name of this number [point to a number on the calendar] and you may go to free play"). If your calendar is magnetic or is designed in a way that something will stick to it (tape on the back of the object works), ask the children to put an object in different spatial configurations relative to a specific number on the calendar. ("Put the circle above the number 21.") This exercise allows you to tap both spatial and numerical concepts. You can modify this form to gather information that is important to you. With an alphabet available, you can pose similar tasks. As children learn the capital letters, introduce the lower-case ones.

RECORDER _____		GENERAL SKILLS CHECKLIST					DATE _____		
					SOCIAL				
CHILD'S NAME	AGE YR./MOS.	LANGUAGE		APPROACH + OR −	ASSERTIVENESS INTERACTION CHILD	ASSERTIVENESS INTERACTION ADULT	MOTOR		
		RECEPTIVE	EXPRESSIVE				SMALL	LARGE	

Key
1 Above average/date   2 Average/date   3 Seems inconsistent/date   4 Needs work/date

Figure 6.2   General Skills Checklist

First decide what skills need to be monitored. Because language skills and motor skills have such widely available norms, I always include those. Then my focus is typically on the social skills that relate to inclusion. I am concerned about whether children approach each other and whether this approach is positive or negative. Another concern is that children have enough assertiveness to hold their own with peers. Often children with disabilities have learned this skill with adults, but are not as confident with peers. Become familiar with the norms in areas with which you are concerned before beginning to use the chart. At the beginning of the year, include the children's ages by both years and months. Be aware of the ages of the children, which will vary by 12 months and perhaps by as many as 18. This span causes a significant difference in skill development.

CHILD'S NAME	UNOCCUPIED	ONLOOKER	SOLITARY	PARALLEL	ASSOCIATIVE	COOPERATIVE

RECORDER _____   TIME _____
DATE _____

QUALITY OF PLAY

Key: Write initials of playmates in space. For cooperative play, note the leader.

Figure 6.3   Quality of Play Form

One goal of inclusive education is to have children play together. It is often useful to know the level at which children are playing to suggest playmates who are more likely to be compatible, and to see whether children can take leadership roles. In addition, the child's level of play is developmental and it is helpful in transition planning. Use a form such as this to make these observations more systematic. *Unoccupied:* Child is not participating in an activity or watching other children. *Onlooker:* Although not participating, the child is actively watching other children. *Solitary:* The child is playing alone with materials that are different from other children's. *Parallel:* The child is playing alone with materials that are the same as other children near by. *Associative:* Children are playing together but the play is not goal oriented and there is no leader. *Cooperative:* Children are playing together and the play is goal oriented and there is a leader.

The advantage of checklists is that they are quick and efficient to use. They can be used on your schedule, and they include all of the children. The disadvantage is that you have to prepare them ahead of time, and it may take a few attempts for you to develop forms that fit your needs.

Work Samples or Portfolios. Work samples or portfolios are another form of assessment particularly applicable to young children and are being viewed as an alternative assessment form for children of all ages (Salvia & Ysseldyke, 1995). Examples of children's work can be writing, art or anything that can be put in a folder. To be useful, the collection of samples needs to begin the first week of school so that you can see growth, and also so the children learn that putting some of their products in the folder is part of the system, both yours and theirs. Items chosen should be tied to the curriculum rather than items that take your fancy. Talk to the children about the portfolio and give them the opportunity to add items and reflect on the items that are included. Establish early that there are to be short- and long-term items for the portfolio. Long-term items would include children's first drawings and paintings of the year, as well as work that illustrates particular skills (or lack of them). Short-term items might be stories that are then replaced by other stories. Use the portfolio with the children. Let them enjoy their personal growth by looking at work they have done earlier and comparing it with what they can do now. Talk about how much they have learned. You might invite a photographer or designer to come to the class and share a portion of their portfolio with the class and explain its use in their profession.

In addition to work that is the outcome of various activities, it is important to include work in the portfolio that helps you focus on specific skills such as language, math, science, and so on. You might design some activities in each area that you do consistently several times each year. For example, make up a short story with some specific details in it at the beginning of the year and then have the children draw a picture about the story. (This is not an art project; it is an assessment project.) Tell the same story about four months later and again at the end of the year. Look for personal growth and also at the level of detail in the drawing across the group. This story should have details, familiar animals and modes of transportation, and a very simple plot. Tell a story something like this:

One day a dog and a cat met. The dog said, "I like to run, I'll race you home." "Okay," said the cat. "One, two, three, go!" The dog raced past the cat. The cat saw a boy on a bicycle. "Can you go fast?" "Yes," said the boy. "Can you catch that dog?" "Sure." The cat jumped on and off they went, up and down hills and across bridges. Finally, they caught up to the dog. The dog was mad. If the cat can play tricks, so can I. He met a horse and asked if the horse could go as fast as the bicycle. The horse said "Yes." The dog jumped on his back, and off they went. They went through the woods, jumped a stream, and finally caught up with the boy on the bicycle. The boy on the bike hit a rock and the cat fell off. The dog raced by on the horse. The cat shook himself off. The dog said to the horse, "I'm glad we don't have to run as fast now." Just then they saw the cat go flying past on an airplane. "Oh, no!" said the dog. And when he got home he said to the cat, "Let's race again tomorrow." "Okay," said his friend the cat.

Feel free to use this story or modify it. By having the children draw pictures about the same story over time, it is easier to see change. It is important that the story be original, as some children might know a published story and others not.

Other areas about which you may begin to gather some systematized data are fine and gross motor skills.

NUMBERS

	Code	Date	Code	Date
0				
1				
2				
3				
4				
5				
6				
7				
8				
9				
10				

LETTER CONCEPTS/CAPITALS

	Code	Date	Code	Date	Code	Date
A						
B						
C						
D						
E						
F						
G						
H						
I						
J						

LETTER CONCEPTS/LOWER CASE

	Code	Date	Code	Date	Code	Date
a						
b						
c						
d						
e						
f						
g						
h						
i						
j						

Key:
a - Recognition (point to the)
b - Identification (what is this letter called?)
+ - Correct
0 - Incorrect
⊕ - Correct with help
NA - Not attempted

SPATIAL CONCEPT

	Code	Date	Code	Date
ABOVE				
BELOW				
BETWEEN				
INSIDE				
OUTSIDE				
BEHIND				
UNDER				
AT THE TOP				
AT THE BOTTOM				
ACROSS FROM				
IN FRONT OF				
UP				
DOWN				
BESIDE				
BENEATH				
NEAREST				
RIGHT				
LEFT				

SHAPES:	RESPONSE	DATE	RESPONSE	DATE
△				
○				
▭				
▢				
⬭				

SIZE:	RESPONSE	DATE	RESPONSE	DATE
SMALL				
SMALLEST				
LITTLE				
LITTLEST				
MEDIUM				
BIG				
BIGGER				
LARGE				
LARGER				
LARGEST				

MATERIALS: THREE SIZES OF THE SHAPES

CHILD'S NAME _____

BODY PARTS:	RESPONSE	DATE	RESPONSE	DATE
ANKLE				
ARMS				
BACK				
CHEEKS				
CHEST				
CHIN				
EARS				
ELBOW				
EYES				
EYEBROWS				
EYELASHES				
FEET				
FINGERNAILS				
FINGERS				
HAIR				
HEAD				
HIPS				
JAW				
KNEE				
MOUTH				
NECK				
NOSE				
LEGS				
LIPS				
TEETH				
TONGUE				
TOES				
THUMB				
WAIST				
WRIST				

Figure 6.4 Grouptime Transitions

The easiest way to do this is to have your own (non-competitive) Olympics. Develop the Olympic events from a criterion-based assessment such as the Hawaii Early Learning Profile (Furuno, O'Reilly, Hosaka, Inatsuku, & Zeisloft-Falbey, 1987) or the Learning Accomplishment Profile (LeMay, Griffin, & Sanford, 1978). For 3-year-olds, the Olympic events (with appropriate norms noted) might include:

- Broad jump (mark off two feet) to the next line.
- Push or pull a wagon to the next line (10-foot distance).
- Walk (10 feet) on a 4-inch-wide taped line.
- Catch a ball thrown from 5 feet away.
- Put the ball down, take two steps, and kick it.
- Gallop back to the starting line.

These are all skills that 3-year-olds are expected to be able to do. The Olympics provides the motivation and learning opportunities that make this part of the curriculum as opposed to doing this as a check list. You have made it fun and interesting as well as informative for you.

You now have some of the informal data you need to confirm or disconfirm your concerns about a particular child, as well as to monitor the growth of all the children in your classroom.

Making assessment part of the curriculum allows early childhood educators to regularly monitor children's progress to enhance programming.

Use this information in two ways: First, to look at the growth of a particular child over time; second, to compare children to a norm or average for the age level you are teaching. Next, look at the birthdates of the children in the class. If there is a child you are concerned about, find other children who are within a month or two of the child's age and compare their work samples and observational results. The intention is not to make judgments, but to see the range of behaviors and to determine whether a particular child is outside of this range. Then compile information from your behavioral observations, checklists, and the child's portfolio. You may decide at this point that the behavior that caught your attention was unusual for the child and just the result of a temporary adjustment problem; or you may decide that you need additional information, or to reach a decision, you might begin to generate some hypotheses about what is causing the behavior and begin some interventions.

If you are going ahead with interventions documentation is extremely important. You have now made a commitment about your concerns and have developed a plan of action. Put your concerns in writing in whatever form works for you and list your hypotheses about probable causes. Decide on your interventions, the time frame in which you plan to use them, and the outcomes that you expect. If your hunch is right, you will need this documentation for the next step. Note at this point, your concerns may relate to a child who needs additional help in a particular area or a child who appears to be bored and needs enrichment. Document your results. If you feel the concern has been dealt with, continue to monitor the situation intermittently to be sure it stays solved. If the problem is still of concern, there is another decision to make: Is it time to call in additional support or to try different methods of remediation or enrichment?

Intervention Assistance

If your planned interventions were not successful, the next step is to seek assistance. Some educational settings have formal intervention assistance teams that are designed for this specific purpose; other intervention assistance works on friendship patterns or an informal organization. With these additional sets of eyes and insights, new interventions may be suggested and tried and again judged as successful or unsuccessful. If the problem is still of concern, it is time to talk with the parents and share your concerns with them. What you are trying to do in the prereferral stage is to eliminate the environment as the source of the problem. If changing the environment, based on your personal insights and interventions and then the collective wisdom of your colleagues does not solve the problem, then additional assessment information needs to be gathered. Parents need to be told of your concerns about their child and what you have done to deal with these concerns.

Conferencing with Parents

Using the guidelines from Chapter 5, schedule a conference with the parents. Explain your concerns, how you have reached your conclusions and why you believe the child will benefit from a formal screening. You need the *information* an evaluation provides (not the *label*) to meet this child's needs in your program planning. If the parents do not agree with your concerns and conclusions, this process may take several conferences and some structured observation. Some parents may never agree.

If the parents agree to diagnostic assessment, the exact procedure depends on the age of the child, whether or not the child is in a public or private school, and the nature of the problem itself. The child may be assessed by the school psychologist, educational diagnostician, child find specialist, or other professionals. If concerns are more medical in nature, their physician would do an initial assessment and necessary referrals.

Your role (with parental permission) is to share your written observations with the specialists of their choice; and to support that person's observations in your classroom. If parents do not agree, your role is to continue to individualize programming in your class and to use your informal support network for additional ideas and interventions. If parents do agree to screening, you move into a set of decisions related to entitlement.

Entitlement Decisions

Entitlement decisions are made to determine whether or not children are eligible for certain types of services. The first step in entitlement decisions is screening.

Screening

Screening is the process of collecting information to decide whether or not additional assessment is necessary. Screening is an organized, goal-directed process. The underlying assumptions behind screening are that children can be divided into two categories, those who are at risk and those who are not at risk for whatever it is that you are screening for. For example, at birth, infants are screened for phenylketonuria (PKU) by testing the level of phenylalanine in their blood. (PKU is a form of mental retardation that is preventable if a specific diet is followed.)

We have all been screened at one time or another. Children are frequently screened when they enter kindergarten. Scheduled hearing, visual, and often dental screenings are done throughout the school years. Screening instruments vary. Some require highly trained professionals; others use trained volunteers. Screening has its origins in medicine, and we often use medical terminology in evaluating screening measures. The goal of a screening instrument is to identify all children who have a certain characteristic (these are called "hits") and none of the children who don't. Children identified as being at risk, but who do not actually have the characteristic being screened for are called false positives. Concern here is that we have caused parents to worry and put children though an unnecessary experience. The opposite problem is when we fail to identify children who truly are at risk: false negatives. In this case children who could truly profit from intensive individualized attention are denied this help.

For young children, screening should consist of a range of activities that include information about the child's health, physical and motor development, social interactions, emotional expressions, social competence, concept development, and adaptative skills (NAEYC, 1991). It should also include an interview with the child's parents so that relevant information about the child's medical history, family health concerns, and the parents' perception of the child's development and their concerns, if any, are available. Screening is a brief assessment designed to identify children who may have a condition that requires further diagnosis. Screening should not be used as a diagnosis, particularly not with children who have limited abilities in English (NAEYC, 1991).

If the screening determines that a child is at risk, further assessment is designed to confirm or refute the existence of a problem. (This should sort out the children who were mistakenly identified.) Sometimes development is more a matter of degree rather than a yes or no answer. For example, a child with 20/30 vision may not profit from wearing glasses; a child with 20/100 probably would. The question really becomes, Is the problem serious enough to require remediation? Diagnosis also is designed to clarify the nature of the problem. (That is, is a hearing loss the result of fluid in the ear canal or nerve damage or both?) Formal diagnosis is a long process.

Children enter the assessment process in different ways. Some physicians have concerns about children and encourage parents to have them assessed. Some parents themselves are concerned and initiate the screening process. The National Collaborative Infant Project (reported in Neisworth & Bagnato, 1987) found that most parents suspected a problem by 6 months of age, but the time lag between suspicion and medical confirmation for severe problems was 6 months, and for more subtle dysfunctions was up to 45 months.

If the results of the screening test indicate that a child is at risk, a referral to a multidisciplinary team is recommended to the parents. The *referral* is a formal process and requires that parents fill out specific forms requesting assessment by a team of professionals to determine whether the child's academic, behavioral, or physical development qualifies for special education services. This team is frequently called a Child Study Team. The makeup of the assessment team varies depending on the age of the child, the particular concern, and how the child entered the screening process. For example, if the early childhood educator expressed the concern to the parents she would be on the team. However, if the parents were just following up on their own concerns, there might be an early childhood educator on the team but that educator would not be the child's teacher if the child were not in a preschool program.

One decision that the assessment team must make is whether or not the child meets the state's eligibility criteria for services by either having a documentable disability or for being gifted and talented. State criteria differ. This is especially true for children birth to 3. Additionally, the team must decide that the child has special learning needs. Students can have a disability and not have special learning needs. Likewise, children can have special learning needs and not meet the state criteria for special services. Children must meet both criteria to receive mandated services. The team typically administers a battery of standardized tests to determine eligibility and may rely heavily on prereferral interventions as the basis for deciding whether or not the child has special learning needs. Educators are rarely expected to give tests at this stage of the referral process, but they are expected to interpret the results and to help parents understand the basis for selecting certain measures.

Standardized Tests

As professionals in the field of early childhood, you need to make decisions about standardized tests, in particular, how to select and evaluate standardized tests appropriate for your purposes, how to interpret the results of standardized tests and how to interpret these results to others (NAEYC, 1988). Educators should have a course in assessment; this chapter is not meant as a substitute for such a course, but rather to highlight the role of assessment in the educator's decision-making process.

Standardized testing is complex—there are many different types of tests for different purposes. The tests you are most likely to encounter fall into two broad areas: *norm-referenced* and *criterion-referenced.*

In a norm-referenced assessment, a child's performance is evaluated in terms of other children's performance. We use norm-referenced tests to compare the performance of a child to the normative sample. To the extent that the children in the sample were representative of the population as a whole and the test was designed for the purpose we are using it, the test results should provide valuable information for decision making (Salvia & Ysseldyke, 1995).

Criterion-referenced measures rely on an absolute standard for determining scores. Children are asked to perform certain tasks and the score is based on the level at which they respond. Criterion-referenced measures are usually more useful for program planning purposes. It is more helpful to know a child can put together a three-piece puzzle or stack three cubes than it is to know that she has a developmental quotient (DQ) of 90.

The measures you encounter also fall into categories depending upon the purpose of the test. *Developmental tests* are age-related, norm-referenced measures of skills and behaviors that compare the scores of children of a given age. They typically have DQs, the norm for which is 100. Children taking this test are compared to the norm. Those scoring more than 100 are considered to be developing faster than the norm and those with DQs less than 100 are developing slower than the norm. The norm was established by testing and retesting many children. Developmental norm-referenced tests are used in most diagnostic work-ups.

Readiness tests are designed to assess a child's level of preparedness for a particular type of program or level of instruction. They may be used in conjunction with developmental tests and achievement tests.

Achievement tests measure the extent to which a child has mastered a certain body of knowledge after having received instruction in that area.

Many different approaches and techniques are used in assessment. All, however, are contingent on the examiner's developing rapport with the child and the family. The assessment measures chosen are likely to reflect the theoretical perspective of the examiner or program. In general, how a person believes children develop and learn influences what she wants to know about a child, the techniques used to get this information, and how she interprets the results (Benner, 1992).

Assessment provides us with baseline data and the capacity for prediction. If one wishes to monitor change, the first thing that has to be established is change *from what.* The initial assessment provides this starting point. The second purpose of assessment is prediction. We not only want to know what the child is doing now, and at what rate he is learning, we also want to be able to predict how the child will be learning when he enters school or at some other future time. Prediction assumes continuity, representativeness, and a lack of external intervening factors (Cicchetti & Wagner, 1990). The assumption is that if the assessment is in fact representative of the child's behavior, then the child will continue to develop at a certain rate. If, however, an external force (early intervention or child abuse) impacts the child, the principle of continuity does not hold and the assessment will not accurately predict behavior.

Regardless of the philosophy of the examiner or team, Benner (1992) notes seven strands to the assessment process. She sees these as a continuum and focuses on describing the end points of the continuum to provide an understanding of the range:

1. *Formal to informal assessments.* Formal assessments use standardized tools and structured, systematized observation. Informal assessments are very similar to the record keeping described previously.

2. *Norm-referenced to criterion-referenced assessments.* Measures that are based on comparing children within age groups with each other are referred to as norm-referenced. The question asked is What does the "average" child do at this age? These criteria have limited usefulness in program planning, but provide useful information for placement and transition. For example, if a child with Down syndrome is being placed in a classroom, a norm-referenced test might help you focus on the particular challenges that child will face. Criterion-referenced tests give information about the specific skills a child can perform within a developmental range. For example, you might learn that a particular child can jump from the bottom step with both feet together, but cannot jump forward a distance of two feet keeping his feet together. This type of information has application to program planning and gives useful information in knowing skill progression. One must be careful, however, to remember that the curriculum should be based on more than improving test scores.

3. *Standardized to adaptive-to-disability assessment.* Standardized tests have specific procedures that must be followed precisely for the administration of the test to be valid. These may be as subtle as whether or not you drop your voice at the end of a list of numbers. If the person giving the assessment varies these procedures, the test is no longer a valid measure. Some of the standardized procedures put

children with diverse abilities at a disadvantage and may not measure their potential. Sattler (1988) recommends a technique known as "testing of limits" to explore the child's abilities. This is used only after the entire test has been given using the standardized procedures. The examiner can return to failed items and give additional time and/or provide additional help or cues. The examiner might probe for additional information, or ask the child to explain how he went about solving a particular problem. The examiner might change the modality from a written response to an oral one. The procedure allows you some insight into the child's potential but does not produce a valid score for the test. Some tests are designed to be altered for use with children with disabilities and include information on adapting them to various situations.

4. *Direct to indirect assessment.* Direct assessment involves the examiner having face-to-face contact with the child. This typically involves both observing the child and using assessment measures. Indirect assessment relies on others to provide information, primarily the parents or educator. If sources differ, it is important to explore the discrepancies. In many cases, a combination of these techniques is used with young children. Observation and assessment of the child is supplemented by information gained from parents and educators to develop an overall picture of the child's performance.

5. *Naturalistic to clinical observations.* Observation of children during their play interactions is naturalistic observation. Observers can look at the entire setting or focus on specific types of behavior that are of interest (prosocial behavior) or concern

(aggression). Although it is often interesting to know what is happening for the entire class time (and videotaping has taken the tedium out of this task), one often gets more material than is useful, and it takes time to quantify and categorize the information.

It is often more useful to decide what specifically you need to know and how to gather that information most effectively. If, a child's temper tantrums are the concern, it might be more useful to focus on them rather than on the entire day. You might use event sampling to note the time of day, physical setup of the classroom, people present, and the frequency and duration of tantrums. The goal is to find the commonalities in the observation of these events.

Other methods of focused observation include time sampling, where you record what is going on in the classroom at specific time intervals, such as every five minutes. This method is useful for behaviors that occur frequently, such as child-to-child contact or teacher-child contact. (Figure 6.1 is a good form for time sampling techniques.) Category sampling involves recording a number of different behaviors in a particular category (social initiations such as smiling, touching, verbal requests, and so on). These observations are all naturalistic.

Most clinical observations are done in settings where the examiner can control the environment. Typically, the observation is set up to optimize the occurrence of the behavior that the professional wants to see. A combination of information from both the controlled environment and the naturalistic setting leads to the most complete and accurate picture of a child.

When assessing disruptive behavior, include information about the children involved as well as the circumstances that precipitated the event.

6. *Product-oriented to process-oriented assessment.* A product-oriented approach to assessment produces scores or other final products much like a report card with grades. These test scores are usually easily understood, quickly communicated, and useful in transition planning. Process-oriented assessment is concerned with the child's ability to learn the task as well as the success or lack of success in completing the task. For children who are severely involved, this may be the most appropriate assessment.

7. *Unidisciplinary to team approaches.* A unidisciplinary team is made up of professionals in a single field. The unidisciplinary approach is appropriate when children have a single specific presenting condition. However, most children with diverse abilities have a variety of concerns and some other services are needed.

A variety of assessment tools as well as other pre-assessment information is used to make a determination. If the child is eligible for special educational services, decision making moves into the next realm.

Post-Entitlement Decisions

For children to be identified during early childhood, some aspect of their behavior brought them to the attention of adults. When children ages 5 to 9 are identified as needing services, it is frequently because of lack of academic progress. For younger children, it is more likely the failure to reach developmental milestones at the appropriate time. These differences are what must be addressed in program planning. There are a variety of decisions that need to be made: What to teach (content), how to teach it (methods, teaching techniques, or strategies), and realistic expectations (Salvia & Ysseldyke, 1995). Consideration also needs to be given to the setting in which instruction will take place, and the additional support necessary for success.

In the 1990s, the expectation is that children with diverse abilities will be placed in a regular classroom with some type of additional support. The choice of setting may be a difficult one, as will decisions surrounding what are necessary supports. Agreement must also be reached on how to evaluate progress or learning on a regular basis.

Accountability Decisions

Assessment includes program assessment. Programs must be regularly evaluated to determine whether or not they are meeting their goals and whether children and their families are benefiting (NAEYC, 1991). That is, how is a particular class doing compared to others in educating all children, including those with diverse abilities.

As with assessing children, it is important that multiple indicators of progress be used. (Standardized group-administered multiple choice achievement tests are *not* valid measures of learning in early childhood.) It is also important to evaluate all components of a program. Parents and legislators are increasingly concerned about how well educational settings are doing in educating the young citizens of the country, particularly those at risk. Without accountability assessments, it is difficult to know which aspects of a program are doing well and which are not. Accountability decisions are usually made at the district, state, or national level.

Issues in Assessment

Assessment is a hot topic in the 1990s for all children, and as assessment and curriculum are inextricably tied together, curriculum is part of the issue.

Goals 2000

As a nation we are concerned about what our children are learning (or not learning) and have stated goals for the year 2000. The passage of the Goals 2000: Educate America Act in March 1994 signified the overall concern about education at the federal level. It focuses on "upgrading academic achievement and preparing students for the world of work" (U.S. Department of Education, 1996). The concern is focused on competency in all subject matter areas, particularly mathematics and science. There is concern about national standards and outcome based education. If standards are set and outcomes are to be measured, then the whole area of assessment is part of the fray. The federal government sees assessment as a critical part of improving instruction and holds states accountable. As academic standards have risen, new assessments need to be developed to see whether or not the standards are met. Federal assessment development grants are being used to develop assessment in areas in which states were having problems. For some states, this assessment was focused on the assessment of children with diverse abilities or with limited English proficiency.

The way we have educated children with disabilities is being challenged by new educational philosophies emphasizing inclusion, participation in the regular education curriculum, and being part of the regular assessment process (Individuals with Disabilities Education Act [IDEA], 1997). With a new educational paradigm, we must reassess old assessment practices and find new alternatives.

Early childhood education is also one of the focal points of Goals 2000. The first national education goal is that by the year 2000 "All children in America will start school ready to learn" (U.S. Department of Education, 1996, p. 1). How will we determine whether or not children are *ready* to learn? Assessment. Concern about the use and abuse of assessment is not new and it stems from many different areas: the tests themselves, the testing process, and the use of the test results. Concern about the assessment process is primarily focused on the use and misuse of standardized tests and testing procedures.

Standardized Testing

Standardized tests are used in many ways in current educational practice. Your scores on a standardized test may have influenced whether you were accepted or rejected from the college of your choice or they may influence whether or not you got into kindergarten. Many question the role of standardized tests in refusing children admission to kindergarten or deciding if children have a disability.

Overreliance on standardized testing is viewed as a major problem. Although there are many alternatives to standardized tests they are used because they are the same everywhere and so allow comparison (but not responsivity to different program goals), they are inexpensive, and they are relatively fast to give. When properly designed and used, they give unbiased information about groups of children that can be compared to a standard (Hill, 1992). They also tend to make assumptions about learning. For example, they are designed to view learning as incremental; that is, a child first learns the name of one color, then a second, and so on. They do not account for a child's discovering that colors have names and properties and becoming intrigued with learning the names, so that one day the child does not know any colors but a few days later may be able to name 20 colors; depending on the day the test was given, the results would be very different for this child. Because young children change quickly and their growth may be uneven across domains, standardized tests may over- or underevaluate what is learned. Therefore, the results of standardized tests may be misleading for some children.

Psychometric issues relate to the quality of measurement of the characteristics that are being measured. The question here is how one differentiates between "good" measures or tests and "bad" ones. There are some basic characteristics about tests that determine the quality of the tests regardless of what they are measuring.

Reliability focuses on the consistency of a measure, that is, the degree to which the scores are consistent, dependable, or repeatable. One way of determining if a measure is reliable is to give it again and compare the results. If the measure is reliable, the results should be the same or very close to the same. The child who obtains a score of 100 on Tuesday should get the same score or one very close to it on Wednesday. The underlying question is to what extent differences in scores on a given test can be attributed to actual differences in the individuals taking the test or to errors of measurement in the test itself. If tests are not reliable, we do not know whether differences are related to the children being tested or the test itself.

Validity has to do with whether or not a test measures what it claims to measure. Reliability is related to validity. If you cannot consistently get the same results each time you measure something (reliability), it cannot be valid. On the other hand, just because you can consistently measure something doesn't mean that it is valid or even worth measuring. There are degrees of validity, and so the question really is whether or not it is valid for a particular use (Smith, 1990). Actually, tests themselves don't have validity; rather, it is how the test is used that determines whether or not it is valid. There are many aspects to validity. *Content validity* is concerned with the relationship between the items in the test and the intended use of the test. If the course you are taking uses this text and your midterm examination consists of 20 math problems, you would question the content validity of the examination. With children, we are frequently concerned with the relationship between a test and the content of the curriculum.

Achievement tests are designed to measure the content children have learned as a result of instruction. That is, the content of the test ought to reflect the content of the curriculum. There is concern that this sometimes works the other way around; that is, the content of the curriculum is driven by the content of the test. If educators believe they will be judged by how well the children in their class do on achievement tests, they may "teach the test." They may also put pressure on the teacher in the previous age/grade level to have children come to their class better prepared. This has resulted in many kindergartens becoming "watered-down" first grades, which are developmentally inappropriate for 5-year-old children (Bredekamp, 1987). In a trickle-down effect, programs for 3- and 4-year-olds may be designed to get children ready for kindergarten. Children who don't come to school "ready" influence later test results and hence are denied admission until they are ready, or, alternatively, they are placed in a readiness class where, in the past, their scores were reported separately.

With young children, we are also concerned with *predictive validity*. Predictive validity is concerned with the ability to predict the same or related characteristics in the future. We are concerned with how children will perform in the future and how their diverse abilities will impact that future. This is especially important for diagnosis and placement. If we identify a child as having delayed language developmental at age 3, we want to be able to assume that she will have delayed language development when tested again at age 8 without intervention. If, however, the child had a language delay at 3, received no intervention, and was identified as having superior language development at age 8, we would question the validity of the test. This particular issue has arisen in the past with children who did not speak English, for whom it was a misuse of the test. Much of early intervention is based on the predictive validity of assessments given at young ages.

Objectivity is important in the administration and interpretation of tests. To the extent that the requirements of a specific measure are not adhered to and that subjective assessments are used, a test is less valid or reliable. A related issue is *bias.* There is concern about individual bias in a testing situation and cultural bias in the test itself. If clean, attractive, cooperative, and highly verbal young children consistently score higher than children who are dirty, poorly dressed, shy, or disruptive, bias might be operating. Cultural bias can occur if all children taking a particular test have not had equal exposure to the material.

There is concern about standardized testing and its use and misuse. Therefore, it is important to use multiple information sources for important decisions such as enrollment, retention, and eligibility for special services. The following guidelines are useful in making decisions about standardized measures:

- Use only standardized tests that meet the technical standards of test development and that are reliable and valid.

- Use tests only for the purpose for which they were intended.

- Be knowledgeable about testing, and interpret test results accurately and cautiously.

- Achievement tests (and other evaluative types of tests) should be selected on how well they match locally determined theory, philosophy, and program objectives.

- Individuals giving tests to young children should be both qualified to administer the test and knowledgeable about the development of young children.

- Testing must be sensitive to individual diversity (adapted from NAEYC, 1988, pp. 44–46).

Some concerns over the misuse of assessment have led to court cases and litigation. One issue contested was the misclassification of children from non-European-American backgrounds.

Litigation and Assessment

In the mid-1960s, a suit was brought against the Washington, DC, schools because of the disproportionate number of African American children assigned to lower-ability groups or tracks. Judge Skelly Wright ruled that "Because these tests are standardized primarily on and are relevant to a white middle-class group of students, they produce inaccurate and misleading test scores when given to lower-class and Negro students" (*Hansen v. Hobson,* 1967, p. 514). After this ruling, both ability grouping and standardized testing came under scrutiny.

In *Diana v. The Board of Education* (1970) the concern was with misclassifying children as mentally retarded who were non-native English speakers (primarily Hispanic American and Asian American), or because of cultural differences. The cases were settled out of court and California agreed to a number of actions to correct the problems.

A lengthy case that began in 1971 was *Larry P.* v. *Riles,* which dealt with the disproportionate number of African American children classified as educably mentally retarded. The 1979 ruling forced the state of California to stop using standardized intelligence tests to place Black children in special education, to re-evaluate all those who were thus classified, and to monitor or eliminate these disproportionate placements. Again, standardized tests were felt to be biased. A similar case, *PASE v. Hannon* in Chicago in 1980, received a different ruling. After a detailed analysis of the items on the test the judge ruled that there were too few "biased" items to result in misclassification; therefore, standardized tests should continue to be used for classification purposes.

In 1993, the *Larry P. v. Riles* case was revisited, as African American parents felt the previous ruling was discriminatory in that their children were kept from receiving needed services. Because California was barred from giving African American children standardized intelligence tests, and one criterion for being identified as having learning disabilities was a discrepancy between ability and achievement, no African American children could be classified as having a learning disability. The judge ruled in favor of the parents and African American children in California can again be given intelligence tests.

One of the best known cases after the passage of P.L. 94-142, *Mattie T. v. Holladay,* was filed on behalf of all children who were classified as disabled in Mississippi. The charge was that the Mississippi Department of Education failed to meet the requirements of P.L. 94-142. As a result, Mississippi's assessment procedures and timelines had to be reworked.

These cases were briefly highlighted to show some of the concerns and complexity related to assessment issues. The cases also suggest why the decision was made to classify young children as having a developmental delay rather than a specific disability. Some people feel that full inclusion would eliminate some of the problems related to the misuse of assessments.

Although the law cannot dictate what specific assessment measures are used, it can and does dictate that more than one measure must be used and that decisions related to assessment are so important that a single individual cannot make this decision. Based on this, we have teams that make decisions relative to the assessment of young children. Teams vary relative to membership, the roles that members play, and what they are called.

Assessment Teams

If more than one professional sees a child, it can be considered a team approach. However, the amount of collaboration varies greatly among teams. In some cases, members of a team are not aware of who else is on the team. Consequently, parents often end up trying to coordinate and to figure out *who* to consult about *what* problem *when.*

The role you as educator will play on the team is largely determined by how the team defines itself, but your role is extremely important. You have the opportunity to talk both formally and informally with families on a regular basis and you see the child almost every day. Few other team members will have that amount of contact.

Although team assessment is necessary, professionals may choose to operate in several ways: as a multidisciplinary team, an interdisciplinary team, or as a transdisciplinary team.

Multidisciplinary Teams

The multidisciplinary team sorts the child's condition into component parts. The parents typically take the child to the various required professionals for assessment and intervention, and the professionals then funnel their input back to each other and to the parents (and hopefully the service coordinator), who must sort it out. A strength of this model is that people from different disciplines are involved and parents have more input in the choice of team members (for example, they can choose the physical or occupational therapist they like best). However, separate disciplinary assessments, reports, and goals written by each professional may contribute to confusion, fragmented services, and lack of coordination of services to children and their families (McGonigel & Garland, 1988).

It is not unusual for the professionals to present conflicting diagnostic and intervention strategies. As team members may not meet together, it is often left up to parents to decide what to do, who to believe, or what further information they need. Despite the obvious drawbacks, with strong, knowledgeable parents, this type of team has the potential for providing good programming for children. In some cases, this is the only approach available to families, especially those who live in rural areas. For professionals, this is the least time-consuming type of team. No time needs to be allocated for interacting with team members and for many privately employed professionals; that is an important consideration.

Interdisciplinary Teams

Traditionally, interdisciplinary teams have specified members as a core team and add members as needed. They meet on a regular basis (for example, once a month). With young children who are severely involved, the service coordinator is frequently a developmental or pediatric nurse. As children get older the service coordinator may be the early childhood special educator.

It is possible for such a team to function in an interdisciplinary fashion with some specialists who do not actually meet with the group but send in written reports. Drawbacks to this method include problems in communication and interaction when team members do not have comprehensive understanding of the expertise of other team members. The scheduling of meeting times is also frequently a problem.

Transdisciplinary Teams

Transdisciplinary teams have the highest level of coordination and integration. All members of the transdisciplinary assessment team, including the parents, provide information regarding the child's strengths and needs. Ideally, this process helps each discipline see the interrelationships among developmental areas. What emerges is an individualized program based on the child as a whole that can be implemented in a setting following the regular routines.

Once the child is assessed, the team develops an integrated service plan and decides on one team member to carry out the plan with the family. One major concept in the transdisciplinary approach is that of *role release.* Role release involves the sharing of information and skills and also coaching other professionals to function in a variety of roles. For example, the physical therapist may coach the speech and language therapist on working with positioning a particular child and thus function in both roles in this instance. Role release requires trust that another professional will follow through and seek more advice when necessary. "Role release is a conscious, carefully planned process that allows transdisciplinary team members to exchange information, knowledge, and skills across disciplines and to work as an integrated team" (McGonigel & Garland, 1988, p. 14). All professionals need to learn something about each other's field. For example, a developmental psychologist may work with a child in the areas of occupational and speech therapy in addition to the areas of therapy traditionally associated with developmental psychology. This does not mean that the developmental psychologist has become an instant speech therapist, but rather that the skills necessary to intervene with this particular child can be transmitted to the psychologist so that the child and family need interact with only one individual and yet receive three types of therapy in an integrated approach.

The potential for more communication and a more accurate diagnosis exists because parents and professionals can question each other during the assessment process than on the basis of written reports or recollections based on information gained earlier. As you might guess, this highly desirable approach is also a costly one. Considerable time needs to be allocated for sharing, planning, coordinating, and training team members. Coordinating schedules so that all are available at the same time necessitates an ongoing regular commitment. However, more and more agencies are seeing the worth of this model. From parents' perspective, one possible drawback is that once they choose the team, they lose the ability to choose individuals, so that if there is one member of the team they do not like or respect, they must adapt.

Being Part of the Team

As part of the assessment team, you will often find yourself in the position of needing to get or give information about a particular child. There are several points to remember when you are part of an assessment team. Without meaning to, other professionals may use terms which are unfamiliar to you. Stop and ask them to define words that you don't understand. If you disagree with something that other professionals have written or said, ask them to talk a little more about it and ask why they made that particular determination. Often if you pair something that you like about what they did or said with something you are concerned about, they will listen more attentively. For example, "I'm very pleased with the progress Victor's been making since he began physical therapy, but I don't understand why it is so important for him to sit this particular way during group time."

Remember that you know the child well. You certainly see the child more often than the specialist you are talking with, and you have important information to share. It is helpful to be specific when possible and to base your comments on direct observations of the child and your written records. For example:

- When you know that a child can perform some skills that specialists report she did not perform during the assessment or testing period, share that information with them. They may still want the child to perform the particular skill for them as well, but your input is helpful.

- Whenever you notice dramatic changes in a child, it is important to report them to the child's parents and other professionals on the team. Especially after a change in medication, tell the child's parents if you notice changes in a child's behavior. (Also, ask that others inform you if a child's behavior or medication has changed.)

- Keep other team members informed when you've observed that a child is able to master goals written on her individualized plan. This will let others know that it may be time to write some new goals and suggest some new activities.

- A child's needs are best met when all individuals working with the child, including parents, educators, doctors, therapists, and child care providers, are well informed.

Diagnostic and Assessment Instruments

Diagnostic and assessment tools are used to identify the developmental skills, strengths, and needs of the child that will have an impact on learning. Information gained through these assessment instruments should be supplemented by personal contacts with family

By talking, being close, and placing her hands over the younger child's, an adult can promote self-esteem, safety, and inclusion.

When support is not close by, a similar experience can be frightening for young children. Assessment procedures need to take the environment into account.

members who can describe what the child does at home and indicate whether the child's behavior during the assessment was typical or atypical.

Many issues surround the assessment of young children with disabilities. One is that assessment tools are usually standardized on nondisabled children, so the validity of using those same tests on children with disabilities is questioned. These tests assume that children have had equal opportunities to learn, which may not be accurate. Traditional assessments may also result in little information on functional skills. For instance, a child with severe motor problems may not be able to use his hands well enough to manipulate objects. Because many items assessing development at young ages require this type of fine motor coordination, the child would not be fairly assessed. Assessments need to be given and used heeding these cautions.

The following pages list a variety of assessment instruments. The list is not exhaustive, but is intended to give information about the types of assessment tools that are available in different categories. The first group of measures are those that are designed to screen or categorize large groups of children into those who are at risk for developmental delays and those who are not.

Screening measures such as the *Denver II* (Frankenberg & Dodds, 1990) and the *Miller Assessment for Preschoolers (MAP)* (Miller, 1988) are used to decide which children receive further testing and which ones don't.

Developmental *norm-referenced* measures often form the core of the diagnostic work-up for infants and young children. Examples include the *Battelle Developmental Inventory (BDI)* (Newborg, Stock, Wnek, Guidubaldi, & Svinicki, 1984), and the *Bayley Scales of Infant Development, 2nd Ed.* (Bayley, 1993). These measures are used to get an overall picture and to determine whether further, more specialized assessment is necessary. Given the lack of high quality screening measures for young children, norm-referenced measures may also serve a screening purpose. These measures are standardized and require a trained examiner.

For preschool and older children tests such as the *Wechsler Preschool and Primary Scale of Intelligence-Revised (WPPSI-R)* (Wechsler, 1989) or the *Wechsler Intelligence Scale for Children-III* (Wechsler, 1991) and the *Stanford-Binet Intelligence Scale: Fourth Edition* (Thorndike, Hagen, & Sattler, 1985) would be used as core assessment tools.

Criterion-referenced measures are typically the most useful in program planning and in measuring smaller increments of development. These are often used after screening and diagnosis has been completed. Measures such as the *Brigance Diagnostic Inventory of Early Development (Revised)* (Brigance, 1991), the *Learning Accomplishment Profile-Diagnostic Edition (LAP-D)* (LeMay et al., 1978), and *The Hawaii Early Learning Profile (HELP)* (Furuno et al., 1987) cover traditional developmental domains: social and emotional development, language and communications, cognition, fine and gross

motor skills, self-help skills, general knowledge and comprehension, written language, and math.

Specialized measures are designed for particular populations that are difficult to test, such as children who are severely involved. Other specialized assessment instruments look at particular areas of development or interaction patterns. Some specialized measures are noted below, and additional specialized instruments are included in the relevant chapters.

The *Carolina Record of Individual Behavior (CRIB)* (Simeonsson, Huntington, Short, & Ware, 1982) was designed to be used with children with severe disabilities who function below 3 years of age. It is useful in organizing the environment to appropriately stimulate severely involved children. The Parent/Caregiver Involvement Scale (P/CIS) (Farran, Kasari, Comfort, & Jay, 1986) measures the adult's involvement and the quality of that involvement in play interactions with the child from 2 months to 5 years. *The Vineland Adaptive Behavior Scales (Revised)* (Sparrow, Balla, & Cicchetti, 1985) have several different versions; the Survey Edition is probably most appropriate in the area of early childhood. Its focus is on personal and social competence. It assesses four domains: communication, daily living skills, socialization, and motor skills. It can be used from birth to age 18. This measure is useful for severely involved children as adults can answer questions about the child's abilities.

Multicultural Issues in Assessment

The impact of a child's cultural environment cannot be overlooked in the assessment process. The devaluation of culture seems to have its greatest impact on young children (Benner, 1992). It is imperative to use a broad framework when assessing children from culturally diverse backgrounds. Using only a narrow concept of standard English language proficiency to assess communication competence biases views of children's abilities. Language barriers can be formidable. Even when interpreters are available, test results may be questionable, and the tests may not provide a picture of the child's abilities in the school setting. Viewing the child within the context of the family and environment, even at an informal level, may lead to insights that make placement and programming decisions more relevant and meaningful for all.

Summary

Assessment is part of the referral process that is used to identify children who are eligible for special educational services. The referral process typically begins informally with parents or educators having concerns about a child. They use interventions that they think will help the child and may call in colleagues for additional ideas. If these interventions are not successful, a more formal process is used that typically begins with the administration of screening measures and may be followed by standardized tests. Information from these measures and the information gained from the prereferral process is used to determine whether or not a child is eligible for special educational services. If the child is eligible, a team that includes the parents makes a decision about the instruction and placement that will best meet the child's needs.

Assessment is also concerned at a broader level with the quality of education for all children and whether or not educational settings are being accountable to the public and legislature in the quality of education they are presenting to all children. There are concerns about how standardized tests are used, particularly with children from minority groups and children with disabilities.

Overall, the assessment process provides the basis for eligibility for special educational services and the individualized program planning that is part of these services. Because of the great importance of the assessment process no single person or test is used to place children, but rather an assessment team is assembled. Assessment teams are organized in a variety of ways depending on the particular team members and the roles that various professionals play.

Educational Resources

American Psychiatric Association
1400 K Street, NW
Washington, DC 20005
   Produces the Diagnostic and Statistical Manual of Mental Disorders (DSM-IV), *which is the standard by which many disabilities are diagnosed.*

American Psychological Association (APA)
750 First Street, NE
Washington, DC 20002
   The APA publishes journals and holds annual conferences that relate to assessment as well as other developmental issues.

References

Bayley, N. (1993). *Bayley scales of infant development* (2nd ed.). New York: Psychological Corporation.

Benner, S. (1992). *Assessing young children with special needs: An ecological perspective.* White Plains, NY: Longman.

Bredekamp, S. (Ed.). (1987). *Developmentally appropriate practice in early childhood programs serving children from birth through age 8.* (Exp. ed.). Washington, DC: NAEYC.

Brigance, A. (1991). *Brigance diagnostic inventory of early development* (Rev. ed.). North Billerica, MA: Curriculum Associates.

Cicchetti, D., & Wagner, S. (1990). Alternative assessment strategies for the evaluation of infants and toddlers: An organizational perspective. In

S. Meisels & J. Shonkoff (Eds.), *Handbook of early childhood intervention* (pp. 246–277). Cambridge, MA: Cambridge University Press.

Diana v. State Board of Education of Monterey County, No. C-70-37 (N.D. Cal., Feb. 5, 1970) (unreported).

Education for All Handicapped Children Act of 1975, Pub. L. 94-142, 89 Stat. 773-796, 20 U.S.C. 1400.

Farran, D., Kasari, C., Comfort, M., & Jay, S. (1986). *The parent/caregiver involvement scale.* Honolulu, HI: Center for the Development of Early Education, Kamehameha Schools/Bishop Estate, Kapalama Heights.

Frankenberg, W. K., & Dodds, J. B. (1990). *Denver II.* Denver, CO: Denver Developmental Metrics.

Furuno, S., O'Reilly, K., Hosaka, C., Inatsuku, T., & Zeisloft-Falbey, B. (1987). *The Hawaii early learning profile.* Palo Alto, CA: VORT.

Goals 2000: Educate America Act of 1994. Pub. L. 103-227, 108 Stat. 125.

Hill, T. W. (1992). Reaching potentials through appropriate assessment in S. Bredekamp & T. Rosegrant (Eds.), *Reaching potentials: Appropriate curriculum and assessment for young children* (Vol. 1, pp. 43–63). Washington, DC: National Association for the Education of Young Children.

Hobson v. Hansen, 269 F. Supp. 401 cert. Dismissed, 393 U.S. 801 (1967).

Individuals with Disabilities Education Act of 1997. Pub. L. 105-17, 111 Stat. 37-157 Sect. 901, 20 U.S.C. 1400.

Larry P. v. Riles, 495 F. Supp. 926 (N.D. Cal. 1979) and 37F 3d 485 (9th Cir 1994).

LeMay, D., Griffin, P., & Sanford, A. (1978). *Learning accomplishment profile—Diagnostic edition.* Lewisville, NC: Kaplan School Supply.

Mattie T. v. Holladay Edu. Handicapped L. Rep. Dec. (LRP) 551:109 (N.D. Miss. Jan. 26, 1979).

McGonigel, M. J., & Garland, C. W. (1988). The individualized family service plan and the early intervention team: Team and family issues and recommended practices. *Infants and Young Children: An Interdisciplinary Journal of Special Care Pediatrics, 1*(1), 10–21.

Miller, L. (1988). *Miller assessment for preschoolers manual* (Rev. ed.). San Antonio, TX: Psychological Corporation.

National Association for the Education of Young Children. (1988). NAEYC position statement on standardized testing of young children 3 through 8 years of age. *Young Children, 43*(3), 42–47.

National Association for the Education of Young Children. (1991). Guidelines for appropriate curriculum content and assessment in programs serving children ages 3 through 8. *Young Children, 46*(3), 21–38.

Neisworth, J., & Bagnato, S. J. (1987). *The young exceptional child: Early development and education.* New York: Macmillan.

Newborg, J., Stock, J., Wnek, L., Guidubaldi, J., & Svinicki, J. (1984). *Battelle Developmental Inventory.* Allen, TX: DLM Teaching Resources.

PASE v. Hannon, 506 F. Supp. 831 (N.D. Ill, 1980).

Salvia, J., & Ysseldyke, J. E. (1995). *Assessment* (6th ed.). Boston: Houghton Mifflin.

Sattler, J. (1988). *Assessment of children* (3rd ed.). San Diego, CA: Sattler.

Simeonsson, R., Huntington, G., Short, G., & Ware, W. (1982). The Carolina record of individual behavior: Characteristics of handicapped infants and children. *Topics in Early Childhood Special Education, 2*(2), 43-55.

Smith, J. K. (1990). Questions of measurement in early childhood. In E. D. Gibbs & D. M. Teti (Eds.), *Interdisciplinary assessment of infants: A guide for early intervention professionals* (pp. 3-14). Baltimore: Brookes.

Sparrow, S., Balla, D., & Cicchetti, D. (1985). *Vineland adaptive behavior scales.* Circle Pines, MN: American Guidance Service.

Thorndike, R. L., Hagen, E., & Sattler, J. (1985). *Sanford-Binet intelligence scale.* Chicago: Riverside.

U.S. Department of Education. (1996, Fall). *Goals 2000: A progress report.* Washington, DC: Author.

Wechsler, D. (1989). *Wechsler preschool and primary intelligence scale—Revised.* New York: Psychological Corporation.

Wechsler, D. (1991). *Wechsler intelligence scale for children* (3rd ed.). San Antonio, TX: Psychological Corporation.

Chapter 7

INDIVIDUALIZING PLANNING

I left for the meeting alone at 7:00 A.M. Jack wanted to come with me, but with three kids, someone had to get them off to school. I arrived at the school for my first IEP meeting. I wasn't sure what to expect, but I knew there would be a lot of *them*. Having gone through all the assessment and evaluation procedures, we were convinced that Charlene had a learning disability. More specifically, she was probably dyslexic.

After the introductions (Where was her classroom teacher?), they gave me the IEP. I was appalled, I thought this was something we did together. I would talk about what Charlene could do, liked to do, and so on and then we would figure out how to use what she could do to help her learn to read. It seemed clear that they did not want my input because the form was typed and there were seven copies of it. This is one page of what they gave me is shown at the top of page 119.

I tried to get myself back together and at least look at the information on the form. The annual goal was fine. We too wanted her to improve her reading skills. The rest of the form made little sense. It was like a code that teachers use to keep parents out. How could I ever tell if she mastered the critical objectives for her grade when they were given as 01,02, and so on. When I looked at the evaluation procedure it said that she was to get at least a 75 percent accuracy. Why not a 100 percent? How were they going to teach her to read: Structural analysis, phonics, and kinesthetics. How individualized was that? What had they been doing up till now, trying osmosis? I was not a happy camper. Then I looked at who was responsible. Staff! What if I have a question. Do I call up the school and say, "Hello, I'd like to speak to staff to see if my daughter is mastering her cm 04s yet." Again, I tried to get my act together.

I asked them what they liked most about my daughter. There was silence. The educational diagnostician finally spoke up. She was the only one in the room who would even recognize Charlene. I asked where Charlene's classroom teacher was. They said she wasn't necessary as they began to explain why Charlene would be better off in a special education class. I explained that my husband and I had both observed in this class and didn't find it appropriate for our daughter. After some discussion, they said that there was a marvelous teacher at another school in the district who would just love to have a girl like Charlene in her class and they were sure it could be arranged to bus her to that school. At this point, the meeting seemed pointless. As I got up to leave, one of the individuals reminded me that I hadn't yet signed the IEP. I left the meeting and I didn't sign the IEP. I wondered if that meant that Charlene didn't have a disability.

Changes in the 1997 reauthorization of the IDEA are designed to decrease the likelihood of situations like this happening again. Parents have a variety of reactions to the IEP process depending on what they expect and the process they enter into. In the past, we did not consider parents full members of the team and did not value their insights or input. The 1997 reauthorization of the IDEA clearly supports the role of parents and the interest in keeping children in regular education as much as possible.

The process of individualizing planning is part of what all early childhood educators do for all children some of the time. It is part of developmentally appropriate practices and good teaching. Individualization is not dependent on the formal assessment and identification process, but rather on the ability of an educator to adapt and modify activities and curriculum based on the individual needs of children that vary by the day, hour, and even minute.

Individuals with Disabilities Education Act

Identification of children as being eligible for formal individualized programs is based on federal guidelines. The procedures are similar to the way a responsive teacher works with all children on a daily basis but the process is more systematic and follows the dictates of the federal law. The Individuals with Disabilities Education Act (IDEA, 1997) requires that all

STUDENT _Charlene_		SCHOOL _West End_				Page _2_ of _____	

ANNUAL GOAL _1.0 To improve reading skills_

SHORT TERM OBJECTIVE	CRITERIA AND EVALUATION PROCEDURES	SPECIFIC EDUCATIONAL SERVICES	DATES		STAFF RESPONSIBILITIES	
			Begin	End	Name	Position
1.0 Charlene will master the critical objectives for grade. Reading Vocabulary Comprehension VC 01 CM 01 02 02 03 03 04 04 05 05 06 06 07 Study/ References Sentences SR 01 SN 01 02	1.0 – Teacher Test ⎤ at least – Textbook Test ⎬ 75% – Observation ⎦ accuracy – Other Methods to include: – Structural Analysis – Phonics – Kinesthetic	Level I	9/98	6/99	Staff	

PARENT'S SIGNATURE	TEACHER'S SIGNATURE _Mo. Jones, E.D._

Figure 7.1   Annual Goal Form

children identified as being eligible for services under the IDEA have an individualized plan for their education. This plan is an acknowledgment that each identified child needs special educational services and supports to learn. Families have goals and expectations for their children that are part of the plan. For children ages 3 to 21, the plan is called an Individualized Education Program or an IEP. For children from birth to 3, the plan is called an Individualized Family Service Plan, or an IFSP. In some cases, children ages 3 to 5 may have an IFSP instead of an IEP, but all children will have a plan.

The initial requirements for the IEP were part of P.L. 94-142 which was passed in 1975, the requirements for the IFSP were part of P.L. 99-457 which was passed in 1986. We learned a great deal as we used the IEP and IFSP. Many of these changes are reflected in the 1997 amendments to the IDEA. Because the IDEA and its amendments play such an important role in individualizing programming as well as establishing eligibility criteria, who is required to be part of the teams, and so on, a synopsis of the parts of the law that affect children birth through 8 is given.

Individuals with Disabilities Education Act

Purpose. The purpose is to assure that all children with disabilities have available to them, within the time periods specified, a free appropriate public education (FAPE) that emphasizes special education and related services designed to meet their unique needs, to assure that the rights of children with disabilities and their parents or guardians are protected, to assist states and localities to provide for the education of all children with disabilities, and to assess and assure the effectiveness of efforts to educate children with disabilities.

The act defines key terms and concepts and sets minimum federal standards that must be met in order to achieve compliance. The following definitions apply to children from birth through 8 and those who educate and care for them. This information is organized conceptually here rather than as it actually appears. You should read P.L. 105-17, the 1997 Amendments to the IDEA. These definitions are quoted from the law to give you a flavor for how laws read and are organized:

Definitions.

(A) IN GENERAL—The term "child with a disability" means a child—

(i) with mental retardation, hearing impairments (including deafness), speech or language impairments, visual impairments (including blindness), serious emotional disturbance (hereinafter referred to as "emotional disturbance"), orthopedic impairments, autism, traumatic brain injury, other health impairments, or specific learning disabilities; and

(ii) who, by reason thereof, need special education and related services (Section 602 (3)(A)).

This section of the law defines what the term "child with a disability" means relative to the disabilities included under that law and the stipulation that, in addition to having a disability, the child must also need special education and related services. Part (B) of this section gives the states the discretion of identifying children ages 3 through 9 as developmentally delayed rather than requiring a more specific diagnosis, such as mental retardation:

(i) experiencing developmental delays, as defined by the state and as measured by appropriate diagnostic instruments and procedures, in one or more of the following areas: physical development, cognitive development, communication development, social or emotional development, or adaptive development; and
(ii) who, by reason thereof, need special education and related services (Section 602 (3)(B)).
(5) INFANT OR TODDLER WITH A DISABILITY.—The term "infant or toddler with a disability"—
(A) means an individual under 3 years of age who needs early intervention services because the individual
(i) is experiencing developmental delays as measured by appropriate diagnostic instruments and procedures in one or more of the areas of cognitive development, physical development, communication development, social or emotional development, and adaptive development; or
(ii) had a diagnosed physical or mental condition which has a high probability of resulting in developmental delay; and
(B) may also include, at a State's discretion, at-risk infants and toddlers (Section 632 (5)).
(1) AT-RISK INFANT OR TODDLER.— The term "at risk infant or toddler" means an individual under 3 years of age who would be at risk of experiencing a substantial developmental delay if early intervention services were not provided to the individual (Section 632 (1)).

Although services for infants and toddlers remain at the discretion of the states, in 1999, all states had statewide systems of early intervention. Each state defined the term *developmental delay* and how it carries out programs based on that definition. States are being encouraged to expand systems of early intervention to include the at-risk population. The law defines both special education and related services:

(25) The term *special education* means specially designed instruction, at no cost to parents, to meet the unique needs of a child with a disability, including
(A) instruction conducted in the classroom, in the home, in hospitals and institutions, and in other settings' and
(B) instruction in physical education (Section 602).
(22) The term *related services* means transportation, and such developmental, corrective, and other supportive services (including speech-language pathology and audiology services, psychological services, physical and occupational

therapy, recreation, including therapeutic recreation, social work services, counseling services, including rehabilitation counseling, orientation and mobility services, and medical services shall be for diagnostic and evaluation purposes only), as may be required to assist a child with a disability to benefit from special education, and includes the early identification and assessment of disabling conditions in children (Section 602).

Other important definitions include:

(8) The term *free appropriate public education* means special education and related services that—
(A) have been provided at public expense, under public supervision and direction, and without charge;
(B) meet the standards of the State educational agency;
(C) include an appropriate preschool, elementary, or secondary school education in the state involved; and
(D) are provided in conformity with the individualized education program required under section 614 (d) (Section 602).

The increasing role of assistive technology in supporting children with disabilities is acknowledged as is the need for educational institutions to both provide and maintain these devices as well as provide training on their use:

1. The term *assistive technology device* means any item, piece of equipment, or product system, whether acquired commercially off-the-shelf, modified, or customized, that is used to increase, maintain, or improve functional capabilities of a child with a disability.

2. The term *assistive technology service* means any service that directly assists a child with a disability in the selection, acquisition, or used of an assistive technology device.

Other important definitions are given where they are discussed in the text.

Important Concepts of the IDEA

Sections of the IDEA require states to do a variety of different things to ensure that children with disabilities are provided with the services they require and the safeguards they need. The following highlights some of these requirements:

Identification. States must make extensive and well-publicized efforts to screen and identify all children and youth with disabilities.

Parent's Role. The parent or guardian must be members of any group that makes decisions about whether or not a child has a disability as defined by the law and the educational placement of their child.

Least Restrictive Environment (LRE). Children must be educated in the least restrictive environment that is consistent with their educational needs and as much as possible with children without disabilities.

Individualized Education Program (IEP) and Individualized Family Service Plan (IFSP). A written individualized education program (ages 3 to 21) or an individualized family service plan (birth to 3) must be developed for each child identified as being eligible for services.

Nondiscriminatory Evaluation. Children must be evaluated by a multidisciplinary team in all areas of suspected disability and in a way that is not biased by the child's language, cultural background, or disability.

Due Process. Parents' informed consent must be obtained before a child is evaluated, labeled, or placed. Parents who disagree with the school's decision have the right to mediation and to an impartial due process hearing.

Confidentiality. Results of evaluations must be kept confidential. Parents and guardians have the right to see the records, and they can give permission for them to be released.

Personnel Preparation. Teachers and other staff working with children with disabilities (including regular education teachers) must be provided training in meeting the needs of children with disabilities.

Children Without Disabilities. Children without disabilities may benefit from the services and support provided with federal special education funds to children with disabilities in the regular classrooms.

Recommended Practice in the Development of the IEP and IFSP

Although the IEP and IFSP are different in some respects, the underlying process is similar. The underlying principle is empowerment. The family is the decision maker in the process, and the process itself is critical. Ideally, the process is dynamic, informal, and responsive to the preferences of the family while being supportive of the family as a whole. The process and corresponding documents must also be responsive to change (Turbiville, Turnbull, Garland, & Lee, 1993).

The Role of the Family. The role of the family is critical. Best practice sees the family as the ultimate decision maker about their role in the process and what they want for their child. This doesn't mean that families make all the decisions, but it is their right to choose which decisions they want to make and which

decisions they defer to others. Families may make all, part, or none of the decisions, but they have the right to decide what role they want to play and to alter that decision.

What happens when families themselves don't agree? Many parents disagree on issues related to their children. Best practice hasn't really addressed this issue directly. You might consider adding to your repertoire skills consensus building, mediation, and the ability to keep the best interests of the child and family at the fore.

There are many decisions to make during the IFSP/IEP process which often begins as a follow-up to the identification and assessment process. Families may just have learned that their concerns about their child's development were justified. Although assessment results still serve as the foundation for meeting eligibility criteria and determining relative areas of strength, the families are the ones who decide what they want for their children and give input into the process.

Individualized Education Program Team

The individualized education program team (IEP team) is responsible for the identification, assessment, design, and implementation of the individualized program. The federal law provides information about the individuals who need to be on this team and their respective roles and necessary skills.

The IEP team for each child with a disability includes: The parents of the child, at least one regular education teacher, one special education teacher, a representative of the local educational agency (LEA), an individual who can interpret the instructional implications of evaluation results, the child (if appropriate), and, at the discretion of the parent or the agency, other individuals who have knowledge or special expertise regarding the child (IDEA, 1997).

The IEP team is a formidable group. Parents have an extremely important role. The requirement for a regular education teacher is new. Because these children were being included in regular classrooms, those teachers felt they should be active participants in this process. The federal government agreed. The special education teacher or consultant has traditionally been part of the team. Someone must be on the team who has the authority to commit resources. If the team wants something, such as an assistive device included in the IEP, someone has to have the authority to say the school system will pay for it. There is a requirement that individuals on the team know specific instructional techniques for this particular child as well as individuals who are knowledgable about the general curriculum. Someone on the team must understand and be able to interpret evaluation results. There is an option for others to be part of the team at the request of either the parents or the educational setting. The goal is to have all the stakeholders on the team.

Additional IEP team members frequently include specialists who work with the child, but they can also include advocates, representatives of agencies and community programs that their child has attended or might attend, friends, previous teachers, parents of children with disabilities, or anyone the family feels would provide emotional support and practical assistance.

Families are equal members of the IEP team and are invited to all team discussions of their child and also receive all the reports and background materials so that they can actively participate in the process. Therefore, documents need to be jargon free (or, at least necessary technical terms should be defined) so all team members can understand. Families need to know the current laws that regulate this process and what is considered best practice in the field.

The Role of the Team

One of the initial responsibilities of the IEP team is to be sure parents understand the process itself and their rights under the law. Team members have responsibilities to talk with families about the range of services and service delivery settings available, and to arrange for meeting times and locations that are convenient for parents and other team members. Responsibilities also include developing individualized criteria for assessing progress toward outcomes or goals and giving family-initiated outcomes, goals, and objectives priority.

Individualized Education Programs

When a child between the ages of 3 and 21 is identified as having a disability, certain procedures and requirements must be followed. Many of these are determined by federal and state laws. Because all states are now required to individualize programming for eligible children with disabilities beginning at age 3, we will begin with this group.

The law requires that an individualized education program (IEP) be designed *in writing* for each child with a disability, and, as we have noted, the program must be developed *jointly* by the teachers, specialists, the parents or guardians, and, if possible, the child. Putting the program in writing is meant to ensure that it will be carried out and that agreement has been reached by all members of the IEP team about its content.

Parents have the right to examine all relevant school records regarding the identification, evaluation, and educational placement of their child. This right enables parents to examine the data that decisions are based on. Parents are now entitled, on request, to see test results and receive copies of reports.

The school district must provide the parents with information *in writing,* in a language they can understand, about the identification, evaluation, and placement of their child. The parents must be notified in writing of contemplated program changes as well. In the past, some parents were not informed when their children were placed in or removed from special education classes.

In developing a child's IEP the IEP team considers the strengths of the child, the concerns of the parents for enhancing the education of their child, and the results of the evaluations of the child (IDEA, 1997).

The federal government uses the following definition and requirements for the IEP developed for each identified child with a disability:

The "individualized education program" or "IEP" means a written statement for each child with a disability that is developed, reviewed, and revised in accordance with this section and must include—

(1) A statement about the child's present levels of educational performance including—

(i) How the child's disability affects the child's involvement and progress in the general curriculum; or

(ii) For preschool children, as appropriate, how the disability affects the child's participation in appropriate activities;

(2) A statement of measurable annual goals including benchmarks or short-term objectives, related to—

(i) Meeting the child's needs that result from the child's disability to enable the child to be involved in and progress in the general curriculum; and

(ii) Meeting each of the child's other educational needs that result from the child's disability;

(3) A statement of the special education and related services and supplementary aids and services to be provided to the child, or on behalf of the child and a statement of the program modifications or supports for school personnel that will be provided for the child—

(i) To advance appropriately toward attaining the annual goals;

(ii) To be involved and progress in the general curriculum in accordance with paragraph (a)(1) of this section and to participate in extracurricular and other nonacademic activities; and

(iii) To be educated and participate with other children with disabilities and nondisabled children in the activities described in this paragraph;

(4) An explanation of the extent, if any, to which the child will not participate with nondisabled children in the regular class and in the activities described in paragraph (a)(3) of this section

(5) (i) A statement of any individual modifications in the administration of State or district-wide assessment of student achievement

that are needed in order for the child to participate in the assessment; and

   (ii) If the IEP team determines that the child will not participate in a particular State or district-wide assessment of student achievement (or part of such an assessment), a statement of—

    (A) why that assessment is not appropriate for the child; and

    (B) How the child will be assessed;

  (6) The projected date for the beginning of the services and modifications described in paragraph (a)(3) of this section, and the anticipated frequency, location, and duration of these services and modifications; and

  (7) A statement of—

   (i) How the child's progress toward the annual goals described in paragraph (a)(2) of this section will be measured; and

   (ii) How the child's parents will be regularly informed (through such means as periodic report cards) at least as often as parents are informed of their nondisabled children's progress of—

    (A) Their child's progress toward the annual goals; and

    (B) The extent to which that progress is sufficient to enable the child to achieve the goals by the end of the year (IDEA, 1997).

This may begin to sound overwhelming. As you are learning the elements of an IEP, the fine points of writing good objectives or benchmarks, or how to work well with specialists, you may ask yourself, "Is this worth the effort for just one or two children?" Yes! In the process of complying with these legal requirements, you can learn a great deal about individualizing instruction for all children and about getting the maximum benefit from the resources you have. For the other children in the class, especially any about whom you have some concerns, you can incorporate into your customary planning the principles used to design IEPs.

Introduction to the IEP Form

There are at least as many different IEP forms as there are states in the United States. All of them must conform to the guidelines stated in the 1997 Amendments to the IDEA, but they may include information not required by law. The following generic IEP form was developed for illustrative purposes. You can adapt the information to the form you are required to use.

An IEP is a working portfolio that holds information and planning materials. If you think about it this way it is not only a required document, but a useful planning tool. The purpose of the portfolio is to collect and save information that will be helpful to the parents and other members of the IEP team as the child embarks (or continues) on his school career. This is an individualized programming form that meets the federal guidelines for the IEP. I have chosen to call it an Individualized Planning Portfolio to acknowledge its ongoing role in planning for the child and as a place to keep important documents related to the child's education. As more children are included in regular education, I think that individualized planning is part of the normative way of educating all children. This individual portfolio follows federal guidelines.

Part 1 at the top of the page, has space for child and family *identification and information.* Often children are in more than one educational setting (public school and after school care, or child care and a specialized preschool program) so it is useful to have two blanks so that all settings are included. The school district the child attends needs to be noted. Have two separate spaces for parents or guardians available (with the number of children in divorced and remarried families and foster care you may need to contact parents or guardians in different settings). Likewise, it is important to know what the custody arrangements are so you know who to contact (if joint custody is held, you need to contact both parents) as well as the child's living arrangements (some children move between settings). Some families do not have telephones, but will list one for emergency purposes. It is useful to know the location you are calling so you can frame your request.

Part 2 provides information about the process that led up to the IEP meeting. This may require additional space. Or the information can be appended. The first part of the process was probably observational data that led to the initial concern. This may include the informal observations of others in addition to the teacher. This may have been followed by an informal teacher assessment to further quantify the concerns. Information from these two processes would have led to interventions and accommodations. To the extent that these adequately responded to the child's needs, there would be no need for the IEP. When these interventions and accommodations are not successful, there is a need for a parent conference. The outcome of this conference might be a request for evaluation, or trying additional interventions and accommodations.

Part 3 looks at the status of the IEP. Although it may seem a bit premature to put this on the first page, for compliance purposes, it is a good thing to have it there. The date of the initial IEP is given as well as the date on which it will be reviewed and a date for revisions. Because an IEP may be written in May to begin the next September, the initiation date is noted as well as the ending date of this IEP. In some instances, a temporary placement may be necessary and also is noted. (This can occur because of summer vacation or for other reasons.) The recommended permanent placement is also noted.

Part 4 provides information about the child's present level of performance based on formal assessments. It includes space for both medical/clinical information and developmental/educational information. This is also the space to include a summary of the current test data, including data from state and district assessments. Information that is relevant but

1. Child and Family Identification and Information

Child's Name: _____ D.O.B.: ___/___/___ CA: ___/___/___

Current Educational Settings: _____ _____

School District: _____

Parent/Guardian/Surrogate Parent: Parent/Guardian/Surrogate Parent:

_____   _____

_____   _____

Address: _____

_____   _____

_____   _____

Telephone (location if not in home):   _____

_____   _____

Custody Status: _____

Living Arrangements: _____

2. Record of Informal Assessments

Observations (include date, observer, location, purpose, summary):

_____

_____

_____

_____

Informal Assessments (include date, assessment, purpose):

_____

_____

_____

_____

Interventions and Accommodations (include date, intervener, intervention, outcome):

_____

_____

_____

_____

Parent Conference (date, time, location, who attended, outcome):

_____

_____

_____

_____

_____

3. IEP Status

IEP: _____ Initial: ___/___/___ Annual Review: ___/___/___

Revised: ___/___/___ Initiation: ___/___/___ Ending: ___/___/___

Temporary Placement (Date begun: ___/___/___) (Expected change: ___/___/___)

Recommended Placement: _____

Figure 7.2   Individualized Planning Portfolio

4. Record of Formal Assessment

Developmental/Educational Information (include dates, tests, and results (attach) Most recent evaluation: _____/_____/_____	Medical/Clinical/Specialist Information (include dates, tests, and results (attach) Most recent evaluation: _____/_____/_____

5. Child's Strengths, Family Concerns, Implications of Formal and Informal Assessments

_____

_____

_____

_____

6. Eligibility

Meets eligibility criteria: (yes) _____ (no) _____   Disability(ies): _____

(1) Participate in statewide assessment: (yes) _____ (no) _____

(2) Assistive technology evaluation: (yes) _____ (no) _____

(3) Specialized transportation: (yes) _____ (no) _____

(4) Discipline/behavior plan: (yes) _____ (no) _____

(5) Extended school year: (yes) _____ (no) _____

Necessary Accommodations: Rationale: (note number)

_____

_____

_____

_____

7. Transition   Formal Plan attached: (yes) _____ (no) _____   Informal plan: (yes) _____ (no) _____

Contact person _____

8. Program Supports

Regular Education (area)	Supports (paraprofessional, consultation); Other	Specialized Educational Services (area)
Time (hours/week): _____	Time (hours/week): _____	Time (hours/week): _____
Location: _____	Location: _____	Location: _____

Rationale for time not in regular education:

_____

_____

_____

Figure 7.2   *Continued*

9. Related Services

Area	Type*	Frequency	Time	Location

*I = Individual, G = Group, C = Consultative
Rationale for services not provided in regular education:

_____

_____

_____

10. Participants Attending Meeting and Role

Name	Role*	Signature	Date
	Parent/guardian/surrogate		
	Parent/guardian/surrogate		
	Regular ed teacher		
	Special ed teacher		
	Rep LEA (curr/resources)		
	Implication of evals for ed		
	Child		
	Transition contact		
	Others		
	Others		

*Service coordinator or contact person designated. Phone: _____

11. Parental Participation and Safe Guards

1. I acknowledge that I have received a copy of the procedural safeguards. I have read the information and my due process rights under those procedural safeguards have been explained to me so I feel comfortable making a decision.
2. I agree/disagree (circle one) with the IEP as written or amended in this document.
3. I agree/disagree (circle one) with the placement decision as written or amended in this document.

_____   _____ / _____ / _____

_____   _____ / _____ / _____

(Parent/Guardian/Surrogate Signature(s))

4. If I disagree, the options available to me have been explained to me and resources have been given to me so I can follow through on my decision.

_____   _____ / _____ / _____

_____   _____ / _____ / _____

(Parent/Guardian/Surrogate Signature(s))

12. General Accommodations

1. No accommodations needed. _____
2. Accommodations:

_____

_____

Figure 7.2   *Continued*

13. Annual Goals, Benchmarks/Objectives

Child's Name: _____   Date: _____   Page ___ of ___

Developmental/Educational Area: _____

Annual Goal _____

_____

_____

PLP _____

_____

_____

Date	Status	Benchmark/Objective	Materials/Methods Action/Strategy	Person Responsible
PLP				
11/98				
1/99				
3/99				
5/99				

Signatures: _____   _____
                     Parent/Guardian   LEA

Status Code: 1 = implementation not yet begun   2 = outcome partially accomplished with physical support
3 = outcome partially accomplished with verbal support   4 = outcome partially accomplished,
performance intermittent   5 = outcome predictably accomplished

Figure 7.2 *Continued*

14. IEP Revisions   Page ___ of ___

Date: ___ / ___ / ___   Date: ___ / ___ / ___   Date: ___ / ___ / ___

Modifications to Annual Goals:

_____

_____

_____

_____

_____

_____

_____

Modifications to Benchmarks/Objectives:

_____

_____

_____

_____

_____

_____

_____

_____

Other Modifications:

_____

_____

_____

_____

_____

_____

_____

_____

Signatures: _____   LEA _____

Notes: _____

_____

_____

_____

_____

_____

_____

_____

Figure 7.2 *Continued*

too extensive can be included in the portfolio as an attachment. The most recent evaluation is noted. For school age children, educational test information is usually stated in grade-level equivalents (1–5; first grade, fifth month); for younger children developmental information is given in age equivalents (AE 4.7; 4 years, 7 months).

In many cases, the examiner's remarks indicating the quality of the child's behavior are as helpful as the test results themselves. They will often not only tell you about a child's strengths, but also give information about cooperation, motivation, response to failure, persistence, and so on.

Part 5 is designed to tie the previous information together with the child's strengths and the parent's concerns. Although some of the previous information could be filled in before the IEP meeting, this section cannot. Parents need to be participating team members and their concerns need to be part of the formal planning process as well as their perceptions of their child's strengths. This section needs discussion by the IEP team.

Part 6 focuses on eligibility and the various areas of services the child is eligible for. Decisions need to be made about whether or not the child does have a disability based on federal and state guidelines and what that disability is (for most young children it will be developmentally delayed), and whether or not there is a co-occurring or secondary disability that will influence a child's educational programming. A decision also must be made as to whether the child will participate in the statewide assessments, if so, are accommodations necessary, and what is the rationale. Has the child had an assistive technology assessment, again, if not, why. Some children will need specialized transportation. Some children have an individualized discipline or behavior plan that is part of their IEP. Some children will meet the criteria for an extended school year. This area is a reminder that all these things should be thought about and considered. For some children, they may be relevant at one time and not at others.

Part 7 focuses on the transition plan. An informal transition plan should always be part of a child's move from one teacher or grade level to another. This plan should be formalized when a child moves from the birth to 3 program into programming for children 3 to 6. This is especially true if the service provider changes.

Part 8 addresses the format of the child's educational program. The expectation is that the child will be in regular education with the necessary supports specified as well as receiving specialized educational services. (These specialized services may include a paraprofessional who comes in for 15 minutes four times a day to help with toileting, or a sign language interpreter, 4 hours each day.) The number of hours per week a child receives these supports and the location are noted. Any time that the child is not in regular education should be noted with a rationale. Some school provide pediatric medical personnel, social workers, home-school visitors, and other special services. If they are used, it should be noted here.

These are the supports that are available to help the child remain in the regular classroom. It may be that one necessary support is to reduce class size or for the teacher to receive some specialized training before a child enters her classroom. If a child needs specialized help in a subject matter area such as reading or math, that is noted in the far right column with time and location noted.

If the child is also in another setting, such as child care, does an early childhood consultant need to provide some training to the early care and education personnel and visit on a regular basis? If so, it needs to be noted.

Part 9 looks at the related services the child will be provided (this includes occupational therapy, physical therapy, speech and language therapy, and so on). The particular area is noted (fine motor, gross motor, speech, and so on), the type of services provided whether it is individual, group, or whether the specialist serves as a consultant for the teacher, and the frequency, time, and location. (This may be an area of contention because parents often want children to receive more individualized services than local agencies.) The available specializations and the amount of time specialists can devote to children vary from child to child and school to school but whatever they are, they need to be agreed upon and put in writing on the form.

Part 10 details the names of those individuals who attend the meeting and their respective roles. In some instances, an individual may play more than one role. For example, the individual who comes with the knowledge base to translate the implications of the evaluations may also represent the local educational agency and would sign in both places. (The designations are given to ensure that all the individuals required by federal law do attend the meeting.) A service coordinator is required for children birth to 3, and it is always useful to have that individual's phone number. Likewise, it is useful for parents of children over 3 to have a designated contact person with a phone number.

Part 11 ensures that parents have been informed of their rights under the law and that they feel they understand them. They have the right to agree or disagree with the IEP and/or the placement of the child. If they disagree, they need to be provided with information about their rights and advocates to contact such as the mandated parent information centers in each state and the Protection and Advocacy System (see Educational Resources).

Part 12 provides a place to list general accommodations that are necessary for a particular child, such as allowing a child more time to complete a test or assignment. These may deal with related but not necessarily educational issues such as closing the windows if they are cutting the grass or not going outside during certain weather conditions. They are conditions that allow the child to be available for learning.

Part 13 is the Annual Goals and Benchmarks/Objectives. This part of the plan requires a strong developmental understanding of children as well as synthesis, creativity, and perseverance. Here the

When individualizing programming, children's likes and dislikes as well as their strengths and challenges need to be taken into consideration.

year's individualized plan for the child is laid out. The programming task involves stating annual goals, benchmarks, or instructional objectives, and then choosing activities to accomplish the goals. The child's name is at the top, and the parent or guardian and a member of the local education agency also signs. There may be only one annual goal, but that would be unusual. Part 13 is repeated for each annual goal. The number of benchmarks, or objectives, will vary with the goal.

- *Writing annual goals.* These are statements of long-range, but measurable goals. They are based on the child's strengths and areas of need and on both informal and formal assessments of the child, developmentally appropriate practice, knowledge about the child's developmental profile, and regular educational standards. Annual goals relate to a particular developmental/educational area such as gross or fine motor development, language arts and literacy, mathematics, and so on. Within that domain, they are more specific. Although an annual goal in the area of mathematics could be *To improve math concepts;* a better one would focus on an aspect of mathematics such as *To improve knowledge of patterns and relationships.*

- *Present level of performance (PLP).* Annual goals are to be the focus for a year so they are

broad but measurable. Where does one begin? The only way to answer that question is to know what the child is able to do at the present time. With older children, achievement tests are often used to provide this information, with younger children it is more of a challenge. If we go back to the annual goal of *To improve knowledge of patterns and relationships,* we need to find out if a child can continue a simple pattern. (If you start a pattern of black, white, black, white . . . and then ask the child to continue the pattern, can he? If not, check to be sure he can match the colors.) If he can match the colors but cannot repeat the pattern, his PLP is *can match colors but cannot identify simple repeating patterns.* This information tells you where to place your first benchmark or objective.

- *Benchmarks and instructional objectives.* Annual goals are further broken down into benchmarks or objectives for instructional purposes. Benchmarks clarify what a particular goal means, provide a way of monitoring attainment, and are matched to the child's present level of performance. Like anything else, once you know how to write benchmarks or instructional objectives it is not difficult. (Information on how to do this follows.) The number of pages of annual goals will depend upon the number of developmental/educational areas that are being planned for. There may be only one page of annual goals or, more frequently, three or more pages. The length is dependent upon the child and the district and state guidelines. Both parents and a representative of the local educational agency need to sign each of these pages.

Part 14 is the final portion of the plan. It is designed to both acknowledge and make possible revisions to the plan. These changes also need signatures.

Think of this plan as a useful system of keeping track of information about a child. Help parents to think about it that way as well. As you talk about annual goals and benchmarks, discuss with parents what you will do in the classroom to ensure the child meets the goal and the types of *doing* experiences parents might do at home that would enhance the child's learning. This is a team effort and all members of the team should be committed to helping the child reach the agreed upon goals.

Annual Goals, Benchmarks, and Instructional Objectives

Benchmarks or instructional objectives form the backbone of the individualized plan.

Annual Goals

Annual goals are, by law, measurable and are usually based on the regular education curriculum. National standards and state developed performance indicators provide the guidance for the broad base for this curriculum. The annual goals in this text are based on the national standards developed by the various professional organizations and detailed in Chapter 18. These goals are also the basis for the activities in Chapters 19 to 23.

Comparing Benchmarks and Instructional Objectives

Benchmarks are broader than instructional objectives; one benchmark could be a source of many instructional objectives. The specific benchmarks used are determined by how benchmarks are defined and at what level of generality benchmarks are given. "Benchmarks do not describe trivial or 'easy' knowledge or skills for the developmental level at which they are found. They are not descriptions of knowledge and skill that have been narrowed through behavioral objectives or by a translation into an instructional objective" (Kendall & Marazano, 1996, p. 25). Appropriate benchmarks are determined by the content area, the time interval between benchmarks, the developmental level (or grade) of the program and the projected rate of growth of the individual child.

Benchmarks have a lower and upper limit and they describe behaviors that take time to master.

"Uses spelling that demonstrates some letter/sound associations" might be a benchmark at the kindergarten level in the area of writing literacy. The key to writing benchmarks is developmental knowledge. The language skills needed to frame the developmental information is easy to learn. Because objectives are so specific, it requires many of them to cover a content area (Kendall & Marazano, 1996). This gets cumbersome if all are included or parts of a content domain may be missed if objectives are left out. Benchmarks provide necessary guidance without the burden of developing so many objectives. Some professionals, especially with a strong behaviorist base, will prefer to use instructional objectives. The federal law allows the use of either benchmarks or instructional objectives.

Regardless of whether benchmarks or instructional objectives are used they need to be based on the child's present level of performance. And, the key to both is sequential learning. As procedures for writing instructional objectives is more clearly laid out let's begin there.

Writing Instructional Objectives

Instructional objectives focus on the sequenced prerequisite skills that are necessary to attain an annual goal. These skills are written in such a way that anyone can tell whether the child has learned the skill and is making appropriate progress toward attaining the goal. To help satisfy this empirical requirement, there are rules for writing these objectives.

Mager (1962) described behavioral objectives as having three components: a target behavior, a description of conditions under which the behavior is to be demonstrated, and a criteria for acceptable performance. Instructional objectives are based on this principle but add a few twists.

The first step in writing an instructional objective is easy. You must decide who is going to implement the action: the child, the teacher, or the parent. Second, determine what is going to be done. This is more difficult because you must be able to measure (see) what is done. This means that some words—such as *understand, know, appreciate, try, feel, discover,* and *think*—cannot be used. Early childhood educators have more difficulty with this step than other educators because young children have a smaller repertoire of behaviors that traditional words—such as *write, list, translate, read, predict,* and *compare*—represent skills the children in their class may not yet have achieved. A starter list of "doing" words might include the following:

point to	match	select	tell	order
say	label	repeat	name	pick out
choose	find	color	copy	dramatize
dictate	set up	state	arrange	locate
define	look at	draw	circle	hop
run	jump	walk	cut out	count

In the third step of writing instructional objectives, state the object of the action. Fourth, impose conditions to make the task easier or more difficult. Here is what a sample objective might look like so far:

> Tinea *(doer)*/will hop *(action)*/on left foot *(object)*/for 10 feet *(condition)*.

The conditions may also determine what will or will not be available to the child. They can be set forth at the beginning or end of the instructional objective. This is usually a matter of the writer's style and how the sentence best makes sense.

The fifth and final step is to develop an evaluation criterion. How well or how often does this objective need to be achieved for you as the teacher to decide that it has been mastered? Examples of criteria include: using at least two colors within 10 seconds, two out of three times, or 80 percent of the time. Because of human variability, it is unwise to anticipate a 100 percent performance, even when you think this can be achieved. For a variety of reasons, children often decide not to comply with requests. You need to build flexibility into your evaluation criterion. You also need to give some thought to what you specifically need to do to test whether or not the instructional objective has been met. How will you know it is 80 percent of the time unless you allow the child at least 5 trials (you can convert 4 out 5 trials to 80 percent, if you choose 90 percent you have to use 10 trials). Will this get "old" for you and the child? Think about it before you write it down.

Putting it all together then, an instructional objective might look like this:

> Given paper and crayons, the child will draw a picture using at least two colors.
>
> *Condition:* Given paper and crayons
>
> *Doer:* the child
>
> *Action:* will draw
>
> *Object:* a picture
>
> *Evaluation:* using at least 2 colors

For the purpose of illustrating the process of writing an instructional objective, we have used a concrete and very specific example. In practice, your objectives can often benefit by being more general, however, if an objective is too general, it will be difficult to verify empirically. Also, the objectives or benchmarks as a group should support the annual goal in such a way that the attainment of each progressively more difficult objective should ensure the attainment of the goal.

Objectives with enough flexibility to allow for individual differences lend themselves more readily to variety in programming. For example, to improve a child's social skills with peers, you may want to have that child interact with others. Your objective may read:

> Given paper and watercolor paints, Cathy will paint a mural of a rainy day with two other children for 10 minutes.

However, you have put a lot of wasted thought and time into Cathy's IEP if she happens to hate painting, and hates painting rainy day scenes most of all. A more general objective that achieves the same purpose reads:

> Given the appropriate materials, Cathy will participate in an activity with at least two other children for 10 minutes.

This gives you and the child the option of using playdough, fingerpaint, cornstarch, and so on to fulfill the objective. It also provides the potential for varying the conditions, instead of art, you could use blocks or dramatic play, increase the number of children to three and even make some statement about their level of participation (that is, how much interaction you expect).

Several things may become apparent as you review this procedure. It is much simpler to write trivial objectives than important ones. Furthermore, some of the qualities you value most are almost impossible to put into behavioral terms, for example, empathy, creativity, cooperation, joy, and interest. Finally, it is clear you will have to develop a system of record keeping to determine whether or not these objectives have been fulfilled.

Objectives should be arranged from simple to more difficult, as well as from high to low priority. For example, if your annual goal is to improve listening skills, your objectives may include skills in auditory discrimination. Perhaps you decide you want the child to distinguish between a bell and a siren. This is a relatively easy task—providing the child's present level of performance includes auditory identification of these objects; that is, that the child can identify each sound by itself. To test the child on auditory identification, ring the bell and ask, "What is this?" Sound the siren and ask the question again. Repeat the sounds behind a screen. Can the child identify the sound without a visual cue? If so, the child can auditorially identify the bell and the siren. This does not mean, however, that he or she can distinguish between the two sounds when played together. Once the child demonstrates the prerequisite skills, you may proceed with more difficult tasks. Be sure you have included enough objectives, in terms of both quantity and scope, to attain your goal. It takes many objectives to cover a developmental/educational area.

Setting priorities, deciding what to do first, is sometimes difficult. Parents' choices and children's preferences are a primary consideration. However, parents may not be aware of how the objectives you have chosen lead to the accomplishment of the particular goal. If parents want their child to read, yet the child cannot identify letters and letter-sound relationships, you need to be prepared to help parents understand why these are important prerequisite skills. This doesn't mean that goal isn't appropriate, it means it may take a long time to reach and you and the parents need to be clear about how the objectives chosen develop prerequisite skills that lead to the attainment of the goal. If you don't have guidance from the parents about priorities, ask yourself about each annual goal: How difficult will it be in the future if the child doesn't learn _____? The more the child will need this skill, the higher the priority you could assign the annual goal and the more time designated to work on the objectives to meet this goal.

Your knowledge of child development, the child's condition and capacity, and your assessment of the difficulty of the task, are reflected in the objectives you choose. Whether using objectives or benchmarks, evenly spaced objectives/benchmarks show progress toward a goal in a way that supports feedback to both the parents and the teacher and may coincide with when report cards are traditionally sent home:

> *Annual Goal:* Stan will name primary and secondary colors.
>
> *Present Level of Performance (PLP):* Stan cannot receptively or expressively identify primary colors.
>
> *11/98:* Given an easel and paints in three primary colors, Stan will point to the correct color when named 3 out of 4 times.
>
> *1/99:* Given an easel and paints in three primary colors, the child will name the colors on request 3 out of 4 times.
>
> *3/99:* Given an easel and paints in 3 primary colors, Stan will mix 2 colors to make another color and name the colors 3 out of 4 times.
>
> *5/99:* Given an easel and paints in three primary colors and black and white, Stan will mix colors to make 3 secondary colors and shades of 3 primary colors and name the colors 3 out of 4 times.

The law requires that the progress of children with disabilities be reported with the same frequency as children without disabilities. This streamlines the reporting process and is congruent with the philosophy of normalization. In most cases, the date you pick will be your best guess as to when the child will be able to perform that particular task. Some tasks are easier than others. Also, our assumption is that learning is linear. That is, a child learns the color red, then adds blue, then yellow, and so on. This doesn't take into account the child who suddenly learns that colors have names and learns 20 colors in a week.

Likewise, we assume if a child can already point to one color, during the fall the child will learn others. If, however, you only expect the child to point to colors in June of the following year, a parent may question your teaching ability and the point of spending a year on learning to point to colors. Setting dates requires you to think through typical child developmental patterns, what you will teach a child, and how many opportunities in a day, week, or month the child will have to practice the skills you are teaching.

The dates you choose and the difficulty of the task will depend on the individual child.

Writing Benchmarks

A benchmark related to the visual arts would probably frame the annual goal differently as well as using benchmarks:

> *Annual Goal:* To understand and apply different art media, techniques, and processes
>
> *(PLP):* The child cannot receptively or expressively identify primary colors.
>
> *11/98:* The child will explore different art materials, techniques, and processes including color.
>
> *1/99:* The child will discover how different materials, techniques, and processes, including color, cause different effects.
>
> *3/99:* The child will investigate how different materials, techniques, and processes, including color, communicate meaning.
>
> *6/99:* The child will use color in different materials, techniques, and processes to convey meaning.

The process feels different. The benchmarks don't state that the child will learn the names of the colors, rather, that the names will be learned in the process of learning broader concepts in the visual arts.

Think about where you are the most comfortable. Then stretch yourself a little. Regardless of the process you use, you must ensure that your everyday programming includes enough opportunities to practice that the necessary learning takes place.

Matching Activities to Benchmarks or Objectives

The next step in the process is the most challenging. It involves choosing and adapting activities that meet the objectives or benchmarks you have set. You need to think in terms of the underlying principles of how children learn, developmentally appropriate practices, and how you plan for children. Activities to support benchmarks or objectives and annual goals must fit in these parameters. To program inclusively, you must meet the learning needs of all children not just those for whom you have annual goals. As you choose activities to support objectives/benchmarks, remember:

1. Choose activities that use as many senses as possible (vision, taste, touch, hearing, smell).

2. Choose activities that reinforce the goal but have many variations. Repetition helps children master a concept but repeating the same activity is boring. If you are working to improve measurement concepts, have children measure both wet and dry materials (water, sand, beans, bird seed, coffee grounds or beans, cornmeal, and so on).

This provides a broad base for learning about a variety of concepts including measurement as well as fitting into a variety of themes that support generalization and contextual learning.

3. Use variety when presenting the same information. Color, for example, can be shown through clothing, painting, bingo, gelatin, and nature walks, to name just a few.

Part 3 of this text is designed to implement this aspect of the requirements. For example, if your goal were *To improve sensorimotor integration* and you looked in the Activity Index at the back of the book, you would find 47 activities listed that implement this goal. You would have to decide which activities to use in what particular progression and how to vary them to meet the child's needs. Part 2 of the text provides guidelines for adapting activities you already do to include children with diverse abilities.

Record Keeping

Good record keeping is indispensable for implementing an IEP. Much of your record keeping will be the same as that described in Chapter 6 on assessment. However, for children with an IEP, in addition to the records that you keep on all the children, you must focus some record keeping on annual goals.

Quick notes or anecdotal records jotted down throughout the week will help your memory; for example, 9/28 J. & Sally, blocks 5 min.

A one-page outline that corresponds directly to the child's IEP will be a reminder to be sure children have many opportunities and that you are keeping track of their progress on a regular basis. In an outline report, numbers and key words identify the goals and objectives (see Figure 7.3). Check, plus, and minus signs are also helpful shorthand for daily notes.

	9/15	10/15	Evaluation criteria 11/15
Tinea B.			
1. Fine Motor			
1.1 beads	✓–	✓–	5 of 10 correct
1.2 copy forms	✓–	✓+	3 of 5 correct
1.3 5 block tower	✓	✓	4 blocks
2. Language Concepts			
2.1 colors	✓	✓	5 of 8 receptive
2.2 numbers	✓	✓+	1–5 expressive
2.3 prepositions	✓–	✓	on, under beside, in/recep.
KEY: NA	No attempt		
✓–	Attempted, little success		
✓	Attempted, shows progress		
✓+	Attained criterion		

Figure 7.3   Weekly Report (Outline)

John H.11/15/82
   Fine Motor: J. is still demonstrating needs in this area. He can now build a four-block tower and copy 3/5 (three out of five) forms, including _____, ○, □ . Bead stringing is still very difficult for J.
   Language: J.'s language quality has improved since September. He is now speaking in 4–5 word sentences and nearly always expresses himself in full sentences. He can identify 5/8 colors and can recite the numbers 1–5. He can follow a one-step direction containing the following prepositions: on, under, beside, in.

Figure 7.4   Weekly Report (Anecdotal)

Figure 7.4 shows how anecdotal notes can be used for record keeping. The choice of how you keep records is yours, but you must keep records.

Working with Specialists

In the process of writing and implementing an IEP, you will work as part of a multidisciplinary IEP team that includes parents, other educators, administrators, and specialists who may work with the child either within or outside the classroom.

Understanding a child's pattern of behavior in the context of developmental norms and the environment is essential in developing an individualized educational plan for a child.

Writing the IEP

Knowing the requirements for filling out an IEP and actually doing it for a specific child are two different things. Full-time special educators and specialists who work only with children with disabilities may write anywhere from 8 to 90 full or partial IEPs a year, depending on their case load. Depending upon the child and the situation in which you work you may have a major responsibility in drafting the IEP, you may only be expected to write one or two annual goals, or you may be expected to react to the *draft* IEP. Note the word *draft*. Hopefully incidents such as the one at the beginning of this chapter will not occur again. If you give a parent a typed IEP with seven carbons it doesn't look like a draft. Nor is there the expectation that each person walks in the room with a blank piece of paper. When preparing for the IEP conference, you must organize your thoughts and ideas in writing. Instead of shuffling through notes and reports, have one sheet of paper outlining the essential information you already have and pointing out information you need to obtain at the meeting as well as a draft of some annual goals and benchmarks or objectives.

A Sample Case

Everyone, including the parents, should come to the IEP meeting with the following information: the parents or guardians perceptions, assessments, observations, records, documented interventions, and reports by specialists. The purpose of this IEP

Psychological Evaluation

Student: Joanna P.   Date of birth: 8/2/93
Examiner: Mrs. F.,   Date of evaluation: 1/25/98
  School Psychologist   Age: 4 years 6 months

Reason for referral: Unpredictable behaviors (varies between physical aggression and withdrawal). Poor peer relationships.

Assessments used: Peabody Picture Vocabulary Test (PPVT), Form A; McCarthy Scales of Children's Abilities (MSCA); Observational data (classroom observation)

Background Observation:
This four-and-a-half-year-old girl was referred for a psychological evaluation by her child care provider, who felt her behavior was "aggressive at times and withdrawn at other times." An occupational therapist's evaluation was also recommended by this examiner and has been scheduled. It is reported that Joanna is an asthmatic who has attacks when she is upset. It is also reported that she may feign attacks on occasion. The family has moved three times in the past two years.

A classroom observation by this examiner was conducted prior to testing. Some aggression noted by this examiner seemed to occur immediately following activities that may have been frustrating for Joanna. One example: After being unable to snap a doll's dress in the housekeeping corner, Joanna hit another child while having a tantrum. A contrast to this behavior was seen on the day examinations were administered, when Joanna's mother brought her to this examiner's office.

Rapport was quickly established. She separated easily from her mother, offering her hand and a shy smile. The quality and intelligibility of her speech were good, but she spoke very little spontaneously. Near the end of the evaluation, she said "I want my mommy" several times. When allowed to see her mother, she immediately returned to the testing area quite happily. She did begin to tire, however, as the testing drew to a close. She became so tired that, when her mother was talking afterward, she fell sound asleep on the mother's lap. Joanna was generally cooperative and attentive throughout testing.

Intellectual Functioning:
As measured by the PPVT, this child's receptive vocabulary is at a "high average" level, being equivalent to that of a child of 5.0 years. Her general cognitive ability, as assessed by the McCarthy Scales, is equivalent to that of a child of 4.0 years, a delay of six months. Her most highly developed skills are in verbal expression and understanding. Quantitative and memory skills fall within the average range. Her perceptual performance and motor skills are lower, falling in the borderline range. Her relational thinking ability is at a "high average" level as measured on the Opposite Analogies subtest, being equivalent to that of a child of 5 years 10 months. Her ability to count and sort blocks is "average." Her memory skills and understanding of quantitative words are "average."

Conclusions and Recommendations:
Although this child's general level of functioning at the present time is only equivalent to the mental age of a child 4 years and 4 months, there is evidence that her intellectual potential may be higher. Her perception of spatial relationships and manipulative skills, rated on the Block Building subtest, are her least developed abilities. These problems could be dealt with in a prekindergarten program with occupational therapy included.

Also, it is recommended that Joanna be evaluated by her physician for possible attention deficit hyperactivity disorder and that she participate in counseling to enhance her peer relationships and help her deal with her frustrations.

Mrs. F.
_____
(Signature)

Figure 7.5 Sample Psychological Evaluation

team meeting is to organize and evaluate the information to develop a program that meets the priorities of the family and ensures that the child will have the accommodations in place to make adequate progress in mastering the general curriculum to the best of her ability.

The IEP team, then (1) confirms their interpretation of the test results, (2) relates these interpretations to the parents' priorities and to the additional observations and information about the child, (3) determines the significance of the data for the child's education, and (4) develops the IEP with teaching strategies and support services designed to implement the child's learning. Figures 7.5–7.7 are sample reports typical of those you may receive about a child. They illustrate neither extremely good nor bad reports, but are average.

You now have a little more information about Joanna. You can see that this child has as many nonclinical "special considerations" as she has tested clinical needs. And although you have a general idea of Joanna's low frustration level, you could benefit from information on what she specifically dislikes.

Looking at the strengths and you can determine some skills that she can work on to develop a more positive self concept and others that need practice to match her developmental level.

Joanna does not appear to have good peer relationships; and, she may feel she doesn't have much control over her environment (extrapolation based on the moves and the asthma). These can begin to frame some of what you want to program for. The next step is to think about general developmental/educational areas that work toward her overall development—working through her strengths to meet her needs. For example:

Social Awareness

To improve self-esteem

To increase awareness of roles people play

To increase inclusion

To increase awareness of individual differences and similarities

To improve problem solving skills

Occupational Therapy Evaluation

Student: Joanna P. Date of birth: 8/2/93
Examiner: Mr. M., Date of evaluation: 1/30/98
 Occupational Age: 4.6
 Therapist

Joanna P. was seen for an occupational therapy evaluation on 1/30/98. Scores from a recent psychological examination indicate weakness in motor skills and perceptual performance.

Joanna P. was brought to the evaluation by her mother. She went readily with the examiner. During the evaluation she tended to wander from the task and had to be repeatedly refocused to the testing. She exhibited some testing behavior, such as scratching her nails on the blackboard and then looking to the examiner for a reaction. Joanna worked best with manipulative materials.

The examiner administered a developmental assessment and the Developmental Test of Visual Motor Integration.

Results:
Joanna's performance on the tactile portion of the developmental assessment indicated that she has awareness of touch and pressure input and can localize tactile input (for example, she knows which finger is touched). Joanna was able to identify correctly four out of four basic textures.

Joanna's gross motor performance was found to vary from that of a 3- to 4-year-old. Response to vestibular input was within normal limits, but Joanna fell off the nystagmus board following rotation. This response suggests that Joanna has difficulty stabilizing her body in dynamic movement experiences. Joanna tended to use each hand on the same side of the body, suggesting inadequate postural flexibility or difficulty in crossing the

midline. For drawing tests, Joanna preferred her right hand, and all graphic reproductions were shifted to the right side of the paper—further evidence of inadequate flexibility. Gross motor planning was found to be adequate.

Fine motor planning activities, such as tapping sequence, were stressful for Joanna. Joanna was able to use both sides of the body together in a coordinated fashion.

During block manipulation tasks, Joanna was able to build a cube bridge and a tower of nine blocks (36-month skills). She was unable to copy an oblique bridge (42-month skill).

Visual motor performance was at the 36-month level, a year and a half below age expectancy. Visual-perceptual performance was also below Joanna's chronological age. She is beginning to use insight to nest and stack rings and blocks. She was unable to nest cans or tower blocks (36- and 42-month skills). She was able to sort blocks according to big-little (42-month skill).

Joanna holds a pencil high on the shaft and does not have a refined, adult-like grasp.

Summary and Recommendations:
Joanna's sensorimotor needs include the following:

1. Improve postural stability and flexibility
2. Improve fine motor planning
3. Improve visual-perceptual performance

Occupational therapy is recommended to meet these needs. It is also recommended that she be placed in an extremely structured program that will provide firm behavioral controls.

Mr. M., O.T.R.

Occupational Therapist

Figure 7.6 Sample Occupational Therapy Evaluation

Child Study Team Report   2/5/98

Student: Joanna P.

In attendance: Mrs. P., mother; Mrs. F., psychologist; Mr. M., occupational therapist; Ms. L., early childhood educator; Mrs. R., early childhood consultant.

Joanna P. is a 4-and-a-half-year-old girl who recently moved to this suburban area from a rural setting. Joanna's father has obtained a job as a salesman with a local firm. Prior to this, Joanna's family moved quite often, three times in the past two years, as Mr. P. was transferred frequently.

Records from Joanna's former preschool identify her as a problem child. Joanna also has asthma. Joanna does not have a current IEP, but testing was completed. The report in the file states that Joanna was referred because of extreme moodiness and frequent physical aggression. Observations by the school psychologist and by the teacher confirm this, reporting both elation or withdrawal. Her mother stated that she was a very difficult infant unlike her sister and brother. The psychological report notes that Joanna is easily frustrated and frequently cries and throws temper tantrums when she cannot do something. One example is a temper tantrum after Joanna could not snap a doll's dress in the housekeeping corner.

Testing was completed by the psychologist in one session, during which Joanna was cooperative and attentive. Aptitude testing identifies Joanna as being average in ability with some variation in test scores. Pencil and paper tasks and those requiring concentration (such as block designs and motor skills) were more difficult for Joanna. She seemed to enjoy more verbal subtests, such as vocabulary and even digit span (repeating digits presented orally).

At the request of the psychologist, Joanna's parents scheduled an appointment with her pediatrician Dr. Mark, for a thorough evaluation to determine whether Joanna might have ADHD, and to see if some of the newer asthma treatments might help control Joanna's asthma better. (Dr. Mark has not yet completed his evaluation.) During the occupational therapy evaluation session, Joanna was slightly more resistive. Tactile development and gross motor planning were adequate, while gross and fine motor performance and visual motor performance were below age level. Occupational therapy was recommended.

Joanna, according to her former teacher's reports, was frequently absent from school. (She had several asthma attacks at school, which seemed to increase in frequency when Joanna learned the family was moving.) The other children generally did not respond well to Joanna due to her unpredictable behavior, and because they did not want to provoke an asthma attack. Joanna feigned attacks when she didn't get her way with the other children. Joanna enjoyed one-to-one attention from adults and older children. She worked best in a small group and needed a lot of verbal praise and affection. The teacher felt Joanna needed to learn ways to express frustration, anger, and fear. She also felt Joanna needed to develop healthy peer relationships. Based on the preschool teacher's observations as well as her own, the psychologist recommended family therapy.

Joanna lives at home with her father, mother, older sister, and younger brother. Mr. P. plans to remain in the area longer than his previous job allowed.

Figure 7.7   Sample Child Study Team Report

To increase adaptive skills

To express feelings

Language and Literacy

To improve expressive communication

To increase vocabulary

To improve reading literacy

Developmental Physical Education and Sensorimotor Skills

To improve sensorimotor integration

To improve fine motor manipulative skills

To increase body awareness

Although there might be more, these seem representative. Until you get input from Joanna's family it is difficult to prioritize them. However you might think about a rational for your choices:

Social Awareness. You always need to start with the child. A child who doesn't feel good about herself isn't likely to develop the skills to reach out to others. The first skill is to increase Joanna's awareness of herself and what she can do. She needs to see herself as a problem solver, she needs to develop adaptive skills to increase her independence (including the asthma) and to become more aware of her feelings. She needs to be included and learn to include others.

Language and Literacy. The expressive communication and vocabulary were chosen because if Joanna could express herself better she might learn ways to join groups as well as talk about what she finds frustrating. Writing is an area that may be difficult and we need to think about ways to make it intriguing.

Developmental Physical Education and Sensorimotor Skills. Joanna needs to increase her awareness of her body, how it moves, and when these movements relate to the asthma. As she becomes more in tune with her body, she will be aware sooner of her needs in this area. She needs to work on sensory motor integration (in addition to what the occupational therapist will do). Likewise, she needs to practice her fine motor manipulative skills. These latter two are not areas she is particularly interested in so the impetus to participate must come from the teacher designing intriguing activities rather than forcing the child into a drill and practice situation.

Now you are prepared for the IEP conference. The actual IEP should be filled out at the conference. Parents need to have input and decide upon their priorities. Their suggestion and involvement is a mandated part of the IEP process.

An example of what part of an IEP might finally look like is shown in Figure 7.8. Rather than give you all the goals and objectives, one annual goal using objectives and a similar one using annual goals *and* benchmarks are shown.

What you have been given is the ideal way the IEP should be developed. In reality, the process may be different. Some IEPs are generated from a computer with parents and teachers having little input. Some educators are told that they can have only one or two goals, regardless of the needs of the child. After the IEP is filled out, you may find that you hold the illegible sixth copy of the form. This is tremendously discouraging as far as paperwork is concerned; however, if your goal is to appropriately individualize programming for children, do not be discouraged, but finish the process for the child, the family, and yourself. The law sets *minimum* requirements that can be exceeded by state laws and individual educators. Our hope is that your goal for yourself is to be an optimal teacher and go beyond the minimal requirements.

The law sets different requirements for individualized planning when children are between birth and age 3.

Individualized Family Service Plans

The Individualized Family Service Plan (IFSP) is one component of Part C of P.L. 105-17, the 1997 Amendments to the IDEA. Infants and toddlers (0–3) will have an IFSP. Children 3 through 5 can have either an IFSP or an IEP. The purpose of the IFSP is to identify, organize, and facilitate the attainment of families' goals for themselves to support their children. The process of interacting and joining with families in their exploration of their strengths and goals for themselves and their children may be more important than the IFSP itself. The IFSP requires professionals to add new skills to their repertoire and to go beyond the traditional boundaries of their disciplines. It acknowledges families and enables them to use or develop the competencies necessary to capitalize on their strengths and those of their children (Dunst, Trivette, & Deal, 1988).

The central idea of an IFSP is that services should be family-centered instead of child-centered. Every IFSP will look different in this regard. The IFSP will change as the family and child change because the process and resulting product are *family-driven.*

Families decide what they want as outcomes on the IFSP. They may make an informed decision to allow professionals to implement plans to reach those outcomes, but they *decided* to do that.

Although it is the process that is important, sometimes the product tells us about the process. Because infants and toddlers are not the same as *small preschoolers,* the IFSP should not bring to it the behavioral, child-focused approach of the IEP.

Principles Underlying the IFSP Process

The following set of ten principles underlying the IFSP process have been adapted from those identified by Johnson, McGonigel, and Kaufmann (1989):

1. Infants and toddlers are dependent upon adults for survival; because of this dependency, a family-centered approach is essential.

2. The definition of "family" must reflect a diversity of family patterns and structures. We must expand our definition of family beyond biological ties.

3. Families are diverse; each must be respected for its structures, roles, values, beliefs, and coping styles.

4. Early intervention service delivery systems and strategies must respect and be congruent with the racial, ethnic, and cultural diversity of families.

5. Families are the decision makers. Families choose the early intervention program and how they want to be involved with it.

6. Professionals need to develop skills that promote mutual respect and partnerships with parents.

7. Service delivery systems must be flexible, accessible, and responsive to family needs.

8. Infants and toddlers and their families should have access to services that allow them to function in as "normal" an environment as possible; that is, they should be included in the neighborhood, school, and community as equal partners.

9. Partnerships and collaboration between families and professionals are necessary to successfully implement the IFSP process.

10. A team approach to planning and implementing the IFSP is necessary as no one agency or discipline can meet the needs of infants and toddlers with disabilities and their families.

Content of the IFSP

Much like the IEP, the content of the IFSP is determined by law, which specifies that the early intervention services must include a multidisciplinary assessment and a written Individual Family Service Plan (IFSP) to be developed with the family.

1. Child and Family Identification and Information

Child's Name: _Joanna Price_   D.O.B.: _8_ / _2_ / _93_   CA: _4_ / _6_ / _8_

Current Educational Settings: _Headstart_   Report Date 2/10/98

School District: _Christiana_

Parent/Guardian/Surrogate Parent: Parent/Guardian/Surrogate Parent:

Mr. & Mrs. Price

Address:

2009 Indian Rd.   _NA_

Newark, DE 19716

Telephone (location if not in home):

_302-833-1920_

Custody Status: _biological parents_

Living Arrangements: _lives at home_

2. Record of Informal Assessments

Observations (include date, observer, location, purpose, summary):

Teacher: New child seems to be out of control a lot. Temper tantrums without provocation, high level of frustration, some adjustment

problems. (10/15/97) (See notes from psychologist observation. Headstart; concern about behavior)

Informal Assessments (include date, assessment, purpose):

We really didn't know what to do.

Interventions and Accommodations (include date, intervener, intervention, outcome):

We tried to have playdough out a lot but she didn't like that. We talked to her about feelings and why children cried when she hit them.

We told her we were worried when she sat in her locker. Nothing really changed. (Nov. to Dec. 1997)

Parent Conference (date, time, location, who attended, outcome):

We decided to wait until after the holiday to talk to her parents. Her mother came to conference on 1/5/98 and we told

her our concerns about Joanna's emotional problems. We talked about the asthma, too, but that wasn't our major concern. Her mother

agreed to the evaluations.

3. IEP Status

IEP: _✓_   Initial: _2_ / _10_ / _98_   Annual Review: _2_ / _10_ / _99_

Revised: _/ /_   Initiation: _2_ / _10_ / _98_   Ending: _6_ / _15_ / _98_

Temporary Placement (Date begun: ____ / / ____) (Expected change: ____ / / ____)

Recommended Placement: _Continuation at Headstart, Kindergarten in Fall at Cape, regular placement._

Figure 7.8   Completed Individualized Planning Portfolio

4. Record of Formal Assessment

Developmental/Educational Information (include dates, tests, and results (attach) Most recent evaluation: ___/___/___	Medical/Clinical/Specialist Information (include dates, tests, and results (attach) Most recent evaluation: _1_/_30_/_98_
MSCA 10/10/97 Some variation in scores; strengths in verbal area — weakness in perceptual, visual motor	OT Eval 1/30/98 Therapy recommended to improve postural & visual–perceptual and motor performance
	Psy 1/25/98 counseling
	See physician for possible AD/HD.

5. Child's Strengths, Family Concerns, Implications of Formal and Informal Assessments

Joanna's verbal skills are good as is her vocabulary. She is really positive on a one-to-one basis. She seems to have a poor self concept; change is difficult for her; she has some challenging emotional responses, and her visual perceptual skills are low. Parents are most concerned about her emotional outbursts especially relative to her younger brother. They would like these brought under control.

6. Eligibility

Meets eligibility criteria: (yes) ✓ (no) ____ Disability(ies): _Developmentally Delayed_

(1) Participate in statewide assessment: (yes) ✓ (no) ____
(2) Assistive technology evaluation: (yes) ____ (no) ✓
(3) Specialized transportation: (yes) ____ (no) ✓
(4) Discipline/behavior plan: (yes) ____ (no) ✓
(5) Extended school year: (yes) ____ (no) ✓

Necessary Accommodations: Rationale: (note number)

Note: At this time we do not feel the need for a specialized Discipline/Behavior plan but that may be necessary in the future.

7. Transition

Contact person: _Ms. Hense_

8. Program Supports

Regular Education (area)	Supports (paraprofessional, consultation); Other	Specialized Educational Services (area)
All areas	Behavioral consultant will give 1 hr to support behavioral plan.	Social worker will talk with family about family therapy.
	Early childhood specialist will consult with Headstart.	
Time (hours/week): _all_	Time (hours/week): _1 hour/2 weeks_	Time (hours/week): _1 hour_
Location: _regular classroom_	Location: _Headstart_	Location: _Lexus Center_

Rationale for time not in regular education:

NA

Figure 7.8 *Continued*

9. Related Services

Area	Type*	Frequency	Time	Location
Occupational	I	1 hr every 2 weeks	9:00 Thursday	Headstart classroom

*I = Individual, G = Group, C = Consultative
Rationale for services not provided in regular education:

Note: Teacher is willing to learn from OT.

10. Participants Attending Meeting and Role

Name	Role*	Signature	Date
Mrs. Price	Parent/guardian/surrogate	Mrs. Price	
	Parent/guardian/surrogate		
Ms. Jones	Regular ed teacher	Ms. Jones	
Mr. Lucas	Special ed teacher	Mr. Lucas	
Ms. Klinzing	Rep LEA (curr/resources)	Ms. Klinzing	
Ms. Lowe	Implication of evals for ed	Ms. Lowe	
	Child		
Ms. Hense	Transition contact	Ms. Hense	
Ms. Agazidian	Other	Ms. Agazidian	
Mr. Hartman	Other	Mr. Hartman	

*Service coordinator or contact person designated. Phone _____

11. Parental Participation and Safe Guards

1. I acknowledge that I have received a copy of the procedural safeguards. I have read the information and my due process rights under those procedural safeguards have been explained to me so I feel comfortable making a decision.
2. I agree/disagree (circle one) with the IEP as written or amended in this document.
3. I agree/disagree (circle one) with the placement decision as written or amended in this document.

Ms. Pamela Price _____   2 / 10 /98

_____   / /

(Parent/Guardian/Surrogate Signature(s)

4. If I disagree, the options available to me have been explained to me and resources have been given to me so I can follow through on my decision.

_____   / /

_____   / /

(Parent/Guardian/Surrogate Signature(s)

12. General Accommodations

1. No accommodations needed. _____
2. Accommodations:

Close windows when mowing. Nurse can take her to emergency room if she can't breathe. Replace shag carpet.

Remove rabbit from classroom.

Figure 7.8   Continued

3. Annual Goals, Benchmarks/Objectives

Child's Name: _Joanna P._   Date: _9/20/98_   Page ___ of ___

Developmental/Educational Area: _Social and Emotional Development_

Annual Goal _To identify and appropriately express feelings_

PLP _Joanna can identify basic emotions (happy, sad) but not more complex emotions (worried, curious). She often displays her emotions in a situationally inappropriate way_

Date	Status	Benchmark/Objective	Materials/Methods Action/Strategy	Person Responsible
11/98	1	Joanna will participate in more complex emotional relationships with peers and teachers (sociogram 2/98, 5/98) Direct teaching of labels for emotions	Adult scaffolding in free play (hospital, circus, doctor's office) Roleplay after relevant literature	Ms. L
1/99	1	Joanna will use more varied, complex and flexible expressions of feelings (Baseline 2/98, compare 3/98, 4/98, 5/98)	(Continue above) Focused questions, play-by-play, refined understanding, generating hypotheses, generalization.	Ms. L.
3/99	1	Joanna will represent her emotions through language, play, fantasy (Baseline 2/98, compare 3/98, 4/98, 5/98)	(Continue above) Comparing own emotions with others in literature, peers, and play.	Ms. L.
5/99	1	Joanna will reflect on her feels and those of others (anecdotal notes beginning 2/98)	Continue above in greater depth with more complex emotions.	Ms. L.

Signatures _____   _____
                Parent/Guardian   Ms. L.

Status Code: 1 = implementation not yet begun   2 = outcome partially accomplished with physical support 3 = outcome partially accomplished with verbal support   4 = outcome partially accomplished, performance intermittent   5 = outcome predictably accomplished

Figure 7.8 *Continued*

INDIVIDUALIZED EDUCATION PROGRAM:
GOALS AND OBJECTIVES

Child's Name: _Joanna P._   Date: _9/20/98_   Page ___ of ___

Developmental/Educational Area: _Social and Emotional Development_

Annual Goal _To increase feelings of group belonging/inclusion_

PLP _Plays alone most of the time, does not participate in large or small groups_

Date	Status	Benchmark/Objective	Materials/Methods Action/Strategy		Person Responsible
PLP					
2/98 3/98 5/98	1	Joanna will participate in large group time	Music, storytime, parachute games, puppets, visitor	1/5 days per week 3/5 days per week 4/5 days per week	Ms. L
2/98 5/98	1	Joanna will participate in structural games (inside and out) as requested with at least 2 other children.	Team games, creative movement,	1/2 of the time 3/4 of the time	Ms. L.
2/98 3/98 4/98 5/98	1	Joanna will participate in "freeplay" with 2–4 other children each day with teacher support	Teachers will actively support this group initially in Blocks, Dramatic play, etc., whichever area Joanna chooses	5 minutes 10 minutes 15 minutes 20 min	Ms. L.
2/98 4/98 5/98	1	Joanna will participate in freeplay with 2–4 other children each day without teacher support	Teachers will only assist when necessary	5 min 10 min 15 min	Ms. L.

Signatures _____   _____
                        Parent/Guardian   Ms. L.

Status Code: 1 = implementation not yet begun   2 = outcome partially accomplished with physical support
3 = outcome partially accomplished with verbal support   4 = outcome partially accomplished,
performance intermittent   5 = outcome predictably accomplished

Figure 7.8   *Continued*

The 1997 Amendments to the IDEA stipulate the following in the area of assessment:

- (a) (1) a multidisciplinary assessment of the unique strengths and needs of the infant or toddler and the identification of services appropriate to meet such needs;

- a family-directed assessment of the resources, priorities, and concerns of the family and the identification of the supports and services necessary to enhance the family capacity to meet the developmental needs of the infant or toddler; and

- a written individualized family service plan developed by a multidisciplinary team, including the parents.

The time frame for review and implementation acknowledges how quickly young children change:

- The individualized family service plan shall be evaluated once a year and the family shall be provided a review of the plan at 6-month intervals or more often when appropriate based on infant or toddler and family needs.

- The individualized family service plan shall be developed within a reasonable time after the assessment is completed. With the parents' consent, early intervention services may commence prior to the completion of the assessment.

The content of the plan specifies that the individualized family service plan shall be in writing and contain—

(1) a statement of the infants' or toddlers' present levels of physical development, cognitive development, communication development, social or emotional development, and adaptive development, based on objective criteria;

(2) a statement of family's resources, priorities, and concerns relating to enhancing the development of the family's infant or toddler with a disability;

(3) a statement of major outcomes expected to be achieved for the infant or toddler and the family, and the criteria, procedures, and timelines used to determine the degree to which progress toward achieving the outcomes is being made and whether modifications or revisions of the outcomes or services are necessary;

(4) a statement of specific early intervention services necessary to meet the unique needs of the infant or toddler and the family, including information about the frequency, intensity, and methods of delivering services.

(5) a statement of the natural environments in which early intervention services shall appropriately be provided, including a justification of the extent, if any, to which the services will not be provided in a natural environment;

(6) the projected dates for initiation of services and the anticipated duration of the services;

(7) the identification of the service coordinator from the profession most immediately relevant to the infant's or toddler's or family's needs (or who is otherwise qualified to carry out all applicable responsibilities under this part) who will be responsible for the implementation of the plan and coordination with other agencies and persons; and

(8) the steps to be taken to support the transition of the toddler with a disability to preschool or other appropriate services.

The IDEA stipulates also that the contents of the individualized family service plan shall be fully explained to the parents and informed written consent from the parents shall be obtained prior to the provision of early intervention services described in such plan. If the parents do not provide consent with respect to a particular early intervention service, then the early intervention services to which consent is not obtained will not be provided.

The IFSP Process

Although all agencies will have slightly different procedures, eligibility criteria, and organizational frameworks, it is expected that the process will be something like this:

1. Families are referred by a physician, agency, or are self-referred to early intervention services.

2. Families then talk about their likes and dislikes, wants and needs, preferences and priorities. This may be first time some families have had any interaction with early intervention. It may also be the first time they have been asked what *they* want for their family as well as their infant or toddler. They may need support to think about the needs of the family instead of just the child. This process may take more than one meeting. As the families' preferences set the stage for the IFSP, it is vital.

3. Assessment planning then analyzes the information-gathering process. It clarifies the family's preferences for involvement and their priorities for both the family and child. Information about the infant or toddler's characteristics and additional information from other assessments should be included.

   One role of the service coordinator is to help support the family in the level of participation and role they decide upon. They should have an active voice in the assessment process, giving input into when the assessment will be, the assessment measures to be used, and when and how the assessment information will be shared (Johnson et al., 1989). Planning the assessment around the parents' work, the child's most alert time, and the schedule of professionals can be a real challenge. Parents need to make the decisions as their participation in the process will make the assessment itself more accurate.

4. Before formal child assessment begins, it is imperative to determine the parents' perceptions of their infant or toddler. What do they consider the child's strengths and needs, the infant or toddler's likes and dislikes, what are their specific areas of concern, and what do they want for their child? It is often useful to find out what a typical day is like in the family; be sure to include all family members to understand how they share roles as well as the role the infant or toddler plays in the family.

5. Child assessment serves different functions at various points in the process. Initially the assessment focuses on diagnosis. It is necessary to determine whether or not the child meets the eligibility criteria for the program. Information is also necessary to develop the IFSP.

6. Identification of family values and preferences involves clarifying with families what aspects of their family life they feel are relevant to helping their child grow and develop. There are a variety of measures available to help families identify their strengths, needs, resources, and supports. These measures come in many different formats. However, the most efficient way to learn about what families want and how they want to participate is to ask them. If they want further clarification offer them some options.

7. Developing outcomes to meet child and family needs requires the interpretation and synthesis of formal and informal assessment information in light of the family's priorities. It may involve some rethinking, and certainly will necessitate choices among strategies, activities, and services that will meet these outcomes. It is critically important to remember that there may be greater diversity within groups than between groups. Do not assume that all families with a child with Down syndrome have the same needs, wants, desires, or values.

The IFSP, unlike the IEP, does not require behavioral objectives or benchmarks. Its expected outcomes are the changes that families want for themselves or their child. The IFSP does require a statement of what is going to occur to produce the desired outcome.

This collaborative development of the IFSP with parents requires new skills for professionals. The IFSP should reflect the values and priorities of the families, not the professionals. The role of professionals is to look at families from a systems perspective to help families identify relevant strengths. Professionals will need to use listening and interviewing techniques as well as negotiation skills. They also need to know the resources available in the community.

Implementing the IFSP requires another round of decision making. Families need to know the range of options available to them and decide which of the options best fit their needs. This range should start with the options that the family would choose from if the

child did not have a disability. If the parents' first choice is that the toddler be in a family day-care home that his older sister went to, then, that should be the first option explored. If this setting is chosen, the question for the team becomes how to support the toddler in that setting. Assistance might include the provision of necessary related and support services as well as training, technical assistance, and perhaps specialized equipment.

Different families have different desires. For some, placement in an early care and education setting is most appropriate; for others a home-based program or even a segregated early intervention program will best fit family needs. Or, families may find that a combination of these options works best. The role of the professional, particularly the service coordinator, is to ensure that families make choices from the full range of options in both settings and service providers. Facilitating linkages among professionals, available resources, and program options is a major role. Creativity is required to meet the needs of today's families.

Young children change quickly. Informal IFSP reviews need to be made on an ongoing basis, and more formal ones should be called for when necessary. At the beginning, reviews need to be made early for trouble shooting if necessary. As placements stabilize, a formal review every six months is required.

Case Studies and the IFSP

Families are different. Two case studies have been included to help to clarify these differences and the roles necessary for positive interaction. Because the IFSP process is more flexible than the IEP process, rather than give one complete IFSP, we have used a variety of formats so you can see which ones most suit your needs and you feel most comfortable with. You might even ask families what format they feel most comfortable with. These case studies are based on real families, but the names and identifying information have been changed.

The Dee Family

The Dee family consists of a single mother with six children. The mother, a full-time homemaker, is pregnant with twins. The two oldest children have been classified as having learning disabilities and receive special education services. Alvin is 1 year, 8 months old and attends a child-care center full time, along with his 2½-year-old brother. Alvin was observed informally at the child-care center where staff were holding an in-service training. Upon learning about developmental norms, a child-care worker became concerned about Alvin and asked if she should talk to his mother. Alvin was not walking, standing, eating independently, or talking. He had strong temper tantrums. He had to be fed and used a bottle. He had limited social interaction skills and few purposeful play skills.

Public Health nurses are involved with the family. They make appointments for the family, but the mother does not keep them (sometimes appointments conflict with one another, sometimes she forgets). The mother reports all children are behavior problems. The family lives in a rural area and transportation is sometimes a problem. The mother reports feelings of being overwhelmed. The father is available but reported not to live in the home.

The amount of child support payments make the family ineligible for the Aid for Dependent Children program; however, payments are at least six months late. While there is no money for utilities, heating bills are $400 monthly. The children experience frequent illnesses, but the mother cannot locate a doctor willing to treat the children because no local doctor will accept new Medicaid patients; therefore, illnesses go unattended.

A graphic outline of the coordination services facilitated by the staff between the family, day-care, and service providers is shown. Initial involvement with this family required assisting the mother in meeting her priorities, including getting financial assistance for child care, food, and utilities. This assistance was gained through agencies listed under the economic category, and included accessing emergency utility funds and budgeting help, applying for special needs day-care funding, and accessing the regional food bank program.

Once some basic resource issues were attended to, the mother became more receptive to tackling child issues. Arrangements were made to have the two young boys assessed for intervention purposes. The family was channeled to the Early Childhood Center for an evaluation. Developmental evaluation results indicated Alvin was functioning at half his age expectations, and his brother had a significant language delay. The Early Childhood Center assisted in the provision of speech and language therapy and behavioral intervention. Therapy was provided at the child-care center. Behavioral intervention was provided at home with day-care consultation. The Public Health system was accessed for evaluations including the hearing clinic, vision clinic, and medical clinic. Transportation was arranged when possible, and efforts were made to prevent appointment conflicts.

Meetings were set up between the day-care center and service providers to facilitate a coordinated intervention program. The day-care center was able to implement activities involving language stimulation and behavioral management. If the mother did not come to the meeting, the early childhood consultant made a home visit to gain input and share the information. The result of these efforts was a coordinated intervention system for Alvin (Figure 7.9).

Service coordination for the Dee family was complex. It required an unusual variety of skills on the part of the service coordinator in addition to a broad knowledge of available community resources, far beyond that expected of most early childhood educators (Figure 7.10).

CHILD'S NAME: Alvin Dee   DOB 4/8/97   Date 10/10/98

Child's Strengths and Functioning Levels:

Alvin is a relatively happy undemanding child who seems to be able to occupy himself. His mother reports that he enjoys watching television but has a "terrible temper" like the other children in the family. She has not encouraged him to stand or walk because he is easier to care for when he stays put in the playpen. He likes his bottle so she has encouraged him to use it. He shows some initial interest in toys but this is only momentary and if in the crib he throws them out. At the child care center he can focus on toys for 2 to 3 minutes with adult support. He can hold his bottle and will crawl toward it when hungry.

Family's Strengths, Concerns, and Priorities:

Alvin's mother is a full time homemaker. She is concerned about all the children but her priorities now relate to basic needs rather than whether or not Alvin has a developmental delay. She is concerned about them turning off the utilities as it is getting cold. The children need warm jackets. She wants to keep the two younger children in child care but is afraid her benefits will run out and with her pregnancy she doesn't have the energy to care for them all day. She needs money for some basic expenses and information on money management as well as the services she might have available. She would like to focus on skills that will make Alvin more independent as she is worried about the time she will have to devote to his care once the twins are born.

Child Assessments

Note: There have been few assessments as Alvin's mother's priorities are in other areas at this time.

Skill Area Language	CA	Functional Level	Skill Area Developmental	CA	Functional Level
Receptive	18 m	12 m (9–13)	Mental Age	18 m	13 m (11–16)
Expressive	18 m	8 m (6–9)	Motor Age	18 m	9 m (6–11)

Figure 7.9 Individualized Family Service Plan

CHILD'S NAME: Alvin Dee		Date 10/10/98				
MAJOR OUTCOMES	**SUPPORTS/ RESOURCES**	**ACTION PLAN**	**COMMENTS**	**FAMILY EVAL.**		
				DATE	**STATUS**	
Alvin's receptive language will improve	*Mrs. Dee, Siblings, Ms. T (Teacher) Mr. J (Service Coordinator)*	*Mrs. Dee and his teachers Ms. T. will make a list of words and concepts that would be most useful for Alvin to understand. Then Ms. T. will develop a plan. Mr. J will show Mrs. Dee and the other children how to use it at home.*				
Alvin's expressive language	*Mrs. Dee, Siblings, Ms. A (Speech Therapist) Mr. J*	*Mrs. Dee and Ms. A (speech theapist) will generate a list of words based on Mrs. Dee's priorities and Ms. A will refine the list based on the difficulty of the words and sounds and suggest alternatives for important ones if necessary. Ms. A will develop a plan and Mr. J will convey, model, and monitor the plan at home and in the child care setting.*				

Family Evaluation Status: 1 = implementation not yet begun   2 = outcome partially accomplished continue current strategies   3 = outcome partially accomplished but need different strategies   4 = outcome partially accomplished but needs practice   5 = outcome predictably accomplished to family's satisfaction

Figure 7.9   *Continued*

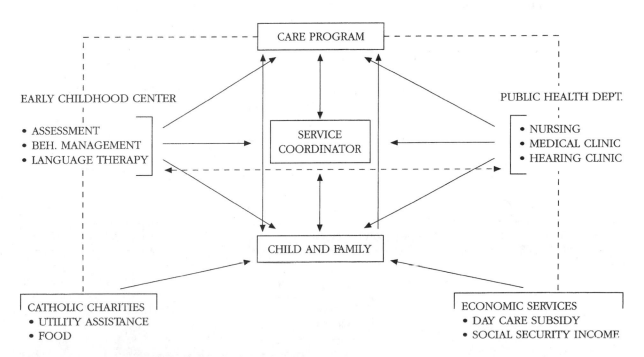

Figure 7.10   Dee Family Service Coordination

For some families service is complex. It requires the service coordinator to know not only about early childhood special education, but also about the available resources, public and private. When service needs are complex it is important that parents set the priority of what needs are more important. Until their basic needs are satisfied, it is unlikely that the child's needs will be a priority.

The Monroe Family

The Monroe family consists of a dual-earner, professional couple and their two biological children and one daughter from the husband's previous marriage. Their youngest child Cathy was diagnosed with Down Syndrome (Mosaic Trisomy 18). Cathy was enrolled in the program in April when she was 25 months old. She is severely delayed in all areas of development, currently functioning at levels of 12 to 14 months in all areas. The Monroes heard about the early intervention program from another parent at a workshop sponsored by the Parent Information Center and contacted the program staff. When services were begun, the Monroe family had their daughter enrolled in a child-care center, but were not satisfied with the level of care she was receiving. They thought the center was too large. The Monroe family located a family day-care provider who agreed to participate in training and also enrolled their daughter in an early intervention program two afternoons a week. (Transportation provided by the early intervention program made this possible.)

This family is functioning well. The parents are aware of their daughter's disability and are seeking ways to provide her with the best opportunities possible. Their concerns have been to find the best public school option for Cathy and to plan wisely for her future. Staff provided the family with information on financial planning for families with children with disabilities. The staff person attended the family's meeting with the school district as part of the transition process to public school services as well as observing in potential classrooms and talking with the teachers.

The service coordinator made a few visits to the early intervention site to coordinate the services Cathy was receiving there with the care she received at the family day-care provider's home. She also arranged for Cathy's physical therapist to visit the family day-care provider to demonstrate positioning and carrying techniques. In the beginning, monthly home visits were scheduled, but once the program for Cathy was firmly in place, the visits were replaced by monthly telephone contacts at the family's request (Figure 7.11).

Some families need far less coordination. They are aware of their personal resources and those in the community. However, they, too, need to have a service coordinator available, especially as children transition from one setting to another. Such families might find an informal narrative statement of their strengths/resources and desired outcomes the most workable for them. Figure 7.12 is an example of a plan that might work for the Monroe family.

Family Goals

Some families do not want family goals as part of the IFSP; others feel having stated outcomes for the family can help them justify what they need for themselves but frequently neglect. Figure 7.13 shows family goals for a mother who wants to return to work.

Transition Planning

Moving from one educational setting to another can be stressful. Increasingly, kindergarten is not the first educational setting that young children encounter. Most children have had previous experience with "school." Based on the requirements of the IDEA and

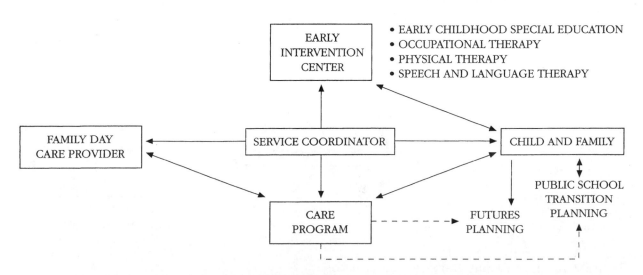

Figure 7.11 Monroe Family Service Coordination
Some families need far less coordination. They are aware of their personal resources and those in the community. However, they too, need to have a service coordinator available, especially as children move from one setting to another.

Families have the right to decide how much and in what ways they want to participate in their child's Individualized Family Service Plan. Educators need to listen to and respect parents' concerns and to incorporate parents' priorities into the child's program.

Individualized Family Service Plan

Family's Strengths, Concerns, and Priorities
   The parents are aware of Cathy's disability and are actively planning for her present and future. They are willing and able to read and understand complex material and participate actively in both short- and long-term planning for Cathy.
   Their long-term goal is to find the best public school placement for Cathy. Their other major concern relates to long-term financial planning.
   Because they both work they would like the service coordinator to coordinate services between early intervention and the family day care provider. More specifically to help the family day care provider understand the importance of positioning for Cathy. They would also like her to provide some references on long-term financial planning.

Figure 7.12   Sample IFSP for the Monroe Family

Family Goals

Outcome: Lee and Joe will spend more time together as a couple.
Objective: They will be together alone for an outing 1/month
   Strategies: Ask Joe's mom or friend to babysit
   Persons Responsible: Lee and Joe
   Criteria: They go out 1/month
   Review Date: 1 month

Outcome: Lee will be provided with more information on prognosis of microcephaly
   Objective: To obtain information about microcephaly and on children with microcephaly, especially long-term effects.
   Strategies:
   1. Ask questions of medical personnel involved with Justin (i.e., pediatrician, pediatric neurologist, or early intervention program).
   2. Provide reading material on specific disability.
   3. Provide phone number of parent information center, where Lee may talk with other parents as well as get information she wants
   Persons Responsible: Lee and Celeste (service coordinator)
   Criteria: Parent is satisfied with information she obtained
   Review Date: 3 months

Figure 7.13   Individualized Family Service Plan

common sense, we have begun to look more critically at the transition from one setting to another and what this means to children, parents, educators, and related service providers. Because planning for the transition from infant and toddler programs to preschool programming is a common one, and has regulations in the law it will be used for examples in the text. However, the principles underlying transition planning are the same for transitions between other settings such as preschool settings to a kindergarten placement.

   Smooth transitions require planning. This planning involves children, parents, educators and specialists from both educational settings. The critical goal for children is to provide the support and skills necessary for them to have a successful experience in the new setting. Children should approach preschool with motivation and openness to a new experience that is a validation of their growing achievement and confidence.

   If children are to approach this setting positively, parents, too, must feel confident about their child's ability and the ability of this setting to meet their child's needs. They need confidence in their ability to communicate with educators and to feel they can become partners with the educational system.

The IDEA sets forth its transition requirements for children moving from infant and toddler programs into the mandated programs that begin at age 3:

- to ensure a smooth transition for toddlers receiving early intervention services under this part to preschool or other appropriate services, including a description of how the families of such toddlers will be included in the transition plans; and the lead agency designated or established will—notify the local educational agency for the area in which such a child resides that the child will shortly reach the age of eligibility for preschool services.

- in the case of a child who may be eligible for such preschool services, with the approval of the family of the child, convene a conference among the lead agency, the family, and the local educational agency at least 90 days (and at the discretion of all such parties, up to 6 months) before the child is eligible for the preschool services, to discuss any such services that the child may receive; and in the case of a child who may not be eligible for such preschool services, with the approval of the family, make reasonable efforts to convene a conference among the lead agency, the family, and providers of other appropriate services for children who are not eligible for preschool services under part B, to discuss the appropriate services that the child may receive;

- to review the child's program options for the period from the child's third birthday through the remainder of the school year; and

- to establish a transition plan (IDEA, 1997).

The written process might look something like Figure 7.14. For teachers to support the transition they need to know the individual child and the differences and similarities between their program and the one the child will enter (or has been in).

Key elements to successful transitions for young children include the following:

- Providing program continuity through developmentally appropriate curricula,

- Maintaining ongoing communication and cooperation between staff,

- Preparing children for the transition, and

- Involving parents in the transition.

To the extent that the programs are developmentally based, the transition between the two is easier.

TRANSITION PLAN

Child: _____   Expected transition date: _____

Service Coordinator: _____   Target receiving site: _____

Reason for transition: _____

TRANSITION EVENT	PERSON RESPONSIBLE	DATES ACHIEVED	COMMENT
1. Parents informed of possible options	Service Coordinator		
2. Receiving agencies contacted	Parents Service Coordinator		
3. Parents visit agencies	Parents Service Coordinator		
4. Transition conference to determine appropriate placement	Parents/Service Coordinator Receiving Agency/ Intervention Team		
5. Transfer of records	Receiving and Sending Agencies		
6. Written transition plan developed	Parents/Service Coordinator Receiving Agency		
7. Placement	Parents/Child/ Receiving Agency		
8. Follow-up	Sending Agency/ Service Coordinator		

Figure 7.14 Transition Plan

It is also easier to meet the individual needs of children with disabilities because this type of programming allows for a wide range of developmental differences within the same class. To the extent that the preschool has a very academic orientation, the transition is likely to be more difficult.

Even preschools with a developmental base have some significant differences from most programs for infants and toddlers. Because preschool children are older, they are able to do more things. Increasingly, they are interested in the broader community, they have better gross and fine motor skills, they are more interested in cooperative play, and play for longer periods.

Other differences also exist. Preschools that include children with disabilities may be part of the public school system and be located in community schools which include Head Start centers that also contain older children. The group size is typically larger and the number of teachers is smaller. Time schedules may be more strictly adhered to because there may be only one time when specific age groups of children can use the playground, or they may have a schedule for "specials" such as gym or music.

Transition planning begins the prior September and October, not June. To support children in transitions, infant and toddler and preschool teachers need open communication patterns throughout the year. If possible, teachers (as well as children) should visit the other program. Joint inservice workshops can facilitate the development of both informal networks as well as the exchange of information.

As developmentalists, you can prepare for the transition process by visiting preschools, perhaps sharing snack with the children, or by making a videotape of what happens in preschool. It is important that you show children several different preschools if you do not know the school or class they will be entering or if children will go to different preschools. Because teachers may be moved or hired in August, this exposure is a good idea even if you feel confident you know what will happen. Talk about the differences and similarities between preschool programs and between preschool and infant and toddler programs.

Encourage parents to visit preschool classes where they would like their child to attend. They may want to visit early in the year (October) to get a feel for the expectations teachers have of incoming children and then perhaps all the classes during the latter part of the school year to look at teaching styles. Some schools are responsive to suggestions from parents about particular teachers with whom they feel their child would do well, others are not. Most are, however, willing to listen to why certain teachers might be a mismatch.

Talk with parents about what records they want forwarded and those they do not. Tell parents about the other children in your class or children that you know who will be attending the same setting as their child. Encourage parents to invite that child over to play and perhaps arrange a time when parents could get together to talk as well. Be sure that parents know what their rights are and help them stand up for them, if necessary.

Summary

Over the past two decades, we have learned much about individualized programming. We started by requiring the Individual Education Program to meet the specific needs of children with disabilities. This solved some problems, but did not succeed in getting the parental participation desired. Increasingly, we saw the efficacy of including families and the needs of the family instead of focusing solely on the needs of the child, especially with younger children. For younger children with disabilities, an Individualized Family Service Plan is required. It is a family-centered plan that focuses on the strengths and resources of the family as well as the child.

Because children are receiving intervention services earlier, they are moving from one program to another. Transition planning has become an important and vital part of the IFSP/IEP process.

Educational Resources

Disability Directory
http://www.igc.apc.org/pwd/
Resources and information of many types of disabilities, listed by type of disability.

Disability Rights Education and Defense Fund
(DREDF)
2212 6th Street
Berkeley, CA 94710
(510) 644-2555, (510) 644-2626
ADA Hotline: (800) 466-4232
e-mail: 75452.120@compuserve.com
Provides information, technical assistance, and referrals on laws and rights.

TASH: The Association for Persons with Severe Handicaps
29 West Susquehanna Avenue, Suite 210
Baltimore, MD 21204
(410) 828-8274
An advocacy organization who disseminates information to improve the education and independence of these with sever disabilities.

References

Dunst, C., Trivette, M., & Deal, A. G. (1988). *Enabling and empowering families: Principles and guidelines for practice.* Cambridge, MA: Brookline Books.

Individuals with Disabilities Education Act of 1997. Pub. L. 105-17, 111 Stat. 37-157, 20 U.S.C. 1400.

Johnson, B. H., McGonigel, M. J., & Kaufmann, R. K. (Eds.). (1989). *Guidelines and recommended practices for the individualized family service plan.* Washington, DC: National Early Childhood Technical Assistance System and Association for the Care of Children's Health.

Kendall, J. S., & Marazano, R. J. (1996). *Content knowledge: A compendium of standards and benchmarks for K-12 education.* Auora, CO: Mcrel

Mager, R. F. (1962). *Preparing instructional objectives.* Palo Alto, CA: Fearon.

Turbiville, V., Turnbull, A., Garland, C., & Lee, I. (1993). IFSPs and IEPs. In DEC Task Force on Recommended Practices, *DEC recommended practices: Indicators of quality in programs for infants and young children with special needs and their families.* Reston, VA: DEC, CEC.

Chapter 8

PROGRAM PLANNING IN INCLUSIVE SETTINGS

We in education know the impossible is our everyday agenda. There are many ways to reach our destinations. Sometimes, the way prescribed is not the way that succeeds. We have our educational goals, our directives, our curriculum guidelines. Often, we are given preset ways to accomplish those goals. Sometimes those ways don't work. We mustn't think there is only one approach. But if goals, approaches, and curriculum grow out of children's ages, stages, interests, and feelings, they are more likely to work. Even so, we mustn't think there is only one approach. (Chenfeld, 1987, p. 29)

Developing a program that (1) meets the needs of all the children in your classroom, (2) falls within the guidelines of your current work place, (3) follows the dictates of both state and federal laws, and (4) fits your personal philosophy and beliefs is a difficult task at best. To do it on a daily basis, year after year, may seem impossible. Given the importance of the task, it is necessary not only to do it well, but also to do it efficiently, in a flexible manner that allows for both short- and long-term change, and to do it creatively, so that the classroom experience is enjoyable for you and the children.

Program planning involves decisions about how children learn, when learning takes place, and what is to be learned. "... good curriculum must be individually appropriate to the needs and interests of the children in a program. In addition, it must be culturally salient and locally relevant and meaningful in the context of a specific community" (National Association for the Education of Young Children [NAEYC] and the National Association of Early Childhood Specialists, 1991, p. 23).

Some children with diverse abilities will find it more difficult to learn some concepts than their peers do. They need activities that are self-motivating within a prescribed set of goals. Additionally, planned activities must cover all the strands that are traditionally part of the developmental domain (cognitive, physical, social, and emotional) and also part of the general curriculum (mathematics, science, language and literacy, and so on). Where possible, activi-

ties need to teach more than one skill at a time. For example, to print, children need to develop finger strength in their dominant hand, particularly in the thumb and index finger. You could ask each child to open and close a pinch-type clothespin 100 times each day to develop this strength. You could even call it math if the child counted the number of times she opened and closed the pin. However, this is *boring* for both you and the child. Part of an educator's roles is to motivate children, to entice them into learning with activities that are so intriguing that children may not realize how much they are learning. And the activities should set them up to want to learn more. Washing doll clothes and hanging them on the line or having a felt alphabet and placing letters on the line to spell words or to match a pattern or just for fun, develops the same finger strength and supports additional learning as well.

Developing a Philosophy

Have you ever gone into a classroom, knelt down, and looked around? If not, give it a try. If you were a child, would you like to learn in this space? Does it look warm and inviting? What does the space tell children is important here? Is it safe? Does it invite them in? Can they be alone as well as with others? What do they do here?

You have a philosophy for working with children. It might not be well articulated, but it influences how you set up your room, the number and type of activities you choose, the amount of teacher-directed time versus child-directed time you allocate, and how you work with parents. It is important to know what your philosophy is, how it developed, and to evaluate and modify it continually with your personal growth. Because your philosophy is such an important variable in how you teach, you need to bring it up to a conscious level so you can take a look at it. You need also to see where children with diverse abilities fit into it. By clarifying your philosophy, you can decide for yourself what you believe. This is true whether this is your first teaching experience or if you have been teaching for 30 years.

Begin thinking about your preparation for teaching. Who taught you? What did they believe? Your training experiences, in conjunction with the experiences and values that you brought with you, shaped your initial approach. As you interacted with children you began to evaluate your philosophy and modify it based on what worked for you and what didn't. In job interviews, you may have decided that there were places you wouldn't want to work even if they offered you a job, while other places seemed well matched to your style.

The philosophy each of us has about teaching is obvious, whether or not it is directly labeled "philosophy." Reflect on Chenfeld's philosophy about teaching children given at the beginning of this chapter. What does she believe? Some of the issues your philosophy will include are given below. As you will note, these areas overlap and influence each other. Our philosophy is certainly reflected in the following sections.

Purpose of Education

What is the purpose of education? This important question is rarely asked. Is it solely to learn to read, write, and do arithmetic? Is the purpose of education to prepare citizens to live in a democracy. What you believe about the purpose of education influences how and what you teach. If education is about citizenship, then all citizens need to be represented, including those with diverse abilities, and everyone needs to be aware of the needs of all the citizens including their abilities and disabilities. How do the responsibilities of educating for citizenship influence your curriculum? Is your program congruent with these goals?

The Learning Environment

What is the best learning environment for young children? All children need to learn in places where they are safe, feel secure, and can master the skills they will need as adults. This environment must be designed with the children's biological needs in mind. Children should not be expected to sit, to listen to adults talk, or to do rote paperwork for long periods of time. They need periods of activity followed by periods that are more restful. They need to have their culture and values acknowledged and respected.

Content and Process

The relative importance of content and process has been debated for years. The conclusion is that they are both necessary and important. In reality, content and process support each other. If children are going to write (process), they need something to write about (content) (Bredekamp & Copple, 1997). Content defined as isolated skills learned through drill and practice is inappropriate at all ages. Relevant content integrated across a broad range of activities supports learning. This is not a new insight, but a reaffirmation:

The most crucial implication of Dewey's research and demonstration school at the turn of the century was that for reading, writing, and mathematics to be meaningful to children they must be built on a strong foundation of experiences, activities, and related language. The 3 Rs must be taught in a context relevant to the interests and understandings of the children. Subject matter cannot be digested well and easily by young children if it is broken down into isolated drill work that has no connection to children's lives and experiences at home, in the community, and at school. The less middle-class experience—which is what school work is based on—children have had, the more this is true. (Borden, 1987, p. 15)

Planning must be integrated across developmental and subject matter areas to be meaningful.

Theoretical Perspective

There are many different theories about how children learn and develop. The author of this text has been most influenced by the work of Piaget (1952/1963), Vygotsky (1933/1978), and Bandura (1992). We have used parts of these theories to build our own eclectic view just as all developmentalists borrow ideas and operationalize them to fit their needs.

Piaget introduced the idea that there were different kinds of knowledge that children construct: *logicomathematical knowledge* and *physical knowledge.* Knowledge is based on the focus of the child. If children are focusing on the organization of their actions, their order, and what happens when they act on objects, they are learning about logicomathematical knowledge. If, on the other hand, they are concentrating on the properties of the object itself, they are learning about physical knowledge (Sinclair, Stambak, Lexine, Rayne, & Verba, 1989). Children are active learners and need opportunities to construct their own knowledge base. Telling is not the same as doing. Planning must be designed to provide repeated experiences for children to construct knowledge (Bredekamp & Rosegrant, 1992). Think of planning as variations on a theme.

According to Vygotsky's theory (1987), cognitive development occurs because of social interaction with more competent partners. This adult guidance, called *scaffolding,* facilitates learning. More mature partners who dialogue with young children support the children's cognitive and language learning by expanding and extending their knowledge base (Meadows, 1993). The support provided by adults is most effective if children can use the same strategies to solve similar problems themselves (Berk, 1994). For example, if a child is trying to force a triangle into a form board, it is more useful to suggest he turn the triangle or try it in another place than it is to say that it is a triangle and doesn't go there.

Another important concept that Vygotsky (1987) has contributed to the field is the zone of proximal development (ZPD). This refers to the range of tasks that a child cannot yet accomplish alone but can accomplish with the help of adults or more competent peers. Learning cycles consist of ZPDs in different experiential domains.

To find the ZPD, the adult must assess the child's abilities, plan activities that are slightly in advance of the child's development, and then provide the necessary scaffolding for the child to perform the task. As the child's competence increases, the adult takes less responsibility for the task and allows the child more.

Vygotsky's importance to us lies in what his theory says about the role of educators. We must know the children because as a teacher we are active participants in the learning process, not in dispensing knowledge, but in adapting the knowledge base to individual children to extend and expand their learning.

There is a third body of knowledge that children need to learn but cannot construct themselves. Piaget refers to this as social-conventional knowledge, Vygotsky as school-learned concepts. This knowledge base must be taught and is culturally dependent. The knowledge is arbitrary and includes such conventions as labeling one color red and another green, as well as learning conventional greetings and social interactions that are culturally appropriate.

Social learning theory provides useful information about how to teach this conventional knowledge. Bandura (1992) suggests that social learning occurs through observation, modeling, vicarious reinforcement, and self-regulated behavior. Children need to see pictures of children from different ethnic/cultural groups as well as some children who wear glasses and others who use wheelchairs. They need male and female dolls to celebrate many different holidays, and to make more than one Mother's Day surprise. Bandura thinks that information such as this provides social learning for children. It provides children with information about whether they are likely to be included or not and how differences are dealt with. Whether children with disabilities are respected and enjoyed for the additional learning they provide or is the approach a "color blind" one with differences ignored.

Social learning theorists believe that children will learn more if they are interested in what they are learning and motivated to discover knowledge. For an educator, this means that an important aspect of our role is to motivate children. We need to develop a curriculum that is developmentally sound and compellingly interesting. We want children to wake up in the morning and be so excited that they can hardly wait to get to school to find out what we are going to learn today. We want them to whirl around and have a difficult time trying to decide what to do first because it all looks so intriguing. And, under the excitement are developmentally appropriate practices based on group and individualized goals for children and out of these goals has grown a theme and activities that are absorbing.

Children need teachers to plan their curriculum. However, the content of this program should reflect what interests children. This means that planning a year's curriculum in September and implementing it a week at a time is inappropriate. There is a general curriculum that children need to learn. However, they can learn it best when the knowledge is embedded in the curriculum based on the children's interests and in a way that is responsive to their individual and group needs.

Child-Initiated and Teacher-Initiated Instruction

The proportion of time allocated to teacher-directed versus child-directed tasks is an area of concern and one in which early childhood educators and special educators often disagree. Early childhood educators frequently believe that children increase their own knowledge by acting on their environment and, with adult scaffolding, reacting and organizing the feedback. They use many child-initiated activities with the adult acting as facilitator. Many early childhood special educators feel that teachers should teach, not facilitate and that they should be the ones to initiate activities and the children should respond to their directions. Children do learn a great deal from adults. Socioconventional and school-learned content is more teacher-initiated instruction. When education is concerned with the processes of constructing physical/logical-mathematical knowledge, the teacher's role is more of facilitating learning, with children initiating the instruction. A more relevant issue may be the relationship between the type of learning and the educator's role.

Inclusion and Segregation

Including children with diverse abilities in regular classrooms begins with a legislative base. However, your personal feelings about inclusion will influence how you proceed. Once you are clear about your feelings, you can move on to the next stage and look at the strategies you will use to be inclusive and the personal supports you need to make inclusion a positive experience for all the children.

There may be some children and some disabilities that you find easier to include than others. While all of us like to think we like all children equally, this is rarely true. We may treat children equally, but personal feelings are different. Try to move yourself away from the specifics and figure out the generic aspect of the child or disability that influences you— the part that will be repeated with other children. Overall, "the goal for the teacher is to serve as a catalyst and to allow each child to feel that she is a capable learner" (Borden, 1987, p. 17).

Developmentally Appropriate Practice

Developmentally appropriate practice focuses on the development of the child, the learning environment, partnerships with families and the community, and guidelines for practice (NAEYC, 1998). The uniqueness of each child is appreciated while the universals in developmental patterns are acknowledged. This is influenced by multiple social and cultural contexts especially the child's family and heritage (NAEYC, 1998).

Learning is an active experience for children and what is learned needs to be meaningful to the child. Learning is done in the context of meaningful relationships. For educators to support children's learning, they must continually make decisions. Some of these decisions are routine, others complex. All are designed to move children toward an educational or developmental goal and must be evaluated within this context (NAEYC, 1998).

Educating children with diverse abilities requires partnerships and the underlying skills to maintain these relationships. Educators need to be clear about their preferences and have the ability to communicate them. They need to negotiate with parents and other professionals and they have to be open to learning and changing (NAEYC, 1998).

The guidelines that support developmentally appropriate practice include the creation of a caring community of learners, teaching to enhance development and learning, constructing appropriate curriculum, assessing children's learning and development, and developing reciprocal relations with families (NAEYC, 1998).

Principles Underlying Developmentally Appropriate Practice

What is developmentally appropriate practice? How do you know it when you see it? The answer has been an undercurrent throughout this book and, although defined, it probably hasn't been explained thoroughly enough for you to truly use it. To explain what is developmentally appropriate, the National Association for the Education of Young Children developed a position paper and guidelines in 1986 and 1987. The principles were revised in 1996 to reflect new knowledge, particularly in neurobiology; the inclusion of children with disabilities in regular classrooms; and the increasing number of infants and toddlers in group care (Bredekamp & Copple, 1997).

The principles underlying developmentally appropriate practice are based on what we reliably know about child development and learning. The principles are presented in italics. An explanation follows each principle. These principles influence beliefs and philosophy about education for all children.

Principles of development and learning that inform developmentally appropriate practice (Bredekamp & Copple, 1997, pp. 9–15):

> Domains of children's development—physical, social, emotional, and cognitive—are closely in-

tertwined. Development in one domain influences and is influenced by development in other domains.

To understand development, scholars have tended to separate it into component developmental and skill areas. Although this separation makes the developmental process easier to conceptualize, it overlooks the interrelatedness of developmental areas. The long-term consequence of this disaggregation approach is that assessment, treatment, and intervention have focused on particular developmental areas as if they could be treated in isolation. For example, a child with cerebral palsy would probably be referred to physical and/or occupational therapists to help him achieve motor milestones that he was slow in reaching. It is unlikely that the child would be referred to a mental health professional to support the motivational and internal mental organization needed to perform motor tasks. In general, the younger the child the closer the curriculum must be tied to the child's experiential base. Real life is not organized by subject matter areas.

Recently, scholars have focused more on functional interrelationships among the different domains. They are not referring to the obvious overlap between social and emotional development, but rather the role emotions play in the cognitive, language, and motor domains (Hyson, 1994). This multidomain approach increases the complexity of viewing children's development, which is further complicated by the need to look at the child as part of a family system that embraces certain cultural values and who lives in a specific geographic area at a particular time:

> Development proceeds at varying rates from child to child as well as unevenly within different areas of each child's functioning.

All children are unique, yet they share many commonalities in their sequence of growth and development. Children come into the world "prewired" to grow and develop in a certain predictable pattern. Understanding these patterns allows us to plan for children in developmentally appropriate ways and to make some predictions about whether future growth and development will fall within the normal patterns.

Most children follow a predictable pattern of development, some follow at a slower or faster rate; a few do not follow the pattern at all. Growth itself in asynchronous. One may have a spurt in one area and lag in another. Some variations are related to family and cultural background and some are related to the uniqueness of each individual. It is important to value this uniqueness in all children as it provides a framework for including children with diverse abilities and respecting different cultural and ethnic backgrounds.

When assessing how a child is progressing, a pattern is typically more useful than looking at isolated behaviors. Rather than only looking at "walking independently" and deciding whether or not a child's behavior is on target, we might look at the progression of walking. For example, we would expect the following pattern of walking: Walks holding on to furniture; walks with both hands held; walks with one hand held; walks alone two to three steps; walks without support.

If a child were in the slower range in walking, holding on to furniture (9 months), we would expect that he would continue this "slower" pattern and not expect him to walk without support until about 15 months. At the upper end of the normal range of independent walking, an infant on the fast track walks without support by 12 months or earlier. (Furuno et al., 1991). However, we cannot assume that the child who is on the slow track for walking is also on the slow track for talking. In fact, the opposite may be true.

We use the information about developmental patterns to decide what types of materials to use with children of various ages, as well as to determine whether children are showing delayed or atypical patterns of development. Planning needs to take into account children's patterns of growth and development.

Early experiences have both cumulative and delayed effects on individual children's development; optimal periods exist for certain types of development and learning.

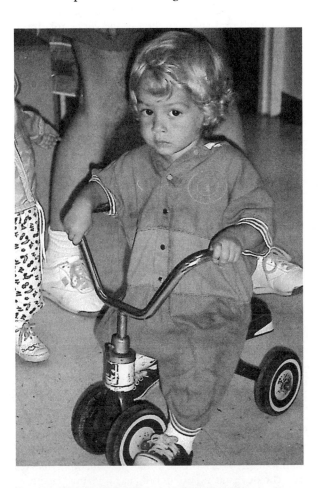

Some children enter the early childhood environment tentatively. This may be related to their temperament or to their past experiences at home, school, or in the community.

Children's early experiences, both positive and negative, affect their development. As with patterns of development, isolated events may have a minimal impact, but frequently occurring events can have powerful lasting effects. Research supports the idea of broadly conceived *sensitive periods and cycles* when the child is more susceptible to change or where the impact of events is more pervasive than at other times (Thatcher, 1994).

Early childhood is a sensitive period. "By the age of 3, the brains of children are two and a half times more active than the brains of adults and they stay that way throughout the first decade of life" (Shore, 1997, p. 21). There are both short- and long-term gains from early intervention (Consortium for Longitudinal Studies, 1983; Ramey et al., 1992; Seitz, Rosenbaum, & Apfel, 1985). These gains are measured by a variety of indices: better cognitive achievement, higher IQ scores, positive social behaviors, fewer years in special education, less delinquency, fewer repetition of grades, better school attendance, and others. By necessity, these are longitudinal studies; the results of studies begun in the 1980s are just beginning to appear. There are indications that over time, the benefits of early intervention are cumulative (Carnegie Task Force, 1994).

There is concern that early environmental stressors not only shape the brain's representation of those experiences, but also sensitize the development of the neural network and influence future development. We have known for many years that children who experience chronic stress during early childhood are at risk for developing a variety of cognitive, behavioral, and emotional problems (Trickett & Kucznski, 1986). We are beginning to understand why. We can identify both risk and protective factors. A strong secure attachment to a nurturing caregiver is a protective factor and may mediate some of the effects of adverse environments. Chronically stressful environments can activate the hormone cortisol which adversely affects the functioning of the brain (Shore, 1997).

Young children who experience maltreatment may have more permanent and lasting problems than we had previously thought: ". . . the psychiatric consequences of early maltreatment may not be exclusively psychological in nature, but may also emerge due to the effects of traumatic experience on the developing brain" (Cicchetti & Tucker, 1994, p. 546). That is, as early experience interacts with the self-regulatory system of the brain, some of the synapses that are pruned may be related to traumatic experiences. Early childhood settings need to provide positive experiences for children and consciously promote prosocial behavior (Honig & Wittmer, 1996):

Development proceeds in predictable directions toward greater complexity, organization, and internalization.

Children learn through their senses. As they enhance their knowledge base with hands-on experiences, they begin to acquire symbolic knowledge and move into thinking that can take place in not only the present but also the past. They grow in the ability to regulate their own behavior. The adult's role is to respond to this increasing growth by presenting a curriculum that motivates and challenges children. Knowledge of the universals in development and the uniqueness of each child supports this curriculum:

Development and learning occur in and are influenced by multiple social and cultural contexts.

Changing patterns have influenced families and hence the lives of children with diverse abilities born into these families. Today, more than half of mothers with young children work. This means that increasing numbers of young children are spending large parts of their day with adults other than their parents. Other patterns relate to the high divorce rate, single-parent, and remarried families.

The diverse makeup of the population of children is rapidly changing, forcing us to investigate the roles of nature, nurture, culture, and the complex intersections of these dimensions. By 2030 "There will be 5.5 million more Hispanic children; 2.6 million more African-American children; 1.5 million more children of other races; and 6.2 million fewer white, non-Hispanic children" (Children's Defense Fund, 1989, p. 116). These changes are attributed to higher birth rates among non-European-American women, as well as increased immigration, and more women of childbearing age in this group (Hanson, Lynch, & Wayman, 1990). Consequently, we must become more aware of culture and the role it plays in early growth and development and assure that planning is based on this knowledge.

Particularly for children with diverse abilities, what is considered best practice has changed greatly over the past 40 years:

Children are active learners, drawing on direct physical and social experience as well as culturally transmitted knowledge to construct their own understandings of the world around them.

We know that infants come into the world seeing, hearing, feeling, tasting, and smelling. We don't think they come "knowing"; but rather, they must interact with their environment to make it meaningful to them. Through generating and testing out hypotheses, they must construct a knowledge base. It is less clear whether learning is continuous, linear, incremental, or whether knowledge is discontinuous and stage-based, sometimes spurting ahead and becoming qualitatively different from previous knowledge, or some combination (Feldman & Snyder, 1994; Meadows, 1993).

Environments that support children in becoming active learners encourage the construction of knowledge by offering experiences that are at the edge of children's knowledge base and that encourage them to test out their hypotheses. New experiences are needed to help children modify, adapt, expand, and reorganize their working model of the world. When educators help children to plan, act, and then reflect on experiences, this process is enhanced.

This is another area where early childhood education and early childhood special education have had some differences. Although both areas acknowledge the utility of direct teaching of certain information at certain points in time, early childhood special educators are frequently more comfortable with far more direct instruction than are those in early childhood education. To the extent that children must construct their own understanding of the world, reliance on direct instruction interferes with the child's active learning.

Development and learning result from interaction of biological maturation and the environment, which includes both the physical and social worlds that children live in.

Probably the only "pure genetic moment" is at conception. From that moment on, there is an interaction between the organism and the environment. The nature-nurture model is no longer adequate to describe development; the focus is on the *interaction* of nature and nurture.

Information about the relationship between early experience and the brain has focused on the early childhood years as the "prime time" for development. Neurons create synapses more easily and efficiently at this time (Shore, 1997). An enriched environment helps brain cells form *synapses* and stabilizes these connections to support learning. During the first year, "the number of synapses increases twentyfold, from 50 trillion to 1,000 trillion" (Carnegie Task Force, 1994, p. 7). The development of the brain is more susceptible to environmental influences than had been thought previously. Early experiences with abuse or trauma also impact the development of the brain; particularly the subcortical and limbic areas which can result in extreme anxiety, depression, and attachment problems. These adverse experiences can also interfere with cognitive processing and problem solving (Shore, 1997).

The brain has more nerve cells (neurons) and synapses than it needs. This overabundance holds the potential for development that responds to vastly different lifestyles as well as individual personality and temperament. During prenatal development, neurons are pruned, whereas in infancy, it is the synapses that are pruned (Cicchetti & Tucker, 1994). *Pruning,* or technically, *parcellation,* is the process by which the brain eliminates general neurons and synapses as part of the process of achieving the specificity of the mature brain. (Brown, 1994). The pruning process appears to be use-dependent; that is, synapses that are used stay, and those that are not used are eliminated (Brown, 1994). An early responsive stimulating environment prevents the pruning of valuable synapses and the devastating effects of "hard wiring" inappropriate synapses particularly those that relate to violent behavior (Shore, 1997).

Genetics may establish the upper and lower limits to development of a specific trait but environment determines where within this range a trait falls:

Play is an important vehicle for children's social, emotional, and cognitive development, as well as a reflection of their development.

A majority of early social interactions center around play and play activities. The quality and type or level of interaction that occurs among children in play activities develops sequentially, increasing with age and maturation. As children's play develops, their social interactions move away from caregiver to peer relationships. The child is developing both motor skills and cognitive ability to decenter, that is, to focus on more than one aspect of an object, which allows for the manipulation of toys and objects in a social context. Increasingly, children participate in reciprocal relationships with peers (Smilansky & Shefatya, 1990). As children gain sophistication, planning plays a more important role. Children decide what they are going to do and how they will go about doing it before they actually do it (Gowen, 1995). The ability to participate in symbolic play has cognitive underpinnings:

Development advances when children have opportunities to practice newly acquired skills as well as when they experience a challenge just beyond the level of their present mastery.

Programming continually moves from what children know to the acquisition and consolidation of new knowledge that requires the support of adults. Children come to learning experiences with different backgrounds; some have had a variety of experiences, others relatively few. It is important to meet all children where they are and provide the scaffolding for them to take the next step. Planning and activities need to be flexible and allow for different learning experiences with the same activity. Activities must be modified (both easier and more difficult) to meet the needs of children with diverse abilities:

Children demonstrate different modes of knowing and learning and different ways of representing what they know.

Children come to understand their world in different ways. Most infants begin with a tactile kinesthetic base to learn about their world and add information from the other senses. Over time, children develop preferred learning modalities and different styles of learning. They represent their world differently. They are good at different things. Sometimes, this is because of a sensory impairment.

Knowing how children represent their world, teachers can present information in ways that make it easier for children to learn; likewise, they can give children opportunities to strengthen areas that may not be as strong. Gardner (1983) feels that all individuals have a unique blend of seven multiple intelligences. This broad definition of intelligence includes areas such as verbal/linguistic, musical/rhythmic, logical/mathematical, visual/spatial, body/kinesthetic, intrapersonal and interpersonal intelligence (Gardner, 1983; George, 1995):

Children develop and learn best in the context of a community where they are safe and valued, their physical needs are met, and they feel psychologically secure.

Children need to be in environments where they can develop trusting relationships with adults, establish their autonomy, and be empowered to continue to learn. Children need to feel safe in school both psychologically and physically. Prosocial behavior needs to be supported; full-time child care beginning in infancy may be associated with increased aggression and noncompliance (Honig, 1993). The increasing amount of war play and superheros and the inclusion of younger children in this play causes consternation for many (Carlsson-Paige & Levin, 1987).

There is increasing concern about the emotional and social functioning of young children. Some very young children who see and are the victims of violence, become so accustomed to violence that they readily take the aggressor role and do not empathize with the victim (Osofsky, 1993/1994).

Young children watch an average of four hours of television a day. In low-income homes, this figure increases to six hours (Miedzain, 1991). When television viewing is not based on developmentally appropriate programs, there is concern that instead of establishing a sense of trust and safety, infants learn that the world is dangerous, enemies are all around, and that weapons are needed to keep one safe (Levin & Carlsson-Paige, 1994). Instead of helping children develop a sense of autonomy and connectedness to each other, television portrays autonomy as being related to fighting, and the use of weapons, helplessness, and altruism are related to connectedness. Other concerns revolve around empowerment and efficacy, gender identity, appreciation of diversity, and morality and social responsibility (Levin & Carlsson-Paige, 1994).

The principles that inform developmentally appropriate practice are a useful foundation for making curriculum decisions for children from birth through 8. They are, however, broadly based principles, and it is up to you to make them more specific and individualized, and to incorporate them into your philosophy and program planning.

Implications of a Philosophy on Program Planning

At this point, you have examined your philosophy. What does this really mean on the first day of school? To the extent that you control how your day is scheduled, it can mean a great deal.

Time Allocation.   Think about your day with children, whether it is a half day, a full day, or extended care. The first broad plans you develop divide the day into purposeful segments. How you allocate time reflects your philosophy. In a two-and-a-half-hour program for 4-year-olds, one teacher may designate an hour for free play and another designates 15 minutes, that is a statement. Look at the length of group times. Are they appropriate for the age/developmental level of the children? How much time is allocated for individual versus group work?

Number of Activities. How many activities are available for children to choose from? Are all the children participating in art at the same time and making the same project, or are some at the easel, some working with Playdough, and some building with blocks? Are some children in the dramatic play area, while others are at the writing center, at the water table, or working on the computer? Do children choose their centers or are they assigned? Must they stay a specific amount of time, or can they come and go?

Balance of Activities. Look at your activities to see the balance between active and passive activities and teacher- and child-directed activities. Do these match your philosophy? How complex are the activities you offer? Do children who are cognitively advanced as well as those who learn more slowly both have choices?

Your philosophy is the first step in program planning. It influences how you teach and what you teach.

Strategies for Individualizing Learning

Regardless of content or age, there is a cycle of learning that takes place as new information becomes part of a child's repertoire. This learning framework has four broad aspects: awareness, exploration, inquiry, and utilization (Bredekamp & Rosegrant, 1992).

1. *Awareness* is the initial stage in the cycle of learning. Awareness grows out of experience. As children notice differences among themselves, questions arise: "Why does Juan have those things on his legs?" "Why is my skin black and Justine's white?" When children are at an awareness level, they want a simple, straightforward answer. "Juan's legs aren't strong enough to hold him so he needs braces to help" may be all the child wants to know. Often we tell them more than they really want to know.

2. *Exploration* is the next level and requires children to observe and try to make sense out of an event or experience by exploring materials, gathering additional information, poking, prodding, or doing whatever seems to make sense to the child. Although it is tempting to "explain" the situation,

Children in this classroom have many choices among the materials with which they work, as well as the peers and adults with whom they interact. This fosters inclusion and allows children to make decisions and become problem solvers.

it is rarely useful; children need to find their own meaning for information. Explaining fosters dependency. Asking open-ended questions is more useful.

3. *Inquiry* involves the understanding of classes of information, the ability to generalize information, and to call up previous learning for comparison. Adults can help children with more focused questions at this stage.

4. *Utilization* is a functional level of learning where information can be used in a variety of settings and applied to new information and situations. Children who understand the concept of counting not only can count objects accurately but can utilize that information to decide that six chairs are necessary for six children to sit on.

This learning cycle occurs again and again as children learn. It is important to know where individual children are in the cycle. When a child encounters information for the first time, he begins at an awareness level. Children with previous experiences may be generalizing the information. Some children with diverse abilities will have less broad experiential backgrounds. They need to be given time to experience and explore before they can be expected to participate in higher level skills. Programs must be designed that allow children to profit from experience at all places in the learning cycle. With new knowledge, the cycle begins again.

Young children encountering a wheelchair for the first time will go through these stages. Initially, they will be curious about the wheelchair and they might want to sit in it and see how it works. This is exploration; they need this time. When they have their own understanding of the wheelchair, try to broaden and generalize this information so they can figure out what activities are difficult or easy to do in a wheelchair and the relationship among wheelchairs, crutches, and walkers. As they integrate this information, have them think about the world outside the classroom, the utility of curb cuts, why bathrooms can be difficult to negotiate, and the problem with table heights.

Teacher-Supported Learning

As the teacher, you play a vitally important role in supporting the learning of children. It is often tempting to let children play by themselves or with other children without being directly involved yourself. Although it is good for children to learn to play independently and with other children, they will learn more if they spend some time with a supportive adult who can provide the scaffolding that children need to learn in the zone of proximal development.

There are three kinds of support adults can give children: environmental support, nonverbal support, and verbal support:

1. *Environmental support.* Set up the space in the center to allow all children to participate in activities. Your support includes providing adaptive equipment that can be explored and used by children. This may mean adding pillows and bolsters to the rug to help a child sit, putting a block under a chair, or even adding a seat belt. Your support requires providing a sufficient quantity and variety of materials to meet children's needs. Include books about children with diverse abilities, that contradict gender stereotypes and accurately represent cultural and ethnic groups. Support children by planning an environment that stretches children's understanding of their world.

2. *Nonverbal support.* You can encourage children's play by watching what children do with materials and listening to what they say. Place yourself at the children's eye level. If the child is sitting on the floor, then you sit on the floor, too. If the child is standing, kneel down to be at her level. Use materials yourself, but don't get so involved that you are no longer paying attention to the children. Imitate children's actions. Use your body to express interest. Accept children's statements and explanations even when they appear to be blatantly contrary to reality. Young children rarely consciously lie, their concept of reality is simply different from adults'. Instead of contradicting them, ask questions to draw their attention to inconsistencies in what they have said. Remain calm in the face of children's "mistakes" such as spilling water, dropping a puzzle, or toppling a tower of blocks. Children need support in following through to clean up or pick up the pieces or rebuild the tower if needed.

3. *Verbal support.* Verbal interactions encourage children's language, self-esteem, and problem-solving as well as social skills. Talk with children about what they are doing, acknowledge their actions and choices. Ask questions that relate to their play. Refer children to one another for problem-solving suggestions and additional conversation. Encourage children to answer their own questions by asking "What do you think?" Converse with children who are not verbal and for whom English is a second language whether or not you receive a response.

Children are curious about each other. It is important to encourage and verbally support this curiosity even if it feels uncomfortable by adult standards. You can stop children from asking questions, but not from being curious. Help children satisfy this curiosity. Honestly talk with children about differences and answer their questions. (In a conversation with a woman using a wheelchair, a 4-year-old asked, "How did you get out of your mother's tummy with that thing?" Her response: "I haven't always used a wheelchair. I was born just like you were. I don't think it would have fit do you?" Both laughed.) Support their exploration of differences and build acceptance of others. When children express concerns, respond to them as real and provide the children with information and experience to cope.

Children who receive developmentally appropriate support from adults during their play will learn more (adapted from Whitehead, 1989).

Continuum of Teaching Techniques

Teaching techniques need to be adapted to meet children's learning needs. These can range from directive to nondirective, with many degrees in between. The goal is to match the technique to the material being learned and the child who is learning. *All* teachers need *all* of these techniques. Starting from the least directive to the most directive, the techniques are as follows (adapted from Bredekamp & Rosegrant, 1995):

- *Withholding attention* or planned ignoring is frequently used when adults know a child can accomplish a task without assistance, or as part of a behavior strategy for handling undesirable but nondangerous behavior. It can also be employed during the latency period between making a request and the child's response. Be sure to give young children enough time to respond.

- *Acknowledging* is used to reinforce children's behavior, particularly when the goal is to have the behavior continue. Done intermittently and for pointing out specific aspects of behavior, it is a useful way to shape behavior. When overused or when acknowledgment is too general, it is less useful.

- *Modeling,* whether conscience or unconscious, is a way of teaching children which behaviors are appropriate and which are inappropriate. By their actions, adults show children how to interact with others or how to use a new material.

- *Facilitating* involves providing temporary assistance to a child. This can involve verbal support, such as providing a suggestion for a different way of approaching a problem or reattaching a piece of paper that has come loose. It is specific and time-limited and enables a child to continue on independently.

- *Supporting* is similar to facilitating, but it is more general and lasts longer. The goal is independence, but the expectation is that it will take longer to achieve.

- *Scaffolding* is associated with Vygotsky's work and implies working on the edge of a child's knowledge base. It provides the link between what a child can do independently and what he can accomplish with adult help. It is more directive than the previous techniques in that the adult provides more focus for the child's activity.

- *Coconstructing* involves actually doing a project with or collaborating with a child. This is a more

Facilitation in this situation involves holding the bowl so the child can continue smashing the apples. When the educator also tells the child *why* she is holding the bowl, she promotes learning new strategies and teamwork to achieve a goal.

directive technique and one that is useful when children don't know how to use particular materials. It is also useful to join with children. One can move momentarily from scaffolding to coconstruction and back.

- *Demonstrating* is more directive than coconstruction as the teacher does the project and the children typically watch. There are times when this is extremely useful and appropriate and other times when children can appropriately construct their own knowledge. Demonstrating is often followed by less directive techniques. The problem with demonstrating is that children often assume that there is only one way to do an activity rather than actively constructing a method of approaching a task.

- *Directing* involves telling a child specifically what to do. It also implies that there is one correct way to do something and that there is one outcome desired. This technique is frequently used when less directive techniques have not taught a desired task.

An educator's philosophy reflects how much time she plans to spend at each end of the teaching continuum. Early childhood educators are frequently criticized for being too nondirective to meet the needs of children with diverse abilities whereas special educators are criticized for being too directive. The solution is to be aware of the continuum, and your personal philosophy, and to continually move from nondirective to more directive techniques as children need more direction in learning, but then to move into less directive strategies as children begin to master tasks. The goal is an appropriate match so that the strategy that provides the most learning for the child is employed.

Contextual Planning

Planning is dependent upon your philosophy, the setting you work in, the age of the children you teach, and the children who are included in your class.

Planning around a theme or unit helps focus activities. Themes provide a context that supports conceptual development. However, like all good ideas, themes can be reduced to the trivial and mundane. As you think about long-range planning, start with brainstorming, include parents and children. Gather ideas; you will focus and narrow them later. If you need more structure, start with the seasons as a foundation. Traditional themes for young children include the senses, transportation, community helpers, and so on. There is nothing wrong with these themes, but sometimes it is fun to stretch yourself. Whatever the theme, be sure it has internal validity. (Don't have children plant seeds outdoors in the fall!)

Implementing an IEP/IFSP in a Theme Plan

The next step in planning is to decide how to implement the theme. It requires "deciding upon theme goals, listing the vocabulary associated with the topic, agreeing on a 'main event,' listing materials needed, describing parents' and children's involvement, and planning evaluation" (Nunnelley, 1990, p. 25). If you are excited about a theme, the children will be as well.

There are a variety of ways to incorporate individualized planning in a theme or unit. One way is to make a chart. Put each of the child's annual goals in the middle and the areas around the room at the sides. If the theme was *transportation* and two of the annual goals were *to improve receptive and expressive language,* the chart would look something like Figure 8.1 for 4- to 5-year-olds. It is not difficult to incorporate individualized planning in a theme; but it is necessary to think it through and plan it. The emphasis would be very different if the annual goal was concerned with improving fine motor skills.

In many ways, the theme makes some of the planning easier. The vocabulary to stress is more obvious and is more easily reinforced because it is maintained for at least a week. As children expand their concepts, use analogies from one form of transportation to another to help them learn. The purpose of theme-based planning is contextual learning. Children can

learn more, faster, and in greater depth if materials are related and relevant.

The principles of contextual learning can be applied to the home as well. If parents want to work on language concepts at home, use the house as your context. Have parents decide what they will do in each room of the house to help children learn contextually. Make a chart similar to Figure 8.1, but instead of having areas of the classroom have rooms of the house. In the bedroom, children might learn the names of various parts of clothing; in the kitchen, eating utensils and foods; in the living room, furniture and so on. Parents are more likely to remember if they can put the sheet of paper on the refrigerator instead of in a notebook. Change charts as children master concepts.

Transitions

In program planning, there are certain events or times that are often forgotten or ignored that are crucial. Transitions are one such time.

Some times of the day have unique opportunities for growth as well as challenges to educators. Transition is the time between the end of one event and the beginning of another. This can be the time between activities, the beginning and end of the day, before and after lunch, or moving from inside to outside. Transitions are particularly difficult times for children, as well as adults. At home, the times before meals, bedtime, and the like are stressful. As there are many transitions in a single day, and the stress created in these transitions can carry over into the next event, it is important to carefully plan transitions to both increase learning and decrease stress.

The younger the children, the wider the age group of children, or the more children with severe disabilities, the more likely it is that transition periods will be longer. (Compare the time it takes for a 5-year-old versus a 3-year-old to put on boots and a snow suit.) With younger children, the transitions may be more obvious to the adult than to the child.

Transitions are important learning times for children, as many tasks involve self-help skills. Teaching these skills (dressing and undressing, toileting, hand washing, eating, and settling for a nap) consumes a large portion of the day. It is sometimes tempting to just do things for the children rather than support them in learning these skills. Learning skills is a legitimate part of the curriculum and should be planned and valued in that light, not just as a daily necessity.

Transitions are difficult for a variety of reasons:

- *Boredom.* Transitions often involve waiting. Children who have "nothing to do" will usually find something to do, and it is rarely what you would choose.

  To *combat Boredom:* Eliminate as much waiting time as possible. When you can't eliminate it, help children by singing a song with them, doing a finger play, telling or reading a story. Do not move from an activity until you

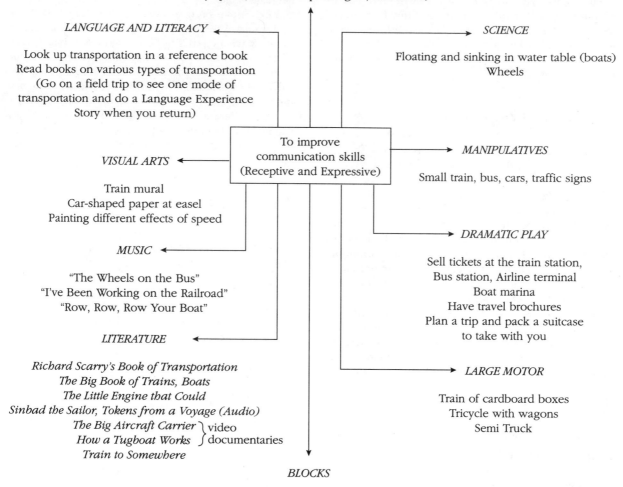

MATH

Identify and classify modes of transportation
Compare size of modes of transportation
Count and order different modes
(by speed, number of passengers, and so on)

LANGUAGE AND LITERACY

Look up transportation in a reference book
Read books on various types of transportation
(Go on a field trip to see one mode of
transportation and do a Language Experience
Story when you return)

SCIENCE

Floating and sinking in water table (boats)
Wheels

To improve
communication skills
(Receptive and Expressive)

VISUAL ARTS

Train mural
Car-shaped paper at easel
Painting different effects of speed

MANIPULATIVES

Small train, bus, cars, traffic signs

MUSIC

"The Wheels on the Bus"
"I've Been Working on the Railroad"
"Row, Row, Row Your Boat"

DRAMATIC PLAY

Sell tickets at the train station,
Bus station, Airline terminal
Boat marina
Have travel brochures
Plan a trip and pack a suitcase
to take with you

LITERATURE

Richard Scarry's Book of Transportation
The Big Book of Trains, Boats
The Little Engine that Could
Sinbad the Sailor, Tokens from a Voyage (Audio)
The Big Aircraft Carrier ⎱ video
How a Tugboat Works ⎰ documentaries
Train to Somewhere

LARGE MOTOR

Train of cardboard boxes
Tricycle with wagons
Semi Truck

BLOCKS

Add trains, buses, airplanes, cars, boats to unit blocks

Vocabulary
Types of transportation
Train (station), bus (station), airplane (terminal, hanger), car (garage), boat (marina, slip, dock)
Freight train, passenger train
School bus, city bus, long distance bus
Sedan, station wagon, convertible
Speedboat, tanker, tugboat, sailboat

Figure 8.1   Theme Plan: Transportation

have the next one prepared. That is, do not dismiss children from group time until the activity centers are prepared. Don't always wait until all the children are present before starting an activity. Often slower children speed up if they think they are missing something. Know your children; if some children are perpetually slow, start them first.

• *Change.* Children, like adults, like to change activities when they are finished, not by the clock.

To m*ake Change Easier:* Warn children before they are expected to make a change. "In five minutes it will be clean-up time." Have a schedule that you follow. If some children have particular problems with change, warn them several times. Young children cannot tell time so it does not matter if you allow activities to run a little longer or shorter, but rather that you follow the same sequence of events (see Figure 8.2). Have a simple picture schedule to show children the order of events. This is particularly helpful for

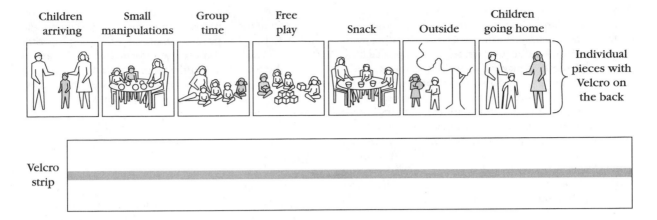

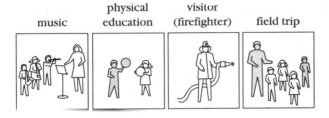

Figure 8.2 Daily Schedule

children who are having problems adjusting, as they can see that the final picture is going home. Encourage children to think about what will happen next. Make a sequencing task out of your daily schedule by having pictures of the activities and having the children arrange these in order. It is particularly important to do this at the beginning of the year and when schedules change or if your daily schedule is variable.

- *Rules.* Children may feel uncertain about the rules or expectations for them during transition times.

  To *make Rules Easy to Follow:* Help children understand exactly what you expect of them during transition times. Provide specific instructions and practice transition behavior. When cleaning up, be sure children know how and where to put materials away. You may even want to have a picture or outline of the item on the shelf where it needs to be returned to a particular place. Expect some testing behavior at transition time. Children need to feel secure and know that there are rules and that an adult is in control. A calm but firm response to children is reassuring.

- *Lack of planning.* Transitions are an important part of the day and need to have a purpose as well as advanced planning to make them work.

  Plan for Transitions: Transitions are a great opportunity for learning as well as a necessary part of the day. Help increase body awareness by having "children with long hair" or "children with brown eyes" or "children wearing stripes"

and so on leave first. Be creative and have children pretend they are cleaning up for a party, or as they move between activities have them jump like kangaroos, move as softly as a feather in the wind, march or tiptoe to the next location (ideas adapted from Davidson, 1988).

Social Competence

Interpersonal competence is established in the first few years of life (Guralnick, 1988). Children with diverse abilities are often expected to have this interpersonal competence because of their experience with a wide variety of adults. However, children may be competent with their parents and adults on a one-to-one basis because adults do the compensating and adapt their expectations. The same compensating rarely occurs with peers (Guralnick, 1988).

Competence with peers is important. Success with social tasks such as making friends and gaining entry into groups is imperative not only now but for later adjustment. Inclusion of all children in the same classroom makes this more of a challenge, yet inclusive settings provide opportunities for many levels of play, including more complex play behavior (Guralnick & Groom, 1987). The predictive value of a child's ability to establish peer relations over the long term is true for all children including those with disabilities (Guralnick, 1988).

Social competence is the key to social acceptance. Peers make judgments based on data (Johnny can't climb, looks funny, and so on). Children enter a new group with a clean slate, but they develop a personal social history within the group. Children with diverse abilities often use strategies of approaching other children that make it difficult to make friends. They are often less socially competent. As clusters of children form, more complex entry skills are required to join groups; for children lacking these skills, a reputation for lack of social competence is established, and a pattern of social separation and reduced social status results (Guralnick & Groom, 1987). Social networks become even narrower and more difficult to enter as children get older, therefore, it is imperative that children learn these skills early.

Intervention aimed at supporting the social integration of children with diverse abilities has been approached from two very different frameworks. Educators with strong developmental backgrounds have assumed that physical proximity to other children, plus using more open-ended, process-oriented activities in a free play setting would result in social integration. This has not been the case. Others, from a more behavioral orientation, have observed the lack of social competence and have developed very structured skits and specific exercises for children to repeat (Strain, 1990). For example, children are paired, and one child says, "Hello, my name is Dayonn. I like your shirt." The other child responds, "I'm glad to meet you. My name is Min." Dayonn then responds with "I'm glad to meet you." Other than using different names, all of the children in the class use the same procedure and the same words. The exercise might be repeated several times. Activities such as these have resulted in increased integration, but have not generalize to nonstructured situations and are not representative of how young children interact with each other in the real world. The problem is that the structured behavioral approach is an overly narrow solution to a complex problem. It is viewed as developmentally inappropriate by some early childhood educators. They find it stilted and not easily incorporated into their existing teaching style.

Successful social inclusion of children with diverse abilities requires thoughtful planning and programming. Think about social inclusion as you do math or language and literacy. Think about the learning cycle and use this to plan for social inclusion: work from awareness to exploration to inquiry to utilization. Start by increasing the awareness of all children about differences including cultural and ethnic differences and disabilities. Children are grounded in the real world and they try to incorporate new information into what they know about the world.

Children need first-hand experiences to learn about their world. Allocate time for children to ask questions, explore, and experiment. If this involves a simulation, do not have the child with a disability play the part of the child with the disability. He already knows what it is like. The goal is for others to learn, he might, however, be a good coach.

Have children discuss the feelings they had during the simulation and have them evaluate the strategies they used to cope. Help them decide what was easy and what was difficult. Discuss how these would vary from the classroom, to home, and in the community. Repeat the process on another day, helping children generalize and use the information they learned from before. Help children generate additional solutions as well as alternative explanations for behaviors. Again, try to encourage children who are ready to think in a broader context.

Discipline

Conflict and its resolution are at the core of many of society's problems. The conflict between the child's growing need for autonomy and the adult's need to inculcate values and socially acceptable behavior is classic. This inherent conflict may be viewed as a continuum. Individuals often feel very differently about where on this continuum one should interact with children.

Complete autonomy ———————— Complete submission

Conflict appears first in toddlerhood, and parents and caregivers make a conscious or unconscious choice about where they stand. The issues that need to be resolved in toddlerhood are the forerunners of the conflicts in adolescence and perhaps even in later adult life. When put in perspective, especially if one believes that conflict resolution patterns with toddlers set the groundwork for adolescence, some solutions become more useful than others.

Many of us use the words discipline, guidance, or punishment as though they were interchangeable synonyms. However, each means something slightly different, and their use affects children differently. Gartrell (1987) defines discipline as behavior that is designed to encourage self-control. Any actions or words that help children learn to self-monitor their own behavior so that it is appropriate and acceptable is discipline. Discipline is a form of teaching. One assumption is that young children misbehave out of lack of knowledge. Discipline supplies information regarding appropriate actions.

Punishment and guidance are two forms of discipline. Punishment involves the infliction of a negative consequence for a behavior that is inappropriate or wrong (Gartrell, 1987). Punishment usually succeeds in stopping behavior that is unwanted, but it may have negative effects on some children. Children may learn that they can "get away" with negative behavior without the presence of the controlling adult. Or, they may come to fear adults as harsh and uncaring.

Guidance, or positive discipline, facilitates the development of self-esteem, prosocial behaviors, and an ability to control one's own behavior (Gartrell, 1987). It is a process approach to guiding children's behavior rather than an isolated act of punishment. Positive discipline involves awareness of children's feelings, developmental levels, and the ability to set and keep sensible limits. When children do something that is unacceptable, they are presented with the logical consequences of their behavior in a way that preserves their self-esteem. As children learn there are consequences for their behavior—positive ones when they are acting appropriately, and negative ones when they act inappropriately—they begin to learn to act responsibly and control their own behavior.

Typically, adults begin to discipline children at the end of the first year, when children become mobile. Young children behave—they don't misbehave. Misbehavior is an interpretation by adults. Setting limits is part of an adult's commitment to a child, not just a reaction to the child's immediate behavior. The discipline should fit the child and should be accompanied by a conviction that setting limits is an important part of caring for young children. When caring accompanies discipline, it is guidance; when there is no caring, it is simply punishment.

The goal of discipline is to help children learn socially acceptable limits and develop internal controls to implement these limits. As such, discipline involves facilitating children's social development and prosocial skills (Lawton, 1988). The objectives of discipline are two-fold. One is immediate: to stop inappropriate behavior as it occurs. The second involves the development of inner controls for behavior. Adults can facilitate the development of these inner controls in children if they use positive discipline effectively.

Some techniques are useful in preventing behavior that will require discipline:

- Respond positively when children are acting appropriately, or making attempts to please: "You worked hard putting away your toys today. You must feel very proud." If children trust and like a teacher, they are more likely to respond to her suggestions and directions.

- Set up physical space that encourages appropriate behavior. Avoid long running areas, shelves that can tip, and congested areas.

- Move close to children who are having problems. Support your words with gentle physical prompts.

- Give children choices, but make sure they are appropriate choices you are willing to support.

- Be consistent in setting limits so children will learn what is expected of them: if children need to stay at the snack table while eating, remind them and reinforce that behavior with all the children.

- Let children know that you care for them and are proud of who they are and what they can do. For example, "Byung, I'm so proud of you. You put the blocks away all by yourself."

- Provide sufficient interesting activities to keep children actively involved in constructive play. Keep transitions smooth, with minimal time wasted in waiting.

- Speak in a natural tone of voice using short sentences and words children can understand. Maintain eye contact and be on the child's level when making an imperative statement.

- Minimize rules. Rigid environments cause more problems than they prevent. A simple rule to follow is: Children may not hurt themselves, each other, or the toys. You may need no other rules. If you have additional rules, be sure the adults model appropriate behavior for children. If children are not permitted to sit on the tables, adults should not either.

- Know your children. Keep a watchful eye on children who hurt others. If they seem frustrated, intervene as quickly as possible.

You are a model for the children and provide security for them. Step in to reframe and modify behavior that might lead to something more major.

- Show and tell children what you want them to do if they are doing something that is not appropriate: "The fence is not for climbing. I'll walk you to the jungle gym."

- Provide reasons for the limits you set for children: "Bobby, you need to walk carefully inside. The floors are slippery."

- Avoid long-winded explanations, but give children a reason for your direction: "Keep the sand in the sandbox. If you throw sand, it might get in someone's eyes and hurt him."

- When children are doing something inappropriate, state your directives positively. Tell children what they can do rather than what they can't:

Say:	Don't Say:
"Walk inside, it's safer."	"Don't run."
"Sit on your bottom."	"Don't stand on the chair."
"Amber is playing with that now. When she's done you may have a turn."	Don't grab that out of Amber's hands. That's not nice."

Sometimes by telling children what not to do you actually give them ideas of doing things they've never thought of.

- Distract or divert children's attention when they are acting inappropriately. If a child wants another's toy, offer him a similar one.

- Provide alternative appropriate behaviors. If a child is splashing water out of the water table, give him an egg beater to make waves.

Use situations to label feelings and to help children develop the verbal skills to talk about differences:

- Accept children's feelings: "If you are angry with Jasmine, tell her. It hurts when you hit her."

- Help children label their feelings verbally when they are upset, angry, or hurt. You might say, "Brooke, you're really angry because Justin took your doll."

- Support young children in using words to solve problems. This may not occur to them, as language competence is relatively new. You may need to assist younger or more inexperienced children with the words to say at first, but eventually they will learn how to "talk out" their problems. An example, "Jimmy, tell Renee you don't like it when she hits you."

- Let children know when you are angry and model appropriate ways to handle that anger. For example, "Rosa, it makes me angry when you hurt Shauna. You need to go to another activity."

- Help children realize that their actions and words affect others: "Peter, did you see Mark's face? He was really upset when you knocked down his blocks."

- Avoid using labels such as "bad girl" or comparing children with each other. Comparing children leads to competition among them.

When it looks as though there will be problems:

- Step in early. Imagination and a "new" activity may solve the problem.

- If a child is having a bad day, give her some space to work out those feelings. Adding playdough or water play to the day's activities often provides a good outlet.

- If a child has a tantrum, allow him to calm down in a safe place. Being out of control is scary for the child, so an adult should be nearby. Tell the child, in a soothing voice, that as soon as he is calm the two of you can talk about the problem. Do not try to reason with a child who is screaming and thrashing.

- It is important to comfort a child who is hurt, but it is also important that the child who does the hurting has your support. He needs your guidance for his growth. He also needs to learn prosocial behaviors.

Discipline is influenced by several factors, including what the adult knows about how the child usually acts or responds to social situations. Children's temperaments and the goodness of fit between adult and child may be particularly important when considering young children with disabilities. Keogh (1982) found that teacher perceptions of the teachability of a child with a disability was significantly related to the child's temperament. That is, those children whose temperaments were rated as easy were more likely to be rated by teachers as successful in the preschool environment. She suggests that the child's temperament may influence the teacher's expectations of the child, and thus influence instructional and disciplinary decisions.

In addition to the child's temperament, his disability, care demands, behavior problems, and social responsiveness play a part in how adults handle discipline situations. Those children whose care involves more demands may cause more stress for caregivers.

Praise versus Encouragement

A positive, appreciative atmosphere is more helpful for children's growth than a setting where negative, blaming comments are made frequently. Children with diverse abilities, in particular, have already heard a great deal about what they cannot do. We usually think about praise as being positive, general, and implying some judgment or evaluation of the individual's performance. Some examples of praise are "Nice job, Alexis" and "Charday is being a good listener." We use praise because we want children to feel good about themselves, to learn, and to promote appropriate behavior. Praise does not always have these effects (Hitz & Driscoll, 1988).

Praise can sometimes have negative effects if not used appropriately. The technique of praising one child to get others to behave similarly is often not effective and may cause the other children to resent the praised child. Inappropriate praise may also influence children to rely on others' opinions rather than judging for themselves. (They have become externally rather than internally motivated.) It thus encourages dependence on adults rather than independence (Hitz & Driscoll, 1988).

What are the alternatives? Certainly a positive climate is important for children. Encouragement

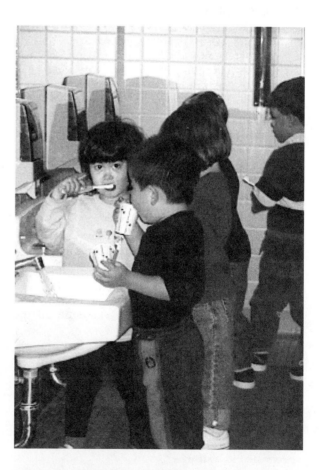

For younger children, transitions take up proportionately more of the day. However, they are an essential way of teaching adaptive skills.

may be more appropriate than praise. Encouragement refers specifically to responses to children's efforts and/or specific aspects of their work or play. Encouragement does not place judgment. ("You used a lot of colors in your painting.") Encouragement also focuses on the child's efforts rather than on an evaluation of a finished product ("I noticed that you played for a long time with the dress-up clothes today" or "You look like you enjoyed digging holes in the sand"). Encouragement is designed not to compare child but rather to note improvement and progress for that individual child. ("You stacked more blocks today than you've ever done before.")

If our goals are to have independent, self-motivated, happy children, it appears that encouragement, rather than praise, may best foster the desired positive growth and development.

Program Evaluation

Once both individual and class programs are in place, it is necessary to determine whether or not they are effective. In the past, it was often simply assumed that if children went to school they were learning. But teaching, like other professions, must be accountable—not to only principals and other administrators, but to children, their parents, tax payers, and the legal system as well. Evaluation is an integral part of teaching and learning.

Program evaluation has two major aspects: the purpose of the evaluation and the process of carrying out the evaluation.

Purpose of Program Evaluation

The major reason for evaluating a program is to provide information to those involved with the program about what it is doing well and what needs attention (Barnard, 1986). One obvious question is, Does the program meet the needs of the people it serves? The answer to this question requires information. What are the characteristics and needs of the children and families served in the program? Different children in different types of families have different needs, although they may all be in the same program or classroom. Program evaluation needs to be sensitive to both group and individual differences.

Sometimes program evaluation is used to help solve a particular problem a program or class is having. This type of evaluation focuses on a single aspect of a program or a classroom that has been identified as a problem. Although the problems may vary, the procedure for evaluation is frequently similar:

1. Identify the problem in a way that it can be solved. "They should not have violence on children's television shows" is not a solvable problem. It is a value judgment. Instead: "Some children watch superheroes on television and come to school and play out what they have seen. How can I set up my classroom to discourage superhero play? What rules do I need to develop to regulate this play?" is a solvable problem.

2. Review the relevant literature and talk to people in other programs or classes to see how they have dealt with similar problems. (Although problems may seem unique, it is unlikely that you are the first person to encounter the problem.)

3. Develop a system for dealing with the problem. Share this system with all those involved (especially parents) and gather their input. Modify the system.

4. Field-test the system for an appropriate period of time (perhaps two to four weeks).

5. Evaluate the results, modify the system if necessary, and retest or keep the system in place.

You may have used this procedure informally when you were coping with superhero play and not realized that in reality you evaluated your program as having a problem, explored the dimensions of the problem, looked at what others had done and developed a system to solve the problem, evaluated that solution, and modified your approach.

Some program evaluation is extensive and ambitious. You may be asked to participate in evaluation projects by providing specific input. Some evaluation projects are long-range as well as short-range. It is important to know at the beginning the purpose of the evaluation. When the evaluation is being done to decide whether to continue a program or eliminate it, those involved may have very different agendas.

If the purpose of the evaluation is to determine whether or not early intervention decreased the number of children requiring special education services, then the data necessary for evaluation are very different than if the purpose of the evaluation is to decide which is more effective, full- or half-day kindergarten. Without having decided on the purpose of the evaluation, one cannot proceed in any meaningful way.

Sometimes evaluation is very long-term. Knowing long-term goals for children can help focus a curriculum in early childhood. United Cerebral Palsy cites a number of long-term goals for children with disabilities and their families. Programs for early childhood might evaluate their program planning in light of these goals:

- Independence;

- A sense of self-worth, including adjustment to the disability, use of talents and abilities and constructive ways of dealing with feelings of helplessness and frustration;

- Inclusion of the child with a disability into the community at large;

- Positive inclusion into the family;

- Development of family's ability to deal constructively with their feelings about the child; and

- A parental sense of competence (Barnard, 1986, p. 6).

The Process of Program Evaluation

People who fund programs want to know how effective they are, and administrators may need the information to defend programs or to get additional programs or classrooms. Educators, however, may feel threatened by the evaluation process or feel that it is not relevant to them. You may feel that the obligations of teaching are already enough. "You hired me to teach, leave me alone and let me teach!" Program evaluation is not likely to succeed without teacher support.

At the very least the process of evaluation describes the population you serve and exactly what you are doing. At a minimal level, all programs and individual classrooms need this information. If you are not clear about what you are doing and why you are doing it, you cannot effectively present your classroom to parents or administrators.

Evaluation is essential to improve programs. Administrators need to know how you evaluate your program and how satisfied you are with your job. To the extent that you are not an active participant in the process, things that do not satisfy you are unlikely to change, and you may be unhappy in your job. Know that you are one of the stakeholders; you have a

vested interest, and you need to know enough about the evaluation process to make it work for you and your program. You also need to be sure the evaluation process does not interfere with your teaching.

The less intrusive and less burdensome the evaluation process is for teachers, the more likely it is to go smoothly and to be completed (Barnard, 1986). You need to remind others this is a primary consideration, not a secondary one. Data collected must be used, and the people who collect the data need to be informed of its use. If you perceive the information you collect going into a "black hole," you are unlikely to continue collecting it in a careful manner, if at all.

When children have individualized programs with measurable goals or outcomes, these need to be evaluated as well. According to Barnard (1986), individualized plans should be grouped for evaluation, and you should aim for an 85 percent achievement rate. A higher rate may show that you aren't stretching yourself or the families; a rate of 50 percent or less means that expectations are not realistic or the program is not effective.

The most commonly asked question of programs is: Are children different because they received this service or participated in this program? This was the question asked of early intervention years ago, and researchers developed experimental designs to try to answer it. Overall, the conclusion was that early

Program evaluation looks at patterns of interactions among children. To the extent that some children are consistently excluded, the planning needs to be evaluated and changed to include all the children.

intervention was effective both economically and as a method for improving the quality of life of the children served in both the short and long term.

Today, we need to ask different questions because we no longer must "prove" the efficacy of early intervention. We are now fine-tuning the system. We need to learn about the effectiveness of different models of programming for different populations: "What types of services, in what combinations, using what models are most effective?" Applied research is concerned with why a program works or fails to work and for whom it works.

Summary

Program planning is complex and challenging. It requires examining one's philosophy about teaching and where children with diverse abilities fit into that philosophy. It requires looking at the relationship between one's personal philosophy and the principles underlying developmentally appropriate practices and, finally, looking at how one's philosophy is reflected in the classroom setting.

Program planning involves consideration of both contextual and theme/unit based planning. Issues deserving special concern are inclusive settings that involve social competence, transitions, and discipline. Program evaluation grows out of these concerns. In the past, we asked whether or not children with diverse abilities should be part of regular classrooms. Now we are asking questions about the most effective way to plan programs to include all children.

Educational Resources

Child Care Settings and the ADA
http://TheArc.org/faqs/ccqa1.html
Questions and Answers about the ADA written in understandable terms. Covers a lot of basic definitions used in the ADA.

Special Education Programs
http://192.239.34.2/pubs/TeachersGuide/pt19i.html
A teacher's guide to the U.S. Department of Education—Fall 1995.

References

Bandura, A. (1992). Social cognitive theory. In R. Vasta (Ed.), *Six theories of child development* (pp. 1–60). England: Jessica Kingsley.

Barnard, K. (1986). Major issues in program evaluation. In *Program evaluation: Issues, strategies and models* (pp. 4–7). Washington, DC: National Center for Clinical Infant Programs.

Berk, L. E. (1994). Vygotsky's theory: The importance of make-believe play. *Young Children, 50*(1), 30–39.

Borden, E. (1987). The community connection—It works. *Young Children, 42*(4), 14–23.

Bredekamp, S., & Copple, C. (Ed.). (1997). *Developmentally appropriate practice in early childhood programs* (Rev. ed.). Washington, DC: NAEYC.

Bredekamp, S., & Rosegrant, T. (1992). *Reaching potentials: Appropriate curriculum and assessment for young children* (Vol. 1). Washington, DC: NAEYC.

Bredekamp, S., & Rosegrant, T. (1995). Reaching potentials through transforming curriculum, assessment, and teaching. In S. Bredekamp & T. Rosegrant (Eds.), *Reaching potentials: Transforming early childhood curriculum and assessment* (Vol. 2, pp. 15–22). Washington, DC: NAEYC.

Brown, J. W. (1994). Morphogenesis and mental process. *Development and Psychopathology, 6,* 551–563.

Carlsson-Paige, N., & Levin, D. E. (1987). *The war play dilemma: Balancing needs and values in the early childhood classroom.* New York: Teachers College Press.

Carnegie Task Force on Meeting the Needs of Young Children. (1994). *Starting points: Meeting the needs of our youngest children.* New York: Carnegie Corporation of New York.

Chenfeld, M. (1987). The first 30 years are the hardest: Notes from the yellow brick road. *Young Children, 42*(3), 28–32.

Children's Defense Fund. (1989). *A vision for America's future.* Washington, DC: Author.

Cicchetti, D., & Tucker, D. (1994). Development and self-regulatory structures of the mind. *Development and Psychopathology, 6,* 533–549.

Consortium for Longitudinal Studies. (1983). *As the twig is bent: Lasting effects of preschool programs.* Hillsdale, NJ: Erlbaum.

Davidson, J. I. (1988). *Dealing with transitions.* Unpublished manuscript. Newark, DE: Delaware Department of Services for Children, Youth and Their Families, Day Care Licensing Services.

Feldman, D. H., & Snyder, S. S. (1994). Universal to unique—Mapping the development terrain. In D. H. Feldman (Ed.), *Beyond universals in cognitive development* (2nd ed., pp. 15–38). Norwood, NJ: ABLEX.

Furuno, S., O'Reilly, K., Inatsuka, T., Hosaka, C., Allman, T., & Ziesloft-Falbey, B. (1991). *HELP chart: Gross motor, fine motor.* Palo Alto, CA: VORT.

Gardner, H. (1983). *Frames of mind: The theory of multiple intelligences.* New York: Basic Books.

Gartrell, D. (1987). Punishment or guidance? *Young Children, 42*(3), 55–61.

George, D. (1995). *Gifted education: Identification and provision.* London: David Fulton.

Gowen, J. W. (1995). The early development of symbolic play. *Young Children, 44*(6), 11–16.

Guralnick, M. J. (1988, November). Keynote address, presented at the International Early Childhood Conference on Children with Special Needs, Nashville, TN.

Guralnick, M. J., & Groom, J. M. (1987). The peer relations of mildly delayed and nonhandicapped preschool children in mainstreamed play groups. *Child Development, 58,* 1556–1572.

Hanson, M. J., Lynch, E. W., & Wayman, K. I. (1990). Honoring the cultural diversity of families when gathering data. *Topics in Early Childhood Special Education, 10*(1), 112–131.

Hitz, R., & Driscoll, A. (1988). Praise or encouragement? New insights into praise: Implications for early childhood teachers. *Young Children, 43*(5), 6–13.

Honig, A. S. (1983). Evaluation of infant/toddler intervention programs. In B. Spodek (Ed.), *Studies in educational evaluation* (Vol. 8, pp. 305–316). London: Pergamon Press.

Honig, A. S. (1993). Mental health for babies: What do theory and research teach us? *Young Children, 48*(3) 69–76.

Honig, A. S., & Wittmer, D. S. (1996). Helping children become more prosocial: Ideas for classrooms, families, schools, and communities. *Young Children, 51*(2), 62–70.

Hyson, M. C. (1994). *The emotional development of young children: Building an emotion-centered curriculum.* New York: Teachers College Press.

Keogh, B. K. (1982). Temperament: An individual difference of importance in intervention programs. *Topics in Early Childhood Special Education, 2*(2), 25–31.

Lawton, J. T. (1988). *Introduction to child care and early childhood education.* Boston: Scott, Foresman/Little, Brown College Division.

Levin, D. E., & Carlsson-Paige, N. (1994). Developmentally appropriate television: Putting children first. *Young Children, 49*(5), 38–44.

Meadows, S. (1993). *The child as thinker: The development and acquisition of cognition in children.* London: Routledge & Kegan Paul.

Miedzain, M. (1991). *Boys will be boys: Breaking the link between masculinity and violence.* New York: Doubleday.

National Association for the Education of Young Children. (1998). *The leading edge: A national video conference/seminal on developmentally appropriate practice in early childhood programs.* NAEYC.

National Association for the Education of Young Children and the National Association of Early Childhood Specialists in State Departments of Education. (1991). Guidelines for appropriate curriculum content and assessment in programs serving children ages 3 through 8: A position statement. *Young Children, 46*(3), 21–39.

Nunnelley, J. (1990). Beyond turkeys, santas, snowmen, and hearts: How to plan innovative curriculum themes. *Young Children, 46*(1), 24–29.

Osofsky, J. D. (1993/1994). Introduction. In J. D. Osofsky & E. Fenichel (Eds.), Hurt, healing, hope: Caring for infants and toddlers in violent environments. *Zero to Three, 14*(3), 3–6.

Piaget, J. (1963). *The origins of intelligence in children.* New York: Norton. (Original work published 1952)

Ramey, C. T., Brandt, D. M., Wasik, B. H., Sparling, J. J., Fendt, K. H., & SaVange, L. M. (1992). The infant health development program for low birth weight, premature infants: Program elements, family participation, and child intelligence. *Pediatrics, 89,* 454–465.

Seitz, V., Rosenbaum, L. K., & Apfel, N. H. (1985). Effects of family support intervention: A ten year follow-up. *Child Development, 56*(2), 528–539.

Shore, R. (1997). *Rethinking the brain: New insights into early development.* New York: Families and Work Institute.

Smilansky, S., & Shefatya, L. (1990). *Facilitating play: A medium for promoting cognitive, socio-emotional, and academic development in young children.* Gaithersburg, MD: Psychosocial & Educational Publications.

Sinclair, H., Stambak, M., Lexine, I., Rayne, S., & Verba, M. (1989). *Infants and objects: The creativity of cognitive development.* San Diego, CA: Academic Press.

Strain, P. S. (1990). LRE for preschool children with handicaps: What we know, what we should be doing. *Journal of Early Intervention, 14,* 291–296.

Thatcher, R. W. (1994). Psychopathology of early frontal lobe damage: Dependence on cycles of development. *Development and Psychopathology, 6,* 565–596.

Trickett, P. K., & Kucznski, L. (1986). Children's misbehaviors and parental discipline strategies in abusive and nonabusive families. *Developmental Psychology, 22*(1), 115–123.

Vygotsky, L. S. (1978). The role of play in development. In M. Cole, V. John-Steiner, S. Scribner, & E. Souberman (Eds.), *Mind in society: The development of higher psychological processes* (pp. 92–104). Cambridge, MA: Harvard University Press. (Original work published 1933)

Vygotsky, L. S. (1987). *Mind in society: The development of higher psychological processes.* Cambridge, MA: Harvard University Press.

Whitehead, L. (1989). Adult-supported learning. In P. Deiner, L. Whitehead, & C. Prudhoe (Eds.), *Technical assistance: Information sheets for day care providers and families of children with special needs.* Unpublished manuscript. Newark, DE: University of Delaware.

PART TWO

Educating Children with Diverse Abilities

Chapter 9

CHILDREN WITH
EMOTIONAL AND
BEHAVIORAL DIFFERENCES

I wonder about Julie. She used to be such a happy, outgoing little girl, and now it seems like she'd rather sit in her locker than do anything else. Even the other children notice it. They ask me what's wrong with Julie. I'm probably over-reacting; after all, what could be wrong with a 4-year-old?

That's a good question. What could be bothering a 4-year-old? As you contemplate your own problems and worries, the things that might bother a 4-year-old seem so inconsequential that you may decide the child's concerns are not worth worrying about. Therefore, you tell the child not to worry. That is like a millionaire telling you not to worry about your inconsequential rent, bills, and so on. Your response would probably be a silent or spoken "You don't understand."

To go back to Julie, she has lost interest in everything, including playdough, which used to be her favorite activity. Trying to interest Julie in the playdough is one way you show you don't understand. Julie has been spending more time just sitting in her locker, and that worries you. Rather than enticing her away, show concern by saying, "Julie, *I'm* worried because you are sitting in your locker and not playing with the playdough and talking with your friends the way you usually do." Compare the preceding statement with this one: "Julie, *you* shouldn't be sitting here in your locker, especially when I put out your favorite activity." In the first instance, you make an "I" statement, which reflects your concern about the situation. It requires nothing of Julie, not even a response. In the second statement, you seem to be both judging and blaming Julie for her behavior. "*You* shouldn't" really means "*she* shouldn't because *I* don't want her to." You would be better off admitting your discomfort than blaming it on her. After expressing concern, give the child permission to talk about her feelings: "Sometimes when I'm sad I want to be alone. I wonder if you're sad about something now?" While still expressing concern, you can offer an opportunity, or invitation, for Julie to talk.

Whether or not she responds, the next move is to tell her how you are willing to help while giving her some control over the situation: "Would you like to talk about how you feel? (Pause) I can listen now. I'd like to come and sit beside you for a few minutes whenever I can. Is that OK with you?" Be careful not to make an offer you can't follow through on. Don't offer to sit beside the child all morning even if you think that would be helpful. Your duties as a teacher make an "all morning" offer impossible to fulfill.

The question is, is Julie just having a temporary bad time? Is this the teacher's imagination or intuition? Is there, in fact, something wrong with Julie? Let's look at Julie to see what signs or characteristics are significant. Children themselves may be at risk, or the environment in which they live can increase or decrease their developmental vulnerability.

Increasingly, children come to educational settings bringing with them the stress that is part of living in families who are themselves struggling. These families may be living in poverty, going through a separation or divorce, or just too stressed to cope with life due to situational or maturational crises. Educators have the opportunity to help children by modifying the learning environment to meet children's needs as well as helping children develop skills to cope with these diverse situations.

Helping children deal with dysfunctional problems has not traditionally been a school responsibility. However, current thinking is that all school personnel should be part of a team engaged in an effort to help children develop coping skills to live with stressful situations. Teachers are key figures because they see the child daily. They need the training to provide psychological first aid to children. However, this is no longer enough. There needs to be a follow-up system to open lines of communication between the home and school.

Teachers need to be supported in looking at experiences as teaching opportunities: The teachable moment is no longer just related to reading readiness, but includes opportunities to teach coping and adaptive skills, stress management and decision-making skills, as well as to build self-esteem.

Stress, Coping, and Crisis

Many psychologists look at stress, coping, and crisis together. Causes of stress are difficult to define, as what is stressful for one child is not stressful for **175** another, and what creates stress at one point in a child's life may not be stressful at other points.

Children and Stress

Stress can be viewed as an event or a "pileup" of events that is perceived as a threat and that the individual does not have the resources to cope with (McCubbin & Patterson, 1982). Developmentally, events that are stressors to young children might be coped with by older children, and adults may be even less sensitive to stressors in young children. Sensitive adults can serve as mediators in lessening the impact of stress on children (Finkelhor, 1995). Stressors can be caused by a variety of different situations. The definition is determined by the individual, and the impact of the stress is related to the coping strategies and resources of the individual. For example, one might believe that a child who has just moved with his mother to an apartment because of a marital separation would feel stressed. If they moved because the father was abusive and now they feel safe, this actually may have reduced stress.

Stress for young children can be *internal,* arising from such factors as gas pains in a colicky infant, a painful ear infection in a young child, or the episodic pain of a child with juvenile rheumatoid arthritis. Stress can also result from *external* factors such as being placed in child care, the arrival of a new sibling, domestic violence, or living in a distressed neighborhood (Honig, 1986).

Stress can be *unique* based on a single situation such as an injection, a single incidence of sexual abuse, or a fire. Stress can also be *habitual, chronic,* and *cumulative* based on living in poverty with a parent who consistently uses drugs or alcohol or abuses the child. A child with a chronic illness may have pain so continually that others tend to see it as the norm and forget that it is still real and stressful to the child.

Stress can be overt or covert. *Overt* stress, such as a home fire or a death in the family, may create fewer problems as others are aware of the situation and are a potential resource for helping the child to cope with the problem. Children can talk about their fears and others can respond. When stress is *covert* others may not know about it. It may be a family secret. Habitual abuse of a child is typically not talked about with others. If children are threatened, particularly by adults they are entrusted to, they have no one to mediate the situation and few resources to cope. Sometimes it isn't clear whether stress is real or imaginary. From the standpoint of the child, that is irrelevant: The child's perception of stress is very real (Pittman, 1987). For children, stress may result in irritability and disorganization. Crisis involves the interaction between the stressor(s) and the vulnerability of a child to that particular stressor (Pittman, 1987).

Children and Crisis

To provide a framework for understanding children and stress, we have borrowed from and adapted Hill's (1958) ABCX model and McCubbin and Patterson's (1982) double ABCX model of family crisis and coping:

a factor—the stressor. This is the event or situation that produces the stress. This can be a single life event or a chronic situation that causes disequilibrium in the child; for a child, this may be a visit to the doctor, unexpectedly confronting a large dog, being yelled at by an adult, being hit by a sibling, being physically abused, or the approach of a hurricane. One also looks at the hardships associated with the stressor event such as pain, separation from a loved one, and so on.

b factor—resistance resources. What skills or resources does the child have to cope with the stress? These can be internal resources such temperament, creativity, or having observed someone else in a similar situation.

c factor—the child's definition of the stressor. Children view events differently from adults, and what adults see as stress children may not and vice versa. Likewise, different children view different events as being stressful. This is a subjective view of the situation, in which a stressor can be viewed as a challenge or a crisis.

x factor—the crisis. The interaction of abc produces tension that must be managed. If the situation cannot be managed, stress or distress is the result. Stress is the state that arises from an actual (or perceived) difference between the demands of the situation and the capacity of the child to respond. Stress moves to distress when the changes that are necessary are defined as undesirable and/or unattainable. Distress is an unpleasant, disorganized state.

All these factors influence whether the event continues as a stressor event or moves into a crisis. Stress may never become a crisis if the child has the resources to cope with the stressor event. When the stressor is a single traumatic event, this model works well as a framework for understanding stress. In McCubbin and Patterson's (1982) variation, they acknowledged that stressors for families (and children) rarely come one at time:

aA—The double *A* acknowledges the pileup of stressors. This pileup is not uncommon in real life. Children who are chronically poor, physically abused, and homeless may view stressors differently from the child who, though her father died, still goes home to a predictable routine.

bB—Although the child may not have the resources to cope, this *bB* acknowledges that additional resources can be brought to bear on a stressor. Being placed in child care among caring adults can mediate the stress for a child. This offers the potential for change in a positive direction.

cC—The child now views the original stressor and his perception of it in light of both the pileup of additional stressors and also the potential resources that caring adults can bring.

xX—The hope is that rather than crisis, we now have coping and the potential for a more positive outcome, although there is also the potential for more negative outcomes without intervention.

These models provide a framework for understanding crisis events and why children both perceive and react to these events differently. It also holds the potential for helping children add resources (bB) with the aid of caring adults to help them cope.

Children and Coping

There are two broad categories of coping: problem-focused and emotion-focused. *Problem-focused* coping centers on confrontation or planful problem solving, whereas *emotion-focused* coping ranges from expressing and sharing feelings to self-blame, avoidance, denial, and wishful thinking (Compas & Epping, 1993). Young children seem to use problem-focused strategies, perhaps from modeling adults because these adult strategies are more obvious. With increasing age, children use more emotion-focused coping strategies (Compas & Epping, 1993).

To understand crisis and the traumatic events that happen to children, we try to categorize events as a way of understanding their impact. We classify traumatic events based on their frequency of occurrence. Acute or *Type I traumas* are traumatic events that occur singly, as the ABCX model depicts. Chronic or *Type II traumas* involve long-standing situations and are more like the double ABCX. The child's assessment of the situation is important, particularly the degree to which the child feels her own life is in danger (Keppel-Benson & Ollendick, 1993). Children's previous experience with stressful events will impact their coping. A second trauma tends to bring back the memories of the first trauma. Even when children themselves are not involved, hearing about a similar event may trigger memories (Keppel-Benson & Ollendick, 1993). Additionally, the child's condition prior to the event will impact the child's perception of the event. A child who has separation anxiety is likely to respond differently to being told that her parents are divorcing from a child who is securely attached. Children's level of cognitive and language development also influences their responses.

Children who have been exposed to chronic traumas have different reactions from those who have been exposed to acute traumas. They are likely to express sadness or dissociation, be detached from others, have a restricted range of affect, and may experience long-term problems. Rather than vivid, their memories of the events may have become blurred over time (Keppel-Benson & Ollendick, 1993).

Children come to stressful events with a very different knowledge base than adults. Children may not be aware of the implied harm in a situation nor have a complete understanding of the implications of an event. They may view sexual assault as an act of violence only and not be aware of the sexual aspect of the attack until middle childhood. Preschool children may expect powerful others like superheros to swoop down and help them, or have unrealistic expectations of what adults can do in situations. They may show more internalizing behaviors in response to stress: separation anxiety, social withdrawal, and somatic complaints (headache, stomachache) (Eth & Pynoos, 1985).

Children frequently look to significant adults to decide how to deal with situations in which they feel stressed. This is called *social referencing*. If the parents show emotional stress, the child is likely to do so as well. In some situations, such as sexual abuse, the stressor itself is only the beginning of the crisis. Children may have to cope with physicians, police, lawyers, and others. This may become a situation of "secondary victimization" as the child ends up bearing the social stigma of the event (Ayalon, 1983).

Stress is related to the extremely complex issue of victimization. In the broadest sense, when thinking about victimization, both direct and indirect, one should consider the many ways in which children are victimized and the particular characteristics that make them prone to victimization.

Children and Victimization

To move beyond the literature that focused solely on child abuse and neglect and to find a developmental framework for viewing situations in which children are at risk, Finkelhor (1995) proposed the concept of "victimization." He saw the need to develop a means for understanding social traumas within a developmental framework.

The initial thrust was to develop a typology of child victimization. Using national statistics, researchers grouped victimization into three broad categories: pandemic, acute, and extraordinary. *Pandemic victimizations* occur to a majority of children in the course of growing up, yet they receive very little public or professional attention. These include such events as assault by siblings or peers and physical punishment by parents. Children are far more likely to be hit by someone than to be abducted, and in fact, children worry more about this because of its alarming frequency and the influence it has on their everyday lives (Finkelhor & Dziuba-Leatherman, 1994). Children with diverse abilities are frequently on the receiving end of this type of victimization. The probability of peer violence increases for children in child care settings.

Acute victimizations, which affect far fewer children, include physical abuse, neglect, and family abductions. Finally, *extraordinary victimizations,* which affect even fewer children yet receive a great deal of attention, include homicide, child abuse homicide, and nonfamily abduction (Finkelhor & Dziuba-Leatherman, 1994).

Children are disproportionately victims of violence. The National Family Violence Survey (Straus, Gelles, & Steinmetz, 1980) found that children were the victims of severe violence (beating, kicking, hitting with a fist or object) twice as frequently as an adult partner. With the frequency of siblings and peers assaulting younger children, it appears clear this is an area where children in many homes experience stress, perhaps even chronic stress.

As children grow and develop, they both acquire and lose characteristics that put them at risk for victimization. Because young children are dependent on adults in their world to fulfill their basic needs, they are vulnerable in ways that older children are not. The most clearly dependency-related form of victimization is neglect (Finkelhor, 1995). And parents are responsible for such neglect.

When adults are victimized they often display *posttraumatic stress disorder,* which is relatively short term and primarily affects the behavior associated with the experience. Whether children experience or witness an acute trauma, they too experience posttraumatic stress disorder. In young children, this is often expressed by disorganization and agitated behavior. The young child may participate in repetitive play in which themes or aspects of the trauma are reenacted, or actually reenact the trauma. Children may have symptoms such as fearfulness, nightmares, and avoidance of violence on television. They may try to avoid places associated with the event and show hyperalertness in similar places or with similar individuals (American Psychiatric Association [APA], 1994; Finkelhor, 1995). Almost all traumatic situations result in some increased sense of fearfulness. In addition to posttraumatic stress symptoms, in very young children victimization can interfere with normal developmental processes (Shirk, 1988).

Assessing the results of victimization of young children differs from assessing adults. Although specific developmental problems vary, the effects of victimization can result in impaired attachment; problems relating to others; poor peer relationships, often in the form of aggression toward peers with lack of remorse; and problems coping with stress and anxiety (Briere, 1992; Cicchetti & Lynch, 1993).

This view of victimization uses the disruption of developmental tasks of childhood as a basis for understanding vulnerability. Development of attachment to a primary caregiver is a major social task of infancy. When abuse is perpetrated by the caregiver, the result is insecure attachment, and the expectation is that the effects of this insecure attachment will be carried into later phases of development and other relationships (Cicchetti & Lynch, 1993). There may also be physiological alterations in endocrine functioning and neurological processes that permanently affect the brain itself as well as cognitive and behavioral development (Putnam & Trickett, 1993).

As children develop and are capable of mental representation, they develop the ability to dissociate. They do this by fantasizing, developing imaginary playmates, and denying things they clearly have done (Putnam, 1991). Children victimized as 2-year-olds or preschoolers use dissociation as a defense mechanism and develop chronic patterns of dissociation, which may include memory loss, a tendency for trance-like behavior, and auditory or visual hallucinations.

The child's level of cognitive development impacts victimization. Cognitive appraisal (what a child

believes about what happened) may mediate the victimization experience (Rutter, 1988). This process is believed to work differently in young children than in adults. Young children do not have the cognitive maturity to objectively assess all situations; therefore, parents can reframe the experience and model behaviors to buffer some of its negative impact (Kendall-Tackett, Williams, & Finkelhor, 1993). When parents are part of the victimization process, the results are not mediated.

Child Abuse and Neglect

Child abuse and neglect encompass all forms of child mistreatment. Honig (1986) identifies four kinds of abuse that occur to young children: "Severe *physical abuse* leaves bodily scars and results in death for several thousand children annually; some children suffer from *psychological unavailability* of the mothering one; some are *neglected* and hungry; and some are *emotionally scarred* by bitter hostility, shaming, chronic verbal abuse, and criticism" (p. 49).

It is estimated that children with disabilities are at one and half times greater risk for a single incident of abuse, and at even greater risk for multiple victimizations, perhaps two to five times as high for severe forms of physical abuse and multiple victimizations of the same child (Sobsey, 1994). Although we separate abuse into categories, they overlap, and children often experience more than one type of abuse.

Physical abuse is nonaccidental physical injury to children. It includes excessive corporal punishment, slapping, hitting, burning, smothering, restraining (physical or chemical), and torture as well as misguided attempts at teaching children (Bear, Schenk, & Buckner, 1992/1993). It accounts for 25 percent of substantiated cases of abuse (McCurdy & Daro, 1994). For infants, physical abuse often takes the form of being shaken by adults, most frequently because the infants will not stop crying. Parents' inability to be successful with their infants causes some to strike out at the infant.

Some parents harm their children as they attempt to teach them certain behaviors. They might burn the child's fingertips as a way of teaching that stoves are hot and he or she shouldn't touch them. These parents will readily admit what they have done, but they do not see it as abuse and may be offended that you consider it as such.

Some parents use physical punishment rather than reasoning with children in the belief that it takes physical measures to make children into good people. Injuries that result from this are typically bruises, welts, and cuts. Parents who discipline children may agree that the punishment is excessive but remain convinced that the child may grow up to be a delinquent if she does not learn right from wrong in this way.

Some children are battered. These are often children who are 4 or younger and have parents with very unrealistic expectations of children; for example, parents may expect an infant to quit crying when told to do so. Children with disabilities represent a disproportionate number of battering victims. Injuries vary from bruises to severe trauma. In addition to the person who actively participates in the abuse, some adults enable the behavior to continue by not preventing or reporting it.

The abuser of children with disabilities is most often the child's caregiver. The child may not live up to parental expectations and be viewed as adding stress and tension to the family. The caregiver just "snaps" and physically abuses the child out of frustration, stress, or lack of understanding. In families where a child with a disability is abused, other siblings are also likely to be abused. One sibling, often the oldest female, may take a protective role toward the child (Morgan, 1987).

Emotional maltreatment is the most subtle and often unrecognized form of abuse. It constitutes only 4 percent of the substantiated cases of abuse (McCurdy & Daro, 1994). Emotionally maltreated children are perceived and portrayed negatively by the parents; the children may see themselves in the same light and describe themselves as "bad." There may be delays in emotional development and immaturity that result in behavioral problems and antisocial behavior (Bear et al., 1992/1993). Children may feel unwanted and unloved and may become cruel or abusive of younger children.

Neglect is the most commonly reported form of abuse, constituting 47 percent of reported cases (McCurdy & Daro, 1994). One broad definition of child neglect is the failure of the parents or caregiver to provide the child with one or more of the following: basic physical needs, emotional needs, or educational needs (Starr, 1988). Families that are chronically neglectful typically have multiple problems and lack knowledge, skills, and tangible resources. Parents simply may not have the money to buy enough food and clothing for their children, or their priorities for spending money may not include necessities for the child. Sometimes, young children remain home alone while their parents are at work because the parents cannot afford child care or no child care center will take the child. In many cases, neglect is the result of a larger dysfunctional pattern that includes adult drug abuse. In these cases, all the family income is used to buy drugs. Unfortunately, problems associated with drug-related abuse and neglect are frequently compounded by the child's prenatal exposure to drugs and alcohol. This condition, plus a neglectful or abusive environment, increases the child's risk for multiple social problems.

Children who have been neglected show an array of problematic behaviors:

- Poor hygiene and personal care skills.

- Short attention span, which may be related to hunger or lack of stimulation at home.

- Low self-esteem and few interpersonal skills.

- Behavior problems in the classroom, which become more problematic with increasing age.

- Insecure attachment to caregiver.

- Lower scores on all measures of school performance.

The long-lasting effects of neglect on academic achievement may be greater than other forms of maltreatment (Eckenrode, Laird, & Doris, 1993).

Child sexual abuse is any activity between a child and an adult (or much older child) that sexually excites or satisfies the adult's needs or desires. Both boys and girls are victims. Children rarely report what has happened, as the perpetrators usually try to convince the children that it was their fault and that no one will believe them anyway. Sexual abuse is further complicated because the most frequent perpetrators are live-in partners, stepparents, adoptive and foster parents, and family members (Faller, 1989). Abuse by nonfamily members is the least frequent type. Some behaviors can serve as warning signs of sexual abuse:

- Play or conversation that suggests sexual knowledge unusual for the child's age.

- Frequent masturbation.

- Increases in hard-to-prove illnesses such as headaches and stomachaches.

- Frequent crying or depression.

- Extreme changes in behavior and eating patterns.

- Reluctance to go home.

Although by law, educators are required to report cases of child abuse or neglect, this is very difficult to do. In many instances, parents figure out who made the report and are very confrontational. In other situations, the child may quit coming to school. It is difficult to develop long-term positive relationships with parents who abuse or are abused.

Families that are the most vulnerable to abuse are those without telephones, cars, and an informal social support network. Abuse is a complex situation and needs trained professionals for intervention. The family should be encouraged to seek such intervention.

Children who have been abused or neglected need a school environment that accepts them and offers them emotional support and reassurance. It is important to make the children feel secure by providing a gentle, understanding, and consistent environment. Help them reframe themselves within the early care and education environment. Take a positive quality of the child and stress that aspect. Parents need to see this aspect of the child so they, too, can begin to build a more positive image of the child's abilities. If parents lack knowledge of appropriate and effective forms of discipline, you might encourage them to observe in the class where you can demonstrate these. Parents can also see appropriate ways of teaching children. Unless you are a trained counselor, family therapy should not be attempted.

Children who have been sexually abused may find it difficult to trust adults. They may have low self-esteem and many self-doubts. Show interest in the child and make encouraging, supportive statements, but also allow the child space to join at her own rate. Children who have been abused may not interpret adult behavior in the same way as other children. This child may interpret a supportive hug as having sexual overtones. Move slowly and build trust through consistency and caring. Respect the child's need for greater personal space.

Teachers of young children have many opportunities to help prevent child abuse and neglect: first, as a role model; second, in knowing the indicators and risk factors of potential danger; third, in helping families obtain the supports they need to stop abusive patterns. Your first alliance is to the child. You must report patterns of circumstances or behaviors that indicate abuse and neglect. Provide a curriculum strong on prosocial behavior. Teach behaviors such as sharing, turn taking, cooperation, and expressing empathy to break the cycle of violence.

Temperament

Some characteristics of children themselves may put them at risk of being abused and neglected and may also be initial indications of emotional, behavioral, or learning problems that will occur later. Temperament is one of these.

All children are different. Shortly after birth, infants have identifiable temperaments. Part of a child's personality is his temperament. Some children smile all the time, no matter what happens, and some children are difficult to soothe once they are disturbed or frustrated. Some children are shy around strangers, and some feel comfortable and secure wherever they are. A child's temperament influences how he reacts to the people in his world and how those people respond in turn.

Just as adults respond to situations in fairly predictable ways, so too do young children. It is the predictable pattern of responses and preferences that makes up a child's temperament. Temperament includes the child's general mood (happy, fussy); activity level (adventurous, cautious); adaptability (flexible, routinized); intensity of reactions (appropriate or not); persistence; distractibility; reactions to new situations; and regularity of sleeping and eating cycles. Using these traits, we can classify children as "easy," "slow-to-warm-up," or "difficult." Although it is not particularly useful to label children as difficult, it is important to acknowledge that some children are easier to cope with than others. Some children have behavior that is not just difficult, but disordered. As early intervention is important, you need to be able to identify these children.

Dimensions of Temperament

All children exhibit the following characteristics to some extent; it is the extremes in these areas that characterize children who show emotional and behavioral vulnerability. Thomas, Chess, and Birch (1968) collected data from parent interviews and child observations and identified nine dimensions and three styles of temperament that they felt had

stability over time. These particular characteristics are useful to observe. Soderman (1985) also described these characteristics and observations in young children. It is the pattern of these dimensions that make up temperament.

Activity Level. This refers to the amount of time a child is active or not active. Children who are always on the go and can't sit still are at one end; children who are inactive and just sit are at the other extreme.

Regularity. Children have an internal biological clock that can be either regular or unpredictable. For those children who are *very* regular (they get up at the same time, eat at the same time), it is important to look at the match between adult expectations, programmatic demands, and the child's typical pattern. To the extent these mismatch, this child can be more difficult than the unpredictable child.

Approach/Withdrawal. Children have a typical response to new experiences. The extremes are to approach without caution or to avoid at all costs through crying or clinging to adults. Most children approach new experiences with some degree of caution. For children who have had many or recent new encounters that were painful, the avoidance response may be predominant.

Adaptability. Some children find it easy to adapt to change, others find it very difficult. Young children who are change resistant may find new routines, a different caregiver or teacher, a new sibling, or even a new child entering the class extremely stressful. Especially at celebrations, holidays, and transitions, slow-to-adapt children need extra time and support.

Physical Sensitivity. Some children are aware of slight changes in the environment; others respond only to major physical changes. Children who are highly sensitive can become overstimulated by too much noise, touch, light, and so on. They need support in regulating their environment.

Intensity of Reaction. Many situations evoke reactions in young children; it is the intensity and length of the response in relation to the event that needs to be evaluated. One child may cry violently for 20 minutes when another child takes a toy, whereas another child may fuss only briefly.

Mood. Children have a range of moods that are a balance of happy and less positive moods. Some children are in a predictable mood most of the time; others vary considerably. Children who are predictably negative may make adults feel guilty or angry. Rather than receiving the extra attention, love, and support they need, these children may be avoided.

Persistence. Persistence is the amount of time a child attends to or persists with a task. It is related to how difficult the task is and how interested the child is in the task.

Resistance/Distractibility. Resistance measures the ability of the child to return to an activity after an interruption. Resistance focuses on longer breaks for such things as toileting. Distractibility relates to momentary interruptions and how the child reacts to extraneous stimuli. Do distracting sights and sounds cause the child to lose concentration or does she continue?

Temperament Styles

Thomas et al. (1968) have organized these dimensions of temperament into three basic temperament categories or styles (see Table 9.1) (*Typical children* [35 percent] did not fall into any of these categories.):

1. *Easy children* are those who rate moderate in intensity, adaptability, approachableness, and rhythmicity, and have predominantly positive moods. They are usually calm and predictable and tend to eat and sleep on a schedule, although they can adapt the schedule to some extent. They smile frequently, typically approach new experiences positively, and show little negative emotion. They tend to be easygoing and highly sociable. They adapt quickly to change, and have low to medium intensity of reactions. Their biological rhythms are regular and they are (or were) easy to toilet train and sleep through the night. Chess and Thomas (1977) classified about 40 percent of their sample as easy children. Some see these as *flexible* children.

2. *Difficult children* are at the other end of the temperament scale. Difficult children often display negative emotion: they cry a lot and are fearful or withdrawn in the face of new experiences. They are unpredictable, have mood shifts, and are easily distracted. Although they set their own eating and sleeping schedule, they do not have a predictable schedule (Chess & Thomas, 1990).

They shift states quickly and may go from sleeping to screaming in seconds. These children are slow to adapt and change, are nonrhythmical, have intense reactions, and often have negative moods. Their biological rhythms are irregular and they are difficult to train to sleep through the night; toilet training also is a challenge. They are also movers: They crawl, walk, or run, rarely staying in the same place for long. They are less sociable than other children. Chess and Thomas (1977) found about 10 percent of their sample to be difficult children. These children are more positively characterized as *feisty*.

3. *Slow-to-warm-up children* share some of the characteristics of difficult and easy children. They initially appeared to have the characteristics of difficult children but did not show the intensity or persistence. Initially, their response to new events was negative, but, given time, they did in fact "warm up," although it took them longer to adapt than easy children. They have negative moods but the intensity is low or mild. They can have either regular or irregular biological rhythms. Fifteen percent of Chess and Thomas's (1977) sample fell into this category. Some refer to these children as *fearful* or shy.

A child's temperament is sometimes a challenge to adults. Some parents find it comforting to know that children come with different temperaments and that they are not the cause of their child's temperament. Temperament affects the child's development because it impacts how the child approaches her environment, as well as how the environment responds to the child (Brazelton, 1992). Difficult children and easy children evoke different responses from adults. However, they don't get the same response from all adults. The key is the interaction pattern between the child and the adult, or the "goodness of fit" (Thomas & Chess, 1980).

TABLE 9.1 ASSESSMENT OF TEMPERAMENT

Activity Level	Active	1	3	5	Quiet
Regularity	Regular	1	3	5	Irregular
Approach/Withdrawal	Approach	1	3	5	Withdrawal
Adaptability	Adaptable	1	3	5	Slow to adapt
Physical Sensitivity	Not sensitive	1	3	5	Not sensitive
Intensity of Reaction	High intensity	1	3	5	Low intensity
Mood	Preditable	1	3	5	Not predictable
Mood	Positive	1	3	5	Negative
Persistence	Long attention	1	3	5	Short attention
Resistance	Returns to task	1	3	5	Doesn't return
Distractibility	Highly distsractable	1	3	5	Not distractable

Temperament Style: Flexible (40%); Feisty (10%); Fearful (15%); Typical (35%)

Using Table 9.1, observe and record the behavior of a particular child for three days or longer to establish a pattern. Have other adults observe, and determine if there is congruence. Ask parents to fill out the chart as well, and compare behavior at home and at school for patterns.

Goodness of Fit

The concept of goodness of fit looks at the match between the expectations and interactions of the adult and the child's behavior in relationship to these expectations. A parent or educator who is up and on the go, wants to do things and not sit around, and isn't disturbed by crying and temper tantrums might be delighted with a difficult child and find an easy child boring. A parent or educator who has a cautious approach to new ideas and patience may find a slow-to-warm-up child enchanting, whereas with either a difficult or easy child, she may feel overwhelmed or unnecessary. It is not possible to evaluate child outcome on temperament alone. Chess (1983) stresses that the interaction between adult's expectations and child's responses is a key factor in assessing the quality of the adult-child relationship. Concern focuses around children who are slow-to-warm-up and those with difficult temperaments who need extra adult understanding but who may actually receive fewer positive responses from adults who do not understand and know how to work with these children. Consider the following two scenarios:

1. Nadine is a 3-year-old who is fearful, shy, and cautious. She has never been in a group child care setting before. One morning, her mother wakes her up earlier than usual, feeds her breakfast with admonitions to hurry, and, without telling her where she is going, takes her on a bus. She and her mother arrive at a strange building into which her mother, who is in a hurry, pulls her. When Nadine is not moving fast enough, her mother picks her up and carries her into a room with eight other 3-year-olds and two unfamiliar adults. The other children are playing with toys and the adults are talking to each other. Nadine's mother takes her over to the adults and says, "Here she is." Nadine tries to cling to her mother, but she loosens her grasp and hurries away. One of the adults takes Nadine over to some blocks and tells her to play with three other children.

2. Nancy is another 3-year-old who is fearful, shy, and cautious. She has never been in group care either. One morning, her mother gets her up earlier than usual. While she is eating breakfast, her mother reminds her that this is the day she is going to stay with Miss Irene and the other children while Mommy goes to work. Nancy knows Miss Irene because her mother has taken her there for short visits to see her and the other children two other times. This time, her mother explains that she will stay until lunch time, which is when her mother will come back to get her. While Nancy and her mother ride the bus to the center, her mother talks about what Nancy will be doing during the morning. When they walk into the room, they see eight other 3-year-olds and two adults, all of whom look familiar to Nancy. Miss Irene comes over to Nancy and her

mother and tells them how happy she is to see them. She then mentions several activities that Nancy might join if she would like to. Nancy's mother sits in one of the chairs for about 10 minutes before telling Nancy that she will be back to get her at lunch time. She then leaves. (Adapted from Franyo, 1996)

The first scenario is an example of *poorness of fit*. The child was being pressured into adjusting in a way that was incompatible with her temperament. The situation makes demands on the child it is not possible for her to adapt to and meet successfully. The second scenario is an example of *goodness of fit*. The adults in the child's world adapted to help the child have a successful experience. Children who experience a pattern of poorness of fit in their environment are likely to develop behavior problems.

Go back to Table 9.1 and rate yourself on the scale. What is your temperament style? Which children do you like to teach most? Which children are you most comfortable working with? Which children are most difficult for you? Which children have the greatest goodness of fit in your teaching? Once you know this, do some hard thinking about children who may not fit as well. The adult and the environment need to be as flexible as possible to include children of all temperament types.

All children (and adults) have bad days. Sometimes, it is difficult to tell if a child is having a bad day or week, has a difficult temperament, is having a short-term behavior problem or one that is long term. It is hard to decide if the child is going through a "stage" or responding to environmental stress. The next part of this chapter looks at emotional and behavioral problems you may encounter. This is followed by a section on more serious emotional and behavioral disorders.

Emotional and Behavioral Problems

Diagnosis has two components: categorical and functional. At a categorical level, we focus on labeling a particular problem and its severity. At a functional level, we determine where the child is functioning developmentally. Emotional and behavioral development focuses on the emergence of an accurate and positive sense of self and the ability to develop and maintain meaningful relationships with other children and adults. Children with emotional and behavioral problems experience an abrupt break, a slowing down, or a delay in the development of these processes (Lasher, Mattick, & Perkins, 1978). It is the level and duration of disruption that distinguishes between emotional and behavioral problems and disorders. Emotional and behavioral actions are difficult to classify accurately. Some children have not had the opportunity to learn the expected social and school-related skills. Other children have had to learn early how to fend for themselves to survive in their environment. Some families have values and expectations for their children different than the traditional white middle class because of their cultural and ethnic heritage. Children's emotional and behavioral development needs to be evaluated in the context of their early environment. Children with emotional and behavioral problems and disorders occur in all ethnic groups and at all socioeconomic levels.

The IDEA (1997) changed the term "serious emotional disturbance" to "emotional disturbance" in an effort to take away some of the stigma of this diagnosis and also to acknowledge that the manifestation of emotional and behavioral disturbances changes with increasing age. We have used the term problems to refer to less serious emotional and behavioral situations that are very real but would probably not meet the requirements of the law. The section on emotional and behavioral disorders describes those that meet the requirements of the law.

Emotional and behavioral problems can be divided into two broad categories: externalizing and internalizing. *Externalizing* behavior involves striking out against others. Children often display aggressiveness, destructiveness, temper tantrums, attention-seeking behaviors (hitting and biting), and so on. Children exhibiting *internalizing* behaviors show withdrawal, anxiety, crying, depression, unresponsiveness, shyness, timidity, and isolation (Achenbach, 1985).

Some behavioral problems are more common at certain stages of development. When they appear during expected periods, they are considered normal behaviors. When these behaviors persist beyond expected ages and/or the behaviors become excessive in nature, they are considered emotional and behavioral problems.

As behaviors that are classified as externalizing are usually the first focus of attention, they are discussed first.

Externalizing Emotional and Behavioral Problems

Before deciding whether or not you think a child has a behavioral problem, look at the child's environment and particular lifestyle. There is a difference between being "streetwise" and having an emotional and behavioral problem. Some children may have *learned* to be aggressive as a way of surviving. We have taught children who would not have made it safely home if they had followed the same rules we enforced in our classrooms. This is the time to emphasize the situational aspects of behavior:

A 6-year-old inner-city boy once told me: "Lady, you wouldn't last one hour on my block." I responded, "Germane, you're right. In fact, I probably wouldn't last five minutes."

Aggressive and Antisocial Behavior. Assertiveness is a valuable asset for children. When it moves into aggressiveness, it causes concern, particularly if it becomes the child's *typical* way of interacting with others. Aggressive children hurt others with or without provocation. Some children become aggressive under stress or when they cannot get what they want and seem to explode. They use aggression as a means of communication, but what are they trying to communicate?

Children who are aggressive may be fearful and anxious and use aggression as a way of responding to an inner self that also feels hateful and suspicious. These children often have poor self-images. Trying to identify the situations that provoke aggressive behavior is one place to start. However, it isn't useful to waste time on what you cannot change. You can, however, control whom the child sits beside or plan to have more space for large motor activities when it rains. You need to set and enforce the boundaries of acceptable behavior in your classroom.

Start by gathering information by behavioral observations, including information about the situation as well as specific characteristics relative to behavior: duration, latency, context, frequency, intensity, and time (Salvia & Ysseldyke, 1995). You want to answer the questions: When, where, and how often does the behavior happen? and What causes or triggers the behavior? You will also need to answer questions that are more specific to the particular situation:

Who is the victim? Is the victim anyone who happens to be there, or is it usually a particular child or a certain few children? If it is a variety of children, check if they are mostly boys or girls; bigger or smaller; older or younger; aggressive or shy, timid. Or are the victims adults?

How does the child act after the behavior? Does the child deny the behavior or admit that it was done? Is the child upset by the victim's crying (if that is what happened)? Does the child get upset if the victim returns the behavior (bites or hits back)? Does the child look to see if an adult is watching before proceeding with the behavior? Does the child walk away? Or does the child apologize and show concern for the victim?

We are particularly concerned about aggressive behavior in early childhood. Children who are aggressive in early childhood are at risk for loneliness and lack of peer support. A high level of aggression is predictive of serious problems in adulthood. Children with these behaviors may continue a cycle of violence, including severe punishment of their own children, domestic violence, and antisocial and violent criminal behavior (Huesmann, Eron, Lefkowitz, & Walder, 1984). Victims of aggression can develop patterns of learned helplessness that increase their risk for continued victimization and depression (Straus, 1995). Other victims become aggressors (Straus, 1991). Bystanders (children who witness aggression) may provide social support by just being there, or they may actively take sides and contribute to the escalation of the aggressive behavior (Slaby, Roedell, Arezzo, & Hendrix, 1995).

We can no longer ignore violence and expect it to go away. Violence that children are likely to face in the world outside must be discussed in the classroom, at the same time providing them a safe place to talk about their fears. There must be follow-up to the discussion. Early childhood educators can intervene in some ways (Slaby et al., 1995):

- Help children to identify violence and its consequences.

- Recognize and talk with children about real-world violence.

- Recognize and respond to children's traumatic reactions to violence.

- Train children in basic violence-related safety and self-protection.

- Help reduce "disciplinary" violence toward children.

- Support families in helping children to cope with violence. (pp. 8–9)

Biting, Pinching, Hitting, and Throwing Objects. The violence that is most prevalent in early childhood is peer violence. Some of this violence is developmental, some learned.

Aggressive children lack self-confidence and when approaching a new material such as clay, they may throw it rather than explore its properties. Their unpredictable behavior makes friendships difficult. You need to convey to children your confidence that they can learn self-control and that you will help them in this process by acknowledging the effort is long and difficult, that you will try to protect them from hurting others or being hurt, and that as they gain control over their own behavior, you will give them more freedom (Lasher, Mattick, & Perkins, 1978).

Many young children between one and three years of age go through a stage during which they bite, pinch, or hit others. Developmentally, children at this stage are still very egocentric, thinking only of themselves. They don't share space, toys, or favorite adults well. They notice other children, but see them as objects, not people. There is frequent tension over possession of objects. Often, biting, pinching, and hitting are useful in getting things. Language skills are still developing, and children do not yet have a good repertoire of words to express anger or frustration in acceptable ways. It is during this time that biting and pinching most frequently occur.

Children need support redirecting their anger in socially appropriate ways. Children need to be clearly told "I don't like it when you pinch me. If you are angry tell me with words. I'll help you find the words." It is when children persist in biting and pinching well past the expected ages, or when the behaviors are excessive (biting that breaks the skin), that the behavior becomes of concern to adults.

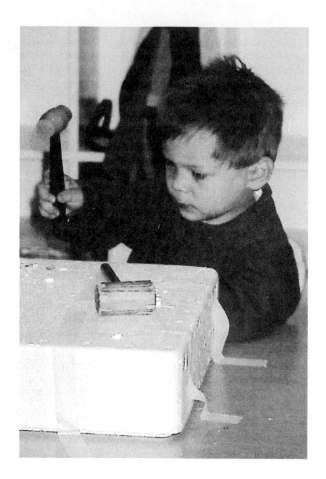

For most children, pounding pegs into styrofoam is a developmentally appropriate activity. However, if children throw mallets because of frustration and anger, they can become very dangerous. Know children's developmental level and behavior patterns before introducing objects that could become weapons.

Biting in particular is distressing to parents and teachers and, obviously, the child who is bitten. A child who bites will probably do it more than once. If the child bites more than once a day for more than a week, something needs to change. Biting a child back should not be used as a consequence. You are a model for all the children. At this point, you have looked for patterns related to situation, time, and victim. If this information is not helpful, look at your program. How can you change the program to decrease the number of children in a group at a given time? That is, how can you create more space for each child? Can half the group go outside and half stay in, half eat lunch while others play, and then change? Think about how you can change the program.

Think also about how you can better monitor the child who is biting. If the biting is severe, you may need to assign a teacher, paraprofessional, or rotating shift of adults as the child's constant companion. If an adult cannot be with the child, then the child needs to be in a safe place such as a playpen (provided he cannot crawl out) and told "I am putting you here for a few minutes because I can't be with you and I don't want you to bite. I will be back as soon as I can so we can play." If biting can be prevented for two weeks, it frequently drops out of the child's repertoire (Legg, 1993).

When talking to parents of the child who was bitten, it is helpful to empathize with them about how stressful it is when a child is bitten, but don't apologize. An apology implies that you could have prevented it (Legg, 1993). Parents are interested in how you handled the situation. Tell them "I picked Julie up and put ice on her cheek and held her until she quit crying. I then asked her what she wanted to do and we went over to the dramatic play area." Do *not* tell them the name of the child who did the biting (the grapevine may, but you shouldn't). Assure parents that biting is common for children of this age, and talk about what you plan to do to decrease the occurrence. Also, it is not useful to tell the parents of the child who bit unless you feel you need to change the child's routine (such as assigning an adult to monitor the child's behavior). Adults react to biting far more then hitting or even throwing.

If you have a class in which the occurrence of children throwing things is high, you need to reevaluate your environment. Toys often used by young children, such as mallets, can cause physical damage if they are thrown at other children.

Crying. Although a pattern of excessive crying is considered a symptom of stress, increasingly, crying is being viewed in a more positive light. Some view crying as the natural repair kit all individuals are born with and consider it an important and beneficial physiological coping mechanism. Crying not only reduces tension but also removes toxins from the body (Solter, 1992). Emotional crying is a response to "the straw that broke the camel's back": Tension has been building, and at some point, something triggers the tears. It is difficult to figure out specifically what caused the crying if the event that was the direct antecedent of crying was trivial. The emotional buildup may have been coming on for a long time.

Although crying is viewed as potentially positive and healthy, just as shouting for joy is, there are times and places when children need to learn to control their emotional expression. This becomes increasingly true as children get older. Adults sometimes have problems accepting children's crying. They see their role as keeping young children happy, and when they cry, adults may feel that they are not doing their job well. They may try to make crying children "happy up" by telling them not to cry or, conversely, threatening to give them something to cry about. In reality, "crying is not the hurt, but the process of becoming unhurt" (Solter, 1992, p. 66). Crying is the solution, not the problem.

Tantrums. Sometimes, crying turns into rages and tantrums. If others are likely to be hurt, the behaviors need to be stopped. The goal is to stop violence while encouraging the expression of feelings. Firm but patient contact with a child having a tantrum can often move the behavior into crying. Children with delayed language skills often continue tantrum behaviors after others have stopped; physical outbursts of emotions are one of the few ways available for them to express anger or frustration.

Most children at one time or another display tantrum behavior without being physically hurt or hurting others. The tantrums are usually strong expressions of anger characterized by crying, screaming, and perhaps hitting, kicking, or destroying materials. Older children may hit others or use language to express frustration. Prior to developing adequate language abilities, children use tantrums as a way to vent pent-up tension or to get attention.

Tantrums can also be attention-seeking behaviors, especially for children raised in environments severely lacking in social stimulation. Reinforcing appropriate behaviors, while providing consequences for negative behaviors, has been the accepted method for dealing with tantrums. Reinforcement includes physical and social rewards for good behavior. Consequences can include loss of freedom (not being able to do something until an adult is available, a thinking chair, and verbal statements about the feelings related to the behavior).

As children develop better language skills, they are able to use speech rather than tantrums as a way to express frustration and anger. It helps to say to a child, "In this class, we use words, not feet, to show someone how we feel." Adults play an important role in helping children learn socially appropriate methods of releasing anger and tension. Modeling appropriate behavior is one way children learn. It may be necessary to teach children what is acceptable behavior without inhibiting their release of anger. This may mean hanging a punching bag in the classroom and saying to a child, "You may punch the punching bag as hard as you want to, but you may not hit me." Teach children skills for interacting with each other.

Internalizing Emotional and Behavioral Problems

All children like and need to be alone some of the time. Children who are alone most of the time or who seem uncomfortable when they are with groups of people cause concern.

Shyness. Occasional shyness is expected, and typical of slow-to-warm-up children. It is characterized by an ambivalent approach/avoidance quality (Hyson & Van Triest, 1987). Shyness is different from wariness and social disengagement; those behaviors do not share the ambivalent characteristics of shyness. In young children, shyness is often in response to new adults and is often characterized by thumb sucking or alternately smiling and hiding (Izard & Hyson, 1986). Avoidance of gaze, an unwillingness to respond to friendly social overtures, and even blushing are also associated with shyness (Honig, 1987). Cultural differences may account for some shyness.

Some children are active and risk takers from an early age; other children are much more quiet and tentative. A child's temperament determines how she approaches new situations and type of support she will need from adults.

Some aspects of shyness are learned by children, some appear to be culturally based, and others are genetic. When shyness is a temporary solution to a novel or overwhelming social situation, it may well be adaptive. Extreme shyness may be related to poor self-image or lack of social skills. Shy children may not be noticed and may not have the opportunities or skills to interact with other children or to gain an adult's attention. Elective mutism in school may be an extreme form of shyness, if the child displays different behavior in the family setting (Honig, 1987).

Shy children need to be given time to warm up in new situations. They may need to be taught skills for joining peer groups and support in feeling good about themselves and the talents they have to offer. They need the subtle support of caring adults who encourage them but don't take over and act for them.

Shy children may need to learn skills to gain access to groups and maintain group membership. Children who grow up in authoritarian families are more likely to be shy. Caregiving styles that support democratic decision making and respect may help young children. Shyness can be helped by making children

feel attractive, supporting them in small groups after having taught them social entry skills, and even by teaching them muscle relaxation games (Honig, 1987).

Withdrawal. Children differ in how introverted or extroverted they are. Children who are introverted need more time to be alone, whereas children who are extroverted like lots of social interaction. Respect the rights of children to be introverts, but be wary of a pattern of excessive withdrawal, characterized by the inability to develop relationships with parents or peers, inactivity, excessive social isolation, and lack of affect. Children may have a favorite place in the room where they feel safe. When approached, they may *react* by moving away and not interacting. If these characteristics occur individually or in combination, there is a cause for concern. Children may need to be taught social skill techniques and reinforced for all social initiatives. Consistent lack of interaction will cause a child to miss experiences that lead to improved social competency, better self-esteem, and increased overall development. Settings that emphasize warmth, caring, and consistency can help children overcome feelings of insecurity. Children who are withdrawn learn from observation. If they are not part of the group, ascertain what they can see from their vantage point and maximize their opportunity for learning.

Fearfulness and Anxiety. All children have times when they are anxious or fearful. Sometimes this begins with a single incident such as being frightened by a dog. This fear may then generalize to all dogs and perhaps to all animals; in extreme cases, even to pictures of animals or animal crackers. When the focus is on a single object, place, or situation (dogs, school, going to a sleepover) it can be the beginning of a phobia. These passing fears are normal in children; it is their persistence and ability to limit the child's daily routine that are of concern.

For other children, anxiety is more generalized. They worry, become upset easily, and may become extremely anxious about participating in new activities. They may be worried that they can't do things right and actually become perfectionists. They may have more problems than other children at their developmental level in distinguishing between the real world and the one that is make believe. Monsters may be very real and a threat to them. Transitions and unstructured situations may increase their anxiety. Their anxiety to try new experiences may delay their mastery of new skills and interfere with their memory and concentration. Help anxious children by giving them clear explanations of what is expected and reassuring them about what is happening and your confidence in their ability to cope. They need praise and support and may be oversensitive to criticism.

Eating. All children go through stages in which eating certain foods is problematic, often more a problem for adults than for children. Typical eating problems involve "finicky" eaters who go through phases when they will eat only certain foods like hot dogs, peanut butter and jelly, and candy. They may refuse to eat most table foods, and they may eat on the run, grabbing an apple slice and cracker. For most children, these finicky habits are just phases that they experience and pass through.

For some children, eating problems are more severe and can lead to nutritional problems that affect development. Some infants develop a pattern in which they refuse to eat, turning their head away from nursing, the bottle, and cereal. Some of these children fall into a category of "failure-to-thrive" babies. They develop a pattern of refusing to eat or drink and refusing social interaction. Their weight can suddenly drop dramatically and necessitate medical intervention, including intravenous feeding. Treatment may include slowly enticing the child to begin eating again. This can be a long process.

As we are learning more about children's eating behaviors, it appears that food allergies may play some part in the child's behavior. Infants who are allergic to milk or soy formulas may be diagnosed as failure-to-thrive, when in reality the child is having an allergic reaction to the food offered. More children seem to be developing severe food allergies as reactions to the preservatives, dyes, and additives in food. Children may react to the amount of sugar and caffeine in foods.

If children have eating problems, a medically based approach such as blood tests to determine food allergies should be suggested. If the child is allergic to particular foods or additives, a special diet can be recommended. Ensuring that children are not hungry, reinforcing appropriate eating habits, establishing consistent eating routines, and suggesting behavior modification techniques can help to overcome most eating problems.

Distinguishing Between Emotional and Behavioral Problems and Emotional and Behavioral Disorders

Before deciding an emotional or behavioral problem might be a disorder, see if there are changes occurring in the child's life. Is there a new sibling, a grandparent visiting, a parent away because of travel, separation, or divorce? Don't reach a conclusion too quickly. Talk with parents about how characteristic the behavior is. If possible, have them come in and observe, or make a videotape to show them, and make a home visit.

The identification of young children with emotional and behavioral disorders is especially difficult. Peterson (1987, p. 226) lists seven identifiers to help distinguish between normal behavioral patterns and behavioral development that is problematic:

1. The situations in which the behaviors are exhibited.

2. The developmental ages at which the behaviors appear and continue to be manifested.

3. The intensity of the behavior (excess or deficiency).

4. The duration or persistence of the behavior.

5. The extent to which others can alter the behavior.

6. The extent to which the behavior interferes with progress in other developmental areas.

7. The extent to which the behavior interferes with the lives of others.

All children have emotional and behavioral problems sometimes; it is the length, severity, and unacceptableness of the behavior that determines whether or not it is a disorder. Some behavior problems are learned behaviors that affect children's ability to participate in activities with adults and other children. They are considered situationally specific responses; examples include attention-seeking behavior, pinching, and temper tantrums. Behavioral and emotional disturbances involve pervasive changes in the child's behavior and mood states that are exhibited across many situations and settings. They interfere with interpersonal relationships and with development and learning. They can be harmful to the child and others (Peterson, 1987).

Classification of Emotional and Behavioral Disorders

There are no universally accepted criteria for determining which children have emotional and behavioral disorders. This chapter acknowledges the emotional aspect of the problem but focuses on the disordered behavior (see Table 9.2). As you might assume, if we cannot define the term we do not have a good idea of how many children fit the definition. Much of what is diagnosed is a matter of the degree to which behaviors occur. It is almost always subjective and falls in the category of "clinical judgment." Kazdin (1989) estimates between 6 to 10 percent of school-age children fall in this category. The American Psychiatric Association (1994) documents from 2 to 16 percent of children exhibiting an oppositional defiant disorder (a pattern of negative, hostile, defiant behavior in response to adult requests). This usually begins gradually, emerges first in the home and is evident before age 8. It may be a developmental precursor to a conduct disorder (a pattern of violating the basic rights of others or societal rules). The prevalence of conduct disorders varies from 2 to 16 percent. In both disorders during early childhood, males outnumber females; less severe behaviors emerge first, and the number of children identified is increasing. Children with this disordered behavior also may be identified as having attention-deficit/ hyperactivity disorder as well as learning and communication disorders. Rates also vary depending on the setting (rural or urban), the population sampled, and the methods used.

TABLE 9.2   RED FLAGS OF EMOTIONAL/BEHAVIORAL DISORDERS

Medical/Physical

History of abuse and/or neglect

Does not like being touched

Behavioral

Shows little or no impulse control

Hits, throws, bites, or kicks as first response to frustration

Engages in excessive self-stimulation

Preoccupied with own inner world

Withdrawn

Anxious and fearful

Interpersonal

Great difficulty separating from parents

Relates only to adults

Withdraws from people; does not accept affection

Hurts others deliberately; shows no remorse

Cognitive/Language

Does not seem to recognize self as a separate person or refer to self as "I"

Conversations do not make sense

Has many fears

Cannot follow a classroom routine

Cannot focus on activities; does not complete activities

Professionals concerned about emotional and behavioral disorders are primarily in the field of mental health (for example, psychologists and psychiatrists). The focus of mental health for young children has been on prevention and an attempt to identify long-term risk factors (Edme, Bingham, & Harmon, 1993). This is a fast-growing field and one that is different from adult mental health. From its inception, the field has been multidisciplinary.

One of the challenges to the profession is the task of classifying problems in this area. Problems must be classified with a developmental orientation because young children change so quickly that what is normal at one time may be atypical at another. Classification must also be done with an understanding of the dynamic exchange among the young child, the family, and the environment. This requires a systemic and multigenerational point of view.

Several different organizations have developed classification systems, including the American Psychiatric Association (APA), the World Health Organization (WHO), and the National Center for Clinical Infant Programs (NCCIP). The APA (1994) has a section devoted to disorders usually first diagnosed in infancy, childhood, or adolescence. This text uses the categories developed by the APA and the NCCIP. Only the most prevalent disorders are discussed.

Pervasive Developmental Disorders

These disorders are characterized by extremely atypical development within the first three years. Many basic psychological functions are affected, such as attention, sensory perception, mood, intellectual function, and motor movement (Rapoport & Ismond, 1996). Pervasive developmental disorders include autistic disorder, Rhett's disorder, childhood disintegrative disorder, and Asperger's disorder. Regardless of the diagnosis, children with these disorders have problems reaching developmental milestones—perceiving the world, forming relationships, using their body, and receiving and giving information.

Autistic Tendencies and Autistic Disorder. Autism (also called infantile autism, or Kanner's syndrome) is the most severe pervasive developmental disorder and involves impaired social interactions and lack of appropriate responsiveness. Autism affects 4 to 5 out of 10,000 individuals, with males outnumbering females (APA, 1994). At birth, the infant with autism appears similar to other children and often shows normal developmental patterns. Some warning signs such as stiffness when being held and lacking or infrequent eye contact are subtle and often recognized only in hindsight. Between 18 and 36 months, the signs of autism manifest themselves prominently, and this is when a diagnosis is likely. About 70 percent of individuals with autism function at a mentally retarded level (APA, 1994). Some children display some but not all of the characteristics of autism, hence the term autistic tendencies.

As early as 6 months, infants with autism may begin to withdraw and be unresponsive and unaffectionate. Children may develop some functional speech, though children with autism typically use repetitive, jargony speech patterns or rely on gestures or repeated motoric actions. There is an absence of peer interaction. Children may exhibit stereotyped behavior such as spinning objects, hand whirling, rocking, echolalic speech, or excessive orderliness. They often engage in excessive repetition of body movements, including head banging and rocking.

Rapoport and Ismond (1996, p. 87) describe the characteristics as:

> Lack of nonverbal behaviors, such as eye contact, facial expression, body postures and gestures.
>
> Failure to develop peer relationships appropriate to developmental level.
>
> Lack of spontaneous sharing of experiences with others.
>
> Lack of social or emotional reciprocity.

Because of difficulty in testing, cognitive abilities are difficult to assess accurately. However, regardless of the general intellectual level of the child, the profile of cognitive skills is usually very uneven. In many high-functioning children with autism, expressive language is better than receptive language. This is the reverse of the typical pattern in early childhood. Children with autism may have a range of behavioral symptoms, including hyperactivity, impulsivity, short attention span, aggressiveness, self-injurious behaviors, and, especially in young children, temper tantrums (APA, 1994). Children may display unusual responses to sensory stimuli such as being under- or oversensitive to sound or to being touched. They often lack what we consider to be common sense; they may be fearful of objects that can cause no harm and lack fear in response to real danger.

The exact etiology of autism is unknown, although there seems to be agreement that autism is caused by an abnormality in or damage to the brain (Mauk, Reber, & Batshaw, 1997). This probably happens early in development, during critical cell migration (Rakic, Bourgeois, & Goldman-Rakic, 1994). Previously, researchers felt that autism was caused by cold, uncaring "refrigerator" mothers. Current research rejects this finding, but many families still feel the stigma.

Early intervention has been shown to be very effective in dealing with autism. Intensive behavior modification, individual attention, and structured learning environments are essential components for a successful early intervention program for children with autism. From the parents' perspective, many readjustments in lifestyle are necessary, as the young child with autism displays unpredictable behaviors, many of which are potentially life-threatening. There is little doubt that these families have increased stress levels. A respite of a few hours away from the child is often a big help in coping.

Early intervention begins as soon as a child is diagnosed. Effective programs are intensive, continuous, highly structured, multidisciplinary, and have small teacher-to-child ratios. They focus on teaching social and communication skills (Mauk et al., 1997). Behavioral interventions are designed to decrease maladaptive behaviors. Language skills, in particular the ability to communicate verbally, and overall intellectual ability are the strongest predictors of success (APA, 1994).

Other Disorders of Childhood

This category is used for emotional/behavioral disorders that don't fit other categories.

Reactive Attachment Disorder of Infancy or Early Childhood. The main characteristic of this disorder is the lack of social relatedness that occurs before the age of 5. There are two different types. In the inhibited type, the child does not express age-appropriate signs of social responsibleness. The child does not respond appropriately to social interactions and may be excessively inhibited, hypervigilant, or show approach/avoidance response. In the disinhibited type, the child is indiscriminately social, relating to strangers with excessive familiarity but showing no selectivity in attachment figures (Rapoport & Ismond, 1996).

The reactive attachment disorder is caused by extreme neglect and grossly inadequate or inappropriate caregiving. Children with this disorder respond well to positive nurturing and caregiving. Intervention focuses on relationships and developmental disturbances. Although the emphasis in intervention is typically on infant-parent relationships, it is possible that a child who is distressed in a child care setting would show a disorder in this category. Adults can be helped to read children's cues more accurately and respond to them quickly as well as to increase the order and predictability in the young child's environment and the availability of a primary caregiver.

Schizophrenia and Other Psychotic Disorders

Psychotic disorders are relatively rare in early childhood. They are marked by loss of ego boundaries and an impaired sense of reality. The child cannot evaluate the accuracy of her perceptions and thoughts and makes incorrect assumptions about reality (Rapoport & Ismond, 1996). Because schizophrenia is so rare in children, there is concern about misdiagnosis.

Schizophrenia is a thought disorder characterized by hallucinations or delusions. Children affected may also exhibit impulsivity, aggression, affect instability, and learning or communication disorders (Rapoport & Ismond, 1996). The presence of disorganized speech may be misdiagnosed as a communication disorder. Other characteristics overlap with autism.

Overall, children with pervasive developmental disorders and phobias are either too sensitive or not sensitive enough to the stimuli in their world. Their sensory systems over- or underreact to stimulation, and sometimes do so inconsistently. Their functional development is uneven, that is, they may walk within the normal range but not talk. Children who talk may have an appropriate vocabulary, but not use it to convey meaning in a conventional sense. They may confuse words that are associated (hat and coat) or use unique code words when most children have replaced this with conventional words. They may have favorite toys they want to use and find it difficult to use others or to change tasks. Their body language communicates isolation and confusion, often lacking a social smile, eye contact, and social approach skills. They may use their bodies in strange ways (rocking, flapping) but also as a way of comforting themselves. Some children also use their bodies to express strong feelings by banging their head against the wall or floor and hitting or biting themselves until they are stopped. They don't seem to function in an integrated way. It is difficult to develop an accurate picture of these children as they are difficult to assess. Educators need to be firm and kind and, above all, consistent. Keep routines the same and favorite toys and materials in the same locations. They need to be honest with the other children in the classroom.

Feeding and Eating Disorders of Infancy and Early Childhood

These disorders are characterized by persistent eating and feeding disturbances. However, some children may actually search for nonfood objects and substances to ingest, such as paint chips, chalk, paper, or other objects. Before behavioral aspects of this disorders are considered, medical reasons for the disorder such as food allergies need to be ruled out.

Pica. Pica involves the eating of nonnutritive substances inappropriate to the developmental level of the child or the culture. It typically occurs between 12 and 24 months. The problem is usually with children who are poorly supervised or children who have cognitive deficits (APA, 1994). Improved caregiving and supervision of children typically solves the problem.

Rumination Disorder. This is a relatively frequent and well-defined disorder. The essential feature is that children repeatedly regurgitate partially digested food, which is then chewed, spit out, or swallowed (Rapoport & Ismond, 1996). It may begin during the first year but is seen more often during the first three years. The condition is not related to a physiological condition. This disorder is potentially fatal because of weight loss and malnutrition. It may be viewed as a failure to thrive. Behavior modification is used to change the child's behavior.

Anxiety Disorders

An acute anxiety state is an overwhelming sense of fear and dread that incapacitates a child. Generalized anxiety is more pervasive. Anxiety in early childhood is more prevalent than had previously been thought; however, these disorders are difficult to diagnose (Rapoport & Ismond, 1996).

Separation Anxiety Disorder. As the name suggests, anxiety results from separation from familiar people, usually parents, or leaving home. The reaction is excessive and usually occurs regardless of the general intellectual level of the child. Separation anxiety and generalized anxiety are strongly associated (Rapoport & Ismond, 1996). Separation anxiety may be a precursor to adult anxiety.

All young children react to separation. Some children cry, others want their mothers to stay, some withdraw and some act out, some hesitate to enter a new setting and, when left, keep returning to the door, some look stressed, and some bring attachment objects. It is recurrent excessive distress on separation and persistent and excessive worry about losing

or having harm befall the attachment figure that characterize this disorder. It may involve sleep disturbances, both not wanting to go to sleep as well as having nightmares about separation. It may involve physical symptoms such as vomiting, headaches, or nausea upon separation or knowledge of separation (APA, 1994). The condition must last at least four weeks to be considered a disorder.

Young children want a sense of predictability and control over their world. Explaining to young children what is going to happen before the parent leaves gives them this information but may produce a predictable separation reaction. Children whose parents try to "sneak out" to avoid this reaction are likely to have increased separation anxiety. Even young children who initially seem to separate easily may experience separation anxiety with the birth of a sibling or if the parents leave the child for a weekend.

Children can use symbolic play with adult guidance to play out the separation situation. This involves games of having objects disappear or hide and then reappear. These games, along with sensitive verbal support, help children cope with fear of abandonment. The major issues involved are whether or not the parent will return and when and who will care for the child in the interim. Children need reassurance on both of those issues.

Symbolic play also offers children the opportunity to play out their feelings about being left. Many young children think they are placed in early care and education settings because they were "bad." Parents may inadvertently support this idea by telling children they are going to child care because they got "so big" (Gottschall, 1989). Young children may play out this theme (sending things away because they get too big) as a way of coping with separation anxiety. Explaining to children that they are in care so their parents can work is rarely useful and doesn't address the child's concerns or misconceptions.

Many children use attachment objects as a way of coping with separation. As young children become attached to people, other objects that are part of the child's daily life also become vested with meaning. Eventually, the child develops an emotional tie for the object (Jalongo, 1987). This transitional or attachment object gives them visual, tactile, and olfactory memories of comfort. Children often want additional security at naptime or bedtime, which is why blankets or "blankies" are the traditional attachment object. Attachment objects are most important to toddlers; the need peaks between 2 and 3 years as they provide portable comfort when children encounter new situations (Jalongo, 1987). Teachers need to be empathetic and supportive of children's need for an attachment object. The attachment object is not something to be shared. When it is placed in a locker or cubbie, children often check on it periodically, just as a younger, securely attached child checks on the presence of a valued adult.

Attachment objects help children make transitions more easily. They serve as a home base for young children venturing out into the world. Disparaging

Some children use attachment objects to help bridge the gap between home and school. Attachment objects are very personal and should not have to be shared. Initially, a child may keep the object with him; then it may stay in a cubby or locker so it is available. Eventually, the object will not be needed.

remarks by adults about the object typically only increase the child's need for it and fear of losing it. As children's confidence and competence grows, the need lessens. As children become more familiar with a new setting, some are willing to replace the attachment object with a visual reminder of their family. Children can be encouraged to bring photographs to school as reminders of home rather than the attachment object (Jalongo, 1987).

The question then becomes, When does the reliance on an attachment object become atypical? The principles are the same that we use for other areas of development: duration, intensity, and emotional distress.

Posttraumatic Stress Disorder. This disorder describes a child's fear reaction to a specific experience of extreme stress or psychological trauma when the situation involves actual or threatened death or serious injury (Rapoport & Ismond, 1996). Increasing numbers of children are experiencing these situations. The symptoms were described earlier in the chapter.

Disorders are classified as related to a single event (acute, single event) or a connected series of traumatic events (chronic, repeated). A child who was in an automobile accident and broke her arm and had to be taken to the emergency room would be expected to have short-term disturbances such as nightmares and probably be fearful of riding in cars for a time. A child who is repeatedly abused or neglected is at risk for more pervasive interference with developmental tasks (Finkelhor, 1995).

Disruptive Behavior Disorders

As the name implies, these are a pattern of behaviors that disrupt and infringe on the rights of others.

Conduct Disorder. Conduct disorders have increased in frequency over the past decade. They are higher in males (6 to 16 percent) and lower in females (2 to 9 percent) for individuals under the age of 18. Childhood onset is a criterion for diagnosis: The symptoms must appear before the age of 10 (APA, 1994).

Conduct disorders are diagnosed when there is a repetitive, persistent pattern in which the basic rights of others or age-appropriate social norms are violated. Behaviorally, this typically takes the form of aggression, destruction of property, deceitfulness, theft, or serious violation of rules. In young children, it frequently involves initiating physical fights; bullying, threatening, or intimidating others; being physically cruel to people or animals. It might involve stealing while confronting a victim or using a weapon to hurt others. Relative to property, it might include setting fires or deliberately destroying property in some other way (APA, 1994). When behavior such as this occurs at young ages, there is concern for continuation into adulthood.

A conscious effort needs to be made to promote and internalize prosocial behavior in all children. Young children struggle with sharing, turn taking, and ownership. Teachers who promote prosocial behavior specifically identify these behaviors: "I like the way you and Connie are taking turns using the markers." Comments should be specific; however, they should not be used to the point that the purpose of prosocial behavior becomes receiving an external reward rather than establishing an internal standard.

To promote prosocial behavior, adults often help children take the perspective of another child, especially in situations where one child hurts another: "She's crying because you hit her. What can you do to help her feel better?" This both points out the consequences of the behavior as well as helps children understand what might make a distressed child feel better. Children need to be able to accurately identify the emotional state of other children before they can act in a prosocial way toward them (Wittmer & Honig, 1994). Most toddlers respond prosocially to peers in distress; however, toddlers who have been abused are impassive or react with anger. Vulnerable children need support in developing prosocial behavior.

Prosocial behavior does not just happen—it must be learned. Modeling prosocial behavior sets the tone for young children. Empowering children by giving them choices enhances their prosocial behavior. Likewise, making them conscious of other children and their feelings promotes prosocial behavior.

Oppositional Defiant Disorder. This disorder is characterized by a recurrent pattern of defiant, negativistic, disobedient, and hostile behavior toward authority figures (for at least six months). Prevalence rates range from 2 to 16 percent, depending on the population (APA, 1994). Transient oppositional behavior is very common in preschool children, but should not be diagnosed at this age unless it is persistent and well beyond what is developmentally expected.

Children with this disorder often lose their temper, argue with adults, and defy or refuse to comply with adult requests or rules. They deliberately annoy people and are easily annoyed by others. They often blame others for their mistakes, and are angry and resentful, spiteful and vindictive. These behaviors interfere with their social and academic functioning (APA, 1994).

Unlike those with conduct disorders, these children are defiant but not aggressive toward others. Given the long-term consequences, it is important that children learn to value their autonomy as well as to comply with important rules. Evaluate your rules; keep those that relate to safety but reconsider the others. Rules that are kept need to be consistently reinforced.

Disorders of Infants and Toddlers

The NCCIP describes two broad areas that apply to children from birth to age 3.

Regulatory Disorders. Infants need to regulate their behavior to adjust to the world around them. Infants with trouble doing this are often referred to as "fussy." Sometimes these behaviors go beyond fussy; then infants need help in regulating themselves. Regulatory disorders are characterized by disturbances in sensory, sensorimotor, or organizational processing (Edme et al., 1993). Infants in this category have trouble regulating their states, gaining control over sensory input, and having efficient motor functioning and may have some problems in social relatedness (Edme et al., 1993). Six specific types of regulatory disorders are identified: Hypersensitivity type, underreactive type, active-aggressive type, mixed type, regulatory-based sleep disorder, and regulatory-based eating disorder (NCCIP, 1991). These subcategories help focus on the specific area of the disruption and allow one to identify disorders in the area of sleeping and eating/feeding as infant disorders rather than as symptoms of other disorders that are more typical of older individuals.

Treatment is very individualistic. However, infants are typically helped to regulate their states by swaddling, rhythmic music, massage, and self-comforting techniques. Speech and language therapists work with children with feeding disorders to find textures, consistencies, and techniques that increase the likelihood of consumption.

Adjustment Reaction Disorders. Concerns in this area focus on the length of time it takes infants to adjust to change. If the adjustment takes more than four months, infants may be having more problems than expected. An infant or toddler who cannot adjust to child care after four months would fall in this category. Specialists in infant mental health may have to be consulted to work with infants and their caregivers to provide support and guidance to work through these problems.

Guidelines

Children with emotional and behavior disorders, whether temporary or long term, need a warm, relaxed, and secure environment. They need to be accepted as they are, not as you would like them to be, while focusing on the behavior that needs to be modified. Allow children to work at their own pace. Until children can cope with the world, they may not have the energy to forge ahead academically, even if tests show they have the ability.

One important thing you can do for these children is to help them accept themselves as good individuals with behaviors that need to be changed. The most effective ways to do that are to teach children to control the behaviors that cause other children to avoid them and to provide successful experiences for them.

Prevention

The simplest solution for preventing unwanted behavior is to arrange the environment to decrease the likelihood of such occurrences.

1. Structure the environment for behavioral success. Have a sensory area with water, sand, or other materials to relax a tense child. Make available a punching bag and playdough to release aggressive feelings. Arrange traffic patterns to prevent congestion and long runs; make lighting less harsh; remove toys or objects that create problems. (Make a rule that if a child brings a gun-like toy from home, it must stay in the child's locker.) Balance active and passive activities. Give children choices and warn them before changes.

2. Maintain consistent rules and discipline. Set limits and enforce them. Children need to know what your expectations are for them. Write them down for yourself, tell the children, and post them both in writing and in picture form. For ex-

ample, draw a stick figure of a child with a block in a raised hand and put a large X over it. Place the picture in the block area. Your reminders for yourself might be to be positive and to say "You may build with blocks, but you cannot throw them." If necessary, add "If you throw a block again, you will need to pick something else to play with." If the child throws the block again, follow through. Physically guide the child to pick up the block and return it. Then remove the child from the block area and help her choose another area to play in. Repeat the rule: "Blocks are for building, *not* throwing." Make as few limits as possible, but if children violate these, there need to be natural and logical consequences.

3. Have a consistent plan that all educators and caregivers use to respond to particular types of behavior. Deal with situations directly and at the time they occur. Don't ignore the situation.

4. Communicate clearly, using language the child can understand. Be clear about your expectations. A child's definition of sharing the blocks may be very different from yours. Ask questions to determine the child's perceptions. Be specific. For example: "Which blocks are you sharing with Misha?" (The child points to three small blocks.) "You need to give him some of the big blocks, too, so that you each have some. Help me count yours. Now help me count Misha's."

5. Teach children to distinguish between feelings and behavior and provide them with socially acceptable outlets that are easily accessible. Teach prosocial behavior and social interaction skills. Support children in practicing these skills with small groups of children who accept different behaviors. Use stories, dramatic play, and puppets to teach ways of expressing positive and negative feelings.

6. Learn more about the children in your class. Watch how each child waits for a turn, plays with others, and interacts in a small group. Learn to read children's body language. Be aware of who is sitting beside whom. Some combinations of children provoke trouble. Intervene before a conflict occurs. Some teachers tape Xs or even children's names on the floor to cope with both spacing and particular combinations of children.

7. Control children's behavior by obtaining and maintaining eye contact, standing close by, or gently touching the child. Use positive, firm, supportive language. Give children choices.

8. If a child cannot cope with a situation, take her out of it early, before it worsens. If children are having problems playing together and your several solutions to sharing aren't working, say, "There are too many children in the dramatic play area now. Who would be willing to play in another area?" If no one volunteers, ask a child. If that doesn't work, close down that area for the day. This is a way of preventing the need for more drastic measures.

9. If you have planned a long story or listening time and some of the children are having problems listening, change the pace. Break for something active; for example, have the children stretch as high and as low as they can, then come back to your quiet activity.

10. Keep waiting times to a minimum. When it is unavoidable, make waiting interesting by singing songs, doing fingerplays, and so on. Often, behavior problems develop when children are unoccupied and expected to wait for long periods.

11. Evaluate the structure and sequence of the class day, especially if children seem to have problems at the same time each day. If large group time is at 10:30 and this is a bad time for the child, consider rearranging the schedule so that the class is outside at 10:30 and in group time at 9:30 or 11:00.

12. Evaluate yourself and the children objectively. Are there particular behaviors that "bug" you? What is your temperamental style? What is the match or mismatch between the children you find most difficult and your temperament? What can you change about your own behavior?

13. Mediate. Children rarely think about how what they do affects others. Children need to be told that being hit with a block hurts and perhaps told that other children might not want to play with them if they do that.

14. Make four positive statements for each negative or corrective one. Count! It may seem to you that you are being positive, but the reality may be different. Make positive statements to children's parents on a regular basis.

15. Be patient. Changing is difficult, both for children and adults. When you become discouraged, try to think of *one* time when the desired response occurred. If even that doesn't work, pretend it did and think through the result. The struggle is long and hard, but the development of children is worth it.

16. Overall, simplify, shorten, and structure activities. Plan to specifically teach skills other children might learn informally. Make learning meaningful and be respectful of children's work.

There is one area that we think should be part of the guidelines, but we feel conflicted about it. Many people feel that a child who hurts another child should apologize. Our problem is this: When a child tells us he isn't sorry he hurt Johnny and he'd like to do it again, we are not clear what to do. If we make him apologize, then we are teaching him to ignore his own feelings. On the other hand, we believe that an apology is an appropriate response. Our compromise has been to find out what the child is sorry about and require the apology, but not the expected one. For example, "I'm sorry I have to sit in the thinking chair because I hit you." A compromise, but consider it.

Classroom Management

Your goals are to strengthen or reinforce appropriate behavior and to redirect inappropriate behavior. Let's start with the strengthening goal. It is easy to reinforce children who do the right things. A smile, a "thank you," a hug, or even a token reward works, but with children who don't do the right things, where do you start? Start with a principle called *successive approximation*. Reinforce the child at each step that brings him closer to the goal. For example, if a withdrawn child like Julie sits in her locker and cries during group time, encourage her when she doesn't cry. Then encourage her when she progresses to sitting on a chair beside her locker, a chair at a table, a chair nearer the group, a chair behind the group, then on the floor a little separate from the group, and finally with the group. Reward each stage, but don't expect her to go directly from the locker to the middle of the group. This process may take days, weeks, or perhaps months. You might try discussing with Julie where she'd like to sit. After you and she reach an agreement, reinforce behavior that conforms to the agreement. As children do things closer to what you want, keep intermittently rewarding that behavior until you achieve the goal.

Modeling—demonstrating behavior in situations— is also effective, but can be doubled-edged. Children tend to model meaningful people, which in a classroom means they will probably model you over classmates or volunteers (and model parents over you). You are always on display. If you combat aggression with aggression, you may then serve as an aggressive model for children regardless of your intentions. Be a good model by behaving in a way you would like the children to copy. If you don't want children to hit each other but to use their voices to solve problems, then you must demonstrate this. Likewise, if you don't want children to yell at each other, then you need to talk in a normal voice even when you are angry.

Cuing—warning children before they are expected to do something—is another effective means of changing behavior. You use cuing when you flick the lights to tell the children it is cleanup time. More specifically, if Amy looks longingly at John's truck, warn her by saying, "Ask John if he is using the truck." Don't wait until Amy has clobbered John and then say, "John was using the truck. It hurts him when you hit him." If you can anticipate that the child is about to do something undesirable, try to act *before* it happens. When you sense trouble, just moving into the area may prevent a child from misbehaving. Giving a child a "teacher look" is another way to cue a child that something the child is doing or plans to do is not appropriate. These nonverbal techniques (frowns, eye contact, throat clearing) are most effective when a child is just beginning to act out. To work, they require a relationship with the child and eye contact.

When children have emotional and behavioral problems or disorders it is important to fine-tune your classroom management techniques. Be consistent, set clear limits, and state the necessary rules as briefly and directly as possible. However, be prepared to enforce rules that you have. Make children aware of both positive and negative consequences. *If you don't think you can enforce a rule, don't make it.*

If a rule states that everyone who plays with the blocks must help to clean them up, you need to know who played there. If one child is reluctant to help, you need to say, "Mae, you played with the blocks, so you need to help clean them up." If there is no response, you might make an offer: "It's time to pick up the blocks. Do you want to do it by yourself, or would you like me to help you?" If necessary, physically help Mae by opening her hand, placing a block in it, closing her hand, walking with her (or carrying her, if need be) to the block shelf, and helping her deposit the block in the right place; then thank her for helping. The rule was not that children had to clean up *all* the blocks. Time and physical limitations might make such a rule unenforceable. The children are only required to *help,* and even one block put away is a help.

When a child does something that you want continued, reinforce the child's behavior. Decide what specific behavior you want to reinforce (such as sitting through group time). Tell the children they can have or do something they value if they do the specific behavior you've decided on. The trick in using reinforcement is to discover what is rewarding to a particular child. Encouragement, attention, a hug, or some time alone to read in the book corner may be the answers for different children. Make your best guess and then try it out. (If the positive behavior continues, you are doing something rewarding.)

When dealing with children with emotional and behavioral problems, be cautious about being demonstrative at first. Some children find this frightening, and some find it difficult to handle praise. Some children may not consider a hug or praise at all rewarding. An obvious ploy is to ask children what they find rewarding and do what they like. Some children will prefer rewards that you don't personally like. Start with rewards you both agree are acceptable until the behavior is established. Then decide how to change the reward system. If the child finds candy rewarding and you want to use encouragement, use the following procedures: When Doyle does well, praise him, then give him candy; gradually stop giving the candy. Present the new reward just before you present the old one that you know works but that you want to change.

The problem in an inclusive setting is how to deal with the other children. What if another child complains that when he paints a lovely picture, all he gets is a hug? You need to talk about differences. You need to talk about the fact that for some children, some things are difficult that for other children are easy. Then enlist the children to find rewards that are reinforcing for all. If what Sean really wants to do is play with Steven, will Steven play with him for 10 minutes? This can be a win-win situation and inclusion rather than exclusion.

Reward children's behavior each time only until the behavior becomes established, then reward randomly. This is the way to have desired behavior continue. If you *always* reward behavior, then forget a few times, the child will decide you don't want that behavior to continue—if you did, you would keep rewarding it as in the past. (Note that the child's age and cognitive level will influence your decision about reinforcement. Some children who are young either chronologically or developmentally may not "get it." Be prepared to be flexible.) Random reinforcement is a proven method for establishing a new behavior. (Regretfully, the same principle works in reverse for setting limits. If you uphold the limits sometimes and not others, the children will *always* test them. It is important to always reinforce limits!)

If you think a child is acting out to get attention, purposefully ignore the behavior—*providing the behavior isn't dangerous to the child or other children.* Make a mental note to give attention when the child does something that is desired. Give the child cues for acceptable ways of getting your attention: "If you want me to watch you while you use the computer, you need to ask and I'll come over."

When these approaches don't solve the behavior problem, you need to take a more systematic approach to changing the behavior. Write down the information that you gathered through informal observation. Then check with the parents to see if the behavior is happening at home. Gather some baseline data on frequency. That is, if hitting is the problem, wear an apron with a pocket and keep a paper and pencil in it. Put a mark for each time the child hits during the day. (This can be adapted for whatever behavior is the problem.) You can get more elaborate and write down the time, place, victim, and reaction if you want. However, the first step is determining how often this behavior occurs. Do this for three days in a week and put it on a chart. Mark where you begin to intervene. By using a chart such as Figure 9.1, you can tell if you are making a difference. If necessary, you can show the parents your documentation of the problem.

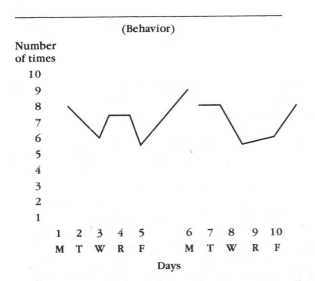

(Behavior)

Number
of times

Figure 9.1

Intervention

To be effective, all teachers and paraprofessionals must use the same procedure when someone is hurt. Consistency works and must be established before the behavior becomes a problem. One scenario might look like this:

1. Quickly check on the victim. If possible, have another adult do this.

2. Tell the aggressor firmly but quietly that you will not tolerate the behavior (think through this statement so you know exactly what you will say ahead of time). For example, as you are walking with the child to the thinking chair, say, "I will not allow you to hurt other children." Ask the child how long she needs to sit in the thinking chair to get herself back together. (Children have little concept of time, so some of their responses may not make a lot of sense, but you want the children to learn techniques of getting in control of themselves and this is part of the process.) If the child's response is unrealistically long, state that you will set the timer for a specific time to come and check on her.

3. Note the time or set a timer, turn your back on the child, and walk away. Do not talk to the child or make eye contact with the child during this time. If other children approach the child, simply state, "TR needs to be alone for a few minutes. He needs to thing about what he has done."

4. Thinking time needs to be developmentally appropriate for the child. A useful guideline is one minute for each year of the child's age: two minutes for a 2-year-old, four minutes for a 4-year-old, and so on. (Although this seems like a short time to adults, a child's perception is very different. It is far better to keep it short than to deal with the child's behavior during a long "thinking time"). In addition to chronological age, children who have developmental delays may need shorter times as well.

5. When the time is up, go to the child and ask, "Are you ready to get up now?" If yes, talk with child about what happened very explicitly. If no, give the child another minute or two. If the answer is no again, tell the child you will help her get ready. Then take the child to a private area and talk about what happened. This is the time to talk about the incident. It is imperative that children know exactly what they have done wrong and why it is not allowed. The incident needs to be addressed. The goal is to bring closure to the incident so that both you and the child can continue your day without this hanging over you.

If particular children are especially difficult, remember that you can get help: You don't have to solve all problems on your own. Sometimes, someone outside of your setting can be more objective about the situation than you are. Ask another teacher or an administrator to observe the situation for a while and offer suggestions. Or seek the advice of a school or community resource person.

Positive behavior management requires respectful treatment of all children. Your consistent modeling of respect for the children in your care is probably the most powerful behavior management tool you have. Positive relationships between adults and children and among children are the foundation for each person's feeling good about herself. Children who feel loved and respected are more likely to help and follow your rules.

Curriculum Adaptations

The number and degree of adaptations depend on each child's needs. Your awareness of short-term needs will do a lot toward the child's long-term adjustment.

Social Awareness: Self-Esteem, Inclusion, Social Studies, Health and Safety

For children with emotional and behavioral disorders, this area is paramount. Some children may not be tuned into the world around them, and they need to be. They often lack social skills and perhaps even an unwillingness to approach others, and because they do not deal with reality well, they may be safety risks. The classroom and community need to become familiar and safe places for them. Do a lot of preparation for field trips as well as follow-up. Make sure you have plenty of adults on trips so that all of the children can be safely supervised. Children may temporarily forget health and safety rules and may need reminders. Take care to keep these routines a consistent part of the program for all children.

Self-Esteem. Children need to feel good about themselves. Before children can learn to control their feelings, they must become aware of their emotions and how they respond to them. It is important to ask a child how he feels: "When I see you wondering around the classroom, I wonder how you are feeling." Don't tell a child "You're lonely"; the child may not be lonely—he may be sad or angry. Help children learn that they are the only ones who know how they feel. Once children are aware of feelings, they can be taught to express them. If you, as a teacher, accept the feelings and don't judge them, then the children will probably continue to talk. If children are told that it is silly or stupid to feel the way they do, they are likely to quit talking about how they feel.

1. Talk about individual children and their similarities to other children; at the same time, talk about what makes them unique (hair and eye color, type of shoes and clothing, and so on).

2. Write children's names on the chalkboard and discuss names and nicknames of the children and members of their respective families.

3. Include children's names in songs and stories.

4. Have children share some of the great things that happen to them. (Children may need support in sharing and these great things may need your help to happen at school.)

Inclusion. It may seem clear to you by this point that including some children with emotional and behavioral disorders will be a challenge. You are right.

Children need help to feel that they are part of the group. They need to be aware of individual differences, know the other children, and know that they too are accepted and belong even when they are isolated or have conflicts with others. Plan some activities that don't demand a great deal of social interaction yet allow children to see themselves as part of the group. For example, have each child paint or color an area of a mural, or have each child contribute a page to a class book.

1. Talk to children about aggressive or withdrawn behavior (or whatever specific problem you have) and discuss the dimensions of that behavior: the ways people behave when they feel different ways. The purpose is to discuss the behavior, not the child.

2. Ask all the children to think about times when they felt or acted this way (aggressive, withdrawn). If they don't respond, ask them to pretend what it would be like. Encourage them to role-play the different general behavior patterns.

3. Then ask them how they felt when they were role-playing the behaviors. (They will usually say "lonely," "angry," "mad," and so on.)

4. Ask them what they really want from others when they feel that way. Talk about how children can help each other. Give them the words: "I'm feeling lonely, may I play with you?" Some children may not be willing to include others in the play. Help them with the skills of negotiation: "You can play when we finish this game"; "You can watch and we'll talk to you." All children need skills to include others and to request inclusion.

Social Studies. As children move into the preschool and elementary years, interaction with peers and the community at large becomes more important.

1. Some adjustment problems have their basis in the family. Talk about many different types of families: those with one or two children, those with many children, those with single parents, step or blended families, families with relatives living in the home, mixed racial families, families that are cohabitating, and families with adopted or foster children. Emphasize the functional components of families.

2. Expand the concept of families by talking about different roles family members have: mother, friend, daughter, teacher, sister. Help

the children see their own various roles: son, friend, brother, pupil.

3. Talk about the many roles of community helpers. (Note that some children may be frightened of police because of previous experience with them.) They may need a neutral ground to learn about the variety of roles community helpers play. Role-play such situations as being lost, seeing a fire, and visiting a friend. Follow this up with having some helpers visit the class (children usually like the K-9 police squad the best).

Health and Safety. Help children learn that your classroom is a basically safe place when they understand how to handle things and when to exercise caution.

1. Help children develop independence and self-esteem by teaching adaptive (self-help) skills. To teach dressing, use buttoning and zipping frames as well as natural opportunities such as coming and going home from school or outside or when playing with large dolls. Teach children hygienic toileting behaviors: Be sure children learn to wipe themselves, flush, and wash and dry their hands after using the toilet.

2. Provide children with a variety of experiences with different foods for snacks or lunches to help them learn to use different eating utensils.

3. Use cleanup time to help all children feel that they are contributing parts of the group. Create a sense of responsibility for keeping the room neat.

Language and Literacy: Speaking, Listening, Reading, and Writing

The language arts area can help children develop the language skills to talk about situations they find difficult and the feelings these situations bring about. Through literature, children learn how other children have dealt with similar feelings and situations. Children with emotional and behavioral disorders require a vocabulary that helps them verbalize their feelings and communicate with others.

Some children may have learned to tune out their environment because it seemed negative, irrelevant, or scary. They will need your help in learning how to tune you in and listen again. These children may find reading and writing less threatening than field trips or spoken language. They can expand their knowledge at a time when other options are not available. Allow them time to do these activities. Writing and illustrating are potential outlets for feelings and expression. Help children take advantage of these.

Speaking. Although children with emotional and behavioral disorders speak, they may not use speech to communicate with others. They need to learn to use speech for social interaction.

1. Teach vocabulary for expressing feelings. Use words the child can understand: *mad, sad, happy, tight, ready to hit, tense, excited.*

2. Encourage children to use words to solve problems: "May I play in the hospital with you? I could be the nurse."

3. Demonstrate words, especially those associated with feelings. Pretend to be a statue or fashion model. Have the children tell you how to arrange yourself to show a specific emotion. If necessary, give them some clues about the areas to address: "I'm angry. Should my hands be open or closed? Should I look up or down? How should my mouth be?"

Fingerplays are beneficial for children because they provide opportunities for peer group acceptance and positive role models.

1. If a child has a characteristic behavior such as hand waving, incorporate it into a fingerplay or a set of motions done to music. Do this in a way that helps the child feel part of the group but that doesn't draw attention to the child: "Shake, shake, shake your hands, shake your hands together." Then do something else that is incompatible with hand shaking: "Clap, clap, clap your hands, clap your hands together." Ask for other suggestions.

2. Use fingerplays to "settle" children. Practice fingerplays ("Open Shut Them") that finish with the hands in the lap. Whether a fingerplay merely quiets the children or has them keep their hands in their lap, they will be less likely to poke others.

Listening. Use listening to increase children's awareness of their behavior.

1. Give children short, simple, and specific directions until they can predictably follow them.

2. Reassure children with your words and your tone of voice.

3. Tell children what to do, followed by what not to do. Children with emotional and behavioral problems often need both.

4. Give children feedback about their behavior: "Walk more slowly. You are walking too fast." (Put a hand on the child and walk with him.)

5. If children seem to listen but not understand, think about the content and whether the child has the experiential background for understanding.

Groups. As many listening experiences happen during group time, be aware of some of the inherent problems for children in groups.

1. Interestingly, aggressive children are often fearful of attack by others. This is particularly true when their personal space is invaded by sitting next to others. Try to seat these children between the most nonthreatening children in the

classroom. However, keep a careful eye out for warning signs of aggression. (Always placing a child next to an adult externalizes their control and contributes to dependency.)

2. Frequently call on a child who is very active, or just mention the child's name; this helps focus attention. (Do this for all the children, but mention that child's name more frequently, if necessary.) Don't focus undue attention on the child. Keep activities short and focused, give directions frequently, and intersperse physical activities with those that require only listening.

3. Children who are anxious may be afraid of talking in front of the whole class. Give them the opportunity to talk, but don't force them to respond. If this is a concern to them, tell them that you will not call on them unless they give a particular signal such as raising a hand.

4. Children who are withdrawn may not participate in the group at the beginning. Initially, they may need to watch and listen from the fringes. As children show signs of becoming part of the group, encourage them as well as their participation.

5. Children with pervasive developmental disorders may need an adult with them during group time. Group interaction is one of their most challenging skill areas. Continually reevaluate their behavior. By the end of the year, they may make many contributions.

Reading. Mastering reading readiness skills requires the child to make fine auditory and visual distinctions. Although here the needs of all children are similar, choose subject matter that is relevant to the adjustment needs of the child.

1. Distinguish and label facial features. Play Lotto by matching faces. Even in simple line drawings,

Figure 9.2

focus attention on the face and help children attach feelings to expressions.

2. Have children discuss moods. Write language experience stories using moods as themes. Discuss what might happen to make children feel different ways. With older children, move beyond the obvious happy and sad.

3. Cut pictures of people and situations out of magazines (those with obvious themes are easiest). Have the children make up a story about what might have happened and how the people involved may have felt. Invent a variety of endings and discuss which aspects of situations could change.

Use stories to help children increase skills in dealing with themselves and others.

1. Read stories dealing with angry feelings and peer conflict.

2. Select stories that have problem situations pertinent to the child's.

3. Tell stories about a child who learns to deal with feelings: "Once upon a time, there was a girl named _____ who . . ." (Be careful not to pinpoint a particular child or emotional/behavioral problem.)

Writing. Like other fine motor activities, writing is problematical with some children. Focus on the process, not the product. Some children may find it is easier to convey ideas graphically than verbally.

1. Have a variety of materials available, especially large paper and large markers and crayons.

2. Help children focus on the communicative aspect of writing as opposed to fine motor skills or art.

3. Praise their efforts and call children authors and/or illustrators. Any attempts they make at communication in any media need to be encouraged.

4. Securing paper with a clipboard or taping it to the table may be helpful.

Discovery: Mathematics, Science, and Computers

Children need positive, successful learning experiences. Praise participation and the process regardless of the outcome. Break tasks down into small steps that can be done in a short amount of time. Science and mathematics demand little social interaction, yet they hold the potential for it. Children with emotional and behavioral disorders may be willing to participate in small groups in these areas. The emphasis on discovery may make this area less threatening for them. Choose computer software that allows children to be in control.

Mathematics. Math skills can be taught for their own sake, but when taught as part of other activities, they can also be used to increase a child's general awareness.

1. Use math to point out likenesses and differences and to create a sense of group belonging: "There are *three* boys with brown hair, but only *one* boy with brown hair and a plaid shirt."

2. Incorporate math skills into turn taking and sharing: "You can play with the truck for five minutes, then it is Stan's turn." (Set a timer.) "You can ride the trike around the play yard four times, then give it to Frances." (Incorporate children into the waiting process by helping them count the four trips.)

3. Use simple card games like Fish to encourage peer interaction.

Science. A discovery approach has great potential for teaching science to children with adjustment problems. They can be doing what they prefer, yet still be included in the group.

1. Help children to understand cause-and-effect relationships as they learn the physical properties of materials: "Snow melts when it gets warm."

2. Encourage children to make predictions about experiments before they actually do them: "What will happen to the balance when you put the cup on it? Let's try it and see." Eventually, you can expand this skill to personal situations: "What might Brad do if you take his book?"

Computers. Computers offer the potential for communication without the need to cope with people. For some children, this is much less threatening.

1. Start with simple programs where the children are in control and a single key stroke makes something happen. Talk with them about what they are doing. Help them begin to focus their behavior and make it more purposeful. If necessary, adjust the touch of the computer keys to make them easier to control.

2. Children can work with the same software with little need (but many opportunities) for personal interaction.

Developmental Physical Education and Sensorimotor Skills: Large Motor, Small Motor, Sensorimotor Integration

Motor activities help develop gross and fine motor skills and provide opportunities for peer interaction and opportunities to learn spatial and temporal concepts. Help children learn to monitor their level of activity. Children with emotional and behavioral disorders can use large motor activities as a way of venting energy and participating in a group experience. A noncompetitive organization allows you to individualize activities without focusing attention on a particular child. Participation in large motor play from a young age helps children develop the trunk muscles that are necessary for the stabilization that precedes the development of fine motor skills. Provide many intriguing fine motor activities, as children may need encouragement to use and develop these skills.

Children need to become more aware of their body and the relationship between their feelings and what their body does. They need help learning how to recognize tension in their body and how to release that tension in a way that doesn't infringe on the rights of others. Children need to know how their body feels just before aggressive interactions; once this knowledge is attained, you can help children learn to substitute other behaviors. (It is much like toilet training in that respect.) Children need to become aware of their body before they can control it.

Large Motor. Large motor activities should not be equated with being out of control. Teach children to use large motor play to run off excess energy and frustration. The benefits are obvious to adults who clean house or jog or work out in a gym when angry. Children have yet to learn this. Prevent the need for time out by encouraging children to run, climb, or ride trikes. Encourage them to play hard until they are tired but not exhausted.

1. If children have a long ride to school, plan to do some large motor activities early in the day.

2. Large motor play may let an aggressive child be part of a group and accepted in this role.

3. Consider adding a punching bag or an inflatable Bobo doll to your room. When children feel like hitting something, encourage them to hit the punching bag—hard. Comment positively on this behavior: "You really can hit that punching bag hard." (A commercial punching bag that is on a spring attached to a wooden base can be moved to different locations, even outside. Be sure to develop rules about its use.)

4. Use light, large, cardboard blocks. They are less of a problem than wooden blocks when a conflict arises.

5. Have children throw Velcro-covered ping-pong balls at a bull's-eye, beanbags at a target, or plastic horse shoes at a stick. (These are good things to do outside.)

Small Motor. Be aware of the timing of small motor activities for children with emotional and behavioral disorders. If a child is already feeling frustrated, problems connected to small motor development may increase the frustration. However, children shouldn't just avoid what they find frustrating; rather, the educator needs to provide motivation, encouragement, and support for the child.

1. Encourage the independent use of small motor toys on children's good days or at good times of the day. At other times, promote success by making the activity more interesting or easier or shorten the time expectation.

2. Use a wide varieties of toys, including some of the *large* small motor toys designed for toddlers.

3. If a child appears frustrated by a toy or activity, help the child finish the step of the task that she is doing, label for the child what this step is ("After you add the eyes, we'll put the puppet away"), and then tell the child that she can finish it another day. Children need to understand that they need to finish tasks (often they don't), so start by completing one part and on another day a little more until the project is completed. They learn both self-control and a sense of completion.

Sensorimotor Integration.   Children need practice integrating sensory information. Some children with emotional and behavioral disorders are hyper- or hyposensitive to touch, sound, or other sensory input.

1. Some children are hypersensitive to touch. Allow them to wear a sweater or jacket when contact is likely. Designate personal space, and be sure all children know the rules of the game before you start. Stop the game, if necessary, to remind all children of the rules. It is imperative the children feel safe.

2. Avoid competitive games, especially chase-type games. Add a cooperative, or at least noncompetitive, component to games.

3. Adapt games so children are not eliminated. If you play musical chairs, don't remove any chairs. When the music stops, all children will have a place to sit.

4. Be sure children have good control of their hands and fingers before expecting them to control tools. Build this strength through using clay, spray bottles, hole punches, holding on while swinging, and so on.

5. Warm water has a calming effect on children and is useful for children who are hypersensitive. For children who are hyposensitive, use cold water and add ice cubes for variation.

6. A large bubble wand with soap and water provides large bubbles for children to catch.

Creative Arts: Visual Arts, Music, Creative Movement, and Dramatic Play

Encourage children with emotional and behavioral disorders to use art as a way of expressing feelings. Strong feelings can be expressed through the use of bold colors, pounding clay, and tearing paper.

Draining angry feelings in these ways helps the children keep themselves in control. Use music to help children relax (play soft music at rest time) and to release feelings (encourage them to beat a drum to express anger). Provide plenty of movement and large motor activities to help them express pent-up emotions. Movements that at other times might be thought unusual may be included here. As long as there is no right or wrong movements, children can participate and learn about their body. Dramatic play can help children work through their fears and anxieties about specific issues. If talking directly about situations produces anxiety, have the child dress up and pretend to be someone else or talk through a puppet. Blocks can be a solitary or group experience; there are no right or wrong buildings. Encourage both boys and girls to use this area, but establish clear safety rules with both words and pictures.

Visual Arts.   Art can teach children about their bodies and how to express their feelings.

1. Use activities that incorporate the child's body or name. Make body pictures. Trace the outline of the child on a large sheet of paper. Have the child color and cut it out to make a life-sized paper doll. Use water to paint the child's shadow on the sidewalk. Use face- or body-shaped paper for painting or coloring. Make a Name Book, a book about the children and what each child does and likes. Make posters or books using pictures of the children in the class. Do foot or hand printing or painting.

2. Help children use three-dimensional art media such as clay to work through feelings. Let them pound, roll, and tear clay.

3. Encourage children to paint their feelings and to use the paintings to talk about these feelings.

4. If children seem reluctant to try messy activities, start with some "clean" messy activities.

Music.   Music can be used to teach the relationship between feelings and sound. Combined with movement, it is good for energy release.

1. If children are particularly wound up and you need to calm them down, start out with a vigorous tune and work toward a slow one. Make a tape of selections ranging from very loud and active to quiet and restful. Tape only a part of each piece rather than the whole piece so that the tape is not too large.

2. Once children have learned songs, use them often to promote a sense of predictability in a changing world. Teach new songs after singing old favorites.

3. The motion of the record player, tape recorder, or compact disk player is fascinating to some children. When not in use, they need to be stored out of reach.

4. Particular rhythms can be very enjoyable to children with emotional and behavioral disorders. A child may be encouraged to request a particular song.

5. Talk about the different moods that music conveys and how different music can make children feel.

6. Music can be exciting to children. Be sure to use quiet music at the end if you expect children to participate in quiet activities.

Creative Movement. Children need to learn to control their bodies, be aware of their internal feelings, and develop socially acceptable behaviors that respond to these feelings. Help children learn to tense their body like wooden soldiers and to relax like a rag doll. Adult assistance may be necessary.

1. Some children may have to be helped to "move through" the activity. (Although, by most standards, this is not creative, it is a beginning for inclusion.)

2. Add movement to make music time more than just a listening experience.

3. Movement requires space. Music activities with movement are good for helping children learn how much space they require to avoid bumping into each other.

Dramatic Play. Dramatic play can be used to help children build successful peer relations and work out fears about specific issues.

1. If a child wants to play with another child or a group of children but does not know how to join the group, you might join the group with that child, play until the child becomes involved, and then slowly lessen your own involvement.

2. If a child is afraid to join in the play when many children are present, arrange some times when only two or three children may use a specific area at one time.

3. Let children see how they fit into the various roles and relationships in a family, school, store, hospital, or fire station. Let them try different roles.

4. Help children reenact fearful experiences in the more supportive class atmosphere, where they can come to grips with the experience. Read children the story of the "Three Little Pigs." As children play the role of a pig, have them make a safety rule when the wolf knocks on the door; for example, never answer the door without asking who it is (look through a window); call 911 if the Big Bad Wolf is breaking into the house or hurting someone; don't take candy (drugs) from the Big Bad Wolf (stranger); don't run off with the Big Bad Wolf (stranger). Videotape the role play and encourage children to draw or paint it.

5. Encourage the children to talk about things they are afraid of and discuss what to do in various situations such as seeing a snake or getting stung by a bee. You may need to include some areas that you will need some preparation for, such as what to tell children about domestic violence and drug dealing and how to remain safe when drugs and alcohol are being abused in the family. This helps children gain some control and some strategies as well as the knowledge that they are not alone.

6. Use puppets as a way for children to talk indirectly about experiences.

7. Have toy telephones available. Children may talk more freely when not face to face with their partner. Encourage them to write, type, or draw feelings and share them with someone.

Transitions

Transitions are the most difficult time of the day for many children. Consider the number of transitions in the day. Can any of them be eliminated (for example, can you have an "open" snack that is available during free play rather than a time specified when all children must participate)? Keep transitions to a minimum. Provide warnings before they happen and support for children who have difficulty with them.

1. Follow a regular routine for arrivals, departures, and moving among activities. If the adults are disorganized, the children will feel even more confused.

2. Gradually reduce the support you offer during routines to match the child's learning.

3. Some children, particularly children who exhibit psychotic behaviors, have a difficult time coping with noise and movement and have little internal sense of time. For them, transitions may be incomprehensible and overwhelming. Adult support is necessary during these times until the child adjusts.

4. When possible, limit the number of transitions and have the same adult assist the child.

5. Use transitions to single out children and build their self-esteem. When you dismiss children from large group time or while you wait for others to join the group, try:

Singing the children's names.

Calling last names or initials (children often are not aware there are so many different ways of referring to themselves).

Calling the child who lives at (address).

Describing an important event or fact about the child.

Calling children by hair color, eyes, or type of clothing.

Summary

We live in a complex world where children are being asked to cope with a variety of situations from very young ages. Some of these situations are stressful to families, children, and early childhood educators and caregivers. Whether or not this stress turns into crisis is dependent on the child and the child's perception of the situation, the stressors, and the resources the child has to cope with stress.

Increasingly, children are victimized because of their dependency and lack of cognitive skills. Children come into the world differently: Some children are easy and flexible, some children are slow to warm up and fearful, others may be difficult and feisty. A child's temperament plays a part in how well the child fits in and adapts to the family and the educational setting.

Because of genetic and environmental factors, some children have emotional and behavioral problems or disorders. Problems are roughly divided into those emotions and behaviors that are externalizing, such as aggression and antisocial behavior, and internalizing problems that include shyness, withdrawal, and eating problems. In general, the behavior that distinguishes an emotional and behavior problem from a disorder relates to the duration and intensity of the behavior.

When children's behavior is consistently disruptive, they are identified as having a disorder. Emotional and behavioral disorders are classified in different ways by different organizations, but they are usually related to broad behavioral areas. Some childhood disorders focus on anxiety or excessive fear of separation. Like adults, children who have experienced or witnessed traumatic events can have post-traumatic stress disorder.

Guidelines focus on preventing situations from occurring and methods for supporting children's awareness of feelings and emotions and for being included in the group. Curriculum adaptations are designed to increase personal awareness, becoming more aware of behaviors and feelings, and learning the language to express this awareness.

Educational Resources

American Academy of Child and Adolescent
   Psychiatry
3615 Wisconsin Avenue, NW
Washington, DC 20016-3007
(202) 966-7300, FAX (202) 966-2891
http://www.aacap.org/web/aacap
   They have publications on children's mental health. Their Web page has information in English, French, and Spanish. There is also information about the organization and other links.

American Association of Psychiatric Services for
   Children
1133 15th Street, NW, Suite 1000
Washington, DC 20005
   Provides information on diagnosis and services.

Center for Attitudinal Healing
19 Main Street
Tiburon, CA 94920
   Offers free help to children and adults with life-threatening diseases or traumatic accidents. Deals with peace of mind and elimination of fear. Pain and death are discussed.

Mental Health Net
http://www.cmhc.com/mhn.htm
   This Web page allows one to search for any mental health topic and find information and links about that topic.

National Alliance for the Mentally Ill (NAMI)
200 North Globe Road, Suite 1015
Arlington, VA 22203-3754
(800) 750-NAMI, TDD (703) 516-7991,
   Front Desk (703) 524-7600, FAX (703) 524-9094
http://www.nami.org/vikings/nami/index.html
   NAMI is a nationwide network for family advocates on behalf of individuals with severe and chronic mental illness. Has local chapters and also publishes and annotates books and pamphlets. Their Web page is for networking people working to improve lives of those with mental illness; many are resources available.

The National Association for Mental Health
1800 North Kent Street
Rosslyn Station
Arlington, VA 22209
   The national office refers individuals to local affiliations, directs a research program and a public information program, and acts as a liaison with governmental and private organizations.

The National Center for Mental Health Services
   (NCMHS)
Knowledge Exchange Network (KEN)
PO Box 42490
Washington, DC 20015
(800) 789-2647, BBS (800) 790-2647,
   TDD (301) 443-9006, FAX (301) 984-8796
http://www.mentalhealth.org/about/index.htm
   Provides information about mental health.

The National Clearinghouse on Child and Abuse and
   Neglect Information
http://www.calib.com/nccanch
   Provides information, statistics, reports, and answers to frequently asked questions.

The National Committee to Prevent Child Abuse
http://www.childabuse.org
   Offers information useful in working toward the prevention of child abuse.

National Consortium for Child Mental Health
   Services
1424 16th Street, NW, Suite 201A
Washington, DC 20036
   Serves as a forum for exchange of information on child mental health services.

National Society for Autistic Children
621 Central Avenue
Albany, NY 12206

The national headquarters makes referrals to local chapters and works for programs of legislation, education, and research for all mentally ill children.

The Pendulum Pages
http://www.pendulum.org
This page contains information on bipolar mood disorders.

References

American Psychiatric Association. (1994). *Diagnostic and statistical manual of mental disorders (DSM-IV)* (4th ed.). Washington, DC: Author.

Achenbach, T. (1985). *Assessment and taxonomy of child and adolescent psychopathology.* Beverly Hills, CA: Sage.

Ayalon, O. (1983). Coping with terrorism: The Israeli case. In D. Meichenbaum & M. E. Jaremko (Eds.), *Stress reduction and prevention.* New York: Plenum Press.

Bear, T., Schenk, S., & Buckner, L. (1992/1993). Supporting victims of child abuse. *Educational Leadership, 42–47.*

Brazelton, T. B. (1992). *Touchpoints: Your child's emotional and behavioral development.* Reading, MA: Addison-Wesley.

Briere, J. (1992). *Child abuse trauma: Theory and treatment of the lasting effects.* Newbury Park, CA: Sage.

Chess, S. (1983). Basic adaptations required for successful parenting. In V. Sasserath (Ed.), *Minimizing high-risk parenting* (pp. 5–11). Skillman, NJ: Johnson & Johnson.

Chess, S., & Thomas, A. (1977). Temperamental individuality from childhood to adolescence. *Journal of Child Psychiatry, 16,* 218–226.

Chess, S., & Thomas, A. (1990). The New York longitudinal study (NYLS): The young adult periods. *Canadian Journal of Psychiatry, 35,* 557–561.

Cicchetti, D., & Lynch, M. (1993). Toward an ecological/transaction model of community violence and child maltreatment: Consequences for child development. In D. Reiss, J. E. Richters, & M. Radke-Yarrow (Eds.), *Children and violence* (pp. 96–118). New York: Guilford Press.

Compas, B. E., & Epping, J. E. (1993). Stress and coping in children and families. In C. F. Saylor (Ed.), *Children and disasters* (pp. 11–28). New York: Plenum Press.

Eckenrode, J., Laird, M., & Doris, J. (1993). School performance and disciplinary problems among abused and neglected children. *Developmental Psychology, 29,* 53–62.

Edme, R. N., Bingham, R. D., & Harmon, R. J. (1993). Classification and the diagnostic process in infancy. In C. H. Zeanah, Jr. (Ed.), *Handbook of infant mental health* (pp. 225–235). New York: Guilford Press.

Eth, S., & Pynoos, R. (1985). Developmental perspectives on psychic trauma in childhood. In C. R. Figley (Ed.), *Trauma and its wake.* New York: Brunner/Mazel.

Faller, K. (1989). Why sexual abuse? An exploration of the intergenerational hypothesis. *Child Abuse and Neglect, 13,* 543–548.

Finkelhor, D. (1995). The victimization of children: A developmental perspective. *American Journal of Orthopsychiatry, 65*(2), 177–193.

Finkelhor, D., & Dziuba-Leatherman, J. (1994). Victimization of children. *American Psychologist,* 173–183.

Franyo, G. (1996). *Temperament: Recognizing, respecting, and responding.* Unpublished manuscript. Newark, DE.

Gottschall, S. (1989). Understanding and accepting separation feelings. *Young Children, 44*(6), 11–16.

Hill, R. (1958). Social stresses on the family. *Social Casework, 58,* 139–150.

Honig, A. S. (1986). Stress and coping in children. In J. B. McCracken (Ed.), *Reducing stress in young children's lives* (pp. 142–167). Washington, DC: NAEYC.

Honig, A. S. (1987). The shy child. *Young Children, 42*(4), 54–64.

Huesmann, L. R., Eron, L. D., Lefkowitz, M. M., & Walder, L. O. (1984). The stability of aggression over time and generations. *Developmental Psychology, 20,* 1120–1134.

Hyson, M. C., & Van Triest, K. (1987). *The shy child* (Eric Digests). Urbana, IL: ERIC Clearinghouse on Elementary and Early Childhood Education.

Izard, C. E., & Hyson, M. C. (1986). Shyness as a discrete emotion. In W. H. Jones (Ed.), *Shyness.* New York: Plenum Press.

Jalongo, M. R. (1987). Do security blankets belong in preschool? *Young Children, 42*(3), 3–8.

Kazdin, A. (1989). Developmental psychopathology: Current research, issues, and directions. *American Psychologist, 44,* 180–187.

Kendall-Tackett, K. A., Williams, L. M., & Finkelhor, D. (1993). Impact of sexual abuse on children: A review and synthesis of recent empirical studies. *Psychological Bulletin, 113*(1), 164–180.

Keppel-Benson, J. M., & Ollendick, T. H. (1993). Posttraumatic stress disorder in children and adolescents. In C. F. Saylor (Ed.), *Children and disasters* (pp. 29–43). New York: Plenum Press.

Lasher, M., Mattick, I., & Perkins, F. (1978). *Mainstreaming preschoolers: Children with emotional disturbance.* Washington, DC: U.S. Department of Health and Human Services.

Legg, J. (1993). What's a bite among friends. *Exchange,* (7), 41–43.

Mauk, J. E., Reber, M., & Batshaw, M. L. (1997). Autism and other pervasive developmental disorders. In M. L. Batshaw (Ed.), *Children with disabilities* (4th ed., pp. 425–448). Baltimore: Brookes.

McCubbin, H. I., & Patterson, J. M. (1982). Family adaptation to crisis. In H. I. McCubbin, M. B. Sussman, & J. M. Patterson (Eds.), *Family stress, coping, and social support.* Springfield, IL: Thomas.

McCurdy, K., & Daro, D. (1994). *Current trends in child abuse reporting and fatalities: The results of the 1993 annual fifty state survey* [Working Paper No. 808]. Chicago, IL: National Committee to Prevent Child Abuse.

Morgan, S. R. (1987). *Abuse and neglect of handicapped children.* Boston, MA: Little, Brown.

National Center for Clinical Infant Programs. (1991). *Diagnostic classification study manual.* Arlington, VA: Author.

Peterson, N. L. (1987). *Early intervention for handicapped and at-risk children: An introduction to early childhood special education.* Denver, CO: Love.

Pittman, F. S. (1987). *Turning points: Treating families in transition and crisis.* New York: Norton.

Putnam, F. W. (1991). Dissociative disorders in children and adolescents: A developmental perspective. *Psychiatric Clinics of North America, 14,* 519–531.

Putnam, F. W., & Trickett, P. K. (1993). Child sexual abuse: A model of chronic trauma. In D. Reiss, J. E. Richters, & M. Radke-Yarrow (Eds.), *Children and violence* (pp. 96–118). New York: Guilford Press.

Rakic, P., Bourgeois, J. P., & Goldman-Rakic, P. S. (1994). Synaptic development of the cerebral cortex: Implications for learning, memory, and mental illness. In J. vanPelt, M. A. Corna, H. B. M. Uylings, & P. H. Lopes da Silva (Eds.), *The self-organizing brain: From growth cones to functional networks.* Elsevier Science BV.

Rapoport, J. L., & Ismond, D. R. (1996). *DSM-IV training guide for childhood disorders.* New York: Brunner/Mazel.

Rutter, M. (1988). The role of cognition in child development and disorder. *Annual Progress in Child Psychiatry and Child Development, 21,* 77–101.

Salvia, J., & Ysseldyke, J. E. (1995). *Assessment* (6th ed.). Boston: Houghton Mifflin.

Shirk, S. R. (1988). The interpersonal legacy of physical abuse of children. In M. B. Straus (Ed.), *Abuse and victimization across the life span* (pp. 57–81). Baltimore: Johns Hopkins University Press.

Slaby, R. G., Roedell, W. C., Arezzo, D., & Hendrix, K. (1995). *Early violence prevention: Tools for teachers of young children.* Washington, DC: National Association for the Education of Young Children.

Sobsey, D. (1994). *Violence and abuse in the lives of people with disabilities.* Baltimore: Brookes.

Soderman, A. (1985 July). Dealing with difficult young children: Strategies for teachers and parents. *Young Children, 40*(5), 15–20.

Solter, A. (1992). Understanding tears and tantrums. *Young Children, 47*(4), 64–68.

Starr, R. H., Jr. (1988). Physical abuse of children. In V. B. Van Hasselt, R. L. Morris, A. S. Bellack, & M. Hersen (Eds.), *Handbook of family violence* (pp. 119–155). New York: Plenum Press.

Straus, M. A. (1991). Discipline and deviance: Physical punishment of children and violence and other crime in adulthood. *Social Problems, 38,* 101–123.

Straus, M. A. (1995). Corporal punishment of children, adult depression, and suicide ideation. In J. McCord (Ed.), *Coercion and punishment in long term perspective* (pp. 59–77). New York: Cambridge University Press.

Straus, M. A., Gelles, R., & Steinmetz, S. K. (1980). *Behind closed doors: Violence in the American family.* Garden City, NY: Anchor Press.

Thomas, A., & Chess, S. (1980). *The dynamics of psychological development.* New York: Brunner/Mazel.

Thomas, A., Chess, S., & Birch, C. (1968). *Temperament and behavior disorders in children.* New York: New York University Press.

Wittmer, D. S., & Honig, A. S. (1994). Encouraging positive social development in young children. *Young Children, 49*(5), 4–12.

Chapter 10

CHILDREN WITH LEARNING DIFFERENCES: ATTENTION-DEFICIT/ HYPERACTIVITY DISORDER AND LEARNING DISABILITIES

In the 1960s, we thought in terms of children who *wouldn't* behave and *wouldn't* learn:

> At the beginning of the school year, 4-year-old Sam was "acting out." He hit other children without provocation. He would neither print his name nor remember where his locker was (despite the animal sticker on it). He wouldn't sit still during group time, but would wander around the room being disruptive. He was reminded so often that "it hurts when someone hits you" that by the end of the school year, no matter where he was in the room, if a child cried, Sam would go up to that child and say, "I'm sorry I made you cry." He believed he caused others to cry even when he wasn't responsible.

We wonder if Sam was a child who *wouldn't* behave or *couldn't* behave and who *wouldn't* learn or *couldn't* learn with the methods we were using. We didn't have a label for attention-deficit/hyperactivity disorder then; there were only "difficult" children who were "behavior problems." Sam was in fact diagnosed as having a learning disability after he had repeated first grade and was having trouble in second grade. By then, he had not only a learning disability but also a poor self-concept. Sam is only one of the children we wonder about. We have had others; perhaps you have, too. This chapter is designed to help you identify and teach the children who "can't" but who "should be able to."

Defining Learning Differences

Learning differences is a term we have chosen to use as an umbrella term to include attention-deficit/hyperactivity disorder (ADHD), attention deficit disorder (ADD), and specific learning disabilities (LD). This area is confounded by definitional problems, which are compounded by federal regulations that determine the labels that can be used to obtain special educational services for children. Learning disabilities frequently coexist with attention-deficit/hyperactivity disorder. Additionally, many of the characteristics and interventions overlap during the early childhood years.

Learning disabilities were recognized by the federal government in 1969 as a group of disabilities requiring special educational services. It is one with the least agreement over the nomenclature. The confusion results from past terms and definitions among four different fields—educational, legal, psychological, and medical.

More than 90 terms have been used to describe what the federal government refers to as learning disabilities. Some include minimal brain dysfunction, information-processing disorder, central nervous system disorder, brain damage syndrome, and on and on. Most fell short of defining the "problem." The focus of many of the definitions was on the central nervous system, as it was assumed that learning disabilities were caused by damage or injury to the brain. Although children showed the behavioral signs of children with brain damage, there was rarely neurological evidence of the damage. The agreement seems to be that children have a central nervous system *dysfunction*.

The problem remained to try to figure out why some children with normal intelligence were not receiving the education they needed. Initially, we focused on these children as "underachievers" and "slow learners." However, these were accurate descriptions for some areas but not others. Some of the children who were not learning at the expected rate showed behavioral and personality problems; others did not. And it was not clear whether these behavior and personality problems were the cause of or result of the learning differences. As parents became more active, they clearly wanted the focus of the definition to be on their children's academic achievement. Hence the term "learning disabled" (Hallahan & Kauffman, 1994), initially proposed by Samuel Kirk in the early 1960s.

Definitional Issues Related to Learning Disabilities

All now agree that there are children (and adults) with learning differences. There is, however, less agreement on the definition of what a learning disability is and how it should be assessed. Some aspects **205** of the definition of learning disabilities are more controversial than others.

IQ-Achievement Discrepancy. One way we identified children with learning disabilities was to look at the difference (discrepancy) between a child's IQ on a standardized intelligence test and the child's academic achievement. This was done by comparing the child's mental age from the intelligence test to the grade-age equivalent of a standardized achievement test. If the child's achievement scores were two years below mental age, the child was identified as having a learning disability. There are three problems with this practice. The first is that a two-year lag is more significant at some ages than others. Achieving two years below grade level in grade 9 is less severe than achieving two years below grade level in grade 2. The second problem was a lack of agreement as to what was the necessary *discrepancy* between IQ and achievement to have a disability (Hallahan & Kauffman, 1994). Also, this two-year discrepancy requirement makes it virtually impossible to identify young children as having a learning disability. Additionally, IQ scores are not good predictors of a child's ability to recognize words and do phonological decoding, the basic skills involved in reading (Church, Lewis, & Batshaw, 1997).

Overlap with Other Disabilities. Some definitions exclude children whose learning problem is based on a sensory impairment, behavior or emotional disorder, mental retardation, or environmental disadvantage. That is, a child could not have a hearing impairment and a learning disability. Many believe it is possible for both of these conditions to exist. Let us look, then, at definitions of learning disabilities.

Definitions of Learning Disabilities

The federal government's definition of learning disabilities governs academic programs and determines our estimates of the number of children with learning disabilities:

Specific learning disability

The term means a disorder in one or more of the basic psychological processes involved in understanding or in using language, spoken or written, that may manifest itself in an imperfect ability to listen, think, speak, read, write, spell, or do mathematical calculations including such conditions as perceptual handicaps, brain injury, minimal brain dysfunction, dyslexia, and developmental aphasia.

Disorders not included. The term does not include learning problems which are primarily the result of visual, hearing, or motor disabilities, of mental retardation, of emotional disturbance, or of environmental, cultural, or economic disadvantage. (Individuals with Disabilities Education Act [IDEA], 1997)

The National Joint Committee on Learning Disabilities (1989) was dissatisfied with the federal definition, and has an alternative definition:

Learning disabilities is a generic term that refers to a heterogeneous group of disorders manifested by significant difficulties in the acquisition and use of listening, speaking, reading, writing, reasoning, or mathematical abilities. These disorders are intrinsic to the individual, presumed to be due to a dysfunction of the central nervous system. Even though a learning disability may occur concomitantly with other disabling conditions (e.g., sensory impairment, mental retardation, social and emotional disturbance), or environmental influences (e.g. cultural differences, insufficient/inappropriate instruction), it is not the direct result of those conditions or influences. (p. 1)

This definition acknowledges that the impairments exist beyond childhood, that they have a heterogeneous nature, that culture may play a role, and that learning disabilities can coexist with other disabilities (Church et al., 1997).

The federal law specifies subtypes of specific learning disabilities, including the ability to *listen, think, speak, read, write, spell,* or *do mathematical calculations.* Practically, specific reading disability (dyslexia) is the most common type of learning disability, with some feeling it accounts for approximately 80 percent of children categorized as having LDs (Roush, 1995).

Definition of Attention-Deficit/Hyperactivity Disorder

The relationship between learning disabilities and ADHD is interesting. Some feel that ADHD and other disabilities such as reading disorders are a subset of learning disabilities; others feel that they are different disabilities that co-occur (Shaywitz, Fletcher, & Shaywitz, 1994).

Accumulating evidence indicates a significant overlap between learning disabilities and ADHD. ADHD is not considered a learning disability, but a disability associated with learning differences (Silver, 1990). Both ADHD and LD are assumed to stem from neurological dysfunction. Current estimates are that a significant proportion of children with ADHD (perhaps 30 percent) also have LD (Shaywitz & Shaywitz, 1988).

Children with ADHD do not meet the criteria for special educational services because they are diagnosed with ADHD. It must be shown that they also have an inability to learn using regular educational methods. To be eligible for special educational services under IDEA, children may be categorized as learning disabled; if their behavior interferes with their ability to learn, they might receive services as children with emotional disturbances; or they might meet the criteria for "other health impairments." These criteria are:

> [I]f the ADD or ADHD is determined to be a chronic health problem that results in limited alertness that adversely affects educational performance, and special education and related services are needed because of the ADD or ADHD. (The note clarifies that the term "limited alertness" includes a child's heightened alertness to environmental stimuli that results in limited alertness with respect to the educational environment.) (IDEA, 1997)

Younger children would have to meet the criteria of developmentally delayed to receive services.

The American Psychiatric Association (APA) in their *Diagnostic and Statistical Manual of Mental Disorders (DSM-IV)* provide information on the distinguishing features in attention deficit disorder with or without hyperactivity. They identify three separate subtypes of ADHD:

> *ADHD, Combined Type*—which requires six or more symptoms of inattention and six or more symptoms of hyperactivity

> *ADHD Predominately Inattentive Type*—which requires six or more symptoms of inattention and with fewer than six symptoms of hyperactivity–impulsivity.

> *ADHD Predominately Hyperactive-Impulsivity Type*—which requires six or more symptoms of hyperactivity–impulsivity and with fewer than six symptoms of inattention.

In all cases the symptoms have persisted for at least 6 months to a degree that is maladaptive and inconsistent with the child's developmental level and that the behaviors happen frequently (American Psychiatric Association [APA], 1994, p. 83).

The symptoms related to *inattention* include failing to give close attention to details or making careless mistakes; difficulty sustaining attention in tasks or play activities; not seeming to listen when spoken to directly; not following through on instructions and failing to finish work; difficulty organizing tasks and activities; avoiding tasks that require sustained mental effort; losing things necessary for tasks or activities; being easily distracted by extraneous stimuli; and being forgetful of daily activities (APA, 1994).

The characteristics of *hyperactivity* include fidgeting with hands or feet or squirming in seat; leaving seat when expected to remain seated; running or climbing excessively in situations where it is inappropriate; difficulty playing or engaging in leisure activities quietly; being "on the go" or acting as if "driven by a motor;" and often talking excessively (APA, 1994).

The characteristics of *impulsivity* include blurting out answers before questions have been completed;

having difficulty awaiting turn; and interrupting or intruding on others (APA, 1994, pp. 83–85).

When developing a framework for working with young children with ADHD it becomes essential to focus on the *cognitive processes* that affect the child and the educational and social implications. ADHD affects both behavior and thought and it impacts academic and social skills:

- The disorder is developmental. It begins before 7 years of age. The child is often described by parents as unusually active, needing constant supervision, and requiring a great deal of attention from caregivers.

- It is a congenital, chronic, long-term condition. ADHD persists throughout childhood and into adulthood. Although for some it will improve in adulthood, for many there is never a point when it is outgrown.

- The hallmark trait is the inability to attend. When compared to peers, these children have more difficulty attending to materials and following directions. This inability is present to a noticeable degree and is developmentally inappropriate.

- There may be a marked degree of developmentally inappropriate impulsivity. The main feature of this impulsivity is the inability to think before acting. Difficulty in inhibiting, delaying gratification, and following rules leads to problems.

- There may be a marked degree of developmentally inappropriate overactivity. In comparison to peers, these children are described as overly fidgety, restless, and exhibiting inappropriate levels of motor activity. Hyperactivity is a common trait of ADD, but is not always present. The inability to attend is sometimes accompanied by withdrawn behaviors. Although they may sit quietly at their desk, children with attending difficulties without hyperactivity are nevertheless unable to pay attention (girls may be particularly prone to this behavior). These children often go unnoticed, but the effects of the attention problems may be just as devastating.

- ADHD is pervasive. Its characteristics will be present in a variety of situations but are most noticeable in educational setting.

- ADHD may result in a production deficit rather than an acquisition deficit. These children have difficulty finishing an assignment rather than actually acquiring the knowledge to do it. Although a child may have the knowledge to finish a math or reading assignment, the difficulty is completing the assignment to demonstrate this knowledge.

- ADHD is not caused by environmental situations or other conditions such as emotional disturbances, mental retardation, or sensory, language, or motor impairments, although it can co-occur. Program planning begins with the primary disability even if children have co-occurring ADHD.

- It is common for some children with ADHD to have related disabilities such as conduct disorder, clinical depression, anxiety disorders, and LDs. These need to be factored in when planning collaborative interventions (adapted from Dykman & Ackerman, 1993; Forness, Kavale, King, & Kasari, 1995; Landau & McAninch, 1993).

Prevalence of Learning Differences

Obviously, the definitional problems may make prevalence figures unreliable. However, it is clear that there has been an increase in the number of children identified as having learning disabilities. According to the U.S. Department of Education Office of Special Education Programs (1995), about half of all children eligible for special educational services were identified as having a specific learning disability. The number of children identified as having a learning disability has more than doubled since 1976–77 (when the federal government began to keep records

As young children are active, it is often difficult to tell the difference between a normally active child and one who is hyperactive. One often looks at the child's temperament and the purposefulness of the activity in making an initial decision.

on LDs). Some are concerned that this rise is a result of misclassification; others believe that it indicates an improved ability to identify these children and a reflection of the stresses of the times and children's response to these stresses.

The APA (1994) estimates that 3 to 5 percent of the school-age population has ADHD, with a disproportionate number (4:1 to 9:1) of these children being boys. Girls with ADHD have more cognitive and language deficits and greater social liability. Boys tend to show more physical aggression and loss of control (Berry, Shaywitz, & Shaywitz, 1985). Some feel that girls are underidentified as having ADHD as they don't show some of the more disruptive behaviors (Shaywitz & Shaywitz, 1988). Others estimate that ADHD is as high as 10 to 20 percent of the school-age population (Shaywitz & Shaywitz, 1988). Either there are unidentified children with learning disabilities or there is an overestimate of the number of children with ADHD. ADHD coexists with other disorders, primarily learning, behavioral, and emotional disorders, with 30 to 50 percent also showing "disruptive behavior disorders" (conduct disorder and oppositional defiant disorder) (APA, 1994). If the estimates of children with learning disabilities and those with ADHD are combined, they probably constitute about 11 percent of the school-age population (Shaywitz & Shaywitz, 1992).

There are few estimates of how many preschool children have ADHD. The problem exists; it just hasn't been diagnosed. Because learning disabilities are tied closely to school-related problems, particularly reading, we typically use the term ADHD when talking about children younger than school age. Whether or not other disabilities will co-occur may not be apparent until the child is older.

Causes of Attention-Deficit/Hyperactivity Disorder and Learning Disabilities

In many cases, the causes of learning differences are not known, although we do have some clues. Some see learning disabilities as a failure in teaching rather than a failure in learning.

ADHD seems to occur with greater frequency in some families than others, and in males more than females, but the contributions of heredity and environment have not been determined. The most common cause of ADHD is thought to be genetic (Blum & Mercugliano, 1997). However, there are certain conditions that apparently predispose the brain to develop this disorder, including prenatal exposure to lead, alcohol, or cocaine; low birth weight; brain infections; perinatal insult; and certain genetic syndromes (Blum & Mercugliano, 1997). There are apparently many developmental factors that can influence the way the brain organizes information. Increasingly, genetic and imaging research has supported the premise that ADHD is a medical disorder (Safer & Krager, 1992).

The frontal lobe of the brain plays an important role in planning, organization, and feelings. Like the rest of the brain, it requires chemicals called *neurotransmitters* to carry messages between brain cells. At least some children with ADHD have neurotransmitter abnormalities, particularly in the frontal lobe (Lynch & Batshaw, 1997). Some drugs prescribed for children with ADHD are designed to increase the activity of neurotransmitters in certain areas of the brain.

The *reticular activating system/locus ceruleus* in the midbrain region functions to screen out distracting sounds and images so that individuals can concentrate or pay attention to a particular stimulus and not be distracted by others. In children with ADHD, this area of the brain also seems to be problematic (Batshaw, Perret, & Mercugliano, 1992). Although brain scans fail to show abnormalities in the brain itself, positron emission tomographic (PET) screening has revealed decreased glucose utilization in several regions of the brain, including the frontal lobes and basal ganglia (Mercugliano, 1995). The brain uses glucose as its main source of energy. With less glucose, the metabolic rate of the brain is reduced, and it appears to be reduced in the areas of the brain that are important for attention, handwriting, motor control, and inhibiting responses. It may be that malfunctioning in this area makes it impossible for the brain to "rein in" automatic motor responses, thus interfering with the child's attention span (Bower, 1994).

Researchers at the University of California, Irvine, have identified an abnormal gene associated with ADHD. This provides the first direct link to a genetic cause and additional information about why the drug Ritalin works (Maugh, 1996). Researchers feel there is certainly more than one gene involved, but this is a first step.

These are all tantalizing pieces of the puzzle of learning differences, but we have yet to find all the pieces and know what the puzzle will look like when it is complete.

Educational Assessment of Learning Disabilities

There is agreement that assessment must be multimodal. The diagnosis of learning disabilities may be made from the discrepancy between standardized tests of intelligence and standardized achievement tests combined with teacher ratings. The teacher rating scales can be informal or formal rating scales such as the Conners Teacher Rating Scale (CTRS). The CTRS contains 39 items that rate five factors: daydreaming-inattention, hyperactivity, conduct problems, anxiousness-fearfulness, and social-cooperation.

Assessment is likely to include a measure of cognitive functioning, such as the Wechsler Preschool and Primary Scale of Intelligence–Revised (WPPSI-R) or some other measure of general intelligence, and a variety of other tests such as the Bender Gestalt Test for visual perceptual tasks, a comprehensive achievement battery like the Woodcock–Johnson Psychoeducational Battery–Revised, or standardized tests in different subject matter areas such as the Gates-MacGinitie Reading Test and the Key Math–Revised. The actual battery will be determined by the child's pattern of strengths and weaknesses and the examiner's preferences.

Informal methods are also used. For example, areas such as reading achievement may involve having a child read a particular passage that has a known age-grade-level equivalent and noting the mistakes the child makes. In the hands of a skilled educator, this can be a good assessment tool; in the hands of a less sensitive educator, it may be meaningless information.

Additional assessments include trained observers and a behavioral event sampling targeted behaviors in specific situations. Peer rating may also be used, as children with LD often find peer relationships difficult.

Reading Disability or Developmental Dyslexia

Developmental dyslexia or specific reading disability is the most common type of LD, affecting approximately 80 percent of all those identified as learning disabled (Lerner, 1989); it is probably the most common neurobiological disorder affecting children. It is a chronic persistent condition and one that is both familial and heritable (Shaywitz, 1998).

Because so many children with learning differences have problems in the area of reading, this is dealt with in more detail. The assessment typically begins because a child is not reading at age/grade level. A battery of tests is typically done to determine the child's IQ, mental age, and reading age/grade using a standardized reading test. If the child's reading age is significantly below what is expected and this cannot be accounted for by delayed general development or a sensory or communications impairment, the child is usually classified as having a reading disability or as being dyslexic (Doyle, 1996). This method is apparently effective in identifying bright children who have dyslexia but will miss others who are also not reading well. A consensus is building for identifying children who have "unexpected" reading difficulties as having a reading disability and receiving specialized services in this area.

Reading involves two main processes: decoding and comprehension. Children with dyslexia have problems with the decoding process. They seem unable to segment the written word into its phonologic elements (Shaywitz, 1998). The phonologic-deficit hypothesis for dyslexia posits that children with dyslexia have a neurological inability in this area. This is supported by neurologic studies that show differences in the temporo-parieto-occipital brain regions between those with dyslexia and those without (Shaywitz, 1998). This lower-order linguistic block prevents access to higher-order linguistic skills: Until children can decode and identify words, they cannot look at meaning and comprehension. Their skills in other areas of language (syntax, semantics, and so on) are comparable to their peers'.

Usually, children with dyslexia are not identified until they are in third grade (about 9 years old) and have experienced repeated failures in reading. There is great interest in identifying children who are at risk for reading disability at younger ages to provide early intervention. A combination of family and individual history, observation, and testing may provide clues. A history of delayed language development, not paying attention to sounds (such as having trouble with rhyming games), a medical history of repeated ear infections, and a family history of reading problems are important risk factors (Shaywitz, 1998). Additional reading readiness tests that isolate such skills as letter identification, letter-sound association, phonologic awareness, verbal memory, and word retrieval skills are useful.

Observations are made of children's reading to determine if they have more problems reading nonsense or unfamiliar and isolated words than words in a passage (in which words they can decode would allow them to guess at other words). In writing, poor spelling with bizarre mistakes can indicate a learning disorder. The comprehension of children with a learning disability is typically superior to their ability to decode.

Approximately 12 to 24 percent of children with developmental dyslexia also have ADHD (Shaywitz et al., 1994).

Educational Assessment of Attention-Deficit/ Hyperactivity Disorder

As a teacher, you may be the first to suspect that a child may have ADHD. The question becomes, When does a child exhibit enough of the characteristic behaviors for a long enough time for you to talk with the parents? Before approaching parents, look at the cultural background of the family and learn something about the family's expectations for the child. Information about any child needs to be evaluated within the context of the family.

If further information sheds no light on the behavior, observe the child over a span of time to get a representative look at the behavior. Then construct a simple behavioral checklist that focuses attention on areas you are concerned about. First, decide how much a particular behavior describes the child on a given day. Then note the behaviors that you observed to form that opinion. Do this for several days and ask other adults in the classroom to do the same. Your form may resemble Figure 10.1.

Your observations should be systematic and the behavior observed should have necessary detail: "Sheila knocked over the juice while reaching for the crackers with her left hand." Write down the details as you see them. Keep your facts objective. The most important part of observing is to look for patterns. You will have to observe for several days to get enough data for patterns to emerge. Whether or not you decide to talk with the parents about your observations, you will get a more accurate picture of the child. This information is useful in targeting program goals for her.

Medical Diagnosis of Attention-Deficit/ Hyperactivity Disorder

Many factors can cause children to have symptoms similar to ADHD. A number of physical and psychiatric problems should be ruled out before a diagnosis of ADHD is made. Inattentiveness, impulsivity, and underachievement can be found in children with emotional and behavioral disorders and those who are depressed. Children should have a medical examination to rule out medical problems such as thyroid disease, hearing impairments, allergies, and upper-respiratory problems (Ciaranello, 1993). The evaluation team for determining ADHD usually involves the family physician or pediatrician, a child psychologist or psychiatrist, a neurologist, a family counselor or therapist, and a teacher and/or professional in early care and education (Garber, Garber, & Spizman, 1993). Accurate diagnosis is important because it dictates follow-up treatment.

Typically, parents are interviewed to obtain information about the child's developmental, medical, and family history, as well as information about the child's behavior, academic progress, and psychosocial relationships (Blum & Mercugliano, 1997). Measures such as the CTRS as well as observation and peer ratings are typically included in this evaluation. Parents are also asked to fill out rating scales. Additional information would be obtained by interviewing the child and his self-report as well as a medical/neurological examination and a psychoeducational assessment (Blum & Mercugliano, 1997). The psychoeducational assessment may be designed to look for overlap with LDs. Most clinicians use the diagnostic criteria developed by the APA as a starting point for diagnosis.

Intervention Strategies for Children with Attention-Deficit/ Hyperactivity Disorder

There is no cure for ADHD, but just as there is a multimodal assessment plan, there is also a multimodal intervention plan. Intervention typically involves parent education in behavior management, an appropriate educational setting (typically, with a teacher who knows behavior management techniques), individual and family counseling when necessary, and medication when required (Silver, 1990).

Education and training of parents of children with ADHD is an essential component of most intervention

Child's name _____   Date _____

Observer _____

	Actual Occurrence	Perception of Occurrence		
		Often	Sometimes	Rarely
Impulsivity				
Observation				
Distractibility				
Observation				
Short attention span				
Observation				
Inability to follow directions				
Observation				
Hyperactivity				
Observation				
Hypoactivity				
Observation				
Perseveration				
Observation				
General awkwardness				
Observation				
Hands used interchangeably				
Observation				
Conflict with other children				
Observation				

Comments:

Figure 10.1   Observation Form

Use a form such as this to quantify your observations and to add some qualitative comments. In the first column, identify the number of times you actually observe the behavior happening; then estimate whether this behavior happens often, sometimes, or rarely. The space for observations is designed for you to report what you see. If you are inclined to write more, add more space in your form. It is important that you count as well as clarify when the behavior occurs. Any plan of action is dependent on this information. In some cases, you may think a behavior is a problem but the data do not support your conclusion. This insight is helpful in deciding how to approach a situation. That is, perhaps you and the child have a "poorness of fit" situation and you need to evaluate your feelings toward the child.

plans. Informed parents are more likely to comply with medication regimens and pursue effective child management (Williams, Horn, Daley, & Nadeer, 1993). Educators also need training in modifying their classroom behavior management methods. Consistency between home and school is a tremendous asset for the child. Techniques focus on maintaining the child's attention on tasks, improving behavior, teaching organizational skills, and adapting programming to specific learning disabilities if they coexist (Blum & Mercugliano, 1997).

Counseling is an important element in working with children and families. One of the focuses of counseling is to increase the child's probability of experiencing success. Traditionally, children are identified as having ADHD after a history of repeated failures and tension both at home and in an educational setting. Counseling can also provide emotional support for parents, siblings, and the child.

Medication is often part of the intervention program. Psychostimulant medications (central nervous system stimulants) are the most widely used for the management of ADHD. Between 70 and 80 percent of children with ADHD respond positively to these medications (APA, 1994). There is typically a marked improvement in attention span, impulsiveness, and on-task behavior (Pelham, Sams, Vallano, Dixon, & Hoza, 1993). Some children also show improvements in frustration tolerance, compliance, and handwriting as well as relationships with parents, teachers, and peers (McCarney, 1995).

Psychostimulants increase the arousal or alertness of the central nervous system. Children with ADHD tended to respond positively to moderate to high doses of methylphenidate (Ritalin), whereas children with ADD (no hyperactivity) tended to have minimal or no response or did best on low doses of the medication (Lerner & Lerner, 1991).

Some are concerned about the amount of drugs prescribed for children. Antibiotics are by far the commonly prescribed drugs for children, with 47,787,000 prescriptions for children 15 and under in the United States. This is followed by antiasthmatic prescriptions (7,279,000) and Ritalin (1,596,000). Antidepressants (670,000), anticonvulsants (606,000), and chemotherapy (73,000) make up the remainder of the top six prescribed medicines (National Center for Health Statistics, cited in Ubell, 1997). Part of the concern is the potential side effects, some of which are temporary as the child's body adjusts to the medication; others are more permanent.

The most commonly prescribed stimulant for ADHD is methylphenidate (Ritalin). The most common side effect of Ritalin is appetite suppression. To circumvent this, the medication can be taken with meals. It may also cause insomnia and, less frequently, headaches, stomachaches, and dizziness. One side effect may not be temporary: nervous tics including eye blinking, facial twitches, throat clearing, and shoulder jerking. Occasional tics are harmless, but frequent tics may signal the onset of the much more serious condition, Tourette's syndrome (Blum & Mercugliano, 1997). If tics develop, other

medication may be tried. These drugs are classified as controlled substances by the federal government.

Stimulants only last three to four hours, so they must be given several times a day. Decisions need to be made about whether to give the medication on weekends and during the summer; this requires balancing the benefits obtained with concerns about the side effects of the drugs. The short-term benefits seem to be well documented, but questions remain about their long-term efficacy.

Early Identification of Children with Learning Differences

As an educator, your role is most likely to be in the early identification of and planning for children with LD and ADHD. Thus, knowledge of their characteristic behaviors are important. Many symptoms of LD relate directly to specific academic areas (reading, writing, spelling, and mathematics); because of this, some experts feel that learning disabilities cannot be diagnosed during the preschool years. Because of the overlap with ADHD, you may identify children who have characteristics of both disabilities. You will not see some behaviors; however, other characteristics are observable at early ages. Regardless of labeling, children need to learn to control their body and to develop skills for learning. The behavioral characteristics typical of children with learning differences are described below.

0 to 3

It is challenging to accurately diagnose children this age with ADHD because many of the behaviors that are characteristic of ADHD are also age-appropriate for this group. However, those infants with a *difficult* temperament may be at risk. Infants who have a high activity level, do not adapt well to changes in the environment, have intense reactions, have unpredictable routines, and have difficulty sleeping, nursing, and feeding are challenging to even the most competent parents. Some studies have found that over half of these *feisty* infants experience later childhood problems in learning, behavior, and socialization (Goldstein, 1992).

Infants who are difficult may frequently be fussy, cranky, uncomfortable, and unhappy. Additionally, their parents, who are not able to comfort them, may feel a mixture of anger, disappointment, and self-blame at their own inadequacy and incompetence (Kelly & Ramundo, 1993). Once mobile, the toddler may jump, roll, swing, and run into situations with little thought of the consequences. Hyperactive toddlers are more likely to have accidents than others. The distractible toddler is likely to leave toys, clothes, food, and anything else that caught her attention momentarily before going on to something else. Parents are conflicted between keeping children safe and allowing them developmentally appropriate autonomy.

If pediatricians began to routinely screen for children with difficult temperaments, we could begin to provide parents with resources to increase their competence in parenting whether or not the child was later identified as having ADHD. To the extent that parents or caregivers become anxious, irritated, and angry at the child because of their inability to manage the child's behavior, problems will certainly be exacerbated.

As children move into the preschool years, it becomes clear to some parents that the predictable "terrible twos" have continued into the threes and perhaps fours. Power struggles between parents and children escalate. Predictable patterns of eating and sleeping have not emerged, and frequently toilet training has not been completed. As children move into group settings, the child may be labeled immature. The combination of the characteristics of ADHD at this time frequently lead to judgment of immaturity. Whenever this label is used, the question should be asked, "Is the child immature or does he have ADHD?"

3 to 6

Identification of children with ADHD often is suspected or confirmed during this time. Three-year-olds who are very intense in their reactions to the environment, particularly when these reactions are usually negative, are of concern. Also, children who are identified as having speech and language problems are at risk for ADHD. Other at-risk children are those who lack good problem-solving strategies as well as those who cannot delay their response to an inviting stimulus, whether a toy another child has or a cookie. These children don't seem to develop the early skills necessary for making and keeping friends. Children who are impulsive, noncompliant, and fearful may also be at risk (Goldstein, 1992).

The irregular eating and sleeping patterns continue as well as struggles over toilet training. Children seem unable to plan or accept limits. Tantrums continue. Motor clumsiness may become apparent as children take over more responsibility in dressing, tying shoes, cutting, coloring, and writing. Although many difficult children have problems with change, the one reaction to change that is notably absent is separation anxiety.

There are other warning signals in the medical realm. Children later identified as ADHD have frequent ear infections; there is also a high incidence of allergies, asthma, and other respiratory problems. This means that parents of children with ADHD have already spent many hours coping with a difficult child, spent many hours in physicians' waiting rooms, have probably had high medical bills, and have had to cope with sick child care (Kelly & Ramundo, 1993).

Early intervention at this stage is critical if the risk of secondary problems is to be reduced (McCarney, 1995). As many as 70 percent of children with ADHD develop secondary behavioral and emotional problems because they cannot meet the demands of a complex world (Goldstein, 1992). For children this age, the development of self-control is a primary goal. Children need a delicate balance between external support and structure that allows active involvement and exploration and also supports them in learning internal control mechanisms.

Early care and education settings allow and expect a wide range of social, emotional, and cognitive development. A child's inability to master specific age-expected tasks may have been unnoticed or attributed to immaturity. These expectations change as children move into elementary school. Here, the pressure to compete and perform socially and academically is more intense.

6 to 9

As children reach elementary school, some of the characteristics of ADHD become more apparent and the implications more obvious. The demands on children to perform specific skills at specific times and in specific ways may be daunting to the child with ADHD. Teachers give tests and grade them and send the results home on report cards (if they wait that long). Some children do not perform well in school, often fail to finish assignments, may become disruptive in class, may experience poor social relations, and may become easily frustrated. They may have a very short attention span and show some aggressive or even oppositional behavior (Lerner & Lerner, 1991). Children frequently are moved to the lowest math and reading groups. If they become disruptive, they lose instructional time because they are in the principal's office. The hyperactive child may become a bully. The nonhyperactive child may be perceived as weird. Because of impaired social skills, the child with ADD (frequently girls) may be lonely and isolated and lack friends.

During these years, organized extracurricular activities begin to play a role in children's development. For some children, sports such as soccer and baseball may be an opportunity for success and acceptance. For others, it will be another area of failure and rejection.

When children spend tremendous amounts of energy keeping themselves under control during school hours, they may let it all out when they come home. Battles ensue over homework, chores, mealtime, bedtime, and so on. As children get up to face another day, they dawdle to keep from having to go to school while parents are trying to get themselves off to work and other children off to school as well. It may be only 8:30 A.M. but parents may feel that they have already put in a full day's work.

Children need extra attention and time for instructional activity, and classroom teachers may need behavior modification skills to counter some of the disruptive behavior in the classroom. Social skills training may help children learn how to interact more successfully in social situations. They may also need to be taught skills in conflict resolution as well as focusing on self-control.

Until children are identified as having ADHD, the support system is not likely to be in place for them. Often, parents who have children with ADHD are relieved that there really is a problem that is identifiable—and it is not that they are bad parents.

Behavioral Characteristics of Learning Differences

The behavioral characteristics of children with LD and ADHD have been identified; the following discussion operationalizes these definitions.

Impulsiveness—In young children, impulsiveness usually means acting quickly, without planning and thinking about the consequences of actions. Children seem to have a short fuse. They act before they think, and they rarely learn from past experience because they don't give themselves time to reflect on previous experiences and their outcomes.

Distractibility—These children cannot attend to a task. Their attention and even their bodies seem to be drawn elsewhere. They do not have the ability to redirect their attention back to the original task once it has wandered. Children's seeming disinterest and inability to complete tasks is not always a disadvantage; sometimes, they notice new connections and come up with imaginative solutions to problems.

Short attention span—These children do not stay at tasks for long. They rarely finish tasks or get satisfaction from them.

Inability to follow directions—Some children do not seem to understand directions. Others seem to understand initially but forget what was asked.

Hyperactivity—Most young children are active. What separates activity from hyperactivity is that active children usually have activity that is purposeful (at least to them); they can typically stay at an activity for a period of time. Hyperactive children seem to be constantly in motion. Their motion is not goal-oriented, as they seem distracted by and need to respond to all environmental stimuli. Even when sitting, these children are not quiet; they may twitch, jerk, or rock. As they get older, the hyperactivity may be displayed in nonstop talking as well as nonstop moving. The hyperactivity is chronic and unrelated to specific events.

Hypoactivity—Some children with learning differences may be hypoactive. They appear to move in slow motion, *if* they move. They may seem listless, bored, or sleepy. Every movement seems to require a lot of effort.

Perseveration—These children start a task and can't seem to stop. A child rolling a playdough snake may roll snakes all morning long if not interrupted. It is as if the child is not capable of refocusing attention once it has been focused: The child can't change channels. This may be a way of coping with distractions.

General awkwardness—These children are awkward compared to other children their age. They frequently bump into things or people, knock things over, and trip.

Handedness not established—Young children often use their hands inconsistently. However, by the time they are about 5 or 6, a preference is usually established. Children with learning differences are not ambidextrous, they are nondextrous: unskilled with both hands.

Social problems—Given the above characteristics, it is not surprising that these children may irritate others. They are more likely than other children to be in conflict with their peers. They have difficulty recognizing social cues and using social skills. They don't read others' body language accurately and hence make wrong assumptions and act inappropriately.

Family problems—Lack of social skills is apparent in the home as well. Children's frustrations and failure affect families and family relationships. Parents may disagree on how to cope with troubling behavior, causing additional stress on relationships. Siblings may feel that there is a double standard applied to behavior and chores. Even as they understand about ADHD they may feel both guilt and anger (adapted from Hayden, Smith, von Hippel, & Baer, 1978; Kelly & Ramundo, 1993; Silver, 1995).

Problems in the Learning Process

One way to look at learning is to break it down into four different processes. The first step in the process is *input,* recording information in the brain. The second step, *integration,* requires the organization and understanding of this information. The third step has to do with recording and retrieving this information: *memory.* The final step, *output,* requires that the information retrieved be packaged in a way to communicate with others or to be translated into behaviors (Silver, 1995). Problems in any of these areas can cause problems in learning. When you think about a child who isn't learning at the rate you expect, explore the following areas to see if there is a pattern (adapted from Kelly & Ramundo, 1993; Silver, 1995).

Input Problems

Information enters the brain through the senses. For educational purposes, we are primarily concerned with seeing (visual) and hearing (auditory). Perception is the cognitive process in which the information received from the senses is organized and interpreted by the brain. To some degree, perception is dependent on motivation and memory. When there are problems in this area, we refer to these as perceptual problems and identify the sense.

Visual Perceptual Problems. Children who have problems in this area confuse visual input. They have difficulty identifying letters of the alphabet, confusing such letters as *b, d, p* and *q*. They might read *pat* as *tap*. They might have problems copying designs and copying from a vertical surface such as the chalkboard to a horizontal one such as their desk.

Other types of visual perceptual problems relate to organizing the child's position in space. The child might confuse left and right or misjudge distance. Some children have problems with figure-ground distinctions; it is difficult for them to focus on a particular aspect or figure as distinguished from the entire page. In reading, they might skip words or lines. In games where children are to find one object in a picture with many details, they are unlikely to find it.

At a younger age, visual perceptual problems might be displayed in visual-motor tasks such as putting puzzles together, catching or hitting a ball, doing woodworking, jumping rope, and related activities that require visual-motor coordination.

Auditory Perceptual Problems. Some children have difficulty distinguishing subtle differences in sounds and confuse words like *plan* and *plane*, *play* and *place*. They may also have problems focusing on a voice, such as the teacher's, when there is background noise like children talking, a record playing, or even the heating or cooling system running. We

Children with visual perceptual problems feel more comfortable when they can feel boundaries as they roll and experiment safely with how they can move through space.

often accuse these children of not listening or not doing what they are told, when, in reality, they may not have heard us.

Integration Problems. Once information enters the system, it must be placed in the correct order or sequence, it must be understood in the context in which it was used (abstraction), and then it must be integrated with other information that is also being processed (organization) (Silver, 1995).

Sequencing Problems. Children with sequencing problems may hear and understand a story, but they confuse the sequence of events; they don't know what comes first or last. They may be able to say the letters of the alphabet, days of the week, or months of the year in order, but they can't tell you what letter comes after *l*, the day that comes before Wednesday, or the month that follows July. If they can, they will start with the beginning of the sequence and go through it in order until they come to the needed information. They may also have problems with numerical sequences, seeing "35" but writing "53."

Abstraction Problems. At young ages, problems with abstraction are developmentally appropriate. Children live in a literal world. As they approach the elementary school years, this becomes more problematic and they misunderstand jokes and puns. These children literally believe "I have eyes in the back of my head" rather than understanding the message that you are aware of their behavior even when you are not looking at them. Children who cannot make these distinctions are easy victims of teasing because they respond so literally.

Organization Problems. Some children can process information but can't integrate the information to form a whole. As long as they are asked for specific pieces of information, they can answer questions (What was the mother's name?). But they often miss the big picture (What was the story about?). Their lack of organization is frequently general: Their desks are a mess; they forget to take things home or bring them back; they might do work but can't find it to turn it in; they forget their lunch or snack; and so on.

Memory Problems

Once information gets into the system, it must be stored. The mind stores information in different ways. The two most important for learning are short- and long-term memory. Short-term memory is limited temporary storage, perhaps five seconds at most; for example, looking up a phone number and then walking to the phone to dial the number. Distractibility makes short-term memory difficult. Long-term memory is more permanent and seemingly unlimited. Retrieving information from long-term memory requires remembering where the information was stored; for example, remembering what label you put on a document in a file cabinet. Many children with learning differences have a pretty haphazard labeling system. They function better using divergent retrieval (talking about a topic he generated) than convergent retrieval (answering a question). This happens too when someone abruptly changes the topic. Usually, the child's ability to transfer is good. That is one reason why contextual learning is so important; it gives them a system for not only learning but storing information. Rote learning and isolated facts tend to be stored randomly; this may account for the unevenness of responses in memory tasks. Memory may also be affected by whether the input was visual or auditory.

Output Problems

Information is communicated through words or motor activity.

Language Problems. Language is related to the memory situation: When language is spontaneous, the words flow; when the demand is to speak on a particular topic or answer a specific question, the language system may break down. The question may need to be repeated; frequently, children need extra time to search their memory for the needed information before they can answer.

Motor Problems. Children can have either gross motor problems or fine motor problems or both. Children with large motor problems are clumsy, bump into things, have poor coordination, and have problems with skills like learning to ride a bike. Children with fine motor problems have trouble tying, zipping, and buttoning, as well as printing and writing. Handwriting might be slow and difficult to read, with uneven pressure.

Guidelines

The following guidelines should prove generally useful when teaching children with learning differences. Two key words to keep in mind are *consistency* and *preparation*.

1. Be consistent, not only in the class rules you set and your classroom management techniques, but also in the daily schedule and sequence of the program.

2. Prepare children for changes in routine. Announcement of a change will set off a flood of questions. The third time you hear the same question, you might respond, "I hear your concern about the trip to the orchard. You are asking that question a lot. Can you tell me the answer?" If the child cannot give you the answer, give the child the words and then ask her to tell you the answer.

3. It may be necessary to simplify the child's program and make it as concrete as possible. Work very gradually toward a more challenging program.

4. Eliminate as many distractions as possible when it is important that the child concentrate; don't have a group activity in a place where this child can look out the window and see others playing on the playground.

5. Keep the classroom orderly and organized. Use color coding or numbering of bins and shelves to identify groups of materials.

6. Be brief. Break information into small, manageable "chunks" and present the information sequentially, a step at a time rather than all at once.

7. Decrease waiting time.

8. Feedback needs to be frequent. Verbal feedback may be the least salient. Find out what works, but try visual feedback (smiles, stickers) and tactile (a touch, a hug).

9. Begin with simple activities dealing with one concept and move to more complex concepts as the child seems ready; for example, move from *taking turns* to *friendship,* from *counting* to *estimating.*

10. Make directions simple, brief, and clear; state them in a positive manner, with eye contact maintained. If necessary, give them a step at a time. "It's cleanup time" may not be enough. Try "Put the doll clothes back in the drawer"; when that is completed, continue with "Put the dolls in their bed," and so on. When the child has done as you requested, be sure to reinforce the behavior: "I liked the way you folded the doll clothes and put them away." A specific and concrete reinforcement is more effective than one as general as "That's a good job."

11. If a child has problems learning a particular task, check if he or she has mastered the prerequisite skills. For example, if a child can't pick out the square from a group of circles, she probably can't find the *p* among similar-looking letters.

12. As young children begin to reason concretely, be sure to use concrete objects when teaching. For example, count children, fingers, boys, girls, windows, teachers—but don't just count. Count for a purpose that you share with the children.

13. All children have a preferred way of learning information (visual, auditory, or kinesthetic/tactile). It is helpful to know and use the child's preference or use all three:

    Visual: Have a poster in the block corner demonstrating the proper and improper use of blocks.

    Auditory: Tell the child, "Blocks are to build with"; "You may not throw the blocks."

    Kinesthetic/tactile: Take the child to the block corner and show the child what to do, then have the child demonstrate the appropriate behavior to you.

14. Provide numerous and varied learning experiences that teach the same idea in many different ways. Teach body awareness through art, movement, listening, music, and health activities.

15. Provide many activities that encourage movement, especially during large group times. Don't expect children with learning differences to sit as long as some of their peers might.

Group time is often a difficult time for all children; for children with learning differences, it can be extremely challenging:

1. Seat children in a semicircle and place the child with a learning difference across from you where you can easily maintain eye contact. Have children who are good role models sit on either side of the child.

2. Provide directions or demonstrations directly in front of the child, not off to the side.

3. When children are required to sit in chairs, consider assigning the child with ADHD two chairs that the child can move between. Allow the child to sit astride the chair (backwards); this will keep the chair from rocking or tipping and provides a more stable base.

Sometimes, children need more structure in learning tasks than is typically provided in a developmentally appropriate early childhood classroom. Within the context of the classroom, a teacher can provide some structured, individualized learning tasks:

1. Assess the child's knowledge base in the specific area.

2. Describe the procedure, what is going to happen, giving the child a rationale for the procedure.

3. Model the procedure. As you demonstrate, state aloud the procedure and the thought processes.

4. Have the child state the procedure aloud (verbal rehearsal).

5. Have the child practice the "easiest version" of the task with your feedback.

6. Make the task more difficult until it reaches age/grade expectations. Provide feedback.

7. Evaluate the child's learning and begin generalization.

8. Promote generalization so the child becomes aware of situations and strategies for using the learned material.

9. Keep in close touch with the parents. Change can take place daily, and knowing that a child had a "good day" may be the support a parent needs (adapted from Ellis, Deshler, Lenz, Schumaker, & Clark, 1991).

Behavior Management Tools

Discipline, or classroom management, is rarely easy; including children with learning differences presents additional challenges. Because their behavior is inconsistent, it is difficult to know whether these children are refusing or are unable to behave as requested. (Parents have the same dilemma.) The traditional solution is *behavior modification*. This may involve token rewards for appropriate, or on-task, behavior or sitting in a "thinking chair," and loss of token rewards for inappropriate behavior. Others have successfully used *logical consequences*. For example, if a child knocks all the plastic blocks off a table, he needs to help pick them up; if she spills juice, she should help clean it up. (If the child spills juice persistently and purposefully, you might try not giving any more. If the child is thirsty, give him water.) A combination of the two methods works best. You want the child to learn internalized self-control to stop inappropriate behavior.

Ignoring inappropriate behavior (especially when you think that getting attention is the child's purpose) is ideal when it works. However, it doesn't always work, and it is inappropriate if the child is doing something dangerous or is disturbing others. Then, removing the child from the situation is probably the best solution. But that is only the first step in the process.

The use of "time out" for children with learning differences has its proponents and opponents. We prefer the concept of "thinking time," which involves removing the child from the ongoing activities to a specified location off to one side of the room or playground. It is designed to give children time to think about what happened and regain their self-control. It is not a punishment. The space can be designated by placing a chair in a taped-off square. If your system does not seem to be effective, see if there are unexpected snags:

I once taught a little girl who was particularly disruptive during group time. I had a student teacher take her out into the hall when she acted up. Instead of decreasing, the disruptive behavior increased, and it began to occur closer to the beginning of group time. I decided to see what was happening. The next time Andrea created a disturbance, I took her out into the hall. Once there, she told me to sit down, plopped herself in my lap, and said, "This is the book I want to read today." She then hauled out her book, and I read it. Now I knew why this child disrupted my group! The next day, Andrea went to the hall with *no* book, and the student teacher was instructed to ignore her. The following day she sat through most of group time! The point of the story is: Make sure your consequence is not rewarding, or the behavior will continue.

Satiation is another way of dealing with inappropriate behavior. The child is made to continue the behavior when he no longer wants to. This is particularly effective for something physical, like falling off a chair. In one case, I required a child to sit down, fall off, and get up repeatedly for 10 minutes! As you might guess, this behavior lost its charm when I not only encouraged but also required it. To discourage acts that are likely to be contagious in a classroom, satiation is far more effective than ignoring.

An additional method of stopping a behavior is to set up *incompatible alternatives*. I used this technique successfully with a child who frequently masturbated in class. After all attempts had failed in discussing the difference between private and public behavior, reviewing the program to see if the child might be bored, checking to see if his pants were too tight, and asking his mother if he had a rash—I changed tactics, planning a program of messy table activities requiring two hands. It really is difficult to finger paint with both hands and masturbate at the same time!

Curriculum Adaptations

Children with learning differences require some adaptations. The particular adaptations and emphasis is determined by children's individual needs. If you adapt your programs to include children with learning differences and meet their needs during the early childhood years, you may prevent a secondary disability such as a conduct disorder that may be based on repeated social and academic failure. If you help children build necessary academic and social skills, they can meet the continuing challenges of the academic system.

A learning difference is usually not a single problem but rather a combination of problems. Learning differences are diverse: One child's strengths might be another's weaknesses. Be alert to patterns of behavior and clusters of needs that indicate areas to concentrate on. (If a child is clumsy, has poor eye-hand coordination, and has balance and rhythm problems, concentrate on working with this child in the motor skills area.) Keep in mind the developmental level of the child. (Is the attention span really short for a 3-year-old?) Look for uneven development characterized by average to above-average development in some areas, but noticeable developmental lags in other areas. (The child can discuss trains, the roles of the various people on the train, and how trains work, but cannot put a toy train beside, in front of, or above a block.)

Social Awareness: Self-Esteem, Inclusion, Social Studies, Health and Safety

All children need to form relationships with other children and adults. They need to be aware of how they are similar to and different from others. Children with learning differences must be encouraged to use a variety of solutions to problems; they have a tendency to get stuck. They require guidance and practice. The skills of taking turns and sharing are especially critical. The behavior of children with learning differences is variable; they are often unaware of how they feel, and so they need to identify their feelings and learn to control them while developing a sense of self-worth and group belonging.

Self-Esteem. Identifying learning needs early benefits both you and the children. Once children have already experienced failure, you have to deal with poor self-esteem in addition to the learning differences. You can help children become aware of their individual strengths even while working on challenging areas.

Children need to increase their awareness of their own feelings and those of others. They also need experience in differentiating between feelings and behavior: "It's OK to be mad at Chunga; it is not OK to hit her." Help them learn to express both positive and negative feelings in socially acceptable ways. They can run, poke playdough, or hit a punching bag. They need to consciously decide how they will deal with their feelings. They may also need to learn expressions and gestures that show others that they are happy and like them. They need help making and keeping friends.

1. Children with learning differences often show poor knowledge of their own body, whether they are asked to label parts on a doll or identify a body part of their own. Increase body awareness and value the uniqueness of each child.

2. Point out what children do well and the contribution each makes to the class as a whole.

3. Highlight children's creativity and divergent thinking.

Inclusion. All children need to feel they are part of the group. Help children appreciate their uniqueness as human beings and the contributions they make to the group.

1. Help children become aware of the situational aspect of socially acceptable behavior. In the classroom, there are rules that all children need to abide by.

2. Help children develop skills to be part of a group some of the time as well as skills to be and do things alone.

3. Teach children to view events from various perspectives. Increase children's awareness of the uniqueness of *self*.

Social Studies. Social studies can be used to create awareness of other people and the roles they play.

1. Try setting up a "society" in your class based on the strengths and needs of the individual children: "Gina will take the messages to others because she is a good runner. Barbara will print the messages. Kenzi will call us all together because he has a good strong voice."

2. Emphasize group belonging and the courtesy extended to other group members, property rights, space to play, and including others. Discuss how

All children need to feel part of a group. Some children may have to be encouraged to initiate and maintain friendships. Adults can teach these skills by modeling appropriate behavior and through direct teaching.

people feel when they are not included, their toys are taken, or their space is intruded on. Also discuss ways of dealing with these feelings.

3. Explore varied occupations such as plumber, computer programmer, baker, physicist, producer, professional athlete, and pest exterminator. Let the children's interest guide your choices. Be sure to give a nonsexist presentation of occupations.

Health and Safety. This is an important curriculum area for children with learning differences, who, even at this early age, may have seen a variety of specialists, perhaps had an EEG and taken medication, and who may have some fears about health professionals. Because children must cooperate in testing and report their reactions to drugs they may be taking, developing good rapport between children and medical personnel is important. Increase body awareness so the children can successfully locate body parts and then respond about how specific parts feel.

Other important health and safety areas need work:

1. As these children are more likely than others to become lost, teach them to state their name, telephone number, and parents' names early in the year.

2. Work on traffic signs and try to teach the children to control impulsive behavior that may lead to accidents.

3. Talk about injury prevention. Help children see the relationship between actions and results (what may happen if someone runs in front of a tricycle or bicycle).

4. State and post class safety rules, especially those related to situations in which children could be hurt (standing on chairs and tables, walking with scissors, throwing blocks).

5. When children initially engage in some unsafe practice, such as climbing the fence instead of the jungle gym, make your limits clear, but situational: "*At school* you may not climb on the fence. If you want to climb, you may climb on the jungle gym." Be prepared to reinforce this statement physically if necessary: Help the child climb down from the fence and walk over to the jungle gym with her.

6. Integrate food preparation into the curriculum through snack and lunch. Discuss nutrition. Help children learn about the relationship, among growth, food, and health. Be sure to include cultural variations of good food. Use foods that are familiar to the children, as well as some that aren't.

7. Discuss where different foods grow and compare fresh foods with canned or frozen foods. Talk about food additives and food allergies.

8. Talk about the common health problems of children (colds, ear infections, stomachaches, headaches) and ask children to identify the symptoms of each. Talk with children about ways to prevent illness and how illnesses are treated.

Language and Literacy: Speaking, Listening, Reading, and Writing

Communication is important to all children. Children with learning differences will find this a particularly challenging area. Make it a positive experience. However tempting, don't resort to drill and practice as a method of teaching. Most children with learning differences find some aspects of language difficult. Sequencing activities and memory games may be difficult for some; making auditory distinctions is difficult for others. For children with a high activity level, having to *just* listen may seem close to punishment. Children with learning differences will need more practice than others in literacy skills. If these skills are difficult, they may try to avoid them. Emphasize activities that intrigue them while teaching the necessary skills at the same time. Your job is also to provide excitement and motivation.

Speaking. Encourage children to verbalize their feelings as well as to communicate ideas. When they do not have the words, provide them.

1. When possible, support children in their verbalizations with picture cues. Ask children to tell you about specific items in a picture. This helps focus their attention as they talk.

2. Have children name pictures and/or discuss what is happening in pictures. Be sure to give children enough time to answer.

3. Give children a sequence of pictures that display a familiar action, such as getting ready for bed, and have the children tell you what is happening in the sequence.

4. Give children pictures of the sequence of your day at school and have children put these in order and describe the sequence.

5. Play a sentence completion game, such as "I draw with a . . ." To make it more difficult, ask what else they can draw with.

6. Play "Say What I Say." You can make sounds, words, sentences or nonsense.

7. Follow up a field trip with a language experience story to which the children contribute. (If you have two groups, compare the stories.)

Fingerplays are great for children with learning differences. The children are actively involved and able to learn through the kinesthetic/tactile sense.

Also, children whose hands are busy doing fingerplays are less likely to be bothering the person next to them.

1. Use fingerplays to teach concepts.

2. Quiz the children in a way that is fun but that also makes them think about what they are saying. For example, sing "Where Is Thumbkin?", but instead of holding up your thumb when you sing "Here I am," hold up your index finger. Ask them what is wrong with doing it that way. Ask them for another word for thumbkin (thumb), pointer (index finger), tall man (middle finger), ring man, and pinkie. Can the children tell you how the fingers got these nicknames?

Listening. Listening is difficult, especially for children who are ready to move. Listening is made up of many different auditory skills. *Auditory discrimination* is the ability to tell the difference among sounds. Children with learning differences often have trouble recognizing differences in sounds or words; hence they often misinterpret meanings *(rat, rap)*. They also have problems identifying the rhyming elements of words.

Auditory memory requires children to keep in mind what was said. Sometimes, children forget the beginning of a sentence by the time you get to the end of it. The second request in two-step directions may not be remembered. Some children have problems with spacial awareness and the parts of speech in relation to position such as prepositions *(in, on, over, under, beside)*. Give them plenty of practice following your directions using these words; showing what they mean both with their own body and with a block or doll.

Children need to develop auditory skills, so choose topics that are of particular interest to them and reinforce their attempts at communicating. Don't avoid areas that are difficult, but keep the time spent on them short and support children's attempts. Work to increase concentration and attention span. Shorten your sentences and give directions one step at a time.

1. Play games such as "Find the . . ."

2. Play direction-following games such as "Put the block under the table," Simon Says, and Mother, May I? Add steps. Don't eliminate children who make mistakes; they are the ones that need the most practice.

3. Play Musical Chairs. Don't eliminate any chairs; this is a listening game.

4. Use sound tapes and have the children identify the sounds.

5. With the child blindfolded or looking away, have the child guess who is talking or where in the room the person is speaking from.

Stories can be entertaining and enlightening for children. Choose them carefully and read them with interest and expression.

1. Keep stories short. It is better to read a 5-page story that the children sit through attentively than to read a 20-page story with 20 interruptions.

2. During group times, you may want to use physical signals to help children organize their bodies as they listen. A carpet square or X made with masking tape may help. As children become more competent, replace these with verbal reminders. It is important for children to learn to control their body without these cues, so you don't want them to become dependent on them.

3. Use stories that allow participation. Children can move the flannel board characters to follow the story.

4. Occasionally read stories in small groups, where you can individualize the story and your attention.

5. Choose stories that deal with feelings, including hostile or unhappy feelings as well as happy ones.

6. Choose stories that deal with individual differences.

Reading. Because many children with learning disabilities will have problems learning to read, it is imperative to make language arts and literacy both successful and enjoyable. To be motivated, they need to know reading can and *will* be fun. Begin by building strength in literacy skills. Children are expected to be ready to read when they are about 5 or 6 years old. However, some children with learning differences don't seem to be ready when their peers are. This doesn't mean that reading instruction should be delayed: It means it may have to begin in a different place. Check that they have the prerequisite skills. Use activities and observation to determine a child's functional level in literacy. You might even devise an informal checklist to ascertain what skills each child has acquired. This way you can match your teaching to the children's level of skill. Challenge but don't overwhelm children with the necessary visual and auditory skills that are prerequisites to reading. (Note: There are many different approaches to teaching reading. It is beyond the scope of this book to decide among these. However, the basic foundation skills given below are a place to start. A reading specialist will provide additional help.)

During the early development of reading, this means:

1. After reading a story, discuss it. Stop some stories and see if children can anticipate what might happen next. Have children retell stories using the pictures as clues. Have children "play read" books. Share your joy of reading with them and continue to read to them. Read stories at their level of comprehension, not their skill level.

2. Children need to learn about the structure of books and the vocabulary that goes with it. They need to be able to know the title of a book (after you have read it) and to point to it on the book itself. They need to know where the story begins. Additionally, they need to know the front and back of a book, the first and last page, and the bottom and top of the page. Children need to be able to find individual words and to point to words as you read. (This is best done individually, with a child on your lap.)

3. Help children recognize rhyming words. Many nursery rhymes have rhyming words at the end of lines. Change one of the words and see if the children notice. If they understand the concept of rhyming, see if children can generate rhyming words to match those you say.

   Children also need to begin thinking about parts of words and how sounds blend into words. If their name has more than one syllable, this is a place to start. Say the first syllable and pause before saying the second: Mi–chael. Sometimes, compound words help children get the idea: play–ground, bed–room, air–plane. Don't belabor this, but do introduce it regularly.

   Another beginning phonetic skill is the association of initial sounds with objects or pictures. Begin with small objects and initially agree what each is called (apple, cup, key, pencil, toothbrush). Then ask the child to give you the object that begins with the sound /a/ (be sure it is the *sound,* not the letter name). Make it a guessing game: "I'm thinking of something that begins with /p/. What am I thinking of?" Then ask for the remainder of the items. Ask for some more than once, and put the items back so the child cannot use the process of elimination. Then have the child be the "thinker" (teacher) who requests the information. Start with real objects, then use pictures for some sounds that are difficult to find small objects for.

4. Children need to be able to match words and letters by sight. Start with words. Print 5 to 10 words that are visually different (penny, is, mom, train, all) on cards (with duplicates) and ask children to "find one that looks exactly like this one." See if they can accurately match the cards. Play a similar game with letters, starting with dissimilar lower-case letters (a, b, f, g, i). Children aren't expected to name letters, just match them. Ultimately, children should be able to match all the letters. Show children four or five familiar words written on cards (including the child's name and other words he is likely to know) and read the words to the child, pointing to each word as you read it. Mix them up and then have the child read the words.

This information should help you decide in which areas children have strengths and needs. Foundation skills and motivation are important in learning to read. If these skills show mastery, continue to look for the child's level by doing the following:

1. Read a book with a child one-on-one. Choose a simple yet unfamiliar book with clear illustrations.

Ask the child what the book is about. (Does the child use the illustrations and other clues to make a guess?) Read the story together with the child. Can the child use context to make sense of the story? Does the child go back and reread part of a sentence once she has worked out the meaning? Does the child hesitate over misreading? Can the child comment on characters and events in the story? Children need to learn to use contextual cues combined with the knowledge of phonemes to figure out what a word might be. If they don't have these skills, you need to teach them while you read to individual children.

2. Children need to be able to read and write single letter sounds. Particularly look for the following errors: b/d/p/q; u/n; m/w; and f/t. When children have associated sounds with lower-case letters, they need to make the same associations with upper-case. Keep records on the sounds that children know and don't know. (Note: Children also need to know the alphabet names of letters, but for reading, we are concerned about the sound-letter association, not the name-letter association.)

3. Have children put words they can read in a word bank.

It is often difficult for children with learning differences to interpret what they see *(visual perception)*. A child may not be able to judge size, shape, location, movement, and color because to the child these properties keep changing. Because of the difficulty they have in sorting out foreground and background, these children often focus on irrelevant details. It is difficult for them to recognize similarities and differences *(visual discrimination)*. Their problems are magnified when they try to learn to recognize numbers and letters, as the differences are slight. The letters that are reversible are especially difficult *(b,d)*, as are the ones with "tails" *(p, q, j, g)*.

Visual tracking is the ability to focus the eyes on one point and then move them rhythmically from side to side, up and down, and diagonally. Some children have jerky eye movements, or move their whole head instead of just their eyes. Part-whole relationships *(visual closure)* cause problems. The children may have trouble identifying missing parts; a picture of a three-legged chair appears normal to them. They may have trouble remembering what they see. (If you had four objects on the table, covered them, removed one, and asked them to name the missing one, could they?) Poor visual memory also makes it difficult to remember sequences. Needed *memory skills* can be built by games that require children to remember the original order of objects that have been moved.

1. Play visual tracking games by having children follow a flashlight or pointer with their eyes.

2. Hide objects or pictures so they are partially visible and have children find them.

3. Play memory games such as Concentration with increasing numbers of cards. Have children identify and match shapes and colors before they proceed to letters and numbers.

4. Have a set of wooden numbers and letters for children to play with. Encourage children to feel the letters and numbers and match them to outlines of the same letters. Start with letters that look different or those with significance (letters in the child's name).

5. Play sequencing games using picture cards.

6. Help children learn to observe detail. Have children think about the parts of a flower while they are looking at it and then from memory.

7. Encourage children to read by having a wide selection of books available on many different reading levels and on many different topics, including books that have only pictures.

8. Have a quiet reading area that has private soft space for children to get away and to encourage looking at books alone or with others.

Writing. Most young children love to write until someone tells them they aren't "really" writing or that they can't spell. They become discouraged and may stop writing. Seeing oneself as an author during the early childhood years provides some insulation for the future.

Writing involves legibility (someone has to be able to read what is written), fluency (writing flows smoothly without breaks within words), and speed. Some problems in this area relate to lack of stamina (poor muscle strength) and lack of fine motor coordination. Left-handed children have additional problems.

There is disagreement about whether children should begin with script (printing) or cursive (joined writing). Those who favor script look at the relationship between reading and writing and feel that it strengthens this connection. Others feel that if children are likely to have problems writing, one shouldn't waste time on teaching them to print when it is easier to write in cursive (Reason & Boote, 1994). This decision belongs to you and the educational setting for which you work. Our choice is to teach cursive and to teach a method of writing cursive where all the lower-case letters start on the line. This helps children with spacial problems because all the letters start on the line. If they have learned script first, they can print the capital letter and follow with this method of cursive (see Figure 10.2).

1. Set up a writing center and stock it with a variety of writing instruments (pencils, fine and thick colored markers, crayons) and many types of paper to write on (plain and colored, cards, envelopes). Talk about writing.

2. When you read a book, talk about the author who wrote the book and the illustrator who drew the pictures.

Children need many opportunities to write. Writing as a group experience allows children to talk about their ideas and share their expertise. A teacher's role is to reframe judgmental statements made by others into positive ones.

3. Show children books that other children have written. If children say they can only scribble, support their efforts and ask them if they would like to entitle their book *A Book of Scribbles*. (Get children "hooked" on writing. It is a necessary but often difficult skill for them.)

4. If children want to write a book with words, have them dictate it to you and write it for them. They could also "write" it verbally on a tape recorder to be transcribed later.

5. Encourage children to "read" their book to others. Let them know that writing is a process that includes writing, editing, rewriting, and publishing. When children are not pleased with their work, talk about editing. This is a way to deal with spelling, as it is an obvious time to correct it.

6. As children become concerned about spelling in their written work, write out the words they need to spell on cards and develop a spelling bank for them. Put the words in the bank alphabetically so they can find them again if they forget. Or you can help them with the process, but you don't need to write the words again. (Looking words up that are in alphabetical order is

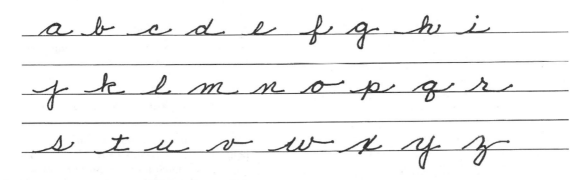

Figure 10.2   Lower-Case Letters
Note how all lower case letters begin on the line.

challenging for children, but it ties together the reading and writing process.)

7. Encourage children to write stories on the computer, spell-check them, and print them. I was initially appalled when a teacher allowed a third-grade student to do her spelling homework on the computer. (She was a very poor speller and had even poorer handwriting.) I predicted gloom and doom. Apparently, the computer pointed out the girl's mistakes again and again without the frustration she and her parents experienced over her continuing problems. The girl's spelling improved.

Be open to trying a variety of different ways to reach children.

Discovery: Mathematics, Science, and Computers

Children with learning differences may not have as much general knowledge as other children. This is especially true in the area of cause-and-effect relationships. They may not understand that it is hotter in the sun than in the shade or that if you don't water plants, they will die.

These children need practice in logical reasoning. Demonstrate first with objects and then by drawing attention to the child's own behavior that it is possible to make predictions about what will happen. In this way, they will gradually improve cause-and-effect reasoning skills. Start with short, obvious examples, such as putting weights on a balance. Work toward tasks requiring higher-level reasoning skills. Include activities in which children can cause change: The harder they press their crayons, the darker the color. Help children learn how they cause their environment to change. Children need skills to understand and organize their world. They need to recognize relationships, classify items, compare and contrast objects, and solve problems. Children need a broad foundation in exploration without their products being judged. They need help learning how to develop compensatory skills that will serve them as math and science become more formalized.

Use real materials and situations. Give the children two crackers: They can count them, see them, touch them, hear you say there are two. Break one in half, count them again, and then consume them—one piece at a time. Computers can be a tremendous aid to children with learning differences, although the initial skills acquisition may be challenging.

Mathematics. Help children develop a sensorimotor experiential awareness of math. *Doing* math, not just looking or hearing about it, is the key.

1. Use concrete objects to teach number sense and numeration, and employ as many variations as you can think of. Use food (raisins, cereal, small crack-

ers) for teaching these concepts: same/different, numbers, sets, equal, one-to-one correspondence, and more/less/same. (Somehow, children learn faster when another child is going to get "more" than they are!)

2. Play number concept games, such as counting objects, naming numbers when shown the number, matching numbers to groups of objects, and games that require matching, sorting, and selecting numbers, colors, or pictures.

3. Provide running commentary whenever possible to help children make connections between mathematics and its use in the real world: "You've had half of your juice"; "You have one cookie yet to eat"; "We have two empty chairs at this table."

4. Create situations where children must use mathematical reasoning to solve problems: "What if you run out of large blocks and you need to make another wall the same length as the first?" Discuss relative length.

5. Play size comparative games with children: "Give me the big ball"; "Give me the biggest triangle."

6. Help children identify, construct, and predict patterns and relationships of colors or objects (shoe, shoe, sock, shoe, shoe, sock).

7. Emphasize the vocabulary children need to communicate mathematical concepts (two- and three-dimensional geometric shapes, relative size, numbers themselves, spatial relations, measurement).

Science. Science activities may create enthusiasm in children with learning differences if a basic discovery approach is taken. Children can use basic science concepts to organize and understand the natural world.

1. Use science to teach general information, such as cause and effect (the relationship between temperature and the state of water: liquid, steam, ice); the relationship between structure and function (how do snakes move?); continuous and discontinuous properties (pitch, and how it changes on various instruments from water glasses to violins); and diversity (how leaves of various trees are alike and different).

2. Let children examine items (orange, cup, mirror) and describe as many details of the item as they can (color, shape, size, texture, function, parts). This is a great way to teach comparison. Two items are alike in some ways and different in others.

3. Cause-and-effect reasoning is important. It may help children develop inner controls and curb impulsivity. Encourage children to answer questions such as "What happens if . . . ?" "What could you do about . . . ?" "Is there anything else you could do?" And, if possible, have them test out their answers.

4. Because children with learning differences often have gaps in their knowledge, remember to repeat the learning cycle (awareness, exploration, inquiry/experimentation, and utilization) when you introduce new ideas and concepts.

Computers. Computers have infinite patience, their energy is inexhaustible, and they don't get upset with children who forget. Some programs are even designed to support children as they get closer to the right answer or have increased their scores, no matter where they started. Computers are under the control of the children who use them. They can be turned off or their plug can be pulled. This is empowering to children who are in charge of so little. Computers can provide personal instruction to children at a speed at which they are ready to learn and in a time frame that accommodates the child's attention span. Children can participate at their own pace.

1. Choose software that is compatible with the child's learning needs, supports her interests, and is open-ended.

2. Although older children might profit from some of the drill and practice in the areas of spelling and math, for younger children, the idea that computers are interactive and that they can learn cause-and-effect reasoning is far more compelling.

3. Becoming comfortable with computers at a young age is critical for children with learning differences. Computers can compensate for poor handwriting, they can check spelling, and as children get older, there are even programs that can analyze their grammar and composition.

Developmental Physical Education and Sensorimotor Skills: Large Motor, Small Motor, Sensorimotor Integration

Children need to refine the movements of both their large and small muscles in addition to coordinating these muscles with information they receive from their senses. Children with learning differences need to develop a physically active lifestyle. It is critical that children develop large motor strength such as trunk stability as a prerequisite for doing fine motor skills. (You can't write if you fall off the chair.) Children who are not good at these activities may avoid them. It is the teacher's role to support children, but also to make activities so intriguing that children want to participate.

Often, children with learning differences have related sensorimotor integration problems. Adaptive skills such as snapping, tying, and buttoning promote sensorimotor integration but are challenging.

Large Motor. Children with learning differences use large motor activities as a means of releasing frustration, tension, and anger. Participating in these activities will help children develop feelings of belonging to a group. Children with learning differences may have been late (or at the end of the normal age range) in reaching developmental milestones such as sitting up, crawling, and walking. Some tend to lack body control and rhythm. While walking or running, these children appear disjointed. They get where they want to go, but they appear inefficient and they don't move smoothly. Some may lack the necessary coordination for hopping, jumping, and skipping.

Some will exhibit problems in tasks that require bilateral movement (using both arms and hands at the same time) such as lifting or throwing. Cross-lateral movements (using opposite arm and leg at the same time) such as crawling may be difficult. It may be hard for them to control their balance while moving, and they may frequently trip, bump into things, or drop things. They may also have poor spatial orientation and may find the relationship of objects to each other difficult to understand. They may not know how high to step to get over an object or how to fit their body under a rope. These children also have trouble catching a ball, especially if it bounces first. It is difficult for them to decide when the ball will reach them and how high the ball will be when it does. Hence, they rarely catch it.

Some children will need your encouragement to participate in large motor activities, especially if others have teased them in the past about their lack of coordination. Plan opportunities both indoors and out for children to practice large motor skills.

1. Help children develop concepts of space and direction by having them pace off distances, or see how far they can run in five seconds compared to walking or crawling.

2. Have children do variations on skills that they already know: walking, jumping, throwing, rolling, and crawling.

3. Include activities that develop the lateral muscles of the trunk: crawling, climbing, and crashing. Children can't control a tool such as a crayon or pencil until the lateral muscles are sufficiently developed.

4. Obtain a punching bag and encourage children who feel like hitting to hit the bag (not just to hit once or tap lightly, but to hit as hard and as often as they can).

5. Provide a large rubber ball for kicking. Encourage children to kick the ball and then run after it and kick it again, or kick the ball and try to hit a target like a bowling pin.

6. Use underinflated beach balls as well as large balls to increase the possibility for successful throwing and catching.

7. Help children learn sequencing by using the large muscles of their body. Design an obstacle course that children must do in order. After the child can successfully navigate the two or three obstacles in sequence, add another obstacle.

8. Support children becoming physically fit.

9. Help children understand and respect differences among children participating in physical activities.

Small Motor. All young children need practice in fine motor skills. Children with learning differences may need extra motivation in this area. They may avoid small motor activities. However, they need the practice, and it is your role to make it fun. Children with poor fine motor skills are clumsy handling small objects that require finger and wrist movement. They may not be able to button and unbutton, snap, or tie. An underdeveloped pincer grip may make it hard to pick up small items. Even speech, which requires coordinated movements of the lips and tongue, may be challenging.

Coloring inside the lines and pasting in a specific area may be very difficult. Cutting with conventional scissors is often close to impossible. Large crayons, large chalk, and simple designs all help. Your concern is to ensure that these children experience success in this area so that they don't quit trying.

1. Pick some activities that may especially intrigue a particular child. If the child likes cars, provide a car drawing to color. (This is not creative art, but rather practice in small motor skills.) Provide a maze for small toy cars to follow. Have the child practice lining the cars up in specified patterns. Magnets can be used to attach metal cars to a jelly roll pan.

2. Have children practice life skills like buttoning, snapping, and tying. Discuss the pride of being able to "do it myself."

3. Encourage children to participate in board games that combine fine motor skills with other skills, such as bingo, dominos, checkers and Chinese checkers.

4. Use hand and finger puppets to increase dexterity.

5. Have a variety of different types of scissors available (including left-handed ones) so children can choose scissors that will enable them to cut.

Sensorimotor Integration. Children get information from their senses—including touch, sight, sound—and from movement, body awareness, and the pull of gravity. The process by which the brain organizes and interprets this information is sensory integration. The integration of this information with motor activities is called *motor planning.* For some children, motor planning is easy and natural, but children with learning differences may find it difficult. When this process is disordered, children may have problems in learning, development, and behavior. They may under- or overreact to touch, movement, sight, or sound; they may be clumsy or appear careless; their activity level may be inappropriate; and this combination may lower children's self-esteem. Motivation plays a critical role in sensory integration. Children must be actively involved and exploring in a

goal-directed way to become an efficient organizer of sensory information.

1. Play Freeze. Play music, and when the music stops, the children must hold the position they are in. Don't stop the music for long.

2. Play Hot and Cold. Hide an object and have the child try to find it by telling the child whether she is hot (close to object), hotter (even closer), or cold (going away from the object).

3. Play Do What I Do. This is a variation on Follow the Leader while sitting still. You do something (clap twice, tap your head with one hand, and hit your thighs with both hands). The children imitate what you do. Play Follow the Leader.

4. Include activities that require children to use both sides of the body at the same time, such as underhand throwing or catching a large ball with both hands, hopping or jumping with both feet together, clapping, and doing jumping jacks.

5. Include activities that require children to use both sides of the body alternately, such as going up steps with alternate feet on each tread, climbing a ladder, riding a tricycle, walking a line or balance beam, running, walking, and skipping. Place a string or tape in various configurations (straight, curved, with angles) and have the children walk on this.

6. Include activities that require children to cross the midline (the imaginary line through the center of the body, which divides it into right and left sides). When playing Simon Says, request children to put the *right* hand on the *left* shoulder and so on. Have children throw balls or beanbags while standing sideways to the target. Have them touch the toes of the opposite foot while standing.

Creative Arts: Visual Arts, Music, Creative Movement, and Dramatic Play

Creative arts provide an opportunity to practice skills in a safe place before using them elsewhere and to learn more about the world. Children with learning differences may find in the visual arts an emotional release and an opportunity to integrate the visual and tactile senses and to make a creation that will not be judged by others as right or wrong. Make sure children understand what is expected of them. Give visual and movement cues to help them understand.

Music can help improve sensorimotor integration; adding creative movement helps children express emotions and increase body awareness. Use dramatic play to help children become more aware of roles and feelings. Help them express caring and happy feelings as well as sad, angry, and unhappy ones. As holidays and special events are stressful for some children, playing them through may help.

Visual Arts. For children with learning differences, the major focus of art should be on the *process,* not the product. Allow children freedom to be spontaneous and creative. When they begin to feel that their work should "be something" or look like something specific, and the emphasis is on a product, the potential for failure is greater.

1. Use three-dimensional materials (clay, playdough). These can be good for releasing tension, and because they are reusable and easily stored, they are available on short notice.

2. Use large paintbrushes; they require less eye-hand coordination than small brushes.

3. Include some art materials that accommodate expansive work. Color or paint on very large paper without restriction or use finger paints on the table, then print the pictures.

4. Colored marking pens are easier to use than crayons, as either light or heavy pressure leaves an impression.

Music. Music contributes to a child's physical, aesthetic, and intellectual development. It provides pleasure and creative experience, develops auditory skills, encourages physical development, and increases the range and flexibility of the voice. There should be a wide variety of musical experiences: listening, singing, moving to music, and playing instruments.

1. Have a variety of different instruments available. Help children explore and evaluate the sound of an instrument when it is held and played in different ways. See if they can identify the instruments they know in a recording.

2. Incorporate music and language experiences; have children make up new verses to songs. Play unusual instrumental recordings and ask children to describe what they imagined while listening.

3. Put stories to music. Have children choose background music for stories; encourage them to think about how the mood of the music relates to their story.

4. Paint to music.

5. Have children make musical instruments (cigar-box guitars, coffee-can drums, wax paper and comb). As they participate in this process, they will gain an understanding of how sounds are made, where they come from, and how to change them. See if they can make sounds with different parts of their body.

6. Introduce children to the concepts and vocabulary of music, including pitch, loudness, tempo, and duration.

7. Sing songs with motions ("My Bonnie Lies over the Ocean," "Hey, Betty Martin") and those that create body awareness ("Put Your Finger in the Air," "Head and Shoulders, Knees and Toes").

8. Expose children to music of various genres, styles, time periods, and cultures.

9. Music can be used to release energy. If bad weather has kept the children indoors, play salsa or a Sousa march. Music also helps children settle down. If the children are excited before a rest period, help them relax with some "easy listening" music.

Creative Movement. Movement that is not judged on quality, but rather on creativity, offers potential to children with learning differences. Children can experiment with movement and their interpretation of what it should be like without judgment. Movement also provides an opportunity for sensory integration.

1. Have the children walk through imaginary substances, such as gelatin, deep sand, flypaper, a swamp, or quicksand. Have the others guess what the substances are.

2. Combine music and movement to give children the opportunity to translate an auditory stimulus (record, music) into movement. Be sure to discuss the mood of the music and what types of action this mood evokes.

3. Encourage children to dance to music with different tempos. Include dances and music from a variety of cultures and those that are stylistically different (waltz, country line dancing, tango). Help children analyze the differences.

Dramatic Play. Dramatic play allows children to try out roles and the potential for working through fearful experiences. It also gives them the opportunity to rehearse new roles and to be in control.

1. Special and unusual events may be stressful. Help children play through field trips, visits to the doctor, and so on. Discuss what could happen as well as what behavior is expected of them. (You gain some insight into what children expect to happen.)

2. Because children with learning differences often have as much trouble expressing pleasure as pain, have them practice being happy and sad. Discuss how others know you are happy. Have the children pretend to open a package that contains something they really want.

3. Encourage children to build structures for various climates and uses. Ask them to suggest additions they need for the construction area, such as fabric, dowels, netting, and so on to build their structures. Have them design:

   A house where it is hot and rainy.

   A school where it is almost always cold.

   A store where the temperature changes.

Transitions

In general, children with learning differences dislike change. Special school events can be stressful, and these children may have trouble handling feelings of anticipation. In addition to the challenge, transitions provide another opportunity for helping children feel the same as others yet unique as individuals. Be sure children understand what you want them to do during transitions, especially at the beginning of the school year. Transitions, a difficult time for many children, making up approximately 15 percent of their day. Structure them well.

1. Plan enough time to prepare children for the upcoming transition; try a warning of "five more minutes" or a song. Let children know about the next activity and the motivating aspects of it. Try code works, songs, or visual cues to help children anticipate transitions.

2. Employ auditory or visual cues to signal change in the daily routine itself. Let children know specifically how and what needs to be done to move to the next activity.

3. Reinforce and acknowledge a child's completion of an activity.

4. Without being obvious about it, dismiss children with learning differences early in the transition; this should be thought of as prevention, not favoritism.

5. Use transitions to increase body awareness and feelings of being part of the group: "All children with brown eyes and black hair may *jump* to their centers."

6. Play the "I'm thinking of someone" game to dismiss children: "I'm thinking of someone with brown hair, brown eyes, and a plaid shirt. Yes. Lisa, you can get your coat."

7. Encourage knowledge of full names and addresses by dismissing children by last name, address, or phone number. (Not all children have a phone number, so you may want to ask parents if there is a phone number for them to learn. Have them learn an emergency number for their area.)

Summary

Children with learning differences are one of the largest categories of children identified as needing special educational services. Learning differences is an umbrella term that includes learning disabilities, particularly developmental dyslexia, and ADHD and others. Many of these learning differences co-occur.

Learning differences are probably present at birth but usually are not identified until later. Infants may have had a difficult temperament. As they increased in age, they had a short attention span and were impulsive, easily distracted, and perhaps aggressive. Academically, their learning was inconsistent and they sometimes didn't remember information, were disorganized, and had difficulty completing projects. Socially, their relationships were difficult with peers, parents, and teachers.

Increasingly, learning differences are tied to a hereditary/genetic base. Although the brain itself appears normal, there appear to be consistent dysfunctions.

Children who have learning differences may need more structure and fewer distractions in their environment and require more direct teacher instruction than other children the same age. Behavior modification techniques are frequently used both at home and at school to modify the children's behavior.

Educational Resources

Association for Children and Adults with Learning
   Disabilities (ACLD)
4156 Library Road
Pittsburgh, PA 15234
(412) 341-1515

ACLD is a nonprofit organization to advance the education and general welfare of children of normal intelligence who have perceptual, conceptual, or coordination related to learning disabilities. They have conferences and write Newsbriefs.

Children and Adults with Attention Deficit Disorder
499 Northwest 70th Avenue, Suite 101
Plantation, FL 33317
(800) 2133-4050, FAX (954) 587-4599
http://www.chadd.org/

An organization founded to better the lives of those with ADD. Emphasizes family and community support, as well as encouragement for scientific research.

Council for Learning Disabilities
PO Box 40303
Overland Park, KS 66204
(913) 492-8755

Publishes the LD Quarterly, *a journal on learning disabilities.*

Division for Learning Disabilities
Council for Exceptional Children (CEC)
1920 Association Drive
Reston, VA 22091-1589
(703) 620-3660, FAX (703) 264-9496
http://www.cec.sped.org/pp/cec_pol.htm

This division concentrates its efforts on learning disabilities, producing a journal and newsletters. They also have state divisions.

Dyslexia Archive
http://www.hensa.ac.uk/dyslexia.html

A Web page that contains information on services provided, links to other sites, as well as opportunities to ask questions and read accounts from dyslexic individuals.

Dyslexia, The Gift
http://www.dyslexia.com/

This page is provided by the Davis Dyslexia Association. It has information about dyslexia and other learning disorders. Great for parents and teachers.

Dyslexia Related Information
http://www.hensa.ac.uk/dyslexia/www
  /remote_servers.html
   This site has many links to pages about dyslexia.

George's Links
http://www.iscm.ulst.ac.uk/~george/subjects
  /dyslexia.html
   This page contains links to other pages, resources, and organizations about dyslexia.

Hyperlexia Association Homepage
American Hyperlexia Association
479 Spring Road
Elmhurst, IL 60126
(630) 415-2212, FAX (630) 530-5909
http://www.hyperlexia.org/index.html
   This page has information about hyperlexia (a set of unusual splinter skills, such as perfect pitch and the ability to perform rapid mathematical calculations, that children with LD, ADHD, or Autism sometime display). It is a good resource for parents and has many other links.

Learning Disabilities Association of America (LDAA)
4156 Library Road
Pittsburgh, PA 15234
(412) 341-1515, (412) 341-8077, FAX (412) 344-0224
http://www.kidsource.com/LDA/index:html
   This is an organization of parents who have children with LD and provides information for parents and professionals. It has information and links on how to get in touch with other parents.

National Center for Children with Learning
  Disabilities
99 Park Avenue, 6th Floor
New York, NY 10016
(212) 687-7211
   Publishes a resource guide to various programs (schools, camps, clinics) that aid children with LDs and their families.

The Orton Dyslexia Society
724 York Road
Baltimore, MD 21204
   Focuses exclusively on helping children with specific reading and language learning disabilities. Has publications for parents, educators, and physicians.

Perceptions, Inc.
PO Box 142
Millsboro, NJ 07041
   Publishes a newsletter that serves as an information source for parents wishing to develop expertise in meeting the educational, social, and emotional needs of children with LD.

Research and Demonstration Center for the
  Education of Handicapped Children and Youth
Box 223
Teachers College
Columbia University
New York, NY 10027
   Addresses the identification of psychoeducational characteristics of learners with a disability

and the development of instructional methods and materials that will be effective in bridging existing gaps between these learners and school tasks.

Wellspring Foundation
http://www.isp.net/wellspring/index.htm
   This organization supports research on dyslexia.

References

American Psychiatric Association. (1994). *Diagnostic and statistical manual of mental disorders* (4th ed.). Washington, DC: Author.

Batshaw, M. L., Perret, Y. M., & Mercugliano, M. (1992). Attention deficit hyperactivity disorder. In M. L. Batshaw & Y. M. Perret (Eds.), *Children with disabilities: A medical primer* (3rd ed., pp. 387–406). Baltimore: Brookes.

Berry, C. A., Shaywitz, B. A., & Shaywitz, S. E. (1985). Girls with attention deficit disorder: A silent minority? A report on the behavioral and cognitive characteristics. *Pediatrics, 76,* 807–809.

Blum, N. J., & Mercugliano, M. (1997). Attention-deficit/hyperactivity disorder. In M. L. Batshaw (Ed.), *Children with disabilities* (4th ed., pp. 449–470). Baltimore: Brookes.

Bowcr, B. (1994). Brain images delve into hyperactivity. *Science News, 145,* 309.

Church, R. P., Lewis, M. E. B., & Batshaw, M. L. (1997). Learning disabilities. In M. L. Batshaw (Ed.), *Children with disabilities* (4th ed., pp. 471–498). Baltimore: Brookes.

Ciaranello, R. D. (1993). Attention deficit-hyperactivity disorder and resistance to thyroid hormone—a new idea? *New England Journal of Medicine, 328,* 1038.

Doyle, J. (1996). *Dyslexia: An introductory guide.* San Diego, CA: Singular.

Dykman, R. A., & Ackerman, P. T. (1993). Behavioral subtypes of attention deficit disorder. *Exceptional Children, 60,* 125–131.

Ellis, E. S., Deshler, D. D., Lenz, B. K., Schumaker, J. B., & Clark, F. L. (1991). An instructional model for teaching learning strategies. *Focus on Exceptional Children, 23*(6), 11.

Forness, S. R., Kavale, K. A., King, B. H., & Kasari, C. (1995). Simple versus complex conduct disorders: Identification and phenomenology. *Behavioral Disorders.*

Garber, S., Garber, M., & Spizman, R. (1993). *If your child is hyperactive, inattentive, impulsive, distractable . . .* New York: Villard Books.

Goldstein, S. (1992, January). *Young children at risk: The early signs of attention-deficit hyperactivity disorder.* CH.A.D.D.er Box.

Hallahan, D., & Kauffman, J. (1994). *Exceptional children: Introduction to special education* (6th ed.). Englewood Cliffs, NJ: Prentice Hall.

Hayden, A., Smith, R., von Hippel, C., & Baer, S. (1978). *Mainstreaming preschoolers: Children with learning disabilities.* Washington, DC: Department of Health and Human Services.

Individuals with Disabilities Education Act of 1997. Pub. L. No. 105-17 111 Stat. 37-157 20 U.S.C. 1400.

Kelly & Ramundo (1993). *Parents of infants.*

Landau, S., & McAninch, C. (1993). Young children with attention deficits. *Young Children, 48*(4), 49-58.

Lasher, Mattick, & Perkins. (1978).

Lerner, J. W. (1989). Educational interventions in learning disabilities. *Journal of the American Academy of Child and Adolescent Psychiatry, 28,* 326-331.

Lerner, J. W., & Lerner, S. (1991). Attention deficit disorder: Issues and questions. *Focus on Exceptional Children, 3,* 1-18.

Lynch, D. R., & Batshaw, M. L. (1997). The brain and the nervous system. In M. L. Batshaw (Ed.), *Children with disabilities* (4th ed., pp. 293-314). Baltimore: Brookes.

Maugh, T. H., II. (1996, May 1) Attention deficit disorder tied to abnormal gene. *The News Journal.*

McCarney, S. (1995). *The early childhood attention deficit disorders evaluation scales.* Columbia, MO: Hawthorne Educational Services.

Mercugliano, M. (1995). Neurotransmitter alterations in attention deficit hyperactivity disorder. *Mental Retardation and Developmental Disorders Research Reviews, 1,* 220-226.

National Joint Committee on Learning Disabilities. (1989). *Modifications to the NJCLD definition of learning disabilities* [Letter]. Author.

Pelham, W., Sams, S., Vallano, G., Dixon, M., & Hoza, B. (1993). Separate and combined effects of methylphenidate and behavior modification on boys with ADHD in the classroom. *Journal of Consulting and Clinical Psychology, 61,* 506-515.

Reason, R., & Boote, R. (1994). *Helping children with reading and spelling: A special needs manual.* London: Routledge.

Roush, W. (1995). Arguing over why Johnny can't read. *Science, 267,* 1896-1898.

Safer, D. J., & Krager, J. M. (1992). Effects of a media blitz and a threatened lawsuit on stimulant treatment. *Journal of American Medical Association, 268,* 1004-1007.

Shaywitz, S. E. (1998). Dyslexia. *New England Journal of Medicine, 338*(5), 307-312.

Shaywitz, S. E., Fletcher, J. M., & Shaywitz, B. A. (1988). Interrelationship between reading disability and attention deficit-hyperactivity disorder. In A. J. Capute, P. J. Accardo, & B. K. Shapiro (Eds.), *Learning disabilities spectrum: ADD, ADHD, LD* (pp. 107-120). Baltimore: York Press.

Shaywitz, S. E., Fletcher, J. M., & Shaywitz, B. A. (1994). Issues in the definition and classification of attention deficit disorder. *Topics in Language Disorders, 14,* 1-25.

Shaywitz, S. E., & Shaywitz, B. A. (1988). Attention deficit disorder: Current perspectives. In J. K. Kavanagh & T. J. Truss (Eds.), *Learning disabilities: Proceedings of the National Conference.* Parkton, MD: York Press.

Shaywitz, S. E., & Shaywitz, B. A. (1992). *Attention deficit disorder comes of age: Toward the twenty-first century.* Austin, TX: Pro-Ed.

Silver, L. B. (1990). Attention deficit-hyperactivity disorder or a related disorder? *Journal of Learning Disabilities, 23,* 394-397.

Silver, L. B.(1995). *ADHD—Attention deficit-hyperactivity disorder and learning disabilities* [A booklet for parents]. Summit, NJ: Ciba-Beigy.

Ubell, E. (1997, October 12). Are our children overmedicated? *Parade Magazine,* (4-6).

U.S. Department of Education. (1989). *Eleventh annual report to Congress on the implementation of the education of the handicapped act.* Washington, DC: U.S. Government Printing Office.

U.S. Department of Education. (1995). *Seventeenth annual report to Congress on the implementation of the individuals with disabilities education act.* Washington, DC: U.S. Government Printing Press Office.

Williams, R., Horn, S., Daley, D., & Nadeer, P. (1993). Evaluation of access to care and medical and behavior outcomes in a school based intervention program for ADHD. *Journal of School Health, 63,* 254-297.

Chapter 11

CHILDREN WITH COMMUNICATION AND LANGUAGE DIFFERENCES

Some children come to school as "talkers." They immediately want to know where the crayons are, why they are in school, why they can't go outside now . . . until you think you may change your profession if you hear one more question. These children stick in your mind from day 1. Then there are the "slow-to-warm-up" children, who appear shy and immature and of whom you probably still won't have a clear picture even after a few weeks. This group is difficult to understand, as it is hard to determine whether these children choose not to communicate or do not have the ability to communicate. A third group is composed of children who have a diagnosed language or communication disorder.

The first question to ask when you suspect a problem is: Can this child communicate in an age-appropriate way that can be understood by others? Then think back over events of the week. When you dismiss the children from group time by the color of their clothes, does this child need to be prompted? When you give simple directions, can this child follow them? How about more complex directions? Does this child seldom volunteer comments to you? Does the child rarely speak up during group time? When this child speaks, can you understand most of the words or only some of them? Given free choice, does this child seek out activities requiring language, or does he avoid them? How can you tell whether the child falls in that wide range called average or has an impairment?

Next consider: Is what you hear typical of the child's speech? Children are very adaptable in their communication styles and use language differently when talking with a peer or an adult, as well as adapting their speech to a variety of situations. Young children's language in school differs from that at home. When at home, the child typically displays more frequent, longer, and more balanced conversations over a wider range of topics than at school. Children who are quiet at school are frequently nonstop talkers at home (Tizard, 1981). Given this, it is important to find out from a child's parents how representative the speech is that you are hearing.

Classification of Communication and Language Disorders

In the introduction to this chapter, we purposefully used language, communication, and speech as if they were interchangeable. Although there is much overlap, there are also some important distinctions. Communication is the broadest level. It includes both verbal and nonverbal communication and human and nonhuman interactions. It involves a sender, who encodes some information, and a receiver, whose job it is to decode the information. Some children, such as children who have autism, have problems in both the linguistic and nonlinguistic aspects of communication. Some children with motor-related problems such as cerebral palsy have communication problems that can be solved or improved through augmentative communication systems (Donaldson, 1995). On the other hand, language has functions other than communication. It is a cognitive tool that is used to organize information and influences thinking and memory skills. Speech is an aspect of language: spoken language. Disorders of spoken language include speech disorders and articulation disorders.

Prevalence of Communication and Language Disorders

Problems with the overlapping of these categories also impact our ability to decide how many children actually have language and communication disorders. Depending on the definition used, children with communication disorders (including speaking, listening, reading, and writing) constitute about a fourth of all children identified for special education services (U.S. Department of Education, 1992). Speech and language therapy is often provided to a wide range of children with other disabilities such as hearing impairments, mental retardation, learning differences, and behavioral and emotional disorders. Language is rarely the only target for intervention in young **231** children (Ensher, 1989). Some young children can have language delays because of a bilingual or multilingual background. This should not be confused with a communication disorder.

Although the preceding comments reflect global data, they don't really pin things down. A study of 5,000 children (Drillien & Drummond, 1994) gleaned more specific information. The study found that 5.7 percent of children between the ages of 2 and 5 had a language impairment sometime during the three-year span. When children with secondary language disorder (for example, children with hearing impairments) were included, the number moved to 7.5 percent. Over half of these language impairments were considered moderately severe to severe. The most frequent problem was an articulation problem (36 percent), followed by an expressive language delay (29 percent), and then children who had both articulation problems and language delays (21 percent).

Table 11.1 highlights behaviors that should make you look more closely at a child's speech and language development.

Language Disorders

Language has a developmental base. What is appropriate for children at one age is inappropriate and considered dysfunctional at other ages. Additionally, language does not develop in isolation, and the interaction between language and cognitive development is difficult to unravel. There are also many ways of classifying language disorders. Some look at the rate and sequence in which language develops, others focus on the cause or related conditions, and still others break language down into subsystems (phonology, morphology, syntax, semantics, and pragmatics). In general, a child's language is impaired when there

TABLE 11.1   RED FLAGS IN SPEECH AND LANGUAGE DEVELOPMENT

Medical
History of ear infections
Mouth seems abnormal

Language
Doesn't talk
Makes no attempt to communicate with words
Has difficulty putting words and sounds in a
   sequence
Dost not appear to understand when others speak
Small vocabulary for age

Speech
Cannot be encouraged to imitate sounds or words
Speech is difficult to understand, words are
   mispronounced
Uses echolalic or parrotlike, repetitive speech
Voice is unusual, breathy, hoarse, loud or soft, high
   or low, or nasal

are deviations in the formation, expression, or understanding of language. Characteristics of impaired language include poor concepts, inability to follow directions, speechlessness, speech confusion, and poor word comprehension.

The American Speech-Language-Hearing Association (ASHA, 1982) is more specific: "A language disorder is the impairment or deviant development of comprehension and/or use of a spoken/written, and/or other symbol system. The disorder may involve (1) the form of language (phonologic, morphologic, and syntactic systems), (2) the content of the language (semantic system), and/or (3) the function of language in communication (pragmatic system)in any combination" (p. 949).

Let's look at this a piece at a time. The initial part of the definition is clear that it includes all aspects of what we traditionally think of as language (expressive, receptive, reading and written language) as well as the cognitive component. The choice of the phrase "deviant development" acknowledges that language is developmental and that the problem can be that the pattern of development is delayed or atypical.

The form of any language is composed of three elements. Starting from the smallest unit of language, we have *phonology. Phonation* is the production of sounds and sound combinations. *Phonemes* are the smallest units of a language that distinguish meaning. They are usually letter sounds. The meanings of c*at* and c*ap* are distinguished by the phonemes /t/ and /p/. Phonology is the sound system of a language and the linguistic rules for using the sounds and sound combinations in a language (ASHA, 1982). One rule of the English language is that *q* is always followed by *u.* Other rules relate to whether vowel sounds are short or long.

The next element in the form of a language is *morphology. Morphemes* are the smallest units of a language that contain meaning. They are usually words or meaningful word parts. Prefixes and suffixes are morphemes. Morphology is the linguistic rule system that governs the internal structure and form of words that form the basic elements of meaning, that is, the structure, classification, and relationship of morphemes. Morphology looks at how adding or deleting parts of words changes their meaning (ASHA, 1982). An example is the difference between *disorder* and *order.*

We have moved from letters to words; the next step is *syntax,* the set of linguistic rules that govern the arrangement of words into phrases or sentences and the relationship among these elements in a sentence (ASHA, 1982). Syntax establishes the requirements that all sentences have a subject and verb, and so on.

Children who have problems with the *form* of a language are considered to have a language disorder. That is, a 5-year-old who uses the telegraphic language of a 2-year-old ("Bring ball" instead of "Bring me the ball") would be identified as having a problem in this area.

The *content* of language can also be a concern. *Semantics* is the psycholinguistic system that governs the relationship between words or phrases and their meanings—the intent and meaning of utterances (ASLHA, 1982). The difference between "Pat played with Max" and "Max played with Pat" is a matter of meaning, or semantics. Sometimes children have problems in this area because of lack of an appropriate knowledge base.

The final aspect of language is *function. Pragmatics* is the sociolinguistic use of language for communication, whether the communication is expressed motorically, vocally, or verbally (ASHA, 1982). This is the use of language in social situations, and the emphasis here is on the function of language rather than the mechanics of it. Children with autism often have problems here.

Speech Disorders

The production of speech sounds involves the manipulation of the mouth, tongue, cheeks, and throat, along with the shaping and control of air, to produce specific vowel and consonant sounds. Problems with any one of these variables can result in atypical sound production or a speech disorder.

In general, a child's speech is impaired when it deviates so far from the speech of other children that it calls attention to itself, interferes with communication, or causes the child to be self-conscious. Again, let us go back to the definition used by the ASHA (1982): "A speech disorder is an impairment of voice, articulation of speech sounds, and/or fluency. These impairments are observed in the transmission and use of the oral symbol system" (p. 949).

A voice disorder involves abnormalities in pitch, volume, voice quality, and/or duration of speech (ASHA, 1982). The cause can be attributed to physical, learned, or psychological problems. Voice disorders occur less frequently than other speech problems. Children's *pitch* should be appropriate for their age, sex, and size; Mismatches can lead to social and emotional difficulties. *Volume* concerns the children's ability to monitor the loudness of their voices; hearing losses can result in a child's using a louder voice than normal. *Quality* refers to the general character of the voice such as hoarse, nasal, breathy, normal. Extremely harsh or hoarse quality speech can be related to vocal cord nodules or excessive screaming; nasal quality speech can be the result of cleft palate disorders. *Duration* refers to how much or little a child talks. Most problems encountered in voice disorders are treatable medically or through speech therapy.

Articulation involves the ability to appropriately produce, orally, any one of a variety of vowels, consonants, and/or vowel-consonant blends. The inability to produce these sounds can be physiological: lack of tongue or mouth control, oral musculature difficulties, or a hearing loss. Articulation errors occur when sounds are omitted, added, distorted, or substituted. Take, for example, *spaghetti:*

paghetti	(*s* is omitted)
spaghettiti	(extra *ti* is added)
speghetti	(*a* is distorted to *e*)
basaghetti	(*ba* is substituted for *p* and put at the beginning)

Articulation errors can happen at the beginning, middle, or end of a word. They may be the result of indistinct articulation. Slow, labored speech and rapid, slurring speech are both articulation problems. Some articulation problems are a natural part of a child's development. Although children may, in fact, outgrow some problems, care must be taken to determine whether therapy is indicated.

One of the primary causes of articulation disorders is middle ear malfunction, resulting from chronic ear infections or ear blockages. This type of hearing loss prevents the transmission of higher-frequency sounds: the consonants. This results in children who hear only the middle parts of words: "-able," "-irl," "-abbi-," "-o wha-." This hearing difficulty causes children to omit sounds when speaking. Some children also substitute sounds to make up for what is missing; "*dirl*-girl," "*wellwo*-yellow," "*w*abbit-rabbit."

Fluency disorders are the abnormal flow of verbal expression characterized by impaired rate and rhythm that may include labored speaking (ASHA, 1982). "Fluent speakers are those who speak easily (without much muscular or mental effort) and continuously (without interruption), at a rapid rate" (Gottwald, Goldbach, & Isack, 1985, p. 9). The most common fluency disorder is stuttering. Stuttering occurs when the normal flow of speech is interrupted by abnormal repetitions, hesitations, and prolongations of sounds and syllables and avoidable struggle behaviors. Associated with stuttering are characteristic body motions such

When a child has problems articulating particular sounds, she may need to see how her tongue, teeth, and mouth are supposed to look as she listens to herself making the sound.

as grimaces, eye blinks, and gross body movements. Occasional dysfluency is common in children 2 through 6.

The most common normal dysfluency is the repetition of whole words: "I want—I want the ball." These occur most frequently at the beginning of sentences. Boys show more repetitions than girls (3 to 1), but both sexes show fewer repetitions with increasing age (http://webpages.marshall.edu/`lynch4/fluency.html, 1997).

Most children become dysfluent between the ages of 2 and 5. In normal dysfluency, there is no struggle and the dysfluency is effortless. Normal dysfluency is also situationally specific: It increases when children talk with someone who speaks rapidly, when language use is more formal, or when they ask questions, use more complex sentences, or use less familiar words (Gottwald et al., 1985). Children who stutter for more than a year and a half or two years are at risk of becoming chronic stutterers (Yairi & Ambrose, 1992). Early intervention is imperative.

Learning theory suggests that children "learn" to stutter because of a cycle of negative reactions and anxiety, that is, as children learn language rapidly, they struggle to find the right words, and if they are nervous, they may become dysfluent. The listener then says "Slow down," and the child struggles to get through the dysfluency and receives more negative feedback; this in turn creates anxiety, which increases stuttering (http://webpages.marshall.edu/`lynch4/fluency.html, 97). Others feel there may be organic or psychological causes. Increasingly, we believe there is a physical/neurological cause (Ahlbach, 1997).

During the preschool years, stuttering is episodic and may occur because the child is upset, anxious, under pressure to communicate, or has a lot to say. Approximately 25 percent of all children go through a stage of development when they stutter. For 4 percent of these children, the stuttering may last six months or more ("Did you know . . . ," 1997). Concern arises, usually during the early elementary school years, when the stuttering is more chronic, more consistent, and not set off by anything (http://webpages.marshall.edu/`lynch4/fluency.html, 1997). The child may begin to see himself as a stutterer. There are danger signs that teachers can detect before children have reached this stage. The first has to do with the frequency of nonfluencies. More than two sound or syllable repetitions or more than one sound prolongation per 100 words spoken is a danger sign (Gottwald et al., 1985). Additional signs include part-word repetitions, especially if these repetitions are repeated more than twice and/or have an irregular rhythm: "Da-daddy," "Da-da-da daddy," or "Da———ddy." Children who are tense and fearful are also at risk for developing stuttering.

As adults, it is important that we give children time to talk and that we learn to listen. Language therapy can help children overcome stuttering, as well as help them learn techniques to diminish the intensity of the stuttering. Table 11.2 provides some useful guidelines.

TABLE 11.2 GUIDELINES FOR WORKING WITH CHILDREN WHO STUTTER

Do not imply that stuttering is a bad habit.

Do not tell stutterers to stop and start over.

Do not tell them to stop and think what to say.

Do not help them with words with which they are having trouble.

Wait for the children to get it out for themselves.

Do not tell them to talk slowly unless they speak too rapidly to articulate.

Do not tell them to talk faster, in a low voice, high voice, to swallow, to take a deep breath first, and so on.

Do not call on them when they don't volunteer or when they are tired and harassed.

If children do not know they stutter, do not call it to their attention.

If they are aware of their stuttering, do not protect them by pretending that their speech is normal.

Try not to make the tempo of home and school life too strenuous.

Do not make children compete for a chance to talk; let them have their turn at activities or during group discussions.

Do not let stutterers or other children feel they can "catch" stuttering. Stuttering is not a disease.

Do not require children to participate in competitive activities that require rapid verbal responses (reading flash cards, spelling bees, etc.).

Adapted from http://webpages.marshall.edu/`lynch4/fluency.html, 97

Communication Variation

There are many differences in communication across groups and cultures. A regional, social, or cultural/ethnic variation is not considered to be a language or communication disorder. Some variations in the use of the English language may relate to learning English as a second language and may reflect the differences between the structure of languages. This is not a communication disorder.

Some children have such severe communication disorders that normal spoken communication is not a long-range option for them. For some, manual communication is an option; others lack the motor coordination. In these cases, a system of augmentative communication needs to be developed. Augmentative communication is an alternative communication system that is used to supplement the communication skills of a child either temporarily or permanently, such as communication boards, computers with speech synthesizers, and so on (ASHA, 1982).

There are both "low-tech" and "high-tech" augmentative communication systems. For young children, a communication board is most likely the first step. Such a communication board consists of pictures of important caregiving events or activities. Children point to the picture of the activity they want to do, or the teacher points to pictures of various activities until the children indicate their preference.

To work effectively, augmentative communication must be designed on an individual level for each child involved. The creative software that is being designed for microcomputers is greatly impacting augmentative communication and has tremendous potential. Even for young children, the use of touch-sensitive control pads can facilitate communication. Voice synthesizers are relatively inexpensive and plug into the printer port of most computers. Rather than printing what is typed, the synthesizer "speaks" it. For example, if the child touches the color red on an adapted keyboard, the word "red" is said.

Early Development of Language and Communication

To determine the nature and extent of a suspected communication impairment, you must first be familiar with the stages of normal speech and language development. In the following sections, the speech production sounds given are based on the age at which 75 percent of the children master sounds. Information is adapted from Herr and Libby, 1990; Liebergott, Favors, von Hippel, and Needleman, 1978; Machado, 1990; and Wang and Baron, 1997.

0 to 3

Young infants respond to speech by looking at the speaker. They respond differently to differences in a speaker's voice (friendly vs. unfriendly). They also turn to sound sources. Near their first birthday, they respond with gestures to words such as "Hi," "Bye-bye," and "Up," as well as with stopping actions when told "No" firmly. Expressively, infants make crying and noncrying sounds. They smile, coo, babble, and repeat syllables (ma-ma-ma-ma). They enjoy taking turns with adults and will vocalize after an adult vocalizes. They can communicate meaning through intonation and the attempts to imitate sounds. Their first word appears at about 12 months. Infants who do not respond to environmental sounds or voices by 6 months should be referred for evaluation as should children who do not make cooing or comfort sounds (but only cry) by 4 months (Wang & Baron, 1997).

Between 1 and 2 years, infants can get familiar objects on request: "Bring me the ball." They begin to understand prepositions such as on, in, and under. They respond to simple commands like "Close the door," and to simple "where" questions: "Where's Jose?" They also enjoy listening to simple stories. About a fourth of their speech is comprehensible to nonfamily members.

Toddlers' sounds become more wordlike and meaningful. They now refer to themselves by name, and they are very clear about the use of "my" and "mine" to indicate possession and are beginning to use the pronouns "me," "I," and "you." Toddlers use successive one-word utterances and begin to make two-word utterances: "All gone." All vowel sounds are learned, plus /h/, /p/, /b/, /m/, /n/. Toddlers can answer routine questions, say the names of familiar objects in pictures, and identify body parts on a doll as well as on their own body. They like to ask "what" questions and have a vocabulary of about 50 words. About half of their speech should be comprehensible to nonfamily members. Children who speak fewer than 10 words and do not seem to comprehend simple directions or requests by age 2, should be referred. By 2-and-a-half, concern arises about children with very limited vocabularies, those who have no phrases of two or more words, cannot answer simple questions, and whose speech is entirely unintelligible (Wang & Baron, 1997).

By 3 years, children can point to pictures of familiar objects when they are named, identify objects when told their use, and understand questions relating to what and where. They also clearly understand the negations "no," "not," "can't," and "don't," and they enjoy simple stories again and again and again.

Expressively, they can now name many common objects and use language as a way of communicating thoughts. They usually enjoy using language, gain satisfaction from expressing themselves and being understood, and show frustration when they are not understood. They understand and use abstract words such as "up," "down," "now," "later." They are beginning to refer to themselves as "me" instead of using their proper name, and they can now state their first and last names. Words are combined into short phrases, and they are starting to ask primitive questions. The consonant sounds /k/, /d/, /f/, /ng/, /y/, /t/, and /w/ have been added to their repertoire, as well as the use of plurals. They use early forms of negation: "No," "No want," "Can't open it." By 3 years, the average child has a vocabulary of 250 to 900 words. Three-year-olds who cannot engage in simple conversation, have no short sentences, and whose speech is largely unintelligible are of concern (Wang & Baron, 1997).

3 to 6

Children's understanding of relationships is increasing. They can use words like "because" and contingencies such as "if" and "when." They also understand size comparatives (large–larger). They are less concrete and are beginning to understand the vocabulary of time (tomorrow) as well as the concept of "pretend." They can carry out a series (two to four) of related directions. Although children often talk to themselves while playing, language is becoming more socially directed. Children are beginning to ask questions for information and for social contacts. They use simple sentence structures and can repeat at least one nursery rhyme. They are beginning to use the simple future tense, "I will," as well as pronouns that refer to others (he, his, and so on).

They have added the consonant sounds /g/, /s/, /r/, /l/, /sh/, and /ch/, and their vocabulary increases rapidly. They love new words. By 4 years of age, all of their words should be intelligible. When four-year-olds have difficulty learning new concepts, explaining events, and following two-step directions, there is concern. Likewise, when their speech is unclear or they are still simply echoing speech with no complete sentences, a referral is indicated (Wang & Baron, 1997).

Children's language skills are increasing in many different areas. They can follow three unrelated commands and they enjoy listening to longer stories. They now understand three levels of comparatives (big, bigger, biggest) as well as the sequencing of events: "First we have group time, then free play, snack, stories, outside play, and then we go home."

Children now talk a lot—not always to tell or ask something important, but to seek attention and companionship. They love silly language. They use a variety of sentence structures and use almost all pronouns appropriately. Now they can explain why they want to do something a certain way as well as asking "when," "how," and "why" questions. The consonant sound /th/ and their vocabulary has grown to about 1,200 to 1,500 words by around age 4.

Between 5 and 6 years, children demonstrate many preacademic skills. Except for the understanding of complex vocabulary, they function at an adult level in understanding communication. They are curious and ask many questions. They use complete sentences and give full information and thus need opportunities to talk with someone who is interested and who will listen attentively. They have added the consonant sound /v/, use different verb tenses, and have a vocabulary of about 2,000 words.

6 to 9

Now children demonstrate academic skills and function at an adult level in understanding communication. They understand more complex vocabulary. The language structures are mastered and are being refined for irregulars. The consonant sounds /z/ and /j/ are added, and their vocabulary had grown to about 2,600+ words. Children are adding reading and writing to their communication.

Language and Other Variables

There are many variables that can affect a child's language and communication development. The child must have an intact sensory system for extracting relevant information from the environment and the capability of processing the information, understanding what was seen and heard, and remembering the important facts. The environment must provide adequate stimulation for the child to learn and be communicatively reinforcing to the child to stimulate further interactions (Peterson, 1987).

Children with a disorder in their sensory system that interferes with their ability to receive relevant information from their environment will very likely encounter language and/or speech problems. Children with hearing impairments may not be able to differentiate among sounds or learn spoken language if they are unable to hear those sounds or how words are used. Children with physical impairments may have difficulty developing language concepts if they cannot interact with materials.

Some children encounter difficulties processing verbal and written information that lead to problems developing a good language base. These processing problems can include how the child perceives the information received; how the child stores the information; and how the child uses the information. A child with poor memory skills may be unable to remember object label names from one time to another, resulting in a poor vocabulary.

The environment plays an important role in the development of language. An environment severely lacking in appropriate materials to facilitate development may have the secondary effect of delaying language development. Experience with a wide variety of materials strongly contributes to children's overall development, which includes language.

Language is essential in learning cognitive skills. If the environment causes the language delay, then it will most likely have the secondary effect of limiting cognitive development. The inability to understand and process what is communicated will interfere with learning. If brain damage is the cause of a language disorder, the damage to the brain may affect cognitive processing as well.

The quantity and quality of social interactions children have also contributes to language development. Children are motivated to communicate when they receive consistent and repetitious, socially reinforcing interactions. The failure of the environment to respond appropriately to children's interactions will eventually result in their not being motivated to interact with others.

An inability to communicate ideas and thoughts can be very frustrating for children. This is especially true for children with intact language systems but unclear speech output. If children know what they want to say but are unable to express their message, extreme frustration and stress can result. This can lead to their developing behavioral problems or to withdrawal from interactions. In either situation, the children need to have alternative means by which to communicate their messages.

Assessment of Atypical Language and Communication Development

Before looking at the assessment process per se, there are some areas that need to be considered.

Cultural Diversity and Age

Language is a very personal thing, and language styles are different depending on the individual and her cultural or ethnic identification. Certainly, we would expect language differences in children who are learning English as a second language. However, there is also much variation in individuals who are native English speakers. Some children who did not speak and write Standard American English have previously been diagnosed as having a language disorder (Salvia & Ysseldyke, 1995). Although there is debate about acceptance of nonstandard English, there is agreement that children who speak nonstandard English should not be classified as having a language disorder. In some instances, there are regional as well as cultural uses of language. Think of such terms as "hot dog," "frankfurter," and "wiener." If only one of these is an acceptable answer on a language assessment, then some children are penalized not for their lack of vocabulary, but for using a regional label.

Language assessment of young children is tied closely to their age. Some sounds and linguistic structures are not part of young children's repertoire.

Subareas of Language

When assessing language, we must look at its five different areas: phonology (speech sounds), morphology (affixes), pragmatics (social skills), semantics (word use), and syntax (word order). In addition, we need to look at each of these areas in the context of both receptive and expressive language (Salvia & Ysseldyke, 1995).

Goals of Formal Language Assessment

The goals of assessment are to determine whether in fact there is a communication and language disorder and in what area or areas this disorder lies. The next step is to determine the goals for intervention and then to establish a plan to meet those goals and implement the plan. The final component is to develop a method for monitoring whether or not the goals are being met.

To determine whether a child has a communication and/or language disorder, we typically use standardized tests. Unlike a global intelligence test, we use tests in many specific areas. For example, the Comprehensive Receptive and Expressive Vocabulary Test (Wallace & Hammill, 1994) is a relatively new individually administered test of vocabulary (semantics) and assesses both receptive and expressive language. The Carrow Elicited Language Inventory (Carrow, 1974) is also individually administered; it is designed to look at morphology (affixes) and syntax (word order) in expressive language. The Arizona Articulation Proficiency Test (Fudala & Reynolds, 1991) is one of the most frequently used tests to assess articulation. You should be aware that standardized testing in language development is related to many specific areas and that several tests may be required to develop a profile.

There are some concerns with the assessment of language. One is whether the formal assessment actually reflects the child's spontaneous language. Testing situations may be new and frightening for children. To the extent that children's response to this situation influences their language, the measure will not be an accurate reflection of their spontaneous language. A second concern relates to the use of standardized tests of language. The step from getting the results of a language test to generating goals and ways to implement them is a large one. Speech and language therapists may want to work on particular articulation problems or other specific areas of language, whereas the early childhood specialist may feel the most appropriate goal is to increase the number, complexity, and length of children's sentences in spontaneous conversation. A third concern of assessment is whether or not the child being assessed has the same characteristics as the sample on which the measure was standardized; in other words, are test norm results valid for this child (Salvia & Ysseldyke, 1995)? If they are not, then it is difficult to figure out what to do. One solution is that early childhood educators often complement the formal assessment with their own informal assessment.

Informal Assessment of Language Development

If you are concerned about a child's speech and language, begin informally. First, look up the child's birth date. This alone might resolve the problem. If this child is one of the youngest in the class and your basis for comparison is the older children, the difference between them may be a developmental one that will disappear with time. In early childhood, even a few months has a considerable effect. As a further check, find out if this child was premature and is developmentally even younger.

If you are still concerned, assign the child to a small group with several others who are close in age. (Don't include children who are cognitively delayed or advanced.) While doing language activities with the children, note who volunteers the most and least often. Take language samples from each child and compare them for sentence length, sentence structure, vocabulary, concepts, and articulation (note omissions, distortions, or substitutions of sounds). An easy way to obtain language samples is by recording small group time. Do this on at least two occasions to allow for a child's having a bad or good day. If the child is in the top to middle of this group, there is probably no cause for concern. If the child is at the bottom, continue gathering information.

As you continue your observations, note how the child uses materials not related to language. How many different materials are used? Are the materials used appropriately? This information will help you decide if the child is delayed in other areas. If so, the child's speech and language problems may have an underlying cause, such as a developmental delay or lack of an experiential background.

The next step is to determine the gap between the child's comprehension and production of language. During the early childhood years, almost all children have a greater ability to understand language than to speak it; you are looking for a significantly wider gap between the two than is expected.

Analyze the child's speech carefully. If the child is having trouble pronouncing words, note exactly which sounds are difficult. Vowels and the consonants /p/, /b/, /m/, and /w/ are easiest for a young child to pronounce, followed by /t/, /d/, /n/, /k/, /g/, /f/, and /v/. The more difficult sounds are /s/, /z/, /l/, /r/, /ch/, /th/, /sh/, /j/, /bl/, and /cr/. If the child only has problems with the last set of sounds, which children normally take longer to learn, reevaluate a few months later. Be sure to look for the obvious. If the child doesn't have front teeth, some sounds will not be possible.

After carefully observing the child alone and with others, if you still feel there is a problem, schedule a conference with the parents. Alert them to your concerns, then accept whatever they say. Your goals in the first conference are to gather more information and to begin to make the parents aware of the problem. Schedule a class visit for them in about two weeks; if this isn't possible, make a videotape to show them. Have them observe (or show them) their own child with an age-mate, just as you did. At your second conference, discuss and compare their observations with your own. (Their opinions may have changed as they became more conscious of their child's speech and language and listened more carefully.)

Consider making a home visit. You will have an opportunity to watch and listen to the family interact more informally. You may learn that the child's speech or language is modeled after the family pattern, which means you are unlikely to convince the parents there is a problem. If you still feel the problem exists, discuss it. Even if parents do not share your concerns, there is still much you can do with classroom programming to foster this child's speech and language development.

If you and the parents agree the child has a problem, you might suggest that the child be assessed. The family physician is probably the best choice to begin, as there may be a medical reason for the problem. The physician might then refer the child to an audiologist to test hearing and to a speech and language therapist, and to a psychologist for testing in social and intellectual development.

No matter how the parents choose to obtain further information about the child's needs, there frequently is a long lag between your initial concern and a final conclusion. Often, as long as a year or two may elapse. Young children can be difficult to assess, test results may be inconclusive, and many times the decision is made to "wait and see." In the meantime, you can develop ideas for helping this child within your classroom.

Guidelines

If the child has been diagnosed, read the child's file. Talk with the parents and gain their perceptions (this is in addition to formal IEP team conferences). Ask the parents' permission to get copies of all the available information if you don't already have it. Find out what the diagnosis means to the child's total development. (Is the language delay part of another disorder?) Ask the child's speech and language therapist when she expects to be in your classroom and the kinds of activities you can do that would be helpful. Whether the child has an official diagnosis or not, you must assess where in the language process the problem is, its severity, and how you will adapt your programming to meet this child's needs. As you listen to children throughout the day, look for their most and least comfortable times with speech. Most children show a pattern. Although each child's situation will be different, the following guidelines will be helpful:

1. Use simple, concrete language and lots of repetition. Simplify your grammar and vocabulary and use shorter sentences. Children will have fewer problems processing the information in this form. Also, if you talk fast, slowing down your rate of delivery may be helpful.

2. Ask few direct questions, especially during group time. This places high demands on a child for speech even when the response requested is just a short one.

3. Use short, simple, clear directions, and ask children to repeat directions. Reward children for following through on the directions given.

4. Plan for language development. Set aside time each day that specifically emphasizes language development. (The activity may vary, but the intent shouldn't.)

5. Increase children's interest in themselves and their environment. Encourage children's desire to communicate.

6. Provide a secure, consistent, well-organized environment.

7. Set up activities to provide noncompetitive peer interaction.

8. Include the child with a language impairment in group activities. The child need not have a speaking role if that is anxiety-provoking. Nonverbal group participation may be a prerequisite to verbal participation.

9. Create a need for speech. If the child uses gestures instead of speech, deliberately (but not obviously) misunderstand briefly and name other objects. Before the child becomes frustrated,

give the child what was requested, but use the word in one or two phrases or sentences. Gradually, over several encounters, increase the number of misunderstandings and incorrect guesses until the child is slightly frustrated by your "stupidity."

10. Give a lot of running commentary. Give a play-by-play description of what either you or the child is doing. Children learn to talk by listening.

11. Be a good listener. Give the child your undivided attention or explain that you can't listen then, but will soon. Arrange to do it as soon after as possible.

12. Reward the child for correct speech, but do not criticize or punish lack of speech or incorrect speech.

13. Model good speech and language.

14. Differentiate between speech and language and reinforce appropriately. For example, you might tell a child, "I'm glad you want to tell me about your picture, but I'm having trouble understanding what you are saying. Can you tell me with different words?" Therapists traditionally teach children to understand the difference between "good language" "poor speech."

15. Reinforce learning through visual and tactile experiences.

16. Structure lessons to provide children with more successes than failures.

17. Use simple, one-step directions; gradually work up to more complex directions. If necessary, have the child repeat or verbally "walk through" the directions before doing an activity.

18. Reinforce spontaneous language independently of the quality of the speech. Respond to the meaning of children's communications.

19. Some children may imitate speech problems or make fun of the way others talk. Do not reinforce the children, and tell them clearly that you find their behavior unacceptable. The imitation problem is usually a short-term one that goes away without reinforcement, but teasing may continue indefinitely. Help children develop the skills to handle this independently.

Language and cognition are related. For children to use their language, they need something to talk about. Expand the children's awareness of the environment. Lack of stimulation may be a factor in underdeveloped language. Use field trips and many hands-on experiences that provide concrete learning experiences and materials to introduce and reinforce concepts. Children cannot be expected to talk about something they have no knowledge of. Given opportunities to explore the environment, children often need several experiences to gain the necessary information. Remember the learning cycle—awareness, exploration, inquiry/experimentation, and utilization—and provide children with opportunities for different levels of learning.

Encourage children to speak, and reinforce attempts to do so. Don't rush children when speaking or criticize the speech. If a child mispronounces a word, don't correct it; instead, use it correctly in a sentence in response. Provide visual cues to speech sounds; if you are asking about a red shirt, point to it. Reinforce newly learned speech patterns.

Curriculum Adaptations

Children with communication impairments require few curriculum adaptations. Rather, they may need some areas of the curriculum expanded to meet their needs. Following are general suggestions organized by curriculum area. This is not a complete list, but it will help you to begin programming.

Social Awareness: Self-Esteem, Inclusion, Social Studies, Health and Safety

Children with communication disorders may not have good skills at joining groups. Help them develop the language necessary to be included. Think about the priorities in language development: Work on the language skills that will increase the child's safety and on auditory identification of warning signals. Broaden language skills through field trips, followed by language experience stories. This sequence supports both the social studies and language aspects of the experience. Include listening skills and following directions: "Show me what you do when you see a red light." Work on vocabulary to go with the actions. As children's vocabulary expands, help them become more detailed and specific in their speech.

Self-Esteem. As children learn more about themselves, their self-awareness improves. Give them the support to use their language skills to communicate their wants and needs. As they build skills, teach them ways to be assertive.

1. Incorporate into your curriculum different ways of communicating to broaden children's background about communications; include different written and spoken languages, American Sign Language, computers with voice simulators, communication boards, and so on.

2. Have children make their own communication board. Discuss what to include. Talk with them about what is important to be able to communicate. Then discuss the limitations and the frustrations of not being understood and especially how the person who isn't understood might feel.

3. Help children learn about their body and how it reacts in different situations and how this impacts their speech and language. (How do they feel when asked a question in a group situation? When someone calls them names?) Talk about

Computers broaden communication experiences for children. Appropriate software supports children in generating written communication, and connecting to the Internet gives children an additional source of reference material.

how children can handle these situations. Initially, the plan may involve your intervention; however, as children learn and grow, they may be able to take increasing responsibility.

Inclusion. Children with communication problems may not seek out other children; they may play alone or near another child. Encourage cooperative play so that children can learn to interact comfortably with peers. When they do play with others, these children are rarely leaders; they often receive instructions from classmates rather than give them, and as they are often reluctant to argue with the leader as others might, they may end up with the least desirable roles. Discourage and, if possible, eliminate teasing (this isn't always easy). It is important for all children to feel they belong. Children need to know they are all similar in some ways and different in others. Language may be an area in which they are different.

1.   Have children play with language, perhaps mispronouncing an unfamiliar word. Ask children how they feel and how they would feel if others criticized or made fun of them. Ask them if they would try to pronounce the word again and how they would feel.

2.   Discuss the importance of turn taking in language as well as on pieces of equipment. Point out that sometimes they may need to wait for others to have time to say what they want to communicate. It is important for them to wait, as well as you.

3.   Use books without words.

Social Studies.   Speech and language skills can be integrated into the social studies curriculum through conversation and role playing. Help the children identify similarities and differences throughout the immediate environment, the region, the country, and the world. Your goal is to promote the concept of diversity. At the same time, you are promoting the children's awareness of differences and similarities in speech and language without making judgments.

1.   Names are different in other languages. Some common names can be discussed that translate well: John in Spanish is Juan; in French, Jacques; in German, Johann. However, there are some names for which there are no equivalents. Discuss these as well.

2.   Make a tape recording of people from different regions in North America (with the characteristic accent). If possible, have them all say the same sentences so that the children can more readily grasp the differences. Make a similar tape of people from different countries or those for whom English is a second language.

3.   Act out situations that require the children to assume roles that have different speech patterns associated with them, for example, cowhand, police officer, father, mother, baby.

Health and Safety.   Speech and language production requires the coordination of muscles from the waist up, the speech organs, and the brain. It is one of the most complicated human processes. Children need to be made aware of the body parts involved. Listening to someone who has nasal congestion helps children learn the nose's function; a sore throat demonstrates the throat's contribution to speech.

Teeth. Discuss how to care for teeth. Invite a dentist to visit the class. As children begin to lose their baby teeth, discuss what sounds become difficult. Have them discover the role teeth play in making sounds.

Jaw. Use scissors to illustrate the hinge-like action of the jaw. Have children use their fingers to feel the bones and muscles as they drop their jaw. Again, experiment with sound as the jaw lowers and rises.

Tongue. Do tongue exercises with the class. Let the children use mirrors to watch their tongue move. Have them pair off and watch each other.

Vocal Cords. Have children place their hands on their throat to feel the vocal cords vibrate. See if they can feel a difference in sounds. Use a rubber band to show how the vocal cords work, stretching it tight for high sounds and only slightly for low ones.

1. Teach children the language of safety: Stop/go (red/green); fast/slow; quickly/slowly; carefully, quietly, and so on. Children not only need to know the words but need to have a sensorimotor understanding of the behaviors.

2. Go on imaginary walks with the children to demonstrate language safety concepts. Children need to know that moving quietly means walking on tiptoes very carefully without talking.

3. Talk about voices and how they are used and where they are used appropriately. Talk about what happens when children shout, scream, or talk loudly for too long.

4. Help children learn about the various health problems related to the speech-producing parts of the body, how to describe their symptoms, and what is typically done about them.

5. Blowing an object like a pinwheel helps develop the muscles of the mouth, gives children practice in closing off the palate and throat, and teaches breath control.

Language and Literacy: Speaking, Listening, Reading, and Writing

The language and literacy curriculum consists of speaking, listening, reading, and writing, and it is the area most emphasized for children with communication and language impairments. Communication skills cannot be viewed in isolation, but rather are related to the acquisition of all language skills. "Children who fail to acquire a complex sentence repertoire are considered at high risk for problems in reading and writing, which are language-based skills" (Garrard, 1987, p. 18).

In particular, these children need to develop and refine listening, attention, and memory skills. Language arts can be used to increase spontaneous language as well as to develop readiness skills. Check with the child's speech and language therapist for specific advice and additional activities. Children with communication and language disorders must concentrate on the development of underlying inner language skills by participating in many firsthand experiences. If children are reluctant to speak, create a need for them to talk: Instead of asking children yes/no questions ("Do you want to play with the blocks today?"), use forms such as "Where do you want to play today?" to elicit more speech. For children who need work on specific speech sounds, read stories and ask questions that require them to practice those sounds. Some children have articulation problems because they do not listen accurately or they don't have good speech models. Their speech reflects what they hear. It is important that you provide a good model for them. Highlight the interrelationship between expressive and receptive language and reading and writing. Children with few skills in listening and speaking may be reluctant to participate in reading and writing literacy activities. Negative feelings about spoken language may carry over into these areas. Children need to be encouraged and rewarded for participation.

Provide the child with firsthand experiences followed by discussions and opportunities for internalizing concepts and expanding key ideas. Using a farm as an example, you might:

> Visit a farm.
>
> Generate a language experience story about the trip to the farm.
>
> Read a book about a farm at story time.
>
> Play farm animal lotto.
>
> Discuss and imitate the sounds that farm animals make.

These suggestions are ordered on the principles that children learn contextually rather than in isolation, they learn the concrete before the abstract, and gradually increasing exposure to a concept increases the depth of learning.

Speaking. Children with communication and language impairments may speak only when absolutely necessary because of the negative feedback they have received in the past: "You talk funny." Speaking in front of others may be a threatening experience for these children. When asked questions in a group situation, they may respond with a shrug or "Don't know." It is easier for them not to know something than to risk ridicule by the other children. Encourage speech in one-to-one situations and in small groups before you work on large groups. Which speech skills to emphasize will depend on the needs of each child; areas include fluency, voice, resonance, and articulation, especially as they relate to intelligibility of speech. Provide many opportunities to practice in nonthreatening situations. Speaking requires practice and the need to communicate information.

1. Use puppets to encourage children to talk. Give the child cues to encourage speaking when necessary. As children become more confident, have them play with each other using the puppets.

2. Have telephones available and encourage children to talk on the telephone with you and with each other.

Fingerplays are good for children with communication disorders. Although done with a group, fingerplays cause children to lose their self-consciousness, in part because they can participate in the motions without speaking. The motions also provide visual cues that help children understand the words. Fingerplays that rhyme are good for ear training. Those that have the sounds the child is working on are also useful.

1. Use fingerplays to stimulate body awareness. Those that involve the face and mouth area especially benefit the child.

2. Fingerplays such as Teensy, Weensy Spider facilitate eye-hand coordination as well as motor and manual control.

Listening.   Provide varied listening experiences to help children discriminate and associate sounds. Describe the child's behavior out loud: "Now you are going up the stairs." Read books to expand the child's world as well as provide an opportunity to practice different sounds. Begin with stories about familiar events, including books about children, families, and animals.

1. Read stories that emphasize specific sounds, ones that are easy or hard for the child, depending on your objectives. *Sammy Snake* is an example of a story emphasizing the *s* sound.

2. Read stories that emphasize rhyming words (e.g., *Each Peach Pear Plum*), voice control ("The Whispering Rabbit and Other Stories"), and listening skills ("What I Hear in My School").

3. To foster ear training, read stories and do fingerplays that have rhymes until the children are familiar with them. Then read the stories with pauses to let the group fill in the rhyming word. The children will also enjoy nonsense rhyming games. You say a word and have the children call out real and made-up rhyming words for you to write on the board.

Reading.   Young children with communication impairments are likely to have difficulty learning to read later. While they are concentrating on pronunciation, their comprehension of the reading material suffers. Their reading rate will be slower than average and their phrasing will be poor. In fact, reading may become so unpleasant they may avoid it whenever possible. Particular care should be taken to develop their reading literacy skills to forestall these problems.

When you teach reading literacy skills, you will most often use visual and auditory means. Children need to see and say letter sounds and blends regardless of where they are positioned in the word. Ear training, the ability to listen well, is one prerequisite that speech- and language-impaired children may find difficult to master, yet, it is essential to the development of literacy and the ability to communicate.

Matching and sorting tasks can be either perceptual or conceptual in nature or combine elements of both. Perceptual matching requires the children to match like letters to each other. They don't need to know what the letters stand for. When the task is a conceptual one, the children are required to abstract

Figure 11.1

the idea and generalize it to another instance, for example, when going from lower-case letters to upper-case letters or when going from script (printing) to cursive. Conceptual matching can be used not only in reading literacy but also in other curriculum areas. Examples of both are presented in Figures 11.1 and 11.2.

A picture file set up in a flexible format allows for later expansion. Divide the file into three sets: beginning consonant sounds, medial (middle) consonant sounds, and ending consonant sounds. Include the consonant blends (*bl*ouse, pum*p*kin, sta*nd*) in each set. Vowels may be omitted because children rarely have problems with them. Organize the sets alphabetically and store them in three file boxes. Once you have developed the three basic sets, you are prepared for a variety of activities.

1. Have children find all the pictures with a specified beginning sound. (When ending an exercise, call out the sounds in alphabetical order. The pictures will automatically be organized for putting away.) Do the same thing for beginning consonant blends. Repeat the process for the middle and final position. When you introduce this activity, you might have the name on the front of the card; the activity is easier when the child can match the initial letters as well as the sound.

2. Set out four picture cards (three of which have the same ending sounds), say the words, then have the children identify the one that is different. Gradually give the children more responsibilities, thereby increasing the level of difficulty. You might have the children say the words, have them create sets for each other, and so on.

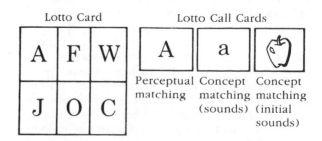

Figure 11.2

3. A more challenging and creative activity is making sound books. Introduce one sound at a time. Write the sound at the top of a piece of paper. Have the children find pictures of objects that have that sound and paste the pictures on the page. When the child has a page for each sound, they can be made into books.

4. Letter Lotto (or variations of bingo) is a fun way to teach letter recognition (see Figure 11.2). When children can match identical letters, add pictures as well as lower-case letters to the game.

5. The development of letter memory or letter sounds can be facilitated by making two sets of the Lotto call cards and playing Concentration. Start by turning four to six pairs of cards face down. If this is too easy, add more pairs.

6. Incorporate reading into other areas where children need to read the directions to complete a project. Support the written word with pictures.

Writing. As in speech, the focus in early writing is on the meaning of children's writing. If the initial focus on written work is on the spelling and punctuation, young writers can become very discouraged. Allowing children to spell creatively (how it sounds or looks to them, regardless of accuracy) increases their fluency and allows writing to serve as an outlet for children who are not comfortable speaking. Correcting children's spelling as they are just beginning to write causes some of the same problems as correcting their speech. If the task becomes onerous, children try not to participate; if children do participate, they take as few risks as possible.

Writing provides both challenges and solutions for children with communication disorders. First, they need to establish the connection between the written and spoken word. Do this informally by pointing out to children that you cannot see words if their hand is over them, or that you cannot read the book if it is upside down. Write down what they say, but do not hesitate to ask them to slow down, pointing out that you cannot write as quickly as they can talk. Use language experience stories and support all of children's attempts at writing, regardless of the quality of the letters or the spelling.

1. Write their names on their papers and point out to children that you do this so they will not get mixed up. Compare two pictures and then explain that if you forget who made them, you can look at the name.

2. Support children's verbalizations by writing down what they say and then reading it back to them. Again, point out the advantage of a written language by reading what the children said at a later date.

3. Discuss writing as a symbol system and point out that the English language uses the alphabet they are familiar with but some other languages do not. Have the children create a syllabary (a type

of dictionary); they can decide on the written configurations that stand for words or syllables. They can use this to write to each other. (In this instance, spelling is irrelevant.)

4. Have a writing center and support writing as a process that involves authorship, illustration, editing, and publishing. Support children in each of these stages of the process.

Discovery: Mathematics, Science, and Computers

For children with only speech problems, the discovery area is not likely to be different from other children in the classroom. Like others, they need concrete experiences to learn best in this area. Emphasize the vocabulary that goes with the experiences of learning math and science: taller, shorter, more, less, the same, equal, one more, one less. Children can learn through science how sounds are made and which parts of the body are involved in making various sounds. They can learn to use objects such as a feather or pinwheel to observe the effect of their breath. Computers offer another opportunity for communicating without the need to speak.

Mathematics. Children with communication problems usually have math skills comparable to their classmates. They often enjoy math, as it can be learned with a minimum of speech. Math, then, can give these children a feeling of achievement.

1. Use math concepts to facilitate speech and language development. Have children count and sort objects that make sounds and objects that don't. Have them count the number of times a sound is made.

2. Make number books by having children cut out a specified number of pictures beginning with the same sound. You might have, for example, one /T/, two /Rs/, three /Ss/, four /Ts/, and so on.

3. Apply the math vocabulary (big/little, more/less, equal) to sounds and body awareness. Tell children to make their bodies as big as they can, then as little. Have them find pictures of an animal with a big tail and of one with a little tail. Do those animals make big/loud sounds or little/soft sounds?

4. Present pictures of geometric shapes and have children draw these shapes in the air with various parts of their bodies. Once they have shown they understand by tracing the shapes with their hands, have them outline the shapes with their jaw, head, tongue, and finally by moving only their eyes.

5. Compare the chest measurements of children after they inhale and after they exhale. This can be done with string or measuring tape, although string is more effective with younger children because they can see which string is longer.

Children need a balance of literacy and creative arts activities. The goal for this literacy activity is reading and following the written directions below. The outcome (boat) shows the children's understanding of the written directions; all of the products should look similar.

3. Decorate paper and glue a stick between the 2 papers.

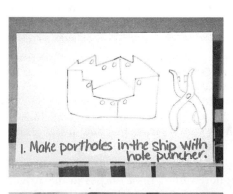

1. Make portholes in the ship with hole puncher.

4. Stick the mast in a lump of playdough in the bottom.

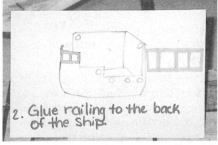

2. Glue railing to the back of the ship.

Science. Science can enhance children's understanding of the mechanics of speech and language. Although fewer verbal skills are required by science than by some other subjects, interest is usually very high and stimulates language use.

1.   Teach some anatomy, especially the organs that produce sound (lips, tongue, teeth, throat, diaphragm).

2.   Use mirrors to help children see the articulatory organs while exploring the concept of mirror images (reversals).

3.   Discuss the sounds different animals make and how they make them. (Crickets, for example, rub their legs together.) Have children experiment making sounds by using different body parts (clap, stomp, slap thighs). Make a tape recording of animal sounds and pair the picture of the animal with the sound.

4.   Talk about how sound is made in nature (thunder, water moving, wind) and how humans make noise (music, talking, working). Discuss how noise cues us to what is happening in our environment. These sounds may be presented on tapes, records, or compact disks. Use pictures when you first present the sounds; the visual reinforces the aural learning.

5.   Discuss the properties of air and its function in speech. Use a beach ball to make air more tangible.

Computers. Computers require no verbal input yet are capable of verbal output. Children who will later depend on computers for communication need to be interacting with them from the preschool years on. Most computers are designed with internal features that can be modified to make them easier for children to use. The manufacturers have this information and willingly share it.

1.   Have a computer with a voice synthesizer in the classroom so children can become familiar with it.

2.   If possible, modify a keyboard to match the child's needs.

3.   Encourage children to learn that computers are part of their life and that they are in control of computers.

Developmental Physical Education and Sensorimotor Skills: Large Motor, Small Motor, Sensorimotor Integration

Sensorimotor activities support the communication process by increasing body awareness. They provide opportunities for communication but are not dependent on it. Supply words for what children are doing in the motor area. Focus fine motor activities on those movements associated with speech, such as breath control and lip and tongue action, in addition to those necessary for visual discrimination, writing, and adaptive skills. Help children increase their body awareness, particularly to learn when they are tense. Many speech problems increase with tension.

Large Motor. Large motor play is usually a pleasure and should be encouraged. Because children's language problems rarely interfere, this may prove to be one of their strengths.

1.   Use large motor play to foster a sense of group belonging.

2.   Help classmates see children's strengths in this area.

3.   Blocks are one activity where speech requirements are few but opportunities for speech are many. As cooperative play increases, children talk more to each other.

Small Motor. Children may need to focus on the small muscles of their body; eye movements are necessary for reading, the hand and fingers for writing, as well as the facial muscles for speaking.

1.   Finger strength is necessary for holding a crayon or pencil. Start with large writing tools, then provide many opportunities for children to pick up small items.

2.   Encourage children to draw or scribble by providing a variety of paper and drawing utensils.

3.   Have children use their breath to do things such as blow up beach balls or make pinwheels turn very slowly or quickly.

Sensorimotor Integration. Children need to develop their ability to listen in coordination with seeing and touching. Sensory integration and eye-hand coordination can be accomplished through small motor play.

1.   Use activities that pair listening skills with visual or tactile skills: "Turn the page when you hear the tone."

2.   Use activities that help establish a hand preference (coloring, turning nuts on bolts, eating). (It is irrelevant which hand is preferred.)

Creative Arts: Visual Arts, Music, Creative Movement, and Dramatic Play

Creative arts offer children the ability to develop skills with much less emphasis on the specific product. Children may become so absorbed in the creative arts that they forget their reluctance to talk as they discover they want to share their work with others. Music can provide a nonthreatening atmosphere for using expressive language. Through music, you can encourage children to attempt speech and to imitate other children and adults. Include songs and activities that concentrate on sounds that are difficult for them to produce. Creative movement allows children to participate without speech and also provides the potential for increasing body awareness. Through dramatic play, children can practice situations before encountering them. They can use puppets, talk on the telephone, or dress up and pretend they are another person as they participate in situations that provide the opportunity for communication.

Visual Arts. Children have the opportunity in the arts to develop fine motor skills. They also get satisfaction from having a product to show for their efforts. Visual art activities provide a nonverbal way of expressing feelings and working off energy.

1. Children can learn to recognize differences in how pencil, crayon, marker, paint, and chalk sound, feel, and look.

2. Encourage children to talk about their pictures (not in response to "What is it?" or, as a naïve graduate student once asked a 3-year-old, "What does this picture represent to you?"). Start out with a comment such as "I like the way you use red in this picture." That's an invitation—you may have shown enough interest to get a response. You might ask, "Does your picture have a story?" Be prepared for the fact that it may not!

3. Make puppets to be used in dramatic play. Often, shy children will vocalize more with puppets.

Music. Music requires children to develop and use different vocal patterns. Blowing instruments and singing stimulate the palate and musculature of the mouth. Because some speech problems don't carry over into singing, this is a vocal activity that can be especially rewarding.

1. Have children make musical instruments to develop listening skills. Make paper plate tambourines filled with beans or rice. They can be played in a group as well as paired according to the different sounds they make. Have children make and use musical instruments that emphasize mouth movements.

2. Children become more aware of their voices as they whistle, hum, and sing high and low, loud and soft. Help them note tension in the lips and the feel of air coming in and out. Help them relate what they learn to speaking.

3. Music is a natural way to teach the concepts of high and low. Reinforce the concepts by having the children stretch their bodies high for the high notes, crouch low for the low notes, and be somewhere in between for the middle notes.

4. Holding notes for long or short periods of time increases breath awareness and improves breath control.

5. Music with movement provides an avenue for interpreting or expressing moods.

6. The rhythm of music also applies to speech and language, especially for children who are dysfluent. Interestingly, these children can often sing things they cannot say. To create more awareness of rhythm, you can have children brush teeth, lower jaws (as if chewing), or even click tongues to a rhythm pattern.

7. Songs with action allow children to participate whether or not they know the words. Actions provide visual cues for learning the words.

8. Records, tapes, and compact disks enhance listening skills, but they should be used with visual aids and an informed adult to help children comprehend the content and purpose.

Creative Movement. Use movement to increase body awareness (especially of speech organs) and to provide relaxation.

1. Have children pretend to be clothes fluttering on the line in a gentle wind. To relax the throat and neck, have the children drop their heads forward (chin toward chest). Have the wind pick up a bit and then die down. Talk with children about the differences. Use a variable speed fan if children seem to have trouble understanding the concept, and hold a piece of clothing in front of it as you change the speeds.

2. Encourage games and movements that use pantomime, like charades, and discuss how frustrating it is not to be understood.

Dramatic Play. Dramatic play provides a safe outlet for energy and an opportunity for children to try out roles without fear of judgment. It also allows children to be a part of a group.

1. At the beginning of the year, the dramatic play area should be an easy, familiar, nondemanding place. Children may drift toward this area, as it represents a tie with home. (This is particularly true of younger children.)

2. Children may be fearful of new situations and the demands this may make on their language skills. Take advantage of dramatic play to have children rehearse the experience beforehand to gain knowledge of what to expect.

3. Puppets encourage speech in a nonthreatening way. Play a recording of characters with very distinctive speech patterns (such as Donald Duck and Mickey Mouse) as a way of reassuring children that puppets can and do sound different.

4. Join children in dramatic play and take a minor role in their play. This allows you to facilitate some children's play without obvious intervention.

Transitions

As children end one activity and prepare to go on to another, there is often some confusion. Turn the confusion into opportunities for learning by taking advantage of transitions.

1. Combine movement and sound to help children get from one area to another: "Walk like a duck and quack as you go to the art area." Ask children to walk as quietly or to make as much noise as they can while going to the learning center of their choice.

2. Increase body awareness and sense of self. Dismiss children by hair and eye color.

Summary

Approximately a fourth of all children who need special educational services either have a primary or a secondary language and communication disorder. For some children, it is a temporary articulation problem, for others a major delay in language development itself, and for still others it is a secondary disorder related to another disability.

Because language has such a strong developmental base, it is sometimes difficult to discern what is problematic and what is part of the normal language development sequence. Assessment of language development is typically broken into specific subareas that have some overlap and also must be understood within the context of both expressive and receptive language.

Children's language development includes several distinct aspects. We are interested in children's ability to make and understand speech and speech sounds, to change meaning, to use language in a social environment, and to understand and use words appropriately.

Language is assessed both formally and informally. When formal assessments are done, they often focus on the separate subareas of language, making it challenging to translate these results into overall goals and planning for children.

Educational Resources

American Speech-Language-Hearing Association (ASLHA)
10801 Rockville Pike
Rockville, MD 20852
(301) 897-5700, (800) 638-8255, FAX (301) 571-0457
Professional society of specialists in speech-language pathology and audiology. Provides a toll-free help line to answer questions about conditions and provides referrals.

Canadian Association for People who Stutter (CAPS)
Association des Begues du Canada Inc.
7801 rue Ste-Claire
Montreal (Quebec) H1L 1v8
(514) 527-1786, (514) 649-0863
http://caps.webcon.net/caps97/step2.html
Offers support and suggestions for students as well as adults who stutter and guidelines for teachers.

Center for Applied Linguistics
1611 North Kent Street
Arlington, VA 22209
Serves as a national and international research and resource center in the application of linguistic science to social and educational problems.

Division for Children with Communication Disorders
Council for Exceptional Children
1920 Association Drive
Reston, VA 22091
A division of the Council for Exceptional Children (CEC) that focuses on communication disorders. It publishes the Journal of Childhood Communication Disorders *as well as a newsletter.*

National Association of Hearing and Speech Agencies
919 18th Street, NW
Washington, DC 20006
Makes referrals to member affiliates and conducts public education campaigns through its bi-monthly magazine and films.

National Stuttering Project
5100 East La Palma Avenue, Suite 208
Anaheim Hills, CA 92807
(800) 364-1677, (714) 693-7480, FAX (714) 693-7554
An organization of individuals who stutter, their families, and those who provide services. They have self-help groups and guides and videotapes as well as conferences.

Specialized Materials

Ablenet
1081 10th Avenue, SE
Minneapolis, MN 55414–1312
(800) 322-0956, FAX (612) 379-9143
Provides a mail order catalogue of communication aids; also produces videotapes and conducts technology workshops.

Jesana Ltd.
979 Saw Mill River Road
Yonkers, NY 10710
(800) 443-4728, FAX (914) 376-0021
Provides a mail order catalogue of speech aids, language software, adapted toys and devices, and other materials for children with disabilities.

Stuttering Foundation of America
PO Box 11749
Memphis, TN 38111-0479

Has a variety of videotapes related to stuttering, including Stuttering and Your Child: A Videotape for Parents *with information on how to help people speak more clearly, as well as self-help guides for parents.*

References

Ahlbach, J. (1997). No easy answers. http://www.mankato.msus.edu/dept/cp,dos/kuster/Infostuttering/ExecDirNSP.html.

American Speech-Language-Hearing Association. (1982). Definitions: Communicative disorders and variations. *ASHA, 24,* 949–950.

Carrow, E. (1974). *Carrow elicited language inventory.* Austin, TX: Learning Concepts.

Did you know . . . (1997). Stuttering Foundation of America. http://www.mankato.msus.edu./dept/cpmdos/kuster/Infostuttering/Didyouknow.html.

Donaldson, M. L. (1995). *Children with language impairments: An introduction.* London, England: Jessica Kingsley.

Ensher, G. (1989). The first three years: Special education perspectives on assessment and intervention. *Topics in Language Disorders, 10*(1), 80–90.

Fudala, J., & Reynolds, W. (1991). *Arizona articulation proficiency test.* Los Angeles, CA: Western Psychological Services.

Garrard, K. (1987). Helping young children develop mature speech patterns. *Young Children, 42*(3), 16–21.

Gottwald, S., Goldbach, P., & Isack, A. (1985). Stuttering: Prevention and detection. *Young Children, 40*(7), 9–14.

Herr, J., & Libby, Y. (1990). *Creative resources for the early childhood classroom.* Albany, NY: Delmar. (http://webpages.marshall.edu/`lynch4/fluency.html, 1997).

Liebergott, J., Favors, A., von Hippel, C., & Needleman, H. (1978). *Mainstreaming preschoolers: Children with speech and language impairments.* Washington, DC: U.S. Department of Health and Human Services.

Machado, J. (1990). *Early childhood experiences in language arts: Emerging literacy* (4th ed.). Albany, NY: Delmar.

Peterson, N. L. (1987). *Early intervention for handicapped and at-risk children: An introduction to early childhood special education.* Denver, CO: Love.

Salvia, J., & Ysseldyke, J. E. (1995). *Assessment* (6th ed.). Boston: Houghton Mifflin.

Tizard, B. (1981). Language at home and at school. In C. B. Cazden (Ed.). *Language in early childhood.* Washington, DC: National Association for the Education of Young Children.

Wallace, G., & Hammill, D. (1994). *Comprehensive receptive and expressive vocabulary.* Austin, TX: Pro-Ed.

Wang, P. P., & Baron, M. A. (1997). Language: A code for communicating. In M. L. Batshaw (Ed.), *Children with disabilities* (4th ed., pp. 275–292). Baltimore: Brookes.

U.S. Department of Education. (1992). *Fourteenth annual report to Congress on implementation of the Individuals with Disabilities Act.* Washington, DC: U.S. Government Printing Office.

Yairi, E., & Ambrose, N. (1992). A longitudinal study of stuttering in children: A preliminary report. *Journal of Speech and Hearing Research, 35,* 755–760.

Chapter 12

CHILDREN WITH COGNITIVE AND DEVELOPMENTAL DELAYS

Watching Andre, you would guess him to be one of the youngest children in the class, yet he is actually one of the oldest. He rarely has much to say, and he doesn't seem to get involved in his play. Most things seems difficult for him. And then, in certain areas, it is as if a light goes on, and he can do things the others can't. His adaptive skills are nearly as good as the other children's, but many things seem to be beyond him. I think about referring him for testing, but I really can't decide if it is just the environment he lives in or if he is not as capable of learning as the others. Or is my program not matching his knowledge base?

This vignette summarizes many of the concerns in the field of early childhood education today. A majority of children who cause concern for teachers look like other children but don't seem to be learning as quickly in one or more areas. We're not as accurate in identifying children with mild delays as we are children with more serious delays. It may not be until a child enters an intellectually demanding environment that adults become concerned about their level of functioning.

Delayed cognitive development is intellectual growth that does not follow the expected rate of cognitive development because of genetic or environmental conditions or a combination of these. Most children with developmental delays follow the same sequence of cognitive skill acquisition as other children, but the rate of acquisition is slower. Some children will not reach the higher level of abstract thinking skills if the brain is not fully developed or is injured.

It is often difficult to identify young children with developmental delays, especially when these delays are mild. Most assessments used with infants and toddlers rely on motor functioning to determine developmental levels. Because these measures don't tap into what we consider cognitive development in older children, we miss children who might profit from early intervention.

Other children who lack motor coordination or have speech and language delays may score poorly on tests. Because of these identification problems and the interrelatedness of growth during the early years, most young children who show delays in cognitive development are referred to as having developmental delays. This acknowledges that their development is delayed but does not imply that it will remain that way. This is a more tentative and general classification than mental retardation and does not carry the same impact. Because it focuses on the child's developmental rate, it leaves the possibility for uneven growth, which assumes the child may catch up developmentally, and alternative diagnoses, for example, language delay or learning disabilities.

In the 1997 amendments to IDEA, the federal government has given states the option to use the term "developmentally delayed" for children birth to 3, birth to 5, or birth to any year they choose up to age 9. Because these options are unevenly accepted, we use the term "cognitively delayed" to focus on this area. We also include information about mental retardation.

Definition and Classification of Cognitive Delays

Cognitive delay is a broad term that can refer to children of all ages and with differing degrees of delayed cognitive development. Within this are two broad categories of children: those who are classified as developmentally delayed (children 0 to 9 years) and those who are classified as mentally retarded.

Professionals today are reluctant to classify young children as mentally retarded. The requirements for this diagnosis are more stringent than they have been in the past. Misdiagnosis is a concern because of the stigma attached to this particular label and because of the overidentification of children from ethnic/cultural minorities (Individuals with Disabilities Education Act [IDEA], 1997). Concern relates to the child developing a poor self-concept, the negative view of others, and the belief that mental retardation is a socially constructed condition (Hallahan & Kauffman, 1994). That is, children who are relatively high functioning do not *become* "mentally retarded" until they enter school. (Many children who in the past were classified as mentally retarded are now classified as 249 learning disabled.) Also, we no longer view mental retardation as a permanent condition.

Mental retardation affects approximately 1 percent of the population (Rapoport, 1996). However, rates differ depending on the definition used, the method of assessment, and the population studied (American Psychiatric Association [APA], 1994). The American Association on Mental Deficiency (AAMD) has developed the most widely accepted definition: "*Mental retardation* refers to substantial limitations in present functioning. It is characterized by significantly subaverage intellectual functioning, existing concurrently with related limitations in two or more of the following applicable adaptive skill areas: communication, self-care, home living, social skills, community use, self-direction, health and safety, functional academics, leisure, and work. Mental retardation manifests before age 18" (American Association on Mental Deficiency [AAMD], 1992, p. 5).

Concerned about labeling per se, and also wary of the assessment process, the AAMD (1992) explains the assumptions behind their definition and how it is to be applied:

1. Valid assessment considers cultural and linguistic diversity as well as differences in communication and behavior factors;

2. The existence of limitations in adaptive skills occurs within the context of community environments typical of the individual's age peers and is indexed to the person's individualized needs for supports;

3. Specific adaptive limitations often coexist with strengths in other adaptive skills or other personal capabilities; and

4. With appropriate supports over a sustained period, the life functioning of the person with mental retardation will generally improve (p. 5).

Previously, the definition of mental retardation was based almost exclusively on IQ scores. Now, although an IQ of 70 to 75 or below is considered below average, there is consensus that additional measures must be used to verify these results and that the results should be reviewed by a multidisciplinary team.

Two elements are important to note here. One is that a child must be well below average in *both* measured intelligence and adaptive behavior. The second is that we no longer regard mental retardation as irreversible, especially for those who are in the mild range. We now believe that with appropriate early educational intervention, some children will no longer be considered mentally retarded, and with early intervention, some children who would have been categorized as mentally retarded will not be so classified (Hallahan & Kauffman, 1994). Hence the use of the term developmentally delayed with young children.

As with many other disabilities, mental retardation is further divided into levels. These are based on the theoretical assumption that intelligence is normally distributed. The levels generally indicate the intensity of services that are needed for the child. The levels are assigned after formal assessment of the child's intellectual and adaptive functioning skills. A traditional breakdown of the levels of mental retardation is given below. Because of the error of measurement of the assessment instruments, we assume that scores can vary by about 5 points, so we use a range (i.e., an IQ of 75 may be 70 or 80, given the error of measurement; see Figure 12.1).

Using only IQ as a way to determine intellectual functioning assumes that 95 percent of the population is in the "normal" range, with 2.5 percent on either end being above or below "normal." Some question the validity of using IQ to determine mental retardation with young children because of the poor predictive validity of infant psychological tests and concerns related to cultural bias. The APA in the *DSM-IV* continues to use IQ scores. The AAMD focuses their subcategories on the patterns and intensity of supports individuals will need. This is a move away from looking at disability to ability. In this text the definitions of the subcategories given combines the two approaches. The designated categories are determined by the *DSM-IV,* but focus on the needed supports.

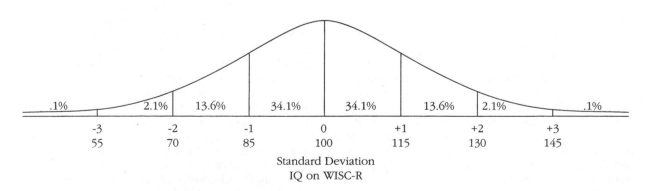

Figure 12.1   Theoretical Distribution of IQ

Mild Cognitive Delays (IQ 50–55 to 70–75)

For educational purposes, children in this category were often referred to as educable mentally retarded (EMR). This category constitutes approximately 85 percent of children with mental retardation (APA, 1994). Children develop sensorimotor, social, and communication skills during early childhood, but these may be consistently at the lower range of the developmental norms. They generally attend regular preschool or child care settings and neighborhood public schools. These children may be identified as needing additional educational services during the early elementary years. Their learning process is usually slower than other children, usually requiring concrete learning procedures. The focus is on learning basic academic skills. Most will be able to live independently in the community with intermittent supports and hold jobs after schooling is completed (APA, 1994).

Because schools have been criticized for improperly identifying minority children as mentally retarded, professionals are now reluctant to identify any children as mildly retarded. As the term learning disabled is more acceptable to both parents and administrators, borderline children are more likely to be placed in this category (Hallahan & Kauffman, 1994).

Moderate Cognitive Delays (IQ 35–40 to 50–55)

This group constitutes approximately 10 percent of the population of individuals with mental retardation. These children are frequently identified during the preschool years because of their delayed pattern of development. They develop sensorimotor and communication skills but at a slower rate. There is increasing focus on the development of their social skills for inclusion. The learning process typically focuses on adaptive skills, functional academic skills, and prevocational skills. Individuals require limited support. Our past expectation was that these children would reach an academic attainment level of about second grade (APA, 1994). Again, as these children are identified during the early years, the success of early intervention makes us question these expectations.

Severe Cognitive Delays (IQ 20–25 to 35–40)

Individuals in this category constitute approximately 3 to 4 percent of this population. Children are identified as infants or toddlers and may not reach early communication and physical/motor milestones until their school years. Their learning may progress to learning some sight words and survival skills. These children need extensive support (APA, 1994).

Profound Cognitive Delays (IQ below 20–25)

Children who are classified as profoundly retarded constitute approximately 1 to 2 percent of individuals with mental retardation. They are delayed in all areas of development and require intensive services and pervasive supports. They usually have an identifiable neurological condition that accounts for the mental retardation. Identification occurs early, and intervention generally focuses on self-help or adaptive skills, mobility, and basic cognitive development. As adults, they can perform uncomplicated vocational tasks and live in supervised settings.

Associated Disabilities

For children with mild mental retardation (those needing intermittent supports), this is often their only impairment. Children needing more supports are also more likely to have other disabilities such as cerebral palsy, speech and language impairments, sensory impairments, seizure disorders, psychological or behavioral impairments, and learning disabilities (Batshaw & Shapiro, 1997). These may make it increasingly difficult to identify children.

Developmental Aspects of Cognitive Delays

Depending on the level of the impairment, cognitive delays are discovered at different times during early childhood and in different manifestations.

0 to 3

We often classify young infants as having a developmental delay rather than trying to pinpoint a specific disability. In the first months of life, concern may arise because of inadequate sucking, floppy or spastic muscle tone, and/or lack of response to visual or auditory stimuli (Batshaw & Perret, 1992). Children may show little interest in the environment and not be as alert as other infants. As infants grow older and approach developmental milestones, it may be determined that the infant is not developing as quickly as most infants his age. It is often unclear whether this is just an individual growth pattern and that the infant will "catch up" in time or whether the delay is of a more permanent nature. Medical consultation can identify some problems early, such as hydrocephalus, for which a shunt can prevent brain damage and educational intervention can promote early development.

The most obvious signs are that these children are slower to talk than other children, may seem immature, and may also have been slower to walk (after 15 months). They may have a short attention span, and some are highly distractible. Language skills are also delayed, as are the acquisition of basic daily living skills (feeding, toilet training, and dressing). Children with more severe delays may lack social interaction skills, motivation, and a striving for independence. Infants and toddlers exhibiting extremely delayed development or for whom there is a known cause or etiology may be diagnosed as developmentally delayed before age 3. Because of the success of early intervention, if you suspect delayed development, talk with parents and support their seeking medical and educational intervention.

3 to 6

Mild delays may not be noticed during the preschool years, although you may begin to suspect something as you watch these children. Perhaps a 4-year-old with a mild delay will act more like a 3-year-old. Preschool children with developmental delays have a slower rate of learning, poor memory skills, poor generalization skills, and lack higher-level learning strategies.

Even at a preschool age, children with moderate cognitive impairments show noticeable delays in mental development, especially speech and language, and motor development. They may need assistance in self-help skills. They may not be toilet trained, or if they are, may not be able to manage taking off and putting on their clothes alone. In some cases, these children will look different from other children (if, for example, they have fetal alcohol syndrome). In other cases, they won't. A 4-year-old needing limited support may act more like a 2-year-old. Most likely, parents will know that their child is cognitively delayed. Children needing extensive support show marked delays in all areas of development and, at the preschool level, have few verbal communication skills. They may still communicate frustration through tantrums.

Increasingly, children needing extensive supports are being cared for and educated in regular settings, particularly in child care and preschool settings. Young children may be in regular settings for part of the day and in a setting designed for intensive early intervention for part of the day. Here, the emphasis is more on developmentally appropriate curriculum and fundamental activities focusing on adaptive skills to support the development of independence. Social skills to foster peer interaction are also stressed.

6 to 9

During the early elementary years, the focus is on early literacy skills and abilities that are prerequisites for later learning. They include behaviors such as learning to sit and attend to teachers, following directions, and learning the names of the letters of the

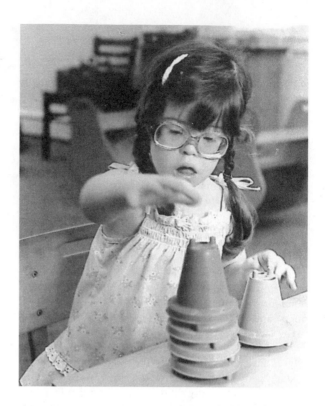

Children with developmental delays also may have visual and physical impairments. Programming must be responsive to the child's overall development.

alphabet. Children with delayed development need support developing small motor skills that are necessary to hold a pencil and cut with scissors. They will need continuing support on adaptive skills and developing skills to interact with peers. The focus is frequently on fundamental academic skills that are necessary in life as well as skills that allow them to communicate in an appropriate way (Hallahan & Kauffman, 1994).

Assessment of Cognitive and Developmental Delays

There are two major aspects in the assessment of cognitive delays: intelligence and adaptive behavior. Adaptative behavior is the ability an individual has for self-care. In young children, we are concerned with self-help skills; in young adults, the ability to understand currency, pay bills, and so on.

Assessment of Intelligence

The assessment of intelligence is a controversial issue. What is intelligence? We can't see it, we can't hear it, and we can't agree on a definition. We use the concept of intelligence to explain differences in behavior. Most individuals who are qualified to give individual intelligence tests have been specially trained and can give many different tests of intelligence.

Assessment of Infant and Toddler Development

Two major dimensions relate to the accuracy of measuring intelligence in very young children; the first has to do with issues relating to the test itself, the second is the challenge of the infant herself. In general, when we talk about intelligence testing for children under age 3, we don't end up with an intelligence quotient or IQ; rather, we talk about a developmental assessment and a developmental quotient or DQ.

One reason for assessing an infant is to determine whether or not there might be long-term problems that could respond to intervention. In this case, the concern is the test's ability to detect problems that have potential long-term negative outcomes. Infant developmental tests do a good job at identifying infants and toddlers with severe and profound delays. They are not as effective in identifying children with mild to moderate delays.

One critical testing issue concerns the relationship between scores obtained on infant developmental tests and intelligence tests given at a later age. What we consider intelligence in infancy is not the same as intelligence in elementary school children or adults; that is, different patterns of cognitive activities constitute intelligence at different ages (Meadows, 1993). Another line of thinking focuses on infant alertness as shown in habituation tasks and attention as a predictor of intelligence test scores in early childhood (Bornstein & Sigman, 1986). Because of the need for longitudinal data to confirm this hypothesis, it will be a while before we know if it is fruitful.

Screening measures such as the Denver II (Frankenburg & Dodds, 1990) are often used to decide which children receive further testing and which don't. Norm-referenced measures such as the Battelle Developmental Inventory (BDI) (Newborg, Stock, Wnek, Guidubaldi, & Svinicki, 1984), and the Bayley Scales of Infant Development, 2nd edition (Bayley, 1993) often form the core of a diagnostic assessment. These measures are used to get an overall picture of the infant or toddler and to determine whether further, more specialized assessment is necessary. Given the lack of high-quality screening measures for young children, norm-referenced measures may also serve a screening purpose. These measures are standardized and require a trained examiner.

Criterion-referenced measures such as the Brigance Diagnostic Inventory of Early Development (revised edition) (Brigance, 1991), the Learning Accomplishment Profile–Diagnostic Edition (LAP-D) (LeMay, Griffin, & Sanford, 1978), and the Hawaii Early Learning Profile (HELP) (Furuno, O'Reilly, Hosaka, Inatsuku, & Zeisloft-Falbey, 1987) are often used after screening and diagnosis have been completed. These measures are useful in program planning and in measuring increments of development.

Regardless of the test, one test alone should never be the only source used to determine whether or not a child has a cognitive delay. This information needs to be included with information from behavioral observations, medical history, and information obtained from the parents to obtain a more accurate picture of the child's functioning.

Assessment of Adaptive Skills

To classify someone as mentally retarded, a test of intelligence and a test of adaptive skills are required. Assessing adaptive behavior is also useful for program planning.

The assessment of adaptive skills relies on the report of a respondent or observer. In the case of young children, this is primarily their parents and caregivers; for older children, a teacher might also be a respondent. The respondent is expected to be both truthful and knowledgeable in answering questions about the child's behavior. Having more than one respondent helps reveal the situational aspects of behavior (home and school) and provides useful information. Because parents have a vested interest, they may be inclined to give their child's accomplishments the benefit of the doubt if they decide they don't want him classified as mentally retarded.

The Vineland Adaptive Behavior Scale (VABS) (Sparrow, Balla, & Cicchetti, 1984) is an individually administered scale for individuals under 19 years of age. There are a variety of forms of this scale that provide an appraisal of the child by a parent, caregiver, or teacher. They vary in the amount of information obtained. All three editions assess communication, daily living skills, motor skills, and socialization. The interviews include information on maladaptive behavior. The reliability of the subdomains varies; the validity appears to be adequate (Salvia & Ysseldyke, 1995).

The AAMD Adaptive Behavior Scale–School 2 (ABS-S2) (Nihira, Leland, & Lambert, 1993) is an individually administered, norm-referenced scale for individuals 3 to 21 years. It looks at five main factors: personal self-sufficiency, social adjustments, personal adjustment, personal-social responsibility, and community self-sufficiency. The scale is new and interrater agreement is weak, but evidence of validity is emerging (Salvia & Ysseldyke, 1995).

Causes of Cognitive Delays

Causes of cognitive delays fall into two overlapping categories. Children who fall in the mild category, those needing intermittent supports, are most frequently from families of lower socioeconomic status and have fewer environmental resources (Batshaw & Shapiro, 1997). Disabilities that require more extensive supports are usually linked to biological causes. There is overlap in these categories. For approximately 30 to 40 percent of children who are classified as mentally retarded, there is no known cause or etiology (APA, 1994).

Children born to women who have fewer resources are more likely to have had poor prenatal care and poor nutrition and are less likely to have received social and cognitive nurturing in early childhood. Women who haven't completed high school are four times as likely to have children with mild developmental delays (Capute & Accardo, 1996). African American children are twice as likely to be categorized as having mild developmental delays; this may be related to the disproportionate number of African American families who live below the poverty line. Early intervention services have improved the expected outcome for children with mild developmental delays (Batshaw & Shapiro, 1997).

When the causes of delay are known, approximately 5 percent are hereditary, such as Tay-Sachs disease, another 30 percent are due to chromosomal changes during the development of the embryo (for example, Down syndrome trisomy 21) or to damage to the embryo due to toxins (such as alcohol, drugs, or infections). Another 10 percent occur during the fetal period and include such problems as malnutrition, trauma, hypoxia (lack of oxygen), and prematurity. After birth, another 15 to 20 percent are related to environmental influences such as neglect and lack of stimulation as well as severe mental disorders such as autism. Approximately 5 percent are related to infections such as meningitis, traumas such as head injuries, and poisoning due to lead (APA, 1994).

Children experiencing cognitive delays are as different from each other as those who have more typical developmental patterns.

Chromosomal and Genetic Causes of Delayed Cognitive Development

Down syndrome and Fragile X syndrome are two of the most frequent forms of delayed cognitive development.

Down Syndrome. Down syndrome was one of the first syndromes to be associated with developmental delays. It is the most frequent chromosomal disorder; however, its prevalence is decreasing. In the 1970s, it occurred in 1 in 700 live births; in the 1990s, it is estimated at 0.92 per 1,000 live births. The most common form of Down syndrome (95 to 98 percent) is trisomy 21 (Down Syndrome Prevalence, 1994; James, 1994). In this disorder, there is a rearrangement of the twenty-first chromosome. This rearrangement almost always results in delayed development, cardiac problems, and some skeletal abnormalities. Down syndrome accounts for about 5 to 6 percent of all cases of retardation (Batshaw & Perret, 1992).

The risks for having a child with Down syndrome vary with maternal age; the probability is 1:1,528 at age 20 and 1:6 at age 50 (James, 1994). There appears to be a critical region in the lower part of chromosome 21 that causes Down syndrome trisomy 21, which results in having three rather than two copies of this chromosome. Initially, it was thought that the problem originated only in the egg. It is now estimated that the problem may lie in the

sperm in approximately 15 percent of cases (Dagna-Bricarelli et al., 1990).

There is no known cure for Down syndrome, but much research has focused on identifying the fetus with Down syndrome by prenatal testing. Levels of alpha fetoprotein are associated with chromosomal abnormalities such as Down syndrome. Approximately 45 percent of fetuses with Down syndrome can be detected using maternal serum alpha fetoprotein levels (Williamson, 1994). These are typically confirmed with amniocentesis. Ultrasound is also used to confirm or deny fetal malformations such as Down syndrome initially suspected because of alpha fetoprotein testing (Harman, 1994). If not detected prenatally, a diagnosis is typically made at birth based on children's distinctive appearance. One reason for the decrease in the number of children born with Down syndrome is the number of women who have decided to terminate pregnancy when the fetus is identified as having Down syndrome (Roizen, 1997).

Children with Down syndrome have characteristic features that include a small, relatively flat head, an upward slant to the eyes that have epicanthal folds at the inner corners, and a broad neck. The ears, mouth, feet, and hands are relatively small, fingers are unusually short and broad, and there is a simian crease on the palm of the hand (Batshaw & Perret, 1992). Chromosome analysis determines if trisomy is an accurate diagnosis or the child has a more rare type of Down syndrome such as mosaic (which is less severe) or a translocation.

Children with Down syndrome have increased risk of abnormalities in almost every organ system (Roizen, 1996). They usually have decreased motor tone and appear floppy. This may result in feeding problems as the tongue is usually thicker. They reach motor milestones later than other children. Some will not walk independently or speak their first words until about age 2. Language delays become evident during the preschool years. Most of the motor problems are overcome by school age, but the cognitive deficits become more obvious. With the success of early intervention and educational inclusion, some children with Down syndrome are doing exceedingly well. They have graduated from high school and are seeking advanced vocational training.

Children with Down syndrome may have other health-related problems. Many have congenital heart disease, gastrointestinal malformations, vision problems such as refractive errors and strabismus, hearing problems (often related to chronic middle ear infections), and dental malocclusions. At elementary school age, concerns relate to short stature and excessive weight gain related to overeating and inactivity. Although this list may sound long and negative, most of the problems are treatable. The vision problems respond to corrective lenses, and most of the problems that relate to the heart and gastrointestinal system are solved through surgery or medication. Most children with Down syndrome are currently included in regular child care centers and in the public schools.

Fragile X Syndrome. The discovery of Fragile X syndrome was accidental and gradual. Researchers in Australia doing chromosomal studies on residents of an institution for the mentally retarded noted that in many of the men, the tip of the long arm of the X chromosome was pinched off or fragile (Batshaw, 1997). Once this was known, other information became clearer. They found that individuals with this syndrome have a characteristic appearance that includes large prominent ears, an elongated face, flat feet, a single simian crease across the palm of the hand, loose joints, and, in adolescent boys, large testicles; also, there is typically a family history of mental retardation (Batshaw, 1997). Most children do not have all of these characteristics, and the manifestation is more subtle in early childhood.

Since its recognition as a genetic disorder, Fragile X is the most frequently diagnosed inherited cause of mental retardation (Down syndrome, although genetic, is not inherited) (Batshaw, 1997). Fragile X is carried on the X sex chromosome and follows X-linked inheritance patterns. The incidence is estimated at about 1 per 1,000 births (Sherman, 1991). It accounts for 6 to 14 percent of males with severe mental retardation, 3 to 6 percent of individuals with autism (Hagerman & Cronister, 1996), and approximately 7 percent of mild retardation in females (Batshaw, 1997). It is believed that Fragile X may account for the fact that more males have cognitive delays than females. Approximately 80 percent of males with this syndrome are mentally retarded, whereas only 33 percent of females are. Children having Fragile X who don't show developmental delays may have learning disabilities or behavior problems (Mazzocco & O'Connor, 1993).

If there is reason to suspect Fragile X because of family history, a DNA blood test can identify children with Fragile X prenatally. A blood antibody test was developed in 1995 that seeks the presence of the gene that causes Fragile X, which allows the identification of children with the full mutation as newborns (Batshaw, 1997). Children with Fragile X may have sensory impairments, orthopedic problems, heart problems, and seizure disorders.

Unless suspected, children with Fragile X are often difficult to identify in early childhood as they may meet developmental milestones; however, their ability to meet milestones on time gradually declines. There are some behavior patterns that are typical of children with Fragile X. Although all the behaviors alluded to below are typical of young children, it is the frequency, duration, and intensity that indicate a problem. When excited or frustrated, children may flap their hands or bite them or have other autistic-like behavior such as fascination with spinning toys or other unusual objects. Speech patterns are unusual, and speech may be high-pitched, repetitious, and cluttered. They may be hyperactive or inattentive, with low levels of frustration tolerance, which can lead to temper tantrums. Some may overreact to light touch. Children with Fragile X may be shy and withdrawn, have difficulty interacting with peers, and make little eye contact (Mazzocco & O'Connor,

1993). A sight word approach to reading, speech therapy with an emphasis on following directions, computer-assisted instruction, and social skills training as well as an emphasis on adaptive skills are recommended (Batshaw, 1997).

Environmental Factors

In the past, cognitive delays that were present at birth were viewed as a given, a nonpreventable disability. Increasingly, causes of cognitive delays are preventable. Some prevention is based on health procedures that ensure that children receive inoculations in a timely manner. Others relate to accident prevention and environmental stimulation. The fastest-growing prenatal causes of mental retardation are preventable.

Cultural-Familial Delays. In the 1990s, this term is used to refer to children with mild retardation or those who need intermittent supports when the cause of the delay is thought to be an unstimulating environment and/or general genetic factors. We are back to the nature-nurture issue but still seem to maintain the position that nature provides the broad parameters in which nurture plays out its role.

Most children being raised in or near the poverty level have fewer opportunities for learning and an increased probability of being exposed to situations that cause developmental delays. According to the U.S. Department of Agriculture (USDA), in 1993, the average annual cost of raising two children for families with incomes between $32,000 and $52,000 was $14,740. The annual earning of a full-time minimum-wage worker in 1993 was $8,840. The maximum Aid to Families with Dependent Children (AFDC) for a mother and two children (median state) was $7,824. The federal poverty line that year was $11,890 for a family of three (USDA Family Economics Research Group, 1994). Middle-class families spend $3,000 more each year raising their children than an entire family of three is expected to live on, and $6,000 more than a full-time minimum-wage earner makes annually (Children's Defense Fund, 1994).

The environment in which a child is raised is a big factor in facilitating the development of cognitive abilities. Some limitations may be present that prevent a child from acquiring specific intellectual skills, such as advanced abstract thinking abilities. However, limiting a child's experiences based on a diagnostic label is a serious and dangerous situation. Many children previously thought unable to function effectively in their environment have accomplished wonders, mostly due to parents who did not let the label of cognitive delay limit the type and range of opportunities and experiences they provided for their children. Appropriate stimulation is a key ingredient to a successful educational program.

Alcohol-Related Birth Defects. Alcohol ingested by a pregnant woman can cause a variety of physical and neurodevelopmental effects on the developing fetus. They range from physical malformation to mental retardation to learning and behavior problems (Batshaw & Conlon, 1997). Alcohol is abused more than any other drug in the United States today. There are approximately 6 million people in the United States classified as dependent on alcohol and another 10 million who drink enough to be considered problem drinkers (Pietrantoni & Knuppel, 1991). Estimates vary on the number of women who are heavy drinkers. Some estimate as low as 1 to 3 percent (Schubert & Savage, 1994); others estimate that between 8 and 11 percent of women of childbearing age are either problem drinkers or alcoholics, and that about 59 to 65 percent of embryo-fetuses are exposed to alcohol in utero (Pietrantoni & Knuppel, 1991). Alcohol intake tends to decrease during pregnancy, but the incidence of binge drinking remains constant or increases (Batshaw & Conlon, 1997).

Although alcohol was known as a teratogen that could cause irreversible damage to the fetus, fetal alcohol syndrome (FAS) was not formally identified until the early 1970s (Spohr, Williams, & Steinhausen, 1993). FAS results in three characteristic anomalies: interuterine and postnatal growth deficiency, including low birth weight and poor muscle tone; facial anomalies (thin upper lip, flat midface, short nose, low nasal bridge, small head, droopy eyes); and central nervous system dysfunction, including irritability, attention deficit, hyperactivity, and mental retardation (Bert, Greene, & Bert, 1992).

Prenatal alcohol use increases the probability of spontaneous abortion and stillbirth. The teratogenic effect of alcohol depends on the amount consumed. Mild FAS, which is characterized by low birth weight, occurs when the daily consumption of alcohol is 1 ounce of absolute alcohol or two standard drinks. The complete syndrome, which affects 30 to 40 percent of the children of alcoholic mothers, is seen when 2 to 2.5 ounces of absolute alcohol are consumed per day during the first trimester (Pietrantoni & Knuppel, 1991). A safe level of alcohol consumption has not been established, and therefore abstinence is recommended.

In the United States and in many parts of Europe, FAS is now the leading cause of mental retardation. It is more frequent than Down syndrome, spina bifida, or Fragile X syndrome (Batshaw & Perret, 1992). Although prevalence varies, estimates are that FAS occurs in 1:300 to 1:2,000 live births in the United States (Schubert & Savage, 1994). Native Americans are particularly at risk as they have decreased activity in the enzyme alcohol dehydrogenase, which may play a role in causing fetal malformations (Batshaw & Conlon, 1997).

FAS can be diagnosed on the basis of a clinical examination of the child. Knowledge of maternal drinking behavior is not essential. When not all of the symptoms are present, an accurate diagnosis cannot be made; this situation is called fetal alcohol effects (FAE) or alcohol-related birth defects (ARBD). The frequency of ARBD is estimated at 3 to 5 per 1,000 live births (Pietrantoni & Knuppel, 1991). Thus, FAS and FAE combined affect approximately 4 to 7 infants

for each 1,000 live births. FAE has a milder impact developmentally and is characterized by growth retardation, low muscle tone, and poor sucking. FAE is probably far more prevalent than FAS yet more difficult to isolate and attribute to alcohol consumption, because low birth weight, for example, can be caused by other factors. In many cases, it is difficult to determine the cause of congenital anomalies; however, some researchers feel that excessive prenatal alcohol exposure (FAS and FAE together) may account for about 5 percent of all congenital anomalies and 10 to 20 percent of all cases of mild mental retardation (Batshaw & Conlon, 1997).

If alcohol abuse occurs during the first trimester of pregnancy, in addition to an increased probability of miscarriage, the physical signs of FAS are likely to be present. Alcohol abuse during the second trimester affects physical and intellectual growth, but there are no physical malformations. If abuse occurs in the third trimester, cognitive development alone is impaired (Batshaw & Conlon, 1997).

Children with FAS will be identified early; those with FAE will not. These children might initially be identified as children with emotional and behavioral disorders. Beyond the physical effects of prenatal alcohol, these children may come from families who are alcoholics. Children of alcoholics are far more likely to be victims of child abuse and neglect than other children (Davis, Allen, & Sherman, 1989). Teachers need to view the child in the context of the family to focus on individual needs.

Infants with FAS and FAE need comprehensive early intervention services with a particular emphasis on language development. They need to work on social skills and behavior. To be effective, intervention may include getting the mother into treatment. Only about 30 percent of children with FAS are in the care of their mothers until they are adolescents (Spohr et al., 1993). Over half of the mothers die during the early years of the child's life from alcohol-related causes such as cirrhosis, car accidents, suicides, and overdoses (Abel & Sokol, 1987).

Environmental Teratogens. Many factors within the environment can greatly affect the developing fetus. Radiation is one commonly occurring factor. Low doses of radiation have not been found to cause harm; however, a mother's excessive or repeated exposure to high levels of radiation has been shown to result in damage to the central nervous system of the fetus. This is why pregnant women should avoid X-rays when possible or wear lead capes to protect the fetus. All women should wear lead capes when exposed to X-rays to protect their supply of eggs from radiation. Other influences include hyperthermia or exposure to high temperatures, especially during the first trimester. Maternal exposure to mercury can lead to severe disabling conditions in the infant. This can affect young children as well. Lead has also been shown to cause brain damage in infants in situations where the mother had a high ingestion of lead during pregnancy and in young children when they have ingested it. Finally, exposure to many environmental pesticides, cleaners, paints, and other toxic substances places the fetus at risk for later problems. It is difficult for women to avoid environmental teratogens that come from industrial pollution. The most common of these are polychlorinated biphenyls, or PCBs. These teratogens were banned in the 1970s but can still be transmitted through the food chain.

Guidelines

Because it takes longer for children with cognitive delays to learn, it is important that you adapt your teaching style to meet the needs of these children.

1. In your teaching, use as many of the senses as possible. Even if you are teaching concepts that are primarily visual, such as colors, have children reinforce the visual with other sensory experiences. Have them: *see* the red ball; *sit on* the red square; *add* red food coloring to the fingerpaint; *eat* a red tomato; and *listen* to a red fire truck. Like most children, they don't learn the first time around, so teach the same concept in different contexts.

2. Keep going over the same concept until they have *overlearned* it, but not to the point of boredom—theirs or yours. Use variations to maintain interest. Because children may easily forget, they need to overlearn and review information until it is firmly established.

3. Teach a concept for a short time each day for many days, rather than for a long period of time on fewer days. Spaced practice is always more effective than massed practice, as those who "cram" for an exam know.

4. Because learning is challenging, determine the learning value of specific materials and use those that are most efficient or those that teach two necessary skills at one time. For example, buttoning sequences where children must duplicate a pattern of colors teaches buttoning, a necessary self-help skill, patterns and relationships necessary for reading and math, as well as color names.

5. Generalizing is difficult. When you teach concepts, try to make them as close to the setting where they will be used as possible. Keep activities relevant, short, and to the point. Be clear with directions. Be wary of cute shortcuts. One school I visited decided to teach children to say "three-teen" instead of thirteen because it was easier. Some of those children are now about "three-teen and five-teen," and their peers make fun of them when they say how old they are.

6. Use many examples when you teach. If you use only one example when teaching the concept red, it is likely that the children who learn this one particular red will have difficulty generalizing to other red objects.

7. Be sure to reinforce appropriate behavior. Set your sights realistically. Reinforce effort and steps accomplished toward a goal. Don't wait until the goal is accomplished, or the child may lose motivation. Reinforce children for zipping up the last part of their jacket; don't wait until they can put the jacket on and get the zipper started.

8. Avoid a watered-down program. Don't try to teach the whole curriculum at a lower, slower, simpler level. Rather, concentrate on what is important for them. What skills will be essential later for the children that need a base developed now?

9. Teach safety and health skills necessary for wellness. Children need to learn to wash hands after toileting, not to get into the path of moving objects, whether swings, tricycles or cars, and to wear clothing appropriate for the weather.

10. Children need the vocabulary to express basic wants and needs whether they learn words or signs or use a communication board. Children need a way to communicate that they are hungry, thirsty, tired, and need to go to the bathroom.

11. Evaluate the progress of children with cognitive delays against their own development, not those of the other children in the class. Choose activities that can be used at many different levels and provide adult scaffolding to help children learn.

Specific Intervention Techniques

In general, teach from simple to complex. Be specific! Where appropriate, simplify information, but not to the point that it loses its meaning. Use a variety of teaching techniques.

Task Analysis. A task analysis is breaking a task down into its component parts, sequencing these, and then teaching them. A great deal has been written on the use of task analysis. However, if you understand the basic principles involved in a task, you can do the task analysis yourself. Start with something the child must do frequently, like putting on a coat. If, after your task analysis, the child still has a problem, review your analysis for both order and possible missed steps. Change it and try again.

Figure 12.2 presents a sample task analysis, including a filled-in chart that shows the child's progress.

Backward Chaining. In some cases, the technique of backward chaining is useful. Using the example of putting on the coat, offer the most help with the first steps and the least help with the last step in the chain. The first step you would expect the child to do without assistance is Step 8 (zip up the coat). This means the child gets some satisfaction for task completion instead of needing help to finish. (Backward chaining is easier when the component parts are of equal difficulty.)

	M	T	W	TH	F	M	T
1. Take coat off hook.	PH	VH	VH	VH	NH	NH	NH
2. Put coat on floor inside up.	PH	PH	VH	VH	NH	NH	NH
3. Stand at neck of coat.	PH	PH	VH	VH	VH	NH	NH
4. Bend over.	PH	PH	PH	VH	VH	NH	NH
5. Put hands in armholes.	PH	PH	PH	VH	VH	NH	NH
6. Flip coat over head, pushing arms into arm holes.	PH	PH	PH	PH	VH	VH	VH
7. Start zipper.	PH	PH	PH	PH	VH	VH	VH
8. Zip up coat.	PH	PH	VH	VH	VH	NH	NH

Be sure to praise the child for his efforts.

Key: PH = physical help
VH = verbal help
NH = no help

Figure 12.2 Task Analysis and Tracking Chart

Modeling. Teachers may need to model the particular behavior while verbally describing it. Provide opportunities for the child to practice and verbalize what the child is doing; also, provide reinforcement and feedback.

Curriculum Adaptations

Adapting the curriculum, in general, consists of simplifying some tasks, focusing on essential tasks and omitting others, and including tasks that other children may learn at home such as toileting, feeding, and early language skills.

Social Awareness: Self-Esteem, Inclusion, Social Studies, Health and Safety

Children learn about themselves and their environment by building on familiar experiences. Begin with them and their immediate surroundings of family and school, then expand to the larger community. Help children evaluate situations, including your classroom, relative to their health and safety. Make good health and safety practices part of their routine. Focus on making all children part of the group and teaching them social skills that will be appropriate throughout their life.

Self-Esteem. All children need to learn about themselves. Teach children the names of their body parts. Use songs as well as direct instruction and questioning to teach this. Remember, you want to include all children: Do not act surprised when a child with cognitive delays can do something.

1. Help develop a positive self-concept by pointing out to the child and others in the room what she *can* do and how much she *has* learned, just as you do with all children.

2. Focus on and support strengths while you continue to work on needs.

3. Support children's expansion of learning at the level at which they are capable.

Inclusion. All children need to be part of society. As you help children join groups, model and teach the skills they need so they will not be dependent on your intervention.

1. Teach children the courtesies of everyday living. Be sure children know how to greet you (say "Hello" and look at you while they say it). They also need to learn to use "Please" and "Thank you" appropriately and not to interrupt conversations.

2. All children need to be contributing members of the class. Give them tasks they can do and praise their accomplishments as you would any other member of your class.

3. Be sure to have easy and hard, but age-appropriate, options available so they can easily participate in group play. Mix age groups for some activities if this is possible.

Social Studies. Like all children, those with cognitive delays need to learn about the community in which they live. When you teach units in this area, concentrate on roles the children may need to know or can readily identify with.

1. Discuss the roles of police, firefighters, and mail personnel. Go on field trips to see them at work, then follow up with role playing. Be practical. Have children mail letters or postcards home to see their address. Talk about the implications of writing the wrong address.

2. Help them learn about many different roles: cafeteria worker, bus driver, therapists they are likely to encounter. Have them play games in a one-on-one situation with a teacher or paraprofessional. Discuss how the teacher also learns from these specialists.

3. Explore varied occupations. Be sure to include *some* occupations that require limited skills (teacher, farmer, baker, factory worker, janitor, clerk, construction worker, worker in fast food chain, and so on). It is important that these occupations be included and that they be valued.

Health and Safety. It is important for children to make good health habits part of their routine. They may not have learned some of the things that seem obvious: toileting; washing hands; blowing and wiping their nose with tissue, not their sleeve; eating with utensils; and grooming.

Help children develop adaptive skills by providing small pitchers for pouring juice and foods with interesting textures. Developing adaptive skills during routines like snack time encourages contextual learning and generalizability.

1. Teach safety skills. Emphasize dangers with the greatest likelihood of occurrence and those that are most dangerous, such as traffic, electrical outlets, and poison.

2. Concentrate on building good food habits. Help children learn to choose healthy snacks like fruit or crackers rather than soda and cookies.

3. Role-play with children what to do if they get lost. Make address and identification cards with a phone number on them.

4. Break complex skills down into simple tasks that the child can do. Teach the necessary skills in different curricula. Toileting, for example, involves the ability to dress and undress oneself, so be sure to teach buttoning and snapping as part of fine motor skills.

Language and Literacy: Speaking, Listening, Reading, and Writing

Language, both expressing and receiving, may be the child's weakest area but one of the most essential. Children with cognitive delays have smaller vocabularies and use simpler sentence structures than their peers. Their language may be difficult to understand and used less frequently than that of other children. Lack of competence in communication can lead to frustration and may result in crying, hitting, or other means of communication.

Children with cognitive delays learn more slowly than other children, so they may need extra repetitions of vocabulary and help generalizing words to a variety of situations. They will spend most of their time mastering the concept of a symbol system and developing a functional vocabulary. They need time to practice literacy skills. They may need to repeat and copy sounds before these become connected to words. These skills may be learned in conjunction with such necessary small motor skills as patterned eye movement (left to right), following a line of print with a finger, and turning pages. Children need to work on these skills, and it is your role to motivate them and capture their interest. Do this in short periods, and be sure prerequisite skills have been attained before going on to more difficult tasks. Children with cognitive delays may just be mastering the initial stages of reading and writing during the early elementary years. If the prerequisite motor skills are not developed, it is useless to continually practice skills such as name writing if they can't effectively use a spoon or cup.

Children who have cognitive delays need first-hand experiences to translate into language and literacy experiences. They need to build a strong experiential base before they can use concepts in language and literacy activities. Start with the concrete and gradually work toward the more abstract. Children need to explore a ball, roll, throw, and kick a ball before reading about a ball makes any sense.

Speaking. Like all children, those with cognitive delays depend on communicating with others to have their needs met.

1. Work on vocabulary. Start with a nucleus vocabulary that focuses on the child. Teaching body parts teaches not only vocabulary but body awareness as well. Next, focus on health care, the family, clothing and aspects of the school and home environments. Emphasize nouns and verbs first. They are essential for communicating needs.

2. Encourage children to communicate in some way. Start conversations with an obvious frame of reference: "I like your hat." Pictures or videotapes taken during field trips can be used later to help children talk about what happened on the trips. The children can also sequence these pictures. A sequence of a trip to the apple orchard might look like this:

   Picture 1: Getting into the cars

   Picture 2: Arriving at the orchard

   Picture 3: Eating apples at the orchard

   Picture 4: Taking off coats back at school, with the apples in the picture.

   Using a camera that provides "instant" pictures allows you to show the sequence immediately without having to wait for the film to be developed.

3. Start with firsthand experiences. Upon your return, show the children pictures of the experience and recall it together. If you are going to set up a grocery store in the dramatic play area, take a field trip to a grocery store so they have this experience to build on. Point out the similarities in the two situations.

4. Use simple nursery rhymes and rhyming in general to develop vocabulary.

Fingerplays can help teach concepts, improve fine motor coordination, and keep children interested and occupied. Using fingerplays also engages the tactile mode for learning and may make the necessary repetition less monotonous.

1. Set aside time to repeat simple fingerplays, songs, and stories.

2. Use fingerplays to teach basic concepts, such as numbers: "Counting Kittens," "Ten Fingers," "Five Little Girls," "One, Two, What Shall I Do?"

3. Use fingerplays to follow stories, field trips, and other activities: "Roly-Poly Caterpillar" and "The Wheels on the Bus."

Listening. Listening is difficult. Where possible, use props. Speak clearly at a normal speed with simple, direct statements.

1. Provide concrete examples of the items that you are talking about so children can both see and hear the information.

2. Give the child practice following one- and two-step directions.

3. Be sure that children understand the interactional quality of listening and speaking and that they don't see it as a passive experience (as they might with television).

At the beginning, use short, simple stories that have a familiar theme. Remember, the group experience may be new to the child.

1. Use stories with repetition, rhythm, and rhyme, such as Dr. Seuss books like *Go Dog Go*.

2. Animal stories with big pictures and few words, alphabet books, and those with simple rhymes are good.

3. Before you read a story, it is helpful to discuss the meaning of some words beforehand. For example, before reading the story "Caps for Sale," establish that caps are hats.

4. Use flannel board stories. They have simple plots and children can participate in the story and repeat it as they manipulate the pieces.

Reading. Children with cognitive delays may require more practice to develop early literacy skills. Build a solid base and do not push children before they are ready or spend so much time on rote drill

and practice that children lose interest in learning to read. First establish basic skills, then use these skills to teach integration of higher-level skills.

1. Read to children. When you read, especially one-on-one, follow the words with your finger so children develop the connection between written words and reading. Make reading fun and exciting. Read more books rather than fewer.

2. Concentrate first on auditory and visual identification. Don't assume that children can label all the sounds and objects in their environment. Then work on discrimination skills. Once identification skills have been established, work on visual and auditory memory. For example, have children first match objects, then alphabet letters, then label them by name or sound.

3. Once some concepts have been mastered, move on to higher-level skills. For example, have children classify objects by color once they understand the colors. Expand this to classification by shape, number, function, and so on.

4. Sitting too long for the sake of sitting, although helpful to the teacher, is not a useful skill for any child. Use fingerplays or listening games while other children are finishing or teach the child to independently get and use readiness materials (puzzles or small motor materials) while they wait.

Writing. Writing begins with marks on the page and ends with the understanding of a complex symbol system. Work initially with the fine motor aspect, as the symbol system will take time.

1. Use large mirrors to encourage children to imitate movements and to make them aware of their own movements.

2. Help children enjoy the process of making marks on paper. Give them a variety of tools (crayons with knob ends, large markers, thick chalk) to mark with and varying sizes of paper, cardboard, and posterboard to mark on.

3. Have large wooden alphabet letters available. Spell out the child's name and have the child trace the letters with two fingers (index and middle fingers of dominant hand).

4. Have children imitate you as you make large arm circles in the air with the dominant arm first in one direction and then the other. As children can make circles, begin to make letters with your arm (it is important that this is a large motor activity). This is air writing.

Discovery: Mathematics, Science, and Computers

Support the discovery approach with verbalizations about the process. Allow time to repeat experiences and to do variations on themes. Children may need help generalizing knowledge or may do so at a lower level than their age-mates. As activities become more difficult, plan some that can be done at different levels. Children with cognitive delays will need concrete experience even after their peers are dealing with more abstract concepts. Use real objects that can be touched and manipulated. Modify the keyboard of the computer or be sure children have prerequisite skills such as the ability to use a single keystroke before expecting them to interact with computers.

Point out similarities and differences within classification systems (e.g., cars and trucks both have wheels). Increase attention span by programming for what the child likes and praising the child for staying with projects to completion. However, don't avoid areas that the child is weak in, as this may be where he or she needs the most practice.

Mathematics. Children with cognitive delays need a foundation in basic mathematical skills to function in society.

1. Teach number concepts, such as counting, with real objects that can be moved or touched. Count children, blocks, chairs, and tables. Use an abacus and relate the beads back to real objects.

2. Choose math experiences that also teach other skills. (Using real objects will help the child's motor development.) Pegboards are useful for facilitating small motor skills while teaching counting and one-to-one correspondence. Pegboards can also be used to teach sequential patterns and relationships. You can make up a pattern and ask the child to copy it, identify the pattern, and then count the number of pegs used in the pattern. Stringing large wooden beads offers a similar opportunity for learning about numbers and patterns while also teaching eye-hand coordination.

3. Use real objects such as cups, napkins, and crackers to teach one-to-one correspondence. A good activity for snack time is to have a child put a glass and cracker in front of each chair (children without something to eat or drink usually make this known, and thus you have a teachable moment).

Science. Science should focus on firsthand knowledge and give information that is relevant for future learning and well-being.

1. Use field trips, especially those dealing with nature and the environment, to teach children about the world around them.

2. Discuss the seasons and the predictable changes that occur with the changes in nature. Discuss how the seasons affect clothing and activities. Whatever you do is dependent on where you live.

3. Encourage children to test simple cause-and-effect reasoning. State a relationship and have the child test it. "The color is darker if you press

harder" may be obvious to you, but children may not realize they cause the change systematically.

4. Plant a garden for firsthand experience with growth and learning the necessary conditions for growth.

Computers. Computers hold great potential for teaching cause-effect reasoning, and their "patience" with repeated learning is infinite. They are an absolute must.

1. Look at various keyboard options and choose one that best meets the child's needs.

2. Choose software carefully. It needs to be developmentally appropriate and simple to operate.

3. Encourage independent use of the computer itself. This is tremendously impressive to others. Parents may be encouraged and surprised that their child can turn on and operate a computer. Some of the skills are easy and sequential, and some software (especially those with picture menus) are very user-friendly.

Developmental Physical Education and Sensorimotor Skills: Large Motor, Small Motor, Sensorimotor Integration

Children with cognitive delays may not be as proficient as other children because their pattern of large motor development may have been slower. Plan activities that are at the child's developmental level, with variations to allow mastery and more challenging ones to provide growth. Children must devote much time to mastering small motor activities, so provide many different opportunities and make these intriguing. They need simple and more complex activities and many opportunities for practice. Begin with relatively large objects with few pieces; program for success. Try to include as many adaptive skills as you can (dressing boards, doll clothes with Velcro fasteners, and so on).

Large Motor. Large motor skills help develop stamina and increase body coordination and awareness. Provide opportunities for children to participate in skills that require locomotion (creeping, running), manipulation (throwing, bouncing, catching) and stability (stretching, rolling, balancing). Encourage children to develop game skills (kicking, throwing, catching, jumping, batting). Participation in cooperative games where no one wins or loses and no one is eliminated works best.

1. Emphasize basic skills and their variations: walking forward, backward, sideways, fast, slow.

2. Help children build physical stamina by daily participation in active games and an active lifestyle.

3. Use large, lightweight blocks, which are easy to manipulate.

Small Motor. When you plan for small motor play, you need to think of the skills that both help the child develop the necessary small muscles in the body and serve as a foundation for later skills, particularly those that relate to eating, dressing, and other self-care skills.

1. Start with beginning grasping and manipulation. Provide a variety of objects so that the child can practice many styles of grasping. Encourage the child to use the pincer grasp (thumb and forefinger apposition) once it has been developed.

2. Use many different activities that require fine motor skills (form boards, pegboards—rubber ones for strengthening finger muscles—plastic blocks or beads that fit together). Start with relatively large, preschool-size objects. Gradually add more pieces and smaller objects (be sure they cannot be swallowed). Use this opportunity to teach color and number skills also. Have children sort and group various materials.

3. Code your sorting and matching tasks by number (use *1* for easy tasks, *2* for more difficult, and so on). This means that all the children can do the same activity but at different levels.

   (a) Sort identical objects from a mix: round beads from crayons or wooden clothespins from small wooden blocks.

   (b) Group the same objects by size: big from small plastic clips or big blocks from small ones.

   (c) Sort the same objects in different colors: red from green beads or red from white Legos.

   (d) Group the same objects with differing shapes: round from square from cylindrical red beads.

   (e) Have a mix of objects that can be grouped in two or more ways. First, demonstrate the system and have the child follow it; later, encourage the child to group and regroup independently. A mix of large and small cars of different colors, large and small blocks of different colors and shapes, and large and small beads of varying colors and shapes may all be sorted into two containers of large and small, three if they sort by object, and more if they sort by color.

   Within each step, you can make the task more difficult by adding more objects, colors, sizes, and shapes. Start with 2 items and work up to perhaps 10. A more difficult version is grouping different objects by color, size, and shape.

4. Often, it is hard for children to hold a pencil or crayon in an appropriate writing grasp. Larger implements are easier to grip. Provide a variety of pencils, crayons, and brushes of different sizes. Add grips, tape, or foam curlers to make them easier to hold. (An occupational therapist can provide advice on these accommodations.)

Sensorimotor Integration. Provide many opportunities for children to use motor skills in coordination with their senses.

1. Provide materials and activities that require the use of two hands: clapping, lacing beads onto string or pipe cleaners, lacing cards with various sized holes (some large and easy to string, others small), putting together snap-construction toys, and placing blocks in containers.

2. Provide puzzles at different levels of difficulty. Puzzles with knobs attached to the pieces are easier to manipulate.

3. Provide activities that require different motions of each hand (one example is a Jack-in-the-Box, where a child must hold the box with one hand while turning the knob with the other). It is easier for children to do the same thing with both hands or to use only one hand. Some fingerplays do this as well.

Creative Arts: Visual Arts, Music, Creative Movement, and Dramatic Play

As long as there is no competition and children are not required to do the "same" thing, children with cognitive delays need little accommodation in this area. Through the manipulation of various art media, they can learn about texture, shape, and size. Expect them to choose to sing favorite songs over and over. They may not show a lot of imagination in moving. If you use costumes, provide realistic ones. Start with large motor movements and encourage children to move their whole body by stimulating them with bold music. Gradually work on small motor movements. The practice of moving and the opportunity to be part of the group is important.

Visual Arts. Art for children with cognitive delays, as with all young children, should focus more on the process than the product. Children learn by doing, especially if a thoughtful teacher is providing guidance.

1. Use a variety of art media.

2. Cutting is often difficult; it may be helpful to use easy-grip or "training" scissors with a loop or a spring handle.

3. Encourage children to participate in the visual arts each day. Provide feedback on what they do and how they are doing it.

Music. Music can be used in a variety of ways. Repetition makes it easier for children to learn songs. Teach the parents the songs so the child can hear and sing them at home as well as in class.

1. Use music to teach basic concepts such as numbers, colors, and body parts.

2. Music can be used to expand a child's vocabulary and to increase auditory memory.

3. Music paired with movement encourages children to move and releases energy. In creative movement, although there is no right or wrong way to move, the music sets the tone of the movements (quiet, slow music means move slowly). Help children connect with these environmental cues.

4. Music can also be used to help children establish a rhythm pattern. Vary the pattern so children can learn to match it.

5. Using songs that call children by name can increase self-esteem and a sense of group belonging.

Creative Movement. Movement is a must for all children. Nonjudgmental movement is an added plus. Support all attempts at movement.

1. Encourage children to move to music that has an obvious beat, but don't require the child to follow the beat.

2. Encourage children to move specific body parts. Be sure to have these parts moved long enough so you are sure the children know the part indicated: "Everybody move your arms in circles."

3. Help children recognize speed by having them move something quickly or slowly. Children gain sensorimotor integration as well as necessary concepts through movement.

Dramatic Play. Dramatic play is a way to make strange experiences more familiar and is a good way to teach appropriate behavior.

1. Visit a real store, then set up a play store (department, grocery, pet). Play through the essential features. Setting it up for one or two days isn't enough; keep adding features throughout the week so it doesn't get boring.

2. Playing with other children in this area might also provide the child with information about how roles are played in society. Children, especially those with disabilities, may be given little realistic feedback, yet feedback is necessary for their development. It can be realistic without being judgmental: "You can't reach that." Acknowledge reality, but help children think about alternatives (a taller friend or a stool might be the solution).

3. Play should be fairly concrete with realistic props. These children are less imaginative than their peers. Have a lot of props available to facilitate play: a garage, for example, needs cars, trucks, a block structure, hose, gas pumps, and so on.

Transitions

Transitions can be used to promote independence and prevocational skills as well as teach colors, numbers, and body awareness.

1. Have a sign in–sign out board. Use this for roll call some days. Either have the children find their own name tag and put it on, or have them move cards from one side to the other. This reinforces name recognition and independence as the children learn to do it more automatically.

2. Children may need more help with toileting and dressing. Dismiss them at a time when they can get the help they need.

3. Use times of transition to reinforce concepts the child has learned.

4. Allow enough time for transitions so that children can be successful. It is easy for children with cognitive delays to get distracted and for you to feel rushed when others are waiting.

Summary

Increasingly, we are seeing cognitive delays as conditions that can be changed or modified through early intervention. Hence, we are reluctant to label children as mentally retarded, and most young children with cognitive delays are classified as having developmental delays. These delays are apparent in infants and toddlers by missed motor and language milestones, the quality of their movements, and lack of interest in the environment. In the preschool years, they are characterized by a short attention span and poor memory skills. By school age, the children may not have readiness skills necessary to pursue further learning. The milder the cognitive delay, the later it is likely to be identified. To be classified as mentally retarded, children must be assessed and shown to have delays in both intelligence and adaptive skills.

There are many different causes of cognitive delays, some of which are unknown. Genetic factors such as Down syndrome and Fragile X cause delays. Environmental factors are related to cultural-familial delays and fetal alcohol syndrome.

Children with cognitive delays may need more repetitions and more direct teaching techniques such as task analysis, backward chaining, and modeling. Teaching goals for children with cognitive delays focus on motor and language skills as well as thinking and reasoning skills, particularly social awareness and adaptive living skills. Adaptations include working from simple to complex and concrete to abstract.

Educational Resources

American Association on Mental Retardation (AAMR)
444 North Capital Street, NW, Suite 846
Washington, DC 20001-1512
(202) 387-1968, FAX (202) 387-2193
http://www.aamr.org/
e-mail: aamr.digex.net
Relevant for physicians, educators, students, and others interested in the general welfare of individuals with mental retardation and the study of the cause, treatment, and prevention of mental retardation. Their page contains information about the association and mental retardation.

Association for Children with Down Syndrome
(ACDS)
2616 Martin Avenue
Bellmore, NY 11710
ACDS has publications for families with young children, including a self-help curriculum, a movement guide, a guide to help children wear eyeglasses, and bibliographies.

Association for Retarded Citizens (ARC)
PO Box 6109
Arlington, TX 76005
(817) 261-6003, FAX (817) 277-3491
http://thearc.org.welcome.html
e-mail: thearc@metronet.com
A strong advocacy group for the needs of those with mental retardation. The ARC Resources Center (246 South River, Holland MI 49423) features practical aids for nonreaders.

Best Buddies Homepage
http://www.gate.net/~bestbud/
This page provides opportunities for individuals with mental retardation to become friends over the Internet.

Children of Alcoholics Foundations, Inc.
PO Box 4185, Department O
Grand Central Station
New York, NY 10163
(212) 351-2680
A voluntary nonprofit organization designed to increase awareness of the problems of children of alcoholics and to promote dissemination of this information.

Children Who Are Mentally Retarded
http://www.psych.med.umich.edu/web/aacap
/factsfam/retarded.htm
This page contains facts for families of children with mental retardation.

Directory of State and Local Resources for the
Mentally Retarded
President's Committee on Mental Retardation
U.S. Department of Health, Education and Welfare
Room 352G
200 Independence Avenue, SW
Washington, DC 20201
(202) 619-0634, FAX (202) 205-9519
A directory of resources on the state and local level. Advises the president and secretary on matters pertaining to mental illness.

Division on Mental Retardation
Council for Exceptional Children
1929 Association Drive
Reston, VA 22091-1589
Publishes a newsletter and a journal, Education and Training in Mental Retardation. *It is also a strong advocacy group for individuals with mental retardation.*

Down Syndrome Association of Ontario
157 Hazelwood Drive
Whitby, Ontario L1N3L9 Canada
Provides materials and guides for parents and teachers, including the development of language and reading.

Down Syndrome Congress
1640 West Roosevelt Road, Room 156E
Chicago, IL 60608
Parents, educators, and health professionals interested in promoting the welfare of persons with Down syndrome. Advises and aids parents with possible help for their child. Acts as a clearinghouse on information about Down syndrome.

Down Syndrome WWW Page
http://www.nas.com/downsyn
This page provides information about and pictures of people with Down syndrome.

The Family Empowerment Network
http://www.downsyndrome.com/
This family-friendly page provides information about mental retardation in a way the whole family can understand.

Family Village
Waisman Center
University of Wisconsin–Madison
1500 Highland Avenue
Madison, WI 53705–2280
(608) 263-5973, TDD (608) 263-0802,
FAX (608) 263-0529
http://www.familyvillage.wisc.edu/
email: rowley@waisman.wisc.edu
This page integrates information and resources on the Internet for people with mental retardation and their families.

National Association for Children of Alcoholics
31706 Coast Highway, Suite 201
South Laguna, CA 92677
(714) 499-3889
A nonprofit organization for children of alcoholics in all age groups. It publishes a newsletter and holds a convention.

National Association for Retarded Children
2709 Avenue E
East Arlington, TX 76011
Supplies general information about programs, facilities, institutions, and careers for the retarded.

National Clearinghouse for Alcohol and Drug
  Information
PO Box 2345
Rockville, MD 20852
(301) 468-2600
   *Provides information about publications, au-
diovisuals, and organizations in the area of alcohol
and drugs.*

National Council on Alcoholism, Inc.
12 West 21st Street
New York, NY 10010
(212) 206-6770
   *A voluntary health agency that provides infor-
mation about alcoholism and alcohol problems
through local affiliates. Some affiliates provide counseling for alcoholics and their families.*

The National Down Syndrome Society
666 Broadway, 8th Floor
New York, NY 10012-2317
(212) 460-9330, (800) 221-4602
http://www.ndss.org
   *The homepage for this organization contains
much information about Down syndrome, including
the topic of inclusion.*

One to One
1 Lincoln Plaza
1900 Broadway
New York, NY 10023
   *Develops community-based alternatives to insti-
tutions for people with disabilities. Provides grants,
interest-free loans, technical assistance, and support
to nonprofit agencies.*

Organizations and Associations Worldwide for Down
  Syndrome
http://www.nas.com/downsyn/org.html
   *Has information about organizations through-
out the world.*

Retarded Infants Service
386 Park Avenue South
New York, NY 10016
   *Service agency devoted to the physical well-
being and development of children with mental
retardation and the mental health of the parents.
Helps families with all aspects of home care,
including counseling, Home Aide Service, and
consultation.*

Siblings: Brothers and Sisters of People Who Have
  Mental Retardation
http://www.nas.com/downsyn/siblings.html
   *Siblings of those with mental retardation have
come together to share a commonality.*

References

Abel, E. L., & Sokol, R. J. (1987). Incidence of fetal alcohol syndrome and economic impact of FAS-related anomalies. *Drug and Alcohol Dependence, 19*, 51-70.

American Association on Mental Deficiency. (1992). *Mental retardation: Definition, classification, and systems of supports* (9th ed.). Washington, DC: Author.

American Psychiatric Association. (1994). *Diagnostic and statistical manual of mental disorders* (4th ed.). Washington, DC: Author.

Batshaw, M. L. (1997). Fragile X syndrome. In M. L. Batshaw (Ed.), *Children with disabilities* (4th ed., pp. 377-388). Baltimore: Brookes.

Batshaw, M. L., & Conlon, C. J. (1997). Substance abuse: A preventable threat to development. In M. L. Batshaw (Ed.), *Children with disabilities* (4th ed., pp. 143-162). Baltimore: Brookes.

Batshaw, M. L., & Perret, Y. M. (1992). *Children with handicaps: A medical primer* (3rd ed.). Baltimore: Brookes.

Batshaw, M. L., & Shapiro, B. K. (1997). Mental retardation. In M. L. Batshaw (Ed.), *Children with disabilities* (4th ed., pp. 335-360). Baltimore: Brookes.

Bayley, N. (1993). *Bayley scales of infant development* (2nd ed.). New York: Psychological Corporation.

Bert, C., Greene, R., & Bert, M. (1992). *Fetal alcohol syndrome in adolescents and adults* (pp. 1-16). Miami: Independent Native American Development Corporation of Florida.

Bornstein, M. H., & Sigman, M. D. (1986). Continuity in mental development from infancy. *Child Development, 57*, 251-274.

Brigance, A. (1991). *Brigance diagnostic inventory of early development.* North Billerica, MA: Curriculum Associates.

Capute, A. J., & Accardo, P. J. (Eds.). (1996). *Developmental disabilities in infancy and childhood: Vols. 1 & 2. Neurodevelopmental diagnosis and treatment and the spectrum of developmental disabilities* (2nd ed.). Baltimore: Brookes.

Children's Defense Fund. (1994). Cost of raising a child. *Children's Defense Fund Reports 15*, 6, 13.

Dagna-Bricarelli, F. D., Pierlugi, M., Grasso, M., et al. (1990). Origin of extra chromosome 21 in 343 families: Cytogenetic and molecular approaches. *American Journal of Medical Genetics, 7*(Suppl.), 129-132.

Davis, R., Allen, T., & Sherman, J. (1989). The role of the teacher: Strategies for helping. *National Association for Children of Alcoholics*, 11-14.

Down syndrome prevalence at birth: United States, 1983-1990. (1994). *Morbidity and Mortality Weekly Report, 43*, 617-622.

Frankenburg, W. K., & Dodds, J. B. (1990). *Denver II.* Denver, CO: Denver Developmental Metrics.

Furuno, S., O'Reilly, K., Hosaka, C., Inatsuku, T., & Zeisloft-Falbey, B. (1987). *The Hawaii early learning profile*. Palo Alto, CA: VORT.

Hagerman, R. J., & Cronister, A. (Eds.). (1996). *Fragile X syndrome: Diagnosis, treatment and research* (2nd ed.). Baltimore: Johns Hopkins University Press.

Hallahan, D., & Kauffman, J. (1994). *Exceptional children: Introduction to special education* (6th ed.). Englewood Cliffs, NJ: Prentice-Hall.

Harman, C. (1994). The routine 18-20 week ultrasound scan. In D. K. James, P. J. Steer, C. P. Weiner, & B. Gonik (Eds.), *High risk pregnancy: Management options* (pp. 661-692). London: Saunders.

Individuals with Disabilities Education Act of 1997. Pub. L. No. 105-17 111 Stat. 37-157 20 U.S.C. 1400.

James, D. K. (1994). Counseling about pediatric problems. In D. K. James, P. J. Steer, C. P. Weiner, & B. Gonik (Eds.), *High risk pregnancy: Management options* (pp. 1215-1225). London: Saunders.

LeMay, D., Griffin, P., & Sanford, A. (1978). *Learning accomplishment profile—Diagnostic edition*. Lewisville, NC: Kaplan School Supply.

Mazzocco, M. M. M., & O'Connor, R. (1993). Fragile X syndrome: A guide for teachers of young children. *Young Children, 49*(1), 73-77.

Meadows, S. (1993). *The child as thinker: The development and acquisition of cognition in children*. London: Routledge & Kegan Paul.

Newborg, J., Stock, J., Wnek, L., Guidubaldi, J., & Svinicki, J. (1984). *Battelle developmental inventory*. Allen TX: DLM Teaching Resources.

Nihira, K., Leland, H., & Lambert, N. (1993). *AAMD adaptive behavior scale–school* (2nd ed.). Austin, TX: Pro-Ed.

Pietrantoni, M., & Knuppel, R. A. (1991). Alcohol use in pregnancy. *Clinics in Perinatology, 18*(1), 93-111.

Rapoport, J. L. (1996). *DSM-IV: Training guide for diagnosis of childhood disorders*. New York: Brunner/Mazel.

Roizen, N. J. (1996). Down syndrome and associated medical disorders. *Mental Retardation and Development Disabilities Research Reviews, 2,* 85-89.

Roizen, N. J. (1997). Down syndrome. In M. L. Batshaw (Ed.), *Children with disabilities* (4th ed., pp. 361-376). Baltimore: Brookes.

Salvia, J., & Ysseldyke, J. E. (1995). *Assessment* (6th ed.). Boston: Houghton Mifflin.

Schubert, P. J., & Savage, B. (1994). Smoking, alcohol and drug abuse. In D. K. James, P. J. Steer, C. P. Weiner, & B. Gonik (Eds.), *High risk pregnancy: Management options* (pp. 783-801). London: Saunders.

Sherman, S. L. (1991). Epidemiology. In R. J. Hagerman & A. Cronister-Silverman (Eds.), *The Fragile X syndrome: Diagnosis, treatment, and research*. Baltimore: Johns Hopkins University Press.

Sparrow, S., Balla, D., & Cicchetti, D. (1984). *Interview edition, expanded form manual, Vineland Adaptive Behavior Scales*. Circle Pines, MN: American Guidance Service.

Spohr, H. L., Williams, J., & Steinhausen, H. C. (1993, April 10). Prenatal alcohol exposure and long-term developmental consequences. *The Lancet, 341,* 907-910.

USDA Family Economics Research Group. (1994). *Expenditures on a child by families, 1993*. Author.

Williamson, R. A. (1994). Abnormalities of alpha-fetoprotein and other biochemical tests. In D. K. James, P. J. Steer, C. P. Weiner, & B. Gonik (Eds.), *High risk pregnancy: Management options* (pp. 643-660). London: Saunders.

Chapter 13

CHILDREN WITH ADVANCED COGNITIVE DEVELOPMENT

Ever since I was a little girl, I have been labeled "bright," "gifted," a "real academic achiever." As a younger child, I enjoyed these labels; they made me feel special and brilliant. However, as I have grown older, these labels have not disappeared, and they continually cause me problems.

I've always had more stress in my life because I was "smarter." Teachers put me in groups with "troublemakers" and "nongifted" children, somehow hoping my influence would encourage them. Extra work and projects were also tasks I had to accomplish because of my status. People ceaselessly expected more of me, which was damaging emotionally. Many children would purposely not interact with me, and if I received a less than perfect grade or score on something, taunts of "Why did you get that grade if you're so smart?" followed.

High school has caused the most critical obstacles. Presently, I have so much responsibility, work, and stress that I feel emotionally unstable—like a nervous breakdown is near. There's a serious problem when you get sick and you're scared to miss school for fear you'll get behind. Enjoyable activities get shoved aside, and the focus becomes school exclusively. It goes without saying that most "bright" students have great motivation and high expectations of their own. This is intensified when well-meaning teachers overwhelm students with pressure.

My generation is completely different from any other in this way. All the fun high school stuff you're suppose to experience, like parties, dating, movies, proms, are pushed away to make additional room for responsibility and work. From what our elders and peers tell us, high school is supposed to be the best years of your life—the final real carefree time before college and the real world. However, for many people my age, this idea is no longer a reality.

I remember one day in my Advanced Placement English/History class when I was so tired and stressed out that my teacher took me out of the room to talk. "Where is our bouncy, happy, eager-to-learn girl?" he asked. "You seem so stressed and uncaring. What is wrong?" I wanted to yell at him, "You took the bounce out of me with your curriculum."

Sometimes, we focus so much on children's differences we forget that, regardless of their ability or disability, they have the same needs as other children. Children with advanced cognitive development are often referred to educationally as gifted and/or talented. "Gifted students are those with a potential to exhibit superior performance across a range of areas or endeavor" (George, 1995, p. 3).

If we are committed to inclusion and equal educational opportunities for all children, then what do we do about children who are advanced in their development? Many see children with advanced cognitive development as a precious national resource that is being wasted (Schwartz, 1994). Others feel that these children will be able to succeed very well without special services (Council for Exceptional Children [CEC], 1996). Gifted education has been criticized as being "elitist," not open to children from diverse ethnic groups, those with disabilities, and those who exhibit gifts and talents in only one area (CEC, 1996).

Definition and Classification of Advanced Cognitive Development

In many ways, what is valued is related to the sociohistorical time and the culture in which one is raised. In a society where people hunted for food, an individual who shot more accurately and from a greater distance than others might have been considered "gifted." In industrialized nations, we value other skills. In the past, we identified individuals as gifted only after they had made major contributions to society (George, 1995). In early childhood education, the goal is to identify children to provide them with a developmentally appropriate education. This is not necessarily a speeded-up curriculum, any more than we try to slow down the curriculum for children with delayed cognitive development. It must be designed to match that child's needs.

Unlike other areas covered in this text, there is no federal mandate for individualized education to meet the needs of this population. Individual states decide whether or not to have programs for them (CEC, 1996). However, the federal government does provide a standard definition in Public Law 95-561, Title IX, the Gifted and Talented Children's Act of 1978: "Gifted and talented children means children, and whenever applicable, youth, who are identified at the preschool, elementary, or secondary level as possessing demonstrated or potential abilities that give evidence of high performance capability in areas such as intellectual, creative, specific academic, or leadership ability, or in the performing or visual arts, and who by reason thereof require services or activities not ordinarily provided by the school" (Education Act Amendments, 1978).

This global definition of giftedness also cites a variety of specific areas in which these unique talents might be displayed. Despite the broadness of the definition, the most frequently used means of identifying gifted children is intelligence tests: the Stanford–Binet (IQ of 130 or higher), the WPPSI-R, or the Wechsler Intelligence Scale for Children III (WISC-III) (Schwartz, 1994).

Some feel that high intelligence alone is not enough, that giftedness is an interaction among above-average ability, creativity, and sustained interest. Currently, we are moving away from using the IQ as the only method of identifying giftedness, just as we are moving away from it as the only way of identifying children with delayed development, to the concept that there are multiple talents or intelligences (George, 1995).

Accelerated Cognitive Development

Throughout this text, we have used terminology and classification to indicate the degree to which a child differs from the norms. Thus, we identify the degree to which children's development is delayed (mild, moderate, severe, or profound) or the level of supports a child needs (intermittent, limited, extensive, or pervasive). An IQ, as a measure of rate of cognitive development, also suggests the degree to which children with advanced cognitive development are developing differently from their peers. For example, a moderately gifted child with an IQ of 133 with chronological age of 6 has a mental age of 9; an exceptionally gifted 6-year-old with an IQ of 160 has a mental age of approximately 11. This first-grader would be expected to be able to understand content at the level of children in sixth grade (Gross, 1993). Some suggest that it would be useful to develop some standardized terminology and classify children based on IQ in the following way:

IQ 130–144   Moderately gifted

IQ 145–159   Highly gifted

IQ 160–179   Exceptionally gifted

IQ 180+   Profoundly gifted

In a normal distribution, approximately 1 child in 20 in a given population would be moderately gifted; 1 in 1,000 highly gifted; fewer than 9 in 100,000 could be classified as exceptionally gifted; and fewer than 1 in a million as profoundly gifted (Gross, 1993). Because the number of moderately gifted children is so much greater than highly, exceptionally, and profoundly gifted children, most school programs for the gifted are designed based on the characteristics, learning styles, and needs of this group (Gross, 1993). These programs rarely take into account that a child with an IQ of 190 is as different in ability level from a child with an IQ of 130 as the child with an IQ of 130 is from the child with an IQ of 70. See Table 13.1 for behaviors that may indicate advanced cognitive development.

Developmental Aspects of Advanced Cognitive Development

Unique gifts and talents appear to be a developmental phenomenon. Young children who display these gifts often show both general and unique patterns of strengths over time. There appear to be three major elements involved in whether or not a child will display gifts and talents: the child's cognitive ability, intrinsic motivation, and a cognitively stimulating environment (Gottfried, Gottfried, Bathurst, & Guerin, 1994). Methods of assessing children vary with the age of the child.

TABLE 13.1 RED FLAGS FOR ADVANCED COGNITIVE DEVELOPMENT

Asks many specific questions and seriously listens to the answers

Has a good memory

Prefers playing with older children

Has a mature and perhaps even subtle sense of humor

Is exceptionally curious

Is interested in cause-effect relationships but may view these relationships differently from adult expectations

Has a long attention span for activities of own choosing

Has a high energy level; may be restless in mind and body

Knows many things that peers are unaware of

Is sensitive to emotional issues at an early age; may have concerns about death, anger, love, pain, and so on

Is eager to try new activities and/or perform familiar activities in new ways

Saunders & Espeland, 1991

0 to 3

Early identification of young cognitively advanced children focuses primarily on early receptive and expressive language development and positive, motivationally relevant behaviors. Identifying children who are gifted and talented is extremely unlikely until close to age 3.

Because children are gifted or talented does not necessarily mean that their growth or development at this age is different from other children. However, because of *uneven* development, young children especially may appear to have deficits when in reality they are developing physically at a normal pace but not at the same pace as their intellectual development or their particular configuration of gifts and talents. Young children with exceptional intellectual resources may have a greater than average need for emotional, social, and other "nonintellectual" capabilities to successfully cope (Howe, 1990). If language develops early, children may discover they can ask others to be their "gofers," and motor skills may appear to lag. When the gofers decide not to perform, the motor skills quickly follow.

We know very little about the developmental course of giftedness until children have actually displayed these characteristics and we consequently identify them. The Fullerton longitudinal study is an exception; it chose a large sample of healthy 1-year-olds. Some of the children at later ages were identified as gifted, others were not. Hence, the study was in a good position to make comparisons between the two groups (Gottfried et al., 1994).

Verbal skills is one area where developmental differences are likely to be most apparent. The Fullerton longitudinal growth study found significant differences between gifted and nongifted children in receptive language at age 1, and differences in both receptive and expressive language were consistent from infancy onward. These were the major differences found in the early years; some questioned whether the high scores in the language area accounted for the differences in intellectual performance that were found at 18 months and continued (Gottfried et al., 1994).

The rate of development of children with advanced cognitive development is different during this period. That is, their particular pattern of gifts and talents develop more rapidly than nongifted children.

Very young gifted children also appeared to be different in the testing situation itself. They showed "significantly greater goal directedness, object orientation, attention span, cooperativeness, positive emotional tone, and responsiveness to test materials" (Gottfried et al., 1994, p. 105). These characteristics are relevant to motivation and might be considered gifted motivational behaviors and be used as one means of identifying young gifted learners. Other indicators include great attentiveness, ability to concentrate, intense interest and curiosity, and delight in the unexpected (George, 1995).

Even during early childhood, it is apparent that some children have skills that are developmentally advanced for their age. Often these skills are in the areas of communications.

3 to 6

Younger children may just hint at potential for exceptional skill that is confirmed during the preschool years. Language proficiency is still a key. Gifted children have large vocabularies that they use accurately and typically speak in entire sentences. Children who read before attending school are often thought to be cognitively advanced. Although parents may claim that this "just happened," that they didn't teach the child, in reality no one (adult or child) can learn to read without instruction. Children cannot teach themselves to read. Someone must draw the child's attention to the particular features and associations that reading requires (Howe, 1990). Young readers have invariably spent a good deal of time being read to by an older child or adult who has informally taught the child. They like books.

They may also have an early interest in and proficiency in drawing, music, or other art forms. They seem to be observant and retain information they learn. They also seem to be able to concentrate for long periods of time. Many have a keen sense of humor. They are also interested in how things work and in cause-effect relationships.

In general, children with advanced cognitive development have physical development that is ahead of same-age children with lower IQs, but this may be due to social class differences more than any other variable (Freeman, 1985b). Their coordination seems similar to their age-mates. To the extent that very gifted children are accelerated in school (for example, starting first grade at age 4), their physical development may appear slower because the comparison group is actually a year or two older. Relating to others in an appropriate way is often difficult, as the child can feel (and is) different. Additionally, their tendency to choose older children as friends focuses attention on their relatively immature physical development (Gottfried et al., 1994). These differences often increase their probability of choosing noncompetitive types of physical activities.

There has been a great deal of interest in the relationship of temperament and intellectual development. The research is decidedly mixed. Some have found gifted children having the ability to concentrate longer and having longer attention spans, being more persistent, happy, and active (Matheny, 1989). Other studies have not substantiated these differences (Gottfried et al., 1994).

Overall, the behavioral and emotional adjustment of children with advanced cognitive development is not distinguishable during early childhood (Gottfried et al., 1994). Advantages in the cognitive realm are not associated with disadvantages in other areas of development, although some display superior social reasoning (but not necessarily social behavior) and adaptive functioning.

There is a great deal of interest in the interaction of these young children with their family and family environment. Research findings in this area have been consistent since the 1920s. Gifted children are predominately firstborn or only children. Most children with advanced cognitive development have been in consistently stimulating environments from infancy through their early elementary years (Gottfried et al., 1994). Their environments respond to the child's demands by providing early culturally and intellectually stimulating activities. Their families are able to provide stimulating environments in part because the families are typically high in socioeconomic status, with highly educated parents. Parents are typically involved, responsive, and nurturing and have high educational aspirations for their children (Gottfried et al., 1994).

6 to 9

Children identified as having advanced cognitive development are significantly more likely to enter school at an earlier age and are not likely to be retained at any grade level through age 8 (Gottfried et al., 1994). Their teachers characterize them as working harder, learning more, and being better behaved than their nongifted counterparts. In general, they are more adapted to the demands of school. Terman (cited in Gottfried et al., 1994) found that at age 7, children identified as gifted and talented were reading an average of seven books per month, whereas nongifted children read very little. Being extensively read to in the early years is consistently associated with advanced cognitive development. Academically, these children excel and frequently skip grades during these years or are placed early into kindergarten or first grade.

As children move more clearly into the academic world, some who were not previously identified will be noted. It is not just what they do, but how they go about doing it. Gifted children seem to grasp the essence of the problem or situation or can relate the situation to an analogous one. They may skip steps in the process or be intrigued by finding alternative

solutions. Again, their persistence, high ideals, self-discipline, and independence are noted (George, 1995).

Children with advanced cognitive development can be more difficult because they don't fit the norm. They are often highly curious, beyond just being interested in things. They are interested in details and ask many questions. They have a broader knowledge base than their peers and may become bored, especially during group instruction. They may be intense and highly critical. They work with information by manipulating it, as opposed to just remembering it. They like mysteries and complexities and enjoy learning. They may have unusual or silly ideas and make keen observations. They often prefer the company of adults or older peers (George, 1995).

They may seem to be more emotionally stable, but they are not invulnerable to life circumstance. However, they are not more likely to be emotionally maladjusted (Freeman, 1985a). They may feel that they are different from others but are not completely aware of the cause of the differences; they may feel superior because they are "smart." They may have fewer skills in peer relationships but deal well with and even prefer adults.

Causes of Advanced Cognitive Development

There is debate about the causes of advanced cognitive development. As in most areas, there are proponents of a genetic view and proponents of an environmental view; most agree it is a combination. The family a child is born into affects the child in two major ways: Families help children gain essential knowledge, skills, and mental strategies, and they transmit values and attitudes related to learning and achievement (Howe, 1990). There are cultural and ethnic differences in the proportion of children who are identified as gifted and talented. This may be related to the bias of IQ tests or to socioeconomic status.

Studies have shown some similarities among parents of young children identified as being gifted or talented (Bloom, 1985). The families placed a high value on achieving. The parents introduced the child at an early age to the area in which he eventually excelled, and it was frequently an area in which at least one of the parents had talent. The child's special skills began developing in the context of home activities through informal parent teaching. Parents were involved in the child's outside activities and made sure that the child practiced.

Advanced Cognitive Development and Unique Talents

We often differentiate between children with advanced cognitive development (gifted) and talented children. Gifted children are those who have the potential to exhibit superior performance across a range of subject matter areas or endeavors. We use the term talented to refer to children with the potential for superior performance in one particular area (George, 1995).

Child Prodigies

A prodigy is a child with the gift of extraordinary developmental potential in one particular area, in contrast to children with advanced cognitive development who possess generalized intellectual abilities that permit high levels of functioning in many cognitive areas. "The prodigy seems to be unique in having an extremely specialized gift that is expressed only under very specific, culturally evolved environmental conditions" (Feldman, 1986, p. 9). The prodigy is a specialist, not a generalist. The child prodigy does not necessarily have a high IQ.

Feldman (1986, p. 16) defines a prodigy as someone capable of "performance in an intellectually demanding field at the level of an adult professional before the age of ten." Prodigies appear in some fields and not others. Using Feldman's definition, prodigies are found primarily in mathematics, musical performance, and chess. Computer science may be another field where prodigies will be found. Prodigies may also be found in sports. To the extent that the prodigy's talent is focused in one area and is not supported by generalized high intelligence, this unevenness can make life extremely difficult. Mozart, for example, was characterized as a relatively simple human being whose wife even cut his meat for him (Feldman, 1986).

Children Who Have Advanced Cognitive Development

In some children, the potential for advanced cognitive development is identified early; in others, it is only apparent later in their development. It is usually identified through standardized intelligence tests. Many children who come from lower-socioeconomic-status homes may not be identified as gifted because they have not had the same learning opportunities as others. The tests may also be biased against children of color. Likewise, children from different cultural backgrounds as well as those with disabilities are more difficult to identify. Tests that focus on divergent thinking and creativity have the potential for identifying some of these children (George, 1995).

Children Who Have Unique Talents

"Talented students are those with a potential to exhibit superior performance in one area of endeavor" (George, 1995, p. 3). Gardner (1983) identifies seven intelligences where special talents may exist. All children have a unique blend of these intelligences; talented children are especially advanced in one (Gardner, 1983; George, 1995; Saunders & Espeland, 1991).

Verbal/linguistic intelligence refers to the ability to appreciate and use language with sensitivity and clarity. Verbally/linguistically talented children:

- Use advanced vocabulary;

- Employ longer and more advanced sentence structures (may use words like "however" and "although");

- Make up elaborate, coherent stories and fantasies;

- Describe experiences with unusual depth and accuracy;

- Memorize and recite stories and poems;

- Prefer books with more words and plot than pictures;

- Have taught or are teaching themselves to read; and

- Are interested in language in its many forms.

Musical/rhythmic intelligence refers to the ability to use musical elements (pitch, rhythm, tone) at an unusually sophisticated level. Some children may have perfect pitch and the ability to identify a wide range of musical scores when only a few bars are played. Musical children are intrigued with and notice sounds in their environment (Gardner, 1983; George, 1995; Saunders & Espeland, 1991). Musically talented young children:

- Enjoy and frequently request music-related activities;

- Respond emotionally to music even without clues from lyrics (might report that certain music makes them happy);

- Can identify familiar songs by hearing the tune;

- Sing in tune or close to it and can match pitch within their range;

- May sing to themselves and often have good pitch;

- Can identify the sounds of a particular instrument;

- Prefer poems with sound and rhythm over narrative stories;

- Dance, move, and clap in time with musical patterns and rhythms.

Logical/mathematical intelligence is characterized by scientific reasoning, a love for abstraction, and an interest in mathematical operations. These children are interested in numbers, counting, and manipulating numbers (Gardner, 1983; George, 1995; Saunders & Espeland, 1991). They are fascinated by how things work. Mathematically talented young children:

- Are interested in maps, globes, charts, calendars, and clocks;
- Are curious about abstract ideas such as time and space;
- Enjoy new, difficult puzzles;
- Like to count, weigh, and categorize objects; and
- Recognize numbers and corresponding objects.

Visual/spatial intelligence is the ability to perceive the visual world accurately and then recreate that visual experience in art or graphics. It involves mental imagery and the ability to manipulate and transform images. These children are adept at puzzles and other spatial problem-solving activities (Gardner, 1983; George, 1995; Saunders & Espeland, 1991). Visually talented young children:

- Draw, paint, or sculpt and show both technical skill and fine detail;
- Remember in detail items, places, and pictures they have seen;
- Have advanced eye-hand coordination;
- Show attention to texture, color, and balance;
- Respond emotionally to photos, paintings, or sculpture; and
- Share feelings and moods through drawing, painting, or sculpture.

Psychomotor/kinesthetic intelligence refers to the ability to control one's body or body parts skillfully. These children move expressively and are good at both informal and organized games and sports (Gardner, 1983; George, 1995; Saunders & Espeland, 1991). Young children with psychomotor talent:

- Enjoy movements such as running, jumping, and climbing as an end in themselves;
- Have an accurate and relaxed sense of both static and dynamic balance (hopping on one foot, walking a narrow line, balancing a bean bag);
- Use gestures, body movements, and/or facial expression to show or mimic feelings;
- Can adapt motor skills in game situations.

Intrapersonal intelligence is the ability to form an accurate model of oneself and use this model effectively to evaluate situations. It involves detecting and distinguishing feelings. These children understand themselves well (Gardner, 1983; George, 1995; Saunders & Espeland, 1991). Young children with intrapersonal intelligence:

- Are aware of their emotional state and the range of emotions, can be very focused and single-minded; and
- May be frustrated when interrupted.

Interpersonal intelligence focuses on the ability to recognize and distinguish the moods, intentions, and motivations of other individuals. These children often emerge as leaders and organizers. They are sensitive to the needs and desires of others (Gardner, 1983; George, 1995; Saunders & Espeland, 1991). Young children with interpersonal talent:

- Interact easily with both children and adults;
- Are sought out by other children for play;
- Are able to enter an already-playing group of children and be accepted;
- Can influence other children toward their goals (positive or negative);
- Understand cause-and-effect as it relates to behavior and consequences;
- Recognize when their behavior yields certain predictable results; and
- Have a sense of justice and fair play for themselves and others.

Because of a lack of uniformity, there may be additional state and local definitions of children who qualify as gifted and talented. How these terms are defined determines who is included or excluded. It is one of the most controversial areas of education and a difficult one. Depending on the definition and method of testing, children with disabilities can be included or excluded from this group.

Assessment of Children with Advanced Cognitive Development

Labels of all kinds are misleading and infer that children can be neatly divided into groups. This applies to children identified as having advanced cognitive development as well as those with delayed cognitive development. Generally speaking, these labels suggest variations along a continuum we refer to as intelligence. All agree that individuals vary in abilities. It is the arbitrariness with which we divide up the continuum and label individuals that fall in particular places that is of concern. This is particularly true when we label young children as either "slow" or "fast" and use this label to project future achievement or lack thereof. In general, we look at children's present level of functioning as a prediction of future abilities. In cases where there are major changes in a child's life, we may not be able to accurately predict future progress (Howe, 1990).

As in other areas, there is general consensus that multimodal testing is necessary to identify those children who are gifted and talented. Most recommend a combination of testing (intelligence, achievement, creativity), observations of parents and teachers, work samples, and so on. A professionally administered individual intelligence test such as the WPPSI–R or the Stanford–Binet Intelligence Scale, fourth edition, is traditionally part of the battery. These measures are well designed, normed, and validated. They allow for observations by a well-trained examiner. It is useful to look not only at the total score, but at the profile. For children who achieve an IQ of 145 with particular strength in verbal and quantitative reasoning, early school entrance might be a consideration.

It is also necessary to evaluate a young child's skills in relation to other children in the class. With the advent of educational television and preschool, many children have academic skills that allow them to test well. This is not necessarily a reflection of their ability to learn, but rather of how they have spent their time. It would be a disservice to these children to advance their placement. Grade-equivalent scores have not yet caught up with this new trend (Robinson & Weimer, 1991).

An IQ score reflects what a child has already learned and hence is a "static" approach to assessment. Another view of assessment tries to assess problem-solving ability, the interactive "dynamic" quality of learning potential. Vygotsky's (1987/1934) theory and methodology focus not on what children can do independently but on what they can do with adult support or scaffolding. He labels this their zone of proximal development (ZPD). To use the ZPD as an assessment paradigm, children are presented a series of analogous problem-solving tasks that they cannot solve independently. The child is asked to solve the first task but is told that assistance will be available. An adult then provides hints, suggestions, and repeated trials necessary for the child to solve the problem. Once the child has mastered the problem-solving strategies, he is presented with similar and increasingly difficult problem-solving tasks. The evaluation then focuses on the child's ability to generalize and adapt the problem-solving strategy. The less the child needs help on the more difficult tasks, the broader the child's ZPD. Children with higher ability have broader ZPDs (Kanevsky, 1992).

Educational Intervention

A variety of strategies are used to meet the needs of children with advanced cognitive development. As with other diverse abilities, professionals support different positions. Some feel that children with advanced cognitive development should be included in the regular classroom to the maximum degree possible and that the role of teachers of the gifted and talented is to support regular teachers in providing an appropriate learning environment for these children (McDaniel, 1993). The key issue here is whether regular classroom teachers can provide an exciting and stimulating environment for children who can achieve at three, four, or five years or grade levels beyond their peers (the same issue we face with all children with diverse abilities). The record from the past in this regard is discouraging. If this *can* be done, it doesn't appear to have been done well, and some feel that separation, especially with increasing age, is de-

sirable. If regular classrooms could be designed to meet the needs of gifted children, theoretically all children would profit. However, we have not yet discovered how to do that (Gallagher, 1993). Although colleges and universities increasingly are requiring education students to take courses on teaching children with disabilities, few require such courses for the gifted and talented. Besides inclusion, additional issues focus on whether educational programming should emphasize acceleration, enrichment, or a combination.

Acceleration

The assumption underlying acceleration is that some children learn at a consistently faster pace than others. As curriculum becomes more rigid, there is the potential for a mismatch between children's abilities and the subject matter presented. Acceleration is a process of moving through an educational program either at a faster rate than usual or at a younger age. There are many different types of acceleration. Children can be admitted to kindergarten prior to the age specified. They can skip a grade. They can be placed in classes where two or more grade levels are combined. They can have subject matter acceleration, that is, be placed at a more advanced grade level for one or more subjects (for example, a kindergartner going to first grade for reading and math (Southern & Jones, 1991).

Because of the range and types of acceleration options, it is difficult to be for or against it. Advocates for acceleration argue that it provides increased efficiency and effectiveness of instruction. They see it as providing bright students with appropriate educational opportunities and continuing challenges that will maintain their enthusiasm and excitement for learning (Southern & Jones, 1991). Those opposed to acceleration are concerned about possible gaps in general knowledge. They are also concerned that children who show academic excellence at young ages may not maintain these advantages, that the accelerated demands may be too great for the young child's experience and sophistication. That is, the programming is not developmentally appropriate. Others focus on the reduced time for age-appropriate activities such as play (Elkind, 1986). There is some concern about later social maladjustment as students reflect on lost opportunities. Some are worried about the effect of acceleration on emotional adjustment, with concern about friendship patterns, increased pressure, and lack of outlets for expression, as well as reduced opportunities for extracurricular activities (Southern & Jones, 1991).

For children identified as having advanced cognitive development during the preschool years, certainly the most frequent option is early admission to kindergarten. This is viewed as the least disruptive option for children who are intellectually advanced and within six months of the usual entry age (Robinson & Weimer, 1991). Studies that focused on children who were *selected* for early school entrance, were within a year of the school-entrance age, and were considered mature for their age performed well (Robinson & Weimer, 1991).

Enrichment

Enrichment refers to broadening the curriculum to include information that is not traditionally part of the curriculum at a particular level. There is no single strategy for enrichment; rather, it is an approach across subject matter areas. George (1995) suggests that one consider the following factors before choosing a method of enrichment:

Is the method flexible enough for children to develop at their own pace?

Does the method support the acquisition of higher-order thinking skills?

Is the method both intellectually stimulating and emotionally protected?

Is the method likely to alienate a child from peers or provide information that will be repeated later?

Does it foster teamwork or individual differences?

Many enrichment programs use a model that increases awareness of higher-order thinking skills. Bloom's (1985) taxonomy, for example, moves from lower-level to higher-level thinking skills: knowledge, comprehension, application, analysis, synthesis, evaluation. The goal in enrichment is to go beyond comprehension to ensure that children have the opportunity to use higher-level thinking skills. That is, it is not enough that a 5-year-old can name several different dinosaurs (knowledge) or make a chart showing the different sizes of dinosaurs (comprehension) or even compare those who are carnivores to those who are

not (application). Children who are gifted and talented need to be challenged to predict what might have happened if dinosaurs had not become extinct (analysis), write a play about life when dinosaurs lived (synthesis), or debate theories of causes for dinosaurs having become extinct (evaluation).

Guidelines

1. Have children with advanced cognitive development develop independent work habits, but don't equate independence with isolation. See if those skills that are best developed independently can be worked on at home. Children come to school to learn with and about other children. Your challenge is to plan activities with a range of difficulty that allows all the children in the class to participate and learn at their particular ability level.

2. Children need to learn socially acceptable ways of dealing with emotions. Many times, they are frustrated if they know they are different and learn things more quickly.

3. Provide a variety of activities and experiences that will allow children to explore and find areas of interest, but also allow children to concentrate their energy in one area if they choose.

4. Provide children with activities that require divergent thinking (for example, have them pretend they are accidentally locked in a bathroom and let them figure out how to get out).

5. Emphasize both how and why something occurs.

6. Emphasize both group and individual problem solving.

There are many ways of encouraging creativity. The easiest is to tell children to be creative—obvious, yet it does work.

1. Regard creativity as a process; do not emphasize the product. Encourage different ways of doing things, regardless of the results (which may look far worse than a classmate's more traditional product).

2. Value creative achievement in comparison to a personal norm, not a universal one. If a product or process is new for a child, it is creative for that child, whether or not society would see it in that light.

3. Reward creativity! Verbally support the child who comes up with a new idea. Ask how things could work in a different way.

4. Encourage children to ask questions and to explore materials.

5. Help children learn by asking questions that stimulate creative thinking. Here are some useful statements:

Program planning needs to be responsive to the needs and interests of children. It must be designed to increase their imagination and problem-solving skills at the same time that it supports peer interactions and social skills.

Start your mind working on this, but don't tell me for a minute:

What (who) do you see of interest?

What can you say about this?

Is there anything worth thinking about?

Do you have any ideas?

Does this remind you of anything?

Let's set up some ground rules for the safety of all.

Stretch your brain a little or a lot.

What can we do with this? What else?

Does this look (sound, feel) interesting?

What else can you make out of this?

What would you like to rearrange?

Do you see any other possibilities?

Can you see some place to start?

Can you find something here (in the room)?

What's funny about this?

Can you change this to make it something else?

Can you use this in a different way?

6. Encourage children to make the commonplace different. Don't always ask what things are or require that products have a specific purpose.

There are a number of practices you should strive to avoid with children who are gifted and talented. You want to encourage creativity, not discourage it. The following responses and procedures are great discouragers.

1. Avoid putting pressure on children for conformity. This does not mean the children should be excused from following class rules, but rather that they should not be judged as strange because they act differently. Discipline that demands abject compliance and discourages understanding and questioning is disastrous for these children. If children must do things "because I said so," they lose the opportunity to learn and create. Tell children why something must be done. Whether gifted or not, children like to have reasons for what must happen, and it increases the probability that the directions of a task will be completed.

2. Avoid emphasis on traditional gender roles. This tends to discourage creativity for both boys and girls because it narrows both roles. All children need exposure to varied nontraditional and non-sexist roles.

3. Avoid pressuring children to succeed. In a success-oriented culture such as ours, failures present problems. Fear of failure prevents many children from being creative.

4. Avoid insistence on regimentation. Having regimented activities that cannot be expanded or contracted, or requiring all children to finish projects in a specified amount of time discourages children with advanced and delayed cognitive development. Be flexible with time limits to allow for the creativity of the process.

5. Avoid highly structured materials. Materials that do it all—that are brightly colored, move, make noise—don't leave as much room for imagination as those that allow the child to create the movement, function, and noise.

6. Avoid using phrases such as: Don't be silly; It won't work; That's not our problem; Don't be so sloppy; Do it the right way; Do it the way I said to; What's the matter with you?

Judging children or their activities often discourages creativity. Parents are also in a position to encourage or discourage creativity.

A group of 4-year-olds were making reindeer out of clothespins, which required them to glue the wooden pieces together as well as add a nose and eyes. Tony proudly displayed his finished product and was asked "Tell me about it." He explained how all the other kids' reindeer had two eyes but he wanted his to only have one. The teacher told him that there was a special name for a race of men giants that had one eye right in the middle of their forehead: Cyclops. They looked it up in the dictionary. Tony went home and proudly told his father about making the reindeer. His father predictably asked, "Where is the other eye? All reindeer have two eyes!" To which Tony responded, "Not mine, mine is a cyclops." The father looked it up in the dictionary and brought Tony and the reindeer into school early the next day.

"We have to speak," he said handing the teacher Tony's cyclops. "What is this? If my son is going to make a reindeer, it has to have two eyes, not one." You could almost feel Tony's hurt feelings. He was crushed that something he was proud of was maligned. Father and teacher agreed that Tony would have time to make another reindeer with two eyes, just like all the other kids. He could keep his cyclops, and the teacher could try to encourage creativity, but he would also conform when necessary. "Well, what about the other kids?" the father asked. The teacher replied that the other children would also be given a chance to make another reindeer and that if they wanted to put three eyes on them, that would be allowed.

Tony was embarrassed after his father left and needed some reassurance. The teacher told him that in life there are different ways to do things. He replied, "Yeah, but with my dad I'll always be making two of something: one for him and one the way I want it to be."

There are times when it is important for children to conform and times when they need the space to be creative. A wise teacher allows time for both.

Curriculum Adaptations

Activities for young children who are gifted and talented need to be more varied, cover a broader range of material, be done in greater depth and with an emphasis on higher-order thinking skills, and offer the possibility for an individualized focus.

Social Awareness: Self-Esteem, Inclusion, Social Studies, Health and Safety

Encourage children to practice developing social skills. Although gifted children may have greater understanding of how to solve interpersonal problems in the abstract, they need practice implementing solutions. Generating solutions and implementing them are different skills. They need practice at both, as many are frustrated when others can't relate to what they are saying.

Self-Esteem. All children need to feel good about themselves. Children with advanced development, although ahead of their peers in many ways, often hold themselves to high standards that are difficult to live up to. Children who are very good in one area may expect to be good in all areas and when they are not, they quit participating.

1. Support children with realistic feedback about their performance.

2. Encourage children to try new activities and take risks in areas where they may not excel.

3. Help them learn the skill of supporting other children in areas of strength and in asking for support from their peers in other areas.

4. Encourage children in all areas of their development, not just those they are good at.

Inclusion. It is difficult and frustrating to be different. All children want to be included and accepted. Highlighting both similarities and differences helps all children belong.

1. Have a small group of children complete the following statements individually and talk about the differences in answers.

    I feel happy when . . .

    I feel sad when . . .

    I am frightened by . . .

    I get angry when . . .

    I feel proud when . . .

    I am like others because . . .

    I am different from others because . . .

2. Children are different. Support this as you include all children in your class. Be willing to talk about both similarities and differences but em-phasize that they are all children and they have strengths as well as limitations.

Social Studies. Social studies can cover traditional and nontraditional roles and occupations and provide information on unusual ways of doing things. Lessons should be designed that give children an understanding of themselves and their role in society.

1. Cook foreign foods and eat them in traditional ways. Tempura and fried rice can be eaten with chopsticks, Pu Pu with two fingers, fondue with a long fork, and so on. Discuss the food and the utensils used and how they are adapted. (Be aware of safety issues. Don't use toothpicks, as they are dangerous for young children.)

2. Explore varied occupations such as plumber, computer programmer, baker, physicist, producer, professional athlete, and pest exterminator. Let the children's interest guide your choices. Take field trips when possible. Be sure to give a nonsexist presentation of occupations and value all occupations.

3. Discuss where different foods grow and compare fresh foods with canned or frozen foods. Introduce some foods that are from other parts of the country or from other countries.

4. Help children make maps of the area around the school and learn the basic elements of a map (such as legend, scale, direction). Have them find a treasure using a map.

5. Show children pictures of different types of housing and houses around the world and discuss how they are adapted to different regions.

6. Discuss the role that rules play in your class and talk about laws and the need for laws, people to obey them, and, if necessary, others to enforce them.

7. Help children learn to take different perspectives. Read books such as *The True Story of the Three Little Pigs*, in which the wolf just got into trouble because he had a cold.

Health and Safety. Health and safety are important for these children because their curiosity and experimentation can lead to problems. The "what happens if I swallow a penny" or "will I bubble like the washing machine if I eat detergent and jump around" syndrome can have dangerous side effects. *So don't do it!* (A trip to the poison control center can be stimulating, but it is best to avoid making it.) Children must learn to develop a pattern of checking with adults before exploring some things. They also need feedback on how to report their specific feelings if they are sick and a clear understanding that this is not the time to be creative.

1. Help children read labels and sort them on the basis of whether or not the contents are safe to play with. Add new things and help children learn

to classify unknown objects as "not to be played with" and "not to be eaten." Don't use food for art. Make sure they realize that unknowns are not always safe and should be checked by an adult for clarification.

2. The safe use of tools should be emphasized. Discuss safe use of simple tools such as hammers and screwdrivers. Have safety goggles available and discuss why they are used.

3. Talk about safety devices (helmets, seat belts, safety glasses) and their use and what can happen if you don't use them.

Language and Literacy: Speaking, Listening, Reading, and Writing

This is an area of special strength for many children who are identified as gifted and talented. It is also a familiar activity for these children, who are frequently read to at home. Because reading is a strength in itself, as well as the basis for learning many academic subjects, it should be encouraged. Your job is to refine, expand, and enrich the child's language skills.

Speaking. Help children use descriptive, colorful, precise speech and make word pictures for people.

1. Encourage fluency and flexibility in verbal interchanges. Encourage colorful phrases, vivid descriptions, and analogies.

2. Visit the library and discuss not only its books and records, but also the events the library sponsors. Discuss how the library is organized and how people get library cards and borrow and return books as well as audio- and videotapes. Set up a lending library in you class. Follow up by sending a note home to parents about your visit and encourage them to join the library if they are not members.

3. Encourage brainstorming. Be sure not to make value judgments or belittle far-out responses because children will then refrain from making comments freely.

4. Help children think creatively and then translate their thinking into expressive language by giving them situations to talk about:

   Describe your life as a 6-year-old bicycle.

   You are a gingerbread mix about to be made and then baked. How do you feel (when made and eaten)?

   You are a camera. What kind of pictures will you take? How do you work?

5. Encourage children to learn new vocabulary words by providing a life perspective that allows for differences; teach concepts such as *some, sometimes, often, frequently, rarely,* as well as *never* and *always.*

6. Encourage children to expand their speaking by *substituting* a person, place, time, or situation. If they were talking about the *beach,* how would the event change if it were the *desert?* Expand children's thinking by having them imagine being in a savannah in Africa or a pass in the Andes Mountains in winter.

Listening. Challenge children's listening skills with more complex comprehension tasks. Fingerplays combine language with motions. They are initially a listening activity that becomes responsive, and ultimately a way for children to express themselves creatively.

1. Have children act out fingerplays with their whole body (this typically takes 10 children). For example, once children know the fingerplay Where is Thumbkin?, see if they can act it out. It is more difficult than it seems.

2. Encourage children to make up their own fingerplays.

3. Teach longer, more complex fingerplays to a small group of interested children.

4. Help children learn signs and sign language as well as finger spelling.

Reading. Read to children even when they are capable of reading independently. Their development is uneven; what conceptually intrigues them is often beyond their reading level. In an inclusive group, it is challenging to find stories that are unusual or creative enough to intrigue all the children in your group. Provide books children can read independently as well as ones with creative illustrations. Read "chapter" books.

1. After reading stories or poems, ask simple questions to evoke creative responses.

2. Have a wide range of recorded books and stories available for independent listening at learning centers. Such materials allow you to individualize programming while supporting inclusion.

3. When reading a new story, stop at a critical point and ask the children to make up an ending. Then compare their ending with the one the author wrote. Have children make up different endings to familiar stories. Pose different circumstances and see if children can make the characters respond to these.

4. Dramatize stories, songs, and poems. Provide props.

5. Have children generate stories to go with the pictures in wordless picture books.

6. Have a box of words that can be made into different compound words (clothes + line = clothesline; sun + light = sunlight). When possible, have drawings on the back.

7. Teach about Braille as a form of reading and writing.

8. Have children match labels on boxes to a shopping list, and categorize boxes and cans of food by type.

Writing. Many children are fascinated by writing and by thinking about themselves as authors.

1. Children may be eager to write their own stories but lack the necessary motor skills. Have a tape recorder available for them, or write stories they dictate. Some children may want to type or word-process their stories. Support creative spelling. However, if the spelling is too creative, you may have to ask the child to "read" the story to you. Sometimes, even a friend can read another child's story, as the friend may be far less confused than an adult in the absence of traditional language conventions.

2. Encourage writing as a joint project. Have children share ideas and help each other as well as providing adult support.

3. Help children make their personal time line and note important events in their lives:

Born	Got a turtle	Sister born	Moved	Started school
1993	1995	1996	1997	1998

4. Make up a word/sign code. Draw a picture on one side of a card and put the word on the other side. Put the "signs" together to make a story. See if others can "read" the story. Use American Sign Language or Braille for the story.

Discovery: Mathematics, Science, and Computers

Discovery is encouraged by exploring the environment in a realistic way. Children can also learn the scientific method of observation, expand to theoretical concepts, and move to more abstract levels. They can learn to use reference materials to encourage independent problem solving.

Mathematics. Math activities should be manipulative and game-like and, at the beginning, should have a concrete experimental base. Once the basics have been established, move with the children in the direction that intrigues them. Help children establish basic number sense and numeration. Help them think about math as a method of problem solving, give them the vocabulary to communicate about math, and help them with mathematical reasoning. Be sure to support boys and girls equally, for stereotyping often discourages girls from developing strong math skills.

1. Help children recognize patterns and relationships in their environment. Teach them the use of "pair" for a single object—pair of scissors, pair of pants, pair of glasses—and explore their ideas about why this label is used.

2. While children are in the process of mastering number and numeration skills, have them count a wide variety of objects: raisins, blocks, children, and so on.

3. When children can count, have them group and count by sorting and classifying: 7 red buttons, 3 yellow buttons. Eventually, help them discover whole number operations such as addition and subtraction, and relate this to hierarchal classification:

Furniture
7 Beds + 5 Chairs + 2 Tables = 14 Pieces of furniture

4. Show them the usefulness of numbers in the real world.

5. Fractions are fun to teach through incidental learning as the occasion arises: half an apple, a quarter of a sandwich. Give children the entire object. They can count the pieces, put them back together to make the whole, and take them apart again. Teach the relationships among fractions and have many different calibrated measuring items. Measuring tasks are easily done at a water table, in the sandbox, or when making cocoa, gelatine, or cookies. Encourage children to think about units of measurement and different ways things are measured (weight, volume, temperature) and how this is done.

6. Use recipe cards with measurements and have children read the recipe and make the item.

7. Introduce children to more complex and different measuring systems: yardsticks, meter sticks, centigrade and Fahrenheit thermometers, tire pressure gauges.

8. Once children understand how easy geometric shapes, teach some of the more unusual ones, as well as the relationship between three-dimensional and two-dimensional ones: oval/egg, circle/ball/globe, combinations (oval and rectangle), cylinder, pentagon, trapezoid. Help them describe, model, draw, and classify these as well as combine them to make different shapes.

9. To facilitate individual work in math concepts, have children use an abacus, Cuisenaire rods, Montessori-type materials (beads of 10), and Unifix cubes. These materials help children discover, experiment, and manipulate information rather than simply memorize facts.

Science. Science often provides the structure for gaining new experience and developing reasoning ability. Start with known concepts and expand on them. Increase the ability of children to hypothesize and make predictions. Present problems that are inherently interesting from the child's perspective. Encourage them to observe closely what they do while solving a problem. Help them learn to apply what they have learned by teaching them to see a pattern or principle (general) and application (particular) in each science activity.

1. Use familiar concepts such as the wind, the sun, and water. On a windy day, make observations of the wind's effects. Draw on the children's experiences with the wind and their reaction to it. Share with them the tingle of the skin, the watering of eyes, the tossing of hair, the bracing and turning of the body to cut through the blowing wind. Have them observe how clothes on a line are pushed by the wind and the differences in the way people walk facing the wind or with the wind at their back. Watch the surface of a pond or puddle as wind blows over it; watch rain change direction when the wind changes; listen to the sound of the wind. Record different wind and blowing sounds. Reenact scenes from a windy day. Have children take a pretend walk on a windy day and have other children guess the direction and strength of the wind. Demonstrate a weather vane or windmill. Discuss machines that create wind such as hair dryers and electric fans. Demonstrate how seeds travel with the wind. Blow a small boat across a pan of water. Blow Ping-Pong balls across the table, then try to blow a tennis ball. Make pinwheels or kites. Talk about the relationship between wind and temperature and the wind chill factor. Read books about the wind and look up wind in reference books. Talk about the role the wind plays in hurricanes.

2. Visit an orchard and pick apples. Explore the parts of the apple. Experiment with the effects of heat and cold on apples. Have children predict what will happen when apples are cooked in different ways and the same way for different lengths of time. Compare the tastes of applesauce, baked apples, apple juice, and apple butter. See how many ways children can use apples. Find out what happens when you drop apples and bruise them.

3. Children often enjoy learning about animals. Provide firsthand experience. Add depth to the experience by talking about where different animals live, how they protect themselves, and how and what they eat and how they are adapted for this. Have children invent animals for particular climates or conditions, such as a light animal with large flat feet to live near quicksand.

4. Help children focus on a particular problem. Encourage them to persist in trying various solutions to the problem. Try to get children to generalize the problem-solving process to new problems. Show them how to use information that was obtained to make increasingly more accurate predictions regarding outcomes.

5. Encourage children to use the scientific method before they actually do a task: State the problem; form a hypothesis; observe, experiment, gather and record data; interpret data; draw conclusion. Have them determine whether their hypothesis was right or wrong, then speculate about why it was right or wrong. Then have children make new hypotheses to further test their thinking.

Computers. Computers hold unlimited potential for children who are advanced in cognitive development. Software can be chosen to enhance the development of children and tailored to their individualized learning needs in a developmentally appropriate way. Computers can provide for independent learning as well as aid abstraction. Computers can provide the necessary scaffolding to enable children to perform tasks they could not master independently. The key is the ability of the adult to choose appropriate software and match it to the needs of the child.

1. Integrate computers into the curriculum—don't think of them as a stand-alone feature. Use creative software that allows children to make choices and be in charge, not merely respond, and to control the flow and direction of the program.

2. Use a speech synthesizer to verbalize each letter or word the child types. Have the child write a story.

3. Encourage children to work at the computer in pairs or small groups.

4. Choose software that becomes increasingly complex as the children learn the basics and move on.

Developmental Physical Education and Sensorimotor Skills: Large Motor, Small Motor, Sensorimotor Integration

Children with unique gifts and talents, unless these lie in the motor area, will have motor skills closer to their chronological age than to their mental ability. Their ability to plan what they want to do may exceed

Computers offer the potential for individualized programming as well as the opportunity to learn and share with other children. If children's fine motor skills do not keep pace with their interests, there are many devices available that will allow them to compensate.

their ability to do it. To develop a well-rounded child, it is important that you encourage the development of motor skills. This is especially true for a child who is the youngest member of the group and whose motor skills may be among the least developed. There is a tendency for children who are not good at motor skills to avoid them. Children need your support to participate when they do not expect to do well.

Large Motor. Help children understand their unevenness in conceptualizing and carrying out activities while being sure they develop necessary skills.

1. Create an imaginary obstacle course. Have a child climb, dodge, or wade while other children try to guess what the obstacles are.

2. Have children walk through imaginary substances, such as mud, deep sand, sticky paper, a swamp, a hot sidewalk. Have others guess what the substances are.

3. Have the children help create an obstacle course either inside or outside. Check for safety before children actually use the course.

Small Motor. Small motor skills may be an area of frustration for children whose fine motor skills have not kept pace with their cognitive abilities. Through creative planning, motivate children to use these skills.

1. Have a wide variety of materials and an abundance of them (two or three sets instead of one) so that children's creations are not limited by scarcity of materials.

2. Encourage planning and prediction by the children after they have mastered the motor skills for manipulating the materials: How many straws do you need to make the foundation?

3. Using short pieces (under 12 inches) of heavy yarn or string, teach children knots and simple macramé.

4. Adding manipulative materials to the block or dramatic play areas will encourage children to create props.

5. Provide old clocks, radios, and other equipment for children to take apart to examine or to compare the sizes and shapes of pieces and basic construction. (Be sure children know they must have permission before experimenting at home, and note the size of the pieces if there is concern someone might swallow one.)

6. Bring in a bicycle and have the children help change the tire and wheel. Discuss air, volume, and shape. Then change the tire on a wheelchair or wagon to expand the concept.

Sensorimotor Integration. Provide opportunities for children to have a variety of experiences that allow motor skills to be integrated with visual, hearing, and kinesthetic experiences. Make activities so intriguing that they want to participate.

1. Introduce children to some unusual sensory experiences that seem to defy logic or change states. Have them help you make goop (equal parts of cornstarch and water) and silly putty (one part liquid starch to two parts glue) and then play with the products they made. Encourage them to think about the processes of making and using these materials.

2. Have children use an eye dropper to mix food coloring with water. Have them dispense only a drop at a time and make predictions about what the additional drops will do to the color of the water.

3. Encourage children to experiment with a variety of media and relate this to their control of the media and the outcome (crayons vs. markers, watercolor vs. poster paint).

4. Using just one medium such as brushes (in varying degrees of thickness), crayons (thin, thick, cone-shaped), or paint (in a variety of densities), encourage them to think about the implications of these shapes or sizes or densities for their final product.

Creative Arts: Visual Arts, Music, Creative Movement, and Dramatic Play

Children can define problems, seek solutions, and grow in their own creative ability.

Visual Arts. Encourage children to explore their world through the visual arts. Introduce activities that allow children to make their own decisions and exert some control over their world.

1. Set up art activities with enough space to enable children to work freely either alone or in small groups.

2. Have children draw themselves as a "creature" who is either very large or very small. Discuss with them what they could do as the creature that they can't do as a human, as well as the drawbacks this creature would have based on size and configuration.

3. Learning in the visual arts is predictably developmental. Younger children are interested more in the process; as they grow older, the product is more complex and more important. Don't stifle creative growth by imposing adult ideas and standards on children however; don't give excessive praise to work that is mediocre for a particular child.

4. When you repeat activities such as easel painting or making collages, vary the shape, size, and kind of paper you use.

5. Encourage children to choose colors (paint or food color) and to predict what new colors will be made by mixing colors. Add white and black

to paint so that children can experiment with shades of color as well.

6. Do some difficult art projects that have several steps, like crayon etching. (Color a design with a light crayon; color over the design with black crayon; etch with a popsicle stick. Use tough paper that resists tearing.) Try again with crayon and paint: light-colored crayon, dark paint. Discuss why the paint doesn't adhere to where the crayon is.

7. Supply a variety of traditional art implements including many colors of wide and narrow crayons and paint brushes in several widths.

8. Origami, Japanese paper folding, is a great activity. It helps them translate ideas into three-dimensional results.

9. Repeat the same activity with many variations and help children explore the differences. Fingerpaint with liquid laundry starch; flour, salt, and water; cornstarch; whipped soap; commercially made finger paint. Add texture to fingerpaint with sand, salt, coffee grounds, fine sawdust, glitter, confetti.

10. Tie-dying is another good problem-solving activity. The children can put small blocks on material (or on a white T-shirt) and then make a knot with short pieces of heavy thread. The complexity of the design will depend on each child. Tie-dye material can later be used in a sewing project. Have the children help pin the fabric together and baste it. Perhaps some can sew it, by hand or machine. Use safety needles and count them to be sure you can account for all of them.

Music. Music can contribute much to a child's physical, aesthetic, and intellectual development. It provides pleasure and creative experience, develops auditory skills, encourages physical activity, and increases the range and flexibility of one's voice. There should be a wide variety of musical experiences: listening, singing, and playing musical instruments.

1. Have a variety of different instruments available. Help children explore and evaluate the sounds of an instrument when it is held and played in different ways. See if they can identify instruments in a recording.

2. Combine music and language experiences; have children make up new verses to old songs. Play short parts of unusual instrumental recordings and ask the children to describe what they imagined while listening.

3. Put stories to music. Have children choose background music for stories.

4. Paint to music.

5. Have children make musical instruments (shoe box guitars, oatmeal box drums, wax paper and comb). As they participate in this process, they will gain an understanding of how sounds are made, where they come from, and how to change them. See if they can make sounds with different parts of their body (clapping hands, stomping feet, putting air in mouth and pressing on it with both hands, strumming finger across lower lip).

6. Introduce concepts of pitch, loudness, and duration by singing echo-type songs.

Creative Movement. Encourage children to take advantage of the creative opportunities in movement to express themselves through their body. Give them the freedom to explore the motor area without fear of failure.

1. Encourage a feeling of group belonging and, at the same time, foster creative movement. Have children "hold up the roof." Children strain together to hold up the roof; they gradually let it down and then push it back up again. They can be ice cubes melting in the hot sun or a balloon deflating. Play "people machines" with or without noises. The children can do this all together or one at a time, slowly or speeding up. Repeat such creative movement experiences until the children are comfortable enough to experiment with their bodies and are interacting with each other.

2. Have two children pretend to be one machine to encourage interaction.

Some children might want to enhance their experiences in music and the creative arts by developing a routine that has props and scenery and then perform their arrangements.

3. Creative movement that combines music and stories is fun and mind expanding. Introduce children to some of the classics such as *The Story of Peer Gynt,* with the recording of the *Peer Gynt Suite* by Grieg; "Cinderella," with the recording of *Cinderella* by Prokofiev; "Hansel and Gretel," with excerpts from the opera *Hansel and Gretel* by Humperdinck; stories about troubadours and Meistersingers, with excerpts from *Die Meistersinger* by Wagner; the fairy tale "Nutcracker King," with Tchaikovsky's *Nutcracker Suite;* and "Mother Goose," with the *Mother Goose Suite* by Ravel.

Dramatic Play. In the dramatic play area, too much may be worse than too little for these children. Use props such as dolls and dishes with few details. Provide enough props to create ideas, then challenge children to create and design props they need. If you provide all the necessary props, children will not improvise and exercise their creativity.

1. Have a small-group planning session to set up a store. Discuss the props that will be needed, how to get them, and when the store should go into business. Create the store and evaluate its success. Use play money and a cash register and/or calculators. Write signs and prices for the store's specials. Make coupons for matching and preliteracy skills.

2. Plan a train or plane trip. Look at maps to determine where to go. Explain how to use a compass. Have the children investigate weather conditions there, how long it will take to get there, what they will do when they get there. Take the class to a travel agency that is willing to answer their questions and provide schedules and brochures.

3. Have children set up their own health food store. They can make veggie burgers, baked potatos, and chicken out of construction paper or papier-mâché. Have them decide who will be the manager, cook, order taker, bagger, and customers. (Obviously, this could be a fast food store, but a health food store presents the opportunity to talk about nutrition.) It can also be tied into cooking and snacking.

4. Help the children set up a small tent (outside, if possible). Discuss aspects of camping and backpacking, including the equipment, and take a "hike."

Transitions

This is a good time to individualize programming while not drawing attention to a specific child.

1. If you are giving directions to others in the class, use multistep directions for these children: "Touch your nose, stamp your foot, and get your coat."

2. Because the child may have more complex projects to clean up, provide an early warning for transitions or agree that some projects don't need to be cleaned up daily but can be set aside to be continued the next day.

Summary

It is often difficult to identify children with advanced cognitive development before age 3. However, early and competent use of receptive and expressive language is one clue. Most agree that there is an interaction between genetics and the environment in the cause of advanced cognitive development. Development of children identified as gifted and talented, however, is strongly affected by their environment. Children who are gifted tend to have a high general intelligence, whereas children who are talented may be talented in only one area.

The field is divided over the best way to educate children who are gifted and talented. Some feel that these children should be accelerated in their education by starting school early, skipping grades, or having advanced placements in some subjects. Others feel that it is more appropriate to enrich their environment and increase the breadth and scope of their knowledge as well as their ability to do abstract thinking. This same division is apparent relative to whether children should be included in the regular classroom or separated into special classrooms.

Educational Resources

American Mensa
http://www.mensa.org/
Members of this group score in the top 2 percent of the population on the standardized IQ test.

Gifted Child Society
190 Rock Road
Glen Rock, NJ 07452
(201) 444-6530
http://www.gifted.org/
This is a nonprofit organization that sponsors activities designed to help gifted children, their families, and educators.

Gifted Resources Mailing Lists
http://www.eskimo.com/~user/zmail.html
This page contains a list of email addresses for parents of gifted and talented children.

Gifted and Talented
http://www.byu/acd1/ed/coe/ulibray/tag.html
This page contains addresses to receive more information on how to help a gifted child.

The Gifted and Talented Resources Homepage
http://www.eskimo.com~user/kids.html and
     http://www.eskimo.com/~user/zorgs.html
This page has information and resources for gifted and talented children.

National Association for Gifted Children
1155 15th Street, NW No. 1002
Washington, DC 20005
(202) 785-4268
http://www.nagc.org/
This is a national advocacy group for gifted children.

The National Foundation for Gifted and Creative
  Children
http://www.nfgcc.oa.net/
This page gives parents information on gifted children and is also a nonprofit organization.

Odyssey of the Mind–Mastery Education Corporation
85 Main Street
Waterwon, MA 02172 USA
Sponsors competitions for gifted children that encourage cooperation and creativity.

Resources in Gifted Education
http://www.ecnet/users/uehunt/mage3.htm
This page has links to resources on the Web.

Talented and Gifted Bibliography
http://klingon.util.utexas.edu/TAG
  /TAG_Bibliography.html
Provides list of books with helpful information about gifted and talented children.

References

Bloom, B. S. (1985). *Developing talent in young people.* New York: Ballantine Books.

Council for Exceptional Children. (1996). Gifted education reaches out to the nontraditional gifted student. *CEC Today, 3*(1), 1, 9, 15.

Education Act Ammendments of 1978. Pub. L. No. 95-561, Title IX, Gifted and Talented Children's Act 92 Stat. 2292 20 U.S.C. 2701.

Elkind, D. (1986). Mental acceleration. *Journal for the Education of the Gifted, 11*(4), 19-31.

Feldman, D. H. (1986). *Nature's gambit. Child prodigies and the development of human potential.* New York: Basic Books.

Freeman, J. (1985a). Emotional aspects of giftedness. In J. Freeman (Ed.), *The psychology of gifted children: Perspectives on development and education* (pp. 247-264). Chichester, England: Wiley.

Freeman, J. (1985b). A pedagogy for the gifted. In J. Freeman (Ed.), *The psychology of gifted children: Perspectives on development and education* (pp. 1-22). Chichester, England: Wiley.

Gallagher, J. J. (1993). Comments on McDaniel's education of the gifted and the excellence-equality debate: Lessons from history. In C. J. Maker (Ed.), *Critical issues in gifted education: Programs for the gifted in regular classrooms* (Vol. 3, pp. 19-21). Austin, TX: Pro-Ed.

Gardner, H. (1983). *Frames of mind: The theory of multiple intelligences.* New York: Basic Books.

George, D. (1995). *Gifted education: Identification and provision.* London: David Fulton.

Gottfried, A. W., Gottfried, A. E., Bathurst, K., & Guerin, D. W. (1994). *Gifted IQ: Early developmental aspects: The Fullerton longitudinal study.* New York: Plenum Press.

Gross, M. U. M. (1993). *Exceptionally gifted children.* London: Routledge & Kegan Paul.

Howe, M. J. A. (1990). *The origins of exceptional abilities.* Cambridge, MA: Basil Blackwell.

Kanevsky, L. (1992). The learning game. In P. S. Klein & A. J. Tannenbaum (Eds.), *To be young and gifted* (pp. 204-244). Norwood, NJ: ABLEX.

Matheny, A. P. (1989). Temperament and cognition: Relations between temperament and mental test scores. In G. A. Kohnstamm, J. E. Bates, & M. K. Rothbart (Eds.), *Temperament in childhood* (pp. 263-282). New York: Wiley.

McDaniel, T. R. (1993). Education of the gifted and the excellence-equality debate: Lessons from history. In C. J. Maker (Ed.), *Critical issues in gifted education: Programs for the gifted in regular classrooms* (Vol. 3, pp. 6-18). Austin, TX: Pro-Ed.

Robinson, N. M., & Weimer, L. (1991). Selection of candidates for early admission to kindergarten. In W. T. Southern & E. D. Jones (Eds.), *The academic acceleration of gifted children* (pp. 29-50). New York: Teachers College Press.

Saunders, J., & Espeland, P. (1991). *Bringing out the best: A resource guide for parents of young gifted children.* Minneapolis, MN: Free Spirit.

Schwartz, L. L. (1994). Educating the gifted: A national resource. In L. L. Schwartz (Ed.), *Why give "gifts" to the gifted?* (pp. 1-7). Thousand Oaks, CA: Corwin Press.

Southern, W. T., & Jones, E. D. (1991). Academic acceleration: Background and issues. In W. T. Southern & E. D. Jones (Eds.), *The academic acceleration of gifted children* (pp. 1-28). New York: Teachers College Press.

Chapter 14

CHILDREN WITH HEALTH IMPAIRMENTS

Mary was diagnosed with Down syndrome shortly after she was born. Like many others, she also had a heart condition, but this was not what would take Mary's life. I had followed her since infancy and visited on a weekly basis. Mary was an only child and both parents loved her very much.

When Mary was about a year old she would pull to stand and then start to cry. Initially, we thought it was because she didn't know how to get down and was afraid to fall. But when we looked at her face, she seemed to be in pain and she would always fall to one side. At first, the physician said this was normal for children with low muscle tone. A few weeks went by and bruises started to appear. The family went back for further medical consultation.

With tears in their eyes, the parents met me at the door; the father had taken off work to share the news. "Mary has leukemia. They say she only has maybe six months to live and we have to decide what type of treatment to do. Please help." I went in and we sat on the couch. Mary greeted me as she always did, with a huge smile, and crawled up in my lap with one of her toys. I'll never forget that day or the ones that followed. We are supposed to accept death as part of life. I had been through the death of other children and I had accepted it. I also realized that what parents and children need is not detachment, but, as the parents pleaded, help. I assured them I would be there to support them through any decision they made, but they would have to make the decisions, not I. Mary would be loved until the day she died, but it was a roller coaster of chemotherapy, radiation, and long hospitalizations, accompanied by many tears, mine included. The hospital staff was wonderful, offering emotional support and counseling for the family, making provisions for visitation whenever possible. When Mary died, her parents called and said that they were going to bury her out of state in a family cemetery and they would call me when they returned.

They did call and wanted me to come for a visit. They said that I had been part of Mary's life since birth and felt it only right that I be part of her life in death. I reluctantly agreed. I dreaded the visit at first, but it was one I'll never forget and always treasure. The parents had taken pictures to share of the funeral and of the grave. Some may think this morbid, but they were so tender and filled with love. Each parent dealt with Mary's death differently. Her mother wanted to take part in the funeral preparation; her father wanted little to do with it. But they respected each other's wishes. They went into detail about the service, and I listened, I cared, I realized that I needed closure as well. And to think that these parents had no obligation to share anything with me. Her mother said, "No one can know if we will be alive tomorrow, but we do know we are alive today. We know that Mary was loved each day of her life and gave that love back in her short life. Thank you for going through the process with us." "You know," added her father, "you have been part of our family through the years as well, and we appreciate your understanding."

We may not be able to change things, but we can sincerely care, and there is nothing wrong with showing that care, while having a healthy balance of detachment when needed. I have learned more from families like Mary's than they probably ever learned from me; but we shared, we cared.

A health impairment interferes with normal growth and development, it continues for a long time, it is likely to have a prolonged convalescence, and it may result in death.

Defining Health Impairments

Health impairment can be defined on two levels: categorical and functional. A categorical definition (for example, juvenile diabetes) determines whether the condition falls within stated guidelines; the functional definition looks specifically at the child and how she is affected. In most cases, the categorical definition is used for reporting purposes and the functional definition for program planning. For example, one could include children with pediatric AIDS in the categorical group, or one could decide that because the functional limitations result in developmental delays, a functional categorization might be more appropriate.

Unlike other disabilities that directly affect the child's ability to gain or process information, most health impairments interfere with the child's learning by decreasing the body's energy, its ability to remove waste, or its ability to grow. Some health impairments shorten the life span, others do not. Many are potentially life-threatening. Some have periods of activity and remission. In some cases, the condition is progressive, getting increasingly worse, or it weakens other body systems, making the child more susceptible to other illnesses.

It is difficult to estimate how many children have severe chronic health problems because there is no common definition of what conditions should be included nor agreement about what "severe" means. Some estimate that between 6 and 12 percent of all children in the United States have a *serious* chronic illness (Hobbs, Perrin, & Ireys, 1984). (Is *serious* the same as *severe*? Your guess is as good as mine, but I tend to think it is.) This population is increasing not only because there are more children with chronic illnesses, but also because they are living longer due to better identification procedures and technological advances. However, health care programs designed to meet these children's ongoing needs are not increasing. Although these conditions vary widely, children with health impairments have some common characteristics that influence their quality of life.

Children with health impairments will miss more school, spend more time convalescing at home, and be in the hospital more frequently than most other children. Health impairments that interfere with the child's ability to learn are covered under the Individuals with Disabilities Education Act (IDEA, 1997): "*Other health impairment* means having limited strength, vitality or alertness, due to chronic or acute health problems such as a heart condition, tuberculosis, rheumatic fever, nephritis, asthma, sickle cell anemia, hemophilia, epilepsy, lead poisoning, leukemia, or diabetes, that adversely affects a child's educational performance."

If the health impairment does not interfere with the child's educational performance, children's civil rights are protected under section 504 of the Rehabilitation Act (1973) and the Americans with Disabilities Act (1990). Children with health impairments cannot be discriminated against in admission to early care and educational settings and *reasonable accommodations* must be made. However, people frequently differ about what they think is reasonable.

Accommodations may mean that a child with asthma is not required to run outside when it is cold or that children with allergies are given different snacks from other children. Class group activities may have to be redesigned so that all children can participate. Because of the progressive nature of some health impairments (such as AIDS and muscular dystrophy), children may not require individualized

programming in the early years but will fall under IDEA as the disease progresses and interferes with their educational progress.

Children who are eligible for accommodations under section 504 of the Rehabilitation Act (1973), but require no special educational services may have a 504 Plan. This child does not have to have an identifiable disability under IDEA but requires some accommodating. (For example, a child with asthma may require only modification in his developmental physical education curriculum. A child allergic to peanuts may require a peanut-free area at lunch and require hand washing for all children.) This plan is far less complex that an IEP or IFSP. Traditionally, it is only one page; however, it requires a team determination, including an administrator or designee, and must be signed by the parents or guardian. The focus is primarily on the modifications or accommodations required and the person responsible for overseeing and/or implementing the modifications. Like the IDEA (1997), section 504 does provide families with the right to a due process hearing if they feel their rights have been violated.

Sometimes, children with chronic illnesses may fall between the cracks in an educational system. Schools that are flexible and responsive may alter a child's day by making it shorter, making breaks for medication unobtrusive, and reducing the demand for physical activity. Episodic illnesses are the most difficult. If a child is in school 10 days, out for 5 days, back for 3, out for 8, and so on, it is difficult to keep continuity in learning. Most schools require that a child be out of school for a particular length of time before being eligible for homebound instruction. A child with an episodic illness may never be out long enough to qualify, yet altogether may miss a great deal of school. Some school districts have an attendance policy that automatically fails children who miss more than a particular number of days. In one district where we lived, if a child missed 28 days in an academic year, that child automatically failed the year. Such policies had several implications for children and parents. The parents may have to be involved with bureaucratic red tape to obtain a waiver of school policy for their child, and they will almost certainly have to add home teaching to their workload.

Characteristics of Chronic Health Impairments

Some characteristics of chronic health impairments interact with a given family in ways that make the illness easier or more difficult to cope with. The age at which an illness is diagnosed impacts the family. When an illness is diagnosed in infancy, the family may more easily integrate into their lifestyle the restrictive diet, complex medication regimen, frequent hospitalization, or dependence on technology (Libow, 1989). The child may know no other way of being in the world because the adjustments made in the family were done when he was so young. Children may have developed relationship and behavior patterns that allow them to adjust well until adolescence. On the other hand, children first diagnosed as having a chronic illness at age 7 may be angry about the ways they must change their activities and interact with their peers.

A child's age also impacts her understanding of the illness and the degree of dependency the child has on her family. Young children rarely have an accurate idea about how their body functions and how the prescribed medical treatment relates to their wellness. We sometimes assume that because children have an illness they are well informed about that illness. In fact, children with chronic illness (and their siblings) are not well informed at all. What they know is a unique blend of what they have been told, what they have overheard, and what they have decided themselves (Lobato, 1990).

The repeated separation and trauma experienced during early childhood affects children both physically and emotionally. The cycles of "good" and "bad" health are often related to stress. Stress may bring on an acute stage of the disease or make an existing acute stage more severe. Children with chronic illness are more vulnerable than other children to having psychological disorders (Davis, 1993).

Typology of Chronic Illness

Rolland (1987) has developed a typology of chronic illnesses and disabilities based on their psychosocial demands. These are broad areas that impact families. In reality, the demands are on a continuum, with the anchor points used for descriptive purposes.

Onset

Illnesses can be divided into those that have *acute* onset (such as a traumatic head injury) and those that are more *gradual* (such as cystic fibrosis). In situations of acute onset, or where a gradual condition was not identified until an acute stage was reached (cancer), the family must rapidly mobilize itself to cope with the situation. All of the decisions and changes that must occur are compressed into a short time span. Families who have flexible roles, good crisis management and problem-solving skills, and who can call upon formal and informal support networks will manage an acute onset chronic illness better than others. When the onset is gradual, families have more time to adjust and accommodate to lifestyle changes.

Course

Chronic illnesses have three predictable patterns: progressive, constant, or relapsing/episodic (Rolland, 1987). A *progressive* illness (cystic fibrosis, muscular

dystrophy, AIDS) is one where the child has symptoms of the illness and these symptoms progress in severity. There are no times when the child is symptom-free, and the progression of the illness requires constant adaptation on the part of the family. There are increasing caregiving demands and requirements to learn new caregiving tasks as the illness progresses. A health impairment that has a *constant* course after stabilization, such as a spinal cord injury, is more predictable. Once a level of functioning has been determined, there is more stability over a time span. Once they have learned the skills needed, family members cope with the particular circumstances; they do not need to learn additional caregiving skills, just adapt these to the growth and development of the child.

Some illnesses, such as asthma and hemophilia, are *relapsing* or *episodic*. Times when the child is symptom-free (or almost symptom-free) alternate with times of flare-up. Strain on the family in this instance revolves around the changing demands of crisis-noncrisis situations and the continual uncertainty of when a crisis might occur. Crisis may be brought on by stress, either positive or negative. Flare-ups may occur at holidays, birthdays, marker events such as the first day of school, and vacations, times when families are already coping with change.

Outcome

The extent to which a chronic illness is fatal or will shorten a child's life span has an impact on families. The expectation is that a child with allergies will live a normal life span, whereas there is the expectation that a child with AIDS will not. Other illnesses, such as cancer, can be life-threatening. Some illnesses such as cystic fibrosis, juvenile-onset diabetes, and hemophilia are likely to shorten a child's life span. In situations where the illness shortens the child's expected life span or holds the possibility for sudden death, families may become overprotective. Children sometimes take advantage of such concerns (as do some parents) (Rolland, 1987).

Incapacitation

The severity of the illness or involvement in more than one area also impacts the family. In young children, we may not be sure of the severity of the particular illness. Incapacitation results from impairments in different domains: cognitive (AIDS), sensory (juvenile diabetes), motor (juvenile rheumatoid arthritis), energy (heart problems), disfigurement (severe burns), and social stigma (epilepsy) (Rolland, 1987).

Knowledge about the attributes of an illness or disability, that is, the onset, course, outcome, and incapacitation, helps early childhood educators work with families and children in a more meaningful way. Regardless of the particular illness, there are predictable phases of an illness.

Phases of Illness

With chronic illness, particularly when the expectation is that the parents will outlive their child, the time phases of the illness are important variables.

Crisis. The crisis phase of a chronic illness begins when symptoms of the illness appear and includes the time when families are struggling to find out what is wrong with their child. It continues through the diagnosis and into the initial adjustment phase (Rolland, 1987). This is an unsettling time when families have to adjust to a new reality. They need to develop skills to work with a health care team, learn a vocabulary to understand their child's diagnosis, and accept the implications of that diagnosis as well as treatment-related procedures. They need to learn illness-related symptoms that accompany acute episodes and develop a flexible family system that is based on an uncertain future.

Chronic. The chronic phase is the time span, long or short, between the initial adjustment period and the time when the issue of terminal illness prevails. This is the long haul. Many parents, when asked, say they live it a day or hour at a time. Some families pull together and reorganize as a normal family in unusual circumstances; other families have less functional responses.

Terminal. The final phase is when the inevitability of death dominates family life. Families then must deal with issues surrounding separation, death, grief and mourning, and the resumption of their family life (Rolland, 1987). Not all chronic illness shortens the life span, so some families may not move into the terminal phase. Different chronic illnesses bring different concerns and impact the child and family in different ways, but the impact of health impairments is always present to some degree. Often, hospitals or community agencies will offer seminars on death and dying which may be helpful for educators and parents to attend. They may also have workshops for children.

Implications for the Family System

Parents play many different roles during the different phases of a child's illness. They are often expected to take on the role of clinician, in addition to the traditional parental role. They perform daily much of the therapy that the specialists prescribe each week or month. They monitor the child's health, seeking medical help in acute phases. When medical treatment is required, they are the ones to chauffeur the child to and from the appointments. The extra work and responsibility may tax the parent-child relationship. Mothers seem to have the most stress. They may become overly concerned about the child's daily activities, along with managing the rest of the family, and become frustrated and angry (Jean, Lawhon, & Lawhon, 1995). Siblings, too, feel the stress and may feel neglected if their relationship with their parents has been disrupted. They may show signs of irritability, social withdrawal, jealousy, guilt, behavior problems, anxiety, low self-esteem, and academic underachievement (Davis, 1993). These problems are very real and exacerbate an already stressful situation. Long-term planning and resource management are major issues in coping with changes.

The family's physical, emotional, and financial resources may be severely taxed as they attempt to cope with the effects and limitations imposed by a child's long-term condition. Families whose income places them just over the eligibility level for assistance programs may find themselves more financially strapped than others who qualify for federal or state aid. Some parents have even been advised to divorce in order to fall within the income limits for single parents. Beyond the strictly medical costs, there are many out-of-pocket costs such as transportation to clinics, meals that are eaten outside the home, babysitting for well children, toys and trinkets after procedures for the child who is ill, long-distance calls to family members, and lodging if hospitals are too far from home to make commuting practical. Additionally, the care requirements may keep one adult family member, usually the mother, out of the job market. Single mothers who work often lose jobs because they miss so much work. Conversely, some family members may feel chained to their jobs because they are afraid if they leave the job the child's preexisting condition will prevent health insurance coverage in a new job.

Siblings are also affected when a child or parent has a chronic illness. Older siblings may be involved in the care and treatment of their younger sibling.

Universal Precautions and Protective Barriers

One challenge in early childhood settings is to keep children healthy and to keep disease from spreading. Because it is not possible to know who is potentially infectious, the following precautions were recommended by the Advisory Committee on Dangerous Pathogens (Dorset Health Authority, 1997). Those that apply to early care and education settings are given below. They are designed to prevent the spread of diseases communicated by body secretions, including hepatitis A, B, and C, HIV infections, bacteria and viruses that cause diarrhea and vomiting, and intestinal parasites such as worms (Humphry, 1996).

Universal precautions should be taken routinely when there is bleeding (such as a nosebleed), a cut from a fall, vomiting, and even when children need to blow their nose.

- Wear disposable gloves when you come in contact with body secretions, including blood, stool, urine, and vomit, and when nonintact skin is anticipated. Avoid hand to mouth/eye contact when finished. Remove and dispose of gloves and wash your hands.

    Children who are sick and vomit need your love and care and attention. Talk to them soothingly and pat their head while someone brings you gloves and probably a blanket. If a sick child is not upset, he can walk to the bathroom; if the child is upset, wrap him in a blanket and carry the child. You need a layer between you and the sick child.

- Wash with disinfectant such as household bleach (1:10 to 1:100 dilution) all toys and surfaces that have come into contact with bodily fluids or stool.

- Cover all open wounds until a scab is formed.

- Use single-use disposable tissues for runny noses and dispose of them immediately in a secure receptacle. Never share tissues.

    Have children deposit used tissues in a waste basket. Don't do it for them, and don't pick them up off the floor. If you need to pick them up, use another tissue and wash your hands.

- Wash your hands when you arrive at the center, when you come in from playing outdoors, and before preparing food, eating, or feeding a child. Wash them after toileting (yourself or a child). When you wash them, use liquid soap, make a heavy lather, and wash under running water for at least 10 seconds, particularly around the nails and front and back of the hands. Rinse by holding hands so the water flows from the wrists to the fingertips. Dry hands with a paper towel, then use the paper towel to turn off the faucet and discard (adapted from Dorset Health Authority, 1997; Humphry, 1996; National Association for the Education of Young Children [NAEYC], 1989).

Using these precautions reduces the risk of spreading communicable diseases.

Classification of Health Impairments

Descriptions of the most common health impairments follow. Remember, you will *not* be expected to be an expert on each impairment, but you do need to be aware of their characteristics and how they will influence your programming. (The impairments are discussed in alphabetical order. Those that you are more likely to encounter are given in greater detail.)

AIDS and Human Immunodeficiency Virus

> I remember not only the day my daughter was diagnosed, but the exact moment in time. I was looking at the clock just before the doctor stepped into the room. It was 2:35 P.M. By the time it was 2:45 P.M., I knew my daughter had AIDS. Therefore I knew I had it also, and I guessed my husband had it since he was the one who used drugs. So at 2:45 P.M., I knew that my whole family was going to die. (Tasker, 1993)

Human immunodeficiency virus (HIV) has caused massive concern in the entire health care and social system. Adult cases of clinical AIDS have increased exponentially, moved into the general population, and, since 1981, are paralleled (although at a lower level) with a rise in pediatric cases. Initially, the HIV pediatric cases were children with hemophilia; today, 90 percent of the children newly diagnosed with HIV infection acquired it from their mother (Rutstein, Conlon, & Batshaw, 1997).

Screening tests are 99 percent effective in identifying HIV in adults. The HIV virus can be transmitted in utero, during delivery, or through breast milk. Women who have no symptoms but have HIV can transmit the virus. Neonates are more difficult to screen as they may retain maternal antibodies for up to 15 months. Pediatric AIDS can begin any time between 2 months and 5 years after the infant is born. From 30 to 65 percent of children born to HIV-infected mothers actually develop AIDS. Many infants born to these mothers are preterm. It is not known whether this is caused by the HIV or whether it is related to other risk factors such as drug abuse. One approach that seems to reduce the vertical transmission of HIV is to give the mother zidovudine (AZT) during labor and delivery and to the newborn for six weeks (Rutstein et al., 1997).

Children with HIV seem to follow two patterns. About a fourth of the children show serious symptoms by about 1 year (infections, not reaching developmental milestones, and slow physical growth). The prognosis for these children is not good, and they are likely to die during the preschool years. It is suggested that these children probably acquired the infection in utero before their immune system was functional (Abrams et al., 1995). The remainder acquire the disease at birth; they are usually asymptomatic during the preschool years and are living into their teens (Rutstein et al., 1997).

Some children with pediatric AIDS show progressive neurological complications, including impaired brain growth, as well as the viral and bacterial infections that typically accompany AIDS (Rutstein et al., 1997). They lose the skills of developmental and intellectual milestones that they have obtained. Other children show patterns more closely resembling ADHD learning disabilities, and expressive language disorders (Rutstein et al., 1997).

Young children face problems of frequent infections, including recurrent bacterial infections, hepatitis, renal disease, gastrointestinal disorder, and pneumonia (Widerstrom, Mowder, & Sandall, 1991). Additionally, the pediatric population displays a variety of cognitive, behavioral, and neurological symptoms; these include mental retardation, neurological impairments similar to cerebral palsy, seizure disorders, and psychotic behavior (Hallahan & Kauffman, 1994). It is estimated that 50 to 90 percent of children with HIV infection have some form of central nervous system dysfunction (Schwarcz & Rutherford, 1989). Their situation is often complicated by parents who may be unable to care for the child because of their health-related problems.

Children with AIDS usually face death (not only their own, but probably also that of a parent). They may be ostracized by other children and even adults. As the disease progresses, the child will be separated from the family unit more and more frequently. For children with AIDS, this separation may be the most devastating aspect of the disease.

With the increasing rate of HIV infection, it is likely that you will have a child with AIDS in your classroom. Because of improvements in medical care and the hope of a vaccine, HIV infection is now considered a chronic illness, not always a fatal disease.

Children with AIDS have much to gain from early education and do not pose a substantial risk to the other children. No case of person-to-person transmission has been documented in early care and education centers (Rutstein et al., 1997). Many believe that the greatest risk is to the infected child, who increases risk of complications through school attendance.

Pediatric AIDS poses a difficult dilemma for the profession, one with many more questions than answers. It is an area that is changing quickly; what is considered "fact" when this book is published may no longer be true when you read the book. Keep informed about both breakthroughs and risks.

Having children with AIDS in your classroom is complex. The child may be coping with the imminent deterioration and death of a parent and at the same time coping with her own health problems and with the social complications of living in a family with

AIDS. You can support the child's efforts to cope with issues surrounding death and dying.

Because of fear of discrimination, many states decided that teachers did not have the need to know whether or not a child had AIDS. The rationale was that the risks to others are not great enough for a family's privacy to be violated. Therefore, you may not know if there is a child with AIDS in your classroom, so that adaptive programming may not be possible.

At one time, we thought that AIDS only affected the immune system. However, especially in children, it appears to affect the brain as well. There is often a marked delay in achieving developmental milestones, especially walking and talking (Schwarcz & Rutherford, 1989). In addition to fragile physical health, the disease may include psychotic behavior, mental retardation, seizures, and neurological impairments (Hallahan & Kauffman, 1994).

Deciding what to tell young children about AIDS is difficult. Information should probably only be provided on a "need to know" basis. For children younger than 8, it is generally felt that the information would be frightening and, with their cognitive capabilities, not useful. For those children who ask, the answers should be simple and direct and in response to what is asked. If children ask, "What is AIDS?," reply that it is something that makes you sick for a long time, and it makes you feel tired and not very good.

Allergies

Allergic and immunologic diseases are one of the leading causes of illness and disabilities. Allergies are the most common health impairment of children. They affect a child's development, behavior, learning, and relationships with others. Allergies account for one-third of all chronic health conditions that occur during the preschool years. Only about 35 percent of children with allergies have been diagnosed and treated. About 10 to 24 percent of the population has serious allergies; another 26 percent experience minor allergies. Immunologic diseases account for nearly 1 out 10 office visits to pediatricians. Most allergies begin in childhood (Kaliner, 1993).

An allergy is a sensitivity to something that most other people find harmless. An allergic reaction is an inappropriate immune response. It works something like this: "The first time the allergy-prone person runs across an allergen such as ragweed he or she makes large amounts of ragweed IgE antibody. The IgE molecules attach themselves to mast cells. The second time that person has a brush with ragweed, the IgE-primed mast cell will release its powerful chemicals, and the person will suffer the wheezing and/or sneezing, runny nose, watery eyes, and itching of allergy" (Schindler, 1997).

You need to find out what parents know about their children's allergies before children come into your classroom. Allergens fall into four general categories:

Airborne (inhalants): These substances are taken into the body through the mouth and nose: plant pollen, fungi spores, mold, dust, feathers (down), animal dander, and perfume.

Foods and drugs (ingestants): These substances are taken into the gastrointestinal tract. Once you know children's allergies, be sure to read package labels. Some oral drugs are common offenders: aspirin, sulfa drugs, and penicillin.

The food allergy that may cause the greatest concern is peanuts and peanut butter. Although very few children have allergies that are severe enough to be life threatening, many children do have reactions that cause swelling and breathing difficulties (an asthma-type reaction). In a severe reaction, an immediate injection of epinephrine will save the child's life. Most children who are allergic to peanuts know it. The problem is in the hidden sources where peanut oil is used in the preparation of products, or peanut butter is used as a thickener—again, a very low level ingredient in a product. Children who are highly allergic can react by breathing the fumes of someone eating peanut butter and also by directly touching someone who has not washed his or her hands after eating peanut products. Some allergists feel that the claims are an overexaggeration, but parents of children are concerned. It is not clear whether a peanut allergy would be covered under the Americans with Disabilities Act and that the necessary accommodations would be required. However, the Federal Department of Transportation has required airlines to set up peanut-free zones (Hartocollis, 1998).

Contact (contactants): These substances come in contact with the surface of the skin: ingredients in cosmetics, starch, wool, and some detergents.

Some drugs and chemicals (injectables): These substances enter the body through the skin: penicillin (injected), mosquito venom, venom from bee stings. Insect bites can be fatal. A bee sting often results in localized swelling and redness, which indicates only a mild allergy. A serious allergic reaction causes more generalized swelling and/or hotness about the face and neck, followed by difficulty in breathing and more severe bodily reactions. A sting to a severely allergic child can result in death if treatment is not immediate. However, if a child is allergic to bees and had never been stung you may be the first to find out. Thus, you need to have an emergency plan for all children.

You will play an important part in diagnosing allergies in young children. Particularly difficult to spot are symptoms that seem to be related to the season or weather (see Table 14.1).

If a child is diagnosed allergic to common inhalants, you should have the classroom scrubbed and vacuumed frequently. Avoid carpet with high pile and read the labels of the chemicals used to clean your room. (Dusting merely redistributes the dust.) If you

TABLE 14.1   RED FLAGS FOR ALLERGIES

Nose
Frequent runny nose, sniffling, rubbing the nose, frequent nosebleeds, frequent sneezing (four or five times in a row), wrinkling up the nose

Mouth
Dry hacking cough, wheezing, mouth breathing

Eyes
Red puffy eyes, rubbing the eyes, dark circles under the eyes

Skin
Skin irritations and rashes

have an air conditioner, be sure the filter is cleaned often. Do the same for the heating system filter. Consider adding a humidifier or air cleaner (Voignier & Bridgewater, 1980).

Be sure to ask all parents whether their children have known allergies of any kind or if they suspect they might, based on family history. The information will help you screen lunch and snack menus, choose a class pet, and prepare in advance against insect bites and other potential allergens encountered during field trips. Find out what reaction the child is

Dustless chalk will allow some children, particularly those with allergies and asthma, to use the chalkboard.

likely to have, what you should do if the reaction occurs, and what the side effects of the child's medication are.

Asthma

Asthma is one of the most common chronic disease of childhood (Asthma, 1997). It is a chronic inflammatory disease of the passageways that carry air to the lungs. The narrowing and inflammation of the airways is characterized by recurrent labored breathing, coughing, shortness of breath, and tightness in the chest (American Academy of Pediatrics [AAP], 1995). More than 13 million Americans have asthma and it affects over 3 million children under the age of 18 in the United States, with most children getting diagnosed by age 5 (Asthma, 1997). The incidence of asthma has increased 60 percent in the past decade (Kaliner, 1993). It is also becoming more severe. Asthma is the leading cause of school absences in young children and accounts for 61 percent of school days lost due to illness or injury (Cook, 1997). It is also one of the main reasons children are admitted to the hospital. (Some 200,000 children are admitted yearly with asthma related illness.) The number of children who have died from asthma has increased and, disproportionately, the children who die are African American (AAP, 1995; Kozol, 1995).

The most common cause of asthma is allergies. Of children under 16, 90 percent are allergic (Cook, 1997). Apparently, poor urban children are exposed to allergens that are triggering asthma. The problem appears to be more social than ethnic. Children living in poverty are exposed to more outdoor and indoor pollutants. When mothers of young children smoke, the risk of asthma more than doubles (Henig, 1993).

Asthma is a respiratory problem caused by an obstruction of the small bronchial tubes that occurs because of a swelling of the tubes themselves or the membrane linings. Asthma can also result from the contraction of the muscles around the tubes or by the plugging of the tubes with mucus. The lungs become enlarged because more air can be inhaled than can be exhaled. The chest expands, the neck muscles strain, and the veins tend to swell. This condition is twice as common in boys as girls. If you don't have asthma but want to know what it feels like, "Pinch your nose closed and breathe through a drinking straw for a few minutes" (Asthma, 1997, p. 1). Children experiencing an asthma attack feel as though they can't get enough air into their lungs.

Symptoms of asthma differ depending on how often, how much, and how fast the airways become narrowed. Coughing may be the first and sometimes only sign of asthma. This is the lungs' attempt to dislodge the mucus. Other symptoms include wheezing (the whistling sound caused by air moving through the narrowed airways), and fast, difficult breathing or breathlessness caused by many swollen, plugged-up airways (AAP, 1995; Asthma, 1997).

One of the most important things for teachers to know is when a child is having an asthma attack and how severe it is. The child's treatment is based on the severity of the symptoms and the degree of the airway obstruction.

In a *mild* asthma attack, the breathing is mildly difficult and only slightly faster than usual; there is some wheezing, coughing, shortness of breath, or tightness in the chest. There is no "drawing in" of the muscles between the ribs; the child is alert and aware of the surroundings, can speak at his typical level, and skin color is good (AAP, 1995).

In a *moderate* asthma attack, the breathing is moderately difficult and faster than usual; there is wheezing, coughing, shortness of breath, or tightness in the chest. There is a slight to moderate "drawing in" of the muscles between the ribs. The child is alert and aware of the surroundings, can speak with difficulty, and skin color is good or may be pale (AAP, 1995).

In a *severe* asthma attack, the breathing is unduly difficult, very fast or very slow and labored, with severe wheezing, coughing, shortness of breath, or tightness in the chest. There is "drawing in" of the muscles between the ribs, neck, and abdomen as the child attempts to breathe. The child may become drowsy, speaks with great difficulty, and skin color is poor (AAP, 1995).

Children with asthma usually have two types of medication: bronchodilators and anti-inflammatories. Bronchodilators offer quick relief by opening up narrow air passages and relieve the wheezing, breathlessness, and tightness in the chest. Anti-inflammatory drugs prevent attacks by reducing the swelling and inflammation of the passageways and increase drainage. The anti-inflammatory drugs need to be taken even if no symptoms are present. These drugs can be given by mouth, by injection, or may be inhaled in an aerosol (mist) form (AAP, 1995).

Bronchodilators are adrenaline-like medications that are fast and effective ways to relieve an attack and may be taken before exercise to prevent exercise-induced asthma. They are most frequently inhaled. The potential side effects include shakiness, rapid heartbeat, headaches, hyperglycemia, anxiety and nervousness, and elevated blood pressure (Asthma, 1997).

Anti-inflammatory medication includes steroids (inhaled and oral). Because of side effects, children are usually given inhaled medication. The device most frequently used with young children is a nebulizer, which children frequently refer to as a breathing machine. It allows them to take the medicine in a mist form and helps produce the right dosage. As children get older, they may use a metered dose inhaler with spacers. The inhaler dispenses a set amount of medication with each puff, making it easy to get the correct dosage; however, children have trouble coordinating their breaths to the burst from the inhaler. The spacers attach to the metered dose inhaler and hold the medication, which allows children to inhale it in a few breaths. Children over 5 also frequently use peak flow meters to measure how air moves in and out of their lungs. This allows medication to be adjusted to prevent an attack (Asthma, 1997). Children who take steroids need to be monitored carefully. The lowest possible dose should be given. Two types of medications, cromolyn sodium and nedocromil sodium, are felt to be safer than steroids. Cromolyn is felt to be safe for infants as well as young children. The potential side effects include cough, sore throat, and bronchospasm, which can be avoided by drinking water and rinsing out the mouth after taking the medication (Asthma, 1997).

Antiasthmatic drugs are the second most frequently prescribed drug for children under 15. There were 7,279,000 prescriptions given to children in 1995, a number exceeded only by the number of antibiotics prescribed (National Center for Health Statistics, 1995).

Asthma has a variety of causes or triggers and interventions, and management involves eliminating the triggers while using the prescribed medication. Asthma is divided into two types: allergic and nonallergic. In the former, the allergen triggers the asthma attack. Children with nonallergic asthma are sensitive to environmental triggers (cold or dry air, changes in the weather, perfumes) or pollutants such as cigarette smoke or irritants in the air. Emotional excitement (good or bad) as well as overexertion or even ordinary activity can trigger an attack. Although these types may seem similar, the allergic reaction produces IgE. One of the chemicals it releases is histamine, which produces the runny nose, watery eyes, and itchy skin. Also, infections of the airways such as pneumonia or any viral infection of the ear, nose, or throat may make asthma worse (AAP, 1995). Both types of asthma are controlled by avoiding triggers and taking medication.

Because asthma attacks occur without warning, they may be frightening to the child who is having one as well as to the other children. Attacks are most likely to come in the early morning hours. Children usually have prescribed medication (in pill or inhaler form) to take. You need to have it available and to know how to help the child use it. Generally, the most comfortable positions for the child having an attack are sitting backwards straddling a straight chair or planting the elbows on the knees. These positions are the easiest for breathing. Lying down is not helpful, and in some cases may actually be harmful.

Most children with asthma are allergic to common allergens. If possible, have the floor of your room damp-mopped rather than swept and eliminate rugs or curtains. If not, have the room vacuumed at night so that dust can settle. Try to balance strenuous activities with less strenuous ones. Develop a system of keeping in contact with the children when they are absent.

Cancer

Cancer is an umbrella term for a group of diseases, related to the uncontrollable growth of cells, all of which produce malignancies in some part of the

For children with asthma, exercises such as running may trigger an asthma attack. Avoid having children with asthma run in freshly cut grass or on very windy days, as they will often be sensitive to pollens or mold spores.

body (skin, muscle, nerve, lining of stomach, and so on). Most commonly affected in children are the nervous system, the genitourinary system, the system of connective tissues, and the blood-forming system. Cancer is treated with surgery, radiation, chemotherapy, or a combination of these. The prognosis depends on how early the disease is detected, what type of cancer it is, and which system is affected.

Leukemia is a type of cancer that can affect any part of the body where white blood cells are found. The white blood cells, or leukocytes, fight infection. In leukemia, the white blood cells do not mature, but they multiply uncontrollably, first appearing in the bone marrow. They begin to take up so much space that the red blood cells spill over from the bone marrow into the bloodstream. The cancer can then grow and infect other organs.

Acute lymphocytic leukemia (ALL) is the most common type of childhood cancer. About 2,000 children are diagnosed each year in the United States. Approximately 70 to 75 percent of the children will be considered cured (no relapse within three years after therapy has stopped) (St. Jude, 1996–1997a). ALL occurs most frequently in children between the ages of 2 and 8 (St. Jude, 1996–1997a).

Childhood acute myeloid leukemia (AML) is a cancer of the blood-forming tissue, primarily the bone marrow and lymph nodes. It affects approximately 500 children in the United States. Children with Down syndrome and children who have been exposed to environmental radiation and certain chemicals are more at risk. The prognosis for this type of leukemia is not as positive, with only 40 to 50 percent of children achieving long-term remissions with chemotherapy (St. Jude, 1996–1997b). Almost all childhood leukemias are acute. The cause of the disease is unknown and treatment varies. There is a higher incidence rate in boys than girls, and among White children than African American children (National Institutes of Health [NIH], 1991). Diagnosis is difficult because the symptoms are similar to less severe infections such as tonsillitis, mononucleosis, anemia, meningitis, rheumatic conditions, and mumps. To get an accurate diagnosis, extensive blood work must be done to rule out other conditions. This is typically followed by a bone marrow biopsy. X-rays may be needed along with a spinal tap (a needle inserted through the back to remove a sample of the fluid that surrounds the brain and spinal column). These are done to determine the location affected (National Cancer Institute, 1997b, 1997c).

Treatment is individualized. The treatment plan is developed by an oncologist, a doctor who specializes in cancer, the parents, and a team of other medical professionals. It may include chemotherapy, platelet and red cell transfusions, radiation, antibiotic therapy, and sometimes surgery (NIH, 1991).

Chemotherapy uses anticancer drugs that are taken as pills, liquids, or injections. For children, the side effects of the chemotherapy can be more devastating than the actual disease. The disease itself is invisible, but bodily changes are very apparent and perhaps even frightening. Children have difficulty tasting food and eat little. They may crave salt and not want meats or sugar products. Because hair follicles are affected by the drugs, their hair falls out. Because of the risk of infection, their activities may be limited (NIH, 1991).

Radiation therapy uses high-energy X-rays; radium and other ionizing radiation sources are used to destroy the cancerous cells. The procedure is not painful; however, the room in which the therapy takes place can be frightening to children. The child is not radioactive during the treatment or after it. Side effects include some skin damage to the treated area, hair loss, nausea or vomiting, diarrhea, sleepiness, and perhaps long-term intelligence loss (NIH, 1991).

The decrease in red blood cells causes anemia, which results in the child's being lethargic, tired, and pale much of the time. Because of the decrease in platelets, the child bleeds excessively and bruises from minor causes. Heavy nosebleeds are frequent. The low "normal" white cell count decreases the child's resistance to infection and makes getting well more difficult.

After the initial diagnosis, a period of intensive treatment follows and then a first remission, in which the child looks well and has energy. This may be when the child is in your program. Discipline should be normal at home and at school. Adequate nutrition for growth is a problem because the drugs decrease appetite. (In some cases, the drugs must be reduced so that the child's appetite can improve.) Be sure your snacks and lunches are nutritious, as this child cannot afford empty calories. School, despite the dangers of infection and possible taunting by peers, has great psychological value to both the child and the family. Instilling realistic hope is the greatest asset a family can have. Being honest and open is important. However, if a child is in a terminal phase and has a prognosis of two months, it is *not* helpful to deny this.

Children need information, but the information they need depends on their age. The main concern of children under 2 is separation from their parents. They understand that they don't feel well, but they don't understand the disease. Children between 2 and 8 are very egocentric in their thinking and try to relate the illness to a particular event or action. They need to be reassured that they did not do anything to become sick and that being sick is not a punishment. It is important to be honest with children, as their imaginations can do more harm than the facts. Answer the questions they ask: Their questions may be very different from the questions you as an adult might have. Use analogies to help children understand that the "good" medicine is fighting the "bad" cells. Children like to be reassured that everyone is trying to make them better (NIH, 1991).

Children typically regress when they are sick. In general, the last task learned will be the first task lost. Parents often find this distressing. Children may have trouble sleeping and display a range of emotions. Providing creative media such as art and dramatic play possibilities that allow them to work through their fears and concerns is helpful. The child is in a world where he feels out of control, so situations where the child can be in control and make decisions are helpful. If possible, let them decide what they want to eat, what they want to play with, and what they want you to help with.

Cystic Fibrosis

Cystic fibrosis is a hereditary chronic disease in which the mucus-secreting and sweat glands produce a mucus so thick and sticky that it interferes with the functioning of the respiratory and digestive systems. It affects boys and girls equally and occurs in about 1 in every 1,600 births. It is far more prevalent in White than in African American or Asian children (Neisworth & Bagnato, 1987).

Cystic fibrosis is diagnosed by analyzing the concentration of sodium and chloride in the sweat. It is difficult to diagnose because it can be confused with asthma, food allergies, failure to thrive, and even maternal overanxiousness, to name a few. Symptoms vary, but common ones are below-average height and weight despite a voracious appetite; frequent coughing (wheezing is common), throat clearing, sinus infections, and respiratory problems; foul-smelling stools; and gastrointestinal problems (upset stomach and diarrhea).

Currently, about 75 percent of children with cystic fibrosis live until middle or late adolescence. This psychological strain is accompanied by a financial one. Estimated cost of treatment ranges from $4,000 to $12,000 per year and is going up. Medication alone can cost over $3,000 per year. The actual treatment and caring for the equipment may take two hours a day. Children's lives depend on their family's ability to put them first.

Support the child who takes prescribed medication before eating. Develop a plan for maintaining contact when the child is sick. See that the child is encouraged to bring up phlegm, not stigmatized for doing so. Some signs of emotional difficulty to look for in the child are depression and withdrawal, fear of death, fear of losing control (dependence), and acting out. Have an emergency plan.

Provide matter-of-fact explanations for other children: "Leroy has trouble breathing, like you do when you have a cold, only Leroy has this all the time. His stomach hurts as well."

Heart Problems

About 8 in 1,000 children are born with congenital heart defects, with an additional 40,000 children identified as having heart defects by their first birthday. Many of these are mild and require no treatment. There are at least 35 different types of congenital heart defects (Neill, Clark, & Clark, 1992); almost all can now be treated successfully. Surgery in infancy is frequently the only necessary hospitalization unless the heart problem is complex.

It is more difficult to identify a heart problem in a child than in an adult. Adults can describe their experience of shortness of breath when they climb stairs or other symptoms; children may not recognize an experience is unusual—it may be the only way they have ever known. Such things as shortness of breath when feeding or crying, tiredness or sweating during feeding, blueness of the lips and fingernails that becomes more obvious when crying or involved in a physical activity, and slow growth are indications of a possible heart problem (Neill et al., 1992).

We know that rubella, enormous amounts of radiation, viruses, and Down syndrome can cause heart defects; however, about 7 out of 10 cases have no known cause (Neill et al., 1992). The most common defects in the heart relate to the flow of blood; blood that should be going into the body is shunted through a defect and reaches the lungs instead.

You may encounter a child with a heart murmur. Innocent heart murmurs are heard in 1 out of 2 normal children (Neill et al., 1992). When listening to the heart through a stethoscope, the normal "lub-dub, lub-dub" is the opening and closing of the heart valves. Sometimes there are extra sounds or "murmurs." These sounds are soft and variable in healthy children, but loud with a specific timing and location when there is heart disease. Heart murmurs are harmless for about half of the children. In other cases, restricted activity or heart surgery may be required.

Children who have either heart or lung problems are frequently given an exercise (stress) test to see whether they can safely exert themselves to the same level as other children their age without showing abnormal heart rhythms or interfering with the supply of oxygen reaching the heart.

Although these children may need some limitations in their activity, this is generally not a problem if you let children rest when they are tired. (Find out the results of the stress test and the medical recommendation for limitations.) If you avoid strenuous competitive games, the children need not exert themselves unduly to win. Children who are subject to blackouts (fainting) should be distracted from excessive activity that causes breathlessness.

It's important for you to be responsive to their needs within a framework that requires the children to learn responsibility. For example, if a child says he is too tired to help pick up the dolls he played with, encourage the child to rest for a minute or two before cleaning up. If the child is genuinely tired, shorten the activity time or increase the variety of less active choices. Children need to both participate and be included. If children are tired, they can sit and hold the box while other children place toys in it, or they can sit and place toys on shelves. Help them find quiet ways to help and be part of the group.

Hemophilia

Hemophilia is an inherited genetic blood disease that usually affects males. Estimates are that 1 in 7,500 males in the United States have hemophilia. It is transmitted by an X-linked recessive gene. There are two types of hemophilia: A and B. Although medically, this distinction is important, for general purposes both are characterized by patterns of chronic bleeding. In hemophilia, the child's blood lacks an essential ingredient for clotting, either Factor VIII or Factor IX. These factors are clotting proteins that create a fibrin clot at the site of an injury (Hoots & Cecalupo, 1994). The old fear was that the child would get a small cut and bleed to death. The real threat is from internal hemorrhaging, particularly inside the cranium; it is the most common medical emergency. Failure to treat this immediately can result in permanent neurological damage or death (Hoots & Cecalupo, 1994). This is now rare. With new treatments, almost all children with hemophilia live into adulthood.

With early diagnosis and treatment, using a clotting factor that can be isolated from blood plasma, many of the dangers of hemorrhaging are eliminated. However, this treatment is not a cure; it must be used whenever hemorrhaging from an injury occurs. Over the long term, bleeding into the joints of the long bones (knees, ankles, elbows) can cause crippling. As you might guess, surgery is not an easy solution to correct these deformities. Even dental work causes concern. This disease can be very painful. Aspirin cannot be used in treating the pain because it further reduces the blood's ability to clot. The expectation is that a child with hemophilia will lead a normal, functional life if some prudence is used. Children need to avoid activities that are likely to produce trauma (physical fighting) and be conscientious about medical care. Concerns about the transmission of bloodborne infections (particularly hepatis and AIDS) appear to be under control with advances in technology (Hoots & Cecalupo, 1994).

Parents, medical professionals, and teachers should decide if there is any equipment the child cannot safely use (for example, a high climber). Find out what the parents want you to do if the child is injured; also, decide how acting out and temper tantrums will be dealt with. If the child is experiencing a lot of pain or seems to be very tired, you might make arrangements for him to go home early. Use noncompetitive physical activities to reduce the dangers of overexertion and injury. Children can run, but don't have them run a race to see who wins.

Insulin-Dependent Diabetes

Insulin-dependent diabetes, or Type I diabetes, is a chronic disease that accounts for 5 to 10 percent of the diabetes in the United States and usually begins in childhood. Its onset in children is usually more swift and severe than it is in adults. It is considered an autoimmune disease because the beta cells in the pancreas that produce the insulin are destroyed by the body's immune system (NIH, 1994c). Children become very sick very quickly, and if treatment does not begin quickly, they will lapse into a life-threatening coma (NIH, 1994b). Diabetes causes the highest rate of hospitalization among White children. Common symptoms are extreme thirst, frequent urination, constant hunger, loss of weight, itching, easy tiring,

When children have diabetes, they need to eat at similar times each day and have predictable food exchanges.

changes in vision, and slow healing of cuts and scratches. However, it is possible for a child to be a diabetic without having all these symptoms, and some children have no obvious symptoms. Once a child is diagnosed, the child needs daily injections of the hormone insulin to survive (NIH, 1994c). The discovery of insulin has literally made the difference between life and death for these children. But insulin does not cure diabetes.

Diabetes is a metabolic disorder that affects the way the body uses digested food for energy and growth. The food we eat is broken down into chemicals, including a simple sugar called glucose. For glucose to get into cells, insulin must be present. Insulin is a hormone made by the pancreas that helps the body use glucose. For most people, the pancreas adjusts its level of insulin production to match the food we eat. In juvenile diabetes, the pancreas produces no insulin at all. As a result, the glucose builds up in the blood, overflows into the urine, and then passes out of the body (NIH, 1994b). The goal is to manage the disease by developing a predictable relationship among the child's diet, insulin, and amount of exercise. Diabetes can lead to many serious medical complications (kidney disease, blindness), as well as a shortened life span.

Insulin injections are necessary for almost all children with diabetes. The injections must be given daily and are probably the most hated part of the treatment. Urine testing (usually before breakfast and dinner) or blood testing may be necessary each day. This procedure is embarrassing for a child striving toward independence. Charting the test results provides the basis for changes in insulin dosage and gives clues to why some diabetics go out of control. When children are old enough, they are encouraged to do this themselves. Diabetic children are allowed to have slowly digestible sweets like ice cream, but are not allowed to eat candy bars and other carbohydrates that burn quickly. (An exception to this rule occurs when the child needs quick sugar to avert an insulin reaction.)

Brittle or "labile" diabetic children are those who are difficult to keep under medical control. In other words, it is difficult to determine the correct amount of insulin to prevent either shock or coma. These children are usually hospitalized until management techniques are worked out.

Although most juvenile diabetics are on a "free" diet, it is by no means unstructured. The free exchange system used by adults is often used with children. This system divides foods into six groups based on calories and grams of carbohydrates, proteins, and fats. Thus, if the child is allowed one bread exchange, the choice of any one of the following could be made: a piece of bread, one-half cup of cereal, two graham crackers, one-half cup of mashed potatoes, or one-fourth cup of baked beans. The number of exchanges are individually determined and parents will tell you what exchanges the child requires. This will affect what you offer at snack and how much the child eats.

The concern is when the child's insulin is out of control. This can happen because the sugar or glucose levels are too high or too low. Diabetic *coma* occurs because the blood glucose (sugar) level is too high and the body has too many ketones (acids). The child is not conscious, the face is flushed, skin and mouth are dry, rapid and labored breathing occurs, pulse is rapid and weak, blood pressure is low, and the breath has a fruity odor (NIH, 1994a). Insulin *reaction* or *shock* occurs when the level of blood glucose drops quickly. The signs are shaking, sweating, dizziness, double vision, convulsions, and collapse. This can occur when a child has injected too much insulin, eaten too little food, or has exercised without ingesting extra food. Taking small amounts of sugar, juice, or food with sugar will usually help within 10 to 15 minutes (NIH, 1994a).

You need to have snack and lunch at about the same times each day. Each should provide about the same food values every day. The child need not eat the same things every day, but the foods should be of equivalent groups and values.

Because of the possibility of insulin reaction, you must always have some quick-burning sugar on hand (pockets are a necessity) to give the child if you suspect a reaction is about to occur. Most children have some warning signs, but young children rarely can identify these. The child may be dizzy, shaky, trembling, or having an emotional outburst before the insulin reaction occurs. Find out in advance what the child's favorite sources of sugar are; you need to offer something especially tempting because the child may not feel like eating at this time. Some traditional quick sugar sources are orange juice, soda, a sugar cube, and small chocolate bars. Always carry one of these on a field trip. If you miss the warning signs and the child becomes unconscious, do not try to get the child to drink, because choking might result. Discuss emergency measures with parents and have a plan for the class and for field trips. (This may include calling the parents, taking the child to the emergency room, and giving the child a shot of glycogen.)

Too much sugar in the body for the amount of insulin is indicated by very frequent urination, thirst, hunger, weakness, drowsiness, vomiting, and finally coma. Call the parents when you notice any of the early signs. This condition can result from eating "forbidden foods," sleeping more, less active playing, or illness. If children know they have done something wrong to bring on the attack, they may be reluctant to tell. An unconscious child must be taken to the emergency room immediately.

The parents supervise and regulate the child's insulin and diet, and they can usually accommodate most situations if they know about them ahead of time. Send them a list of your snacks for the week or month, or at least post them on a bulletin board for the parents to check when they drop off or pick up their child. If another child will have a birthday party with cupcakes, tell the parents. This child can have one too, if it is planned. The child should wear a Medic-Alert bracelet or locket at all times.

Being different is often a problem. Children with diabetes may have low self-esteem and play alone frequently. Remember to work toward improving their self-concept and find ways of including them in play.

Juvenile Rheumatoid Arthritis

Arthritis is an inflammation of the joints. When joints are inflamed, they are painful, swollen, and stiff (Rennebohm, 1994). Juvenile rheumatoid arthritis (JRA) is the most common form of childhood arthritis. It can appear at any age and estimates are that 1 out of 2,000 school-age children have JRA (Cassidy & Nelson, 1988).

In JRA, "the immune system is making a mistake and waging an inappropriate inflammatory attack within the joint(s)" (Rennebohm, 1994, p. 71). Children with JRA will experience joint inflammation until the immune system self-corrects. This generally takes a year or two. Sometimes, this remission is permanent; sometimes, the system makes the mistake again and the child will again have inflamed joints. Occasionally, the mistake is only partially corrected, and in a small number of cases the problem does not correct itself. When the disease is in remission, the joints return to normal or nearly normal size.

We don't really know why some children get JRA and others don't. Some children seem to have a genetic tendency to develop the disease, but it is unique to the child and other family members are not affected (Rennebohm, 1994).

There are three types of JRA: pauciarticular, polyarticular, and systemic onset JRA. In *pauciarticular* onset JRA, there are four or fewer joints involved. The most common scenario is a preschool girl with arthritis in her knee; the knee is stiff and she limps, particularly in the morning. It is usually treated with ibuprofen-like therapy and typically goes into spontaneous remission in a year or two. However, it can persist for years and more joints can become affected; also, it can evolve into polyarticular JRA (Rennebohm, 1994). *Polyarticular* JRA involves five or more joints. This is more serious because more joints are involved, they are more likely to be seriously involved, and it is likely to persist longer. Children may experience chronic tiredness, poor appetite, and low-grade fever (Rennebohm, 1994). *Systemic* onset JRA begins with a high fever which occurs intermittently for days or weeks (another immune system mistake). The spectrum of involvement and severity in systemic onset JRA is broad and difficult to predict at the onset of the disease (Rennebohm, 1994).

The drugs that are used to treat JRA do not turn off the immune system, but help by reducing the quantity and intensity of the inflammation. Mild JRA is usually treated with nonsteroidal anti-inflammatory drugs (ibuprofen, aspirin); more severe JRA usually requires prednisone or other slow-acting antirheumatic drugs. Children are often required to adhere to therapeutic exercise regimens as well as take medication for years (Varni, Rapoff, & Waldron, 1994). Exercising a painful joint is distressing for both children and parents. (The goal is to keep the range of motion in the joints until the JRA goes into remission.) Over time, parents may have trouble paying for the medication; there is often parent-child conflict over the exercise regimen, and parents may burn out.

One of the most disturbing aspects of JRA is pain and the management of the pain. Children may be taught self-regulatory methods such as progressive muscle relaxation, meditative breathing, or guided imagery as ways of managing the pain (Varni et al., 1994).

The child may be tired or irritable and lack muscular strength. Allow the child time to do things. Realize that the child is probably in some pain. (The drugs reduce inflammation and pain but don't cure it.) The child should not participate in competitive sports, in activities that continuously use the same joints, or in jarring, twisting play.

Obesity

Obesity in young children is a serious problem. It affects their health, their self-concept, and the way others feel about them. Obesity is an excessive accumulation of fat, in which body weight exceeds "normal" by at least 20 percent. The number of young children who are overweight and obese is increasing (Harkaway, 1989). Obesity is commonly caused by eating too much. Overeating may result from poor dietary habits or from difficulties in coping with everyday problems. Rarely do inherited disorders or metabolic and endocrine abnormalities contribute to obesity. Few children are referred for medical advice at this age; it is assumed that they will outgrow their baby fat. However, in many cases, they never stop being overweight. Lifestyle changes in the 1990s such as the practice of eating fast foods on a regular basis and the increase in watching television and playing video games are contributing to the problem.

Children who are classified as obese are likely to have one or two obese parents. It is difficult to tell if children become obese because of eating patterns, because of a genetic tendency in the family, or because of a combination (Harkaway, 1989).

Obesity in childhood is difficult to reverse. Overweight children have a difficult time keeping up with their friends. They can't run as far or as fast or climb as high. The social and emotional costs are great. These children are also at risk for elevated blood pressure and, with increasing age, are more susceptible to premature heart attack, diabetes, and arthritis (Epstein & Squires, 1988).

Our society looks scornfully at obesity. Even from 3-year-olds, the taunts of "Tubby," "Fats," and "Fatso" are heard. Overweight children are discriminated against by peers and teachers. They may grow up expecting rejection and usually get it. If they feel isolated and unhappy, they may react by eating more. Some children are obese from lack of activity and they need to be encouraged to participate in more active play.

Children need to get more in touch with their bodies. When children tell us they are not hungry and we require them to eat or finish the food on their plate, we are teaching them not to respond to what their body is telling them. We need to evaluate our own practices related to eating and the nutritional quality of the food served in early care and education settings.

Children who are obese exercise less than other children. They seem to be able to do single, nonrhythmic activities like climbing, but have problems with repeated rhythmic activities like running. Playing loud music with a distinct beat during activities helps them improve this skill. To help burn calories and tone muscles, these children should be encouraged to participate in large motor play. As obese children may be loners, plan special activities to bring them into the group and foster a sense of group belonging. They and their parents also need education on nutrition. Praise and other noncaloric rewards should be used, never sweets.

Seizure Disorder

A seizure is "an abrupt, spontaneous, and time-limited behavioral or psychic dysfunction caused by an abnormal and involuntary electrical discharge from nerve cells in the brain" (Bobele, 1994, p. 177). Seizures are one of the more common chronic medical diseases of childhood and among the most poorly understood. About 8 percent of all children in the United States will have at least one seizure before they are 16 years of age (O'Donohoe, 1994). Most of these are isolated events related to high fevers in childhood. A *seizure disorder* is the condition of having seizures. *Epilepsy* is a type of seizure disorder that involves having recurrent unprovoked seizures (Brown, 1997).

Seizures are related to brain abnormalities, lack of oxygen to the brain, trauma, and infection, all of which also cause developmental disabilities (Brown, 1997). Most seizures are brief, lasting only a few minutes. All seizures are not alike. The effect of the seizure depends on the location of the cells and how far the discharge spreads. Seizures occur more often in children under 6 and in old age. Seizures take many forms, but there are two major types: generalized and partial. *Generalized* seizures involve the discharge of cells in a large part of the brain; as a result, these seizures involve the whole body. *Partial* seizures begin in a localized area (for example, the motor area of one hemisphere), and hence the motor system of the body is involved. Partial seizures are subdivided into *simple partial* seizures (formerly called focal), in which consciousness is not impaired, and *complex partial* seizures (also called temporal lobe or psychomotor seizures), which may cause disorientation, confusion, or total loss of consciousness. Complex partial seizures usually involve parts of the brain that connect to the limbic system or brain stem (Bobele, 1994). Partial seizures may spread and become *secondary generalized* seizures. In this case, consciousness is almost always impaired.

Generalized seizures include tonic-clonic seizures (formerly called grand mal), clonic seizures, tonic seizures, absence seizures (formerly called petit mal), and those that are grouped under minor motor seizures (Bobele, 1994). *Tonic-clonic* seizures, or convulsions, are characterized by the sudden loss of consciousness, loss of posture (which may lead to an unprotected fall), and a stiffening of the extremities (the tonic phase). The jaw may clench tightly (biting the tongue if it is caught between the teeth). This is followed by a rhythmic, symmetric jerking of the extremities with slow and rapid components (the clonic phase) (Bobele, 1994). Respiration may be labored. At the end of the seizure, the jerking stops and the muscles become limp. There may be incontinence of urine or feces. After the seizure, the child is usually lethargic or disoriented and it may be several minutes or hours until full consciousness returns (Bobele, 1994). *Clonic* seizures resemble the tonic-clonic seizures but without the stiffening after the loss of consciousness or the rhythmic movements; the stiffening may begin before loss of consciousness, causing a backward fall. *Myoclonic* seizures are brief, single, rapid contraction of muscles that may be repeated and can involve isolated muscle groups or more general muscles of the trunk and limbs. *Atonic/astatic* seizures are characterized by sudden loss of posture and a forward fall; loss of consciousness is brief and a child may get back up immediately if unhurt (Bobele, 1994). *Absence* seizures occur most frequently in school-age children. They are characterized by an abrupt alteration in consciousness, giving the child a "blank look," and may last 20 to 30 seconds. They may occur many times a day, but there is no loss of consciousness or disorientation afterwards (Bobele, 1994).

About half of children with seizures have no known cause. The remaining seizures are caused by brain trauma or tumors, toxins, metabolic or vascular problems, infections, and genetic disorders, as well as some other causes (Bobele, 1994). Children with seizure disorders have a high incidence of learning disabilities as well as psychological and behavior problems. About half of children with epilepsy have varying degrees of cognitive delays (Brown, 1997).

Seizures themselves are managed in two ways: through the use of particular drugs and by eliminating provoking factors in the environment. A variety of antiepileptic drugs, either singly or in combination, are used to reduce or eliminate seizures. Most childhood seizures can be controlled in this way, and because many children will go into a sustained remission, the drugs can be stopped (Brown, 1997). When these are ineffective, surgery may be considered if the seizures originate from a part of the brain that can be surgically removed and not cause more of a disability than the seizures themselves. Certain environmental factors (such as flashing lights) may precipitate seizures for some children. These need to be eliminated from the environment.

Seizures are both embarrassing and frightening for the child having them and for the children who witness them. Children with seizures may be anxious, have a poor self-concept, and be rejected and socially isolated. In early childhood, the social and emotional consequences of seizures may be the most devastating effect.

Seizures are primarily a medical problem. The management of seizures that may happen in the classroom, however, involves educational decision making. The first thing to do is to talk with the child's

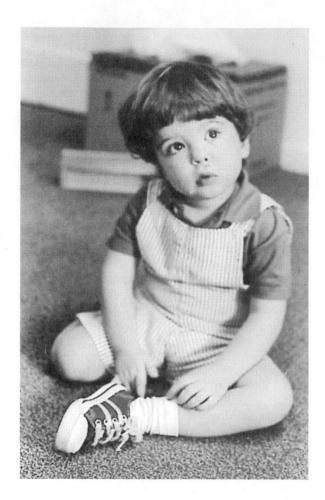

It is difficult to determine if this child is just staring into space or having an absence seizure.

parents and find out as much as you can about the type of seizures the child has, their frequency and length, if they are set off by identifiable environmental stimuli, and how the child reacts when having a seizure.

Obviously, it is important to know the first-aid procedure for seizures: It starts with *stay calm.* You can't stop a seizure once it starts. If the child is upright, help move the child to the floor, loosen clothing, and remove any nearby objects so he doesn't strike head or body against them. Turn the child's face to the side so saliva can flow out of the mouth, but don't otherwise interfere with movements. Don't be alarmed if the child stops breathing momentarily, and don't put anything in the child's mouth. When the movements stop and the child is relaxed, cover the child and allow her to rest or sleep until ready to get up. Notify the child's parents that a seizure has occurred. It isn't necessary to call a doctor unless the seizure lasts more than 10 minutes or a second seizure follows. The child needs to be observed until fully alert, then provide reassurance and comfort and encourage the child to resume activities once recovered (Brown, 1997; Epilepsy Foundation of America, n.d.).

In addition to knowing first-aid procedures, you should note the length of the child's seizure and what the child was doing when the seizure took place. You should know the medication the child takes and its possible side effects; some side effects include fatigue, inattention, irritability, and aggression.

Again, you are the model; to the extent that you are calm and matter of fact, the children will be as well. If children ask you questions, answer them honestly, but simply: "Sometimes Sibyl's brain has too much energy. Her body is affected by this energy. Once the energy is gone, she is tired and wants to rest." Children who have tonic-clonic seizures are obvious to all children in the classroom. Prepare them for this, including the embarrassment of bowel and bladder incontinence during the seizure (Brown, 1997). You should keep a towel and washcloth and a change of clothing for the child in your classroom.

Sickle-Cell Disease

Sickle-cell disease is a painful, inherited blood disorder that primarily affects African Americans. It can be identified at birth through blood tests. Testing is offered to all families in newborn nurseries (Brown, 1997). Red blood cells are normally shaped like a doughnut with a hole in the middle that does not go through completely. In sickle-cell disease, cells take on a crescent, or sickle, shape. This shape impairs the oxygen-carrying capacity of the cells and is also conducive to clogging. The result is pain and chronic fatigue. There is no known cure, and frequent blood transfusions are necessary to replace the destroyed red blood cells. Children with severe forms of the disease may die in childhood or early adult life from a blood clot, which prevents oxygen from reaching the brain.

There is a major distinction between sickle-cell trait and sickle-cell anemia. The trait exists when the child inherits the disease from only one parent, the anemia when it is inherited from both. The child with the trait is not ill, but is a carrier of the disease. The trait occurs in about 1 in 10 African Americans, the anemia in about 1 in 400. The actual proportion of the sickle-shaped cells varies from child to child. The higher the proportion and the earlier the symptoms appear, the more severe the disease is likely to be. Diagnosis is usually made between age 2 and 4. Characteristically, this child will be chronically sick with infections of one sort or another, will be weak, and will experience abdominal pain. The child may also have painful swelling of hands and feet.

Young children with sickle-cell disease are more prone to crisis and hospitalization than are older children. Crises are precipitated by a variety of circumstances: infection, chilling, dehydration, strenuous exercise, sweating, and cold damp weather. Use this knowledge to take preventive measures. These children need a high-protein, high-vitamin, adequate iron diet. You can plan snacks and lunches to meet that need. They also need to drink a great deal of fluid, especially water and juice. Encourage children to drink more by having fluids readily available and ensure that there is easy access to the bathroom.

Fatigue is a major factor, as children tire easily and a general lassitude is often present. Be aware of the balance of active and quiet activities in the classroom. Be sure to alternate these activities and to have alternative activities for those that are physically demanding. Stress cooperation, not competition. Help children build a good self-concept.

Special Health Care Needs

Some children with health impairments have survived very serious medical experiences and may need specialized health care indefinitely. These children are sometimes called "medically fragile." Others are referred to as "technology-dependent." In the past, they received their education in hospital or institutional settings. This is no longer the case.

Technology Assistance. With the passage of Public Law 100-407, the Technology-Related Assistance for Individuals with Disabilities Act of 1988, we began to focus on how technology—devices, equipment, and systems—could improve the capacities of individuals with disabilities. About 2 in every 100 children use this type of assistive technology (Millner, 1991). Devices range from wheelchairs to computers to switches to augmentative communication devices, but all support the inclusion of children in regular classrooms.

In contrast, the number of children requiring medical assistive technology is relative low. The Office of Technology Assessment (1987) views medical assistive technology as a device used by a child who requires substantial daily skilled nursing care to avert death or further disability. Almost half of the children who are medically dependent require some form of respiratory technology assistance: suction, oxygen, tracheostomy care, cardiorespiratory monitoring, or mechanical ventilator support. Other types of medical assistive technology include surveillance devices, nutritive assistive devices, intravenous therapy, and kidney dialysis (Levy & O'Rourke, 1997).

Problems of children with special health care needs raise many questions about the relationship between educational and medical services. Although there is general agreement that medical needs must be stabilized before educational needs can be met, there is disagreement about the proper setting for the children's education. In situations where the child is medically stable but ventilator-dependent, oxygen-dependent, needs nutritional supplements, is on an apnea monitor, or is dependent on other specialized health care, the question of least restrictive educational environment arises. These children qualify for special educational services. However, many teachers and administrators are concerned about issues such as liability, medical support services, and educational barriers.

Teachers of young children must be prepared to support those with special health care needs in the classroom. This may require in-service training and working with medical support staff. The classroom must be made hygienically safe, and adjustments (both individual and group) to the schedule must be made to accommodate learning needs. Teachers need to work closely with parents to gain their input and knowledge as well as allay their fears about school. Clear plans must be in place for medical emergencies as well as school emergencies (fire drills, etc.). Working relations may have to be established between teachers in other settings (hospital- or home-based) to allow continuity. There is little doubt that these children will challenge the capacity of both the system and the teacher.

Guidelines

1. Use activities that allow children to be in control or adapt activities so that children have more control. Let the children decide what color(s) of finger paint they want to use and whether they want one dab or two and where they want these on the paper.

2. Encourage independence and allow the children to do as much as possible for themselves. Actively support age-appropriate independence.

3. Arrange the class schedule so that vigorous activities are followed by less strenuous ones; during strenuous activities, provide rest periods that are built in for everyone.

4. Be flexible in scheduling the children's day so that if they have to leave for medical procedures this can become part of the routine. If you accept the children's therapy and its importance, it will be easier for them. Some children find a full day tiring, especially when they return after an illness. If possible, have them come initially for part of the day.

5. Plan activities that are open-ended and do not require excessive amounts of time to complete, or ones that can be completed at home. Because some children may work more slowly and miss more school than others, they may decide not to start things they may never complete.

6. Be a good observer. Watch for mood changes, as these are often cues to well-being. Be aware of the children's body language. Often, children will grimace or give other signs that will alert you to possible pain or arouse concern about the level of medication the child is taking. Young children have trouble recognizing and verbalizing their needs; you can help them.

7. Find out as much as you can about the illnesses children have and how it affects them. Talk to parents, therapists, and medical personnel, read books on the subject, and check the Internet. Be informed about children's diet, physical restrictions, medication, possible side effects of the medicine, and the behaviors that indicate a chronic illness might be moving into an acute phase.

8. Find out what children have been told about their illness and its implications. Be prepared to respond to comments such as "I don't want to play with you. You have leukemia. You're going to die." You need to know how the parents are dealing with the concept of death and exactly what they call the illness. Even with that knowledge, handling the situation is not easy. Young children are not capable of abstract thinking. Death is not viewed as permanent. This doesn't mean, however, that they are any less fearful of it. Although the child's classmates may seem unfeeling, they are only displaying curiosity and lack of knowledge.

9. Help children learn about the implications of their health problems. Verbalize for them what happens under certain circumstances: "You are allergic to peanuts. If you eat them, it will be hard for you to breathe. There are other things that are crunchy like peanuts that you can eat. These are sunflower seeds. I like them. Do you?"

10. Provide an open atmosphere where children can discuss fears and problems freely. One thing that children know is that if it is taboo, it is bad. Be honest when you do not know an answer; say you don't know and then find out the answer. In general, don't tell children more than they ask. They are the best guide about what they need to know.

11. Develop a plan for keeping in touch with absent children. You could send get-well cards through the mail. Another child could deliver an audio- or videotape. The child could be called on the phone by other children (find out good times to call, or let the child phone school). Send home a "fun bag" or develop a lending library of books and toys. The best plan is one that is tailored to your situation and the child's needs.

12. Certain illnesses require adaptations such as free access to the toilet, extra time for task completion, special food for snacks, scheduling time to take medication, and so on.

13. Classroom stress can bring on crises in some chronic illnesses (asthma, diabetes). Play down competitive games and deadlines. Make the classroom as pressure-free as possible.

14. Special events (holidays, birthdays, field trips) may lead to flare-ups, as there is almost always some psychosomatic element in the timing or severity of acute bouts. Prepare children for events. Talk about what is likely to happen. This is a time to watch for stress-related reactions.

15. Learn to recognize warning signs of emergencies. Discuss with parents what they want you to do in case of an emergency. If you are to call, call when you suspect something is wrong—do not wait for full confirmation. Tape the numbers near the phone you will use. Know the location of the nearest emergency room and the fastest way to get there. Take a first-aid course; be sure it includes the Heimlich maneuver and cardiopulmonary resuscitation.

Curriculum Adaptations

Children with health impairments require few curriculum adaptations as long as they are allowed to work at their own pace. While working in each curriculum area, help children feel included in the group and focus on improving their self-concept.

Social Awareness: Self-Esteem, Inclusion, Social Studies, Health and Safety

Many children with health impairments have been hospitalized. They may have concerns about doctors, hospitals, and being separated from their parents. One of the most frightening aspects of hospitalization is the feeling of being out of control. Helping children learn about health and safety matters as a part of a group is useful. Giving them knowledge of the roles of professionals, including physicians, is empowering.

Children can help prevent some acute episodes by learning to recognize their symptoms and/or avoiding situations that are likely to cause them. This knowledge will in turn make them feel more in control and help them toward independence. They need to develop social skills and methods of keeping in touch with peers when they cannot attend school (telephone, visits after school).

Self-Esteem. Children with health impairments need to become aware of their uniqueness. Because most look like other children, adults may not understand or remember their problems. Because they have periods when they are fine and periods when they are not, others wonder if it is just a game they are playing. They may be misunderstood at school. They may not be able to participate in some strenuous activities. Because of frequent absences, it may be difficult for them to build relationships with other children and to complete projects. Especially if children are experiencing pain or side effects from drugs, they may not be fun to be with. Teachers may have to remind the other children of these circumstances.

Some children who are chronically ill may develop phobias; they may be fearful and anxious, always awaiting the next crisis situation, the next painful experience. They cannot even enjoy their periods of health because of the fear of doing something that will bring on an acute period. They may experience loneliness, boredom, and depression.

For some children, the fear of death and dying is a major issue that may often be on their minds as well as on their parents'. (This seems to be true whether or not they have been told of their life expectancy.)

1. Help children become more aware of their feelings and learn to express them. Give them the skills to work through them.
2. Have children make a list (an adult can write it) of what they can do and like to do. Focus on the positive.
3. Help children think about what makes them happy and how they can use this knowledge when they become depressed and fearful.

Inclusion. Children who have spent a long time in the hospital or at home convalescing may have had fewer opportunities to learn how to play with other children. They may not function at an age-appropriate level in areas such as cooperating with others, sharing, and turn taking. They may have fewer skills in joining and being part of groups.

1. You are a model of the behaviors that are necessary for children to join groups. To the extent that you never join groups, you don't model this behavior and it is more obvious when you try to include a child with a health impairment. Suggest roles that need filling, or parts that they could play. However, accept the reality that this sometimes doesn't work, and openly explain to children that this is the way it is. If this happens frequently, you may need to use a different strategy.
2. Your role should be one that changes over time. Children may initially need your active support. However, supporting them when they have the ability to act on their own creates dependency and decreases growth.
3. Emphasize ways of approaching others.

Social Studies. Although our concerns about children with health impairments focus on medical practice and settings, children spend most of their life in the community. Children need to know and role-play not only traditional occupations but also variations.

1. Help children play the roles of public health nurses who visit homes; itinerant teachers who educate children who cannot attend school; and social workers or others who may serve as a support system to the family.
2. Be sure to include cultural variations and the role of extended family as well as alternative medical sources.
3. Help children understand the interconnectedness of the community in which they live. Include information about water, electricity, and waste disposal and the consequences if the community did not address these needs.
4. Have children help draw and fill in a map of the route from the classroom to the nurse's office (if that is where they go). If hospitalized, remind children that they can learn about an unfamiliar place using the skill they have in map making. Include other significant places in the map.

Health and Safety. Health and safety should be emphasized. Children need to learn about foods, those that are good for them and those they must avoid, as well as safety practices.

Frequent hand washing for children and adults is one of the easiest ways to prevent the spread of contagious diseases.

1. Work on the food groups, which foods are in each, and how the body uses different foods.

2. Using illustrations, explain what happens when people eat food they are allergic to.

3. All children need to be protected from contagious diseases, so it is important that all children cover their mouths when coughing and sneezing, wash hands after toileting, and follow all forms of good hygiene.

4. Emphasize body awareness. Children need to be able to name body parts. As children's understanding increases, include the internal ones. Start with those they can feel (bones) and commonly known parts (stomach).

5. Help children analyze situations for potential injuries and talk about what can be done to prevent injuries.

6. Talk about healthy lifestyles.

Language and Literacy: Speaking, Listening, Reading, and Writing

Children need to be able to communicate. Some children with chronic illness will lack the experiential basis for language because they have spent time in restrictive settings. Parents may have limited children's opportunities both because of the disease itself and because most illnesses weaken children and increase their susceptibility to contagious diseases. In addition to expanding their overall language base, children need to develop the vocabulary to express their fears and concerns and increase their understanding of the situations they may face. They need to be aware of their symptoms and how to label them, know the body parts, and be able to put the two together to give accurate information about their current state of health. Children may have consciously tried not to listen or found that adults did not expect them to listen, so they quit attending. Adults often forget that there may be so much attention to other areas of learning that listening is neglected, or that, although children listen, they may not understand what they hear. Reading offers the child an escape into other worlds of learning. Writing affords children the opportunity to express and share feelings even when those we want to speak with are not present. It also provides a way of remembering important information.

Speaking. Encouraging children to speak about nonthreatening experiences provides the groundwork for talking about experiences that they perceive as frightening or scary.

1. Use field trips to the florist, bakery, post office, radio station, and so on to help children gain the firsthand experiences that may be lacking in children with chronic health needs (be sure the places you plan to visit will not trigger an episode for a child).

2. When the child is home for extended periods, exchange language experience stories. Have children write stories about "Going to the Hospital" or "Things I Can See out My Window."

3. Send a "Get Well Soon" audio- or videotape to the child. Have children who want to share send a message on the tape. If this is set up as an activity area, put a picture of the child beside the tape and encourage the children to talk to her. The child who is ill may wish to send an answer tape back.

4. Encourage children to ask questions. Show children pictures of situations and ask them to describe what is happening in the picture; help them ask questions about what specific objects are, how they are used, and about what will happen next.

5. Show children pictures of scenes (beach, grocery store, hospital, doctor's office, classroom, and so on) and ask them about how they would feel if they were part of the picture. Show pictures with moods that may be interpreted in a variety of ways. After one child has responded, ask if others feel differently and have them describe their feelings. Ask children what they need to change in the picture to change a negative feeling to a positive one (have a parent present, a stuffed animal, and so on).

Fingerplays can be used to teach concepts and are especially good for those who are confined to bed frequently. Fingerplays are active, yet not tiring. Parents can easily learn them and thus form another link with school.

1. Use fingerplays that are repetitive, so children only have to learn minor changes to participate: "Where Is Thumbkin?"

2. Use fingerplays to increase body awareness: "I Put My Finger on My Face."

3. Use fingerplays to teach concepts: "A Little Ball."

Listening. Children frequently are expected not only to listen, but to understand and follow through on adult requests, especially if these come from medical personnel. Children need skills in following directions but also in asking for clarification when they do not understand what is required.

1. Play Simon Says and include requests that frequently occur in medical situations: "Say, ahhh," "Take a deep breath," "Open your mouth wide," and so on.

2. Using similar phrases, put them together and have children perform a series of tasks involving their body: "Open your mouth, take a deep breath, and breathe out slowly."

3. If the child is likely to be hospitalized, make a listening tape of hospital sounds. This will make a strange place a bit more familiar. If the child has to stay in bed, make a listening tape of things one might hear from bed.

Stories are a great way to make the unknown a little more familiar, to help children know they are not the only ones with fears, and perhaps to help them put themselves and their situation into perspective. Choose stories that relate to the specific situation the children you are dealing with might face.

1. Read stories about children in hospitals.

2. Read stories about children or animals who are different.

3. Have a listening center where you have appropriate books as well as tape recordings of those books. Help children develop the skill of independent listening, so that if they are out of school for an extended period, they have a familiar activity they can participate in. Some portable tape players have sound governors, so children can use headphones and safely listen while not bothering others. As your collection of tapes and books is likely to be more extensive than any family's, plan a system of loaning children their favorites.

4. Fatigue and illness can impair listening. If you notice children who are typically attentive listeners not paying attention, consider the appropriateness of what you are doing, but also consider health issues.

5. Read or tape a story that the children are familiar with. Make some obvious mistakes (change words, locations, outcomes, and so on) and have the children find your mistakes.

Reading. Reading requires not only cognitive readiness, but an experiential background so that the reading content makes sense. Part of your role is to develop creative ways to give children the experiential background they need to read and comprehend.

1. Children with health impairments have limited experiences. Take them on field trips; if this is not possible, use the dramatic play area to extend their concepts. Some excellent videotapes are also available that bring experiences to children who cannot participate in field trips.

2. Listen to the child's spoken language. If children have not had opportunities for speaking and listening that others have had, build these skills as part of your literacy program.

3. Help children focus on the relationship between printed and spoken language.

4. Encourage children to gain some control over their world through sequencing activities, especially ones that hurt or are frightening: "First we go to the doctor's office, then I tell them my name, then I wait, then I get the shot, then I wait, then I get checked for a reaction, then I can go home." This makes the injection one of a series of events rather than the total focus.

5. Expose children to a wide variety of written materials. Recite many different types of children's books, poetry, fingerplays, and so on. It is useful, especially if what you are reciting is new to you, to have the words available in case you forget them. Point out to the children that you are doing this and why.

6. Give children opportunities to work with the perceptual skills necessary for reading.

7. Have children match line-drawing faces showing different expressions. Then talk about what these people might be feeling or doing.

8. Play hospital or medical Lotto.

Writing. The goals for writing at this age is to help children develop the small motor skills and eye-hand coordination necessary to write and to build a desire to write.

1. Make writing part of many different curriculum areas; for example, in dramatic play, encourage children to write prescriptions for the dolls who are sick.

2. Have children keep a chart about what happens to the doll who is sick. Discuss with children why they might do this and how this helps ensure accurate information when different people care for the doll.

3. Have some of the children make a picture menu of what the choices are for snack and then let them find out from the other children what they want from the menu. (Be sure you have enough so that children can have what they request.) After each child "writes" his name on his menu, distribute menus to children's places at the table, along with their "orders." Because of the quality of the writing, it is likely that some of the orders will be wrong. Talk about that and the fact that mistakes happen in all restaurants and what to do about them.

Discovery: Mathematics, Science, and Computers

Children need support in investigating the world around them and in making sense out of it. They need to sort, classify, and develop the vocabulary that allows them to express themselves. They need to *do* this, not be told about it. The lives of children with health impairments are linked to medicine and scientific discoveries. Their understanding of the scientific process can help them look at the implications of taking medicine versus not taking it. They can also explore and learn about their body and how it functions. Be sure children know the amounts of medication they need and the time sequence in which they take the medicine. Have them count sips of water. Make math real and relevant. Computers are a frequent aid in home study and may allow children to participate in the same experiences as their classmates.

Mathematics. It is especially important for children who have health limitations to start with a sensorimotor concept of mathematics. This involves active interaction with materials like blocks, Cuisenaire rods, and pegs. Then move on to more abstract number concepts.

1. Use three-dimensional objects like unit blocks to teach basic math concepts; don't rely on rote memory.

2. Use music and rhythmic activities to reinforce math concepts (clap four times).

3. Make math relevant. Children need to know how many pills they must take and when. This is a step toward independence as well as toward learning number concepts.

4. Have children sort and classify familiar pieces of medical equipment (cotton balls, tongue depressors, bandages of different sizes and shapes, gauze).

Science. Because most children take medicine to alleviate symptoms, it is important to develop their cause-and-effect reasoning skills. They need to understand why they should take the medicine even when they feel well.

1. Plant seeds. Discuss conditions for growth. Put some plants in the dark. Do not water some. Discuss the implications of the various conditions and "treatments."

2. Help children make predictions. Help them apply this skill to their particular situation: "I have trouble breathing when I run fast. If I run slower, I can run farther."

3. Help children learn about the seasons of the year, especially if they directly affect their state of health. Discuss with them how we prepare ourselves for seasonal change as well as how this happens in nature. Have children talk about the season's effects on them: "I can't walk as far in the winter when it is cold and windy." They need to develop this type of causal thinking.

Computers. The computer has many applications for children with health impairments. It requires little energy to use; it is hygienic, self-paced, and available when the child wants to use it; and it is potentially portable and interactive.

1. Encourage children with health impairments to become familiar with computers. They need to establish some control over their world, and they can do that with a computer. Regardless of how rudimentary their skills, the potential for cause-effect reasoning is present.

2. There may be times when children with health impairments cannot communicate. Computers equipped with a simple switch and a scanning program can allow children to make their needs known.

3. If children are absent from school, you might be able to loan or recommend to parents software that will help children learn some of the concepts you are teaching.

4. Computers have the possibility for helping children participate in interactive recreation. (Traditional "arcade" games typically require good fine motor coordination, but are timed, which may not be helpful.) Computerized board games such as checkers and Monopoly exist, as well as many other commercially available games.

Developmental Physical Education and Sensorimotor Skills: Large Motor, Small Motor, and Sensorimotor Integration

Many of the sensorimotor activities that you do in the classroom are appropriate for children with health impairments. They, like all children, are individuals with differing needs. Children with health impairments must develop as much strength and endurance as they can. Respect their limits, but encourage them to participate in gross motor play. Young children will rarely overextend themselves, but individualize programming so children can set their own limits. Opportunities for sensorimotor integration are essential. Small motor activities are easily adaptable for quiet play and can be used to pace the day. Try to think of variations and new materials that will keep them interesting. Be aware of the weather, especially when it is windy or very cold or hot. These extremes may cause children to tire quickly. Have some quiet activities outside also.

Large Motor. Children with health impairments may find large motor play challenging. Find ways of allowing different amounts of time for activities if children are not self-regulatory.

1. Keep activities noncompetitive and pressure-free.

2. Emphasize the quality of movement, not speed.

3. Modifications may need to be made to some games. Reduce the distance to be traveled. Slow the pace by having children walk, not run. Institute intermissions. (All children must clap 10 times between events.)

4. Have children jump on a trampoline (or mattress with dust cover). This improves drainage of the respiratory tract.

Small Motor. Small motor play is not physically taxing and can therefore be a potential strength. Many activities that fall into this category use materials that can be placed in jellyroll pans. These can serve as storage trays and can also be used in a wheelchair, on the floor, or in bed.

1. Choose toys that are washable. If one child has a contagious disease, it may be passed to others if the toys cannot be disinfected.

2. Use a variety of fine motor toys. Children need much practice in this area and, without sufficient variety, they may become bored before they acquire the necessary skills.

Sensorimotor Integration. Children need experience coordinating their senses. If they have not had the opportunity to do this, you need to provide more activities that make them aware of their body and where it is in space.

1. Give verbal directions for motor activities and see whether the children can follow them. Once you have ascertained that they can, change the directions slightly.

2. Games with beach balls require little effort but a fair amount of coordination and integration.

3. Beanbags can be tossed, balanced, or caught. They are adaptable to the classroom as well as other settings.

4. Hand clapping is a simple but effective activity. When done to music or in a pattern (sequence)—especially when the hands cross the midline, the right and left hand take turns, and a partner is added—it is a challenging activity that can be used in a variety of circumstances.

Creative Arts: Visual Arts, Music, Creative Movement, and Dramatic Play

Children with health impairments may express concerns and fears through the arts that they are unable or unwilling to express otherwise. The arts also can be used as a way of releasing energy and emotions. Music can provide a good transition between home and school. Use slow music when children appear to be tiring. If a child is out of school for an extended period of time, send a musical greeting or a tape of new songs the children are learning so the child can come back to school knowing the words and thus feel included. Help children use dramatic play to better understand their world and to play through situations that they may find scary. Children may be very competent at role playing and can provide leadership, while at the same time working through some of their own feelings. Have a variety of sizes, shapes, and weights of blocks for them to choose from.

Visual Arts. The visual arts are both a means of creative expression and a tension reliever.

1. Concentrate on the process. If you can convince children to use arms and fingers they might not otherwise use, you are succeeding. As the process becomes easy, focus on variations.

2. Use many three-dimensional art materials. Again, the initial goal is manipulation, not a final product.

3. Use art materials that require varying amounts of fine motor skills.

Music. Music contributes much to a child's physical, aesthetic, and intellectual development. It provides pleasure and creative experience, develops auditory skills, encourages physical development, and increases range and flexibility of one's voice. There should be a wide variety of musical experiences: listening, singing, moving to music, and playing instruments.

1. Have a variety of different instruments available. Help children explore and evaluate the sounds of an instrument when it is held and played in different ways. See if they can identify the instruments they know in a recording.

2. Incorporate music and language experiences; have children make up new verses to old songs. Play unusual instrumental records and ask the children to describe what they imagined while listening.

3. Use music for exercise, self-expression, listening, and keeping time, not just for singing.

4. Introduce concepts of pitch, loudness, and duration.

5. Teach some colors and numbers with songs: "Who Has Red On," "Ten Little Children."

6. Sing songs that call children by name.

7. Use chants, especially if children (or adults) are self-conscious about singing.

Creative Movement. Creative movement helps children internalize their ideas about the world and their ability to respond to it.

1. Have children toss beach balls into the air and hum or sing one note until the ball touches the floor.

2. Do movement exploration activities, especially those that emphasize relaxation skills: "Move like a rag doll," "Move like a flag blowing in the breeze."

3. Put stories to music. Have children choose background music for stories.

4. Paint to music.

5. Music that combines creative movement and stories is fun and mind expanding.

6. Exercise to music. Select a body part (or combination) and have the children move it back and forth at a slow tempo.

Dramatic Play. Dramatic play, given appropriate props, allows children to act out fears and gives them control over frightening situations. Set up situations that chronically ill children may encounter.

1. Emergency room: Discuss and play scenes that might be going on in an emergency room, emphasizing the sense of urgency but allowing the child to be in control.

2. Doctor's office/clinic: Talk about routine visits and visits when children are sick.

3. Surgery: Discuss operations. Allow the children to operate on dolls to "fix" them. Make finger casts so that children can learn that this is not a painful process.

4. Hospital: Set up a hospital. Talk about being scared, about strange hospital sounds, about being left alone.

5. Encourage children to build a hospital, using blocks in conjunction with the dramatic play area.

Transitions

Transitions are often difficult times. Children who are wary of adults and who may not trust them have a particularly difficult time. Reentries into the classroom require separation from important people; after a period of being absent, children may feel uncertain about their acceptance and about you.

They need your support. This may be a time when children feel helpless or abandoned. They may feel hurt that they are being left again or afraid that you will hurt them. A predictable routine helps this transition.

1. Have a predictable arrival schedule, with one adult assigned to be the "greeter." At least during difficult transitions, have that be the same person each day.

2. Have the same adult help the child leave the setting and briefly talk about what will happen the next day, with the expectation that the child will return.

3. As children become more comfortable, encourage more independence—but *not* until the issue over separation has been resolved.

4. As the day is ending, try to make it positive. Find something that you can say about the day that is positive with the expectation that the next day will be even better.

5. If the child with a health impairment moves more slowly than the other children, remind her early about the transition to come. Dismiss that child among the first from the group.

6. Transitions may be a good time to have children take necessary medication. Other children are less likely to notice because there is a lot going on at this time.

7. This is a good time to emphasize similarities: all children with brown hair and blue eyes, all children with plaid shirts, all children with buckle shoes.

Summary

There are a variety of health impairments that can impact the lives of children and their families. Although they are different, some of the characteristics are similar. The age of onset of the disease makes a difference. Children and their siblings may not understand the illness and its implications. Families may have a difficult time coping with the medical requirements, pain, and financial obligations of the impairment.

Health impairments have many different manifestations. Some occur gradually, others all at once, some are acute and go into remission, some are chronic, others episodic. In some cases, there is the expectation that children will die prematurely; in others, that the life span will be shortened; and in still others, that the impairment will not affect the life span. The degree of incapacitation the child will have also impacts the system.

There are many different health impairments; when a child with an impairment is in your classroom, it is important to learn more about that particular impairment, how it affects that particular child, what the child knows about the impairment, and what to do in emergency situations. Adapting the curriculum can help children work through some of their fears and give you information about their perception of the health impairment.

Educational Resources

Allergy Foundation of America
801 Second Avenue
New York, NY 10017
Has national and regional programs and printed literature; gives lists of qualified, practicing allergists in United States.

American Alliance for Health, Physical Education and
   Recreation
Room 422
1201 16th Street
Washington, DC 20036
Provides information and materials on physical education and recreation for people with disabilities.

American Cancer Society
219 East 42nd Street
New York, NY 10017
(800) ACS-2345
National Headquarters refers affiliates for local support; provides information on research, education, patient services, and rehabilitation.

American Diabetes Association (ADA)
1660 Duke Street
Alexandria, VA 22314
(800) 232-3472, In Washington, DC: (703) 549-1500
FAX (703) 836-7439, http://www.diabetes.org
National headquarters has five basic programs in patient education, professional education, public education, detection, and research. Makes referrals to affiliates and answers questions; publishes cookbooks and exchange lists for meal planning.

American Heart Association
44 East 23rd Street
New York, NY 10010
National office forwards inquiries and requests to appropriate local affiliates, which aid in maintaining or developing heart centers and clinics.

American Red Cross
1730 D Street, NW
Washington, DC 20037
(800) 452-7773
Writes and distributes information on a variety of health-related areas, including AIDS.

Asthma and Allergy Foundation of America (AAFA)
1717 Massachusetts Avenue, NW, Suite 305
Washington, DC 20038
Has many basic materials related to these chronic health conditions, including "Allergy in Children," "Tips for Teachers: The Allergic Child," and "Children with Asthma: A Manual for Parents."

The Arthritis Foundation
1212 Avenue of the Americas
New York, NY 10036

Supports clinical research centers; local affiliates provide complete spectrum of care, including diagnosis, treatment, orthopedic surgery, and rehabilitation services.

Association for the Care of Children's Health (ACCH)
3615 Wisconsin Avenue, NW
Washington, DC 20016
(202) 244-1801
A nonprofit organization that addresses the psychosocial and developmental issues in pediatric health care.

Cancer
http://cancer.med.upenn.edu/psychosocial
   /cope/13.html
The ONCOLINK Internet site has a variety of information on the medical profession and the emotional aspects of cancer; provides links to other sites that deal with children's emotions, a newsletter for parents, and support groups.

Candlelighters Childhood Cancer Foundation
(800) 366-CCCF
Provides support groups and counseling for families. Has local chapters worldwide.

Children in Hospitals
31 Wilshire Park
Needham, MA 02192
Tries to minimize the trauma in a child's hospitalization by supporting and educating parents and medical personnel.

Epilepsy Foundation of America (EFA)
4351 Garden City Drive, Suite 406
Landover, MD 20785-2267
(800) 332-1000, (301) 459-3700, FAX (301) 477-2684
Supports research and provides information to families and professionals, including Epilepsy: You and Your Child; *has resources for schools, including videotapes, a comic book, and a poster:* First Aid for Seizures. *Some materials are available in Spanish. Maintains the National Epilepsy Library: (800) 332-4050.*

Home Care of the Dying Child
Children's Hospice International
(800) 242-4453
Provides support for families whose children are dying and who want their child at home.

JDF Canada
89 Granton Drive
Richmond Hill, Ontario L4B 2N5 Canada
(800) 668-0274, (905) 889-4171, FAX (905) 889-4209
Funds research, provides counseling and support services, educates the public; has many local chapters and print material.

Juvenile Diabetes Foundation International (JDF)
The Diabetes Research Foundation
432 Park Avenue South
New York, NY 10016-8013
(800) 533-2873, (212) 889-7575, FAX (212) 725-7259

Leukemia Society of America, Inc.
211 East 43rd Street
New York, NY 10017
(800) 284-4271

National headquarters conducts the research and educational programs and makes referrals to local chapters, which provide many medical services and counseling.

Muscular Dystrophy Association of America, Inc.
1790 Broadway
New York, NY 10019

National headquarters services include payments for authorized services, education of the public, publishing of literature and films, and sponsoring of national conferences.

National Cancer Institute
(800) 4-CANCER
http://wwwicic.nci.cih.gov/clinpdq/pif
/Ch...d_acute_limphocytic_leukemia_Patient.html.

Provides information and publications on cancer; gives information about current treatments for cancer and up-to-date research and studies for the medical profession and patients.

National Cystic Fibrosis Research Foundation
3379 Peachtree Road NE
Atlanta, GA 30326

National headquarters funds research, education, and care; refers inquiries to local chapters and cystic fibrosis centers.

National Health Information Center (NHIC)
Office of Disease Prevention and Health Promotion
PO Box 1133
Washington, DC 20013-1133
(800) 336-4797, In MD (301) 565-4167,
    FAX (301) 984-4256
e-mail: nhicinfo@health.org, http://nhic-nt.health.org

Maintains a library and a database on health-related organizations and provides referrals; has a free publication list to help locate information and resources.

The National Hemophilia Foundation
25 West 39th Street
New York, NY 10018

Assists chapters in developing social service programs; makes referrals to treatment centers; offers publications.

National Kidney Foundation
116 East 27th Street
New York, NY 10010

Makes referrals to affiliates and distributes public and professional educational materials.

National Tay-Sachs and Allied Disease
    Association, Inc.
200 Park Avenue South
New York, NY 10003

Makes referrals for diagnosis and carrier detection and provides information about social services and care.

National Tuberculosis and Respiratory Disease
    Association
1740 Broadway
New York, NY 10019

Makes referrals to affiliates and makes available literature and films.

Ronald McDonald House
(312) 836-7100

Provides inexpensive lodging for families of ill children.

U.S. Centers for Disease Control
1600 Clifton Road, NE
Atlanta, GA 30333
http://www.cdc.gov

Has information on many contagious diseases that it will send free, much of which is available on the Internet.

References

Abrams, E. J., Matheson, P. B., Thomas, P. A., et al. (1995). Neonatal predictors of infection status and early death among 332 infants at risk of HIV-1 infection monitored prospectively from birth. *Pediatrics, 96,* 451–458.

American Academy of Pediatrics. (1995). *How to help your child with asthma: Guidelines for parents.* Elk Grove Village, IL: Author.

Asthma: What is Asthma? (1997). Medical Treatment. http//www.thriveonline.com@IQ. . .th/asthma/seek/omfp.framewhat.html.

Bobele, G. (1994). Seizure disorders: Medical issues. In R. A. Olson, L. L. Mullins, J. B. Gillman, & J. M. Chaney (Eds.), *The source book of pediatric psychology* (pp. 177–184). Boston: Allyn & Bacon.

Brown, L. W. (1997). Seizure disorders. In M. L. Batshaw (Ed.), *Children with disabilities* (4th ed., pp. 553–594). Baltimore: Brookes.

Cassidy, J. T., & Nelson, A. M. (1988). The frequency of juvenile arthritis. *Journal of Rheumatology, 15,* 535–536.

Cook, A. R. (Ed.). (1997). *Allergies sourcebook.* Detroit: Omnigraphics.

Davis, H. (1993). *Counseling parents of children with chronic illness or disability.* Baltimore: British Psychological Society.

Dorset Health Authority. (1997). *Universal precautions.* http://www.dorset.swest.nhs.uk /comm_dis/universal.html.

Epilepsy Foundation of America. (n.d.). *First aid for epileptic seizures.* Landover, MD: Author.

Epstein, L., & Squires, S. (1988). *The stoplight diet for children: An eight-week program for parents and children.* Boston: Little, Brown.

Hallahan, D., & Kauffman, J. (1994). *Exceptional children: Introduction to special education* (6th ed.). Englewood Cliffs, NJ: Prentice-Hall.

Harkaway, J. L. (1989). Childhood obesity: The family context. In L. Combrinck-Graham (Ed.), *Children in family contexts: Perspectives on treatment* (pp. 231–251). New York: Guilford Press.

Hartocollis, A. (1998, September 2). Nothing's safe: Some schools ban peanut butter as allergy threat. *New York Times*, A26.

Henig, R. M. (1993, March 2). Asthma kills. *New York Times Magazine*, 42–52.

Hobbs, N., Perrin, J., & Ireys. H. (1984). *Chronically ill children and their families.* San Francisco: Jossey-Bass.

Hoots, K., & Cecalupo, A. (1994). Hemophilia. In R. A. Olson, L. L. Mullins, J. B. Gillman, & J. M. Chaney (Eds.), *The source book of pediatric psychology* (pp. 145–149). Boston: Allyn & Bacon.

Humphry, T. (1996). Universal precautions for daycare and preschool providers. http://www.morthcoast.com/~thumphry /universalp.html.

Individuals with Disabilities Education Act of 1997. Pub. L. No. 105-17, 111 Stat. 37-157, 20 U.S.C. 1400.

Jean, R. E., Lawhon, T., & Lawhon, D. C. (1995). Stress in families with chronically ill children. *Journal of Family and Consumer Sciences, 87*(1), 47–52.

Kaliner, M. (1993). Asthma deaths. *Journal of the American Medical Association, 269,* 1994–1995.

Kozol, J. (1995). *Amazing grace: The lives of children and the conscience of a nation.* New York: Crown.

Levy, S. E., & O'Rourke, M. (1997). Technology assistance: Innovations for independence. In M. L. Batshaw (Ed.), *Children with disabilities* (4th ed., pp. 687–708). Baltimore: Brookes.

Libow, J. A. (1989). Chronic illness and family coping. In L. Combrinck-Graham (Ed.), *Children in family contexts: Perspectives on treatment* (pp. 213–230). New York: Guilford Press.

Lobato, D. J. (1990). *Brothers, sisters, and special needs: Information and activities for helping young siblings of children with chronic illness and developmental disabilities.* Baltimore: Brookes.

Millner, B. N. (1991). Technology-dependent children in New York state. *Bulletin of the New York Academy of Medicine, 67,* 131–142.

National Association for the Education of Young Children. (1989). New guidelines on HIV infection (AIDS) announced for group programs. *Young Children, 44*(1), 51.

National Cancer Institute. (1997a). *PDQ: Childhood acute lymphocytic leukemia.* Bethesda, MD: National Institutes of Health Publication.

National Cancer Institute. (1997b). *PDQ: Childhood acute myeloid leukemia.* Bethesda, MD: National Institutes of Health Publication.

National Center for Health Statistics (CD-ROM). (1995). Hyattsville, MD: U.S. Department of Health and Human Services, Public Health Services, Centers for Disease Control, and National Center for Health Statistics.

National Institutes of Health. (1991). *Young people with cancer: A handbook for parents* (NIH Publication No. 92-2378). Bethesda, MD: National Cancer Institute.

National Institutes of Health. (1994). *Talking with your child about cancer* (NIH Publication No. 96-2761). Bethesda, MD: National Cancer Institute.

National Institutes of Health. (1994a). The diabetes dictionary. In K. Bellenir & P. D. Dresser (Eds.), *Diabetes source book: Health reference series* (Vol. 3, pp. 3–50). Detroit: Omnigraphics.

National Institutes of Health. (1994b). Diabetes overview. In K. Belllenir & P. D. Dresser (Eds.), *Diabetes source book: Health reference series* (Vol. 3, pp. xiii–xvii). Detroit: Omnigraphics.

National Institutes of Health. (1994c). Insulin-dependent diabetes. In K. Bellenir & P. D. Dresser (Eds.), *Diabetes source book: Health reference series* (Vol. 3, pp. 165–173). Detroit: Omnigraphics.

National Institutes of Health. (1995). *When someone in your family has cancer* (NIH Publication No. 96-2685). Bethesda, MD: National Cancer Institute.

Neill, C. A., Clark, E. B., & Clark, C. (1992). *The heart of a child: What families need to know about heart disorders in children.* Baltimore: Johns Hopkins Press.

Neisworth, J., & Bagnato, S. (1987). *The young exceptional child: Early development and education.* New York: Macmillan.

O'Donohoe, N. V. (1994). *Epilepsies of childhood* (3rd ed.). Oxford, England: Butterworth-Heinemann.

Rennebohm, R. M. (1994). Arthritis. In R. A. Olson, L. L. Mullins, J. B. Gillman, & J. M. Chaney (Eds.), *The source book of pediatric psychology* (pp. 70–74). Boston: Allyn & Bacon.

Rolland, J. S. (1987). Chronic illness and the life cycle: A conceptual framework. *Family Process, 26,* 203–221.

Rutstein, R. M., Conlon, C. J., & Batshaw, M. L. (1997). HIV and AIDS: From mother to child. In M. L. Batshaw (Ed.), *Children with disabilities* (4th ed., pp. 163–182) Baltimore: Brookes.

Schindler, L. W. (1997). Understanding the immune system's role. In A. R. Cook (Ed.), *Allergies sourcebook* (pp. 31–35). Detroit: Omnigraphics.

Schwarcz, S., & Rutherford, G. (1989, Winter). AIDS in infants, children, and adolescents. *Journal of Drug Issues,* 75–92.

St. Jude Children's Research Hospital. (1996–1997a). *Acute lyphoblastic leukemia.* http://www.stjude.org/medical/ all.htm.

St. Jude Children's Research Hospital. (1996–1997b). *Acute myeloid leukemia.* http://www.stjude.org/medical/all.htm.

Varni, J. W., Rapoff, M., & Waldron, S. A. (1994). Juvenile rheumatoid arthritis: Psychological issues. In R. A. Olson, L. L. Mullins, J. B. Gillman, & J. M. Chaney (Eds.), *The source book of pediatric psychology* (pp. 75–89). Boston: Allyn & Bacon.

Voignier, R., & Bridgewater, S. (1980). Allergies in young children. *Young Children, 35*(4), 67–70.

Widerstrom, A. H., Mowder, B. A., & Sandall, S. R. (1991). *At-risk and handicapped newborns and infants: Development, assessment, and intervention.* Englewood Cliffs, NJ: Prentice Hall.

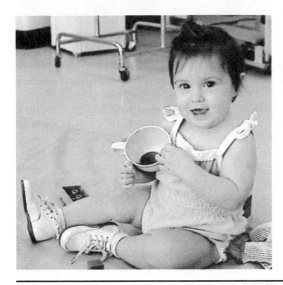

Chapter 15

CHILDREN WITH ORTHOPEDIC IMPAIRMENTS

Sari is one of eight children and a twin. Her mother, Carol, is 25. Carol spends her entire day trying to feed, change, or pick up after the children. The two oldest children are in school. This leaves six at home, including Sari, who has cerebral palsy; she is very spastic. Early intervention began with home visits shortly after her birth. This was difficult, because Sari's mother had little time to pay attention to what I was saying as she tried to watch the other children. Carol's education was limited, and she didn't seem to understand what she had been told about Sari. The only thing she remembered was that Sari had "CP" and she "would never be normal." She sometimes referred to Sari as "the freak"; the other children picked this up and teased her for as long as I can remember.

Because Sari's medical treatment was very involved, she had many appointments for intervention. Many were missed because the family couldn't afford gas for the car, couldn't get a ride with someone, or couldn't find someone to watch the other children. Home visits were the mainstay of her program. Sari was a fussy child and cried frequently, but, interestingly, she almost always cried when her mother yelled at one of the other children. There were few toys and those that were there were broken. As Sari was slow, she could rarely reach a toy before someone else had snatched it up. She didn't lack verbal stimulation or visual variety, for that matter, with the other children around. However, she never had to speak, as someone always spoke for her. By 8 in the morning, when I came each week, Sari's mother was totally exhausted and at her wit's end. Sari had a short attention span, and her mother was happy if she was sleeping and not crying. She had to be fed slowly as she choked easily, and she would usually spill the juice or cereal as her movements were clumsy and shaky and she didn't have a highchair to give her the support she needed.

Although a diagnosis of cerebral palsy had been made shortly after birth, a full evaluation was not completed until Sari was about 6 months. Neither the mother nor I was part of the evaluation team. I came for my regular home visit after Sari's mother had received a copy of the report. Carol was in a deep depression and didn't really want me to come in. I persisted. I wanted to know why things had gotten worse. After a while, she told me. The team had written in their report that Carol "was a mother who neglected the needs of her child." She was trying as hard as she could just to cope through the day. Her husband worked all the time and even when he was home, he was little help. Her family lived out of state; his "could care less." Carol admitted that she had been suicidal at times. We talked more. By the time my home visit was over, my head was splitting and I wondered how anyone could survive such a lifestyle. Carol was doing the best she could with the resources she had available to her. Her parents had divorced when she was young and she had only seen abusive parenting role models. She had no knowledge of other alternatives. About the same age as this mother, I only wondered if I would have done as well in the same situation. To call this "case" a challenge was putting it mildly. I again thought of my job description, which never mentioned this type of family. It was time to become adaptive and creative as well as respectful and compassionate. I could leave and go home to a quiet organized lifestyle and this mother could not.

I wondered about my job description again. What was I really? An early childhood educator, a counselor, a family support network, a referral service, a shoulder to cry on, a person who cares? I guess the answer is "all of the above." I went back to my office and began to make some calls.

Most young children can climb and run, but children with orthopedic impairments may be limited to walking, crawling, or scooting. They may have different firsthand knowledge and experiences than their peers. Children with physical limitations often show an unevenness in physical, sensory, mental, and social-emotional growth related to this limited experience.

Definition of Orthopedic Impairment

Orthopedic impairment is an umbrella term for a variety of different conditions. There are frequently differences relative to definitions. According to the Individuals with Disabilities Education Act (IDEA, 1997), *"Orthopedic impairment* means a severe orthopedic impairment that adversely affects a child's educational performance caused by congenital anomaly (e.g., clubfoot, absence of some member, etc.), impairments caused by disease (e.g. poliomyelitis, bone tuberculosis, etc.), and impairments from other causes (e.g. cerebral palsy, amputations, and fractures or burns that cause contractures)."

Causes of Orthopedic Impairments

Orthopedic impairments can have a variety of causes. Lack of oxygen in the child's brain either while the mother is pregnant or during birth can cause physical impairment. Diseases that affect the brain, such as meningitis and encephalitis, and prolonged high fevers can also cause permanent damage. Poisoning and other conditions that lead to lack of oxygen in the brain, as well as head, neck, and back injuries, sometimes cause paralysis or abnormal movement patterns. Some chronic health problems such as arthritis and muscular dystrophy may ultimately result in physical impairments, but, because such impairments usually occur only after repeated acute attacks, they are less likely to be apparent during early childhood.

Patterns of Growth and Development

Although children are unique, they share many commonalities in patterns of growth and development. Growth refers to the physical changes that occur in children over time, and can be measured in inches or centimeters, pounds or kilograms. Development is concerned with the acquisition of skills, such as walking and talking. Understanding the underlying principles of growth and development allows us to make predictions about whether or not growth and development will fall within the normal patterns. It also provides direction for intervention strategies.

Motor development pervades all areas of development during infancy. It enhances social behavior and benefits from and supports cognitive development. Early motor movements are involuntary and reflexive. Motor development matures eventually to become controlled through voluntary responses. Voluntary movements are deliberate motor responses that are a result of increased higher-brain functioning. Early motor development involves three interrelated aspects: gaining control of the gross or large muscles of the body, developing the fine or small muscles, and then integrating the developing motor skills with information from the senses.

Gross motor development refers to the maturation of the large muscles of the body such as those in the neck, trunk, arms, and legs. These muscles are necessary for all antigravity postures such as sitting, standing, and walking. They also are necessary to stabilize the body as finer movements are performed. Fine motor development involves the child's ability to use the small muscles of the arms, hands, and fingers. The major goal is the precise use of the hands for reaching, grasping, and manipulating objects. Motor skills are often used in conjunction with vision, hearing, and touch. In sensorimotor integration, both sensory and motor components are integrated in the brain to facilitate smooth movement and the ability to learn new skills.

0 to 3

Missed motor milestones is one of the markers we use to identify children with orthopedic impairments. In general, children with increased muscle tone (spasticity) will have delays in all antigravity positions. They may roll over or even "flip over" close to the expected time, but they may not sit unsupported until age 2 or be walking at age 4. Children who have low muscle tone (hypotonic or floppy) may stand with support or cruise holding onto furniture, but they lack the trunk stability for independent walking and so will remain in this stage for a longer time. Because of small motor delays, children may have problems with self-feeding and -dressing. Grasping objects using the pincer (thumb and index finger) is difficult, as is eye-hand coordination (Miller & Bachrach, 1995).

Severely involved children may also experience delays in language and problem-solving abilities. In general, receptive language is better than expressive language (especially if a child's motor involvement prevents him from forming words); however, it is sometimes difficult to tell how much children understand because they may not have the physical ability to complete the requested task. Because so many IQ tests at this age have large motor components, it may be difficult to determine the child's level of cognitive functioning.

One of the challenges most parents and caregivers face during these years is toilet training. Children probably don't have the voluntary motor control to regulate their bowel and bladder movements until about 18 months. Children with orthopedic impairments may be unable to sit on a toilet seat and need an adaptive seat (physical or occupational therapists provide guidance in the selection of these). Many children have fears about losing part of themselves during this process as they see bowel movements flushed away. When children are unsteady on the potty or fall, this fear is exacerbated, and the child may become scared. Some children may not understand the relationship between elimination and the potty. Habit training may be necessary, that is, having them go to the potty on a schedule, perhaps a half hour after each meal, or a schedule determined by their individual elimination patterns (Miller & Bachrach, 1995).

Many children have temper tantrums, and children with physical and motor impairments are no exception. They experience the normal frustrations of growing up as well as additional frustrations when their body doesn't do what their mind tells it to.

3 to 6

Children with physical limitations may have a difficult time keeping up with their peers. Differences are becoming more apparent to the child as well as to the other children. As children get larger and heavier and even more determined to be independent, some of the self-care tasks become more difficult. By this age, most gross and fine motor skill patterns are set, so the aim of intervention is to maximize a child's potential by capitalizing on what the child can do (Miller & Bachrach, 1995). Children may profit from adaptive equipment. If children are frustrated by a lack of ability to communicate, a simple communication board might help (children can show what they want if they cannot tell). Using a communication board does not discourage children from speaking.

It is clear to children this age that they are different from other children. They are also clear about what they can't do, so the emphasis needs to be on what they *can* do, keeping their limitations in perspective.

6 to 9

As children enter elementary school settings they become part of a larger community. Kindergarten and certainly first grade brings a demand for more fine motor coordination. Some children find that computers with some modifications are helpful in compensating for difficult fine motor skills. As sports become important, the emphasis is on what children can do; often, adaptative aquatics is an area with possibilities. Educators need to consider the possibility of learning disabilities, particularly in the area of reading, when children's performance is uneven.

It helps to be honest about abilities and limitations and to praise work that is praiseworthy. Although you can and should support effort, it should be clear that is what you are supporting. Tell a child he worked hard controlling the crayon to make the drawing, but, if he is 6 and the drawing looks like the advanced scribbles of a 3-year-old, don't tell him it is a great drawing. Children need help in developing a positive self-concept at a time when new awareness about differences and the value of a beautiful body are becoming part of the child's social world.

Muscle Tone

Before explaining in detail the implications of various impairments, it may be helpful to look at movement in general. Knowledge of how we move and the importance of muscle tone in movement aids in the understanding of some of the problems children with physical limitations encounter. To move, we increase the tension in specific groups, or patterns, of muscles.

Muscle tone is the amount of tension, or resistance to stretch, in muscles. "Normal" muscle tone is the condition of the muscles at rest. Children with high muscle tone (hypertonic) (typical of children with cerebral palsy) move with stiff, jerky movements. In some cases, depending on the exact area of the brain involved, a child's motor problems are compounded by faulty internal communications. The child may think, "Let go of the cup," but the brain does not send the appropriate message to the muscles in the hand for the child to let go.

Children with low muscle tone (hypotonic) may have problems picking up the cup in the first place. A child who did pick it up successfully may unexpectedly drop it later because it was held too loosely. Grasping very small objects is especially difficult for hypotonic children (it may be difficult for children with high muscle tone as well, but for different reasons).

To get the idea, lie with your back on the floor, tense all of your muscles (make fists, squinch up your face, tense your legs, trunk, and back), and try to sit up. You will find that your movements are jerky and stiff and that you probably cannot sit up. Now relax. Let your arms become floppy as you pretend to be a rag doll. Try to sit up without tensing any of your muscles. That doesn't work either. The first situation will give you an idea of the problems hypertonic children have; the second will help you understand hypotonic children. How do you feel at this point? You have only done this for a short period of time. Particularly, children who have high muscle tone become fatigued.

If children have high, low, or inconsistent muscle tone, you can expect that they have difficulty with many gross motor activities. The biggest issue with young children is establishing trunk stability. Try to write while constantly moving your upper body. To the extent that you move it too far and overbalance, your concern is with not falling, not your penmanship. The focus of much early therapy is in this area.

Children may also be challenged by skills that require rotation, the ability to twist a part of the body. Rotation is of primary importance in learning to write because writing requires rotating the wrist and fingers. For a better understanding of the problem, attempt to take the lid off a container while keeping your fingers and wrists stiff. (Try handling classroom materials and doing all classroom procedures with stiff muscles to see how difficult each task is for children.) In general, hard objects are more difficult to handle than soft, small more difficult than large, and slippery more difficult than rough. Your awareness of the child's strengths and needs and your creativity and willingness to try things that are different are the key to good programming for children with orthopedic impairments. Muscle tone also affects the small muscles of the mouth and face that involve communication. Children's speech may be difficult to understand.

Regardless of the diagnosis, general information on the child's muscle tone and, in the case of muscular dystrophy, muscle atrophy and how this impacts a child's ability to move and how it relates to fatigue is important both to your programming and your expectations.

Classification of Orthopedic Impairments

In general, orthopedic impairments are classified according to three considerations: severity of the impairment, the clinical type of impairment, and the parts of the body that are involved.

Children with a *mild* impairment can walk (with or without crutches, walker, or other prosthetic device), use their arms, and communicate well enough to make their wants and needs known. They may take more time to do things, but with adaptations can do what most other children can. Their problems involve mostly fine motor skills. Children with a *moderate* impairment require some special help with locomotion and need more assistance than their peers with self-help and communication skills. Children with a *severe* impairment are usually not able to move from one place to another without the aid of a wheelchair. Their self-help and communication skills are usually challenging.

Movement Disorders

It is difficult to decide whether or not some children have a motor problem. We are becoming more concerned about clumsy children. Although it is difficult to agree on a definition of clumsy, most of us know a clumsy child when we see one.

Developmental Coordination Disorder

The *Diagnostic and Statistical Manual of Mental Disorders (DSM-IV)* added the category of Motor Skills Disorder in its fourth edition (American Psychiatric Association, 1994), specifically, developmental coordination disorder. This diagnostic category focuses on the relationship between age-expected norms and children who are delayed in reaching motor milestones (walking, running, and so on) or who drop things, are clumsy, do poorly at sports, and often have poor handwriting. As children increase in age, ther is concern about the relationship between coordination and academic achievement and the activities of

daily living. This clumsiness is not due to a medical condition (for example, cerebral palsy) or sensory impairment or cognitive delay. Estimates are that approximately 6 percent of children between 5 and 11 have these coordination problems (APA, 1994). Others feel that the percentage may be higher.

Clumsy children have been a concern to many over the years. Orton (1937), who focused most of his work on dyslexic children, was interested in the problems of physical awkwardness. He decided that lack of motor coordination could reflect a motor planning problem or could be caused by problems with visual perception. He felt that motor dysfunction could be multidimensional, that is, that children who were awkward at running also labored over printing and writing. He was concerned that poor motor coordination also led to feelings of social inferiority and low self-esteem. He believed motor awkwardness to be a most debilitating condition.

One problem is that we look at clumsiness as a "soft sign." Also, some children display generalized awkwardness, whereas others are clumsy relative to only one task, such as writing, balance, and so on (Cratty, 1994). Many agree that the clumsy child syndrome is made up of several subclassifications of children, including those with and without academic problems. In some children, the problem seems to be immaturity; in other children, it may be longer lasting. The literature indicates that early remediation is more likely to succeed than just waiting, mild problems are more correctable than moderate ones, and that given the current state of knowledge, it isn't clear which problems will change because of maturation and which ones will not (Cratty, 1994). If these problems are not dealt with until middle childhood, there may be a negative emotional overlay to the problems themselves. Children may develop negative self-concepts because of constant feedback about dropping, spilling, running into things, knocking things over, and so on.

Some clumsy children are diagnosed as having *developmental dyspraxia*. Praxic behaviors refer to the ability to perform coordinated, complex acts that consist of several parts. To do this, children have to perceive a demonstrated movement accurately or understand verbal directions to move in a specific way; integrate the information and develop a motor plan; and motorically carry out the plan in the correct sequence (Cratty, 1994). Children who are dyspraxic have a disruption in their motor planning abilities at one of these three levels. They either do not understand the request, can't figure out how to do the action, or can't perform the action.

Children who are clumsy need to be encouraged to participate in motor activities. They need experience with motor planning in situations where they are likely to succeed and be supported. In general, to require motor planning, a task must be goal-directed. For example, just walking requires little motor planning, whereas to walk to the other end of the room, put on a hat, and skip back requires far more motor planning. Likewise, an obstacle course requires a child to motor plan. After a referral to their physician, clumsy children are most likely referred to a physical or occupational therapist.

Correctable Orthopedic Impairments

A variety of relatively short-term orthopedic problems are dealt with during the early childhood years to facilitate normal future growth. These conditions usually require surgery, bracing, casting, and physical therapy. The prognosis is generally good if the condition is treated at an early age. If not treated, these problems result in some degree of orthopedic impairment.

Bowlegs and inwardly rotated feet are common when a child first begins to walk. They are usually cured by normal growth. In extreme cases, however, braces, casts, and/or surgery are used to correct the problem. Clubfeet are usually treated with casts, splints, and physical therapy or surgery. Flat feet may be treated with arch supports or corrective shoes. Congenital hip problems result from improper fit of the femur in the socket joint of the hip; they are most often treated by a webbed brace, traction, cast, or surgery. Usually, hip problems are treated in infancy. In severe cases, they can have long-term implications.

The prognosis for these correctable orthopedic impairments is very good, yet from the child's perspective, the restriction of movement is frustrating. Some children need a lot of help expressing this anger. Prepare children for medical procedures; discuss their fears and feelings; help them express emotions while they are physically restricted; give them activities they can participate in; and try to explain the purpose of the medical treatment in terms they understand.

Types of Orthopedic Impairments

Some orthopedic impairments have strong neurological components; others are related more to musculoskeletal conditions. The impairments are discussed below in that order.

Neurological Impairments

One cause of orthopedic impairment is damage to the central nervous system—the brain or spinal cord. In some cases, the damage may be so minimal it is undetected; it can be very specific and focused in a small area, or it can be diffuse, involving a large area of the brain. Depending on the area of the brain affected, children can have cognitive delays, learning disabilities, seizures, or speech and/or orthopedic impairments.

When the spinal cord is damaged, the brain sends the appropriate message to the spinal cord, but the message does not get relayed to the appropriate place. Damage to the spinal cord may mean that the child will lose sensation or be unable to move or feel certain body parts (as in some cases of spina bifida).

Cerebral Palsy. The cerebral palsies consist of a group of motor disorders that come in many varieties and severities. "Cerebral palsy refers to a disorder of movement and posture that is due to a nonprogressive abnormality of the immature brain" (Pellegrino, 1997, p. 499). The neurological mechanisms of posture, balance, and movement are disorganized. Cerebral palsy can be caused by numerous conditions prenatally (genetic abnormalities and infection), adverse conditions during labor and delivery, lack of oxygen to the brain, injury to the brain during the birthing process, premature birth, or injury to a very young child (traumatic brain injury). Although considered an orthopedic impairment, cerebral palsy is more complex than was previously thought and is more appropriately considered a syndrome that can include motor impairment, psychological dysfunction, seizures, behavior disorders, or other related impairments due to brain damage (Miller & Bachrach, 1995). Children are affected to different degrees: from very minimally, so that it is hardly detectable, to so severely the child has little control over his body.

Cerebral palsy occurs in about 2.5 of every 1,000 births (Miller & Bachrach, 1995). The incidence level is relatively constant because medical technology has intervened in a number of difficult births, reducing this as a cause; however, children who previously would not have survived now live, and many have disabilities such as cerebral palsy. Almost 80 percent of these children have spastic cerebral palsy (Miller & Bachrach, 1995).

Cerebral palsy is typically classified by the extremities involved, the type of brain damage, and the motor disability. In *diplegia,* the whole body is involved, though the legs more so than the arms. Diplegic children usually have some head control and moderate to slight paralysis of the upper limbs. Speech can be affected. In *hemiplegia,* there is involvement of the upper and lower extremities on the same side of the body. Hemiplegia is usually of the spastic type. *Monoplegia* involves only one arm or, less frequently, only one leg (this is very rare). In *paraplegia,* the lower extremities are involved. Paraplegia is commonly found among spinal injuries and spina bifida and rarely found in cerebral palsy. *Quadriplegia* involves all four limbs. Head control may be poor and, in cerebral palsy, there is usually impairment of speech and eye coordination. In spinal cord injuries, speech is often not affected. *Triplegia* involves three extremities, usually both lower extremities and one arm. It may also be a combination of paraplegia and hemiplegia.

Although classifications differ, one method looks at the type of brain damage and the resultant motor implications.

Pyramidal Cerebral Palsy (Spastic). In this case, the motor cortex or pyramidal tract of the brain was damaged, resulting in limb muscles that are very tight and are difficult to move (spastic). Spasticity is the inability of the muscles to relax. Spasticity does not mean paralysis (Miller & Bachrach, 1995). Voluntary movements are often jerky and inaccurate. Voluntary motion is present but may be labored. Infants who are hypotonic often later develop spasticity.

Extrapyramidal Cerebral Palsy. Damage outside the pyramidal tracts has different implications. The most common type is called choreoathetoid cerebral palsy and is characterized by abrupt, involuntary movement of the limbs. Here, the problem isn't moving, but rather regulating the movement and maintaining posture. The limb might originally appear rigid, but it can be moved. Because the patterns of muscle tone change from hour to hour, children may have more problems sucking, swallowing, drooling, and speaking than children who have the spastic form (Batshaw & Perret, 1992). Again, the variable muscle tone makes it difficult to develop the stability needed for sitting and walking. Children may have rigid muscle tone while awake and normal or decreased muscle tone in sleep (Pellegrino, 1997).

In addition to choreoathetoid cerebral palsy, some children have rigid, constantly tight muscles, and others have so little muscle tone they are described as hypotonic (atonic). In these cases, there is one predominant type of muscle tone. About 10 percent of children with cerebral palsy fall in to this category (Miller & Bachrach, 1995).

Mixed-Type Cerebral Palsy. Some children have damage to both the pyramidal and extrapyramidal areas of the brain and can have symptoms of both types (that is, rigidity in the arms and spasticity in the legs). Children with mixed types of cerebral palsy also account for about 10 percent of the population (Miller & Bachrach, 1995). Because the brain damage in these children is more extensive, they may also have cognitive delays and other developmental disabilities (Batshaw & Perret, 1992).

Medical classification is based on the type and extremities involved; for example, a child might have spastic quadriplegia. This means that the muscles in both the child's arms and legs are very tight and difficult to move.

Many screening tests that are traditionally used with infants by the medical profession may not identify children with cerebral palsy during the first year. Often, the absence of primitive reflexes, abnormal muscle tone, and resting positions (an extended arched position for high tone and a rag doll position for low tone) give clues to the possibility of cerebral palsy (Pellegrino, 1997). Some children with cerebral palsy also have sensory impairments, speech disorders, and delayed cognitive development. Accurate developmental testing is difficult.

The goal of intervention is to maximize the children's functioning and minimize disability-related problems. Orthotic devices, primarily braces and splints, are used to prevent contractures of specific joints, to help provide stability and control involuntary motion, and to maintain range of motion (Pellegrino, 1997). *Contractures* are an irreversible shortening of muscle fibers that cause decreased muscle joint mobility. (If you always kept your elbow bent and held your hand on your shoulder and kept your arm tight, you might develop a contracture.) Muscles that remain in shortened positions for prolonged periods are at risk of contractures. Splints and braces are used to position limbs and joints to prevent contractures. The most commonly prescribed orthotic is a short leg brace that prevents the shortening of the heel cord (Pellegrino, 1997). Most splints and braces made for young children are custom-made of plastic materials that are molded directly on the child. These must be modified as the child grows, or they can become both nonfunctional and painful.

Positioning is another key to preventing impairment. Because children spend a lot of time sitting, it is important that they sit in the most beneficial position. This is often not the easiest one. If you hold a child with cerebral palsy in your lap, have the child's legs straddle one of yours and hold the child around the middle. If the child sits on the floor, cross-legged, or tailor-style, sitting is not recommended; instead, have the child sit with legs in front and together, bent at the knee if the child has variable muscle tone, straight if the muscle tone is tight. Sitting in a W position with knees forward and a foot on either side is particularly disadvantageous for the child.

Children often find that sitting in a W position increases their stability. Because of the strain it places on the hips, this position should be discouraged for all children. It is particularly dysfunctional for children with orthopedic impairments.

As of 1997, medication has not been found particularly useful in improving muscle tone in young children (Pellegrino, 1997). Nerve-blocking drugs are being explored. Surgery is sometimes the treatment of choice, especially to reduce spasticity in the lower extremities for some children.

One of the major concerns many parents have is whether or not their children will walk. Young children who are expected to walk will usually have ambulation training, which includes a combination of physical therapy, assistive devices (walkers or crutches), orthotics, and perhaps surgery (Pellegrino, 1997).

During the early years, problems related to mobility tend to be focused on and receive the most attention. As children are included in regular elementary school classes, some of the associated learning and sensory problems may receive greater attention and adaptation.

Neural Tube Defects. Neural tube defects is an umbrella term that refers to a group of congenital malformations of the vertebrae, spinal cord, and brain. The three major neural tube defects are spina bifida, encephalecele, and anencephaly (Liptak, 1997). The most common is spina bifida, which is characterized by a split in the vertebral arches. This separation can be isolated; individuals with spina bifida occulta have no symptoms and may not even know they have a split. Sometimes, individuals are born with a membranous covering of the spinal cord called meningocele. As the spinal cord itself is not entrapped, these children too are symptom-free, but identified. It is when the meningeal sac contains part of the spinal cord and the spinal cord is malformed that it is symptomatic and what we call spina bifida. (Technically, it is called meninogomyelcele or myelomeningocele.) The fluid-filled sac (meningocele) protrudes through the spine of the newborn above the defect in the vertebral column; it looks like a flat bubble on the infant's back and contains the malformed spinal cord. The nerves below the protrusion do not develop properly, leading to loss of sensation and paralysis below the site. Surgery is done within several days to remove the bubble, protect the exposed nerves from physical injury, and prevent infection. It does not impact the neurological functioning of the child (Liptak, 1997).

Neural tube defects occur in approximately 1 in 10,000 births in the United States (Liptak, 1997). The problem occurs prenatally by 26 days after conception, when the neural tube has folded over itself to become the spinal cord and vertebral arches. If during this process the neural tube does not close completely and the spinal cord is malformed, neural tube defects result (Liptak, 1997). There appear to be a genetic component and also environmental factors. Treatment with folic acid during the first 12 weeks of pregnancy has been successful in decreasing the occurrences of neural tube defects. Women contemplating pregnancy are urged to take folic acid (Liptak, 1997).

Most children with myelomeningocele also have an associated malformation of the brain, Arnold–Chiari malformation. This interferes with the circulation of cerebrospinal fluid in the brain, putting pressure on the brain tissue itself. Hydrocephalus is caused by excess cerebrospinal fluid on the brain. It is diagnosed by ultrasonography during infancy or magnetic resonance imaging (MRI) in older children. A shunt is usually necessary to drain this fluid, typically into the child's abdominal cavity. A shunt consists of plastic tubing with a one-way valve that provides permanent drainage to relieve pressure on the brain. The shunt needs to be modified as the child grows because it will probably become too short. In young children, shunts frequently become blocked or infected. In infants, this results in excessive head growth and a tense "soft spot" on the top of the head. In children 2 years and older, the bones of the head have fused; symptoms can include severe headaches, lethargy, stomachaches, double vision, vomiting, and irritability (Liptak, 1997). Notify the parents of any of these; failure or infection of a shunt is a life-threatening condition.

There is considerable diversity in the degree of motor delay children will have. Although frequently late to roll over, most use belly crawling as a method of locomotion. Children's mobility is dependent on the location of the lesion. In general, the higher the level of the meningomyelocele, the more muscle weakness and the greater the impairment in ambulation.

The spinal cord is divided into three major areas. Starting from the bottom, there are 4 sacral vertebrae, 5 lumbar vertebrae, 12 thoracic vertebrae, and 7 cervical vertebrae, which are sometimes referred to as S, L, T, and C. The closer to the head, the more severe the injury. Each inch of spine or vertebra is important in bodily function (Conway, 1994). Children with sacral lesions S1, S2 will walk well by age 2 or 3; S3, S4 may need minimal bracing; low lumbar (L4, L5) will walk but may need crutches; midlumbar (L3) will need braces and usually crutches; thoracic or high lumbar (L1, L2) will need extensive bracing at ankles, knees, and hips and crutches or other mobility devices (Liptak, 1997; see Figure 15.1). As children's center of gravity changes in adolescence, some will use a wheelchair. Walking is not easy for many and is more difficult for children who also have cognitive delays. It requires physical therapy and committed parents as well a child who wants to walk.

Children with myelomeningocele are usually incontinent and cannot tell when they are wet. During the preschool years, incontinence is not a significant problem because the child can usually just wear diapers. The parents and surgeons later make some decision about how to manage this problem. This is frequently done with technique called clean intermittent bladder catheterization (CIC). Parents are taught how to do this and it is usually begun at 3 to 4 years of age. Bowel problems are related to ineffective relaxation or contraction of the internal anal sphincter as well as lack of sensation. Parents make the decision of how to handle this, which may include timed potty

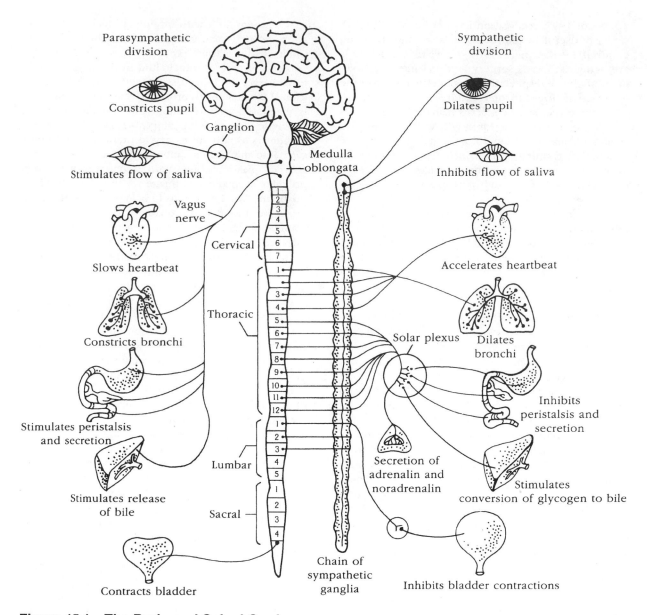

Parasympathetic division

Sympathetic division

Constricts pupil

Dilates pupil

Ganglion

Stimulates flow of saliva

Medulla oblongata

Inhibits flow of saliva

Vagus nerve

Slows heartbeat

Cervical

Accelerates heartbeat

Constricts bronchi

Thoracic

Solar plexus

Dilates bronchi

Stimulates peristalsis and secretion

Inhibits peristalsis and secretion

Stimulates release of bile

Lumbar

Secretion of adrenalin and noradrenalin

Stimulates conversion of glycogen to bile

Sacral

Contracts bladder

Chain of sympathetic ganglia

Inhibits bladder contractions

Figure 15.1   The Brain and Spinal Cord

sitting after each meal (Batshaw & Perret, 1992). Bowel and bladder continence is a realistic and critical part of a child's development. Because of concern over urinary infection, children need to drink more liquids than other children their age. Children with spina bifida may have weight problems due to lack of movement; keep this in mind, along with the need for liquids, when choosing snacks.

Most children with spina bifida will fall within the normal range of intelligence, but many will have learning disabilities. They need to be assessed and planned for individually. Developing a positive self-concept and feelings of autonomy and independence are imperative.

These children have decreased strength and sensations, so special care must be taken to protect their lower limbs. Their bones may not be as strong as they should be and are prone to fractures. Be alert

for things that might cause skin problems, such as water that's too hot, sunburn, and insect bites. Children can develop skin sores or decubitus ulcers on weight-bearing surfaces and not know it, as they are not sensitive to pain. Socks should be worn in wading pools and shoes should be worn if the child is walking or crawling (adapted from Temme, personal communications, December 1991; Liptak, 1997).

Many children with spina bifida are allergic to latex. The reason is unclear, but the reaction can be life-threatening. Toys that contain significant amounts of latex, such as rubber balls, should be avoided and Band-Aids and Ace bandages should not be used. Talk with parents and therapists about alternatives.

Spinal Cord Injuries. Spinal cord injuries are relatively uncommon in young children. When they do happen, they are usually the result of motor vehicle accidents when children have not been wearing seat belts (Conway, 1994).

Some infants are born with malformed spinal cords or conditions where the spinal cord deteriorates. If the spinal cord is not completely cut, some feeling may remain below the lesion, but in general, anyone who has a spinal cord injury is permanently paralyzed and unable to feel pressure or pain below the lesion. The ultimate effect of an injury cannot be ascertained with certainty for about two months.

If a child has movement in the arms and shoulders, work should be done to strengthen these, because future mobility may depend on them—ultimately, the child has to learn to lift his own weight. Another important consideration is the prevention of pressure sores (decubitus ulcers). These seem innocuous, but pressure sore infections can cause death. Sometimes, it takes weeks or months for them to heal, and they may have to be closed surgically. Children with spinal cord lesions generally have poor blood circulation; therefore, injuries are slow to heal and prone to infection.

Spinal atrophy is characterized by progressive degeneration of the motor-nerve cells, resulting in slow weakening of the body's muscle strength. The effects include skill decrease, fatigue, and decreased coordination. Congenital atrophy progresses rapidly, resulting in an early death. Acquired atrophy develops much more slowly, first affecting the legs and then progressing to the upper extremities. Because the child lacks feeling, be concerned about sunstroke, overheating, and frostbite. Insect bites may also occur and not be noticed.

Traumatic Brain Injury. An increasingly frequent cause of orthopedic impairment is head injury. This can occur from automobile accidents, falls off a bicycle, gunshot wounds, or from other accidental causes. The effects of this injury vary widely and can include sensory, motor, emotional, and cognitive impairments. They range from mild to profound and from temporary to permanent.

Each year, 1 child in 25 receives medical attention because of a head injury (Brookes, MacMillan, & Cully, 1990). These range from not being of medical concern to severe brain damage. Brain injury is defined as trauma sufficient to change a level of consciousness or having an anatomical abnormality of the brain. This occurs in approximately 1 in every 500 children (Baker, O'Neill, & Karpf, 1984). Boys are more likely to sustain head injuries than girls. They are more likely to occur in the spring and summer, on weekends, and in the afternoon (Michaud, Duhaime, & Lazar, 1997). Traumatic brain injury (TBI) was acknowledged as a separate category of disability under IDEA in the 1990 reauthorization. There is also an expectation that more children will survive TBIs and be in early care and education settings (Horton, 1993).

Causes of brain injury vary with age. In children under 4, over half of head injuries are caused by falls (55 percent), followed by motor vehicle accidents (19 percent), sports and recreation accounted

(13 percent), assault (7 percent), and all other causes (6 percent). In children between 5 and 9, three causes account for almost all the head traumas: sports and recreation (32 percent), falls (31 percent), and motor vehicle accidents (31 percent); assault (1 percent) and all other causes (5 percent) make up the remainder (Centers for Disease Control, 1990; Division of Injury Control, 1990).

The type of head injury has implications for the impact of that injury on the child's behavior. Although scalp injuries bleed a lot, they do not injure the brain. A linear fracture of the skull also has little impact, but a depressed fracture, when part of the skull is broken and presses into the underlying brain tissue, may cause a weakness or disability (Michaud et al., 1997). Brain contusions, usually the result of direct impact, such as a baseball striking the head, bruise the brain. This can be minor, like bruises to other parts of the body, or may require surgical removal. Epidural hematomas are the most lethal, but also the most treatable. A hematoma is a blood clot, in this case between the skull and the outer covering of the brain. Typically, the child falls or is injured and appears fine, then symptoms begin to develop as the hematoma grows. These lead to headaches, confusion, vomiting, and perhaps even lethargy and coma. If treated quickly, children usually recover completely; if treatment is delayed, there may be physical and cognitive delays and even death (Michaud et al., 1997).

Acute subdural hematomas are blood clots that form beneath the dura or the brain covering and are often part of a more generalized injury to the brain itself. They result from sheering forces applied to the veins (acceleration-deceleration forces) that actually displace the brain from the dura to rupture these membranes (Michaud et al., 1997). A subdural hematoma may cause brain swelling and stroke. A large area of the brain is affected and, although surgery is done to remove the blood clot, the prognosis is not as positive.

In diffuse axonal injury, the concern is not with a blood clot but the nerve fibers throughout the brain that have been damaged, usually by violent motion (as in a motor vehicle accident). The child usually becomes immediately unconscious and stays unconscious for at least six hours (Michaud et al., 1997). Recovery may take weeks to years depending on the amount of damage done. Sometimes children have both diffuse axonal injury and subdural hematomas as a result of accidents.

Because timing is such an important variable, you need to know when head injuries need immediate care and when they don't. If a child hits his head and does not lose consciousness, no treatment is necessary—unless the child develops symptoms of an epidural hematoma (vomiting within an hour or two, lethargy, severe headache). If these develop, the child should be taken to the emergency room (Michaud et al., 1997).

A child who has an injury and loses consciousness and then resumes normal activities may have a mild concussion. If the loss of consciousness is more than momentary, a skull X-ray or computerized tomographic (CT) scan should be done to rule out brain injury. The X-ray shows the bones of the skull, the CT scan the soft tissue of the brain itself (Gronwall, Wrightson, & Waddell, 1990). If a child is unconscious for more than a few minutes, call the paramedics (Michaud et al., 1997).

The seriousness of a brain injury when the child is in a coma is usually rated on the Glasgow Coma Scale, used within the first six hours. This rating looks at the eye opening, motor, and verbal responses. A child with a score of 3 has no eye opening, no movement, no verbal response, and is in a deep coma. A score of 15, the highest score, reflects the ability to spontaneously look around, move limbs on request, and make relevant verbal responses. Severe head injury is a score of 8 or less (Michaud et al., 1997).

After medical problems are stabilized, the goals for the child are to relearn lost skills and to learn new skills to compensate for those that cannot be regained. Almost 95 percent of children admitted to a hospital for a TBI survive (Michaud & Duhaime, 1992). The severity and type of injury to the brain impact the recovery. Predicting how children will fare appears to be more complex than with adults. The brain of the young child is more plastic and hence has the potential for further development. However, brain injury appears to impair new learning more than the retention of old learning, and young children haven't had as much time to build a knowledge base (Michaud & Duhaime, 1992). Most recovery takes place in the first six months after the injury and will take place at a slower rate after that. Some believe that two years after the injury there will be no more recovery; others find that individuals improve for 5 to 10 years (Gronwall et al., 1990).

Whereas adults seem to develop predictable patterns after brain injury, children seem to have different patterns depending on the task. For some tasks, the child shows a progressive pattern of recovery over time; in others, the impairment is constant; in still others, there is no discernible impairment after the injury, but over time a problem appears, a delayed reaction (Horton, 1993).

Children who experienced severe diffuse axonal injuries are likely to have impairments in all areas of functioning, whereas children who had injury in one area of the brain are likely to have more localized problems. Damage to the motor areas of the brain often result in impairments similar to pyramidal cerebral palsy: spasticity, ataxia, and tremors. Feeding disorders may result as well as impaired motor skills, sensory impairments, communication impairments (receptive, expressive, or mixed), and cognitive impairments (Michaud et al., 1997).

Children who have sustained moderate to severe TBIs often experience problems in academic learning. These may manifest themselves in reading or math, but the more pervasive effects relate to attention, problem solving, and speed of information processing (Carney & Shoenbrodt, 1994). Their patterns of learning differences vary from those of children with learning disabilities and ADHD. They demonstrate "highly variable performance within and across academic subjects and continued change over time" (Michaud et al., 1997, p. 608). Behavior changes can also be expected.

Children who sustain TBI must cope with psychological stress. The loss of skills is distressing to children. Families too may be stressed, initially with concern about whether the child will live or die, then in coping with the child himself, and finally, with the financial consequences of paying for the child's treatment (Yeates, 1994).

In cases of TBI, it is important that the transition from hospital to school involves shared information. Children will typically have a difficult time attending for long periods, remembering information they had known before, and learning new information. Their greatest difficulty seems to be in the area of the organization of information. They may also find abstractions and creative thinking challenging. The loss of skills that they could perform before, that other children their age are now easily doing, is a source of frustration. It is important to maintain very close contact with their parents and review their IEP/IFSP every month or six weeks during the early recovery period as rapid changes can take place.

Musculoskeletal Conditions

Absent Limbs. Some children are born with deformed or absent limbs. These disorders can be the result of genetic or chromosomal causes or environmental influences such as drugs or chemicals. When congenital, the insult usually occurs during the early gestation period when limb development occurs. Young children can also have limbs surgically removed because of injury or disease. Prosthetic devices are available to assist in replacing missing limbs. There is a difference in philosophy about the age at which children should be fitted with an artificial limb or prosthesis. Some believe that children should be fitted almost immediately. They feel that the younger a child gets an artificial limb, the easier and more natural the adjustment is. Others feel that children should not be fitted for devices until they are older, when they are better able to use the device, have better control, and can take better care of the device (Peterson, 1987). Regardless, fit is very important, in terms of both comfort and the ability to use the device. A prosthesis must be adapted as the child grows.

You need to have some basic understanding of how the prosthesis works in case the child needs help making adjustments and so that you can plan activities that do not frustrate the child. Being accepted as a whole person is extremely important, so don't refer to this device as the child's "bad" arm or leg. If you notice abnormal postures or motor patterns developing, discuss them with the parents and physical therapist. Exercising the joints nearest an amputation is important; ask for information about that as well from the parents, medical professionals, and occupational and physical therapists.

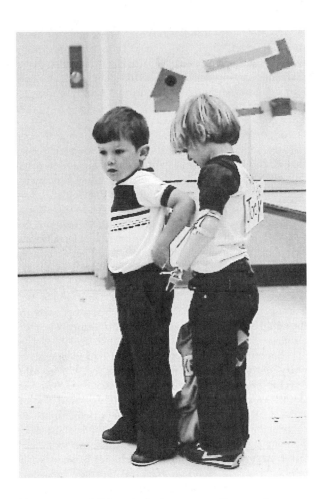

Encourage children to help one another perform necessary transition tasks such as removing name tags before going outside.

Arthrogryposis Multiplex Congenita. Arthrogryposis is a condition that is present at birth and is characterized by stiffness of the joints. It usually affects both sides of the child's body and means that there may be little or no movement in the child's joints. This is caused by thickened joint capsules, shortened muscles, and decreased muscle mass. The arms turn in from the shoulders and the elbow and wrist joints are very stiff. The fingers may also have little useful movement. The legs turn out from the hip and the hips are prone to dislocation. The knees and ankles have only a few degrees of movement. Long leg braces help the child who has adequate trunk control. A walker or crutches may be useful depending on the child's upper body control.

Adaptive skills may be difficult for these children. Independent eating is hard because lack of movement in the elbows and wrists may make it difficult for children to bring their hand up to their mouth. Some children become very adept and graceful at taking food from the plate directly with their mouth. When children use this technique, consider putting the child's lunch box or a plastic box on the table to place the food at a more appropriate height. Children with arthrogryposis may also use their mouth to manipulate objects during play. Dressing and toileting skills may be difficult.

As you assist these children, remember that not only are their joints stiff, their bones are osteoporotic, and so they tend to fracture easily. Keep handling to a minimum and when you do, do it gently (adapted from Albert, personal communications, December 1991).

Muscular Dystrophy. Muscular dystrophy is an umbrella term for a group of chronic, progressive disorders that affect the voluntary muscles. It is an inherited sex-linked disorder, in which the child has a decreased or absent production of the protein dystrophin that stabilizes the muscle membrane during contraction (Dormans & Batshaw, 1997). When this protein is deficient, muscle degenerates. The most common type, Duchenne muscular dystrophy, is not usually detected until a child is between 2 and 5 and begins to fall down frequently due to muscle weakness. It effects approximately 1 in 3,000 males

Adaptive skills are difficult for children with arthrogryposis; however, their creativity and persistence often supports the independence. Educators need to encourage children to be independent as well as asking for help when needed.

(Emery, 1993). The muscles closest to the center of the body, those of the hip and shoulder area, are affected first, with the muscles in the fingers being affected later. The result is gradual weakness and decline in muscle strength and health. The child's intellectual functioning is not affected. The process, which can occur quickly or slowly, leads to increased disability and death (usually by age 20). However, innovative treatments (myoblast transplantation and gene therapy) may change this prognosis (Dormans & Batshaw, 1997).

We do not know how to correct the metabolic disorder or halt the progression of the disease. The earlier the symptoms appear, the more severe the disease is likely to be and the earlier death will occur. Toddlers will have a waddling gait, fall frequently and have trouble getting up, climb stairs with difficulty, and may walk on their toes. They will typically be able to walk during early childhood. As more muscles deteriorate and the child becomes weaker, a wheelchair is necessary. Once the disease has started, there are no remissions and its progress over time is predictable. Patience and emotional support are an essential part of dealing with the everyday frustrations that face the child.

Children with muscular dystrophy have normal feeling in their limbs even though they cannot always move them (unlike a child with a spinal cord injury, who may have little or no feeling in the limbs). They cannot hold onto you very well because of muscular weakness, so be sure you are holding them securely before you pick them up. Don't lift them under the arms; because of weak shoulders, the arms will fall through your hold. Remember that the neck muscles may be very weak, so support the head when going from sitting to lying. Make sure the child has side supports when sitting. Children often depend on armrests to help hold themselves upright. As children get older and heavier, get someone to help you move the child; a two-person transfer is almost always safer for a child with muscular dystrophy. Find out from parents and therapist the most advantageous way to move the child (adapted from Temme, personal communications, December 1991).

Although too much exercise is painful, appropriate stretching exercises are helpful (be sure to consult the parents and physical therapist to find the right exercises). Because the child's physical activities are limited and added weight is a problem, a low-calorie diet is recommended.

Blowing and breathing activities maintain the chest muscles that are essential in coughing. Snacks and lunches should be planned with the child's diet in mind. At preschool age, this child looks weak, not ill, and hence may be made fun of. Work to develop both the child's self-esteem and peer relationships. School, especially at an early age, is invaluable psychologically for both the child and the parents. The children pose few problems at this age. Therapy focuses on minimizing contractures, maximizing muscle strength, and learning to compensate for weaknesses (Dormans & Batshaw, 1997). It becomes progressively more difficult for children with muscular dystrophy to stand and walk. They need to keep their legs well stretched; a goal is to keep the child walking as long as possible. Children may also have learning disabilities and developmental delays and may need individualized educational programming to meet these needs.

Osteogenesis Imperfecta. Osteogenesis imperfecta (brittle bone disease) results in poor bone formation; that is, the bones do not form completely and as a result are short, thin, and prone to breaking. Frequent fractures exacerbate the condition, leading to additional shortening of the limbs compared to the trunk. Although the fractures heal quickly, there may not be good alignment, leading to the curving of long bones between the joints. Related problems may result, such as thinning of the skin, excessive joint mobility, and hearing loss (usually in adulthood). This condition is sometimes misdiagnosed as child abuse because of frequent hospital visits for fractures early in the child's life. The condition usually improves after puberty.

Encourage children to participate in as much activity as their parents and therapists feel is safe and developmentally appropriate. Emphasize fine motor skills, especially eye-hand coordination, and social skills. Children can have problems with constipation, so provide plenty of liquids. Excessive weight may also be a problem, so consider snacks wisely. The children may use some adaptive equipment with which you will need to become familiar (adapted from Albert, personal communications, December 1991).

Specific Intervention Techniques

Regardless of the diagnosis, many children with orthopedic impairments use adaptive equipment for assistance in moving.

Mobility Aids

Most children have a variety of mobility aids; some are very simple, others highly complex. It is important that you know the purpose of the equipment and the relationship among the aids. Organizationally, the equipment starts with the child and what is necessary to implement independent mobility. It then goes on to short- and long-distance mobility aids. Because children use many different types of equipment, an adult must often help them transfer from one to another or to the floor or toilet.

Braces. The purpose of braces is to support the joints in a functional position, that is, ready for use. In general, being upright is better for body growth, respiration, and circulation. Braces are all custom-made by an orthotist (brace maker). There are two basic types of braces: plastic and metal. Plastic braces are lightweight and can be contoured to use on the trunk and legs and occasionally on the arms. (A child with cystic fibrosis may even have a plastic "jacket.") Plastic braces are molded to fit the body part and keep that body part in a position that is ready to function, as well as position it for better growth. Many plastic braces have hinges at the ankles and knees to allow for movement.

Metal braces are used far less frequently today than they were in the past. For legs, braces can be short or long. If they are long, they are hinged at the knee and have locks. Young children do not have the strength or dexterity to make these locks work. The first time you work with these locks you need to do it under the supervision of the physical or occupational therapist or the parent. (The locks require a lot of pressure to change. The pressure you use needs to be against the brace and not the child's body.) When the therapist demonstrates for you how the locks work, that is only the first step. *You* need to be able to work the locks. Ask the therapist to watch and coach you while you try. You need to be able not only to work the locks, but also to put the braces on and off. (A child might get wet at the water table or have a toileting accident, and you will have to change her.) While the therapist is there, do it, and let the therapist coach you. Watching isn't the same as doing.

One of the things you will notice is that the shoes of children in braces frequently look identical, and it may be difficult to tell the right shoe from the left one. Take your handy permanent marker and mark the right and left shoes (or ask the parents to do this). Although the shoes look alike to you, they are individually fitted and feel very different to the child. If a child who is usually cheerful is unhappy or crying and you have gone through your usual repertoire of possible causes, check to see if the child's braces are on the appropriate legs. Molded plastic braces are particularly uncomfortable for the child when placed on the wrong leg. On a hectic morning, parents and teachers may make a mistake.

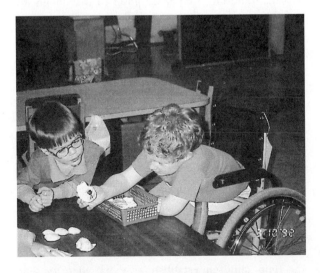

When children use wheelchairs in the classroom, be sure that the tables and other equipment are accessible so all children can be included in activities.

Short-Distance Mobility Aids. Walkers, scooters, crutches, and canes are the most common mobility aids for short distances. Some or all of these may be in your classroom with the child, as they serve slightly different purposes.

Walkers are individualized to the child's ability, size, and functional level. Young children often use walkers before they use crutches. Walkers provide a broader base of support. Children can use the walker for balance and get up to it independently before they can manage the same skills with crutches. The area inside the walker is personal space for the child. If children need adult support to use the walker, place it out of the way when it is not being actively supervised. If children can use the walker independently, it needs to be accessible to the child. Know the child's individual competence level with this, as with all mobility aids. Be sure the walker has a basket so the child can transport books, puzzles, and other items.

Crutches require much better balance than walkers. They are, however, a more normalized system of transportation. They approximate a gait pattern that is similar to independent walking. Children might use crutches in therapy for a long time before they have them for general use. Children will use different types of crutches that are prescribed for them.

Scooters are another set of wheels that children can use for independent mobility. Some are designed to be sat upon, others to lie on. Scooters provide children both independence and exercise when they don't have good sensation in their legs.

Long-Distance Mobility Aids. Strollers and wheelchairs constitute the most common long-distance mobility aids. When children are very young, it is fine to carry them as you would any infant or toddler. However, as children get older, this is developmentally inappropriate, except for short distances or in emergencies. For younger children, specially made strollers are designed for this time slot. These strollers offer the child a little more positioning than regular strollers and are designed for larger children. As children get older, they use wheelchairs.

For young children, a wheelchair can be thought of as a specialized source of assistance. It is necessary for fire drills, for long walks for which the child does not have enough stamina, and sometimes for seating. Wheelchairs are custom fitted to individual children by the physical therapist, physiatrist, or sometimes an occupational therapist, and a representative of the company that makes the wheelchair working together as a team.

Wheelchairs may be totally customized or chosen from modular systems that are put together to meet the needs of an individual child. The wheelchair prescribed is based on the child's abilities, the type of seating the child needs, the level of independence, the child's age and cognitive ability, and how easy it is to get in and out of the wheelchair. Therapists are particularly concerned about children's ability to position themselves. If they can't position themselves well, the wheelchair will need more belts and padding.

All wheelchairs are different, and the expectations for the children who occupy these chairs differ also. However, there is one rule about wheelchairs that transcends types: Put on the brakes before anything else. And, when putting a child in a wheelchair, put on the child's seat belt before taking off the brakes. For your safety and the child's, get a lesson from the child's physical therapist on how to safely transfer the child from a wheelchair and where to put the child after she is out. One obvious but crucial point: Before taking a child out of a wheelchair, know where the child is going. Children cannot stand there and wait for you to decide. In addition, you need to talk with the children before you move them: "I'm going to take you out of the wheelchair and put you on the floor." Some children may be learning to use a transfer board; if so, find out the ability of the child to independently transfer and what your role should be.

In general, young children should not be in wheelchairs in your classroom. They belong on the floor or in chairs like others sit in (with modifications, if necessary). Decide on a place to park the wheelchair, perhaps in the hall outside. Use short-distance mobility aids in the classroom (walkers, scooters, or whatever meets the child's needs) when possible.

Transferring

Transferring is the term used when you move children from one piece of equipment to another. It might be from the floor to the toilet, the wheelchair to the floor, into or out of a chair, and so on. In general, transferring requires two people. One person is in charge of the trunk area and stands behind the child; the other manages the thigh area and stands in front of the child. In the case of *very small* children, perhaps one person could do the transfer. In all cases, work with the therapists on transfers. The particular type of transfer that is most effective for the child and you will be determined and demonstrated by the physical and occupational therapists working with the child. One-person transfers are not recommended for children you wouldn't normally carry, but ask a therapist how to do this in case of emergency.

Transferring happens several times each day from different positions. Use the therapists' knowledge in this area. *Caution:* It is imperative that you know a child's level of competence in mobility. If a child does not have protective reflexes (if when she falls forward she does not put out her hands to protect herself), she needs the constant monitoring of a trained adult in all antigravity positions. Knowing the equipment is very different from knowing the child's ability to use such equipment (adapted from Albert & Chadwick, personal communications, December 1991). Children need to be an active part of the process.

When you put children with orthopedic impairments with other children, you will find that the similarities are far greater than the differences. Other children will be astonished at their creative problem-solving skills.

Guidelines

Early care and education settings can provide a broad range of experiences for children with orthopedic impairments. Children need to be included in first-hand experiences and provided with a wide variety of materials and equipment. Foster independence in any way you can.

1. Children learn early what others can do that they cannot. To motivate them, give them tasks they *can* accomplish.

2. Have "reachers" in your classroom (assistive devices that individuals use to reach high objects; they usually have a grip that controls a pincer or magnet at the top to pick things up) and encourage all children to use them when they can't reach something they want. Be sure to use them yourself.

3. Be sure children get to touch things as well as see them. When necessary, bring things to children so that they can actively explore them.

4. If the child doesn't seem interested, demonstrate how things can be used. Some children really don't know what to do and are simply too shy to ask. Goop may be a new experience for children, and rather then exploring it, they avoid it. Support children through the cycle of learning: awareness (encourage children to poke, feel, and hold the goop); exploration (talk about its properties and support children in exploration); inquiry (encourage children to experiment with media in a variety of ways); utilization (encourage children to compare goop to playdough, to fingerpaint, and so on). Talk about the uses of cornstarch in the context of cooking.

5. Our society is a mobile one that values beauty and strength. Because body image greatly influences self-concept, children with orthopedic impairments need help integrating body image into a healthy self-concept. Be sure you have pictures of individuals using mobility devices on your walls and include these people as visitors in your classroom. Read books about children that encourage diverse abilities.

6. Work on developing language skills, especially those necessary to express feelings and to meet personal needs. Provide many creative activities that help children release energy and work out feelings.

7. Help children establish a sexual identity. For some reason, people with orthopedic impairments are often treated as if they are asexual. An appropriate sex-role identification is important to their development.

8. Keep in contact through get-well cards, audiotapes, videotapes, and visits if the child is out of school for an extended period of time. Send the child messages by e-mail if the child has a computer and access to these services.

For children with orthopedic impairments, the classroom itself needs to be evaluated for accessibility and perhaps modified.

1. Borrow a wheelchair, sit in it, and pretend that you are teaching. Go to the doorway to greet children, take them to their lockers and help them hang up their coats, then help them settle into the routine. Monitor different children at play in different areas of the room. Be sure to include the bathroom on your excursion. Now, reflect on what was difficult for you to do and how you feel (tired, frustrated?). How long were you in the wheelchair? Reevaluate your room to determine how accessible classroom equipment is for children with orthopedic impairments. Check doors and passageways to be sure walkers and wheelchairs can get through and turn easily. Be sure areas around activities and equipment are wide enough for mobility aids. Now, we really don't want children in wheelchairs in the room. How accessible is the class if you were on a scooter or crawling?

2. Tables with legs that allow you to adjust the height of the table and tops that can be angled are useful. If these are not available, a wooden wedge can serve the same purpose.

3. Include some lighter equipment such as cardboard blocks and have a variety of manipulatives that require pushing and pulling with varying degrees of strength. Be sure that large equipment like bookshelves are heavy and stable, as children might lean against them or use them to pull upright.

4. Move sand and activity tables away from walls so that children can get to them from all sides. Evaluate the level of the tables so they are accessible to all children.

5. Be sure there are many different types of chairs children can sit in (if all the chairs are the same except one, it points out difference, not inclusion). If necessary, modify a chair with the help of a physical therapist or physiatrist. An abduction block—a chunk of something padded that the child's legs can straddle—will prevent a child from sliding onto the floor, or you can add a seat belt. If recommended by the child's physical therapist, add a footstool so that the child's feet can be flat (this corrects the angle to obtain trunk stability).

6. Ramps may need to be added to help children enter and leave the classroom.

7. Use nonslip floor coverings (no highly waxed floors, scatter rugs, or shag carpet). If you have carpets with low pile, be sure they are attached by a metal strip so they won't slide and so children don't trip over the edges. Keep toys off the floor when not in use to prevent children from tripping.

8. Toilet cubicles should be wide enough to accommodate a child and a wheelchair and an adult; handrails need to be at the child's height to make the transfer an easy one. A transfer pole (a moveable pole that goes from floor to ceiling) may need to be added. There are also many different types of potty chairs that are designed to solve a variety of problems. Ask parents what word or sign they use for "potty" and how they deal with this issue at home.

9. Shorten and widen the handles on paintbrushes, rackets, and paddles to make them easier for the child with an orthopedic impairment to use. Use rubber tubing or foam around the handles for easier grip. Add a Velcro strap to the handle if children have trouble keeping a grip on the brush.

10. For snacks, use deep-sided bowls instead of plates and two-handled mugs instead of cups. Serve a lot of finger foods. Use cups and plates that have rubber on the bottom (found at boat supply stores). Add rubber tubing to utensils for easier grip. Put plates on Dycem to keep them from moving around.

11. Be aware of the temperature of the food you serve. Some children can't tell when something is too hot, including food, and they could burn themselves.

12. Have bolsters, wedges, and beanbag chairs to provide a change for children, as well as scooters to encourage movement.

13. Be sure walkers have baskets and provide around-the-waist carriers for children on crutches. For small items, a fanny pack works well. Knapsacks also work, but children should wear them in front. Most wheelchairs have their own trays.

14. Use both large and small versions of manipulative toys. Especially helpful are toys that have a built-in tolerance for error (that is, blocks that fit together even if the child doesn't match them perfectly).

15. Remove equipment that is easily overturned such as rolling shelves if they are not stable.

16. With appropriate trunk support, wagons are great for outside and field trips.

17. Use padded lap boards (frequently used in cars for a writing surface) or lap trays for children who may be more comfortable on the floor than sitting in a chair.

18. Use a book or music stand with a page holder to keep pages of a book open. For children who have difficulty turning pages, get a specialized page turner. Have a listening center with headphones.

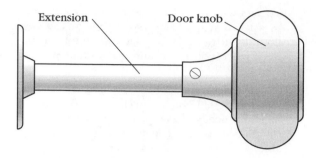

Extension   Door knob

Figure 15.2

19. If doors have knobs, put an extension on the knob to make it easier to turn (see Figure 15.2).

20. Using bicycle gloves may make climbing and pushing a wheelchair easier.

21. Prioritize tasks, putting those that require more energy and concentration first if the child tires easily.

Curriculum Adaptations

The actual physical limitations a child has will determine the number and degree of adaptations necessary. In general, encourage children to do as much as possible independently—but not to the point of frustration. Offer help when you think it is necessary. When you give it, tell the child what you are going to do and, as you do it, what you are doing.

Don't forget that children change and grow. An adaptation that may be necessary at the beginning of the year may not be needed by the middle or end of the year. As you adapt equipment and programming for children, consider whether the adaptation is both developmentally and socially appropriate. Adaptations should be designed to include children, not draw attention to them.

Social Awareness: Self-Esteem, Inclusion, Social Studies, Health and Safety

Children need to learn about the larger world and be part of it. They need both information and skills. Children with orthopedic impairments may not move as fast as others or with the same quality of movement and need to refine skills of speed, distance, and coordination for their own safety. If they have a prosthetic device or braces, they need to be aware of any irritation or pain that may develop, or they might have to do without these aids until the irritation clears up. Children who lack sensation in some body parts must learn to deal with conditions they may not feel. Children need awareness of their bodies not only to

achieve a good self-concept but also to maintain health and safety. Children and adults need to be able to assess what they can do physically.

Self-Esteem. Children need to be accepted for who they are. They need to be accepted for their similarities as well as their differences. They need to build a positive self-concept. Find out from the parents what they have told their child about the disability. Many parents do not talk with children about this, or give children the impression that there is a "cure" for what they have and that when they grow up the disability will be gone. It is important that children integrate their abilities and disabilities into their self-concept in a positive way.

1. Children need to talk about the feelings they have about their disability. Be a good listener.

2. Children need to learn to deal with rejection and discrimination as it happens. Ignoring it or pretending it isn't there doesn't work. Be sure children have the words to respond to comments such as "What's wrong with you?" An appropriate response might be "There isn't anything wrong with me. My legs aren't strong enough to hold up my body, so I wear these braces. What's wrong with you?"

3. A full-length mirror helps develop body awareness and self-concept, as do songs and fingerplays that use body parts.

4. Provide self-help aids such as buttoners and reachers so children can practice self-help skills with these supports.

Inclusion. All children need to feel that they are part of the group. This is especially true when physical distance from other children is sometimes required because of special equipment. Don't exclude activities that children cannot do independently; rather, have a paraprofessional help them do any movement that needs to be done to feel included. If this really isn't possible, have them think about what others are doing and how they might move given the opportunity. Encourage all children to think about how they will move before they actually do it. All children need to be part of the group.

1. Help children acknowledge obvious limitations, yet see other areas as challenges. Be realistic, but not pessimistic: "I can do _____, but I can't do _____." At the same time, help children figure out different ways they can be part of the group.

2. Children need to talk about the feelings they have about their disability. Ask open-ended questions. Children may not be able to tell you how they feel, so ask them to show you with paint or another media. Help children label feelings. For example, "I think if I needed to sit in your chair I might be scared of _____. Do you ever get

scared?" Encourage all children to talk about and label feelings.

3. Talk about their role as part of the group, what they do to help others, and what others do to help them.

Social Studies. Awareness of community is important for children with orthopedic impairments. Start by familiarizing the children with their immediate environment.

1. Get children out into the community so their knowledge is firsthand.

2. If you are doing a unit on transportation, include wheelchairs (nonpowered and electric) in your discussion.

3. Help children personalize their equipment (with parents' permission). Wheelchairs can be decorated with license nameplates, bicycle bells, or horns and streamers. Walkers may be painted or wrapped with ribbon. Casts can be decorated with marking pens or paints.

4. Have appropriate community visitors, including those who play a role in this child's life: osteopath, physical therapist, occupational therapist, orthopedic surgeon, etc.

Health and Safety. Health and safety are especially important for children with orthopedic impairments and can make a difference not only to them but to other children.

1. Teach children to put crutches or other aids in a place where they can have easy access to them. These aids are needed for independence. Teach others to walk around them. These aids belong to the children who use them. They should not be shared. If you want to use mobility aids to increase awareness, borrow or rent them.

2. Help children identify bruises and scrapes and spot pressure sores and show them to an adult. As you care for these, talk about what you do and why you are doing it.

3. Be sure children are familiar with the procedures and the routes to be taken during safety drills. Have your own drills in preparation for the official ones. Use wagons, or if the child is light enough, lift the child up and carry him if fire occurs. Plan ahead as to who will take the child.

4. Keep extra boxes of tissues around for children to use and trash cans that are easy to get to. Distance makes a difference. Have children deposit used tissues in the trash and then wash their hands. If you help them, you need to wash your hands.

5. Children need to sit in chairs with their buttocks at the back of the chair. At this point, put the seat belt on, if necessary; it usually goes around the hips, not the waist. Check that the knees are at 90 degrees and the feet are on the floor also at 90 degrees. Elbows should rest gently on the table.

Language and Literacy: Speaking, Listening, Reading, and Writing

Children develop language by interacting actively with their environment. To the extent that this first-hand experience has been limited, children may need additional experiences to spur language development. Field trips should be followed by stories, both those written by the children about the experience and those written by others to expand the experience. Children with orthopedic impairments may not be as mobile as other children. They need practice in asking for what they want, especially if they cannot reach it. Likewise, adults need practice listening and allowing children to ask rather than doing it for them. Adults particularly need to learn to give precise directions. Reading can broaden the range of experiences available to these children. Writing may offer a particular challenge. Using materials that have some built-in resistance may be necessary, such as writing or drawing in sand or on clay, or using a computer with an adapted keyboard.

Speaking. Because children have physical limitations, they must rely more on speaking to get some of what they need and to convey information to others. The ability to express themselves can help compensate for lack of motor skills.

1. Use puppets to encourage expressive language. Have puppets that talk and move in many different ways. Finger puppets as well as hand puppets can encourage body awareness. If the child favors one hand, encourage using a puppet on each hand and having them "talk" to each other. Sock puppets or puppets on sticks with padding that just need to be moved up and down may be easier for some children to operate.

2. Expand children's utterances, especially when they use "telegraphic speech." If a child says "Get doll," you might respond, "Which doll do you want me to get you? Oh, you want the one with the red dress." When children ask for objects by pointing, help them learn vocabulary by filling in the words they need: "That's the doll." However, if children are able to respond with only "yes" or "no," phrase your questions accordingly: "Do you want the blue one?" not "Which one do you want?"

Fingerplays encourage children to use both hands in a controlled fashion.

1. When you introduce a new fingerplay, encourage children to do only the actions at first, if they need a lot of concentration to follow those. Keep

the actions simple and slow enough for everyone to keep up.

2. Use some fingerplays that allow the child to use the whole hand rather than just the fingers.

3. Remember that children may need the help of a friend to make certain movements. Use a paraprofessional to assist the child if needed to include her in the activity.

4. Some fingerplays that require different motions with each hand may be too difficult. Think of variations that children can do instead. Make these variations available to all children.

Listening. Be sure that books are stored in a place that is accessible. Select stories that have a variety of characters, some of whom have visible diverse abilities.

1. Have all children sit in chairs for group time. If the class sits on the floor and the child needs to sit in a chair, at this time be sure that child is part of the group by having another child or two to sit in a chair also.

2. Read stories and show pictures of children who have orthopedic impairments; choose stories that emphasize the senses the child can use. Present a balance of diverse abilities in your selections. Have a variety of books, including some made of cardboard or other materials that are easier to use.

3. Use flannel board stories made of Pellon to help focus attention and to increase participation.

4. Add background music to stories to enhance the mood for children who haven't experienced the events described (circus music, waves breaking).

5. As you read stories, check the vocabulary for words children might not be familiar with. If possible, add concrete examples to help children understand the story. For example, bring in types of seashells mentioned in the story to show the children.

Reading. Reading skills involving listening, and visual activities can easily be adapted for children with orthopedic impairments.

1. Field trips followed by language experience stories are good initial reading experiences. Help children establish the idea that you can learn about places by reading about them.

2. Children with orthopedic impairments may lack experiences other children have had. Be sure that they can visually and verbally identify objects before you work on discrimination and other higher-level skills.

3. Talking Books are available from the Library of Congress for children who are orthopedically impaired (as well as visually impaired). Introduce children to these as part of their reading program.

Writing. Writing skills can present a challenge for children with coordination problems. All children need to develop trunk control before they can coordinate the small muscles of the hands and fingers necessary for writing.

1. Children may need to start activities without tools. For example, have children draw with their fingers in the sand before giving them a stick. Have them write letters with their fingers before using a marker. Have children use two fingers, both their index finger and the one next to it, for these experiences.

2. The more variety you have in graphic materials and tools, the more likely it is that children will find a match between what they want to do and what the medium will allow them to do. Also, children with orthopedic impairments may have had limited physical experiences, and the variety adds to their knowledge of the world and how they fit into it. Have a variety of sizes, shapes, and types of materials.

3. When teaching fine motor skills, have children use materials that create some resistance, such as a pencil drawing on clay, so that they can feel the resistance as well as see the results. Talk with the occupational therapist about the best adaptations for writing instruments. There are many different cushions or gripper adaptations available.

4. Children may need to warm up their muscles by squeezing clay or dough. They may need to either strengthen or loosen these muscles before using writing instruments.

5. To teach prewriting skills, use activities that require finger and wrist movement, especially rotation with the palm of the hand down.

Discovery: Mathematics, Science, and Computers

This area has potential for children with orthopedic impairments, as the approach supports and encourages the development of skills for problem solving. Concepts that relate to size, distance, and speed are especially important to children with orthopedic impairments. Because they are less mobile than others, they may require more energy to carry out tasks; thus, it is important that they learn to think about tasks before attempting them rather than use a trial-and-error approach. They must learn to predict how long it will take to cross the path to the swings if someone is approaching on a tricycle. Size concepts help them understand where they can easily fit using a mobility device and still turn around. They also need to learn that, like other children, they are growing and their body is changing. They will, with time, get too big for some of their mobility aids. Customized computers offer children ways of communicating that have not been possible before. They need to feel comfortable with this technology at an early age. They must develop cause-and-effect reasoning skills. Help them develop problem-solving skills to compensate for things they may not be able to do; for example, have them think of how many different ways they can get across the room, paint a picture, or play with blocks. Encourage unconventional solutions.

Mathematics. Children with orthopedic impairments have been exposed to many concepts that are classified under the heading of math. They know something about time concepts: It will usually take them longer to do some things than it takes to do others because of different muscle tone or muscle atrophy. They know something about distance and how far they can go before they get tired. Math can help them quantify these experiences.

1. Children need to learn about the relationship between speed and distance (for example, "If I go 20 feet [here to the door] as fast as I can and I'm tired, I can go 80 feet [the length of the room] slowly. It takes longer, but I can do it").

2. Measuring and weighing children helps them understand why braces no longer fit and need to be replaced. Weigh a child's braces and talk about how much they weigh. Bring in weights that can be attached around children's wrists and ankles and have children use these during the day and talk about the difference the weights make in how they feel and can perform tasks and the amount of energy it takes.

3. Discuss shapes that roll and those that don't. Relate them to concepts like brakes and moving: Round shapes are used for wheels; a triangular block of wood can be used to stop a wheel from moving.

Science. Science has great potential because it teaches cause-and-effect reasoning that is necessary for safety and encourages children to devise adaptations to meet their needs.

1. Magnets are fun and potentially useful. Attach a string to a stick, tie a magnet on the end of the string, and go fishing. Catch paper fish that have paper clip mouths. Show children how they can pick up metal objects with a magnet attached to a stick. A child in a wheelchair can then pick up some things without needing help by using a reacher with a magnet.

2. Work on simple casual relationships: "The faster I move my hands on the wheel, the faster the wheelchair moves. If I only move the right wheel forward, I turn left!" If children have electric wheelchairs, they need to learn how to steer them.

3. Help children learn to use simple machines such as wheels and pulleys with ropes as a way of moving objects that they otherwise might not be able to move. Demonstrate how you might use a long foam roll to move a heavy objects (inflatable rollers are used to move boats).

4. Use objects that vary in weight for sorting activities. Set out a Ping-Pong ball, tennis ball, hard ball, empty cup, cupful of cereal, and cupful of rice and see if the children can arrange them in order. Discuss the relationships among an object's weight, the distance someone throws it, and the thrower's strength. Outside, set up a range and have each child throw different balls (Ping-Pong, tennis, hard ball, large rubber ball, and beach ball), mark and measure how far each goes, and relate this back to size, weight, and strength. Then have children kick the rubber ball and beach ball and see which goes farther. The focus is on relative distance, not throwing it the farthest. If children don't want to throw, have them participate in measuring.

5. Use objects that vary in shape, size, and texture. Help children decide the easiest and most difficult to move.

6. Children need to explore basic principles of physics. Use scales and balances and relate this to their body and how far they can lean without unbalancing.

7. Study the concept of energy as part of learning about children themselves and also the natural world. Children with orthopedic impairments have to expend more energy to move, so they get tired more quickly and it may take more concentration to move body parts. Read about energy as well.

8. Learning about the effects of gravity is vital because most of these children will struggle against it as they sit and stand.

Computers. Children need to be exposed to computers early and to think of them as part of their life. Computers can be used by any child who has control over one motor part, whether that is a hand, a big toe, or the tongue. Most computers are designed with adaptations. Call the manufacturer to find out how easy adaptations will be or consult an assistive technology specialist (all states have them).

1. Computers can and should be used by children with muscular, motor, and movement disabilities. Adaptations make computers accessible to these children. Mouses can be larger and adapted to respond to different amounts of pressure. Keys can be slowed down and attached to a voice activation system that tells the child in addition to showing what is happening.

2. Computers can be equipped with foot switches and head switches. They can respond to a sip and puff straw and even the movement of an eyebrow. There are joysticks that can be operated by tongue or head movements. Because of the potential of computers for children, they need to be

part of their educational environment as early as age 3 or 4.

3. As children become more competent on computers, they may be part of the child's individualized program. In this case, adults need to learn how to use the computer and software that has been chosen. This computer is likely to be specially customized and will travel with the child from school to home. Procedures need to be worked out for this to happen without damaging the computer.

Developmental Physical Education and Sensorimotor Skills: Large Motor, Small Motor, and Sensorimotor Integration

Children must be given the opportunity to discover their abilities and challenges in the motor area. Allow children to use all equipment (within realistic limits) and participate in all activities normally provided in your setting, unless you have other directives from the parents, physician, or therapists. If there is *any* doubt, it's best to check with these people. Therapists and parents too, are prime resources for ideas on adapting equipment and activities. Have these people brainstorm with you for ideas about how to adapt activities and materials to include children with orthopedic impairments. Children's particular impairments will determine the extent of their ability to participate in motor play and the strategies that will be most effective. Children whose lower body is most affected need to strengthen the upper body to allow them to use a walker or to transfer from a wheelchair to the floor; at the same time, you don't want to ignore the child's lower body. Children need to have as much functional ability as possible so that muscles don't contract or atrophy. To adapt activities to individual differences, use lightweight plastic objects that are easily manipulated or materials that tolerate some degree of error but still work. Help children control the environment by putting smaller objects in jellyroll pans or trays with edges. Allow children time to participate.

Large Motor. Children need to use and develop their large muscles for strength and endurance.

1. Supervise children carefully. Children with poor muscular control are in danger of falling; someone must be on hand to catch them. Additionally, they need to learn to fall safely, which is vital or their health, well-being, and self-esteem—and not a bad thing for all children to know. Work with the physical therapists and parents to continue this learning process and learn how to help children transfer into unusual equipment (such as a wagon or tricycle).

2. Don't assist children in climbing higher than they can climb independently. Even then, children may climb higher than they realize and be unsure how to get down safely. They may need not only your verbal guidance, but your physical help.

3. If children can use equipment independently (get on and off a trike), encourage them to use it. However, don't assist them in using equipment beyond their skill level unless a therapist has requested this and gives you instructions on how to support the child. Use safety equipment like bicycle helmets for tricycles.

4. Where possible, have children work on vertical surfaces (chalkboard or easel) that are large enough so they can use large muscles both standing and sitting. These are antigravity positions and are necessary for children to integrate the concepts high and low, up and down, and around.

5. If muscular control is unsteady, secure feet to tricycle pedals with giant rubber bands from an inner tube or with toe straps or clips. (Note: This should only be done on the advice of a therapist, as it could be dangerous. A child who falls will have difficulty getting out and could potentially twist a knee.)

6. When you use toss games (beanbags, balls, ring throws), attach the objects to the child's chair with a string so that the child can retrieve them. Initially, keep distances short, and gradually lengthen them as children become more skillful. (Monitor the string carefully and remove it when the child has finished, as it is a potential danger.)

7. If the game cannot be otherwise adapted, allow the child to be scorekeeper with an abacuslike counter or a large key calculator (they make some that even talk). Instances in which an orthopedic impairment can't be accommodated should be rare.

8. Children with poor balance and motor coordination may increase mobility if you have them push something as they move forward, such as a toy carriage weighted with sandbags.

9. Mounting toys on walls at a child's height facilitates hand coordination, balance, and grasping. If a child needs practice standing, mounted objects provide the incentive and the opportunity.

10. Children in wheelchairs can participate with little or no difficulty in any game that requires sitting down. Tossing and catching are skills in which this child needs practice. Use yarn balls or foam for safety; underinflated beach balls are good, too. Scoopers for catching the balls can be made easily from bleach bottles. You can use tossing games to teach concepts such as over, under, low, and high.

11. If children are prone to bump into the edges of the wall, wall guards are necessary; these are plastic or metal strips on the corners or walls so the plaster does not chip off (young children might eat the plastic chips).

Small Motor. Children need a balance of fine and gross motor skills. The ability to grasp, manipulate, and release objects is basic to using materials in the class and to lifelong independence skills. Most self-help skills as well as preliteracy skills require small motor coordination.

1. Magnetic toys are great. Use the front of a conventional teacher's desk for small group work; for individual work, give children cookie sheets with smaller toys.

2. Glue magnets to small toys and blocks such as one-inch cubes, parquetry blocks, and small "people" to make them easier for the children to manipulate. Use these on cookie sheets. If children are younger than 3, be sure the pieces are too large to be swallowed.

3. Blocks that snap together and those that are held together with bristles can be built into structures that are not easily knocked apart unintentionally by children with poor control of their hands. Attach Velcro to blocks to encourage children to use them and to have them cross the midline. Although these blocks are forgiving to put together, they take strength to pull apart.

4. Pegboard play improves the child's ability to grasp, aim, and control involuntary motion. The size, number, and spacing of the pegs should vary according to the child's needs. Holes distantly spaced suit some children because they are less likely to knock over one peg when inserting another. Rubber pegboards with large pegs are good for strengthening fingers because they offer some resistance.

5. Playing with pop beads (both pulling them apart and putting them together) helps develop eye-hand coordination.

A copy of the alphabet, the front of a teacher's desk, and magnetic letters support the development of early reading literacy. The magnetic letters promote fine motor skills and tactile perception, and allow children to make up words when writing is difficult.

6. If a child has trouble holding a lacing card for stringing, you might use a stand-up pegboard or a piece of cardboard that is perpendicular to the table (and therefore does not require wrist rotation). Pegboard from the hardware store comes in all sizes (or get giant lacing cards). Pasting pictures on cardboard helps to make them sturdier. Reinforce the end of the string with tape or glue so that it is stiff, or use shoelaces knotted at one end.

7. Use index cards or old greeting cards for cutting with a variety of adaptive scissors. They are stiffer and easier for children to handle.

8. Use flat, firm shapes such as cardboard or posterboard with large holes for stringing. (The string comes through the hole faster and more easily.) Cover construction paper with clear contact paper to make it stiffer.

9. Clothespins that must be squeezed to open can be put around the edge of a can or used to hang up doll clothes. Their use develops necessary finger strength.

10. Puzzle pieces with knobs are easier to insert and remove. Start with shapes that go in easily (circles before octagons).

11. Get a variety of special scissors such as easy-grip loop scissors (they have a squeezable loop instead of finger holes) or scissors with four holes so that you can help the child cut.

12. Have children stick objects in and take them out of clay and playdough; cookie cutters and rolling pins work well for this.

13. Use a pipe cleaner instead of a shoelace to string beads. Make a loop at one end for an easier grip.

14. Blowing bubbles encourages lung usage, but be sure the bubble liquid is safe if children accidently swallow it.

Sensorimotor Integration. Integrating information that comes from the senses is critical. Give the children unusual stimuli as it helps them focus.

1. Use recipes for playdough that have different consistencies and textures. Support children in using their hands to poke, pull, and roll the dough before adding rolling pins and other tools. Have children use their whole arm to roll the dough. Encourage them to squish the dough between their fingers.

2. Make Freddie the Frog or Katie Kangaroo or some such animal from a beanbag. Put the beanbag on the child's head and see how long it will stay there before it falls (or "jumps"). This is a fun

way to strengthen neck muscles and to help children learn about the position of their head in space.

3. Activities that require performing two separate motions or a different action with each hand are difficult (holding a juice cup while pouring juice). Initially, hold the cup while the child pours with two hands, or have the child hold the cup while you pour. As the child's skill improves, encourage him to try both tasks (but practice at the water table first).

4. Buy or make a tetherball. Using a small table as a base, secure a 30-inch pole in the center and attach a string. Attach a rubber ball to the string. The children try to wind the ball around the pole by hitting it with their hands or a paddle. This game can be played either sitting or standing. It develops the child's eye-hand coordination. This is great outside.

5. For children who have difficulty sitting, a sandbag shaped like a large worm placed around them (like the letter *c*) on the floor provides some support and stability. Have several, so all children can try them.

Creative Arts: Visual Arts, Music, Creative Movement, and Dramatic Play

Creative arts offer the potential to learn about the world and different media. The emphasis is on the process and creativity. Thinking about the final product and how it will be used, the method of achieving a particular result, and the message it conveys is important. Children can use the arts to express feelings, increase body awareness, and practice necessary motor skills. During music and movement, be sure to provide assistance to children so they feel included. Have them help you make up the rules of the game or call out "Simon Says" so they are verbally and mentally, if not physically, included in the play. Make eye contact and tell them that that was "half a stomp" if the leg moved a little. Have the child sit on your lap and gently guide her through motions to a song. Or carry the child as your partner while you play Ring around the Rosie. Help children "visit" some places that may not be accessible to them, or figure out creative ways of increasing accessibility.

Visual Arts. For some children, the visual arts are difficult and discouraging; others find in them a release.

1. Choose activities that require two hands, such as modeling playdough and fingerpainting. Encourage children to use both hands as a way of building strength.

2. Tape drawing paper to the table so that children can concentrate on what they are putting on the paper, not on preventing the paper from slipping. Or use Dycem, a plasticlike sheet that is tacky enough to hold objects where they are placed. (Most office or medical supply stores have it.) Also use it to keep papers and other objects from moving around. When it becomes less tacky, put it on the bottom of the chair to keep children from slipping off.

3. Use washable marking pens. They require little pressure, are easy to grip, and are colorful. Build up thin ones with masking tape or place foam hair curlers or rubber tubing around them so they are easier to use.

4. Adapt drawing materials. For easier gripping, use large pieces of chalk (on sidewalk) and insert crayons wrapped in paper into roll-on deodorant bottles (with the ball removed). Encourage all children to use these variations and comment upon the effect.

5. Make paint jars easier to handle: Put a thick rubber band (or a thin sheet of foam or sponge) around them, and glue sandpaper on the lids.

6. Use large, heavy, adjustable easels. Adjustable easels allow children many options for working. You may need to put sandbags around the legs so they won't fall if someone pulls up on them or bumps into them.

7. Paint on large paper and large objects, like boxes.

8. Outside, have the child "paint" the sidewalk with a bucket of water and a broom (if the child is in a wheelchair) or a large brush. Tape cloth or paper onto the sidewalk and have children roll wheels (wagon, wheelchair, and tricycle) in washable paint, then over the cloth (be sure the wheels are clean before the children go home). You can make tracks with water as well. (Check with parents for precautions.)

9. Make clay, varying the moisture to meet the strength and motor skills of the child (the moister the clay, the easier to manipulate). Use a rolling pin or tongue depressor to mold clay. Be sure to allow adequate time for exploration. This activity will help build strength and coordination.

10. Don't make models for children even when you are tempted. Support their attempts to control the medium, not the final product.

11. Paint with bare feet on paper on the floor (this can be done from a chair or wheelchair). Have children follow each other's footprints or go in the opposite direction.

Music. Use music to increase body awareness and encourage movement. Music can also be used to teach concepts.

1. Sing the song "Put Your Finger in the Air" and substitute words for "finger" and "air." Be sure to take into account the abilities of the children as you adapt this song. Some variations are: nose

on your shoulder, tongue on your lip, and wrist on your cheek. Other songs also teach body awareness.

2. Have children play rhythm instruments to create a mood. This is a nondemanding way for children to be part of a group.

3. Activities that require two hands to be coordinated, such as clapping, are good practice, but may be difficult, so go slowly.

4. If a child has difficulty holding on to specific instruments, adapt them. On finger cymbals, have elastic attachments that go around the hand rather than knobs. If a child cannot hold a stick to tap a xylophone, have the child wear a mitten with Velcro in the palm and glue Velcro to the stick. Weigh down objects like drums or xylophones with beanbags to help them stay in one place.

5. Use short, fat, round sticks to hit together or with the xylophone or triangle, or adapt the sticks as you did the paintbrushes and put a larger, sturdier ring on the triangle.

Creative Movement. Creative movement is just that, creative. Help children see the creative quality to movement. This involves not judging the quality of the movement, but accepting the right of individuals to interpret creatively.

1. Allow for individual differences and creativity. Make your suggestions in relation to the child's abilities.

2. Plan activities where children can move creatively as part of a group. Choose some movements that the children are able to do while sitting on the floor such as swaying to music.

3. Give children time to explore the quality of their movements. Include some times of slow movement and encourage children to do fewer of some movements (one stamp instead of five).

4. Isolate movements, based on children's ability. Have them move their eyes creatively, or arms, or another body part.

Dramatic Play. Children can use this type of activity to play different roles as well as to express fears and concerns. They need to learn to use dramatic play to acknowledge and act out their feelings. They cannot run angry feelings off, and feelings that are denied eventually take a toll.

1. Help other children become more aware of the challenges of being in a wheelchair or on crutches by having these available to play with. These should be borrowed, not the child's.

2. Play hospital with casting tape (available in most drugstores). Have children cast dolls' legs or their own fingers (use blunt-nosed scissors to cut the casts off).

3. Use a full-length mirror to encourage children to explore their individual characteristics. Be sure to show children how you use the mirror to see parts of you that are difficult to see otherwise. (Put a dot or a cutout on each child's back and have the child try to see it in the mirror.)

4. You may have to demonstrate how to play some roles initially, as children may not have been exposed to them and may not know what to do. Your role is to be a coach: You can't play the game for the children, but you can encourage them, spot them, model how to do it, and teach them techniques. In addition to having had fewer experiences, they process less visual and kinesthetic input. They need verbal support and feedback.

5. If children are likely to use equipment to pull up on, such as a stove in the housekeeping area, weigh it down with sandbags so it doesn't fall on the child.

Transitions

Transitions are often confusing. Be sure these children know where they are going and for what purpose.

1. Use transitions to teach simple concepts, such as color and clothing texture.

2. Because these children need more time to move around, dismiss them no later than the middle of the transitional activity.

3. Always tell the children what you are planning to do *before* you begin doing it. Ask children to help in the transfer—they need to be included in the process. If you simply lift them onto the rug, for example, they may become frightened at suddenly being taken out of a secure position. Even if they have limited speech, talk to them, and make them aware of any changes.

Summary

Children come into the world wanting to move. For some children, this is a challenge. One challenge is muscle tone: When children have muscle tone that is too high, their responses are spastic; when too low, it is floppy; when it is mixed, it becomes undependable and a challenge for them to control.

Increasingly, we are becoming concerned about young children who are clumsy, partly because of their developing self-concept but also as it relates to learning differences. There are many different types of orthopedic impairments, roughly divided into neurological and musculoskeletal. Neurological impairments include cerebral palsy, neural tube defects, which are usually present at birth, and injuries to the brain or spinal column that take place in early childhood. With the advent of new technology, increasing numbers of children with TBI are living and returning to educational settings. Musculoskeletal impairments include missing limbs and problems related to brittle bones; other problems such as muscular dystrophy relate to a progressive atrophy of the muscles.

Many children who have orthopedic impairments need mobility aids for locomotion. These aids vary from braces and crutches to wheelchairs. Curriculum adaptations allow children with orthopedic impairments to be included in regular classrooms.

Educational Resources

American Paralysis Association
http://teri.bio.uci.edu:80/paralysis/
This page explains what may occur after an injury, ways of prevention, and reversal.

Camps for Kids with Disabilities
http://www.kidscamps.com/specialty/special_needs/physical.html
Search for a camp that will best fit your child who has a physical disability.

Celebrating Communications Technology for Everyone
http://www.law.indiana.edu/fclj/v47/no2/blanck.html
This site covers issues of telecommunications and other assistive technology; supports the concept of "schools without walls."

Cerebral Palsy: A Multimedia Tutorial for Children and Parents
http://galen.med.virginia.edu/~smb4v/tutorials/cp/cp.htm
This page gives information on the causes of CP and treatments and therapies available.

Cure Paralysis Now
http://www.cureparalysis.org/
This site provides different concepts and research in many fields to help cure paralysis.

Disabilities Sites of Interest
http://www.merrywing.com/newsites.htm
This site contains direct links to many other sites concerning various disabilities of children as well as adults.

http://galen.med.virginia.edu/~smb4v/tutorials/cp/cp.htm
A basic easy-to-understand site on cerebral palsy. It covers causes and types of cerebral palsy as well as equipment and the problems children encounter. It also includes awareness exercises.

Hydrocephalus Association Homepage
http://neurosurgery.mgh.harvard.edu/ha/
This page contains information about this organization and hydrocephalus.

March of Dimes
Public Health Education and Community Services Department
1275 Mamaroneck Avenue
White Plains, NY 10605
(914) 428-7100
Sponsors research, but also provides free public health information sheets on disabilities.

The National Easter Seal Society
70 East Lake Street
Chicago, IL 60601
Administrative headquarters for Easter Seals affiliates that operate direct service programs for children with disabilities; they have an array of print materials on topics from accessibility and attitudes to dental care.

National Head Injury Foundation
Turnpike Road
Southborough, MA 01772
Provides information about teaching children who have had a traumatic brain injury.

National Rehabilitation Association
1522 K Street, NW
Washington, DC 20005
Encourages an interdisciplinary approach and increased public understanding of physical and mental disabilities.

Networking Students with Physical Disabilities
http://calvin.stennet.nef.ca/~cfield/abled.htm
Created in Canada, this page helps people who have an interest in physical disabilities.

Parents Campaign for Handicapped Children and Youth
Closer Look
Box 1492
Washington, DC 20013
Provides a free newsletter about educational programs and special services to parents and professionals who work with children with physical, mental, and emotional impairments.

Services for Crippled Children
U.S. Department of HEW
Bureau of Community Health Services
Rockville, MD 20852
Provides information about programs available for children with physical impairments.

Spina Bifida Association of America (SBAA)
1700 Rockville Pike, Suite 540
Rockville, MD 20852
Provides information and support through local chapters; they have many publications for teachers and parents.

Spinal Cord Injury, Stroke, Paralysis Guide to Support Organizations
http://neurosurgery.mgh.harvard.edu/paral-r.htm
Resources and organizations mentioned provide support for and educate parents.

Traumatic Brain Injury
http://www.neuroskills.com/~ens/tbi/injury.html
This page contains a plethora of information about traumatic brain injury.

United Cerebral Palsy Association (UCP)
1660 L Street, NW
Washington, DC 20036-5602
(800) USA-5-UCP, (202) 776-0406,
TTY (202) 973-7197, FAX (202) 776-0414
http://www.ucpa.org/text/index.html
email: ucpnatl@ucpa.org

National headquarters provides information, guidance, and referrals to local affiliates.

References

American Psychiatric Association. (1994). *Diagnostic and statistical manual of mental disorders (DSM-IV)* (4th ed.). Washington, DC: Author.

Baker, S. P., O'Neill, B., & Karpf, R. S. (1984). *The injury fact book.* Lexington, MA: Lexington Books.

Batshaw, M., & Perret, Y. (1992.) *Children with disabilities: A medical primer* (3rd ed.). Baltimore: Brookes.

Brookes, M., Macmillan, R., & Cully, S. (1990). Head injuries in accident and emergency departments: How different are children from adults? *Journal of Epidemiology and Community Life, 44,* 147–151.

Carney, J., & Shoenbrodt, L. (1994). Educational implications of traumatic brain injury. *Pediatric Annals, 23,* 47–52.

Centers for Disease Control. (1990). Childhood injuries in the United States. *American Journal of Diseases of Children, 144,* 627–646.

Conway, R. (1994). Spinal cord injury: Medical issues. In R. A. Olson, L. L. Mullins, J. B. Gillman, & J. M. Chaney (Eds.), *The source book of pediatric psychology* (pp. 277–281). Boston: Allyn & Bacon.

Cratty, B. J. (1994). *Clumsy child syndromes: Descriptions, evaluation and remediation.* Chur, Switzerland: Harwood Academic.

Division of Injury Control, Center for Environmental Health and Injury Control, Centers for Disease Control. (1990). Causes of traumatic brain injury in children by age and percentage. *American Journal of Diseases of Children, 144,* 627–646.

Dormans, J. P., & Batshaw, M. L. (1997). Muscles, bones, and nerves: The body's framework. In M. L. Batshaw (Ed.), *Children with disabilities* (4th ed., pp. 315–334). Baltimore: Brookes.

Emery, A. E. H. (1993). *Duchenne muscular dystrophy* (2nd ed.). Oxford, England: Oxford University Press.

Gronwall, D., Wrightson, P., & Waddell, P. (1990). *Head injury: The facts.* Oxford, England: Oxford University Press.

Horton, A. M. (1993). *Behavioral interventions with brain-injured children.* New York: Plenum Press.

Individuals with Disabilities Education Act of 1997. Pub. L. No. 105-17, 111 Stat. 37-157, 20 U.S.C. 1400.

Liptak, G. S. (1997). Neural tube defects. In M. L. Batshaw (Ed.), *Children with disabilities* (4th ed., pp. 529–553). Baltimore: Brookes.

Michaud, L. J., & Duhaime, A. C. (1992). Traumatic brain injury. In M. L. Batshaw & Y. M. Perret (Eds.), *Children with disabilities: A medical primer* (3rd ed., pp. 525–546). Baltimore: Brookes.

Michaud, L. J., Duhaime, A. C., & Lazar, M. F. (1997). Traumatic brain injury. In M. L. Batshaw (Ed.), *Children with disabilities* (4th ed., pp. 595–620). Baltimore: Brookes.

Miller, F., & Bachrach, S. J. (1995). *Cerebral palsy: A complete guide for caregiving.* Baltimore: Johns Hopkins University Press.

Orton, S. T. (1937). *Reading, writing, and speech problems in children.* New York: Norton.

Pellegrino, L. (1997). Cerebral palsy. In M. L. Batshaw (Ed.), *Children with disabilities* (4th ed., pp. 499–528). Baltimore: Brookes.

Peterson, N. L. (1987). *Early intervention for handicapped and at-risk children: An introduction to early childhood-special education.* Denver, CO: Love.

Yeates, K. O. (1994). Head injuries: Psychological issues. In R. A. Olson, L. L. Mullins, J. B. Gillman, & J. M. Chaney (Eds.), *The source book of pediatric psychology* (pp. 262–276). Boston: Allyn & Bacon.

Chapter 16

CHILDREN WITH HEARING IMPAIRMENTS

It's hard to know when to push and when to just agree and forget it. When I asked our pediatrician whether Erica might have a hearing loss because of her frequent ear infections, he told me he didn't think so. I wanted her seen by an ear specialist. He told me he thought it was unnecessary but eventually gave the referral I needed. After examining her, the otologist said she seemed fine. I had come this far and I wasn't giving up. I told him that he had only seen her for 15 minutes and I didn't think he could tell by what he had done whether or not she could hear. I told him her preschool teachers said that she was louder than the other children and that she seemed to "not hear" as well as the other children. Reluctantly, he agreed to the screening. I didn't want her to have a hearing loss just to prove I was right; on the other hand, after all this, I wasn't surprised. What did surprise and dismay me was that the loss they found wasn't the traditional one that accompanies fluid in the ears. It was a sensorineural loss. It was forever—it was hearing aids and speech therapy and all that. I wasn't prepared. But I did follow through. Her audiogram was pretty flat, with a loss of about 60 decibels in the speech frequencies.

It was hardest at the beginning. After all this, Erica refused to wear the hearing aids. We put them in, she took them out. She screamed, cried, and threw temper tantrums when we put them in. We tried to acknowledge her feelings, but we made the decision that she was going to wear them. We felt like meanies each time we put them back in. We even taped them in a couple times so she couldn't pull them out. I'm glad we had each other for support during this round. We kept reminding ourselves that if we didn't make her wear them, she would miss out on so much of life. She needed to begin wearing them now as a 4-year-old. We couldn't wait until she was old enough to understand to explain it to her.

It was a war, but we eventually won the first battle. By the time we had gotten all of this sorted out, Erica was about to begin kindergarten. Now putting in her hearing aids is part of getting dressed. Mornings are no longer a war zone. During kindergarten, Erica had a speech and language specialist visit the classroom three times a week; she helped her learn concepts that she hadn't gotten like "front" and "back." She uses both sign and speech reads. She can do this well with the help of her hearing aid as long as she can see the teacher. This teacher was really good. She would ask Erica if the volume of the video was loud enough without singling her out. (One teacher had her in tears, as she kept asking her in front of all the other children.)

We thought we had this together. I could now sign to her and she could hear my husband's voice. We encouraged her independence and her younger brother was feeling as though we had enough time for him. The IEP meeting in May went well. The summer was a relaxing one. Erica was beginning to accept her hearing loss and the hearing aids, as were we. First grade came with a vengeance. At first, the protests were mild but her stand irrefutable. She refused to use the auditory trainer. She said it made things too loud, it hurt her ears, and gave her a headache. We talked, we explained, we tried to convince her what she would miss. None of it worked. We made an appointment to meet with her teacher to talk about the problem. We walked into the classroom and were warmly greeted by a voice that almost blasted us out of the classroom. We should have believed her. Erica did not need an auditory trainer in this classroom! They may not have needed a teacher in the next room or even the next school. Some things like fire drills still worry us. When sounds get really loud, like when there is a fire alarm, her ears get really sensitive and she turns off her hearing aid. She can still hear the fire alarm but not much else. I guess if next year's teacher has a soft voice I'll worry about it then.

Erica now accepts the hearing aids. They are part of her. When she takes them off, she can hear some things, like her dad's voice. It's like a mumble but she can hear it. She can take care of the aids pretty much by herself. When kids she doesn't know ask her "What are those?," she tells them "They're my hearing aids and they help me hear." She says it doesn't bother her when they stare. "If they stare, that's their problem. I just ignore them. I just mind my own business. It's not their fault." When she sees someone else with a hearing aid she just says "Hi." She doesn't say anything about it until she gets to know them.

I think they really are a part of her now. She used to always wear her hair down to cover them. Now she wears it back in a ponytail sometimes. She even asked if she could get her ears pierced.

When a child with a hearing impairment joins your class, you suddenly become aware of the many times during the day that children must listen. They have to listen for their name to be called, for opening exercises, and for directions for activities and cleanup. They must listen for music, story time, and fire drills.

Hearing is important in developing communications skills. Children learn to talk by listening and imitating others and by hearing themselves. The hearing child enters kindergarten with a vocabulary of about 5,000 words. The child with a hearing impairment may understand and speak only a few basic words, and even those few words may be hard to understand. Our society assumes that people can convey their wants and needs verbally. In school, children are expected to ask to go to the bathroom, to tell the teacher if they are hurt, and to talk with their playmates. They are also expected to put away their materials when requested and to line up or come when called. Children with hearing impairments may have trouble following instructions and discussions. Before their hearing impairment is identified, they may be mistaken for children who daydream or choose not to listen. They are sometimes characterized as stubborn, disobedient, and lazy.

Hearing allows a person to gain information about the world. We use hearing to monitor our physical and social environment. Children who cannot hear danger signals may find themselves in hazardous situations that others can avoid. Being out of touch with moment-to-moment ordinary sounds has a social-emotional impact of equal magnitude. Children with hearing impairments must be taught to use other cues to be in touch with their world.

Sound

Before looking at hearing impairments, we need to understand more about sound and the hearing system.

What we hear when we hear a sound is an interpretation of a pattern of vibrations or sound waves. These sound waves have two distinct aspects: loudness (intensity) and pitch (frequency). Sound intensity is measured in decibels (dB). The softest sound the average person can hear has been arbitrarily defined as 0 decibels. The higher the number of decibels, the louder the sound. People can hear sound from 0 dB to about 120 dB. Sounds louder than 120 dB first produce a "tickle," then pain, and beyond that, sensorineural damage. A whisper is about 30 dB,

ordinary conversation falls in the 45 to 50 dB range; chain saws are about 100 dB and rock concerts perhaps even more (Steinberg & Knightly, 1997).

Pitch or frequency is determined by the number of cycles per second the sound wave has. A cycle is the distance between the top of one sound wave to the top of the next sound wave. The closer the sound waves are to each other, the higher the frequency. These are measured in Hertz (Hz): One Hertz is equivalent to one cycle per second. People can hear sounds that are low (about 20 Hz) to those that are very high (about 20,000 Hz). (Dogs can hear frequencies over 40,000 Hz.) The normal speech frequencies fall between 500 and 2,000 Hz, and virtually all speech is between 250 and 6,000 Hz. Middle C is 256 Hz (Batshaw & Perret, 1992). A loss above these frequencies (such as is common with increasing age) may affect one's appreciation of music but does not interfere with communications.

Speech is more complex than a single intensity or frequency. Some sounds, such as vowels, have lower frequencies and are more intense. Some consonants, such as the voiceless h, p, s, and so on, are higher in frequency (Steinberg & Knightly, 1997). The interaction of speech with an individual's pattern of loss may allow some children to hear speech but not understand it because they hear only part of what is said. They may hear "Hey" as /ā/.

The Auditory System

The ear is the organ of the body that we think of when we think of hearing. However, there is rarely a problem with the outer ear or *auricle*. It is one of the least important parts of the auditory system. It does function to keep foreign objects out of the middle ear. The external ear is one of three parts of the ear and the only one that is visible. It is connected to the middle ear and the inner ear (see Figure 16.1).

Sound waves enter the auricle, travel through the *ear canal*, and hit the *tympanic membrane* (eardrum),

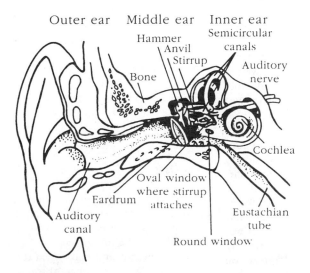

Figure 16.1

causing it to vibrate. The ear canal protects the middle ear by secreting wax that catches debris and keeps it away from the eardrum. The eardrum is attached to one of the small bones in the middle ear, the *malleus* (hammer), through which vibrations are transmitted to the *incus* (anvil) and *stapes* (stirrup). Together, these are known as the *ossicles*. The stapes lies next to the *oval window,* the beginning of the inner ear. The tympanic membrane and ossicles amplify sound by about 30 dB in addition to transmitting it (Steinberg & Knightly, 1997).

The inner ear transforms sound from mechanical energy to electrical energy. It is about the size of a pea. As the vibrations push the oval window (a thin membrane) back and forth, the fluid in the cochlea moves. The *cochlea* is a snail-shaped structure with three chambers that makes hearing possible. The middle chamber, the *organ of Corti,* contains about 20,000 tiny, delicate hair cells. The hair cells near the oval window respond to high-frequency sounds; those in the middle and end respond to low-frequency sounds. These hair cells send electrochemical impulses through the nerve fibers of the ascending auditory pathway and to the auditory cortex in the temporal lobe of the brain. The route to the auditory cortex is complex and includes four transmitting stations. At one of these stations, the nerve fibers cross over, permitting stereophonic hearing; others fine-tune the sound and inhibit background noise. The auditory cortex combines sound with other sensory information and memory and allows perception and interpretation (Steinberg & Knightly, 1997). The auditory cortex isn't needed to hear pure tones, but to interpret language.

In addition to providing hearing, the ear serves two other functions: balance and responding to differences in pressure. The inner ear has three loop-shaped tubes, the *semicircular canals,* that serve to maintain balance (vestibular sense). The *eustachian tube,* a slender tube that runs from the middle ear to the pharynx, equalizes pressure on both sides of the eardrum. When changing altitudes, it is the clearing of the eustachian tube by swallowing or chewing gum that keeps the eardrum from bursting. The ears essentially duplicate each other; the major benefit of having two ears is the ability to localize sound.

At a more global level, the auditory system can be divided into the *peripheral auditory system,* which contains the structures in the outer, middle, and inner ear, and the *central auditory system,* which involves the auditory nerve, the brain stem, and the auditory cortex of the brain.

Modes of Hearing

We hear sound in two different ways: air conduction and bone conduction. *Air conduction* is the most common way we receive auditory input. Sound travels through air; when it enters the outer ear, moves through the middle and inner ear, and ends up at the auditory cortex, we hear. We also hear through *bone conduction,* in which the bones of the head are mechanically vibrated. This vibration causes the hair cells in the cochlea to move and begins the hearing process in a way that bypasses the outer and middle ear. When we speak and hear ourselves, part of what we hear is based on bone conduction. When you hear yourself on an audiotape, you often think that it doesn't sound like you, whereas others claim it is exactly how you sound. The difference is because you are hearing the air conduction aspect of your speaking when listening to the tape.

Hearing Assessment

We would like to be able to identify children in their infancy who have hearing losses. We are particularly concerned about children who are born prematurely, those with complicated prenatal histories, and those with families with a history of hearing loss.

Hearing Screening

The American Speech-Language-Hearing Association (ASHA, 1990) has developed guidelines for the screening process. These involve obtaining a case history of the child; visually inspecting the outer ear, ear canal, and ear drum; pure-tone hearing screening; and tympanometry. ASHA suggests that all children should be screened annually from age 3 until third grade, and high-risk children annually regardless of age.

The case history and visual inspection is often done by a school nurse, speech-language therapist, or an audiologist. If a child has a history of ear infections or if the visual inspection shows abnormalities (excessive ear wax, fluid in the middle ear, and so on), the child is referred for a medical evaluation. (This step is frequently bypassed, as it is time-consuming.)

Hearing screening and hearing threshold testing for children over 3 is typically done using an *audiometer,* an electronic instrument that comes in many different types. The most commonly used in the school setting is a *pure-tone audiometer,* which can be used to screen children and also to determine hearing thresholds. Pure-tone audiometers produce discrete frequencies called *pure tones* at different loudness levels (decibels). In pure-tone testing, the tester places earphones on the child, then the child is given sounds at 20 dBs at frequencies of 500, 1000, 2,000, and 4,000. These are the most important frequencies for speech, and 20 dB is the lower range for what we consider normal hearing. This is purely an air-conduction evaluation. Children who fail to hear at any frequency should be retested. (Before retesting, one should be sure the child understands the instructions.) Children who fail the retest should be referred to an audiologist or otologist for a pure-tone threshold test.

An otologist is a medical doctor who specializes in the diagnosis and treatment of ear diseases. Otologists look at the physical conditions associated with the ears to determine whether or not any medical intervention is indicated. The audiologist is a professional trained in the identification and measurement of hearing impairments and also aids in the rehabilitation of children with hearing impairments.

Hearing-Threshold Testing

A hearing threshold is defined as the lowest hearing level at which the child responds to a minimum of two of three ascending (from inaudible to audible) tones (Salvia & Ysseldyke, 1995). The results of this test are expressed numerically and are plotted separately for each ear on an audiogram. Hearing is assessed for each ear separately, as it is possible to have a severe loss in one ear and not in the other, or have a different configuration of loss in each ear. A bone vibrator is used to measure hearing via bone conduction.

Tympanometry Screening

Tympanometry is designed to detect normal and abnormal conditions of the eardrum and middle ear. As disorders of the middle ear are the most frequent cause of hearing loss during the early childhood years, including this screening is important (Salvia & Ysseldyke, 1995). A specially designed instrument, the tympanogram screener, is inserted into the child's ear canal, an airtight seal is obtained, the ear drum analyzed, and then the screener removed. When the tympanogram screener is returned to its stand, it automatically prints out a tympanogram. Children who have an abnormal tympanogram should be rescreened in four to six weeks or referred for further treatment depending on the abnormality. A normal tympanogram looks something like a narrow pyramid. When children have fluid in their middle ear, the tympanogram is flat. Additional testing is done to aid in further diagnosis and to fit hearing aids.

Testing Young and Difficult-to-Test Children

In pure-tone testing, children have to be able to follow directions, wear the earphones, and be able to indicate the ear the sound was heard in. Children under 4 and those with diverse abilities may not have these skills.

Play Audiometry. For children between about 6 months and 4 years, some form of conditioning is used to first teach the child to respond to a sound and then use that teaching to determine the child's level of hearing. After the tester establishes rapport with the child in a soundproof room, the testing situation is made into a game. Loudspeakers are used instead of earphones. Essentially, the audiologist, working with levels of sound he knows the child can hear, conditions the child to do a particular repetitive activity, such as raising a toy, putting a ring on a stick, or looking at a certain interesting object, whenever the child hears a "noise." Once the behavior is established, the audiologist then uses some sounds that are out of the child's range of hearing to determine the hearing threshold.

Auditory Brain Stem Responses. Auditory brain stem responses are used to test infants and children with multiple disabilities because it does not require their cooperation. EEG electrodes are placed on the sleeping child's forehead and behind the ears and earphones are placed on the ears. This tests both hearing loss and the neural activity of the auditory pathway (Steinberg & Knightly, 1997).

Classification of Hearing Impairments

The most common way to classify causes of hearing impairments is by their location in the hearing process and the severity of the loss. Knowing the exact type of loss has implications for treatment and education, as well as long-term implications.

Types of Hearing Loss

When hearing thresholds are tested, both air conduction and bone conduction tests are done. Differences in the two thresholds have important diagnostic significance.

Conductive Hearing Loss. A conductive loss is one in which the outer or middle ear prevents sound from getting to the inner ear. This can be caused by something lodged in the ear canal, excessive ear wax, or fluid in the middle ear (otitis media). The air conduction threshold indicates a hearing loss and the bone conduction indicates normal hearing. This is called a conductive hearing loss because the problem is in the conducting mechanisms of the outer and/or middle ear (Salvia & Ysseldyke, 1995).

Many young children who experience frequent ear infections have periodic conductive losses, typically running about 60 dB or less (see Figure 16.2). Most conductive losses can be corrected through surgery. This is the most common type of hearing problem in early childhood and the hearing loss is due to fluid in the middle ear.

Impairments of the Middle Ear. Because of the frequency of middle ear disease in young children, its implication for language development, and your role in detection, it is treated in detail here. Middle ear disease, middle ear effusion, middle ear dysfunction, otitis media, and otitis media with effusion are all terms used to describe the same chronic condition: fluid in the middle ear. Most children have one or two ear infections during their early childhood years.

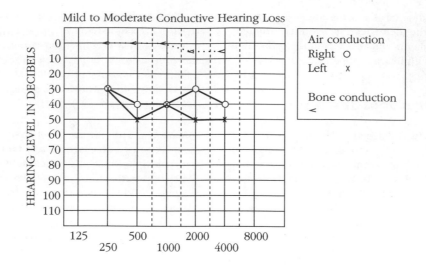

Figure 16.2

In a conductive loss, the bone conduction is within the normal limits, but the air conduction shows a loss.

However, there are usually few long-term implications from these. In fact, earaches are the second most commonly diagnosed disorder in young children during an office visit. It is estimated that over half of all antibiotics given to children are for acute otitis media (Hallahan & Kauffman, 1994). Children who have repeated bouts of otitis media, on the other hand, are at risk of acquiring language skills slowly, of displaying learning disabilities (Denk-Glass, Laber, & Brewer, 1982; Ralabate, 1987), and of developing a permanent sensorineural hearing loss caused by damage to the organ of Corti (Steinberg & Knightly, 1997).

Middle ear disease (MED) is caused by thick fluid in the middle ear that does not drain through the eustachian tubes. Once the middle ear is stopped up, the child experiences a hearing loss (see Figure 16.3). Additionally, this thick fluid is a prime target for bacterial growth. Antibiotics cure the infection, but the fluid may linger on for days or even weeks, causing a hearing loss. The cause of fluid in the middle ear is related to dysfunction of the eustachian tube (Salvia & Ysseldyke, 1995).

It is difficult to accurately measure the prevalence of MED. Some estimates are as high as 50 percent of young children (Denk-Glass et al., 1982). The problem

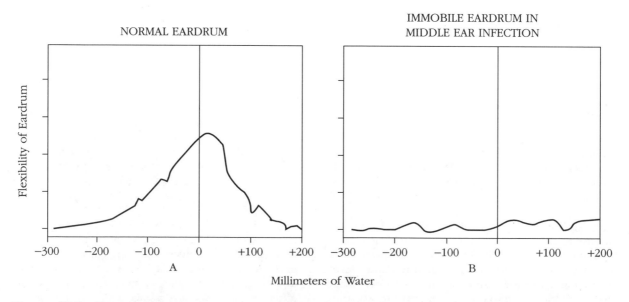

Figure 16.3 Tympanogram

A normal tympanogram is shaped like a triangle. When there is fluid in the middle, the flexibility of the eardrum is decreased and the pattern is flat.

is that MED is often undetected until the child shows signs of physical illness; typically, lethargy, irritability, and inattentiveness are the most visible symptoms. Because of the intermittent nature of the problem, even children who have their hearing checked can be missed: "Up to 60 percent of the children who have MED can be missed by the traditional school hearing screening" (Ralabate, 1987, p. 10).

Initially, MED is treated with antibiotics. When the problem persists, MED is treated surgically by making an incision in the lower part of the eardrum, removing the fluid, and inserting a small plastic tube in the eardrum incision. The small tube, called a *pressure-equalization tube,* takes over the function of the eustachian tube by allowing air to enter the middle-ear space and also allowing fluid to drain (Salvia & Ysseldyke, 1995). The procedure is called a *myringotomy with tubal insertion.*

Parents may not be aware of the implications of ear infections for hearing loss or the risk of speech and language development, attention, and learning disabilities. Research is showing such a link, and parents and teachers need to be cognizant of the possibility (Freil-Patti & Finitzo, 1990). Sometimes, physicians themselves are overcasual about frequent ear infections, making statements like "Don't worry, spring is coming." That is an appealing idea, but not one that is necessarily useful to the child.

More subtle, and even more difficult to diagnose, is *nonsupportive otitis media* or *otitis media with effusion* (OME). This condition often follows infectious otitis media, but it occurs without the infection. This means the child has a conductive loss but no signs of fever or pain. Some feel this is solely caused by the malfunctioning of the eustachian tube, others that it is related to allergies. Fluid may be draining into the middle ear from the mastoid and sinus, resulting in middle ear effusion (Hurst, 1998).

When this is frequent, it interferes with language and learning. "Children with hearing loss secondary to OME constitute the largest group of people with reversible learning disorders in the world" (Hurst, 1998, p. 1). There appears to be enough evidence to investigate the possibility of allergies as a cause and to look for learning differences.

Sensorineural Hearing Loss. A sensorineural hearing loss involves damage to either the inner ear, the nerve to the brain stem, or both. In this case, both the air conduction and the bone conduction tests are abnormal (see Figure 16.4), but the tympanogram is normal. Perceptive impairment, nerve loss, cochlear or neurosensory loss all refer to this type of hearing loss. The hearing loss may be congenital (present at birth) or occur due to illnesses such as mumps, rubella, and meningitis as well as ototoxic drugs, head trauma, or exposure to noise. Sensorineural losses cannot be treated medically or surgically at this time. Typically, a hearing aid is prescribed to make sounds louder. Even with amplification, however, sounds are unclear and distorted to the child. Children with severe sensorineural losses are usually identified in infancy. Losses in one ear, in only the high frequencies, or milder losses may not be detected until the early elementary years (Salvia & Ysseldyke, 1995).

A cochlear implant is a surgical procedure that allows some children who are profoundly deaf and do not profit from amplification to hear sounds they previously could not, such as the ring of a telephone and traffic noises. A cochlear implant is an inner ear prosthesis that restores gross hearing functions by electronically stimulating the nerve fibers in the ear. The implant enables children to speech-read more easily. A learning process is necessary, as the child needs to differentiate and identify sounds he or she hears (Steinberg & Knightly, 1997).

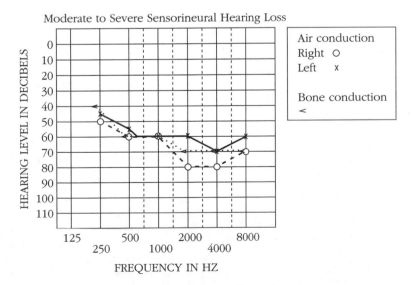

Figure 16.4

In a sensorineural loss, air conduction and bone conduction reflect the hearing loss.

Mixed Hearing Loss. In some cases, children can experience both a sensorineural and a conductive loss. In this case, the conductive problem is treated surgically and the sensorineural problem with a hearing aid. These combined situations are difficult to diagnose.

Central Auditory Hearing Loss. A central auditory hearing loss or central auditory processing dysfunction occurs when children have problems understanding speech when there are distracting noises around. They have additional problems related to short- and long-term auditory memory, auditory sequential memory, sounding out words, and reading comprehension (Salvia & Ysseldyke, 1995). These children are particularly difficult to identify because they pass all the traditional auditory screening tests. Testing is therefore complex, but there are standardized tests designed to identify these children.

Those in the medical field are interested in specifying what intensity of sound (loudness) a child can hear at what frequencies (pitch). Early childhood educators are more interested in practical considerations relative to how the child's hearing impairment will affect performance in the classroom and what modifications will need to be made.

Severity of Hearing Loss

Hearing impairments range from the inability to understand speech even with amplification to problems interpreting faint speech. The effects on the child vary according to not only the type of loss but the frequencies and severity of hearing loss as well. During early childhood years, the severity of hearing losses can be characterized as follows:

Normal limits: 0–25 dB

    No difficulty hearing faint speech

Mild hearing loss: 25–40 dB

    Difficulty with faint speech, no problem with normal speech

Moderate hearing loss: 40–55 dB

    Frequent difficulty with normal speech. Will have a more limited vocabulary than peers. If faced and spoken to within 3–5 feet, will probably understand. If in a large group and voices are faint, may miss as much as half of what is said.

Moderately severe hearing loss: 55–70 dB

    Frequent difficulty with loud speech. Will have a limited vocabulary and may have speech problems. Loud conversations, face-to-face, will probably be understood. Will have a great deal of trouble understanding large-group discussions.

Severe hearing loss: 70–90 dB

    Can understand only shouted or amplified speech. Will have little comprehensible speech. May hear loud voices at a distance of 1 foot from ear. May hear warning signals (alarms, sirens).

Profound hearing loss: 90 dB and greater

    Usually cannot understand even amplified speech. Will have very little if any comprehensible speech. Will be more aware of vibrations than of speech itself. Will rely on vision rather than hearing. (Bess & Humes, 1990)

Keep in mind that the two ears can have different amounts of loss and, typically, the child can function at the level of the better ear. If a child had a 55 dB loss in the right ear and an 80 dB loss in the left, she may function as a child with a moderately severe hearing loss, not a severe hearing loss.

Hearing Loss and Understanding Speech

Measuring a hearing loss and understanding the implications of that loss for understanding speech are different issues. Children with mild to moderate conductive losses hear approximately what you would hear with very tight-fitting ear plugs. It takes strain and much concentration to hear. Try it. Are you startled when people come up behind you quietly? Do you get tired with the effort and concentration it takes to hear? What might you do over the course of several days or months like this? Unless there were some good reasons for you to continue, you might tune it all out.

Children with more severe losses have an even more difficult problem. Although they may be able to hear some speech, they have trouble understanding it, even with hearing aids. They may be able to hear the low-frequency vowel sounds that carry the power of speech but miss the high-frequency consonant sounds that make speech intelligible. Consider the following sentence (Bryan & Bryan, 1979, p. 226):

"Let's go camping in a state park next August."

The child may hear:

"Le o amp n a ar ne Au u."

At the same time, the child may see by speech-reading:

"Let's o ampi in a state par ne t Au ust."

Even using a combination of hearing and vision, understanding is difficult. Try listening to a mistuned radio. You know they are speaking, but it is difficult to figure out what is being said. In classrooms where the teacher's voice is only about 5 to 10 dB louder than the general background noise in the classroom, children with hearing impairments have an extremely difficult time. Improving this ratio helps the child immensely. This can be done by having the teacher talk louder or modifying the classroom to make it quieter by adding carpet, drapes, and so on. Audiologists can provide information on how to improve this situation.

Prevalence of Hearing Impairments

Because of definitional problems, it is difficult to reach conclusions about prevalence. The prevalence rate varies according to the method of testing and the criteria used by the audiologist. Mild hearing losses in particular are not easily detected and, consequently, the child is not referred for testing. The same is true for children who have intermittent conductive losses.

Approximately 10 to 15 percent of preschool and school-age children do not pass the screening test. Most of these children have a transient conductive hearing loss (Steinberg & Knightly, 1997). The estimate is that only about 1.8 percent of children have a persistent hearing impairment (National Center for Health Statistics, 1995). Of those children who have persistent losses, most are mild (40 percent), with the remainder equally distributed among moderate, severe, and profound (Glorig & Roberts, 1977). Another estimate is that between 3 to 5 percent of school-age children have hearing needs severe enough to profit from individualized programming (Bryan & Bryan, 1979). However, the U.S. Department of Education (1989) reported only .12 percent of school-age children having hearing impairments.

Early Identification of Hearing Impairments

Children who are born with a hearing impairment or acquire one before they acquire speech are difficult to identify. Some will go unrecognized into adolescence. There are some signs that should alert you to suspect a hearing impairment (see Table 16.1).

0 to 3

Infants with hearing impairments make noises and babble like other babies up until about 6 months of age. At this point, the reflexive vocalizations diminish and are replaced by an auditory feedback loop. Vocalizations begin to show more variation, express intent, and become reciprocal. By 8 months, those with hearing losses babble less and their babbling is qualitatively different from infants who can hear.

Although they initially babble, children with hearing impairments do not respond to auditory stimuli out of their range of hearing. Parents may be concerned, but the problem is hard to pin down; just when parents think they should be concerned, the infant does something to make them think they are imagining things. Most parents don't want to appear overprotective and look foolish to their pediatricians. Additionally, many parents continually adjust to and

TABLE 16.1   RED FLAGS FOR HEARING IMPAIRMENTS

Speech

Speech and grammar that is delayed and immature

Speech that cannot be understood by nonfamily members beyond expected ages

Speech that is too loud or too soft for the situation

Language

Misunderstands directions or gives inappropriate answers to questions

Asks for information to be repeated or says "What?" a lot

Is hesitant in answering questions or joining conversations

Has difficulty with listening activities

Attention

Is unusually attentive to speaker's face

Short attention span, distractable

Disinterested in many activities, especially those that require listening

Health

Frequent colds, respiratory tract infections, or ear infections

Draining ears, breathing through the mouth

Poor balance, seems clumsy

match their child's emerging skills. As children respond to more visual communication efforts, parents automatically use more gesture and expression. This facilitates the child's language but makes the assessment process more difficult. Those who don't adjust their language may find it difficult to attach to a child who doesn't seem responsive.

In a survey of parents who had children with hearing impairments, Horton (1976) found that in 70

Children with mild or intermittent hearing impairments are difficult to identify at an early age. They have trouble paying attention during group time and may talk louder or softer than their peers.

It is important to know the amount of hearing loss a child has and the gain she gets from aids. Know how to help a child adjust to the hearings aids, if necessary, and then develop expectations to meet her auditory abilities.

percent of the cases, it was the parents who suspected the hearing impairment, and in only 7 percent was it the physician who first noted the problem. Parents who note the problem usually do so because the child does not reach traditional milestones in the area of speech and language. Unless there are other disabilities present, hearing loss itself does not interfere with the attainment of physical milestones such as walking and exploring the environment. One concern is that parents and educators may interpret as a behavior problem the child's unwillingness to verbally take turns, looking away when someone is talking, and not beginning to learn the rules that govern language.

Children who are identified as hearing impaired before language was established are considered prelingually hearing impaired. They have not yet established a language base. This makes it more challenging to learn spoken English. One major decision parents must make is how they are going to communicate with their child. This decision has major implications for the child, the family, and the educational system.

3 to 6

During the preschool years, children with hearing impairments will have delays in speech and language.

They may have developed unusual ways of attaining adult attention. As they can't hear adults, they must engage them physically or visually. Misbehavior is very effective in doing this. For the young child, this may be an attempt at communication. As adults, we rarely view it this way; these children may seem either extremely attentive or inattentive.

It is important that early childhood educators are alert to these signs. You may see the child more than the parents and have more information about how the child responds compared to other children. Alert parents if you are concerned.

6 to 9

As children reach elementary school age, almost all those with moderate to profound losses, sensorineural losses, and conductive losses should have been identified. As children become more dependent on oral communication, those with hearing impairments are at a disadvantage in standard English. Many children with profound hearing impairments have speech that is not or is barely intelligible. One of the outcomes of having speech that is difficult to understand is that children speak less frequently.

Amplification

The ears receive sound waves in the air and convert them into electrical signals the brain can understand. When the ear sends weak or distorted signals, hearing and understanding are impaired. Children, including infants, should be fitted for hearing aids as soon as a permanent loss is confirmed (Steinberg & Knightly, 1997).

Hearing aids have three major components: a microphone that changes sound waves into electrical energy, an amplifier (or amplifiers) that increases the intensity of the signal, and a receiver that converts the electrical signal back to an acoustical signal and projects this amplified sound through the earmold into the ear (Steinberg & Knightly, 1997). Hearing aids are battery powered and have volume controls. They are individually prescribed by audiologists based on the characteristics of the loss, the child's speech and language skills, intellectual ability, situations in which the child will listen, and school performance (Steinberg & Knightly, 1997). Hearing aids are purchased from commercial dealers.

There are four basic categories of hearing aids: behind-the-ear aids, in-the-ear aids, body aids, and bone conduction aids. Because of improvements in behind-the-ear aids, body aids are less frequently used with young children than in the past. Because these were worn on the chest, clothing acted as a baffle against receiving sound; there was the concern that young children would get them wet or fall on them in active play, and they are cosmetically less appealing. Because behind-the-ear aids are larger than in-the-ear aids, they can accommodate more circuitry and controls and allow more flexibility. This flexibility is particularly important when test data for young children are incomplete. The advantage of in-the-ear aids is primarily cosmetic (Steinberg & Knightly, 1997).

Children who have problems with constant drainage into the ear canal and those with long-term conductive losses use a bone conduction aid, which is a vibrator placed over the mastoid and is attached to a headband to keep it in place.

Assistive listening devices such as the FM system are used in combination with hearing aids. They are used in difficult listening situations such as classrooms to reduce the amount of background noise. Some newer amplification systems have an all-in-one hearing aid–FM combination (Steinberg & Knightly, 1997).

A hearing aid amplifies all sounds, not just speech. Because it does not correct distortion, it is not useful for all types of hearing impairments. Using the aids properly requires training. (The child must actually be taught how to listen; speech may be gobbledygook to a child who has never heard it.) Hearing aids are not like eyeglasses, which can correct vision to within normal limits; hearing aids do not correct hearing impairments.

Although a hearing aid is beneficial, that doesn't ensure that the child will willingly wear it. Parents and teachers are frequently frustrated by children who pull out their hearing aids. To young children especially, the aid may feel strange, and they will try to make themselves more comfortable by taking it out. If children were previously unaware of most sounds and speech, the hearing aid may be delivering what to them is meaningless noise. Again, their solution is to remove the aid. Once children see the advantages of hearing with the aid, they are usually willing to wear it; until then, however, encouragement is needed. Don't be in awe of the hearing aid, the parents, or the audiologist. Work out an agreement with the parents about what to do when a child takes off the hearing aid.

You need to develop some skills in working with a hearing aid. You should be able to do certain things younger children may not yet have mastered:

Put the earpiece back in when it falls out or is pulled out.

Check if batteries are dead and replace them. (Keep a supply in the child's locker or with the school nurse.)

Know how to manipulate the controls. When the hearing aid "whistles," ask the child to turn it down or, if necessary, turn it down yourself.

Hearing aids should not be abused, but they are sturdy enough to allow the child to participate in most activities. Try to keep them from getting painted, soaked, or sandy. Remember, hearing aids do not make a child hear perfectly. Be sure the other children understand this. Also, realize that a hearing aid works well for a radius of only 10 feet; even then, it amplifies sounds indiscriminately.

Communication

There are many options available to parents relative to the communication system they choose to use with their child. Their decision is based on many different variables, including the amount and frequency of the child's loss, whether there are other disabilities, what professional advice they have been given, what information they have sought, and their personal preferences. As educators working with children who have hearing impairments, we must understand the options available to parents; if they have not yet made a decision, help provide information about choices, give them information about how the child communicates in the classroom, and learn enough about the chosen communication system to interact with the child.

The *total communication approach* uses the auditory, visual, and tactile senses in combination to provide children with as much information as possible. The goal is communication and to achieve that using whatever combination of methods work. Practically, it relies on a system of spoken language and sign. The sender of the message, or speaker, verbalizes the message while simultaneously signing or finger-spelling the same message. This focus allows a child to speak to hearing persons and systematically

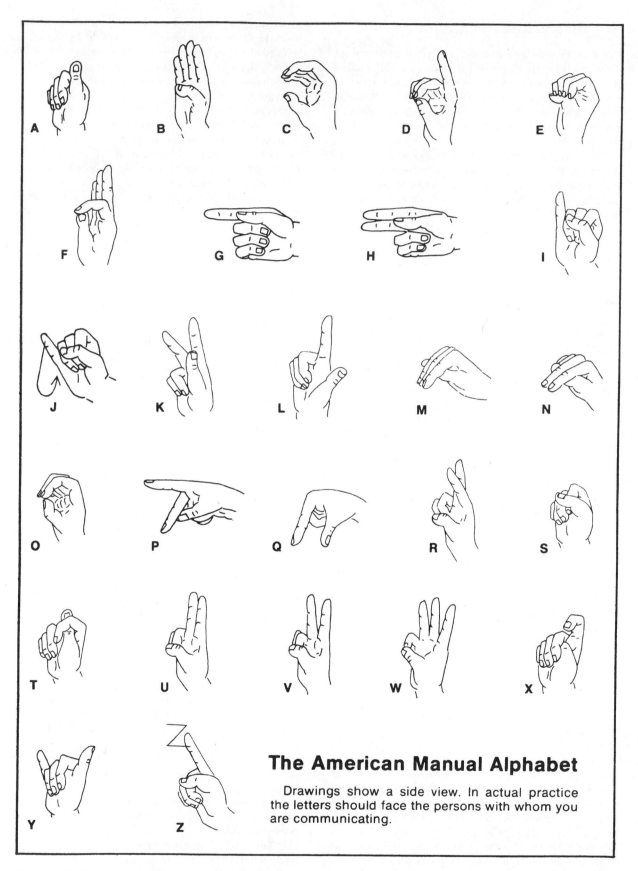

The American Manual Alphabet

Drawings show a side view. In actual practice the letters should face the persons with whom you are communicating.

Figure 16.5

sign to others who do not hear (Gregory, Bishop, & Sheldon, 1995).

American Sign Language (Ameslan or ASL) is a language with a distinct grammar structure that must be learned as one would learn any language. It consists of a set of standard hand signs used in relation to other parts of the body. Each sign represents an idea or concept. It uses finger-spelling for clarifying purposes and for new words that have no conventional signs. Finger-spelling uses 26 different finger configurations, one for each letter of the alphabet (see Figure 16.5 for an illustration of this alphabet). ASL is not a universal language. There is Japanese Sign Language (JSL), British Sign Language (BSL), French Sign Language (FSL), and so on. There is some evidence that children who learn sign language as a natural language during their early childhood years are at an advantage later socially and academically (Marschark, 1997). Many of these children are raised by families who use ASL as their first language.

The *oral approach* uses only spoken language (face-to-face communication), taking advantage of whatever residual hearing there is. Because signing is much easier than speech-reading or talking, the fear is that if children are allowed to sign, they will not develop these skills and hence will be able to communicate only with people who can sign and not the majority of society. Only about 30 percent of auditory information is gained from looking at the lips alone (Schwartz, 1996). Children have to find ways of filling in the missing cues based on their knowledge of the situation, past knowledge, and other cues they can extrapolate from the circumstances. Some children become competent speakers in the hearing world, others become frustrated, lost, and confused (Gregory et al., 1995). The early childhood years are difficult because children are not familiar with language per se and they have fewer experiences to draw from. The *auditory-verbal approach* (AV) is similar to the oral approach, but hearing is stressed. The approach is rigid and demanding. Sometimes, the speaker's mouth is covered so the child cannot depend on visual cues (Schwartz, 1996). Parents who chose this approach may also have chosen to use cochlear implants.

Some parents choose a sign system to communicate with their child. These sign systems are different from ASL in that they use English as the base and essentially are a manual representation of English rather than a language with its own grammar. Although often combined with spoken language, these systems favor signing and finger-spelling with less emphasis on speech-reading or talking than is advocated by total communication. There are a variety of different sign systems and they vary on how closely they are associated with English (Marschark, 1997). Signed English contains the signs from ASL but uses the grammatical structure of English. There are 14 markers that are added to words/signs to communicate the structure (Marschark, 1997). Pidgin Signed English is a mixture of ASL and signed English and is used frequently in the deaf communities. Seeing Essential English and Signing Exact English express

English literally, and it is the listener who must add meaning and context to what is signed (to sign "bird-bath" you would first sign "bird" and then sign "bath") (Marschark, 1997).

Some people feel that *cued speech* is a better system than signing. It can be used in conjunction with speaking and hearing to provide additional cues to what is being said. In this system, a hand motion depicts a particular sound and the speaker says the word as well as cuing it (the sound-related hand shapes help differentiate sounds that appear alike on the lips) (Marschark, 1997). As it is based on sounds in the English language, once those sounds are learned, any word can be cued.

Although you should be aware of the issues that parents face trying to make decisions related to communication, you will not have to take a side in the controversy, as you will teach the child in accordance with the parents' choice.

Guidelines

Some children with hearing impairments know how to speech-read and depend on it to understand communication. Others, with milder hearing impairments, may not have learned speech-reading but will still benefit from picking up cues and by watching lips. Regardless of the type of communication system the child is using, and whether or not there is an interpreter present, it is important that you as a teacher be expressive and congruent in your spoken and body language. Children with hearing impairments will watch you as a way of tuning into their environment.

1. Face the child, and whenever possible, bring yourself to the child's eye level. Sit in front of children when helping them, not beside them. Don't talk to children from another room, while looking in a closet, or while writing on the chalkboard. Don't walk around the room or pace back and forth when you talk.

2. Talk clearly and distinctly. Don't obscure your lips; wear lipstick; shave (or at least trim) a beard or mustache. If your hair is long, tie it back so that it doesn't fall in your face while you talk. Don't talk with your hand over your mouth or anything in your mouth. Don't shout.

3. Monitor light levels. See that there is enough light and that it is not shining in the eyes of the child.

Once you are certain the child can see your face, communication can begin.

1. Attract the child's attention. Before speaking, call the child's name and wait to make eye contact; otherwise, you will have to repeat your first few words.

2. Speak in a normal voice. It is impossible to speech-read when the mouth is distorted. Even

if you whisper loudly, the sounds and lips are distorted.

3. Use gestures. Aid the child's understanding of your speech by using appropriate body language.

4. Reduce background noise. Avoid extra background noise when carrying on a conversation or at activities. When this is not possible, realize that the child is likely to miss much of what you say. (Hearing aids pick up all noises, not just relevant ones.)

5. Repeat information. Some words are more difficult to speech-read than others. If you find different ways of saying something rather than merely repeating the sentences exactly, children will have a better chance of getting the information. It is important to repeat concepts; however, until concepts have been established, be consistent on word usage (cat, not kitty or kitten).

6. Write down key words and short sentences. Children need to develop an early knowledge that there is a relationship between what is said and what is written.

7. Choose activities that facilitate communication. Encourage children to play together based on a theme that sparks discussion.

8. Use imitation for teaching. Demonstrate how to do a specific skill and then have the child imitate what you did. Encourage the child to imitate speech.

9. Let the child take the lead. Observe children and see what interests them. Comment about what is important to the child, what the child wants or needs or is interested in. Watch and interpret the child's gaze, pointing, sounds, and gestures.

Similar principles are reflected in the use of audiovisual aids.

1. Use color codes and pictures. Use as many visual aids as possible as well as words (picture cards for daily routines, charts, and hand gestures).

2. Use closed-caption videos and films. (It is not relevant that the children are not yet reading; you want them to grow up knowing this is a possibility.) Remember also that children may miss much of what is said on TV, films, and videotapes, as the actors often turn their faces away from the camera.

3. Use an overhead projector instead of a chalkboard, if possible. Then you do not have to turn your back to the child.

4. Use filmstrips that do not require words. Try not to talk in the dark during a filmstrip or slide presentation (if the child can't hear you). If this is necessary, seat the child close enough to see you and try to use some spot illumination.

5. Support audio presentations with visual cues. Don't expect the child to react to a tape recorder, record, radio, or intercom just because

you turned the volume up. The child still may not understand.

During group activities, the following adaptations will help.

1. Seat these children where they have the best view of the teacher and class. This is in front of or across from you, not beside you and not facing a window. It is best to use a circle.

2. Call, sign, or cue children's names. During discussion, use signs or gestures so the child will know who is speaking next and can follow the conversation. If the children have hand signs for their names, sign the speaker's name; if the child is using cued speech, cue the speaker's name. When children raise their hands instead of calling out, it is easier for the child to identify who is speaking.

3. Call on the child if he is comfortable. Remember that children may be so intent on catching the main points of the discussion that they cannot think about the concepts at the same time. If you call on a child to participate, give the child extra time to think; don't demand an immediate answer.

4. Summarize and repeat points other children have made. Encourage the children to use gestures, signs, and cues when they talk to this child. Ask them to show the child what they want.

If the child knows how, signing, finger-spelling, and cuing are aids to communication, whether used individually or in groups.

1. Learn to sign, finger-spell, or cue depending on the system that the child's family has chosen.

2. Teach the other children some signs, especially the sign or cues for their name. Learn significant signs (drink, bathroom) and cues. Ask the help of the child and the parents or a teacher of the hearing impaired in making up signs or cuing each child's name. To help yourself, draw these on the back of your roll cards or whatever system you use.

3. If the child has an interpreter, look at the child when you speak and talk the way you would to any other child. Do not say to the interpreter "Ask him if . . ."

Finally, there are two points of caution. Remember that only about 30 percent of speech sounds are visible on the lips. The best speech-reader only gets about one word in four. Children with hearing impairments are great bluffers. They may not want to ask you to repeat; if you ask if they understand, they will often say yes when in fact they do not. Learn to recognize when a child is bluffing; when it is important, ask the child to demonstrate or repeat the instructions.

One of the greatest skills that children with hearing impairments need to learn is to fill in missing information (what they can't understand from words). Developing ideas about their world through generalization and differentiation is difficult for children with hearing impairments because they learn primarily from direct experience. If a child is shown an armchair labeled "chair," the child may not immediately make the generalization that a rocking chair also belongs in the "chair" class. Because of this, it is important that children with hearing impairments be given a large variety of visual stimuli to help them generalize to an abstract concept. For "chair," compare many different chairs. This is the type of thinking children need to do to fill in gaps.

Curriculum Adaptations

The severity of the hearing impairment will determine what, if any, curriculum adaptations need to be made. The less hearing the child has, the greater the reliance on visual and tactile channels of communication.

Social Awareness: Self-Esteem, Inclusion, Social Studies, Health and Safety

All children need to be part of the group. They need to realize they can support each other in many ways. Given information, young children can be incredibly adept at helping each other. Be sure that the child with the hearing impairment is not always receiving the help, but giving it as well. Children with hearing impairments profit from firsthand experiences, followed in the classroom by visual aids to clarify and generalize these experiences. Children may need to be taught nonverbal ways of approaching other children, and others must be made aware that that is what is happening. At an early age, they need to have signs and words that are descriptive of feelings and body parts. Safety procedures must be emphasized. Children must learn to recognize and respond quickly to visual signals of danger. They must be taught visual cues if they cannot hear the warning sounds of a car horn, fire alarm, or a shout.

Self-Esteem. Children need to increase their awareness of themselves as individuals and as part of a group. Previous unsuccessful experiences in interacting with children and adults may cause children to withdraw or to avoid participating with others. Because they are often not aware of the tone of the events taking place, they may have an inappropriate facial expression. When possible, they watch for cues and are often followers, not leaders. In general, these children have usually had more negative experiences, both medical and personal, compared to other children their age. They need to learn to view themselves positively and to develop skills in dealing with others, especially when others are being unkind.

1. Give careful thought to talking about any child's diverse abilities. Talk with the child's parents and the child about how they want this handled. Our choice is, after several days of school, to introduce the concept of similarities and differences. (Children conjure up fantastic ideas about what a child with a hearing impairment will look like. Sometimes, they expect the child to have no ears!) Plan a group-time game emphasizing similarities and differences. For example:

   "Will all the children with hair stand up?"

   "Will all the children with brown hair stand up?"

   "Will all the children with hearing aids stand up?"

   "Will all the children with green eyes stand up?"

   In the process, emphasize that all of the children have hair, some have brown hair, one has a hearing aid, and one has green eyes. Be nonchalant. Answer children's questions directly and honestly.

2. Because of difficulty in communicating with the outside world, children with hearing impairments may have developed self-feedback systems (such as teeth grinding, mouth breathing, masturbation). Such actions result from their need to receive information from other senses. Teach them body awareness and engage them in sensory activities that provide tactile feedback.

3. If a child has an interpreter, be sure that you and all the children talk to the child, not the interpreter.

4. Encourage children to share their style of communication with others. Talk about circumstances where signing or being able to speech-read is preferable to speaking (in a noisy place, if you want to keep something a secret, etc.).

Inclusion. Children with hearing impairments may not reach out to others and may feel rejected. When they do reach out, their approach may be physical and inappropriately vigorous. Help the children develop the skills to approach others and give them cues for roles that they might play. Children need to learn skills for including others as well as skills for approaching others. They need to know that no matter who they are, these skills do not mean that they will be accepted into the group each time they ask. Including children with diverse abilities takes a type of planning you may not have done before.

1. Play games where you whisper or talk to children so softly they have difficulty hearing you; talk about how it feels.

2. Have children wear earmuffs when they play together. Keep them on long enough for children to feel the limitations, not just until the novelty wears off.

3. Discuss differences in families, races, and abilities.

4. Ask all children to talk about things that are difficult for them and what they would like others to do to help.

5. Help children understand how they might feel and behave if they could see people talking but not understand what they were saying. Have them decide what to do to include a child who might feel like this.

6. If children ask questions, answer them simply and honestly. Encourage the child with the hearing impairment to help answer the question, if possible.

> "What's wrong with John?" "There's nothing wrong with John. He can't hear as well as others." "Why does he wear that box?" "To help him hear better." "Does he sleep with it?" "No." "If I play with him, can I catch that?" "No, it isn't like a cold or chicken pox. John was born that way" (or however the impairment occurred). "Can I have a box, too?" "No, ear doctors decide who needs these boxes, just as eye doctors decide who needs glasses. We'll have a box in class someday that you can try out." "I don't like it when John hits me." "I can understand that. John is telling you in his way that he wants to play with you. What could he do that would be better for you?" "Can't he talk?" "He can only say a few words. It is hard to learn to talk when you can't hear other people talk." "I hate John." "Today, that is true for you. Someday, you might like him."

You might also give the children hints on how to communicate: "Be sure John is looking at you when you talk to him." "Can you show him what you want?" "What can he do that doesn't require talking?" "What kind of game do you think John would like?"

Social Studies. The child with a hearing impairment has to learn the skills to cope with a hearing world.

1. Teach children to generalize by using illustrations of diverse families (those with single parents, working mothers, grandparent in the home, and so on).

2. Emphasize firsthand experiences but use follow-up activities as well. Take your class to a police station. Later, read stories about police and use police props in dramatic play; have a police officer visit.

3. Prepare children with hearing impairments for social situations they may encounter. Help all children learn to use social cues to decide how to act.

4. Use family celebrations and holidays to talk about similarities and differences.

5. Making maps is an excellent way to familiarize children with a new situation. Start with maps of known places (the classroom, the play yard) before you branch out into less familiar places.

Health and Safety. Because children with hearing impairments may miss some warning signals, their safety is jeopardized more often than others. Additionally, they may have fewer skills to deal with dangerous situations.

1. Use traffic warning signals outside with the tricycles, wagons, and so on. Teach the meaning of traffic lights (play Red Light–Green Light).

2. Practice crossing streets.

3. Discuss what to do if a child is lost or hurt, then dramatize the emergency (using dialogue) or pantomime it.

4. Use snack or lunchtime to instill good eating habits, and toileting to teach good hygiene.

5. Familiarize the child with the procedure for fire alarms. Incorporate a visual cue (flickering lights or a red flag) into your usual procedure. Keep this child in sight during a fire alarm to ensure the child neither wanders off nor misses later instructions. With older children, use a buddy system as well.

Language and Literacy: Speaking, Listening, Reading, and Writing

Children with hearing impairments often have limited or impaired speech. They often run words together and have a voice quality that is a flat, high-pitched monotone. When they speak, the volume may be inappropriate. They may use gestures to express themselves. Encourage children to speak in small informal groups first, where they feel safe. Be sure to reward their speaking even if it is labored and difficult to understand. Children need support to practice talking; encourage them to attempt this even if their speech is not always understandable. Because they are more dependent on environmental cues than others, they need to fine-tune their ability to use contextual information. They need many hands-on experiences. Children need to use any residual hearing that is available to them. Pair listening with visual or kinesthetic cues. When possible, help the child refine the auditory skills available. Because reading and writing are not as dependent on auditory skills as speaking, children may initially feel more comfortable in these language areas. Language and literacy are difficult areas for children with impaired hearing and require the most adaptation. Nevertheless, language is an area that is extremely important.

Speaking. Help children develop experiential concepts by associating objects with words, the written word with the spoken one. Understanding and talking about abstractions is extremely difficult for people with hearing impairments.

1. Give children enough time to talk without feeling rushed.

2. Always respond to a child's communication. If you understand, reply; if not, try to have the child tell you in a different way or show you.

3. To teach concepts, use materials that interest the child. If you are teaching number concepts to a football fan, you can put the numbers on checkers, set up a checkerboard as a football field with the checkers as players, and then call the plays: "Give the ball to number 3 and have him run around number 5 and then between 1 and 7." The child scores only if she follows the correct pattern. If the child cannot hear or speech-read, use your fingers or cards to show the plays.

4. Use the concrete to demonstrate the abstract. Use conceptual matching cards in Lotto: shoe-slipper, clock-watch, lamp-flashlight, shirt-blouse, jacket-coat.

5. Point out objects in the room that are used in the same way but look different: crayons versus paint, short versus long brushes.

6. Show visual analogies.

7. Have children classify and reclassify objects in different ways. Using small and large shapes, some of which are black and the others white, ask the child to sort them into two piles; when the task is complete, ask the child to sort another way.

8. Teach situationally and describe verbally what is happening at that moment: "I'm sitting in front of you."

Fingerplays are excellent, as all children can participate and the "choral" aspect of fingerplays may reduce their self-consciousness about speaking. This is an excellent way to teach visual memory and sequencing.

1. Choose short, simple fingerplays at first.

2. Demonstrate the actions as you sing or say the words.

3. Encourage the children to imitate you; move slowly so the children can keep up.

Listening. Children with hearing impairments need to develop good listening skills and to use their residual hearing. They may listen with their head tilted, to favor the stronger ear. They may have difficulty understanding the speech of others, especially when in groups, when the speaker is far away, or when the speaker is looking in another direction. Be sure auditory information is presented clearly and loudly enough so that children can hear it. The sequence of developing listening skills is the same for

all children. Children with hearing impairments may need you to help more in matching their skill level. Initially, children need to become aware of sound. They need to pay attention to sound and find its source. Then they need to make gross discrimination among sounds followed by finer ones. Finally, they have to attach meaning to sound. Children who can hear usually go through these stages within the first year of life. Children with hearing impairments may still be learning to distinguish sounds and attaching meaning to them during the preschool years.

1. Help children learn to check during the day that the volume of their hearing aid is at an appropriate level. Active play can change the volume or move the on-off switch.

2. Point out sounds to children when they might hear the sound and can have a visual association: "See the airplane. It went vooooooom."

3. Emphasize the basic vocabulary words in each curriculum area. Post the words where they can be seen or hang them on a string from the ceiling so that all educators use the same vocabulary. If you have a doctor's office, create labels of important words, backing the labels with pictures, as in Figure 16.6 (avoid stereotyping by using several pictures).

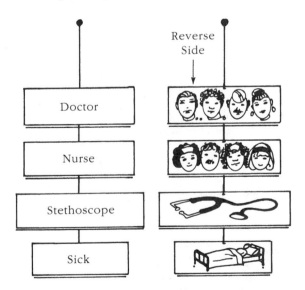

4. Use as many visual aids and gestures as possible to help the child understand.

Stories can expand the child's world. Start with stories about familiar events and descriptive pictures before using more creative ones.

1. Choose books that depict familiar sights and actions.

2. Use illustrations that are simple, large, and uncluttered.

3. Provide the child with auditory cues and visual aids when reading. For example, when reading

"The Three Little Pigs," squeal, change rhythm, and huff and puff. You might even bring in straw, wood, and bricks and let the children huff and puff at them at the science table.

4. Use flannel board stories, as these usually have simple, graphic plots.

5. Have the children act out simple stories.

6. Allow the child with a hearing impairment to preview the story.

7. Place picture books with a clear, sequential story line in the book corner. Include some books without words.

8. Avoid using chalkboard stories. If you draw on the overhead projector, the child will have an unobstructed view of your face.

9. Choose books with realistic, not abstract illustrations when teaching language arts. Abstract illustrations are more appropriate for the visual arts.

Reading. Early reading literacy skills include habitually looking at words and letters from left to right, making fine visual discriminations, and recognizing a sense of pattern (letters vs. spaces). Children with hearing impairments need to replace some of the auditory skills they lack with visual skills. Speech-reading also depends on fine visual discrimination bolstered by visual closure, upon which reading literacy is based. Interpreting signs and finger-spelling is both a visual task and a reading literacy skill. Plan numerous activities that require fine visual discrimination. Introduce variety into activities by using three-dimensional objects, pictures, line drawings, and even people.

1. Demonstrate left to right progression. For example, point a marker or your finger at the left side before starting and move it to the right as you read.

2. When writing stories of the children's experiences, draw or paste in pictures illustrating significant words, as in Figure 16.7.

3. Use activities that require perceptual (visual matching) skills, such as Lotto, bingo, and puzzles.

4. Label everything in the classroom (tables, chairs, lockers, crayons, paints, easel).

5. Emphasize activities that require fine visual discrimination (alphabet-matching Lotto or a Lotto

game using the American Manual Alphabet) because this skill is needed for reading.

6. Play concentration using the American Manual Alphabet.

Writing. Give children a wide variety of writing tools and paper to work with. Children need to explore the media and develop the connection between the written and spoken word before writing will be meaningful. Because children with hearing impairments may be more dependent on writing for communication, it is important that they have a positive view of writing from the beginning.

1. Add stickers to the writing center as well as pictures that can be cut and pasted.

2. Encourage children to use creative spelling in their writing. Support all attempts at writing and illustrating. Emphasize the meaning of writing, until children become fluent writers. Accept the children's creative spelling. It is extremely difficult for children who cannot hear accurately to spell accurately.

Discovery: Mathematics, Science, and Computers

Children need to develop the skills of inquiry, problem solving, and cause-effect reasoning. Children with hearing impairments can learn about the parts of the body concerned with hearing and speech. Children can explore how a hearing aid works by using microphones and by playing with the balance on a stereo and the volume on tape and record players. Because computers are primarily dependent on small motor and visual skills, they are an asset to the child with a hearing impairment. The abstractions in math and science are more logical and data-based than in language and literacy.

Mathematics. Math goals for children with hearing impairments are the same as they are for all children: The initial focus is to develop a concrete base of fundamental math concepts to prepare for abstract concepts that will come later.

1. Use three-dimensional materials (cubes, balls) before progressing to two-dimensional (squares, circles) ones.

2. Develop the language skills that serve as the foundation for math, such as understanding relationships (equal/more/less).

3. Use naturally occurring situations to teach math. Cooking, sand play, and water play provide many opportunities for learning math concepts.

4. Measure with different instruments (ruler, metal tape, cloth tape). Compare relative amounts, using both conventional and nonconventional measures.

Science. Few other curriculum areas have the potential for discovery, satisfaction, and interaction with materials that science has. Provide children with hearing impairments with the right materials and offer well-timed visual hints, in addition to asking questions as you normally would.

1. Help the child generalize by providing abundant materials.

2. Allow plenty of time to process hypotheses and conclusions.

3. Help the child understand that things can exist in more than one state. Compare corn on the cob, frozen corn, canned corn, creamed corn, and popped and unpopped corn.

4. Use visual demonstrations.

5. Have the child go through the action when there are directions to be followed.

6. Use a variety of media. For example, to teach about plants, visit a farm, nursery, or plant store; plant seeds, varying the water, light, and soil; look at books on plants; show a filmstrip on how plants grow; invite a florist to speak to the class.

7. Use regularly occurring natural events like seasonal changes and weather to teach a sense of predictability in the world.

8. Use items made of different materials, such as wood, cardboard, and Styrofoam, to broaden the child's understanding of the concept of matter.

Computers. Computers are very usable for children with hearing impairments. Both input and output are visual and require no hearing. Computers can be used as an interactive teaching tool. They are likely to play an important part in the lives of children with hearing impairments. Computers may be their way of communicating with the world if their speech is difficult to understand.

1. A child can learn cause and effect reasoning easily on a computer: Press a key and the computer does something—instantly. A different key causes something else to happen.

2. Encourage children to use computers. This may be one area where they can work with another child and not be at a disadvantage. The words may be so obvious that they are understood regardless of the quality of articulation.

3. With the help of a modem, the vast resources of the Internet are available to members of the community with computers. Sophisticated computer use may seem a long way in the future for a young child with a hearing impairment, but the computer skills and attitudes learned now will serve that child for a lifetime.

Developmental Physical Education and Sensorimotor Skills: Large Motor, Small Motor, and Sensorimotor Integration

Sensorimotor activities help children learn skills to become more physically fit, be more aware of where their body is in space, and fine-tune the small motor skills that support literacy. Children with hearing impairments may be challenged in this area, as the sense of balance is located in the inner ear and may be part of their impairment. They also have had fewer opportunities to integrate auditory input with motor skills. Children benefit from extra help with activities that focus on body awareness and balancing. Noncompetitive games that require starting, stopping, and turning are good.

Large Motor. There are relatively few restrictions placed on children with hearing impairments when large motor activities are taking place. If there is damage to the semicircular canals, the child may have problems with dizziness, with obvious implications. High climbing should be discouraged (falling on a hearing aid hurts). Rough tumbling may also cause damage. Remember, too, that the child's difficulty in hearing verbal instructions poses some safety concerns. An adult should have an unobstructed view of the child when outside, and you should stay fairly near the child if he is in a relatively dangerous area (near the swings, seesaw, blocks).

1. Choose activities that help develop the child's sense of balance, both dynamic and static.

2. Choose activities that require stopping, starting, and changing directions. (Inability to do these without losing balance is related to the inner ear.)

3. Use activities such as obstacle courses to teach language skills (crawl *through* the tunnel, jump *over* the bar, run *around* the pole).

4. Help the child perfect the skills of crawling, rolling, running, leaping, jumping, skipping, and so on.

5. Have the children imitate animal walks (with pictures as cues) to help them identify different styles of walking.

6. Help the child use large motor skills to safely relieve pent-up energy and frustration.

7. Use props to help children realize the intent of the group if it appears a change of plans has been missed by the child.

Small Motor. Children with hearing impairments interact with the world primarily through vision, touch, smell, and the integration of these senses. Help them develop good fine motor control in conjunction with vision.

Because the vestibular sense (balance) is located in the inner ear, children need practice accommodating to changes in direction or speed of motion. Avoid quick stops and turns to prevent falls.

1. Use activities that require both visual and fine motor skills (puzzles, assorted nuts and bolts to put together, woodworking, bead stringing).

2. Use activities requiring only the sense of touch, such as sorting graded sandpaper or playing with a feeling box.

3. Provide choices among activities to give the child with a hearing impairment opportunities to make discoveries on her own.

4. Use tweezers or tongs to sort cotton balls, blocks, wooden beads, or small toys.

Sensorimotor Integration. Characteristically, when children with hearing impairments explore the environment, they rely more on vision and touch than do their peers. Their visual and tactile skills need to be refined and integrated so that they can gain as much information from the environment as possible.

1. Provide a variety of unusual activities that help in processing movement information in the brain (skating, sliding, walking on different surfaces and angles).

2. Add a ball to activities to help focus concentration, such as having children kick a ball to each

other in a circle game or while doing a crab walk.

3. Have children do various balancing activities with a beanbag.

4. Provide opportunities for the hands to practice working together, such as cutting with scissors (one hand holds, the other cuts), mixing activities, using an egg beater, and so on.

Creative Arts: Visual Arts, Music, Creative Movement, and Dramatic Play

Because the emphasis in creative arts is creativity, children with hearing impairments are not at a disadvantage. Use pictures and realistic props to set the mood. Children with hearing impairments can refine visual skills while playing beside other children in a way that supports yet does not demand high-level language skills. They can learn by watching what others do and seeing what they make while still choosing and using materials in their own way. Music is primarily an auditory experience. For children with hearing impairments, depending on the degree of loss, music activities must be adapted to include experiences that will be meaningful to them and allow them to participate. Include visual cues so the children can clap the rhythm, stamp their feet, and so on. Include hand motions or signs along with your songs so that these children will be able to be involved as well. Use a guitar or auto harp so the children can see the hand movements, or arrange the piano so the child has a good view of your hands. Use creative movement activities that allow children to

If parents decide to use a form of signing as a method of communication, teachers need to learn important signs to communicate with children.

experience rhythm. Have another child or adult mirror-dance with them. Creative movement is an excellent opportunity for children to experiment with movement. Make music and movement a release for emotions, not an emotionally frustrating experience. Help children act out situations they are likely to encounter. Use as many props as you can, and keep them realistic. Help children learn what to do in a given situation through dramatic play. Use accessories to set the mood.

Visual Arts. Art needs few adaptations for children with hearing impairments. Use discussions about art to provide opportunities for language input.

1. Help children with hearing impairments learn to use art as an emotional release. It is an additional outlet that is especially useful in bad weather, when large motor activities are restricted.

2. Have three-dimensional art materials available.

3. The child may tend to overgeneralize as a result of limited experience. Provide time for children to learn the qualities of materials (paint vs. paste) through trial and error as well as from your demonstrations and watching peers.

4. Give clear, simple instructions.

Music. Accompanied by visual cues, music can be a positive experience. Don't eliminate these children from the group because they can't sing.

1. Use percussion instruments (children can feel vibrations and see the beat).

2. Take the front covering off the piano so the children can see how and when the piano hammers strike.

3. Choose songs that incorporate motion so the child can participate in the movement if not in the singing.

4. Show pictures to set the mood for songs and creative movement. If you want the children to pretend they are walking through leaves, use a fall picture with leaves; if they are to be flowers growing, show both buds and flowers in full bloom.

5. Use the piano with a child who has a mild hearing impairment to teach the concepts of high/low, fast/slow, and other types of auditory discrimination. For a child with a moderate to severe impairment, use a more visual method—drums or clapping.

6. When you sing, use your hand to show when the song goes up or down in pitch.

7. Learn to sign some favorite songs. The class may find this more challenging and fun than some fingerplays.

Creative Movement. Keep the focus on the process. If you are trying to convey a mood, use visual props.

1. If children are taking turns, don't call on a child with a hearing impairment first. As other children move, point out the features of the movement that help set the mood.

2. Place the child to best see how others move.

3. Use mirror movement and allow the child to be the mirror first if there is a mood. If there is just movement, be sure the child has equal opportunities to lead.

4. Use rhythmic dance and free dance.

Dramatic Play. Through dramatic play, children with hearing impairments can express feelings and concerns. They can also try out roles (mother, father, teacher, audiologist) without fear of being judged. Dramatic play provides some of the experiences necessary for developing a strong experiential language base.

1. Include a traditional home living area in your classroom initially. (This fosters some sense of security for all children at the beginning of the year.)

2. Use the dramatic play area to expand the children's environment as well as play out situations that are familiar in their life.

3. Provide play props appropriate to the activities.

Transitions

Transition periods are not particularly fun for any child. They can be especially difficult for a child with a hearing impairment, who may not have grasped the verbal directions or the other children's intentions.

1. Be sure children know the daily sequence. Use a picture poster and point to what will happen next.

2. Keep your schedule fairly standard once it is set. Knowing that some things are predictable gives the child with a hearing impairment a sense of security.

3. Use visual signs to announce upcoming changes (one light blink for a five-minute warning, two blinks for cleanup time).

4. Post any rules, adding illustrations and the word "NO" or an *X* through the picture. Also, post pictures of some of the things the child is allowed to do. Visual reminders of how to carry scissors and put paint away will be helpful to the entire class.

5. Demonstrate what is going to happen (start picking up, get your coat, and so on).

Summary

Sound travels in waves that have both frequency and intensity. It is the interpretation of these sound waves that keeps us in touch with the environment and allows communication with others. The auditory system, consisting of the outer, middle, and inner ear, as well as the auditory nerve and auditory cortex, interprets these sound waves.

Because of impairments in the auditory system, some children don't hear sounds as well as others. In early childhood, children are screened annually to determine whether or not they have a hearing impairment. Children who do not pass the screening are given follow-up threshold testing to determine if there is a temporary or permanent impairment, or if the test itself was in error.

There are different types of hearing impairments. A conductive hearing impairment relates to the inability of the outer and middle ear to conduct sound to the inner ear. In young children, fluid in the middle ear is the most frequent cause of a conductive impairment, and drug therapy and surgery are used to remediate this situation. Sensorineural losses are permanent and are the result of an impairment in the inner ear or the auditory nerve. Mixed hearing impairments involve both conductive and sensorineural losses. The conductive part of the loss can be remedied; the sensorineural part cannot.

In addition to interfering with the ability to hear, a hearing loss impacts speaking and the understanding of speech. Parents must make a decision about how their child will communicate; some choose total communication, which involves both verbalizing and using sign language, others use sign alone or only just speaking, and some choose cued speech.

Some curriculum areas such as language and literacy may require many modifications, whereas other areas that are dependent on vision and tactile input and feedback need few.

Educational Resources

The Alexander Graham Bell Association for the Deaf
3417 Volta Place, NW
Washington, DC 20007-2778
(800) 432-7543
Sponsors conferences and workshops and publishes many materials for parents and teachers. They have a special section for parents of children with hearing impairments. Publishes Volta Review.

American Society for Deaf Children (ASDC)
2848 Arden Way, Suite 210
Sacramento, CA 95825-1373
(800) 942-2732
Publishes information on the impact of a hearing impairment on children. Provides resource materials, holds a biennial meeting, and publishes a quarterly newsletter, Endeavor.

American Speech-Language-Hearing Association
10801 Rockville Pike
Rockville, MD 20852
(800) 638-TALK
Provides information as well as posters, buttons, and suggested activities.

American Tinnitus Association
PO Box 5
Portland, OR 97207
(503) 248-9985
Disseminates information about tinnitus; provides referrals; supports research; sponsors workshops for testing and evaluating.

Canadian Hard of Hearing Association
2435 Holly Lane, Suite 205
Ottawa Ontario K1V7P2 Canada
(800) 263-8068 (Canada only), (613) 526-1584,
    FAX (613) 526-4718
A national consumer advocacy group with branches across Canada that offer self-help and educational meetings.

Canadian Hearing Society
271 Spadina Road, Room 311
Toronto, Ontario M5R 2V3 Canada
(416) 964-9595, FAX (416) 964-2066
An advocacy group that provides direct services including screening, counseling, hearing aids, technical devices, and information. They have regional offices throughout Canada.

Ear Research Institute
256 S. Lake Street
Los Angeles, CA 91345
Develops conceptual and technically feasible approaches to resolving hearing and balance disorders through applied research. Conducts research; offers seminars; maintains a library.

Fanlight Productions
47 Halifax Street
Boston, MA 02130
(800) 937-4113, (617) 542-0980, FAX (617) 542-8838
Offers videotape, Interpretations, *on relationship between an elementary-age child with a hearing impairment and her interpreter and her family and friends.*

Gallaudet Bookstore
Kendall Green
PO Box 103
Washington, DC 20002
(202) 651-5380
Has catalogue of curriculum materials designed for students with hearing impairments.

Gallaudet Research Institute (GRI)
(202) 651-5400
http://www.gallaudet.edu/-teallen/kjcole/gri.html
    Conducts research on hearing impairments.

Gallaudet University
800 Florida Avenue, NE
Washington, DC 20002
(202) 651-5000, http://www.gallaudet.edu
Offers special programs for children with hearing impairments, distributes materials, and consults with schools throughout the country.

International Foundation for Children's Hearing
    Education and Research
871 McLean Avenue
Yonkers, NY 10704

Parents and professionals concerned with public awareness of hearing impairments. Supports research; seeks to improve educational facilities for children with hearing impairments.

The John Tracy Clinic
806 W. Adam Avenue
Los Angeles, CA 90007
    Specializes in stimulation programs for infants who are hearing impaired.

Joyce/Ideal
Ideal School Supply Company
11000 South Laverne Avenue
Oak Lawn, IL 60453
    Toys that are adapted to children with hearing impairments.

National Foundation for Children's Hearing
    Education and Research
928 McLean Avenue
Yonkers, NY 10704
(914) 237-2676
    Focuses on public awareness and improving educational facilities within the United States.

National Information Center on Deafness (NICD)
(202) 651-5051, FAX (202) 651-5054
http://www.gallaudet.edu
e-mail: nicd@gallau.gallaudet.edu.

    Located at Gallaudet. This page includes a directory of organizations and a list of publications and prices.

Sign Language Store
8753 Shirley Avenue
PO Box 4440
Northridge, CA 91328
    Has materials on and in sign language.

South Carolina ETV Marketing
Box 11000
Columbia, SC 29211
(800) 553-7752, (803) 737-3441, FAX (803) 737-3503
    Sign language instruction on videotape.

References

American Speech-Language-Hearing Association. (1990). Guidelines for audiometric symbols. *ASHA, 32*(Suppl. 2), 25–30.

Batshaw, M. L., & Perret, Y. M. (1992). *Children with disabilities: A medical primer* (3rd ed.). Baltimore: Brookes.

Bess, F. H., & Humes, L. E. (1990). *Audiology: The fundamentals.* Baltimore: Williams & Wilkins.

Bryan, J. H., & Bryan, T. H. (1979). *Exceptional children.* Sherman Oaks, CA: Alfred.

Denk-Glass, R., Laber, S., & Brewer, K. (1982). Middle ear disease in young children. *Young Children, 37*(6), 51–53.

Freil-Patti, S., & Finitzo, T. (1990). Language learning in a prospective study of otitis media with effusion in the first two years of life. *Journal of Speech and Hearing Research, 33,* 188–194.

Glorig, A., & Roberts, J. (1977). *Hearing levels of adults by age and sex* (Series II, No. 11. U.S. Vital Statistics). Bethesda, MD: National Center for Health Statistics.

Gregory, S., Bishop, J., & Sheldon, L. (1995). *Deaf young people and their families.* New York: Cambridge University Press.

Hallahan, D., & Kauffman, J. (1994). *Exceptional children: Introduction to special education* (6th ed.). Englewood Cliffs, NJ: Prentice Hall.

Horton, K. B. (1976). Early intervention for hearing impaired infants and young children. In T. D. Tjossem (Ed.), *Intervention strategies for high risk infants and young children* (pp. 371–380). Baltimore: University Park Press.

Hurst, D. S. (1998). *Complications.* http://home.earthlink.net/~meear/Complications.html.

Marschark, M. (1997). *Raising and educating a deaf child.* New York: Oxford University Press.

National Center for Health Statistics. (CD-ROM) (1995). Hyattsville, MO: U.S. Department of Health and Human Services, Public Health Services, Centers for Disease Control, and National Center for Health Statistics.

Ralabate, P. (1987). What teachers should know about middle ear dysfunction. *NEA Today,* 10.

Salvia, J., & Ysseldyke, J. E. (1995). *Assessment* (6th ed.). Boston: Houghton Mifflin.

Schwartz, S. (Ed.). (1996). *Choices in deafness: A parent's guide to communication options* (2nd ed.). Bethesda, MD: Woodbine House.

Steinberg, A. G., & Knightly, C. A. (1997). Hearing: Sounds and silences. In M. L. Batshaw (Ed.), *Children with disabilities* (4th ed., pp. 241–274). Baltimore: Brookes.

U.S. Department of Education. (1989). *Eleventh annual report to Congress on the implementation of the education of the handicapped act.* Washington, DC: U.S. Government Printing Office.

Chapter 17

CHILDREN WITH VISUAL IMPAIRMENTS

One of my memories of being in first grade is of Charles, whose mother once asked our teacher whether or not we teased him about his patch. The teacher's startled response was, "What patch?" Charles went out of the house each morning with a patch over his left eye, put it in his pocket, and arrived at school without it. He put it back on before he got home. I don't know if we would have teased him had he worn it, but the fear of being teased or different made him avoid the possibility. It is a very powerful concern that causes a 6-year-old to do that kind of planning and remembering.

Vision helps us interpret the world around us. We form visual images of ourselves and others. Vision motivates us to reach out and touch objects, to climb a hill for the view, and to return a friendly smile. Children whose vision is impaired need to connect with their world using all of their senses.

Including children with visual impairments in your class involves teaching children who wear eyeglasses, lenses, or corrective patches, helping to identify children whose visual impairments have not yet been diagnosed, and adapting your programming for children who have noncorrectable visual problems.

You probably will have a number of questions about children with visual impairments. First, of course, you want to find out from the parents how much functional vision a child has. On a practical note, you want to know if the child can participate in everyday classroom activities you currently have or the types of adaptations that will allow the child to be included. You might have questions about the arrangement of your room and safety concerns about how to best protect the child from injuries. Your role as an educator is to help children use the vision they have and the vision aids they need while being included in the activities of your classroom.

Classification of Visual Impairments

Visual impairments are classified in a variety of ways. They can be labeled according to the legal, medical, or educational implications of the impairment. The legal and medical definitions typically emphasize the acuity of the visual ability, or how clearly the child can see. The educational definition emphasizes the extent to which the child can use visual ability to read printed material for learning (Peterson, 1987).

Vision may be limited in three ways: visual acuity, the field of vision, or color vision. *Visual acuity* is the resolving power of the eye, the sharpness or clarity of the image viewed. We usually measure this by having children identify or match letters or pictures in various sizes while standing a standard distance from the chart; that distance is 20 feet (6.1 meters). A person who can see at 20 feet what most people see at 20 feet has normal or 20/20 vision. For children below third grade, vision of 20/40 or better in each eye or vision of 20/30 or better when using both eyes is considered normal. That is, the young child sees (with one eye) at 20 feet what an adult would see at 40 feet or with both eyes at 30 feet.

A child's *field of vision* can be restricted by lack of peripheral vision. The child may have normal central visual acuity but reduced peripheral vision. This is often called *tunnel vision*. Or the field of vision may be restricted by a scotoma, or blind or dark spot. This dark spot can be of various sizes and be anywhere in the field of vision. If it is in the middle of the eye, the child's central vision will be impaired.

Color vision involves the ability to discriminate three qualities of color: hue, saturation, and brightness. The difference between those with normal color vision and those without normal color vision is that some of the hues that appear different to a person with normal color vision appear similar to those without. *Achromatopsia, color deficient,* or *color blindness* refers to this condition. The term color deficient is technically correct and preferable to use because young children are often frightened by the use of the term color blindness. The total inability to see color is very rare. The most frequent problem is distinguishing between specific colors, usually red and green. For most people, it is possible to distinguish these colors when the object is large (like a car), but they have trouble with smaller items and when the colors are part of a pattern such as a plaid. Children who have color deficient vision rarely know it. As a teacher, you may suspect it when children have difficulty identifying one or more of the primary colors. Color deficiency is an inherited X-linked trait. It affects 8 percent of males and 1 percent of females (Menacker & Batshaw, 1997). We typically don't regard this as a disability as children's visual acuity is not affected, however, it is useful to be aware of it, as you are likely to encounter children with this condition. However, if you are a person who color codes materials for children, you may need to modify your system. If you use the color red, write the letter R or the word red over the color so you are sure all children can use the system.

Blindness

A person is considered legally blind who has a visual acuity no better than 20/200 in the better eye with the best possible correction, or has a field of vision restricted to 20 degrees or less (tunnel vision). The child who is legally blind sees at 20 feet what people with normal vision can see at 200 feet. For educational purposes, children are considered blind if they have a visual loss severe enough so that it is not possible to read printed material and necessitates the use of alternative forms of communication such as Braille. Although children may have light perception that is useful in orientation and mobility, the child's education is dependent on auditory and tactile input.

Blindness is one of the least prevalent disabilities in children. The U.S. Department of Education (1989) identified only .05 percent of the school-age population as blind. The incidence of blindness in children is 1 in 30,000. Of these children, almost half (46 percent) were born without vision, and another 38 percent lost their sight during the first year (Foster, 1988). Of infants born with severe visual impairments, about a fourth have no usable vision, another fourth can distinguish some light, and the remaining half have enough vision that they can read enlarged type (Menacker & Batshaw, 1997). Although the causes of blindness are varied, about half of the cases of infants who are born without sight are due to genetic and chromosomal abnormalities (Gilbert, 1993). Intrauterine infections such as rubella and toxoplasmosis and the use of drugs and alcohol also place the fetus at risk for malformation of the visual system. Although infants can have blindness as their only disability, in about half of these children, there are other developmental disabilities as well (Menacker & Batshaw, 1997).

Terminology is important, particularly being sensitive to people-first language and the needs and wants of children and their families. Ask parents what terms they use to refer to their child's visual impairment. Some parents may tell you that they prefer to use the term blind. Honor their preferences.

Partially Sighted

Children who are partially sighted, or have low vision, have visual acuity between 20/200 and 20/70 in the better eye with the best possible correction (IDEA, 1997). Educationally, children with low vision have enough residual vision to read large print or regular print with special assistance such as magnification. These children should *not* be referred to as blind.

Visually Limited

This term refers to children who are considered sighted children for educational purposes but who are limited in their use of vision. They may need particular light conditions, prescriptive lenses, optic aids, or special materials to aid their vision.

Although it is unlikely (but not impossible) that you will have a child with no usable vision, it is more probable that you will help identify a child with limited vision. Estimates vary widely—from 5 to 33 percent (Salvia & Ysseldyke, 1995)—relative to the number of school-age children who have visual limitations. If 20 percent of the children have a visual limitation, then of every classroom of 25 children, 5 are likely to have vision problems of some sort. Estimates vary because of the definitions used and the screening instruments. (These estimates do not include children who have visual processing problems.)

Early Identification of Visual Impairments

Unless parents have a reason to suspect that a child has a visual problem, it usually doesn't occur to them to take a young child to an ophthalmologist. Children themselves are usually no help, because they assume that whatever vision they have is normal.

As you observe children, be aware of the behaviors and complaints that may indicate vision problems. Preschool children have a tendency to see things better at a distance than they do at close range. When doing close work such as looking at books, puzzles, or games, a child with a visual impairment may blink continually, hold a book (or place self) too close or too far away, keep changing the distance of the book, or over- or underestimate distance when working with puzzles or pegboards. When doing visual work at a distance (such as during group time, films, or slides), the child may seem inattentive or lose interest after a brief time. Other symptoms to look for are the inability to identify parents, friends, or teachers at a distance; not noticing objects from across the room or playground; difficulty in such activities as calendar reading or chalkboard games; bumping into things; and misjudging distances in games (see Table 17.1). If your observations support your suspicion, ask parents if they have considered this; if not, encourage them to observe more closely. After they have observed, share your concerns and encourage them to take the child to an eye doctor (ideally, a pediatric, developmental, or neuro-ophthalmologist).

0 to 3

Many infants and young children with correctable visual problems function as if they had low vision until their vision is corrected. They often show delays in reaching developmental milestones and tend to sit later and may not crawl but hitch. Hitching is a method of moving where the child's bottom is on the floor and she scoots, using the legs for movement. Hitching makes the head less vulnerable. Children will typically walk with a wide stance for added support, but may not walk until age 2 or later. Speech also develops later, with less body and facial expression, and little nonverbal communication.

The infant who is born with no vision not only misses the visual aspects of the environment but the ability to form visual images about the world. Therefore, the child may not be attracted to people,

TABLE 17.1   RED FLAGS FOR VISUAL IMPAIRMENTS

Medical/Physical

Eyes that are red, watery, or have a discharge

Itchy, scratchy, burning eyes

Uncoordinated eyes (one eye remains still while the other follows the object; eyes cross or one eye wanders)

Eyelids that are red, swollen, crusted, or droopy

Swelling of eyes

A white pupil

Frequent or recurring styes

Excessive blinking

Eyes appear out of focus

Behavioral

Frequent frowning, squinting, or eye rubbing

Widens or squints eyes when looking in the distance

Holds books or objects too close

Shutting or covering one eye

Tilting head to one side or the other

Frequent headaches, stomachaches, or dizziness

Not alert to surroundings; few attempts at locomotion or communication

Problems judging distance when using small objects

High sensitivity to light

Failure to respond to or turn to the source of sound

Unable to recognize familiar faces from a distance

objects, or even the exploration of his own body; unless the child can experience these through taste, touch, or sound, he does not know they exist. A conscious effort has to be made to link the child to the environment by building mental concepts through language. Young children who cannot see babble, smile, and laugh when sighted infants do, but infants with sight see the responses that their parents make to these behaviors and they are reinforced. The tonal pattern of voices must convey to young infants what they cannot see. As infants become familiar with the people and objects in their environment, they will form concepts through the senses of hearing and touch. They will recognize the voices and footsteps of family members. This is the time that an infant is building connections. Name whatever these infants touch, whatever they do, and whatever is done for them. Pick out the salient features of the experience and put it into words. Objects that make sounds need to be placed in their hands. They need to learn to touch their nose and toes. They need to learn "up" as they are being picked "up" and obviously "down" in the same way. As first words and associations are difficult, initially use the same objects and the same words during routines. Prolonged periods of echolalia (parroting words) are common among children with low vision. This is true until the child understands self and others as being separate and capable of interacting independently of each other and the environment (Harrison & Crow, 1993).

Infants who do not respond to vision need other stimulation. They need to *feel* a smile; they need sounds and singing as their day progresses. Call infants so they raise their heads; rattle noisemakers in different positions to entice them to move; place them in different positions; call to infants from above, beside, and below them. Encourage infants to move. Place noisemaking objects in their hands and then slightly out of reach to intrigue them to reach for these objects. Prop infants in a sitting position or place them in a contained area where they can sit, and place a variety of noisemaking toys with them. (This makes the toys easier to locate.) Periodically, squeak a toy to help maintain interest. Teach infants to localize and attend to sound. This is a precursor to learning to look at the person who is talking.

Children who cannot see may not want to explore their world. They might become discouraged as they bump into things and it hurts. When children are learning to walk, they can learn about the process of walking by standing on your feet, their back to your front and walking with you. This gives information about bending their knees as well as information that walking is safe.

Walking, although wonderful, poses additional challenges. Children must now rely on their memory of space and hope that things remain in the same place. Initially, rubber soles give security; however, once walking has been mastered, leather soles provide more feedback (Kastein, Spaulding, & Scharf, 1980). Climbing up stairs is easier than down; help by placing their feet on the treads. Use snack time to help toddlers develop hand-mouth coordination. Use small bits of food in a contained area to help children both grasp the food and then eat it. This is messy, but continuing practice works.

Prepare children for new experiences and changes by providing auditory cues. This is not just verbally telling children what will happen next, but consciously thinking about the natural environmental cues that provide information. Before giving infants a bottle, shake the bottle, let the infants feel its warmth, walk "heavy," and talk to the infants to let them know you are near. Perhaps "drop" children's boots in front of them and then say, "You need to put your boots on," or "Listen, I'm pouring your juice," and so on.

Play games in which children need to crawl and eventually walk toward sound sources. Use environmental sounds such as running water in the sink (with comments like, "It sounds as though some of the children are washing their hands") as well as sounds of toys. Then, of course, name the sound, put their hands in the water and help them experiment with turning the water on and off.

Young children with little sight may need to be taught how to explore an object placed in their hands. Teach children to explore the length of a spoon with their fingertips, then the bowl of it, as well as feeling the weight, texture, and temperature. Help them turn it over and feel the bowl from the back. These are the qualities of "spoonness" they must learn, but labeling them as they are trying to learn "spoon" is confusing. Just say the word "spoon."

3 to 6

Until children are about 3, they are usually not aware that others see differently than they do. If they "see" using their hands, they may expect that you see that way as well and give you things to feel (that is, see). The realization begins gradually as children discover discrepant behavior. Others may comment on a child's new watch without feeling the child's arm, or talk about something the child realizes he isn't experiencing. However, at some point during the preschool years, children typically come to an understanding of the meaning of having limited sight. Some children become angry, others depressed (Kastein et al., 1980).

Children need to be helped to put their feelings into words, and adults need to provide acceptance with words as well. Adults need to ask such questions as "Does it make you angry that you can't see the picture the other children are talking about?" Children with visual impairments need support in play skills. Interactive play develops more slowly, and their play tends to lack imagination. Describing, explaining, and helping them experience their world helps them understand it better.

Children with very limited vision rely on hearing as their most important link with the other children; instead of facial expressions, this is how a child knows if another child is serious, angry, or joking. Loud sounds, too much noise, and constant auditory stimulation may cause children to tune out, losing a major source of contact with the environment.

One decision that needs to be discussed during the preschool years is how children will learn to read and write: with Braille, print, or a combination. Children need early instruction in both so that a decision can be made while a child is at an appropriate age to learn the appropriate preliteracy skills. Classrooms should have both large-print books and Braille books available for children.

6 to 9

As children with visual impairments reach school age, they continue to need support with social development and interaction. Their language may be more self-centered than other early elementary school children, as they don't see what others do to talk about it or comment on it. Peers need support in communication. Perhaps the best analogy for children this age is to have them pretend they are talking on the telephone when they communicate with a child who is visually impaired and have them fill in the necessary details in that way. Initial social relationships may be awkward, but with time, children adjust.

Listening skills are extremely important to children with low vision, especially as they move into elementary school where children are expected to follow directions and do many teacher-directed tasks. Children will need extra time to respond, as it takes them longer to make the necessary connections among words, people, objects, activities, experiences, and other sentences (Harrison & Crow, 1993).

A decision must be made at this point about how a child will read and write. Many advances in technology have made the choices greater and, regardless of the choice, have facilitated including children in the regular classroom.

In elementary school, children need access to the content of more formal lessons and this requires adaptations to teaching materials and different teaching approaches. A majority of children can use print. Where regular print cannot be seen, a low-vision aid must be employed. These devices use one or more lenses to magnify the print; all use enlarged photocopies (these can get a bit bulky, depending on the degree of enlargement) (Best, 1993). Some children who need low-vision aids are reluctant to use them because they believe it will draw attention to them. Other problems include skill in using the materials (Best, 1993). Some children read Braille; others use a combination, often writing on a Braille writing machine. With assistive technology, the range of input and output devices has expanded to the point that a specialist in this area is necessary to determine the best match for the particular child and the classroom situation.

Children vary in how good their orientation and mobility skills are. "Orientation is the ability to create and maintain a mental map of one's environment and the relationship of oneself to that environment. Mobility . . . is the ability to travel safely and efficiently through the environment" (Tuttle & Tuttle, 1996, p. 21). Trailing is a method that young children use to learn about their environment, holding the back of their hand at waist level and gently maintaining contact with the walls and furniture as they walk.

Watch for gaps in general knowledge and experience. Children may fail to perceive similarities, differences, and invariances, so they mix up concepts that are perceptually different but functionally the same. For example, a young child who is familiar with house plants might assume that the bark of a large tree is the tree's pot.

Assessment of Visual Impairments

Tests of visual acuity fall into two general categories: those based on an examiner's assessment or eye chart, and those that utilize high technology, which require special training and equipment. Most early care and education settings and elementary schools provide some kind of basic visual screening.

Vision Screening

One common screening test for elementary school children is the standard Snellen Wall Chart. The child is asked to read standard-sized letters at a distance of 20 feet. Although a good screening test, some children may fail or pass this test based on variables other than vision. Children who don't know their letters may not pass the test for this reason. Some children may memorize the order of the letters; some letters of the alphabet are easier to discriminate than others, which leads to guessing. The Snellen E Test is used with preschool children who don't know the letters of the alphabet. The letter E is shown in different spatial arrangements and the child either identifies the direction, points, or holds up the letter E to match the stimulus. Another common screening test used with very young children is the Flash-Card Vision Test, which uses three symbols (apple, house, and umbrella) that can be either verbally or manually matched.

One problem with these tests is that they fail to identify the child with near-vision problems (myopia), the kind most critical for reading. They also miss physical problems related to the eye itself and are ineffective in identifying visual perceptual problems (Salvia & Ysseldyke, 1995).

I was once called by a mother who was concerned because her 18-month-old son only ate what was on the top half of his plate. She found that very strange. I went for a home visit at lunch time. Sure enough, the little boy only ate from the top of his plate. He didn't appear full, but he also didn't touch the food on the bottom of the plate. So, we turned the plate around so that the remaining food was at the top, and that too was then eaten. The mother was baffled. "But why? This makes no sense." I agreed and told her I would think about it. It nagged me. There was something obvious I was missing but for the life of me I couldn't figure out what it was. The child wasn't physically impaired or autistic. It was truly strange. It continued to nag. Then the light broke. I called and said, "I think I have an idea. I think Seth may be farsighted and perhaps doesn't see the food when it is too close to him. Can you take him for an eye examination?" She replied, "Well, I guess, but wouldn't his physician already have noticed this?" I then said, "He needs to see an ophthalmologist, not a pediatrician." She agreed to take him. She called back several weeks later, elated, saying, "Seth now has glasses. He was farsighted. He eats all the food on his plate. I'm so pleased. But, do you think he would ever have learned to read if we hadn't figured this out?"

Scary isn't it?

An ophthalmologist has the technology for following up on children who do not pass visual screening tests and for determining the visual acuity of children who do not give verbal responses or recognize characters. For young children who cannot cooperate in the visual testing process, an ophthalmologist can look through a retinoscope and adjust the combination of lenses until the correct refraction is obtained (Menacker & Batshaw, 1997).

There are many possible reasons for limited vision (acuity, brain function), and these reasons interact with individual differences in other areas (cognition, motor skills) and also with the environment. You should actively think of vision as a potential learning problem when the material to be learned is visual and the child's performance on these tasks seems different from the child's level of performance in other areas.

To program for children with limited vision, it is necessary to have a fundamental understanding of the visual system and the potential problems in this system.

The Visual System

The visual system is very complex. A brief discussion of the visual mechanism follows. Think of the eye as a camera.

When light enters the eye, it passes through the *cornea* (a transparent membrane), the *aqueous humor* (a watery fluid), the *lens,* and the *vitreous humor* (a jellylike substance that fills the eyeball). The amount of light that enters is controlled by the *iris,* a set of muscles that expands or contracts the *pupil,* the hole through which the light enters. The light focuses on the *retina,* a layer of nerves that transmits impulses to the brain through the *optic nerve.* The most sensitive part of the retina is the *fovea;* the only insensitive part is the *blind spot,* where the nerve fibers come together (see Figure 17.1).

The eye does not actually "see" any more than the ear "hears." It receives light, turns light into electrical

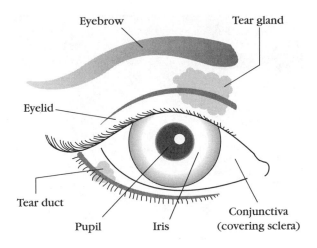

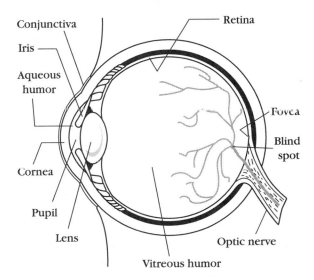

Figure 17.1

impulses, and sends them through the optic nerve to the visual cortex of the occipital lobe of the brain. It is the brain that actually perceives visual images. If the relevant part of the brain that sees is severely damaged, a child may not be able to see, even though the eye is completely normal. Damage in the brain or the optic nerve is not correctable. Defects in the eye itself, however, often are. The purpose of most visual aids is to compensate for defects in the eye so that a correct message can be sent to the brain.

Types of Visual Impairment

Visual impairments are categorized according to the part of the eye involved. There are problems related to the physical mechanisms of the eye, problems with visual acuity, impairments to the muscular structure of the eye, and problems in visual perceptions or the message pathway between eye and brain. Each problem category can be further broken down into specific areas. For many children, problems involving the physical mechanisms, acuity, and muscular structure

can be corrected with medical techniques, eyeglasses or contact lenses, and/or surgery. Problems involving the nerve pathways and brain cannot.

Functions and Diseases of the Eye

Damage to the physical mechanisms of the eye involves the cornea, lens, retina, aqueous chamber, and optic nerve. Damage to any of these parts can affect how light passes through the eye or is transmitted to the brain. Causes have been traced to infectious diseases such as measles, genetic disorders, prescription drugs, environmental hazards, and accidents.

Damage to the eye structure can result in permanent loss of vision. Damage can result from large particles getting into the eye; the longer a particle remains in the eye and the deeper it becomes embedded, the greater the likelihood of permanent damage.

Refractive Errors. For clear vision, the eyeball must be the right length and the cornea must have the proper shape. Errors of refraction occur because the eyeball is either too long or too short or the cornea is elliptical rather than spherical. The most common refractive error of childhood is hyperopia.

Hyperopia (farsightedness) means that the child can see distant things better than relatively close things. When the eyeball is too short or the lens and cornea are too strong, the focused image falls behind the retina. The shorter the eyeball, the more out of focus the image will be and the more convex the lenses in the glasses will be to correct the problem. Often, children can use the eye's power of accommodation to focus the image and have excellent visual acuity (Menacker & Batshaw, 1997).

Myopia (nearsightedness) is the opposite of hyperopia. In this case, the child can't see things that are far away because the eye is too long, causing the image to be in focus before it reaches the retina. Myopia is corrected with the use of concave lenses. There is no mechanism to fine-tune vision for children with myopia, so their distance vision will be blurred without corrective lenses.

An *astigmatism* is an error in refraction caused by the cornea's being more football-shaped than spherical. The image does not focus because the parallel light rays do not come together at one point. Astigmatism can usually be corrected by cylindrical lenses that compensate for the irregular shape. This condition can also occur with other visual conditions. A child can be nearsighted or farsighted and also have an astigmatism (see Figure 17.2).

From a developmental perspective, corrective lenses may not be prescribed for young children if the refractive problem does not interfere with daily functions. It is important to know what children do see and how the demands for vision relate to the child's ability to see.

Correction of refraction errors is described in units called *diopters*. The higher the number of diopters, the stronger the prescription; a minus sign

Myopia, hyperopia, astigmatism, and normal vision.

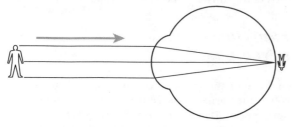

Normal vision

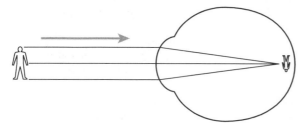

Myopia (nearsighted)

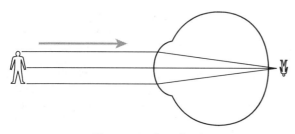

Hyperopia (farsighted)

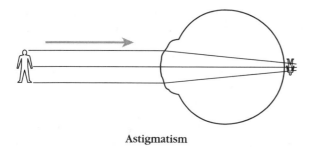

Astigmatism

Figure 17.2

Knobs on puzzles make them easier to use for children with very low vision.

indicates concave lenses, a plus, convex lenses. A prescription for a child who is farsighted might be a +3.5 diopter correction for one eye. The other eye may have a different correction.

The Cornea. Known as "the window of the eye," the cornea protects the lens and the iris. The cornea also focuses images on the fovea centralis, the most light-sensitive part of the retina. It does this by taking the parallel lines of light that reach the surface of the cornea and turning or *refracting* them so the light rays focus on the fovea and a sharp image is sent to the brain (Menacker & Batshaw, 1997).

Cornea damage, usually punctures or scars, results in impaired vision. A cloudy cornea can be caused by birth trauma, inborn errors of metabolism, and congenital glaucoma. It is possible in some cases to have a cornea surgically replaced. This is the only kind of eye transplant possible to date.

The Anterior Chamber. The anterior chamber is behind the cornea and in front of the iris. The pressure in this chamber is kept within normal limits by the drainage of fluid through a canal. If the canal becomes blocked, the intraocular pressure rises and causes glaucoma. Intraocular pressure is measured using a *tonometer.*

In children, *glaucoma* is usually a congenital anomaly, but it may be related to other diseases and syndromes or eye trauma and inflammation. Without treatment, the pressure pushes the optic nerve backward and results in injury to axons and the optic disk becomes cupped. As optic nerve fibers are destroyed, the child develops *scotomas,* or blind spots. These may not even be noticed. If these continue, the child develops tunnel vision and eventually even the central vision may be lost. If detected early, glaucoma can be prevented through the use of eyedrops or microsurgery. Glaucoma causes approximately 4 percent of all blindness in children (Nelson, Calhoun, & Hurley, 1991).

The Lens. The cornea is the first refracting surface of the eye; the second is the lens, located between the cornea and the retina. The lens can change its shape in response to changes in the distance of the focal object: It can be stretched or relaxed. Young children naturally have too-short eyeballs, making them farsighted, but the ability of the lens to adjust allows most of them to compensate and not need glasses (Menacker & Batshaw, 1997).

The major problem with the lens comes from cataracts. *Cataracts* are the clouding of the lens inside the eye, which results in blurred vision. If the lens is clouded, light cannot reach the back of the eye and hence cannot be sent by electrical impulses to the brain. Some children are born with cataracts. A primary cause of congenital cataracts is maternal infection such as rubella. Most cataracts can be removed surgically. If cataracts are small and stable, they may not need to be removed, but if they become larger and more dense, they will inhibit vision. Children with congenital cataracts typically have them microsurgically removed during the first months of life (Menacker & Batshaw, 1997). Children who have had cataracts removed will wear very thick glasses that help bend and focus light rays in place of the missing lens, a contact lens, or an intraocular lens may be used with older children with unilateral cataracts (Menacker & Batshaw, 1997). Cataracts account for about 15 percent of blindness in children and occur in about 1 in 250 births (Nelson et al., 1991).

The Retina. Images are focused on the retina and then sent to the brain. The retina has two types of sensory cells or photoreceptors: cones and rods. *Cones* are needed to see colors and for detailed vision (such as numbers and letters). Each cone is sensitive to one of three colors: red, green, or blue. (Color deficiency involves a disorder of the cones.) *Rods* function in low-light conditions and are necessary for night vision (Menacker & Batshaw, 1997).

Detached Retina. Injury can cause the retina to come loose from the back of the eye. As a result, the retina loses its ability to function. This can be corrected by burning the retina back onto the eye with a laser beam. There will be a permanent blind spot where the laser beam reattaches the retina, but vision will be restored.

Retinopathy of Prematurity (ROP). Previously called retrolental fibroplasia, ROP occurs primarily in premature infants. Although the rates of ROP have remained constant, the number of premature infants surviving has increased the number of children with ROP. ROP is caused by an interruption of the development of blood vessels in the retina and involves the formation of scar tissue behind the lens of the eye. Excessive tissue can result in detachment of the retina from the optic nerve. The greater the scar tissue, the greater the visual impairment. One factor in ROP is the level of oxygen used to treat infant's respiratory problems. The lowest concentrations of oxygen that are necessary for the infant's survival are used to help prevent ROP; however, prematurity itself may be a contributing factor. We cannot prevent ROP, but there are techniques that reduce the likelihood of the retina's detaching and hence the incidence of blindness (Menacker & Batshaw, 1997).

The Optic Nerve. Over a million nerve cells join at the *optic disc* (blind spot) to form the optic nerve. Because there are nerve fibers here, not cones and rods, there is no vision (Menacker & Batshaw, 1997). One optic nerve is joined to each eye. At one point along the path to the brain, some of the nerve fibers cross over *(optic chiasm)* on their way to the occipital lobe.

Damage to the optic nerve itself is usually associated with the incomplete development of the optic nerve or damage to it from disease or trauma. The optic nerve carries the electrical impulses from the eye to the brain for processing. If this nerve is not developed properly, it will not be possible for signals to get to the brain so the child can see. The effects on vision vary depending on the amount and place of the damage.

The Visual Cortex. All visual information received through the eye passes through the optic nerve and to the visual cortex in the occipital lobe of the brain. There, the messages are decoded and action taken if necessary. For some children, the visual process appears to work accurately until the message gets to the brain. These children have cortical visual impairments, most commonly caused by oxygen deprivation, infection, or brain trauma and hydrocephalus (Menacker & Batshaw, 1997). Premature infants who survive because of advances in neonatal care have increased the number of children with cortical visual impairments.

A *visual perceptual disorder* is the inability of the child to identify, organize, and interpret what is sensed by the eye. This may not be noticed until children encounter learning tasks. These children may have problems in the area of spatial relations. They are often uncoordinated and clumsy. In visual discrimination tasks, they have difficulty classifying, sorting, and matching. The children usually have difficulty recognizing objects when only a part of the object is visible.

The Eye Muscles. Muscular problems involve the inability of the six muscles controlling the eyes to work in coordination with each other to result in clear vision. Clear vision is produced by the action of the eye seeing two images fused into one. Correct fusion of these images depends on the eyes being straight and moving in synchrony. Disruption in either causes visual problems.

In *strabismus,* the eyes are not able to focus simultaneously on one point. One or both eyes squint all or some of the time. This is usually identified by about age 3. There are two main forms of strabismus. In *esotropia,* the eyes (or weak eye) turns in toward the nose (cross-eyed), whereas in *exotropia,* the eyes (or weak eye) turns away from the nose (wall-eyed). This condition may be present all the time or only when the child tires. If it is only present intermittently, it is not likely to cause damage. If it is not dealt with, it can lead to visual loss and amblyopia.

Strabismus can be the result of several problems: in the nerves supplying the eye muscles, abnormality in eye focusing, or in the brain itself (Menacker & Batshaw, 1997). Depending on the cause of the problem, it is dealt with by corrective eyeglasses, orthoptic training (exercise that works on developing the eye muscles), or surgery. Strabismus occurs in about 3 to 4 percent of children and is as high as 15 percent in infants who have been born prematurely (Nelson et al., 1991).

Amblyopia (sometimes referred to as "lazy eye") is a reduction in visual acuity that only occurs in children under the age of 9 and is a consequence of long spans of time when there are no retinal images or blurred ones. Congenital cataracts, for example, obscure vision, so there is very little stimulation in the cortical visual pathway. As a result, nerve cells die, a loss that is permanent. If the cataract is removed within two months, the child's visual acuity may be decreased, but she will not be blind (Menacker & Batshaw, 1997).

Amblyopia can also be caused by a muscle imbalance. If the eyes do not focus on the same image, the brain, seeing a double image, will turn off the vision of the weaker eye to compensate. If this imbalance is not treated by the time the child is about 6 years of age, the vision in that eye will be limited for the rest of the child's life.

Amblyopia is treated by surgery, by wearing an occlusive patch or lens over the stronger eye to force the weaker eye to work, and by wearing glasses or contact lenses in the weaker eye. Amblyopia occurs in about 2 percent of the population (Stager, Birch, & Weakley, 1990).

Assistive Technology

Increasingly, technology is being used to help those with limited vision. Depending on the amount of vision a child has, a ViewScan may be helpful. This is a machine that uses a camera to project an image. It is able to project the pages of a book in many sizes of print and contrast (Jan & Robinson, 1989). An Optacon is a device that scans print and converts it into patterns transmitted by 144 tactile pins that produce an image of the letter that can be felt against a finger. Another system, VersaBraille, can convert information from the computer into Braille. Other computer programs provide speech capacity to a personal computer, and computer printouts can be converted into speech by using a Kurzweil Reading Machine and Total Talk. There are even talking calculators, talking watches, and talking clocks. This is all in addition to talking books and other individualized tools that children can profit from.

Guidelines

The modifications that you will need to make in your classroom depend on the needs of the particular children you have. The following guidelines are divided into two sections. The first deals with techniques to encourage children to use corrective

vision aids. The second section provides guidance in how to modify your room for children whose corrected vision still qualifies them as being partially sighted or blind.

Corrected Visual Impairments

When you are working with a child with correctable vision problems, the dilemma is that you want the child to wear the patch or glasses *and* to enjoy learning. You can't afford to be cast in the role of the villain who *makes* the child wear these things. First check with the parents or, if necessary, the ophthalmologist to be certain of what the child is supposed to do. Then the trick is to make the child *want* to do what she is supposed to.

1. Find out from the parents when and for how long visual aids should be used. For example, are the glasses to be worn at *all* times? Sometimes the correction is for specific use only. A nearsighted child wears glasses to see at a distance, but because this correction may distort the child's vision for close work, it would be inappropriate to keep the glasses on during close work.

2. Observe the child's behavior with visual aids. Does the child continually take the glasses off or look over them? Such actions may mean the correction is not helping and further consultation is necessary.

3. If a child refuses to wear glasses, try to create a situation in which the child needs to wear the glasses to succeed. How you actually do this depends on the problem. If, for example, a child is farsighted, find an intriguing book or game that requires close vision. Then, depending on the circumstances, say something like "Before you got your glasses, we couldn't have played this," or "I'd like to play this game with you, but you forgot your glasses. If you wear them tomorrow, we can play." You might also make appropriate statements like "You've learned to do this so much faster since you got your glasses," or "I like the way you look with your glasses." The child will feel rewarded not only by the activity, but also by your attention.

4. Create a need to see. For example, if a nearsighted child will not wear glasses, you might have that child sit as far away from you as possible during group time. Then, when the child realizes that there is a need to see (in the middle of a story with pictures or during a fingerplay), have the child get the glasses if that won't disrupt the group; otherwise, have someone bring the child's glasses.
   This sounds like a manipulative thing to do, and the child will have a harder time learning, but if you and the parents agree that it is important to wear the glasses, you must create a definite need and then reinforce the change in behavior that occurs. This process may have to

be repeated many times before the behavior is established. Be careful to do this subtly and in a matter-of-fact way so as not to focus the group's attention on the child. But you also have to be realistic and say "Tommy, you can't come any closer, but you can see better if *you* get your glasses." You may need to remind him where the glasses are, but you want him to be responsible. It is your job to make the activity so enticing that the child will want to get his glasses or he'll miss something others are enjoying. However, don't let this become a power struggle. If he chooses not to comply, he won't see as well. Some children who don't want to wear glasses may purposefully lose them. One frustrated parent tells this story:

> I know to the teachers I must have seemed like a witch, but it got to me. I got his eyes tested like they said and he needed glasses. I got the first pair. They were lost in a week. The kids called him "Four Eyes." He lost them. They sent letters home. I got another pair, not as pretty, but it was all I could afford. He lost them on the way to school. I can't keep doing this. I bought another pair and they were broken on the playground in two days. I can't get him any more glasses until the beginning of the month. They don't even need him to come with me anymore to have them fitted. They know his size. All I have to do is pay and I'm all out of money. And I'm all out of patience. I know what my responsibility is in this: I pay. But what is your responsibility?

> What is your responsibility? The question is a real one.

5. A unit on sight may also help all children better understand how they see. Discuss the sense of vision as well as a variety of visual problems. Simulating various visual needs creates awareness and is educational as well.

6. Don't fall into the trap of saying, "I'll bet you can see much better since you got your glasses." A child who doesn't want to wear glasses will probably respond, "No, I can't," even when you know he can. Sometimes, reality is irrelevant. Remember, if it is important that a child learn a particular thing, such as safety rules, make sure the child can learn it with or without glasses.

Uncorrected Visual Impairments

Some children with uncorrected visual impairments will have limited vision, others little or no usable vision.

Children with Low or Limited Vision. Some children who have visual impairments need accommodations. Fostering visual skills means encouraging children to use their vision in a way most advantageous to them. Remember, *children will not hurt their eyes through use.*

1. Within their ability to see, teach children visual discrimination. Start with gross discrimination paired with tactile reinforcement, then progress to finer distinctions. Some children may miss details, so work on visual closure. It will help them make better guesses about what is missing.

2. Help children compensate for reduced vision by regulating the light levels in the room. Be aware of lighting conditions and sources of light. Use shades or Venetian blinds to regulate the amount of natural light in your room. (Ideally, illumination should be between 70 and 100 foot-candles.) Light switches with dimmers can be helpful (but most cannot be used with fluorescent lights). Don't stand or sit with your back to the light source or in outside doorways; there is too much contrast between the bright light of outside and the figure.

3. Arrange seating so that the lighting condition favors those who need it most. (Check the eye specialist's report. For some children, maximum

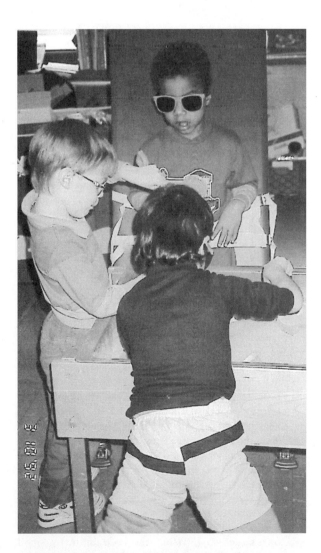

Children may require different visual adjustments. Some may need tinted lenses to adjust to different lighting situations while others do not.

illumination is best, and for others lower-than-normal levels are optimal.) Some children use tinted lenses to reduce glare.

4. Use photographs with matte or flat finishes and nonglare glass or contact paper on framed pictures.

5. Light-colored tables (or dishes) should have a dull finish; glare is fatiguing.

6. Change or improve color contrast. Where possible, paint the rims of bookcases, tables, and door frames with a lighter or darker color that will make the edges easier to see. Use a dark light switch against light-colored walls so it will stand out.

7. Use a heavy black marking pen to outline the boundaries of the paper so that the child knows where the edges are.

8. Look at the books you have in your reading area. Make sure that some of them have clear, simple pictures, and large print.

9. Try to use materials with distinctive shapes and textures and bright, high-contrast colors.

10. Keep the general noise level down. A child with low visual ability relies on auditory cues, and these will be masked by noise.

11. Avoid excessive detail on bulletin boards. Be aware of the child's vision when you display the children's work. The work of children with partial sight should be hung at their eye level so they can see it displayed and can point it out to others.

12. Think about what you do to reinforce children's behavior. Do you rely on smiles, gestures, body cues, and eye contact? These are visual cues. With children who have partial sight, you need to talk and touch for reinforcement in addition to using visual cues. You may need to draw attention to the visual cues with words and gestures.

13. Enlarge images and objects. Print information large. Regularly use different types of magnifiers.

Children with Little or No Vision. Children who have very little or no usable vision need additional accommodations.

1. A well-arranged classroom helps all children but especially those with severe visual impairments. Eliminate clutter and confusion! Keep things neat and make sure that toys are picked up as soon as children are finished with them. Be sure that chairs are pushed under the tables. Eliminate unnecessary obstacles in the classroom. Be aware of protruding objects such as puzzles or blocks that have been placed on a shelf but still stick out. Rearrange these so they no longer protrude. Consolidate items where possible. (Have one large wastebasket rather than many small ones.) Keep doors fully open or completely shut. Even children with excellent vision tend to run into partly opened doors. Round tables are safer than rectangular ones because there are no corners to bump into. If rectangular ones are all you have, pad sharp edges with foam. If you are a person who likes to arrange and then rearrange your classroom, *don't!* It takes a while for children to establish permanent reference points and feel comfortable in a room. If possible, give children a chance to become acquainted with the arrangement of the room before the other children come in by having them visit the classroom before school starts or in the evening when other children are not present. Verbally describe the classroom and spatial relationships as children explore. Then ask the children for specific feedback: "Can you show me where we keep the puzzles?" Don't assume that just because you told children and they had time for free exploration that they will understand and remember.

Use auditory, olfactory, and tactile cues to structure the room. The bubbling of an aquarium might identify the science area; a rug could mark the story area; wind chimes could indicate that the outside door is open, and so on.

2. Encourage independence. When you assign lockers or coat hooks, be sure to give these children ones that are easy to locate, perhaps one on the end, out of the traffic pattern. Don't move objects around after children have placed them without telling the children. Moving something two inches may mean that it is "gone" if children can't visually scan the area.

3. Use a label maker to put raised labels on materials where possible. It is more important to label favorite toys with something easy to find than to make a descriptive label. (A puzzle of different types of fruit might have just the raised letter *f* on it rather than the entire title.) Make sure materials are put away so that the label is facing out. With older children, use rubber bands as labels on round objects. Put one rubber band on the red paint, two on the blue, and three on the yellow. This helps children with color deficiencies also. Using rubber bands with children under 3 is not safe, as they might swallow them.

4. Use props children can feel throughout the classroom. Be careful not to give children *unnecessary* special treatment. Before you give these children help you would not give others, ask them if they need it. Do offer help, but don't take over or allow other children to do the task for children with visual impairments. Teach the other children in the class how to offer help as well.

5. Your teaching techniques may have to be modified. Identify yourself when you enter a room or area, especially if the child is alone. Tell the child specifically where you are: "I'm standing behind your chair." Encourage the other children to do the same. Also make it clear when you leave, especially if you are wearing soft-soled shoes—it is rarely necessary with clogs! Use children's names during group time and when they

are playing in small groups. Teach children in the group to do this as well. Have you ever talked to an unidentified person on the telephone who assumes you know who is speaking? It's disconcerting until you identify the person. It is important for children with visual limitations to know who is present, especially at the beginning of the year. Use auditory cues—a short tune, a chord on the piano, or a song—to signal regular activities, such as cleanup time. Be consistent in using the signals, so the children learn to associate the activities and cues. Help out with an ongoing monologue about what is happening during an activity. If the class is making cookies, say, "Susie has finished sifting the flour, and now Harry is going to beat the batter." Include children by asking, "Oh, Jesusa, what are you doing now?" This also helps the child learn to identify sounds and encourages all children to participate in the experience.

6. When talking to this child, keep your voice within normal limits. (Some assume that those who don't see well also don't hear well.) Give careful attention to the tone of your voice. Talk directly to a child, not about her. Don't ask Pat's father if she wants to play in the block area: Ask her. (Her father may answer, but that is a different problem.) Don't eliminate the words "see" and "look" from your vocabulary—use them when they are appropriate. Make directions clear and concise. Use characteristics that can be felt, heard, or counted rather than seen.

   Address the child by name before giving instructions and make sure that the instructions you give really help. "It's right over there" is not enough. You have to name places and specify ways of doing things. It helps if the child knows right from left. If not, have the child wear something (rings, bracelet, watch, ribbon) on one hand or arm so that you can say, "Reach up with the hand with the bracelet on it."

7. Learning directions is important. Teach children the concepts of left and right early. Use the word "correct" when something is accurate, not "right," as this is confusing. Children also use the image of a clock for location. Use this image to identify where items are located: "The cup is at 2 o'clock." This is also useful when children are sitting in a circle. If the child knows that the teacher is at 12 o'clock and the child is at 3 o'clock, it is useful to say "Jason is sitting at 6 o'clock."

8. When walking with a child who has very limited vision, you walk in front, never behind. If you walk alongside, let the child hold your arm or wrist; don't hold the child's. This allows a greater sense of the movement of your body, especially when you turn or go up or down steps. As you walk, be sure to describe what you are passing: "Now we're going by the swings. Can you hear Marie and Syma talking while they swing?"

9. Provide children with visual impairments many opportunities to learn to ask questions. Because they don't see objects to say "What is that?," they ask questions less frequently. If adults always anticipate their needs, they don't have the opportunity to ask questions and hence may not gain this skill.

10. Always give accurate feedback. Because a child may not be able to evaluate his own work, the child is dependent on you for this information. If feedback is always positive, the child may not have an incentive to improve and may build a false sense of confidence.

Coping with Teasing and Name Calling

A unit on feelings may be necessary to increase other children's awareness and openly talk about taunting and teasing. At first, you may have to lead the discussion and state some typical reactions, but you should gradually help the child to speak up. Perhaps a session on assertiveness training will help. Children must learn to say, "I don't like it when you call me Four Eyes."

One child described her experience this way: "I don't mind wearing glasses. I am the same on the inside, in my heart. Everyone has something she has to go through sometimes. I just pretend they aren't on my face, and my friends don't even notice them. Some kids teased me at first—but now no one cares."

Curriculum Adaptations

The amount of functional vision a child has will determine what, if any, curriculum modifications have to be made. The less vision the child has, the more the auditory and tactile channels must be used and the use of any residual vision encouraged.

Social Awareness: Self-Esteem, Inclusion, Social Studies, Health and Safety

All children need to be part of the group and learn about the strengths and needs of others. As adults, we are familiar with aids to vision such as glasses; younger children may not be as familiar, and they need to learn. Personal worth and adequacy is a fundamental need for all children. They need to develop a strong, healthy self-concept as a prerequisite to self-esteem. Self-esteem is a personal judgment of worthiness that children feel about themselves; it is shaped by self-perception and the perception of others (Coopersmith, 1967).

Self-Esteem. Children with limited vision tend to develop body awareness more slowly because of lack of confidence and having fewer examples to emulate. Visual memory is the basis for such things as pretend play (Bishop, 1991). Because children may not have visual memory, alternative ways of developing it need to be explored. They may learn words without having a clear understanding of their social significance. Many social skills are learned through observation. If they cannot see others, they may need to be taught.

1. Children with visual impairments need role models who wear glasses and use other optical devices. They need to be encouraged to use the correctable vision they have and to learn the skills to explain to others why these particular devices help them. Look around your classroom and be sure the pictures include children with visual impairments and visual aids.

2. Sometimes, children with visual impairments make faces that are socially unpleasant. These faces offend both children and adults and my be followed by teasing and name calling. Address the problem directly. Describe the problem: "When you move your tongue like that, you look unpleasant (or silly). Do you want to look silly now? If not, please put your tongue back in your mouth."

3. Often, children with visual impairments have fewer facial expressions and less obvious body movements. They may turn their face away when others are talking and appear inattentive when in reality they are listening carefully. Reinforce them when their face is more expressive and tell them "I like it when your face is turned toward me when I speak to you."

4. Help children label their body parts. Use exercises and songs in naming body parts and discuss the ways these parts move. Hold the child's hands in your own as you point and demonstrate, but tell them what you are going to do before you do it.

5. Teach children the vocabulary to explain how they feel as well as how to use auditory cues to understand others' emotions.

6. Encourage children to explore a variety of methods of moving from place to place. Have them talk about when they could use these different methods. They need to become more aware of their body in relation to their surroundings.

7. Confidence and positive self-esteem come from learning age-appropriate adaptive skills. This is an important part of group acceptance and motivates further exploration. Give children time and opportunity to develop these skills.

8. Provide an environment of acceptance and experimentation that will build children's self-confidence.

Inclusion. Your expectations of a child with a visual impairment will set the tone for the class. If you do not require the child to clean up, or if you are apprehensive or overprotective, the other children will quickly pick this up.

1. Teach children to identify themselves when they begin a conversation; otherwise, the child's energy is spent on figuring out who the speaker is rather than what that person is saying.

2. Explain to other children the impact of having limited vision; sometimes, children do not approach children with visual impairments because they seem unresponsive and to lack curiosity.

3. Encourage children to invite a child with low vision to play by suggesting or bringing specific toys and materials for both of them to use.

4. Children with low vision often learn about their environment through their tactile/kinesthetic senses. They may want to touch their classmates. Help them find acceptable ways to work this out.

5. As children get older, have them use blindfolds or masks that simulate various visual impairments. Support children in pretending they have different visual impairments and give them specific tasks to do (go specific places in the room, find particular objects, write their name, eat a snack). Discuss with the child how this felt. If teasing is an issue, bring it up as part of this experience.

Social Studies. All children need to learn about the world around them, and field trips are a pleasant and effective way to accomplish this. Children with visual impairments can use many hands-on experiences to make accurate generalizations. Even children who have fully corrected vision have spent some portion of their life without optimal vision. (If corrective lenses were worn at age 3 and the child is 6, that is *half* of the child's lifetime.)

1. Plan many field trips with *small* groups of children so each of them can participate in the experience. It isn't enough just to see a cow, especially if the child can't see it well. The child has to feel it and feel enough of it to form an accurate perception of a cow.

2. Provide follow-up activities with stories and dramatic play after field trips. Have the children describe with all their senses what they remember. Drink milk, smell and handle hay, make farm sounds, and sing farm songs.

3. When naming objects for a child, differentiate between the representation and the real thing: "We saw a real cow on the field trip. This is a toy cow. How are they different?"

4. Records and tapes can help children expand their social world. Children may be more sensitive to auditory signals than visual ones. However, these must be linked to meaningful experiences if they are to expand the child's knowledge base.

5. Help children become aware of the role the medical profession plays in assessing visual acuity

and prescribing corrective lenses. This can be done with a field trip, a visit from an eye doctor, and follow-up dramatic play.

6. If you know a person with a visual impairment who would be comfortable with the children, have the person visit. (A seeing eye dog always makes an impression and provides an important learning experience.)

Health and Safety. Health and safety is an important and difficult area of learning for all young children. It requires them to consciously inhibit their spontaneous curiosity and think through the implications of actions *before* doing them. For children with low vision, the possibility of falling or bumping into things or stooping over and hitting something is greater than for other children, yet the price of overprotection is great also. Greater coordination problems exist when learning skills because these children are more dependent on tactile and auditory cues for learning than on visual ones. They may not see another child riding a tricycle toward them or the swing in motion. They need to use their residual vision and hearing to compensate.

1. Help all children develop independence in adaptive (self-help) skills. Use buttoning, lacing, and snapping frames to teach these skills. Montessori materials are excellent, but you can make your own fairly easily. Keep soap, paper towels, and the wastebasket in the same places in the bathroom and at a level the child can reach.

2. Teach safety, looking, and listening skills. Make sure children can identify such sounds as cars, sirens, and fire bells and know what to do when they hear these sounds.

3. Teach children to do deep knee bends as a way of getting down to pick things up. It is especially important when they lift heavy objects, and it decreases bumped heads.

4. When children are playing very actively, have those wearing eyeglasses use a safety strap to keep the glasses from falling off.

5. In outdoor play areas, fence in the swings, seesaws, and any other heavy moving equipment. Keep tricycles and wagons on specified paths. Add bells to moving objects (tricycles, wagons, even balls) so the child can hear them and avoid their path.

6. Teach children with limited vision to use their sense of touch to determine if they have rashes or cuts or to tell if their hands are clean.

Language and Literacy: Speaking, Listening, Reading, and Writing

The area of language and literacy is challenging yet essential for children with visual impairments. Language is their major source of acquiring knowledge, of "seeing" the world, and of communicating with others. Children with visual impairments usually depend on verbal skills to communicate and listening skills to learn about their environment. If they can't find a needed object, they may ask others. They need practice in both giving and following directions with children and adults. They are more dependent on auditory cues and rely more on auditory memory. Children who have visual losses miss some of the nonverbal qualities of attending and eye contact. They need help in focusing on intonation patterns, volume, and speed of language for additional cues. They may require an individualized literacy program. Encourage children to refine the visual skills they can use.

Speaking. Children with visual impairments may rely more on auditory cues to learn speech, whereas other children can more easily see and imitate movements of the lips, mouth, and jaw. Encourage children to ask what things are and help them to broaden their understanding of labels used. Encouraging feedback from the children about their perceptions will enable you to clarify misunderstandings and foster increased verbalization.

1. Following verbal directions is an important language skill. Start with simple one- or two-step directions. Remember to keep them concrete.

2. Children with visual impairments depend more on words to express or understand feelings. Help them learn these words.

3. Many young children talk to themselves; this is normal for all children. Children with visual impairments may also talk to imaginary friends. This is fine unless they become more interested in imaginary friends than real ones.

Fingerplays incorporate language as well as fine motor skills.

1. Begin with simple, short fingerplays that have more large than small movements. (Teach "Head, Shoulders, Knees, and Toes" before "Thumbkin.")

2. For children who aren't picking up the details and sequence, write down the fingerplay and send it home to the parents. Teach the parents the fingerplays so the children can practice them at home or while traveling. (If you don't demonstrate the fingerplay, you can get some amazing variations.)

3. Children with low vision find fingerplays difficult because they can't see some of the finer details. When teaching fingerplays to these children, have a paraprofessional or volunteer help the child respond at the appropriate time so that the child begins to associate the movement with the words.

Listening. Children who have visual impairments have a greater need for understanding speech because they are often dependent on verbal information to perform certain tasks. Even children with corrected vision problems don't always wear their glasses. It is important that they learn to identify and discriminate among sounds. Help children develop better skills in this area through differentiating similar sounds and listening to tapes.

1. Because children with visual impairments may not be able to see the speaker, they may not look at the person speaking. Encourage them to look by saying "Please look at me." Give them an opportunity to respond. If they don't, say "I'll help by turning your head so it faces me. People like it when you look at them when they are speaking." Then gently turn it.

2. Children need practice locating sounds. Play listening games. Make a sound and see if the child can locate the source of the sound. Once the source is located, the child needs to feel the object that makes the sound and tell how it is used.

3. Have children match sounds by placing objects in pairs of film containers (with taped lids) and shaking them.

4. Children have to learn fine auditory discrimination. Describe and explain what children hear but cannot see. Use this as a game (describe noises and their implications and have the children guess the source from your description).

5. Use tapes and records of stories and music for classifying sounds (long, short, high, low) and for identifying who or what might make that sound and in what situations.

6. Where possible, give children replicas of what you are talking about. Don't worry about size relationships at this point—you can describe those verbally—but clearly identify the object as a toy so children know it is not the real thing.

7. "Where," "why," and "what" are difficult for all children to comprehend. Demonstrate, where possible, the meaning of these words. If possible, take the child to a location, or let the child feel "what" is making the sound.

8. The most difficult words for children to use and understand are those that cannot be experienced through the senses such as colors, the sky, and so on. Use these words in context so children have additional cues. Literature often does this well.

9. Use language to help children focus their vision, as well as to get feedback: "Can you see that wheel? Do you see what's inside the wheel? Those are spokes. Can you count them by touching each one?"

10. Use words that refer to things that can be smelled, touched, heard, seen, tasted, or experienced directly. Try to make the words you use as concrete as possible, using real examples whenever you can. Then move on to more abstract language concepts such as "time," "friendship," and so on.

11. Use functional definitions of objects as well as descriptive ones. "A ball rolls" or "a ball bounces" should be used in addition to the definition "a ball is round." Reinforce the concept by letting the child roll and bounce the ball.

12. To move freely, the child with low vision needs to be able to follow verbal directions. Words like "stop/go," "high/low," "big/little," "in/out/on," and "hard/soft" are useful. Other important spatial terms include "side by side," "back to back," "full turn, half turn, quarter turn," "top/bottom," "in front of," and so on. Games like Simon Says, May I, Hokey Pokey, and Follow the Leader, work well for teaching directions.

Stories can expand the children's world, provided you start with themes children are familiar with. It is preferable to use pictures that illustrate the story's major points in a simple way. Point out to children the relationship of the picture to the story. Create a need to see within their ability to discriminate.

1. When you read stories, pass around small replicas of the major objects (rabbits, carrots, trains) for the children to look at and feel. Do the same with textures and smells.

2. Use cassette tapes or records of books at a listening center. These allow more individualization and choice in the books available. Make your own recordings of favorite books, and bring in blank cassettes so children can dictate their own books.

3. Have books with large type and in Braille. Even if the child does not require Braille, it broadens the range of experience and understanding to develop the idea that Braille is a form of writing. Sometimes refer to books on tape as "talking books" to expand children's ideas about books (available from the American Foundation for the Blind at little or no cost).

Some children with low vision may need to be very close to objects to see them.

Reading. In the area of reading literacy, one emphasis is on developing and refining visual discrimination skills. Children with visual processing problems will also have trouble developing these skills.

1. Start with large objects that have gross distinctions. Simple shapes are fine, such as circles, triangles, and squares. Encourage children not only to label and distinguish among shapes, but also to point out salient characteristics (a circle doesn't have any corners, a triangle has three). Have children trace the shapes with their index and third finger to gain a kinesthetic as well as a visual sense of these distinctions.

2. When children can make gross distinctions, work on finer ones. Even when you teach these, try to point out significant features. Use large wooden letters and have the children trace them with their index and third fingers. Teach them that *A* has straight lines, *O* has curved lines, and *P* has straight and curved lines. Teach by contrasting *A, O,* and *P* and use other contrasting groups of shapes before you have the children attempt to differentiate among letters such as *N, M,* and *W,* for example, which have only straight lines.

3. Children with low vision may have to combine their usable vision with tactile skills to develop reading readiness. If the amount of usable vision decreases, the need for more tactile discrimination will increase because this is a pre-Braille skill. Among the things that can be used to help these children develop these skills are sandpaper letters and texture cards (for matching practice). For example, glue six different three-inch fabric squares to a piece of cardboard and have the six matching pieces glued to three-inch square pieces of cardboard. Have the children match the fabric squares to the larger cardboard. Encourage children with sight to do this blindfolded. Have children match and grade sandpaper from course to fine.

Writing. All children need to develop the link between the ability to speak a word and the ability to write it so others can understand. The form this takes depends on the child.

1. For children who are partially sighted, choose wide black markers so they can easily see what they are marking.

2. If the child cannot use visual feedback, then you need to employ media with more tactile feedback. Start without tools. Have children write in the air. Encourage them to hold their two writing fingers together (the index finger and longest finger of their dominant hand), then, using their whole arm, write letters. (This gives them body feedback.)

3. Provide children with sandpaper or wooden letters that they can trace with two fingers. Provide

auditory cues to support the visual or tactile experience.

4. Use writing media that have different tactile properties. Have children "write" on sand in a jellyroll pan, and mark clay that has been rolled flat, or, using their finger, "write" on black felt on which you have taped white lines (narrow masking tape is fine).

5. As children get older, they will probably use a word processor for written work. Provide children with experiences for learning the position of letters on the keyboard; if necessary, use a Braille keyboard. A speech synthesizer and appropriate software provide children with auditory feedback about their key strokes.

6. A good way to prepare for reading and writing Braille is using pegs and a pegboard. First, allow a child to explore the entire pegboard feeling the holes. Then, cover with tape or cardboard all except the line you want the child to use. If it is a horizontal line, have the child move from left to right; if vertical, top to bottom. Children who are right-handed should use the index finger of their left hand as a guide to find the hole and the right hand to place the peg into the hole. They find the next hole with their index finger and continue. Work to the point that children can copy adult patterns (Kastein et al., 1980).

Discovery: Mathematics, Science, and Computers

Discovery experiences need to start with the familiar and concrete and work toward the less familiar and abstract. Start with natural situations and real objects that are meaningful to the children: two socks and two shoes, one coat with two arms, and so on. Help children feel round balls and square boxes. Use sandpaper outlines of circles and squares. Help children pace off and count distances to and from various places in the room: 5 steps from the locker to the circle area, compared with 10 steps from the locker to the blocks. Provide additional time for children to touch the equipment and materials. Be sure to include equipment that magnifies. Computer literacy is an excellent long-term resource for children. Computers can be designed to have large print, speech, or Braille output. Computers with a voice synthesizer are extremely useful. Learning to make predictions about what will happen under a specified set of circumstances is important as a way of developing independence and creating a sense of predictability in the world.

Mathematics. Number concepts are necessary for all children to learn. The fun is in using them creatively to help children explore and classify their world. For children with low vision, the tactile-motor aspect of learning these concepts can be added with a few modifications.

1. Teach children to tactilely discriminate and match materials of various shapes, sizes, and weights. Have children sort matching buttons into ice cube trays.

2. When teaching number concepts and geometric shapes, start with real objects. Food works well. Everyone gets *1* carton of milk, *2* crackers, *10* raisins, and so on. An abacus is also useful for counting. One can both see and feel the placement of the beads and check back if necessary. Encourage children to count.

3. Matching together large dominoes with indented dots is a good activity that teaches fine motor skills as well as number concepts. Play dominoes.

4. Have children use their body and other devices to measure. Record these measurements. Special modifications should be made to help children with low vision understand distances: an arm's length, two paces, three hand spans. Glue pieces of string on the paper or use glue lines to make graphs that can be felt.

5. Use physical boundaries to delimit the block area, and put the blocks in a tub so the child can locate them easily. Show and tell the child the dimension of the blocks in the tub. Start with individual block building.

6. Teach children about patterns and relationships by using a variety of repeating tactile patterns (rough, smooth, rough, smooth; rough, rough, smooth, and so on).

7. Provide children with many experiences matching, sorting, categorizing, sequencing, and patterning with a wide variety of materials.

Science. Science helps children learn about the sense of vision and the other senses as well as the natural world. Emphasize creative problem solving, decision making, and discovery.

1. Help children learn about the eye and how it works. Get a model of the eye and use the concept of a camera to help children understand.

2. Talk about the purpose of lenses. Have a variety of magnifying glasses and binoculars available in the science area. Talk about the difference in the amount of detail that can be seen with the naked eye and with magnification.

3. Have children participate in experiences in which materials change form, such as making butter or melting ice. Be sure to let children with low vision feel the changes as well.

4. Discuss the weather and appropriate dress for different types of weather. Talk about and feel fabrics used in warm versus cold weather clothing. Experiment with materials designed for specific uses (rain, sun, cold).

5. Help children develop thermic (temperature) and baric (weight) sensitivity by sequencing and matching plastic bottles full of water of differing temperatures and containers of varying weights.

6. Children need to refine their senses to identify pleasant and unpleasant tastes and smells. These are important cues. Some smells might mean that something is going bad (like sour milk), some provide environmental information (damp earth means it rained recently), some are clues to locations (flowers are near a garden), and so on. Other smells indicate whether something or someone is clean or dirty, such as smells of clothing and babies. Children can refine these senses by matching sets of film containers filled with fragrances (spices such as cinnamon, cloves, basil, nutmeg, ginger) and tasting a variety of foods.

Computers. Initially, computers may be difficult for young children with visual impairments because so much of computing is visual. For children with enough vision to see the keyboard and the monitor, the problems are few. Most adults with visual impairments have learned touch typing and to use a numeric keypad. This learning begins when children are young.

1. Use a voice synthesizer with the computer.

2. Use a 25-inch monitor so the letters displayed on the screen are large. Programs are also available that enlarge the type on the screen. It may be easier to read a video screen than a piece of paper because the source light is coming from the letters on the screen and is not reflected light.

3. Computers also allow us to change text and background colors. Some children with partial sight do better with certain color combinations. Find the best combination.

Developmental Physical Education and Sensorimotor Skills: Large Motor, Small Motor, Sensorimotor Integration

Although vision may be limited, the coordination of hearing and tactile/kinesthetic senses provides an avenue of learning combined with available vision. Children with visual impairments are dependent on motor skills and also have more limited opportunities for practice. They need to learn where they are and to develop safe ways of moving through unknown spaces. This requires sensorimotor integration. Children who lack the visual aspect of sensory integration need to learn ways of compensating for, as well as refining, their residual vision. The refinement of fine motor skills will aid Braille reading (if needed). Body awareness and motor planning are an integral part of orientation and mobility training. Children with limited vision need encouragement and a safe place to practice developing skills. Outdoor activities may be a challenge. With temperature changes, glasses sometimes fog up, so have tissues handy to wipe them off. For children with low vision, watch for safety concerns. Be sure that paths for moving vehicles are well delineated and that there is a low fence around swings, seesaws, and other moving equipment so that children cannot accidentally walk into them.

Large Motor. Using the large muscles of the body is one way for children to increase their knowledge of their own bodies, as well as a way to explore their environment. Children who have recently had visual correction and those with low vision will probably have less refined skills in this area than their age-mates. They may need encouragement as well as practice.

1. Balancing "tricks" are especially useful. Start with static balance: The child stands or sits still and balances a particular object. (Bean bags are easier to start with than books.) For dynamic balance, have the children walk, jump, or crawl while balancing an object on their head or other body part. As children become more skillful, see how long or how far they can balance objects. Walking on a balance board or beam is also useful.

2. Relay races where children run, walk, jump, hop, or skip while holding hands with a partner are great for developing both large motor skills and cooperating with peers.

3. Walking between the rungs of a ladder placed flat on the ground or floor helps children establish spacing, and they learn to realize whether or not they are walking in a straight line.

4. Encourage children to do motor tasks blindfolded and talk about the implications of not being able to see.

5. If children are having trouble conceptualizing a particular movement, have them feel the outline of an adult's body (or that of a willing peer) before they do a movement. The adult may still need to help children position their body until they get the feel of it.

Small Motor. The development and refinement of fine motor skills and eye-hand coordination requires practice. Start with experiences that are likely to be successful so children don't get discouraged. Success is especially important for those who are just learning to use corrective visual aids. They may tell you they can do it better without the aids and, if they have learned good compensatory skills, they may be right!

1. Fit-in puzzles (those with large pieces that go into specific places) and knob puzzles are good for teaching fine motor skills.

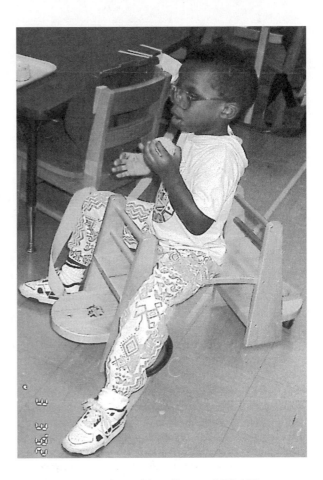

Moving toys, such as this, allow a child with a visual impairment to safely explore his environment. The riding toy is stable and close to the ground.

2. Three-dimensional building toys are very helpful (but get the type that interlock in some way, so they won't fall apart when bumped). Encourage children to start with larger pieces and work toward using the smaller ones. Keep the pieces in a tray so that children can keep track of them.

3. Sewing cards with large holes around the perimeter of the image allow a child to both feel and see the outline of the images. These cards can be easily made by pasting pictures on cardboard and using a hole punch.

4. Teach children to discriminate among textures. Begin with pleasant-feeling textures such as satin and velvet. Then move on to wool, leather, and so on. These fabrics can also be used for texture-matching games. Try different grades of sandpaper, which the children can try to arrange in order of fineness.

5. Tracing shapes will help the child progress from using actual items to learning to represent them. Children can begin by tracing the actual shape (using a piece of very heavy cardboard) and can then fill in the space with colors.

Sensorimotor Integration. If children do not have accurate visual feedback, they need to develop a motor memory for moving their bodies through space.

1. An obstacle course that requires children to crawl over, under, and through different sized obstacles is a great way to teach spatial orientation. You might start a human obstacle course, where the "course" itself can provide help and support.

2. Use the vision children have, but be aware that it may vary from day to day. Children who are anxious or tired may not have as much ability to focus their vision as they do when they are relaxed and rested.

Creative Arts: Visual Arts, Music, Creative Movement, and Dramatic Play

Creative arts provide children with the opportunity to explore their world in a safe way. They can gain experiences inside the classroom that prepare them for what will happen outside. Children can participate without fear of doing it wrong. Children with visual impairments may need obvious boundaries for work on paper, such as a thick black line marking the outside of the paper, or a larger, high-contrast piece of paper underneath the paper being worked on. As long as the emphasis is on process, there are few limitations on what children can do. It is often useful to add textured materials to paint and playdough. Three-dimensional materials such as clay and dough are particularly good because the children can feel the results.

Music can be used to enhance listening skills and auditory discrimination. Moving to music is an excellent way to acquire body awareness, but be sure to have an area without physical obstacles. Give the children boundaries they can trust, such as two adults who can cue them if their movements are too large. Creative movement supports orientation and mobility skills. Children with limited vision must learn a variety of ways of moving safely. Have children move with partners. Use music to help them localize sound and distinguish one voice from another. Let them feel vibrations of instruments and voices. Sound will be vital in the life of these children, so use music to train their hearing.

Children with visual impairments, like those with hearing impairments, profit from acting out situations and having realistic props. Be sure to keep the props in the same place so they will be easy to find.

Visual Arts. Although children with very little residual vision face limitations in some areas of art, there are many highly tactile materials that allow a great deal of manipulation. The potential that art activities and materials offer for the release of emotions makes them doubly valuable experiences for all children with visual impairments.

1. Use a variety of modeling materials to provide different tactile experiences. Among the most popular materials are playdough (made of salt and flour), clay (use the powdered type and let the children help mix it), cornstarch, papier-mâché, and plastic-coated wire.

2. Have children fingerpaint right on the table if they are using actual fingerpaint. You can then print the picture when a child makes one he wants to keep. In addition, try fingerpainting Ivory Snow Flakes (a clean feeling for those who are reluctant to get dirty) or laundry starch. Fingerpainting to music is another good variation.

3. Add textured materials such as sand or sawdust to easel paint and fingerpaint. Make the paint thicker so that it can be more easily felt and controlled.

4. Make textured boundaries for work areas. (This is a good idea for any child who tends to use too much space.) Use masking tape to divide the table into areas, depending on your needs. Use place mats to define each child's space: Put glue around the outside edge of a sheet of paper and sprinkle a little sand on it as a tactile boundary.

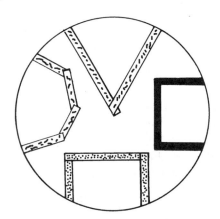

5. If you are using white paper on the easel, first cover the easel with dark construction paper so that the child can easily see where the paper ends. If the child cannot see, use a textured material for the board, such as coarse sandpaper or cork so the child can feel the boundaries.

6. Use a thick, dark marking pen to print names on papers and remember to *print big.*

7. Hang the child's artwork in a place where the child can find it easily, see it, and point it out to others. Hang it low and near the beginning or the end of the line.

8. Make a texture collage with a specific theme; for example, for *nature,* use feathers, pine needles, leaves, and grass.

9. Tape paper to the table so it stays in one place.

Music. Music is usually a particularly enjoyable activity for children with low vision and, with the number of famous musicians who are visually impaired (such as Ray Charles, Stevie Wonder, and Joaquin Rodrigo), it is not difficult to find encouragement to do well in this area. However, don't assume that children with visual impairments will automatically be good at music. Music study develops finer auditory discrimination and facilitates the development of memory skills.

1. Play an instrument or ring a bell and have the children (who have their backs to you and eyes closed) guess what area of the room you are in. A variation of this is to have them search for a ticking kitchen timer or music box.

2. Teach the concepts of *high* and *low* with music pitch games. Have children practice using *loud* and *soft* volume as cues to distance (for example, for finding a hidden object). *Fast* and *slow* are also easily taught through musical games: The faster the music, the closer the child is to the hidden object.

3. Songs that have motions teach names, actions, and labels. Extra time, however, must be devoted (at school or home) to teaching children with low vision the motions that go with songs.

4. Sing songs that promote body awareness and songs that describe what children are doing: "This is the way we put on our boots/climb the stairs/ride our trike" and so on. Adapt and make up songs to fit your needs.

5. Use a variety of musical instruments and allow children plenty of time to experiment with them.

6. Have children move around the room while music is being played. When the music stops, the child has to follow the teacher's directions: "Make yourself into a ball"; "Make yourself as tall (or as short) as you can"; "Be as still as you can."

Creative Movement. Combining movement and an idea helps children learn abstract concepts. It is also a way of finding out about a child's concepts of the world. If you ask children to be a leaf blowing in the wind, you will see their interpretation of what this is like. It can serve as the foundation for some future planning.

1. Start with ideas that are simple and familiar to children and provide props that support these ideas, but do not dictate how an activity is done. Talk about being a group marching in a parade and play music to march by.

2. When you ask children to move in a particular way, be sure to verbally discuss "how" this will happen and to give clear, precise details about the event the children are portraying. Using the example of leaves, ask children what would make the leaves fall, then talk about how they would move in response to falling off the tree versus being blown by a strong wind.

3. Talk about personal space and how to figure out where they can move without bumping into each other.

4. Provide props such as scarves, hats, to make an experience more concrete. Props help set the stage for children who cannot see well. They can expand on an idea that has been established.

5. Moving creatively to music encourages a variety of movements and gracefulness, and there is no right or wrong. Dancing, from the waltz to the twist to the macarena, is good exercise and great for developing coordination.

Dramatic Play. Dramatic play allows children to learn about, experience, and control situations. They can make new experiences more familiar by playing through them first. Working through potentially frightening experiences may make them easier to handle.

1. Provide a lot of props. Be sure that at least some of them give obvious cues (tactile as well as visual) about the activity going on. For example, teacups and saucers mean a tea party; adding a tea pot and appropriate clothing sets the mood.

2. When children dress up, check to be sure there are no dangling belts or scarves that could cause tripping.

3. Set up an optometrist's office and have children test each other's vision.

4. Be sure to include eyeglasses frames as props.

Transitions

Transition times are difficult for all children because a lot of movement and change occurs.

1. Use nonvisual cues as one means of dismissal, for example, "Everyone with a shirt that buttons can get their coats." You can use types of clothing, fabrics, or the first letters of names.

2. Dismiss children with visual impairments either early or late, when there will be the least amount of confusion.

3. Allow enough time for children to use their adaptive skills. If children are slow or need more help, provide additional support.

Summary

The visual system is a complex one, and disease or injury to the system can cause visual impairment. Early signs of a visual impairment include lack of attention to objects, holding objects too close or too far away, and inattention. The degree of the impairment determines the accommodations that are needed. Problems in different parts of the visual system have different implications for the child and his learning.

For educational purposes, we are concerned with the amount of usable vision a child has. Children with little functional vision are dependent on auditory and tactile sources for learning. Children with low vision need accommodations such as larger print or particular lighting. There are many assistive devices that are available to children with visual impairments to help compensate for their lack of vision.

Young children are difficult to assess visually, and some of the standard screening testing such as the Snellen tests are unlikely to identify children who are myopic. This is a drawback, as we are most concerned about children who lack the near vision necessary for reading and other close work. Children have a variety of needs depending on the amount of vision they have available to them. Some activities must be modified to allow them to participate: other concerns relate to safety.

Educational Resources

American Alliance for Health, Physical Education, Recreation, and Dance (AAHPERD)
PO Box 10375
Alexandria, VA 22310
Provides suggestions for helping infants and young children to grow and learn while using their bodies.

The American Council of the Blind
1155 15th Street NW, Suite 720
Washington, DC 20005
(800) 424-8666, (202) 476-5085
http://abc.org/
This page has general information about the council and contains issues of their monthly publication The Braille Forum.

American Foundation for the Blind (AFB)
11 Penn Plaza, Suite 300
New York, NY 10001
(800) 232-5463, In New York: (212) 502-7657, FAX (212) 502-7774
http://www.igc.apc.org/afb/
Serves as a clearinghouse for information on visual impairments. Call for their publications catalogue. Their Web page has information on blindness, Braille, reviews of books, links to laws passed, and additional information.

American Printing House for the Blind (APH)
1839 Frankfort Avenue
PO Box 6085
Louisville, KY 40206-0085
(800) 223-1839, (502) 895-2405, FAX (502) 895-1509
A resource for educational materials in large print and Braille; sells children's Braille books; manufactures and sells equipment and assistive devices for the visually impaired.

Association for Education and Rehabilitation of the Blind and Visually Impaired (AER)
206 North Washington Street
Alexandria, VA 22314
(703) 548-1884, FAX (703) 683-2926
An organization concerned with education, guidance, vocational rehabilitation, and occupational placement.

Blind Links
http://www.seidata.com/~marriage/tblind.html
This page has links to topics including adaptive technology, advocacy training, employment, and medical information.

Blindness Resource Center
http://www.nyise.org/text/blind.htm
This page, through the New York Institute for Special Education, has information on organizations and other resources.

Canadian National Institute for the Blind (CNIB)
1929 Bayview Avenue
Toronto, Ontario M4G 4C8 Canada
(416) 480-7580, FAX (416) 480-7677
Provides rehabilitative services and counseling for any degree of visual impairment, including deaf-blind; provides literature and addresses of provincial and local CNIB offices.

Library of Congress National Library Service for the Blind and Physically Handicapped
1291 Taylor Street NW
Washington, DC 20542
(800) 424-8567, (202) 707-5100, FAX (202) 707-0712
(800) 424-8572 (Reference), (800)424-9100 (Application)
http://lcweb.loc.gov/nls/nls.html
The service provides talking and large print books for individuals with visual or physical impairments. All services and publications are free. Their Web page contains information on how to find Braille books and talking books.

Lions World Service for the Blind
http://www.rollanet.org/~rlions/lwsb/
This home page explores the rehabilitation center, which provides services for the blind.

National Association for Parents of the Visually Impaired (NAPVI)
PO Box 562
Camden, NY 13316
Provides practical suggestions for teaching games and activities to young children and information about resources.

National Association for the Visually Handicapped
22 West 21st Street
New York, NY 10010

Provides information and resources for and about individuals with partial vision.

National Society for the Prevention of Blindness, Inc.
79 Madison Avenue
New York, NY 10016

The society and affiliates carry out a program for service, education, and research dealing with blindness prevention.

NCIP Library
http://www.edu.org/FSC/NCIP/Library_VI_TOC
.html

This page lists resources that relate to the blind, including products, research, organizations, and publications.

Videos and Materials

Blind Children's Center
4120 Marathon Street
PO Box 29159
Los Angles, CA 90020-0159
(800) 222-3566, In California: (800) 222-3567,
(213) 664-2153
FAX (213) 665-3828

Provides resources and support to parents, with many practical low-cost publications.

National Braille Press
88 St. Stephen Street
Boston, MA 02115
(617) 266-6160, FAX (617) 437-0456

The Children's Braille Book Club inserts Braille pages into standard print children's books.

Touch Toys
PO Box 2224
Rockville, MD 20852

Information on tactile toys and how to construct them.

Visually Impaired Preschool Services
1229 Garvin Place
Louisville, KY 40203
(502) 636-3207, FAX (502) 363-0024

Produces a series of five videotapes, Can Do Video Series, *about preschool children and their families.*

References

Best, A. R. (1993). Access to the curriculum for children with visual impairments. In A. R. Fielder, A. R. Best, & M. C. O. Bax (Eds.), *The management of visual impairment in childhood* (pp. 157–162). London: Mac Keith Press.

Bishop, V. E. (1991). Preschool visually impaired children: A demographic study. *Journal of Visual Impairment and Blindness, 85,* 69–74.

Coopersmith, S. (1967). *The antecedents of self-esteem.* San Francisco: Freeman.

Foster, A. (1988). Childhood blindness. *Eye, 2*(Suppl.), S27–S36.

Gilbert, D. (1993). In A. R. Fiedler, A. B. Best, & M. C. Max (Eds.), *The management of visual impairments in childhood* (pp. 180–208). London, England: Mac Keith Press.

Harrison, F., & Crow, M. (1993). *Living and learning with blind children: A guide for parents and teachers of visually impaired children.* Toronto, Ontario: University of Toronto Press.

Jan, J. E., & Robinson, G. C. (1989). A multidisciplinary program for visually impaired children and youths. *International Ophthalmology Clinics, 29,* 33–36.

Kastein, S., Spaulding, I., & Scharf, B. (1980). *Raising the young blind child: A guide for parents and educators.* New York: Human Sciences Press.

Menacker, S. J., & Batshaw, M. L. (1997). Vision: Our window to the world. In M. L. Batshaw (Ed.), *Children with disabilities* (4th ed., pp. 211–239). Baltimore: Brookes.

Nelson, L. B., Calhoun, J. H., & Hurley, R. D. (1991). *Pediatric ophthalmology* (3rd ed.). Philadelphia: Saunders.

Peterson, N. L. (1987). *Early intervention for handicapped and at-risk children: An introduction to early childhood-special education.* Denver, CO: Love.

Salvia, J., & Ysseldyke, J. E. (1995). *Assessment* (6th ed.). Boston: Houghton Mifflin.

Stager, D. R., Birch, E. E., & Weakley, D. R. (1990). Amblyopia and the pediatrician. *Pediatric Annals, 19,* 301–305, 309–315.

Tongue, A. C. (1987). Refractive errors in children. *Pediatric Clinics of North America, 34,* 1425–1437.

Tuttle, D. W., & Tuttle, N. R. (1996). *Self-esteem and adjusting with blindness: The process of responding to life's demands* (2nd ed.). Springfield, IL: Thomas.

U.S. Department of Education. (1989). *Eleventh annual report to Congress on the implementation of the education of the handicapped act.* Washington, DC: U.S. Government Printing Office.

Warburg, M., Frederiksen, P., & Rattleff, J. (1979). Blindness among 7,720 mentally retarded children in Denmark. *Clinical Developmental Medicine, 73,* 56–67.

PART THREE

Curriculum
and Activities
for Inclusion

Chapter 18

CURRICULUM FOR INCLUSION

The first part of this text dealt with the *hows* of educating and including children with diverse abilities and with basic information about diverse abilities and their potential impact on learning. It didn't discuss *what* to teach, that is, content. As leaders have focused on what children know and what they need to know, they are becoming increasingly concerned about standards and the content that children should learn at various ages. Before 1998, there was less concern about the struggles that regular education was having with regard to issues related to the scope, purpose, and nature of education. Many individuals in early childhood education had focused on young children and had not really been part of the standards movement, nor had those in special education. As of 1998, in the United States, *all* children are expected to take part in the regular education curriculum, including the assessment process, with accommodations if necessary, unless an exemption can be justified.

The federal government has supported the effort to develop national standards (Bredekamp & Rosegrant, 1995). This standards movement is part of the National Education Goals, known as Goals 2000. As of 1998, it does not have a great deal of popular support, which may be related to the complexity of the issue and the fear of federal judgments and interference in the educational process. But it is a movement to do something about improving all levels of education.

Standards in and of themselves are neither good nor bad. However, these standards can transform the early childhood curriculum. Before 1998, there was little concern about standards in special education, as these children were exempt from both standards and the assessment practices that looked at how standards were being met. As children with diverse abilities are now included in regular classes, they will also be included in the standards and the assessment process.

Early childhood educators face additional challenges. They not only have to teach children in a developmentally appropriate way, but must find ways to support children to meet recognized standards, whether the standards are those developed by professional organizations, the federal or state government, or the school district. These standards, plus the 1997 amendments to IDEA, will influence the development of IEPs and IFSPs. The goals for individualized programs, developmentally appropriate practices, and national standards, and the benchmarks to meet these standards must be seen as guiding and building on each other to develop successful programs for all children in early care and education settings.

Standards

Different people mean different things by *standards*. Not only can we not agree on what standards to support, but there is not real agreement on what standards are.

Content or Performance

Some see standards in terms of specific content based on subject matter areas; others see it as the ability to perform certain tasks. In reality, the two are intrinsically related (Kendall & Marzano, 1996). Content standards specify what children should know and be able to do; performance standards specify at what level children need to know and demonstrate their understanding of the concept to meet the standard, that is, the quality of the child's performance. In elementary school, report cards typically indicate how a child is meeting performance standards.

The emphasis of this book is on content standards. The expectation is that content standards will be used to determine the annual goals that are on children's IEP, and benchmarks related to these standards will include both subcomponents of the goal and performance standards to judge competency.

Literacy or Expertise

One way of looking at standards is by looking at the expectations one has relative to the content to be mastered and the level at which it must be mastered to reach the standards. Does everyone have to be an expert at everything? Literacy and expertise form a continuum of competence, with literacy being the minimum that all students need of knowledge and skills in a particular area to continue moving toward becoming competent adults of the twenty-first century. Expertise includes the level of mastery and content options that should be available to children who want to become mini-experts in a field (Kendall & Marzano, 1996). This text focuses on the literacy end of the scale, the skills that all children need to attain.

Thinking and Reasoning

Virtually all content areas require (or should require) skills related to thinking and reasoning. The question is how these skills should be articulated in the standards. Some standards developed by professional organizations have specifically included these standards: Math standards include mathematics as problem solving, communication, reasoning, and connections (National Council of Teachers of Mathematics, 1989). Others are implied in the standards themselves, such as in the visual arts: choosing and evaluating a range of subject matter, symbols, and ideas (Consortium of National Arts Education Associations, 1994). The standards are written by different groups, and they include these skills in ways each group feels are most appropriate.

When you try to use the standards in program planning, it is clear that they have some commonality that transcends content areas. For this text, we have made these generic thinking and reasoning skills rather than tied them to a content area. For example, one science goal is "to improve cause-and-effect reasoning"; this goal can relate to safety and traffic signs, magnets, or the different textures of playdough. Some types of thinking and reasoning should transcend content areas, just as building self-esteem and increasing inclusion happens across the curriculum. We professionals often have a particular area of expertise; we may need to draw back from standards and try to gain a more holistic approach to the curriculum and be sure that we do not forget the child in the struggle over the standards the child should meet.

Benchmarks and Objectives

Benchmarks are subcomponents of a goal or standard and can be identified for all age/grade levels (Kendall & Marzano, 1996). In the public schools, the major benchmarks are assessed at grades 3 or 4, 7 or 8, and 11 or 12. Obviously, these are *major* benchmarks that provide direction, but for the most part, they are used for assessment and accounting purposes.

Regardless of the discussion about standards, there is a need to have appropriate content in all content domains, a method for determining the order in which this content should be presented, some parameters for the scope of what content is covered, and the determination of some minimal level of performance. At the least, the standards can guide our thinking about curriculum and what we like and dislike about the standards. They provide the impetus for continued reflection about what are developmentally appropriate practices during the early childhood years.

Using the Standards

The educational standards developed by professional organizations are included by content area. In some cases, just an abstract of the standard is used; in other cases, more details are given. This was done because of the complexity and applicability of some of the standards and because some standards did not include children below kindergarten. We strongly recommend that you read the standards developed, not to jump into the fray over their use, but as part of your reflective learning and growth and to clarify what you believe is important. As a field, early childhood has not strongly embraced content. We need to give it some serious thought before we discover we are expected to include content we feel is developmentally inappropriate.

Because of the link between curriculum standards and activities, the order below reflects the organization of the activity chapters. Where there are more holistic standards (for example, self-awareness), they have been included. Some areas do not have standards (for example, self-esteem).

Thinking and Reasoning Goals

Some skills are necessary in all areas of learning. Because we are combining and adapting many sets of standards, we have classified them as thinking and reasoning skills and grouped these skills together.

To Improve Problem-Solving Skills

Living and working with others, children have to learn to negotiate, mediate, and compromise. Young children know about "yes" and "no" and "mine," but they need to be taught ways of taking turns, sharing, and developing rules that all can abide by. They also need to have some knowledge of exceptions to rules and why and how these exceptions are made. Because we live in a world of diminishing natural resources, children need to learn about conservation and the interaction between people and their environment. (We use paper for drawing. Paper comes from trees. If we use both sides of the paper, we will have to cut down fewer trees.) These children will face many problems as they grow older, they need to see themselves as problem solvers from an early age.

To Increase Vocabulary

All fields have a vocabulary that is essential to understand; thus, increasing vocabulary must be considered part of all areas of the curriculum. Children need to both understand and speak to make their needs and wants known. They need to know the words to use to be clear and specific in their requests. The number of words children both understand and can use needs to be expanded. Children must learn to speak with accuracy and precision. To do this takes a large vocabulary, and they need to tie this vocabulary to what they are learning and doing.

To Follow Directions

Following directions is an important aspect of education in general. Children need practice in following increasingly complex directions. They need feedback on how well they are following the given directions. They need practice in giving directions, another related and necessary skill.

**To Improve
Memory Skills**

Children need to remember what they learn in all areas. Unless children can remember what they have learned in the past, they do not have a solid foundation for future knowledge. Contextual learning and variations help children group information and see connections. It also helps children retrieve this information.

**To Improve
Cause-and-Effect
Reasoning**

Children need to learn that they affect their world. Cups don't usually spill on their own—something causes the cup to spill. Children need to know about their actions and begin to learn how to make changes. At the beginning, children usually use a trial-and-error approach and may even need an adult to point out that they were responsible for the change. They need to establish a broad base of understanding before they can move into systematically testing hypotheses. They need to think broadly about causes and effects. They need to establish some control over their world.

**To Improve
Generalization
Skills**

Generalization is the application of thinking skills to other areas. It provides the basis for future learning. It allows children to have a base from which they can make more accurate predictions and structure their world. They can begin to make predictions based on information. We can't experience everything, and the ability to generalize experience and information allows children to learn from analogies and to make predictions about their world.

**To Improve
Problem Solving**

Creativity will be needed to find solutions to some of the problems confronting humanity today. The process of seeking unconventional solutions starts in early childhood. Children with disabilities face challenges that others do not. They need to seek innovative solutions to keep themselves in the mainstream.

**Social
Awareness**

For young children, social awareness is necessary to understand and function in the world in which they live.

Self-Esteem

Before one can reach out to others and the world, one needs to learn about oneself. During their early childhood years, children are developing their values and attitudes about themselves, other children, and adults in their family and community. They are developing their concept of self. It is important that they have a broad range of experiences and are exposed to people and materials without gender, racial, or cultural bias. People with diverse abilities must be portrayed accurately, including both their abilities and disabilities.

Inclusion

From an early age, children need to become aware of individual differences and learn to respect these differences. Children need to better understand how differences affect children and how children can interact with each other in light of these diverse abilities. Ignoring differences is not effective. Stories can be useful, but children learn best by doing.

Examine your feelings about children with diverse abilities, children from different ethnic backgrounds, and your expectations based on gender to discover if you have personal values that might make working with certain children challenging. Check out your verbal language and body language to see if they reflect an antibias message (Derman-Sparks & the ABC Task Force, 1989).

As children begin to be aware of how they are different from each other, the skill of a sensitive teacher can help determine the long-term outcome of this awareness. Children look to you as a model. If you pity children with diverse abilities or are overprotective or condescending toward them, the children will react the same way. If you celebrate only holidays that a majority of the children participate in, those who have different beliefs may feel excluded. If you always choose boys to go to the block area and expect girls to use the dramatic play area, you are supporting stereotypic gender differences.

Awareness is important for *all* children; a child with a physical impairment cannot be expected to have any more understanding of what it is like to have a visual impairment than any other child in your class. Children need help in learning to view events from others' perspectives early in life, without making judgments about whether that perspective is good or bad. Activities in the area of inclusion are not easy; they are rarely part of the everyday curriculum. They require special planning, thinking, and sensitivity on your part. They also have special payoffs, to you and to all the children in your class.

Provide an atmosphere in which issues about race, gender, disability, and violence can be discussed. Young children are very aware of differences. Support diversity in your classroom through activities, materials, and program planning. Children may need to be taught specific ways to handle people who stare, make unkind remarks, or are physically aggressive. Find out how parents cope with these issues and support and expand on their techniques, or if necessary, support children in learning different ways of responding. Children may wonder how to talk to a child who stutters or what questions it is appropriate to ask about a prosthesis. They will use your behavior as a model. Children may need help in finding roles to play and adaptations and accommodations and allow all children to play together.

Social Studies

Social studies is a subject with specific activities and learning, but also one in which observation and modeling are important learning tools. National standards have been developed for three social studies areas—geography, civics and government, and history—in *Geography for Life, National Standards* (Geography Education Standards Project [GESP], 1994); *National Standards for Civics and Government* (Center for Civic Education [CCE], 1994); and *National Standards: History for Grades K-4: Expanding Children's World in Time and Space* (National Center for History in Schools [NCHS], 1994).

Some of the social studies standards are problematic for young children. The history standards are written with an understanding of young children, but standards for geography and civics are numerous and require mastery of abstract concepts that most children between 3 and 8 are not capable of. Even if children master some of these concepts at a superficial level, the difficulty of mastery may well do more to discourage them than to pique their interests as global citizens (Seefeldt, 1995). Although the standards may need revision, the concepts themselves are sound and can be used for guidance in increasing children's awareness and exploration of ideas. They provide guidance regarding areas to be covered, but it is up to early childhood educators to match the appropriate methods and materials to use to cover them in a developmentally appropriate way.

The geography content standards for grades K through 4 are abstracted below:

> The World in Spatial Terms: Children need to use maps and other geographic representations as tools to learn about people, places, and environments and their distribution on the earth's surface. They need to use mental maps to organize this information.

Places and Regions: Children must learn the physical and human characteristics of places, including culture and experience. People create regions to interpret earth's complexity.

Physical Systems: Physical processes shape the earth's surface, and different ecosystems exist.

Human Systems: Humans are part of geography. Their numbers, migration, and settlement patterns and culture impact the earth's surface. Human systems are economically interdependent on earth's surface, and cooperation and conflict influence the division and control of earth's surface.

Environment and Society: Our actions modify the physical environment, and these changes influence natural resources, which in turn influence our lives.

The Uses of Geography: Geography skills help interpret the past and present and plan for the future (GESP, 1994).

Young children's study of geography begins with digging in sand, being fascinated by the stars, and getting wet from the rain. The standards are given so you have a feel for the range of content areas in geography. The process of *doing* geography can guide the curriculum. The skills are asking questions and acquiring, organizing, analyzing, and answering these questions (Seefeldt, 1995).

The Center for Civic Education has 29 content standards, which are daunting and require concepts few young children understand. However, the questions that they used to develop these standards provide useful guidance for the area. These questions related to what government is and what it should do; the basic values and principles of American democracy; the relationship of the United States to other nations and world affairs; and the roles of citizens in our democracy (CCE, 1994). Seefeldt (1995) has translated these into principles that also provide useful guidance for early childhood:

A willingness to participate in improving the quality of life in the community, the nation, and the world;

The ability to take the perspective of, cooperate with, work with, and respect others; and

Knowing the mechanics of rule setting and voting, and balancing personal interests with the common good.

The history standards are divided into two broad areas: historical thinking skills and historical understanding. The standards are abstract and we strongly recommend using literature to make the knowledge meaningful to young children (Seefeldt, 1995).

Historical Thinking Skills: These skills include chronological thinking, historical comprehension, analysis and interpretations, issues and decision making, and research capabilities.

Historical Understanding: This understanding includes knowledge about family life now, in the recent past, and long ago; knowing about the history of the community and how communities were different long ago; the people, events, problems, and ideas that created the history of each state; how democratic values came to be and are exemplified; the reasons people move now and did so long ago and the folklore and culture that helped form our heritage; the development of various societies throughout the world and the impact of science and technology on development.

Taken together, these social studies standards and principles require early childhood educators to take a very close look at how they present the social studies curriculum. This is an area that is frequently neglected in early childhood but has more standards than other areas. It will take a skillful teacher to implement social studies standards in a developmentally appropriate way.

In early childhood, social studies is usually taught through daily organization and decision making: deciding what to name the new goldfish, what to do when someone knocks down the blocks, and how to share special materials. This is all part of the social learning that occurs at this age.

As children and their families enter your classroom, they will learn something about how you teach social studies. They will look at the pictures and bulletin boards to see if they represent the culture and language of the children you teach as well as those in the community. They will look at the books on display to see if they support a bias-free approach or if they reinforce racial and gender stereotypes. They will evaluate the room to determine whether or not it allows diversity in play. As their eyes wander, they will note whether the dolls represent diverse cultures reflective of the children in the classroom. They will look for the possibility of language differences, not only Spanish, but American Sign Language and Braille. They might even note whether there are pictures and books about children with diverse abilities. All children need to feel they are part of the class. It is important that they become aware of themselves both as unique human beings and as people who are similar to, as well as different from, others. Children can learn that they are all members of the class even though some of them are boys and others girls, some like art and others don't, and some wear glasses and others don't.

Children learn through social studies about the situational aspects of behavior. Behavior that is appropriate in one situation or time is not necessarily right in another. Children in the process of learning to take turns wonder whether or not they will actually get their turn if they postpone it or let

Children need to have caring adults to talk to about problems and concerns. Educators need to listen to children and talk with them about options for constructive resolution.

someone ahead of them. If they do lose their turn, they will be less likely to take turns in the future.

As children with diverse abilities are increasingly included in regular classrooms and community activities, it is important that they learn more about these environments. Start with your setting. Help children feel comfortable knowing their way around both indoors and out. Take short walks in the area. Focus some part of your curriculum on the community itself as well as communities in general—why we have them, what they do, and how they help the people who live there. Discuss the differences between rural and urban communities.

Field trips are one of the most common ways of making abstract ideas concrete to young children. Resource people can be invited to visit and resource media such as film, television, videotapes, compact disks, and the Internet can also be used to include the social studies standards in your curriculum.

Health and Safety

Health and safety are areas of study as well as states of being. When young children become aware of what it means to be unhealthy and have the knowledge and vocabulary to describe their symptoms, there is less likelihood of serious, undetected illness. When they have learned to recognize signs of danger and act appropriately, the environment will be less threatening to them. Children need to refine their awareness and skills in these areas. Only children who are healthy and feel safe are free to enter into your program fully. Children learn basic health practices as part of a routine (such as washing their hands after toileting and before snack).

The Joint Committee on National Health Education Standards (1995) developed the National Health Education Standards: Achieving Health Literacy. Young children achieve health literacy through experience and learning activities related to personal health (Hendricks & Smith, 1995). The abstracted standards include concepts relating to health promotion and disease prevention; accessing health information, products, and services; practicing health-enhancing behaviors and reducing health risks; using interpersonal communication skills to enhance health; learning skills in setting goals and making decisions to enhance health; and advocating for personal, family, and community health.

In early childhood, most of the emphasis is placed on the development of a healthy lifestyle, including good hygiene and the prevention of infectious diseases and injuries. Safety education focuses on self-awareness and the prevention of injuries in the classroom and at home. Accidents are the leading cause of death for children under 14 (Children's Safety Network, 1991). Common accidents for young children include falls, burns, eating small, sharp objects or poisonous substances, choking, smothering, traffic accidents, and water accidents. Children need skills to avoid these situations and to cope if they have not avoided them.

Proper nutrition is an important part of being healthy. Infants come into this world preferring sweet over bitter and sour tastes. Too many sweets in the diet contribute to dental caries and to excess weight. As a teacher, your role is to choose snacks wisely, offering foods that are low in fat and salt and high in complex carbohydrates. Because 22 percent of children's caloric intake comes from snacks (Rogers & Morris, 1986), choose them wisely. When you make snacks with the children as part of your programming, make sure they adhere to the same standards. Find ways of celebrating special events that do not always include cupcakes and candy.

Management of health-related problems is part of the programming for young children. Allergies are the most common chronic health problem of children. However, current concerns focus on developmentally appropriate drug and alcohol abuse prevention and AIDS prevention as well.

Social Awareness Goals

This is a very broad area that has recently witnessed the development of sets of standards that impact the goals we set for children. It is necessary to integrate these standards to develop goals that both meet the standards and are developmentally appropriate for *all* children as well as meeting the individualized needs of some children. Social awareness begins with self-awareness.

To Improve Self-Esteem

How children feel about themselves may influence the risks they are willing to take in trying out new materials and meeting new people. Children with positive self-concepts evaluate information from that perspective; a bad experience is just that. Children with low self-esteem have difficulty differentiating between the bad experience and themselves. Children need to experience many successes.

To Increase Awareness of Roles People Play

When children enter an early care and education setting, they may have had little experience with adults other than their immediate family and caregivers. They need to broaden their experience with the roles that adults play as well as the authority structure that exists. They need information about the helping professions. Children can begin to learn which occupations sound interesting to them. People's occupations require different skills and preparation. They need a perspective on roles that presents neither gender nor racial bias. They need to know about the educational setting and the roles that the people they see play and how educators and others are different from parents.

To Broaden Concepts of Families

Children start out very egocentric, believing that all children are like them and all families are like their families. They need to become aware of individual and family differences without making judgments that "different" is "bad." Learning about the functions of families and the roles they play, including an international perspective, is the beginning of citizenship. They need to know that some families have only one parent and some have parents of the same sex; that some children move between families and that some children live in homes of heterosexual adults that are not married; that some families have more than one generation living together; that families live in a variety of different types of housing; and that families have existed through generations.

To Increase Inclusion

If this is the children's first school experience, they may have had little experience with peers other than siblings. Some children learn how to get along with each other easily, without conscious effort on the teacher's part; others need to be taught this just as much as they need to be taught math and literarcy skills. Children may need to be taught specific skills to help them become part of the group, and special activities may need to be created that include all children in the group. Children need to learn how to join groups and be included as well as the skills of including others. Part of learning how to include others is awareness of how people are the same and different.

To Increase Awareness of Individual Differences and Similarities

Children need to become aware of how others are both like and different from them. They must learn to acknowledge, but not judge, others by these differences. Sensitivity must be taught through firsthand experiences with adult input to help clarify feelings. Children also need to learn skills to accommodate differences.

To Improve Adaptive Skills

The development of independent functioning and self-sufficiency is important not only as a motor accomplishment, but for self-esteem as well. Focusing on motor activities that promote autonomy serves both functions.

To Understand Geography Concepts

Children need to learn about the world in which they live, and they need to start by understanding their near world. They can understand concepts of mapping by mapping the classroom or the way to the nurse's office. They can understand locations and climates and know that there are different areas of the world that have climates that are different from theirs. They can learn about the physical characteristics of the environment, starting with the yard they play in. Children need a solid grounding in concrete geography concepts before they venture into the abstract ones.

To Participate in Democratic Process

Children learn by doing. They need to be part of a democratic process before they can understand why it is important. Class roles and procedures need to be framed in a way that helps children see them as part of the democratic process. Children need to learn skills to help reach consensus, and this may be most appropriately done in figuring out what to name the class pet. When educators have group times with children, they need to point out the principles on which they make decisions such as who to call on and why.

To Increase Health Literacy

Health and safety patterns must be conscientiously taught to young children. Children must learn to make good judgments about what is and is not safe for them to do. They must learn to think through the implications of actions *before* they decide to do something and then evaluate the consequences in terms of whether or not it is a safe thing to do. Children must be taught ways of compensating for diverse abilities and be aware of ways to be safe and healthy.

Language and Literacy

Learning to communicate and understand communications is one of the major tasks facing all young children. Learning language is a dynamic process that is affected by the language heard in the environment and the way that adults respond to the development of speech. In situations where children have rich language models and are supported in producing speech, they are more open to new opportunities to expand their language skills. In addition to a strong experiential base to provide something to talk about, children also need to feel the urge to communicate. If no one listens and responds, children are unlikely to talk. Children who spend long hours watching television have little incentive to talk because television is a non-interactive media.

Speaking, listening, reading, and writing are the major components of the language and literacy curriculum. Although this chapter highlights them individually, overall program planning sees them and other curriculum areas as interrelated and interdependent. Likewise, although there are designated language and literacy activities, the language and literacy curriculum should be part of all program planning. And the goals for language and literacy, such as increasing vocabulary, appear in the math and science area as well as the language area.

The standards for the English language arts were developed by the International Reading Association (IRA) and the National Council of Teachers of English (NCTE). These 12 standards are developmental and appropriate for emerging literacy, yet they are not prescriptive; there is ample room for innovation and creativity. A synopsis follows (IRA/NCTE 1996, p. 3):

Children need to be exposed to a wide range of print and nonprint texts to acquire information about themselves and the world they live in. Texts should include works or fiction and nonfiction as well as classic and contemporary works. These works should be from many periods in many genres. They need to develop a wide range of strategies to use texts including knowledge of the English language and life experience. Children need to learn the structure and conventions of language and to adjust their language usage (written and spoken) to their purpose and audience. They need to use a variety of resources (library, electronic, video, and so on) to gather information and the skills to synthesize and organize this data and to use data in research. They need to respect diversity in languages. They need to use spoken, written, and visual language to accomplish their purposes.

Speaking

Speaking, or expressive language, is a major component of the early language and literacy curriculum. To match language and literacy activities to the level of the children in your class, it is important to know each child's present level of language functioning, what the average child of that age can say, and types of activities that are likely to help the child move from his current level to the next one.

Although most children have the ability to speak, it is not necessarily wise to set up a situation in which you *require* them to speak. This social demand may make them feel uncomfortable or even frightened, especially if it is in front of a group (French, 1996). You can create a no-win situation if you demand and the child refuses. Speaking under these situations is developmentally inappropriate for children who do not volunteer.

There is some professional debate about the role language plays in learning. Some focus on children's active role in language learning as they construct language (and knowledge) for themselves to meet their needs to communicate. The child is viewed as a producer of knowledge, not a recipient of it (Piaget, 1967). The process itself is interactive. Others place more emphasis on the social function of language and view speech as a vehicle for self-organization (Vygotsky, 1978). The core of young children's language and literacy development is to convey meaning through speaking and writing and to interpret meaning through listening and reading (Whitmore & Goodman, 1995). Whether children invent language or use it as a vehicle for social interaction, it is an important part of the development of communication and knowledge. The role of the teacher is to ensure that children have a rich base on which to build communication skills.

Expansion and extension are two techniques that encourage the use of more complex language structures. *Expansion* is the process of extracting the meaning of a child's utterances and putting them into a more complex form. With a younger child using telegraphic speech such as "Me go," the expansion might be "Where do you want to go?" or "Are you ready to go now?" The objective is to provide a language model, not just an answer that says "O.K." As children get older, expansion can help them be more specific in their word usage and structural complexity. If the child says, "I want that," respond with "Do you want the one with the red flowers or the one with the green stripes?" Your objective is to encourage the child to give you a more descriptive response in return.

Extension involves putting the child's statement in a broader context, that is, extending the meaning of the child's phrase. If the child says, "I want to go out," you might respond, "If you want to go outside and play, you need to put your coat on." Using these techniques is particularly effective, because children are prepared to listen to the response because it is meaningful to them.

Sometimes, it is helpful to rephrase what you say if the child does not appear to understand or comprehend your words. This is also useful if you don't understand the child. Or ask the child, "Tell me in different words." This way, both you and the child have a second chance to process the information.

Remember that you are *always* a language model for the children, not just when you are specifically teaching a language lesson. Whether you are addressing a child, talking to the child's peers, or talking to other adults in the classroom, you are a language model. The richer and more descriptive your language is and the greater the variety of syntactic forms you use, the better language model you will be for the children.

It is imperative that children have a vocabulary large enough to express their wants and needs and to enable them to understand the wants and needs of others. They must also learn the rules that govern how language is used. Understanding language enables them to function effectively in their environment. They also need to learn that language can be both spoken and written.

Listening

Listening is a relatively recent addition to the language and literacy curriculum. It was obvious to most people that children learned to talk and must be taught to read and write, but listening was taken as a given. The belief was that all children knew how to listen; they just needed to "pay attention."

Listening is a complex component of learning. It involves hearing that allows for auditory identification and discrimination. There is both a short- and long-term memory component. Listening or auditory processing is also part of attending and sensorimotor integration. If you ask a child "What is your name?", the child must hear the message, interpret the meaning, formulate an answer, and respond to the question (Jalongo, 1996). We do not assume children are listening unless they respond to our requests.

Listening, or at least making sense out of what is heard—taking in information—has a developmental base. It is the role of the adult to match the language base of the child. Use of expansion and extension can improve listening skills. Listening moves from a point when an infant can gain no meaning from words themselves to where children can listen to information about places they have not been to and experiences they have never had:

No information intake via language: Initially, the verbal aspects of language (words) have no meaning for children; they use nonverbal cues by looking at what is being done or the tone of the voice to gain information.

Information intake if language is redundant with the experience. This is like the play-by-play broadcast: Adults put in words what children are seeing or experiencing.

Information intake if language compliments or extends the ongoing experience.

Information intake if language compliments or extends the context of the experience, that is, paints a broader scene.

Information intake if language compliments or extends a topic or activity a child has initiated.

Information intake if language reminds the child of past familiar experience and extends that experience.

Information intake if language is about a new topic the child has no experience with nor any particular interest in (adapted from French, 1996).

Much teaching in public schools is about new topics some children may have had little experience with, and perhaps no interest in. If children have not had the previous developmental experiences, they may not gain information through listening.

As with speaking, children are most likely to develop good listening skills if you are a good model. If you always repeat what you say, children learn *not* to listen the first time. When you are listening to a child, *listen*. Also, expect that children will listen when you are talking to other adults. Don't talk about children as if they are not there. Children seem to listen better when we don't want them to.

Although we don't often think of listening as a school subject, children spend more of their school time listening than doing any other single task. They listen to the teacher, they listen to peers, they listen to the intercom, and they listen to recorded sounds. For younger children, we have finger-plays that help them "zip their mouths closed" so they can listen, or they put on their "listening cap." The goal is to have the children be quiet. Despite the preparation for listening, the focus is still on speaking rather than the skills involved in listening. One of the questions we as teachers must evaluate is how much of what we say is worth listening to? Would we be willing to sit spellbound for several hours each day listening to boring information? For children to practice good listening skills, they need something stimulating to listen to. Interest helps them to focus on listening as a process (Jalongo, 1996).

Just as in other areas, it is helpful to develop rules for listening. For children to listen, they must pay attention. Teachers usually have a signal to focus

Listening is an active skill; like any other, it requires practice.

children's attention on listening. Common listening rules have to do with taking turns, not interrupting, raising your hand, and so on. You might add some speaking rules as well, such as talking loud enough to be heard and speaking clearly. You don't want children not to participate, yet you can't expect them to listen when it is not possible to hear. Helping them fine-tune their listening skills means that children will get more useful information from their environment.

There are a variety of auditory skills that are part of the listening process:

Auditory identification is the process of getting meaning from what is heard. Some of the first words children learn to identify are their name and those of their family, favorite toys, and pets. Later, children learn to identify sounds in the environment such as a car horn, running water, and other familiar sounds. The ability to identify specific sounds and to attach meaning to these sounds allows children to get more cues about their environment.

Auditory discrimination involves distinguishing likenesses and differences in sounds. Children learn to distinguish between a fire alarm and a jingle bell (gross discrimination) and the *p* and *b* sounds (fine discrimination). Children learn from listening who is talking and even something about their mood based on their speech patterns, volume, and choice of words. Once children can identify a variety of sounds, they begin to make finer distinctions. They may know without concentrating that the teacher is calling roll, but they must listen carefully to know whether to respond to "Kenny" or "Denny." Rhyming words help sharpen children's ability to identify similar and dissimilar sounds in words and build vocabulary at the same time.

Auditory memory involves remembering what was heard a few moments ago, such as the directions for who could get their coats, as well as the story *Whistle for Willie* that was read last week.

Auditory closure involves using grammatical rules (tense, pronouns, and so on) and picking out speech patterns and rhyming words. For example, "Sugar and spice and everything . . ." Children learn what category of word is missing as well as the particular word. They know the sentence, "We swim in the . . ." might be completed by "pool" or "lake" but not "her," as the sentence requires a noun, not a pronoun.

Auditory association and comprehension are higher-level processing skills. *Auditory association* involves understanding what is heard in the context of past experience and knowledge. This is a high-level process that uses analogies (at night it is *dark*, in the day it is . . .), categorization and classification skills, and the ability to associate behavior with words: "What do you do when you hear the fire alarm?" It also involves generalizing about how things are alike and different: "How are a bell and a siren alike? How are they different?"

Auditory comprehension requires children to bring together all the previously learned skills and use them to understand and focus on what is being stated. This involves thinking up a title for a story or making up a beginning or ending for a story. The more complex the material, the more difficult the task.

It isn't necessary for you to think about each of these processes as a separate entity, but rather to be aware of them and to be sure that your range of programming in the area of listening covers all of them. And, if children have problems listening, figure out what the particular problem is. Good auditory processing provides a solid foundation for other language skills.

Reading

Educators are becoming more and more interested in and concerned about reading literacy. Although there is no general agreement on the best method for teaching reading, almost all agree that it must be done with a phonetic base. There is also agreement that the teacher is an important variable. Your enthusiasm for reading and your valuing it as a skill are important as children struggle to learn this complex task. Although the formal teaching of reading usually begins in first grade, early literacy skills set the foundation for beginning reading. Developing reading literacy is a broad process that includes field trips, followed by stories dictated by the children to help them recall trips, and children's illustrations of their trip.

Some children have difficulty learning to read. Although this book suggests many activities to make learning the small steps of reading more fun, it is your role to put the magic in reading. The best way to do that is to read to children. Read literature, poetry, and plays. Read to children even after they can read. Their ability to read and what they enjoy as literature may be on different levels. My favorite third-grader announced after the first week of school that she liked all her teachers but one, the librarian. When asked why, she said, "She doesn't read to us." Reading is difficult; it requires many skills and complex tasks. These should be learned because of the elation of reading, not the drudgery and discipline of learning letter sounds and blends.

There are basic skills that children need to learn to read. Children must learn to see small differences. Using *visual identification* skills, they must learn that objects (letters, words) have consistent labels and these labels stand for or symbolize the objects. More specifically, they must learn the names for the letters of the alphabet and the sounds they make and know that these names and sounds are consistent, based on phonetic rules. They must also distinguish among various objects by looking for similarities and differences *(visual discrimination)*. To read, children need to be able to make fine distinctions between letters and patterns of letters and spaces between words. This is an extremely difficult task built on simpler tasks such as discriminating shapes and learning about patterns and relationships. Children must not only learn to discriminate letters, they must remember what the symbols stand for. Eventually, they not only need to remember the sound of the letter, the sequence of the letters, and how this sequence influences sound. The sequence in which letters appear determines what word is formed *(mat* versus *tam)*; thus, sequential memory is an essential reading skill.

Visual closure involves recognizing objects or pieces of visual information without seeing the whole or through a quick scan. For example, it is possible to recognize a rabbit even if one ear is missing; a quick scan might not even pick up the missing ear but would register the rabbit. Eventually, children learn to look at word configurations instead of looking only at the individual letters in each word.

Higher-level skills, such as *visual association,* require children to understand what is seen in the context of past experience and knowledge. If you show children a snow scene and ask them about the temperature, they should be able to tell you it is cold. If you place a girl in a swimsuit in the snow picture and ask what is wrong, the children should point out that her clothing is inappropriate. This visual association skill includes the ability to abstract function. Children can pair a lamp and a flashlight based on their function of giving light.

Visual comprehension involves bringing together previously learned skills and using them to interpret visual information. If you show children a picture and ask them, "What's happening in this picture?", they use visual comprehension to tell a story about it. This skill includes summarizing the main points or ideas of something that has been seen.

Most professionals feel that children use their own language system to make guesses about words they cannot read. The more specific and complex their spoken language is, the better their guesses will be as they learn to read.

Writing

A classroom that provides the space, materials, time, and rewards for writing is a classroom in which children will write. Although we think of writing as beginning later than other communication skills, such thinking is due more to our inability to interpret the writing of children than to their lack of interest. From the time a toddler picks up a marker and puts the first stroke on the page, that child has become an author. Over time, with appropriate materials and encouragement, that author will go from scribbling, to drawings that may contain letters or words or tell a story, to writing words using invented spellings, to fluent writing that may involve editing and publication.

One of the first things that children want to write is their name. However, even before children can write, they need to see you write. As you write, verbalize for the children why you are writing: "I am writing your name on the paper so I know that it is yours"; "I am making a list of the things we need at the store so I don't forget"; "I am writing a note to your mother so that she knows why you have a bandage on your finger." Children need to be aware of the purpose of writing from an early age (Waring-Chaffee, 1994). If a classmate is sick, suggest that the children write a note so the child knows she is being thought of. In the age of the television and the telephone, it is important that children appreciate the value of writing.

Writing, like most other skills, progresses through developmental stages. Thus, writing a name, for example, typically progresses as follows: "scribbling a name; writing a name in mock letters; copying a name; writing a name that is illegible; writing a first name legibly, but misspelled; writing a first name correctly with some letter reversals; writing a first name correctly; writing a first name with last initial; writing a first and last name legibly and correctly spelled" (Lamme, 1985, pp. 48–49).

The requirements necessary for writing vary with age. Very young children need both stand-up and sit-down places to write (Lamme, 1985). For young children, a chalkboard with large chalk, an easel with thick markers, or just a large piece of paper taped to the wall or any other flat surface can make a mural so that writing is a social event.

Although children can write almost anywhere, having a designated place in your classroom increases the likelihood that they will do so. Choose a table large enough for at least two and no more than four children. Tape on the alphabet letters that the children are using so that each child can see them as she writes. Think of writing as a social process, not an isolated experience. Children will ask each other questions related to what they are writing. After writing, children need an audience for their written work if they choose to share it. An author's chair, where children can read to others what they have written, is part of the process.

As children become more experienced writers, the tools needed increase. The center should be equipped with a variety of paper: manila paper, wide-lined paper that covers the entire sheet as well as some that covers only half the sheet (which then allows for illustrations), plain white paper. Add paper that is folded in half, small notepads, paper cut into interesting shapes, colored paper, and even stationery. Rubber stamps allow children to print their own stationery. Almost any light-colored paper will do; it is having a variety that is important. The writing tools need to be selected to match both the paper and the children using them. The youngest children (18 months to about 3 years) need water-soluble markers and large crayons or crayons with knobs on the top. They also need large paper. As children gain experience and proficiency, add thin markers and pencils that have erasers, as well as a supply of interesting erasers. Obviously, a pencil sharpener is a must; the small handheld ones are fine if they don't "walk home." Colored pencils add interest also. As children get older, you might add some of the writing and illustrating media that are more difficult to control, such as oil pastels, chalk used on paper, watercolors, and charcoal. One solution is to place the writing center near the art area so that children can freely use art materials to illustrate their writing.

Children need to think of writing as a process, and certain materials can help make that possible. Rewriting is often slow for children, so they need to have scissors and tape available for changes. Glue or paste is also helpful, as well as a stapler, hole punch, and brads to hold pages together (provided there are not younger children around). Add a ruler, gummed stickers, cards, and other accessories. Although you might have all of these materials available, it is not necessary to have them all out at any one time. The particular materials and accessories used can vary with the theme or unit that is being studied and even the season of the year.

After children have completed a writing project, it is important that you show your appreciation of it and value it. Many children like to have writing portfolios where they keep all their work. Display some of it. Don't, however, hang up only the work that has the neatest penmanship, as this may be more a deterrent than an incentive to writing for some children.

Language and Literacy Goals

Language and literacy curriculum goals are similar for all children. These goals are measurable and are based on national standards. They provide the broad base for the regular education curriculum and for the activities that follow.

To Increase Expressive Communication

Create opportunities for children to talk. Be sure to ask questions that require more than a "yes" or "no" answer. Reinforce children when they use language appropriately. Be a good language model: Your speech should reflect a wide variety of verbs, nouns, adjectives, adverbs, and pronouns. Increase the specificity of words that depict what is happening in the environment: "He hobbled over to the table" versus "He went over there." Verbally label the environment.

To Improve Listening Skills

Vary your method of presentation to include some times for listening. Tell a story instead of reading one; use a compact disk, record, or tape; give children verbal directions. Children need to be exposed to situations that require active listening. We frequently pair listening with visual cues (reading a story with illustrations) and listening while doing something physical (dancing or movement). Listening provides cues that activities are changing and sets a moods through background music. Listening skills need to be isolated and refined, as well as paired with other sensory inputs.

To Improve Receptive Communication

Children need to not only listen, but to process the information they receive. They need to figure out which sounds carry meaning, interpret that meaning, and, often, act on the information.

To Increase Comprehension

The purpose of speaking, listening, reading, and writing is to convey meaning and elicit comprehension. Expand the meaning of words that children already know (orange is a color and also a fruit). If you expand children's speech, they learn new grammatical structures and vocabulary. Comprehension involves more than understanding what is said or read; it requires children to interpret nonverbal communication as well. Children need to become aware of the intonation patterns, tone, and rhythm of speech as clues to its meaning. They should become aware at an early age of their own body language and gain some skills in interpreting others' body language. Skills without comprehension are meaningless. Check for comprehension on a regular basis and be sure that children have a solid experiential base from which to comprehend.

To Increase Knowledge of the Structure of Language

Children need to develop a working knowledge of the systems and structures of language, not necessarily to label them but to use them. Children need to learn conventions related to grammar, spelling, and punctuation. They need to learn about parts of speech and how they work together. At a broader level, they need to learn how to convey mood and content using language. This is a goal that goes through a broad evolutionary process during the early childhood years: from lack of knowledge of words, to using nonconventional words, to understanding and using conventional words, to inventive spelling, to conventional spelling. Children need to learn to critique their own work and that of others.

To Respect Diversity in Modes of Communication

Individuals use many different ways of communicating, both verbal and nonverbal. Children speak many different languages, and they need to learn about and respect these languages and some of the problems confronting children who are learning English as a second language. Children also need to learn how children can communicate through sign language, communication boards, and Braille. Children need to learn to respond to and respect all types of communication.

To Improve Reading Literacy

Learning to read is a complex task. Children must develop skills in the area of visual identification, discrimination, and memory as well as higher-level skills in association and comprehension. These skills must be paired with auditory skills involved in labeling not only letters, but specific sounds of letters, and blending these into words.

To Improve Sequencing Skills

Recognizing and understanding sequences is an important element in reading, science, and math. Spacing sequences differentiate words and the configuration of letters in words.

To Improve Writing Literacy

We don't expect children to write extensively at early ages, but the underlying skills must be developed. Early scribbling, the use of writing tools, and understanding that writing is a symbol system are precursors to writing. Supporting children's writing through illustrating, editing, and publishing are part of an early writing program.

To Use Diverse Print and Nonprint Sources and Genres

Children need to be exposed to a variety of print and nonprint sources about people who are like them and people who are different because of culture, age, gender, abilities and disabilities, and life circumstances in the past and present. Children need to learn about a variety of technical and information resources such as libraries, videos, and electronic sources. Children also need to be exposed to poetry, short and long stories, plays, and so on.

Discovery

Discovery describes both a curriculum and an approach to a curriculum area. The approach is one of *doing* math, *doing* science, and *working* with computers. This is not drill and practice but developing an understanding of the underlying concepts.

Mathematics

Mathematics is an area that causes concern for many people. When children have trouble remembering math facts at whatever level, adults usually try to intervene, perhaps by getting flash cards or writing numbers for children to count, copy, add, or subtract. Such an approach is rarely effective, even though the facts are reviewed over and over again.

The National Council of Teacher of Mathematics (NCTM, 1989) discussed their ideas about math in a document called *Curriculum and Evaluation Standards for School Mathematics*. They identified 13 curriculum standards for children in kindergarten through fourth grade. The first four standards focus on mathematical thinking: mathematics as problem solving, as communication, as reasoning, and as connection. These relate to basic thinking and reasoning and are underlying skills that should be applied to all subject matter areas. This text looks at these as broad-based skills and not at skills that relate just to math, as they are equally important in science, social studies, and literacy. The remaining nine standards focus on the content of mathematics: estimation, number sense and numeration, concepts of whole number operations, whole number computation, geometry and spatial sense, measurement, statistics and probability, fractions and decimals, and patterns and relationships (NCTM, 1989).

Children are viewed as active learners as they interact with mathematics. They are *doing* math, not *drilling* math. Math is a way of thinking, a tool for children to use to understand their world. These standards are "big ideas" that are encountered at many levels of complexity during early childhood.

Although young children can often count up to 10 or higher, they rarely understand the relationships among the numbers that they are counting; that is, they do not realize that 6 is one more than 5 or that 7 is two fewer than 9. The names children give to numbers are referred to as "tags." Children experience some predictable problems with counting and tags. The first relates to keeping track of the number of objects counted versus the number yet to be counted, a partitioning error (Schickedanz, York, Stewart, & White, 1990). Children often forget where they started to count, especially when the objects are not in a straight line. Coordination errors involve having too many tags for the number of items counted, that is, counting objects more than once (Schickedanz et al., 1990). Although errors such as these are often declared carelessness, Kamii (1985) believes that it is more than a mechanical or attention problem, but really involves the child's lack of understanding of ordering items.

Many children understand the relationship among numbers up to 10 during kindergarten and can often count as high as 100. They may not understand, however, that in our base 10 system, there are eight 10s in 80, although they may be able to count to 100 by 10s. All of this is to say that understanding mathematical concepts requires far more than arithmetic, and young children need many concrete mathematical experiences.

Children write numbers less frequently than they write letters or words, so their skill in this area may be lower. Reversals of numbers in the preschool years are common, with the numbers 2, 3, 6, 7, and 9 the most frequently reversed. These numbers continue to be reversed even after children are consistently writing all of their alphabet letters correctly (Lamme, 1985). Left-handed children are more likely to have reversals than right-handed children.

In addition to signaling inadequate left-right orientation, reversals may be one sign of a problem with patterns and relationships. In this instance, "before and after" games with numbers are especially useful. Just playing "What number comes before or after X" is helpful, as is having children reproduce sequences or patterns. Patterning can be done with silverware, coins, markers, or anything that you have enough of to manipulate. Children enjoy counting backward as well as forward, especially if it is tied to an event such as jumping off or "blasting off."

Board games in which children toss dice or spin to determine the number of spaces to move help establish knowledge of patterns and relationships, especially if one can be "sent back." Card games such as Fish, War, Hearts, Solitaire, Concentration, Skipbo, and Uno are also fun and great ways to learn. Having children put all the cards in order to see if there is a full deck is another useful activity, especially if the cards have fallen. Dominoes and Double Nines are other excellent ways to teach matching, patterns, and addition.

Children learn basic geometric shapes during the preschool years. By kindergarten, children can usually identify basic shapes such as triangles, circles, squares, and rectangles, although the latter two are often confused. Although children can see differences in types of triangles, they cannot usually articulate these differences. With experience, they can discover the relationships among these figures and what makes each unique. Children need exposure to many different shapes: plain, colored, large and small, and even embedded in each other to sort out the qualities that remain stable.

Understanding relative size and the vocabulary that goes with it is a necessary math skill. The vocabulary of size is part of all of our lives. We want a "little" more to drink and the "largest" piece of pie. Children are curious about how "big" they were when they were born and how "tall" they are now. All children like to see how they are growing by comparing their height over a span of months and years. However, children grow slowly compared to

Children learn about rules of both language and math by playing games.

bulbs and seeds that can also be sized, measured, and charted. Have children predict whether things will be bigger or smaller than others and then have them check out their estimates.

Basic concepts of measurement are another focus of early mathematics. Children can measure length, weight, area, and volume. Before children can be expected to use standard units of measurement, such as feet and inches or meters and centimeters, they need to understand that measuring involves describing something in small increments. Children can use their hands, feet, books, popsicle sticks, blocks, or whatever is handy to measure length; scales and balances are used for weight; squares for area; and marbles or liquids to ascertain volume. Standard measures hold little meaning for children. It is only when two children measure the same item and get different results that the need for a standard becomes apparent. One child may claim that the water table is 11 hands long, another that it is really 13. Obviously, their hands are different sizes.

Intriguing children with measuring the dimensions of rooms and objects by a variety of means is also good. Encourage children to use a traditional yardstick, a meter stick, a ruler, paces, their feet, hands, and so on as tools of measurement. Getting the exact measurement is not the initial goal, but developing skills of estimating and checking.

Children need to learn number and measurement concepts before they can understand basic time concepts. (Telling time usually is not taught until the end of the early childhood years.) Children can begin to learn underlying time concepts by the use of a calendar and by discussing time sequences for class activities: "We will have a snack, go outside, and then it will be time to go home."

Money is another difficult concept for young children. They can, however, learn to recognize and name common coins and bills. Then they will learn the value of each. Somehow, 10 pennies seems like more than a dime, and the fact that a nickel is larger than a dime ought to make it worth more. These are difficult conceptual realities for young children. Again, it is not until the early elementary years that most will understand that four quarters and a dollar are the "same."

Mathematics for young children must be concrete and experiential. Adults can be a tremendous aid when they have an appropriate level of expectation for the children. They can expand math and make its usefulness in life apparent.

Because math requires few formal props, play math games while waiting or during transitions. Children can learn as much from activities that are fun as from those that seem "academic." The arithmetic problems that we so commonly associate with school are a formalization of experiences that relate to numbers, geometry, measurement, time, and money.

Science

Science, or sciencing, is a process, a way of knowing about the world. Science facts may change at a fast pace, but the process of generating these facts is relatively stable. Science is both knowledge about specific phenomena and the strategies or processes used to collect and evaluate the information. The application of science to human problems (technology) is also part of science (American Association for the Advancement of Science, 1989; National Center of Improving Science Education, 1990; National Research Council, 1994).

Three goals are recommended for *sciencing* with young children:

To develop each child's innate curiosity about the world;

To broaden each child's procedural and thinking skills for investigating the world, solving problems, and making decisions; and

To increase each child's knowledge of the natural world (National Center of Improving Science Education, 1990).

Children need to develop a respectful curiosity about the beauty, orderliness, and balance of the world. They need to develop skills to gather data; this requires observation. The next step requires that these observations be organized in some useful way so that information can be classified and hypotheses can be generated. These hypotheses need to be tested through experimentation and, typically, the results recorded. The last step in the process is the application of the knowledge gained.

Think about a simple problem such as what sinks in water and what doesn't. First, children experiment and discover that in fact some things float and others do not. The children then observe objects and try to predict which will and which will not sink. There should be a place to list the sinkers. Children may even note that some sink faster than others. They may try dropping objects from different heights or laying them gently in the water. They may ask that the water be made deeper. Slowly, their guesses become more accurate. They might even be able to figure out that they can make a paper clip float by putting it in the middle of a piece of cardboard. Although children may not be able to articulate facts about density, they have started to use the scientific process to investigate sinking.

Although the major focus of science is on process, the learning process does not take place in a vacuum: Facts are also important. The knowledge base works from the familiar to the unfamiliar. Science for young children moves from concrete to abstract. The content of science varies with the interest of the teacher, the children, and the setting. Children who live near the ocean may classify and learn about seashells. They may seine for sea life to put in their saltwater aquarium. Such a marine theme would be inappropriate for young children in a school in an urban area or the Midwest. Science activities need to be relevant to the children's interests and environment.

Children need the opportunity to explore materials on their own, with minimal adult supervision. Initially, children need to be asked questions such as "What do you think will happen?" "What else could you try?" and so on. Such questions aid children in exploring materials and learning about their properties. Your goal is to have children discover as many properties as they can and to encourage their discovery of more subtle aspects of the materials. Your role is to give as little guidance as possible to promote the most learning. Children are not just learning facts; far more important, they are learning how to learn.

Just exposing children to informal science and experiences is not enough to build the necessary concepts. But it is a necessary first step. This means that many activities in this area require at least two days and often more. The second time the materials are out, some children will continue to explore the materials; others will need more structure to expand their explorations. It is important that children view science as part of their world and that they see the cause-and-effect relationships rather than "teacher magic."

Computers

Computers are part of today's life. The question is how to make their use developmentally appropriate and an optimal learning experience for children. The computer offers children a potential source of communication and a way of exerting some control over their environment. Children can make a plan, carry it out, and see the outcome of their actions.

Work in adapting computers to serve as a resource for children with diverse abilities is an important part of the field's growth. Computers can be customized for children with severe physical or sensory impairments using switches, voice and music synthesizers, robots, and other peripherals.

Whether or not you have computers available in the classroom or you use them only for administrative tasks, children can and must learn computing skills during the early childhood years.

The key to using computers appropriately in early childhood is selecting appropriately designed software and modifying the hardware to be responsive to the developmental needs of the child. The criteria for evaluating software set forth by Haugland and Shade (1990) offer some guidance in the selection process:

1. *Age appropriateness:* Think about the age of the children. Regardless of the computer, would you expect children to do these types of activities? The software should support your curriculum.

2. *Child control:* Does the computer request responses from the child or does the child control the computer? The computer is only a tool. The control should be with the child.

3. *Clear instructions:* How easy are the instructions? Young children do not read. To the extent that directions are dependent on the teacher's reading to the children, children are being taught dependence in a medium that should foster independence.

4. *Expanding complexity:* Software should start where the child is and grow with her. It should be designed to provide increasingly challenging tasks, not solely repetition.

5. *Independence:* The goal of computers is to make children independent of adults. The software must be selected to support this. Using a computer independently or with peers supports self-esteem, confidence, and learning.

6. *Process orientation:* Computers are discovery-oriented media; the reward is in the process. Printing a product should be a reminder of a pleasant process, not a goal.

7. *Real-world model:* In the real world, houses are larger than children and eyebrows fit on faces. Look at the software to see if the images on the screen reflect this orientation.

8. *Technical features:* Graphics and sound should support the program. Cluttered designs and too much sound detract. The program should load quickly, and the disks need to be sturdy.

9. *Trial and error:* Children need the opportunity to make decisions and test them. They need a program that allows them to generate hypotheses and make their own decisions about what they like, not what is right or wrong.

10. *Transformations:* Computers have the potential for making changes at the stroke of a key. Children can make designs and re-create them without the redrawing necessary in other media (adapted from Haugland & Shade, 1990, p. 21).

Much of the software that is on the market today for young children is not developmentally appropriate. The developmental software criteria set forth by Haugland and Shade (1990) bring this issue into focus as well as evaluating specific software designed for young children.

To make traditional computers work, children must be able to implement a single key stroke. Without this skill, typing looks like this: *ppppppppppppppp*—and the computer cannot interpret it (the sensitivity of the keyboard can be controlled to make this easier). Once children can make a single key stroke, they need to build keyboarding skills. These skills involve learning to locate keys, reading and selecting from a menu, and giving commands. Additionally, children need to learn about the computer itself and how to make it run (Davidson, 1990). They also must develop the necessary fine motor and sensory integration skills.

Computers have tremendous potential for positive change for children with diverse abilities. They need adult scaffolding to make the system work. As we begin to think about the area of computing with children, it too has suggested levels of goals for the use of the Internet. The expectation is that by the first or second grade, children should be able to recognize a Web site and work in that site using links. They also should be able to use the basic tools of a browser to go forward, back, and home. By grades 3 or 4, they can be expected to recognize the components of a URL (Web site address) and to access a Web site by using a URL. They should be able to use a children's search engine (such as Yahooligan) to find information. Additionally, they should be able to send and receive e-mail (http://www.online schoolyard.com). Appropriately used, computers hold potential for helping all young children. Your role is to help children see computers as a natural part of everyday life.

Discovery Goals

Discovering is what it is all about. In many areas, the language of discovery may sound as though it should be happening in the high school. It does, but it also needs to happen in early childhood. The concepts and ideas are sound; we as early childhood educators must adapt to the new semantics. The goals that follow are measurable and are based on national standards. They provide the broad base for the regular education curriculum.

To Improve Number Sense and Numeration

All children must learn to count, match numbers, and understand that numbers stand for quantities in math and in the real world. Encourage children to count and to write numbers. By counting real things that have a purpose, children learn the utility of math. As the opportunity arises, provide a natural check on one-to-one correspondence.

To Improve Geometric and Spatial Sense

Recognizing, labeling, combining, and dividing shapes is a part of geometry, which is both a part of math and a reading readiness skill. Children need many experiences with both three- and two-dimensional shapes. The skill involves identification of what is relevant in symbols and learning that specific configurations of lines have names. Children need to recognize geometric shapes in the real world and the implications and utility of these shapes.

To Improve Measurement Concepts

Start by measuring the children themselves—not just their height, but the size of their feet, hands, and heads. Then measure familiar spaces. They can use their hands or feet to measure. As children participate in the cooking process, talk about the importance of measuring accurately and the implication for the final product. Have children pour and measure a variety of substances (beans, rice) so they understand that measurement concepts are unrelated to what is being measured.

To Understand Fractions and Decimals

Children need to develop a working model of our number system and how it works. They need to develop the concept of units of 10 that make up hundreds. Then they need to learn the implications of a decimal point as it relates to units of 10. They also need to learn about parts of objects and relationships. Children can easily learn the size of a cup and the resulting fractions that are common measures. They can learn about half a cookie and other fractions as part of learning about their world.

To Identify and Understand Patterns and Relationships	Children need to be able to identify, describe, and extend the patterns and relationships they see or hear. They also need to be able to create their own patterns. They need to learn to predict what will be the next item. In early childhood, these start with the stripes on a shirt, the colors in a plaid, or the pieces of fruit on a fruit kabob.
To Improve Estimation Skills	Children need to learn to think about estimating in a broad sense. They need to estimate how many steps it will take them to get from one side of the playground to the other—and then do it. Estimation ought to become an integral part of what they do, part of how they think about the world, and they should check out their estimation. As children become more dependent on technology (such as calculators), it is easy to make a mistake. One way that children know they have made a mistake is if they know about what the answer should be: if they have estimated.
To Understand Concepts of Whole Number Operations and Computations	During the childhood years, children need to learn the basic foundation of mathematical operations including addition, subtraction, multiplication, and division. They also need to figure out when to use these operations. Children also need to be familiar with calculators and how they work.
To Improve Knowledge of Statistics and Probability	Children need to learn to collect, organize, and describe data. In early childhood, this may be how far they can throw different types of balls or the distance they can run in a certain amount of time. Children need to think about ways to make data understandable and useful.
To Improve Observation Skills	Observation is one of the most basic skills in science. It uses the senses (seeing, hearing, touching, tasting, and smelling) to learn about the environment. Observing is more than looking: It requires children to describe information in detail. If children find an earthworm, have them look at how it moves, watch its movements under a magnifying glass, listen to see if it makes any sound, set up a mark and see if it goes there and how long it takes, see what happens to the dirt when it makes a hole, and so on. This is too much for one observation, but children must be supported in refining their observation skills. It also involves quantifying these data in a useful way.
To Improve Classification Skills	Classifying information makes order out of chaos. Children need to learn to classify in many ways, depending on the properties involved. They need to learn that differing categories change what is included. They also need to be exposed to classification systems and the logic that underlies the system. They can learn that animals include dogs, cows, and bears, and that in each category there are many different types of dogs, cows, and bears.
To Make Predictions	Often, the difference between exploration and just messing about is purposefulness. Making predictions focuses children's attention on what they expect to happen. It makes a project more goal-directed and learning more relevant. Children learn whether or not the prediction is accurate. When their prediction is not borne out, they need support in figuring out why. It is

possible that the prediction was inaccurate or that some steps in the process were not completed. It is important that adults offer guidance at this stage.

To Increase Knowledge of the Natural World

Children need to learn about the world they live in. They need to know how to investigate problems and to seek solutions. This requires them to not only experience this world but to explore it and the impact that they have on it, and it on them.

To Improve Computer Skills

Children need to learn that computers are simply a more complicated tool than a pencil, good for some things and not for others. Children need to learn how to operate the computer, the names of the parts of the computer, and what they do. They must develop keyboarding and menu-reading skills. Computer skills can be developed whether or not you have computers in your classroom.

Developmental Physical Education and Sensorimotor Skills

The first several years of life are characterized by a multitude of new motor behaviors. The first year sees rapid growth in motor development. The next several years are devoted to fine-tuning these motor skills. Ultimately, children participate in intricate motor processes. Much of what we consider to be motor development occurs as a result of experience and practice.

The National Association for Sport and Physical Education (NASPE) published its national education standards in 1995. The standards are for *all* children. The role of the teacher is to include *all* children in meeting the standards. The content standards for a physically educated kindergartner are as follows:

Demonstrates competency in many movement forms and proficiency in a few movement forms;

Applies movement concepts and principles to the learning and development of motor skills;

Exhibits a physically active lifestyle;

Achieves and maintains a health-enhancing level of physical fitness;

Demonstrates responsible personal and social behavior in physical activity settings;

Demonstrates understanding and respect for differences among people in physical activity settings; and

Understands that physical activity provides the opportunity for enjoyment, challenge, self-expression, and social interaction.

The content standards are the same at the early childhood age level; the assessment guide reflects increasingly complex motor activities and thinking.

Large Motor

To help children develop appropriate large motor skills, you need time, space, and the proper equipment. Children are often more capable in this area than we are willing to allow them to be. Their motor skills need to be progressively challenged. As their sense of balance improves, children can progress from walking, to walking on a line taped on the floor, to walking on a balance beam. You might even consider time for power walking.

You must provide space and objects for children to push, pull, carry, and lift to help them develop strength in the trunk area. Children need safe places to slide and swing. Skipping and dancing are part of large motor planning.

Turn on the music and encourage children to dance either alone or together. This is not ballet; this is moving! There are some records that encourage children to exercise. Use these regularly, especially when you cannot go outside. Encourage children to participate in games that require physical activity. Figure out games where all the children can be active.

Children need physical activities year-round, day in and day out. There is real concern about the physical fitness of young children and the increasing number of them who are obese, a condition to which lack of exercise contributes.

Small Motor

Fine motor development involves the child's ability to use the small muscles of the arms, hands, and fingers for reaching, grasping, and manipulating objects. Muscle and joint stability is a prerequisite for fine motor control. It is difficult for children to perform fine motor tasks such as writing without the necessary trunk stability. Fine grasp involves the independent use of the fingers and the ability to use the thumb and index finger together to pick up small objects. Experience with finger foods, large crayons, and large wooden beads facilitates the development of these skills. Again, the children need to develop motor planning to pick up these objects precisely and to release them when finished. Catching and throwing beanbags and under-inflated beach balls helps develop these skills. Variations help perfect skills.

Sensorimotor Integration

Sensorimotor integration combines information from the senses with motor responses. It is necessary to run an obstacle course, to pick up tiny objects, to draw pictures, to cut with scissors, and to perform many adaptive activities such as buttoning and snapping. Reading, writing, arts and craft activities, and many sports are dependent on the development and refinement of sensorimotor integration. Problems in this area are frequent with children with diverse abilities.

Bissell, Fisher, Owens, and Polcyn (1988) list nine separate components involved in sensorimotor integration:

Auditory processing involves the ability to understand what is heard. It is not hearing per se, but rather the ability to sort, remember, and sequence auditory information.

Body awareness requires the interpretation of sensations that come from the muscles and joints of the body, enabling you to know your body position without visually scanning yourself.

Coordinating body sides is necessary for the development of a dominant hand and also for the hands to work independently of each other on a given task. Such coordination is needed for one hand to hold a piece of paper and the other to cut it.

Fine motor control in the hands is necessary before children can be expected to use tools such as crayons or pencils.

Motor planning is the cognitive conceptualization of how a skill is performed that occurs before movement. Children need motor planning skills to figure out how to climb a tree or how to build a tower. It is important in learning new skills.

Ocular control is the ability of the eyes to smoothly track objects. It underlies all activities requiring eye-hand coordination and is a necessary prerequisite for reading.

The *perception of movement* requires the processing of vestibular information originating in the inner ear. Children who don't process enough information about movement may have trouble maintaining balance and may even need to spend conscious energy just to sit in a chair. Those who process too much movement information may become overstimulated. Vestibular information helps to regulate attention as well as posture and balance.

The *perception of touch* involves both a protective aspect and a discriminative touch. The protective tactile system is what makes us withdraw our hand quickly from a hot surface. Children can either overreact or underreact to touch. Children who are hyposensitive may not feel pain from bumps and bruises and may not be able to manipulate materials well. Children who are hypersensitive may avoid tactile input by not participating in messy activities such as art or sand and water play. Such children are sometimes labeled "tactile defensive."

Visual-spatial perception involves assessing the relative distance between one's body and a particular object as well as between objects.

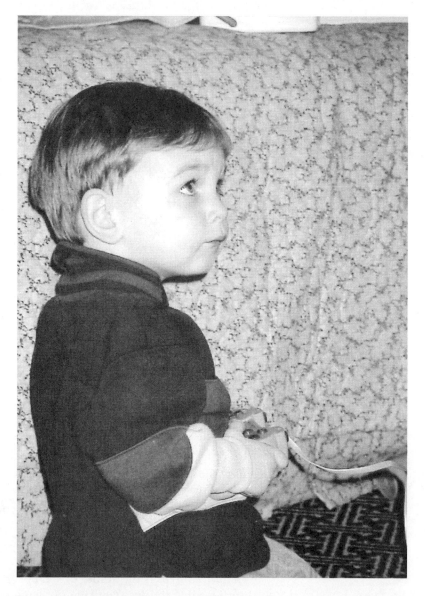

Today, children often spend time playing video games. If this is a small part of their activities, it isn't a problem. However, if this is how they spend most of their time, some of the large motor skills as well as peer communication skills may lag.

Children with deficits in visual-spatial perception may bump into objects and have trouble adjusting their gait to go down or up steps. Letter and number recognition may be difficult, and reversals common, for this child. Going from a vertical to a horizontal plane (copying from the chalkboard or the computer monitor) may also be difficult. These children need to establish spatial concepts through physical experiences (adapted from Bissell et al., 1988).

Children who have problems in sensorimotor integration to the point that it interferes with behavior and learning in the classroom need to be referred to an occupational therapist. A teacher's awareness of the importance of observing sensorimotor integration in children is an important first step. Regularly including activities that require sensorimotor integration can facilitate learning in this area.

Developmental Physical Education and Sensorimotor Goals

Goals in the sensorimotor area relate to locomotion, manipulation, and stability (Gallahue, 1995).

To Increase Body Awareness

Children need to control their body and move in ways they desire. They need to know where their body is in relation to objects. Children must learn to vary their posture, strength, and amount of force exerted to meet required tasks. All dynamic activities with antigravity postures require body awareness: running, cycling, skating, and dancing. Children also need feedback in static activities such as holding a position or an object without losing balance.

To Increase Physical Fitness

Children need to develop an interest in physical fitness from an early age. Although we think of young children as always being on the move, they often do not participate in activities frequently enough or for a long enough sustained time span to develop physical fitness. Activities that develop flexibility, strength, and endurance are necessary for fitness.

To Improve Locomotor Skills

To attain movement literacy, children must be able to carry out locomotor activities skillfully. Children need to practice locomotor skills regularly so coordination increases. They need to move from the basic elements of walking, running, leaping, jumping, and hopping to skills that require a combination of elements such as skipping and galloping. Children must be challenged with increasingly more demanding and complex activities to refine these skills.

To Improve Motor Planning

Motor planning is the ability to think about, organize, and execute a sequence of movements. It is the first step in acquiring new motor skills. Motor planning occurs as children are given variations of familiar activities. Varying the sequence of familiar actions, such as in an obstacle course, also requires motor planning.

To Improve Gross Motor Manipulative Skills

Gross motor manipulative skills are those that most of us associate with competitive games. They involve such things as throwing and catching, kicking, striking, bouncing, and rolling an object (usually a ball). They are the underlying skills developed during the early childhood years in a noncompetitive

Some children find fine motor skills dull. Using tongs provides a
challenge and by making it into a sorting or classification game,
enhances the potential for learning.

environment. Children need to experiment with these fundamental movements to develop skill.

To Improve
Stability Skills

Children need to be able to control their body in static and dynamic antigravity positions. They need to bend, twist, and stretch as well as swing and
turn while maintaining balance. They also need to hold a balanced upright
position, including when they start, stop, and dodge. They also need to control their body as they roll either sideways or in a somersault.

To Improve
Fine Motor
Manipulative
Skills

Children also need opportunities to develop and refine the small muscles in
their body. Children need many and varied opportunities to strengthen their
hand and finger muscles to allow ease in using tools.

To Improve
Sensorimotor
Integration

Sensorimotor integration involves the organization of the senses and muscles
of the body to perform both gross and fine activities. Children need to be
able to move in response to their environment and environmental feedback.

To Improve Eye-Hand Coordination

Good eye-hand coordination is part of sensorimotor integration, but it serves as a foundation for so many activities that it has been singled out as a specific goal. It is a requirement in most adaptive skills as well as many motor tasks, from using a pencil to catching a ball.

To Improve Tactile Skills

Tactile skills are particularly important to children who have sensory impairments. We rarely pay much attention to tactile feedback because we have so much visual and auditory stimulation; thus, it is important to bring attention to this area.

Creative Arts

All children are creative. Some are more creative than others. Some children are more creative in one area than in other areas. As children interact with the environment, and the response they get to their creative efforts plays a large part in their creative development.

As children get older, they are increasingly rewarded for convergent thinking. Children also need to be supported in divergent thinking. The world is changing too quickly to predict the kinds of knowledge children will need in 20 years. They need to develop processes that allow many potential solutions and methods for figuring out how to solve problems. This approach to problem solving begins now. Children who know only how to acquire facts and who are rewarded for conformity and neatness may not be equipped to solve tomorrow's problems.

What is creativity? Creativity is a process of thinking, acting, or making something that is new or different. It doesn't mean that a person has to be the first one to produce a product, but it does mean it is a new experience for that particular person.

The creative process can be thought of in two stages. The first is the thinking or idea stage: Children play with what they want to do in their mind. The second stage is the implementation stage. This is the "doing" stage: Children try out their ideas. This process is probably best thought of as a circular rather than a linear process, as children change their thinking and actions as they get feedback from the process.

Children gain many benefits when their creativity is fostered. Rewarding creativity helps develop a positive self-concept. It supports children's finding alternative solutions to problems and expressing their own ideas. Children learn to take risks to develop new skills and also learn about their own uniqueness.

Educators can support creativity in two major ways in children: by supporting the creative process itself, and by providing the time, space, and materials necessary to foster creativity. The Consortium of National Arts Education Associations (1994, pp. 122–127) developed national standards for arts education. The standards for students in the Visual Arts in kindergarten through grade 4 follow:

Understanding and applying media, techniques, and processes;

Using knowledge of structures and functions;

Choosing and evaluating a range of subject mater, symbols, and ideas;

Understanding the visual arts in relation to history and culture;

Reflecting on and assessing the characteristics and merits of their work and the work of others; and

Making connections between visual arts and other disciplines.

The arts are a mainstay in the early childhood curriculum (Thompson, 1995). The visual arts offer opportunities for individual participation as well as for being part of a group.

Visual Arts

The visual arts for young children is messy, fun, and exploratory. It ranges from squashing sponges and watching how much paint drips, to rolling and pounding playdough; from gluing paper, cloth, and macaroni, to coloring or scribbling with water-based markers, chalk, or crayons. Art is actively engaging materials. It is not making something that looks like everyone else's; nor is it gluing precut objects in the same place as does everyone else. Art is an experience, a process. The best art may never hang on the refrigerator door. It may remain in the child's mind.

Art helps young children understand the properties of materials. Children's first response to any new medium is one of exploration: What can it do? What are the limits? What do I like to do with it? Curiosity abounds. Allowing children to explore these differences and helping them figure out the variables to test is far more useful than explaining to them that objects stuck with glue will stay when turned upside down, whereas paint is unlikely to hold objects together. They also learn that thin paint is more likely to run down a page than thick paint.

At about 12 months, children can begin to do simple art projects. By 3 years, these patterns begin to have more structure and children are willing to tell you about them. With increasing age, products become more important, and this is the time when reinforcing the process aspect is imperative. If children decide they don't draw well, they may decide not to draw. Some children will have better products than others. However, the process is as important as the product.

To support the visual arts in your program, you need to do the following:

Schedule time for children to paint, draw, glue, color, and use dough or clay each day.

Do *not* provide a model for the children to copy. When children request a model, help them visualize what they want to draw and emphasize the process, not the product.

Differentiate between art and fine motor development. Keep art activities for art. Teach academic tasks like letter printing or coloring within the lines for other times.

Show interest in what the children are doing and display everyone's original art work regardless of quality.

Instead of asking "What did you make?" say "Tell me about your picture."

The arts provide a lifelong means of expressing feelings and gaining enjoyment that is essential for all people. It allows children to be part of a group, while at the same time expressing their feelings and creativity without being judged different or strange. At the same time, children can react to art and talk about the characteristics that appeal to them or do not in a particular work as well as in their own art. Children can explore materials and express themselves in a visual form, and they can look back at past artwork and see how they have changed.

Audiovisual equipment can be used both as a source of creativity and as a method of capturing creativity so that it can be shared or viewed at a later time. Consider videotaping a creative movement experience or the dramatic play area and then showing it to the children. Children can use simple cameras and record the events of a field trip with snapshots. Encourage children to record their voices and play them back, or record the group singing and then listen. Children are intrigued with media. Use them to encourage and support creativity.

Music

Music can be soothing or stimulating; it can promote social activity, and it can be used anytime anywhere. Traditionally, music has not been integrated with the rest of the curriculum. It has been restricted to a "music period" and taught without any goal beyond the vague one of teaching children music. But music can be used to meet a number of educational needs. It can teach and/or reinforce skills that are part of other curriculum areas.

Music is, however, also an academic field in and of itself, with its own standards established by the Music Educators National Conference (1994a). This organization has a very child-centered approach to learning. Their standards are based on the following beliefs:

All children have musical potential.

Children bring their own unique interests and abilities to the music learning environment.

Very young children are capable of developing critical thinking skills through musical ideas.

Children come to early childhood music experiences from diverse backgrounds.

Children should experience exemplary musical sounds, activities, and materials.

Children should not be encumbered with the need to meet performance goals.

Children's play is their work.

Children learn best in pleasant physical and social environments.

Diverse learning environments are needed to serve the development of many individual children.

Children need effective adult models (Music Educators National Conference, 1994b, p. 9).

As with other areas of the arts, music educators have included children below kindergarten in their standards. Content standards for children 2 through 4 years are:

Singing and playing instruments,

Creating music,

Responding to music, and

Understanding music (Music Educators National Conference, 1994b, pp. 10–11).

Content standards for children 5 through 8 years include:

Singing, alone and with others, a varied repertoire of music;

Listening to, analyzing, and describing music;

Performing on instruments, alone and with others, a varied repertoire of music; and

Reading and notating music (Andress, 1995, pp. 105–106).

Music is a multisensory experience. Music can be used to foster learning skills without sacrificing the goals and objectives or the standards of a music education program. The goal of music is to "acquire a disposition for lifelong musical interest" (Andress, 1995, p. 107). Children can learn new words and develop memory as they recall songs or parts of songs from one time to the next. They can develop a sense of rhythm as they sing and listen to music.

Musical experiences need to match the developmental level of the child. At about 1 year, children begin to become active participants in music. They clap and hit drums or xylophones in a purposeful way. They like to dance, but they seem to dance for their own pleasure, as they will often continue after the music stops (Mayesky, 1990). About age 2, children enjoy learning simple songs, especially those that include movement. Songs need to be short. By 3, children may have favorite songs and can recognize some tunes. They may want to add words or motions to songs for a new verse. They can learn longer songs. By age 4, children can participate in singing games and more actively participate in selecting musical experiences. With increasing age, children are able to sit longer and enjoy songs and dances that have rules (Mayesky, 1990). By 7 or 8, children can read the words to songs, and some become interested in more formalized music training.

The overlap of music and necessary listening skills is obvious. Children can learn to differentiate pitch, rhythm, and intensity. As children become older, they enter into some of the more visual aspects of music, such as visually discriminating the musical notes and symbols and then integrating this information into auditory output. Pairing music with movement can use both gross and fine motor skills and supports sensory integration. The mood of the music can set the pace for the movement. Music also supports language development. As children vocalize sounds and words, they may create new verses to familiar songs. Music is also a social experience. Be sure to include music of other cultures, folk music, and contemporary selections. As a creative experience, music allows free expression.

Music can be incorporated into your daily schedule or routine in a number of ways.

1. Sing a song at a particular time of the day to let children know it is time to move to another activity. For example, at the time for cleanup, sing the same song every day and children are likely to join in both the singing and the cleanup. The tune can be simple, such as:

    Time to put the toys away, toys away, toys away,
    Time to put the toys away, for another day.
    (Sung to the tune of "Mary Had a Little Lamb.")

2. Play records or cassette tapes at a variety of times throughout the day. Children's songs will be enjoyed, but classical or popular tunes may be appreciated as well. Fit the music to the activity.

3. Sing simple songs throughout the day. You can make up the words. Children especially enjoy having their name included in the song.

4. Set aside special time aside for music as children get older.

Creative Movement

Movement helps children become aware of their body. This awareness in turn can help them express feelings and moods, improve self-control, and help them learn how to relax at will. Movement exploration helps children discover ways to relax and to work off excess energy. Movement activities help develop rhythm and balancing techniques. Such activities can provide sensory integration and offer an opportunity for creativity and expression.

Creative movement is not a child-sized version of calisthenics with a "no pain, no gain" philosophy. It is the way young children learn how their bodies work. Creative movement is a personal statement about one's inner self. This is what differentiates it from functional movement, which usually has a practical purpose such as running to get a ball.

Movement can be integrated with other activities, especially music, and done in small or large groups. Pair creative movement with poetry, literature, and science. Read "What Makes the Wind?" by Laurence Santrey and have the children be the wind on a warm beach or a winter blizzard. Have them move as a gentle breeze, a strong wind, a gale, and a tornado. Help children understand the life cycle of the butterfly using movements for each stage. The more freely and easily children can move in their world, the more opportunities they will have for exploration and active involvement with materials of all kinds.

Dramatic Play

Dramatic play is spontaneous, self-expressive play through which children can learn to understand themselves and their relation to others and to the world around them. In dramatic play, children construct a world in which they can make up for defeats and frustrations and experiment with different ways of working out fears, feelings, and uncertainties. Dramatic play can help children grow in social understanding and cooperation; it provides a controlled emotional outlet and a means of self-expression.

You, the teacher, can use dramatic play as an index to measure the growth and development of children. Through observations you can assess small and large motor coordination, speech development, social-emotional growth, and concept formation. There are developmental progressions in dramatic play: Young children who have not had much experience playing with others often play alone; this is called solitary play. Regardless of age, all children participate in solitary play, but young children have that as their total repertoire. Next, children learn to participate in parallel play. That is, they play beside another child using the same materials but don't interact in a way that focuses on a cooperative venture.

In most dramatic play in early childhood, children start out with what they know the best: domestic scenes. Children cook, clean, care for younger children, leave for work and return, have visitors, and so on. They begin with roles they are most familiar with. A second theme is superimposed upon the first and involves a rescue mission. The baby is sick, someone has fallen and broken a leg, and the children focus their play around solving the problem presented. Once solved, a new "problem" is likely to occur. The third theme is sudden threat. A monster appears to carry off a victim, wild animals threaten to attack, and villains must be beaten off (Kostelnik, Whiren, & Stein, 1986).

Children reenact these themes over and over again. The setting changes, and with increasing age, the play becomes more sophisticated, but the themes remain. The play itself, however, often is chaotic, violent, noisy, and difficult to manage (Kostelnik et al., 1986). It sometimes involves children who "don't want to play" as unwilling victims. It has some unquestionable advantages, but it needs firm guidelines to work for all the children in the class.

"Superhero" is a specialized form of dramatic play that occurs frequently in early childhood settings. Its appeal to children is obvious. The superhero is the epitome of good; villains are just as clearly bad. Even more appealing, superheroes are powerful. They can take control of problems with their supernatural powers; they are always in control and they always win. Children who have little power in a world of adults identify with these characteristics. Superheroes provide children with clear models and predictable themes for play.

Blocks are another aspect of creative play that deserves special mention. A set of blocks is essential for the early childhood classroom. Blocks can be used in a variety of ways by children of varying ages. Children learn about cause-and-effect relationships by knocking down block towers: When they hit the tower with their hand, the tower falls and makes a loud sound. They may want to build towers over and over again as they test to see if the same thing happens each time.

As children make more complex structures, encourage them to work on them for more than one day. Have children design communities with blocks and accessories. Blocks allow children to obtain three-dimensional feedback about their ideas. They learn what to do when their building isn't complete and there are no more long blocks, and they learn about gravity. This is all hands-on learning. As they build together, they learn about social relations and sharing.

Creative Arts Goals

Art is a process of creation. To develop art concepts, children need to explore a wide range of art materials.

To Use Different Art Media, Techniques, and Processes

To understand the differences among art media, children must explore them and try out different techniques. The role of the teacher is to help them describe how these materials are different and how they cause a different effect. As children get older, they become more planful in their approach; they consciously decide what they want to convey in their art and how they will do this.

To Understand the Structures and Functions of Art

Children need to learn how they as artists as well as other artists use color, shape, materials, size, and so on to convey messages or to serve a purpose.

To Understand Art in a Cultural and Historical Context

The visual arts are a part of history, and the culture and times in which artists live play a part in the art they produce. Often, children's first introduction to the art of others is through the illustrations in children's books. Use these illustrations to place art in a historical and cultural context for children.

To Reflect on One's Own and Others' Works of Art

Although the goal is not to judge children's art, help children think about their idea and how well what they did conveyed it. Encourage children to reflect on this and to help them explore alternatives such as different media, techniques, or processes that might work better for them. Expose children to art and talk about it. Take children to museums to look at art.

To Use a Range of Subject Matter, Symbols, and Ideas

The capacity to use and create representative symbols emerges during the preschool years. Drawings that represent something appear. Once this stage is reached, children begin to think about their drawings before actually doing them.

To Connect the Arts and Other Disciplines

All content areas are interrelated. This goal acknowledges this connection, yet at the same time, seeks to retain art as a discipline in and of itself. The visual arts and other disciplines are enhanced by this connectedness, not diminished.

To Listen, Analyze, Describe, and Respond to Music

Music can teach children to differentiate pitch, rhythm, and intensity. Children can express their feelings and moods through music. They can become aware of cultural aspects of music and how different music is selected for different occasions.

To Read and Interpret Music

With increasing age, children experience some of the more visual aspects of music such as musical notes and symbols and integrate this information into auditory output. They become aware that music is also a written language with symbols they can read.

To Perform on Instruments Alone and with Others

As children learn to play instruments, they learn causal relations—beating a drum harder makes a louder sound. They can learn rhythm patterns and identify the sounds of different instruments. They can also learn about the different instruments that are used in different cultures.

To Sing Alone and with Others

Young children often enjoy singing and improvisation. They like to hear their name sung and to respond. They have favorite songs and can remember their names and lyrics.

To Appreciate a Varied Repertoire of Music

Children need to be exposed to a wide variety of music during the early childhood years, from the classics to rock to traditional children's songs from both the past and present. They need to hear and talk about lullabies and tangos. When music and movement are combined, children can interpret music as they explore the relationship of music and movement.

To Develop Creative Movement

In addition to becoming more aware of their bodies, children can, through movement, become a tree in the wind, a flower ready to bloom, or a fish swimming against the current. By actually acting out their interpretations of these events, they can learn about nature and themselves. Creative movement allows children to compare their body when it is tight and tense to when it is limp and relaxed and to compare an open, stretched position to a tightly curled position.

To Increase Creativity

Creative arts focus on a process of thinking, acting, or making something that is new or different. Children don't have to invent a new idea; they just need to participate in an experience that is new for them. Encourage children to "do their own thing," not what another child does. Help them experiment with techniques, methods, and media.

To Express Feelings

Children need to become aware of their feelings, label these feelings, and then find constructive outlets for expressing them. If these skills are learned as children, they have lifelong usefulness. It is important for children to be in tune with their feelings and to develop socially acceptable ways of venting them.

Integrating the Curriculum

Although it is important to highlight each curriculum area individually, it is also impotent to integrate the curriculum to provide a context of learning.

As diversity in the classroom has increased, you have been called on to use more care in planning your work. In choosing goals and activities for your class, you have to analyze the needs, strengths, likes, and dislikes of each child. Although some of the children in your class will have particular strengths and diverse abilities, you must choose activities that teach concepts, develop skills, and satisfy the requirements of the general education curriculum and are of interest to *all* the children in your class.

Activities and Record Keeping

In addition to designing a curriculum and choosing appropriate materials for the children in your classroom, you will want to develop a record-keeping system that helps you track children's learning and chart their progress. When you think about developing or refining your record keeping, first decide *why* you need to keep the records. If activities are chosen to support a goal on the IEP, then a relatively simple system can identify the goal with space to show the activities you have chosen as well as space to note the duration and quality of the child's behavior. If you keep this to one page, you should note increasing competence and children meeting benchmarks to show they will accomplish the goal.

Before you pick the activities you will use, review your information about where the child spends time and what she likes to do. Choose activities that both provide information on the goals you are concerned about and are in an area the child enjoys. The trick is to figure out how to teach what the child needs to learn in such a way that the child will want to learn it. Before reaching any conclusions about a particular child, use several different activities that include a range of skills. This is where the activities and the indexes that follow come in. The indexes at the beginning of the curriculum areas list the activities within those areas by goal. The index at the end of the book lists all the activities in the book that are designed to meet a particular goal and specifies the curriculum area for each activity. Using these indexes effectively will help you plan your general education curriculum as well as assure that you are meeting a child's individualized needs through an IEP.

Organization of Activities

The activities in the remaining chapters are organized by developmental/curriculum areas such as social awareness, and within each chapter these are broken down into smaller areas (for example, self-esteem, inclusion, social studies, and health and safety). Activities are numbered and presented in terms of the particular goals and objectives they meet. The goals are stated as annual goals, which can be used in individualized planning with supporting measurable objectives.

The numbers of the activities for each curriculum area are given at the beginning of each chapter and organized by the goals. When activities have more than one goal, they appear in the index under each goal. For example:

CHAPTER 20

Goal	Activities
To improve expressive communication	53, 54, 55, 56

If you look up activity number 53 you will find that it is called "Synonyms." (An index for all the activities in the book is at the end of the book.)

The organization of the activities section is designed to aid you in record keeping as well as day-to-day programming. The activities have a standard format, and the procedure includes information for modifying or adapting the level of difficulty of the activity. This can be done to adapt for individual children or to expand the age range of the activity. The standard format is:

Curriculum Area: Small (or Large) Group (or Individual)

(NUMBER) ACTIVITY NAME

GOALS

OBJECTIVES

MATERIALS

PROCEDURE

INTEGRATION

Using Activities
in the IEP

If a child has an IEP, look at the annual goals or outcomes in the plan, locate these goals and related ones in the index, and use the activities listed to implement the IEP.

    If you are in charge of writing the IEP, use the goals and activities to help you write the plan. To adapt the specific activities to an IEP format that requires goals and objectives, use the following example:

Small Motor: Individual

157 BUTTONS

GOAL   To improve fine motor manipulative skills; to improve sensorimotor integration; to improve tactile skills

OBJECTIVE   The child will identify the objects and pair them by touch.

MATERIALS   12 pairs of buttons (with tactile differences), a bowl or bag, an egg carton or ice cube tray, a blindfold

    The goals are already stated as annual goals. The objective and materials are combined to become an instructional objective. An appropriate evaluation is added: Given an egg carton, 12 pairs of objects, and a blindfold, the child will correctly match 10 of the 12 pairs of objects using only the tactile sense.

    You have now reformatted the activity to meet the requirements of an IEP. Look up other activities that also improve fine motor coordination. You now have not only the IEP but also a variety of activities you can use to implement it. These activities are also based on the general education curriculum so that activities chosen will help the child progress in this area.

Using Activities
in the IFSP

If a child has an IFSP, the activities are also useful for those outcomes that relate to the child. The format of the IFSP varies more than for the IEP. However, the same system of reformatting applies. Objectives can be written, as can outcomes.

    Activities designed for infants and toddlers are in Chapter 24, although some of the activities in other chapters can be used with younger children. Share these activities with families if that is compatible with their wishes.

Using the
Activities

Some of the activities in this book are familiar ones given a twist to make them especially useful for children with diverse abilities (Circus, Alphabet Lotto). Others are new activities designed to fulfill a specific purpose (Audiologist, Slings). However, if you refer to the goals at the beginning of the activities, you will see that each activity is designed to meet the needs and help develop skills in all the children in the class. Feel free to adapt these activities to suit your class, and use them as a springboard to make up your own. If you want more ideas for activities the Educational Resources after each activity chapter provides additional sources.

    As an educator of young children, you have much to keep in mind. Because you have the strengths and needs of all the children in your class to consider, you must find activities that foster the strengths of children with diverse abilities but are appropriate and enriching to all. You must use school as a world in which all children feel safe, belong, and have appropriate work to do. But, most of all, you must remember that you are a model for the children. Your behavior toward children—your acceptance, consideration, and respect—will speak louder to the class than anything you deliberately set out to teach. We hope these varied activities will be a stimulating resource for your teaching programs.

Guidelines for Adapting Activities for Children with Diverse Abilities

Tables 18.1–18.9 summarize the methods used to include children with diverse abilities, who were discussed in prior chapters.

TABLE 18.1   GUIDELINES: EMOTIONAL AND BEHAVIORAL DIFFERENCES

- Remove toys that might be dangerous or cause problems (hammers or mallets that might be thrown).
- Analyze the structure of your day to determine if an adjustment would be beneficial to all children.
- Remove children from situations if they are unable to cope and it appears that the situation will escalate. Give the child time to think (two minutes), talk about what happened and what the child can do to get back in control.
- Set clear, precise expectations: "In this class, we use words to say how we feel."
- Teach the difference between feeling and behavior. All children have feelings and should be in touch with them. The way they express their feelings (behavior) should not hurt themselves or others.
- Be alert to when adult intervention may be necessary. If possible intervene before the situation becomes a problem.
- Arrange the environment to enhance learning. Balance your schedule with active and less active times. Provide quiet alternatives when children need them.
- Keep noise levels reasonable.
- Develop a plan for dealing with aggressive behavior and follow it.
- Simplify, shorten, and structure activities when necessary.
- Utilize and arrange space to enhance your goals and prevent problems.
- Plan to specifically teach skills others might learn informally.
- Make learning meaningful and be respectful of children's work.
- If possible limit the number of transitions.

TABLE 18.2   GUIDELINES: LEARNING DIFFERENCES

- Be consistent.
- Establish a consistent routine so the child can anticipate what will happen next (snack, free play, outside).
- Provide enough time for and plan for transitions. Prepare children for changes by giving them a 5 to 10 minutes warning.
- Eliminate distractions. Keep noise levels down and confusion to a minimum.
- Make eye contact, keep directions short, simple, and clear: "Stan, you need to sit in your chair now."
- Confirm that a child has the prerequisite skills before teaching new skills.
- Start teaching with concrete objects (let the child explore a ball before talking about its properties).
- Begin with children's preferred way of learning (visual, tactile, or auditory), but don't exclude other modalities; instead, work to strengthen them.
- Provide numerous learning experiences with interesting planned variations.
- Teach prosocial skills.
- Motivate children to attempt challenging activities.
- Support child's interest and comprehension by reading to them as they are learning decoding skills.

TABLE 18.3   GUIDELINES: COMMUNICATION DIFFERENCES

- Simplify your grammar and vocabulary. Use shorter sentences, but don't "talk down."
- Be a good communications model by using clear diction and correct grammar.
- Include children in group activities, but don't call on a child unless he volunteers.
- Set aside a specific time each day for language and literacy but also incorporate language into routines and other activities.
- Encourage children to communicate by increasing their self-confidence and interest in their environment.
- Select activities that support noncompetitive peer interaction.
- Create a need for speech. Don't always respond to a child who is just pointing if that child can speak.
- Talk with children about what they are doing.
- Reinforce learning through visual and tactile experiences.
- Be an attentive listener.
- If you can't understand a child's speech, reinforce the child's attempts at communication and then be honest and say, "I'm having trouble understanding you. Can you tell me in different words?"

TABLE 18.4   GUIDELINES: DELAYED COGNITIVE DEVELOPMENT

- Use as many senses to teach as possible.
- Help children overlearn concepts by presenting interesting variations of principles.
- Teach a concept for a short time each day for many days rather than a long time for a few days.
- Evaluate the utility of materials, tasks, and skills and begin with the essentials. Learning should be essential, fun, or both.
- Teach concepts that are relevant and familiar first, then work toward the less familiar.
- Use several examples to teach a concept (*red:* apples, balls, books, crayons).
- Sequence learning from simple to complex.
- Use a task analysis to break down complex tasks into their component parts.
- Use backward chaining so children have the satisfaction of completing a task.
- Support the child in learning at a rate that is possible for that child, at the same time including him in group activities and planning.
- Encourage children to participate in the same activity at different levels.

TABLE 18.5   GUIDELINES: ADVANCED COGNITIVE DEVELOPMENT

- Plan activities that children can work on together but at different levels of complexity.
- Avoid pressure to conform by asking open-ended questions, not yes-no questions.
- Teach socially acceptable ways of handling emotions.
- Model acceptance. Smile, clap, use verbal praise, but do support children.
- Provide a variety of activities and experiences that encourage exploration of interests and allow depth and concentration.
- Increase complexity by adding materials and expanding the time frame.
- Provide activities and problems that require divergent thinking.
- Emphasize how and why things occur and what children (or others) can do to change things.
- Make up new endings for stories, take a different perspective, and so on.
- Emphasize group and individual problem solving and brainstorming.
- Encourage children to do activities in different ways and reflect on the differences.
- Allow children to choose some themes.

TABLE 18.6   GUIDELINES: HEALTH DIFFERENCES

- Find out as much as you can about a child's health (diet, physical restrictions, medication and its possible side effects, and behaviors that indicate an illness is becoming acute).
- Find out what children have been told about their illness and its implications.
- Use activities that allow children to be in control or adapt activities so that children have more control.
- Encourage age-appropriate independence and allow the children to do as much as possible for themselves.
- Arrange the schedule so that vigorous activities are followed by less strenuous ones. If necessary, provide short breaks for everyone.
- Organize your routine so that children can leave for medical procedures. Treat these departures as you would any transition.
- Allow children returning from an illness to come initially for part of the day, working back up to a full day.
- Plan some open-ended activities and some that can be completed at home if necessary.
- Observe children. Watch for mood changes and body language indicating pain, fatigue, or reactions to medication.
- Help children learn about the implications of their health problems. Verbalize this for them.
- Provide an atmosphere where children can discuss fears and problems.

TABLE 18.7   GUIDELINES: ORTHOPEDIC DIFFERENCES

- Learn about the child's particular disability and the general objectives of therapy. Know the child's competence in independent mobility and transferring.
- Learn how to safely lift and transfer a child with another adult and alone if necessary.
- Learn how wheelchairs work in general and how the particular wheelchair a child uses works. Regardless of type, *put on the brakes* before you place a child in or take a child out of a wheelchair.
- Learn what equipment children can use for variety in positioning and how to use it (beanbag chairs, bolsters, wedges).
- Attach baskets to walkers or have bags with shoulder straps or knapsacks available to carry materials.
- Have assistive devices available to reach objects, turn pages, and so on.
- Have large versions of manipulative toys and puzzles with knobs.
- Keep toys and materials picked up and off the floor.
- Encourage tactile exploration.
- Demonstrate how to explore new materials. Support children in learning about new materials and exploring them.
- Provide spaces wide enough for activities and movement, including space for mobility aids.
- Evaluate classroom doors, bathrooms, and passageways for accessibility as well as for the building itself. Do this for field trips, too.

TABLE 18.8   GUIDELINES: HEARING DIFFERENCES

- Face the child, and bring yourself to the child's eye level.
- Make your lips clearly visible (wear lipstick, trim or shave mustache).
- Keep bright lights out of children's eyes. Avoid flourescent lights if possible.
- Attract the child's attention *before* you begin speaking. Make eye contact or use a visual signal or touch to get the child's attention, but don't scare the child.
- Speak in a normal voice to aid speech reading.
- Use appropriate expressive body language, including gestures and pointing.
- Reduce background noise; ask other children to talk or play more quietly. Remember that a hearing aid does not correct a hearing impairment.
- If you repeat a word that is not understood, try a different one.
- Use as many visual aids as possible.
- If a child cannot see to read your lips when you are using audiovisual aids, have an interpreter and be sure the child sits close to the sound source. Use closed-captioned aids if possible.
- In group activities, place the child across from you (where she has the best view), with the child's back to the windows.
- Learn significant signs or cues to communicate with the child.
- Learn how to work with and use an interpreter.

TABLE 18.9   GUIDELINES: VISUAL DIFFERENCES

Corrected Visual Impairments
- Find out when and for how long corrective lenses must be worn.
- Observe and record the child's behavior with the visual aids (removing eyeglasses, position relative to materials, headaches), and share these with parents.
- Create a need to see and a reason for a child to wear glasses to see better.
- Support children wearing glasses. Discuss name calling and alternatives.

Visual Limitations
- Find out the level of a child's usable vision.
- Use verbal and tactile supports and rewards.
- Be aware of lighting conditions; arrange seating to benefit from lighting. Use natural light but regulare with blinds.
- Light-colored tables should have a dull finish.
- Use black marker to outline paper; other surfaces that need to stand out should be high contrast.
- Have a variety of books, including some with large print, and Braille.
- Use materials with distinctive shape and textures that have high contrasting colors.
- Keep furniture in the same place and materials picked up.
- Have children practice giving and following directions.
- Teach location by using the numbers on a clock face.

Summary

There is a concern about the level of educational attainment that all children are achieving in schools. In response to this concern, many professional organizations have developed national standards for children in a variety of areas. The standards will impact education for *all* children. As children with diverse abilities are included in regular classrooms, they are part of the groups that will be assessed in these areas.

Social awareness is a broad area that looks at the child and the world he lives in. There are three different sets of standards that are applied to social studies, an area of social awareness. The geography and civics content standards may require skills that young children do not yet have. The principles underlying history standards are more developmentally appropriate, but challenging. However, the content areas themselves help focus the curriculum. Language and literacy is an area that permeates other curriculum areas. The mathematics and science curriculum focuses a hands-on approach to learning not only content but also the underlying principles of the discovery process. Computers are part of the technology that supports discovery. Applying principles of developmentally appropriate practices with computers can make them an integral part of the curriculum. Movement underlies many activities in early childhood as children learn to master the large and small muscles of their bodies and integrate these movements with sensory information. In addition to movements themselves, there is an emphasis on an early commitment to physical fitness. Creative arts has long been a focus of the early childhood curriculum. The standards in the visual arts support creativity and experiencing many different media. Music standards emphasize that all children have musical ability. The combination of music and movement leads to an integration of sensory experiences.

When these area standards are translated into activities that are flexible enough to meet the needs of all the children in the classroom and they are placed in the context of a relevant, developmentally appropriate theme or unit, the integrated curriculum emerges.

Educational Resources

Bredekamp, S., & Copple, C. (Ed.). (1997). *Developmentally appropriate practice in early childhood programs. Revised edition.* Washington, DC: NAEYC.

Provides information on developmentally appropriate practices for children birth through 8.

Bredekamp, S., & Rosegrant, T. (1992). *Reaching potentials: Appropriate curriculum and assessment for young children, Vol. 1.* Washington, DC: NAEYC.

Serves as a guideline for interpreting appropriate curriculum and assessment. More focus on process of teaching than content.

Bredekamp, S., & Rosegrant, T. (Eds.). (1995). *Reaching potentials: Transforming early childhood curriculum and assessment* (Vol. 2, pp. 5–13). Washington, DC: NAEYC.

Has information on national standards for curriculum areas as well as information on the role of assessment. Focuses more on the content of the curriculum.

Cool School Tools!
http://www.bham.lib.al.is/cooltools/
This is an index to the World Wide Web and other Internet resources for kindergarten through twelfth grade.

ERIC Clearinghouse on elementary and early childhood education.
http://www.ericps.ed.uiuc.ed/ericeece.html
Covers timely topics such as the project approach, families, and technology, and provides links to other cities.

Interesting Places for Kids.
http://www.crc.ricoh.com/people/steve/kids.html
A compilation of pointers to Web sites that might be of interest to children including art, literature, math, and other curriculum areas. Web pages are set up by (or for) children.

Jones, E., & Nimmo, J. (1994). *Emergent curriculum.* Washington, DC: NAEYC.
Focuses on the interaction of responsive teaching to children's interest in planning the curriculum.

Kids Web.
http://www.npac.syr.edu/textbook/kidsweb
An extensive list of Web sites related to curriculum areas as well as links to other sites for children.

Little Explorers.
http://www.enchantedlearning.com
Provides many on-screen activities as well as an alphabet Web crawler. Clicking "H" brings you to Haiku.

Ultimate Children's Internet Sites.
http://www.vividus.com/ucis.html
A link to other children's Web sites by school age as well as links for parents and teachers.

Yahooligans.
http://www.yahooligans.com
A searchable, browsable index of the Internet that focuses on content designed for children.

References

American Association for the Advancement of Science. (1989). *Science for all Americans: Project 2061 report on literacy goals in science, mathematics, and technology.* Washington, DC: Author.

Andress, B. (1995). Transforming curriculum in music. In S. Bredekamp & T. Rosegrant (Eds.), *Reaching potentials: Transforming early childhood curriculum and assessment* (Vol. 2, pp. 99–108). Washington, DC: NAEYC.

Bissell, J., Fisher, J., Owens, C., & Polcyn, P. (1988). *Sensory motor handbook: A guide for implementing and modifying activities in the classroom.* Torrance, CA: Sensory Integration International.

Bredekamp, S., & Rosegrant, T. (1995). Reaching potentials through national standards: Panacea of pipe dream? In S. Bredekamp & T. Rosegrant (Eds.), *Reaching potentials: Transforming early childhood curriculum and assessment* (Vol. 2, pp. 5–13). Washington, DC: NAEYC.

Center for Civic Education. (1994). *National standards for civics and government.* Calabasas, CA: Author.

Children's Safety Network. (1991). *A data book of child and adolescent injury.* Washington, DC: National Center for Education and Maternal Health.

Consortium of National Arts Education Associations. (1994). *National standards for arts education.* Reston, VA: Music Educators National Conference.

Davidson, J. I. (1990). *Children and computers together in the early childhood classroom.* Albany, NY: Delmar.

Derman-Sparks, L., & the A.B.C. Task Force. (1989). *Anti-bias curriculum: Tools for empowering young children.* Washington, DC: NAEYC.

French, L. (1996). Language, listening, and literacy. *Young Children, 51*(2), 17–20.

Gallahue, D. L. (1995). Transforming physical education curriculum. In S. Bredekamp & T. Rosegrant (Eds.), *Reaching potentials: Transforming early childhood curriculum and assessment* (Vol. 2, pp. 125–144). Washington, DC: NAEYC.

Geography Education Standards Project. (1994). *Geography for life, national standards.* Washington, DC: National Geographic Research & Exploration.

Haugland, S., & Shade, D. (1990). *Developmental evaluations of software for young children.* Albany, NY: Delmar.

Hendricks, C., & Smith, C. J. (1995). Transforming health curriculum. In S. Bredekamp & T. Rosegrant (Eds.), *Reaching potentials: Transforming early childhood curriculum and assessment* (Vol. 2, pp. 65–79). Washington, DC: NAEYC.

International Reading Association, & National Council of Teachers of English. (1996). *Standards of the English language arts.* Newark, DE: International Reading Association.

Jalongo, M. R. (1996). Teaching young children to become better listeners. *Young Children, 51*(2), 21–30.

Joint Committee on National Health Education Standards. (1995). *National health education standards: Achieving health literacy.* Atlanta, GA: American Cancer Society.

Kamii, C. K. (1985). *Young children reinvent arithmetic: Implications of Piaget's theory.* New York: Teachers College Press, Columbia University.

Kendall, J. S., & Marzano, R. J. (1996). *Content knowledge: A compendium of standards and benchmarks for K–12 education.* Auora, CO: McRel.

Kostelnik, M., Whiren, A., & Stein, L. (1986). Living with He-Man: Managing superhero fantasy play. *Young Children, 41*(4), 3–9.

Lamme, L. (1985). *Growing up writing.* Washington, DC: Acropolis Books.

Mayesky, M. (1990). *Creative activities for young children* (4th ed.). Albany, NY: Delmar.

Music Educators National Conference. (1994a). *Opportunity-to-learn standards for must instruction: Grades preK–12.* P. Lehman (Task force chair). Reston, VA: Author.

Music Educators National Conference. (1994b). *The school music program: A new vision.* P. Lehman (Project director). Reston, VA: Author.

National Association for Sport and Physical Education (NASPE). (1995). *Moving into the future: National physical education standards: A guide to content and assessment.* Reston, VA: Author.

National Center for History in Schools. (1994). *National standards: History for grades K–4.* Los Angeles, CA: Author.

National Center of Improving Science Education. (1990). *Getting started in science, a blueprint for elementary school science education* (A report for the National Center for Improving Science Education). Colorado Springs, CO: Author.

National Commission on Social Studies in Schools. (1989). *Charting a course: Social studies for the 21st century.* Washington, DC: Author.

National Council of Teacher of Mathematics. (1989). *Curriculum and evaluation standards for school mathematics.* Reston, VA: Author.

National Research Council. (1994). *National science education standards* (Draft). Washington, DC: National Academy Press.

Piaget, J. (1967). *The language and thought of the child.* Cleveland: World.

Richardson, K., & Selkeld, L. (1995). Transforming mathematics curriculum. In S. Bredekamp & T. Rosegrant (Eds.), *Reaching potentials: Transforming early childhood curriculum and assessment* (Vol. 2, pp. 23–42). Washington, DC: NAEYC.

Rogers, C., & Morris, S. (1986). Reducing sugar in children's diets: Why? How? *Young Children, 41*(5), 11–19.

Schickedanz, J. A., York, M. A., Stewart, I. S., & White, D. A. (1990). *Strategies for teaching young children* (3rd ed.). Englewood Cliffs, NJ: Prentice-Hall.

Seefeldt, C. (1995). Transforming curriculum in social studies. In S. Bredekamp & T. Rosegrant (Eds.), *Reaching potentials: Transforming early childhood curriculum and assessment* (Vol. 2, pp. 109–124). Washington, DC: NAEYC.

Thompson, C. M. (1995). Transforming curriculum in the visual arts. In S. Bredekamp & T. Rosegrant (Eds.), *Reaching potentials: Transforming early childhood curriculum and assessment* (Vol. 2, pp. 81–98). Washington, DC: NAEYC.

Vygotsky, L. S. (1978). *Mind in society.* Cambridge, MA: Harvard University Press.

Waring-Chaffee, M. B. (1994). "RDRNT . . . HRIKM" ("Ready or not, here I come!"): Investigations in children's emergence as readers and writers. *Young Children, 49*(6), 52–55.

Whitmore, K. F., & Goodman, Y. M. (1995). Transforming curriculum in language and literacy. In S. Bredekamp & T. Rosegrant (Eds.), *Reaching potentials: Transforming early childhood curriculum and assessment* (Vol. 2, pp. 145–166). Washington, DC: NAEYC.

Chapter 19

SOCIAL AWARENESS ACTIVITIES: SELF-ESTEEM, INCLUSION, SOCIAL STUDIES, HEALTH AND SAFETY

Social awareness for young children is designed to help them understand and function in the world in which they live. During their early years, children are developing their values and attitudes about themselves, other children, and adults in their family and community. They are developing their concept of self. It is important that they have a broad range of experiences and are exposed to people and materials without gender, racial, or cultural bias. People with disabilities must be portrayed accurately, including both their abilities and disabilities.

TABLE 19.1   ACTIVITY GOALS AND REFERENCE NUMBERS

Goals	Activities
To improve self-concept	1, 2, 3, 4, 5, 6, 10, 12, 34, 35, 36, 37, 38
To increase awareness of roles people play	1, 2, 4, 6, 10, 31, 32, 33, 34, 35, 36, 37, 38, 39, 40, 41
To broaden concepts of families	1, 2, 3, 4, 5, 33
To increase inclusion	6, 7, 11, 12, 13, 14, 15, 16, 17, 18, 19, 20, 21, 22, 23, 25, 26, 27, 28, 29, 30, 31, 32, 35, 36, 37, 40, 41, 42
To increase awareness of individual differences and similarities	7, 11, 14, 15, 16, 17, 18, 20, 21, 22, 23, 24, 25, 26, 27, 28, 29, 30, 31, 41
To increase cultural awareness	3, 24, 33
To increase adaptive skills	39, 44, 45, 46, 48, 49, 50, 51, 52
To improve health literacy	44, 45, 46, 47, 48, 49, 50, 51, 52
To understand geography concepts	13, 32, 42, 43
To encourage problem solving	7, 8, 9, 38, 42, 43, 52
To increase thinking and reasoning skills	8, 11, 52
To express feelings	12, 17, 18, 19, 21
To increase vocabulary	34, 47
To improve expressive communication	8, 10
To improve reading literacy	40
To increase respect for diversity in modes of communication	9, 15, 16, 22, 24, 29
To improve observational skills	9, 25
To improve cause-and-effect reasoning	5, 13, 20, 39, 43, 45, 46, 48, 49, 50, 51
To improve locomotor skills	26, 28
To increase body awareness	27, 30, 47
To improve tactile skills	23
To use the arts to express a range of subject matter, symbols, and ideas	19

1   PHOTOGRAPH STORY

GOALS   To improve self-concept; to broaden concepts of family; to increase awareness of roles people play

OBJECTIVES   The child will identify the individuals and state at least two roles the person in the picture can play.

MATERIALS   Pictures of the children in your class and several familiar people, including teachers in your school and even you, in a variety of roles: a teacher with the children in the class; an adult daughter with her mother; a father with children and stepchildren; a child with siblings; a wife with her husband; a student taking a course; a child with friends; a child with parents and stepparents

PROCEDURE   Start with yourself and show the children pictures of you with them and with your family. Then show pictures of children and the roles they play. (Invite children to bring pictures from home to share as well. Ask that the roles and identification be placed on the back.) Note the similarities and differences among the roles that children and adults play. It is important at the beginning to use pictures of familiar people so children understand the concept of multiple roles. Be sure to include many different relationships. Add pictures of famous people and occupations: the president of the United States, astronauts, movie stars. All may be husbands, wives, sons, daughters, siblings, aunts, uncles, and so on.

INTEGRATION   Children need to gain a perspective on adult roles. They need to see medical personnel and related service providers as playing other familiar roles. They also need to see that they themselves have many roles.

2   FAMILY MAP

GOALS   To improve self-concept; to broaden concepts of family; to increase awareness of roles people play

OBJECTIVES   The child will make a map of her family.

MATERIALS   Manila paper, crayons, circles and squares of different sizes made from construction paper

PROCEDURE   Give children construction paper and tell them that they are going to make a map of their family. For this map, all the females in the family will be circles and the males, squares. The children can choose the circles and squares and place them on the page where they choose or draw them (see Figure 19.1). Encourage children to decide who is part of their family and where they should go on the page. Help children identify family members and mark them. Have children designate in some way who the squares and circles represent. Be sure to allow for pets if children want to include them. They can put a boundary around the family, or not, as they choose. Some children may be part of more than one family and the map can represent this. Encourage children to think more about families and how they are connected. Help them develop a key to show relationships among family members.

INTEGRATION   This activity helps children see different family configurations. It also can give you insight into the child's perception of her family.

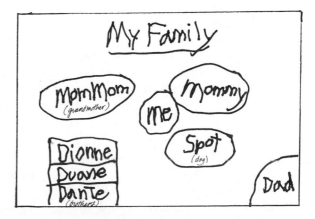

Figure 19.1   Family Map

Self-Esteem: Large Group

3   CELEBRATIONS

GOALS   To improve self-concept; to broaden concepts of family; to increase cultural awareness

OBJECTIVES   The child will share with the group information about a particular occasion and how his family celebrates this special occasion or holiday.

MATERIALS   None (unless the child wants to bring in something)

PROCEDURE   Talk with children about how their families celebrate particular holidays. Then choose one or two children to act this out for the group. Include different holidays, birthdays, and celebrations. Be sure to discuss feelings, excitement, and expectations. Discuss how families have different ways of celebrating as well as different occasions that are celebrated. Encourage children to have their parents or others come to talk about the celebrations as well. Plan some special activities and snacks that support the learning experience.

INTEGRATION   Be aware that there might be children in your class who do not celebrate holidays. Find out from them and their families how they want to share this information with their classmates.

Self-Esteem: Large Group

4   ROLES

GOALS   To improve self-concept; to broaden concepts of family; to increase awareness of roles people play

OBJECTIVES   The child will state at least three different roles an individual can have in a family and three roles the child has in her family.

MATERIALS   Flannel board and Pellon figures: 4 boys, 4 girls, 2 women, 2 men, 2 older men, 2 older women

PROCEDURE   Have a group discussion about the variety of roles that children play. Use flannel board figures to help clarify these roles for the children. Explain such roles as: brother/sister, stepbrother/stepsister, friend, grandfather/grandmother, boy/girl cousin, daughter/son, stepdaughter/stepson, man/woman, nephew/niece, husband/wife, grandson/granddaughter, father/mother, stepfather/stepmother.

Explain that one person can play many roles. Start with roles that children are most familiar with. Be sure to include all the relationships that children in your classroom might have. When the children have identified their various roles, describe roles to see if the children can guess whom you are talking about: "I'm thinking of a girl who has one sister who is younger than she is and no brothers. Who am I thinking of?" Increase the complexity of relationships you talk about. Include great-aunts, second cousins, and so on.

INTEGRATION   All children have a variety of roles. Discuss family change and roles that change with changing situations (marriage, husband-wife roles) and those that don't change (parental). Your mother is still your mother even if she no longer lives with your father. *Note:* This may be a sensitive issue for a child whose family is changing (through divorce, death, birth, and so on). Be sure to include acquired kin as well (favorite friends that become "aunts and uncles"), as well as godparents and others who are important in some cultures.

Self-Esteem: Small Group

5   FOOD FORMS

GOALS   To improve self-concept; to broaden concepts of family; to improve cause-and-effect reasoning

OBJECTIVES   The child will identify food in different forms and state who in a family eats it in those forms and why.

MATERIALS   A variety of whole foods, a baby food grinder, baby food jars of the same foods, a knife, a scraper, a hot plate, a masher

PROCEDURE   Pick one or several foods (carrots and apples are traditional favorites; peaches and squash also work well). Have the children feel the food whole and cut up into different shapes:

CARROT

whole—curls (cut long and thin and put in ice water)

pieces—cubes (cut at an angle), coins

Put some of the carrots in a saucepan to cook. (It's fun to cook some whole carrots as well as the cut-up ones. Set a timer and have the children see which is softer after a specified time period.) When the carrots are cooked, experiment again with different forms:

whole carrots	pureed carrots (if you have a blender)
carrots cut as coins	ground carrots (in baby food grinder)
mashed carrots	

Compare these to baby food in jars. Discuss the taste of the different forms and how some are the same or almost the same and others different. Experiment by adding salt. Talk about who would eat the various forms (babies who don't have teeth, children getting permanent teeth, and people with braces or false teeth) and why (variety, need, individual preference). Have children taste the different forms. As children become experienced, use less familiar foods and a greater variety of vegetables and fruits.

INTEGRATION   Children may not be aware of what causes food to change. Explain to children what being on a "soft" diet means. Be sure to include vocabulary about the states of food: soft, hard, crisp, mushy, and so on.

Self-Esteem: Small Group

6   GET WELL CARDS

GOALS   To improve self-concept; to increase awareness of roles people play; to increase inclusion

OBJECTIVES   The child will talk about being sick, make a get well card for a classmate, and talk about why cards are sent.

MATERIALS   Construction paper, crayons or markers

PROCEDURE   Have the children make drawings or paintings of their choice on a folded piece of construction paper. They can make either two pictures (front and inside of card) or one picture with a written message. Talk with the children about the particular illness the child has and the kinds of activities that child particularly likes. Encourage children to write (or dictate) a message.

INTEGRATION   Make the first card for a specific child; then start a collection of get well cards so you will always have a card to send when the occasion arises. After a while, the children may notice that certain members of the class are absent more often than others. Talk about this.

Self-Esteem: Small Group

7   NO WORDS

GOALS   To increase awareness of individual differences and similarities; to increase inclusion; to encourage problem solving

OBJECTIVES   The child will pantomime an instruction and state how she feels about communicating without words, what strategies she used to make others understand, and how it felt if others didn't understand.

MATERIALS   None

PROCEDURE   Have a discussion about how animals and people communicate without using words.

bees	dance to help other bees find honey
dogs	bark, wag tails
birds	chirp, sing
people	gesture

Give one child in the class instructions for a task the group must perform. Have this child get the other children to carry out the task without using words. Initially, all the children could do the same thing, for example, go to the bathroom and wash their hands. Make the tasks easy and have a pair of children convey the message. As the children get better, assign more difficult tasks.

INTEGRATION   Discuss the differences between using nonverbal "language" and words, especially in relation to how long it takes to convey information without words. Lead this into a general discussion of communication and how difficult it is to express yourself when you don't know the right words to say. Point out examples of nonverbal body language people use.

Self-Esteem: Small Group

8   ONE MORE

GOALS   To encourage problem solving; to improve expressive communication; to increase thinking and reasoning skills

OBJECTIVES   The child will state at least four different possible solutions to a given problem.

MATERIALS   None

PROCEDURE   Make up hypothetical situations or use actual problems that have occurred in the classroom. The situations can relate to peer relationships, sharing materials, time with the teacher, and so forth. For example, if two children want the same toy, ask them for a solution, then ask, "What else could you do?" See if children can generate at least four different alternatives to consider. Don't give children solutions or judge their answers as inappropriate, although they may seem outlandish to you—unless they are dangerous. It is important that children learn to generate alternatives as a way of coping. Expand the scope of the problems. Help children evaluate the probable outcome of each solution and decide which they might try first.

INTEGRATION   The more complex situations children are in, the more likely they will need to find solutions to problems. They may need to try several options before they find one that works. Give them the foundation for generating solutions to problems and thinking them through.

Self-Esteem: Large or Small Group

9   CHARADES

GOALS   To encourage problem solving; to increase respect for diversity in modes of communication; to improve observational skills

OBJECTIVES   Without using words, one child will act out an object or action for the others to guess and actively participate in guessing others' actions.

MATERIALS   Pictures of people, animals, or objects; pictures of someone doing something: getting a drink, going outside, getting a cookie, getting in the car, putting on a coat

PROCEDURE   Give the child a picture or tell the child what to pantomime. Give hints and suggestions to both actors and guessers until the children catch on. Make the pictures more difficult. Include titles of books that children know. Teach them some of the codes that charade players have developed.

INTEGRATION Encourage awareness of nonverbal communications and how hard it is to communicate accurately without speech. Begin to introduce children to some conventions that people have developed to share meaning without words. Expand this into a discussion of American Sign Language.

Self-Esteem: Individual

10   BE THE TEACHER

GOALS To increase awareness of roles people play; to improve self-concept; to improve expressive communication

OBJECTIVES The child will imitate the teacher by giving directions to the children.

MATERIALS None

PROCEDURE During group time, pick one child to help you give instructions. Pick a routine that you have done frequently, such as the calendar or dismissing the class. Coach the child to give specific directions: "All children who have plaid shirts may go to free play." Initially, have the child do part of the task; that is, you decide how the children will be dismissed, and this child says it, or vice versa. Give children greater responsibility for a longer time.

INTEGRATION Children need practice in leadership when they can be successful; however, this too is a skill that needs to be taught and practiced in a variety of circumstances. It is very different to be in charge and ask questions than it is to answer them. Talk with children about how they felt being in charge.

Inclusion: Large Group

11   I'M THINKING OF

GOALS To increase inclusion; to increase thinking and reasoning skills; to increase awareness of individual differences and similarities

OBJECTIVES The child will guess the person or object.

MATERIALS None

PROCEDURE This is a variation of the game '20 Questions' but is used as a teaching tool to help children realize when they don't have enough information. Start with obvious cues.

> *Teacher:* I'm thinking of someone with brown hair. Who am I thinking of?
> *Child:*   Me.
> *Teacher:* I could be thinking of you, but you can't be sure. Listen. I'm thinking of someone with brown hair and a plaid shirt. Who am I thinking of?
> *Child:*   Sam.
> *Teacher:* I could be thinking of Sam, but who else has brown hair and a plaid shirt?
> *Child:*   Tom.
> *Teacher:* Listen then. I'm thinking of . . .

As children become more proficient, make the clues more subtle to help children develop the skills of classification and observation. Give children two or more characteristics to consider at one time: "I'm thinking of someone who has blond hair, who loves to paint, and whose last name starts with J."

INTEGRATION This activity is designed to create a sense of group belonging; children learn that they are all both similar to and different from each other. Children can participate verbally or nonverbally. Do not pick out stereotypic characteristics, such as "I'm thinking of someone in a wheelchair."

12   SHARE YOUR FEELINGS

GOALS   To increase inclusion; to improve self-concept; to express feelings

OBJECTIVES   The child will share a feeling with classmates.

MATERIALS   None

PROCEDURE   After the children have discussed feelings and expressions, ask them to share a feeling with the other children, for example, liking. Some ways the children might share this are to hold hands, kiss, hug, say "I like you," and so on. Support children in expressing feelings with their peers and knowing that they are valued members of the class. Give children the vocabulary they need to express their feelings accurately. Help children think of a variety of ways to share feelings, both verbal and nonverbal.

INTEGRATION   Sharing feelings is not usual in some cultures. At first, older children might feel self-conscious doing this, but if you demonstrate and support them, they may learn that, at least at school, feelings can be shared.

13   WHEELS

GOALS   To increase inclusion; to improve cause-and-effect reasoning; to understand geography concepts

OBJECTIVES   The child will state the function of wheels in moving objects and traverse a designed course in a wheeled object.

MATERIALS   Pictures of familiar objects with wheels: inline skates, wagons, tricycles, roller skates, toy cars, wheelchair, creepers, scooters

PROCEDURE   Discuss the function of wheels and encourage children to experiment moving on or using things with wheels. If you have shelves on wheels, compare moving those shelves with shelves not on wheels. Help children experiment by using rollers to move objects. When you are outside, keep the wheels of a tricycle or wagon from turning by putting something through the spokes and discuss how this affects its movement. Be sure to include a wheelchair. Talk about brakes and the function they serve. Encourage children to experiment with a wheelchair to see how it works. Encourage them to use a wheelchair on a ramp to see the difference in energy it takes to go up and to go down. (Have an adult with the child in the chair.) Map out a course that requires turns, and have children use wheeled objects to traverse the course. Ask about what is easy and difficult for them.

INTEGRATION   Children can learn about the functions wheels play in moving and become aware of the implications of using a wheelchair, of curb cuts, and so on.

14   CUTTING CARDBOARD

GOALS   To increase awareness of individual differences and similarities; to increase inclusion

OBJECTIVES   The child will try to cut the cardboard and state her feelings about cutting it.

MATERIALS   Scissors, cardboard (from the back of writing tablets)

PROCEDURE   Draw intricate designs on cardboard and have the children try to cut out the design. This task will be difficult. Discuss children's feelings about not being able to accomplish this task. Talk about how it feels to do things that are hard. Ask how they felt while attempting the task: if they wanted to leave and do something else; wanted to get help from the teacher; wanted to talk to their friends; and so on.

Have them talk about which things are easy and hard for each of them and how they can help each other with difficult tasks (don't do it for someone, don't tease, don't tell them to hurry up, and so on).

INTEGRATION   This activity is designed to help children gain some insight into the frustrations that result from attempting a task that is too difficult. Talk with the children about how they might feel if everyone else thought the task an easy one and they couldn't succeed. Discuss what they would like people to say and what wouldn't be helpful.

Inclusion: Small Group

15   FINGER-SPELLING LOTTO

GOALS   To increase awareness of individual differences and similarities; to increase inclusion; to increase respect for diversity in modes of communication

OBJECTIVES   The child will match the letters of the alphabet with the appropriate finger-spelling letters.

MATERIALS   Alphabet Lotto cards with Ameslan signs for each letter

PROCEDURE   Make a Lotto game using the letters of the alphabet and the manual signs for those letters. Encourage the children to make the sign with their hands as they match the cards. Start with the signs that have some visual resemblance to the letters they represent (for example, *c, d, I, l, m, n, o, v*). Have the children finger-spell their names.

INTEGRATION   This activity shows children a potential avenue of communication and another representation of language.

Inclusion: Small Group

16   MUFFLERS

GOALS   To increase awareness of individual differences and similarities; to increase inclusion; to increase respect for diversity in modes of communication

OBJECTIVES   The child will discuss how it feels to have trouble understanding speech while playing with others.

MATERIALS   Ear muffs or cotton balls, record player and records *or* tape recorder and tapes

PROCEDURE   Set up the dramatic play area in the usual way. Have the children wear ear muffs or put cotton balls in their ears and tell them to whisper while playing instead of talking out loud. Have a record or tape playing in the background to make it even harder to hear the speech. Follow this activity with a discussion at group time. Start your discussion by talking very softly while the music is playing. If the children get frustrated or restless, go back to your normal style. Talk about how hard it is to cooperate with others and to pay attention when you can't hear.

INTEGRATION   Children can begin to better understand the implications and frustrations of not being able to hear or understand what is going on around them.

Inclusion: Large Group

17   NEW DOLL

GOALS   To increase awareness of individual differences and similarities; to increase inclusion; to express feelings

OBJECTIVES   The child will tell how she feels about the new doll and what could be done differently.

MATERIALS   A child-size (4′) doll dressed in typical clothes

PROCEDURE   Bring the doll into the classroom and give it special privileges: Let it sit beside you during group time, point out how well it is dressed and how special it is, but don't let the children touch it for fear they will break it or get it dirty. When they are allowed to touch it, tell them how careful they must be. Have presents for the new doll: clothes, books, and so on. Then discuss with the children how they feel about this new doll and its privileges and whether or not they want the doll to visit again. Discuss ways of dealing with these feelings. Then, have a baby visit. Discuss the good and bad points of new babies. Read stories on this subject. Discuss how having a baby is different from having a doll (more time-consuming, messier).

INTEGRATION   Children appreciate a chance to talk about their feelings of neglect when they have a new sibling or a family member who takes up a disproportionate amount of time. Help children think about how they can cope with these feelings.

Inclusion: Large or Small Group

18   NOISY TASKS

GOALS   To increase awareness of individual differences and similarities; to increase inclusion; to express feelings

OBJECTIVES   The child will state how it feels to work in a noisy environment under pressure and make some suggestions about how things could be changed.

MATERIALS   Record and record player *or* tape and tape player, noisemakers

PROCEDURE   Have the children do some task that requires a lot of concentration (coloring intricate designs, lacing a paper plate). Tell them you want them to do this task as fast as they can without making mistakes. Time them (two minutes is about right). Spend another two minutes in the same activity, either before or after, but provide as many distractions as possible: Turn the lights on and off; talk loudly to an aide; bang some things together; open and shut the door; stomp around; and so on. Have the children count how many holes they laced or squares they colored under each set of circumstances. You could graph the results for the whole class if you choose. Talk with the children about how easy or difficult it was for them to work with lots of distractions. Then explain to the class that for some children, even small distractions prevent them from working well.

INTEGRATION   Talk about distractions, such as the TV at home, traffic noise, loud music, and so on. Help children think back to this activity as a reminder of how difficult it is for some children to work with distractions that are relatively minor.

Inclusion: Small Group

19   FEELINGS

GOALS   To use the arts to express a range of subject matters, symbols, and ideas; to increase inclusion; to express feelings

OBJECTIVES   The child will draw a picture of a situation in which he felt a particular negative emotion and talk about the experience.

MATERIALS   Paper, crayons, markers, scissors, old magazines

PROCEDURE   Have children make a book of situations in which they were sad (or angry, unhappy, or mad). When the children have put in several entries, have a group discussion and talk about how children might feel if a lot of sad things happen at one time, how hard it would be to be happy, and how they might even be scared and expect sad things to happen. Talk about what children can do to make themselves feel better when they feel sad. Encourage children to talk in greater depth and to distinguish short- and long-term emotions. Have them discuss how the actions and reactions of others influence their response.

It is normal for children to want and need to be alone some of the time. However, if a child is primarily spending time alone, an educator needs to encourage inclusion into small and large group activities. Even young children learn social skills through interacting with others.

INTEGRATION   This helps all children realize that all people, including adults, have some bad days. Help them differentiate a bad day from a pattern of negative emotions that might cause children to either withdraw or become aggressive.

Inclusion: Large or Small Group

20   TIRED

GOALS   To increase awareness of individual differences and similarities; to increase inclusion; to improve cause-and-effect reasoning

OBJECTIVES   The child will name at least two activities she doesn't want to do when tired and two reasons why someone might be tired.

MATERIALS   None

PROCEDURE   Encourage children to run or jump very actively until they are tired (they could run or jump in place if the weather is bad). Then have them list the activities they wouldn't want to do right away (run more, climb fast) and those they would do (listen to a story or music). Talk about how children differ in how easily they get tired and how it isn't fun to play actively when you're tired. Encourage children to talk about the difference between what they don't want to do because of lack of energy and tasks they just don't like (cleaning their room, picking up in general). Ask them if they ever use being tired as an excuse. Do they ever not believe others who say they are tired?

INTEGRATION   All children know how it feels to be tired. They need to learn that others may feel tired when they don't and some of the reasons why (reactions to medicine, not feeling well, and so on). Encourage children to tell each other when they are tired and suggest things they can still do together.

21   TONGUE TWISTERS

GOALS   To increase awareness of individual differences and similarities; to increase inclusion; to express feelings

OBJECTIVES   The child will state how he feels after saying a difficult tongue twister fast.

MATERIALS   None

PROCEDURE   Teach children some tongue twisters, then encourage them to say them fast. This often results in both laughter and the realization that some things are difficult for all of us to say. For example:

> The bootblack brought the book back.
>
> Beth brought a big blue bucket of blueberries.
>
> Big black bugs buckle and bulge beneath the big blue bundle.
>
> Betty Balder bought some butter for her bread batter.
>
> Greek grape growers grow great grapes.
>
> Peter Piper picked a peck of pickled peppers.
>
> Suzy sells seashells down by the seashore.
>
> The sixth sheik's sixth sheep's sick.
>
> Red roosters read riddles rapidly.

Have children make up their own tongue twisters.

INTEGRATION   This activity promotes an understanding that speech can be difficult for some children. Done slowly, it is an interesting way of practicing specific initial sounds.

22   VOICELESS ROLL CALL

GOALS   To increase awareness of individual differences and similarities; to increase inclusion; to increase respect for diversity in modes of communication

OBJECTIVES   The child will respond to her name in an appropriate way.

MATERIALS   None

PROCEDURE   Call the children's names but mouth the names instead of speaking them out. Discuss how difficult voiceless roll call is, especially how hard it is to keep paying attention. When the children get the idea, tell them voicelessly what activities are available and ask them to make choices.

INTEGRATION   You may have to practice a bit before you are comfortable calling roll this way. Discuss how difficult it is to pay attention when you can't hear and why it might be impossible for a child who has a visually impairment to participate. Help them decide how this child could be included.

23   WHO IS IT?

GOALS   To increase awareness of individual differences and similarities; to increase incision; to improve tactile skills

OBJECTIVES   The child will describe a classmate's features and identify him by touch.

MATERIALS   A blindfold

PROCEDURE   Blindfold one child and have him touch another child. You will have to give some guidance at first on the appropriate ways to touch another person. You might even guide the child's hand to feel the length of hair, height, type of shoes and clothes, facial features, and so on. Help the child by stating what to feel for: "Let's see. Who is about as tall as you are? Who has long, straight hair, and high cheek bones? Who is wearing a sweatshirt and tie shoes?" (Children may have to use clothing as clues until they become more precise in their ability to touch.) Initially, choose a child to identify who has very obvious features or one that is a good friend. Have the child talk. As children become more proficient, give fewer clues.

INTEGRATION   This activity gives children the experience of "seeing" with their hands as a child who is blind might. It also shows them some of the difficulties such children face. Encourage children to look in the mirror and try to figure out what would feel different about different faces (bone structure, how deeply set the eyes are, shape of the nose, and so on).

Inclusion: Large or Small Group

24   FOREIGN LANGUAGES

GOALS   To increase awareness of individual differences and similarities; to increase cultural awareness; to increase respect for diversity in modes of communication

OBJECTIVES   The child will understand that people of the world speak many languages and will recognize when speech is in English and when it is not.

MATERIALS   Cassette tape, tape recorder

PROCEDURE   Sing or play a cassette of a familiar song in a foreign language. Ask children what the words mean and discuss how some words are the same or similar in several languages. Then teach the English version. "Frère Jacques" is one of the most familiar songs. Discuss with the children how hard it is to listen and pay attention when you don't understand. Have children work on differentiating English from non-English. Use a variety of languages if possible so children understand that there are many different languages. If children or their families speak another language, invite them to come and talk to the class; be sure they talk about the culture as well. If there is a Spanish or French TV or radio station in your area, ask the children to listen to it, or use an audiotape of a foreign language. Help children become more aware of other languages and how difficult it is to learn another language—and also how valuable.

INTEGRATION   Encourage children to think about their dependence on language to communicate and what the problems are when you do not speak the language of the people around you. Have a children's picture dictionary that labels pictures in two languages so they not only hear that the language is different but see it as well.

Inclusion: Small Group or Individual

25   SIMULATED GLASSES

GOALS   To increase awareness of individual differences and similarities; to increase inclusion; to improve observation skills

OBJECTIVES   The child will state what she sees using various types of glasses and how it feels to move around wearing different glasses.

MATERIALS   Glasses frames or sunglasses, gauze, half-face Halloween masks, cellophane, adhesive tape

   To simulate visual conditions, you can use inexpensive sunglasses or Halloween masks. When you cover the eye holes, put the cellophane over the inside opening or make sure the sticky side of the tape faces outward (see Figure 19.2).

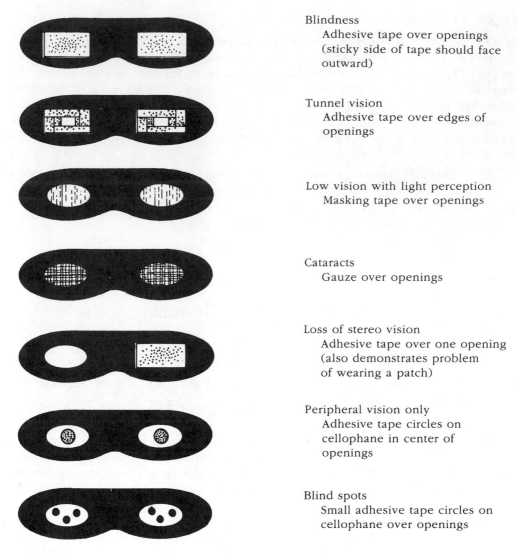

Blindness
Adhesive tape over openings
(sticky side of tape should face outward)

Tunnel vision
Adhesive tape over edges of openings

Low vision with light perception
Masking tape over openings

Cataracts
Gauze over openings

Loss of stereo vision
Adhesive tape over one opening
(also demonstrates problem of wearing a patch)

Peripheral vision only
Adhesive tape circles on cellophane in center of openings

Blind spots
Small adhesive tape circles on cellophane over openings

Figure 19.2

PROCEDURE Have children talk about what they can and cannot see with the glasses. Encourage them to wear the glasses and then do what they usually do during the day. Talk with them about what is easy to do with the glasses and what is difficult.

INTEGRATION Have the glasses available for several days so children can continue to experiment with them. Children can progress from being aware of what a particular visual impairment means to the implications this has for daily life. Encourage children to use magnifying glasses and binoculars and talk about the changes these make in what they see.

Inclusion: Small Group

26 CREEPERS

GOALS To increase awareness of individual differences and similarities; to increase inclusion; to improve locomotor skills

OBJECTIVES The child will move around the classroom on the creeper or dolly and state what is easy or difficult to do.

MATERIALS   Several creepers, mechanic's dollies, or anything on wheels several inches from the floor and propelled by the children's hands and feet

PROCEDURE   Focus first on the mechanics of using a creeper. Then have the children explore the room from the dolly and think about how much energy it takes, how tired they get, what they can and can't reach, and how their body feels after a while. After the novelty has worn off, discuss with the children the limitations involved in moving around this way. Ask children to perform specific tasks such as getting a puzzle and putting it together, getting something from the locker area, and so on.

INTEGRATION   It is important to have children stay on the dolly long enough to realize the limitations, not just experience the novelty of moving in a different way. Encourage them to be creative and think about how they might get things they can't reach and so on.

Inclusion: Small Group or Individual

27   MITTENS

GOALS   To increase awareness of individual differences and similarities; to increase inclusion; to increase body awareness

OBJECTIVES   The child will state how he or she feels when trying to use small manipulatives with mittens on.

MATERIALS   Mittens, a variety of small objects and typical small manipulatives (puzzles, blocks that join together, and so on)

PROCEDURE   Have the children bring mittens to school or provide them. They can be worn throughout the day or used just to demonstrate fine motor skills such as stacking small blocks, interlocking shapes, eating snacks, stringing beads, coloring, and so on. Allow the children to take off the mittens if they become frustrated. If they take the mittens off, ask why and discuss how they felt before and after. However, encourage them to put them on again when they change tasks. Have children discuss how they feel after an activity.

INTEGRATION   As children become more aware of how useful their fingers are, they also gain an appreciation of the difficulties faced by children with fine motor coordination problems.

Inclusion: Large or Small Group

28   MOVING IN THE DARK

GOALS   To increase awareness of individual differences and similarities; to increase inclusion; to improve locomotor skills

OBJECTIVES   The child will show how she can move safely in the dark.

MATERIALS   Blindfolds

PROCEDURE   Make up a story about a child who has to go somewhere in the dark and is afraid of hitting her head. Have the children think of ways the child could move to avoid getting hurt, then demonstrate these. Make it relevant to the children by suggesting they could get up in the night to try to find something. See if they can learn specific techniques for moving safely when they cannot see. (Encourage children to put on blindfolds and try out their techniques. Have others provide feedback so the technique can be modified.) Create some obstacles the children have to go around or through to add interest. Ask children to think about how having another person around would be helpful.

INTEGRATION   This activity helps children's awareness of their heads in space and the need to protect them. It also illustrates the problem of moving when you can't see and what others can do that is helpful and not as helpful.

29 TALKING

GOALS To increase awareness of individual differences and similarities; to increase inclusion; to increase respect for diversity in modes of communication

OBJECTIVES The child will talk about the implications of talking in different ways and about how it feels when others have difficulty understanding her.

MATERIALS None

PROCEDURE In a small group, give a child a specific thing to say and then tell the child how to use her mouth. If you don't think they will understand, demonstrate for the children the various ways of talking before asking them to do each one. For example:

Keep your teeth clenched while you talk.

Keep your lips closed.

Keep your tongue behind the lower teeth.

Have the children continue trying to make themselves understood until they experience some frustration. Discuss how it feels when others don't understand your speech. Help children focus on the function of the various parts of their mouths in speech. Help them specify how speech changes based on the parts of the mouth that they cannot use.

INTEGRATION This activity can be varied by having each child talk into a tape recorder, then listen to herself.

30 SLINGS

GOALS To increase inclusion; to increase body awareness; to increase awareness of individual differences and similarities

OBJECTIVES The child will state why slings are used and at least three things that are difficult to do using only one arm.

MATERIALS A piece of material or scarf for each child, large enough to be made into a sling

PROCEDURE During group time, talk about what it is like to be able to use only one arm. (Some children are born with only one arm, others break their arms.) Have the children guess what things are difficult to do with just one arm, and encourage them to participate in activities with one arm in a sling. Help children who participated talk about the feelings and difficulties they had. If they become frustrated and take the sling off, use their experience of frustration to make your point. First, put the child's nondominant arm in the sling; to gain further understanding, put the child's dominant arm in the sling.

INTEGRATION Children can gain perceptions of what kinds of adaptations having only one arm might require. Encourage them to think of adaptive devices that might help, some of the skills they would have to develop, and what they might do differently.

31 VISITOR

GOALS To increase awareness of roles people play; to increase awareness of individual differences and similarities; to increase inclusion

OBJECTIVES The child will state what the adult does in the community and how the adult chose this profession.

MATERIALS   None

PROCEDURE   Invite adults from the community to come into the class. Pick people who are comfortable with children. Have them talk briefly about what they do and answer the children's questions. Choose people who will broaden the children's understanding of the community, as well as reduce sex-role stereotyping. For example:

photographer	Red Cross staff	farmer
businessperson	waitress/waiter	plumber
Welcome Wagon staff	male nurse	builder
female medical doctor	female lawyer	musician
female engineer	real estate agent	
construction worker	computer programmer	

Include visitors who use wheelchairs. There is no doubt that a service dog makes a positive impression of independence. Educators and children need to learn their value and use in society.

Start with occupations the children are familiar with and keep the large-group discussion short. Have those children who are particularly interested follow up the large-group experience with a small-group discussion. The visitor can go into greater depth about the profession as well as answer additional questions. Follow this up by visiting the person at work as well as by dramatic play in the classroom incorporating that theme.

INTEGRATION   Children often have a restricted view of the community. This activity can extend their understanding and make them feel more a part of the community. Be sure to include visitors who represent a variety of cultural and ethnic groups and include those who have disabilities.

Social Studies: Small Group

32   OUR TOWN

GOALS   To increase inclusion; to increase awareness of roles people play; to understand geographic concepts

OBJECTIVES   The child will construct a block structure that makes a contribution to the community and state what this contribution is.

MATERIALS   Masking tape, blocks and accessories

PROCEDURE   In the block corner, use masking tape to map out a road and building lots. Assign each child a lot and have them construct buildings. Begin with a few building lots and more actively help children decide what they will build. Ask children to decide what kinds of buildings (houses, restaurants, hospitals, firehouses, gas stations) their community needs and who is going to build them. Leave the construction style up to each child. Pose questions such as, "Where would someone go if he got sick?" Expand the children's ideas if necessary. Emphasize group problem solving and a sense of community spirit. As children gain skill, have them map out the roads and plots. Expand the block area and leave the structures up for several days. Talk about whether or not the structures are handicapped-accessible and how they might be adapted if they are not.

INTEGRATION   This provides a more concrete way for children to think about communities and how they work and support the people who live in them.

Social Studies: Large Group

33   INTERNATIONAL SNACK

GOALS   To broaden concepts of families; to increase awareness of roles people play; to increase cultural awareness

OBJECTIVES   The child will identify and taste the snacks and make one statement about the region it comes from.

MATERIALS   An international snack: flour tortillas, pupu, fondue, crêpes, Irish soda bread, pita bread

PROCEDURE   As one activity for the day, make a snack that is not traditionally American. Start with foods that, although from other countries originally, are familiar to many of the children (tofu, pita bread, and crêpes), then work in foods that are increasingly different. Discuss what the foods are made of and where they come from, then eat them. Include children in the preparation and discuss the foods used, the culture, and the people. Use parents and relatives as a resource.

INTEGRATION   Help children think of differences without judgment. Have them look at the broad geographic features of a region such as temperature, rainfall, and elevation, and look at the foods eaten in relation to those variables. Children will often participate in experiences with food at school that they would not try at home, especially if they participated in its preparation.

34   MEDICAL TOOLS

GOALS   To increase awareness of roles people play; to improve self-concept; to increase vocabulary

OBJECTIVES   The child will identify the equipment, match it to the correct body part, and state its function.

MATERIALS   Medical equipment, or pictures of medical equipment, and pictures of the parts of the body where these are most commonly used:

mouth	tongue depressor	arm	blood pressure cuff
throat	throat swab	eyes, ears, throat	small flashlight
knee	rubber hammer	lungs, heart	stethoscope
arm	intravenous system	bottom	needle and syringe

PROCEDURE   Demonstrate how the tools are used on a child or doll. Begin with the most familiar ones. Have the children match the pictures of medical equipment to pictures of the appropriate body parts. This often leads to discussion about doctors and medical procedures. Discuss in detail the equipment and how it is used. Include information on what doctors look for and why. Have a medical dictionary available so you can look up information.

INTEGRATION   Be sure to use the equipment the children in your class are most likely to encounter. This activity should help make all children's contact with the medical profession less frightening, and also help them realize that some of their classmates must see doctors more frequently than they do.

35   PATIENT IN THE HOSPITAL

GOALS   To increase awareness of roles people play; to improve self-concept; to increase inclusion

OBJECTIVES   The child will participate in and discuss the roles and purpose of the people the "patient" comes in contact with.

MATERIALS   None

PROCEDURE   Adapt the song "The Farmer in the Dell" to your specific purposes relative to the medical profession:

There's a child who is sick,
There's a child who is sick.
Hi Ho the Office O.
There's a child who is sick.

"There's a child going to the doctor" and "There's a child going to the hospital" can also be used. In the following stanzas, the child chooses someone to accompany him or her to the hospital (mother, father, grandmother, aunt); that person chooses the doctor; the doctor chooses the nurse (or specialists). Then:

They all stand together,
They all stand together.
Hi Ho the Office O.
Until the child gets better.

Have the children hold a picture or equipment (stethoscope, thermometer) as a clue to their role. You might follow the song by talking about some of the various specialists and what they do. Include the speech and language, occupational, and physical therapists, psychologist, family therapist, different types of doctors (pediatrician, neurologist, surgeon, and so on).

INTEGRATION Children encounter many members of the health profession. This activity helps make the interaction fun rather than threatening. Let the children choose whom to include.

Social Studies: Large and Small Group

36 AUDIOLOGIST

GOALS To increase awareness of roles people play; to increase inclusion; to improve self-concept

OBJECTIVES The child will state what an audiologist does and why, and play the role either of the audiologist or the patient.

MATERIALS Props for an audiologist's office: bells, ear muffs, a box with knobs, buzzers

PROCEDURE During group time, introduce the concept of an audiologist and what he or she does. Talk about how and why people get their hearing tested. Explain that there is an audiologist's office set up. Use a box with knobs on it; bells, buzzers, or anything that makes noise; and ear muffs for earphones. Have the children "test" each other's hearing. They can raise a hand when they hear a noise or they can do a task, such as stack a circle on a stick, each time they hear a noise. Once children understand the process, erect a barrier so one child can't see what is happening and has to rely on sound to respond. Ask children to identify the sound.

INTEGRATION Use this activity to prepare all children to have their hearing tested by a school nurse. Allow children for whom this is a common practice to take a leadership role and work through any feelings that they have about the procedure.

Social Studies: Large and Small Group

37 EYE DOCTOR

GOALS To increase awareness of roles people play; to increase inclusion; to improve self-concept

OBJECTIVES The child will state what an eye doctor does and why, and play the role of either the eye doctor or the patient.

MATERIALS Props for an eye doctor's office: vision chart, card with a "three-legged table" to be matched to the chart (see Figure 19.3), glasses, index card, frames, pointer, mirror

PROCEDURE During group time, discuss eye doctors and what they do. Explain that you have set up an eye doctor's office. Encourage one child to be the doctor and point to the letters, another to be an

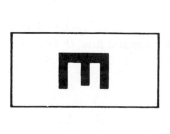

Card

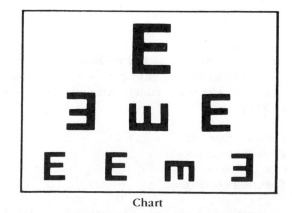

Chart

Figure 19.3

assistant and help with glasses and the testing process. To become familiar with the procedure, initially concentrate on the matching aspect of this experience at a distance where you are sure children can see. Have them talk about these roles and how they feel about them. Encourage children to experiment with the relationship between distance and seeing, and have them find where in the room they can no longer see accurately. They can measure this distance.

INTEGRATION   Follow this activity with vision screening by a nurse or other qualified person. Eye Doctor teaches children how doctors help people see better and may help identify children who need visual follow-up.

Social Studies: Small Group

38   EMERGENCY ROOM

GOALS   To increase awareness of roles people play; to encourage problem solving; to improve self-concept

OBJECTIVES   The child will state what an emergency room is and why one might go there, and play the role of either a medical professional or a patient.

MATERIALS   An emergency room setup: table, paper, chairs, pencils, bandages, lab coat

PROCEDURE   Set up the emergency room. During group time, talk about the reasons for going to the emergency room: a broken bone, a bad cut or burn, as opposed to a headache or a cold. Talk to the children about what would be likely to happen: Someone would ask for their name and insurance number, and they would have to wait. Also discuss what they could do while they wait, what the doctor might do, and the possibility that they would not know the doctor. Emphasize that you go here in an emergency. Stress the importance of time, and how those with life-threatening conditions are treated first, regardless of when people arrived.

INTEGRATION   The purpose of this activity is really to familiarize the child with a set of procedures so that the fear of the emergency room is not added to the medical problem. Try to have an element of realism as well as creativity. See this as a variation on the doctor's office, although the element of time, the reasons for going to the emergency room, and the other people in the waiting room are different.

Social Studies: Large or Small Group

39   WHO AM I?

GOALS   To increase awareness of roles people play; to improve cause-and-effect reasoning; to encourage adaptive skills

OBJECTIVES   The child will state the purpose of the head covering, who might use it, and demonstrate its usefulness.

MATERIALS   Characteristic hats:

firefighter's hat	fishing hat	rain hat
police officer's hat	cowboy hat	sunbonnet
hardhat	woman's hat	
stocking cap	football helmet	
hats from other areas and cultures	baseball hat	
	baby's bonnet	

PROCEDURE   Show the collection of hats to the children. Start with what children know: What hats do they wear and why? Have them figure out what person would wear each hat and demonstrate the purpose of the hat. At first, use hats that are specific to one role, then use some to broaden ideas; that is, a woman's hat could be worn by a mother, teacher, secretary, or lawyer. Talk about the characteristics of the hats that make them suitable for the people who wear them. Help children understand the efficacy of hats and how they are different based on when and where you wear them. Look at the subtle differences among similar hats (football, motorcycle, baseball, and bicycle helmets) and help children understand why they are different.

INTEGRATION   This is a different way of approaching community helpers as it uses one clue and leaves the rest to the child. Be sure to talk about the purpose of hats in general. Teach the basic safety and health aspects of hats for use on bicycles, as protection from the sun, and to stay warm.

Social Studies: Small Group

40   LIBRARY

GOALS   To increase awareness of roles people play; to increase inclusion; to improve reading literacy

OBJECTIVES   The child will select a book, explain why she chose that book, check it out of the library, and return it.

MATERIALS   Props for a library: books, cards, posters

PROCEDURE   Set up a library in your room with a collection of children's books that can be categorized by the pictures on the front; use books about the country, animals, people, and so on. Encourage children to look over the selection and ask for the books they want. Be sure some children are librarians and some patrons. Have the children categorize the books in the library by topical area of interest and mark them so they know the area. Encourage the other children to ask for books on specific topics. Talk with them about the role of a reference librarian. Encourage them to develop a system for checking the books in and out and, of course, talk about overdue books.

INTEGRATION   This helps children understand that libraries are parts of communities and their family can use this resource. It also helps children become familiar with library procedures. Follow up with a trip to a library and encourage parents to take their children to the library.

Social Studies: Small Group

41   CAST IT

GOALS   To increase awareness of roles people play; to increase awareness of individual differences and similarities; to increase inclusion

OBJECTIVES   The child will state the purpose of a cast, who puts them on, the problems people with casts have, and put a cast on either a doll or a classmate.

MATERIALS   Plaster tape (available at most drug stores), water, scissors without points, dolls, broken chicken bone, X-ray

PROCEDURE   Talk about broken bones; show one from an animal and talk about what a cast does for a bone. Set up the dramatic play area with plaster tape (just soak it in water to use it), a bucket of water, and dolls. First, have the children experiment with a doll. Some children may just explore the plaster tape as an art medium. Then, have them put a cast on a thumb or finger. The cast will slip off, but have some blunt-nosed fingernail scissors so you can cut off any stubborn ones. Discuss with the children that breaking bones hurts, but casting doesn't. Bring in an X-ray of a broken bone and show it to the children. Help them understand the purpose of setting and casting broken bones.

INTEGRATION   Warn parents about this project so they will know their child's thumb isn't really broken if he wears the cast home. Children who know how and why casts are put on and taken off are less fearful when they need an actual cast. If most of the children put casts on their thumbs, you can make an art project out of decorating the casts.

Social Studies: Small Group

42   MAPS

GOALS   To increase inclusion; to encourage problem solving; to understand geography concepts

OBJECTIVES   The child will find two paths to a designated location and describe them.

MATERIALS   A simple laminated map of an area that includes the school and familiar places, crayons, or erasable marking pen, tissue

PROCEDURE   Introduce the concept of maps and their purpose. Start with a map of the classroom and have children use the map to go to a certain area. Then introduce the map of the area. Set the map on a table with several crayons beside it. Encourage the children to pick a location and work together to trace a path from school to that location and then to find an alternative route and compare them (see Figure 19.4). Use the tissue to erase the crayon. Help children map out a walk or field trip. Encourage children to find alternative routes.

INTEGRATION   This activity is a way of increasing children's understanding of their community and of what is near the school. It also helps them learn about alternatives.

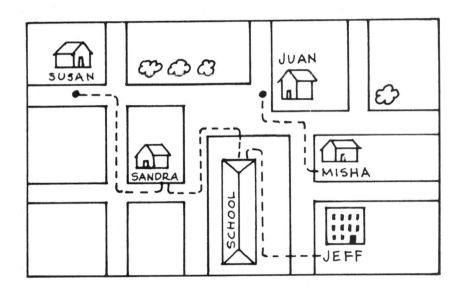

Figure 19.4

Social Studies: Large or Small Group

43   WHO HAS BEEN HERE?

GOALS   To encourage problem solving; to understand geography concepts; to improve cause-and-effect reasoning

OBJECTIVES   The child will describe who would make the designated footprints and give a reason for that choice.

MATERIALS   Water-based paint, paper (8 ½″ × 11″), a variety of footwear in different sizes and for different purposes:

baby shoes	high heels	sneakers
baseball spikes	hiking boots	roller skates
ice skates	clogs	golf shoes
ballet slippers	toe shoes	riding boots

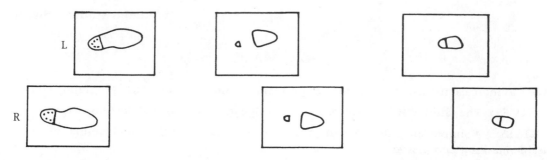

Figure 19.5

PROCEDURE   Make footprints by putting the bottom of the shoes in paint, then printing each one on a sheet of paper. Make at least six footprints with each pair of footwear.

First, use only one type of shoe, differing only in size (for example, sneakers). Have children match the shoe to the print. Start by showing the children footprints that are about the size they would make. Ask them to arrange the prints as if someone were walking (see Figure 19.5). Ask the children to describe the size of the person and where the person might be going. Have the children walk on the prints (after they are dry) to see if the spacing is right; help them correlate the size of footprints with the spacing between footprints. Add the more specialized footwear. Then help the children match the shoes to the prints and decide under what conditions this type of footwear would be most useful.

INTEGRATION   Thinking skills are both challenging and fun. You might have children design shoes for various environments (swamp vs. desert). Be sure to include shoes from a variety of places: moccasins, thongs, clogs, and so on. Use textured paint so the children can feel as well as see the prints. Have a specialty footwear store; the children can describe the circumstances and activities they want shoes for.

Health and Safety: Small Group

44   NOT TO EAT

GOALS   To increase awareness of individual differences and similarities; to increase adaptive skills; to improve health literacy

OBJECTIVES   The child will state which substances are edible and which are not.

MATERIALS   A variety of substances, some edible (crackers, juice, milk, peanut butter, nuts) and some not (soap, playdough, sand)

PROCEDURE   Put the substances on a table and talk about which ones the children can eat and which ones might make them sick. Then talk about individual differences in things people can't eat. Children with allergies, for example, must avoid some foods. Mention the particular allergies of children in your class. Talk about what happens when children have food allergies. Start with obvious things that cannot be eaten. State the rules about how to decide what to eat. Add foods that are eaten by animals (bird seed, dog food). Talk about the differences in what animals and people eat.

INTEGRATION   Children must learn which foods they can and cannot eat and that some children cannot eat some foods that others like. They may not be able to eat some foods they really like. Discuss the temptation of "sneaking" these foods and the implications of that behavior. The rules about what is edible and what is not need to be kept very clear for children with diverse abilities. Don't confound issues they may be struggling with by using pudding as fingerpaint and making peanut butter into playdough. This is very much a health and safety issue: What is edible must be separate from what children can play with.

45   SEASONAL CLOTHING

GOALS   To improve health literacy; to increase adaptive skills; to improve cause-and-effect reasoning

OBJECTIVES   The child will state in what season various items of clothing are worn and why.

MATERIALS   Articles of clothing or pictures of them, pictures of scenes of the four seasons labeled by season, pictures of events that happen in various seasons

PROCEDURE   Have the children sort the clothes or pictures into piles by season. Include fabric swatches to sort as well. Be sure to discuss why certain clothes and fabrics are chosen for different seasons:

SPRING	SUMMER	FALL	WINTER
long pants	swimsuit	long pants	snowsuit
sweater	sleeveless top	jacket	mittens
jeans	cotton shorts	kneesocks	boots
flannels	eyelet	knit	fake fur
terry cloth	gabardine	wool	velvet

Be sure to agree that some clothes for cool weather can be worn in spring or fall or all seasons. It is the reasoning that matters. Start with characteristic clothing from the season that you are currently in (for example, a snowsuit in winter). Compare this to a swimsuit. Start with the most obvious comparisons. Have the children try on the clothing and sort it into boxes. Make comments to support children's choices: "When you put mittens on, I can't see your hands. Mittens keep your hands warm."

Have children classify the events and also include appropriate clothing to be worn at the events. Use pictures of events to be classified as well:

SPRING	SUMMER	FALL	WINTER
trees bud	people swim	school starts	animals hibernate
birds build nests	people take vacations	leaves change colors and drop, apples and pumpkins are harvested	snow falls, people ice skate

INTEGRATION   This activity is an opportunity for children to talk about the predictability of seasonal change and how seasons are different in various climates. Children need to learn to be responsive to the weather as they choose their clothing. They can also learn about the protective quality of clothing. *Note:* This activity is most appropriate for places where there are four seasons. In places where there are rainy and dry seasons or where climate is determined by altitude, those would be obvious divisions. Relate the activity to the climate where you are.

46   SMELL CUES

GOALS   To improve health literacy; to increase adaptive skills; to improve cause-and-effect reasoning

OBJECTIVES   The child will state what the smell is, what the situation might be, and what to do after smelling the container.

MATERIALS   Small containers, each holding a cotton ball saturated with a familiar-smelling substance (paint, food, perfume, liquid smoke, and so on)

PROCEDURE   Have the children guess what the smells are, in what situations they would find them, and how they could respond:

> paint, wet paint, don't touch
>
> food, mealtime, set the table
>
> smoke, danger, leave
>
> ammonia, cleaning time, pick up toys
>
> perfume, going out, say good-bye

A variety of behaviors is possible in all these situations. Support all appropriate behaviors and help children think of many different ways to respond. Tell children to just smell (caution them not to taste the substances); initially, use only substances that would be safe if ingested. When children are familiar with the procedure, increase the variety of smells under careful supervision. Where possible, include smells of dangerous substances. Be very clear that these are dangerous. Obviously, this activity needs close supervision.

INTEGRATION   Because of experience and visual association, small cues are meaningful to us, but they are not necessarily meaningful to children or those who have sensory impairments. These children may need to be specifically taught when a situation is dangerous. Some children are more curious and less cautious than others. They must learn that there are some things in the environment that are not safe to experiment with, and that one cue about this is smell.

Health and Safety: Small Group

47   SYMPTOMS

GOALS   To improve health literacy; to increase vocabulary; to increase body awareness

OBJECTIVES   The child will state what her symptoms are and where in her body they are occurring and how severe they are.

MATERIALS   Dolls

PROCEDURE   Help children develop the vocabulary to describe their symptoms and to give some information on the area and degree of the "hurt."

BODY PARTS	MEDICAL TERMS	DEGREE TERMS	
tummy, stomach	vomit, throw up	swollen, puffy	small, little
head	dull pain	a little dizzy	blood, bleeding
arms, legs	sharp pain	a lot	large, big
knee, neck	sore	cut	hot, cold

Role-play situations in which a child who is "hurt" tells you or another child what's wrong. Decide what to do in the case of various symptoms (dizzy—lie down; cut—wash it; swollen part—put ice on it). Use both the child's body and a doll to teach body parts. Role-play the most likely events a child might encounter (a cut or a stomachache). Help children learn more internal body parts as well as where they are located.

INTEGRATION   This activity provides useful information for a child to have *before* she becomes ill. Be sure to include specific terms that children may need, depending on their impairment. Be sure that children understand that their objective is to be accurate, not creative.

48 TRAFFIC SIGN HUNT

GOALS To increase adaptive skills; to improve health literacy; to improve cause-and-effect reasoning

OBJECTIVES The child will state what to do in response to each sign shown.

MATERIALS Story traffic signs (see Figure 19.6)

PROCEDURE This is an adaptation of the bear hunt. Go over each sign with the children before you begin an imaginary walk and be sure they know what to do. Initially, make the walk slower and shorter. Start "walking" by putting your palms on your thighs in a rhythm. Change the rhythm in response to the signs.

Anyone want to go on a traffic sign hunt? OK, let's go. Close the gate (close with hand motions). We're coming to a corner. I see a sign (hold up a stop sign). What do you think it is? A stop sign! What do we have to do? (Stop. Hold up palms toward children.) OK, look both ways. (Look.) No cars. Let's cross the street. Hurry. (Increase beat of hand.) You don't wander across streets, but you don't have to run either. Oh, what's this? This is a railroad crossing sign. (Hold up.) See the tracks? Be very careful. Look both ways. Are the gates up or down? Listen, do you hear anything? Are there any lights flashing? OK, let's cross. Look again and let's go. Oh, there really are a lot of signs to look at when you go for a walk. What's this one? (Hold up yield sign.) What shape is that? What should we do? It's a little like a stop sign; we don't have to stop, just slow down (slow rhythm) and look around. If we see anyone, then we have to stop.

Look, do you see anything? Hey, I see an elephant. Do we have to stop? Yep. The elephant has the right of way. We have to yield. Go very slowly. OK, he's gone. That was a nice rest. I wonder what other kinds of signs we'll see. Hey, that one has lights. It's green and yellow and red. What is it? (Hold up traffic light.) We have the green; now what do we do? We can go. I am beginning to get

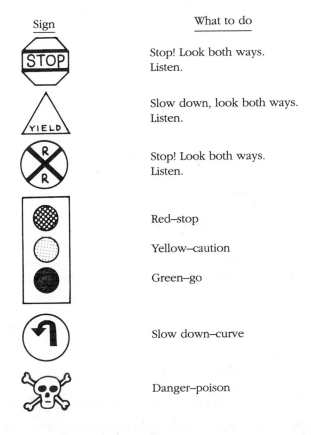

Sign	What to do
STOP	Stop! Look both ways. Listen.
YIELD	Slow down, look both ways. Listen.
RR	Stop! Look both ways. Listen.
(traffic light)	Red–stop Yellow–caution Green–go
(curve)	Slow down–curve
(skull)	Danger–poison

Figure 19.6

tired; how about you? No? Well, there is another sign. That's for a curve. Lean left or you'll go off the road. Do you think we're on a mountain? Let's slow down. Oh, what's that sign? (Hold up skull and cross blood, bleeding bones sign.) Danger. Let's get out of here. As fast you can, lean right, hurry back over the curve. Now, oh, there's the light; what color is it? Red. Stop.

OK, now it's green; let's go. There's the yield; is there anything coming? (Look.) We're OK, good, keep going. What will it be next? Oh, the railroad. Stop. Look. Listen. Any trains? Let's go. Hurry, oh, there's the stop sign; everybody stop. Look, let's go. Open the gate; shut it. Whee, it's good to be back here in our classroom.

As children get better, add more signs, make the walk longer, go faster, and add more drama.

INTEGRATION Use your imagination and be dramatic. The children love it at the end when you go fast. This is good practice and yet fun. Children can participate at different levels. Children also enjoy bear hunts or lion hunts, and can learn about different terrain, but run home once the prey is spotted.

Health and Safety: Large Group

49 WARNING SOUNDS

GOALS To increase adaptive skills; to improve health literacy; to improve cause-and-effect reasoning

OBJECTIVES The child will identify sounds and state what to do when he hears a specific sound.

MATERIALS Videotape of objects making warning sounds, VCR, audiotape with warning sounds, tape recorder

PROCEDURE Make a videotape of warning sounds and the objects making them. Talk about what the children should do in these circumstances. Start with the safety sounds they are most likely to encounter. Then make an audiotape recording of various warning sounds children might hear and have them identify these without visual cues. Include a broad range of sounds:

fire alarm	truck's beep (when backing up)	telephone sound when left off the hook
shouts of alarm		
bell buoy (boats)	fire siren or whistle	police siren
train whistle	fog horn (boats)	car horn
microwave timer	calling a name	oven timer
clothes dryer timer	"Fore" (golfers)	"Watch out"
smoke alarm	"Timber" (tree falling)	

When the children can identify these sounds, have them name a sound and tell where they might hear it and what they should do if they hear it. Use more unusual sounds and ones that are more difficult to discriminate but that nevertheless are important.

INTEGRATION Children need to depend on their auditory cues for safety. They will hear a siren before they see the fire truck and they need to be able to identify the sound. This activity helps them determine what is happening in their environment whether or not they can actually see what is going on.

Health and Safety: Small Group

50 STOP AND GO

GOALS To increase adaptive skills; to improve health literacy; to improve cause-and-effect reasoning

OBJECTIVES The child will stop when red is held up and go when green is held up.

MATERIALS Red, green, and yellow pieces of paper; tricycles

Learning at a young age about safety concerns, such as wearing a
helmet while riding a tricycle or bicycle, is an important part of safety
and prevention of head injuries.

PROCEDURE   Adapt the traditional game of red light/green light by having the children walk or ride when you hold up a piece of green construction paper and stop when you hold up a piece of red paper. Once children learn the process, increase the time between changes from red to green, and make some times very short so the children must pay close attention. Initially say the word "stop" with red and "go" with green. Using this procedure, introduce the concept of caution to children. When holding up the yellow paper, have them walk or ride more slowly and be ready for change. Have a child be the traffic director and regulate the tricycles with the red, yellow, and green "lights."

INTEGRATION   Stop and Go is an important safety concept for all children to learn. Children need practice learning to wait for the signal to change as well as identifying the basic relationship between the color and what they should do.

Health and Safety: Small or Large Group

51   WARNING SIGNS

GOALS   To increase adaptive skills; to improve health literacy; to improve cause-and-effect reasoning

OBJECTIVES   The child will identify each sign and demonstrate appropriate behavior when the sign is held up.

MATERIALS   Pictures of familiar warning signs (stop, yield, one way, railroad crossing, traffic lights, walk signals, and so on)

PROCEDURE   Introduce the various warning signs; be sure to include the ones near your setting. Focus first on the signs that are necessary for survival. Discuss with the children what the signs mean and what the children should do when they see them. Have the children role-play situations. Use the signs outside in the play yard to direct traffic flow. Be sure to change the locations and directions frequently so children really do have to look. Follow this with a walk in the community and have children identify the signs. Include more signs such as those that give information about places to camp, sleep, eat, and buy gas. Have children help make up signs to add to the play yard that include additional information about the area (swinging, no trikes, picnic area, and so on). Encourage children to think of significant ways of portraying the information they want to convey.

INTEGRATION   Obeying safety signs is necessary for all children. Those with sensory impairments may need specific help learning the cues; others may have difficulty waiting for the sign and readjusting when the signs change. This is an important experience for all children. Help children pair sounds with warning signs for additional information.

Health and Safety: Large or Small Group

52   WHAT WOULD YOU DO IF?

GOALS   To improve health literacy; to encourage problem solving; to increase thinking and reasoning skills

OBJECTIVES   The child will identify the situation and state four possible solutions to the problem.

MATERIALS   None

PROCEDURE   Think of a variety of problems a child might encounter and ask the children: What would you do if:

> you cut your finger?
>
> you smelled smoke or saw a fire?
>
> you broke a glass?
>
> you got lost?
>
> you fell down and couldn't get up?

The usual response is to tell an adult. Support children in that response but continue to question the children: "What if there weren't an adult around?" As children solve the problem, change the situation slightly: "I'd go outside." "What if the doors were locked?" Get children to think of as many solutions as possible. Place some restrictions on them, such as not being able to speak, to see how they might help others solve the problem. Discuss the implications of various solutions. Have children role-play some of the situations. Continue to talk with children when the more obvious solutions have been suggested.

INTEGRATION   It is especially important for children to know what to do if they are lost. In a real situation, they would probably be scared as well. Having practiced solutions may help if the problem arises. Foster thinking that supports children's seeking solutions to problems until something works.

Summary   Social awareness activities cover a broad range and are useful to all children in learning about themselves, the world they live in, how to include others who may be different than they are because of the way they look, move, or talk, and how to keep themselves safe and healthy.

Educational Resources

Bisson, J. (1997). *Celebrate! An anti-bias guide to enjoying holidays in early childhood programs.* St. Paul, MN: Redleaf.

A framework for assessing and developing appropriate celebrations in early childhood programs while honoring cultural diversity.

Charney, R. S. (1997). Habits of goodness: Case studies in the social curriculum. Greenfield, MA: Northeast Foundation for Children.

Different from discipline, this book focuses on bringing civility, caring, and nonviolence into the early childhood classroom.

Classroom Connect's Acceptable Use Policy FTP Site
ftp://classroom.net/wentworth/Classroom-Connect /aup-faq.txt

Policies and safety for children and the Internet.

Derman-Sparks, I., & Phillips, C. B. (1997). *Teaching/learning anti-racism: A developmental approach.* New York: Teachers College Press.

Provides a conceptual framework for implementing an anti-racist course for educators.

Global School Network's Guidelines and Policies for Protecting Students
http://www.gsn.org/web/

More information on establishing guidelines for children's use of the Internet.

Intercultural E-Mail Classroom Connection
http://www.stolaf.edu/network/iecc/

A listserv to encourage partnerships with classrooms for the exchange of international and cross-cultural electronic mail.

Link Library—Resources for Teachers
http://www.hmco.com/hmco/school/links /index.html

Provides links to art, math, social studies and cross-cultural curriculum themes and areas.

Multicultural Opportunities: Walk a Mile in My Shoes: Multicultural Curriculum Resources
http://www.wmht.org/trail/explor02.htm

A source of curriculum ideas to enhance multicultural understanding.

Native American Indian Resources
http://indy4.fdl.cc.,m.us/~isk/mainmenu.htlm

Information about Native American tribes and their beliefs with ideas for program planning.

Social Studies: History/Social Studies Web Site for K–12 Teachers.
http://www.execpc.com/~dboals/boals.html.

Provides information and plans for teaching social studies.

Chapter 20

LANGUAGE AND LITERACY ACTIVITIES: SPEAKING, LISTENING, READING, WRITING

Learning to communicate is one of the major tasks facing all young children. Learning language is a dynamic process that is affected by the language heard in the environment and the way that adults respond to development of speech. Speaking, listening, reading, and writing are the major components of the language and literacy curriculum. These skills are interdependent.

TABLE 20.1   ACTIVITY GOALS AND REFERENCE NUMBERS

Goals	Activities
To improve expressive communication	53, 54, 55, 56, 57, 58, 59, 60, 61, 63, 64
To improve listening skills	54, 67, 68, 69, 70, 71, 72, 73, 74, 75, 76, 77, 78, 79, 84
To increase knowledge of the structure of language	55, 62, 63, 84, 85, 91, 96
To improve receptive communication	53, 65, 67, 69, 70, 71, 72, 74
To increase vocabulary	53, 58, 62, 66, 83
To increase respect for diversity in modes of communication	82
To use diverse print and nonprint sources and genres	56, 57, 99, 100, 101, 102, 103
To improve reading literacy	62, 82, 83, 84, 85, 86, 87, 88, 89, 90, 91, 92, 93, 94, 95, 97, 100, 101, 102, 103
To increase writing literacy	89, 93, 96, 97, 98, 99, 100, 101, 102, 103
To increase comprehension	65, 66, 68, 71, 72, 73, 74, 80, 85, 86, 96
To improve sequencing skills	80, 81
To follow directions	63, 65, 88
To increase inclusion	55, 57, 61, 64, 94
To improve memory skills	80, 87, 90
To improve number sense and numeration	77
To identify and understand patterns and relationships	77, 81, 87, 88, 91
To improve geometric and spatial sense	60, 78
To improve classification skills	54, 60, 73
To improve cause-and-effect reasoning	59, 75, 76, 81
To make predictions	75, 76, 78, 79, 90, 92
To improve generalization skills	82, 92
To improve fine motor manipulative skills	89
To improve sensorimotor integration	86, 93, 95, 98, 99
To increase body awareness	83
To encourage creativity	56, 58, 59, 66, 67
To improve self-concept	64, 79
To express feelings	61, 95
To improve concentration	68, 69, 70

53 SYNONYMS

GOALS   To improve expressive communication; to improve receptive communication; to increase vocabulary

OBJECTIVES   The child will learn the concept of synonyms and label an object or concept in at least two different ways.

MATERIALS   Pictures or objects that have more than one name (see synonyms below)

PROCEDURE   Define synonyms: words that mean the same thing but sound different. Then present children with the objects or pictures of these objects, and see how many synonyms they can think of. It is not important that these be exact synonyms in a dictionary sense. The point is for the children to know that one object can have several different names. Start with familiar objects in your classroom and community:

rug/carpet/floor covering	store/shop	chair/seat
couch/sofa/davenport	road/street	bed/cot
scissors/shears	bathing suit/swimsuit	shirt/top

INTEGRATION   Children need to know that objects often have several names even in the same language. Discuss how some names are different in various regions of the country. Subs, hoagies, and grinders or soda and pop all are regional variations. Show children a thesaurus and how and why it is used.

54   SAME AND DIFFERENT

GOALS   To improve expressive communication; to improve listening skills; to improve classification skills

OBJECTIVES   The child will state what objects or concepts are the same or how they are different and classify these by function.

MATERIALS   A variety of books, markers, pens, pencils, crayons, chairs, articles of clothing, eating utensils, and dishes

PROCEDURE   Go around the class and have each child state what is and is not his or her name: "My name is Jay. My name is not Lynn." When the children have the idea, begin to joke with them and have them correct you: "Sam is a chair!" "No, Sam is not a chair. Sam is a boy." Be sure to use the negations. Once children realize how the negation works and that there can be numerous names that are not theirs, add objects and other items: "Sam has blue hair," "These books are the same," and so on, using is/is not, has/has not, does/does not, same/not the same. Then use simple concrete objects that are the same and not the same. Choose objects that look different from each other. Be sure children have the idea of negation before introducing the idea that something is different. That is, teach the children *the same/not the same* before teaching *the same/different*.

As children become more proficient, use materials that are alike in some ways and not alike or different in other ways, then ask how they are not the same or how they are different. It is challenging to use objects that are conceptually alike and perceptually (visually) different, such as a red and a blue book, a flashlight and a lamp, and so forth.

INTEGRATION   Helping children grasp underlying concepts of same and different is at the core of inclusion. As children understand that individuals are the same and different, they can begin to make accommodations for differences while at the same time acknowledging the underlying similarities. This concept is also the foundation for compare and contrast questions in many areas.

55   NEVER

GOALS   To improve expressive communication; to increase knowledge of the structure of language; to increase inclusion

OBJECTIVES   The child will use absolute and relative adjectives and adverbs appropriately.

MATERIALS   A variety of clothed dolls of different races and both genders, blocks, yarn

PROCEDURE   Teach children to make absolute and relative comparisons. Make a circle with the yarn. Place all the blocks in the circle and ask the children to move the blocks so some (a few, many, most, none, and so on) of the blocks are in the circle. After children are comfortable with negations, introduce the concept of opposite and discuss how opposites are only part of the negation. Then introduce some of the other words that allow for comparison, such as:

ABSOLUTE	RELATIVE	
always	sometimes	often
never	frequently	few
all	many	some
none	usually	occasionally
nothing	rarely	
everything		

Group and regroup the objects on both relative and absolute characteristics.

Have children make up sentences using the absolute words. When appropriate, challenge the concept and encourage children to use a more relative word. If a child says, "I *always* clean up the block corner," question the child: "Has there been *one* day when you haven't?" Help the child choose another word that more accurately represents reality: "I *often* clean up the block corner."

INTEGRATION   Although this may seem like belaboring a point, prejudicial statements are usually absolute ones: "John can't do *anything*"; "ALL people with disabilities are *helpless*." The skill of using words that allow for exceptions needs to be developed as a language skill so that absolute, prejudicial statements can be avoided in social situations.

56   BE IT

GOALS   To improve expressive communication; to use diverse print and nonprint sources and genres; to encourage creativity

OBJECTIVES   The child will tell a creative story about a familiar object.

MATERIALS   Common objects: shoes, winter coat, roller skates, ring, tricycle/bicycle, chair, brick, towel, cotton ball, stone

PROCEDURE   During group time, discuss the difference between animate and inanimate objects and have children imagine what objects might feel if they had feelings. Give them an example:

Shoes: I have pretty buckles and I am red. This morning I was sleeping in a dark closet very peacefully when someone turned on a bright light and stepped on me. I creaked a little, but that didn't stop her. She wiggled her feet into me and then ran down a flight of stairs. I then was stood on in the kitchen for 20 minutes. Finally, there was some relief. . . .

Start with familiar objects that have numerous visual cues, such as a hat with flowers on it. Prompt the child with cues such as "What happened then?" or "How did you feel then?" or more obvious ones, such as "What color are you? What do you look like?" Expect only a sentence or two. Encourage children to tell stories in small groups.

Then, use objects that have fewer visual cues and are less well-known to the children. Encourage children to write and illustrate their story, or record it on a tape recorder or a video recorder. This way children can share their stories with their families.

INTEGRATION   This activity can easily be adapted to most units and themes. For example, if you have a circus theme, have the children be the tightrope or the safety net or the lion tamer's shoes. This is a good game for parents to play in a waiting room; the child could be the dentist's mirror or even the drill. Pretending to be the object may help a child think about it in a different way, especially if the child is apprehensive about it.

Speaking: Small Group

57   SHOE THEATER

GOALS   To improve expressive communication; to use diverse print and nonprint sources and genres; to increase inclusion

OBJECTIVES   The child will participate in developing and producing a play using unusual objects as puppets.

MATERIALS   Pairs of shoes (men's, women's, children's, baby's), pairs of socks (men's, women's, children's, baby's)

PROCEDURE   Have the children pretend the objects are puppets. Use one hand for each shoe or sock and have a shoe or sock theater. Help less skillful children find roles that allow them to participate but require less language, such as a visiting pair of shoes or the baby's shoes. Children can develop a script for their play and dictate it into a tape recorder or write (or have someone write) it down. Encourage them to make props and scenery.

INTEGRATION   Because shoes really suggest no particular theme, this activity encourages creativity. Roles are undefined, so it is easy to include children with varying skill levels. Help children learn about the ways in which plays are different from other types of literature and the many different roles people have to support a play (prompter, set designer, and so on).

Speaking: Large Group

58   IDEAS

GOALS   To improve expressive communication; to increase vocabulary; to encourage creativity

OBJECTIVES   The child will name conventional and nonconventional uses for an object.

MATERIALS   Common objects with few details, such as block, plate, scarf, sock, book, chair, cup/glass, table

PROCEDURE   Choose an object and ask the children to identify it. First ask them to describe the usual uses for the object. Then ask them to think of different ways to use the object. (The block could keep the door open; you could paint a face on it and use it as a doll; step on it to reach something.) List the children's suggestions. Once children are familiar with the procedure, include objects from places that might be threatening, such as a doctor's office or hospital. Start with tongue depressors, masks, and flashlights, then work your way up to dentist's drills and needles for injections. Have children think of different uses for these objects.

INTEGRATION   Children may be able to look at items in a different way and broaden their concepts of tools, as well as tap into their creativity.

59   DIVERGENT

GOALS   To improve expressive communication; to improve cause-and-effect reasoning; to encourage creativity

OBJECTIVES   The child will state at least two ways in which life would be different without a particular thing and how we could adapt.

MATERIALS   Paper, clothing, pencils, chair

PROCEDURE   Have a discussion related to a particular theme or topic (wheels, chairs, television, paper). Start off simply asking the children to name objects they have or use. Then ask them to imagine what it would be like if we didn't have the objects. Show children objects that they use in the classroom and then expand these into categories. Show them a piece of paper and then talk about all the paper used in the classroom and ask how it would be different not to have this particular object. Give children hints, such as, "What would we write on if we didn't have paper?" and "What would we sit on if we didn't have chairs?" Expand this concept to have children think about how life would be different if they didn't have hands, eyes, ears, and so on. (Scrupulously avoid references that could hurt or offend a particular child or family situation.) Pose questions as to how they would do certain things, and demonstrate these.

Expand the examples into social and public services such as medicine, electricity, water, and so on. Talk about natural events, asking what it would be like if the sun didn't set.

INTEGRATION   This activity is particularly appropriate when studying cultures such as Native Americans or units referring to the past such as dinosaurs, or holidays such as Thanksgiving. This is also a time for children with some disabilities to show off. Children with sensory impairments might share with others how they compensate. "Joan has a great way of looking for things when her locker gets rearranged. Can you show the class how you search for things? What is she doing?" Build children's self-concepts by pointing out how they compensate either for disabilities or for situational conditions such as being too short to reach something they want. As children realize the principles behind their skill, it will become easier to apply them in other situations.

60   BRING ME

GOALS   To improve expressive communication; to improve geometric and spatial sense; to improve classification skills

OBJECTIVES   The child will get a requested object or state that he can't bring it.

MATERIALS   None

PROCEDURE   The teacher requests various objects, and the child must either get the object or say, "I'm sorry, I can't bring you X because . . ."

CHILD COULD BRING	CHILD COULDN'T BRING
block	wall
shoe	sky
piece of paper	elephant

When children get the idea of the game, the child who can't bring the requested item can name something she can bring instead. Start with easy, obvious requests. Ask for objects that are either more difficult to find or more difficult to transport so they may need to have a friend help.

INTEGRATION   This request game requires some logical reasoning skills to play. It also offers a great opportunity to use humor.

61   WEEKEND NEWS

GOALS   To improve expressive communication; to increase inclusion; to express feelings

OBJECTIVES   The child will share with others events that are important to him.

MATERIALS   None

PROCEDURE   During group time, give each child (or a designated smaller group of children) an opportunity to talk about things that happened to him over the weekend. Write down briefly what the children say and encourage them to look at it during the day. As you write, be sure to include each child's name. For example,

> "Paige said, "Mary Beth slept over at my house."

> "I saw a fire," Don said.

When children have gotten comfortable sharing what happened to them over the weekend, ask them to talk about the best and worst things that they encountered. Because children's time lines are not very well defined, they may relate events from longer ago than asked for. The variety of comments is likely to be tremendous:

WORST	BEST
coming to school	going out to dinner
falling down	staying up later than usual
hearing a scary noise at night	having a special food
Inti hit me	Nana's coming to visit
being teased or yelled at	playing with Mommy
a sibling's birthday	getting my hair cut

These topics can lead to general discussions about the concerns of all children. Children are surprisingly candid about and responsive to this. With the help of sensitive adults, the activity provides a safe place for children to talk about their worst experiences without shame or ridicule and perhaps gain ideas for how to handle future problems. They also learn that all people have best and worst things, including you.

For variation, have the children draw pictures of what happened to them over the weekend and talk about their picture individually. Children can also "write" their weekend news and read it to the class.

INTEGRATION   Having children talk about what has happened to them, especially when they discuss the best and worst events, can help others see that children with diverse abilities have many of the same problems they do.

62   RHYMING WORDS

GOALS   To increase vocabulary; to improve reading literacy; to increase knowledge of the structure of language

OBJECTIVES   The child will give at least one rhyming word for the one the teacher presents.

MATERIALS   None

PROCEDURE   Define rhyming words—words that end with the same sound. Give lots of examples before asking the children for words. Read stories such as Dr. Seuss's *Green Eggs and Ham* and point out the rhyming words to the children. See if they can generate some as well. Say familiar fingerplays that use such rhyming words. List both real and nonsense words. Praise the children for finding a rhyme, even if it is a nonsense word, but point out that it isn't a real word—look it up in a children's dictionary.

ACE	DARE	HEAD	BUMP	COW	BED
brace	care	read	stump	now	fed
trace	stare	bread	lump	how	led
pace	care	dead	jump	pow	red
place	bare	tread	grump	plow	sled

Use the opportunity to expand the children's vocabularies by asking them to define the words. Have the children repeat the rhyming words quickly and slowly. Encourage children to make a "Have You Seen a . . ." book of rhyming words they can illustrate: Have you seen a red bed, bare mare, cow plow, fake cake.

Help children explore the structure of language using different parts of speech and longer words that rhyme. Make cards with pictures of words that rhyme (red, bed, sled) and see if you can help children isolate the initial sound and add the rhyme.

INTEGRATION   Rhyming is a good way to dismiss children. As each child leaves, ask the child to give a word that rhymes with yours: "Jose, give me a word that rhymes with cat." "Sat." "Sally, another word." "Hat." You can also make up words that rhyme with their names. Be sure you can do this with all the children before you start.

Speaking: Large Group

63   OBJECT HUNT

GOALS   To improve expressive communication; to follow directions; to increase knowledge of the structure of language

OBJECTIVES   The child will both give and follow directions and correctly guess what the object is.

MATERIALS   None

PROCEDURE   Choose an object in the classroom. Give easy-to-follow directions to find it. Once children understand the procedure, let a child give the directions to a searcher. The searcher can only ask questions that can be answered yes or no.

> *Direction Giver:*   Go to the block area. Stand beside the longest blocks. Look up.
> *Searcher:*   Is it a window?
> *Direction Giver:*   No. Turn around . . .

As children become more skillful, choose objects in difficult locations that require fine discriminations for both the direction giver and the searcher.

INTEGRATION   Children can play this in pairs or small groups, inside or outside. It provides good feedback on how difficult it is to give accurate directions and the frustration of trying to give and follow directions.

Speaking: Large Group

64   INTERVIEWS

GOALS   To improve expressive communication; to increase inclusion; to improve self-concept

OBJECTIVES   The child will answer questions in front of a group of children.

MATERIALS   A play microphone

PROCEDURE   Do a takeoff on some of the popular talk shows: "Good morning, today is Tuesday, February 2, and we are delighted to have as our guest today Miss Suling. Suling, can you tell our listeners some of the things that you really like to do? Do you have any favorite foods?" If children are hesitant, make the questions easy, and keep the interview short. Be sure to have a "mike" as a prop. You might even explain that this is Suling's first appearance and she might be a bit shy. If they are more comfortable, encourage children to talk about particular interests they have and want to share.

INTEGRATION   It is great for children to feel special and to highlight what is unique about them. If you really get into it, you can take questions from the "audience" and also share with the "audience" what you find so special about this particular child and why you "invited" her.

Speaking: Small or Large Group

65   IMAGINARY WALK

GOALS   To increase comprehension; to follow directions; to improve receptive communication

OBJECTIVES   The child will walk following the directions given and perform appropriate movements.

MATERIALS   None

PROCEDURE   As the children take a walk around the room or outdoors, help them imagine they are somewhere else. Initially, make the walk slower paced, shorter, and have one-step directions only. Call out commands, such as:

> Stop! There is a big step. Go up it. Oh, the sidewalk is hot. Tiptoe fast. There is a little step. Go down. Wait. Listen. OK. Walk forward. Stop. There is a wall. Walk sideways. Oh, there is a small hole. Trace it with your hand. Will you fit? Now, wiggle through it. Lean back against the wall. Be careful, it's not very sturdy. Take a deep breath. Sit down and relax.

As children's skill increases, make the walk longer, and ask the children how to circumvent various obstacles you invent.

INTEGRATION   The skills in this activity are basic to learning many activities. Help children learn solutions to problems and think about how they might go about dealing with issues.

Speaking: Small or Large Group

66   WORD ASSOCIATIONS

GOALS   To increase comprehension; to increase vocabulary; to encourage creativity

OBJECTIVES   The child will name an associated word and explain why it occurred to him.

MATERIALS   None

PROCEDURE   Teach the children the game of word associations: "I'll say a word, and I want you to tell me what other words you think of." Start with something easy, such as colors—red: fire, hot, tomatoes, anger. Have children look around the room for ideas if they are having problems. Encourage children to say as many things as they can think of that they associate with the color. Use more obscure ideas and see what children come up with. Listen especially to their rationale for why they associate those words. Encourage them to think of several associations. If children don't say some of the obvious words you want to explore, say, "It reminds me of . . ." Then share with them your rationale.

INTEGRATION   This encourages and supports divergent thinking. Children need to have many solutions to problems and learn that there are many ways of dealing with a particular situation.

67   MAGICIAN

GOALS   To improve listening skills; to improve receptive communication; to encourage creativity

OBJECTIVES   The child will make the noise requested by the adult and identify at least two noises made by classmates.

MATERIALS   None

PROCEDURE   The adult plays the magician and "changes" a child into a noise-making object by whispering into the child's ear what object he is to be or gives the child a picture of the object. The child then pretends to be the object by making the noise, and the other children guess what the object is. Initially, use sounds that are phonetically different yet conceptually related, such as vehicles, outside sounds, sounds of animals, or kitchen sounds. Have the objects or pictures of the objects in sight. In addition to making the sound, have the child pretend to be or use the object; for example, for a snake, have the child hiss as well as squirm on the floor if the sound is not initially guessed. Have the listening children shut their eyes.

INTEGRATION   Children need to tune into their environment and need support gaining the skills to do this.

68   SOUNDS OF SILENCE

GOALS   To improve listening skills; to increase comprehension; to improve concentration

OBJECTIVES   The child will listen and name one thing he heard.

MATERIALS   None

PROCEDURE   Ask the children to be silent. Explain that they are going to listen and figure out what they can hear when they are absolutely quiet. First, help children relax their bodies, then have them listen for one minute. Make a list of what they heard. The list might include clocks ticking, heating sounds, blinds moving, and birds chirping. Keep the period of silence short as children are learning the procedure, then have longer silent periods. Help children write a poem or short story about the "Sounds of Silence." Talk about night and the sounds they hear while going to sleep. Encourage them to talk or write about this.

INTEGRATION   The world is full of so much stimulation for children, they rarely concentrate on listening for very small sounds. This is a concentration and identification activity.

69   WHISPER

GOALS   To improve listening skills; to improve receptive communication; to improve concentration

OBJECTIVES   The child will act out the whispered task.

MATERIALS   None

PROCEDURE   This is a takeoff on the party game Telephone. Pick a command such as "Touch your head." With the children sitting in a circle, whisper this to the first child, have the first child whisper to the second child, and so on around the circle until the child at the end performs the task. Start with fewer people and simpler commands and whisper louder. As children become more skillful, increase the length of the task so that they must remember longer commands: "Go to the door and open it, then come back and sit down."

INTEGRATION   Have a sense of humor about this. Whispering is a fun way for children to see the outcome of misarticulation.

70   SAY IT

GOALS   To improve listening skills; to improve receptive communication; to improve concentration

OBJECTIVES   The child will correctly imitate the sound made by the adult.

MATERIALS   None

PROCEDURE   During group time, say various words or sentences and have the children imitate you. Using the same words, change your voice pitch, intonation, speed, or stress.

> SENTENCE VARIATIONS
>
> I like juice. (normal, loud, soft/whisper, fast, slow, puckered mouth)
>
> *I* like juice. (stress)
>
> I *like* juice. (stress)
>
> I like *juice.* (stress)
>
> raise your voice for a question
>
> hold your nose

As the children imitate you and change their voices, verbalize for them what you (they) did: "Great, you all said it as loud as I did." Explore with children the impact that tone and intonation pattern have for meaning. Discuss where you might use different voices. Ask children how they would say something at a sports event as compared to group time. Have children use longer and more challenging sentences and have other children imitate them and give them feedback about different intonation patterns.

INTEGRATION   Because so much of meaning is passed through the nonverbal aspect of language, it is important that children are aware of it from an early age.

71   LISTENING WALK

GOALS   To improve listening skills; to increase comprehension; to improve receptive communication

OBJECTIVES   The child will identify a sound he hears on the walk, describe the sound, and say what makes it.

MATERIALS   None

PROCEDURE   Before you take the children outside, ask them to listen carefully and identify sounds, but to talk very little to others during the walk. Tell them to try to figure out what is making each sound. When they return, have them describe and imitate the sounds they heard. The other children have to decide what might have made the sound. A child might say, "I heard a peck, peck, peck. What is it?" rather than "I heard a bird." Vary the walk by having the children first walk making a lot of noise and then very little noise and compare what they hear. Point out sounds on the walk. If possible, encourage children to pick up something to help them remember the sound when they return to the classroom. Take small groups of children on the walk again. Be quieter, pause more frequently, and walk more slowly. Compare what was heard on the first walk with the second.

INTEGRATION   Focusing on listening in a variety of situations helps children generalize underlying skills.

Listening requires concentration and, when paired with visual stimuli, it requires sensory integration.

Listening: Large Group

72 NOISY AND QUIET

GOALS To improve listening skills; to increase comprehension; to improve receptive communication

OBJECTIVES The child will identify sounds and events that are typically either noisy or quiet.

MATERIALS Construction paper, crayons, pencils

PROCEDURE Play the game "I'm thinking of something noisy," and have the children guess what you are thinking of. Respond to them in one of three ways: "Yes, it is noisy, but not what I'm thinking of"; "That is quiet; think of something noisy"; or "Yes, that's it." Do the same thing with *quiet.* Make a list of the ideas the children generate of what is noisy and what is quiet. Ask children to think of noisy holidays, foods, animals, instruments, and so on. Ask children to fold a piece of construction paper in half and draw a noisy picture on one side and a quiet one on the other or write a story using noisy or quiet words. Help children use objects in the classroom and decide whether they are noisy or quiet. Point out times when the class is noisy or quiet.

INTEGRATION It is important to point out that noisy and quiet are different, not to make judgments that noisy is "bad" and quiet is "good." Children need to associate sounds and the environmental cues they can offer.

73   SOUND AND TELL

GOALS   To improve listening skills; to increase comprehension; to improve classification skills

OBJECTIVES   The child will identify the sound.

MATERIALS   A screen (could be a rectangular table on its side); a paper bag for each child in the class; a noisemaker (an object from class or one brought from home):

whistle	dishes	bell
two blocks	spoons	pen that clicks
timer	scissors	book (to close or drop)

PROCEDURE   Ask each child to bring a noisemaker from home or to find an object in the classroom that makes a noise and can fit in a bag. The other children can then guess how the sound was made. Give each child a bag in which to hide the noisemaker. Have each child go behind the screen and make the sound. The other children guess what it is. Then have the child make the sound so that all can see. While hidden, have children make noises with various body parts behind the screen (e.g., clap, stomp). Once the noises have been identified, have two children go behind the screen and make a pattern of noises that the children must identify. Make a chart classifying the various sounds. Classify noises as loud, soft, sharp, and so on. Discuss the properties of objects that make noise and those that do not.

INTEGRATION   Classifying sounds helps children become more aware of the environment and personal safety.

74   SOUND CUES

GOALS   To improve listening skills; to increase comprehension; to improve receptive communication

OBJECTIVES   The child will identify the sound and the actions the sound describes.

MATERIALS   Tape recorder, tapes of sounds, pictures of items making the sound

PROCEDURE   Record a variety of sounds. Have the children identify them. Then have them decide where they might hear each sound and what might be happening. Indoor sounds might include:

mixer: cooking

vacuum cleaner: cleaning

toilet flushing: going to the bathroom

washing machine: washing clothes

This can also be done with street noises:

brakes: stopping

engine: starting

car door closing: getting in the car

seat belt clicking: putting on seat belt

horn: warning of danger

If this is difficult, first give the child a choice of two pictures of objects, one of which actually made the sound. Increase the choices to three, then five, and then see if the children can discriminate without the visual cues. Then, using the car noises as an example, see if the children can sequence the sounds of events as they might normally happen in the act of coming to school in the car. Give the child a tape recorder and have the child record sounds in the classroom and outside and have others identify them.

INTEGRATION   Identifying sounds of musical instruments is challenging, but a fun activity. Start with widely different instruments, such as a piano and a guitar, and add from there. Have some instruments available for the children to explore.

Listening: Small Group

75   SOUND EGGS

GOALS   To improve listening skills; to improve cause-and-effect reasoning; to make predictions

OBJECTIVES   The child will find the pairs of containers that sound the same and explain the relationship between the material shaken and the sound.

MATERIALS   5 or 6 pairs of containers (plastic eggs, juice or milk cartons, yogurt containers—nothing transparent); materials that can be used to make a sound (enough for two containers): rice, paper clips, pebbles, macaroni, bells, shells, dried beans/peas/lentils, ball bearings
    Partially fill each pair of containers with the chosen materials. Mark the bottoms of the pairs of containers with pairs of letters or numbers so the child can check to see if he or she has made a pair.

PROCEDURE   Ask the child to shake the containers and match the pairs by sound. At first, use fewer containers and materials that have very different sounds. Put duplicate materials in cups (rice, macaroni, etc.). See if the children can figure out what is inside the pairs of closed containers by looking at the possibilities. Then make predictions about the sound it makes. Help them make their own noise-making containers. Encourage children to experiment with sound and quantity of materials as well as style of shaking.

INTEGRATION   Children enjoy exploring the process of what makes sound and how they can control it.

Listening: Small Group

76   WATER TONES

GOALS   To improve listening skills; to improve cause-and-effect reasoning; to make predictions

OBJECTIVES   The child will state whether the tapped glasses sound the same or different.

MATERIALS   2 sets of water glasses with varying amounts of water in them, tapper

PROCEDURE   Fill one set of glasses with different amounts of water. Start with three glasses, two nearly full and one almost empty. Help the children classify their sounds as the same or different. Gradually introduce more glasses. Allow the children to examine the glasses and the sounds they produce. Help them discover the relationship between the amount of water and the pitch. Have children arrange the glasses by pitch. Blindfold children and have them match the glasses and then put them in order of pitch from high to low. Encourage children to predict what will happen as they experiment by adding or subtracting water to make different pitches.

INTEGRATION   Children can both hear and see the differences produced. Help them make finer discriminations while talking about the underlying principles.

77   NUMBER TAPPING

GOALS   To improve listening skills; to improve number sense and numeration; to identify and understand patterns and relationships

OBJECTIVES   The child will make a requested number of taps and identify those made by others correctly.

MATERIALS   Piano, drum, table, tambourine, tapper

PROCEDURE   Have a child tap a number or tap it yourself. Tap slowly on the same instrument in a steady pattern. Start with only low numbers. Have the class state the number, hold up the right number of fingers, or call on one child to answer. Tap a nonrhythmic pattern or tap very quickly. Tap each rhythm on a different object or instrument. Have the children close their eyes. Ask the children to repeat the pattern back to you. Use different patterns.

INTEGRATION   The activity requires the integration of auditory, tactile, and verbal skills to learn number concepts. Initially, tap dramatically so that the children can use visual as well as auditory skills.

78   WHERE IS IT/WHO IS IT?

GOALS   To improve listening skills; to make predictions; to improve geometric and spatial sense

OBJECTIVES   The child will point to the general area from which the sound is coming.

MATERIALS   None

PROCEDURE   Have the children sit facing a wall with their eyes shut. Ask one child to walk to a specific area of the room. As the child is walking, tell the children to listen and then point to or name the area where the child stops. Then have them open their eyes and check if they are right. If this is difficult, have the child hit a tambourine or drum and stay in one place. Naming the area is difficult because the children have to remember the various parts of the room and visualize their location. Children might also try to identify the walker by the sound of the footsteps. Help with some initial questions: "What kind of shoes is the child wearing? Is the walk heavy or light, fast or slow?" This is not a good variation with a rug, and sneakers are challenging.

INTEGRATION   Children can learn to fine-tune their listening skills, but it requires practice.

79   TAPE IT

GOALS   To improve listening skills; to improve self-concept; to make predictions

OBJECTIVES   The child will identify his own voice and predict who else is talking based on a rationale.

MATERIALS   Video recorder, videotape, pictures of children

PROCEDURE   Over the course of several days, videotape each child talking about what he is doing for about a minute or two. Using only the audio portion of the tape, have a small-group listening time when the children try to predict who is talking and explain their rationale (It's a boy, voice quality, etc.). If this is difficult, give children pictures of several classmates who might be talking and ask them to choose which one it is. Have children try to disguise their voices. Encourage children to identify the features in a voice that make it recognizable. Then turn on the video portion so they can see if they are right.

Children need a variety of literacy experiences. This particular chart is part of a survey the class is doing to determine its next thematic unit. The writing, supported with illustrations, helps children understand what they are voting for; each child can have a first, second, and third choice. The outcome of the survey is tallied and children have learned something about the democratic process.

INTEGRATION   Send this tape to a child who has been out of school for a while. The child can practice identifying voices at home as well as keep in touch with classmates. Encourage children to send videotaped messages to friends who are not in school and have them returned. You can do the same thing with an audiotape, but it is not as effective with younger children.

Listening: Large or Small Group

80   GOING TO THE BEACH

GOALS   To improve sequencing skills; to increase comprehension; to improve memory skills

OBJECTIVES   The child will remember at least three items that she is taking on a trip to the beach.

MATERIALS   Flannel board, pictures of objects drawn or glued onto Pellon that children would be likely to take to the beach

PROCEDURE   Discuss the beach and what people do there. Then play the game "I am going to the beach and in my suitcase I'm going to take a *swimsuit*." The child must repeat the sentence and add another item. Initially, have a suitcase and real items that the children actually pack. If children have trouble remembering the items, give them functional cues (for example, "What will we sit on?"). Then have children choose from the pictures available. As each child chooses, place the chosen picture on the board, as in Figure 20.1.

Write the name of each item below its picture. When the children have used up all the pictures, take the cards down in order and see how many they can remember. When this becomes easy, see if they can remember the pictures in the order in which they were hanging.

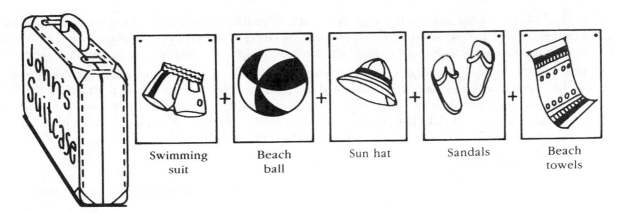

Figure 20.1

INTEGRATION   This sequencing activity can be adapted to many themes and units. The class can go for a picnic and pack their lunches; they can pack for a trip to the jungle, desert, North Pole, hospital, grandparents, and so on. Encourage children to discuss why specific items are necessary.

Listening: Small Group

81   NATURAL SEQUENCING

GOALS   To identify and understand patterns and relationships; to improve sequencing skills; to improve cause-and-effect reasoning

OBJECTIVES   The child will place the pictures in the correct sequence and state the relationships the pictures portray.

MATERIALS   Pictures of a naturally occurring sequence

PROCEDURE   As these are naturally occurring sequences, begin by having the actual objects there and match the stages with the sequences. That is, get roses in different stages of bloom, put them in warm water, and watch how they open, or burn a candle down (be sure to talk about fire safety if you use a candle) and have the children match the sequence at each stage. Draw pictures of naturally occurring sequences on cards. Have the children place these pictures in order and explain why the sequence is occurring (see Figure 20.2).

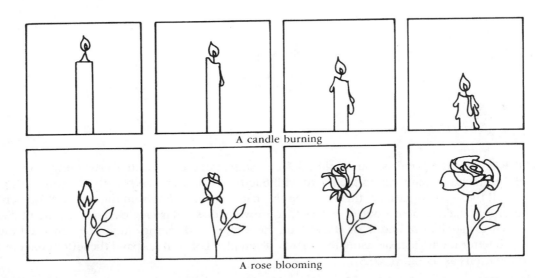

A candle burning

A rose blooming

Figure 20.2

Choose more complex but familiar sequences, such as getting dressed or brushing teeth. Then work up to sequences that are less familiar but logical, such as going on a trip in a car or plane. See if children can work out the sequence, draw or write it, and then do the activity to check their accuracy.

INTEGRATION   Be sure the sequences do not always show objects going from little to big. You do not have to be a terrific artist to make these, provided you pick concepts that are simple to illustrate (a pencil getting used up, a pine tree growing, etc.). Pictures are available commercially. Natural sequencing is a good follow-up after a field trip. Children with limited experience often see events individually, without developing the connections that language and experience allow.

Reading Literacy: Individual

82   ALPHABET LOTTO

GOALS   To improve reading literacy; to improve generalization skills; to increase respect for diversity in modes of communication

OBJECTIVES   The child will match the letters to the Lotto board.

MATERIALS   Alphabet letters: Divide pieces of posterboard (9″ × 12″) into 6 rectangles (4″ × 4½″). Print a letter of the alphabet (not necessarily in order) in each rectangle. Make 4 cards with different letters on each (see Figure 20.3).

Figure 20.3

Cut 24 4″ × 4½″ pieces, also out of poster board. Print a letter on each small rectangle to match the larger boards. (*Note:* Because our alphabet has 26 letters, two will be missing. If you make two sets like this, omit different letters from each one.) If children are having trouble matching particular letters, design cards to meet these problems. For example, for lower-case letters, make a card with reversible lines and curves (see Figure 20.4).

Figure 20.4

PROCEDURE   Play the game as you would any Lotto game. Put the individual letters into a box to draw from so children can match them to the board with 6 letters. Children can play this as a matching game alone. With all these combinations, there will be five cards for each letter on the board. When children are just learning, make a board out of letters that are very dissimilar (for example, *A, W, O, S, T, D*). Don't have letters such as *M* and *W* or *O* and *C* on the same board, as they might be confused initially. First work on letter identification using the boards. Then play Lotto. To expand the letter concept, make Lotto combinations as in Figure 20.5.

INTEGRATION   Add the American Sign Language alphabet and the Braille alphabet as well as sandpaper letters.

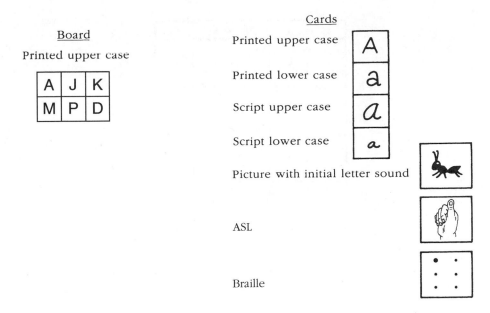

Figure 20.5

Reading Literacy: Small Group

83   BODY SOUNDS

GOALS   To improve reading literacy; to increase vocabulary; to increase body awareness

OBJECTIVES   The child will decide which words for body parts have the same initial sound.

MATERIALS   None

PROCEDURE   Name a part of the body and then ask the children to name a part that has the same beginning sound (or letter). Initially, have children choose between two parts that you name or allow them to name things in the room or anything they can think of that has the same initial sound or letter. Encourage children to think of less obvious body parts (internal ones) such as muscles, joints, and blood vessels. Give them functional clues.

toe: teeth, tongue, tendons

eye: elbow, eyebrow, ears, earlobe

hearing: hand, head, heart, hips

fingers: fingernails, foot, forearm, follicle

legs: lips, lungs

INTEGRATION   This is a fun way of teaching children the names of body parts and the functions they serve. Children need the vocabulary to talk about their body with precision. Use pictures or models to help children learn about parts they cannot see.

Reading Literacy: Large Group

84   SOUND BINGO

GOALS   To improve reading literacy; to improve listening skills; to increase knowledge of the structure of language

OBJECTIVES   The child will identify the letter by its sound (/b/—/b/ as in ball).

B	I	N	G	O
a	u	r	b	o
s	h	b	c	i
w	y	free	g	v
m	j	n	l	d
e	f	t	p	z

Figure 20.6

MATERIALS　Bingo cards with letters rather than numbers (see Figure 20.6)

PROCEDURE　Using a regular bingo game format, play the game and ask children to identify the letters as you call them out. As you move to letter sounds, pair the children so they can work together. A few letters will have to be eliminated, as they sound the same as others (/c/ and /k/), or give words that start with that sound as a clarifying clue. Have the children put a marker on the letter for each sound as it is called out. The winner is the first child to have a horizontal, vertical, or diagonal row. Continue to play until most children have completed a row. Instead of letter sounds, call out words and have the children mark the initial letter sound. This can also be done with the final letter sound, but you need to check the words for silent letters and those that are misleading, such as *penny,* where the *y* sounds like an *e.*

INTEGRATION　As you work toward developing words for games such as this, you begin to appreciate the problems in learning English, which has so many exceptions to rules. Talk with children about why some sounds can't be used in this game.

Reading Literacy: Large Group

85　TITLE

GOALS　To improve reading literacy; to increase comprehension; to increase knowledge of the structure of language

OBJECTIVES　The child will choose an appropriate title for the story.

MATERIALS　A made-up story or a printed story with the title hidden

PROCEDURE　Read or tell a simple story or use a paragraph from a longer story. Explain that it has no title and that you want their help in deciding on one. Ask them to suggest titles and write them down. Talk with the children about the titles and have them explain which titles would be good or not as good as others. Use more complex stories as children become more proficient.

INTEGRATION　Appropriate titles require high-level abstract reasoning skills. Challenge children to think this way.

86   LETTER DAY

GOALS   To improve reading literacy; to increase comprehension; to improve sensorimotor integration

OBJECTIVES   The child will identify the letter through vision, hearing, and touch.

MATERIALS   Letters of the alphabet made of sandpaper and wood, objects that begin with each letter

PROCEDURE   Pick a letter of the alphabet. Expose the children to that letter in as many ways as you can: With the letter *P*; trace a sandpaper letter *P*; feel your breath with your hand as you say /*P*/; point to *P* in a group of letters; think of words that start with *P*; make cookies or clay in the shape of *P*; eat *pretzels* for snack.

Emphasize the sound of the letter as well as letter identification. This is particularly important for letters that have more than one sound, such as *g* (*George* vs. *Gary*), as well as long and short vowel sounds.

INTEGRATION   You can do any letter. Granted, *X* is a challenge! If you plan to do all the letters, start with the vowels and leave the most difficult consonants until last. Be sure to use both upper- and lower-case letters if you extend the activity.

87   CHANGING OBJECTS

GOALS   To improve reading literacy; to identify and understand patterns and relationships; to improve memory skills

OBJECTIVES   The child will put three objects in their original order after they have been rearranged.

MATERIALS   Small objects such a blocks, doll furniture, and cars, and a screen

PROCEDURE   Put three objects in a row and ask the children to look at them. Put a screen in front of the objects and rearrange them. Ask one of the children to put them in the original order. Initially, use objects that are less similar, such as cup/doll/block. For variation, take one object away and have the children name the missing object. As the children improve, increase the number of objects and their similarity:

Easier: red block/blue airplane/green cup/orange crayon

Hard: Red block/blue block /green block/orange block

Harder: Red stocking cap/red baseball cap/red ski hat/red felt hat

INTEGRATION   The objects that you choose can be based on the theme you are working on (hospital: tongue depressor, little flashlight, stethoscope, bandages) or as a way of introducing a topic that has unfamiliar materials or materials that children might be concerned about. Encourage the children to touch and handle the materials.

88   COLOR GRAPHS

GOALS   To improve reading literacy; to follow directions; to identify and understand patterns and relationships

OBJECTIVES   The child will color the designated square a specific color.

MATERIALS   Paper, crayons: Draw a pattern of squares on a piece of paper and duplicate it so each child has one.

PROCEDURE   Give the children directions to follow in coloring in the squares: "Color the first two squares on the top left green. Color the next square red. Color the square below the second green square yellow," and so on.

Move from left to right in your directions. To make it easier, have children color each "car" on the train in order. Make the first square somewhat different as a starting place. Give children additional time to color. As they improve, you can have children skip a particular number of squares, if that is useful, and use more squares. Have the children describe the pattern to you using both color and number.

INTEGRATION   Vary your rate of presentation to match the skill of the children. If you are very creative, the design can be made to look like an object when it is colored accurately.

Reading Literacy: Small Group

89   ALPHABET LINE

GOALS   To improve reading literacy; to improve writing literacy; to improve fine motor manipulative skills

OBJECTIVES   The child will find the designated letter and put it on the clothesline.

MATERIALS   Clothesline, marking pen, paper, pictures, wooden clothespins with an alphabet letter on each

PROCEDURE   Initially, use this as a letter identification task and have the child find the clothespin letter and put it on the clothesline. Then have the children put each clothespin on the clothesline in alphabetical order using a guide, or put up each letter or sound you or another child request. Print the letter or sound on a separate piece of paper. Have the children match the paper letters or initial sounds of pictures to the clothespin, then hang them. Have children make words with the clothespins (you'll need additional letters) or copy words that you have printed on cards.

INTEGRATION   Although simple, this activity is a useful way of developing finger strength while teaching a variety of skills relating to the alphabet. Identifying letters and sounds is essential to reading. It is important to have many ways to do this.

Reading Literacy: Small Group

90   COLOR CONCENTRATION

GOALS   To improve reading literacy; to make predictions; to improve memory skills

OBJECTIVES   The child will remember where the matching color is.

MATERIALS   A set of cards with matching pairs of colors on one side

PROCEDURE   This is a variation of the game Concentration. Lay out the cards face down. Each child takes a turn and chooses two cards. The objective is to turn over two cards that are the same color. Start with four or five pairs of cards. Use primary colors and/or simple shapes. First, have the children match the cards, then demonstrate how the game is played. Gradually add more cards. As children become more proficient, add shades of colors and more cards. You can use a regular deck of cards for numbers, or pairs of pictures of any kind. The more cards you add, the more difficult the activity becomes. Also, the more detailed the pictures, the more difficult the game.

INTEGRATION   This can also be done with letters of the alphabet. You can even match capital and small letters, a more difficult variation.

91   FOLLOW THAT LINE

GOALS   To improve reading literacy; to increase knowledge of the structure of language; to identify and understand patterns and relationships

OBJECTIVES   The child will make a pattern using the squares and explain how she made the pattern.

MATERIALS   Posterboard, markers (red, green, black): Cut posterboard into 3″ × 3″ squares and arrange these squares in a pattern on a large table or the floor. (This is only for your ease in drawing.) Using black, red, and green markers, draw a pattern of lines, stopping and starting colors and using straight and curved lines.

PROCEDURE   To begin, use squares with only one color. When this is mastered, add a second color. Have the children build a track with the cards in a variety of patterns (see Figure 20.7). Talk with the children about punctuation, especially periods, and their function in language. Discuss how the period represented on the cards is also a stop. Encourage them to make a variety of patterns and count the number of stops each color has.

   The more squares you have available and the more colors and patterns, the more complicated the task is. It is also more challenging when children must make a designated pattern. Making the letter *H,* for example, requires a lot of problem solving. Children can also draw their own squares.

INTEGRATION   Punctuation and spacing make important contributions to both reading and writing and are often overlooked as we teach children about the structure of language.

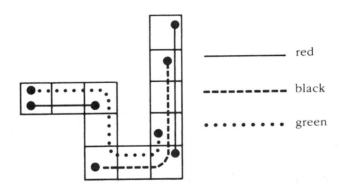

Figure 20.7

92   WHAT IS IT?

GOALS   To improve reading literacy; to make predictions; to improve generalization skills

OBJECTIVES   The child will correctly identify the object while viewing less than 50 percent of it.

MATERIALS   Large (8″ × 10″) pictures of familiar objects, large envelopes

PROCEDURE   Put a picture of a familiar object in an envelope. Pull it out slowly until part of the picture is exposed. Have the children guess what it is. Keep exposing more of the picture until it is correctly identified. Encourage the children to guess and give you the reasons for their guesses. Start with pictures of simple, familiar objects (boats, cars, trains, animals). Pull about half of the picture out before you stop. You can use a screen and gradually push objects out as well. Use 8″ × 10″ pictures of all children in the class to add interest at the beginning of the year. Add pictures of less familiar objects or ones that have more ambiguous cues (an armchair and sofa).

INTEGRATION   Children need to develop skills in the area of visual closure. They need to be able to use partial information to infer what they cannot see. This helps focus on relevant details. Encourage children to talk about guesses they make and their rationale for them.

Reading Literacy: Individual

93   SANDPAPER LETTERS

GOALS   To improve reading literacy; to improve writing literacy; to increase sensorimotor integration

OBJECTIVES   The child will trace each letter of the alphabet and name it and the sound(s) it makes.

MATERIALS   Sandpaper, glue, cardboard, pictures: Cut the letters of the alphabet out of sandpaper and glue each on a cardboard square. Glue a picture of something that begins with that letter on the back.

PROCEDURE   Start with the easiest letters based on the configuration of the letter and the child's knowledge. Have the child trace the letter with index and middle fingers as you talk about the structure of the letter: "This is the letter *A*. It has three straight lines. One, two, three. The third connects the first two in the middle." Show the child the picture on the back to connect the letter with a sound. Then have the child identify the letters blindfolded.

INTEGRATION   The sensory integration aspect of learning the alphabet is good for all children and challenges many.

Reading Literacy: Small Group

94   CHANGES

GOALS   To improve reading literacy; to increase inclusion

OBJECTIVES   The child will name or point to the change.

MATERIALS   None

PROCEDURE   Begin by helping focus the children's attention by picking a category of change—for example, clothing—and have these changes be obvious. It may help if you are "it" first and give some clues. Then, have one child turn around and close his eyes while the child who is "it" changes something about her appearance (unties shoe, rolls up pant leg, removes glasses, or unbuttons shirt). The first child must name or point to the change. As children improve, have them make subtle changes.

INTEGRATION   This activity allows the child who is "it" to be in control of the change and to be part of the group, yet the child doesn't have to speak. Children become aware that they can change some aspects of themselves.

Reading Literacy: Small Group

95   FISHING FOR FACES

GOALS   To improve reading literacy; to improve sensorimotor integration; to express feelings

OBJECTIVES   The child will match the face she catches to a face on a poster and discuss the facial characteristics and what emotion is being expressed.

MATERIALS   Matching pairs of pictures of faces, a shoe box, a poster-sized piece of paper, paste, paper clips, construction paper, a stick (fishing pole) with a string at the end, to which a magnet is tied

PROCEDURE   Paste one of each pair of faces on a fish-shaped piece of construction paper and attach a paper clip at the fish "head." Put the "fish" in the shoe box. Paste the remaining faces on the poster. Have children use fishing poles to fish for the faces in the box. Ask children to match the face they have "caught" to the same face on the poster. Encourage children to talk about their matches, how they made them, and the meaning of the expressions.

INTEGRATION   Children can fish for numbers, letters, or even fish (count the catch). If you want to put the fish in water, make them out of plastic and use waterproof marker for the face.

Writing: Large or Small Group

96   MIND MAPPING

GOALS   To improve writing literacy; to increase comprehension; to increase knowledge of the structure of language

OBJECTIVES   The child will participate in writing/drawing a group mind map and then make one in a small group of children.

MATERIALS   Paper, pencil/marker

PROCEDURE   After a topic has been chosen, encourage children to make a mind map before they begin to write. Start with the topic in the center of the page. Draw a balloon around it. Surround it with related ideas connected to it or to each other with lines. The lines show the relationship between the central theme and the topics mentioned. If there appear to be tangents, put these in the corners of the page. If they eventually become related, attach them; if not, they will not be part of the writing. A mind map of the ocean is pictured in Figure 20.8. Have a small group of children make more complex maps on topics of their choice. Have reference materials available for them.

INTEGRATION   Children need to organize their ideas for writing, but traditional outlines are rarely useful with young children. Mind mapping, or clustering ideas, is more useful and helps set the flow for the writing. Initially, each balloon will probably only be a phrase or sentence.

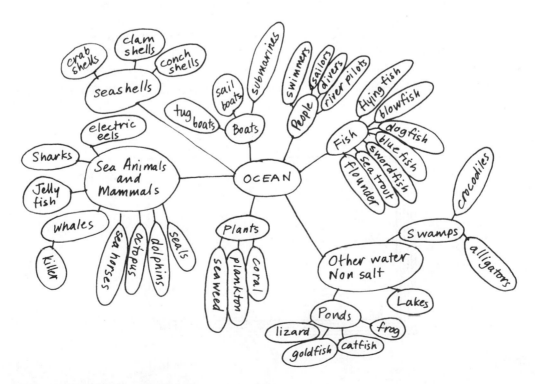

Figure 20.8   Mind Map or Webbing

97 BOOK MAKING

GOALS   To improve writing literacy; to improve reading literacy; to use diverse print and nonprint sources and genres

OBJECTIVES   The child will write, illustrate, and publish a book with a hard cover.

MATERIALS   Cardboard, cloth or wallpaper, scissors, needle and thread, artist's spray dry mount, paper

First, decide how many pages you want in the book and add one additional page. We suggest 6 pages to start.

1. Fold the 6 pieces of paper in half for pages (11″ become 5½″). Make a definite fold.

2. Unfold pages and sew the 6 pages together in the crease with a needle and thread (or use a sewing machine; see Figure 20.9).

3. Cut cloth 10½″ × 16″. This leaves 1′ extra in the width and 2½″ at either end.

4. Cut an 8½″ × 11″ piece of cardboard in half. (The backs of tablets work fine.)

5. Lay cloth flat, wrong side up. Spray cardboard pieces with artist's dry mounting spray. Place them on the cloth, leaving a 1/4″ space between the cardboard pieces to allow the book to open and close (see Figure 20.10).

6. Doing one side at a time, fold corners in; then fold top down and bottom up and hold (you are putting on the book cover).

7. Spray the side of cardboard facing up, including the material that you have folded over (see Figure 20.11). Lay the first of the 6 pages that you have sewn together over the cardboard (this covers over the cloth) and press hard (see Figure 20.12). Repeat 6 and 7 with the back cover, using the 12th page to cover the cardboard.

PROCEDURE   Children can now write and illustrate their book. As children become more familiar with writing, have them include a title page as well as identifying themselves as the author and/or illustrator. Look at their favorite books to see not only the story but the format of a book as well. Have children do increasingly more of the production, with less supervision. Help them choose different fabrics and make books of different lengths and shapes and for different purposes. Encourage them to write longer stories, poems, and plays, and to think about how the cover is related to what they plan to write.

INTEGRATION   Children like these books because they look like "real" books. They learn the steps of bookmaking in the process.

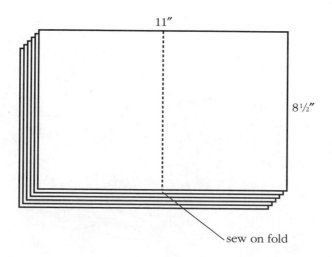

Figure 20.9

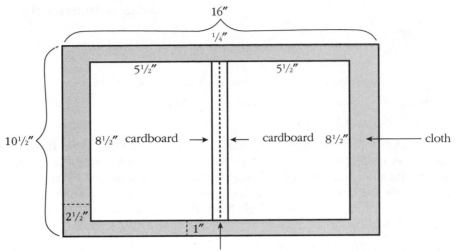

This is where the book will fold in the middle.
That is the only purpose of the space.

Figure 20.10

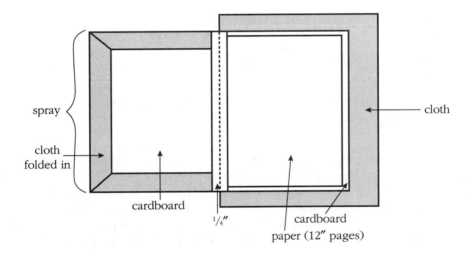

Figure 20.11

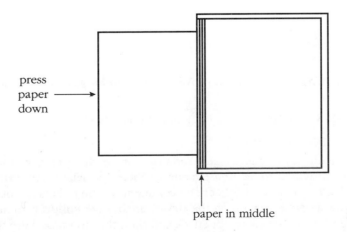

Figure 20.12

98   AIR WRITING

GOALS   To improve writing literacy; to improve sensorimotor integration

OBJECTIVES   The child will write cursive upper- and lower-case letters in the air.

MATERIALS   None

PROCEDURE   Have children write letters and words in the air before they put them on paper. Using the dominant hand, have children keep their elbow straight, point their index finger, and write the letter or word in the air. Be sure children use the large muscles of the arm, not wrist muscles. Write large letters. If necessary, guide the child's arm through the motions or stand next to the child and model the motion while talking about the strokes. Have children write large letters on the chalkboard after writing them in the air, and then on large paper.

INTEGRATION   As children become interested in writing, they need to develop a sensorimotor base. For some children, writing comes easily; others will need help. Children who have trouble writing with paper and pencil may need additional work with their large muscles before practice with a pencil and paper is useful.

99   SAND PRINTING

GOALS   To improve writing literacy; to improve sensorimotor integration; to use diverse print and nonprint sources and genres

OBJECTIVES   The child will print or write letters and words in the sand.

MATERIALS   Jelly roll pan, sand, stick or unsharpened pencil, cards with an individual letter or word printed on each

PROCEDURE   Fill a jelly roll pan (cookie sheet with sides) about 1/4″ deep with sand. Using the index finger of their dominant hand, have children write letters, sounds, their name, or words in the sand. For variation have them use a stick after they have gained skill with their finger. Sort the letters into those that have straight lines, curved lines, and combinations. Give children cards with simple words printed on them. After children have written individual letters, encourage them to copy words in the sand from cards that you have written. Begin with words that are important to the children, yet short.

INTEGRATION   The sand provides some resistance and also leaves a mark so the children can see what they have printed. This provides feedback on fine motor control in an unusual way.

100   TICKETS

GOALS   To improve writing literacy; to improve reading literacy; to use diverse print and nonprint sources and genres

OBJECTIVES   The child will write, distribute, and read tickets.

MATERIALS   Markers, paper, press-on labels

PROCEDURE   Have the children make tickets for snack or lunch using the labels as a base. Tell children that today they need tickets to eat and encourage them to make them. (Have a few extras and a marker for those who don't.) Be sure to collect and comment on the tickets as you distribute snack. Support the children for any writing they do on the ticket. Encourage children to make "identical" tickets (numbers are easiest) and have one ticket for snack and the other to mark were the child is to sit. Then have the children find their place at the table by matching the ticket to the place marker.

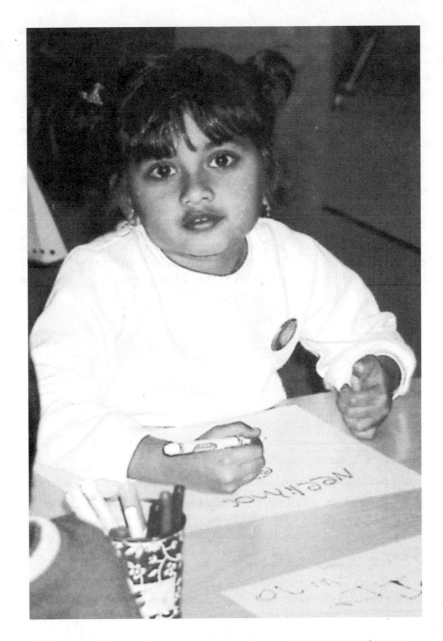

Children need to see themselves as authors and illustrators; from an early age, they will learn to appreciate books and art throughout their lives.

INTEGRATION Children need practice writing, especially numbers. Use an activity such as this to support dramatic play by giving out railroad and airline tickets. Give tickets for using an obstacle course or riding tricycles. There can be tickets for puppet shows, group time, and stories. Children need to learn that writing is an important literacy activity, not a tedious small motor penalty.

Writing: Small Group

101 WRITING CENTER

GOALS To improve writing literacy; to improve reading literacy; to use diverse print and nonprint sources and genres

OBJECTIVES The child will write and illustrate a story, poem, or play.

MATERIALS   Variety of paper: manila paper, wide-lined paper, plain white paper, paper folded in half, small notepads, paper cut into interesting shapes, colored paper, and stationery; writing tools: thin and thick water-soluble markers, pencils and colored pencils, a supply of interesting erasers, a pencil sharpener; copy of the alphabet; writing folder with each child's name

PROCEDURE   Encourage children to think about an experience or feeling they would like to write about. Discuss writing as a process that involves writing, editing, and publishing. When you talk with children at the writing center, use the terms author, editor, and publisher with them. Writing is best thought of as a small-group activity, where children can actively discuss their ideas and try them out on others. It is not a quiet solitary activity. Emphasize the process of writing. Encourage children to work in small groups and support each other in the process. Discuss illustrating and differentiate it from "just drawing." Encourage children to write more detailed and longer stories; increase the variety of writing genres to include poetry and plays. Then have them read their work to others and publish their work. Discuss the different but related aspects of writing, editing, and publishing.

INTEGRATION   As children begin to think about themselves as authors, their interest in writing increases. When they see writing as a process, and the details of editing as separate from writing, they can focus on the aspects of spelling and punctuation that are important in a final product but ought not to interfere with creativity.

Writing: Small Group

102   PUBLISHING

GOALS   To improve writing literacy; to improve reading literacy; to use diverse print and nonprint sources and genres

OBJECTIVES   The child will write, illustrate, publish, and read a book.

MATERIALS   Posterboard or cardboard, three-ring punch, notebook rings, written work

PROCEDURE   Talk with children about the parts of a book and the purposes they serve. Show them a copyright symbol and talk about the meaning of it. Show them copyright pages, dedications, acknowledgments, and indexes. Then write a class book to which each child contributes. The contributions can vary with the ability and interest of the children. Encourage children to use their knowledge of books and their parts in their own writing when appropriate. Help children add additional stories to their book or create new books on other topics. Include photographs as well as illustrations. After children have written the text for their book, have them make a cover out of posterboard and, using a three-hole punch, make holes in the paper and cover and put the book together. Encourage them to use a title page and, if there is more than one story, a table of contents.

INTEGRATION   Children like to think of themselves as authors who produce a product that is called a book that can be kept, read, and placed on a bookshelf. Learning at an early age that one edits and reflects on what one writes is a life-long skill.

Writing: Individual

103   MY DIARY

GOALS   To improve writing literacy; to improve reading literacy; to use diverse print and nonprint sources and genres

OBJECTIVES   The child will write and/or illustrate a diary.

MATERIALS   Pencils and markers, notebook or paper stapled together

PROCEDURE   Talk with children about diaries and why people keep them. Tell them that diaries are personal and that they are usually kept over a long span of time. Include information that diaries are sometimes kept on trips or even about inventions. Ask the children to keep a diary for a week related to the theme that you are using. Support diary writing, not whether or not you can read what is written. Encourage children who are unsure about writing to illustrate their diary. Use the word "illustrate." Have each child choose or put together the paper for his or her diary and label it. Put it in a particular place so they have access to it for at least a week. Encourage each child to spend some time each day writing or illustrating the diary. Continue to make the materials available for the diary and have children expand the content. Allow them to choose what they will write about, but support the writing process.

INTEGRATION   Children need practice writing. An activity that requires children to write for short periods over several days is useful. The emphasis in this activity is the process of writing itself. Inventive spelling and letter reversals are expected during the early childhood years. Children need to learn the many different purposes of writing.

Summary

Language and literacy is an area in itself, yet many other areas of learning are dependent on these basic skills. Young children need to develop the literacy skills for further learning as well as a commitment to continued independent learning.

Educational Resources

Ask the Author
http://www.ipl.org/youth/AskAuthor/
Just as it sounds, the site allows children to ask questions of authors and receive their replies.

Beaty, J. J. (1997). *Building bridges with multicultural picture book for children 3-5.* Upper Saddle River, NJ: Merrill/Prentice Hall.
Profiles how children develop relative to content area. Includes recommended books, techniques, and follow-up activities.

The Children's Literature Web Guide
http://www.ucalgary.ca/~dkbrown/index.html
Provides information about available literature for children with many connections. A good place to begin.

Children and the Media Program
http://www.dnai.com/~children/media/media.html
Advocates for public policies affecting children's media and raises awareness about the needs of children and their portrayal in the media.

Christie, J., Enz, B., & Vukelich, C. (1997). *Teaching language and literacy: Preschool through the elementary grades.* New York: Longman.
Includes case studies and trade secrets as well as a framework to design language learning and assessment activities.

Davidson, J. (1996). *Emergent literacy and dramatic play.* Albany, NY: Delmar Publishers.
Rich with anecdotes, this provides an overview of the nature and value of dramatic play and its connection with emergent literacy.

Dyson, A. H. (1997). *What difference does difference make? Teacher reflections on diversity, literacy, and the urban primary school.* Urbana, IL: National Council of Teachers of English.
Documents the struggle to make writing response to children who use multiple frames of reference to make sense out of their world.

Enchanted Learning
http://www.EnchantedLearning.com/Dictionary.html
A site set up like a children's picture dictionary.

Human Languages Page
http://www.june29.com/HLP/
Contains languages and literature from around the world from Aboriginal to Yiklamu.

International Reading Association
http://www.readingonline.org/
Reading Online is a journal about reading published by the IRA.

Midwest Book Review
www.execpc.com/~mbr/bookwatch
A packed Web site that has links to numerous libraries and sources for book reviews.

Pinnell, G., & Fountas, I. C. (1997). Help America read: A handbook for volunteers. Portsmouth, NH: Heinemann.
A short book that provides basic information and suggestions to volunteers about how to read to children, the importance of letters and phonics as well as creating props.

Sign Language
http://www.gorilla.org
Learn sign language from Koko, a gorilla.

Chapter 21

DISCOVERY ACTIVITIES: MATHEMATICS, SCIENCE, AND COMPUTER

Mathematics, science, and computers are taught as hands-on experiences in the early childhood curriculum. Young children do not think either abstractly or logically at this age. Simply telling them about their world is rarely effective. They need to develop a solid base of internalized experiences as a foundation for later abstract scientific and mathematical thinking.

TABLE 21.1 ACTIVITY GOALS AND REFERENCE NUMBERS

Goals	Activities
To improve number sense and numeration	104, 105, 106, 107, 108, 109, 110, 111
To improve geometric and spatial sense	108, 110, 112, 113, 114, 115, 116, 117, 118
To improve measurement concepts	111, 112, 113, 115, 119, 120, 129, 142
To improve observational skills	121, 122, 123, 124, 125, 126, 127, 128, 129, 130
To improve classification skills	110, 114, 116, 118, 119, 120, 121, 124, 125, 131, 132, 133
To improve estimation skills	107, 120
To identify and understand patterns and relationships	111, 112, 116, 118, 132, 139, 140, 141
To improve knowledge of whole number operations and computations	104
To improve knowledge of fractions and decimals	106
To improve cause-and-effect reasoning	122, 125, 126, 127, 128, 130, 133, 134, 135, 136, 137
To improve generalization skills	123, 131, 132, 136, 138
To increase knowledge of the natural world	121, 123, 124, 131, 134
To make predictions	126, 127, 128, 133, 134, 135
To improve computer skills	129, 135, 136, 137, 138, 139, 140, 141, 142, 143, 144
To increase thinking and reasoning skills	114, 119
To increase inclusion	109
To follow directions	117, 137, 142, 143, 144
To improve reading literacy	104, 105, 107, 108, 117, 138, 139, 140, 141, 143, 144
To increase vocabulary	105, 106
To improve sensorimotor integration	109, 115
To improve eye-hand coordination	130

104   ABACUS

GOALS   To improve number sense and numeration; to improve knowledge of whole number operations and computations; to improve reading literacy

OBJECTIVES   The child will count sets of objects and designate the number of objects that correspond to the written number.

MATERIALS   A large abacus, several small abacuses for individual work, cards with numbers on one side and a picture of the number of beads moved on the other

PROCEDURE   Give the children cards with the number side up. Have them count (move) the specified number of beads and then check their answer by comparing it to the drawing on the other side of the card. Begin by using only the cards with lower numbers and use this as a teacher-directed activity. As children become more competent, give them higher numbers and require more difficult math skills (addition and subtraction).

INTEGRATION   Talk with children about different computation methods and how they are used, including using cubes and other small objects as well as calculators. Help children grasp the relationship between the written number and the number of objects.

105   MATCHING SYMBOLS

GOALS   To improve number sense and numeration; to improve reading literacy; to increase vocabulary

OBJECTIVES   The child will count sets of symbols and match the number of symbols to the corresponding written number.

MATERIALS   Cards numbered 1 through 20, cards with up to 20 symbols

PROCEDURE   Have the children match the number and symbol cards. As children begin, make the cards large and only use the numbers 1 through 5. Initially, use cards to count and identify numbers. Encourage children to point to or touch the symbols as they count. Use cardboard or laminated cards so they are easier to handle. Include sandpaper numbers and symbols (see Figure 21.1).

Add cards that have different shapes or pictures on them (for example, small animal stickers), including cards that have different symbols on the same card (for example, a dot, square, and a sticker) with different spatial arrangements (see Figure 21.2). Encourage children to put all of the cards with the same number of objects in a pile. Help children learn that the number value doesn't change with the specific symbols or their arrangement on the card.

INTEGRATION   Emphasize the language of equivalency—"same as," "equals"—and the concepts "more," "less," and so on. Use sandpaper or felt numbers and shapes to provide tactile cues.

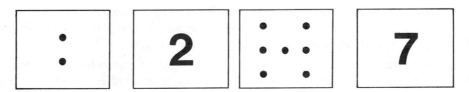

Figure 21.1

Figure 21.2

Mathematics: Small Group or Individual

106   FRACTIONS

GOALS   To improve number sense and numeration; to improve knowledge of fractions and decimals; to increase vocabulary

OBJECTIVES   The child will join the pieces of the objects, count the pieces, and state the fraction.

MATERIALS   Egg cartons; box or bag to contain objects; objects cut in half, thirds, and fourths:

socks	pencil
paper plate	crayon
plastic bottle	straw
piece of paper	glove

PROCEDURE   Let children use the pieces like a puzzle, with fewer pieces and more dissimilar materials. As children get the idea of putting the pieces together, introduce the idea of fractions, starting with half. Use the vocabulary "half" and "whole." Talk about the mathematical properties that make something *half*. When children begin to understand the concept of half, introduce other fractions and have children cut some objects into thirds and fourths. Introduce the term "equals."

INTEGRATION   Use the vocabulary of "whole" and "half" during snack, asking children to eat half of their crackers or raisins. As they consume some, ask them to eat half again to help them see the relative nature of fractions.

Mathematics: Individual or Small Group

107   NUMBER SQUARES

GOALS   To improve number sense and numeration; to improve estimation skills; to improve reading literacy

OBJECTIVES   The child will move the specified number of spaces in the fewest moves.

MATERIALS   Graph paper, pencil, marker

PROCEDURE   Use graph paper or make your own grid. Initially, use only numbers 1 to 5 and a grid with 6 lines down and 6 across; make the grid itself large. Once the children have the idea, move to a grid of about 10 lines down and 10 across. Fill in each box with a number between 1 and 9. Mark the center square and put a marker (e.g., a button) on it (see Figure 21.3). The object of the game is to figure out how to go from the center and land just outside the grid on the last move. Children can play individually or in pairs. You can move in any direction in a straight line (diagonal, left, right, up, down). Choose a number for the first move (or throw die). The number that you land on is the next number of moves you will make (if you land on 3, then you move 3 squares). As children become more adept, increase the size of the grid to 20 across and 20 down, or larger. To play alone, have each child keep a record of the number of moves he or she takes to land outside the grid.

INTEGRATION   It is useful to have several different sizes of grids and to have different number configurations so that children do not see this as a competitive game, but rather one of planning. Have a variety of different grids for children to choose from. Encourage children to challenge themselves.

Mathematics: Individual or Small Group

108   SPACEY DOTS

GOALS   To improve number sense and numeration; to improve geometric and spatial sense; to improve reading literacy

1	2	7	6	1	2	6	7	8	6	2
5	9	3	2	9	8	1	9	3	5	1
4	3	7	7	1	2	5	6	8	6	1
5	1	2	3	5	9	8	7	6	4	2
6	8	9	7	8	5	2	4	3	1	2
2	3	4	1	9	✕	7	6	8	9	5
4	5	2	6	1	7	1	2	5	1	2
7	6	4	3	1	5	7	8	6	4	3
9	2	5	1	3	7	4	1	2	8	9
8	1	6	5	2	7	8	1	3	5	7

Figure 21.3

OBJECTIVES   The child will group together cards that have equal numbers or numerical designations.

MATERIALS   A set of three cards for each number between 1 and 10; each card of the set has an equal number of dots, with different dots arranged in different configurations on each card (see Figure 21.4).

PROCEDURE   Start by using only two sets of cards with 1 to 5 dots. Have children match cards with equal numbers of dots. Ask the child to give you the card that has the same number of dots as the card shown. Count with the child. Encourage the child to touch the dots as she counts. Add sets of cards, including cards with numerals. Have the children describe the markings and where the markings are on the card (center, right-hand corner, top half).

INTEGRATION   Spatial configuration sometimes distracts the child from the concept of numbers. Some children will be helped by tactile cues. Use sandpaper shapes rather than dots or use textured glue to make the dots.

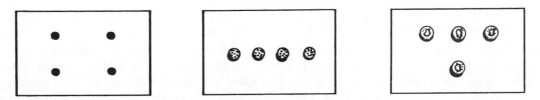

Figure 21.4

109   NUMBER LINE

GOALS   To improve number sense and numeration; to increase inclusion; to improve sensorimotor integration

OBJECTIVES   The child will move the specified number of spaces.

MATERIALS   A 20-foot length of fabric marked into 20 1-foot areas and numbered consecutively from 1 to 20, a spinner or dice

PROCEDURE   Spin a spinner or roll dice and have children move on the cloth the designated number of spaces. Initially, use only one die or numbers up to 6. As children become more competent using the board game format, increase the complexity by having certain numbers be "wild cards" and have a child who lands on an occupied space send the other child back to "start." Ask the children to read the number they are on.

INTEGRATION   This is a variation of a board game, with the children as the playing pieces. Although this may initially be a teacher-directed game, once children learn the rules, encourage them to play independently. Children can gain a sensorimotor feeling for numbers by playing while they participate with peers.

110   VARIATIONS ON BLOCKS

GOALS   To improve number sense and numeration; to improve geometric and spatial sense; to improve classification skills

OBJECTIVES   The child will perform the requested activity.

MATERIALS   A set of unit blocks

PROCEDURE   During clean-up, request that children follow specific directions relative to the blocks:

Pick up all the blocks that are the same as this one.

Pick up all the curved blocks.

Pick up blocks of three different lengths.

Pick up blocks in sets of twos, threes, or fours.

Pick up all of a certain type of block: rectangles, squares, cylinders, and so on.

Place blocks on the shelves in a certain order: top shelf, then middle, then bottom.

Count the number of different blocks in a structure.

Count how many blocks of a certain type were used.

Count the total number of blocks in a structure.

Combine two or three of the above (e.g., request a child put three cylinders on the top shelf).

Or decide that there are only some blocks that children can play with and help them figure out how to make a configuration of their choice under these circumstances.

INTEGRATION   The block area is a great place to learn and reinforce math concepts. Children can learn much just through building and manipulating blocks, providing an adult adds the information about size, shape, and so on. Adding the vocabulary increases the usefulness of understanding mathematics for children and helps them transfer this usefulness to everyday life. Children need many real-world experiences using three-dimensional materials to develop a strong foundation in math.

Blocks offer the potential for learning in many different areas such as eye-hand coordination, counting, and spacial relations.

Mathematics: Individual or Small Group

111   VARIATIONS ON CUISENAIRE RODS

GOALS   To improve number sense and numeration; to identify and understand patterns and relationships; to improve measurement concepts

OBJECTIVES   The child will arrange the rods in the specified order and explain why the arrangement fits the request.

MATERIALS   Several sets of Cuisenaire rods (Do not use with children under 3; the small rods are easily swallowed.)

PROCEDURE   Initially, allow children to explore the rods. Encourage them to sort by length and color. Have them build flat designs as well as vertical structures, and count the rods used in these activities. Help children discover that the same length is always the same color. Support children working as a team to create a theme using the rods, such as building a farm, boat dock, or amusement park, and talk about their creation. When children become familiar with the rods, do the following activities:

Build a person.

Make flat designs.

Make a design using a specified number of rods.

Copy another child's design.

Build staircases.

Outline a simple design on graph paper and color it in, using the rods to determine the colors.

Give children a design on graph paper and have them duplicate it with the rods.

Use smaller rods to measure the larger rods.

Make a repeating pattern with the rods.

INTEGRATION   Cuisenaire rods can be used to teach higher-level skills such as addition, subtraction, and multiplication, as well as more basic skills.

Mathematics: Individual or Small Group

112   AREAS

GOALS   To improve geometric and spatial sense; to improve measurement concepts; to identify and understand patterns and relationships

OBJECTIVES   The child will cover the given shape with a variety of the building pieces, and identify the shapes in the building pieces, their relative size, and number.

MATERIALS   Building pieces made of white posterboard, shapes made of red posterboard

PROCEDURE   Using the patterns shown in Figure 21.5, cut out the designated number of building pieces. Put building pieces together to form new shapes, outline them, and cut them out (see Figure 21.6).

Begin by using only the square and triangle shapes that can be made from them. Use the shapes as if they were puzzles and count how many building pieces it takes to cover each shape. Make more shapes using different configurations of the building pieces. All building pieces are relative in area—1, 2, or ½. Help children "discover" the relationship of the building pieces and use this information to figure out the area of designated shapes.

INTEGRATION   This activity can be used at different levels by varying the complexity of the shapes and the challenges you pose. You can teach measuring and area concepts and have children see the variety of ways they can use the pieces to cover the shapes. You can teach fractions, estimation, and computation. For children who need tactile cues, glue sandpaper to the shapes and put the materials in a jellyroll pan to confine them.

Mathematics: Small Group

113   OBJECT SIZES

GOALS   To improve geometric and spatial sense; to improve measurement concepts

OBJECTIVES   The child will order objects according to size.

MATERIALS   4 sets of measuring spoons and measuring cups (see Figure 21.7), plastic glasses of different sizes, a water or sand table

PROCEDURE   Place sets of objects in the water or sand table. Start with two different-sized containers. Give children time to explore the objects and play with them by just filling and dumping them. As

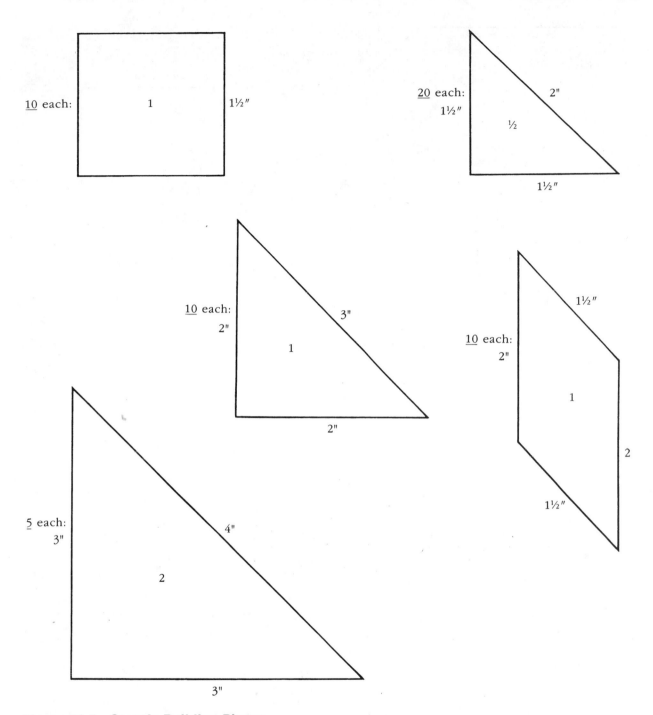

Figure 21.5   Sample Building Pieces

Number inside shape represents relative size.

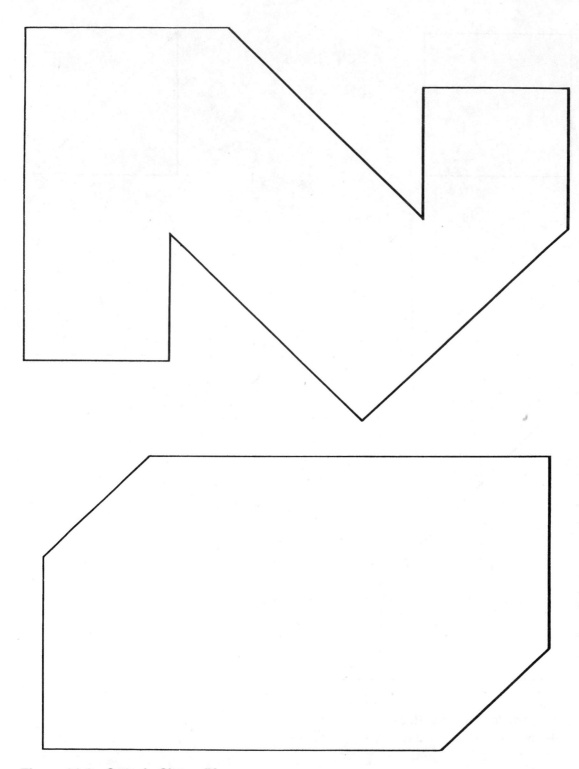

Figure 21.6 Sample Shape Pieces

Figure 21.7

children become aware of differences, ask them to point to or give you the objects in order of size. Help children explore the relative sizes of objects through pouring and measuring. Give them examples for comparisons: "It takes 4 of the smallest cup to fill the big one." Arrange the objects in order of size, and give the children another set to match the first. When this has been mastered, add a slightly different set to be matched (measuring spoons). Have the children arrange both sets from largest to smallest. Then stagger the arrangement. See if the children can remember the relative sizes by having them place the objects in the proper order again. Add containers that are deceptive (tall narrow and short wide ones). Encourage children to make predictions about relative volume and then to check if they are right.

INTEGRATION   Have children measure a variety of different materials so they learn that measurement is a constant. Use cornmeal, oatmeal, rice, beans, birdseed, and so on, depending on the age of the children. This focusing of "dump and fill" has many potentials, including learning adaptive skills. Adult input and questioning varies the activity.

Mathematics: Large or Small Group

114   THINKING SHAPES

GOALS   To improve geometric and spatial sense; to improve classification skills; to increase thinking and reasoning skills

OBJECTIVES   The child will find or name objects in the room that are the designated shape.

MATERIALS   None

PROCEDURE   The teacher will think of objects in the room that are a particular shape, and the children must guess the object. The teacher will answer only "yes" or "no" questions. Initially, accept and support anything that is the right shape and ask the children to find more objects of that shape. Then play the actual game.

> *Teacher:*   I'm thinking of something in this room that is square.
> *Child:*   The record player.
> *Teacher:*   No, the record player is square, but that is not what I'm thinking of.
> *Child:*   Is the square you are thinking of red?
> *Teacher:*   Yes.

The process continues as the children make more guesses. When children can classify objects in the room by two-dimensional shapes, introduce three-dimensional shapes and their names (for example, cube, pyramid, sphere, cylinder). Add objects that are composed of more than one shape. Encourage children to narrow the field categorically before guessing specific objects.

INTEGRATION   This is a good activity to share with parents to use in rooms that are unfamiliar. It gives familiar qualities to them and helps time pass.

115   BOXES AND MORE BOXES

GOALS   To improve geometric and spatial sense; to improve measurement concepts; to improve sensorimotor integration

OBJECTIVES   The child will identify the boxes by size and label her relationship to them relative to distance and space.

MATERIALS   Cardboard boxes of varying sizes, including a very large box (usually from an appliance)

PROCEDURE   Place small, medium, and large boxes in an open area. Encourage children to climb in and out of the boxes. Some children may even enjoy "hiding" for a short time in larger boxes. Allow children to push and pull the boxes. Support children's exploration of the boxes both verbally and physically. Place children in boxes if they need help. Talk about size concepts such as small, medium, and large, and the objects that might be placed in each box. Use language about spatial relations—in, out, in front of, behind, beside—and measurement terms such as near, far, close, and even foot lengths. Given a larger appliance box, children may enjoy having their own private "house." Help them decide where the windows and doors should be placed, how to measure the height and area of each, and how large they should be. Encourage children to use the boxes in imaginative play, such as making a train. Help them arrange the boxes in order by size. Measure the length of the train.

INTEGRATION   This is also a good outdoor activity in nice weather. Children need real-life relevant sensorimotor experience with these mathematical concepts before they can use them in an abstract way.

116   PICTURE SHAPES

GOALS   To improve geometric and spatial sense; to identify and understand patterns and relationships; to improve classification skills

OBJECTIVES   The child will identify relationships and geometric forms in pictures and sort the pictures according to form.

MATERIALS   Geometric shapes cut from cardboard, pictures of common objects with definite geometric shapes mounted on cards (record, house, ice cream cone, bed)

PROCEDURE   Choose pictures with little detail and help children place shapes over the pictures to find a shape in the picture. Then have the children sort the pictures according to shape. Use more complex pictures with several shapes and have children find shapes in a picture containing several shapes.

INTEGRATION   This activity helps children recognize and classify geometry in their world. It requires visual generalization and application of knowledge of shapes to pictures of real objects. Discuss with children why a particular shape is functional for a particular purpose: the pitch of roofs (or angle of a triangle) and the north-south orientation of a structure relative to snow and its weight; a roof overhang to keep the sun from shining in regions that are very hot.

117   SHAPE PICTURES

GOALS   To improve geometric and spatial sense; to follow directions; to improve reading literacy

OBJECTIVES   The child will connect the designated shapes using a crayon or marker.

MATERIALS   Drawings containing arrangements of various shapes (triangles, circles, squares). Within each arrangement, all the shapes of one type, when connected, should form a letter or shape.

PROCEDURE   Begin with designs with fewer shapes and consistent shape and color patterns. Use simple one-step directions and be sure the children are keeping pace with you. Have the children connect the shapes with a crayon or marker and then name the connected shape (see Figure 21.8).

Use more shapes and colors and a greater variety of them in the design. Make the directions more complicated; for example, "Start at the upper right-hand corner (or designate it with a star). Count down one triangle and two circles. Connect this shape to the closest oval, then . . ."

INTEGRATION   Have children count the shapes and colors when they are finished. Interested children might graph this information.

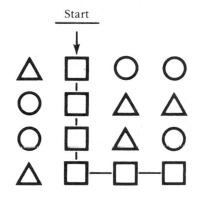

Directions: Connect the squares in order. What letter do the squares make?

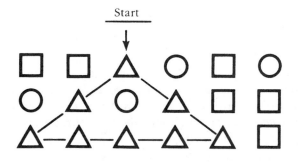

Directions: Connect the triangles so that they make a triangle.

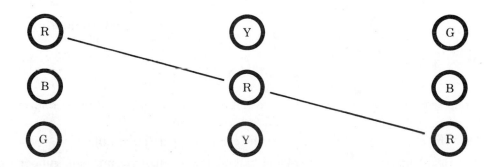

Directions: Connect the colors that will make a straight line.

Figure 21.8

118   BIG AND LITTLE PAIRS

GOALS   To improve geometric and spatial sense; to identify and understand patterns and relationships; to improve classification skills

OBJECTIVES   The child will pair the large and small objects.

MATERIALS   Pairs of objects, one large and one small: tablespoon-teaspoon, large book-small book, adult shoe-child's shoe, large plate-small plate, large piece of paper-small piece of paper; large bag or box to contain the objects

PROCEDURE   Choose the objects so that the large and small objects are the same color and different from other pairs. Have children empty the box and place the large and small versions of objects together in pairs. Encourage children to find other ways of classifying the objects (size, use, color, and so on). Have the children pair the objects using only touch (put a cover over the box). The child chooses one object and then must find its pair using only his hands.

INTEGRATION   There are many variations of this activity. For example, use cards and envelopes of different sizes or boxes and lids of varying sizes.

119   MEASURING TOOLS

GOALS   To improve measurement concepts; to improve classification skills; to increase thinking and reasoning skills

OBJECTIVES   The child will choose the appropriate measuring tool for an activity or event.

MATERIALS   Timer, ruler, food scale, hourglass, stopwatch, tape measure, bathroom scale, alarm clock, yardstick, balance scale, meter stick, paper/pencils

PROCEDURE   Place one group of measuring devices on a table with appropriate suggestions for things to be measured, timed, or weighed. Encourage children to use and explore the tools. Discuss with children the efficiency of their choices, what worked, and what didn't work as well. Encourage children to record and graph their results and to make predictions about other measurements. Have them begin to order objects and events based on principles of measurement.

INTEGRATION   This is a good activity for children working in pairs. It can encourage inclusion as well as teach math concepts.

120   MEASURE IT

GOALS   To improve measurement concepts; to improve classification skills; to improve estimation skills

OBJECTIVES   The child will estimate how far she can throw particular objects.

MATERIALS   Beanbag, tennis ball, Ping-Pong ball, sponges, small rubber ball, rubber rings, horseshoes, whiffle ball, crumpled paper, beach ball, 12″ rubber ball, softball, feather, balloon, towel

PROCEDURE   Have a variety of objects for the children to throw. This is not a contest to see who can throw the farthest, so style of throwing is not important. Have the children help you draw a line or stake a string and then mark it at each foot with a ribbon. Have the children develop a baseline (average throw) with the small rubber ball or a tennis ball. Have other children watch where the ball goes and then stand where it first hits. Determine how far it went. Then have the child who is throwing decide whether the next object will go farther or closer. Measure the distance and classify the objects after they are thrown. Have several children do this and compare the results. Help children understand how to make better predictions. *Note:* For some, this might simply be a motor activity with an understanding that it is easier to throw some objects farther than others.

INTEGRATION This combines math, science, and motor skills. Encourage children to estimate how far they can throw various objects. Have children chart their relative lengths and compare them. Help them determine the properties of objects that influence distance.

Science: Individual or Small Group

121 MY YARD

GOALS To improve observational skills; to improve classification skills; to increase knowledge of the natural world

OBJECTIVES The child will identify at least five items he sees.

MATERIALS A yard of string for each child, binoculars, small sticks or nails. pad and pencil, magnifying glasses of different strengths

PROCEDURE On a warm, sunny, dry day, cut pieces of string a yard long and tie one end to a stick or nail. Have the children push or pound these into the ground. Give each child a magnifying glass and have them explore their "yard." Their "yard" is a circle with a one-yard radius. At first, you may have to help them see the little things: a blade of grass, an ant, dirt. Or have children work in pairs. Point out specific objects to the children. Encourage them to list what they find and even map out the location. Use different degrees of magnification, and note what is seen. Note where the child is and repeat the activity in a different season or move to a different place.

INTEGRATION Be sure to draw the analogy between glasses and magnifying glasses. They are different devices to help people see better. If the ground is damp, have the children sit on something. *Note:* If any children are allergic to grass, these allergies are usually worse just after the grass has been cut.

Science: Individual or Small Group

122 GOOP

GOALS To improve observational skills; to improve cause-and-effect reasoning

OBJECTIVES The child will explore the properties of cornstarch in its various states.

MATERIALS Water, tea, cornstarch, food coloring, flour, sugar, beet juice, bowls or jellyroll trays

PROCEDURE Have children mix approximately equal amounts of cornstarch and water to make goop. Allow children to experiment with the proportions and observe the results. Allow children time to explore the plain goop. If this is the children's first experience, leave the goop white. Later, try adding some natural dyes like beet juice or tea (be careful, these can stain). Help children talk about the different and confusing states of the goop. Then, use equal proportions of flour and water and compare the results to the goop. What happens with sugar and water? Help children learn about the different properties and reactions of materials that look similar.

INTEGRATION Goop is edible and relatively easy to clean up. It is easily used on a bed tray, and it is clean. Goop requires little strength to manipulate and defies coordination. It is a soothing yet intriguing media.

Science: **Individual or Small Group**

123   ANT FARM

GOALS   To improve observational skills; to improve generalization skills; to increase knowledge of the natural world

OBJECTIVES   The child will observe the ants.

MATERIALS   Sets of two clear glass jars (one small enough to fit inside the other), loose or sandy soil, sugar, water, ants

PROCEDURE   Put the smaller jar inside the large one, open side down. Fill the larger one with loose soil—don't pack it down. (You want to be able to see the ants, so you want the space relatively narrow.) Collect ants from one ant colony only for each jar (otherwise, they may fight). Collect about 20 ants, put them in the jar, and screw on the lid. Once a week, feed the ants a few drops of sugar water; add a few

Children need to actively explore the world in which they live with safe supervision by adults.

grains of birdseed, if you wish. Initially, concentrate on the observation process. Point out what is going on in the ant farm. Then make a second ant farm and encourage the children to compare the two. Have them draw the configuration of tunnels. Encourage them to look up ants in reference books and learn about how they live and work.

INTEGRATION   Discuss the needs of animals for survival and how ants are both different and the same as other animals. It is possible to get commercially available ant farms, but the process of making your own is part of the children's learning.

Science: Large or Small Group

124   NATURE BOARD

GOALS   To improve observational skills; to improve classification skills; to increase knowledge of the natural world

OBJECTIVES   The child will identify and classify objects found.

MATERIALS   Objects found on a nature walk, cardboard, glue, small bags, rubber gloves

PROCEDURE   On a nature walk, help the children pick up objects such as nuts, sticks, stones, leaves, twigs, and so on. Start by labeling objects for the children. While you are on the walk, point out obvious relationships: "Look, you found a leaf. Let's look up in the tree and see if there are more like it. I think this leaf fell from this tree. This is called an oak tree. You have a green oak leaf." Try to get at least two of each object. In addition to picking up natural objects, using gloves, pick up environmental pollutants as well: Styrofoam, aluminum cans, plastic bags, cigarette butts. Put these in a separate bag. When you get back to the class, glue each of the natural objects onto a separate, small piece of cardboard. Put the "pairs" to these objects in a bag, and have children see if they can match the designated object. Have children try to remember where they found certain objects and why they might be there, for example, acorns and pine cones under trees. Classify the objects found in as many different ways as possible. Talk with children about pollutants and the problems they cause in the environment. Have them help figure out some solutions to these problems. Have children make a map of the nature walk and draw significant landmarks. Help them mark where objects were found and, if possible, glue some of the objects to the map.

INTEGRATION   Classifying objects makes them more relevant. And it is never too early to begin environmental education.

Science: Small Group

125   SINK OR FLOAT

GOALS   To improve observational skills; to improve classification skills; to improve cause-and-effect reasoning

OBJECTIVES   The child will state which objects will float and which will sink.

MATERIALS   water table, bucket of water, dishpan

paper with illustrations of sinking and floating

objects to put in the water

different shapes and weights of sinkers (that fishermen use) and floats

items from the classroom (paper, cardboard, blocks)

items from the kitchen (silverware, cups, egg cartons)

items from nature (bark, wood, seeds)

PROCEDURE   Fill a water table, bucket, or pan at least three inches deep and allow children to put objects in the water and to both play with them and observe them. Encourage children to make predictions and place objects that sink and float in separate groups. Encourage active exploration. Have children place objects in the water in different ways (upside down, sideways). As they generate hypotheses, support their checking them out. Encourage children to think about why fishermen use different kinds of sinkers (weight and shape). See if children can use floaters to make sinkers float. If they need other objects, for example, a paper clip, penny, or pin, help them find the objects. Discuss where the sinkers are placed on the floater. Have them try variations. Have them categorize materials and try to generate principles for their classifications. (Carefully monitor items that could be swallowed.)

INTEGRATION   Always have an adult present when young children are near water. Repeat this activity with different items.

Science: Small Group

126   COLOR CHANGES

GOALS   To improve observational skills; to make predictions; to improve cause-and-effect reasoning

OBJECTIVES   The child will mix water and food coloring and predict the color of the water.

MATERIALS   Water; measuring cups; spoons; red, blue, and yellow food coloring; eye droppers; clear plastic glasses (about six per child); large container; a set of 64 crayons of varying colors

PROCEDURE   Fill the glasses about half full of water. Give children food coloring and other equipment and allow them to experiment. Have children identify the color in the container. Emphasize the vocabulary of specific colors as well as the relationship between the intensity of the color and the ratio of water to food coloring. Encourage children to predict what will happen before they mix colors. Have them count the number of drops used of each color. If children want to mix more colors, have them empty their glasses into a large container, and at the end put all their colors in, observing the changes with each addition. Using the crayons as a guide, have children pick a crayon and see if they can match it with food coloring. Have them ask others whether or not the color matches and what to add if it doesn't.

INTEGRATION   The activity can help children learn color names in a creative way as well as be a science project. Help generalize this experience to painting and using markers.

Science: Small Group

127   GELATIN

GOALS   To improve observational skills; to make predictions; to improve cause-and-effect reasoning

OBJECTIVES   The child will state the changes that take place in the gelatin during the activity.

MATERIALS   Fruit-flavored gelatin, ice cubes, boiling water, fruit, cold water, bowls, spoons

PROCEDURE   Following the directions on the package, make gelatin with cold water. Then make another batch with ice cubes. Emphasize vocabulary: cold, hot, boiling, melt, thicken, powder, liquid, solid. Initially, concentrate on the vocabulary and the change of state of the gelatin. Add fruit at various stages in the thickening process and discuss sinking and floating. Plan to have the gelatin for snack or lunch. Compare making gelatin with cold water and with ice by timing both processes and predicting when the gelatin will be thick enough so the fruit floats instead of sinking. Make a chart showing how the children's predictions compare with what actually happens.

INTEGRATION   Encourage children with visual impairments to stir the gelatin at various stages to gain tactile feedback about the change from a powder to a liquid and the process of thickening as the gelatin turns to a solid.

These children not only studied the causes of pollution, but became an active part of their community by advocating for recycling. They are learning early that learning goes beyond the classroom walls.

Science: Small or Large Group

128 POLLUTION

GOALS To improve observational skills; to make predictions; to improve cause-and-effect reasoning

OBJECTIVES The child will predict the color of the celery or carnation.

MATERIALS 3 sticks of fresh celery with leaves, or white carnations; 3 glasses of water; red and blue food coloring

PROCEDURE Cut off the bottoms of celery sticks or carnation stems. Put a few drops of red food coloring in one glass of water and blue in a second. Leave the water in the third glass clear. Put one stick of celery (or carnation) in each glass. This can be done early in the day and checked at the end or checked the next day. Cut the celery sticks and see how the ones in colored water are different from the one in fresh water. One needs only observe the carnations to see the effects. The carnations may look beautiful, but it is important that children see beyond the visual effect. Talk with children about pollution in underground water. Tell them how it gets into the plants we eat. Have them begin to think about ways of preventing pollution. Pollution is a relatively abstract concept, and children may learn only about the principle of osmosis. Help children learn more about pollution and how it affects them. Talk about the implications of increasing populations and conservation. Help children generate ideas for actions that could be done at school and at home to decrease pollution.

INTEGRATION Children need to learn about conservation at an early age. It is important to make this global, abstract problem relevant to them.

129 MAPS

GOALS   To improve observation skills; to improve measurement concepts; to improve computer skills

OBJECTIVES   The child will make a map of an area of a room.

MATERIALS   Cardboard, water, paper, crayons, a container, masking tape, papier-mâché, string or yarn

PROCEDURE   Have the children choose an area of the classroom (block, dramatic play) or playground and draw it on cardboard with crayons. Divide the area and paper into quarters. Discuss with the children where things are in their drawing and how they decide where to put them. Make large graph paper for the children (1 inch equals 1 square foot) and use string or yarn to mark off the area the children are mapping in 1-foot-square sections. (If you are lucky, you may have floor tiles that are 1 foot square, so this will be unnecessary.) Have them make another map. Ask the children what in the area is flat and what should stand up from the surface (tables, swings, and so on). Use papier-mâché to have the children's maps reflect these contours. Talk about relative size as it relates to both area and height.

INTEGRATION   This project is best done over the course of several days; they need not be consecutive.

130 BUBBLES

GOALS   To improve observational skills; to improve cause-and-effect reasoning; to improve eye-hand coordination

OBJECTIVES   The child will blow bubbles and catch them.

MATERIALS   Bubble mixture (5 cups water, ½ cup Joy, pail, 2 T. glycerin), bubble-blowing rings, plastic six-pack holder, wire, assorted bubble wands

PROCEDURE   Have some children blow bubbles and other children try to catch or pop them. Encourage children to figure out where the bubbles will go based on the wind. Have them experiment with blowing hard and soft. Encourage children to make their own bubble wands. Help them observe the relationship between the wand and the size and number of the bubbles. Help them experiment with soap and how it reduces water tension, resulting in bubbles, not droplets.

INTEGRATION   This is a good outside activity on a warm day. Encourage children to wash dolls, clothes, and dishes, and to think about the role soap plays in getting things clean.

131 FOOD LOTTO

GOALS   To improve classification skills; to improve generalization skills; to increase knowledge of the natural world

OBJECTIVES   The child will match the sets of pictures correctly.

MATERIALS   A Lotto game with four sets of pictures of fruits or vegetables:

    2 identical pictures of each fruit or vegetable

    a picture of a whole fruit or vegetable as it grows (for example, apple on an apple tree, squash on a plant)

    a picture of a whole fruit (vegetable) to be matched with a picture of the same fruit (vegetable) cut in half a picture of a whole fruit (vegetable) to be matched with a picture of the same fruit (vegetable) in a different state (for example, apple/applesauce; orange/orange juice; pumpkin/pumpkin pie; corn on the cob/corn in a bowl)

the actual fruits or vegetables whole and cut up

PROCEDURE   Let the children first have experience with the actual objects. Encourage children to look and taste the actual fruits or vegetables, then go on to the Lotto game. Start with a traditional Lotto game in which children match the identical pictures. Then have the child match the other sets. This can be done individually or in small groups. Choose less familiar fruits and vegetables (star fruit, yard-long beans, yucca, etc.).

INTEGRATION   You can draw the pictures yourself or find a parent or friend to do it. Otherwise, use seed catalogues. Two or three of the same kind are especially useful. All children may have trouble recognizing the source of less familiar food; this task may be especially difficult for children who have not had experience in growing plants used for food.

Science: Individual or Small Group

132   SORTING

GOALS   To improve classification skills; to improve generalization skills; to identify and understand patterns and relationships

OBJECTIVES   The child will sort common objects and classify them.

MATERIALS   Three containers for each child, blocks, fruits, animals, furniture, vegetables, vehicles, kitchen, utensils, balls, objects that can be sorted into two categories:

OBJECTS	CATEGORY A	CATEGORY B
buttons	rough	smooth
buttons	two holes	four holes
silverware	forks	knives
silverware	big spoons	little spoons
shapes	circles	squares
shapes	oval	rectangle

Anchor three containers to a board or place them in a row (coffee cans with lids work well). Vary the size of the can to the size of the objects to be sorted.

PROCEDURE   Put the objects to be sorted in the middle container. Then have the children sort the objects into the two empty containers. Start with simple objects with obvious differences (blocks and balls) that are large enough to be handled easily and few enough so the task can be completed. Have children sort the objects into categories and tell you the basis for their sorting. Then have them resort the same objects using different classes. Have them sort the objects into three categories.

INTEGRATION   For children who rely on tactile cues, choose objects that are visually very different (black and white) or have tactile cues (rough and smooth, one or two holes).

Science: Small Group

133   MAGNETS

GOALS   To make predictions; to improve cause-and-effect reasoning; to improve classifications skills

OBJECTIVES   Before using the magnet, the child will predict which objects will be attracted by the magnet and which will not.

MATERIALS Magnets of varying sizes, shapes, and strengths

assorted small nonmetal objects (toothpicks, plastic clips)

assorted small metal objects (not aluminum)

paper clips (large and small), nails, washers

safety pins (large and small), staples

shallow box of metal filings covered with plastic wrap

PROCEDURE Give the children a variety of magnets and materials to experiment with. Encourage them to use the magnet both on the top and bottom of the box with metal filings. Ask them to sort objects according to the object's response to the magnet. Allow time for exploration, then ask them to predict whether specific objects will be attracted by the magnet. Have them discover objects in the room that are attracted to the magnet. Teach them to modify objects so that they will be attracted to the magnet (attach a paper clip to a small piece of paper). Encourage children to chart the results of their investigations. Have them explore the strength of different magnets by finding out how many paper clips each magnet can pick up. Introduce paper clips of different sizes and see how many of each size can be picked up. Weigh or balance the different clips. Graph your results.

INTEGRATION Iron filings are available from hardware stores that cut pipes. Encourage children to think of ways that magnets might be useful. Then add a magnet to the end of a stick. Have children sit in a chair and use the tool as an extension of their arm to get things they can't reach. Have them try to pick up paper clips on the floor while sitting in the chair. This activity is an initial step in showing how some devices can help those with physical impairments. *Note:* This activity should not be used if there are children under 3.

Science: Large and Small Group

134 PLANTING

GOALS To make predictions; to improve cause-and-effect reasoning; to increase knowledge of the natural world

OBJECTIVES The child will help plant seeds, help put signs on the pots, and make predictions about how well each plant will grow.

MATERIALS Lima beans (dried, soaked in water), damp cotton or paper towel, water, sponge, plastic glasses, seeds (large), potting soil, signs, large pots, paper (to graph results), crayons, popsicle sticks marked at 1″ intervals

PROCEDURE Have each child plant several beans in a plastic container with the cotton or paper towel inside so they can see the bean from the side. This way they can watch the root develop. They can begin to understand that even if they can't see anything happening, things are going on under the surface of the ground. Add a new bean each day to help children see the differences. Be sure to keep the beans damp. When the seeds are sprouted, the sprouts can be planted and observed. Plant seeds in three large pots with soil and a popsicle stick beside each. Make signs that show the conditions under which the seeds will try to grow (see Figure 21.9). Note that all plants need air and food. Have children count and mark the days on a calendar until the first sprout appears. Once they sprout, measure the plants each day, and then graph the results. Be sure to put several seeds in each pot, as some seeds may not grow even under ideal conditions. Choose seeds that are easy to handle and sprout quickly (a combination of rye grass and beans works well).

Expand the concept of planting. Help children notice differences among the seeds. Plant some of the seeds in a pot or garden. Observe the plants at various stages and compare the resulting plants with the picture.

INTEGRATION This project is best done in the spring as part of a general theme on plants and growth. It helps show variations in growth patterns. Send a sprouted seed home to a child who is absent for a long time and compare the growth between the school plant and the home plant.

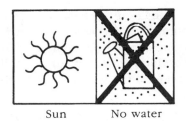 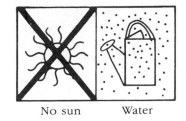 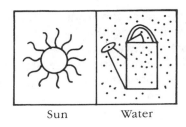

Sun   No water   No sun   Water   Sun   Water

Figure 21.9

Science: Large and Small Group

135   SCRAMBLED EGGS

GOALS   To make predictions; to improve cause-and-effect reasoning; to improve computer skills

OBJECTIVES   The child will scramble an egg and eat it. He will put the unbroken egg, the egg in the bowl, the beaten egg, and the scrambled egg in the right order.

MATERIALS   1 egg per child, cup, pepper, water, fork, electric fry pan, salt, teaspoon, spatula (metal)

PROCEDURE   Have a group of three or four children make scrambled eggs. At each stage of the procedure, have children predict what will happen. Allow each child to crack his or her own egg into a cup and stir it; add 1 teaspoon of water; stir; pour it into an electric fry pan; scramble it with the fork; put it on a plate with the spatula. Then eat it with the other children in the group. When they have finished, show them: an egg in the shell, an egg in a dish, an egg beaten in the dish, and a scrambled egg. Have the children put these different egg states in the correct sequence and discuss the differences among them and the effect of heat on the egg. Encourage children to look at the color of the yolk and see how the color changes as more air is beaten in. Have children beat with a fork or eggbeater, and whip it to see the differences in color and volume. Help them see the analogy of selecting a disk, putting it in the computer and booting the system.

INTEGRATION   Discuss the use of heat in cooking and what it does to different common foods. Encourage children to think about how the raw or unheated food is different from cooked food (bread–toast, potato–baked potato; raw carrots–cooked carrots).

Computers: Large Group

136   INPUT-OUTPUT

GOALS   To improve computer skills; to improve cause-and-effect reasoning; to improve generalization skills

OBJECTIVES   The child will state at least one input and one output.

MATERIALS   Chalkboard, chalk outline of a person

PROCEDURE   Talk with the children about how they learn information. For example, how did they decide what to wear today? If they looked outside and saw the sun was shining, that was visual *input*. If their mother told them what to wear, that was auditory *input*. That input went into their central processing unit (CPU), or brain. They all came with clothes on; that is *output*. Help children think about how they learn in terms of an *input-CPU-output* framework. Ask the children, "Who is absent today?"(input). The children look around, and in their CPU (brain), they compare who they see with their memory of who is in the class. They process the information. Then they decide that Danny is absent (output). Use the chalkboard to draw further illustrations for the children. Using a simple machine such as a drinking straw dispenser. Explain how pressing the lever is an *input,* the movement inside the

CPU causes the straw to fall, and the straw is the *output*. Or turn the handle of the Jack-in-the-box (input), something happens inside (CPU), Jack pops up (output). Encourage children to design their own processors based on the principle of input-CPU-output. Help them think of simple machines that work on this principle (soda and juice machines, jukeboxes). Now help children go a step further and think about the automatic teller at the bank and the computer at the fast-food restaurant. (*Note:* Tell children that they must put money in the bank before they can take it out!)

INTEGRATION   This is a basic introduction to the concepts of input-CPU-output, some basic computer terminology, and also good logical thinking. It is important for children to know that if they don't put anything in the computer, nothing will come out. They can use a software program, but somebody had to put all the information into the computer.

Computers: Small Group

137   ROBOT-CONTROLLER

GOALS   To improve computer skills; to improve cause-and-effect reasoning; to follow directions

OBJECTIVES   The child will give commands that can be carried out by the teacher or another child.

MATERIALS   None

PROCEDURE   Have one child be the controller of a robot and another (or the teacher) be the robot. The controller's job is to command the robot. The robot could initially work like a toggle switch (on or off). If the child says "Jump," the robot jumps until the child says "Stop jumping." When the teacher is the robot, he or she can lead the child into more complexity: "Shall the robot jump fast or slow?" "Shall the robot jump in place or around the room?" If the commands are unclear ("Robot walk"), send back a message: "That does not compute. Robot needs to know whether to walk forward or backward or sideways." The feedback will help children expand their vocabulary and become more specific in their speech, as well as gain practice giving commands. The children take turns so that they get practice in both commanding and following directions. The children need to learn the concept that the computer will not do anything unless they give the commands. They also need to learn that the commands must be specific and that some commands "will not compute," so they need to find ones that will. Then have children give two- and three-step commands at one time and increase the complexity of locational cues and numbers: "Take three steps to the right and then raise your hands and clap twice."

INTEGRATION   The robot-controller can be modified to work in any situation in which someone is in charge and teaching another what to do. You could have an animal trainer in the circus, a dog in (pet) obedience school, ground control to someone in a space capsule, a transportation maze where the navigator verbally, through remote control, steers the car (other child) through the roads, and so on. This activity is an excellent way for children to see the results of commands.

Computers: Individual or Small Group

138   BURIED TREASURE

GOALS   To improve computer skills; to improve generalization skills; to improve reading literacy

OBJECTIVES   The child will find the buried treasure on the first attempt.

MATERIALS   Large flat box with top, or sand table; sand, oatmeal, or rice; string or yarn; masking tape; 9 small treasures; clay; marker; cards with coordinates on one side and a drawing of the treasure in those coordinates on the other

PROCEDURE   Using four pieces of string, divide the box into nine equal segments (or start with two pieces of string and four segments). Tape the string so that it goes on top of the open box. In each segment, put a small piece of clay to keep the treasure from moving around, and stick the treasure in the clay. Add sand to the box, making sure the treasure stays in the designated segment. Divide the top of the box in the same way, using a marker to divide it into sections. Add a narrow section across the left

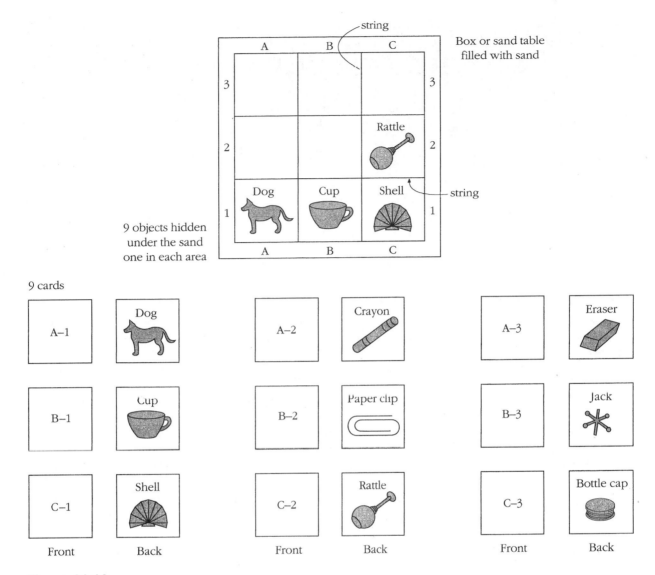

Figure 21.10

side and the bottom: put the numbers 1, 2, and 3 on the left side and A, B, and C on the bottom. Give the children a card with a set of coordinates (2-B) and see if they can find the right treasure. Draw a simple picture of the treasure on the back of the card so they can check themselves (see Figure 21.10). Have children predict what they will find. Then, have children find the treasures. Once they have the idea, bury the treasures and give them a drawing of the area marked off and have them chart the location of the treasures they found.

INTEGRATION   This activity helps children learn to move in a systematic way between vertical and horizontal planes, a skill that is necessary not only for the computer but for copying from the chalkboard. It also helps children learn to read the coordinates of a graph.

Computers: Individual

139   MY KEYBOARD

GOALS   To improve computer skills; to identify and understand patterns and relationships; to improve reading literacy

OBJECTIVES   The child will place the letters and numbers in the correct sequence and identify the function of the control keys.

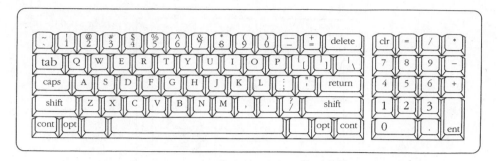

Figure 21.11

MATERIALS   Posterboard, keyboard markers, Velcro

PROCEDURE   Using the computer keyboard as a guide (see Figure 21.11), make a keyboard out of posterboard by using a large piece (12″ × 15″) for the base and smaller pieces (¾″ circles or squares) for the keys. Write the letters and numbers on the keys. Place four 15″ strips of Velcro across the base and attach Velcro to the back of each of the keys. Place the keys in a container and have the children place the keys on the keyboard in the correct order, using a keyboard as a guide. Add a guide strip with the letters or numbers for each row of the computer keyboard for the child. Making the keyboard is a difficult task in itself, but you might add some of the additional keys, such as the return, shift, control, alternate, and delete. Choose keys that are meaningful in the software packages you use.

Place the guide strip above the Velcro. At the beginning, have some of the letters in place so that the children only have to find three or four missing ones. Increase the number of missing letters until the children can place all the letters.

INTEGRATION   Whether or not your classroom has a computer, this activity provides a good foundation in computing and reading literacy. Use discarded keyboards to help children become familiar with the sequences.

Computers: Individual or Small Group

140   SPELL IT

GOALS   To improve computer skills; to identify and understand patterns and relationships; to improve reading literacy

OBJECTIVES   The child will "type" three words.

MATERIALS   Keyboard from My Keyboard with letters and numbers and guide strips in place, 3″ × 15″ posterboard with a 15″ long Velcro piece, basket with children's names printed on posterboard, basket with words printed on cards or posterboard

PROCEDURE   Have children find their name or a word they want to "type" and place it above the keyboard. The children can then take the letters off the keyboard and place them on the blank strip. Encourage children to replace the letters when they are finished. The guide strip is essential for this part of the process. Print words that children request and place them in the basket. Encourage children to work with a friend. As children get better, put short sentences on cards.

INTEGRATION   This activity does not require an actual computer (although having one available is great) and supports reading literacy skills.

141   FRUIT KABOB

GOALS   To improve computer skills; to identify and understand patterns and relationships; to improve reading literacy

OBJECTIVES   The child will make a fruit kabob following the rebus picture menu.

MATERIALS   Wooden skewers, cut-up apples, pineapple cubes, grapes, banana slice, picture menus

PROCEDURE   Design several rebus picture menus (these are pictures designed for nonreaders that resemble international road signs) using varying amounts of fruit (1 apple piece, 3 grapes, 2 pineapple cubes, 1 banana slice) on a skewer or a repeating pattern of fruit (1 apple piece, 1 pineapple cube, 1 grape, 1 apple piece, 1 pineapple cube, 1 grape, and so on; see Figure 21.12). Let children choose the menu they want and make it. Be sure to include a simple picture that uses a simple repeating pattern and with just two different fruits. They then eat the fruit kabob for snack.

Increase the complexity of some of the menus by having additional fruits and more difficult patterns. Have a word menu as an alternative for children who can read.

INTEGRATION   This activity gives children practice selecting from menus and interpreting rebus pictures. Use this procedure for adding fruit to a fruit salad or making trail mix and for other food projects.

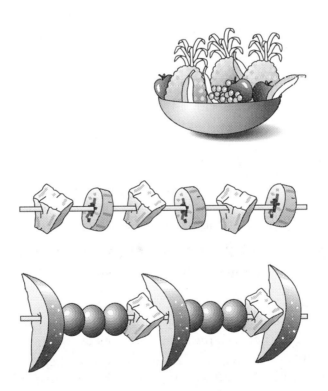

Figure 21.12

142   CEREAL BALLS

GOALS   To improve computer skills; to follow directions; to improve measurement concepts

OBJECTIVES   The child will make the cereal balls following the picture recipe.

Figure 21.13

MATERIALS Honey, measuring cups, peanut butter, large bowl, coconut, small bowl, cereal, mixing spoon

PROCEDURE Write the recipe on large paper (see Figure 21.13). Encourage children to take turns so that all children can participate. Or make this an individual activity by reducing the honey, peanut butter, coconut, and cereal to one tablespoon each and rolling it in ¼ cup of cereal at the end.

INTEGRATION Following sequential, multistep directions is an important computing skill. Using rebus pictures for illustration reinforces the concept as well. Use words that imply the sequence: "First we are going to measure the honey. Second . . . third . . ." *Note:* Be sure no children have allergies, as peanut butter is a common one.

Computers

143 ALPHABET KEYBOARD

GOALS To improve computer skills; to follow directions; to improve reading literacy

OBJECTIVES The child will connect the designated letters using a crayon or marker.

MATERIALS Pictures of the letters and numbers on the computer keyboard, a separate card for each letter of the alphabet and the numbers 0 to 9

PROCEDURE Let children draw their own numbers and letters to control the pace of the activity and match the letters before connecting them. Then, have someone read them after drawing them from a hat. Have the children draw lines between the letters and numbers with a crayon or marker.

INTEGRATION This is another off-computer activity that stresses keyboard skills. Children can connect the letters of their name. They can even color in the connecting shapes.

Computers: Individual or Small Group

144 COMPUTER BINGO

GOALS To improve computer skills; to follow directions; to improve reading literacy

OBJECTIVES The child will place a marker on the designated letters.

Computers are part of the learning environment. Children need to feel comfortable and competent with them from an early age.

MATERIALS   Pictures of the letters and numbers on the computer keyboard, cards with a number and letter designation:

1-Q	2-W	3-E	4-R	5-T to 0-P
1-A	2-S	3-D	4-F	5-G to 0-;

PROCEDURE   First, have children draw their own cards. Then, have the children place a marker on each letter as the caller reads the cards after drawing them from a hat.

INTEGRATION   This is another off-computer activity that stresses keyboard skills. Although structured like bingo, obviously all the children who follow the instructions accurately will "win."

Summary

Young children need a solid foundation in discovery activities. In addition to doing math activities, play math games while waiting or during transitions. Children can learn as much from activities that are fun as from those that seem "academic." The arithmetic problems that we so commonly associate with school are a formalization of experiences that relate to numbers, geometry, measurement, time, and money.

Many activities in this area require two days or more. The second time the materials are out, some children will continue to explore the materials; others will need more structure to expand their explorations. It is important that children view science as part of their world and that they see the cause-and-effect relationships rather than "teacher magic."

Computers have tremendous potential for positive change for children with disabilities. They need adult scaffolding to make the system work. The educator's role is to help children see computers as a natural part of every-day life and to help them develop the skills to use them.

Educational Resources

Children's Software Revue
http://www.micorweb.com/pepsite/revue /revue.html
   Provides timely, accurate, and objective information about children's software and access to many reviews of the software.

Cool School Tools!
http://www.bham.lib.al.us/cooltools/
   An index to the World Wide Web and other Internet resources for Kindergarten through twelfth grade.

Davidson, J. I. (1990). *Children and computers together in the early childhood classroom.* Albany, NY: Delmar Publishers, Inc.
   Helpful information about including computers in the early childhood classroom in a developmentally appropriate way. Good ideas for on-and-off computer learning.

Frank Potter's Science Gems
http://www-sci.lib.uci.edu/SEP/SEP.html
   Provides science lesson plans for educators and links to other sources of lesson plans.

Haugland, S. W., & Wright, J. L. (1997). *Young children and technology: A world of discovery.* Boston, MA: Allyn & Bacon.
   Provides information on choosing software for young children as well as information on new computers and technological advances.

K–12 Science Lesson Plans
http://www.sci.lib.uci.edu/SEP/SEP/html
   More science lesson plans.

National Geographic
http://www.nationalgeographic.com
   A resource for teachers and children, this site is interesting and constantly updated.

Science Museum
http://www.sci.mus.mn.us
   A child friendly, hands-on virtual science museum.

Smithsonian Institution
http://www.si.edu/organiza/start.htm
   Describes exhibits and has places to visit virtually and in person.

Surf School
http://zdnet.com/yil/filters/surfjump.html
   For teachers who are not confident of their computer skills, an easy way to get current.

Thompson, I. (Ed.). (1997). *Teaching and learning early numbers.* Philadelphia, PA: Open Press.
   Includes information on emergent mathematics and how children think mathematically.

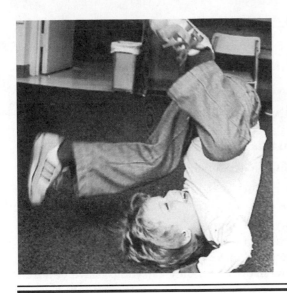

Chapter 22

DEVELOPMENTAL PHYSICAL EDUCATION AND SENSORIMOTOR ACTIVITIES: LARGE MOTOR, SMALL MOTOR, AND SENSORIMOTOR INTEGRATION

Having adequate motor abilities is important for young children. They learn from the sensations acquired through movement. The acquisition of new sensations occurs through active participation in the environment. Because children with diverse abilities, like others, spend increasing amounts of time watching television, they may need encouragement and support to develop necessary motor skills. They need to participate in activities that expose their muscles to demanding tasks. We must resist the temptation to do too many things for children with diverse abilities and must allow them to participate in enough resistance and power activities to develop strength.

TABLE 22.1 ACTIVITY GOALS AND REFERENCE NUMBERS

Goals	Activities
To improve locomotor skills	143, 144, 145, 146, 149, 150, 154
To improve gross motor manipulative skills	148, 152, 153, 155, 156, 168, 169
To improve stability skills	147, 151, 154, 166, 169, 170
To improve physical fitness	143, 145, 149, 150, 154, 155, 156
To improve sensorimotor integration	144, 147, 148, 151, 157, 165, 166, 167, 168, 170, 171, 172, 173, 174, 175
To improve motor planning	144, 145, 146, 147, 148, 149, 152, 155, 156, 165, 166, 167, 168
To increase body awareness	150, 151, 167, 171
To improve fine motor manipulative skills	157, 158, 159, 160, 162, 163, 164, 173
To improve eye-hand coordination	152, 153, 160, 161, 163, 174
To improve adaptive skills	158, 159, 160, 162, 163,
To improve number sense and numeration	161, 164
To identify and understand patterns and relationships	163, 164, 174
To improve estimation skills	143, 146
To improve classification skills	175
To make predictions	153
To increase inclusion	161, 162, 165
To improve self-concept	162
To improve tactile skills	157, 172, 173, 175
To improve listening skills	170
To increase vocabulary	158, 159, 169, 172
To follow directions	171

143   VARIATIONS ON JUMPING

GOALS   To improve locomotor skills; to improve physical fitness; to improve estimation skills

OBJECTIVES   The child will jump for distance, for height, and from height, and estimate the distance and height of jumps.

MATERIALS   None

PROCEDURE   Have the children participate in various styles of jumping. Begin with the easier jumps and support all attempts. Keep the activity short, as it is easy for children to become fatigued. Encourage children to think about the names of some of the jumps and make up new names with a rationale. Have them estimate how long, how high, how far, and how many times they can jump. Have children work in pairs so one can check the estimate. Help children write down this information and then graph it. Put the graph in their portfolio. Encourage them to repeat this activity after several weeks and compare their results.

Pairs jumping: One child faces another and they hold hands; they jump together to the count of 10.

Line jumping: Children jump forward and backward over an imaginary line a specified number of times.

Stair jumping: Children jump from a step to a line on the floor.

Long jump: Children jump forward for a distance from standing position.

Snake jump: Children crouch in squat position and jump up as far as possible.

Kangaroo jump: With feet together, elbows bent, and hands away from body, children do knee bends and jump.

Rabbit jump: Children squat low on heels, palms down and fingers pointing forward, and simulate a rabbit jumping with feet coming forward between hands.

Mattress jump: Use partially filled air mattress; children jump forward and backward without falling. For additional safety, put mattress on a 5′ × 8′ rug with adult spotters.

Jumping jacks: Start with feet together and arms by side; jump so that feet go to each side and arms come up to shoulder height, then jump and return to starting position.

INTEGRATION   Children like to see personal improvement, and by graphing their jumping, they can look at their personal growth as well as have a base from which to estimate when they do the activity a second time.

144   VARIATIONS ON CREEPING AND CRAWLING

GOALS   To improve locomotor skills; to improve sensorimotor integration; to improve motor planning

OBJECTIVES   The child will creep and crawl forward and backward for distance and time.

MATERIALS   Yarn, boxes, barrels, chairs, hula hoops, beanbag chair, carpet squares, welcome mats, bubble packing, blindfold, seesaw, balance board

PROCEDURE   Have the children participate in various types of creeping and crawling activities. Initially, focus on the movement control and coordination then begin with the easier variations for short distances. Encourage children to describe what they feel or predict what will happen next as they proceed. Have children experiment with different techniques of creeping and crawling and encourage children to think up their own variations.

Turtle crawl: Have children creep on their hands and knees with a small beanbag chair on top of the child (the chair looks like a shell over the child). Have children pick a destination when they begin.

Texture crawl: Blindfold children; have them crawl on a path of different textures (carpet squares, welcome mats, bubble packing, etc.).

Snake crawl: Slither with stomach on floor forward and backward using only arms to pull.

Obstacle course: Creep through a course made of boxes or chairs, barrels, boards, and so on.

Yarn trail: Following yarn trails, creep and have someone keep time for each child. Write the time down and have the child decide to do it faster or slower the second time.

Seesaw: Crawl up one side of a seesaw board, maintain balance as board tips down, and then crawl down the board to the ground (be sure to have an adult as a spotter).

Balance board: Crawl forward and backward on a board propped between two blocks.

INTEGRATION   Discuss with children when creeping or crawling might be a useful way to move. Include information related to safety issues such as smoke or fire, gunshots, and if they are trying to move silently and hide. *Note:* In crawling, the stomach touches the ground; in creeping, it is off the ground.

Large Motor: Small Group

145   VARIATIONS ON RUNNING

GOALS   To improve locomotion skills; to improve physical fitness; to improve motor planning

OBJECTIVES   The child will run for distance, varying speeds, and in response to signals.

MATERIALS   Tape, yarn, rope, cones, string

PROCEDURE   Have the children run and try some of the following variations. Initially, keep the length of time and distance children run short and make few variations. Focus on the quality of the child's movement and make individualized suggestions to increase efficiency and coordination. Use variations to motivate children to refine skills as well as build endurance. As children run for longer distances, have them stretch to warm up and walk to cool down. Encourage children to challenge their limits. Repeat an activity and see if they can run faster, slower, and so on. Videotape children and discuss variation differences.

Run slowly; run quickly.

Run and stop on a signal; change direction on the signal; change from running to walking on a signal.

Run as quietly as possible; as noisily as possible; as lightly as possible; as heavily as possible.

Run, walk, run; repeat.

Run slowly and talk to a friend.

Run on a designated path.

Run the variations in pairs, with one child running blindfolded.

Use roller blades, a scooter, or wheelchair to do the course.

INTEGRATION   Encourage children to think about the relationship between speed and endurance and help them decide which is the more important in various situations.

146   OBSTACLE COURSE

GOALS   To improve locomotor skills; to improve motor planning; to improve estimation skills

OBJECTIVES   The child will discuss ways of moving through the obstacle course, estimate how long it will take, and then complete the course.

MATERIALS   Barrels, boxes, boards, chairs, hoops, balance beam

PROCEDURE   Set up an obstacle course (inside or outside) that requires a variety of movement skills and is long enough so several children can participate at the same time. Use obstacles that require children to move over, under, around, and through them. Encourage children to explore the course and talk about it and how they plan to move through the obstacles. Encourage children to watch another child go through the course, pointing out the strategies that child uses. Walk beside children and, if necessary, coach them. As children's proficiency increases, have them go through the course using different movements or blindfolded. Give them more complex activities to do such as picking up a beanbag or walking through a hoop while on the balance beam. Add music to determine the pace of movement. Have them time their trip through the course and estimate their completion time (it's not a race, it's a prediction). Provide auditory cues for children who are blindfolded or visually impaired to help them locate themselves on the course. A rope might also function as a guide. Encourage children to work out adaptations to include scooters and wheelchairs and to try them and decide if they are easier or more difficult.

INTEGRATION   Children have the opportunity to learn about their body and spatial relationships as well as the words for their movements and the shapes of what they are navigating over, under, around, or through.

147   VARIATIONS ON BALANCING

GOALS   To improve stability skills; to improve sensorimotor integration; to improve motor planning

OBJECTIVES   The child will walk the length of the balance beam independently, following the directions given.

MATERIALS   Tape; balance beams: 6″ and 4″ wide, 6″ off the ground

PROCEDURE   Dynamic balance is an important skill for children. Begin by using lines 6″ wide taped on the floor or taping lines 2′ apart and having the children perform the tasks in a scooter or wheelchair. Use a balance beam that is 6″ wide, then 4″. Move the 4″ beam higher off the floor so that you can add 1′ dips. Have children walk across the beam in the following ways:

Walk forward, backward, sideways.

Walk forward, turning at each end.

Walk holding an object (for example, short pole) in hands.

Walk touching heel against toe.

Walk forward and backward without looking at feet.

Walk to the middle and touch the board with hand, then knee.

Walk to the middle and pick up a small object.

Walk to the middle and catch a ball.

Walk over a small object on the balance beam.

INTEGRATION   Learning about oneself in a confined area is valuable. Children redefine straight and narrow and may look at activities they considered easy from a new perspective.

148   VARIATIONS ON DRIBBLING

GOALS   To improve gross motor manipulative skills; to improve sensorimotor integration; to improve motor planning

OBJECTIVES   The child will dribble the ball for height and speed, using each hand in a variety of ways.

MATERIALS   8″ or 10″ balls

PROCEDURE   Begin by having children bounce and catch the ball each time, then do one dribble and catch the ball. Dribbling develops control and coordination. Practice and variations develop consistency, which then allows the skill to be combined with other skills to play games.

Dribble the ball several times and then pass it to someone else.

Dribble the ball while walking, then while running.

Dribble the ball low, high, at waist height.

Dribble the ball with right hand, left hand, alternating hands.

Dribble the ball fast and slow.

INTEGRATION   While children are dribbling, teach spatial references such as fast and slow, high and low, left and right, and so on.

149   VARIATIONS ON JUMPING ROPE

GOALS   To improve locomotor skills; to improve physical fitness; to improve motor planning

OBJECTIVES   The child will jump over the rope for height and timing, with both feet and alternating feet.

MATERIALS   Jump rope 12–15′ long for 2–4 children

PROCEDURE   Rope jumping is difficult for young children. Initially, move the rope slowly to give children more time to react. Alert them verbally to jump as the rope approaches. Turn the rope faster, encourage children to jump for longer times, or have them jump to music. Teach children traditional rhymes to chant as they jump.

Rope line: Children jump from side to side over length of rope, forward then backward.

High water: Two children hold a rope between them (loosely in hands). The third child attempts to jump over the rope forward, backward, sideways, and at progressive heights.

Snake: Two children hold a rope between them (loosely in hands) and move it back and forth on the floor like a snake. The third child attempts to jump over the rope. (Moved vertically, it resembles waves.)

Swing jump: Two children hold a rope between them and swing it back and forth. The third child jumps over the rope. When a child can do this successfully, turn the rope overhead.

Circle: Teacher or child is in the middle of a circle and turns with the rope so that each child must jump as it passes.

Run: Two children turn the rope between them and a third child tries to run through without the rope's touching him or her.

Individual jump rope: A child turns the rope overhead and jumps with both feet, alternating feet, faster and slower.

Rope jumping requires both physical stamina and sensorimotor integration.

INTEGRATION   Talk about the professional sports that require athletes to jump rope (those who play football, tennis, box, and others). Help children think about why they do this (footwork, endurance, discipline).

Large Motor: Small Group

150   VARIATIONS ON HOPPING

GOALS   To improve locomotor skills; to improve physical fitness; to increase body awareness

OBJECTIVES   The child will hop on each foot for height, distance, and time.

MATERIALS   Hopping stones made of tiles or carpet squares

PROCEDURE   Hopping is challenging for young children. Hold the child's hand while he hops. Help the child count the number of hops he or she can make without putting down the other foot. For older children, try more complex variations. Play hopping games on patterns of tiles: The children hop on the tiles in an obstacle course fashion according to your directions. Play hopscotch.

Hop on left foot; right foot.

Hop as quietly as they can; as noisily as they can.

Hop as high as they can; as low as they can.

Hop as far as they can on their left foot; on their right foot.

Hop in one direction as far as they can on one foot, and see if they can hop back on their other foot.

Hop and change feet.

Hop with a partner.

Hop as long as they can (time it, record it, and compare it to the next time).

INTEGRATION   Hopping is a basic locomotor skill that is part of many games. As children gain proficiency, combine hopping with other skills and use them in games.

Large Motor: Small Group

151   VARIATIONS ON BODY ROLLING

GOALS   To improve stability skills; to improve sensorimotor integration; to increase body awareness

OBJECTIVES   The child will roll with hands overhead and then by sides in each direction.

MATERIALS   Beach towel; ball

PROCEDURE   Have the children participate in various types of rolling activities. If children are having trouble coordinating their roll, give them a gentle push on their hip or shoulder. Discuss when rolling might be a useful way to move.

Log roll: Hands extended over the head, feet together.

Ball roll: Hands extended over the head, feet clasping ball.

Torpedo roll: Hands at sides of body.

Windmill roll: One hand above head, one at side.

Towel roll: Start at one end of a beach towel and roll up into it, then reverse and roll out.

Circle roll: Roll in circles while someone holds their ankles.

Downhill roll: Roll down a hill or incline.

Stop, drop, and roll: Combine these three skills.

INTEGRATION   Encourage children to make up variations that include walking, running, hopping, rolling, and so on. There is also a safety aspect to rolling. Talk about fires and Stop, Drop, and Roll. *Note:* These rolls are good for rainy days or as outdoor activities on the grass. Be sure to clear the area of rocks or other potentially harmful objects.

Large Motor: Small Group

152   TARGET BOUNCE

GOALS   To improve gross motor manipulative skills; to improve motor planning; to improve eye-hand coordination

OBJECTIVES The child will bounce the ball on the target. When the ball misses the target, the child will analyze her mistakes and state a different strategy.

MATERIALS Tape, 8″ or 10″ ball

PROCEDURE Tape a target on the floor, large at first (3′ square). Have the children see how often they can hit the target and have their partner catch the ball. Have the children stand about 3′ on either side of the target and bounce the ball to each other, hitting the target with the ball. Encourage children to use both overhand and underhand techniques to hit the target. Establish a rhythm to the bouncing by singing a song. For variation, have children sit in chairs and play. After a number of successful bounces, have them move the chair back 6″. As children become more proficient or have problems, modify the size and weight of the ball and target.

Have children count how often they can catch the ball and/or hit the target. Use a ball that has a bell inside and see if children can catch and throw the ball accurately blindfolded.

INTEGRATION Many games use throwing and catching skills. Help children develop upper body strength and skill to use in games and in combination with other skills.

Large Motor: Small Group

153 VARIATIONS ON THROWING

GOALS To improve gross motor manipulative skills; to improve eye-hand coordination; to make predictions

OBJECTIVES The child will throw different balls for height, distance, and accuracy, and discuss the strategy used.

MATERIALS 8″ or 10″ ball, tennis ball, Nerf ball, beach ball, 15″–24″ wastebasket, hula hoop, cans of varying sizes

PROCEDURE Have the children participate in various types of ball-throwing activities. Discuss the differences in skills required to throw large and small balls. An underinflated beach ball doesn't go far but works well for younger children. Have children measure the distances they throw and make a graph, or count the number of times they can throw and catch a ball with another child. Have children stand increasing distances away from a target or partner as they improve. Have the children try the following variations:

Throw the ball as high as they can.

Throw the ball as low as they can without hitting the ground.

Throw the ball as far as they can.

Throw the ball softly to another child.

Throw the ball in a high arc to another child.

Throw the ball into a round wastebasket from 2′ to 5′ away.

Throw the ball through a hula hoop from varying distances.

Throw the ball at a target of stacked cans.

Encourage children to roll or toss balls as soon as they are able. This helps develop the fine motor skills of releasing and grasping that are necessary for writing and skills of daily living.

INTEGRATION   Encourage children to play ball-throwing games with others so they practice both throwing and catching. Have some balls available with bells inside. *Note:* These activities are most easily done outside.

Large Motor: Individual

154   FITNESS COURSE

GOALS   To improve physical fitness; to improve locomotor skills; to improve stability skills

OBJECTIVES   The child will perform the designated number of exercises at each station.

MATERIALS   Cards with a picture of the exercise to be done and cards with numbers of repetitions:

5 bent knee sit-ups	10 knee lifts
4 toe touches	count to 15 running in place
3 push-ups	10 double leg jumps

PROCEDURE   Place cards around the room or an outside area and have children go to each area and perform the activity. Vary the activities and the number of repetitions to meet the needs of the children. Coach some children as they perform the activities, and modify activities to meet the needs of the child. Increase the number of activities, the number of repetitions, or choose more difficult activities for more advanced children.

INTEGRATION   Talk with children about the role of the coach and what a coach does. Encourage children to think about physical fitness as part of their lifestyle. Have children keep a fitness log so they can see how frequently they "work out."

Large Motor: Small Group

155   BADMINTON

GOALS   To improve gross motor manipulative skills; to increase physical fitness; to improve motor planning

OBJECTIVES   The child will hit the ball or bird over the net with the racket with increasing accuracy.

MATERIALS   Balls, birdie, badminton rackets, string or net

PROCEDURE   Have children hit Wiffle balls or yarn balls with another child. As they become more proficient, add a net or string and use a birdie instead of the balls. Help them make predictions about how far or how often they can hit the ball. Explore the causal relationships among how hard they swing, the angle of the racket, and where the ball goes. Help them swing overhand for high shots and underhand for low ones.

INTEGRATION   Badminton can be played indoors or outdoors (if not windy). It requires skill but not strength. Children can play sitting as well as standing. Although children may eventually play competitive games using tools such as bats and rackets, it is useful to learn the skills early in a noncompetitive atmosphere.

Large Motor: Large Group

156   CIRCLE BALL

GOALS   To increase physical fitness; to improve gross motor manipulative skills; to improve motor planning

OBJECTIVES   The child will hit the ball with hands or feet.

MATERIALS   8″ to 12″ ball

PROCEDURE   Initially, place the children in a circle sitting on their bottoms, using both feet to hit the ball to someone. As they understand the game, have them move onto their stomachs, facing the inside of the circle. The children roll the ball to each other using two hands. As they tire, have them hit the ball with only one hand. The objective is accuracy, not force. This activity strengthens the muscles of the upper back.

INTEGRATION   Children will increase their body awareness as they realize that some positions make tasks more difficult. Encourage children to think up variations, such as standing and kicking the ball, bouncing it, tossing it to a child while calling the child's name, and so on. Be sure the variations children decide on include all the children. Circle games are noncompetitive and allow all children to be part of the group.

Small Motor: Individual

157   BUTTONS

GOALS   To improve fine motor manipulative skills; to improve sensorimotor integration; to improve tactile skills

OBJECTIVES   The child will identify the objects and pair them by touch.

MATERIALS   12 pairs of buttons (with tactile differences), a bowl or bag, an egg carton or ice cube tray, a blindfold

PROCEDURE   Collect pairs of buttons that feel different from each other. Put one button of each pair in an egg carton or ice cube tray section and put the other in a bowl or bag. Initially, choose buttons that are larger and more dissimilar. Allow children to match the buttons visually before doing so by touch. Then, have the children match up the pairs while blindfolded. (If children don't like blindfolds, put the buttons in a bag and have the child decide which button it matches before looking at it.) As they become proficient, use smaller, more similar buttons.

INTEGRATION   This procedure can be used with fabric, textured wallpaper discs, or small objects. We often neglect to isolate the tactile sense, and it provides children with a lot of feedback if they fine-tune this sense.

Small Motor: Small Group

158   PROGRESSIVE DRESS-UP

GOALS   To improve fine motor manipulative skills; to improve adaptive skills; to improve vocabulary

OBJECTIVES   The child will put on the various parts of clothing and describe what he is wearing.

MATERIALS   Adult clothing: sweaters, sweatshirts, pants, shirts, skirts, shorts, dresses, socks, shoes

PROCEDURE   Divide the clothing into three piles: tops, bottoms, and footwear. Put the piles in three different places. Have the children walk, jump, or skip to each pile, find and put on that article of clothing, and then go on to the next pile until they are "dressed." Then have each child describe his outfit. Include some oversized clothing without buttons and with cut-off sleeves, as well as clothing that is closer to the children's actual size. Add accessories such as gloves, ties, scarves, and hats. Have children dress for a particular occasion, particular weather, or a particular profession, and discuss why they chose those clothes.

INTEGRATION   Help children focus on aspects of clothing that make it more or less difficult to put on, to think about how clothing for young children is different from that for older individuals, and how some clothing is adapted for individuals with disabilities and why this is done. Encourage children to experiment with these ideas.

159   TOOLS

GOALS   To improve fine motor manipulative skills; to improve adaptive skills; to improve vocabulary

OBJECTIVES   The child will pick up small objects using tools, name the tools, and discuss the characteristics of the tools that make them easy or difficult to use.

MATERIALS   Tub with rice, small and tiny objects, chopsticks, spatula, spaghetti spoon, pierced serving spoons, tongs, tweezers, needle-nose pliers, magnifying glass

PROCEDURE   Place small objects in the tub with rice and have children use their hands to find the objects. Then add the spoon and finally more complex tools. Now have the child retrieve the objects using different tools. Then have children pick up very tiny objects using the tweezers. Once these objects have been picked up, encourage children to explore them under a magnifying glass, turning them with tweezers. (Don't make objects so small that they get lost in the rice.) When children find them, encourage the children to describe and classify the objects and tools.

INTEGRATION   Children need practice using many different tools.

160   LOCK BOX

GOALS   To improve fine motor manipulative skills; to improve eye-hand coordination; to improve adaptive skills

OBJECTIVES   The child will open all the locks or follow other procedures to open the box or demonstrate all the functions.

MATERIALS   A busy box (see Figure 22.1)

PROCEDURE   Buy or make a variety of busy boxes. All require fine motor skills, but some teach more needed skills and are more intriguing than others. Start with a busy box that requires little skill so children learn the concept. Then choose or make more difficult busy boxes. Our most successful one was a "lock box." It had a variety of locks and keys (attached by 9″ strings so they don't get lost).

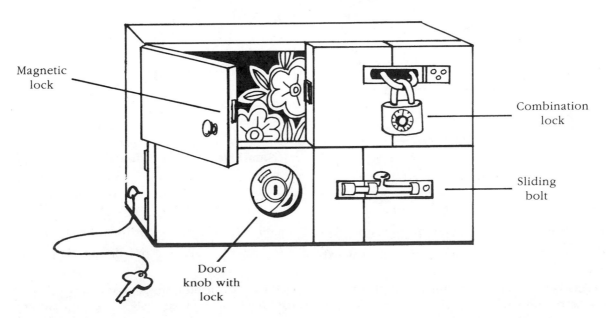

Magnetic lock

Combination lock

Sliding bolt

Door knob with lock

Figure 22.1

The combination lock was challenging. Place pictures inside the doors for children to see. Request that children open the locks in a specific order or time them to see how quickly they can open all the locks.

INTEGRATION   After using the lock box, talk with children about the purpose of locks, from the perspective of both privacy and safety. Talk about when to unlock doors and when not to. Talk about locks on car doors. Talk about how locks might keep you safe. Also talk about getting locked in a place like a bathroom and how you might be able to get out of locked places if you had a key; discuss how someone might get the key to them.

Small Motor: Small Group

161   GAME BOARD

GOALS   To improve eye-hand coordination; to increase inclusion; to improve number sense and numeration

OBJECTIVES   The child will help make a game board, determine the rules for the game, and play the game with others.

MATERIALS   A cookie sheet or jellyroll pan, magnets, string or 20–30 straws, paper plates, glue, felt dots, black construction paper, brads

PROCEDURE   Have the children help make the game board (see Figure 22.2): Glue the string and/or straws to the pan in a ladderlike track. Add environmental cues to support the theme. Make a spinner out of a paper plate; use felt dots to signify the number of spaces to move. Use an arrow attached by a brad as the pointer. Use magnets as markers. *Note:* Children can make a variety of games in this way.

As children learn to play board games, focus on the prosocial behaviors of taking turns and playing a game with rules. As they understand basic rules, help children decide on and write the rules for their game. Have children try to play the game blindfolded. Discuss how this impacts the rules, if at all.

INTEGRATION   Children enjoy and learn a lot from playing games. Having them make the board themselves and make up the rules gives them a different perspective. The tactile cues allow children to feel the game board.

Figure 22.2

Small Motor: Individual or Small Group

162   MY PUZZLE

GOALS   To improve fine motor manipulative skills; to increase inclusion; to improve self-concept

OBJECTIVES   The child will pose for an individual and group picture and put the puzzle picture together.

MATERIALS   An 8″ × 10″ full-length picture of each child and the group, scissors or jigsaw

Take pictures of all the children in class doing something they enjoy as well as a group picture. Keep a small picture for a class collage. Have an 8″ × 10″ enlargement of each child made. Laminate it or cover it with clear contact paper and glue it to heavy cardboard. Draw lines on the back and cut it with heavy scissors or a jigsaw. No matter how you cut it, it will fit back together. (Put the child's initials on each piece so the children can put the puzzles back together if they get mixed up. Number the pieces of the group puzzle.)

PROCEDURE   Encourage children to put the puzzles together in small groups and discuss how they are each similar and different and what each child enjoys doing. Have several different puzzles of the group and encourage children to name others in the group and talk about what each likes to do.

INTEGRATION   This activity can also be done with children's drawings, or you can buy blank puzzles that are already cut and have children draw on them. These often have many pieces, however.

Small Motor: Individual

163   CATERPILLARS

GOALS   To improve fine motor manipulative skills; to improve adaptive skills; to identify and understand patterns and relationships

OBJECTIVES   The child will construct a caterpillar by following a designated pattern and verbally describe the sequence.

MATERIALS   2″ square fabric pieces of different colors and/or textures, with a button on one end and a buttonhole on the other

Decide on the shape (or shapes) you want to use and cut them out of different fabrics (felt, leather, velvet, wool, terry cloth). Put a button on one end and a buttonhole on the other (see Figure 22.3). Finish the edges so they don't ravel. (Felt is good because it doesn't need finishing and you can make a slit for the buttonhole.)

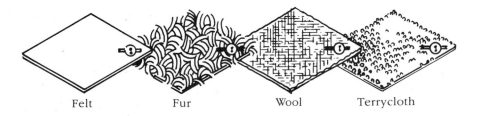

Felt   Fur   Wool   Terrycloth

Figure 22.3

PROCEDURE   Initially, let children just practice buttoning or fastening the material together, then use a short sequence with only two materials (e.g., fur, felt, fur, felt). If some children find the buttoning difficult, use Velcro instead of buttons. As children understand the concept of patterns, button the materials together in a sequence to make a caterpillar and have the children copy it. Increase the length and complexity of the caterpillar by varying both color and texture in the pattern (see Figure 22.4). If you want to emphasize the adaptive aspect of the activity, use hooks and eyes, snaps, and other closures as well as varying the size of the buttons used.

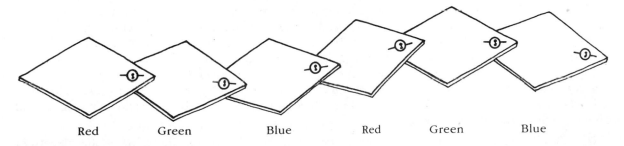

Red   Green   Blue   Red   Green   Blue

Figure 22.4

INTEGRATION   This activity provides good tactile feedback for children as well as some essential reading readiness and math skills.

Small Motor: Small Group

164   PLAYDOUGH BEADS

GOALS   To improve fine motor manipulative skills; to identify and understand patterns and relationships; to improve number sense and numeration

OBJECTIVES   The child will make a bead necklace with a repeating pattern, describe the pattern, and count the number of beads.

MATERIALS   1 cup cornstarch, 2 cups baking soda, 1½ cups water (food coloring can be added if desired), yarn for stringing

Mix ingredients. Cook until mixture looks like mashed potatoes and begins to form clumps. Turn onto a plate and cool. Knead when cool. Roll into a "snake" and cut off pieces (be sure these are large enough to allow for a hole) or roll out flat and cut into shapes with kitchen knife or small cookie cutters. Make holes for stringing by inserting a cut-off straw in each piece. Dry in sun or heat oven to warm. Turn oven off, then put beads in to dry. Flip over to dry other side. (The drying process may take a day or two.)

PROCEDURE   Have children color the beads with watercolor markers if they have not yet been colored. Provide yarn for stringing. (Taping one end of the string or dipping it in glue and allowing the glue to harden makes stringing easier.) Have children color and string only one kind of bead or make a simple pattern on the table before stinging the beads. Encourage children to design repeating patterns that have two or more beads. Encourage them to count the number of patterns and to make more complex ones.

INTEGRATION   Children can solidify concepts from math and science while sharing an experience with others.

Sensorimotor Integration: Small Group

165   HAND CLAPPING

GOALS   To improve sensorimotor integration; to improve motor planning; to increase inclusion

OBJECTIVES   The child will duplicate the designated clapping patterns in a small group and with a partner.

MATERIALS   Record, cassette, or CD player; record, cassette, or CD

PROCEDURE   Have children clap slow and fast, loud and soft, and then to a rhythm as they master the coordination necessary to clap patterns consistently. When children can predictably do this, progress to a two-step sequence: clap hands, clap thighs, clap hands, clap thighs. (You can choose other body parts such as head, feet, shoulders.) Now make the pattern itself more difficult: clap hands twice, clap thighs twice, repeat. Or do it three or four times. Another variation is to have the children clap hands and then clap their left thigh with their right hand, clap hands, clap their right thigh with their left hand. (The objective is to cross the midline of the body, not to be concerned about right and left.) Have children try clapping hands with a partner, repeating the patterns given for individual clapping. These are ordered in increasing levels of difficulty; that is, start clapping your own hands, clap partner's hands, clap your own hands, and so on. The most difficult pattern is clapping the partner's right hand with your right hand and vice versa.

INTEGRATION   Many traditional children's songs and games are enhanced by higher levels of clapping.

166   BALANCE IT

GOALS   To improve sensorimotor integration; to improve stability skills; to improve motor planning

OBJECTIVES   The child will balance the beanbag on the body part requested and participate in the designated physical activity for the allocated time period.

MATERIALS   Beanbags, books, paper plates, paint brushes, feathers, crayons, plastic drinking glasses

PROCEDURE   Have children balance a beanbag on their head. Encourage them to stand up and sit down, walk fast and slow while balancing it. Give children feedback about their posture and guidance about how to move to make balancing easier. Then have them balance the beanbags using other body parts: shoulders, elbow, knee, foot. Have them get down on the floor, feet in the air, and balance it on the bottom of one foot and then catch it.

Encourage children to experiment with balancing a variety of objects and have them predict how long they can balance each object, or whether or not they can sit down and stand up twice without its falling off.

INTEGRATION   These activities require both static and dynamic balance and concentration.

167   MIRRORING

GOALS   To improve sensorimotor integration; to improve motor planning; to increase body awareness

OBJECTIVES   The child will both initiate and follow (mirror) the movement with a partner.

MATERIALS   String

PROCEDURE   Have the children work in pairs facing each other. (Choose carefully the children you match.) Have one child start as the initiator of the movement; this is easier. Encourage the children to use slow, simple movements. Tell them to pretend they are looking in a mirror. One child initiates a movement, and the other child mirrors it. As the children become more skillful, the movements can be faster and more subtle (such as facial movements). This can be done to music. Blindfold one child and have them touch hands gently while they move together. Tie a 12″ string between the children's wrists and have them move gently to respond to the pressure on the string.

INTEGRATION   Mirroring requires the child to look at another child, not his or her own body, to figure out what to do. It requires a child to "read" and respond to another child's body language.

168   VARIATIONS ON TOSSING

GOALS   To improve sensorimotor integration; to improve motor planning; to improve gross motor manipulative skills

OBJECTIVES   The child will increase the accuracy of her tossing through practice and the self-analysis of errors.

MATERIALS   beanbag, tennis ball, Ping-Pong ball, sponges, small rubber ball, rubber rings, horseshoes, Wiffle ball, crumpled paper, cups, targets, milk cartons, Velcro-covered Ping-Pong ball

PROCEDURE   Have the children participate in the various types of tossing activities listed below. Discuss how the activity feels, where they can safely throw objects and where they shouldn't, and which objects are harder to throw and which are easier. Encourage children to analyze their misses and to verbalize how to increase the accuracy of their tossing. Begin with short distances and large targets, and make the object being tossed one of the bigger and heavier options. Be sure to assign retrievers who take turns with the children tossing, and be aware of safety needs all the time. These activities are good both indoors and outdoors depending on the objects you use.

Texture ball toss: Use a sponge or texture ball (Wiffle ball). The children begin with underhand tossing to a person close by. Gradually extend the distance and use overhand throwing.

Basketball toss: Use a shoe box with the bottom removed. Tape it to the wall for an indoor game. Toss a tennis ball.

Dodge ball: Divide the class into teams and play dodge ball.

Ring toss: A variation of horseshoes with rubber rings, this game requires a different set of tossing skills.

Beanbag toss: Toss beanbags through large holes in a target or into empty coffee cans.

Paper toss: Crumple paper into balls and toss them into a wastebasket.

Tennis ball toss: Toss the tennis ball so it bounces once between two children; help children to cup hands together to catch the ball if it is low.

Milk carton toss: Use plastic milk cartons stacked in pyramids. Knock the structure down with a tennis ball.

Bucket toss: Use a bucket or wastebasket for catching balls. First set it on the floor, then raise it on a chair or box.

Empty box throw: Place a bottomless cardboard box on its side on the ground or on a chair. The object is to toss a ball through the box without hitting the sides.

Tennis toss-back: Throw a tennis ball against a brick or cement wall and catch it before it bounces (an outside activity on a wall without windows).

Target toss: Use the Velcro-covered Ping-Pong ball and toss it at a target with Velcro pieces attached. Vary the distance from the target and the size of the target.

Sponge toss: Make a cardboard target with holes of various sizes, or see if they can throw the sponges through suspended hula hoops. On a hot day, you might throw wet sponges.

Ping-Pong ball toss: Have children stand arm's length apart, toss a Ping-Pong ball, and catch it in a plastic or paper cup.

INTEGRATION   Children can chart their accuracy in tossing. They will probably need your help in setting up the chart, as there are a variety of variables (distance, target, object).

Sensorimotor Integration: Small Group

169   FOAM

GOALS   To improve stability skills; to improve gross motor manipulative skills; to increase vocabulary

OBJECTIVES   The child will perform the designated activities and describe how performing them on the foam differs from performing them on the floor.

MATERIALS   A piece of 4"- or 5"-thick foam or mattress

PROCEDURE   Put the foam on the floor in the center of a piece of carpet. Initially, have children perform only simple tasks such as walking across the foam and offer to hold the child's hand. Then have children walk, roll, jump, and so forth on the foam. Encourage them to experiment by doing these activities on the floor and then on the foam. Encourage children to perform more difficult tasks involving both dynamic and static balance. When they are successful, see if they can articulate how they compensated with their body. *Note:* Be sure to have spotters.

INTEGRATION   Encourage children to combine skills that involve locomotion (such as walking), axial stability (bending, twisting), static stability (upright balancing), and dynamic stability (rolling) into a routine that they write down in sequence and repeat.

170   FREEZE

GOALS   To improve stability skills; to improve sensorimotor integration; to improve listening skills

OBJECTIVES   The child will listen, stop at a given signal, and maintain his position.

MATERIALS   Drum, gong, or record, cassette, CD; record, cassette, or CD player

PROCEDURE   Have the children move around the room (walking, skipping, hopping, jumping, spinning). Play music or beat a drum or gong, then stop suddenly. You might initially call out "Freeze" until they get the idea. At the silence, the children should freeze in their position. As you unfreeze the children (by touching them), talk about the positions they are in. Touch children who are having trouble balancing first. Encourage children to move in more difficult ways that will be harder to hold when frozen. Talk about these. As a variation, have all the children melt to the ground before the music is started again. This provides good practice in static balance. For variation, use a visual signal, such as flicking the lights or waving your hands.

INTEGRATION   Help children understand some of the basic principles of balance and why some postures are easier to hold than others. Have them experiment with block designs and see which ones are more stable, and help them draw analogies.

171   TENSE ME

GOALS   To improve sensorimotor integration; to increase body awareness; to follow directions

OBJECTIVES   The child will tense and relax the designated body parts.

MATERIALS   None

PROCEDURE   Have all the children lie or sit on the floor. (Sitting is easier because both you and they can see better). Have children tense and relax both arms and then both legs. You may need to touch the tensed part to see if the child understands the request. Then have the children make a tight fist or muscle in one arm and feel that arm with the other hand. Tell them that feeling is *tense*. Ask if they can squeeze harder and make it more tense. Have them hold it to a count of five. Then tell them to see how loose (relaxed) they can make that arm. Again, have them feel it with their other hand. Discuss the difference in feeling. Encourage them to make the arm even floppier. Repeat with the other arm. On another day, do different body parts such as legs and face. Words like "tight," "loose," and "floppy" may work better than the words "tense" and "relax," but be sure to use these too. Use your voice to mirror both the tension and relaxation. Move to other body parts, particularly facial parts. See if the children can learn to isolate parts of their body and tense just the part requested. Can they tense their right fist and keep the left fist relaxed? Before children can voluntarily relax, they need to learn the feeling of what relaxation is. Otherwise, they won't know what they are striving for.

INTEGRATION   Children need to become in tune with their body as a way of self-knowledge and also as a way of monitoring their own behavior. They need to learn the relationship between body tension and behavior and what they do when they are tense. Teach them how to recognize this tension in themselves.

172   FEELY BAG

GOALS   To improve sensorimotor integration; to improve tactile skills; to increase vocabulary

OBJECTIVES   The child will identify objects by feel and describe their characteristics.

MATERIALS   Several small fabric bags; 2 each of objects that can be identified by feel: cups or glasses, cars and trucks, blocks, doll furniture, balls, dishes

PROCEDURE   Place one object in the bag and have the children feel through the bag to figure out what the object is. Use only one object per bag. Place a duplicate set of objects on the table and ask the child to point to or name the one she feels. As children improve, choose objects that have to be felt systematically to be identified. Encourage children to talk about the objects they feel and their descriptive characteristics. Almost anything in your room that will fit in the bag and has obvious tactile features can be used. For variation, have children put their hand in the bag to feel what is there. This allows you to add items like a snake skin, feather, and other objects that are not easily felt from the outside. Avoid sharp objects.

INTEGRATION   Touch can provide children with additional information, provided they link what they are feeling with possible explanations for what might be happening and the implications for what they ought to do.

Sensorimotor Integration: Small Group

173   DRAW IT ON

GOALS   To improve sensorimotor integration; to improve tactile skills; to improve fine motor manipulative skills

OBJECTIVES   The child will draw and interpret a design.

MATERIALS   Paper and markers; cards with simple shapes, numbers, or letters

PROCEDURE   Have children sit in pairs front to back. Demonstrate the procedure by having an adult tap out numbers or finger-draw simple designs (square, circle, triangle) on a child's back. Then give the child in back a card with a design. Using his finger, this child draws the design on the card on the back of the child in front. The child in front draws the design on the paper with a marker. The children then compare the design drawn with the one on the card. Add more difficult designs or a series of designs (letters or numbers) or simple words. Have four children sit in a line, sequentially drawing on the back of the child in front. This is an interesting, quiet activity that requires unusual concentration and attention to detail.

INTEGRATION   Children need to integrate information received from all parts of their body. This is an unusual way to identify and draw geometric shapes, numbers, and letters.

Sensorimotor Integration: Individual

174   FOLLOW THAT LIGHT

GOALS   To improve sensorimotor integration; to improve eye-hand coordination; to identify and understand patterns and relationships

OBJECTIVES   The child will repeat or follow a pattern using a tool.

MATERIALS   2 flashlights

PROCEDURE   Make the room as dark as possible. Turn on two flashlights. Initially, have an adult use one flashlight and move it slowly in a simple pattern for the child to follow. Then give a flashlight to each of two children. Have one child make simple designs with the light on the wall, floor, or ceiling, and have the other child repeat the design when it is completed or "shadow" the design as it is being done. As skills improve, make the designs more complex and move the flashlight faster. Encourage children to use the button on the flashlight to make long and short flashes in a repeating pattern. *Note:* This is an interesting way to look at patterns for children who are in bed.

INTEGRATION   Talk about patterns that are auditory, such as Morse code, and signal lights and how patterns of light are used for communication on ships. Show children these symbol systems.

175   PICK-A-PAIR

GOALS   To improve sensorimotor integration; to improve tactile skills; to improve classification skills

OBJECTIVES   The child will describe the textures and match them.

MATERIALS   Fake fur, cardboard, flannel, felt, sandpaper, sponge, nylon, corduroy, dotted Swiss, wool, silk, ultrasuede

Cut each piece of fabric in two 2″ × 2″ pieces. Glue one piece of each fabric on cardboard. Place the matching piece of fabric in a feely bag or box.

PROCEDURE   Choose a piece of fabric on the cardboard and ask the child to find that piece in the feely bag and match it. Initially, make the differences among the materials obvious (e.g., use cardboard, fake fur, and nylon) and have fewer materials to choose among. Have the children look carefully at the textures and classify them in some way: woven/not woven, soft/hard, rough/smooth, and so on. Have them explain how they know they have a match. As children become more skillful, use 2″-square pieces of sandpaper of different grades. Have them order these from coarse to fine.

INTEGRATION   Talk with children about fabric and the qualities of different fabrics. Ask them which fabrics might make the best towels and which the best bathing suits. Help them think about the qualities of materials that relate to their use.

Summary   Developmental physical education and sensorimotor activities support the development of large and small motor skills and the integration of these skills with sensory information. For very young children, mastering sensorimotor skills is a large part of their development. For all children, having a physically active lifestyle is part of health and wellness. Variations on activities allow for practice in a skill while learning to adjust to different conditions. The basic skills learned form the foundation for participation in sports as well as the precision of movement necessary for academic activities such as writing.

Educational Resources

Gabbard, C., Leblanc, E., & Lowy, S. (1987). *Physical education for children: Building the foundation.* Englewood Cliffs, NJ: Prentice-Hall.

Information on developing a physical education program for children.

Luvmour, S., & Luvmour, J. (1990). *Everyone wins: Cooperative games and activities.* Philadelphia, PA: New Society Publishers.

An emphasis on non-competitive games and ways to modify competitive ones.

Pica, R. (1995). *Experiences in movement with music activities and theory.* Albany, NY: Delmar Publishers Inc.

Provides information on physical fitness in young children and plans for movement education for toddlers through early elementary school including modifications for children with disabilities.

Chapter 23

CREATIVE ARTS ACTIVITIES: VISUAL ARTS, MUSIC, CREATIVE MOVEMENT, AND DRAMATIC PLAY

All children are creative. Some are more creative than others. Some children are more creative in one area than in other areas. As children feel the impact of the environment, the response they get to their creative efforts plays a large part in their creative development. Educators have an important

TABLE 23.1 ACTIVITY GOALS AND REFERENCE NUMBERS

Goals	Activities
To use different art media, techniques, and processes	176, 177, 178, 179, 180, 181, 182, 183, 184, 185, 186, 187, 188
To understand the structures and functions of art	178, 180
To understand art in a cultural and historical context	177
To use the arts to express a range of subject matter, symbols, and ideas	177, 179, 181, 182, 183, 189, 190
To connect the arts and other disciplines	176, 186, 187, 188, 190,
To listen, analyze, describe, and respond to music	191, 192, 195, 196, 197, 200, 201, 207
To read and interpret music	193
To perform on instruments alone and with others	193, 194
To sing alone and with others	197, 199, 202
To appreciate a varied repertoire of music	195, 196, 198, 199, 200, 202
To develop creative movement	191, 192, 203, 204, 206
To encourage problem solving	178, 187, 208, 209, 210, 211,
To encourage creativity	180, 182, 183, 207
To improve self-concept	184, 189, 208, 213
To express feelings	189, 190, 191, 209, 210
To follow directions	193
To increase comprehension	195, 196
To improve classification skills	185
To improve cause-and-effect reasoning	176, 179, 185, 194, 203, 211, 212
To increase body awareness	204, 205, 206, 213
To improve sensorimotor integration	192, 199, 200, 201, 204, 205, 207
To increase inclusion	184, 186, 202, 203, 206, 213
To increase awareness of roles people play	209, 210, 211, 212
To increase awareness of individual differences and similarities	188
To improve memory skills	198
To improve sequencing skills	198
To identify and understand patterns and relationships	181, 197
To use diverse print and nonprint sources and genres	205
To participate in democratic process	208, 213
To understand geography concepts	212

role in the development of creativity. They can actively support creativity (see Table 23.1) or squelch it by concentrating only on the product that emerges. And they can enhance the experience by having children think more about the process as it will impact the product.

Visual Arts: Small Group

176   CREATURE

GOALS   To use different art media, techniques, and processes; to connect the arts and other disciplines; to improve cause-and-effect reasoning

OBJECTIVES   The child will design and make a creature and describe its environment and how it is adapted to live there.

MATERIALS   Balloons, papier-mâché: Tear newspaper into very small pieces and pour a little boiling water over it. Stir until it forms a pulp. Cool. Then add about 6 tablespoons of wheat paste for every 2 cups of pulp. Mix first with a spoon, then with the hands.

PROCEDURE   Let the children mold the papier-mâché into some creature-like form. Covering an inflated balloon with papier-mâché is a good way for older children to begin. Initially, have the children create the creature and then help them think of the environment it would be most adapted for. Talk about this creature during the process so that the children think about how it moves, what and how it eats, where it lives, and so on. Then see if they can adapt the creatures to the environment they create. When the creatures are dry, encourage the children to use the construction area to build an environment for them. Help children focus on adaptations people make to the environment: Mobility aids, prosthetic devices, and eye glasses are all adaptations.

INTEGRATION   Precede this activity by discussing how people and animals are adapted to their environments (a monkey's tail is for climbing; polar bears are white for protective coloration; a cheetah's is for catching prey). Monitor balloons carefully if you use them.

Visual Arts: Small Group

177   CRAYON RUBBING

GOALS   To use different art media, techniques, and processes; to use the arts to express a range of subject matter, symbols, and ideas; to understand art in a cultural and historical context

OBJECTIVES   The child will choose an object to rub, make predictions about what it will look like, do the rubbing, and discuss the ways rubbings are used.

MATERIALS   Paper, masking tape, thick crayons, objects with various textures

PROCEDURE   Talk to children about rubbings and how people rub tombstones, temples, and other interesting objects as mementos. Show children examples of rubbings that have been done on either cloth or paper. Talk about various surfaces that the children touch and how they would describe them (soft, furry, scratchy), then about surfaces that they see (shiny, hairy, has ridges or patterns), and then about the two combined (something that feels bumpy and looks rough). Demonstrate rubbing techniques to the children. Help children rub the edges of objects first to determine their shape. Initially, encourage children to pick objects that have distinctive shapes as well as textures. Either have them search the room to find their own textures to rub or provide a variety of textured objects on a table. Tape the corners of the paper to the table with the object under it. The tape keeps the paper from moving as the children rub. Write the name of the article rubbed on the other side of the paper. During group time, ask the children to look at the papers and guess what article was rubbed. (The name on the back helps for those "creative" rubbings.) As children gain experience, have them predict how a rubbing will look before they begin and then see if they were accurate.

INTEGRATION   This requires little coordination, yet helps develop finger strength and sensorimotor integration and gives the children feedback about how hard they are pressing the crayon. It is an interesting way to include aspects of history and culture into the curriculum in a very concrete way. You might show children rubbings from other cultures that are done of fish (Japanese). Talk about fossils and how these relate to rubbings.

Visual Arts: Small Group

178   CORRUGATED COLLAGE

GOALS   To use different art media, techniques, and processes; to understand the structures and functions of art; to encourage problem solving

OBJECTIVES   The child will make a collage on corrugated paper and discuss how the corrugations influenced the process and product.

MATERIALS   A 6″ x 9″ or larger piece of corrugated paper (such as a box divider or packing separator), a variety of yarns, glue or paste, cloth materials, popsicle sticks, pipe cleaners, crayons and markers

PROCEDURE   Initially, give children time to just experience the new medium and talk about how it is different and what would happen if they were to color or glue the surface. Allow children to experiment and then have them make collages with a piece of corrugated paper, some glue, and materials to be glued. Help the children see that the glue goes naturally into the corrugations, where it is easy to glue the yarn but much more difficult to glue the cloth. As the children gain experience and better motor control, you might have them try doing this blindfolded. This then becomes more of a sensory experience than an art activity.

INTEGRATION   The corrugated paper provides an interesting and challenging change and expands children's experience with different media. It gives children with visual impairments tactile feedback and a definite boundary as they work.

Visual Arts: Individual or Small Group

179   TEXTURE PAINT

GOALS   To use different art media, techniques, and processes; to use the arts to express a range of subject matter, symbols, and ideas; to improve cause-and-effect reasoning

OBJECTIVES   The child will describe the texture of the paint, how he plans to use it, and how it influenced his ideas.

MATERIALS   Add texture to easel paint with one of the following:

flour: lumpy (don't stir it too much)

sugar: shiny, grainy (use right away)

salt: shiny, grainy (table or Epsom salt)

salad oil: oily

sawdust: rough

syrup: sticky

sand: gritty

PROCEDURE   Have the children experiment with various textures. Focus on the process and verbalize the change in texture. Experiment with making different colors and different textures on the same day. Focus on the cause-effect relationship in the materials added and the resultant texture. Talk with children about how the change in the paint will change their picture (outcome). Have them think about what this means to what they will choose to do.

INTEGRATION   This activity provides both tactile and visual variations of a familiar substance.

180   CLAY

GOALS   To use different art media, techniques, and processes; to understand the structures and functions of art; to encourage creativity

OBJECTIVES   The child will explore and then mold the clay for a particular purpose.

MATERIALS   Dry clay, rolling pins, water, blunt knife

PROCEDURE   Make, or have the children make, clay from powder. Vary the amount of moisture with the strength and motor skills of the children (more moisture: easier to manipulate). Allow adequate time for exploration. Encourage children to use rolling pins and blunt knives as well as hands to mold the clay. (When the clay is used as an emotional release or a means for developing finger strength and coordination, plan to put it back in the crock when the activity is completed.) As children gain experience, help them focus on a particular idea that they want to convey with the clay and talk with them about how they will symbolize their idea with the clay. Explain that you will allow the clay to dry or fire it in a kiln and they will paint it. (Be wary of objects that are supposed to fit together when they dry; they rarely do.) Have children paint the object after it is dry and talk about their initial idea and how they conveyed it.

INTEGRATION   Clay offers potential for many levels of development. Because playdough and plasticine are so readily available, we often forget about clay, but it has potential that the other media don't have.

181   STENCILS

GOALS   To use different art media, techniques, and processes; to use the arts to express a range of subject matter, symbols, and ideas; to identify and understand patterns and relationships

OBJECTIVES   The child will design and use a stencil to make a repeating pattern of one or two colors.

MATERIALS   Construction paper (5″ × 5″), scissors, paint, posterboard, cotton ball, colored chalk, crayons

PROCEDURE   Give the children several pieces of posterboard. Have them cut holes or designs in the posterboard. If they want a symmetrical design (for example, heart, flower, person), it is easiest if they fold the paper in half first. Encourage them to think about their choice and how and why they made it. After they have finished making the stencil, use tape or bits of adhesive to keep the stencil in one place as the children color it. Have them use colored chalk to color the opening or rub the colored chalk with the cotton ball. Working from the stencil to the center of the opening, have them color until they have a clear print. Crayons can be used in the same manner. Have children print a scene or make a card using this process.

INTEGRATION   Talk with children about the purpose of stencils and how they can use single or multiple stencils to make repeating patterns and designs. Show them stencils that have been commercially made and show them how they are used. If they want to use more than one color, explain how this is done. Posterboard is sturdier, but construction paper is easier to cut and make designs.

182   STRING PAINTING

GOALS   To use different art media, techniques, and processes; to use the arts to express a range of subject matter, symbols, and ideas; to encourage creativity

OBJECTIVES   The child will talk about the characteristics of string as an art medium, then make a string painting reflecting these ideas.

MATERIALS   Pieces of string, yarn, or cord of various thicknesses approximately 12″ long, paper, 2 or 3 colors of tempera paint in pie pans

PROCEDURE   Give the children a variety of pieces of string, cord, or yarn, help them think about what their design will look like. Show them how to dip the string in the paint, and allow them to make a design by applying the paint on paper with the string. (Put the yarn or string through an empty spool to make it easier to grip.) If very thick paint is used, the children will be able to feel the ridges the string makes. The children can also match the ridges to the thickness of string used. Help children identify differences in techniques, for example, holding string taut between two hands versus holding one end and swirling. Encourage children to use different thicknesses of string in the same picture and to compare different techniques.

INTEGRATION   This is a creative visual process and children can feel the picture when it is dry. Help children compare string painting with other types of painting relative to the control they have and the outcome.

Visual Arts: Small Group

183   TORN PAPER FLOWERS

GOALS   To use different art media, techniques, and processes; to use the arts to express a range of subject matter, symbols, and ideas; to encourage creativity

OBJECTIVES   The child will plan and make a picture of a chosen topic by tearing and pasting paper.

MATERIALS   A pot or vase of flowers, construction paper, colored paper scraps, paste, crayons

PROCEDURE   Show the children the flowers. Discuss the parts that make up the flower (stem, petals, leaves, and so on). If children have had little experience in this area, start by having them just tear the paper and paste it. Then help them experiment with pieces of different sizes and shapes for different purposes. Have them paste paper petals and other flower parts. (If flowers aren't interesting to the children in your class, make something that is.) Once the children know the technique, allow them the freedom to make *their* flower. Provide crayons and markers to complete details. Encourage children to both cut and tear the paper and show them how to curl the paper around a pencil so it curls away from the paper to add depth.

INTEGRATION   Tearing is satisfying for children who have trouble cutting. Yet it too is an artistic technique that offers a potential for three-dimensional pictures. Show children pictures of art that have used this technique.

Visual Arts: Large Group

184   HAND PRINT MURAL

GOALS   To use different art media, techniques, and processes; to improve self-concept; to increase inclusion

OBJECTIVES   The child will participate in a mural by making a handprint and will identify her handprint and compare it to the prints of others in the class.

MATERIALS   Paint, butcher paper, paint brush, construction paper

PROCEDURE   Decide on the purpose for the mural. Will it be a get well card, part of a bulletin board display, or a thank you card for a past field trip? Have the children generate an appropriate message. Then take the mural paper to a separate table. Have children put on their handprint and name. The easiest way to do this is to put the paint on a sponge and have children press their hand on the sponge, then print it. Encourage interested children to be creative with the handprint. Help them look closely at their hand and perhaps paint the palm one color and the area between each knuckle another. Supply additional small paper so children can try out their print first or make another project. Have children add fingerprints and look at both hand- and fingerprints with a magnifying glass.

INTEGRATION   The concept of printing is different from finger painting. Show children prints and discuss how they are made. For some children, this will be new. This project is an easy one for children to participate in and, if hung on the wall, a reminder that all children are part of the class.

Visual Arts: Small Group

185   TEXTURED PLAYDOUGH

GOALS   To use different media, techniques, and processes; to improve classification skills; to improve cause-and-effect reasoning

OBJECTIVES   The child will identify the different doughs and classify them as rough, smooth, soft, or grainy.

MATERIALS   Playdough made with 7 parts flour to 1 part salt (about 1 Tbsp. vegetable oil); playdough made with 2 parts flour to 1 part salt (about 1 Tbsp. vegetable oil)

PROCEDURE   Have the children help make the playdough so that they can see the difference in the quantities of flour and salt. Start with gross discrimination, then see if the children can make finer distinctions. Help them verbalize: The more flour, the smoother the dough; the more salt, the grainier it is. Vary the texture of the playdough by changing the ratio of flour to salt; use 7 parts flour to 2 parts salt; 7 to 3; 7 to 4; 7 to 5; and 7 to 6 to see how well the children can make tactile discriminations. Color code the different mixtures if necessary.

Have children classify the playdough by touch. Talk about uses for the different textures. Have children make other recipes by adding sawdust, sand, and so on. Use small quantities, as some of the products might not be appealing.

INTEGRATION   This activity helps develop and refine tactile skills. Because children participate in the process of making the dough, they can begin to understand the relationship between the amounts of the ingredients used and the outcome.

Visual Arts: Small Group

186   FINGER PUPPETS

GOALS   To connect the arts and other disciplines; to use different art media, techniques, and processes; to increase inclusion

OBJECTIVES   The child will design and then make a finger puppet and use it in a small group.

MATERIALS   Papier-mâché (see Activity 176, Creature, for recipe)

PROCEDURE   Help children focus on what they want their puppet to do or be when the puppet is finished. Help them think about how this influences the size and shape of the puppet, and how they will dress it. After the children have molded their creation, have them insert their finger to make the finger hole. Wait for the puppets to dry and then have the children paint and dress them. Have children take them into the dramatic play area and use them together. Encourage children to think about the roles they envisioned for each puppet.

INTEGRATION   Finger puppets require less manipulation than other puppets, and children have to supply more of the dramatic energy. They especially enjoy using a puppet they have created. This also helps children connect the visual arts to other areas. Talk about how dramatic productions need set design as well as the puppets to perform. Perhaps they even need a narrator or someone to write a script. (They may then discover that they need to make additional finger puppets.)

187   WHAT SHALL WE MAKE?

GOALS   To connect the arts and other disciplines; to use different art media, techniques, and processes; to encourage problem solving

OBJECTIVES   The child will design and make an appropriate piece of doll's clothing.

MATERIALS   Linen, corduroy, needles, thread, wool, gabardine, patterns, gingham, scissors, cotton, denim, chiffon, velvet, tape, vinyl, pins, fur, knit, felt, stapler and staples, trims, Velcro (with sticky back), simple patterns for male and female doll clothes

PROCEDURE   Have the children decide on the type of clothing they want to make, choose a pattern, then pick the material to make the desired clothing. Help them think about the relationship between the garment and the cloth. Help the children pin or tape on the pattern, cut it out, and sew up the seams with a large needle and heavy thread. For some children, just choosing the material and cutting it out will be enough. However, those who want to continue could staple the garment together or have a volunteer help with the sewing. Talk about their choices of material relative to the style and weather, when it will be worn, and so on. Encourage children to choose more difficult patterns and materials to work with. Add fasteners such as buttons, snaps, and hooks and eyes. Talk about aspects of clothing (arm holes, sleeves, neck hole, and so on) and how they are part of the pattern. Discuss with them the relationship between size and closures, and where these are placed relative to ease of dressing. Encourage children to add trims to their garment to make it unique.

INTEGRATION   Encourage children to make up a story about the occasion for which the clothing will be worn, dress the doll, and role-play the occasion.

188   TRACING PICTURES

GOALS   To use different art media, techniques, and processes; to connect the arts and other disciplines; to increase awareness of individual differences and similarities

OBJECTIVES   The child will make a picture with a tactile boundary and trace the boundary with his fingers.

MATERIALS   Paper, glue, crayons, sand, salt shaker

PROCEDURE   Have the children draw a simple shape (circle, triangle, square), pattern, or picture (kite, table, cup, balloon, maze) on heavy paper. Tell the children to put glue around the outline (try to avoid ending up with puddles of glue that take days to dry) and then have them sprinkle sand on it. Putting the sand in a large salt shaker makes it easier to control. Point out where the sand stays and where it doesn't. When the glue is dry, shake off the excess sand and have the children trace the object with their fingers or lightly color in the object using the sand as a boundary. Encourage children to make more complex shapes or designs on the paper and to trace the outline blindfolded and color the picture that way as well.

INTEGRATION   Talk to the children about the tactile boundaries of the picture they have created. Help them think about how they could share this picture with a person who can't see.

189   MOOD MONTAGE

GOALS   To use the arts to express a range of subject matter, symbols, and ideas; to improve self-concept; to express feelings

OBJECTIVES   The child will create a mood montage and talk about the mood it conveys and why he believes it conveys that mood.

MATERIALS   Pictures and/or magazines, scissors, crayons, paper, glue or paste

PROCEDURE   Give the children pictures, magazines, and crayons. Have them pick a mood or feeling, find pictures that match or create that mood, and paste the pictures on pieces of paper. They can use the crayons to personalize and finish the pictures. Encourage children to "write" a book on "The Many Moods of Me." Children can illustrate the moods as well as write about them. The illustrations in the book should help set and convey a mood too. Discuss some of the color stereotypes (fire engine red: hot; sky blue: cool; white: aseptic, clean, sterile).

INTEGRATION   Encourage children to talk about their pictures. Help children become more aware of moods and some of the situations in which these moods may occur as well as how they can convey moods through the visual arts, music, and movement.

Visual Arts: Small Group

190   MOOD COLORS

GOALS   To use the arts to express a range of subject matter, symbols, and ideas; to connect the arts and other disciplines; to express feelings

OBJECTIVES   The child will choose an appropriate color theme and setting to express the mood of a picture and explain why it is appropriate.

MATERIALS   A short story, tempera paint or crayons, paper

PROCEDURE   Read (or tell) the class a story with a definite mood. Have the children draw pictures about the story in dark and/or light colors. Use obvious moods until children get the idea. Talk about the relationship between moods and colors and how one uses color. As children become more aware, make the moods a bit more subtle. Have them consider the different reactions and moods of each character in the story and how these might be portrayed. Talk with children about how their mood influences what they want to do.

INTEGRATION   This helps children use visual environmental cues for information as well as expression. It may also help children realize that all people have moods and that moods vary.

Music: Large Group

191   MOOD SONGS

GOALS   To listen, analyze, describe, and respond to music; to develop creative movement; to express feelings

OBJECTIVES   The child will move in a way that is congruent with the tempo, dynamics, meter, and style of the music she hears.

MATERIALS   Record, tape, or CD player; records, tapes, CDs

PROCEDURE   Choose songs that have a specific mood: lullabies, jazz, rock, easy listening, as well as more traditional children's music. Start with only familiar, obvious songs until children get the idea. Help children focus on the mood of the music before they begin to move. Have them demonstrate what they will do. After moving to a song, talk about when they might want to listen to this type of music. Then, have them sing a familiar song the "wrong" way (a loud, fast lullaby). As children become more skillful, use songs that are not familiar to the children. Have children identify some of the musical characteristics that are used to create the mood. Help them identify how different instruments contribute to the mood.

INTEGRATION   Children learn to become more aware of their own moods and can perhaps match music to these as a way of learning to control them. Children need to develop the skills of analyzing and describing music.

192   RHYTHM WALK

GOALS   To listen, analyze, describe, and respond to music; to develop creative movement; to increase sensorimotor integration

OBJECTIVES   The child will describe the beat, the variations of patterns of beats after moving to the beat, and how the music made him feel.

MATERIALS   Drum or piano

PROCEDURE   Set up a path around the room (or outside) and have the children walk to the beat that you play. (If you don't play, use a record or tape.) Initially, warn the children before changing: "Listen, I'm going to change now. Is it faster or slower?" Be sure the children can see you and the beat; play dramatically. Then, vary the beat and see if the children change with you. As children's skill increases, make the changes more quickly. Don't let the children see what you are doing; this takes away the visual cue. Sometimes beat slowly enough for their movements to become a balancing activity.

INTEGRATION   Instead of walking, children can participate in many different movement activities. Use music from different cultures that have different beats and moods. Talk about these differences both in rhythm and culture.

193   CONDUCTOR

GOALS   To read and interpret music; to perform on instruments alone and with others; to follow directions

OBJECTIVES   The child will give (or follow) visual musical symbols and directions for playing instruments.

MATERIALS   Rhythm band instruments, videotape of a concert

PROCEDURE   Teach the children some of the simpler hand signals that musical directors use:

softer: palms toward the group (up and down)

louder: palms toward you (large gesture)

slow: waving slowly (circular)

fast: waving fast (circular)

expand: pass arm in front of body parallel to floor

staccato: cut in the air (vertically)

Your signals don't have to be the actual signals, but you and the children should agree on their meanings. Make a picture of the signals, with the word written below.

Start with the teacher being the "director." Use sounds like *me, me, me, me; la, la, la, la; see, see, see, see.* Then go to two or more syllables. Names are always fun: *Ja*—expand (use horizontal hand movement), *mie*—staccato (vertical hand movement). Be sure a child knows the process before choosing her to be the conductor. If children cannot make the hand motions, have them point to the cards that show the hand signals. Play a short videotape of a concert and point out to the children the motions the conductor uses to direct the orchestra. Encourage them to figure out what happens with each different motion. Then have the children use their instruments with a conductor. Instruments are far more challenging to control than voices.

INTEGRATION   Even if children discover only that the other children will start and stop on their hand signals, this can be a positive experience.

Music: Small Group

194   REEDS

GOALS   To perform on instruments alone and with others; to improve cause-and-effect reasoning

OBJECTIVES   The child will make two horns of different pitches, play them, and state why they make different pitches.

MATERIALS   Plastic drinking straws, scissors

PROCEDURE   Flatten about 1 inch of a plastic drinking straw, creasing it so it stays flat. Using scissors, cut a V in that end. This becomes the reed. The children put this in their mouth behind their lips and blow. First, have children make short straws and see if they can get a noise out of the straws. Then encourage them to make several reeds of different lengths and see if they can discover the relationship between length and pitch. (The shorter the straw, the higher the pitch.) Shorter straws are easier to blow. Have children make a series of tuned reeds and arrange them by pitch.

INTEGRATION   Expand children's understanding of pitch by having someone play a guitar or violin and talk about how they are tuned and how they change the pitch.

Music: Small or Large Group

195   BUMBLEBEES

GOALS   To appreciate a varied repertoire of music; to listen, analyze, describe, and respond to music; to increase comprehension

OBJECTIVES   The child will listen to "Flight of the Bumblebee," make a bumblebee, and then talk about why the music and the bumblebee go together.

MATERIALS   "Flight of the Bumblebee" by Rimsky-Korsakov; record; cassette, or CD player; toothpicks; wax paper; construction paper; glue; black pipe cleaners; crayons or markers; pictures of bumblebees; yarn, yellow and black cut into strips; Styrofoam balls

PROCEDURE   Talk with children about bees, their characteristics and function. Be sure to include information about bumblebees' flying. Listen to "Flight of the Bumblebee." Talk about the music with the children. Give the children the materials to make a bumblebee and encourage them to talk about the music while they make their bumblebee. Encourage the children to use the materials creatively. Whether or not the children's product looks like a bumblebee is not important. Listen to "Flight of the Bumblebee" again and have children pretend they are bumblebees and dance to the music. Talk in more detail about bumblebees, what they look like and how they move.

INTEGRATION   We rarely think about using classical music with young children, but some selections fit in well. Encourage children to talk about why this is not called "Flight of the Hawk" or other birds they might have some knowledge of.

Music: Small or Large Group

196   CLOUDS

GOALS   To appreciate a varied repertoire of music; to listen, analyze, describe, and respond to music; to increase comprehension

OBJECTIVES   The child will move like a cloud to the music and talk about how this feels and why the music is titled as it is.

MATERIALS   Record, cassette, or CD player; "Nuages" (Clouds) by Claude Debussy; *The Cloud Book* by Tomie DePaola; cotton balls; paste; construction paper; crayons, pencils, or markers

PROCEDURE   Read *The Cloud Book* before playing the selection. Discuss clouds with the children. If possible, go outside and have the children lie down on the ground and watch the clouds as they listen to "Nuages." Play only a portion of the selection if the children get restless. Have some of the children listen a second time and move as if they were clouds. Encourage children to make pictures of clouds and write about their feelings.

INTEGRATION   Children can develop another way of enjoying and thinking about nature. They can begin to tie sound, whether in nature or as an interpretation of nature, into a context.

Music: Large Group

197   BONNIE

GOALS   To listen, analyze, describe, and respond to music; to sing alone and with others; to identify and understand patterns and relationships

OBJECTIVES   The child will identify the pattern and change positions on every other *Bonnie.*

MATERIALS   None

PROCEDURE   Sing the song "My Bonnie Lies over the Ocean" with everyone standing. Each time you sing the word *Bonnie,* if the children are standing, they squat; if they are squatting, they stand. Use other songs that have this repetitious quality (for "The Ants Go Marching," move up on *hurrah,* down on *hooray*) and encourage the children to decide on other patterns of movements (for example, raising and lowering their hands). If you sing but don't move with the children, it is more difficult for them.

INTEGRATION   Activities such as this help children think about the patterns within music and how they repeat.

Music: Large Group

198   SEQUENCING SONGS

GOALS   To appreciate a varied repertoire of music; to improve memory skills; to improve sequencing skills

OBJECTIVES   The child will understand the concept behind the sequence and remember at least three items in the sequence.

MATERIALS   None

PROCEDURE   Sing songs that require the children to remember a particular sequence. Initially, you may need to make pictures for the different words the children have to remember and hold them up as visual reminders. For "Old MacDonald," these would be pictures of the different animals. When you sing "Old MacDonald," pause after "and on his farm he had a . . ." to see if they can remember the sequence without your help. As children become more skillful, add more words for the children to remember.

INTEGRATION   Use additional songs that have many verses, such as "This Old Man," "If You're Happy," "I Know an Old Lady Who Swallowed a Fly," and "Hush, Little Baby."

Music: Large Group

199   MOVEMENT SONGS

GOALS   To appreciate a varied repertoire of music; to sing alone and with others; to improve sensori-motor integration

OBJECTIVES   The child will sing and follow the motions stated in the song.

Songs with a sequence of motions such as "Head, Shoulders, Knees, and Toes" allow children to participate at many different levels.

MATERIALS   None

PROCEDURE   Sing the song "Put Your Finger in the Air." Once they know the song, help the children explore their bodies by putting their finger on their knee, cheek, shoulder, ankle, and so on. Then go on to various other combinations, like "Put your nose on your shoulder, on your shoulder." In the third line, you need to be creative and have a rhyme in mind: "Put your nose on your shoulder, leave it there until you're older." The repetition in the songs makes them easy for children to learn. Sing the song more slowly and dramatically. Or modify some songs by having the children put an object (e.g., bean-bag) on the body part named: "Put the beanbag on your knee, on your knee," and so on. Other songs de-signed to increase sensorimotor integration include "Heads, Shoulders, Knees, and Toes" (tune: "Oats, Peas, Beans"); "My Head, My Shoulders, My Knees, My Toes" (tune: "Mulberry Bush"); "Where Is Thumbkin?"; "Clap Your Hands"; "The Hokey Pokey"; "The Wheels on the Bus"; "Eensey-Weensey Spi-der"; "Johnny Hammers with One Hammer"; "I'm Being Swallowed by a Boa Constrictor." When chil-dren know the songs, have them sing with their eyes closed.

INTEGRATION   These songs teach body parts, use both auditory and tactile senses, and provide an opportunity to experience success and a sense of group belonging.

Music: Large or Small Group

200   MUSICAL COLORS

GOALS   To appreciate a varied repertoire of music; to listen, analyze, describe, and respond to music; to improve sensorimotor integration

OBJECTIVES   The child will name the color and the shape he lands on.

MATERIALS   A variety of colored shapes, one for each child, mounted on cardboard, including shapes in shades of colors (pink, violet, and so on) and more difficult shapes (oval, cross, trapezoid, and so on) and placed in a circle

PROCEDURE   Play music and have the children move around the outside of the circle of colored shapes. When the music stops, have the children sit on the nearest shape. Ask them to name the color and the shape. As a variation, use numbers and letters instead of colors and shapes. Have children move like various animals around the circle.

INTEGRATION   This is an adaptation of musical chairs based on color/shape recognition but without the mad scramble. As speed is not important, all children can play.

Music: Large Group

201   TEMPO

GOALS   To listen, analyze, describe, and respond to music; to improve sensorimotor integration

OBJECTIVES   The child will match the speed of his or her movements to the tempo of the music and be able to verbalize the changes.

MATERIALS   Drum or piano

PROCEDURE   Have the children lie down on the floor, spaced so that they can stretch and not touch each other. As they are lying there, tell them that you want them to listen to the beat and move according to how fast or slow the beat is. They can move any body parts they want in any way as long as they remain in one place on their back. Start with a slow beat so you can watch and make comments to the children about their movements. Initially, warn children before you change the tempo, then abruptly change to a fast beat. If they move with you, make finer gradations to your changes. Change the beat more frequently and introduce some intermediate tempos. Also, vary the loudness and sometimes use more difficult rhythms or patterns: soft but fast or loud but slow. See if the children can focus on the tempo.

INTEGRATION   This activity can be used to quiet excited children. Pace your periods of vigorous beat so that the children don't become too tired. Unless you want excited children, be sure to end on a slow tempo.

Music: Large Group

202   MY SONG

GOALS   To sing alone and with others; to appreciate a varied repertoire of music; to increase inclusion

OBJECTIVES   The children will look at the named child while singing and respond to their own name in song.

MATERIALS   None

PROCEDURE   Sing songs in which you can substitute the name of a child from your group, or adapt a song to include a name. Initially, point to the child whose name you are singing. Then add songs that require the children to sing back a response, such as "Here I Am."

"Bingo"

There was a farmer had a son
and Michael was his name—O.
M-I-C-H-AEL
M-I-C-H-AEL
M-I-C-H-AEL
And Michael was his name—O.

"Paw-Paw Patch"

Where, oh, where is pretty little Sherry?
Where, oh, where is pretty little Laura?
Where, oh, where is handsome Juan?
They're in the block corner
picking up blocks.

"Hey Betty Martin"

Hey, Jenny Gilbert
tippy toe tippy toe.
Hey, Dante Turner
tip toe fine.

"Who Has Red On?"

G.L. has a red shirt,
red shirt, red shirt,
G.L. has a red shirt
in school today.

INTEGRATION   These songs are great at the beginning of the year, when children are getting to know each other. Also, use them when you are trying to get a group together and you have a few wanderers ("Hey, Natalie Beers, come join us").

Creative Movement: Large or Small Group

203 BE IT

GOALS   To develop creative movement; to improve cause-and-effect reasoning; to increase inclusion

OBJECTIVES   The child will move his body to show how an object moves and discuss how the object is adapted to different environments.

MATERIALS   Pictures of objects that move: airplanes, windmills, trains, helicopters, birds, worms, kites

PROCEDURE   Show the children the pictures and discuss how they might make their body move like the objects in the pictures. Talk about the environment in which the animal (or object) lives (or is used) and discuss why their movements are particularly useful. Point out salient characteristics of the objects that give hints to how it moves (fast, slowly, in air, on water, over land). Encourage creativity by pointing out differences in the children's interpretations and by not making judgments. Add pictures of unusual objects (hovercraft) or objects from other cultures and encourage children to figure out how they move and why they are useful.

INTEGRATION   This activity requires children to integrate visual and auditory stimuli and translate them into active physical movement. Have an appropriate way to stop the children's movements: airport, train station, heliport.

Creative Movement: Small or Large Group

204 RAG DOLL

GOALS   To develop creative movement; to increase body awareness; to improve sensorimotor integration

OBJECTIVES   The child will identify body tension and relaxation and move in a loose, relaxed manner or a tight one and verbalize the differences.

MATERIALS   Rag doll

PROCEDURE   Show the children a rag doll and demonstrate how it moves. Start with the children lying down and show them what happens to the rag doll when the legs and arms are lifted. Then go around the class and check out your collection of "rag dolls." Raise limbs an inch or two and see how floppy children can be. (Don't drop a leg very far or the children will tense!) This activity is difficult for some children.

As the children learn to relax lying down, see if they can gain skill in locating just the muscles they need; that is, they can sit up while keeping their arms and head relaxed. Then have them try standing. Eventually add music. See if children can alternate between being floppy rag dolls and tense, marching tin soldiers on your command. Call out to the children what you want them to be. Help children learn to relax specific body parts on command.

INTEGRATION   Tension increases pain, so anything you can teach children about relaxing is useful. Tension may also be the precursor to aggression, and that also is useful for children to get in touch with.

205   RELAXATION STORIES

GOALS   To increase body awareness; to improve sensorimotor integration; to use diverse print and nonprint sources and genres

OBJECTIVES   The child will relax her body while listening to the story.

MATERIALS   None

PROCEDURE   Have the children lie down and shut their eyes. Begin by using this activity to teach body parts and lightly touch the parts as you talk or have someone else do that. Tell them a story while they listen and relax. The actual content of the story may vary with what your class has done and the experiences your children are familiar with. An example follows:

> There was a little boy who was tired, but he couldn't go to sleep; he had the wiggles. Every time a part of him was tired, another part would start to wiggle, and he'd giggle, and then he couldn't go to sleep. So he decided to tell himself a sleepy story. He started with his toes and said, "Toes, don't wiggle," but they kept wiggling. Then he said, "Toes, we're going to the beach and we are going to walk through so much sand that you'll be glad not to wiggle." And he walked and he walked and he walked and finally he was so tired that he sat down and his toes weren't wiggling. They were too tired. His ankles were tired and so were his knees. They felt heavy. Even his legs felt heavy. It just felt nice to be sitting down. Maybe even lying down. Oh, stretch out. . . . Umm. Rest your head back, get comfortable, close your eyes. . . . Oh, relax those tired feet again, all the way up the leg. Now your hip. Now your middle. Let your shoulders touch the floor if they want to; your elbows too. Now your hands. Uncurl your fingers. Even that little finger is heavy. Now let's go back up. The wrists, elbows, and shoulders are all heavy and relaxed. Move your head up and lay it down; roll it a little to find a comfortable place. Open your mouth. Now close it. Yawn. Close your eyes. (Pause.) Breathe deeply. (Pause.) You're waking up. Roll your head, open your eyes. Sit up and wiggle just a little.

As children learn the process, increase the length of the pauses and incorporate more visual images. Make a recording of the story and encourage children to make up their own stories. Point out the relevant variables of pace and tone as well as content.

INTEGRATION   The relaxation portion of this is best spoken in a slow, placid monotone. At first, make your pauses short. In addition to providing a tone of relaxation, it exposes children to another type and use of storytelling.

206   MOVEMENT EXPLORATION

GOALS   To develop creative movement; to increase body awareness; to increase inclusion

OBJECTIVES   The child will move his body in response to directions given and discuss the adaptations he is making and how easy or difficult it is.

MATERIALS   None

PROCEDURE   Ask the children to move in unusual ways:

> Use any 3 parts of your body to move across the floor: 1 hand, 2 feet; 2 hands, 1 foot; 1 hand, 2 knees.

> Hold your feet with your hands and pretend they are connected: How many ways can you move across the floor?

> Can you move across the floor without touching your feet on the ground?

After one child has responded to a request, see if children can respond to the same request in a different way.

INTEGRATION   Given appropriate choices, all children may be very skillful in moving in different ways. With discussion, others may become aware of the challenges of not being able to use one or more limbs.

Creative Movement: Large or Small Group

207   WEIGHTY MOVEMENTS

GOALS   To encourage creativity; to improve sensorimotor integration; to listen, analyze, describe, and respond to music

OBJECTIVES   The child will identify the beat and demonstrate appropriate movements.

MATERIALS   Record, cassette, or CD player; records, cassettes, or CDs; drum

PROCEDURE   Talk to the children about the way they move. Talk about the weight of their movements. Ask them to stomp across the floor, then tiptoe across the floor. Have them label which was light and which was heavy. Have them demonstrate other heavy and light movements. Then have them combine heavy and light movements in a rhythmic fashion, using heavy movements to accent the beat (light, light, heavy, light, light, heavy). Add music and see if they can accent the beat with their movements. Initially, count out the beats for the children: ONE, two, three, FOUR, five, six, ONE, two, three, FOUR, five, six. Count slowly. Use dance music with a definite beat, such as a tango, and see if they can accent the beat with their movements. Use rhythm patterns that represent different music and cultures.

INTEGRATION   This activity emphasizes the rhythmic nature of movement, especially when it is paired with music. It shows children a repeating pattern that is not related to pitch or loudness.

Dramatic Play: Large Group

208   NO NAME

GOALS   To encourage problem solving; to improve self-concept; to participate in democratic process

OBJECTIVES   The children will agree on a name for the doll and discuss the naming process.

MATERIALS   A doll that has not been in the classroom before

PROCEDURE   During group time, show the children the doll. Explain that it is new to the room and doesn't have a name. Ask the children how they think you should go about naming the doll—not what, how. Note their suggestions, then suggest that if they want, they can play with this doll in the dramatic play area. At the end of the day, the class can actually name the doll or make suggestions that will be finalized the following day. When the group meets again, talk about the method used to reach a decision as well as the decision reached. Then ask them about their own names and why they think their parents chose those names. As the doll can have only one name, have the children discuss *how* they will decide on the name, in addition to choosing one.

INTEGRATION   This activity can be used for a class pet or anything in the classroom that can be named. Children need to focus on ways to participate in a group process and understand the underlying principles.

209   DENTIST'S OFFICE

GOALS   To increase awareness of roles people play; to encourage problem solving; to express feelings

OBJECTIVES   The child will play the roles of both dental office personnel and patient and discuss the role of the dentist and her feelings about going to the dentist.

MATERIALS   Props for a dentist's office:

dental floss	lab coat	cloth for around neck
table	tongue depressors	small mirrors
cups	pretend drill	rubber gloves
mask	chair	

PROCEDURE   Set up a dentist's office. Allow children to play the dentist, dental hygienist, nurse, receptionist, patient, parent of patient, and so on. Encourage them to explore the different materials and how they are used. Also talk about why it is important to go to the dentist. Precede (or follow) this with a trip to a dentist's office and some information on teeth and food. Talk about the care of the teeth and mouth area as well as their function in speech. Support children in cooperative play and role taking. Provide them with pictures and additional equipment. Have them use the mask and rubber gloves and talk about why these are used. Talk about the dentist and their feelings about going. Add a listening tape of the sounds of the dentist's office.

INTEGRATION   Some children may not have been to the dentist's office. They might have many questions. For children who are fearful of trips to the dentist, this activity might help them work through

Children need props to support dramatic play. If the theme is the seashore, the children need books about the beach as well as masks, bathing suits, boats, and shells to count and classify.

some of their concerns. Be sure that all materials that might get into children's mouths are disinfected and disposable ones thrown away immediately.

210   DOCTOR'S OFFICE

GOALS   To increase awareness of roles people play; to encourage problem solving; to express feelings

OBJECTIVES   The child will take the roles of the doctor, nurse, and patient and talk about each role.

MATERIALS   Props for a doctor's office: stethoscope, lab coat, flashlight (without batteries), syringes (without needles), dolls, tongue depressors

PROCEDURE   Set up the dramatic play area as a doctor's office. Have the children examine "sick" dolls and/or classmates. Be sure to include information on routine procedures, such as immunization and regular checkups, in addition to sick calls. Allow the children time to explore the equipment. It is sometimes useful to have the same equipment available for several days, as after initial exploration, children participate in higher-level play. Give children information on different types of medical specialties. Talk about a pediatrician, surgeon, ophthalmologist, family practice physician, and allergist, and how you might need several doctors to handle a particular problem. Include the specialties that are most relevant to your classroom.

INTEGRATION   The doctor's office will probably be a familiar setting because most of the children will have been to the doctor for a checkup. Introduce this activity with a story or a visit from a doctor. Be sure to discuss why people go to doctors. You can expand this activity into a hospital setup. Be sure to talk to the children about the differences. Use this to talk about health and staying healthy as well.

211   SHOE STORE

GOALS   To encourage problem solving; to improve cause-and-effect reasoning; to increase awareness of roles people play

OBJECTIVES   The child will select and buy a pair of shoes appropriate for her stated purpose.

MATERIALS   Shoes for different purposes:

walking shoes	baby shoes	bowling shoes
baseball shoes with cleats	high heels	toe shoes
shoes with steel toes	winter slippers	hiking boots
sandals	thongs	golf shoes
running shoes	boots	
clogs	ballet slippers	

PROCEDURE   During group time, discuss with the children the functions of shoes and how some situations require certain types of shoes. Have some examples and talk about how these shoes make it easier. Use obvious examples:

steel toes: won't hurt if something gets dropped on the toes

baseball cleats: get better traction running, less likely to slip

sandals: cooler

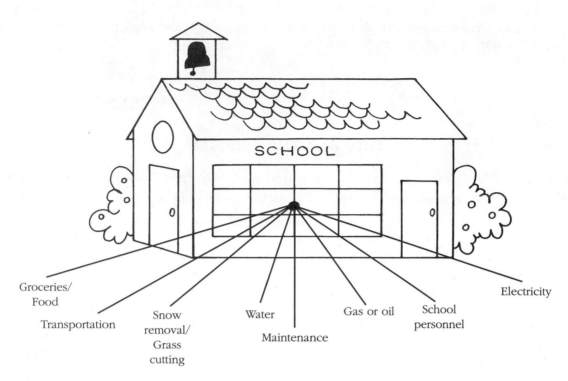

Figure 23.1

Once children have grasped the idea, have them use it in dramatic play to choose the shoes they need. Use the concept of shoes to help children think of a variety of ways we can adapt to changing situations.

INTEGRATION   This activity not only teaches the principles of buying and selling but also teaches specialized ways of coping with environments. For children who rely on visual cues, add pictures of the places where the shoes might be used and have children match the shoes to the picture.

Dramatic Play: Large or Small Group

212   CONNECTIONS

GOALS   To improve cause-and-effect reasoning; to understand geography concepts; to increase awareness of roles people play

OBJECTIVES   The child will make one statement about what will happen when a connection is cut.

MATERIALS   String, wide marking pen, paper of various colors, scissors, 8″ × 8″ squares of construction paper, tape

PROCEDURE   Pick a familiar place (the children's school) and draw a large picture of that place. Help the children think through the places in the city or services the school is dependent on. As each is mentioned, write the name on a piece of paper, attach string with a piece of tape, give this to a child, and secure the other end of the string to a central location in the picture (see Figure 23.1).

Talk about what each connection signifies. Then take a pair of scissors and cut one string (e.g., water). In addition to cutting the string, explain to children the implications of what happened: "There is no water. What do we do if we are thirsty, have to go to the bathroom, and so on?" Help them experience the problem and generate possible preventive measures or solutions. Ask the children how the school would be different without electricity and what they could do to compensate; for example, if there are no lights, you can use flashlights or lanterns. Talk about different places and environments and how connections are not necessarily the same in all places around the world.

INTEGRATION   Help children see the interdependency of services as well as alternatives for services. Talk about what might happen if the workers were unhappy and decided to go on strike.

Dramatic Play: Large Group

213   CIRCUS

GOALS   To improve self-concept; to increase body awareness; to participate in democratic process, to increase inclusion

OBJECTIVES   The child will participate in setting up the circus and in at least one event.

MATERIALS   Props for a circus: hats, balance beam, scarves, stuffed animals, costumes, mats

PROCEDURE   Read a story about the circus and talk about animal trainers, acrobats, tightrope walkers, and so on. Encourage children to decide how they will organize their circus, how many events they will have, and in what order they will appear, the events themselves, necessary props, and so on. Include some acts that are less demanding. Provide children with alternative roles if they are uncomfortable performing (that is, handing out tickets). Be sure everyone is included.

INTEGRATION   This provides an opportunity for children to practice skills of negotiating and participating in a group process that needs a resolution that includes all children.

Summary

The creative arts are an integral part of the early childhood curriculum. They provide children with life-long skills as well as a way of learning about themselves and others in an atmosphere of exploration.

Educational Resources

American Orff-Schulwerk Association
http://pen.1pen.k12.va.us/~jneill/aosa.html
   Emphasizes the integration of music throughout the curriculum, including whole language and reading.

ArtsEdNet
http://www.artsednet.getty.edu/
   Provides lesson plans and curriculum ideas.

Aunt Annie's Craft Page
http:/ww.auntannie.com
   Good craft ideas that are simple, but work.

Children's Music Web
http://www.childrenmusic.org/
   An index of Web sites related to music for children.

Goldberg, M. (1997). *Arts and learning: an integrated approach to teaching and learning in multicultural and multilingual settings.* New York: Longman.
   Illustrates the connection of the arts to other curriculum areas and how they can serve as a powerful motivator in helping children apply knowledge.

Isenberg, J. P., & Jalongo, M. R. (1996). *Creative expression and play in the early childhood curriculum* (2nd ed.). Englewood Cliffs, NJ: Merrill/Prentice Hall.
   A good sourcebook for information about all the creative arts especially music.

Chapter 24

PROGRAM PLANNING AND ACTIVITIES FOR INFANTS AND TODDLERS

I nfants and toddlers are not simply younger preschoolers, in the same way that preschoolers are not miniature adults. Although young infants have a limited repertoire of skills, they do have them, and the objective of planning is to enjoy infants themselves and support the development of their skills.

Infants from birth to 8 months are dependent on adults not only to plan activities but also to take the activity to the infant and often play on a one-to-one basis. Activities for infants this age are designed as lying or sitting activities. For infants with emerging mobility (8 to 18 months), the focus is on motion. They need both incentives to move and something to do when they get where they are going. Moving still requires concentration and effort, and children's skills develop at differing rates; the competent crawler may be late in walking or find it inefficient as a mode of transportation. Planning is still very individualized. Toddlers and twos (18 to 36 months) are reliably, independently mobile. They can actively choose what they want to do because they can seek out the activities that they want to participate in and leave when they are finished. Planning is divided into these three age ranges.

Planning for Nonmobile Infants: Birth to 8 Months

Planning for nonmobile infants is very individualized and developmentally based. Activities are usually one-on-one, are planned for a particular infant, and are executed when that infant is interested. Because of the individualistic nature of planning, including young infants with disabilities requires few adaptations. Infants, especially when very young, have such a small repertoire of behaviors that a single activity with slight variation is often repeated until the infant reaches another developmental level. For example, an activity such as Teethers can be repeated many times, simply using different teethers and talking about their characteristics.

Planning for infants is more holistic than planning for older children. Their ability to attend to a task is dependent on their state and your ability to choose the appropriate time and activity to engage them. The ability to excel as a teacher is dependent on accurate observations of the infant, knowledge of development, and the ability to bring these two sets of information together.

The best materials are those that encourage active involvement of the infant. Active involvement differs; just looking is active involvement for a very young infant, but not for an older infant. A major part of the day for very young infants is taken up in routine care and transitions. The challenge is making these experiences smooth and enjoyable and taking the opportunity to spend time with and enjoy each infant.

The learning environment changes during the day as infants play on the floor, are picked up and carried, are rocked in a rocking chair, are walked outside in a stroller, and bask on a blanket in the sun on the grass. Infants need a variety of learning environments. Their environment should contain both soft and hard elements; they need pillows and mirrors. Infants like bright, high-contrasting colors and interesting patterns to look at. They need cheerful, friendly pictures of infants, children, and adults hung at different levels. These pictures should depict a variety of ages and ethnic groups. Infants need space to be quiet by themselves and space to interact with other children. They need space to pivot, roll over, and crawl, as well as sturdy furniture to practice pulling to standing. The learning environment should include equipment and materials that are developmentally appropriate, and these materials should be organized in a useful way so that they are readily available, but are rotated so they are not all out at once.

The interaction of development, experiences, and learning is the foundation for planning for young infants. The infant's development is the given; the adult selects experiences or activities within the infant's zone of proximal development, and when the match is accurate, learning takes place. This learning is then "grooved" to a level of mastery through variations of the experiences, and new and more complex experiences are introduced with adult scaffolding.

There are two schedules that impact the day: infant and adult. Each infant has an individual schedule that responds to her physical and biological needs. This schedule changes over time (older infants sleep less than younger infants). Some infants have relatively regular internal schedules and settle into a routine easily, whereas others do not seem to have a pattern. With increasing age, almost all infants develop more predictable routines. Adults must develop a schedule that coordinates the caregiving for each infant (Wilson, 1990). The key to schedule planning is *flexibility* and organizing general time blocks that respond to infants' needs. Ideally, timing is flexible, but sequences are predictable. This helps infants learn what will happen next. The younger the infant, the more imperative it is to respond to that infant's biological clock.

Much of the time spent providing care to infants is made up of important and essential routines such as changing diapers, preparing meals, giving bottles, or helping infants settle down for a nap. These routines offer an opportunity for spending time individually with an infant and provide chances to communicate how much you like that infant by making eye contact, talking, singing, imitating the infant's sounds, or reciting nursery rhymes. Routines give infants a sense of security and trust, as their most basic needs are being met in a consistent caring manner. Thinking about routines as part of the learning environment allows planning to be incorporated into the physical care aspect of the routine situation.

Infants learn through their senses: looking, listening, touching, smelling, and tasting. They need materials that can be held, dropped, thrown, mouthed, and shaken. They need materials of different textures, colors, weights, and sizes. Adults must choose appropriate materials to support infant learning. Table 24.1 depicts this process of materials-methods interaction.

Including Nonmobile Infants with Developmental Delays

Some infants are born with disabilities that are identifiable at birth. Others are born at very low birth weight or are classified as having a developmental delay and need individualized programming planned by an early intervention team. Early intervention increases the probability that premature infants will catch up to their peers and no longer be classified as having a developmental delay and that those with disabilities will reach their potential. As with all infants, planning is based on developmentally appropriate practice. Initial judgments are made about age/stage appropriateness. For young infants, gestational age may be most useful in planning. That is, an

TABLE 24.1   MATERIALS-METHODS/ADULT-INFANT INTERACTION

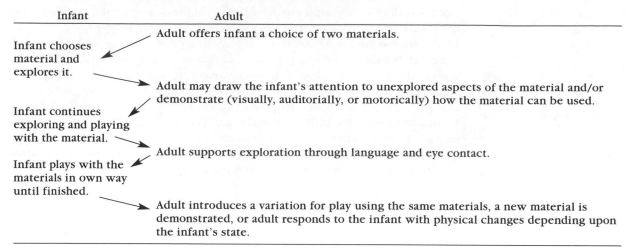

Infant	Adult
	Adult offers infant a choice of two materials.
Infant chooses material and explores it.	
	Adult may draw the infant's attention to unexplored aspects of the material and/or demonstrate (visually, auditorially, or motorically) how the material can be used.
Infant continues exploring and playing with the material.	
	Adult supports exploration through language and eye contact.
Infant plays with the materials in own way until finished.	
	Adult introduces a variation for play using the same materials, a new material is demonstrated, or adult responds to the infant with physical changes depending upon the infant's state.

infant who is currently 5 months old who was born two months prematurely may be more appropriately planned for as a 3-month-old. Individual appropriateness supports the adaptation and modification of planning and programming to meet infants' needs.

Infants with developmental delays often have an especially limited repertoire of skills, so a variety of materials at the same developmental level is particularly important. Although many very low birth weight infants catch up with their peers, at this young age there are predictable differences. The cues that these infants give are often subtle, and the task of interpretation and response may not be easy. With practice, these can be interpreted and responded to.

- Infants may have trouble establishing a pattern of wake and sleep; their cry is often more high-pitched and frequent.

- A disorganized, premature infant often cries six hours a day. (Full-term newborns often cry two to three hours a day for several months.) Colicky crying typically begins right after feeding, and frequent burping is useful. Random patterns of crying are difficult to interpret. They may be just a discharge of excess energy, boredom, or overstimulation.

- Many premature infants have a low tolerance for stimulation, and a setting with as much going on as in child care may tax their system. When they become fussy and irritable, try less, as opposed to more, stimulation.

Planning for Crawlers and Walkers: 8 to 18 Months

Planning for crawlers and walkers is different from planning for either infants or 2-year-olds. This is a transitional time emphatically marked by developmental milestones: the first step and the first word! Children have a growing sense of self and an increased interest in their peers. They are interested in listening to adult language but may not be happy around unfamiliar adults. Sitting is old hat; crawling is being replaced by creeping and standing. Walking is emerging, to be followed by trotting and even walking backwards.

Receptive language far outstrips expressive language, although the child may say several words. There are often long, babbled sentences that "ought" to make sense, but it is as if they are in a different language. Self-help skills are emerging and children want to dress and feed themselves, although they may be happier undressed and self-feeding is often very messy. Emotions are becoming more specific. There are smiles and hugs for affection, anxiety at

As children begin to crawl, they need to be placed in a prone position and given toys to play with that will strengthen their upper body. Activities need to be responsive to their changing interests and to stimulate their emerging locomotion.

separation, and anger at both people and objects that don't do what they are "supposed" to do. Crawlers and walkers have a heightened awareness of the world around them and the ability to get to more of that world, but they lack experience. Much of the emphasis in planning is on consolidating emerging skills and building a foundation of trust in the world around them.

Adults are responsible for setting the stage for children's play. To provide quality play experiences for crawlers and walkers, adults must arrange time, space, materials, and preparatory experiences (Johnson, Christie, & Yawkey, 1987). A schedule for children 8 to 18 months includes time for free play, inside and outside, and for routine events such as eating and napping. Toddlers need space to play. A good program should have areas for them to create messy artwork, a dramatic play corner for simple thematic play (primarily, variations on housekeeping), a block corner for constructive play, a cozy book and language area for quiet reading, a fine motor manipulative area, and a sensory area for exploring sand (rice, oatmeal, beans) and water.

Crawlers and walkers need a variety of materials to choose and use. Adults must provide enough materials for each child, have duplicates of popular toys, and provide enough space for toddlers to use materials. Teachers should select toys for crawlers and walkers that are safe, durable, cleanable, appealing to them, realistic, versatile, and developmentally appropriate (Johnson et al., 1987).

Some crawlers and walkers may need preparatory experiences to help them understand how to play certain roles. For example, a child with experience accompanying parents on grocery shopping trips can usually act out the roles of shopper and clerk to some degree. But the child who has never been to the grocery store may have difficulties. That child might carry out the role Mommy or Daddy plays when the groceries are brought home, that is, storing them or preparing food to eat, rather than the clerk and shopper roles. Field trips are good ways to expand the repertoire of real-life experiences upon which the toddler can draw (Johnson et al., 1987).

Including Crawlers and Walkers with Developmental Delays

With increasing age, differences among children become more apparent. Children with developmental delays may require some modifications in your planning and activities, but these are minor and usually easy adaptations. Peterson (1982) has found that to successfully include children with disabilities, adults must be aware that social interactions do not occur spontaneously. Adults frequently must take the responsibility to facilitate positive social interactions between crawlers and walkers with disabilities and those without. Some ways to encourage positive interactions include:

Highlighting the achievements of all children,

Pairing children for short time periods or tasks,

Modeling appropriate play behavior for the child with a disability, and

Encouraging empathy and prosocial behaviors in all the children.

Beckman, Robinson, Jackson, and Rosenberg (1985) suggest that to meet the educational needs of crawlers and walkers with disabilities, adults need to:

- Be responsive to cues from the child that indicate understanding, interest, frustration, or fatigue.

- Provide appropriate verbal information that highlights the child's attempts at behaviors and positive reinforcement successes.

- Maximize the child's opportunities to manipulate and explore objects and materials. For some children with physical disabilities, this may be difficult, but the adult is responsible for helping the child discover adaptive skills.

- Provide activities that are developmentally appropriate for the skills and goals of each child in the program.

- Simplify your language and use short directions.

- Offer more difficult activities in small steps (if you are using pop beads, have all except one together).

- Demonstrate what you want the child to do. Give the child a turn and encourage attempts at imitating you. After watching the child's response, modify your demonstration and take turns.

- Once a child has developed a skill, work on variations of that skill; that is, if a toddler has learned to pound a red block to make a noise, vary the color and size of the block.

Keep activities short, and expect crawlers and walkers with developmental delays to have shorter attention spans than others and to need more support and redirection as they move among activities. They may need more cues to interact with materials.

Planning for Toddlers and Twos: 18 to 36 Months

The changes that occur between 18 and 36 months are dramatic. Toddlers move from tentative walking to running, climbing, jumping, and twirling around. They learn to throw and sometimes catch a ball, to pick up small objects with their fingers, to scribble, and to feed themselves. They learn to dress themselves in easy-to-put-on and -take-off clothing and most learn to use the toilet.

Toddlers are also beginning to talk and put words together. They use two-word phrases and finally full sentences. By their second year, most children are capable of holding conversations with adults. With the advent of language skills, play becomes richer and more imaginative. They begin to "pretend play" with toys and imitate the adults in their world, often playing "Mommy" or "Daddy."

They begin to understand themselves as separate individuals with rights and privileges; however, they are only beginning to see that others have these same rights. They are more aware of their own feelings and the feelings of others. This is the stage of increasing independence and possessiveness. You'll hear exclamations such as "Mine!", "Me do it", and "No!" as children try to assert control over their environment. They notice other children in their world and struggle with building social play skills, sometimes eager to share toys with another child and sometimes hoarding all toys.

They are emotional beings. They are learning to identify, label, and demonstrate their feelings. They display a range of emotions, from pure delight to utter frustration and sadness, from open curiosity and gregariousness to extreme shyness, from happy cooperation to obstinate noncompliance, and from tender loving to hurtful anger.

Physical development has slowed down, but language, cognitive, social, and emotional development are in full swing. It is a period of rapid changes and amazing growth. Toddlers need adults who can accept the inconsistencies in their behavior with loving care and serenity.

Toddlers and twos are challenging to adults in different ways than are infants. Some adults feel very comfortable working with toddlers. For these adults, it is like being able to watch a person unfold and develop, with all of the trials and tribulations that are inherent in the process. Others prefer to work with infants; they like the dependency and the caring of this age more than the budding autonomy of toddlerhood.

Although developmentally based, planning for toddlers is typically activity-related and organized along traditional subject lines. A good toddler curriculum provides toddlers with choices of activities. Toddlers play with what interests them at any given moment. If given choices, they can choose what they want to play with from the preselected, developmentally appropriate activities the adult has provided. This is most easily accomplished by having low, open shelves with safe toys that children can use. Choices also provide toddlers with the opportunity to assert their independence and autonomy. Choosing for oneself builds self-esteem.

Good toddler planning provides activities that are self-paced and open-ended. A toddler is finished playing when she wants to leave an area. Forcing or coaxing a 2-year-old to "finish" an art project only causes frustration for the adult and the toddler. Some toddlers will paint for 20 minutes, others for 20 seconds. The same child might paint for a long time one day and not show any interest in painting the next.

Good planning provides toddlers opportunities to learn through sensory, creative, physical, and problem-solving activities. Activities are the building blocks of planning. As you think about the activities, think about areas of development and how these can be incorporated into your plan. Space should be allocated for water play, easel painting, creative arts, play-dough, simple dramatic play, books, blocks, music, language, and manipulative activities.

Toddler activities are designed for children who can get to places and can choose what they want to do. Use variations for making activities more difficult.

Including Toddlers and Twos with Developmental Delays

As toddlers become aware of the ways in which they are different from each other, it is the skill of a sensitive teacher that determines the long-term outcome of this awareness. Children look to you as a model.

Adults can successfully facilitate the toddler's inclusion into their programs if they plan to meet the individual needs of all the children in their group. Sometimes, special toys or materials will be needed to allow the toddler with disabilities the opportunity to learn a new skill. Often, the special toys can be used by other children in the program.

Involve toddlers actively in the learning process but expect to repeat this process many times with variations for learning to take place. You may need to use more directive teaching, rather than just assuming the toddler will discover what to do or learn from simply observing others.

Including toddlers and twos with disabilities requires more individualized planning. Adults need to plan to meet the needs of all the children in their group as well as the individual needs of a particular child. Typically, these needs are very compatible and need only variations on the general plans. Most of the recommendations for including toddlers with developmental delays are good for all toddlers; however, they are necessary for toddlers with developmental delays to be included in the group.

By including young children with disabilities in a setting, there is potential gain for all children in the classroom. Some suggestions for including toddlers with disabilities follow:

- Provide an atmosphere where issues about race, gender, and disability can be freely discussed. Young children are becoming aware of these differences. Toddlers learn respect and caring for others who are different from themselves by modeling adults' interactions with the child.

- Support diversity in your classroom through activities, materials, and program planning. Toddlers learn about differences by first-hand experience. If a toddler wears braces, the other children may want to try on the braces. Under supervision and perhaps with the support of a physical therapist, children can explore and experiment with braces and other adaptive equipment, but it should not be the child's actual aids. Toddlers generally dislike blindfolds, so it is probably unwise to simulate a visual impairment. The goal is to create awareness and to have a positive, rather than a negative, experience.

- Teach toddlers specific ways of handling situations involving staring or making unkind remarks. Make toddlers and twos aware of how children who are stared at feel. Teach all children socially acceptable ways of learning about others.

Because planning for young children is so individualized, a child's IFSP goals can easily be incorporated in the program plan.

- Teach children specific skills to use in approaching others and entering groups. If other children tease or make unkind remarks about the toddler with a disability, serve as the child's ally. Stop the teasing and explain that words can hurt people's feelings. Give correct information: "Camille is not stupid. It just takes her longer to learn new things." Over time, help children build the skills necessary to stand up for themselves.

- Help toddlers find roles to play and facilitate adaptations and accommodations that allow all children to play together.

- Encourage older children in a multiage group to help the toddler with a developmental delay as needed. Make sure, however, that this is not a constant responsibility. Also, pair the child with another, perhaps younger toddler, so that child, too, has the experience of helping.

- Keep a consistent daily schedule so toddlers will know what will happen next. Provide a picture chart to support the schedule.

- Limit choices to two or three activities during free play.

- Limit the potential for distraction, especially during small group times, by seating the child close to you and facing away from busy areas. If you have group activities, they should be limited to 5 to 10 minutes.

- Add cues such as carpet squares to indicate where toddlers should be.

- Provide safe outlets for the release of excess energy and feelings. Toddlers may need punching bags or silly time when they are encouraged to use up excess energy.

- Sequence tasks from easy to hard and match the toddler's developmental level. Use backward chaining where appropriate.

- Be specific about rules for activities and post these with pictures. Show the toddler the rules as well as telling him or her.

- Help toddlers organize their activities. For example, say, "What will you do first? . . . What comes next?"

- Use a variety of teaching techniques, including modeling what you want the child to do. Toddlers and twos often learn appropriate behavior by imitating others. Those with developmental delays may have a limited repertoire of behaviors, and modeling can increase this repertoire.

- Help shape a toddler's behavior by breaking an activity down into smaller steps and then leading the toddler through progressively more of the steps, providing many prompts until she can do it independently.

- The opposite technique of shaping is fading. As the toddler begins to master a skill, gradually give fewer cues and less information so that she becomes more responsible for doing the skill independently. Activities for infants, toddlers, and twos are so different from those for preschool children that they are included in this chapter.

Adapting Materials for Children with Developmental Delays

Most of the toys and materials you would use for any child can be used with children who have disabilities; others may require minor modifications. If there are major modifications, parents or specialists will typically provide this equipment. If there is no need to modify an activity, don't. When modifications are necessary, the toys and materials should be appropriate for the child's developmental level and chronological age, promote age-appropriate social and communication skills, and not interfere with regular routines or call undue attention to the child (McCormick & Feeney, 1995). Although specific alternative activities may be used, they should be interesting, varied, and available to other children in the class as well. Many simple adaptations such as adding Velcro, handles, magnets, and so on as well as the suggestions below will be useful for any child who is challenged by an activity.

- Slightly deflated beach balls are easier than regular rubber balls for toddlers and twos to grasp, throw, and catch.

- Toys can be hung above a child who is not moving independently but is interested in looking at and/or reaching and grasping the toys. Toys can be hung from the upright handle of an infant seat, above a changing table, or (if you are really ambitious!) you can attach a pulley to the ceiling and hang toys from a rope. Use of the pulley allows you to easily adjust the height of the toys for various children. If toddlers are grasping toys and pulling them, be sure that this equipment is strong enough to be safe.

- Toys with several parts (such as simple puzzles) can be adapted by gluing magnetic strips onto the back of each piece. A cookie sheet can be provided on which children can move the pieces. Just moving the pieces and taking them on and off the cookie sheet provides some resistance at first.

- If the child has difficulty grasping small handles, such as those on a Jack-in-the-box, pop beads can be cut at their opening and pushed over the handle to make it easier to hold onto. Likewise, foam hair curlers can be placed over paint brushes or crayons to make them easier to hold.

- Experiment with different materials to see what works, and remember that children change and grow quickly, so adaptations have to be monitored and evaluated on a continuing basis to be sure that they are developmentally and socially appropriate (adapted from Langley, 1985).

Although children with disabilities are more similar to those without disabilities than they are different, they still have unique needs.

Selecting Activities for an IFSP

Once you have a child's individualized plan with its goals and outcomes, you need to select activities to meet those goals. The IFSP should be written so that activities can be carried out within the regular routine of the child's program. Most of the needs of infants and toddlers and twos with disabilities can be met with minimal rearrangements of daily routines and schedule. Many toys can be used effectively without any adaptations.

- Suction-cup toys are valuable because they stay put more easily when a child who is working on eye-hand coordination tries to manipulate them.
- Velcro wrist bracelets can aid a child who is unable to hold a rattle independently.
- Pop beads or bristle blocks are usually thought of as being good for putting things together, but for a child who needs to work on strength, pulling them apart is great.
- Inflatable toys that haven't been inflated all the way are easier to grasp.
- Place Dycem (a nonslip plastic) on the table so toys don't roll away and cups and plates stay anchored. You can also put Dycem on chair seats to keep children from slipping off.

Questions to ask yourself include:

- Is this toy appropriate for children who are functioning as infants, toddlers, or both?
- What skills can you facilitate/encourage with this toy?
- What kinds of activities can you do with this toy?
- How can you adapt this toy (if necessary) so a child with a disability can use it?

Sometimes, major adaptations from a specialist are necessary. At other times, what appear to be major adaptations can actually be just a matter of hooking up a toy to a capability switch (a device the child uses to manipulate something. The child activates the switch and something happens, encouraging cause-and-effect reasoning). Capability switches are very sensitive and will respond to slight movements from any body part. Switch selection should be based on the child's or toddler's most consistent and reliable body movement. There are switches that will respond to sipping or puffing, voice, sideswipes, pinches, touch, tongue movements, chin, nose, and so on. Some switches are lighted for children with hearing impairments, others are gravity-sensitive so that tilting by any body part will activate them. Photosensitive switches are activated by any body movement that creates a shadow. Switches can control robots, trains, fire engines, pigs, bears, and rabbits. They can be attached to music boxes, toy radios, toy TVs, and tops. They allow children with disabilities to gain control over their world.

Curriculum and Assessment for Children with Developmental Delays: Birth to 3

Individualized planning is a circular process. It starts with a designated outcome: what it is you want the child to be able to do. For example, you might want a toddler to increase his receptive vocabulary. You then incorporate the words you want the child to identify into a theme to increase contextual learning. If you are interested in children learning household words, you might set up the dramatic play area as a house, choosing the specific household items based on the vocabulary you plan to teach. Then consider how you will incorporate the teaching into the play. You might begin by labeling the objects for the child and demonstrating what each does. Support the child using the objects and again verbally labeling the objects and what the child is doing. Finally, request that the child discriminate between the desired object and others: "Show me the blanket." "Can you wrap the baby in the blanket?"

Based on your observations, you either continue this procedure or modify it. When you have reached some conclusion about the technique, you tell the team that you are making progress toward the desired outcome or that you need ideas from the team to modify your procedure or reevaluate the outcome because it is not appropriate. Figure 24.1 depicts this process.

Implementing an IFSP in Infant and Toddler Programming

Because so much of infant and toddler programming is individualized, incorporating the goals of the IFSP into your daily plans is relatively easy. As you work from the IFSP, you may find it useful to develop your own format for planning.

Sometimes, the easiest way to individualize programming is to work it into your daily routine on a regular basis. This process ensures that it is done and supports contextual learning. Serving a gelatin snack is an easy way to help children practice using a spoon. Likewise, talking about body parts and pointing to objects is easy when a child is arriving: "You needed to wear a sweater today to keep your arms warm. Please hang your sweater in your locker." "Show me what you have on your feet. What are these?" You can easily incorporate these steps in your planning, but you need to remain deliberate about what you are doing and why. Schedule when you will work on specific outcomes with a toddler. Short-spaced work is more effective than attempting to sit a toddler down for half an hour and "do it all."

Because routines take up so much of the day, it is often useful to develop a chart that focuses your attention on the goals themselves as well as when you plan to implement them. This can be generalized to home if parents are interested.

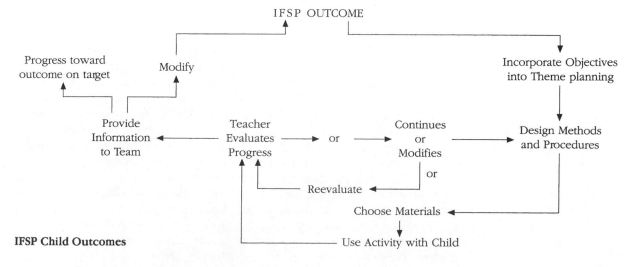

Figure 24.1 IFSP Child Outcomes

Child _____   Date _____

ROUTINES

Outcomes	Arrival	Morning Snack	Diapering	Play	Lunch	Special Time	Play	Outside
Point to or touch named objects	X	X		X		X		
Touch and name body parts	X		X		X	X		
Follow simple directions	X			X	X	X		X
Use a spoon		X			X			
Drink from a cup		X			X			

X indicates when you plan to work on the desired outcome behavior.
Progress toward attaining outcome:
AS - Attempted successfully
A - Attempted with some success
AU - Attempted very little success
NA - Not attempted
General Comments:

Figure 24.2 Goals Chart

When individualizing programming, it is often useful to take advantage of naturally occurring opportunities to facilitate skill development. As so much of infant/toddler programming revolves around routines, it is often useful to decide how to incorporate IFSP outcomes into these routines. A chart such as this one makes it clear when individual outcomes will be worked on.

Another useful format is to write one or more daily activities to work on with each child on a calendar or plan book. A calendar is helpful because you can post it where you can see it. Figure 24.3 shows a sample calendar for toddlers for April. You can send a copy of your plan home to the parents so they are aware of what you are doing.

Some areas need particular attention for most young children with disabilities and frequently appear as goals on the IFSP. These include adaptive/self-help skills and developing the senses.

Adaptive/Self-Help Skills. The development of self-help skills is important for the independence of the growing child and also to reduce the amount of time parents spend in caregiving. Parents often have conflicts regarding self-help skills. They want their children to be able to do more activities independently, yet logical times for learning these skills are often stressful,

April 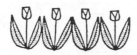 Ideas for daily activities

Mon., Ap. 3	Tues., Ap. 4	Wed., Ap. 5	Thurs., Ap. 6	Fri., Ap. 7
stack and knock down large cardboard or milk carton blocks.	Find pairs of big & little objects (spoons, socks, trucks). Talk about big & little.	Use scarves while dancing to music.	Play with soapy water. Add small sponges & plastic dishes.	Play with nesting cups (or try boxes or cans).
Mon., Ap. 10	**Tues., Ap. 11**	**Wed., Ap. 12**	**Thurs., Ap. 13**	**Fri., Ap. 14**
Take a walk outside. How can you tell Spring is here?	Read a simple book about spring.	Tape record the children singing and talking. Listen to the tape.	Play with dirt! Use large containers & scoops, small shovels or large spoons.	Plant seeds in dirt.
Mon., Ap. 17	**Tues., Ap. 18**	**Wed., Ap. 19**	**Thurs., Ap. 20**	**Fri., Ap. 20**
Make an obstacle course for riding toys.	Talk about pictures or toys of farm animals. Make sounds of those animals!	Sing "Old MacDonald had a farm".	Brush paint with water outside on sidewalk or driveway.	Play with pots & pans & lids. See if children match lids to their containers or stack lids or pots.
Mon., Ap. 24	**Tues., Ap. 25**	**Wed., Ap. 26**	**Thurs., Ap. 27**	**Fri., Ap. 28**
Have children line up chairs to make a pretend train.	Whisper as you read a quiet story, such as "Goodnight Moon".	Sing "Open, shut them".	Finger paint with soap paint.	Have children make simple snack (spread peanut butter on cracker).

Figure 24.3   Activities Calendar

especially in two-earner households. Children could learn to dress themselves in the morning before going to school, but this is a high demand time for parents and, although they may value self-dressing, they may also find early morning time spent teaching dressing skills adds great stress to daily routines. This doesn't mean that parents don't value dressing skills. It means they need your help in finding another time and way to support dressing.

Adaptive skills in general are repetitive and tend to be highly predictable in how they are done effectively. They might require adaptations for particular children, but overall, the procedure is similar. Children with disabilities often find these tasks difficult, especially at a time when someone is always trying to "hurry" them. It is helpful to have children experience success with each small part of a task rather than being expected to complete the whole task before feeling successful. One of the most effective ways of teaching these skills is through a task analysis. This breaks down a task into its component parts. Because self-help skills are so necessary and predictable, there are many commercially available sources for this information. One old standby is the *Guide to Early Developmental Training* (Wabash Center for the Mentally Retarded, Inc., 1977). Before going to a source such as this, it is useful to try to create one yourself. Pick an area such as hand washing and write down the steps involved. Number each step.

Now, wash your hands using the steps. Did you forget anything? Does your chart look like this?

1. Turn on water.
2. Press the liquid soap container.
3. Rub soap on hands.
4. Rub hands together.
5. Rinse hands.
6. Turn off water.
7. Dry hands.
8. Throw paper towel away.

Knowing the parts of any task is the first step involved in teaching it. The next step is chaining.

Chaining refers to the process of taking a task analysis and deciding where to begin teaching. Chaining can be forward (start at the beginning of the task and work through it step by step to the end) or backward (start with the end of the activity and work backward through the steps to the beginning). In backward chaining, a child can feel successful after having to complete only the last step in the process. Gradually, earlier steps are added until the child is able to complete the entire task. For backward chaining, then, you would *help* the child turn on the water, *help* use the soap, *help* rinse, and *help* dry hands. You would then say something like, "Amie, now put the towel in the trash. Great job! You did that by yourself." Praise the child for doing it well. To begin at step 1 is discouraging because the teacher, not the child, accomplishes the final step. Task analysis is useful in making you aware of the steps involved in a particular task. It also becomes clear what the prerequisite skills are. If a child lacks the prerequisite skills, it is doubtful that the task will be completed.

Sensory Stimulation. Infants and toddlers learn about their world through their senses: looking, hearing, touching, tasting, and smelling. The development of these senses increases the amount of input children receive. Children with sensory impairments and those who have not had rich environments because of restrictions due to chronic illness or their living conditions need many different daily experiences with sensory materials to encourage learning. With your support, children with sensory impairments will optimize their use of a sense that is impaired and strengthen and adapt their other senses to compensate. Compensation is not an automatic biological response, it needs a lot of practice and adult support.

Older toddlers are interested in doing things for themselves. Although still playing alone most of the time, they can participate in organized group experiences, provided the groups are small and the time is short (about 5 minutes).

The Infant/ Toddler Curriculum

Underlying all programming for infants and toddlers, especially those with disabilities, is respect. Young children need activities that help them establish some control over their environment. This security builds a sense of efficacy and self-esteem, difficult issues for infants and toddlers with developmental delays. To facilitate this development, talk directly with the infant. Tell children what is going to happen; even if the child cannot talk, still consult with the infant before taking action and explain to the children the purpose of your actions. (You might ask the infant, "Are you ready to be picked up?" The child's nod or tensing might be your answer.)

Social Awareness   Infants first need to develop self-awareness, then awareness of others and the roles those significant others play in their lives. They learn about their family and caregivers. As they enter a group setting, they must expand their awareness of roles of adults to include teachers. Likewise, they will need to develop methods of interacting with peers. Through this process, they are learning about themselves.

Inclusion. Social awareness begins with self-awareness. Adults can help infants develop self-awareness in a number of ways. For infants to interact, they must be in a quiet, alert state, calm *and* aware of what is going on around them. In young infants, this state lasts for only a few seconds or minutes at a time. Ways you can help infants develop self-awareness follow:

- When the infant begins to stir from a nap, begin to talk in a soothing voice. Try to catch and maintain eye contact.

- When the infant cries, lift the infant to your shoulder, rub his or her back, and help the infant focus on an interesting object or your face.

- As the infant notices her hands and has fun making them move, play a gentle game of pat-a-cake or peek-a-boo using the child's hands.

- When you are changing the infant, take the opportunity to develop body awareness by massaging arms, legs, and feet with gentle pressure and light touches.

With increasing age, self-awareness grows. Toddlers can tell you their name; they know the members of their family and their ethnic background. They learn where they live. Toddlers also become aware of ways in which they are similar to and different from others. They are becoming aware of their strengths and limitations. They learn about themselves by the way others respond to them.

Toddlers who feel good about themselves can accept themselves as they are. They can also accept others, for social awareness also involves the child's growth as a member of a group. To be part of the group, toddlers must learn to share materials, take turns, listen at appropriate times, work independently, and also join the group.

Toddlers may need to learn new ways to be with adults when they enter an early childhood program. They must learn the different expectations of educators and caregivers and parents and understand the expectations of the center versus home. They need to find ways of sharing adult attention. These are difficult areas of growth, especially for infants and toddlers with disabilities.

Include materials that encourage awareness of self and others, such as toys with mirrors, dolls, and puppets. Provide materials for cuddling, such as stuffed dolls and toys, as well as a cozy area to cuddle in. Build self-esteem.

Social Studies. Infants and toddlers gradually become aware of their near environment, their home, and the early care and education setting, and then the community in which they live. They do this by taking short field trips around the school, going to the store, and visiting others. They see people who look different from themselves and adults performing many different tasks. Social studies helps children learn about the complexities of their environment.

Young toddlers will spend most of their social studies time reenacting adult roles that they are most familiar with and situations that are meaningful to them. As their awareness of the environment expands, new roles will be incorporated into play. After a visit to a fire station, for example, domestic play scenes may be interrupted by firefighters who come to put out the fire.

Health and Safety. As children become more independently mobile, issues of health and safety take on new importance in the curriculum. As you venture out into the community with young children, they will learn that red means stop, and that they must hold hands or a rope while crossing streets. Even before infants can walk, you can begin to teach these concepts by verbalizing what you are doing as you push the stroller or pull a wagon: "The light is red. We have to stop until it turns green." "I'm looking both ways before we cross the street."

As children learn to label their body parts and become more aware of their bodies, they can take a more active part in their health care. Toddlers can learn some health routines early, such as washing their hands before eating and after toileting.

Language and Literacy

Learning to talk is a major task for infants and toddlers, requiring listening skills and someone to listen to. As infants learn to talk, they are also learning to use language as a way of internalizing and organizing information.

Listening and Speaking. Infants begin the process of learning to talk at birth. In the first few months of life, infants learn to distinguish different sounds, that is, noise versus the human voice. By 1 month, they respond differently to speech than to other sounds and even begin to show awareness of the different speech sounds that people make. By the time infants are about 1 month old, they begin to practice sound formation by cooing and are babbling by 4 months. Talking to them and imitating their babbling are good ways to foster language during this stage.

As infants begin to babble, they also initiate verbal contact with others. Infants need verbal stimulation at this time. You can support language development by responding to an infant's attempts at conversation (babbling). Introduce new words, but take turns with infants. Infants are continually learning how to say new sounds and eventually new words. Language development evolves into learning the meaning of words.

Around 1 year, infants begin to form easy words from the sounds they have been babbling. Da-da-da-da becomes "dada" or "daddy"; ma-ma-ma becomes "mama" or "mommy." The sounds become meaningful and consistently applied. Other common first words are action words or words that the child hears frequently, such as "cup," "juice," "bye-bye," and "ball."

Usually, those first words carry a lot of meaning. When a toddler says "ball," it is usually easy to understand from the situation whether the child means "Get me the ball," "Catch the ball," or "Look what I found: a ball!" It is not until about 18 months that toddlers begin to string words together, such as "Juice all gone," or "Daddy up!" Toddler conversations are different from adult conversations; adults must rely on situational cues to understand the meanings of words (and to fill in gaps).

Children's language, as their other skills, develops at different rates. Some children are early talkers and some are not. All children have problems with pronouncing certain sounds or words. Developmentally, children cannot make all the sounds necessary for the English language until about age 6 or 7.

Offer infants and toddlers a wide range of experiences and talk with them during and following these experiences. Experiences as simple as a stroll around the block, a trip to the grocery store, or looking and touching a visiting pet are very important. Point out the flowers you pass on your walk, name the bananas as you place them in the grocery cart, and label the kitten's fur as "fluffy" while the children pet it. Other ways of supporting language development follow:

- Model good language skills when you talk with children.

- If a child mispronounces a word, repeat the word correctly in your next sentence. For example, if the child says, "Here's a poon," you might say, "Oh, you found the *spoon.*"

- When giving toddlers a choice, encourage them to tell you which one they want, not just "yes" or "no."

- For very young children, point to what you are talking about so the children can learn the names of objects.

- Keep sentences simple; use "motherese" to talk with infants, but modify and expand your language as children get older.

- Listen to what toddlers say. Having someone listen encourages their talking.

- Provide materials that encourage talking: toy telephones, puppets, books, and so on.

Reading. Very young children learn best from concrete experiences. They learn more about the concept of "apple" when they can see, touch, smell, and taste a real apple rather than when they just see a picture of one. However, when concrete experiences with objects are accompanied by appropriate books, learning can be further enhanced.

Programs specifically aimed at helping children become good readers when they are infants and toddlers are controversial. Indeed, programs that encourage parents to use an academic approach, such as letter and word flash cards, with infants and toddlers, have been criticized for placing undue pressures on children and for not letting them "be children" and learn through play experiences. It is, however, appropriate to set the stage for reading, even with infants.

Read aloud to infants and toddlers. Have a daily time for reading. Infants enjoy sitting on your lap as you slowly turn the pages in a book and name pictures on the pages. The close physical contact provided is often as important as the book itself. Independently, toddlers may mouth or chew on books, attempt to turn the pages, squeal and slap pages, or carry books with them as they toddle about. Even such playful manipulations of books provide positive early experiences, which enhance learning language and preparation for reading.

When selecting books for infants and toddlers, bear in mind the following:

- Choose books with bright, colorful, appealing pictures.

- The simpler the pictures, the better. Books with one picture per page are good for the very young.

- Encourage toddlers to talk about the pictures.

- If there are words, the language should be simple and brief.

- Select durable books. Many infant/toddler books are available with pages of heavy coated cardboard, cloth, or plastic.

- Expect toddlers to bring their favorite book to you to be looked at or read again and again.

Writing. In the area of writing, the major objective for toddlers is to introduce them to the concept of a written language and for them to understand that there is a connection between written and spoken words.

Provide writing materials. With supervision, they love coloring and drawing on blank paper. You can introduce words informally as you write their name on their paper. (Say something like "This says Tiki" each time you write his name.) As children begin to label their drawings, for instance, calling their scribbles a "ball," write their label on the paper whether or not it looks anything like what they say it is. This, too, will help children make the beginning connection between spoken and written words.

Discovery

Infants and toddlers need to learn about the world they live in. They need many real-life experiences as a foundation for concept development. From birth until about 24 months, infants move from reflex-dominated behaviors to voluntary, planned responses to objects or events in the environment. For this learning to take place, infants need to be actively engaged with their environment and must have a variety of experiences from which they can abstract ideas.

Adults need to provide opportunities for learning as well as the language labels that make these experiences more meaningful to children. This combination of experience and language is necessary for children to develop scientific and mathematical thinking. For example, the young toddler first learns that soft, green things outside are called plants. Later, the child discovers that not all green things outside are plants, but can be other things such as cans, cars, trees, and so on. Further, he or she learns that there are different types of plants: some that you can eat, some that hurt, and some that look pretty. Later, the child learns that small, green things called plants outside are also called plants when inside. Finally, the child learns that different plants have individual names, which distinguish one plant from another. In each case, the child adapts previously learned information into a new category of information. The child does this by experiencing his world with the support of adults.

Mathematics. There is no expectation that infants and toddlers will learn complex math skills, rather, that they will be aware of numbers and the concept of counting. They will have heard songs and nursery rhymes that include numbers. They will be familiar with words that designate quantity and size.

With increasing age, toddlers can make size distinctions between what is big and what is little. They can put large pegs in pegboards as adults count them. They can sing counting songs. They may be able to "count," but it is unlikely that they will have number concepts at this age. They can do simple (three-piece) form boards and puzzles.

Science. Science for infants and toddlers involves investigating the world they live in. The process of learning to find answers is more important than the answers themselves. It is the basis for a way of thinking. For children this age, science is mostly informal; that is, it is nondirected, free investigation by the infant and toddler. The adult's role is to plan an intriguing environment that invites exploration.

Beginning at about 4 months, infants become fascinated with what objects do. Infants now explore materials to see what they can do. Previously, the goal was simply motor action. Now, an infant who discovers she can make a toy rattle will repeat the shaking action again and again to hear the rattle. This is the beginning of means-end behavior. This is also science.

Means-end describes the ability to use a means or procedure to achieve a desired end or goal, for example, pulling a string to get a ring that is out of reach. This behavior starts as trial and error in the middle of the first year, but becomes more purposeful by the end of the year.

To facilitate this learning, infants need sound toys: shakers, bells, rattles, clackers. Show infants a xylophone and help them make a noise with it. Give them spoons or blocks to bang. They need a variety of toys and time to experiment. Include materials that involve cause-and-effect relationships: wind-up toys, "busy boxes," and Jack-in-the-boxes.

The first signs of the concept of object permanence begin about the middle of the first year. Object permanence is the knowledge that allows infants to remember that objects exist even when they are not in sight. Infants at this age will search for and may find a toy that is partially hidden. If the toy is completely hidden, the child loses interest and will not search for it. By the end of the first year, the infant will search for objects that he sees you hide. However, if the object is not where the child initially searched for it, the child will stop looking. By the middle of the second year, the infant searches beyond the initial uncovering place and begins to search in new places for hidden objects. He must, however, still see the object hidden to know what to look for.

As infants and toddlers are developing the concept of object permanence, play games with them that involve forms of looking for objects and hiding and seeking. Drop objects and see if the child looks for them and then retrieves them. Hide toys for the infant to find, play peek-a-boo, disappear and reappear in the same or different places. Talk to the children when you are out of their sight.

By about age 2, toddlers can begin to solve problems in their mind, without going through the physical actions of the external problem-solving process. They can mentally represent objects and actions without needing to see them. They can invent new means to get objects, without relying on the trial-and-error process. They can find hidden objects that are identified verbally.

Between 2 and 3, toddlers begin to use mental representations and symbolic thought. Words become signifiers of objects and events. Toddlers can classify based on function. The child's play skills expand into more creative activities.

Infants and toddlers acquire information by experimenting with materials, objects, and events. Active learning experiences allow toddlers the opportunity to practice, refine, and revise previously learned skills. They need a safe environment, with materials that encourage exploration and experimentation.

Sensorimotor

Infants and toddlers need activities that encourage the development of motor skills and provide opportunities for integrating these skills with sensory input. They need a variety of materials that encourage all types of movements and reflect a developmental progression for skill building.

Large Motor. Activities for young infants are designed to use the large muscles of the body, such as those in the neck, trunk, arms, and legs. These muscles are necessary for all antigravity postures, such as sitting, standing, and walking. They also are necessary to stabilize the body as finer movements are performed. The pattern in which they develop serves as a guide for matching activities to children:

*   Infants gain head control first, then arm coordination, and finally control of their legs. Coordination of motor skills first develops close to the center of the body, with control of the neck and the shoulders. Then control of body parts moves further away from the midline to the arms and, eventually, the fingers.

- The acquisition of more complex motor skills builds on simpler motor skills. Young children must acquire the ability to control their head before they acquire the ability to sit.

- The sequence of motor development is overlapping between skills. Mastery of one skill is not necessary before others can begin, although it does need to reach a functional level. Children begin to experiment with new motor skills as they are fine-tuning others.

- The development of motor abilities involves the breaking down of gross movements into finer, coordinated, and voluntary motor responses.

- Children differ in the rate at which they acquire motor skills, but the progression of development is the same.

Developing and using the large muscles of the body is one of the tasks of infancy and early childhood. The pattern of motor development dictates that gross motor development precedes fine motor development. Children who cannot pick up a large ball and lift it over their head cannot be expected to print their names recognizably, regardless of the amount of time spent practicing.

To support large motor development, children need materials that encourage movement: soft, easily grasped balls, small riding toys, push and pull toys, and objects to climb.

Small Motor. Fine motor development involves the child's ability to use the small muscles of the arms, hands, and fingers. Reaching begins with gross movements of the arm and progresses to directed, precise touching of objects. Grasping proceeds from swiping at and missing objects to accurately picking up small items. Fine motor development involves three concepts that underlie skill maturity:

- Initially, the infant's hands are used palm down. As the wrist muscles strengthen, the hand can rotate so that the child can accept objects with palms up.

- Skill development (reaching) occurs close to the midline of the body and slowly moves to the outer extremes.

- The infant develops grasping skills first using the little finger side of the hand and hand pad. As hand muscle strength increases, this action moves to the thumb side. The child progresses from raking up objects with the whole hand to picking up objects with the tips of the thumb and index finger.

The development of fine motor skills is dependent on other related skills. Although vision is not a prerequisite for fine motor development, the ability to see objects motivates children and directs their reaching. Reaching is also dependent on the child's head and trunk control and adequate balance. Reaching is a prerequisite to grasping and picking up objects. An infant must be able to pick up and release objects for finer eye-hand coordination skills to develop.

Children need interesting toys to reach for and grasp. They need materials with pieces that fit together or stack, such as shape boxes, simple puzzles, blocks, and stacking rings. Also useful are materials that require pressure to put together or take apart, such as bristle blocks, rubber pegboards and plastic pegs, rubber puzzles, and pop beads.

Sensorimotor Integration. Motor skills are often used in conjunction with vision and hearing. In sensorimotor integration, both sensory and motor components of behavior are integrated in the brain to facilitate smooth movement and the ability to learn new skills. Use materials with varied textures (textured rattles and blocks, fuzzy puppets, playdough made from different recipes) to facilitate sensorimotor integration.

Creative Arts

Children are unique. Each has her own special way of being in the world, her own style of working, learning, and creating. Creativity is dependent on the developmental level of the child and the child's past experience with media. That is, what is creative for infants is not creative for toddlers, and what is creative for children who have never experienced a particular medium is not creative for children who have much experience with it.

Visual Arts. Art for toddlers is a sensory experience. They randomly make marks on paper. They may be just as interested in getting crayons out of the container or the tops off markers as they are in making marks. Because of their lack of concern about the product, the boundaries of paper are seen as arbitrary and are rarely acknowledged. Toddlers need large, sturdy crayons, chalk, and paint brushes. The paper, too, needs to be large enough to accommodate broad movements. Toddlers need to explore and use many different art media. They can paste collage materials and they can help tear them into pieces. They enjoy finger painting as well as using thick tempera paint, clay, or playdough. Toddlers are interested at first in exploring the medium itself.

At some point, children discover the connection between their movements and the marks on the paper. They are now in control. The product may not look different, but the experience is different for the toddler. The control is motivating. It is also generalized; if they know they made a mark on the page, they also know their finger made the hole in the dough. Although children differ, this usually happens around age 3.

Music. Very young infants respond to quiet singing and rocking, which is soothing and sets the tone for sleep. When infants develop means-end behavior (beginning about 4 months), moving rattles and hitting bells are initial musical experiences. At about 8 months, infants can use tools to produce sound. They can hit the xylophone with a mallet or the piano with their fingers to produce sound. The toddler experiments with sound by hitting different instruments with different objects to discover different sounds. By about 18 months, toddlers enjoy music and dancing. By 2 years, they can learn simple songs and will want to sing them again and again. They like simple songs and nursery rhymes that you can sing or chant together.

Creative Movement. As movement comes more under toddlers' control, they begin to experiment. At about age 2, they like songs with motions and moving to music. They do, however, need frequent breaks. They are not up to prolonged periods of strenuous movement. While movement is still being mastered, children are not as free to be creative.

Dramatic Play. Young toddlers use dramatic play to consolidate adult roles that they are most familiar with. These are usually roles that revolve around the home. Child care, cleaning, and cooking are typical "housekeeping" themes. Toddlers also play through situations that are meaningful to them. One can often learn about toddlers' feelings by watching and listening to their play.

Teaching Strategies

Although some children between birth and 3 are referred to as developmentally delayed, it is often clear there are specific areas in their development that are lagging more than others. When this is obvious, the following strategies are useful.

Young children with *communication* delays need experiences that help them to communicate more effectively. Teachers must give clear instructions, provide opportunities for conversation, and model good language skills. Books that are on the child's developmental level are always important. Learn the gestures toddlers with *hearing* impairments use for communicating. Be sure to use hand signs, gestures, and body language while you talk with these children. Provide stimulation through their senses of vision, smell, touch, and taste. Establish eye contact before you begin interactions. Imitate the sounds to encourage continued babbling and respond enthusiastically to all vocalizations. Let toddlers feel your lips and throat vibrate as you talk or sing. Use a mirror so infants can watch themselves make babbling sounds. Infants and toddlers with *visual* impairments need high-contrast materials (such as black and white combinations) to use their residual vision. Offer stimulation through their other senses (sounds, smell, touch, taste). When you talk to infants or imitate their babbling, let them feel your lips move. Help infants identify and locate the source of sounds they hear. Some infants with visual impairments rock themselves back and forth for self-stimulation. Distract them by providing them with an interesting activity or toy. Use words to tell toddlers what you are doing and pair words with motions or activities. For example, pair the word "up" with the action of picking up the child. Sensory activities help children learn the meaning of words when adults pair words with the way the materials feel. Be sure to tell toddlers the names of foods and drinks. They will learn what peanut butter is by the smell, texture, and taste of it, even if they can't see it.

You will rarely encounter an infant or toddler that is thought specifically to have an *emotional and behavioral* problem or ADHD. You are more likely to encounter children with *difficult* temperaments or children who seem very active. Later testing, when children are between 5 and 8, is necessary for classification.

For infants and toddlers with *orthopedic* impairments, provide toys to look at and listen to. Be sure to bring to children objects that they can't get themselves. Positioning is very important. Be sure to consult with the occupational or physical therapist for specific information.

You will encounter children with *health* impairments. Those that are diagnosed may be children who are medically fragile or technology-dependent. The medical profession will typically provide guidance on how to care for these children and their health-related concerns.

The term *developmentally delayed* is used to include children

>   (i)   experiencing developmental delays as defined by the State and as measured by appropriate diagnostic instruments and procedures: in one or more of the following areas: physical development, cognitive development, communication development, social or emotional development, or adaptive development; and
>   (ii)   who, by reason thereof, need special education and related services. (IDEA, 1997)

Because each state defines developmental delay, the definitions are not uniform. This category is available for children from birth to age 9 at the discretion of the state. Children with developmental delays will have very mixed characteristics at this age. It is useful to look at assessments to determine areas of strength and need.

Children with overall developmental delays need a great deal of repetition. Give short directions one step at a time. Offer challenging activities in small steps. Use demonstrations and modeling to help children learn.

Encourage children's effort as well as their achievement. Expect children to have a very short attention span. Emerging language skills may be best encouraged with a short picture book with one picture per page, which you verbally label for the child. It is likely that developmental skills will be more difficult for children with developmental disabilities to master, and they will develop at a later time than they do with other children.

Activities for Infants and Toddlers

Activities for infants, toddlers, and twos are designed and modified for individual children as they grow.

TABLE 24.2   ACTIVITY GOALS AND REFERENCE NUMBERS

Goals	Activities
To increase social awareness	214, 215, 216, 217, 223, 224, 225, 253, 254
To increase language and communication skills	214, 215, 216, 218, 219, 220, 221, 222, 223, 224, 225, 226, 234, 240, 241, 252
To increase cognitive development	227, 228, 229, 230, 231, 232, 233, 234, 242, 243, 244, 245, 246
To increase sensorimotor skills	214, 215, 216, 217, 219, 220, 221, 222, 223, 228, 229, 230, 231, 232, 233, 234, 235, 236, 237, 238, 239, 240, 241, 242, 243, 244, 245, 246, 247, 248, 249, 250, 251, 252
To increase creative development	226, 247, 248, 249, 250, 251, 252, 253, 254

Social Awareness: Small Group

214   CLEANING HOUSE

GOALS   To increase social awareness; to increase language and communication skills; to increase sensorimotor skills

OBJECTIVES   The child will use the house cleaning materials appropriately.

MATERIALS   Toy vacuum cleaner, broom, dust cloth, sponge, dust pan

PROCEDURE   Let children "vacuum" the floor or rug. Encourage them to work together with the broom and dust pan. Talk about cleaning and how you are all helping to get the room cleaner. Make vacuum sounds. Use different actions (such as several pushes and pulls, a long push, a twist around a corner) and encourage children to imitate. Make a path with tape or paper for children to follow around a room. Demonstrate how different cleaning tools work and help children use the materials.

INTEGRATION   Children often enjoy imitating the work of adults. Because you don't really care how effectively the children are cleaning, you can concentrate on the process. But while you are at it, slip in a few words about safety.

Social Awareness: Small Group

215   DOLLS

GOALS   To increase social awareness; to increase language and communication skills; to increase sensorimotor skills

OBJECTIVES   The toddler will play with the dolls in a variety of ways.

MATERIALS   Dolls

PROCEDURE   Encourage exploration of the dolls. Help children to gently feel the dolls' hair, eyes, and clothing, and to move body parts. Name body and clothing parts for children. Encourage them to play with dolls in different ways. Children may want to carry, cuddle, bottle-feed, sing to, or rock the baby. When they are ready, introduce new ways of playing with the doll. Encourage two children to play together and talk about what each is doing and why. Encourage them to think about what the baby might want or need. See if children can imitate more difficult skills, such as pretend feeding with a spoon, sprinkling powder or rubbing lotion on body parts, and combing the doll's hair. Help children use their imagination with the doll. Take the doll for a walk in a wagon or stroller. Wash the baby in a small tub, using soap and a washcloth, then dry the doll with a towel. Help children develop adaptive skills by practicing undressing and dressing, not only themselves, but also a doll. Remember, undressing is a skill that comes before dressing.

INTEGRATION   Children may need to be taught caregiving skills. They are often more willing to practice adaptive skills in play.

Social Awareness: Individual

216   MIRROR

GOALS   To increase social awareness; to increase language and communications skills; to increase sensorimotor skills

OBJECTIVES   The child will look at himself or herself in the mirror.

MATERIALS   Unbreakable mirror (about 12″), or large, mounted mirror

PROCEDURE   Hold children one at a time in your lap with a mirror in front so they can see themselves. Talk about what they see in the mirror: "Look, there's Dantea! I see you!" Or place children in front of a large mirror where they can more easily see themselves. Point to and name the child's facial parts when he or she looks in the mirror. Ask children to point to or name facial parts, as they are able. Have them play imitation games in the mirror, such as opening and closing their mouth, patting their head, tugging their ear, and making silly faces!

INTEGRATION   Children enjoy looking at themselves in the mirror. This activity shows children what they look like.

Mirrors can increase children's self-awareness and self-esteem as an adult points out their body parts and tells them how great and special they are.

217 WASHING DISHES

GOALS To increase social awareness; to increase sensorimotor skills

OBJECTIVES The toddler will play with objects in a basin.

MATERIALS Plastic dishes, basin, water (lukewarm)

PROCEDURE Put objects in the basin. Help children explore the dishes. Encourage them to put the dishes in the basin, swish the water, and take them out. Talk about their actions. Ask them questions. Have at least two basins so that children can interact. Say "out" as you take a dish out and "in" as you put the dishes in. Physically guide the child's hand, if needed. Say, "Good, you took it out!" Fill the basin with a small amount of water and add a small amount of soap. Let children "wash" dishes. Add a sponge or handled scrubber for them to wash dishes. Have several towels available to dry dishes. Encourage appropriate actions, that is, placing cups on saucers, pouring, and stirring the cup with a spoon. Have children sort utensils in a storage unit. Encourage them to match items by color. Have children set the table and use dishes to serve snack.

INTEGRATION Even young children enjoy pretending with familiar objects. The lukewarm water is soothing.

218 BOOKS

GOALS To increase language and communication skills

OBJECTIVES The child will attend to the book.

MATERIALS: Child's picture book (one picture per page)

PROCEDURE Place the child on your lap. Look at one page at a time. Name the picture. Encourage the child to touch or pat the picture. Ask the child to repeat some of the easy words. Then let the child explore the book while sitting on your lap or close by. Comment on the picture the child is looking at; for example, say, "Look at the bear. He is climbing a tree." If the child's attention continues, keep talking about the major details of the picture, pointing out colors and familiar objects. When the child loses interest, stop.

Then, open the book so two pictures are visible. Ask the child to show you the bear, for example. If the child points to the wrong picture, say, "Here's the bear. That is a cat." Place the child's hand on each picture as you are naming it. Later, move on to having the child name the picture you point to. Look for chances to use the words in the book in your later verbal interactions with children. For example, say, "There's a cat. We saw one like that in our book."

INTEGRATION Children enjoy books at an early age, even if they can attend to only one picture. Use black and white books with young infants, but increase the complexity of the book as children get older and have more experience with books.

219 DRESSING BOOK

GOALS To increase language and communications skills; to increase sensorimotor skills

OBJECTIVES The toddler will point to the articles of clothing named and attempt to name them.

MATERIALS A book about dressing

PROCEDURE   Begin by using children's clothing and ask children to point to the part of themselves or you that the clothing would cover. If necessary, give children a choice. Then point to the picture and back to the clothing as you name each. Read the book while the child is sitting on your lap or near you. Name and point to the articles of clothing. Ask the child to point to the correct picture as you name each article. Then ask children to name the article of clothing shown in the picture and find the piece of clothing on themselves if they are wearing that article.

Encourage children to "read" the book to you. Then ask them to show you where each article goes, for instance: "Where do the shoes go? Yes, that's right! Shoes go on your feet!"

INTEGRATION   This activity fosters adaptive behavior as well as language development. There is no expectation that young infants will dress themselves, rather, that their awareness is increased and that they frame these experiences as positive.

Language Development: Individual

220   FEED THE FACE

GOALS   To increase language and communication skills; to increase sensorimotor skills

OBJECTIVES   The toddler will put the tops in the designated opening.

MATERIALS   Shoe box, paper, markers, tape or glue, tops from baby food jars or small blocks

PROCEDURE   Cover a sturdy shoe box with paper and draw a clown face on the front. Decorate the face. Then cut openings for the mouth, eyes, and nose. (Laminating the face or putting clear Con-Tact paper over it increases its durability.) If children are younger or have difficulty, increase the size of the holes in the clown. Some children may not be ready to put items in but may enjoy removing the lids from the shoe box. Demonstrate how the jar lids fit into the clown's mouth, eyes, and nose and encourage toddlers to try. Then ask children to put a lid in the facial part that you name. Ask them to point to their corresponding facial part. Ask them to name the parts of their face as you point first to your face then to the child's face. Talk about how hungry the clown is today and count the number of lids the clown "eats." Have children decide what the clown's favorite foods are.

INTEGRATION   This is a fun way to practice eye-hand coordination with the opportunity for a lot of language input.

Language Development: Individual

221   FOOD

GOALS   To increase language and communication skills; to increase sensorimotor skills

OBJECTIVES   The child will put the pictures of the food in the tub.

MATERIALS   Laminated pictures of foods, tub with lid (slotted), plastic food: fruits, vegetables

PROCEDURE   Start by taking the lid off the tub and let children put the plastic food in and take it out of the tub. Then put the lid on the tub and encourage children to explore the tub. Demonstrate how to put laminated picture food into slot. Talk to children about what food they are putting into the tub, especially foods that are most familiar to them. As children become more proficient, add more laminated food pictures and ask children to find a certain food you name: "Can you find the grapes?" Ask children to name the picture they choose to place in the tub. Have children name foods at snack and meal time. When possible, give children a choice of foods to eat.

INTEGRATION   Food is a familiar and relevant concept to children. Using the pictures, however, is more difficult than using the food itself or a three-dimensional representation.

222   HATS OFF

GOALS   To increase language and communication skills; to increase sensorimotor skills

OBJECTIVES   The toddler will put the hat on and take it off upon request.

MATERIALS   A hat for each child, large mirror

PROCEDURE   Show the children your hat. Say: "This is my hat. Now it's *off*. I'm going to put it *on*." Put it on. Then tell the children to put their hats on and then take them off. Do this several times. Be dramatic! Have the child stand in front of a mirror and put on and take off the hat on request.

    This activity can be used as a simple Simon Says game by just putting the hat on and off: "Simon says put your hat on." (Hats go on.) "Take it off." (Hats should stay on.) Have children put the hat on another body part, for example, the hand, foot, or knee.

INTEGRATION   This activity involves both following directions and understanding the concepts on and off. Be sure to reinforce these concepts by telling children that they are "on the cot" or that they just jumped "off the bench."

223   MY BOOK

GOALS   To increase language and communication skills; to increase sensorimotor skills; to increase social awareness

OBJECTIVES   The toddler will make and read a book.

MATERIALS   Sandwich-size plastic bags that zip closed, magazines, markers, construction paper, paste, yarn, rings, paper scraps

PROCEDURE   Cut construction paper to fit inside the plastic bag. Encourage the children to draw or paste on the paper and then help them put it inside the bag. Write their name on one piece of paper and put that in a bag for the beginning of the book. Children can make as many or as few pages as they wish. Put each page in a separate bag. Put holes through the pages (and bags) and fasten them together with small rings or yarn. Support children in marking or gluing objects on the construction paper. You may have to put the pages into the plastic and help make the book while the child observes.

    Encourage children to make additional pages. Help them decorate both sides of the paper. They might have a theme for the book, such as color, and they could have a different color of paper on each page and paste pictures of that color on the paper.

INTEGRATION   Children can enjoy looking at these books. Encourage parents to make similar books with pictures of family members or as a way of reminding children of a special event.

224   PUPPETS

GOALS   To increase language and communication skills; to increase social awareness

OBJECTIVES   The infant or toddler will interact with the puppet and use it.

MATERIALS   Duck puppets (or other animal puppets)

PROCEDURE   With the puppet on your hand, talk to the child and encourage the child to talk with the duck or bunny: "I'm a duck. I say 'quack, quack.'" Encourage the child to imitate sounds, words, or actions. Then let the child experiment with putting the puppet on his own hand. Use the puppet to have a "conversation" with the child. Give the child time to respond.

INTEGRATION   Encourage older children to use puppets with younger children. Talking with puppets may encourage peer interaction as well as foster development of language skills. Simple puppets that use whole-hand movements are the best.

Language Development: Small Group

225   TELEPHONE

GOALS   To increase language and communication skills; to increase social awareness

OBJECTIVES   The toddler will "talk" on the telephone.

MATERIALS   2 telephones

PROCEDURE   Make phone noise: "Ring, ring." Pick up the phone, hold it to your ear, and say, "Hello, Oh, it's for . . ." Hand the phone to the child and encourage conversation. Praise any sounds or words made. Help the child explore the telephone. Show the child how the buttons can be pushed. Model holding the receiver up to your ear and talking. Encourage the child to do the same. Guide the child's hands and fingers, if needed. Then allow the child to explore independently. With a second telephone, call the child, asking simple questions: "Hi, how are you today?" "What are you doing today?" "Did you eat breakfast?" "What did you have?" Allow the child time to respond to each question. Give an answer if the child does not respond: "Oh, yes, I had warm oatmeal to eat." Say "Good-bye" and that you will call again before the child loses interest.

INTEGRATION   Use blocks or tubes as a pretend telephone. Encourage two or three children to talk on the pretend telephones with some help from you. Children enjoy telephones and may have had vast experience with them. Have a variety of telephones for children to use both with cords and cordless.

Language Development: Individual

226   HOUSE

GOALS   To increase language and communication skills; to increase creative development

OBJECTIVES   The toddler will develop imaginative skills and increase language concepts.

MATERIALS   Large doll, dollhouse, doll furniture, *or* build a house with blocks

PROCEDURE   Sit down with the child and encourage exploration of the dollhouse. Encourage imaginative play. Stimulate conversation with the child and talk about what is happening. Talk about activities in the house as the child plays. Talk about concepts like open and close, up and down, in and out. Introduce new vocabulary while encouraging creativity. Lay the doll on the bed. Say: "He's tired. Go to sleep." Seat the doll at the table. Say: "Time to eat! I'm hungry." Encourage the children to imitate your actions and words. Ask a child what a particular "person" is doing in the house. Give directions, such as: "The boy looks sleepy. Can you put him to bed?"

INTEGRATION   Small people pieces are not recommended for children under age 3 due to concerns about choking. Choose dollhouse accessories and people that are too large to choke on. This is a familiar setting for most children, and they enjoy working through routines.

Cognitive Development: Individual

227   HIDDEN TOYS

GOALS   To increase cognitive development

OBJECTIVES   The infant or toddler will find the toy after it has been hidden.

MATERIALS   A small toy, several cloths

PROCEDURE   Get the child intrigued with a toy. Then cover the toy completely with cloth and say, "Oh, where did the toy go?" Encourage the child to find it. Start by only partly covering the toy with cloth. Encourage the child to find the toy. If the child doesn't attempt to get it, point to the toy and again encourage the child. If the child still doesn't find it, take the cloth off dramatically and say, "Here it is!" If the child is willing, play the game again. If the child does not find it, partly uncover the toy and again encourage the child to look. If the child finds the toy, hide it first under one cloth, then move it to the other, covering the toy completely. Initially, expect that the child will hunt under the first cloth and then go to the second.

INTEGRATION   Activities such as this help children develop the concept of object permanence. Be sure to also play peek-a-boo and other games that focus on hiding and finding.

Cognitive Development: Individual

228   BIG OR LITTLE

GOALS   To increase cognitive development; to increase sensorimotor skills

OBJECTIVES   The toddler will identify the big and little toys and put them in the appropriate places.

MATERIALS   Objects that are large and small, 2 containers, dolls, books, cars, blocks, shoes

PROCEDURE   Put out the two containers and the toys to be sorted. Start with just one type of object, shoes. Tell the child to put all the big shoes in one container and the little shoes in another. Coach the child by asking each time for information about size and the appropriate container. If necessary, work only on identification skills and omit the sorting. Show the child a shoe and say, "Is this big or little?" When the child correctly identifies it, have her put it in the appropriate container. If the child forgets which container is for big, remind him or her to look at the shoes already in the container. Have children sort two types of objects, such as shoes and cars, into two containers. See if the children can figure out additional ways to sort the objects (shoes by type, cars by color, etc.).

INTEGRATION   Size and classification concepts are the foundation for many later skills. Younger children may only be interested in putting the objects in and taking them out of the can.

Cognitive Development: Individual

229   NESTING TOYS

GOALS   To increase cognitive development; to increase sensorimotor skills

OBJECTIVES   The child will pull the toys apart and renest them.

MATERIALS   Stacking/nesting cups

PROCEDURE   Offer the cups to the child nested together. Let children play with and discover what they can do with these objects. If the child doesn't pull them out of the nested position, show him how to do so. At another time, let the child play and experiment by dumping and filling the cups with water, sand, cornmeal, and so on. Then take out every other cup and encourage the children to build a tower. Let them knock it down. Encourage children to nest the containers themselves. Begin by offering a small number of loosely fitting cups. (If the set has five cups, take out the second and fourth ones.) Give prompts as needed. (Pointing, say, "Put this cup in.") Gradually increase the difficulty by offering more cups. Continue to provide some time for children to play in their own way with the cups. Talk about size, using first only the largest and smallest cups. Say, "Give me the big one." Gradually offer more choices.

INTEGRATION   Nesting toys that are cubes are easier for young children, as they do not roll away, yet circular ones are easier to nest. Provide both.

230 NOISY ROLLERS

GOALS To increase cognitive development; to increase sensorimotor skills

OBJECTIVES The child will roll the toy to make a noise, retrieve it, and roll it again.

MATERIALS Toy that makes noise when rolled and pulled

PROCEDURE Encourage reaching for and grasping the toy. Then show the child what happens when you roll the toy, and then give the toy to the child. Encourage the child to imitate your actions and also to explore the toy in various ways; that is, shake it or roll it to see if the child discovers the relationship between her behavior and the noise the toy makes. Then add toys that may be pulled or pushed. Encourage the child to try different toys to listen for different sounds. Help the child notice the different sounds, based on how quickly or slowly she moves the toy as well as the noises made by the toys themselves.

INTEGRATION Activities in this category support a variety of motor and cognitive skills and can be used at many different levels. For visual stimulation, be sure the rollers are clear plastic so they can see objects move.

231 RATTLE

GOALS To increase cognitive development; to increase sensorimotor skills

OBJECTIVES The infant will shake the rattle to make a noise.

MATERIALS Rattle or toy that makes a noise when shaken or poked

PROCEDURE Shake the rattle and offer it to the child. Demonstrate how to shake the rattle or poke the toy. Help children explore the toy or manipulate it for them so they can see and hear how it works. Talk about what you are doing and the relationship between what you do and the sound. Use a Velcro bracelet to help children hold the rattle if they have difficulty doing so. Tie a sturdy string (less than 12″) onto the rattle and attach it to a highchair. When the toy falls off the tray, encourage children to pull the string to get the toy. Offer help if needed. You can also encourage children to imitate your behavior with the object; for example, make two sounds and see if the child can make just two sounds. Make short or long sounds, loud or soft, and see if the child can follow your lead.

INTEGRATION Use dolls, blankets, bottles, and other accessories that rattle or make noise for pretend play. For visual stimulation, use clear rattles. *Note:* Use the string only with direct adult supervision. The child should not be left alone with string, and it should never be more than 12 inches long.

232 SHAPE SORTER

GOALS To increase cognitive development; to increase sensorimotor skills

OBJECTIVES The toddler will place the shapes in the correct places.

MATERIALS Shape sorter

PROCEDURE Present a toy to the child and encourage the child to lift the top off, remove the blocks, and then replace the top. Encourage children to place the blocks in appropriate holes. If needed, demonstrate how the shapes fit in the holes. If this is difficult, allow children to put in and take out blocks from the container without the lid. Then cover one or two spaces with your hand or a piece of cardboard or tape so children have fewer choices and can be successful more easily. As children become more skillful, use a shape sorter with more shapes, name the shapes, and ask children to put in the shapes you name.

INTEGRATION   Help children learn about the shapes in their environment. Play a game by looking around your room for shapes that are round, square, or triangular. A doorknob, a ball, a book, and blocks are examples of items you may find.

Cognitive Development: Individual

233   SUCTION CUP TOYS

GOALS   To increase cognitive development; to increase sensorimotor skills

OBJECTIVES   The infant will purposefully move the suction cup toy.

MATERIALS   Toys with suction cups

PROCEDURE   Place the suction cup toy on a highchair or walker tray or other smooth surface where the infant can easily reach it. Encourage children to hit it to watch the movement and listen to the sound it makes. Slowly move the top of the toy in different directions so infants can follow its movement visually. Gently guide the infant's arms from the shoulder to help the child either reach and grasp the toy or bat at it. Move the toy in a pattern and see if the child can repeat your pattern.

INTEGRATION   Toys such as these provide a variety of feedback to the young child. Once children learn the underlying principle, they can use this toy independently.

Cognitive Development: Individual

234   TAKE-APART TOYS

GOALS   To increase cognitive development; to increase language and communication skills; to increase sensorimotor skills

OBJECTIVES   The child will take the toy apart and put it back together.

MATERIALS   Toys (animals) that come apart

PROCEDURE   Present the toy to children to explore. If they don't take it apart on their own, show them how. Talk about the toy's body parts. Ask "Where's his head?" and so on. Use the toy to stimulate language development while you do the more difficult taking apart and putting together. Ask "Is this where the head goes?" Or ask the child to show you where the head goes and then you put it on. Take off one part at a time, such as the head or tail. Encourage the child to replace that piece. Gradually remove more and more pieces for children to replace or encourage children to pull the toy apart themselves. Help put the toy back together as needed.

INTEGRATION   This activity helps children think about body parts as well as part-whole relationships.

Sensorimotor Development: Individual

235   KEYS

GOALS   To increase sensorimotor skills

OBJECTIVES   The infant will reach for and grasp the keys, crossing his midline.

MATERIALS   Plastic keys

PROCEDURE   Call the child's name and shake keys. Gently place the keys in the child's hand. Help the child mouth, look at, or shake keys, if necessary. Keep the keys close to the midline. Then offer keys to the child to reach and grasp from different angles (up, down, right, left). Encourage feeling, looking, mouthing, and shaking. Try to get the child to reach across his midline to get the keys. (This can be encouraged by having the child hold a toy in one hand while you offer the keys.) Increase the distance the keys are from the child so that it is a long reach. Put the keys out of the child's field of vision and call, "Get the keys," so that the child has to turn and reach.

INTEGRATION   Any small toy that intrigues the child can be used. Children need to reach across the midline of their body to do many activities; initially, they need encouragement to do this.

Sensorimotor Development: Individual

236   MOBILES

GOALS   To increase sensorimotor skills

OBJECTIVES   The infant will look at the mobile.

MATERIALS   Mobile with few details and highly contrasting colors

PROCEDURE   Secure mobile tightly on crib out of the child's reach. The mobile provides something interesting and visually stimulating for a child who cannot yet coordinate movements to reach and grasp objects. Place the mobile in different places on the crib every few days to encourage the child to look in different directions. Talk to, look at, or help focus the child's attention on the mobile. Remove the mobile when the child can reach for and grasp it. Mobiles are for infants to look at and can present a danger if the infant grasps and pulls them. Provide safe rattles or other toys when children are ready to use them.

INTEGRATION   Children enjoy the stimulation of a mobile for about the first 4 months. Children with developmental delays use them longer. They are not designed to be grasped, so for safety, remove them when children begin to grasp objects.

Sensorimotor Development: Individual

237   ROLLING BALLS

GOALS   To increase sensorimotor skills

OBJECTIVES   The child will explore and roll the ball.

MATERIALS   Beach ball

PROCEDURE   While sitting on the floor, roll the ball toward the child. Encourage children to get the ball and examine it. Initially, take some of the air out of the ball so it is easier to grab. Hold the ball in the child's line of vision. Say, "Get the ball." If children do not reach for the ball on their own, put the ball in their hands. Place the ball a few feet from the child who is sitting on the floor and pat the ball. Say, "Get the ball," as you encourage the child to creep or crawl toward it. Provide smaller balls and toys of other textures for rolling. The child can experiment with rolling objects of different weights and sizes.

INTEGRATION   Children need firsthand experience to discover that balls roll but cubes do not.

Sensorimotor Development: Individual

238   TEETHER

GOALS   To increase sensorimotor skills

OBJECTIVES   The infant will hold and mouth the teether.

MATERIALS   Teether

PROCEDURE Encourage children to reach, grasp, and mouth the teether. Say "This is a foot (if teether is foot-shaped). Do those toes taste good?" Touch the child's foot and toes and say "Here's your foot. I have your toes!" If the child has problems, gently guide the child's arm from the shoulder area to help grasp the teether. Help grasp and mouth if needed. Talk to children and tell them about your actions as well as theirs. Encourage them to explore the teether in other ways, such as banging, shaking, and dropping. Try to support children in simple imitation skills.

INTEGRATION This activity uses a natural form of exploration (teething) to interest the child and then expands on this.

Sensorimotor Development: Individual

239 YARN BALLS

GOALS To increase sensorimotor skills

OBJECTIVES The child will explore and play with the ball.

MATERIALS Yarn ball

PROCEDURE Let children feel and touch the ball. Roll the ball on children's arms, legs, and stomach. Name their body parts as you touch them. Suspend the ball from the crib or other frame. Encourage children to move the ball with their arms or legs and to explore the ball. Hold it so children can grasp it. Encourage children to transfer it from one hand to the other. (If necessary, model this behavior.) Take turns giving and receiving the ball with the child. Toss the ball into a container and retrieve it. Encourage children to do same. Use a sturdy cardboard tube and encourage children to move the ball along the floor by pushing it. This activity encourages tool usage skills.

INTEGRATION Yarn balls are extremely forgiving, easy to hold, easy to make, and washable, and they don't break objects when they stray.

Sensorimotor Development: Individual

240 INFLATABLE ANIMALS

GOALS To increase sensorimotor skills; to increase language and communication skills

OBJECTIVES The infant or toddler will explore the toy.

MATERIALS Plastic rabbit or other plastic inflatable animal

PROCEDURE Offer the toy to children slightly beyond their reach. Say, "Get the bunny." Allow children to explore the toy with hands and mouth. (Be sure to wash it if children put the toy in their mouth.) If a child doesn't respond to the toy, call the child's name and touch the child's hand with the toy to catch her attention. If the child doesn't try to grasp the toy, gently squeeze it to make a sound. Move the toy out of the child's line of vision and squeeze the toy again. Say, "Where's the bunny?" and watch to see if the child turns her head. Encourage imitation by squeezing the bunny and then saying, "Now you do it." Talk about some of the bunny's body parts such as ears, eyes, and tail. Say "I'm touching the bunny's ears. Can you touch the bunny's ears?" If children can squeeze the toy to make a sound, provide more complex objects for manipulation: Give them a busy box or cash register with buttons to push.

INTEGRATION Children sometimes need stimulation to encourage them to explore their environment.

Sensorimotor Development: Small Group

241   MOVING LIKE THE ANIMALS

GOALS   To increase sensorimotor skills; to increase language and communication skills

OBJECTIVES   The toddler will move like an animal.

MATERIALS   Pictures of familiar animals

PROCEDURE   See if children can identify the animals in the picture. Help them decide if the animals are large or small and how they move. Have the children move as they think the animal would move. Make sure the children have enough space and encourage movement of any kind. As children become more proficient, choose animals that are less familiar but have obvious movement patterns. Talk about the animals and where they live.

INTEGRATION   This activity helps children learn more about the world in which they live and even think about it differently.

Sensorimotor Development: Individual or Small Group

242   BLOCKS

GOALS   To increase sensorimotor skills; to increase cognitive development

OBJECTIVES   The child will participate in block play at a developmentally appropriate level.

MATERIALS   Large cardboard blocks

PROCEDURE   Sit on the floor with the child and begin stacking blocks. Give the child a block and encourage him to join you. Let the child knock down the blocks you've stacked. Then encourage the child to put one block on top of another. Praise any attempts, whether they are successful or not. Let the children do most of the building. Provide other materials to extend the children's block play, such as cars or toy people. Begin to build simple structures such as roads and so on. Roads can be built easily by laying blocks side by side and "driving" a car over them. Say, "Look! I made a road!"

INTEGRATION   Blocks have the potential for building both mathematical and creative problem-solving skills for young children. At this age, large, light blocks are preferable. Those made out of two milk cartons forced together with the triangular ends cut off are fine.

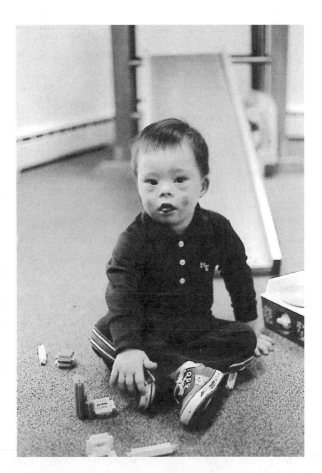

After toddlers have had experiences with blocks, add props to expand their play.

Sensorimotor Development: Individual or Small Group

243   DUMP AND FILL

GOALS   To increase sensorimotor skills; to increase cognitive development

OBJECTIVES   The toddler will fill the container and then dump it.

MATERIALS   Dishpans, rice, sand, oatmeal, beans, plastic measuring cups, measuring spoons

PROCEDURE   Put about 2″ of rice, oatmeal, or beans in a dishpan. Add a variety of cups and spoons. Help the children explore the medium itself. If necessary, place their hands in the container and help them explore the medium. Encourage them to fill the container with their hands. Then encourage the children to fill up the containers and dump them. Have the children dump the contents from one container into another. Help them establish a basic relationship between size and volume of contents.

INTEGRATION   This activity is a precursor to pouring liquids, but far less messy. It has the potential for simple exploration as well as for building concepts about measurement and size.

Sensorimotor Development: Individual

244   GRAB IT

GOALS   To increase sensorimotor skills; to increase cognitive development

OBJECTIVES   The infant will grasp the block and explore it.

MATERIALS   A variety of small blocks of different sizes

PROCEDURE   With the child in a sitting position, hold a small block just outside of the child's reach and see if she will reach for it. If not, place the block close to the child's midline or preferred hand, if that has been established. If the child takes the block, offer a second and then a third to see what the child does. Vary where you place the block for reaching. Sometimes place it close to the center of the child's body, sometimes more to the right or left so the child has to maintain balance while reaching. Give the child two blocks of different sizes and keep two blocks that match the child's. Clap them together and see if the child will imitate you or bang them on the tray.

INTEGRATION   Some children need to be encouraged to reach and grasp and imitate.

Sensorimotor Development: Individual

245   PUZZLES

GOALS   To increase sensorimotor skills; to increase cognitive development

OBJECTIVES   The toddler will place the puzzle pieces correctly.

MATERIALS   Wooden puzzle (1 to 6 pieces)

PROCEDURE   Start with easier shape-matching activities, such as shape sorters or puzzles with circles, squares, and triangles. Cover one side of the puzzle so the child has fewer spaces from which to choose. Encourage the child to remove and replace puzzle pieces. Verbally label pieces as children use them; encourage children to say the name of each piece. Hide puzzle pieces in oatmeal, cornmeal, or another medium. Have children find the puzzle piece and put it in the correct place. Hide puzzle pieces around the room while the child watches. As the child finds one, he replaces it and finds another. Provide a variety of whole-piece puzzles. When children successfully complete several, add puzzles with more pieces.

INTEGRATION   Sturdy wooden puzzles are a good early learning experience for toddlers. They provide children with feedback about their movements yet hold up to their lack of precision.

246   WHOLE-PIECE KNOBBED PUZZLES

GOALS   To increase sensorimotor skills; to increase cognitive development

OBJECTIVES   The toddler will put the puzzle together.

MATERIALS   Whole-piece knobbed wooden puzzles

PROCEDURE   Have the puzzle available for children to manipulate and experiment with on their own. If children are not familiar with this type of puzzle, remove a piece by lifting the knob. Encourage children to pick up the puzzle pieces. If a child doesn't try to imitate, help her: Place the child's fingers on the knob and help lift the puzzle piece. Place all but one of the pieces in the puzzle. Then, ask the child to place the final piece. Offer help as needed, but be sure to first let children try to replace the pieces on their own. Use puzzles with more pieces. Remove all puzzle pieces and have children replace them. When children can identify the puzzle pieces, ask them to replace the piece you name.

INTEGRATION   This activity is the first step in helping children work with puzzles. The knobs help emerging small motor skills and provide variety in practicing these skills.

Creative Arts: Small Group

247   DANCING

GOALS   To increase creative development; to increase sensorimotor skills

OBJECTIVES   The toddler will dance to the music.

MATERIALS   Record, cassette, or CD player; record, cassette, or CD

PROCEDURE   Play music for toddlers to dance to in their own ways. Use many different types of music. If toddlers don't dance, dance with them or pair them with other children who have the idea. Focus children's attention by talking about the beat and the concepts of fast and slow before they begin to dance. Add scarves.

INTEGRATION   Moving to music is a lifelong skill. Clap the beat dramatically so children will have visual clues as well.

Creative Arts: Small Group

248   DRESS-UP

GOALS   To increase creative development; to increase sensorimotor skills

OBJECTIVES   The toddler will put on and take off the clothing.

MATERIALS   Hats, shoes, shirts, blouses, skirts, dresses, pants, jackets, scarves, ties

PROCEDURE   Encourage children to dress up in the clothing. Talk with them about where they are going and what role they are playing. Focus on the self-help aspect of the play and encourage children to put on and take off the clothing. Be sure clothing is large enough to go on easily. As children become more competent, encourage them to play together with complementary roles.

INTEGRATION   Most toddlers enjoy a familiar level of pretend play.

Creative Arts: Individual or Small Group

249   PAINTING WITH WATER

GOALS   To increase creative development; to increase sensorimotor skills

OBJECTIVES   The child will paint with water.

MATERIALS   1″ and 2″ paint brushes, buckets, water

PROCEDURE   On a warm day, fill the buckets with water and encourage children to paint the sidewalk or house. Encourage the children to draw faces or pictures and then watch as the sun makes them disappear.

INTEGRATION   This is a clean painting activity. Children are free to experiment with the water and brush.

Creative Arts: Small Group

250   PRINT IT

GOALS   To increase creative development; to increase sensorimotor skills

OBJECTIVES   The child will make a finger painting print.

MATERIALS   Finger paint, washable table, finger paint paper

PROCEDURE   Put finger paint directly on the table (one color or two at most). Let the children finger paint directly on the table. You may have to model this behavior by showing the children how to get started. Encourage them to experiment. When they are finished, ask if they want to print their painting. If so, put the paper over the painting and smooth your hand over the paper to print the painting. Have the children paint directly on the finger paint paper.

INTEGRATION   Finger painting is a messy activity. It requires aprons for the children and a pan of soapy water or ready access to a bathroom for hand washing. Finger paint paper is expensive. While children are experimenting, using the table as a surface works well.

Creative Arts: Small Group

251   STAMPS AND STICKERS

GOALS   To increase creative development; to increase sensorimotor skills

OBJECTIVES   The toddler will place the stamps or stickers on the paper.

MATERIALS   Paper, stamps (free ones), stickers, markers

PROCEDURE   Show the children how to lick the stamps to make them stick to the paper. Then encourage the children to lick them and put them on the paper. Include stickers and markers for children's use. You may need to show the children how to take the stickers off the backing. Larger stamps are easier for them to handle. Let children participate in the process: Help children draw a simple figure, such as a circle or triangle, and then put the stamps on the design.

INTEGRATION   As you are sent stamps in the mail for advertising purposes, save them and let the children use them when you have a collection. Children may not have had much experience with stamps. For younger children, use clean contact paper, sticky side out, and have them attach small items.

252   TEXTURES

GOALS   To increase creative development; to increase sensorimotor skills; to increase language and communications skills

OBJECTIVES: The child will explore the textures.

MATERIALS   Squares (6″) of different textured cloth: dotted Swiss, satin, cotton, wool, terry cloth, knit fabric, Lycra, fake fur

PROCEDURE   Put the fabric squares on the table, and let the children explore them. Gently rub a piece of fabric on your arm and talk about how it feels. Gently rub the fabric on the arms or legs. Talk about how it feels. Encourage older children to stroke the fabric. Talk about its texture. Compare the fabrics. Add additional fabrics.

INTEGRATION   This increases children's awareness of different textures and builds language skills.

Creative Arts: Small Group

253   BIG PICTURES

GOALS   To increase creative development; to increase social awareness

OBJECTIVES   The toddler will mark the paper.

MATERIALS   Large sheet of newsprint, water-based markers, large crayons, large chalk

PROCEDURE   Cover a table with the paper; tape it down so it won't move. Be sure that each child has her own space to work in, with her own markers, crayons, and chalk. Encourage the children to work together and to talk. Make the picture part of a theme and have the children scribble something related to that theme. If the children desire, label the scribble and write what they say about it.

INTEGRATION   Leave the paper out long enough so that children can leave it and then come back. Young children often leave an activity and return to it later.

Creative Arts: Individual or Small Group

254   DOG WALKING

GOALS   To increase creative development; to increase social awareness

OBJECTIVES   The toddler will walk an animal.

MATERIALS   String, stuffed animals

PROCEDURE   Use the string to make a leash for the toy dogs (or other animals). Have one animal for each child who participates. Talk about taking the dog for a walk. Expect the children to walk with the dog and not participate in the creative aspect of the play. Walk around the room or outside, pulling the animal with the string. Talk about why we walk dogs and what you see on the walk. Make the walk a little longer and make more detailed observations. See if the children will pretend with you.

INTEGRATION   Don't forget to take off the leashes when you bring the dogs home. If you take an outside walk, be sure the animals are washable and expect to wash them.

Summary

Infants change and grow rapidly, from a stage where they are not mobile and teachers must present activities to them, to crawling and walking so that they can get to some activities, to toddlers and twos who are interested in exerting their independence and choosing activities that intrigue them.

For all very young children, program planning is individualized and dependent on the child's schedule and that of the adult. With increasing age and development, young children increase their repertoire and level of skill. They become increasingly interested in others and in learning about the world around them.

Educational Resources

Cryer, D., Harms, T., & Bourland, B. (1987). *Active learning for infants*. Menlo Park, CA: Addison-Wesley.

    A spiral bound activity book for infants.

Cryer, D., Harms, T., & Bourland, B. (1987). *Active learning for one*. Menlo Park, CA: Addison-Wesley.

    Activities for walkers and crawlers.

Cryer, D., Harms, T., & Bourland, B. (1987). *Active learning for twos*. Menlo Park, CA: Addison-Wesley.

    Even more activities to meet the child's developing skills.

Deiner, P. L. (1997). *Infants and Toddlers: Development and Program Planning*. Fort Worth, TX: Harcourt Brace College Publishers.

    Provides developmental information on children from birth to age 3 and activities to support development and learning.

Picks for Parents
http://nucleus.com/parent.html

    Links to information about infant development and products for young children as well as to other search engines.

References

Beckman, P. J., Robinson, C. C., Jackson, B., & Rosenberg, S. A. (1985). Translating developmental findings into teaching strategies for young handicapped children. *Journal of the Division for Early Childhood, 10*(1), 45–52.

Bruder, M. B., Deiner, P. L., & Sachs, S. (1992). Models of integration through early intervention—Child care collaborations. In S. Provence, J. Pawl, & E. Fenichel (Eds.), *The zero to three child care anthology 1984–1992* (pp. 46–51). Arlington, VA: National Center for Clinical Infant Studies.

Division for Early Childhood. (1996). *Developmental delay as an eligibility category: A concept paper of the division for early childhood of the council for exceptional children*. Reston, VA: Council for Exceptional Children.

Individuals with Disabilities Education Act of 1997. Pub. L. No. 105-17, 111 Stat. 37-157, 20 U.S.C. 1400.

Johnson, J. E., Christie, J. F., & Yawkey, T. D. (1987). *Play and early childhood development*. Glenview, IL: Scott, Foresman.

Langley, M. B. (1985). Selecting, adapting, and applying toys as learning tools for handicapped children. *Topics in Early Childhood Special Education, 5*(3), 101–118.

McCormick, L., & Feeney, S. (1995). Modifying and expanding activities for children with disabilities. *Young Children, 50*(4), 10–17.

Peterson, N. L. (1982). Social integration of handicapped and non-handicapped preschoolers: A study of playmate preferences. *Topics in Early Childhood Special Education, 2*(2), 56–69.

Ross, D. D. (1982). Selecting materials for mainstreamed preschools. *Topics in Early Childhood Special Education, 2*(1), 33–42.

Segal, M. (1988). *In time and with love: Caring for the special needs baby*. New York: Newmarket Press.

Wabash Center for the Mentally Retarded, Inc. (1977). *Guide to early developmental training* (Rev. ed.). Boston: Allyn & Bacon.

Wilson, L. C. (1990). *Infants and toddlers: Curriculum and teaching* (2nd ed.). Albany, NY: Delmar.

CHILDREN'S BIBLIOGRAPHY

The books in this section were specifically chosen to reflect the content of this book. They are organized topically and the organization follows this introduction. Many of the books are relatively new and reflect a body of children's literature that focuses on children—their diverse abilities, their similarities and differences, the implications of changing demographics, and cultural diversity.

The bibliography is designed as a resource for you and one that you might share with parents. When difficult topics arise in the classroom, it is often easier and wiser to initially approach them through literature. This provides the frame that what is happening is not solely focused on one child but is rather something that also happens to others. It offers the opportunity to lead into a general discussion rather than a specific one.

This bibliography allows you to expand your classroom to include diversity that does not naturally occur. Children can learn about other cultures and ethnic groups whether they are represented in the class just as they can learn about the implications of various diverse abilities.

These are not necessarily easy books to use in the classroom. Plan to read the books over several times before sharing them with children. Be clear why you are reading the book and how you will frame the discussion. These books offer many ways to expand a child's world when read by thoughtful caring adults.

Awareness of Emotional and Behavioral Differences

Hahn, M. (1996). *Following my own footsteps*. New York: Clarion.

(6–8) Gordy, a trouble maker, and his family move to live with his grandmother after his abusive father is arrested. An inspiring story of a grandmother's love and discipline.

Thompson, M. (1996). *Andy and his yellow frisbee*. Bethesda, MD: Woodbine House.

(6–8) Andy's talent and fascination with spinning his frisbee makes his classmates curious. Rosie, a protective sister provides information about autism as well as a siblings perspective.

Watson, E. (1996). *Talking to angels*. San Diego, CA: Harcourt.

(3–6) A story about having a sister with autism and her siblings understanding of how they are both similar and different.

Wells, R. (1995). *Edward unready for school*. New York: Dial Books for Young Readers.

(3–6) Edward, a timid bear, resists going to nursery school. He has problems separating and he is unhappy, vulnerable, and fearful. Other books by the same author discuss his first night at a friend's house (*Edward's overwhelming overnight*) and a swimming party (*Edward in the deep end*). Although these seem negative, they allow children to identify with emotions and educators and parents to acknowledge that some children are not ready for particular experiences.

Awareness of Learning Differences

Dunn, K. B., & Dunn, A. B. (1993). *Trouble with school: A family story about learning disabilities*. Bethesda, MD: Woodbine House.

(6–8) Allison and her mother take turns telling their sides of the story about discovering and dealing with Allison's learning disability.

Moss, D. (1989). *Shelly, the hyperactive turtle*. Bethesda, MD: Woodbine House.

(3–8) Shelly has a hard time sitting still. During a doctor's visit he learns that he is hyperactive and is given medicine to control his wiggly feelings. He begins to feel better about himself.

Gehret, J. (1992). *The don't-give-up-kid and learning differences*. New York: Verbal.

(6–8) Alex receives special attention to help his dyslexia. May serve as a stimulus for discussion but has some misconceptions (analogies of wearing braces and allergies) as well as some concepts young children might not understand.

Janover, C. (1997). *Zipper, the kid with ADHD*. Bethesda, MD: Woodbine House.

(6–8) Zipper (a.k.a. Zachary Winson) is always annoying someone. He is bright but his impulsive behavior gets him into trouble at school and at home. **595**

He earns a drum set by becoming more organized and learning to control his actions.

Awareness of Language and Communication Differences

Aliki. (1993). *Communication.* New York: Greenwillow Books.

(3–6) A picture book that introduces ways we communicate with one another with emphasis placed on talking and listening.

Andersen, H. C. (1988). *It's perfectly true.* New York: Holiday House.

(6–8) An innocent, jesting remark about losing a feather, made by a respectable white hen, is repeated, misconstrued, elaborated upon, distorted, and believed by the other birds.

Baer, E. (1980). *Words are like faces.* New York: Pantheon.

(3–8) A tiny-sized book of a lovely poem about words and what they do for us.

Chaplan, R. (1991). *Tell me a story, paint me the sun.* New York: Magination Press.

(3–8) A young girl feels the stress when her father loses his job and becomes despondent.

Hutchin, P. (1986). *The surprise party.* New York: Macmillan.

(3–6) A message about a party is passed from animal to animal, getting more confused each time.

Keats, E. J. (1983). *Louie.* New York: Greenwillow Books.

(3–6) Louie, a silent child, makes his first friend, a puppet, and is allowed to keep it for his very own.

Leventhal, D. (1998). *What is your language?* New York: Puffin Books.

(3–6) A boy travels around the world asking each person he encounters the same question, "What is your language?" Many languages are represented including Spanish, German, and Arabic.

Rahaman, V. (1997). *Read for me, Mama.* Honesdale, PA: Boyds MIlls.

(3–8) A young boy is unhappy because his mother never has time to read to him. She is distressed because she is illiterate.

Salt, J. (1991). *First words for babies and toddlers.* New York: Random House.

(B–3) A chunky picture book of objects familiar to young children.

Awareness of Developmental Differences

Berkus, C. W. (1993). *Charlie's chuckle.* Bethesda, MD: Woodbine House.

(3–8) Charlie, a boy with Down syndrome, has an infectious giggle that wins people over.

Litchfield, A. B. (1984). *Making room for Uncle Joe.* Morton Grove, IL: Whitman.

(3–8) Three children adjust when a relative with mental retardation comes to stay with them.

Prall, J. (1985). *My sister's special.* Danbury, CT: Children's Press.

(6–8) A seven-year-old boy describes his family life with his sister who has brain damage.

Robinet, H. G. (1980). *Ride the red cycle.* Boston: Houghton.

(3–8) Jerome, who has brain damage wants to ride his new red tricycle.

Awareness of Special Gifts and Talents

Carrier, R. (1991). *The boxing champion.* New York: Tundra.

(3–8) Young Rock wants to go into training so she can become a powerful boxer.

Caseley, J. (1990). *Ada potato.* New York: Greenwillow.

(3–8) Ada deals with being teased about playing the violin.

dePaola, T. (1979). *Oliver Button is sissy.* New York: Harcourt.

(3–8) People think Oliver is a sissy until he shines in a talent show as a fine tap dancer.

Fern, E. (1991). *Pepito's story.* New York: Yarrow LB.

(3–8) A young boy who likes to dance overcomes the teasing of his friends.

Gauch, P. L. (1992). *Bravo, Tanya.* New York: Putnam.

(3–6) Young Tanya encounters difficulties when she begins taking ballet lessons.

Hanft, P. (1991). *Never fear, Flip the dip is here.* New York: Dial LB.

(6–8) Flip learns baseball skills so she will be able to play with the older kids.

Hoffman, M. (1991). *Amazing Grace.* New York: Dial Press.

(6–8) Grace, an African American girl, wants to play the part of Peter Pan in the school play. Because of her gender and color she is denied the part. With encouragement from her grandmother she persists.

Isadora, R. (1979). *Ben's trumpet.* New York: Greenwillow.

(6–8) A young black boy dreams of becoming a trumpet player and eventually is taken to a jazz club by a musician.

McPhail, D. (1988). *Something special.* Boston: Little, Brown.

(3–8) Everyone in the family does something special except Sam.

Spinelli, E. (1993). *Boy, can he dance!* New York: Macmillan.

(6–8) Tony's father wants him to become a chef, but for Tony dancing is his world.

Awareness of Health Differences

Almonte, P., & Desmond, T. (1991). *Diabetes.* New York: Crestwood.

(6–8) A book written to present diabetes to young readers.

Bergman, T. (1989). *One day at a time: Children living with leukemia.* Milwaukee, WI: Gareth Stevens.

(6–8) A photo-essay following two children, ages 2 and 3, through eight months of treatment.

Chamberlain, S. (1990). *My ABC book of cancer.* New York: Synergistic Press.

(3–8) An A-B-C description of cancer.

dePaola, T. (1981). *Now one foot, now the other.* New York: Putnam.

(6–8) Bobby helps his grandfather recover from a stroke.

Gaes, J. (1988). *My book for kids with cansur.* Aberdeen, SD: Melius & Peterson.

(3–8) Jason, an 8-year-old with cancer, describes the various treatments he's received and which one is worse. He tells children what to bring to the hospital and addresses feelings of fear and the pain of treatment. This book is written with creative spelling.

Harrison, T. (1998). *Aaron's awful allergies.* Buffalo, NY: Kids Can Press.

(3–6) Aaron loves animals but is allergic to them. He is unhappy until his mother gives him a surprise.

Hausherr, R. (1989). *Children and the AIDS virus: A book for children, parents, and teachers.* Boston: Houghton.

(6–8) The author explains AIDS and tells about two children with the virus.

Kaufman, C., & Kaufman, G. (1985). *Rajesh.* New York: Atheneum.

(6–8) Rajesh, a boy missing both legs and one hand at birth, tells the story of his first day of kindergarten and the acceptance of his classmates.

Krisher, T. (1992). *Kathy's hats: A story of hope.* New York: Westcott.

(3–8) When Kathy undergoes chemotherapy for cancer, she finds a new reason to wear her hats.

Kuklin, S. (1986). *Thinking big: The story of a young dwarf.* New York: Lothrop, Lee, & Shepard.

(3–8) An 8-year-old achondroplastic dwarf tells of her life with her normal-sized parents and brother.

London, J. (1992). *The lion who has asthma.* Morton Grove, IL: Whitman.

(3–8) In his imagination, Sean, the lion, becomes a variety of animals to suit different situations.

Moss, D. M. (1989). *Lee, the rabbit with epilepsy.* Bethesda, MD. Woodbine House.

(3–8) While fishing with her grandfather, Lee, a young rabbit has her first epileptic seizure.

Ostrow, W., & Ostrow, V. (1989). *All about asthma.* Morton Grove, IL: Whitman.

(6–8) A book that explains the disease and reassures children who have this chronic disability.

Pollack, E. (1992). *Whisper whisper Jesse, whisper whisper Josh.* New York: Advantage.

(6–8) Jesse's uncle, Josh, who is dying of AIDS, comes to stay with Jesse's family.

Rogers, F. (1988). *Going to the hospital.* New York: Putnam.

(3–8) A book that describes in simple language what to expect when going to the hospital.

Verniero, J. C. (1995). *You can call me Willy: A story for children about AIDS.* New York: Magination Press.

(3–8) The book shares the hopes and fears of 8-year-old Willy as she copes with AIDS and still wants to play baseball.

Awareness of Orthopedic Differences

Bergman, T. (1991). *Going places: Children living with cerebral palsy.* Milwaukee, WI: Gareth Stevens.

(3–8) A black and white photo-essay of Mathias, a 6-year-old boy with cerebral palsy and a hearing impairment.

Brown, T. (1984). *Someone special, just like you.* New York: Henry Holt.

(3–6) A black and white photographic book that shows children with disabilities doing the same activities as others.

Burns, K. (1989). *Our mom.* New York: Watts.

(3–8) A mother with paraplegia writes her story through the voices of her four children. Includes black and white photos and explanations on how she dresses, drives, shops, and so on.

Carlson, N. (1990). *Arnie and the new kid.* New York: Viking.

(6–8) When Arnie has an accident, he realizes what life is like for newcomer Philip, who is in a wheelchair.

Caseley, J. (1991). *Harry and Willy and Carrothead.* New York: Greenwillow.

(3–8) Shows how a young boy copes with having only one hand.

Emmert, M. (1989). *I'm the big sister now.* Morton Grove, IL: Albert Whitman and Co.

(6–8) A young girl describes what life is like with a sister with cerebral palsy.

Holcomb, N. (1992). *Andy finds a turtle.* Series: Turtle Books.

(3–8) The story of Andy, a young boy with cerebral palsy.

Lakser, J. (1980). *Nick joins in.* Morton Grove, IL: Whitman.

(3–8) Nicky, who uses a wheelchair, wonders what will happen to him when he goes to a regular school.

Rab, B. (1981). *The balancing girl.* New York: Puffin.

(3–8) Margaret, a girl with paraplegia, delights in balancing things.

Smith, E. S. (1988). *A service dog goes to school: The story of a dog trained to help the disabled.* New York: Morrow.

(3–8) The story of a dog, Licorice, trained to help a boy who is paralyzed. Includes the background and training of the dog.

Waddell, M. (1990). *My great grandpa.* New York: G. P. Putnam's Sons.

(3–8) A little girl talks about her experiences with her great grandpa and how she can push his wheelchair and help care for him at home.

Awareness of Hearing Differences

Adler, D. A. (1990). *A picture book of Helen Keller.* New York: Holiday House.

(3–8) A book with pictures and descriptions of Helen Keller's life and accomplishments.

Ancona, G., & Miller, M. B. (1989). *Handtalk zoo.* New York: Four Winds.

(3–8) Using words, color photographs, signs, and finger spellings, this book presents animals and children at the zoo, translating the written English into sign language.

Arthur, C. (1979). *My sister's silent world.* New York: Talbot.

(6–8) An older girl tells about her sister Heather who is deaf.

Fain, K. (1993). *Handsigns.* San Francisco, CA: Chronicle Books.

(B–6) A classic ABC book that contains no words, but the alphabet letter, a clear sign, and an illustrated picture of an animal that begins with that letter of the alphabet.

Lee, J. M. (1991). *Silent lotus.* New York: Farrar, Straus & Giroux.

(6–8) A Cambodian girl who cannot hear or speak is unhappy and lonely until she learns to communicate through movement and dance.

Litchfield, A. B. (1980). *Words in our hands.* Morton Grove, IL: Whitman.

(3–8) Michael describes his life with his deaf parents.

Okimoto, J. D. (1995). *A place for Grace.* Seattle, WA: Sasquatch Books.

(3–8) Grace, with the help of her friend Charlie, who is hearing impaired, graduates from training school for hearing dogs and becomes Charlie's life long friend and hearing helper.

Peterson, J. W. (1977). *I have a sister, my sister is deaf.* New York: Harper LB.

(3–8) About a young girl's adjustment to deafness.

Rinkin, L. (1988). *The handmade alphabet.* New York: Dial Books.

(B–6) Each page is filled with a clear sign and beautiful illustrations. There are no words, simply an alphabet letter on each page.

Riggio, A. (1997). *Secret signs: Along the underground railroad.* Honesdale, PA: Boyds Mills.

(3–8) An intriguing, suspenseful story about a young boy with a hearing impairment who carries a message to the next safe house when his mother is detained.

Awareness of Visual Differences

Brown, M. (1979). *Arthur's eyes.* Boston: Little, Brown.

(3–8) Embarrassed by his new glasses, aardvark Arthur tries to lose them.

Hoban, T. (1996). *Just look.* New York: Greenwillow.

(3–8) This picture book provides a visual mystery as children attempt to identify a photograph through a small hole cut in each page. Children can be encouraged to make predictions and also talk about the problems of only being able to see a small part of something.

Keller, H. (1987). *Cromwell's glasses.* New York: Greenwillow.

(3–8) Friends make fun of Cromwell's "goggles."

Moon, N. (1994). *Lucy's picture.* New York: Dial Books.

(3–6) Lucy makes a collage that her grandfather, who cannot see, can enjoy through touch.

Raskin, E. (1989). *Spectacles.* New York: Macmillan.

(6–8) Iris Fogel misinterprets everything she sees until her myopia is corrected.

Yolen, J. (1977). *The seeing stick.* New York: Harper LB.

(6–8) By carving pictures on a stick, an old man helps a blind girl to "see" in this tale set in ancient China.

Awareness of Diverse Abilities

Bunnett, R. (1993). *Friends in the park.* New York: Checkerboard.

(3–6) Shows children with disabilities enjoying all the activities that children like.

Dwight, L. (1992). *We can do it.* New York: Checkerboard.

(3–8) A photographic book that shows the abilities of five children with diverse abilities including spina bifida, Down syndrome, cerebral palsy, and blindness with their families and friends. Available in Spanish.

Thompson, M. (1992). *My brother, Matthew.* Bethesda, MD: Woodbine House.

(3–8) A young boy describes the ups and downs of life when his brother is born with a disability.

Awareness of Families and Their Diversity

Albert, L. (1992). *You and your dad.* New York: Whispering Coyote Press.

(3–6) Colorful pictures compliment the rhyming tale of the different activities fathers do

Children need to be read to at home and at school. Older children can influence younger siblings by reading to them and encouraging them to read.

with their children. There is a wide representation of cultural groups and occupations.

Anholt, C., & Anholt, L. (1998). *Catherine and Laurence Anholt's big book of families.* Cambridge, MA: Candlewick Press.

(3–8) Poems, letters, and illustrations that celebrate the entire family.

Bailey, D. (1992). *My mom.* Toronto: Annick Press.

(B–3) A board book with pictures of multicultural young children doing things with their mothers. If you like this book it is part of a series of similar books. About five words per page.

Ballard, R. (1992). *My father is far away.* New York: Greenwillow.

(3–8) A lonely girl imagines that her father is having an amazing adventure.

Bauer, C. F. (1981). *My mom travels a lot.* New York: Frederick Warne.

(3–6) A little girl and her father cope well when her mother needs to be away on business.

Browne, A. (1986). *Piggybook.* New York: Knopf.

(3–8) When Mrs. Piggot unexpectedly leaves one day, her family begins to realize just how much she did for them.

Bunting, E. (1991). *A perfect Father's Day.* New York: Clarion Books.

(3–6) Susie, age 4, treats her father to some special activities for Father's Day; they happen to be her own favorite things.

Bunting, E. (1994). *Flower garden.* New York: Harcourt Brace.

(3–6) An African American girl goes with her father to buy flowers to make a window box for her mother's birthday.

Davol, M. W. (1993). *Black-white, just right.* Morton Grove, IL: Albert Whitman.

(3–6) A young girl comfortably narrates this story about a loving interracial family.

Glassman, P. (1994). *My working mom.* New York: Morrow Junior Books.

(3–8) This book describes a girl who, although she does not like having a working mom, she cannot picture her mom any other way.

Hoberman, M. A. (1995). *Fathers, mothers, sisters, brothers: A collection of family poems.* Morristown, NJ: Silver Bardett Ginn.

(3–8) A delightful collection of humorous and serious poems about families.

Hurwitz, J. (1991). *School's out.* New York: Morrow Junior Books.

(6–8) Lucas is worried that his summer will be ruined when he learns that his mother has hired a French baby-sitter to take care of him and his siblings.

Joosse, B. M. (1995). *Snow day!* New York: Clarion Books.

(3–6) When school is canceled because of snow, Robby and his family enjoy the day together.

Leedy, L. (1995). *Who's who in my family?* Orlando, FL: Harcourt Brace.

(3–8) Because of a class project children explore family membership including stepmothers, cousins, aunts, and grandparents and all the relative relationships.

Porter-Gaylord, L. (1992). *I love my mommy because.* New York: Dutton.

(B–6) Many mother-child animal pairs are illustrated that convey the link of caring.

Porter-Gaylord, L. (1992). *I love my daddy because.* New York: Dutton.

(1–3) Many father-child animal pairs show caring fathers and what being a baby animal is like.

Simon, N. (1993). *All kinds of families.* Chicago: A. Whitman.

(3–8) Families have many configurations and life styles but all can support their children.

Steig, W. (1996). *The toy brother.* New York: HarperCollins Juvenile Books.

(3–8) Yorick is always annoyed by his younger brother. Then one day when experimenting, Yorick shrinks himself. He needs his younger brother's help to find an antidote. As they struggle together, they begin to learn what being brothers is all about.

Williams, V. B. (1990). *"More more more," said the baby.* New York: Greenwillow.

(B–6) This book contains short stories about three multiethnic babies who want more attention. A mother, father, and grandmother lovingly respond.

Yolen, J. (1987). *Owl moon.* New York: Philomel Books.

(3–6) A young child and her caring father take a nighttime stroll through the winter woods looking for owls.

Awareness of Extended Family

Bat-Ami, M. (1993). *Sea, salt, and air.* New York: Macmillan.

(3–6) During a summer visit to her grandparents at the beach, a young girl ponders how she will develop in the future.

Blegvad, L. (1993). *Once upon a time and grandma.* New York: Macmillan.

(3–8) Grandma shows her grandchildren the house she lived in when she was a girl and her many memories growing up there.

Bunting, E. (1994). *Sunshine home.* New York: Clarion.

(6–8) Timmie's grandmother is in a nursing home recovering from a broken hip. At first everyone in the family seems happy then Timmie helps them express their feelings and that makes the family express their sadness despite the name of the home.

Butterworth, N. (1991). *My grandma is wonderful.* Cambridge, MA: Candlewick Press.

(3–6) Clear, realistic drawings and easy humor describe the reasons a child loves his grandma and the special things they do together.

Carlson, N. (1991). *A visit to grandma's.* New York: Puffin Books.

(3–8) A family visits grandma to find she has changed. She no longer sits home knitting, she is taking aerobics. The comical style of the book helps eliminate stereotypes about grandmothers.

Chorao, K. (1994). *Annie and cousin Precious.* New York: Dutton.

(3–8) This book portrays the ambivalent affection close young relatives share.

dePaola, T. (1993). *Tom.* New York: Putnam.

(6–8) Aside from having the same name, Tommy and his grandfather Tom share a sense of humor.

Karkowsku, N. (1989). *Grandma's soup.* New York: Kar-Ben.

(3–8) Several children gradually adjust to the fact that their grandmother has Alzheimer's disease.

Pinkney, G. J. (1992). *Back home.* New York: Dial.

(6–8) Eight-year-old Ernestine returns to visit relatives on the North Carolina farm where she was born.

Rodowsky, C. (1992). *Jenny and the grand old great-aunts.* New York: Bradbury Press.

(6–8) Although Jenny is a bit apprehensive about spending the day with her great-aunts, she finds herself pleasantly surprised.

Shecter, B. (1996). *Great-Uncle Alfred forgets.* New York: HarperCollins.

(3–6) Emily spends a day with her great-uncle who is showing sings of Alzheimer's disease. Although he sometimes forgets her name, he tells great stories.

Wild, M. (1994). *Our granny.* New York: Ticknor & Fields.

(3–8) A charming book that shows that grandmothers come in all sizes, shapes, colors, and styles.

Awareness of Adoptive and Foster Families

Banish, R., & Jordan-Wong, J. (1992). *A forever family.* New York: HarperCollins.

(6–8) This photo essay takes 8-year-old Jennifer after 4 years of living in many different foster homes into adoption.

Barracca, D., & Barracca, S. (1990). *The adventures of taxi dog.* New York: Dial Books for Young Readers.

(3–8) Maxi recalls his days as a stray and his adoption by Jim, the taxi driver.

Gabel, S. (1989). *Where the sun kisses the sea.* New York: Perspectives.

(3–6) A sensitive young Asian boy is adopted by a white American family.

Girard, L. W. (1991). *Adoption is for always.* Morton Grove, IL: A. Whitman.

(6–8) Celia is old enough to understand what adoption really means and she isn't sure she likes it.

Keller, H. (1991). *Horace.* New York: Greenwillow Books.

(6–8) Horace, an adopted child, realizes that being part of a family depends on how you feel and not on how you look.

Maclachlan, P. (1992). *Mama one, mama two.* New York: Trumpet Club.

(6–8) When mama one becomes severely depressed, Maudie goes to a foster parent until her mother gets well.

Pelligrini, N. (1991). *Families are different.* New York: Holiday.

(3–6) Two Korean girls gradually adjust to their new American adoptive family.

Turner, A. (1990). *Through moon and stars and night skies.* New York: Harper.

(6–9) An Asian boy recalls all of the steps in being adopted into his happy American home.

Awareness of Families and Separation

Abercrombie, B. (1990). *Charlie Anderson.* New York: Margaret K. McElderry Books.

(3–8) A cat lives in two houses. In one he is known as Charlie, the other Anderson. He is loved and cared for in both. A gentle story about custody.

Pristine, J. (1996). *Mom and dad break up.* St. Paul, MN: Redleaf Press.

(3–8) A boy deals with his feelings and the reality of his parents separation.

Van Leeuwen, J. (1996). *Blue sky, butterfly.* New York: Dial.

(6–8) After the separation, Twig's mother sits and does nothing. Twig, an 11-year-old, assumes responsibility for the family. Her grandmother arrives and gradually the family begins to rebuild.

Awareness of Families and Divorce

Amos, J. (1991). *Annie's story.* Chatham, NJ: Raintree.

(6–8) Annie talks about her feelings when her father does not come home anymore and having to visit him. (Discussion questions are included.)

Ballard, R. (1993). *Gracie.* New York: Greenwillow.

(3–8) The realities of divorce are dealt with in simple language.

Brown, L. K., & Brown, M. (1988). *Dinosaur's divorce: A guide for changing families.* Boston, MA: Little, Brown.

(3–8) These dinosaurs are green and somewhat crocodilian and they demonstrate all the feeling and problems children encounter with divorce in the family.

Christiansen, C. B. (1989). *My mother's house, my father's house.* New York: Anthenum.

(3–8) A positively written book about the realities of children's lives including divorce, childcare and working mothers.

Girard, L. W. (1987). *At daddy's on Saturdays.* Morton Grove, IL: Albert Whitman.

(6–8) Katie is afraid she will never see her father when her parents get divorced but she soon realizes he will always be there for her even if he doesn't live with her.

Schindel, J. (1995). *Dear daddy.* Morton Grove, IL: Albert Whitman.

(6–8) Jesse's father lives across the country from him, but his letters bring them closer.

Spelman, C. (1998). *Mama and daddy bear's divorce.* Morton Grove, IL: Albert Whitman.

(3–6) Dinah Bear feels sad and scared when her parents say they are getting a divorce.

Rogers, F. (1996). *Let's talk about it: Divorce.* New York: G. P. Putnams Sons.

(3–6) Through pictures and easy reading, Mr. Rogers talks about divorce and the concerns of children. This book can provide the impetus of helpful talk and careful listening.

(3–8) A little girl adapts to a joint-custody situation.

Vigna, J. (1987). *Mommy and me by ourselves again.* Morton Grove, IL: Whitman LB.

(3–8) Mother and daughter are alone after the divorce, and it's a lonely birthday until relatives arrive again.

Awareness of Remarried Families

Best, C., & Palmisciano, D. (1996). *Getting used to Harry.* New York: Orchard Books.

(6–8) Cynthia is left home when her mother and stepfather Harry go on their honeymoon. When they return, Harry is home all the time. Cynthia wants Harry to go home, but remembers—he is home.

Boyd, L. (1990). *Sam is my half brother.* New York: Viking.

(3–8) Hessie finds that she is no longer the center of attention when her half brother is born.

Boyd, L. (1989). *The not-so-wicked stepmother.* New York: Puffin Paper.

(3–8) A story about Hessie, who must spend the summer with her father and his new wife.

Casley, J. (1995). *Priscilla twice.* New York: Greenwillow Books.

(6–8) Priscilla has two of everything, but what she really wants is one family. This is a heartwarming and funny story of Priscilla as she realizes there's more than one kind of family and what makes a family is love.

Cook, J. T. (1995). *Room for stepdaddy.* Morton Grove, IL: Albert Whitman.

(6–8) The more Joey's stepdad tries to connect with him, the more Joey misses his dad. After seeing the positive relationship between his mommy, daddy, and stepdaddy, Joey realizes that there's room for them all.

Day, N. R. (1995). *The lion's whiskers: An Ethiopian folktale.* New York: Scholastic.

(6–8) Fanaye, a stepmother, desires her stepson's love and fulfills an awesome task imposed by a medicine man to reach him.

Leach, N. (1993). *My wicked stepmother.* New York: Macmillan.

(6–8) At first, Tom hates his stepmother, but when he deliberately hurts her and she cries, his hate turns to love.

Han, O., & Plunkett, S. (1996). *Kongi and Potgi: A Cinderella story from Korea.* New York: Dial.

(3–8) After Kongi's mother dies, her father marries the wicked stepmother. But through the help of a variety of animal friends, Kongi goes to the prince's ball and eventually marries the prince.

Hines, A. G. (1996). *When we married Gary.* New York: Greenwillow Books.

(6–8) A warm and understanding story of a second marriage seen through the eyes of a child.

McAfee, A. (1985). *The visitors who came to stay.* New York: Viking.

(3–8) At first, Katy objects to Mary and her son Sean when they move into her house.

Sherman, C. (1996). *Eli and the swampman.* New York: HarperCollins.

(6–8) Eli leaves the home of his mother and stepfather to visit his father in Alaska. As he travels through an old swamp, he develops a brief relationship with the swampman who helps him understand that two fathers are better than none.

Awareness of Single Parent Families

Harrison, T. (1995). *The long weekend.* London: Red Fox.

(3–8) For his birthday, James wants a long weekend. He and his mother spend the time together at the beach creating sand castles and memories.

Lindsay, J. W. (1994). *Do I have a daddy? A story about a single-parent child with a special section for single mothers and fathers.* Buena Park, CA: Morning Glory Press.

(3–8) Erik has not seen his father and wants to know why. His mother answers his questions simply and honestly. Also in Spanish.

Awareness of Gay and Lesbian Families

Elwin, R., & Paulse, M. (1996). *Asha's mums.*

(3–8) When Asha brings a form signed by two mothers, the teacher is confused until Asha and her mothers explain. Milford, CT: LPC/InBook.

Heron, H., & Maran, M. (1991). *How would you feel if your dad was gay?* Los Angeles: Alyson Publications.

(6–8) Jasmine faces problems with her classmates because she has three dads: her stepfather, her natural father, and his lover.

Newman, L. (1991). *Heather has two mommies.* Los Angeles: Alyson Publications.

(3–6) Three-year-old Heather sees nothing unusual about having two mommies. When she joins a play group and discovers "daddies" her confusion is dispelled by a caring adult and other children who describe their families.

Newman, L. (1989). *Gloria goes to Gay Pride.* Los Angeles: Alyson Publications.

(3–6) Gay Pride day is fun for Gloria and her two mothers. The day is described from a young girl's point of view.

Valentine, J. (1991). *The duke who outlawed jelly beans and other stories.* Los Angeles: Alyson Publications.

(6–8) Five fairy tales, colorfully illustrated, about the adventures of children who happen to have gay or lesbian parents.

Wilhoite, M. (1990). *Daddy's roommate.* Los Angeles: Alyson Publications.

(3–8) A simple, honest depiction of the everyday life of a boy with a gay father.

Wilhoite, M. (1996). *Daddy's wedding.* Los Angeles: Alyson Publications.

(6–8) When daddy and daddy's roommate decide to get married, Nick gets to be the best man. While everybody is celebrating the big day, the dog Clancy, has a big surprise, too.

Awareness of Families and Their Cultures

Bartone, E. (1993). *Peppe the lamplighter.* New York: Lothrop, Lee, Shepard Books.

(6–8) This is a story about an Italian immigrant family at the turn of the century. Peppe, the son works as a lamplighter and tries to win his father's respect.

Breckler, R. K. (1992). *Hoang breaks the lucky teapot.* Boston, MA: Houghton.

(3–8) A young Vietnamese-American boy believes his family will have bad luck after he breaks his grandmother's precious teapot.

Garza, C. L. (1990). *Family pictures/Cuadros de familia.* San Francisco: Children's Book Press.

(3–8) Shows pictures of a Mexican-American family and helps children learn about this culture and how families are both the same and different.

Garza, C. L. (1996). *In my family/En mi familia.* San Francisco: Children's Book Press.

(3–8) A collection of paintings showing family experiences and customs in Mexican-American culture. In English and Spanish.

Johnson, T. (1996). *Fishing Sunday.* New York: Tamborine.

(3–8) An American-born grandson comes to appreciate his Japanese grandfather's uniqueness and the charm of his old fashion ways.

Kuklin, S. (1992). *How my family lives in America.* New York: Macmillan.

(6–8) Three children, one an African American, one a Chinese American, and one a Chinese American, talk about their families and their pride in their ancestors.

Nomura, T. (1991). *Grandpa's town.* New York: Kane/Miller Books.

(6-8) A young Japanese boy, worried that his grandfather is lonely, accompanies him to the public bath.

Ricklen, N. (1994). *My family/Mi familia*. New York: Aladdin Books.

(B-3) A photographic book of pictures of families from many cultures in English and Spanish.

Say, A. (1993). *Grandfather's journey*. Boston: Houghton Mifflin.

(3-8) Through water color illustrations, this book takes a look at a Japanese immigrant and how he feels torn between his family in America and his old life in Japan.

Awareness of Cultures

Anholt, C., & Anholt, L. (1991). *All about you*. New York: Scholastic

(3-6) A simple book that introduces concepts related to multiculturalism as it shows individuals in many cultures doing familiar things such as eating, sleeping, and dressing. It invites children to think about themselves and their feelings. This book also has an accompanying audio cassette.

Badt, K. L. (1994). *Greetings*. Chicago: Children's Press.

(6-8) Shows the many different ways people greet each other throughout the world.

Badt, K. L. (1994). *Hair there and everywhere*. Chicago: Children's Press.

Each chapter explores different regions and hair styles with color photographs to illustrate.

Baer, E. (1995). *This is the way we eat our lunch: A book about children around the world*. New York: Scholastic.

(3-6) Takes children on a journey using rhyming verse to show a variety of different children and the lunches they eat.

Baer, E. (1990). *This is the way we go to school: A book about children around the world*. New York: Scholastic.

(3-8) Shows the many different ways children get to school.

Dooley, N. (1991). *Everybody bakes bread*. Minneapolis, MN: Carolrhoda Books.

(3-8) Carrie samples many different kinds of bread (including chapatis, challah, and papasas) as she goes through her diverse neighborhood looking for a three-handled rolling pin. (Recipes included.)

Dooley, N. (1996). *Everybody cooks rice*. Boston: Houghton Mifflin.

(3-8) Carrie searches the neighborhood for her brother and discovers that although the families are from different places all are eating rice. (Recipes provided. Also available in Spanish.)

Greene, C. (1982). *Holidays around the world*.

(6-8) A photo essay that explains the when, where, and why of different celebrations.

Jackson, M. (1995). *Homes around the world*. Austin, TX: Steck-Vaughn.

(3-6) A mixture of illustrations and photos show a variety of homes around the globe.

Kissinger, K. (1994). *All the colors we are: The story of how we get our skin color*. St. Paul, MN: Redleaf Press.

(3-6) This book of engaging photographs helps children understand skin color as part of their uniqueness. Book is in both English and Spanish.

Morris, A. (1993). *Bread, bread, bread*. New York: Mulberry Books.

(3-8) Photographs of bread and people making and eating it around the world.

Morris, A. (1996). *Shoes, shoes, shoes*. Carmel, CA: Hampton-Brown Books.

(3-8) Photographs of shoes and people wearing them around the world. Some are for dancing, walking, playing, some for ice and snow, and some are made of wood or cloth.

Awareness of African and African American Culture

Adlerman, D. (1996). *Africa calling, nighttime falling*. Danvers, MA: Whispering Coyote.

(3-8) African wild animals are depicted in their habitats and described through poetic text.

Chocolate, D. (1996). *Kente colors*. New York: Walker.

(3-8) Illustrations and verse explain the meanings of colors and patterns in this beautiful cloth from West Africa. (Author's notes provide further explanations.)

Farris, P. J. (1996). *Young mouse and elephant: An East African folktale*. Boston, MA: Houghton Mifflin.

(3-8) A mouse claims to be the strongest animal in the forest. The wise grandfather cautions him that he could be wrong. The book is the story of quest. It provides insight into Sudanese culture.

Hru, D. (1993). *Joshua's masai mask*. New York: Lee & Low LB.

(6-8) By playing the kalimba, an African musical instrument, in his school's talent show, Joshua gains self-esteem.

Mennen, I. (1990). *Somewhere in Africa*. New York: Dutton Children's Books.

(3-6) This book compares wild Africa to a modern city in Africa using modern art illustrations.

Stewart, D. (1996). *Gift of the sun: A tale from South Africa*. New York: Farrar Straus Giroux.

(3-6) As a farmer tires of his chores, he sells his cow to buy a progression of other animals and eventually sunflower seeds.

Vigna, J. (1992). *Black like Kyra, white like me*. Morton Grove, IL: Whitman.

(6-8) Christy tells what happened after the family of her black friend Kyra Kirk moves into her all-white neighborhood.

Awareness of Hispanic and Hispanic American Culture

Castaneda, O. (1993). *Abuela's weave.* New York: Lee & Low Books.

(6-8) In Guatemala, a young girl and her grandmother take their handcrafts to sell at a fiesta.

Garay, L. (1997). *Pedrito's day.* New York: Orchard.

(3-8) Pedrito is a shoeshine boy in Latin America who is working to save money for a bicycle. While doing an errand he chooses to play soccer and loses the money for the errand. He repays it himself and the family rewards his honesty and maturity.

Guy, G. (1996). *¡Fiesta!* New York: Greenwillow.

(3-6) A counting book in English and Spanish about children buying candy and toys for their pinata.

Havill, J. (1992). *Treasure map.* Boston: Houghton.

(3-8) Alicia hears the story of how her great grandmother left Mexico and came to the United States.

Johnston, T. (1996). *My Mexico—Mexico mio.* New York: Putnam.

(3-8) A bilingual poetry book with one or two poems on a page in both Spanish and English. Topics offer a flavor of Mexican culture.

Kleven, E. (1996). *Hooray, a pinata!* New York: Dutton.

(3-6) Clara's family prepares for her 6th birthday by having a party with a pinata. She chose a dog pinata and her family saves Lucky from being smashed.

Mora, P. (1996). *Confetti: Poems for children.* New York: Lee & Low.

(3-8) A blend of English and Spanish, the poems linguistically integrate both cultures. (A glossary provides information on pronunciation and meaning.)

Mora, P. (1996). *Uno, dos, tres: One, two, three.* New York: Clarion.

(3-8) Two sisters shop for the perfect birthday present for their mother in a Mexican market. The rhyme helps all children learn to count in Spanish. (Includes an author's note and pronunciation guide.)

Nodar, C. S. (1992). *Abuelita's paradise.* Morton Grove, IL: Albert Whitman.

(6-8) Marita remembers the stories her grandmother told her about growing up in Puerto Rico.

Roe, E. (1991). *Con mi hermano (with my brother).* New York: Bradbury Press.

(3-8) A little boy admires his big brother and aspires to be like him when he is older. Done with simple watercolor illustrations and text in both English and Spanish.

Wainwright, R. M. (1991). *Mountains to climb.* New York: Family Life.

(6-8) During his two-year stay in the United States, a young Ecuadoran boy gradually wins his classmates' acceptance.

Zapatar, B. (1993). *Fiesta!* New York: Simon & Schuster.

(6-8) Chucho and his family, from Columbia, plan a fiesta in their home in America.

Awareness of Asian and Asian American Culture

Friedman, I. R. (1991). *How my parents learned to eat.* Orlando, FL: Harcourt Brace Jovanovich.

(3-8) A delightful book about an American soldier who learns to use chopsticks and his Japanese fiancee who learns to use a knife and fork.

Garland, S. (1997). *The lotus seed.* San Diego, CA: Harcourt Brace Jovanovich.

(3-8) A story about a woman and her possession of a lotus seed which also conveys the history of Vietnam, a land she had to flee.

Heide, F. P., & Gilliland, J. H. (1990). *The day of Ahmed's secret.* New York: Macmillan.

(3-8) Ahmed waits all day to show his family that he has learned to write his name (in Arabic).

Ho, M. (1996). *Hush.* New York: Orchard.

(3-6) As a Thai mother puts her baby to sleep she quiets all the animals that surround her thatched roof house until the only one who remains awake is, of course, the baby.

Kimmel, E. (1996). *One eye, two eyes, three eyes: A Hutzul tale.* New York: Holiday.

(3-8) The Hutzuls are an ethnic group in the Ukraine. The folk tale is about Larissa, a mistreated heroine and the goat that helps her complete her impossible requirements and the winning of the prince.

Levine, E. (1989). *I hate English!* New York: Scholastic.

(3-8) Although Mei-Mei feels comfortable in Chinatown, she resists learning the English language or American ways.

Knoll, V. (1994). *Pink paper swans.* MI: William B. Eerdmans.

(6-8) A young girl discovers the art of origami from her Japanese neighbor.

Machizuki, K. (1993). *Baseball saved us.* New York: Lee & Low LB.

(6-8) A Japanese-American boy gains acceptance playing an excellent game of baseball while an intern during World War II.

Awareness of Native American Culture

Ancona, G. (1993). *Powwow.* San Diego, CA: Harcourt Brace Jovanovich.

(6-8) The story of the Crow Fair in Montana and the Plains Indians who celebrate their customs and history at this event.

Haley, G. E. (1996). *Two bad boys: A very old Cherokee tale.* New York: Dutton.

(6-8) Wild Boy tries to influence his sibling to make trouble with him. Their parents, upset, require

Children need to have a variety of print media to choose from. Provide pop-up books, books without words, reference books, and books in large print and braille.

the boys to hunt for and plant their own food which is why all people must work. (Background information also provided.)

Jackson, E. (1997). *The winter solstice.* Brookfield, CN: Millbrook Press.

(6–8) Explains how people have celebrated the shortest day of the year and the customs that are associated with the celebration including the Cherokee creation myth.

Medaris, A. (1991). *Dancing with the Indians.* New York: Holiday House.

(6–8) The story of a young girl who visits the Seminole Indians with beautiful illustrations and clear text. It tells the traditions of this Native American tribe.

Nashone. (1989). *Where Indians live: American Indian houses.* Sacramento, CA: Sierra Oaks.

(3–8) Illustrations of 15 different Native American dwellings and information about the many different lifestyles among Native Americans.

Awareness of Other Cultural and Ethnic Groups

Ammon, R. (1996). *An Amish Christmas.* New York: Atheneum.

(3–8) This story portrays how this private religion celebrates the holiday. It includes many details about contemporary Amish life.

Charles, F. (1996). *A Caribbean counting book.* Boston: Houghton Mifflin.

(3–8) A collection of rhymes of Spanish, Dutch, and French origin. Children rhythmically count mongoose, mosquitos, and centipedes.

Ikeda, D. (1993). *Over the deep blue sea.* Morton Grove, IL: Whitman.

(3–6) The friendship between three children on a tropical island becomes strained because of racial prejudice.

Kuskin, K. (1993). *A great miracle happened there.* New York: HarperCollins.

(6–8) A Christian boy joins his friend's family for the first night of Hanukkah.

Kimmel, E. A. (1996). *The magic dreidels: A Hanukkah story.* New York: Holiday House.

(3–8) Jacob drops his new dreidel into a well, fortunately the home of a sympathetic goblin who turns it into a magic dreidel, a neighbor tricks him out of it, but eventually the dreidel is recovered before Hanukkah.

Polacco, P. (1992). *Mrs. Katz and Tush.* New York: Bantam Books.

(6–8) Mrs. Katz and Larnel become friends because he gives her a scrawny cat without a tail. Through their friendship they share their great suffering and pride because of his African American heritage and her Jewish background.

Polacco, P. (1998). *The keeping quilt.* St. Petersburg, FL: Spoken Arts.

(6–8) A handmade quilt ties together four generations of an immigrant Jewish family as a symbol of their love and faith.

Body Awareness

Archambault, J. (1987). *Here are my hands.* New York: Scholastic.

(B–6) A multicultural book showing children with each of their body parts described in a rhyming phrase.

Bentley, N. (1991). *I've got your nose.* New York: Doubleday.

(3–6) A witch with a button nose sets out to steal a nose more in tune with her profession.

Blegvad, L. (1986). *This is me.* New York: Random House.

(B–3) A simple rhyming book that moves from morning until night and shows body parts, clothing, and children's possessions.

Borton, M. R. (1988). *Tails, toes, eyes, ears, nose.* New York: Harper & Row.

(3–6) A brightly colored, simple, animal guessing game. Children must identify the animal when only parts are shown on one page, with the answer illustrated on the other side.

Caple, K. (1985). *The biggest nose.* Boston: Houghton Mifflin.

(3-8) Elephant Eleanor is so embarrassed at having the biggest nose in her school, she ties it in a knot.

Carle, E. (1997). *From head to toe.* New York: HarperCollins.

(3-6) Colorful animals ask children to perform different body movements.

Cole, B. (1989). *No more baths.* New York: Farrar.

(3-6) A dirty little girl runs away in disgust when her mother wants to give her a bath.

Parnall, P. (1988). *Feet!* New York: Macmillan.

(3-6) A book illustrating many feet from the animal kingdom.

Rose, D. (1993). *Where's your nose?* New York: Simon & Schuster.

(B-3) A rhyming book with photographs of infants and their body parts on sturdy cardboard.

Wantanabe, S. (1991). *How do I put it on?* New York: Putnam LB.

(B-6) How to dress oneself; told in simple terms.

Awareness of Child Abuse and Neglect

Anderson, D., & Finne, M. (1986). *Liza's story: Neglect and the police.* Parsippany, NJ: Silver Burdett Press.

(6-8) This book presents a case of child neglect in which the police become involved as it demonstrates the positive effects of reporting abuse to caring people.

Anderson, D., & Finne, M. (1986). *Michael's story: Emotional abuse and working with a counselor.* Parsippany, NJ: Silver Burdett Press.

(6-8) Because his parents continually berate him, Michael considers himself stupid as well as unloved.

Anderson, D., & Finne, M. (1986). *Robin's story: Physical abuse and seeing the doctor.* Parsippany, NJ: Silver Burdett Press.

(6-8) Robin's mother hits her causing a serious wound. The two go to counseling to improve their relationship.

Boegehold, B. (1985). *You can say "no."* New York: Western.

(6-8) A book about protecting your body.

Girard, L. W. (1984). *My body is private.* Morton Grove, IL: Whitman.

(3-6) A mother-child conversation introduces the topic of sexual abuse and ways to keep ones body private.

Katz, I. (1994). *Sarah.* West Hills, CA: Real Life Story Books.

(6-8) Sarah is saddened and shocked when Uncle Jack hurts her and touches her in private places, but with the help of Dr. Good she finds the strength to tell.

Lowery, L. (1994). *Laurie tells.* Minneapolis, MN: Carolrhoda Books.

(6-8) When her mother doesn't believe her, Laurie tells a supportive aunt that she is being sexually abused by her father.

Powell, S. (1991). *Daisy.* Minneapolis, MN: Carolrhoda Books.

(6-8) A realistic story of a girl and her father who abuses her both physically and verbally.

Spelman, C. (1997). *Your body belongs to you.* Morton Grove, IL: Albert Whitman.

(3-6) This book tells children that their body belongs to them and gives them ideas about what to say to someone who touches them, particularly their private parts.

Awareness of Feelings

Aliki. (1984). *Feelings.* New York: Greenwillow Books.

(3-8) Cartoon-like illustration help children describe and identify feelings such as jealousy, grief, frustration, and so on.

Avery, C. E. (1992). *Everybody has feelings/Todos tenemos sentimientos.* New York: OpenHand.

(3-8) Photographs of children illustrate a wide range of human emotions with a brief bilingual text.

Baker, A. (1987). *Benjamin's portrait.* New York: Lothrop.

(3-8) Benjamin, a hamster, sketches and then paints himself on canvas, with amusing and messy results.

Berlan, K. H. (1993). *Andrew's amazing monsters.* New York: Macmillan.

(3-8) The monsters that Andrew draws come to life and have a party.

Berry, J. (1988). *Being selfish.* Danbury, CT: Grolier.

(3-6) Children Katie and Sam learn to be unselfish.

Berry, J. (1988). *Complaining.* Danbury, CT: Grolier.

(3-6) Reading about Amy and Tami and looking at the cartoons will help children understand and deal with complaining.

Gardner, R. A. (1990). *The girls and boys book about good and bad behavior.* New York: Creative Therapeutics.

(3-6) This book talks about ethics and values.

LeShan, E. (1992). *What makes you so special?* New York: Dial Books.

(6-8) Such issues as self-esteem and psychology discussed in an informal way.

Awareness of Loving, Caring, and Sharing

Cooney, B. (1982). *Miss Rumphius.* New York: Viking.

(3-8) Miss Rumphius wonders how she can make the world more beautiful.

Joosse, B. M. (1991). *Mama, do you love me?* New York: Chronicle Books.

(3-6) A child living in the Arctic learns that a mother's love is unconditional.

McBartney, S. (1995). *Guess how much I love you.* New York: Candlewick Press.

(3-8) Little Nutbrown Hare plays around with the feeling of affection. This story describes how he deals with and displays his affections.

MacLachlan, P. (1994). *All the places to love.* New York: HarperCollins.

(3-8) A quiet family story shows males and females who are comfortable with loving feelings.

Pfister, M. (1992). *The rainbow fish.* New York: North-South.

(4-8) This colorful book tells a story of a fish who finds life to be much nicer when she shares.

Awareness of Loneliness

Bogart, J. E. (1992). *Daniel's dog.* New York: Scholastic Paper.

(3-8) To compensate for feeling left out because of his new baby sister, a young African-American boy invents a dog.

Burningham, J. (1992). *Aldo.* New York: Crown LB.

(3-8) A lonely young girl creates an imaginary friend in Aldo, a rabbit.

Awareness of Fears

Angelou, M. (1993). *Life doesn't frighten me.* New York: Stewart, Tabori & Chang.

(6-8) Boldly illustrated, this poem speaks of many of the fears children experience growing up.

Bradbury, R. (1993). *Switch on the night.* New York: Alfred A. Knopf.

(3-8) A young boy is afraid of the dark until a girl introduces him to the wonders of the night and he is able to join the children playing.

Cooper, H. (1993). *The bear under the stairs.* New York: Dial.

(3-8) William imagines that there is a fearful grizzly bear living in the storeroom beneath the stairs.

Gorbaty, N. (1986). *Tiger is a scaredy cat.* New York: Random House.

(3-8) Tiger is afraid of everything, even mice. When a baby mouse is lost and needs help, Tiger gathers his courage and returns the mouse to its home.

Henkes, K. (1996). *Sheila Rae, the brave.* New York: Greenwillow.

(3-8) Sheila Rae is not afraid of anything. Her sister on the other hand, is not quite so brave. One day when caught in a bind, her little sister helps her out and proves she is not a "scaredy cat" after all.

McCully, E. A. (1992). *Mirette on the high wire.* New York: G. P. Putnam's Sons.

(3-8) Mirette helps a famous tightrope walker overcome his fear and realizes her own dream to walk on the wire.

Polacco, P. (1997). *Thunder cake.* New York: Putnam & Grosset.

(3-8) A young girl's Russian grandmother helps her conquer her fear of thunderstorms as she collects the ingredients necessary to make a thunder cake.

Simon, N. (1989). *I am not a crybaby.* New York: Puffin Books.

(3-8) A multicultural group of children describe their worst fears and hurts, which include a broken leg, bad dreams, divorce, first day of school, death of a pet, getting a hearing aid, and parents fighting.

Waddell, M. (1988). *Can't you sleep little bear?* New York: Candlewick Press.

(3-6) When bedtime comes, Little Bear is afraid of the dark, until Big Bear brings him light and love.

Winthrop, E. (1987). *Maggie and the monster.* New York: Holiday House.

(3-6) Maggie is not afraid of the monster she sees each night, but wishes she would go away. After talking with her mother she asks the monster what she wants.

Awareness of Anger

Berridge, C. (1992). *Hannah's temper.* New York: Scholastic.

(3-8) A story about a child's anger when everything goes wrong.

Everitt, B. (1992). *Mean soup.* San Diego, CA: Harcourt Brace.

(3-8) The story of a child's anger and getting help from an adult.

Jahn-Clough, L. (1994). *Alicia has a bad day.* Boston: Houghton Mifflin.

(6-8) Alicia tells what it's like to have a bad day and nothing she does makes her feel better.

Preston, E. M. (1978). *Temper tantrum book.* New York: Puffin Books.

(3-8) Using animals, children are presented with situations "I hate it when . . ."

Shapiro, L. A. (1994). *The very angry day that Amy didn't have.* King of Prussia, PA: Childswork/Childsplay.

(3-8) About a child's anger and the problem solving that helps her cope.

Awareness of Separation

Berry, J. (1990). About dependence and *separation.* Danbury, CT: Children's Press.

(6-8) A combination of large easily understood cartoon pictures and easily read text deals with separation due to childcare and other occasions. (There is an appendix for adults.)

Brown, M. (1994). *Arthur's first sleepover.* Boston: Little, Brown.

(3–8) This is a good book for children who may be preparing for their first overnight stay.

Butterworth, N. (1995). *All together now!* Boston: Little, Brown.

(1–6) This book has hidden animals getting ready for a picnic. The reader has to lift the flaps to find all the animals.

Cannon, J. (1993). *Stellaluna.* New York: Harcourt Brace.

(3–8) A story about a baby fruit bat who gets separated from her mother and ends up in a bird's nest. Stellaluna tries to make the best of it but she misses her mother and is not very happy. Finally she is reunited and the two of them are very happy.

Henkes, K. (1993). *Owen.* New York: Greenwillow.

(3–6) Owen cannot part with his fuzzy yellow blanket until his mother comes up with a solution to solve the dilemma, just in time for school to start.

Hoff, S. (1994). *Duncan the dancing duck.* New York: Clarion Books.

(3–6) Duncan dances his way to celebrity status but eventually misses home and goes back to his pond.

Wells, R. (1996). *Edward's overwhelming overnight.* New York: Dial Books.

(3–6) Describes a new experience for young children—sleeping over at a friend's house.

Yee, P. (1995). *Baby lion.* New York: Viking Press.

(1–3) A sturdy board book where a baby lion gets a surprise shower from a baby elephant, but returns home safely.

Yee, P. (1995). *Baby penguin.* New York: Viking Press.

(1–3) On a swim a baby penguin meets a baby whale, but returns home safely.

Awareness of Perspective

Celsi, T. (1992). *The fourth little pig.* Madison, NJ: Steck Vaughn.

(3–8) An extension of the folk tale, the sister of the three little pigs persuades her brothers to overcome their fears and rejoin the world.

Coles, R. (1995). *The story of Ruby Bridges.* New York: Scholastic.

(6–8) The true story of an African American girl who, at age 6, braved the mobs to go to an all-white school.

Scieszka, J. (1989). *The true story of the 3 little pigs.* New York: Puffin Books.

(3–8) This version of the traditional tale is written from the point of view of the wolf who has a cold and doesn't truly mean to huff and puff.

Trivizas, E. (1993). *The three little wolves and the big bad pig.* New York: Margaret K. McElderry Books.

(3–8) The three little wolves try to build a secure structure, but the big bad pig outwits them. An unforseen solution turns enemies into friends.

Use with other stories of the three little pigs to help children gain perspective.

Waddell, M. (1992). *Farmer duck.* New York: Candlewick Press.

(3–6) The farmyard animals join together to give the slothful farmer his just reward and save Farmer Duck.

Awareness of Laughing at, Teasing, and Bullying

Barbour, K. (1989). *Nancy.* New York: Harcourt Brace Jovanovich.

(3–8) Four best friends shun and tease the new girl in the neighborhood until she invites them to her extraordinary birthday party.

Bourgeois, P. (1993). *Franklin is bossy.* New York: Scholastic.

(3–8) A story about a boy who tries to get what he wants by being bossy, but it doesn't work.

Boyd, L. (1989). *Baily the big bully.* New York: Viking Press.

(3–8) A book about bullies and how to deal with them.

Henkes, K. (1991). *Chrysanthemum.* New York: Greenwillow Books.

(3–8) Chrysanthemum loves her name until she gets to school and the girls tease her unmercifully. An empathetic teacher, who is also named for a flower, helps.

McMullan, K. (1995). *Hey! Pipsqueak.* New York: HarperCollins.

(4–8) On the way to a party, a boy must outwit a troll to cross a bridge.

Martin, B., Jr. (1994). *A beautiful feast for a big king cat.* New York: HarperCollins.

(3–8) A little mouse taunts a big cat. His mother always comes to the rescue, except for one day when the tiny mouse has to get himself out of trouble.

Reider, K. (1997). *Snail started it!* New York: North-South.

(3–6) Snail starts by calling Pig fat, and the chain starts as the animals make derisive remarks about each other. They then apologize.

Schwartz, A. (1988). *Annabelle Swift, kindergartner.* New York: Live Oak Media.

(3–6) Annabelle's older sister Lucy has prepared her for kindergarten. Still, all the children end up laughing at her when she tried to solve problems. Once Annabelle overcomes her mistakes, she surprises the class including the teacher.

Wilhelm, H. (1988). *Tyrone the horrible.* New York: Scholastic.

(3–8) A book about dealing with bullies.

Ziefert, H. (1994). *Pete's chicken.* New York: Tambourine Books.

(3–8) Pete, a rabbit, has a lot of self-confidence until his classmates make fun of his drawing of a chicken. Even his mother's support is not enough.

After a struggle, Pete decides it is okay to be his own person.

Awareness of Being Different

Cannon, J. (1997). *Verdi*. San Diego, CA: Harcourt Brace.

(3-6) A young interestingly yellow snake decides he does not want to turn green and slow down like his elders. Through his adventures he learns some of the values of being green.

Imai, M. (1994). *Lilly's secret*. Cambridge, MA: Candlewick Press.

(3-6) Lilly, a cat, feels she cannot be friends with Joe because of her peculiar paws. He feels differently.

Johnson, A. (1993). *The girl who wore snakes*. New York: Orchard Books.

(6-8) An African American girl loves snakes and wears them wherever she goes. She defends her rights and finds an aunt who shares her passion.

Lester, H. (1994). *Three cheers for Tacky*. Boston: Houghton Mifflin.

(3-8) Tacky, a penguin, is different but ends up stealing the show because of his own special abilities.

Mitchel, R. (1993). *Hue boy*. New York: Dial Books for Young Readers.

(6-8) Hue boy is so slow in growing that he worries about remaining small forever.

Quinsey, M. B. (1986). *Why does that man have such a big nose?* Seattle, WA: Parenting Press.

(3-6) Answers questions about people who look different in a matter-of-fact positive way. Invites discussion of uniqueness.

Shannon, M. (1993). *Elvira*. New York: Ticknor & Fields.

(3-8) Elvira is different and doesn't want to do dragon-like things. She would rather make daisy chains. She runs away to join the princesses and ultimately discovers she can be herself.

Awareness of Friendships and Making Friends

Aliki. (1982). *We are best friends*. New York: Greenwillow.

(3-6) When Robert's best friend Peter moves away, both are unhappy, but they learn that they can make new friends and still remain best friends.

Blegvard, L. (1985). *Anna Banana and me*. New York: Margaret K. McElderry Books.

(3-8) A timid boy relates the story of his friendship with a daring and intrepid girl.

Carlson, N. (1994). *How to lose all your friends*. New York: Viking Press.

(3-8) This hilarious book tells children exactly what to do if they want to end up with no friends.

Carlsson-Paige, N. (1998). *Best day of the week*. St. Paul, MN: Redleaf Press.

(3-8) Two children who live in a big city find a card table that is left for the trash. Both want it, but have different ideas about how it should be used. Their methods of conflict resolution can lead to good discussion.

Henkes, K. (1989). *Jessica*. New York: Greenwillow.

(4-8) Ruthie does everything with her imaginary friend Jessica; and then on her first day of kindergarten, she meets a real new friend with the same name.

Hess, D. (1994). *Wilson sat alone*. New York: Simon & Schuster.

(3-8) Wilson is shy and lonely until a new girl comes to school. She plays monster and roars at Wilson who roars back. He is then accepted as part of the group.

Holabird, K. (1988). *Angelina and Alice*. New York: Crown.

(4-8) Angelina finds her friendship with Alice becomes bumpy because of problems in gymnastics class.

Hutchins, P. (1993). *My best friend*. New York: Greenwillow Books.

(3-6) Two African American girls are best friends, each with her own special strengths.

Kelly, T. (1990). *Day-care teddy bear*. New York: Random House.

(3-6) Anna is afraid to enter day care. Bringing her teddy bear makes the process easier. The book depicts the activities of a typical child care setting.

Kroll, V. (1994). *New friends, true friends, stuck-like-glue friends*. Orlando, FL: Harcourt Brace.

(3-6) Illustrates many different friendship patterns including cross-gender friends.

Lionni, L. (1994). *The extraordinary egg*. New York: Knoff.

(3-6) Jessica, a frog, befriends the animal that hatches from an egg she brought home, thinking it is a chicken.

Malone, N. L. (1988). *A home*. New York: Bradbury Press.

(3-8) Molly finds a new friend in her new neighborhood.

Nikola-Lisa, W. (1994). *Bein' with you this way*. New York: Lee & Low.

(3-6) An African American girl gathers a diverse group of friends and they discover that their similarities are more important than their differences. They celebrate their friendship and cooperation.

Polacco, P. (1992). *Chicken Sunday*. New York: Philomel Books.

(6-8) A moving story about cross-gender, cross-cultural, and intergenerational friendships play out as a white girl and two African American brothers earn money for a gift for the grandmother.

Raschka, C. (1993). *Yo! Yes*. New York: Orchard Books.

(3-6) Describes a friendship between children of different races.

San Souci, R. D. (1995). *The faithful friend*. New York: Simon & Schuster.

(6-8) A story of two devoted friends.

Stevens, J. (1992). *Tops and bottoms*. New York: Harcourt Brace.

(3-8) The humorous retelling of a tale of the ups and downs of a partnership and the work ethic.

Waddell, M. (1993). *Let's go home little bear*. New York: Candlewick Press.

(3-6) When little bear is frightened by the noises he hears while walking in the snowy woods, his friend Big Bear reassured him.

Waddell, M. (1996). *You and me LITTLE Bear*. New York: Candlewick Press.

(3-6) Little Bear helps Big Bear gather wood, fetch water, and tidy the cave so that they can play together.

Wormell, M. (1995). *Hilda Hen's happy birthday*. New York: Harcourt Brace.

(3-8) Hilda Hen finds birthday presents even in places her farm friends did not intend.

Awareness of Illness

Brandenberg, F. (1976). *I wish I was sick, too*. New York: Greenwillow.

(3-6) A cat sister is envious of her brother's illness until she catches it herself.

Cherry, L. (1988). *Who's sick today?* New York: Dutton.

(3-6) Captivating colorful illustrations of animals with ailments, from beavers with fevers, to cranes with pains.

Gao, R. L. (1989). *Adventures of Monkey King*. New York: Victory Paper.

(3-8) With medical help, Andrew is gradually able to control his bowel movements.

Hathon, E. (1994). *Let's go to the doctor*. New York: Grosset & Dunlap.

(1-3) A picture story about a toddler going to the doctor and getting an inoculation. A small board book.

LeGuin, U. K. (1988). *A visit from Dr. Katz*. New York: Atheneum.

(3-6) When Marianne gets the flu and has to stay in bed, her brothers Philip and The Bean known together as, "Dr Katz," keep her company and make her feel better.

Marino, B. P. (1989). *Eric needs stitches*. New York: Harper.

(3-8) A book that describes in reassuring terms how a young boy has to go to a hospital emergency room.

Awareness of Death and Dying

Bohlmeijer, A. (1996). *Something very sorry*. Boston: Houghton Mifflin.

(6-8) A tragic car accident takes the life of Rosemyn's mother and the rest of the family have serious injuries. Rosemyn's inner turmoil and emotions are shared.

Brown, M. W. (1989). *The dead bird*. New York: Harper LB.

(3-8) After finding a dead bird, children give it a solemn burial.

Carson, J. (1992). *You hold me and I'll hold you*. New York: Orchard LB.

(3-8) A little girl confronts death when she and other family members attend a memorial service for Aunt Ann.

Cohn, J. (1987). *I had a friend named Peter: Talking to children about the death of a friend*. New York: Morrow LB.

(3-8) Betsy's story about her friend Peter, who was killed in a car accident.

Cohn, J. (1994). *Molly's rosebush*. Morton Grove, IL: A. Whitman.

(6-8) When her mother has a miscarriage Molly becomes sad and confused. Her grandmother finds ways to comfort her.

Douglas, E. (1990). *Rachel and the upside down heart*. Los Angeles, CA: Price Stein Sloan.

(3-8) The story of a child coping with the death of her father.

Keller, H. (1987). *Goodbye, Max*. New York: Greenwillow.

(3-6) Ben has to mourn the death of his dog Max before he can accept the new puppy.

Lanton, S. (1991). *Daddy's chair*. New York: Kar-Ben.

(3-8) Michael cannot believe that his now dead father will never sit in his favorite chair again.

Madensky, M. (1991). *Some of the pieces*. Boston: Little, Brown.

(3-8) On the first anniversary of his dad's death, a young boy tells how it feels and what he remembers.

Old, W. (1995). *Stacy had a little sister*. Morton Grove, IL: A. Whitman.

(6-8) When Stacy's baby sister dies of SIDS she has many fears and questions. Her parents, although sad, are reassuring and loving.

Powell, E. S. (1990). *Geranium morning*. Minneapolis, MN: Carolrhoda Books.

(3-8) A young boy feels loss and grief at the death of his father.

Rogers, F. (1988). *When a pet dies*. New York: Putnam Paper.

(3-6) A simple discussion of this emotional experience.

Spelman, C. (1996). *After Charlotte's mom died*. Morton Grove, IL: A. Whitman.

(3-8) Because of her mother's death Charlotte feels mad, sad, and scared. She and her father visit a therapist to help express their feelings.

Willner-Pardo, G. (1996). *Hunting grandma's treasures*. New York: Clarion.

(6–8) Seven grandchildren try to enjoy a family vacation but it doesn't seem the same since their grandmother died. They discover that she has left one last treasure.

Wright, B. R. (1991). *The cat next door*. New York: Holiday House.

(3–8) A young girl grieves for her grandmother who has died. The cat's gift helps her recall the good times and accept this death.

Awareness of Children Coping with Adversity

Bernstein, S. C. (1991). *A family that fights*. Morton Grove, IL: A. Whitman.

(3–8) A quiet story about three children where the father hits their mother and threatens them when he is angry.

Borton, L. (1997). *Junk pile*. New York: Philomel.

(3–6) Jamie, an Appalachian child, doesn't seem to notice her poverty. Others notice but are converted by her ingenuity and imagination. Watercolor and blackline illustrations.

Bunting, E. (1991). *Fly away home*. New York: Clarion Books.

(6–8) Andrew and his father live in an airport because they have lost their apartment. They are trying to save money for a home. Andrew almost gives up hope until he sees a trapped bird find its freedom.

Calhoun, M. (1997). *Flood*. New York: Morrow.

(3–8) A picture book that describes a young girls experiences preparing for and dealing with a devastating flood (based on the 1993 floods in the Midwest).

Lyon, G. E. (1990). *Come a tide*. New York: Orchard Books.

(6–8) When grandma predicts a flood, everyone leaves with feelings of sadness and dread. They return to begin the chore of cleaning up.

Guthrie, D. (1996). *A rose for Abby*. Nashville, TN: Abington Press.

(6–8) A great story about a young girl who is tired of seeing people homeless and gathers the neighborhood to open a soup kitchen.

Rathmann, P. (1995). *Officer Buckly and Gloria*. New York: Putnam.

(3–8) The children at Napville Elementary School always ignore Officer Buckly's safety tips, until a police dog named Gloria accompanies him when he gives his safety speeches.

Vigna, J. (1990). *I wish Daddy didn't drink so much*. Morton Grove, IL: A. Whitman.

(3–8) A story about a father's alcoholism.

Vigna, J. (1990). *My big sister takes drugs*. New York: A. Whitman.

(3–8) A story about an older siblings involvement with drugs and alcohol.

Butterworth, O. (1993). *A visit to the big house*. Boston: Houghton.

(3–8) Along with her mother and younger brother, Rose visits Dad in prison.

INDEX OF ACTIVITIES

Activity Goals and Reference Numbers

Social Awareness

To improve self-concept   1, 2, 3, 4, 5, 6, 10, 12, 34, 35, 36, 37, 38, 64, 79, 144, 184, 189, 208, 213

To increase awareness of roles people play   1, 2, 4, 6, 10, 31, 32, 33, 34, 35, 36, 37, 38, 39, 40, 41, 209, 210, 211, 212

To broaden concepts of families   1, 2, 3, 4, 5, 33

To increase inclusion   6, 7, 11, 12, 13, 14, 15, 16, 17, 18, 19, 20, 21, 22, 23, 25, 26, 27, 28, 29, 30, 31, 32, 35, 36, 37, 40, 41, 42, 55, 57, 61, 64, 94, 109, 161, 162, 165, 184, 186, 202, 203, 206, 213

To increase awareness of individual differences and similarities   7, 11, 14, 15, 16, 20, 21, 22, 23, 24, 25, 26, 27, 28, 29, 30, 31, 41, 44, 188

To increase cultural awareness   3, 24, 33, 104

To improve adaptive skills   39, 44, 45, 46, 48, 49, 50, 51, 52, 158, 159, 160, 162, 163

To improve health literacy   44, 45, 46, 47, 48, 49, 50, 51, 52

To encourage problem solving   7, 8, 9, 38, 42, 43, 52, 178, 187, 208, 209, 210, 211

To understand geography concepts   13, 32, 42, 43, 212

To participate in democratic process   208, 213

Language and Literacy

To increase expressive communication   8, 10, 53, 54, 55, 56, 57, 58, 59, 60, 61, 63, 64

To improve listening skills   54, 67, 68, 69, 70, 71, 72, 73, 74, 75, 76, 77, 78, 79, 84, 170

To improve receptive communication   53, 65, 67, 69, 70, 71, 72, 74

To increase comprehension   65, 66, 68, 71, 72, 73, 74, 80, 85, 86, 96, 195, 196

To increase knowledge of the structure of language   55, 62, 63, 84, 85, 91, 96

To increase vocabulary   34, 47, 53, 58, 62, 66, 83, 105, 106, 143, 158, 159, 169, 172

To increase respect for diversity in modes of communication   9, 15, 16, 22, 24, 29, 82

To use diverse print and nonprint sources and genres   56, 57, 97, 99, 100, 101, 102, 103, 205

To improve reading literacy   40, 62, 82, 83, 84, 85, 86, 87, 88, 89, 90, 91, 92, 93, 94, 95, 97, 100, 101, 102, 103, 104, 105, 107, 108, 117, 138, 139, 140, 141, 143, 144

To increase writing literacy   89, 93, 96, 97, 98, 99, 100, 101, 102, 103

To improve sequencing skills   80, 81, 198

To follow directions   63, 65, 88, 117, 137, 142, 143, 144, 193

To improve memory skills, 80, 87, 90, 198

To improve concentration   68, 69, 70

Discovery

To improve number sense and numeration   77, 104, 105, 106, 107, 108, 109, 110, 111, 161

To improve geometric and spatial sense   60, 78, 108, 110, 112, 113, 114, 115, 116, 117, 118

To improve measurement concepts   111, 112, 113, 115, 119, 120, 129, 142

To improve observational skills   9, 25, 119, 120, 121, 122, 123, 124, 125, 126, 127, 128, 129, 130

To improve classification skills   54, 60, 73, 110, 114, 116, 118, 119, 120, 121, 124, 125, 131, 132, 133, 175, 185

To improve estimation skills   107, 120

To identify and understand patterns and relationships   77, 81, 87, 88, 91, 111, 112, 116, 118, 132, 139, 140, 141, 163, 164, 174, 181, 197

To improve knowledge of whole number operations and computations   104

To understand fractions and decimals   106

To improve cause-and-effect reasoning   5, 13, 20, 39, 43, 45, 46, 48, 50, 51, 59, 75, 76, 81, 122, 125, 126, 128, 130, 133, 134, 135, 136, 137, 176, 179, 185, 194, 203, 211, 212

To improve generalization skills   82, 92, 123, 131, 132, 136, 138

To increase knowledge of the natural world   121, 123, 124, 131, 134

To make predictions   75, 76, 78, 79, 90, 92, 126, 127, 128, 131, 132, 133, 134, 135, 153

To improve computer skills   129, 135, 136, 137, 138, 139, 140, 141, 142, 143, 144

To increase thinking and reasoning skills   8, 11, 52, 114, 119

Developmental Physical Education and Sensory Motor

To improve locomotor skills   26, 28, 143, 144, 145, 146, 150, 154

To improve gross motor manipulative skills   148, 152, 153, 155, 156, 168, 169

To improve stability skills   146, 147, 151, 154, 166, 169, 170

To increase physical fitness   143, 145, 150, 154, 155, 156

Creative Arts

Goals and Activities for Infants and Toddlers

INDEX OF SUBJECTS

INDEX OF NAMES

K

Kahn, A. J., 88
Kaliner, M., 289, 291
Kamii, C. K., 401
Karmerman, S. B., 88
Karpf, R. S., 319
Kasari, C., 115, 208
Kastein, S., 360, 361, 373
Kauffman, J., 16, 18, 28, 205, 206, 249, 250, 251, 252, 289, 340
Kaufmann, R. K., 84, 142
Kavale, K. A., 208
Kazdin, A., 187
Keith, V. M., 62
Kelly, 212, 213, 214, 216
Kendall, J. S., 131, 384
Kendall-Tackett, K. A., 178
Keppel-Benson, J. M., 177
Ketterlinus, R. D., 88
King, B. H., 208
Klein, A. G., 15
Klein, T., 91
Klein, N., 42
Knightly, C. A., 337, 338, 339, 340, 341, 343, 345
Knuppel, R. A., 256
Kontos, S., 34, 43, 75
Kostelnik, M., 417
Kotsch, L., 55
Kozol, J., 291
Krager, J. M., 208
Kreiger, R., 93
Kryden-Coe, J. H., 90
Kucznski, L., 157

L

Laber, S., 340
Laird, M., 179
Lamb, M. E., 88
Lamme, L., 398, 401
Landau, S., 208
Langley, M. B., 565
Lasher, M., 182, 184
Lassiter, S., 69
Law, T. C., 86
Lawhon, D. C., 287
Lawton, J. T., 167
Lawhon, T., 287
Lazar, M. F., 319
Lee, I., 121
Lee, J., 92
Lee, R. V., 49
Lefkowitz, M. M., 183
Legg, J., 185
LeMay, D., 105, 253
Lerner, J. W., 209, 212, 213
Lerner, S., 212, 213
Levee, Y., 55
Levin, D. E., 159
Levy, S. E., 299
Lewis, M. E. B., 206
Lexine, I., 154
Libby, Y., 235
Liebergott, J., 235
Lin, S., 87
Liptak, G. S., 317, 318
Lobato, D. J., 286
Loeb, P., 7
Lombardi, J., 44
Lorenz, F. O., 90
Lynch, D. R., 209
Lynch, E. E., 93, 94
Lynch, E. W., 158
Lynch, M., 92, 178

M

Machado, J., 235
Mager, R. F., 131
Malach, R. S., 69
Maluccio, A. N., 93
Marazano, R. J., 131, 384
Marschark, M., 347
Mason, E., 49
Mattick, I., 182, 184
Mauk, J. E., 189
Mayesky, M., 416
Mazzocco, M. M., 255
McAninch, C., 208
McCarney, S., 212
McConnell, S., 23
McCormick, L., 564
McCubbin, H. I., 176
McCurdy, 178, 179
McDaniel, T. R., 273
McDonnell, A., 10
McDowell, J., 60
McGoldrick, M., 50, 58, 59, 62, 69, 70, 86, 84, 94, 113, 142
Meadows, S., 154, 158, 253
Menacker, S. J., 359, 362, 363, 365, 366
Mercer, R., 89
Mercugliano, M., 208, 209, 210, 212
Michaud, L. J., 319, 320
Miedzain, M., 159
Miller, L., 115
Miller, F., 312, 313, 315, 316
Miller. S., 76
Millner, B. N., 299
Mirowsky, J., 75
Mokuau, N., 67
Molnar, J. M., 90, 91
Morgan, S. R., 179
Morris, S., 390
Moulton, J., 30
Mowder, B. A., 289
Mullen, R. C., 18
Music Educators National Conference, 415

N

Nadeer, P., 212
National Association for Sport and Physical Education, 408
National Association for the Education of Young Children, 10, 29, 34, 37, 100, 288
National Cancer Institute, 293
National Center for Health Statistics, 4, 292, 343
National Center for History in Schools, 387
National Center of Improving Science Education, 403, 404
National Coalition against Domestic Violence, 92
National Commission on Social Studies in Schools, 387
National Council of Teachers of English, 392
National Council of Teacher of Mathematics, 384, 401
National Information Center for Children and Youth with Handicaps, 19
National Institutes of Health, 293, 295, 296
National Joint Committee on Learning Disabilities, 206

National Research Council, 403
Needleman, H., 235
Neill, C. A., 294
Neisworth, J., 107, 293
Nelson, L. B., 364, 366
Newachek, P. W., 89
Newborg, J., 115, 253
Nisivoccia, D., 93
Nitz, K., 88
Nordhaus, 93
Nugent, J. K., 93
Nunnally, E. W., 76
Nunnelley, J., 163

O

O'Connor, T. G., 86
O'Neill, B., 319
O'Reilly, K., 105, 253
O'Rourke, M., 299
Ollendick, T. H., 177
Olson, D. H., 55, 56, 57, 64, 66
Orton, S. T., 314
Osofsky, J. D., 91, 159
Owens, C., 409

P

PACER, 6
Palkovitz, R., 53
Panitz, P., 43
Paquio, L., 54
Patterson, J. M., 176
Pearpoint, J., 27, 31
Pelham, W., 212
Pellegrino, L., 315, 316, 317
Perkins, F., 182, 184
Perret, Y. M., 209, 251, 254, 256, 285, 316, 318, 337
Peters, D. L., 15
Peterson, N. L., 187, 320, 358, 560
Piaget, J., 22, 23, 154, 393
Pietrantoni, M., 256
Pine, B. A., 93
Piotrkowski, C. S., 58, 60
Pittman, F. S., 176
Pizzo, P. D., 44
Polcyn, P., 411
Pope, S. K., 88
Portner, J., 55
Powell, D. R., 45, 85
Pransky, J., 8, 9, 10
Presser, H. B., 54
Proctor, T. J., 30
Putnam, J. W., 3
Putnam, F. W., 178
Pynoos, R., 177

R

Rabideau, G., 92
Ralabate, P., 341
Raley, R. K., 87
Ramey, C. T., 157
Ramundo, 212, 213, 214, 216
Rapoff, M., 296
Rapoport, J. L., 188, 189, 190, 191, 250
Rasch, B. W., 32
Rayne, S., 154
Reason, R., 222
Reber, M., 189
Rennebohm, R. M., 296
Reynolds, W., 237
Reynolds, M. C., 32
Riley, R. W., 3